THEOLOGICAL DICTIONARY
OF THE
OLD TESTAMENT

THEOLOGICAL DICTIONARY
OF THE
OLD TESTAMENT

EDITED BY

G. JOHANNES BOTTERWECK

AND

HELMER RINGGREN

Translator

DAVID E. GREEN
(Graduate Theological Union)

Volume IV

זְאֵב-חמץ

z^{e}*'ēbh–ḥmṣ*

WILLIAM B. EERDMANS PUBLISHING COMPANY
GRAND RAPIDS, MICHIGAN

Theological Dictionary of the Old Testament

Translated from
Theologisches Wörterbuch zum Alten Testament
Band II, Lieferungen 4–9
Published 1975–1977 by
Verlag W. Kohlhammer GmbH Stuttgart, W. Germany

Library of Congress Cataloging in Publication Data

Botterweck, G Johannes.
Theological dictionary of the Old Testament.

Translation of Theologisches Wörterbuch zum Alten Testament.
Includes rev. ed. of v. 1–2.
Includes bibliographical references.
1. Bible. O.T.—Dictionaries—Hebrew.
2. Hebrew language—Dictionaries—English.
I. Ringgren, Helmer, 1917- joint author.
II. Title.
BS440.B5713 221.4′4′0321 73-76170
ISBN 0-8028-2338-6 (set)
Volume IV 0-8028-2328-9

Printed in the United States of America

CONTRIBUTORS

G. W. Ahlström, Chicago
G. André, Uppsala
C. Barth, Mainz
A. Bauman, Wolfsburg
J. Bergmann, Uppsala
K.-M. Beyse, Halle
G. J. Botterweck, Bonn (Editor)
A. Caquot, Paris
H. Cazelles, Paris
R. E. Clements, Cambridge, England
J. Conrad, Leipzig
W. Dommershausen, Trier
H. Eising, Münster
S. Erlandsson, Uppsala
H.-J. Fabry, Bonn
D. N. Freedman, Ann Arbor
J. Gamberoni, Paderborn
M. Görg, Bamberg
H. Haag, Tübingen
V. Hamp, Munich
G. Hasel, Berrien Springs
F. J. Helfmeyer, Cologne
F. Hesse, Albachten
H. A. Hoffner, Chicago
W. T. In der Smitten, Niederkrüchten
A. Jepsen, Greifswald
B. Johnson, Lund
A. S. Kapelrud, Oslo
B. Kedar-Kopfstein, Haifa
D. Kellermann, Tübingen
K. Koch, Hamburg
M. Krause, Münster
B. Lang, Paris
J. Lundbom, Berkeley
R. Mosis, Eichstätt
H.-P. Müller, Münster
G. Münderlein, Helmbrechts
A. Negoită, Bucharest
R. North, Rome
M. Ottosson, Örebro
H. D. Preuss, Neuendettelsau
H. Ringgren, Uppsala (Editor)
J. Scharbert, Munich
K.-D. Schunck, Rostock
K. Seybold, Kiel
L. A. Snijders, Beetsterzwaag
S. Steingrimsson, Uppsala
S. Tengström, Uppsala
M. Tsevat, Cincinnati
S. Wagner, Leipzig
G. Wallis, Hale
B. Wiklander, Uppsala

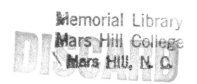

CONTENTS

ABBREVIATIONS

AANLR	*Atti dell' Academia Nazionale dei Lincei, Rendiconti,* Rome
AASOR	*Annual of the American Schools of Oriental Research,* New Haven, Ann Arbor
AAWLM	*Abhandlungen der Akademie der Wissenschaften und der Literatur Mainz,* Wiesbaden
AB	*The Anchor Bible,* Garden City, N.Y.
ABAW	*Abhandlungen der Akademie der Wissenschaften,* Berlin
ABL	R. F. Harper, *Assyrian and Babylonian Letters,* Chicago, 1892-1914, 14 vols.
ABR	*Australian Biblical Review,* Melbourne
abs.	absolute
acc.	accusative
AcOr	*Acta Orientalia,* Copenhagen
AcOrASH	*Acta Orientalia, Academiae Scientiarum Hungaricae,* Budapest
act.	active
adj.	adjective
ADOG	*Abhandlungen der Deutschen Orient-Gesellschaft,* Berlin
adv.	adverb
AER	*American Ecclesiastical Review,* Washington
ÄF	*Ägyptologische Forschungen,* Glückstadt
AFNW	*Arbeitsgemeinschaft für Forschung des Landes Nordrhein-Westfalen,* Cologne
AfO	*Archiv für Orientforschung,* Graz
ÄgAbh	*Ägyptologische Abhandlungen,* Wiesbaden
AHAW	*Abhandlungen der Heidelberger Akademie der Wissenschaften*
AHw	W. von Soden, *Akkadisches Handwörterbuch,* Wiesbaden, 1959-
AJSL	*The American Journal of Semitic Languages and Literatures,* Chicago
Akk.	Akkadian
AKM	*Abhandlungen zur Kunde des Morgenlandes* (Leipzig), Wiesbaden
ALUOS	*Annual of the Leeds University Oriental Society*
AMT	R. C. Thompson, *Assyrian Medical Texts,* London, 1924-1926
AN	J. J. Stamm, *Die akkadische Namengebung. MVÄG,* 44 (1939)
AnAcScFen	*Annales Academiae Scientarum Fennicae,* Helsinki
AnBibl	*Analecta Biblica,* Rome
AncIsr	R. de Vaux, *Ancient Israel: Its Life and Institutions,* New York, trans. 1961
ANEP	*The Ancient Near East in Pictures,* ed. J. B. Pritchard, Princeton, 1954, ^{2}1969
ANES	See *JANES*
ANET	*Ancient Near Eastern Texts Relating to the OT,* ed. J. B. Pritchard, Princeton, ^{2}1955, ^{3}1969
AnOr	*Analecta Orientalia,* Rome
AO	*Der Alte Orient,* Leipzig
AOAT	*Alter Orient und AT,* Neukirchen-Vluyn
AÖAW	*Anzeiger der Österreichischer Akademie der Wissenschaften,* Vienna
AOB	*Altorientalische Bilder zum AT,* ed. H. Gressmann, Berlin, Leipzig, ^{2}1927
AOBib	*Altorientalische Bibliothek,* Leipzig
AOS	*American Oriental Series,* New Haven
AOT	*Altorientalische Texte zum AT,* ed. H. Gressmann, Berlin, Leipzig, ^{2}1926
AP	A. E. Cowley, *Aramaic Papyri of the Fifth Century B.C.,* Oxford, 1923
APNM	H. B. Huffmon, *Amorite Personal Names in the Mari Texts,* Baltimore, 1965
Arab.	Arabic
Aram.	Aramaic
ArbT	*Arbeiten zur Theologie,* Stuttgart
ARM	*Archives Royales de Mari,* Paris
ArOr	*Archiv Orientâlní,* Prague

ARW	*Archiv für Religionswissenschaft,* Leipzig, Berlin
ASAW	*Abhandlungen der Sächsischen Akademie der Wissenschaften in Leipzig*
Assyr.	Assyrian
ASTI	*Annual of the Swedish Theological Institute in Jerusalem,* Leiden
AT	Alte Testament
ATA	*Alttestamentliche Abhandlungen,* Münster
ATD	*Das AT Deutsch,* ed. V. Herntrich-A. Weiser, Göttingen
Aug	*Augustinianum,* Rome
AuS	G. Dalman, *Arbeit und Sitte in Palästina,* Gütersloh, 1928-1942, repr. 1964
Bab.	Babylonian
BAfO	*Beihefte zur Archiv für Orientforschung,* Graz
BASOR	*Bulletin of the American Schools for Oriental Research,* New Haven, Ann Arbor
BASORSup	*Supplement to BASOR*
BAss	*Beiträge zu Assyriologie und semitischen Sprachwissenschaft,* Leipzig
BAT	*Die Botschaft des ATs,* Stuttgart
BBB	*Bonner Biblische Beiträge*
BBLAK	*Beiträge zur biblischen Landes- und Altertumskunde,* Stuttgart
BDB	*Brown-Driver-Briggs, A Hebrew and English Lexicon of the OT,* Oxford, 1907
BE	Babylonian Expedition of the University of Pennsylvania, Philadelphia, *Series A, Cuneiform Texts,* ed. H. V. Hilprecht, 1893-1914
BeO	*Bibbia e Oriente,* Milan
BETL	*Bibliotheca Ephemeridum Theologicarum Lovaniensium,* Paris, Gembloux
BEvTh	*Beiträge zur Evangelische Theologie,* Munich
BHHW	*Biblisch-Historisches Handwörterbuch,* ed. L. Rost and B. Reicke, 1962-1966
BHK	*Biblia Hebraica,* ed. R. Kittel, Stuttgart, ^{3}1929
BHS	*Biblia Hebraica Stuttgartensia,* ed. K. Elliger and W. Rudolph, 1966-1977
BHTh	*Beiträge zur Historischen Theologie,* Tübingen
Bibl	*Biblica,* Rome
BiblRes	*Biblical Research,* Chicago
BIES	*Bulletin of the Israel Exploration Society,* Jerusalem
BietOr	*Biblica et Orientalia,* Rome
BIFAO	*Bulletin de l'institut français d'archéologie orientale,* Cairo
BiLe	*Bibel und Leben,* Düsseldorf
BIN	*Babylonian Inscriptions in the Collection of James B. Nies,* New Haven, 1918-
BiOr	*Bibliotheca Orientalis,* Leiden
BJRL	*Bulletin of the John Rylands Library,* Manchester
BK	*Biblischer Kommentar zum AT,* ed. M. Noth and H. W. Wolff, Neukirchen
BL	*Bibel-Lexikon,* ed. H. Haag, Einsiedeln, 1951, ^{2}1968
BLe	H. Bauer-P. Leander, *Historische Grammatik der hebräischen Sprache,* Halle, 1918-1922, repr. 1962
Bo	Unpublished Boğazköy tablets (with catalog number)
BRL	K. Galling, *Biblisches Reallexikon,* Tübingen, 1937
BRM	*Babylonian Records in the Library of J. Pierpont Morgan,* ed. A. T. Clay, New York, 1912-1923
BS	*Bibliotheca Sacra,* Dallas
BSAW	*Berichte über die Verhandlungen der Sächsischen Akademie der Wissenschaften zu Leipzig*
BSt	*Biblische Studien,* Neukirchen
BT	*The Bible Translator,* London
BTB	*Biblical Theology Bulletin,* Rome
BuA	B. Meissner, *Babylonien und Assyrien,* Heidelberg, I, 1920; II, 1925
BWA(N)T	*Beiträge zur Wissenschaft vom Alten (und Neuen) Testament,* Stuttgart
BWL	W. G. Lambert, *Babylonian Wisdom Literature,* Oxford, 1960
BZ	*Biblische Zeitschrift,* Paderborn

BZAW	*Beihefte zur ZAW,* Berlin
BZNW	*Beihefte zur ZNW,* Berlin
CAD	*The Assyrian Dictionary of the Oriental Institute of the University of Chicago,* 1956-
CB	*Coniectanea Biblica, OT Series,* Lund
CBC	*Cambridge Bible Commentary on the New English Bible,* Cambridge
CBQ	*Catholic Biblical Quarterly,* Washington
CChr	*Corpus Christianorum,* Turnhout
CD A,B	Damascus Document, Manuscript A, B
CH	Codex Hammurabi
ChrÉg	*Chronique d'Égypte,* Brussels
CIG	*Corpus Inscriptionum Graecarum,* ed. A. Boeckhius, Berlin, 1828-1877, 4 vols.
CIS	*Corpus Inscriptionum Semiticarum,* Paris, 1881-
CML	G. R. Driver, *Canaanite Myths and Legends,* Edinburgh, 1956
CO	*Commentationes orientales,* Leiden
ComViat	*Communio Viatorum,* Prague
ConBibOT	*Coniectanea Biblica. OT series,* Lund
conj.	conjecture
const.	construct
ContiRossini	K. Conti Rossini, *Chrestomathia Arabica meridionalis ephigraphica,* Rome, 1931
Copt.	Coptic
COT	*Commentaar op het OT,* ed. G. C. Aalders, Kampen, 1955-1957
CRRA	*Compte Rendu de . . . Recontre Assyriologique Internationale*
CSEL	*Corpus Scriptorum Ecclesiasticorum Latinorum,* Vienna, 1866-
CT	*Cuneiform Texts from Babylonian Tablets . . . in the British Museum,* London, 1896-
CT	*The Egyptian Coffin Texts,* ed. A. de Buck and A. H. Gardiner, Chicago, 1935-1947
CTA	A. Herdner, *Corpus des Tablettes en Cunéiformes Alphabétiques Découvertes à Ras Shamra-Ugarit,* I/II, Paris, 1963
CThM	*Calwer Theologische Monographien,* Stuttgart
CTM	*Concordia Theological Monthly,* St. Louis
DB	*Dictionnaire de la Bible,* ed. F. Vigouroux, Paris, 1895-1912
DBS	*Dictionnaire de la Bible, Supplement,* ed. L. Pirot, A. Robert, H. Cazelles, and A. Feuillet, Paris, 1928-
DBTh	X. Léon-Dufour, *Dictionary of Biblical Theology,* trans. E. M. Stewart, New York, ^{2}1973
DHRP	*Disertationes ad historiam religionum pertinentes,* Leiden
dial.	dialect
DISO	C. F. Jean-J. Hoftijzer, *Dictionnaire des Inscriptions Sémitiques de l'Ouest,* Leiden, 1965
diss.	dissertation
DJD	*Discoveries in the Judean Desert,* Oxford, 1955-
DMOA	*Documenta et Monumenta Orientis Antiqui,* Leiden
DN	name of a deity
DÖAW	*Denkschriften der Österreichischer Akademie der Wissenschaften,* Vienna
EA	Tell el-Amarna Tablets
EDB	L. F. Hartman, *Encyclopedic Dictionary of the Bible,* New York, 1963
Egyp.	Egyptian
EHAT	*Exegetisches Handbuch zum AT,* Münster
Einl.	Einleitung
EJ	*Encyclopedia Judaica,* ed. J. Klatzkin-I. Elbogen, Berlin, 1928-1934, 10 vols.
EMiqr	*Entsiqlopēdiā Miqrāʿīt-Encyclopaedia Biblica,* Jerusalem, 1950-

EncBib	*Encyclopaedia Biblica,* ed. T. K. Cheyne, London, 1800-1903, ^{2}1958
EncBib Barc	*Enciclopedia de la Biblia,* ed. A. Diez Macho-S. Bartina, Barcelona, 1963-1965
EnEl	Enuma Elish
Eng.	English
ErfThSt	*Erfurter Theologische Studien*
ErJb	*Eranos-Jahrbuch,* Zurich
EstBib	*Estudios Biblicos,* Madrid
ÉtB	*Études Bibliques,* Paris
Ethiop.	Ethiopic
ETL	*Ephemerides Theologicae Lovanienses*
EvTh	*Evangelische Theologie,* Munich
ExpT	*The Expository Times,* London
FRLANT	*Forschungen zur Religion und Literatur des Alten und Neuen Testaments,* Göttingen
FuF	*Forschungen und Fortschritte,* Berlin
FzB	*Forschung zur Bibel,* Stuttgart
GaG	W. von Soden, *Grundriss der akkadischen Grammatik. AnOr,* 33 (1952)
gen.	genitive
GesB	W. Gesenius-F. Buhl, *Hebräisches und aramäisches Handwörterbuch,* Berlin, ^{17}1921
GHK	*Hand-Kommentar zum AT,* ed. W. Nowack, Göttingen
Gilg.	Gilgamesh Epic
GK	W. Gesenius-E. Kautzsch, *Hebräische Grammatik,* Halle, ^{28}1909 (=Kautzsch-Cowley, *Gesenius' Hebrew Grammar,* Oxford, 1910)
Gk.	Greek
GLECS	*Comptes Rendus du Groupe Linguistique d'Études Chamito-Sémitiques,* Paris
GSAT	*Gesammelte Studien zum AT,* Munich
HAD	*Hebrew and Aramaic Dictionary of the OT,* ed. G. Fohrer, London, trans. 1973
HAT	*Handbuch zum AT,* ed. O. Eissfeldt, 1st series, Tübingen
Ḫatt.	Ḫattic
Heb.	Hebrew
HG	J. Friedrich, *Die hethitischen Gesetze. DMOA,* 7 (1959)
Hitt.	Hittite
HNT	*Handbuch zum NT,* ed. G. Bornkamm, Tübingen
HO	*Handbuch der Orientalistik,* ed. B. Spuler, Leiden, 1952-
HSAT	*Die heilige Schrift des ATs,* ed. E. Kautzsch-A. Bertholet, Tübingen, ^{4}1922-23
HSS	*Harvard Semitic Series,* Cambridge, Mass.
HThR	*Harvard Theological Review,* Cambridge, Mass.
HUCA	*Hebrew Union College Annual,* Cincinnati
IB	*The Interpreter's Bible,* ed. G. A. Buttrick, Nashville, 1951-1957
IDB	*The Interpreter's Dictionary of the Bible,* ed. G. A. Buttrick, I-V, Nashville, 1962; *Supplement,* ed. K. Crim, 1976
IEJ	*Israel Exploration Journal,* Jerusalem
ILC	J. Pedersen, *Israel: Its Life and Culture,* Copenhagen, 1926, repr. 1973, 4 vols. in 2
impf.	imperfect
impv.	imperative
In	*Interpretation,* Richmond
inf.	infinitive
in loc.	on this passage
Introd.	Introduction
IPN	M. Noth, *Die israelitischen Personennamen. BWANT,* 3/10, 1928, repr. 1966
Ja	Enumeration according to A. Jamme (Old South Arabic)
JANES	*Journal of the Ancient Near Eastern Society of Columbia University,* New York

JAOS	*Journal of the American Oriental Society,* Boston, New Haven
JAOSSup	*Supplement to JAOS,* New Haven
JBC	*Jerome Biblical Commentary,* ed. R. E. Brown-J. A. Fitzmyer-R. E. Murphy, Englewood Cliffs, 1969
JBL	*Journal of Biblical Literature,* New York, New Haven, Philadelphia, Missoula, Ann Arbor
JBR	*Journal of Bible and Religion,* Boston
JCS	*Journal of Cuneiform Studies,* New Haven, Cambridge, Mass.
JE	*The Jewish Encyclopedia,* ed. I. Singer, New York, 1901-1906, 12 vols.
JEA	*Journal of Egyptian Archaeology,* London
JNES	*Journal of Near Eastern Studies,* Chicago
JPOS	*Journal of the Palestine Oriental Society,* Jerusalem
JQR	*Jewish Quarterly Review,* Philadelphia
JSS	*Journal of Semitic Studies,* Manchester
JTS	*Journal of Theological Studies,* Oxford
K	Tablets in the Kouyunjik collection of the British Museum
KAI	H. Donner-W. Röllig, *Kanaanäische und aramäische Inschriften,* Wiesbaden, I, ^{2}1966; II, ^{2}1968; III, ^{2}1969
KAJ	E. Ebeling, *Keilschrifttexte aus Assur juristischen Inhalts. WVDOG,* 50, 1927
KAR	E. Ebeling, *Keilschrifttexte aus Assur religiösen Inhalts. WVDOG,* 28, 1915/19
KAT	*Kommentar zum AT,* ed. E. Sellin, J. Herrmann, Leipzig, Gütersloh
KAV	O. Schroeder, *Keilschrifttexte aus Assur verschiedenen Inhalts. WVDOG,* 35, 1920
KB	*Keilinschriftliche Bibliothek,* ed. E. Schrader, Berlin, 1889-1900
KBANT	*Kommentare und Beiträge zum Alten und Neuen Testament,* Düsseldorf
KBL	L. Koehler-W. Baumgartner, *Hebräisches und aramäisches Lexikon zum AT,* Leiden, ^{2}1958, ^{3}1967–
KBo	*Keilschrifttexte aus Boghazköi. WVDOG,* 30, 36, 68–70, 72–. Leipzig, 1916-1923; Berlin, 1954–
KEHAT	*Kurzgefasstes exegetisches Handbuch zum AT,* ed. O. F. Fridelin, Leipzig, 1812-1896
KHC	*Kurzer Handcommentar zum AT,* ed. K. Marti, Tübingen
KlPauly	*Der Kleine Pauly,* ed. K. Ziegler-W. Sontheimer, Stuttgart, 1964–
KlSchr	*Kleine Schriften* (A. Alt, 1953-59, ^{3}1964; O. Eissfeldt, 1963-68; K. Elliger, 1966)
KTU	*Die Keilalphabetischen Texte aus Ugarit,* I, ed. M. Dietrich-O. Loretz-J. Sanmartin. *AOAT,* 24 (1976)
KUB	Staatliche Museen zu Berlin, Vorderasiatische Abteilung (later Deutsche Orient-Gesellschaft), *Keilschrifturkunden aus Boghazköi,* 1921–.
Lane	E. W. Lane, *An Arabic-English Lexicon,* London, 1863-1893, repr. 1968, 8 vols.
LAS	D. D. Luckenbill, *Annals of Sennacherib. OIP,* 2 (1924)
Lat.	Latin
Leslau, *Contributions*	W. Leslau, *Ethiopic and South Arabic Contributions to the Hebrew Lexicon,* Los Angeles, 1958
LexÄg	W. Helck-E. Otto, *Lexikon der Ägyptologie,* Wiesbaden, 1972–
LexHebAram	F. Zorrell, *Lexicon Hebraicum et Aramaicum Veteris Testamenti,* Rome, 1966
LexLingAeth	A. Dillmann, *Lexicon Linguae Aethiopicae,* Leipzig, 1865
LexLingAram	E. Vogt, *Lexicon linguae aramaicae Veteris Testamenti documentis antiquis illustratum,* Rome, 1971
LexSyr	C. Brockelmann, *Lexicon Syriacum,* Halle, 1928, ^{2}1968
LidzEph	M. Lidzbarski, *Ephemeris für semitische Epigraphik,* Giessen, 1900-1915
LidzNE	M. Lidzbarski, *Handbuch der nordsemitischen Epigraphik,* Weimar, 1898
lit.	literally

LSS	*Leipziger Semitistische Studien*
LTP	*Laval Théologicue et Philosophique,* Quebec
LUÅ	*Lunds Universitets Årsskrift*
LXX	Septuagint
MAOG	*Mitteilungen der Altorientalischen Gesellschaft,* Leipzig
MdD	E. S. Drower-R. Macuch, *Mandaic Dictionary,* Oxford, 1963
MedHab	Epigraphic Expedition, *Medinet Habu. OIP,* 8 (1930), 9 (1932)
MEOL	*Mededeelingen en Verhandelingen van het Vooraziatisch-Egyptisch Gezelschap "Ex Oriente Lux,"* Leiden
MGWJ	*Monatschrift für Geschichte und Wissenschaft des Judentums,* Breslau
MPL	J. P. Migne, *Patrologia Latina,* Paris, 1844-1864, 221 vols.
ms.	manuscript
MSL	*Materialen zum sumerischen Lexikon,* Rome, 1937-
MT	Masoretic Text
MThZ	*Münchener Theologische Zeitschrift*
Mus	*Le Muséon, Revue d'Études Orientales,* Paris
MVÄG	*Mitteilungen der Vorderasiatisch-Ägyptischen Gesellschaft* (Berlin), Leipzig
NAB	*New American Bible,* Paterson, N.J., 1970
NAWG	*Nachrichten der Akademie der Wissenschaften in Göttingen*
n.d.	no date
NEB	*New English Bible,* Oxford, 1961-1970
NFT	*Nouvelles Fouilles de Tello,* Paris, 1910-14
NKZ	*Neue Kirkliche Zeitschrift,* Erlangen, Leipzig
N.S.	New Series
NTS	*New Testament Studies,* Cambridge
obj.	object
OECT	*Oxford Editions of Cuneiform Texts,* ed. S. Langdon, 1923-
OIP	*Oriental Institute Publications,* Chicago, 1924-
OLZ	*Orientalistische Literaturzeitung* (Leipzig), Berlin
OMRO	*Oudheidkundige Mededeelingen uit het Rijks-Museum van Oudheden te Leiden*
Or	*Orientalia,* Rome
OrAnt	*Oriens Antiquus,* Rome
OrBibLov	*Orientalia et biblica lovaniensia*
OSA	Old South Arabic
OTL	*The Old Testament Library,* Philadelphia
OTS	*Oudtestamentische Studiën,* Leiden
PÄ	*Probleme der Ägyptologie,* Leiden
PAAJR	*Proceedings of the American Academy for Jewish Research,* Philadelphia
par.	parallel/and parallel passages
pass.	passive
PBS	University Museum, University of Pennsylvania, *Publications of the Babylonian Section,* Philadelphia
Peake	*Peake's Commentary on the Bible,* ed. M. Black-H. H. Rowley, New York, 1962
PEQ	*Palestine Exploration Quarterly,* London
perf.	perfect
Phil.-hist. Kl.	Philosophische-historische Klasse
Phoen.	Phoenician
PJ	*Palästinajahrbuch,* Berlin
PN	name of a person
PNPI	J. K. Stark, *Personal Names in Palmyrene Inscriptions,* Oxford, 1971
PNU	F. Grondähl, *Personennamen der Texte aus Ugarit,* Rome, 1967
prep.	preposition
PRU	*Le Palais Royal d'Ugarit,* ed. C. F.-A. Schaeffer- J. Nougayrol, Paris
ptcp.	participle

PThS	*Pretoria Theological Studies,* Leiden
Pun.	Punic
PW	A. Pauly-G. Wissowa, *Real-Encyclopädie der classischen Altertumswissenschaft,* Stuttgart, 1839-; supplements, 1903-1956, 11 vols.; 2nd series, 1914-1948
Pyr.	K. Sethe, *Die altägyptischen Pyramidentexte,* Leipzig, 1908-1922, 4 vols.
QuaestDisp	*Quaestiones Disputatae,* ed. K. Rahner-H. Schlier, New York, 1959-
R	H. C. Rawlinson, *The Cuneiform Inscriptions of Western Asia,* London, 1861-1909
RA	*Revue d'Assyriologie et d'Archéologie Orientale,* Paris
RAC	*Reallexikon für Antike und Christentum,* ed. T. Klauser, Stuttgart, 1950-1978, 10 vols.
RÄR	H. Bonnet, *Reallexikon der ägyptischen Religionsgeschichte,* Berlin, 1952
RB	*Revue Biblique,* Paris
RdM	*Die Religionen der Menschheit,* ed. C. M. Schröder, Stuttgart
RE	*Real-Enzyklopädie für protestantische Theologie und Kirche,* ed. A. Hauck, Leipzig, ^{3}1897-1913
RÉg	*Revue d'Égyptologie,* Paris
repr.	reprint, reprinted
RES	*Revue des Études Sémitique,* Paris
RES (with number)	*Répertoire d'Épigraphie Sémitique,* Paris
RevQ	*Revue de Qumrân,* Paris
RGG	*Die Religion in Geschichte und Gegenwart,* Tübingen, ^{2}ed. H. Gunkel-L. Zscharnack, 1927-1931, 5 vols.; ^{3}ed. K. Galling, 1957-1965, 6 vols.
RHLR	*Revue d'Histoire et de Littérature Religieuses,* Paris
RHPR	*Revue d'Histoire et de Philosophie Religieuses,* Strasbourg, Paris
RHR	*Revue de l'Histoire des Religions,* Paris
RIH	J. de Rougé, *Inscriptions hiéroglyphiques copiées en Egypte. Etudes égyptologiques,* 9-11, Paris, 1877/78, 3 vols.
RivBibl	*Rivista biblica,* Rome
RLA	*Reallexikon der Assyriologie,* ed. G. Ebeling-B. Meissner, Berlin, I, 1932; II, 1938; III, 1957-1971; IV, 1972
RS	Ras Shamra
RSO	*Revista degli Studi Orientali,* Rome
RVV	*Religionsgeschichtliche Versuche und Vorarbeiten,* Halle
Ry	Enumeration in G. Ryckmans, *Inscriptions sudarabes* I-XVII. *Mus,* 40-72 (1927-1959)
Sab.	Sabean
Saf.	Safaitic
SAHG	A. Falkenstein-W. von Soden, *Sumerische und akkadische Hymnen und Gebete,* Zurich, 1953
SAOC	*Studies in Ancient Oriental Civilization,* Chicago
SAT	*Die Schriften des ATs in Auswahl,* trans. and ed. H. Gunkel, *et al.,* Göttingen
SBS	*Stuttgarter Bibel-Studien*
SBT	*Studies in Biblical Theology,* London, Chicago
ScrHier	*Scripta Hierosolymitana,* Jerusalem
SEÅ	*Svensk Exegetisk Årsbok,* Lund
Sem	*Semitica,* Paris
Seux	J. M. Seux, *Epithètes Royales Akkadiennes et Sumériennes,* Paris, 1968
SGL	A. Falkenstein, *Sumerische Götterlieder,* Heidelberg, 1959
SgV	*Sammlung gemeinverständlicher Vorträge und Schriften aus dem Gebiet der Theologie und Religionsgeschichte,* Tübingen
SHAW	*Sitzungsberichte der Heidelberger Akademie der Wissenschaften*
SIDA	*Scripta Instituti Donneriana Åboensis,* Stockholm

SNumen	*Supplements to Numen,* Leiden
SNVAO	*Skrifter utgitt av det Norske Videnskaps-Akademi i Oslo*
Soq.	Soqoṭri
SPIB	*Scripta Pontificii Instituti Biblici,* Rome
SSAOI	*Sacra Scriptura Antiquitatibus Orientalibus Illustrata,* Rome
SSN	*Studia Semitica Neerlandica,* Assen
StANT	*Studien zum Alten und Neuen Testament,* Munich
St.-B.	H. L. Strack-P. Billerbeck, *Kommentar zum NT aus Talmud und Midrasch,* Munich, 1922–1961, 6 vols.
StBT	*Studien zu den Boğazköy-Texten,* Wiesbaden
StDI	*Studia et Documenta ad Iura Orientis Antiqui Pertinentia,* Leiden
StFS	*Studia Francisci Scholten,* Leiden
StJLA	*Studies in Judaism in Late Antiquity,* Leiden
StOr	*Studia Orientalia,* Helsinki
STT	*The Sultantepe Tablets,* London, I, O. R. Gurney-J. J. Finkelstein, 1957; II, O. R. Gurney-P. Hulin, 1964
StTh	*Studia Theologica,* Lund, Aarhus
StUNT	*Studien zur Umwelt des NTs,* Göttingen
subj.	subject
subst.	substantive
suf.	suffix
Sum.	Sumerian
SVT	*Supplements to VT,* Leiden
Synt.	C. Brockelmann, *Hebräische Syntax,* Neukirchen, 1956
Syr.	Syriac
Syr.	*Syria. Revue d'Art Oriental et d'Archéologie,* Paris
TAik	*Teologinen Aikakauskirja,* Helsinki
TAPhS	*Transactions of the American Philosophical Society,* Philadelphia
TCL	*Textes cunéiformes du Musée du Louvre,* Paris, 1910–
TDNT	*Theological Dictionary of the NT,* ed. G. Kittel-G. Friedrich, Grand Rapids, trans. 1964–1976, 10 vols.
TDOT	*Theological Dictionary of the OT,* ed. G. J. Botterweck-H. Ringgren, Grand Rapids, trans. 1974–
TGI	K. Galling, *Textbuch zur Geschichte Israels,* Tübingen, 1950, ²1968
Th.	Theologie
ThArb	*Theologische Arbeiten,* Berlin
THAT	*Theologisches Handwörterbuch zum AT,* ed. E. Jenni-C. Westermann, Munich, 1971–1976, 2 vols.
ThB	*Theologische Bücherei,* Munich
ThEH	*Theologische Existenz Heute,* Munich
Theol.	Theology (of)
ThLZ	*Theologische Literaturzeitung,* Leipzig, Berlin
ThPh	*Theologie und Philosophie,* Freiburg
ThR	*Theologische Rundschau,* Tübingen
ThSt	*Theologische Studien,* Zurich
ThV	*Theologische Versuche,* Berlin
ThViat	*Theologia Viatorum,* Berlin
ThZ	*Theologische Zeitschrift,* Basel
Tigr.	Tigrīnya (Tigriña)
TigrWb	E. Littmann-M. Höfner, *Wörterbuch der Tigre-Sprache,* Wiesbaden, 1962
TR	P. Lacau, *Textes Religieux Égyptiens,* I, Paris, 1910
trans.	translated
TrThSt	*Trierer Theologische Studien*
TrThZ	*Trierer Theologische Zeitschrift*

TüThQ	*Theologische Quartalschrift*, Tübingen, Stuttgart
UCPNES	*University of California Publications, Near Eastern Studies*, Berkeley
UET	*Ur Excavations. Texts*, London, 1928-
UF	*Ugarit-Forschungen*, Neukirchen
Ugar.	Ugaritic
Urk.	*Urkunden des ägyptischen Altertums*, Leipzig, 1903-
UT	C. H. Gordon, *Ugaritic Textbook. AnOr*, 38 (1965)
UUÅ	*Uppsala Universitets Årsskrift*
VAB	*Vorderasiatische Bibliothek*, Leipzig, 1907-1916
VAS	*Vorderasiatische Schriftdenkmäler der königlichen Museen zu Berlin*
VD	*Verbum Domini*, Rome
VG	C. Brockelmann, *Grundriss der vergleichenden Grammatik der semitischen Sprachen*, Berlin, 1908-1913, repr. 1961, 2 vols.
vo.	verso, on the reverse of a papyrus or tablet
VT	*Vetus Testamentum*, Leiden
Vulg.	Vulgate
WbÄS	A. Erman-H. Grapow, *Wörterbuch der ägyptischen Sprache*, Leipzig, 1926-1931, repr. 1963, 5 vols.
WbMyth	*Wörterbuch der Mythologie*, ed. H. W. Haussig, Stuttgart, 1961-
Wehr	H. Wehr, *A Dictionary of Modern Written Arabic*, ed. J. M. Cowan, Ithaca, 1961
Whitaker	R. E. Whitaker, *A Concordance of the Ugaritic Literature*, Cambridge, Mass., 1972
WMANT	*Wissenschaftliche Monographien zum Alten und Neuen Testament*, Neukirchen
WO	*Die Welt des Orients*, Göttingen
WTM	J. Levy, *Wörterbuch über die Talmudim und Midraschim*, Leipzig, ^{2}1924, repr. 1963, 4 vols.
WuD	*Wort und Dienst*, Bielefeld
WUS	J. Aisleitner, *Wörterbuch der ugaritischen Sprache. BSAW*, Phil.-hist. Kl., 106/3, 1963, ^{4}1974
WVDOG	*Wissenschaftliche Veröffentlichungen der Deutschen Orient-Gesellschaft* (Berlin), Leipzig
WZ	*Wissenschaftliche Zeitschrift*
WZKM	*Wiener Zeitschrift für die Kunde des Morgenlandes*
YJS	*Yale Judaica Series*, New Haven
YOSBT	*Yale Oriental Series, Babylonian Texts*, New Haven, 1915-
ZA	*Zeitschrift für Assyriologie* (Leipzig), Berlin
ZÄS	*Zeitschrift für Ägyptische Sprache und Altertumskunde* (Leipzig), Berlin
ZAW	*Zeitschrift für die Alttestamentliche Wissenschaft* (Giessen), Berlin
ZB	*Zürcher Bibelkommentare*, Zurich, Stuttgart
ZDMG	*Zeitschrift der Deutschen Morgenländischen Gesellschaft* (Leipzig), Wiesbaden
ZDPV	*Zeitschrift des Deutschen Palästina-Vereins* (Leipzig, Stuttgart), Wiesbaden
ZEE	*Zeitschrift für Evangelische Ethik*, Gütersloh
ZKTh	*Zeitschrift für katholische Theologie*, Innsbruck
ZNW	*Zeitschrift für die Neutestamentliche Wissenschaft* (Giessen), Berlin
ZThK	*Zeitschrift für Theologie und Kirche*, Tübingen
→	indicates cross-reference within this *Dictionary*

TRANSLITERATION OF HEBREW

VOWELS

◌ַ	a
◌ֲ	ª
◌ָ	ā
◌ֶ	e
◌ֱ	ᵉ
◌ֶי	ey
◌ֵ	ē
◌ֵי	ê
◌ְ	ᵉ
◌ִ	i
◌ִי	î
◌ָ	o
◌ֳ	ᵒ
◌ֹ	ō
וֹ	ô
◌ֻ	u
וּ	û
◌ַי	ai
◌ָיו	āv
◌ָ	āi
הּ	h

CONSONANTS

א	ʾ
בּ	b
ב	bh
גּ	g
ג	gh
דּ	d
ד	dh
ה	h
ו	v, w
ז	z
ח	ch, ḥ
ט	ṭ
י	y
כּ	k
כ	kh
ל	l
מ	m
נ	n
ס	s
ע	ʿ
פּ	p
פ	ph
צ	ts, ṣ
ק	q
ר	r
שׂ	ś
שׁ	sh, š
תּ	t
ת	th

זְאֵב z^{e}'ēbh

Contents: I. Etymology. II. Ancient Near East: 1. Egypt; 2. Mesopotamia; 3. Arabia and Palestine. III. Old Testament: 1. Characteristics; 2. Symbolizing Benjamin; 3. Symbolizing Enemies; 4. Symbolizing Social Classes; 5. Peace among Animals; 6. z^{e}'ēbh as a Personal Name.

I. Etymology. The root *z'b* is found throughout the Semitic world (except for Ugarit) and in Egypt, but its precise meaning cannot be given. The earliest occurrences are in the Egyptian pyramid texts, where *s3b* refers to one of the canidae,[1] probably the "jackal."[2] Neobab. *zību* sometimes means "jackal,"[3] sometimes "vulture."[4] The translation "fox"[5] has not found support. The meaning "jackal" (→ תן *tan,* "jackal"), according to W. von Soden[6] and others, has been confirmed by a prism inscription of Sargon,[7] according to which dogs (*kalbū*) and *zi-i-bu* skip about like lambs (*dakāku* II[8]); this cannot apply to vultures. Neither can the "wolf" be referred to, since it is mentioned separately a bit later (*nēšū ū barbarū,* "lions and wolves").[9] The *zi-i-bu a-ki-lu* mentioned in an incantation[10] is likewise to be understood as a "greedy jackal." Here, too, as in *MSL,* VIII/2, 17, 140f., the vulture cannot be meant. The *zību*

---

z^{e}'ēbh. F. S. Bodenheimer, *Animal Life in Palestine* (Jerusalem, 1935), 110f.; *idem, Animal and Man in Bible Lands,* I (trans. Leiden, 1960), 44, 100; G. Bornkamm, "λύκος," *TDNT,* IV, 308–311; G. J. Botterweck, *Die Tiere in der Bildersprache des AT unter bes. Berücksichtigung der äg. und akk. Literatur* (inaug. diss., Bonn, 1953), 21, 173f.; E. D. van Buren, *The Fauna of Ancient Mesopotamia as Represented in Art. AnOr,* 18 (1939); G. Cansdale, *Animals of Bible Lands* (Exeter Devon, 1970), 119–121, 124–26; Dalman, *AuS,* VI (1939), 219, 233–35; K. Elliger, "Das Ende der 'Abendwölfe' Zeph. 3, 3 Hab 1, 8," *Festschrift A. Bertholet* (1950), 158–175; J. Feliks, *The Animal World of the Bible* (trans. Tel Aviv, 1962), 35; *idem,* "Wolf," *BHHW,* III (1966), 2180f.; H. Grapow, *Vergleiche und andere bildliche Ausdrücke im Ägyptischen. AO,* 21/1-2 (1920); B. Landsberger, *Die Fauna des alten Mesopotamien nach der 14. Tafel der Serie ḪAR-RA = ḪUBULLU. ASAW,* 42/6 (1934), 68, 78f.; Meissner, *BuA,* I, 224; II, 307, 381; A. Schott, *Die Vergleiche in den akkadischen Königsinschriften, MVÄG,* 30 (1926); H. G. Tristram, *The Natural History of the Bible* (London, [3]1873), 152–55; H. Wildberger, *BK,* X/1 (1972), 455–462; H.-J. Zobel, *Stammesspruch und Geschichte. BZAW,* 95 (1965), 25, 107f.

[1] H. Kees, *RÄR,* 41.
[2] *WbÄS,* III, 420.
[3] Landsberger, 78f.
[4] *CAD,* XXI, 106.
[5] E. Ebeling, *Kritische Beiträge zu neueren assyriologischen Veröffentlichungen. MAOG,* 10/2 (1937), 43.
[6] Private communication.
[7] C. J. Gadd, "Inscribed Prisms of Sargon II from Nimrud," *Iraq,* 16 (1954), 192, 53ff.
[8] *AHw,* I, 151b.
[9] Gadd, lines 71f.
[10] *STT,* II (1964), 230, 16ff.

that is identified with *barbarū*[11] is the West Semitic word for "wolf." The word *zibû* also appears as a disputed term for a "bird" or a "locust."[12]

In West Semitic the predominant meaning is "wolf": Aram.,[13] Syr.,[14] Heb. and Middle Heb. (*z^{e}'ēbhāh* used to designate the nurse of Romulus and Remus[15]), Mand. *diba*[16] and *zabia,* "wolf,"[17] as well as Pahl. *dyb',*[18] and Arab. *ḏi'b,* "wolf, jackal," with the denominative verb *ḏa'iba* X, "be wolflike, be fierce or cruel like a wolf."[19]

In modern Syriac dialects, the word sometimes means "fox."[20] In Old South Arabic, *z'b* is attested only in personal names.[21] In the later dialects, the meaning "wolf" (like Ethiop. *zĕ'ĕb*[22]) is rare; more commonly, as in Tigré and Amharic, it means "hyena."[23] Eilers attempts to explain *ḏi'b,* "wolf," as an abstract noun expressing the notion "banishment."[24]

II. Ancient Near East.

1. *Egypt.* From the outset, no clear distinction was made in Egypt between the wolf (*Canis lupus*) and the jackal (*Canis lupaster*). Along with the desert dog they belong to the genus *Canis,* sacred since time immemorial to several gods. It was not until late that the wolf (also called *ỉśhb, wnš,* and *wnšyw* as a symbol of cowardice[25]) became associated with the war-god Up-wawet.[26] But the jackal (the heraldic animal of the nome of Cynopolis), as representative of the canidae called *s3b,* became the sacred animal of the "jackal gods,"[27] the gods of the dead Anubis and Khenti-amentiu, because jackals roamed the fringes of the desert, made their dens in the caves of the necropolises, and burrowed in the burial sites. "These habits of the Canidae... were reinterpreted in such a way that Anubis became the guardian of the dead."[28] Anubis,

---

[11]Malku, V, 44; now in B. Landsberger, *The Fauna of Ancient Mesopotamia, 2d Part: ḪAR-ra = ḫubullu Tablets XIV and XVIII. MSL,* VIII/2 (1962), 74, 44.

[12]*CAD,* XXI, 105.

[13]Levy, *WTM,* I, 370.

[14]Brockelmann, *LexSyr,* 65.

[15]*WTM,* I, 507.

[16]*MdD,* 106a.

[17]R. Macuch, *Handbook of Classical and Modern Mandaic* (1965), 34, 174.

[18]E. Ebeling, *Das aramäisch-mittelpersische Glossar Frahang-i-Pahlavik im Lichte der assyriologischen Forschung. MAOG,* 14/1 (1941), 21.

[19]Wehr, 307.

[20]A. J. Maclean, *Dictionary of the Dialect of Vernacular Syriac* (Oxford, 1901), 59a.

[21]G. Ryckmans, *Les noms propres sud-sémitiques. Bibliothèque de Muséon,* 2 (1934/35), I, 68; ContiRossini, 127.

[22]Dillmann, *LexLingAeth,* 1056; S. Grébaut, *Supplément au Lexicon Linguae Aethiopicae de A. Dillmann* (1952), 308.

[23]*TigrWb,* 499; W. Leslau, *Hebrew Cognates in Amharic* (1969), 44, 86, 92.

[24]W. Eilers, "Zur Funktion der Nominalformen," *WO,* 3 (1964/66), 132, n. 1.

[25]H. Grapow, *Die bildlichen Ausdrücke des Ägyptischen* (1924), 74.

[26]*WbMyth,* 334.

[27]*RÄR,* 674f.

[28]B. Altenmüller, "Anubis," *LexÄg,* I/3 (1973), 327-333; cf. *RÄR,* 40-45.

"lord of the necropolis," is the judge of the dead;[29] from the Old Kingdom onward the jackal hieroglyph stands for "judge"[30] as an official or honorary title. Other animal fables bear witness to this same aspect of the jackal.[31] On account of their facile manner, they function as servant figures in myth and story;[32] in mythology, jackals represented the "servants of Horus,"[33] sometimes pulling the sun boat. There is evidence that a jackal cult persisted even in the late New Kingdom.[34] We read that the enemies of Seti I "lie in their caves by day like wolves."[35] When hunting, Rameses III looks upon bulls and lions "as though they were wolves."[36] Apparently the cowardice of the small Egyptian wolves (*wnš*) is the point of the simile.

2. *Mesopotamia.* In Mesopotamia the wolf and jackal are not considered symbols of any gods; neither do they have any particular significance in representational art. E. D. van Buren mentions a picture of a wolf from the Jemdet-naṣr period;[37] F. S. Bodenheimer cites in addition a North Syrian Aramaic amulet from Arslan Tash, dating from the seventh century.[38] Archeological finds illustrate jackals, alone or in packs. The jackal is occasionally shown playing a musical instrument in an animal orchestra.[39] That the order of nature was still intact at the dawn of history can be inferred from scenes illustrating paradisal peace among the animals. According to the poem Enmerkar and the Lord of Aratta, "Once upon a time, there was no snake, there was no scorpion, there was no hyena, there was no lion, there was no wild dog, no wolf, there was no fear, no terror, man had no rival."[40] According to the story of Enki and Ninhursag, "In Dilmun the raven utters no cry . . . the lion kills not, the wolf snatches not the lamb, unknown is the kid-devouring wild dog. . . ."[41]

Alongside lions, hunger, and pestilence, wolves were also considered a plague to man; apparently, however, wolves were considered a lesser evil, since Ea berates Enlil for having brought on the deluge rather than afflicting men with wolves.[42] In a hymn to Ishtar, Ishtar is described as follows: "You are a wolf sent forth to snatch away a

---

[29] Pyr. 157c.

[30] *WbÄS*, III, 421.

[31] E. Brunner-Traut, *Altägyptische Tiergeschichte und Fabel* (^{2}1968), 52.

[32] *Ibid.*, 18.

[33] *Urk.*, VII, 56; Pyr. 2011.

[34] *RÄR*, 674f.

[35] J. F. Champollion, *Monuments de l'Égypte et de la Nubie: Notices descriptives* (Paris, 1844-1889), 100.

[36] *MedHab*, 338.

[37] Van Buren, 13.

[38] Bodenheimer, *Animal and Man*, 44; cf. *ANEP*, 662.

[39] Van Buren, 13f.

[40] S. N. Kramer, *Enmerkar and the Lord of Aratta* (1952), 15, lines 136–140; *idem, History Begins at Sumer* (1958), 297.

[41] *Idem, Enki and Ninhursag. BASORSup*, 1 (1945), 11, lines 13-17; *idem, History*, 196; H. Gross, *Die Idee des ewigen und allgemeinen Weltfriedens im alten Orient und im AT. TrThSt*, 7 (1956), 19.

[42] Gilg. XI, 190f.

lamb.''[43] Wolves (*barbarū*[44]), lions, leopards, panthers, etc. were among the game hunted by the king and the nobles of the empire. An amulet from Arslan Tash depicts the ''lamb-slayer,'' a she-wolf with the tail of a scorpion, in the act of devouring children.[45] Lamashtu is called a ''she-wolf'' (*barbarat*); she is the demon of childbed fever and murders suckling infants.[46]

Parts of a wolf's body play a role in the preparation of drugs.[47] In omens, too, the wolf has various functions.[48] The wolf plays an important part in Wisdom Literature.[49]

3. *Arabia and Palestine*. In Arabia and Palestine, the wolf was feared on account of its dangerous attacks on flocks. In periods of drought, wolves would invade the settled regions from the Syrian desert or Transjordan. The danger they presented is described by Oppian: ''A sheep trembles even when the wolf is dead.''[50] Wolves hunted during the night, hiding in the rocks during the day.[51] Despite the fact that wolves were dangerous and bloodthirsty, a shepherd was expected to be able to ward off the attack of a single wolf on his flock; thus according to Jewish law he was liable for any losses in this case. Only if the flock was attacked by two wolves, or by a lion, a bear, or the like, was he absolved of liability.[52]

Arabic traditions in Kazwīnī and Ibn al-Baiṭar mention medicinal and superstitious uses of portions of wolves' bodies.[53] The South Arabian tribe *al-ḏi'āb*, ''the wolves,'' was feared as a wild and rapacious tribe throughout all of South Arabia. Its leaders are called *Abu*, ''father.''[54] The Mandeans consider the wolf as dangerous as lions, thieves, fire, and flood. It symbolizes the enemy of the faith. Finally, an apostate is punished by ''being delivered to the wolves.''[55]

III. Old Testament.

1. *Characteristics*. The wolf is considered fierce (*chādhadh*), ravenous (*ṭāraph*, Gen. 49:27; Ezk. 22:27), and devouring (Gen. 49:27). It sheds blood (*shāphakh dām*), destroys lives (*ʿābhadh n^e^phāshôth*), gets dishonest gain (*bātsaʿ betsaʿ*, Ezk. 22:27), and destroys (*shādhadh*) its prey (Jer. 5:6). Along with the panther, lion, and eagle/

---

[43] *KB*, VI/2 (1915, repr. 1970), 118f.

[44] Cf. *AHw*, I, 106b.

[45] Cf. Akkadian Lamaštu, *WbMyth*, 276.

[46] *AHw*, I, 106b.

[47] Cf. *KAR*, 186, 35; *CAD*, II, 109b.

[48] A. Goetze, *Old Babylonian Omen Texts*. *YOSBT*, 10 (1947), 56, III, 3; CT 40, 42d, 15ff.; further references in *CAD*, II, 109.

[49] Cf. *BWL*, 186; 194 r, 13; 196, 17; 207, 13; 216, 22; 218, 55; for a wolf in a Namburbi ritual, see R. Caplice, ''Namburbi Texts in the British Museum II,'' *Or*, 36 (1967), 17.

[50] *Cynegetica* iii.282ff.

[51] Bodenheimer, *Animal Life*, 110.

[52] *AuS*, VI, 233f.

[53] J. Ruska in *Enzyklopädie des Islam*, I (1913), 998.

[54] J. Schleifer, in *ibid.*

[55] Mandean Book of John 47:8.

vulture, it symbolizes a nation that is bitter (*mar*), hasty (*nimhar*), dread (*'āyôm*), terrible (*nôrā'*), and violent (*chāmas*) (Hab. 1:8; cf. Jer. 5:6). According to Zeph. 3:3; Ezk. 22:27, the wolf symbolizes the violent and greedy judge or official.

The so-called "wolves of the evening" (*ze'ēbhê ʿerebh,* Hab. 1:8; Zeph. 3:3) are the product of textual corruption: instead of *ze'ēbhê ʿerebh,* Hab. 1:8 should be read *ze'ēbhê ʿarābh* or *ʿarābhāh,* following the LXX (*lýkoi tḗs Arabías*); cf. Jer. 5:6. Zeph. 3:3 should also be read "wolves of the desert," or, following Elliger's suggestion, *ze'ēbhîm lō' ʿāzebhû gerem* [*labbōqer*].

2. *Symbolizing Benjamin.* In the tribal oracle Gen. 49:27, Benjamin is "a ravenous wolf, in the morning [still] devouring the prey, and at evening [once more] dividing the spoil." The ravenous (*ṭāraph*) wolf, greedy for prey (*ʿadh*) and spoil (*shālāl*), is so successful that he has food for the whole day and even has spoil left over to divide in the evening. This ravenous, rapacious, insatiable, and successful wolf is obviously meant to point up certain ideals or virtues of the tribe of Benjamin: courage, aggressiveness, success in spoliation (*shālal*), and generosity in distributing the spoil. Formal, substantial, and historical considerations have rightly led scholars to ascribe the tribal oracle to a very early period: the nomadic period,[56] the period of the judges,[57] or before the battle of Deborah, around 1200 B.C.[58] Benjamin's military prowess is well attested (Jgs. 3:15ff.; 20:3ff.; 2 S. 2:15f.; etc.); it is hardly likely that particular reference to raids on caravans is intended.[59] The generous distribution of spoil, like that described in 1 S. 30:26ff., where David's generosity to the elders of Judah is told, is probably to be interpreted as meaning that Benjamin wished thereby "to be looked upon as the military leader of the tribes and perhaps to be recognized as prince."[60] Whether the animal metaphors in the tribal oracles derive ultimately from totemistic ideas is uncertain; equally hypothetical is the derivation of the tribal oracles from self-predications used in celebrations of the tribal league or amphictyony.[61]

3. *Symbolizing Enemies.* In Jer. 5:1-6, an announcement of judgment upon Jerusalem and its rulers, the punishment is executed by enemy troops, symbolized by wild beasts: "Therefore a lion from the forest shall slay them (*hikkām*), a wolf from the desert (*ze'ēbh ʿarābhôth*) shall destroy them (*yeshādhedhēm*), a leopard is watching (*shōqēdh*) against their cities; every one who goes out of them shall be torn to pieces (*yiṭṭārēph*)" (Jer. 5:6a). The multitude of their transgressions (*rabbû pishʿêhem*) and the greatness of their apostasies (*ʿātsemû meshûbhôthêhem*) are mentioned explicitly as the reason for the punishment (v. 6b).

According to the oracle in Hab. 1:5-11, Yahweh is "rousing the Chaldeans, that

---

56 G. Fohrer, *History of Israelite Religion* (trans. 1972), 32.

57 O. Procksch, *Genesis. KAT,* I (2,3 1924), 285.

58 Zobel, 25, 107f.

59 Gunkel, Gressmann.

60 Zobel, 26; cf. 107f., with additional bibliography.

61 A. Weiser, *Psalms. OTL* (trans. 1962), 489, n. 1; cf. A. H. J. Gunneweg, *ZAW,* 76 (1964), 247, 254.

bitter and hasty nation (*haggôy hammar vᵉhannimhār*), . . . dread and terrible (*'āyôm vᵉnôrā'*)'' (vv. 6f.). In their rapid and sudden raids, attacks, and incursions, the forces of these conquerors resemble beasts of prey: ''Their horses are swifter than leopards (*nᵉmērîm*), more fierce than the 'desert' wolves (conj. *zᵉ'ēbhê ʿᵃrābhāh*); their horsemen press proudly on . . . like an eagle (*nesher*) swift to devour (*chash le'ᵉkhôl*)'' (v. 8). Leopard, desert wolf, and eagle/vulture conjure up a vivid picture of the ''bitter,'' ''hasty,'' ''dread,'' and ''terrible'' character of this nation and its violence (*chāmās*).

4. *Symbolizing Social Classes.* Zeph. 3:1-4 is an invective against the various classes of the rebellious and oppressing (*mōrᵉ'āh, yônāh*) city of Jerusalem. In v. 3 the officials (*śārîm*) are called ''roaring lions'' and the judges (*shōphᵉṭîm*) ''wolves that leave no bone'' (conj. *zᵉ'ēbhîm lō' ʿāzᵉbhû gerem*[62]) or ''desert wolves that gnaw bones until morning'' (*zᵉ'ēbhê ʿᵃrābhāh garᵉmû labbōqer*). Since the lion is restricted to the first-named higher officials (*śārîm*), the rebuked judges (*shōphᵉṭîm*) are identified with wolves. The imagery of beasts of prey—lions, wolves—is intended to characterize the violence and greed of these officials and their abuse of power and office with respect to the less powerful, although this is not stated explicitly.

Ezk. 22:23-31 presupposes a knowledge of Zeph. 3:1-5, 6-8, elaborating freely on the invective. Of the five corrupt classes, the princes (conj. *nᵉśî'îm;* Zeph.: *śārîm*) are compared to roaring lions (v. 25) and the officials (*śārîm;* Zeph.: *shōphᵉṭîm*) to wolves tearing the prey (*kiz'ēbhîm ṭōrᵉphê ṭāreph*) (v. 27), ''shedding blood, destroying lives to get dishonest gain.'' In substance, both the princes (*nᵉśî'îm*) and the officials (*śārîm*) are accused of the same thing: injustice and corruption; both are therefore compared to ''ravenous'' beasts of prey. In line with their social rank, the lion image is reserved for the *nᵉśî'îm,* while the subordinate officials (*śārîm;* Zeph.: ''judges'') are castigated by means of the lower-ranking image of the wolf. These wolfish officials were violent (*ṭāraph*); in their greed (*bātsaʿ*) they did not shrink from shedding blood (*shāphakh dām 'abbēdh nᵉphāshôth*). In this retrospective discourse on the different classes, directed against princes, priests, officials, prophets, and rural nobles, Ezekiel (or one of his pupils?[63]) seeks to bring the exiles, suffering God's judgment, ''to real humility under God's righteous judgment.''[64]

5. *Peace among Animals.* In Isaiah's description of the peaceful messianic kingdom (Isa. 11:1-10), there recur many ancient Near Eastern notions of an idyllic period at the beginning of history, a time when there were as yet no snakes, scorpions, hyenas, lions, wild dogs, and wolves, no fear, no terror.[65] In the paradisal land of Dilmun, the lion does not kill, the wolf does not snatch the lamb, and the wild dog does not devour the kid.[66] According to Isa. 11:6-8, the peaceful kingdom of the future king

---

[62]Elliger, 173f.; *idem, ATD,* XXV (⁶1967), 75.
[63]W. Zimmerli, *BK,* XIII (1969), 522.
[64]*Ibid.,* 523.
[65]Enmerkar and the Lord of Aratta, lines 136-140; see II.2 above.
[66]Enki and Ninhursag, lines 15-17.

of salvation will find visible expression in the restoration of the original order of creation, including harmony between man and beast, and thus security.

> 6 The wolf shall dwell with the lamb, and the leopard shall lie down with the kid; the calf and the young lion shall "fatten" (conj. *yimreʾû* for *ûmerîʾ*) together, and a little child shall lead them. 7 The cow and the bear shall be friends (conj. *tithrāʿeynāh* for *tirʿeynāh*); their young shall lie down together; and the lion shall eat straw like the ox. 8 The sucking child shall play over the hole of the asp (*pethen*), and the weaned child shall put his hand on the adder's (*siphʿônî*) den. 9 They shall not hurt or destroy in all my holy mountain. . . .

According to Lev. 26:3ff.; Ezk. 34:25, 28; and Isa. 35:9; 65:25, the wild beasts will be exterminated so that men may dwell in safety. In this idyll of peace among the animals those very beasts that now endanger domestic animals and men are singled out as living in harmony: the deadly and ravenous wolf will dwell with the lamb, the leopard with the kid, the young lion with the calf, the bear with the cow. Is it the prophet's purpose to declare that the coming age of peace will witness a real transformation of animal nature and instinct, that the lion will really eat chopped straw? Hardly! What is crucial is the promise of total peace, the cosmic scope of which is represented in the vivid picture of peace among the animals. The righteousness and peace of the messianic age of salvation will also bring "quietness and trust" (Isa. 32:17). While the ancient Near East visualized the ideal primordial age as a cosmos without wild beasts, without danger and anxiety, hope projected this primordial age into the coming eschaton of peace. Isaiah, however, did not draw the logical conclusion that there would be no wild animals at the eschaton; instead he interpreted the age of peace as including a new harmony between the wild animals (wolf, leopard, young lion, bear, adder, and viper) and the domestic animals, and even the suckling child. The prophet's concern is for the ideal situation in which "they shall not hurt or destroy" any more (v. 9). According to Trito-Isaiah (Isa. 65:16b–25), in the coming age of salvation "the former troubles will be forgotten and hid . . ." (v. 16b); the sound of weeping and the cry of distress will no longer be heard (v. 19b); men shall be "the offspring of the blessed of Yahweh" (v. 23). This picture of the age of salvation (vv. 19b–24) concludes with a slightly altered quotation of Isa. 11:6 from the more detailed idyll of peace among the animals (11:6–9, secondary).

6. *zeʾēbh as a Personal Name*. The name *zeʾēbh* (LXX *Zēb*) is attested for a Midianite prince (Jgs. 7:25; 8:3; Ps. 83:12 [Eng. v. 11]); cf. Old Bab. *Zibu*, Nab. *zʾbw*(?), and OSA *Dʾb*. According to an ancient local tradition (Jgs. 7:25), the two Midianite princes Oreb ("raven") and Zeeb ("wolf") were killed by the Ephraimites at "raven rock" and "wolf wine press."

Botterweck

זָבַח zābhach; זֶבַח zebhach

Contents: I. 1. Etymology; 2. Verb; 3. Noun; 4. Related Terms. II. Background: 1. Origin; Ancient Near East; 2. Pagan *zebhach* in Israel. III. Forms: 1. The Ancient Festival Ritual; 2. The Simple Ritual; 3. Concluding Sacrifice. IV. History: 1. The *zebhach* at Rural Sanctuaries; 2. The *zebhach(-sh^{e}lāmîm)* in the Jerusalem Temple; 3. Modern Sacrificial Practice. V. Significance: 1. The Meal and its Preparation; 2. Sacrificial Motifs: Honor, Thanksgiving; 3. Effect of the *zebhach*: the Presence of Yahweh, Good, Joy, Propitiation, Appeasement; 4. Myth and Ritual; 5. Social Significance. VI. Punishment at the Hands of Yahweh.

I. 1. *Etymology*. The root *zbḥ* is found in all Semitic languages; the extrabiblical occurrences are semasiologically more or less similar to Heb. *zbḥ*. Several cognates cannot be defined precisely: the Akkadian noun *zību* (verb *zebû*), the majority of whose

---

zābhach. A van den Branden, "Lév 1-7 et le Tarif de Marseille, CIS I. 165," *RSO*, 40 (1965), 107-130; W. Burkert, *Homo necans. RVV*, 32 (1972), 10-14; J. Casabona, *Recherches sur le vocabulaire des sacrifices en Grec* (Gap, 1966); A. Charbel, *Il sacrificio pacifico* (Jerusalem, 1967); *idem*, "La portata religiosa degli š^{e}lāmîm," *RivBibl*, 18 (1970), 185-193; *idem*, " 'Shelamim' nei documenti di Elefantina," *BeO*, 12 (1970), 91-94; K. W. Clark, "Worship in the Jerusalem Temple after A.D. 70," *NTS*, 6 (1959/60), 269-280; F. Crüsemann, *Studien zur Formgeschichte von Hymnus und Danklied in Israel. WMANT*, 32 (1969); K. Elliger, *Leviticus. HAT*, 4 (1966); L. R. Fisher, ed., *Ras Shamra Parallels*, I. *AnOr*, 49 (1972); O. H. Gates, "The Relations of Priests to Sacrifice before the Exile," *JBL*, 27 (1908), 67-92; L. Ginzberg, *The Legends of the Jews*, I-VII (1909-1938); G. B. Gray, *Sacrifice in the OT* (1925, ^{2}1971); A. Guttmann, "The End of the Jewish Sacrificial Cult," *HUCA*, 38 (1967), 137-148; H. Haag, *Vom alten zum neuen Pascha. SBS*, 49 (1971); M. Haran, "The Uses of Incense in the Ancient Israelite Ritual," *VT*, 10 (1960), 113-129; *idem*, "The Passover Sacrifice," *Studies in the Religion of Ancient Israel. SVT*, 23 (1972), 86-116; H. Hubert, *Sacrifice, Its Nature and Function* (trans. 1964); J. Jeremias, *Die Passahfeier der Samaritaner. BZAW*, 59 (1932); K. Koch, "Wesen und Ursprung der 'Gemeinschaftstreue' im Israel der Königszeit," *ZEE*, 5 (1961), 72-90; R. Kriss and H. Kriss-Heinrich, *Volksglaube im Bereich des Islam*, I-II (1960-1962); S. Łach, "Antiquité du rituel des sacrifices (Lev. 1, 1-7, 35)," *Rozniki Teologiczno-Kanoniczne*, 14 (1967), 19-38; *idem*, "Le sacrifice zebaḥ-š^{e}lamîm," *Folia Orientalia*, 11 (1969), 187-197; *idem*, *Rozwój ofiar w religii starotestamentowej. Sprawy Biblijne*, 24 (Poznán, 1970); J. C. Lawson, *Modern Greek Folklore and Ancient Greek Religion* (1910, ^{2}1964), x, 265f., 322f., 326; W. Leslau, *Falasha Anthology. YJS*, 6 (1951); B. A. Levine, *In the Presence of the Lord. StJLA*, 5 (1974); D. Lifchitz, "Un sacrifice chez les Falachas, Juifs Abyssins," *La Terre et la Vie*, 9 (1939), 116-123; A. Loisy, *Essai historique sur le sacrifice* (1920); V. Maag, "Erwägungen zur dtr Kultzentralisation," *VT*, 6 (1956), 10-18; J. Milgrom, "The Alleged Wave-Offering in Israel and in the Ancient Near East," *IEJ*, 22 (1972), 33-38; A. de Nicola, "La Pasqua dei Samaritani," *BeO*, 13 (1971), 49-56; M. P. Nilsson, *A History of Greek Religion*, I (trans. ^{2}1949); W. O. E. Oesterley, *Sacrifices in Ancient Israel* (1937); A. F. Rainey, "The Order of Sacrifices in OT Ritual Texts," *Bibl*, 51 (1970), 485-498; R. Rendtorff, *Studien zur Geschichte des Opfers im Alten Israel. WMANT*, 24 (1967); L. Rost, "Erwägungen zum israelitischen Brandopfer," *Von Ugarit nach Qumran. Festschrift O. Eissfeldt. BZAW*, 77 (^{2}1961), 177-183 = *Das kleine Credo und andere Studien zum AT* (1965), 112-19; *idem*, "Weidewechsel und altisraelitischer Festkalender," *ZDPV*, 66 (1943), 205-215 = *Das kleine Credo*, 101-112; R. Schmid, *Das Bundesopfer in Israel. StANT*, 9 (1964); J. Sint, "Schlachten und Opfern," *ZKTh*, 78 (1956), 194-205; L. Sirard, "Sacrifices et rites sanglants dans l'AT," *Sciences Ecclésiastiques*, 15 (1963), 173-197; N. H. Snaith, "The Sprinkling of Blood," *ExpT*,

occurrences suggest the use of incense;[1] Ya'udic *zbḥ*;[2] Saf. *ḏbḥ*;[3] both the latter suggest animal sacrifice. Phoen.-Pun. *zbḥ* is more distantly related to Heb. *zbḥ*: only

82 (1970/71), 23f.; *idem,* "The Verbs zābaḥ and šaḥaṭ," *VT,* 25 (1975), 242-46; W. B. Stevenson, "Hebrew 'Olah and Zebach Sacrifices," *Festschrift A. Bertholet* (1950), 488-497; R. J. Thompson, *Penitence and Sacrifice in Early Israel Outside the Levitical Law* (1963) (cf. the review of P. Wernberg-Møller in *JSS,* 10 [1965], 89-92); R. de Vaux, *Studies in OT Sacrifice* (trans. 1964); J. Wellhausen, *Reste arabischen Heidentums* (²1897, ³1961); R. B. Wright, *Sacrifice in the Intertestamental Literature* (diss., Hartford Seminary Foundation, 1966); E. Zenger, *Die Sinaitheophanie. FzB,* 3 (1971).

On II: A. Bertholet, *Die Stellung der Israeliten und der Juden zu den Fremden* (1896), 152-176; A. Capuzzi, "I sacrifici animali a Cartagine," *Studi Magrebini,* 2 (1968), 45-76; A. Caquot, "Un sacrifice expiatoire à Ras Shamra," *RHPR,* 42 (1962), 201-211; A. Charbel, "Il sacrificio di communione presso i Cartaginesi," *BeO,* 12 (1970), 132-37; *idem,* "Sacrificio di communione presso gli Assiri-Babilonesi?" *BeO,* 13 (1971), 135-140; *idem,* "Il sacrificio di communione in Ugarit," *BeO,* 14 (1972), 133-141; M. Dietrich and O. Loretz, "Beschriftete Lungen- und Lebermodelle aus Ugarit," *Ugaritica,* VI (1969), 165-179; W. Eisenbeis, *Die Wurzel* שלם *im AT. BZAW,* 113 (1969), 8f., 293f.; R. Frankena, *Tākultu; de sacrale Maaltijd in het assyrische Ritueel. CO,* 2 (1954); *idem,* "New Materials for the Tākultu Ritual; Additions and Corrections," *BiOr,* 18 (1961), 199-207; D. Gill, "Thysia and šelamim," *Bibl,* 47 (1966), 255-262; J. M. Grintz, " 'Do not Eat on the Blood,' " *ASTI,* 8 (1972), 78-105; H. Kümmel, *Ersatzrituale für den hethitischen König. StBT,* 3 (1967); E. Lipiński, "Banquet en l'honneur de Baal," *UF,* 2 (1970), 77-88; S. E. Loewenstamm, "mṣd," *UF,* 3 (1971), 357-59; J. C. de Moor, "The Peace-Offering in Ugarit and Israel," *Schrift en Uitleg. Festschrift W. H. Gispen* (1970), 112-17; M. Noth, *Leviticus. OTL* (trans. ²1977); M. H. Pope, "A Divine Banquet at Ugarit," *The Use of the OT in the New and Other Essays. Festschrift W. F. Stinespring* (1972), 170-203; E. Townsend-Vermeyle, *Götterkult. Archaeologia Homerica,* III/5 (1974), 95-100; L. Ziehen, "Opfer," *PW,* XXXV (1939), 579-627; P. J. van Zijl, *Baal. AOAT,* 10 (1972), 88-92.

On IV: G. Amadon, "Important Passover Texts in Josephus and Philo," *Anglican Theological Review,* 27 (1945), 109-115; G. Bornkamm, "Lobpreis, Bekenntnis, und Opfer," *Apophoreta. Festschrift E. Haenchen. BZNW,* 30 (1964), 46-63 = *idem, Geschichte und Glaube. BEvTh,* 48 (1968), 122-139; A. Caquot, "Purification et expiation selon le ps LI," *RHR,* 169 (1966), 133-154; A. Charbel, "*Todah* como 'Sacrifício de Açâo de Graças,' " *Atualidades Bíblicas. Festschrift J. J. Pedreira de Castro* (Petropolis, 1971), 105-114; R. Dobbie and H. H. Rowley, "Sacrifice of Morality in the OT," *ExpT,* 70 (1958/59), 297-300, 341f.; R. Dussaud, *Les origines cananéenes du sacrifice israélite* (Paris, 1921, ²1941); H. Gunkel and J. Begrich, *Einl. in die Psalmen. GHK,* sup. vol. (1933); M. Haran, "Zebaḥ hayyamim," *VT,* 19 (1969), 11-22; *idem,* "*Zbḥ ymm* in the Karatepe Inscription," *ibid.,* 372f.; H.-J. Hermisson, *Sprache und Ritus im altisraelitischen Kult. WMANT,* 19 (1965); J. Jeremias, *Kultprophetie und Gerichtsverkündigung in der späteren Königszeit Israels. WMANT,* 35 (1970), 125-27; O. Keel, "Erwägungen zum Sitz im Leben des vormosaischen Pascha und zur Etymologie von פֶּסַח," *ZAW,* 84 (1972), 414-434; P. Laaf, *Die Pascha-Feier Israels. BBB,* 36 (1970); M. Möller, "Gebet und Kerygma in den Psalmen," *ThV,* 3 (1971), 11-29; S. Mowinckel, *The Psalms in Israel's Worship* (1962), II; E. Olávarri, "El calendario cúltico de Karatepe y el Zebaḥ Hayyamym en I Sam," *EstBíb,* 29 (1970), 311-325; J. M. Robinson, "Die Hodajot-Formel in Gebet und Hymnus des Frühchristentums," *Apophoreta. Festschrift E. Haenchen. BZNW,* 30 (1964), 194-235; H. H. Schmid, *Gerechtigkeit als Weltordnung. BHTh,*

continued on p. 10

[1] *CAD,* XXI, 84, 105f.

[2] *KAI,* 214.15-22.

[3] G. Ryckmans, "Le sacrifice ḎBḤ dans les inscriptions Ṣafaïtiques," *HUCA,* 23 (1950/51), 431-38.

one text refers to animal sacrifice;[4] elsewhere *zbḥ* is a general term for sacrifice, so that a priestly title can also be derived from it.[5] On the other hand, Ugar. *zbḥ* is very similar to Heb. *zbḥ*: the verb and the noun refer to a sacrificial ritual comprising slaughtering, a libation, and a meal[6] or a festival meal at which meat was consumed.[7] Hebrew and Ugaritic also share corresponding word pairs such as *dbḥ/ʿšrt* = *zbḥ-mʿśr*.[8] A polyglot vocabulary[9] equates Ugar. *da-ab-ḫu* with Sum. *ezen,* "festival"; like Ugar. *dbḥ,* Akk. *isinnu* refers to both cultic festivals and noncultic festivities characterized by lavish banquets.[10]

---

40 (1968), 100–102; F.-E. Wilms, *Das jahwistische Bundesbuch in Ex 34. StANT,* 32 (1973), 170f.

On V: P. A. H. de Boer, "An Aspect of Sacrifice," *Studies in the Religion of Ancient Israel. SVT,* 23 (1972), 27–47; H. Cancik, "Das jüdische Fest," *TüThQ,* 150 (1970), 335–348; A. Charbel, "Virtus sanguinis non expiatoria in sacrificio *šelāmîm,*" *Sacra Pagina, I. BETL,* 12–13 (1959), 366–376; J. Heller, "Die Symbolik des Fettes im AT," *VT,* 20 (1970), 106–108; W. Herrmann, "Götterspeise und Göttertrank in Ugarit und Israel," *ZAW,* 72 (1960), 205–216; K. Kerényi, "Die griechische Idee des Opfers," in *Antike Religion* (1971), 124–137; G. Klinzing, *Die Umdeutung des Kultus in der Qumrangemeinde und im NT. StUNT,* 7 (1971), 34–41; L. Köhler, *OT Theol.* (trans. 1957); E. Kutsch, "Das sog. 'Bundesblut' in Ex 24, 8 und Sach 9, 11," *VT,* 23 (1973), 25–30; *idem, Verheissung und Gesetz. BZAW,* 131 (1973); B. A. Levine, "Prolegomenon," in G. B. Gray, *Sacrifice in the OT* ([2]1971), vii–xlvi; A. Lods, "Israelitische Opfervorstellungen und -bräuche," *ThR,* 3 (1931), 347–366; A. Loisy, "La notion de sacrifice dans l'antiquité israélite," *RHLR,* N.S. 1 (1910), 1–30; E. W. Nicholson, "The Interpretation of Exodus XXIV 9–11," *VT,* 24 (1974), 77–97; *idem,* "The Antiquity of the Tradition in Exodus XXIV 9–11," *VT,* 25 (1975), 69–79; F. Nötscher, "*Das Angesicht Gottes schauen*" (1924, [2]1969), 98–119; W. J. O'Rourke, "Israelite Sacrifice," *AER,* 149 (1963), 259–274; L. Perlitt, *Bundestheologie im AT. WMANT,* 36 (1969), 181–203; E. L. Peters, "Aspects of the Family Among the Bedouin of Cyrenaica," in M. F. Nimkoff, ed., *Comparative Family Systems* (1965), 121–146, esp. 123, 139; N. Rabban, "לפני ה," *Tarbiz,* 23 (1951/52), 1–8; G. von Rad, *OT Theol.,* I (trans. 1962), 250–262; J. Reindl, *Das Angesicht Gottes im Sprachgebrauch des AT. ErfThSt,* 25 (1970), 24–36, 219–225; F. Schnutenhaus, "Darstellung der Theophanie in Israels Gottesdienst durch Töne, Rauchwolke, und Licht?" *Jahrbuch für Liturgik und Hymnologie,* 8 (1963), 80–83; E. Schürer, *A History of the Jewish People in the Time of Jesus Christ* (trans. 1891), II/1, 299f.; W. R. Smith, *Lectures on the Religion of the Semites* ([3]1927) (cf. Thompson, 1–18; E. O. James, *Sacrifice and Sacrament* [1962], 17–20); N. H. Snaith, "Sacrifices in the OT," *VT,* 7 (1957), 308–317; A. B. du Toit, *Der Aspekt der Freude im urchristlichen Abendmahl* (1965); G. Wehmeier, *Der Segen im AT. Theol. Diss.,* 6 (1970), 152f.; A. Wendel, *Das Opfer in der altisraelitischen Religion* (1927).

On VI: P. D. Hanson, "Zech 9 and the Recapitulation of an Ancient Ritual Pattern," *JBL,* 92 (1973), 37–59; A. Lods, "Eléments anciens et éléments modernes dans le rituel du sacrifice israélite," *RHPR,* 8 (1928), 399–411; H.-M. Lutz, *Jahwe, Jerusalem und die Völker. WMANT,* 27 (1968), 71–74, 84–91; L. Sabottka, *Zephanja. BietOr,* 25 (1972), 33–35.

[4] *KAI,* 26.

[5] *DISO,* 71: זבח III: Sacrificer=Sacrificial priest.

[6] *CTA,* 14 [I K], 71–78, 160–170; cf. RS 24.260 = *Ugaritica,* V (1968), 586–88.

[7] *CTA,* 15 [III K], VI, 5; 1 [VI AB], IV, 28.

[8] *CTA,* 16 [II K], 39–41; Dt. 12:6, 11; cf. Fisher, *s.v. zbḥ.*

[9] RS 20.123 . . . = *Ugaritica,* V, 244f.

[10] *AHw,* I, 388; *CAD,* VII, 195–97; J. Renger, "*isinnam epēšum*: Überlegungen zur Funktion des Festes in der Gesellschaft," *CRRA,* 17 (1970), 80–85; H. G. Güterbock, "Some Aspects of Hittite Festivals," *ibid.,* 175–180.

Likewise similar to Heb. *zbḥ* are OSA *ḏbḥ,* "offer animal sacrifice,"[11] and Ethiop. *zabḥa,* "slaughter, sacrifice."[12] The root is still current in Arab. *ḏabaḥa,* "slaughter, sacrifice."

2. *Verb.*

a. The verb *zābhach* occurs in the qal 113 times: 25 in legal contexts, including 9 in Leviticus and 10 in Deuteronomy, 5 times with *zebhach* as the object and 7 times absolutely; 88 in nonlegal contexts, 28 times with *zebhach* as the object and 38 times absolutely.[13]

The verb occurs 22 times in the piel, never in a legal context. Once it has *zibhchê-shᵉlamîm* as its object (2 Ch. 30:22); 19 times it appears absolutely.

b. In the sense of "slaughter (an animal)," the verb can refer to both what a butcher does (Dt. 12:15, 21; Ezk. 34:3) and what is done by someone who slaughters an animal as part of a religious ritual.

The course of a *zebhach* ritual is described in 1 K. 19:21 (cf. Dt. 16:6f.): the animal is "taken" (*lāqach*) and "slain" (*zābhach*); its flesh is "boiled" (*bšl* piel), "given" (*nāthan*), and "eaten" (*'ākhal*); the people "arise" (*qûm*) and "go" (*hālakh*). Dt. 27:7 contains the series *zābhach, 'ākhal,* and *śāmach,* "rejoice." The vocabulary of the ritual also includes:[14] *qārā',* "call, invite (to the sacrificial meal)" (Gen. 31:54, etc.);[15] *shāphakh,* "pour out (the blood)" (Dt. 12:27). Lev. 3 describes the *zebhach-shᵉlāmîm* ritual as follows: the animal is "brought" (*qārabh* hiphil) to the place of sacrifice; hands are "laid" (*sāmakh*) upon its head; it is "killed" (*shāchaṭ*); its blood is "thrown" or "sprinkled" (*zāraq*) against the altar;[16] pieces of its fat are "burned" (*qṭr* hiphil).[17] In addition, *zābhach* (as well as the paronomasias *zābhach zebhach* and *zābhach zᵉbhāchîm*) can refer to the totality of what the participants in the ritual do: "sacrifice" an animal or "offer sacrifice." As a rule, this refers to performance of the *zebhach* ritual. But the verb can also be used for the performance of more complex rituals (Ex. 5:3 following Ex. 24:5)[18] and for other types of sacrifice (Ex. 20:24; Josh. 8:31); it can even refer to human sacrifice (Ezk. 16:20; Ps. 106:37f.) and murder (1 K. 13:2; 2 K. 23:20; see VI).

Details: In Ex. 20:24, *vᵉzābhachtā* has to be rendered twice in translation: "You shall 'celebrate'... your *ʿōlôth* and your *shᵉlāmîm,* you shall sacrifice your sheep and your oxen." In Ex. 23:18, *zābhach* appears to be limited to what is done with the

---

[11] M. Höfner, *WbMyth,* I, 520f.; G. Ryckmans, "Sud=arabe m ḏ b ḥ t = hébreu m z b ḥ et termes apparentés," *Festschrift W. Caskel* (1968), 253-260.

[12] *LexLingAeth,* 1048f.

[13] Somewhat different statistics will be found in R. Schmid, 20, 23f.

[14] Rendtorff, 145-48, 153-161; Oesterley, 90-94.

[15] Cf. C. Rabin, "Etymological Miscellanea," *ScrHier,* 8 (1961), 399.

[16] Cf. Snaith, "Sprinkling."

[17] Cf. Sirard, 180f.; Haran, "Uses," 116-18.

[18] Cf. Zenger, 136.

blood: " 'offer' the blood of my sacrifice" (Haran translates instead: " 'celebrate' my bloody *zebhach*"[19]). In the piel, *zbḥ* means "sacrifice regularly or repeatedly, be given to sacrificing,"[20] or "hold sacrificial meals (repeatedly)."[21] It refers to the practicing of an illegitimate cult (19 times, especially in the Deuteronomistic condemnation formula in 1 K. 22:44 [Eng. v. 43b]; 2 K. 12:4[3]; 14:4; 15:4, 35; cf. 1 K. 3:2f., etc.) and the regular activity of the Levites in performing the *zebhach-sheʾlāmîm* (2 Ch. 30:22). According to Jenni, the piel in 1 K. 8:5 (= 2 Ch. 5:6) cannot be explained iteratively; Schmid makes reference to the size of the sacrifice and suggests an intensive meaning for the piel.[22]

3. *Noun.*

a. There are 160 occurrences of *zebhach,* 53 of which are in legal contexts, including 34 in Leviticus. Among these, *zebhach-sheʾlāmîm* occurs 29 times. The sacrificial list in Num. 7 uses *zebhach-sheʾlāmîm* 13 times.[23] The following compounds occur: *zebhach-sheʾlāmîm,* "peace(?)-offering," 48 times; *zebhach-tôdhāh,* "thank-offering," 6 times; *zebhach-hayyāmîm,* "yearly sacrifice," 3 times; *zibhchê-tsedheq,* "right sacrifices," 4 times; *zebhach-mishpāchāh,* "family sacrifice," 1 S. 20:29; *zibhchê-mēthîm,* "sacrifices offered to the dead," Ps. 106:28; *zibhchê-theʾrûʿāh,* "sacrifices with shouts of joy," Ps. 27:6; *zibhchê-rîbh,* "feasting(?) with strife," Prov. 17:1.

b. The word *zebhach* is the name of a specific ritual, namely, animal sacrifice, but it can refer also to the celebration of the ritual (sacrificial festival or meal) or the animal sacrificed (or its flesh). Only in Ex. 10:25; 18:12; Ezk. 40:42; 44:11 does the word refer to the animals while they are still alive. Only in 2 Ch. 7:12 (*bêth zebhach* in the sense of "temple") is *zebhach* used for "sacrifice" or "cult" in general. Everywhere else the notion of sacrifice is expressed by a series of specific rituals (or ritual objects, as in Hos. 3:4) comprising at least two members: Lev. 7:37; Dt. 12:6; Isa. 1:11; Prov. 15:8; etc. In particular, the doublet *ʿôlāh-zebhach* occurs frequently (Ex. 10:25; Dt. 12:6; 1 S. 15:22; Hos. 6:6; etc.).[24] In the priestly literature, we almost always find the combination *zebhach-(hash)sheʾlāmîm;* of its 48 occurrences, only 6 are outside P.[25]

Details: In Ex. 24:5, either *zeʾbhāchîm*[26] or *sheʾlāmîm*[27] is secondary. The fat of the slaughtered animals is referred to by *zebhach-hashsheʾlāmîm* in Nu. 6:18, by *zeʾbhāchîm* in 2 Ch. 7:1. In 1 S. 11:15 *sheʾlāmîm* is not original.[28] In Prov. 17:1, *zibhchê-rîbh* means "sacrificial meat with strife," the meat having been taken home.[29]

---

[19]Haran, "Passover Sacrifice," 98.
[20]E. Jenni, *Das hebräische Piʿel* (1968), 205-207.
[21]H. W. Wolff, *Hosea* (trans. 1974), 86.
[22]R. Schmid, 24.
[23]For detailed statistics, see R. Schmid, 20, 25f.
[24]Rendtorff, 57f.; R. Schmid, 26.
[25]Rendtorff, 149-151.
[26]*Ibid.,* 150f.
[27]Zenger, 75.
[28]Rendtorff, 150.
[29]Cf. Philo *Quaest. in Gen.* i.62.

Others translate the phrase as "feasting with strife."[30] Hos. 13:2 is a *crux interpretum.*[31]

4. *Related Terms.* The root *ṭbḥ* and *šḥṭ* are semasiologically related to *zbḥ*. The verb *ṭābhach* means "slaughter (animals), slay (men)"; it never appears in a cultic context. In Isa. 34:6, *zbḥ* and *ṭbḥ* are used in parallelism. The verb *shāchaṭ* means "slaughter (animals)," almost always in a cultic context; more rarely, it means "slay, execute (men)" or "sacrifice (children)." In Lev. 17:1-7; Isa. 66:3; Ezk. 44:11, *zābhach* and *shāchaṭ* stand in juxtaposition. The regulations governing priestly sacrifice in Leviticus use *shāchaṭ* 34 times as a sacrificial term, *zābhach* only 7.

II. Background.

1. *Origin; Ancient Near East.*

a. The question whether Israel practiced *zebhach* sacrifice as early as the nomadic period or introduced it after settlement cannot be decided with certainty: animal sacrifice belongs as much to pastoral culture as to the culture of the Canaanite towns. The period without sacrifice in the wilderness mentioned in Am. 5:25 and Jer. 7:22[32] is to be understood in the context of Deuteronomistic theology,[33] not historically. The Canaanite *zᵉbhāchîm* mentioned in the OT are also known from Ugaritic and Phoenician texts. Pagan *zᵉbhāchîm* are mentioned in the Yahwistic, Elohistic, and Deuteronomistic histories: Nu. 25:2f. (cf. Ps. 106:28; Hos. 9:10); 22:40; Jgs. 9:27(?); 16:23; 2 K. 10:18-27.[34]

b. Egyptian has an extraordinary wealth of sacrificial terminology.[35] The most important words are: *ʿ3b.t,*[36] "offerings, contributions," usually for the gods, often a large sacrifice, "hecatomb"; *wdn.(t),*[37] "offering," used for both the concrete offerings and the general action; *ḥby.t,*[38] often used as a superscription for offerings, something like "festival offering," with the stipulation *n.t ỉmny.t,* "perpetual offering"; *ḥnk.t,*[39] a special form of sacrifice (particularly at cornerstone layings) consisting of two jugs of water and animal heads, also used in the general sense of "offering."

---

[30]See W. A. van der Weiden, *Le livre des Proverbes. BietOr,* 23 (1970), 70; *CTA,* 4 [II AB], III, 19f.; Homer *Odyssey* xx.311-19.

[31]Cf. the commentaries; R. Schmid, 24, n. 13; Fisher, No. II, 408.

[32]Cf. Ginzberg, VI, 94f.

[33]W. Thiel, *Die deuteronomistische Redaktion von Jeremia 1-25. WMANT,* 41 (1973), 121-28.

[34]For the subsequent history, see Sozomen's *Ecclesiastical History* ii.4.

[35]Cf. *WbÄS,* VI, 114.

[36]*WbÄS,* I, 167.

[37]*Ibid.,* 392.

[38]*WbÄS,* III, 61.

[39]*Ibid.,* 118.

The most important term, used in the stereotyped offering formula and in the common sacrificial ritual, is *ḥtp(ṭ),*[40] "offering slab, altar."

Information about the Egyptian sacrificial system in the funerary cult and temple cult is found primarily in the following sources: offering lists, i.e., written lists of tributes offered to make enduring magical provision for the material needs of the dead and the gods; endowment lists, lists of offerings in kind, which are called "donation inventory" or "property summary"; offering slabs of stone or metal, often decorated with representations of the various offerings; mortuary and temple reliefs with scenes depicting the presentation of offerings, sometimes accompanied by texts; festival calendars, especially the detailed specimens in the Ptolemaic temples, which list the particular offerings of the festival liturgies. The enormous variety of sacrificial worship under Rameses III is detailed in the long endowment lists of the great Papyrus Harris; it must be remembered that these endowments were also meant to provide security for the immense temple personnel.

Egyptian sacrifice is by nature a meal.[41] Three times a day "the god is brought to his food," corresponding to the three daily meals already attested in the Pyramid texts.[42] The most important is the morning offering, which takes place in the temple after the image of the god has been cleansed and adorned; there is a roughly similar ceremony in the mortuary cult.[43] The "laying of the offerings" on the altar ("lifting of the offerings" in the mortuary cult), accompanied by the invitation "Come to this your bread, come to this your roast," etc., is followed by a concluding censing and aspersion of the offerings, having the character of a consecration. On the offering table (which developed out of the small offering slab and survives as an altar in the temple[44]) are found all kinds of breads, cakes, fruits, roast geese, etc., which constitute the daily food of the gods and of the dead. Even in the Old Kingdom a large variety of sacrificial animals is attested: cranes, geese, ducks, doves and all kinds of young birds, oxen, cows and calves, oryxes, gazelles, ibexes, stags, hyenas, hedgehogs, and rabbits.[45] A sequence of six or seven scenes illuminates the way the animals were slaughtered; especially popular are representations of the severing of an ox's foreleg, which was considered the choicest sacrificial portion of the animal. The extremely frequent pictures of the killing of geese recall the fact that geese were the animals most commonly sacrificed. The larger animals were slaughtered in special "abattoirs" on the temple grounds; geese and smaller animals were apparently killed in front of the offering table. Whole-offerings of animals were probably made only on the major feasts, while normally selected pieces were offered, especially the head, foreleg, and ribs.

The slaughtering is associated with a symbolism that becomes the primary focus in the late period: the killing of the animal is interpreted as the destruction of an evil being.[46] Thus the sacrificial animals are understood as embodying enemies of the gods.

---

[40]*Ibid.,* 183.
[41]*RÄR,* 547ff.
[42]Pyr. 404.
[43]*RÄR,* 554ff.
[44]*Ibid.,* 557ff., 15ff.
[45]L. Klebs, *Die Reliefs des Alten Reiches. AHAW,* 3 (1915), 120.
[46]H. Junker, "Die Schlacht- und Brandopfer und ihre Symbolik im Tempelkult der Spätzeit," *ZÄS,* 48 (1911), 69–77.

An ancient saying that accompanies the sacrifice of a bull in the presence of Osiris reads: "For you I strike him who struck you, as an ox."[47] All kinds of features associated with Seth (e.g., red color) are ascribed to the sacrificial animals. In this context we find even sporadic sacrifices of swine, which were normally prohibited.[48] The various representations of "striking the enemy," with the sacrifice depicted as a kneeling man (or as a group of kneeling persons), apparently attest the same symbolism. Whether these representations reflect the actual practice of human sacrifice in the historical period is a matter of debate.[49] In the majority of cases, both interpretations of the sacrifice can be combined: the victim represents both nourishment and the enemy of the god. The meal of the god consists of his slain enemy. When special emphasis is placed on the destruction of the enemy, true burnt-offerings are found.[50] Only on extraordinary occasions is the entire animal burned; for most burnt-offerings, certain portions only are burned or merely roasted. In either case, furthermore, the smell can have a beneficent effect ascribed to it. A text from Edfu[51] attests ambiguity of sacrifice in the late period: "The slaughtery is furnished with the enemy in the form of all the beasts of the desert in order to make your altar festive, so that their burning fat may rise to the limits of the heavens."

In the interpretation of sacrifice, two different tendencies are at work. On the one hand, even in the earliest texts almost all concrete offerings are interpreted mythologically as the eye of Horus, the vital organ of the god. On the other hand, especially in the later period, we find symbolic offerings such as an image of *maat,* a symbol of life, etc. In both cases the cosmic function of the offering is emphasized.

It is the most important duty of the king to establish and multiply the offerings, both for the gods and for his royal ancestors. The very order of the cosmos depends on his performance of this function. In all the temple scenes, therefore, the pharaoh appears as the only legitimate agent of the sacrifice; according to the formula *ḥtp dỉ nśw.t,*[52] every offering, even in the mortuary cult, is viewed as a royal offering. Sacrifice serves as a necessary link between the divine and human worlds, between the realm of the living and the realm of the dead. The offering scenes in the temple emphasize in word and picture that sacrifice is an element in the constant interaction between the divine world and the pharaoh, the human world. One and the same offering is to be understood as a simultaneous expression of obligation, thanksgiving, expectation, and promise.[53] The entire context is illuminated greatly by the *maat*-offerings, which contain in microcosm the highly specialized offerings of the late period.[54]

The cheerfulness and joy that naturally mark the sacrificial situation and are espe-

---

[47]H. Kees, *Ägypten. Religionsgeschichtliches Lesebuch,*[2] ed. A. Bertholet, 10 (1928), No. 60.

[48]Cf. Book of the Dead, chap. 112.

[49]Junker, *loc. cit.; RÄR,* 452ff.

[50]*RÄR,* 123ff.

[51]*Urk.,* VII, 102.

[52]See W. Barta, *Aufbau und Bedeutung der altägyptischen Opferformel. ÄF,* 24 (1968).

[53]Cf. S. Morenz, *Egyptian Religion* (trans. 1973), 95ff.

[54]J. Bergman, "Zum 'Mythus vom Staat' im Alten Ägypten," *The Myth of the State,* ed. H. Biezais. *SIDA,* 6 (1972), 83ff.

cially emphasized, for example, when the offerings involve wine, beer, or musical instruments, find expression in vocal and instrumental music, as well as in dancing.[55]

In wisdom instructions and idealized biographies, sacrifice is often mentioned as a meritorious action. We read simply the command, "Sacrifice to your God,"[56] or, in greater detail, "Provide richly for the libation table, and offer many loaves; increase the regular offering; this will benefit him who does so."[57] In Merikare we also find a passage that is strikingly reminiscent of Hos. 6:6, but shows at the same time that we are not dealing with an either/or: "The thoughts of the man whose attitude is right are more acceptable than the ox of the man who does wrong. Do something for God, that he may do the like for you, through great offerings that richly furnish the altar. . . ."

Bergman

c. There are no comprehensive monographs devoted to the Babylonian sacrificial system; some fundamental questions therefore still are unresolved. The following points serve only as a preliminary survey. The common Akkadian word for "sacrifice" is *niqû* (noun) or *naqû* (verb).[58] The basic meaning was probably "libation" or "pour out." Nevertheless, the substantive is used primarily of offerings that are not liquid.[59]

Since blood did not play any role in the Mesopotamian cult,[60] this usage cannot refer to the spilling of blood in the course of a sacrifice. The word *nindabû* refers to grain-offerings, bread-offerings, or freewill-offerings.[61] The term *naptanu* refers to sacrifice as a (festal) meal of the god.[62] The word *zību,* which is connected etymologically with *zebhach,* and the verb *zebû* are comparatively rare; according to Zimmern,[63] it is a West Semitic loanword, while *CAD* treats it as originally Akkadian.[64] It is found as early as Hammurabi, being used as a synonym of *mākālû,* "foodstuffs."[65] There are also other terms for sacrifice, e.g., *qurrubu,* "bring near, present," and *šumḫuru* or *muḫḫuru,* "offer." "Slaughter" is *ṭabāḫu,* rarely *nakāsu.*[66]

As can be seen from the word *naptanu* (and another word, *tākultu,* from *akālu,* "eat"), sacrifice was viewed primarily as provision of food for the gods. Gilg. XII, 162 tells how, after the deluge, the hungry gods gather like flies about Utnapishtim as

---

[55]H. Kees, *Der Opfertanz des ägyptischen Königs* (1912).

[56]Wisdom of Ani, 7, 12.

[57]Merikare, 65f.

[58]*AHw,* II, 744f., 793.

[59]For Old Assyrian, see H. Hirsch, *Untersuchungen zur altassyrischen Religion. BAfO,* 13/14 (^{2}1972), 62-64.

[60]A. L. Oppenheim, *Ancient Mesopotamia* (1964), 365, with reference to the *CAD* article *damu.*

[61]*AHw,* II, 790.

[62]*Ibid.,* 741f.

[63]H. Zimmern, *Akkadische Fremdwörter als Beweis für babylonischen Kultureinfluss* (^{2}1917), 66.

[64]*CAD,* XXI, 105f.

[65]CH § 3, 22, 33f.; § 4, 36f.

[66]*AHw,* II, 721a; for a general discussion, see also G. Furlani, *Il sacrificio nella religione dei Semiti di Babilonia e Assiria* (Rome, 1932).

he offers sacrifice. A late ritual from Uruk[67] describes the daily feeding of the god: two courses each morning and evening, the "large meal" and the "small meal." Like human meals, the sacrificial meal comprised meat, fish, beverages, and fruit.[68] As sacrificial animals oxen, calves, sheep, goats, and (rarely) gazelles are mentioned, as well as various birds and fish. Certain restrictions were also in force: birds, for example, could not be offered to the chthonic deities.[69] The meal included wine, beer, and other intoxicating beverages, as well as milk, honey, oil, and butter. Dates, onions, figs, grapes, and various baked goods are also mentioned.

The animals were slaughtered, their flesh was prepared (roasted or boiled), and it was set out ready to eat before the god on a table (or occasionally an altar). The drinks were poured out on the ground or into vessels. Only exceptionally were portions of the sacrifice burned. Incense and aromatics accompanied the meal. Obviously it was thought that the deity in some mysterious way drew sustenance from the offerings, either by looking at the foods presented or by having them moved back and forth before him.[70] Apart from the daily meals of the gods, there were special sacrifices offered by particular classes of priest (seers, incantation priests) or on particular occasions. Sacrifice was also offered to demons, the deified king, and the dead; the significance of ancestor sacrifices in Babylonia, however, remains unclear. The ritual texts collected by Thureau-Dangin describe a variety of different sacrifices.[71]

There is no evidence that those who offered the sacrifice shared table fellowship with the gods.[72]

In certain cases the sacrificial animal could be considered a substitute (*pūḫu, dinānu*) for the person offering it; in this way the wrath of the deity was appeased and sickness or disaster averted.[73]

Ringgren

d. In certain Phoenician texts,[74] *ṣwʿt* appears to correspond to *zebhach*. Ugar. *dbḥ* is an animal sacrifice including a sacrificial meal.[75] In *CTA*, 32, 34, 32f., *dbḥ* occurs in the context of a propitiatory ritual; Caquot supposes that in this case the entire animal was burned. The banquets of the gods that are called *dbḥ* also take the form of sacrificial meals.[76] At Ugarit, as in Israel, we find in addition to the *dbḥ*/*zbḥ* sacrifice

---

67F. Thureau-Dangin, *Rituels accadiens* (Paris, 1921), 74f.

68F. Blome, *Die Opfermaterie in Babylonien und Israel,* I (Rome, 1934).

69Oppenheim, *Ancient Mesopotamia,* 191.

70*Ibid.,* 191f.

71*Rituels accadiens.*

72Oppenheim, *Ancient Mesopotamia,* 191; Dhorme, however, claims to find traces of actual participation in sacrificial meals (*La religion assyro-babylonienne* [1910], 231f.); cf. Frankena, *Tākultu.*

73E. Dhorme, *Les religions de Babylonie et d'Assyrie. Mana,* I/1 (1945), 229f.

74*KAI,* 69 and 74; de Vaux, 45f.; Capuzzi, 64-72; Charbel, "Il sacrificio di communione presso i Cartaginesi."

75See I.1; Lipiński, 80; van Zijl.

76RS 24.258 = *Ugaritica,* V, 545-551; *CTA,* 1 [VI AB], IV, 28; Loewenstamm, Pope.

an obviously related *šlm(m)/šlmym* sacrifice.[77] The Ugaritic texts provide no clue as to whether the *dbḥ* included the burning of a portion for the deity.

From Ugarit to the Nabateans we find evidence of a cultic institution called *mrzḥ*.[78] These were sacrificial feasts in which wine played an important role; they were sponsored by cultic fellowships. Sifre Num. 131 on Nu. 25:2f. and possibly 1 S. 20:6, 29[79] suggest that these feasts mentioned in Am. 6:7 and Jer. 16:5 were related to or identical with the *zebhach*.

Additional parallels might be cited,[80] but the clearest is the ancient Greek sacrifice called *hiereíon* or *thysía,* "slaughtering, sacrifice, feast,"[81] because, like the *zebhach,* its ritual included the burning of portions of the sacrificial animal.[82] According to Rost and de Vaux,[83] *zebhach* and *thysía* are rooted in a common earlier culture, but R. Schmid[84] and Gill marshal considerable arguments in favor of a Greek origin for the Israelite practice of burning a portion of the sacrifice.

During the second century B.C. the Greek *thysía* gained a foothold in Palestine. To orthodox Jews, it was an abomination to partake of the flesh of pagan sacrifices (4 Macc. 5:2f.). They refused to eat the internal organs, part of which the Greeks ate themselves,[85] on the grounds that these belonged to Yahweh; therefore in 2 Macc. 6:7f., 21; 7:42[86] Greek sacrifice is called *splanchnismós,* "sacrificial meal," literally "eating of internal meats (offal)." In Christianity the partaking of sacrificial flesh (*hieróthyton;* in polemic, *eidōlóthyton*) was a point of controversy (Acts 15:29; 21:25; 1 Cor. 8; 10:14ff.; Rev. 2:14, 20).[87]

2. *Pagan zebhach in Israel.* Israelites are forbidden by sacral law to take part in pagan *z^ebhāchîm* (Ex. 34:15; cf. Ex. 22:19[20]; Lev. 17:7); but Ex. 18:12 speaks of cultic fellowship with the Midianites. The prohibition is a consequence of the exclusive worship of Yahweh. Transgressions of this law are mentioned only in rebukes from Deuteronomistic tradition (Dt. 32:17, 38; Ps. 106:28, 37f.; Bar. 4:7; cf. 1 Cor. 10:20), but these are probably based on historical fact. Equally justified are the charges of

---

[77]Eisenbeis; Charbel, "Il sacrificio di communione in Ugarit"; Fisher, No. I, 1; de Moor; Levine, *StJLA,* 5, 8-20.

[78]Pope, 190-94; J. Teixidor, "Bulletin d'épigraphie sémitique, 1971," *Syr,* 48 (1971), 458, 481.

[79]J. C. Greenfield, "Un rite religieux araméen et ses parallèles," *RB,* 80 (1973), 48f.

[80]For Mesopotamia, cf. F. Nötscher, "Sakrale Mahlzeiten vor Qumran," *Lex tua veritas. Festschrift H. Junker* (1961), 156-165 = *Vom Alten zum Neuen Testament. BBB,* 17 (1962), 91-100; Charbel, "Sacrificio . . . Assiri-Babilonesi?" For ancient South Arabia, cf. J. Ryckmans, "Le repas rituel dans la religion sudarabe," in *Symbolae biblicae et Mesopotamicae F. M. T. de Liagre Böhl dedicatae. StFS,* 4 (1973), 327-334. For a general presentation see G. Widengren, *Religionsphänomenologie* (trans. 1969), 303-320.

[81]Casabona, 28ff., 126ff.

[82]Ziehen, Burkert, Townsend-Vermeyle.

[83]De Vaux, 48-51.

[84]Pp. 90-94.

[85]Homer *Odyssey* iii.461; Ziehen, 616-19.

[86]M. Hengel, *Judaism and Hellenism* (trans. 1974), I, 299; II, 202.

[87]F. Büchsel, "εἴδωλον," *TDNT,* II, 375ff.; G. Schrenk, "ἱερόθυτος," *TDNT,* III, 252f.

having adopted pagan practices: the eating of blood along with meat, for which the Philistines are rebuked in Zec. 9:7, is spoken of in 1 S. 14:32–34 and Ezk. 33:25 (cf. Acts 15:29); Canaanite sexual rites are mentioned in Ex. 32:6; Hos. 4:14; 5:6f. In addition, the removal of sacrificial sites outside Jerusalem was not carried out by all (Josh. 22:23–29; Ezk. 18:6, 11, 15; 20:28; 22:9; 2 Ch. 33:17). The rejection of pagan sacrifice accounts first for P's extension of Israelite ritual to resident aliens (Nu. 15:14–16),[88] and then for its extension to other peoples and the postulate of its universal validity (Isa. 19:21; 56:6–8; Zec. 9:6f.).

The following texts involve particular problems of interpretation:

a. In Lev. 17:1–7, the utopian legislation that requires *all* animals to be slaughtered at the temple is supported by stigmatizing the contrary practice as an impious cult[89] or by rejection of the cult attested in 2 K. 23:8.[90] Rendtorff[91] takes a different approach, arguing that the purpose of the text is to convert the *zebhach,* which exhibits pagan features, into the legal *zebhach-sh^{e}lāmîm* at the temple.

b. According to Grintz, Lev. 19:26 refers to a *zebhach* that is associated with the practice of divination. He likewise includes Lev. 17:5 and 1 S. 14:34 in this category and makes reference to corresponding Greek sacrifices to chthonic (1 S. 14:32: *'ortsāh*) powers, worshipped at night (1 S. 14:34: *hallaylāh*). M. Saebø interprets 1 S. 14:32–34 differently, as an abrogation of the illegitimate custom in time of war of eating beasts of burden with their blood.[92]

c. The *zibhchê-mēthîm* of Ps. 106:28 may be *z^{e}bhāchîm* in the context of a mortuary cult (cf. Dt. 26:14 and RS 24.323);[93] but it is also possible that here the term already has its later meaning of "sacrifice to idols" in general.[94]

d. Prov. 7:14ff. probably does not presuppose any connection between *zibhchê-sh^{e}lāmîm* and some sexual rite; the young man is merely invited to eat the rest of the sacrificial meat and come to bed.[95]

III. Forms.

1. *The Ancient Festival Ritual.* Any reconstruction of how a *zebhach* was actually carried out must be fragmentary and in part hypothetical. Because there is no detailed description of an actual sacrifice, we are forced to rely on sources of varying nature

---

[88]Bertholet.
[89]Elliger.
[90]Noth.
[91]P. 120.
[92]M. Saebø, *Sacharja 9-14. WMANT,* 34 (1969), 198f.
[93]Dietrich and Loretz, 172f., 176.
[94]*Aboth* iii.3; *Aboda zara* ii.3; Jub. 22:17; Sib. 8:384.
[95]B. Lang, *Die weisheitliche Lehrrede. SBS,* 54 (1972), 91-96; Thompson, 105f., 227f.

(legal, narrative, and poetic texts) and varying date. An attempt to reconstruct a model based on what is recorded in 1 S. 1-2 yields the following sequence: Elkanah goes from Ramathaim to the cultic center at Shiloh, about a day's journey. He takes his whole family with him: his two wives, along with all his sons and daughters. They have with them a three-year-old bull, together with a sack of flour and a skin of wine (1 S. 1:24). They have already performed certain preparatory rituals, among which sexual abstinence plays a major role (1 S. 16:5; 21:5f.[6f.]). At Shiloh, Elkanah slaughters the bull at the sanctuary and throws its blood[96] against the altar, which stands outdoors. With the aid of the priest or his assistants, who are merely sanctuary attendants, several rituals are performed: specified fat portions (cf. Lev. 3:3f., 9f., 14f.; 7:3f.; the fat tail of the sheep was a later addition[97]) are removed and burned on the altar.

What additional rites were performed (the burning of a cereal-offering, incense, and libation are suggested by Lev. 7:12f.; Nu. 15:1ff.;[98] prayers, blessings, hymns, and music are mentioned in 1 S. 9:13; Ps. 27:6; Am. 5:23[99]) and what part the priest played[100] are not known precisely. The flesh is boiled in vessels of earthenware or metal (Lev. 6:28; cf. Ezk. 24:3-5). The priest receives a portion of the boiled meat, and perhaps bread as well (Lev. 7:12-14). Then Elkanah distributes the meat to his family (including his wives and children, Neh. 12:43) and perhaps also to the needy as well (Ps. 22:27[26]; Philo *De spec. leg.* i.221; Ep. Jer. 27;[101] cf. also the Koran, Sura 22:28, 36). The meat is eaten at once, in halls near the temple (1 S. 1:9 conj.; 1:18 LXX?; 9:22[102]). The meal includes wine and beer (1 S. 1:13-15). It is joyful in character (*śmḥ*, Jgs. 16:23; Dt. 12:7; 1 S. 11:15; Philo *Quaest. in Gen.* i.63[103]); the cultic rejoicing probably begins with the meal (cf. Isa. 22:13; 65:13; Eccl. 3:12f.; 8:15). Two passages mention the number of guests (*qᵉrûʾîm,* "those invited"): 30 in 1 S. 9:22 and 200 in 2 S. 15:11 (cf. the 3000 in Jgs. 16:27). A man would have to be very rich to sponsor a large sacrificial feast (Dt. 33:19). The feast probably came to an end the next day; whatever was left of the sacrificial flesh was burned on the spot (Lev. 7:16f.).

The sacrificial animals mentioned include cattle (→ בקר *bāqār*) and small livestock (→ צאן *tsōʾn*), including both sheep and goats (*gᵉdhî,* 1 S. 10:3).[104] Bulls (*shôrîm*) are mentioned only in Hos. 12:12(11), possibly in the context of pagan sacrifice.[105]

2. *The Simple Ritual.* For many *zᵉbhāchîm* in the OT we can postulate the ritual attested in 1 S. 1-2; Gen. 31:54; Nu. 22:40; 2 Ch. 18:2. Above all, the festivals in

---

96 Rendtorff, 145-47.
97 Elliger, 52.
98 Haran, "Uses," 113f.
99 Sirard, 181-86.
100 Rendtorff, 164f.; Gates; Ginzberg, VI, 219.
101 Ginzberg, II, 231.
102 J. P. Brown, "Mediterranean Vocabulary of the Vine," *VT,* 19 (1969), 153-53.
103 Cf. H. Conzelmann, "χαίρω," *TDNT,* IX, 362f.
104 Rendtorff, 148f., 161f.
105 D. Grimm, "Erwägungen zu Hosea 12:12 'in Gilgal opfern die Stiere,'" *ZAW,* 85 (1973), 339-347.

whose context a king was acclaimed belong in this category (1 S. 11:15 [cf. 9:12f.]; 16:3, 5; 2 S. 15:12; 1 K. 1:9, 19, 25). For many other occasions, however—entertainment of guests (1 S. 28:24; 1 K. 19:21), social occasions[106] (Ex. 5:8)—we should think in terms of a simpler ritual. The simplest ritual probably consisted only of pouring off the blood[107]—everything else was omitted. This simple ritual was preserved following the Deuteronomic reform as the code governing secular slaughtering (Dt. 12:15f., 21-25; 15:22f.): a cultic law became a cultural law.

3. *Concluding Sacrifice*. In the Priestly Document, we find the *zebhach(-sh^e^lāmîm)* as the concluding sacrifice of the Feast of Weeks (Lev. 23:19f.), of ordinations (Ex. 29:19-34; Lev. 8:22-32[108]), of a new priest's first official function (Lev. 9), and of the ceremony marking the completion of a Nazirite's separation (Nu. 6:14-20). These rituals consist of the sequence: sin-offering, burnt-offering, *zebhach-sh^e^lāmîm;* we may therefore presume that this was the structure of public sacrificial observances.[109] While only priests took part in the sacrificial meal of the Feast of Weeks, the concluding *z^e^bhāchîm* on other occasions provided food for all the participants in the celebration (1 K. 8:62f.; 1 Ch. 29:21f.; 2 Ch. 7:4f.; 30:24). It is possible that Lev. 23:37 and Ex. 23:17f. presuppose such sacrificial celebrations (although Ex. 23:18 could refer to Passover[110]).

IV. History.

1. *The zebhach at Rural Sanctuaries*. In the period before centralization of the cult, the ancient festival ritual[111] was undoubtedly practiced at all the rural sanctuaries. The *zebhach* was usually the private sacrifice of small groups (as an annual sacrifice, sacrifice of the first-born, thank-offering). But we also read of larger sacrificial feasts involving larger groups: Dt. 33:19 (peoples or tribes); 1 S. 9:12 (a city); perhaps 2 K. 10:19 should be included here. Presumably these larger feasts had a more complex ritual than the private sacrifices (cf. 2 K. 10:24f.). A special form of *zebhach* is the *pesach* sacrifice celebrated in small groups.

a. An annual sacrificial festival of a clan or family is attested in 1 S. 1:21; 2:19; 20:6, 29, the *zebhach-hayyāmîm,* "yearly sacrifice," or *zebhach-mishpāchāh,* "family sacrifice."[112] Here we should perhaps also include 1 S. 9[113] and Am. 4:4.[114] The clan as a sacrificial community is also attested in *KAI* 69.16. It is reasonable to suppose

---

[106]Nilsson, 145; Casabona, 30, 143.
[107]Wellhausen, 117f.; Loisy, *Essai,* 454f.
[108]Leslau, xxiii.
[109]Rainey, 497f.; H. Ewald, *Die Alterthümer des Volkes Israel* (1848), 135-37.
[110]See IV.1.d.
[111]See III.1.
[112]Rendtorff, 134f.; Haran, "Zebaḥ."
[113]Haran, "Zebaḥ," 17-19.
[114]H. W. Wolff, *BK,* XIV/2 (1969), 259.

that the sacrifice was celebrated at an arbitrarily chosen new moon (1 S. 20:18, 24;[115] cf. Isa. 1:13; Hos. 2:13[11]; → חדשׁ *chādhāsh*).

Diverging from this view, most scholars think *zebhach-hayyāmîm* was a term for the Feast of Booths.[116] Olávarri's attempt, on the basis of *KAI* 26, to interpret *zebhach-hayyāmîm* as a name for the Canaanite New Year Festival is disputed.[117]

b. According to Dt. 12:17f.; 14:23-26; 15:19-23 (and Gen. 4:4?[118]), the male firstlings of cattle were slaughtered and eaten as *zebhach*.[119] Later, the firstlings were treated as a temple tax, i.e., the worshipper does not receive any of the sacrificial flesh (Nu. 18:17-19; Neh. 10:37[36]).

c. From the Psalms[120] and other texts (Lev. 7:11-21; 22:21; 2 S. 15:7f.) we know of the *zebhach-tôdhāh*, "thank-offering" (of an individual), along with its variants, the *n^edhābhāh*, "freewill-offering," and *nēdher*, "vow."[121] Here belong also the private *z^ebhāchîm* on the occasion of religious festivals (Zec. 14:21; 2 Ch. 29:31-35; Neh. 12:43).

d. In Ex. 12:27; 34:25; Dt. 16:2-6 (and perhaps also Ex. 23:18[122]), the → פסח *pesach* is treated as a *zebhach* sacrifice; and the Chronicler's history assumes that the *pesach* was celebrated as a *zebhach-sh^elāmîm* (2 Ch. 30; 35:1-19; Ezr. 6:19-22)[123] with the burning of pieces of fat (2 Ch. 30:15; 35:12; Jub. 49:20; Mishnah *Pesaḥim* v.10; vi.1). Therefore *pesach* and *zebhach-sh^elāmîm* could be easily confused.[124] It remains uncertain whether the *pesach* began as an apotropaic blood ritual against demons and turned into a *zebhach* after Israel settled in Canaan,[125] and whether the burning of pieces of fat was part of the original ritual[126] or a later addition.[127]

2. *The zebhach(-sh^elāmîm) in the Jerusalem Temple.* The forms of the *zebhach* described in the preceding section were also practiced in the Jerusalem temple; until its destruction, they were celebrated in its outer court (Ps. 65:5[4]; 100:4; 116:19) as the private sacrifices of small groups.[128] Jeremiah appears to have celebrated such a private sacrifice with a Rechabite family, with the meal being held in a hall on the temple

---

[115]Lifchitz, 116.

[116]Cf., e.g., *AncIsr*, 495.

[117]Haran, "ZBḤ"; Teixidor, "Bulletin," 470f.; J. C. de Moor, *New Year with Canaanites and Israelites* (1972), II, 29f.; Levine, *StJLA*, 5, 132-35.

[118]Cf. Ginzberg, V, 137.

[119]Gray, 34f.; Stevenson, 496.

[120]See IV.2.d.

[121]Rendtorff, 135-37, 152f.

[122]Haran, "Passover"; Wilms.

[123]Laaf, 94-100, 139-141; Haag, 97-107.

[124]Mishnah *Pesaḥim* v.2; Maimonides *Mishneh Torah* viii/v.18.12; Amadon.

[125]Laaf; Keel; cf. Haran, "Passover," 89f.

[126]Rost, *Das kleine Credo*, 104; Haran, "Passover," 112-14.

[127]G. Beer, *Pascha. SgV*, 64 (1911), 48.

[128]Mishnah *Zebaḥim* v.6; H. Gese, "Ps 22 und das NT," *ZThK*, 65 (1968), 17ff.

grounds (Jer. 35). But great sacrificial ceremonies were also celebrated at the Jerusalem temple, with the *zebhach* as the conclusion.[129] In this case all the people took part in the sacrificial meal. The Feast of Weeks was an exception: at its concluding *zebhach* the entire cultic community acted as a sacrificial fellowship but not as a table fellowship: only the priests participated in the sacrificial meal (Lev. 23:20; Maimonides *Mishneh Torah* viii/v.1.4).

During the late monarchy, the *zebhach* became restricted by cultic law (Dt. 12; 2 K. 23) to the Jerusalem temple. "The ancient pastoral ritual had taken final refuge in the temple at Jerusalem; throughout the countryside it was now abolished."[130] (The *zᵉbhāchîm* in the Jewish temple at Elephantine constitute an exception.[131]) The ritual was modified through increased participation of the priests. The sources provide the following picture:

a. According to the draft of the law in Ezk. 40–48, performance of the *zebhach* ritual is a function of Levites (44:11) and temple ministers (46:24). The layman who comes to offer sacrifice merely hands over his animal and is given the cooked meat.[132]

b. In P, radical changes are observable: the name of the ritual is usually *zebhach-shᵉlāmîm;* the layman takes care of the slaughtering and dismembering of the sacrificial animal, while the priest takes over the sprinkling (→ זרק *zāraq*) of the blood; the portion for the priest is larger, and now includes the breast and right thigh (Lev. 7:28–36);[133] the *zebhach-shᵉlāmîm* occurs not only as an independent ritual, but as a component of more complex rituals.[134] The ritual of the *zebhach-shᵉlāmîm* is recorded in Lev. 3 and 7.[135]

While earlier writers[136] considered *zebhach, shᵉlāmîm,* and *zebhach-shᵉlāmîm* different terms for one and the same ritual, Rendtorff and Łach have suggested a more differentiated approach: The *zebhach-shᵉlāmîm* came into being through a combination of the *zebhach* and *shᵉlāmîm* rituals. In the process, the *zebhach* took on features of the solemn *shᵉlāmîm* offering, which had previously been exclusively royal and national.[137] The ritual of the *shᵉlāmîm* offering, however, can be reconstructed only hypothetically. It is always associated with the *ʿôlāh;* Rendtorff[138] takes it as the concluding sacrifice of the *ʿôlāh* and leaves open the question whether the sacrificial animal was burned or eaten. Łach,[139] on the contrary, thinks in terms of a sacrificial meal; in his view, the *shᵉlāmîm* offering was the public counterpart to the *zebhach.*

---

[129]See III.3.
[130]Maag, 17.
[131]Cf. *AP,* 30, 28, *ʿlwh wdbḥn*; Charbel, "Shelamim."
[132]As among the Falasha: Leslau, xxvii.
[133]Van den Branden, 116f.; Milgrom.
[134]See III.3.
[135]Rendtorff, 153-161.
[136]De Vaux, R. Schmid.
[137]Levine, *StJLA,* 5, 45-52.
[138]Pp. 123-133.
[139]Łach, *Roswój,* 82.

c. According to the Chronicler's history, *z^e^bhāchîm* took place as private sacrifices at the Jerusalem temple (2 Ch. 29:31; probably Neh. 12:43[140]). The Levites took part in the slaughtering (2 Ch. 30:17, 22). At public *z^e^bhāchîm* the entire cultic community took part in the sacrificial meal (1 Ch. 29:21; 2 Ch. 7:1-7; 33:16). Twice we find the term *zebhach-sh^e^lāmîm* instead of *zebhach* (2 Ch. 30:22; 33:16).

d. Following Dussaud[141] and Gunkel, most scholars assume that the *Sitz im Leben* of the individual thanksgiving hymns (such as Ps. 30; 118:5-19; 138; Isa. 38:10ff.; Jonah 2:3-10[2-9]; Sir. 51:1ff.) was the celebration of the *zebhach-tôdhāh* (Lev. 7:11ff.). (The *ʿôlāh* as a thank-offering is less common: Ps. 66:13, etc.[142])

The thank-offering is called *zebhach-tôdhāh* (Ps. 107:22; 116:17) or simply *tôdāh* (Ps. 50:23; 56:13[12]; 95:2; 100:1, 4). Besides the thank-offering, we find two other very similar types of sacrifice: the *nēdher,* "vow" (Ps 22:26[25]; 50:14; 56:13[12]; 61:9[8]; 65:2[1]; 66:13; 116:14, 18), and the *n^e^dhēbhāh,* "freewill offering" (Ps. 119:108; cf. 54:8[6]). The *zibhchê-th^e^rûʿāh,* "sacrifices with shouts of joy" (Ps. 27:6), are identical with the thank-offering.[143] What the *zibhchê-tsedheq,* "sacrifices of righteousness" or "right sacrifices" (Ps. 4:6[5]; 51:21[19]; Dt. 33:19; Sir. 7:31; semantically analogous to *zibhchê-rîbh,* Prov. 17:1, and *zibhchê-th^e^rûʿāh?*), are, we do not know;[144] perhaps we are dealing with *z^e^bhāchîm* celebrated with the correct intention (cf. Mal. 3:3).

The psalm was recited by a temple minister[145] or even by the layman offering sacrifice after an introductory libation (Ps. 116:13)[146] or when the sacrificial animal was given to Yahweh (cf. the *tôdhāh* formula in Ps. 30:2[1]; 118:21; etc.).[147]

The relationship between sacrifice and song underwent a transformation. Initially the song accompanied the sacrifice (Ps. 22:26f.[25f.]; 66:13-15); finally it took the place of the sacrifice (Ps. 69:31[30]; 1QH 2:20).[148] Alongside the tendency of the spoken word to supplant the *zebhach,* we also find it supplanted by keeping the commandments (Sir. 35:1-4) and a "broken heart" (Ps. 51:18f.[17f.]). The reasons for the subjective transformation of the private cult[149] in Ps. 51 can only be guessed; perhaps the distance of the temple in the Diaspora[150] or the inability of sacrifice to expiate capital offenses[151] played a role. From the Psalms we learn a few details about how sacrifice was understood: the worshipper knows that he is in communion with God and

---

140 Cf. Rendtorff, 142f.

141 Pp. 104-107.

142 Crüsemann, 265f.

143 H.-J. Kraus, *BK,* XV ([4]1972), *in loc.*

144 Cf. the commentaries; Dobbie; Koch; H. H. Schmid; Levine, *StJLA,* 5, 135f.

145 Mowinckel, 33f.; Maimonides *Mishneh Torah* viii/ii.3.2.

146 Mowinckel.

147 Cf. the *tôdhāh* formula in Ps. 30:2(1); 118:21; etc.; Crüsemann, 267-274.

148 Cf. Hermisson, 29-64; Möller, 15-19; Robinson.

149 Bornkamm, 54.

150 Caquot, "Purification."

151 H. H. Rowley, "The Meaning of Sacrifice in the OT," *BJRL,* 33 (1950/51), 98ff. = *From Moses to Qumran* (1963), 94ff.

is the recipient of God's grace (Ps. 4:6–9[5–8]; 22:27[26]; 23:5f.; 36:9f.[8f.]; 65:5[4]); sacrifice without an ethical stance on the part of the person offering it does not suffice (Ps. 40:7[6]);[152] to assume that Yahweh needs sacrificial flesh for nourishment is mistaken (Ps. 50:12f.).[153]

e. The use of *z^e^bhāchîm* in the intertestamental literature is discussed elsewhere.[154]

3. *Modern Sacrificial Practice.* The Jewish sacrificial system has survived only to a limited extent among the Samaritans in Palestine and the Falasha in Ethiopia. The Samaritans celebrate Passover as a sacrifice;[155] the Falasha have continued to practice a more extended sacrificial system down to the present.[156] In both groups we find the essential rituals of the biblical *zebhach.* There are survivals of ancient Greek and Arabic animal sacrifice in Islam[157] and in the churches (!) of the Near East.[158] A portion for the deity is never burned, but manipulations with blood frequently play a role.

V. Significance. The question of how the priests and worshippers conceived the significance of the individual rituals and the effect of the *zebhach* is difficult.[159] Ritual texts[160] do not provide any interpretation; apart from cryptic phrases like "Yahweh comes and blesses" (Ex. 20:24),[161] narrative and poetic texts likewise give no interpretation and leave open "a realm of silence and secrecy in respect to what God works in sacrifice."[162] Sacrifice refuses to allow for a simple analysis, because the conservative ritual embodies differences of place and time in the understanding of sacrifice, and also because each specific occasion contributes to the meaning of the sacrifice.

1. *The Meal and its Preparation.* The cultic celebration takes place *liphnê yhvh:* the worshippers sacrifice (*zabhach,* 1 S. 11:15), eat (Dt. 12:7), and rejoice (Dt. 12:12) "before Yahweh," i.e., within the temple precincts and in the presence of the deity.[163] "Eating in the presence of Yahweh" means being Yahweh's guest (semantic parallels: 2 S. 11:13; 1 K. 1:25): God is the *hestiátōr,* "host."[164] Fellowship with Yahweh presupposes the removal of uncleanness (Lev. 7:20; 2 Ch. 30:17; Jub. 49:9), conti-

---

152 Crüsemann, 258–263.

153 Hermisson, 35f.; J. Jeremias.

154 Cf. J. Behm, "θύω," *TDNT,* III, 186f.; O. Schmitz, *Die Opferanschauung des späteren Judentums und die Opferaussagen des NT* (1910); Oesterley, 252–267; Wright; Clark; Guttmann.

155 J. Jeremias; de Nicola.

156 Lifchitz, Leslau.

157 Cf. Koran, Sura 22:34–37.

158 Kriss and Kriss-Heinrich; Burkert, 16; Lawson; R. Schmid, 55–57; Haag, 54–57.

159 Cf. von Rad and the investigations of Lods, O'Rourke, and Levine.

160 Lev. 3 and 7; Philo *De spec. leg.* i.212–225; Mishnah *Zebaḥim.*

161 See F. Schnutenhaus, "Das Kommen und Erscheinen Gottes im AT," *ZAW,* 76 (1964), 18f.

162 Von Rad, 260.

163 Nötscher; Oesterley, 157–168; Rabban; Reindl.

164 Philo *De spec. leg.* i.221.

nence (1 S. 16:5; 21:5f.[4f.]), and if necessary fasting (cf. Jgs. 20:26), moral uprightness (Prov. 15:8; Hos. 8:13), and careful observance of the ritual (Lev. 7:18; 22:31f.). Only so will the sacrifice and the worshipper be acceptable to Yahweh (Ezk. 20:41; 43:27).[165] In complex rituals like Nu. 6:16f.; Ezk. 43:25-27; Ginzberg, III, 195-209, sin-offering and burnt-offering prepare for fellowship with Yahweh;[166] in the simple *zebhach,* purification and burning of the fat suffice.

The fat and the blood constitute the portion owed to Yahweh (Lev. 7:23-27).[167] The significance of pouring out the blood and burning the pieces of fat is unknown.

The earlier period thought of the blood and fat as food and drink for Yahweh (Lev. 3:11, 16; Dt. 32:38; Isa. 43:24; Ps. 16:4(?); Ps. 50:13),[168] but such an interpretation was later rejected (Ps. 50:12f.).[169]

Modern interpretations: Blood and fat are the focus of the animal's life and therefore belong to Yahweh;[170] the fat is a substitute for the entire animal, which belongs to Yahweh, and redeems it for use as food;[171] the pouring off of the blood was not a propitiatory ritual, but was probably only a way of getting rid of it;[172] it is unnecessary to suppose a primitive fear that spilled blood cries out for vengeance.[173]

The focus of the ritual is the meal, which is preceded by a table blessing (1 S. 9:13).[174] Whoever eats the holy (consecrated) flesh (*b^e śar qōdhesh,* Jer. 11:15; Hag. 2:12) boiled in "sacred" vessels (Zec. 14:21) has fellowship with Yahweh (cf. 1 Cor. 10:18-22); therefore participation in pagan sacrificial meals is forbidden. The flesh must be consumed within a specified sacred period (Lev. 7:15-18). Alongside the notion of holy food (also involved in the bread of the Presence, 1 S. 21:5-7[4-6]),[175] we also find the notion of the divine presence,[176] symbolized by the fire of the altar (Lev. 9:24; 2 Ch. 7:1)[177] and the rising smoke (Ex. 19:18).[178] God and man are mutually present: God acknowledges man, man acknowledges God—thus there comes into being a relationship of protection[179] and "friendship with God";[180] the worshipper knows that he is united with God and receives God's gifts (see IV.2.d).

In the history of exegesis, the *b^e rîth* concept has played an important role: every *zebhach* is interpreted as a covenant ceremony with Yahweh.[181] This notion, the theory

---

165 On the acceptance terminology of → רצה *rātsāh, rātsôn,* cf. Rendtorff, 253-260.

166 Rainey, 497f.; expiation-sanctification-fellowship; cf. Philo *Quaest. in Ex.* ii.32.

167 Snaith, 310-12.

168 Hermann, Heller.

169 A common motif: Clement of Alexandria *Strom.* vii.30-34; Origen *Contra Cels.* iv.32; Koran, Sura 22:37.

170 R. Schmid, 33f.

171 G. Gerleman, "Die Wurzel šlm," *ZAW,* 85 (1973), 12f.

172 Charbel, "Virtus"; Rendtorff, 146.

173 Maag, 15f.

174 Wehmeier.

175 Cf. de Boer, 27-36.

176 Wendel, 111f.; Kerényi, 132.

177 Levine, "Prolegomenon," xxxiii; Sirard, 186-190.

178 Zenger, 147; but cf. Schnutenhaus.

179 Köhler, 183.

180 Hugo Grotius on Lev. 3.

181 Wellhausen, 124.

maintains, is historicized in Ex. 24:1-11;[182] it appears in the postulated covenant festival of Ps. 50:5 and terminologically in the idiom *kārath b^e^rîth*, "cut a covenant," i.e., "dismember the sacrificial animal."[183] More recent interpretations of Ex. 24[184] and *kārath b^e^rîth*[185] no longer support this hypothesis. Only in Ps. 50 can *zebhach* probably be understood as an act of commitment to Yahweh.[186] The use of salt may have been understood as a commitment ritual.[187]

2. *Sacrificial Motifs: Honor, Thanksgiving.* A *zebhach* honors Yahweh (*kbd* piel, Isa. 43:23; Ps. 50:15, 23; 1 S. 2:29). As a form of private worship,[188] the *zebhach* is a natural expression of private devotion (cf. Ps. 4:6[5]: *bāṭach*); in addition to special occasions for sacrifice, it is always possible to worship Yahweh spontaneously with a *zebhach* (Lev. 7:16). Whoever acknowledges Yahweh expresses his devotion by celebrating *z^e^bhāchîm* (2 K. 5:17);[189] even a pagan might honor Yahweh at least outwardly with a *zebhach*.[190] Yahweh is also honored by a *zebhach* in response to a divine encounter experienced in a miracle (Jgs. 2:1-5; Ex. 3:18; 5:3) or in divine aid in one's personal life (votive offering: Lev. 7:16; 2 S. 15:7ff.).[191]

3. *Effect of the zebhach: the Presence of Yahweh, Good, Joy, Propitiation, Appeasement.* The *zebhach* effects Yahweh's presence in a special way. Yahweh gives benefits to the worshippers, although his gifts are not defined more closely; Ps. 4:7(6) refers to them as *ṭôbh*, "good, well-being."[192] The atmosphere of joy so emphasized in Deuteronomistic tradition[193] is both the rejoicing of a banquet and also rejoicing over the presence of Yahweh, which frees men of their cares (Ps. 4:6-9[5-8]; Plutarch *Ne suav. vivi posse sec. Epic.* 1101e-1102d). The meal is an expression of thanksgiving and of harmony with Yahweh,[194] just as fasting is a sign of lament, remorse, and petition (Jgs. 20:26; 1 S. 7:6; Neh. 1:4).

Other effects of the *zebhach* are occasionally attested:

a. Yahweh's presence may be invoked[195] so that he can be a witness to an agreement (Gen. 31:54)[196] or bring a revelation in a dream (Gen. 46:1f.; 1 K. 3:4f.).

---

[182] R. Schmid, 33; Loisy, "Notion," 14f. (but later rejected: *Essai*, 268f.).
[183] Dussaud, 217.
[184] Perlitt, 181-203; Kutsch, "Bundesblut"; Nicholson.
[185] Kutsch, *Verheissung*, 40-50.
[186] *Ibid.*, 98-101; cf. Sirard, 195.
[187] Lev. 2:13; Test. Levi 9:14; Lifchitz, 122; Elliger, 46; A. Jirku, *Von Jerusalem nach Ugarit* (1966), 185-88; → ברית *b^e^rîth*, IV.1.
[188] Wendel, 199-209.
[189] See II.2.
[190] Schürer.
[191] Thank-offering: see IV.2.d.
[192] See IV.2.d., Koch.
[193] See III.1.
[194] Du Toit, 11f., 56; Cancik, 344f.
[195] Wendel, 111f.
[196] Perlitt, 187f.

b. In Ex. 29:33 (concluding sacrifice following a *chaṭṭā'th* ritual), 1 S. 3:14 (unless one follows the NEB and translates "their abuse of *zebhach* and *minchāh* shall never be expiated"), 1QM 2:5, and 1QS 9:4,[197] a propitiatory effect is ascribed to the *zebhach*. As in Ezk. 45:15-17,[198] these passages appear to express a tendency to ascribe a propitiatory effect to all sacrifices.

c. In Ex. 5:3 (cf. 2 S. 24:25), the *zebhach* has an apotropaic or appeasing effect; this may be explained by the motif of the angry god (Canaanite Reshef), characteristic of the Yahwist.[199]

4. *Myth and Ritual*. The OT says nothing of any myth that establishes the *zebhach* and through which the *zebhach* ritual is performed. Like the sacrifices of the Arabs, the *zebhach* is noteworthy for having no associated mythology. Particular animal sacrifices, however, did not remain unassociated with myth. In Israel, Passover recalls the exodus; among the Arabs, the sacrifices of Abraham (Gen. 22)[200] and of Abel (Gen. 4)[201] are recalled. The sacrificial site, too, can be associated with mythological symbolism, e.g., being marked off by four stones that Moses ordered brought from the Red Sea.[202]

5. *Social Significance*. Frequently the texts lend expression only to the social aspect of the *zebhach*.[203] The table fellowship represents the solidarity of a group such as the clan,[204] a festal assembly,[205] or a group of conspirators.[206] The *zebhach* establishes solidarity with guests[207] and reconciles enemies (Gen. 31:54); therefore refusal of political fellowship implies refusal of table fellowship (Ex. 34:15).

The seating arrangement (1 S. 9:22; cf. Prov. 25:6f.; Lk. 14:8-11) and distribution of meat (1 S. 1:4f.; 9:23f.; cf. Homer *Odyssey* xiv.437-445) are determined by the social rank of the participants.

VI. Punishment at the Hands of Yahweh. In four texts *zbḥ* is used metaphorically of punishment at the hands of Yahweh.

a. In Jer. 46:10, *zābhach* means "slaughter, massacre," and is synonymous with the more frequent root → טבח *ṭābhach* (Jer. 12:3; 25:34; 48:15; 50:27; 51:40; Lam. 2:21; Ezk. 21:15, 20[10, 15]; Isa. 65:12). Both words designate total annihilation in

---

[197] Klinzing.
[198] Thompson, 233.
[199] Zenger, 136, 146.
[200] Koran, Sura 37:99-107; T. P. Hughes, *A Dictionary of Islam* (London, 1885), 193; M. Gaudefroy-Demombynes, *Le pèlerinage à la Mekke* (Paris, 1923), 277f.
[201] Kriss and Kriss-Heinrich, I, 199.
[202] Lifchitz, 119.
[203] Cf. *AuS*, VI (1939), 70-74; Smith, 265; Peters.
[204] See IV.1.a.
[205] See III.3.
[206] See III.2.
[207] *Ibid*.

war according to the practice of the ban (→ חרם *ḥrm* II), which is mentioned in the context (Jer. 25:9; 50:21, 26; 51:3).

b. In Isa. 34:6; Ezk. 39:17, 19; Zeph. 1:7, *zebhach* is used as a sacrificial term: the description of Yahweh's punishment mixes military images with images from the *zebhach* ritual. The images from the ritual are the killing of animals (Isaiah), and the inviting of guests followed by killing (Ezekiel, Zephaniah). The fertilization of the soil with blood and fat (Isa. 34:7)[208] and the exposure of corpses as carrion (Ezk. 39:17-20; cf. 2 S. 21:1-10; 1 K. 14:11; 16:4)[209] likewise have a ritual background. The images from the ritual are distorted; the guests "invited" by Yahweh to the feast are the soldiers "called up" against his enemies (*qārā'* in a double sense: Zeph. 1:7; Lam. 2:22);[210] it is not animals but men that are killed. In Isa. 34:6, Yahweh slaughters like the warlike goddess 'Anat,[211] but there is no close correspondence between the scenes.[212]

Lang

[208]Hanson, 47.
[209]Wellhausen, 121; Lods, 406.
[210]Sabottka.
[211]*CTA*, 3 [V AB], II, 17-41.
[212]Cf. Sabottka, 34.

זְבֻל *z^e bhul*

Contents: I. Etymology; Use in Ugaritic. II. Old Testament.

I. Etymology; Use in Ugaritic. There is no apparent semantic continuity between the Akkadian[1] and the Hebrew use of the root *zbl*. The Mari documents mention a

z^e bhul. W. F. Albright, "Zabûl Yam and Thâpiṭ Nahar in the Combat between Baal and the Sea," *JPOS*, 16 (1936), 17-20; *idem*, "The Psalm of Habakkuk," *Studies in OT Prophecy, Festschrift T. H. Robinson* (1950), 1-18; M. Dietrich and O. Loretz, "Zur ugaritischen Lexikographie, II," *OLZ*, 62 (1967), 533-552; G. R. Driver, "Ugaritic and Hebrew Words," *Ugaritica*, VI (1969), 181-86; M. Görg, "Die Gattung des sog. Tempelweihspruchs (1 Kg 8, 12f.)," *UF*, 6 (1974), 55-63; M. Held, "The Root ZBL/SBL in Akkadian, Ugaritic and Biblical Hebrew," *Essays in Memory of E. A. Speiser* (1968), 90-96; M. Limbeck, "Beelzebul-eine ursprüngliche Bezeichnung für Jesus?" *Wort Gottes in der Zeit. Festschrift K. H. Schelkle* (1973), 31-42; J. van der Ploeg, "Notes sur le Psaume XLIX," *OTS*, 13 (1963), 137-172; W. von Soden, "Die Fürstin (*zubultum*) von Ugarit in Māri," *UF*, 4 (1972), 159f.; M. Wagner, "Beiträge zur Aramaismenfrage im alttestamentlichen Hebräisch," *Hebräische Wortforschung. Festschrift W. Baumgartner. SVT*, 16 (1967), 355-371; W. A. Ward, "Notes on Some Semitic Loan-Words and Personal Names in Late Egyptian," *Or*, 32 (1963), 413-436, esp. 425f.

[1]Cf. Held, 90; *APNM*, 146f., 186; Wagner, 362-64.

zubultum, probably to be understood as the princess of Ugarit.[2] At Ugarit, the noun *zbl* stands in apposition before compound terms for various gods: *zbl b'l 'rṣ* (esp. common, par. *'l3yn b'l*),[3] *zbl mlk šmm,*[4] *zbl mlk 'llmy* (par. DN *ḥyly*);[5] before the name alone: *b'l,*[6] *yrḫ,*[7] *ym;*[8] after the name alone: *yrḫ zbl,*[9] *ršp zbl,*[10] and perhaps also *ḥyly zbl.*[11] It also appears as a genitive epithet of the (divine) throne: *kḥt zblk/hm.*[12] It also appears as a place name;[13] as an element, possibly theophoric, in two personal names, one Phoenician and the other Punic;[14] and as a frequently postulated *zbl* II, meaning "sick" or "sickness."[15] None of these latter usages has any bearing on the use of *z^ebhul* in the OT.

As a stereotyped epithet of the gods and as a designation of their "majesty," *zbl* signalizes the honor of the pantheon. The translation "prince" or "princess" should be taken in this sense.

II. Old Testament. Apart from a few personal names, *zbl* appears 5 times in the OT as a noun and once as a verb. In 1 K. 8:13 (par. 2 Ch. 6:2), *bêth z^ebhul lākh* stands in parallel to *makhôn l^eshibht^ekhā.* The only other occurrences of the phrase *mākhôn l^eshibht^ekhā* are in the (Deuteronomistic) prayer spoken by Solomon at the dedication of the temple (1 K. 8:39, 43, 49 [par. 2 Ch. 6:30, 33, 39]), Ps. 33:14, and Ex. 15:17. In Solomon's prayer, Yahweh's throne is expressly located in heaven; the context of Ps. 33:14 also places it there. Even where finite or infinitive forms of *yāshabh* or *mākhôn* are used of God, they point to a location beyond the earth either explicitly (Ps. 2:4; 123:1) or by context (1 K. 22:19 [par. 2 Ch. 18:18]; Isa. 40:22; Ps. 9:5 [Eng. v. 4]; 22:4[3]; 29:10; 47:9[8]; 102:13[12]; Lam. 5:19; cf. Ob. 3, with reference to arrogant power). Terms that are geographical, historical, architectural, and the like (Zion, the temple, cherubim, etc.) serve to focus the active presence of God (2 S. 6:2; Ps. 80:2[1]; 99:1; Isa. 6:1; Joel 4:12[3:12]; Ps. 9:12[11]; 68:17[16]; 132:14; cf. the polemic against misconstruing these expressions in a limiting sense in 2 S. 7:6 [par. 1 Ch. 17:5]; probably the only "neutral" example is 2 Ch. 2:2[3]). Ex. 15:17 expresses the same meaning in terms of ancient notions already attested at Ugarit.[16]

---

[2]Von Soden, 159f.

[3]See *UT,* No. 815; *WUS,* 878.

[4]*CTA,* 13, 26f.

[5]*CTA,* 22 [III Rp], B, 10.

[6]*CTA,* 2 [III AB], I, 38; IV, 8; 9 vo., 10.

[7]*CTA,* 19 [I D], 164.

[8]*CTA,* 2 [III AB], III, 8, 16, 21, 23; in the last passage, parallel to *ṯpṭ nhr,* cf. *UT,* No. 2727; Held, 91.

[9]*CTA,* 15 [III K], II, 4.

[10]*CTA,* 15 [III K], II, 6.

[11]*CTA,* 22 [III Rp], B, 9f.; cf. *CML,* 89.

[12]*CTA,* 2 [III AB], I, 24, 25, 28, 29; 16 [II K], V, 25.

[13]*PRU,* II, 84, 13.

[14]*KAI,* 34.4; 67.1f.; cf. *IPN,* 123.

[15]Cf. *UT,* No. 816; *WUS,* 878; Dietrich-Loretz, 538f.

[16]Cf. F. M. Cross and D. N. Freedman, "The Song of Miriam," *JNES,* 14 (1955), 237-250, esp. 249f.

The expression in 1 K. 8:13 is traditional (cf. the LXX and its setting in a quotation), using *z^ebhul* as a ceremonious term for Solomon's temple. The words *bānāh* and *bayith* refer to the material temple. Like *mākhôn l^eshibht^ekhā, z^ebhul* expresses its special relationship to God (cf. *zbl* at Ugarit!). The sun in the heavens, God in darkness (8:12; *ʿ^arāphel* is an element of the theophany; cf. the LXX of 8:53), the cloud and the *k^ebhōdh yhvh* (8:10f.), the description of the outward ceremonies in terms that render them absolute (8:1-9), exaggerate them (8:54-66), and expand on them (2 Ch. 6:41-7:1) exalt by literary means the temple built by human hands. Solomon's prayer (8:22-61) is a piece of associated casuistry. These heterogeneous sections all interpret the nucleus in 8:13 (cf. Ps. 24:7, 9; Isa 6:1).[17]

In Isa. 63:15, similarly, *z^ebhul* is interpreted by the parallel *shāmayim* (cf. Ps. 2:4; 80:15[14]; 102:20[19]; Job 35:5; Lam. 3:50) and by the two coordinate defining genitives: *qodhsh^ekhā v^ethiph'artekhā*. In Isa. 64:10, the same genitives occur with *bêth* in a lament over the earthly temple, in other words, in an historical context, but now with the 1st person plural suffix, referring to the lamenters. In Hab. 3:11, *z^ebhul* designates the place of the moon, the divine mythological enemy of Yahweh (cf. Josh. 10:12f.).[18] In a mythological context, therefore, *z^ebhul* designates the realm of the gods, as it does at Ugarit.

In Ps. 49:15(14), a crux, *z^ebhul* may be understood as arrogated divinity, the exalted status that the wicked delight to claim for themselves through lavish buildings (cf. Ezk. 28:1-19, esp. 2-9, 12f., 18; Am. 3:15; 5:11; Mic. 2:2, 4; Isa. 14:13-15; 22:15-19; Jer. 51:53; Ps. 73:9). The word *yizb^elēnî* in Gen. 30:20a is perhaps to be understood in this general context. For the barren and neglected woman, children are a sign of God's special favor (Gen. 29:32, 34; 30:20); she would like to see them honored by her husband. Since the interpretation of *yizb^elēnî* as meaning "to present gifts" is hardly convincing, despite the proximity of *zbd,*[19] the interpretation "glorify" or "exalt," following the analogy of the noun, would fit reasonably well in the context.

As a verb, then, the root is attested only as a secular term in the context of family life (Gen. 30:20). As a noun, it stands for blasphemous hubris (Ps. 49:15[14]), for the dwelling place of the mythological enemy of Yahweh (Hab. 3:11), for the temple of Jerusalem, inasmuch as heaven and earth meet there (1 K. 8:13; 2 Ch. 6:2), and finally for the heavenly throne of God (Isa. 63:15).

Gamberoni

---

[17] M. Metzger, "Himmlische und irdische Wohnstatt Jahwes," *UF,* 2 (1970), 139-158; Görg, 56.

[18] Albright, "Psalm," 8-11, 16; S. Mowinckel, "Zum Psalm des Habakkuk," *ThZ,* 9 (1953), 1-23; J. H. Eaton, "The Origin and Meaning of Habakkuk 3," *ZAW,* 76 (1964), 144-171.

[19] Held, 90; for a different view, see Dietrich-Loretz, 539.

זָהָב zāhābh; חָרוּץ chārûts; כֶּתֶם kethem; סְגוֹר s^eghôr; פַּז paz

Contents: I. Linguistic Data: 1. *zāhābh;* 2. Synonyms. II. Gold in the Ancient Near East. III. Old Testament: 1. Nature and Use; 2. Value; 3. Metaphors. IV. Religious Significance: 1. In the Cult; 2. Valuation.

I. Linguistic Data.

1. *zāhābh.* In the OT (as well as Sirach and the Qumran texts), *zāhābh* is the commonest word for the precious metal gold; it is used 385 times. Use of its synonyms is more restricted, both qualitatively (almost exclusively poetic or late) and quantitatively (fewer than 30 occurrences). Outside of Hebrew it appears with variants of the voiced dental (Protosem. *ḏ*):[1] Arab. *ḏahab* (OSA *ḏhb,* "gold[?], bronze,"[2] "spice"; Tigr. *zahab*); Aram. *d^ehaḇ* (Zenjirli Inscription: *zhb*[3]). It is not found in Akkadian, Ugaritic, or Phoenician, where words cognate with Heb. *chārûts* (see below) serve as terms for "gold." The word *zāhābh* occurs only in the singular.[4] It can be used in the construct[5] and take pronominal suffixes.[6] A cognate root *ṣhb* is used only twice: to describe the color of a leper's hair (Lev. 13:30ff.) and of a bronze similar to gold (Ezr. 8:27; the text

---

zāhābh. A.-G. Barrois, *Manuel d'archéologie biblique,* I (Paris, 1939), 372, 398-402; H. Blümner, "Gold," *PW,* VII, 1555-1578; R. J. Forbes, *Studies in Ancient Technology,* VIII (Leiden, 1963/64), 151-192; R. Forrer, *Reallexikon der prähistorischen, klassischen und frühchristlichen Altertümer* (1907), 292ff.; A. Guillaume, "Metallurgy in the OT," *PEQ,* 94 (1962), 129-132; P. Haupt, "The Hebrew Terms for Gold and Silver," *JAOS,* 43 (1923), 116-127; R. de Langhe, "L'autel d'or du Temple de Jérusalem," *Bibl,* 40 (1959), 476-494, esp. 491-94; W. F. Leemans, H. Otten, J. Boese, and U. Rüss, "Gold," *RLA,* III, 504-531; G. Loud, *Megiddo II* (1948), Plates 213f.; A. Lucas, *Ancient Egyptian Materials and Industries* (London, ³1948), 257-268; H. E. del Medico, "Zahab Parwayim," *VT,* 13 (1963), 158-186; J. A. Montgomery, *Arabia and the Bible* (1934), 38f.; W. M. F. Petrie, "Gold, Goldsmith," *A Dictionary of the Bible,* ed. J. Hastings (1923), II, 225f.; H. Quiring, "Das Gold im Altertum," *FuF,* 18 (1942), 55-58; G. Rawlinson, *History of Phoenicia* (London, 1889), chap. 10; J. Reider, "Contributions to the Scriptural Text," *HUCA,* 24 (1952), 100f.; G. Ryckmans, "De l'or(?), de l'encens et de la myrrhe," *RB,* 58 (1951), 372-76; S. Yeivin, "זהב," *Lešonenu,* 7 (1936), 47-51.

1 *VG,* I, 128.

2 A. Jamme, "Sabaean Inscriptions," *JAOS,* 77 (1957), 32f.

3 *KAI,* 215.11.

4 In contrast to *k^esāphîm* (Gen. 42:25, 35); *shibh'āh z^ehābhîm,* "seven kinds of gold" (Talmud *Yoma* 44b); cf. Jerome's comm. on Jer. 10:9: "Gold is called by seven names among the Hebrews."

5 On the form of the *regens* (*ûz^ahabh*), cf. *BLe,* § 208r; as *nomen rectum* it indicates the material used (*VG,* II, 249).

6 Also in Hos. 8:4, *z^ehābhām,* "their gold," contra N. H. Tur-Sinai, *Die Entstehung des semitischen Sprachtypus,* I (1916), 86ff., who considers the suffix a fossilized adverb and translates the word "(made) of gold."

is suspect: according to the Peshitta, this is a "Corinthian" bronze of copper, gold, and silver). A precise definition of the color cannot be ventured (possibly "golden yellow" [cf. the LXX], or more likely "brilliant red" [cf. Mid. Heb. *ṣhb*, "red with anger"]). Above all, it is impossible to decide whether *zāhābh* derives from this root and is thus to be understood as "that which is bright red" or whether *ṣhb* should be considered a denominative ("gold-colored"). On the derivation of *zāhābh* from *zûbh*, see below (III.3).

2. *Synonyms*. The context, especially poetic parallelism, and linguistic analogy disclose various synonyms, but methodological difficulties stand in the way of defining them precisely. There is a mixture of oppositions both diachronic and dialectic, geographical and qualitative, technical and poetic, borrowed and native Hebrew.

In individual cases it is still a matter of debate whether we are dealing with a term for "gold" at all,[7] and whether a word commonly used as an attribute of "gold" should be considered a synonym in ellipsis (*s^e ghôr* for *zāhābh sāghûr; 'ôphîr* for *kethem 'ôphîr*). In addition, there are lexical and textual obscurities: *zāhābh parvayim, kethem 'ûphāz,* and the like.

With these reservations, we shall here list briefly those synonyms that will be included in our discussion of the concept "gold."

a. *kethem*. Scholars have attempted to derive *kethem* from the root *ktm* (Akk. *katāmu,* "cover up, close";[8] Aram. "hide"), so that, like *sāghûr* (see below), the word would mean "that which is hidden (in treasure chambers)." Other suggested explanations include gold as being "massive" or "red." On the other hand, there is not likely to be any connection between *kethem* and Sum. *kù-dím,* Akk. *kutimmu,* "goldsmith,"[9] since Egyptian texts (as early as the 20th dynasty) mention a kind of gold called *ktm.t.*[10] In biblical usage the word designates neither origin (Ophir is often added explicitly: Isa. 13:12; Ps. 45:10 [Eng. v. 9]; Job 28:16) nor quality (cf. the additional attributes in Job 28:19; Lam. 4:1). It occurs nine times in late poetic texts, parallel to *zāhābh* (Job 31:24; Prov. 25:12; Lam. 4:1), *paz* (Isa. 13:12), and a whole series of other precious materials (Job 28:16ff.; Ps. 45:9f.[8f.]).

Contrary to Ibn Ezra, Luther ("gülden Kleinod"), and others, the word *mikhtām* in the superscriptions to the Psalms (16, etc.) does not derive from our word.

b. *paz*. Scholars who assume a Hebrew etymology for *paz* connect it either with *pzz,* "be agile, leap," so that it would mean "that which glitters," or with *pzr,* "unalloyed."[11] If the verbal form *mûphāz* (*zāhābh*) (1 K. 10:18) were certain (glossed

[7] According to Tur-Sinai, הלשון והספר, I (1948), 46; II (1950), 87f., *betser* and *paz* actually mean "strength, means."

[8] *CAD,* VIII, 298-303; *AHw,* I, 464.

[9] *CAD,* VIII, 608; *AHw,* I, 518.

[10] *WbÄS,* V, 145, 6-13; see T. O. Lambdin, "Egyptian Loan Words in the OT," *JAOS,* 73 (1953), 151f.

[11] E. König, *Hebräisches und aramäisches Wörterbuch zum AT* (1910), 360.

in the par. passage 2 Ch. 9:17 as *zāhābh ṭāhôr*), we could assume the meaning "pure gold" for *paz*. Here, too, however, we must reckon with the possibility of borrowing from a non-Semitic language. Ugar. *pḏ*[12] and Arab. *fiḍḍah*, "silver," are disputed in their relationship to our word; Dravidian *pačču*, "yellow," Skt. *pita*, "golden stone," are more likely related to Heb. *piṭdāh*, Gk. *tópazos*, "topaz." The Talmud[13] in fact interprets the word as a precious stone, but textual evidence (e.g., Job 28:17) suggests the meaning "gold, pure gold" (*mûphāz* is either denominative or a textual error for *mēʾûphāz;* cf. Dnl. 10:5). The word occurs nine times in poetic language, usually in parallel with *zāhābh, chārûts*, or *kethem* (Ps. 19:11[10]; Prov. 8:19; etc.).

The asyndetic phrase *kethem pāz* occurs in Cant. 5:11 (LXX and Theodotion with copula); it can be taken as apposition or pleonastic hyperbole.

c. *chārûts*. A Semitic etymology is not out of the question. If it derives from the root *ḥrṣ*, "cut, dig," it could refer to gold in the stage of production;[14] associated with Arab. *ḥariḍa*, "be yellow," it could be considered originally a color term. It has been suggested that Gk. *chrysós* likewise derives from this root,[15] but it is more likely that the Greek word, and hence also the Semitic, is borrowed from the Hurrian *ḫiaruḫḫe*.[16] The word *chārûts* (cf. Akk. *ḫuraṣu*, literally "that which is yellow," Ugar. *ḫrṣ*, the usual term for gold) occurs only seven times in the OT (as well as Sir. 14:3; 34:5); five of its occurrences are in Proverbs. It always stands in parallel with *keseph*. (In the difficult verse Prov. 12:27, contrary to the Targum and Vulg., which translate "gold," the homonym meaning "diligent" is to be preferred.) In view of the common Akk. *kaspu uḫurāṣu*[17] and Canaanite *ksp . . . ḥrṣ*,[18] apparently here a foreign stereotyped phrase has been borrowed. The two occurrences outside of Proverbs are Zec. 9:3, which is describing Tyre, and Ps. 68:14(13), in a psalm full of Canaanisms. In the latter verse, our word is preceded by the attribute *yᵉraqraq*, which may describe beaten gold as "gleaming yellowish-green" or refer to gold leaf (Ugar. *yrq, yrq ḫrṣ*[19]). OSA *wrq* means "gold"; in Arabic, the same word means "silver"; in Geʿez it refers to both precious metals.

d. **betser* (Job 22:24f.; *bᵉtsār?* Job 36:19). Whether this is actually a word for "gold" cannot be determined.[20] Context (par. *ʾôphîr* and *keseph*) and etymology (*bṣr*, "cut off"; Arab. *baṣrat*, "lump containing precious metal") reveal only that we are dealing with gold or silver ore.

---

[12] *CTA*, 2 [III AB], I, 19, 35.

[13] *Yoma* 44b.

[14] Cf. Diodorus Siculus iii.12; according to Haupt, the term refers to gold obtained by mining as opposed to panning (*zāhābh* from *zûbh*).

[15] H. Lewy, *Die semitischen Fremdwörter im Griechischen* (1895), 59f.

[16] *CAD*, VI, 179.

[17] *AHw*, I, 454b.

[18] *KAI*, 13.4f.; *CTA*, 24 [NK], 20f.; etc.

[19] *CTA*, 4 [II AB], IV, 6, 11; 14 [I K], 126, 283.

[20] So rendered by many commentaries since Ibn Janaḥ; the Syriac and Ibn Ezra, however, translate "silver."

e. *s^e^ghôr*. This word occurs in Job 28:15 as an elliptical term for the more frequent *zāhābh sāghûr* (1 K. 6:20, etc.), which resembles Akk. *ḫurāṣu sagru*. It means "pure (hidden) gold"[21] or "gold enclosed in quartz."[22]

Analysis based on actual usage reveals that the use of particular terms for "gold" does not suggest technical distinctions, but is based on stylistic considerations. Thus the LXX and Vulg. basically render *zāhābh* and its synonyms without distinction as *chrysós* and *aurum*, respectively, but are forced when these words occur in sequence (as in Job 28:15-19) to turn to closely related realms (e.g., precious stones, metals) for translations.[23]

II. Gold in the Ancient Near East. From earliest times gold has been highly valued for its metallurgical and aesthetic qualities. It was extracted at many sites from auriferous rock (*ʿaphrōth zāhābh,* Job 28:6)[24] and from secondary deposits in alluvial sand (cf. the Edomite name *mê zāhābh,* Gen. 36:39; also 1 Ch. 1:50). Originally cut to shape in its natural state (with silver, copper, or iron), later hammered, pure gold has been produced by various techniques ever since the transition from the Neolithic to the Bronze Age (*bāchan, tsāraph,* "refine, try," Prov. 17:3; Zec. 13:9; Job 23:10; Isa. 40:19; *zāqaq,* originally probably "filter," cf. Job 36:27; 28:1, later "refine," Mal. 3:3). "Refined gold" (*zāhābh m^e^zuqqāq,* 1 Ch. 28:18), also called "pure gold" (2 Ch. 3:4) or "fine gold" (2 Ch. 3:5, 8), was then alloyed with other metals, usually to achieve greater hardness. When alloyed with copper it took on a reddish tint; alloyed with silver it was yellowish. In certain proportions, the latter alloy is what is called electrum, possibly Heb. *chashmal* (Ezk. 1:4, etc.). Gold was used to make ornaments and jewelry, and later also to make coins.

The Egyptians obtained gold (*nb*) primarily from Nubia, which took its name from the metal, but also from Arabia,[25] and used it for the cult and court. Gold ingots of fixed weight as monetary standards were already in existence in the first dynasty.[26] Gods, especially the sun-god, were called "gold" metaphorically. The body or skin of the gods was gold.[27] The "house of gold" played an important role in the temples as well as in the mortuaries: here statues of the gods and sarcophagi were covered with gold and thus brought to life—since "gold" stands for "life." In temple architecture, too, gold played a prominent role. Besides Re, whose nature was "gold," and the king

---

[21] *GesB,* 536.

[22] Haupt.

[23] The term *obrizum* used by the Vulg. in 2 Ch. 3:5 and elsewhere refers to a process used in assaying gold (Pliny *Hist. nat.* xxxiii.3.19 § 59) and thus means "gold of exemplary quality" (Job 31:24).

[24] Against *challāmîsh* (Job 28:9) as "veins of quartz" (*EncBib,* II, 1749f.), cf. W. von Soden, "Kleine Beiträge zum Ugaritischen und Hebräischen," *Hebräische Wortforschung. Festschrift W. Baumgartner. SVT,* 16 (1967), 297ff.

[25] Inscription of Rameses III.

[26] Blümner.

[27] *RÄR,* 217.

as his earthly representative, Hathor in particular was "the golden one," i.e., life and bestower of life.[28]

The Sumerian royal tombs, dating from the middle of the third millennium B.C., contained various types of golden jewelry.[29] In Semitic Mesopotamia a complex nomenclature bears witness to a many-sided occupation with the precious metal. Besides its usual uses, it was employed in medicine and magic. In Middle Babylonian it was the standard of value; it was used as a term for one's most valued possession ("from chaff to gold"). Metaphorically it stood for the property of endurance.[30] Among the Hittites the technique of working with sheets of gold was known at an early date.[31] In Canaan the use of gold jewelry since the early Bronze Age is attested through archeological finds. At Gezer two pieces of gold in the form of a circle and tongue were discovered.[32] The Amarna letters bear witness to the great demand for gold and its use for gifts, tribute, and international exchange.[33]

The relative value of gold and silver in the ancient world constitutes a special problem. In Egypt, and perhaps elsewhere as well, silver was the scarcer and therefore more valuable until the late period.[34] This does not hold true, however, for Mesopotamia and Canaan. In the time of Hammurabi, gold was six times as valuable as silver, later ten times; in the Assyrian and Neo-Babylonian period it was worth twelve times as much. Cf. also the story of Wen-amon.[35] For the conversion of gold shekels to silver shekels, cf. *BRL,* 379.

III. Old Testament.

1. *Nature and Use*. In the Canaanite area there are no gold deposits, although there may have been some east of the Arabah (cf. the place name *dî zāhābh* in Dt. 1:1).[36] The Israelites knew gold as an exogenous commodity, typical of Ishmaelite caravan traders (Jgs. 8:24), or as booty (Josh. 7:21). Gold was brought from far away by the ships of Tarshish (Isa. 60:9). Various points of origin are indicated, whose location, however, remains unclear: Havilah (Gen. 2:11, possibly India; Gen. 10:7, 29 suggest a region of Cush or Arabia near the Red Sea), Ophir (1 K. 9:28, etc.; conceivably India or southern or eastern Africa; possibly southern Arabia). The latter became practically synonymous with gold (Job 22:24). An ostracon found at Tell Qasileh contains the words *zhb* *'pr*.[37] Parts of Arabia are mentioned in 1 K. 10:1ff.; Isa. 60:6; Ezk. 27:22; 2

---

[28]F. Daumas, "La valeur de l'or dans la pensée égyptienne," *RHR,* 149 (1956), 1-17.
[29]H. Schmökel, *Ur, Assur und Babylon* (1955), 37.
[30]*CAD,* VI, 245ff.; *RLA,* III, 504ff.
[31]I. Benzinger, *Hebräische Archäologie* (^{3}1927), 51, 220.
[32]*BRL,* 379.
[33]J. A. Knudtzon, *Die El-Amarna-Tafeln. VAB,* II (^{2}1964), index *s.v. ḫuraṣu,* 1417f.
[34]Singer, Forbes; cf. also O. Schrader, *Sprachvergleichung und Urgeschichte,* II (^{3}1906), 45.
[35]*AOT,* 75ff.
[36]F.-M. Abel, *Géographie de la Palestine,* II (1938), 307.
[37]Dating from the ninth century B.C.; B. Mazar (Maisler), "Two Hebrew Ostraca from Tell Qasîle," *JNES,* 10 (1951), 266.

Ch. 9:14. The following terms are totally obscure: *'ûphāz* (Jer. 10:9; Dnl. 10:5), which was sometimes taken as a geographical name (LXX and Vulg. in Jer. 10:9 [although Jerome translates *obryzum* in his comm. *in loc.*]; Cant. r. 3:13; Qimḥi), sometimes as a kind of gold (Aquila; Vulg. in Dnl. 10:5; *Yoma* 44b; Ibn Ezra). Some scholars have suggested correcting it to *mûphāz* (see below) or reading *'ôphîr,* following Syriac.

The word *parvayim* (2 Ch. 3:6) was taken either as a geographical name (LXX; Rashi; Qimḥi) or as a kind of gold (Vulg., Syr., Jer. *Yoma* iv.4). It has also been interpreted as deriving from the Egyptian word for "gold houses" or treasuries[38] or as meaning "gold of fertility."[39] Once we read: "Out of the north comes *zāhābh*" (Job 37:22). Emendation (*zōhar*) is unnecessary, but the statement should not be interpreted realistically (the north as a gold-producing region).[40] The passage is poetry tinged with mythology (theophany!): the palace of Baal in the north is also of gold.[41]

The Hebrews were familiar with the technology necessary for producing and working gold.[42] Gold was hammered (*miqshāh,* Ex. 25:18, etc.), beaten (*zāhābh shachûṭ,* 1 K. 10:16), soldered as granulation (Isa. 41:7), hammered out (*rqʿ,* Ex. 39:3; cf. Isa. 40:19) to form gold leaf (*pachê hazzāhābh,* Ex. 39:3), or drawn into gold thread for brocade (Ex. 28:6, 15; Sir. 45:10). It was used for making valuable objects (Ex. 11:2; 1 S. 6:8, etc.) and jewelry (listed in detail in Ex. 35:22; Nu. 31:50; also 2 S. 1:24; Prov. 25:12; Jgs. 8:26), above all for women (Gen. 24:22f.; Jer. 4:30; Ezk. 16:13; Cant. 1:11). In the form of sheets, gold was used to cover figures or objects made of wood or base metal (Isa. 30:22; 1 K. 10:18; 2 K. 18:16; on the exaggerated statements in 1 K. 6:20-22 and 2 Ch. 3:5-9, see below).

Gold also served as a medium of exchange, albeit much less commonly than silver and often alongside the latter. The Gibeonites reject David's offer of reparations by saying, "It is not a matter of silver or gold" (2 S. 21:4); for the healing of his commander, the Syrian king offers, among other things, 6000 shekels of gold (2 K. 5:5); tribute is paid in gold (2 K. 18:14; 23:33).[43] Gold is carried in purses (Isa. 46:6); it circulates in the form of bars (*lāshôn,* Josh. 7:21) and rings of specific weight, i.e., value: shekel (Gen. 24:22, etc. [understood when no other weight is specified]), mina (1 K. 10:17), and talent (2 K. 18:14). These are reweighed for inspection. During the Persian period, the daric, an actual gold coin, was introduced (Ezr. 2:69, etc.; 1 Ch. 29:7 is clearly an anachronism!).

2. *Value.* All the evidence suggests that gold was rarer than silver and the most valuable metal throughout the entire biblical period (Isa. 13:12: *paz;* commenting on this passage, Jerome says: "Pretiosum autem dicitur omne quod rarum est"). It was used in making the most valued objects associated with the cult[44] and with the royal

---

[38] A. S. Yahuda, "Hebrew Words of Egyptian Origin," *JBL,* 66 (1947), 87.
[39] Del Medico.
[40] Cf. Herodotus iii.116.
[41] *CTA,* 4 [II AB], VI, 33ff.
[42] See the citations above.
[43] Cf. *ANET,* 301.
[44] See below.

court (scepter and crown, Est. 4:11; 8:15; overlay for the throne, 1 K. 10:18ff.). In contrast to silver, it appears not only alongside other metals (Ezk. 27:12; Nu. 31:22), but alongside precious stones (1 K. 10:2; Ezk. 27:22) and other precious materials (Job 28:15ff.) as well as fine apparel (Ezk. 28:12f.; Ps. 45:10-14[9-13]). Gold is offered in smaller quantities than silver (Nu. 7:14; 2 K. 5:5; 18:14; 23:33; Ezr. 1:9ff.; 8:26). When abundant, silver can lose its relative value (1 K. 10:21), but not gold.

This conclusion appears to be at variance with the fact that in earlier texts silver is mentioned before gold (Gen. 24:35; Nu. 22:18 [JE]; Josh. 6:19; 2 S. 21:4; etc.), whereas later the opposite sequence becomes more common (Ex. 25:3 [P]; Ezk. 16:13; Est. 1:6; etc.): cf. 2 S. 8:10 with its parallel 1 Ch. 18:10. It is hardly appropriate to cite purely stylistic considerations for the sequence "silver . . . gold," for example, placing the shorter[45] or commoner[46] word first, possibly for the sake of climax (Dt. 29:16[17]). Passages like 2 S. 8:10 ("silver . . . gold . . . bronze") argue the contrary. It is nevertheless reasonable to conjecture that the earlier idiom preserves archaic evidence of a time when gold was less valuable.

Gold promises prosperity (Job. 42:11). Its possession is the preeminent mark of wealth and—often in combination with silver—becomes practically synonymous with riches (Gen. 24:53; Prov. 22:1; Eccl. 2:8; Sir. 29:11). It is a mark of independence (1 K. 20:3, 7) and signifies the honor of princes (Job 3:15) and kings (1 K. 10:14; Ps. 72:15). It is the most precious of gifts (Gen. 24:22; 1 K. 10:2), the currency of political bribery (1 K. 15:19), tribute levied for an offense (2 K. 18:14; 23:33), and coveted booty (Josh. 7:21; 2 S. 1:24; 2 K. 25:15: *zāhābh zāhābh*, "pure gold"[47]). It is "means" in the strict sense of the word: it provides power (Ezr. 1:6; Sir. 40:25). Even when other values are ranked above gold (Psalms, Proverbs, etc.[48]), the high esteem enjoyed by this precious metal is implicit.

3. *Metaphors*. The properties of gold appear frequently in metaphorical use. Golden oil is called *zāhābh* (Zec. 4:12).[49] The same may be true of wine (Jer. 51:7).[50] Above all, however, the properties of gold employed metaphorically are its beauty (Prov. 11:22; Cant. 5:11: *kethem paz*), its perfection of form (Prov. 25:11), its purity (Mal. 3:3; Prov. 27:21; Job 23:10), its nobility (Lam. 4:1), its rarity and value (Isa. 13:12; Sir. 28:24f.).

The interpretation of individual verses sometimes raises difficulties. Cant. 5:11 cannot refer to the color of the beloved's hair (cf. v. 11b!), nor, most likely, to the color of his face browned by the sun; in the light of vv. 14f.; Lam. 4:1; Sir. 50:9, the gold must be taken as a general metaphor for attractiveness and charm. In Prov. 25:11,

---

45 H. Ehelof, *Ein Wortfolgeprinzip im Assyrisch-babylonischen*. *LSS*, 6/3 (1916), 3.

46 M. Held, *Studies in Ugaritic Lexicography and Poetic Style* (diss., Johns Hopkins, 1957); cited in R. G. Boling, " 'Synonymous' Parallelism in the Psalms," *JSS*, 5 (1960), 223f.

47 *GK*, §123e.

48 See below.

49 Already so interpreted by medieval Jewish commentators; Rost's derivation from *zûbh* is unlikely; L. Rost, "Bemerkungen zu Sacharja 4," *ZAW*, 63 (1951), 219 = *Das kleine Credo und andere Studien zum AT* (1965), 67.

50 Qimḥi; Ehrlich; but Ugar. *yn bks ḫr*[*ṣ*] (*CTA*, 4 [II AB], IV, 37) speaks against this interpretation.

tappûchê zāhābh (possibly to be read *pittûchê zāhābh?*) can hardly refer to fruit (apricots? [modern Heb. "oranges"]), but rather to an ornamental motif. Prov. 27:21 means that a man is tried in the opinion of others as gold is tried in the furnace. In Lam. 4:1, the "gold" may be the temple gold; but v. 2 suggests a metaphor for the inhabitants of Zion.

The metaphorical use of gold makes it a standard of value. Judicious speech (Prov. 20:15), wise exhortation and attention to it are as valuable as gold and jewels. A faithful friend, a gracious woman (Sir. 7:18f.), charity (Sir. 29:11; Tob. 12:8), a good name and favor (Prov. 22:1), and above all wisdom (Job 28:15ff.; Prov. 8:10, 19; Wisd. 7:9), its acquisition and profit (Prov. 16:16; 3:4)—all are more valuable than gold. The breath of life is more valuable (Sir. 13:15), and life itself can be called *gullath hazzāhābh* (Eccl. 12:6). Whether the image is that of a lamp (v. 6a) or a pitcher does not matter in this context. At death the "golden bowl"[51] is broken.

IV. Religious Significance.

1. *In the Cult.* Many cultic objects were made of solid gold (mercy seat, vessels, lampstand, Ex. 37:6, 16f.; Ezr. 1:9, 10; Zec. 4:2) or overlaid and ornamented with gold (ark, table, incense altar, Ex. 37:2, 11, 26; parts of the tabernacle, Ex. 36:34; cf. 1 K. 6:20ff.). Gold also played a role in the priestly vestments (ephod, breastpiece, bells, crown plate, Ex. 39:2f., 8ff., 25, 30; crown, Zec. 6:11).

The descriptions are far from trustworthy in detail. According to 1 K. 6:18ff., the cherubim were wooden statues overlaid with gold; according to Ex. 37:7 (P), however, they were of pure gold. The abundant gold overlay on the temple structure (1 K. 6:20ff.; even more extravagantly described in 2 Ch. 3:5-9) appears to be a fiction; at least it is never mentioned in the frequent lootings on the part of enemies (1 K. 14:26; 2 K. 14:14; 16:17; 18:16; 25:15). These additions, too, attest the place of gold in the value system.

In the case of the "golden altar" (1 K. 7:48, etc., probably identical with the incense altar of Ex. 30:1ff.), it is possible to assume the meaning "spice, incense" for *zāhābh* (as in OSA) and translate as "incense altar." This hypothesis is plausible in Isa. 60:6 (*zāhābh ûl^e bhônāh*) and possible in Ps. 72:15 (*z^e habh sh^e bhāʾ*).[52]

The use of gold may at one time have been associated with magical or mythocosmic ideas: the golden bells, for instance,[53] may have been apotropaic in nature (Ex. 28:35b);[54] the golden plate on the crown[55] may have symbolized the sun disk.[56] The account in 1 S. 6:4 describes a bit of apotropaic magic based on the modelling of a diseased member in gold; it is ascribed to non-Israelites, but was clearly familiar to the author as an Israelite practice. In Ex. 32:20 the motif of a magical potion of gold has been woven skillfully into the narrative of the golden calf, with the gold representing

[51]So translated on the basis of Akk. *gullu, gullatu; CAD,* V, 129; *AHw,* I, 297.
[52]Cf. Ryckmans.
[53]See above.
[54]Cf. *RLA,* I, 122.
[55]See above.
[56]Benzinger, 359.

the people's sin. (This interpretation also disposes of Gressmann's metallurgical comment: "Gold cannot be burnt or . . . ground to powder."[57]) But these primitive ideas have faded into unrecognizability. The reason gold is used in the service of God is its value (Josh. 6:19; 1 K. 15:15). An offering of gold evidences the spirit of reverence and devotion (Ex. 36:36; Ezr. 8:25; 1 Ch. 29:4, 7). On the other hand, gold becomes consecrated by being lifted up and swung before Yahweh (Ex. 35:22; *zᵉhabh hattᵉnûphāh,* 38:24; *zᵉhabh hattᵉrûmāh,* Nu. 31:52).

At the same time, gold used in alien cults is spurned. It is only natural that there would be disagreement as to whether it should be dedicated to Yahweh or destroyed (cf. 2 S. 5:21; Dt. 7:25; 1 Ch. 14:12; also Josh. 6:19, 24; 7:1, 21ff.; 2 S. 12:30). Images of Yahweh were known to early Israel (Jgs. 17:4; 18), as we may also conclude from the polemic against them (Ex. 20:23, which can hardly refer only to costly images). The later view equates these images of gold and silver with idols (Hos. 2:10[8]; Dt. 29:16[17]; Isa. 30:22; 31:7). Gideon, a faithful devotee of Yahweh, makes an ephod out of the gold he has captured (Jgs. 8:26f.); v. 27b condemns his action as idolatry. After the prohibition against images was in force, any cult to be rejected could be attacked schematically as gold (and silver) fetishism (Jer. 10:3f.; Hab. 2:18f.; Ps. 115:4; 135:15); gold in the approved cult could be interpreted as mere ornament. An instructive example is the difference between the verdicts of Judahite theology on two legitimate cult objects of Yahwism: the (Jerusalemite) cherubim[58] and the (Ephraimite) calf (Ex. 32; 1 K. 12:28ff.). This polemic, however, paves the way for the idea of God's absolute incomparability (Isa. 46:5-7) and his infinite superiority to the splendor of golden idols (Isa. 2:18-21).

2. *Valuation.* Possession of gold is a clear blessing from God (Dt. 8:13; Josh. 22:8; 2 Ch. 1:15; Hos. 2:10[8]; Ezk. 16:17); it is taken away as a divine punishment (Ex. 11:2; Ps. 105:37; Nah. 2:10[9]; 2 Ch. 25:20, 24). This is also the sense in which we are to understand the eschatological descriptions in which the foreign nations are to bring tribute of gold to the Israelites and Judahites (Isa. 60:9, 17; Zec. 14:14); here we are dealing primarily with the return of property taken as booty (Joel 4:5[3:5]; Ezk. 38:13; cf. 39:9f.). But possession of gold also involves spiritual dangers: it leads to arrogance (Ezk. 16:17; 28:13ff.; Dt. 8:13f.) and idolatry (Isa. 2:7; Hos. 2:10[8]). Therefore Israel is warned against excess (Dt. 17:17) and avarice (Sir. 31:5ff.). The intelligent and upright man does not trust in his possessions (Job 31:24), but submits to the divine will (Nu. 22:18). Gold and silver have no power to save a man (Ezk. 7:19; Zeph. 1:18). The word of God is more valuable than any gold (Ps. 19:11[10]; 119:72,127).

Hag. 2:8, "The silver is mine, and the gold is mine, says Yahweh of hosts," is to be understood primarily in an eschatological sense;[59] but the echo of Lev. 25:23 ("The land is mine") suggests that gold, too, is bestowed on men only conditionally.

Kedar-Kopfstein

---

[57] *SAT,* I/2, 62.
[58] See above.
[59] See above.

זָהַר *zāhar*; זֹהַר *zōhar*

Contents: I. Occurrences: 1. Extrabiblical Evidence; 2. Biblical Data. II. "Neutral" Use. III. Theological Relevance: 1. Use Outside the Prophets; 2. Ezekiel. IV. Eschatological Meaning.

I. Occurrences.

1. *Extrabiblical Evidence*. Outside the OT, the root *zhr* is attested as yet only in a few (late) West and South Semitic dialects.[1] The spectrum of occurrences (Arabic, Syriac, Aramaic) exhibits both verbal (e.g., Arab. *zahara*, "shine") and nominal (e.g., Arab. *zuhrat*, "brightness") use. Aram. *zîhᵃrāʾ*, "moon," and Ethiop. *zᵉhura (zᵉhora)*, "Venus" ("an Arabic loanword" according to Leslau[2]), clearly refer to the brightness of the heavenly bodies. Tigr. *zāher*, "evident,"[3] with the implication of transparency, likewise exhibits a semantic connection.

Whether Ugar. *ḏhrt*[4] is related to the root in question is definitely still open.[5] If *ḏhrt* turns out to be a variant of *ḏrt* with anything like a comparable meaning ("dream, vision"[6]), a semantic relationship to *zhr* might be seen in the related meanings "vision" and "brightness, splendor," just as according to *UT* No. 725 a "semantic connection" between Ugar. *hdrt*, "dream," and Heb. *hdr*, "splendor," may be indicated by the "equation" majesty=theophany=dream.[7] At this point, however, caution is advisable.

Yet another early Canaanite occurrence is attested indirectly. A Syro-Palestinian deity with the name *Ḏhr* is mentioned in Egypt during the Ramesside period (19th/20th dynasty),[8] appearing alongside another deity *Nqphn:* it is stated of both that "they ravish maidens and emasculate the gods."[9] According to Stadelmann, the text "characterizes the deities mentioned according to their actions."[10] If *ḏhr* (*ḏ3h3r* in

---

zāhar. P. Auvray, "Le prophète comme guetteur, Éz XXXIII, 1-20," *RB*, 71 (1964), 191-205; W. Eichrodt, "Das prophetische Wächteramt; zur Exegese von Hes 33," *Tradition und Situation. Festschrift A. Weiser* (1963), 31-41; H. Graf Reventlow, *Wächter über Israel; Ezechiel und seine Tradition. BZAW*, 82 (1962); R. Stadelmann, *Syrisch-Palästinensische Gottheiten in Ägypten. PÄ*, 5 (1967); P. Volz, *Die Eschatologie der jüdischen Gemeinde im neutestamentlichen Zeitalter* (1934; ²1966); R. B. Zuck, "Hebrew Words for 'Teach,'" *BS*, 121 (1964), 228-235.

[1] Cf. *KBL*³, 254f.

[2] Leslau, *Contributions*, 18.

[3] *TigrWb*, 493.

[4] According to *UT*, No. 735, "a scribal error for *ḏrt*."

[5] Cf. M. Dahood, *Psalms*, I. *AB*, XVI (1965), 124.

[6] Cf. L. Fisher, *Ras Shamra Parallels*, I. *AnOr*, 49 (1972), chap. 2, No. 192.

[7] Cf. H. Donner, "Ugaritismen in der Psalmenforschung," *ZAW*, 79 (1967), 331ff.; → הדר *hādhār*.

[8] Cf. A. Massart, *The Leiden Magical Papyrus I 343 + I 345* (1954), 56.

[9] Recto, II, 9; vo., IV, 4; cf. Massart, 52f.

[10] P. 125.

syllabic orthography) is a Semitic loanword,[11] a connection with *zhr* is possible in principle, since Semitic *z* can also be represented by *ḏ*.[12] Perhaps we are dealing with an astral deity not otherwise attested so far in Canaanite literature, whose name is based on the effect emanating from him. Helck[13] transcribes the name as *śa-ha-r,* thus committing himself to a vocalization that the syllabic orthography does not define absolutely. It is also conceivable that the name is based on a *qātil* participial form, suggesting in our case a characterization of the deity as "shining" or "radiant." Here, too, however, we must proceed with the caution demanded by the diachronic evidence.

2. *Biblical Data.* According to Palache,[14] the root *zhr* is "similar to many other roots with *-hr*" in bearing the meaning "shine, gleam, be bright." A connection with *ṣhr* ("and probably *ṭhr*"[15]) is likely.[16] The meaning of the hiphil forms in Dnl. 12:3 (Sir. 43:9 Rd) and the nouns in Ezk. 8:2; Dnl. 12:3 appears to differ from the meaning conveyed by the root elsewhere in the OT (verb only; 8 times in the niphal and 15 in the hiphil, including conjectures), where its semantic component is "warning" rather than "shining." This observation has led to the hypothesis of two different roots. The semantic development "make shine, enlighten" > "teach" is possible,[17] however, and would necessitate only a single root. Analysis of the position and function of the individual occurrences will be undertaken independently of these etymological considerations.

II. "Neutral" Use. The position of the hiphil form in 2 K. 6:10b (suf. conjugation) is formally distinct from the narrative in v. 10a; the subject shifts to the "man of God,"[18] who "warned" the king of Israel to "disregard"[19] a strategically important position of the Syrians. To determine the semantic force of the form in question, we must therefore refer back to the words of the man of God in v. 9 as well as to the results of his words ("so that he was on his guard there"[20]); we must also take into account the explicit statement that the event took place frequently (v. 10b). We are dealing with repeated "briefings" in the past, characterized by the context as "warnings."

According to a conjecture by Rudolph,[21] Jer. 4:16a contains a hiphil imperative of *zhr* in parallel with *hashmîʿû* (16b), obviously in the sense of an enlightening an-

[11] Cf. already M. Burchardt, *Die altkanaanäischen Fremdworte und Eigennamen im Ägyptischen,* II (1910), No. 1242; *WbÄS,* V, 605.

[12] Cf. Burchardt, *Fremdworte,* I (1909), §153.

[13] W. Helck, *Die Beziehungen Ägyptens zu Vorderasien im 3. und 2. Jahrtausend v. Chr. ÄgAbh,* 5 (^{2}1971), 468.

[14] J. L. Palache, *Semantic Notes on the Hebrew Lexicon* (1959), 25.

[15] *Ibid.*

[16] Cf. *GesB,* 675f.

[17] Palache, 25.

[18] According to H. C. Schmitt, *Elisa; traditionsgeschichtliche Untersuchungen zur vorklassischen nordisraelitischen Prophetie* (1972), 155, "it cannot be demonstrated with certainty that the 'man of God' of the original narrative stratum referred to Elisha."

[19] On the translation, cf. *ibid.,* 216.

[20] *Ibid.*

[21] W. Rudolph, *HAT,* 12 (^{3}1968), 34; *BHS.*

nouncement that the south is threatened by a danger explained in greater detail in the words that follow. Thus Rudolph correctly translates: "Give warning to Benjamin!"

The proverb in Eccl. 4:13b gives preference to a poor but wise youth over an old but foolish king, who does not understand (*ydʿ*) any longer "how to take advice." The niphal infinitive does not necessarily imply the notion of "warning" on the part of the adviser; the foolish king is simply not open to enlightenment. A similar semantic neutralization obtains in the case of the hiphil imperative in Eccl. 12:12: the son should "be advised." That ultimately a "warning" is involved becomes apparent only from the content of the admonition that follows. The "neutral" use of the root *zhr* thus reveals initially some "information" or "instruction" about a subject that need not involve specific theological reflection.

III. Theological Relevance.

1. *Use Outside the Prophets.* In Ex. 18:13-27, a "smooth, self-contained narrative sequence,"[22] probably Elohistic, v. 20 begins with the hiphil of *zhr* in climactic suffix conjugation (here in the sense of a certain future), continuing an exhortation on the part of Moses' father-in-law. The advice pertains to a future function of the mediator between the people and God (v. 19), who is also to be the mediator between God and the people (v. 20). A double object here characterizes the force of the verb: what is meant in the first instance is undoubtedly the function of "informing" the people (*'ethhem*) about "statutes" (*ḥuqqîm*) and "decisions" (*tôrôth*) of God. More can be learned by comparing v. 20b with 16c: 20b continues the discourse with the commission to make the people (*lāhem*) know (*ydʿ* hiphil) the practical consequences of this information; according to v. 16c, Moses includes among his previous functions making known (*ydʿ* hiphil) the "statutes" and "decisions" of God, without specific mention of the people addressed. It may even be suggested that with the commission in v. 20a a commentary on the "statutes" and "decisions" is meant, in the sense of a clarification. In any case, Moses' adviser expects him to exercise the function of a "teacher" who is required to do more than merely make formal pronouncements. The terms *zhr* (hiphil) and *ydʿ* (hiphil) now stand in correspondence (v. 20): "enlightening" instruction parallels making known the way men must walk and act.

The hiphil form in Lev. 15:31a (suf. conjugation) must be taken as representing the same aspect (certain future). It is clear that the word must be a form of the root *zhr*; if *vᵉhizzartem* (MT) is not emended to *vᵉhizhartem,* it should be understood as the latter form with late suppression of the weak gutteral rather than being derived from *nzr*.[23] In the immediate context, v. 31 stands as a secondary "parenesis"[24] addressed to Moses and Aaron; it picks up the commission formula in 15:2a and separates the caption from the body of the text. According to Elliger,[25] v. 31 belongs to the work of

---

[22]M. Noth, *Exodus. OTL* (trans. 1962), 146.

[23]K. Elliger, *HAT,* 4 (1966), 192.

[24]*Ibid.,* 196.

[25]*Ibid.*

the redactor responsible for the position of chaps. 11–15 (laws dealing with what is clean and unclean). Here, too, "instruction" is demanded; this time its theme is the absolution of the Israelites from their uncleanness (*miṭṭumʾāthām*), which could be their undoing should they defile the *mishkān* of Yahweh.

The structure of 2 Ch. 19:10 is related to that of Lev. 15:31 in that here, too, the force of the verb (*hizhartem*) introduces a negated clause of purpose. The judges in Jerusalem are to "instruct" their "brethren" who bring legal questions to them so that they may not incur guilt before Yahweh and suffer the punishment of God's wrath. The reference is probably not so much to attempts at bribery as to false testimony.[26] But the parenesis, composed by the Chronicler on the basis of Deuteronomic formulations (cf. Dt. 16:18–20; 17:8–13), undoubtedly has as its subject matter information addressed to all parties concerned (both plaintiffs and judges) about the norms that must be observed "in the fear of Yahweh" (v. 9). In the light of Ex. 18:13ff., furthermore, it would probably not be misleading to posit the institution (later restored?) of detailed "instructions in the law" within the framework of the Israelite judicial process.

In Ps. 19B, a late hymn in praise of the law, *zhr* (niphal) appears in the suffix conjugation with an explicit subject, apparently in the sense of a universal statement: the "servant of Yahweh," too, is "instructed" by the *mishpᵉṭê yhvh* (v. 12 [Eng. v. 11]). Nor is Yahweh's instruction given unconditionally even to the elect: he must "keep" it.[27] Here, too, the "instruction" mediates a sense of the *fascinosum et tremendum* of divine authority. It can take on the concrete form of "enlightenment" as well as "warning."[28]

2. *Ezekiel*. Two passages in Ezekiel (3:16b and 33:1–9) exhibit a unique concentration of verb forms derived from *zhr* (all hiphil except for the niphal forms in 3:21; 33:4, 5[two], 6), which justifies separate treatment.

According to Zimmerli,[29] Ezk. 3:17–21 prove "thematically and syntactically to be a composite exposition; these verses expand the watchman statement of 33:7–9 by the addition of ideas from chap. 18."[30] According to Reventlow,[31] the "thematic and formal points of contact" with Ezk. 18 "are by no means limited to 3:20–21; they are also clearly marked, for example, in 33:9." Zimmerli conjectures that 3:16b–21 represent "an expansion of the call narrative during the phase of redaction that gave the book as a whole its present form."[32] Reventlow assumes that "the present position of 3:16b–21 is the result of a purely text-critical cause such as a displaced page."[33] Ezk. 33:1–9 turn out to be an organized unit comprising an "allegorical section" (vv. 1–6) and an

---

[26] K. Galling, *ATD*, XII (1954), 125.

[27] According to J. Kraus, *BK*, XV/1 (⁴1972), 159, we are dealing with "a kind of declaration of loyalty."

[28] Cf. Dahood, *Psalms*, I, 124.

[29] W. Zimmerli, *BK*, XIII/1 (1969), 87.

[30] *Ibid.*, 88.

[31] Reventlow, 129.

[32] Zimmerli, 88.

[33] Reventlow, 130.

"application" (vv. 7-9);[34] according to Zimmerli,[35] they are "styled in the form of a casuistic lawsuit," which is "depicted in narrative style by a series of actions" (vv. 2-4), then recapitulated in concise factual language "with a perceptible parenetic purpose" (v. 5), followed by "an interruption of the neutral legal discourse by God's personal words" (v. 6), and concluding with an "appointment oracle" (vv. 7-9) marked by elements of casuistic style.[36]

Both passages contain the key term, which characterizes the "function of the watchman."[37] In 3:16b-21, with a single exception (v. 17), the LXX translates the verb with *diastéllein,* while in 33:1-9 additional verbs are chosen, without any consistency and without any equivalent in v. 7. Examination of the syntactic position of the Masoretic verb forms reveals more particulars.

The statement of the case in 33:3 uses the hiphil of *zhr* in the suffix conjugation, followed by a complement (*hāʿām*). This accentuates, in terms of the prophet's commission, the certainty with which the *hizhîr* must take place in the future, whether it meets with response or not. This is followed by inverted suffix conjugations in the niphal, elucidating in negative (vv. 4,5a,6) and positive (v. 5b) terms the punctilious aspect of the possible response. In 5b, we should probably follow Zimmerli in construing the verb as referring to the person warned.[38]

An almost parallel structure is revealed by the sequence of occurrences in 33:7-9 and 3:17-19. In each case the appointment of the prophet as "watchman" is coupled with his commission, stated, together with additional details, by means of the suffix conjugation (certain future) (33:7 par. 3:17), and repeated indirectly in the following "protasis" by an infinitive construction (33:8 par. 3:18); this function is also performed in 3:18 by the initial addition of a negated form in the suffix conjugation. Finally, in the positive case (33:9 par. 3:19), the punctilious aspect of the response is formalized by means of the inverted suffix conjugation.

The expansion in 3:20f. discusses the case of the righteous man threatened by sin. The aspect of contingency is expressed formally in suffix conjugations: the negation (v. 20) and the personal pronoun (cf. 3:19; 33:9) in inverted position,[39] together with a retrospective motivation within the framework of "apodosis" (v. 21b), where the only niphal found in this context also occurs, make clear the punctilious perspective of the incident.

Dominating the dichotomous context and at the same time determining the semantics is the expression *vᵉhizhartā ʾōthām mimmennî* (3:17 par. 33:7), the last element of which Zimmerli interprets as meaning "about me, against me."[40] The related constructions in 3:18; 33:8f.; Lev. 15:31 suggest "instructing away from me," i.e., "warning against me." Yahweh is a harsh judge; the people must be warned against him. According to

---

[34]Cf. *ibid.,* 129f.
[35]Zimmerli, 798.
[36]*Ibid.,* 799.
[37]Reventlow, 129.
[38]P. 795.
[39]In v. 21a, *hizhartô* should undoubtedly be read *hizhartā* (Zimmerli, 87).
[40]*Ibid.,* 86.

Reventlow,[41] "this warning function of the watchman is to be viewed in form-critical association with the proclamation of the law during the covenant festival recorded in chap. 18." Even if caution must be enjoined on this point, it is probably reasonable to conjecture that the prophet has in mind the office of a (sacral) instructor in the law.

IV. Eschatological Meaning. The use of the root as a noun in Ezk. 8:2 appears to stand in total isolation from its use as a verb elsewhere in Ezekiel. Zimmerli even conjectures that the "strikingly vague *kmr'h zhr* is secondary."[42] Nevertheless, comparison to an "appearance of brightness" is appropriate for a visionary figure, probably that of the "heavenly messenger."[43] This forges the link to the impression given by the use of the root as a verb: the "instruction" of the prophet is grounded in the *zōhar* of Yahweh. Ezekiel's role as watchman is totally committed to Yahweh.

A paronomastic construction in Dnl. 12:3 compares the eternal "shining" of the "wise" (syntax indicating the aspect of a certain future) to the *zōhar* of the firmament (cf. Sir. 43:9).[44] According to Volz, this passage "announces eternal life for the individual, or, more precisely, certain individuals."[45] The "wise" have a favored position in the hierarchy of the blessed.[46] That it is the wise who will "shine" at the eschaton is undoubtedly because they may be considered both "instructed" and "instructors." Thus the eschatological relevance of *zōhar* does not stand in isolation from tradition; at the same time, it prefigures the later importance of the concept in Cabalism.

Görg

[41]P. 129.
[42]P. 191.
[43]*Ibid.*, 210.
[44]*KBL*[3], 254.
[45]P. 402.
[46]Cf. *ibid.*, 399.

זוד* *zûdh; זִיד *zîdh;* זֵד *zēdh;* זָדוֹן *zādhôn*

Contents: I. Etymology; the Root in Other Semitic Languages. II. OT and Sirach: 1. Verb; 2. Nouns. III. Qumran. IV. LXX. V. Semantic History; Theological Use.

I. Etymology; the Root in Other Semitic Languages. Hebrew lexicons record a root *zwd*[1] or *zyd*[2] with the fundamental meaning "boil," "be hot," on account

zûdh. G. Bertram, "'Hochmut' und verwandte Begriffe im griechischen und hebräischen AT," *WO*, 3 (1964/66), 32-43, esp. 36f.; *idem*, "ὕβρις. B. Old Testament," *TDNT*, VIII, 299-302.

[1]*GesB*, 195, but alongside *zyd*.
[2]*KBL*[3], 257 and *HAD*, both with reference from *zwd;* Zorell, *LexHebAram*, 207.

of the hiphil in Gen. 25:29 and the noun *nāzîdh,* "boiled food." Probably, however, *zûdh* and *zîdh* should be distinguished.

For *zwd,* the Arabic dictionaries give the meaning "provide food for oneself," and for *zâd,* "provisions (for a journey)."[3] The Aramaic and Syriac dictionaries give similar meanings for the pael and ethpaal of *zûdh* and the noun *zûdhā'*. To this root probably belong Heb. *nāzîdh,* "food" (Gen. 25:29, 34; 2 K. 4:39f.; Hag. 2:12), and the hiphil *vayyāzedh* in Gen. 25:29, "he prepared some food." There is no evidence for any basic meaning such as "boil" or "be hot."

For *zîd,* the Arabic dictionaries give such meanings as "increase," "surpass," "outdo," V "exaggerate," "lie," X "demand more," "make great claims"; the Ethiopic dictionaries give the meaning "surpass" for *zēda.* Here belong the Biblical Aram. haphel inf. *h^{a}zādhāh* (Dnl. 5:20) and Jewish Aram. *zîdh,* "be or act petulant, arrogant," with the nouns *z^{e}dhônā'* and *z^{e}dhānûthā'*, "arrogance, insolence," as well as Heb. *zîdh* qal and hiphil (similar in meaning) and the nouns *zēdh,* "insolent, arrogant," *zādhôn,* "insolence, pride, arrogance," and *zêdhôn,* "raging, overwhelming" (of flood waters in Ps. 124:5).

The roots *zûdh* and *zîdh* are not attested in other Semitic languages. Akk. *ṣâdu,* "whirl" and "melt,"[4] is not related.[5]

II. OT and Sirach.

1. *Verb.* The verb appears in the qal only twice (Ex. 18:11 [E] and Jer. 50:29), nine times in the hiphil; there is no discernible difference in meaning. The construction with the qal and with the hiphil in Neh. 9:10 is: *A* (the Egyptians, Babylon) *yāzîdh ʿal/'el B* (Israel, Yahweh). The meaning is that a foreign nation arrogates to itself rights over Israel or Yahweh as protector of Israel to which it is not entitled (forced labor, deportation). In religious usage, the indirect object can be omitted with the hiphil when the arrogance transgresses divine law; the translation of *A yāzîdh* is thus "A acts arrogantly." In Dt. 1:43 and Neh. 9:16, 29 Israel is the subject and the hiphil of *zîdh* is expanded in greater detail: the people or their fathers did not hearken to Yahweh or Moses. The hiphil participle is used similarly in Sir. 3:16: a man who forsakes his father is a *mēzîdh;* that the injured party is not the father but God is shown by the parallelism: "Whoever angers his mother is an aggriever (*makhʿîs*) of his Creator." The Aramaic haphel infinitive in Dnl. 5:20 has similar force: the king's "heart was lifted up (*rim*) and his spirit was hardened so that he dealt proudly/arrogantly. . . ." Insolent or arrogant conduct can be further specified by means of *l^e* or *l^{e}bhiltî* + infinitive. In Dt. 18:20 it consists in a false prophet's claim that something not spoken by Yahweh is the word of Yahweh. In similar fashion, *ʿāśāh bh^{e}zādhôn l^{e}bhiltî* is used in Dt. 17:12f. of one who ignores the decision of the priest or judge. Such a man is sentenced to death; then "all the people shall hear, and fear, and not act arrogantly again (*v^{e}lō' y^{e}zîdhûn ʿôdh*)." In what is probably the earliest occurrence of the hiphil, Ex. 21:14 (Covenant Code), the emphasis of the verb was not on arrogance toward God and his moral order, but rather

---

[3] E.g., Wehr, 385.
[4] *CAD,* XVI, 57-59.
[5] Contra *GesB,* 195; *LexHebAram,* 207.

on the premeditation of the illegal action in contrast to the lack of premeditation described in v. 13: "But if a man presumes willfully to attack another to kill him treacherously. . . ." Thus in early legal usage the verb appears to have referred to a premeditated disregard of the law, a presumptuous offense against law and morality. After the development of Israel's sense of nationality, *zîdh* took on the meaning of an arrogant transgression of Israel's basic rights on the part of heathen nations (Ex. 18:11; Neh. 9:10). In religious usage since Deuteronomy (Dt. 1:43; 17:13; 18:20), the verb acquired the sense of a presumptuous, premeditated offense against God and his religious and moral order (Jer. 50:29; Dnl. 5:20; Neh. 9:16, 29; Sir. 3:16). The qal and hiphil can therefore be translated the same: "act arrogantly, presumptuously"; with *ʿal* or *ʾel*, "treat someone arrogantly"; with *lᵉ*, "have the arrogance or presumption to do something forbidden."

2. *Nouns*. Of the nouns, only *zēdh* and *zādhôn* have theological significance. The noun *zēdh* appears in the singular only in Prov. 21:24 and Sir. 12:4(7). In Prov. 21:24, the conduct of the *zēdh yāhîr* is described as *ʿāśāh bᵉʿebhrath zādhôn,* and he himself is termed a *lēts,* "blasphemer." We might translate: "The presumptuous and arrogant man, . . . he acts with unrestrained arrogance." In Sir. 12:4(7), *zēdh* stands in parallelism with "the ungodly" (*raʿ*) and in contrast to "the humble" (*makh*). Here, too, the meaning is probably "arrogant."

All other occurrences involve the plural. In Sir. 11:9, the *rîbh zēdhîm* in which the wise man will not interfere is probably a conflict between individuals who insist uncompromisingly on their own exaggerated claims. Thus in the usage of Wisdom *zēdh* is a term of secular ethics: "the arrogant man, the man who presses exaggerated claims," or the like. In Ps. 86:14, on the other hand, there are echoes of religious ethics: the devout worshipper feels threatened by *zēdhîm,* who are mentioned in parallelism with "a band of ruthless men"; we are dealing with men who claim rights over against the devout man to which they are not entitled. The situation is similar in Ps. 119:51,69,78,85,122; in vv. 78 and 122 the conduct of the "presumptuous" is described as subversion (*ʿivvēth*) and oppression (*ʿāshaq*). In Ps. 119:21 and later prophetic texts (Isa. 13:11; Jer. 43:2; Mal. 3:15, 19), finally, the *zēdhîm* are those who, like the wicked (*rᵉshāʿîm*), transgress God's commandments and disregard the words of the prophets: "presumptuous men" who claim in their arrogance the ability to defy God himself.

The word *zādhôn* underwent a similar development from secular everyday usage to purely religious usage. In 1 S. 17:28 it is part of the vocabulary of common invective: the elder brother is furious with his immature younger brother for interfering in matters that do not concern him while neglecting his job (guarding the flock). He shouts at him: "I know your malice and insolence."

In the language of Wisdom, *zādhôn* is arrogance, the presumptuous and headstrong conduct of the fool (Prov. 21:24), which can only lead to wrangling and ultimately to disgrace, in contrast to the wisdom of the humble, those who accept advice (Prov. 11:2; 13:10). Ben Sira holds that someone who cannot "put aside arrogance" is unfit to rule (Sir. 7:6), and advises against being disturbed by the arrogance of a successful careerist, whose humiliation is coming (9:12). Arrogance is simply unbecoming in one who is "born of woman" (10:18). Windbags and "arrogant men" (*'anshê zādhôn*) can never attain wisdom (15:7), and "better than the end of an arrogant life" (*'achᵃrîth zādhôn*) is death without children or wealth (16:3).

In Deuteronomy and the prophets, this noun, too, takes on a religious meaning. Someone who disregards the decision of a priest or judge spoken in the name of Yahweh "acts presumptuously" (Dt. 17:12), and a prophet who falsely appeals to the word of Yahweh "speaks presumptuously" (Dt. 18:22). In the days of Ezekiel, "injustice" (read *hammuṭṭeh*) and "pride" "blossom" in Jerusalem (Ezk. 7:10). Jer. 49:16 and Ob. 3 threaten Edom with a consuming judgment of Yahweh on account of the "pride of their heart," which consists in having attacked hapless Judah. Jer. 50:31f. personifies the pride of Babylon, which consists in seeking to destroy Israel. Under the influence of Deuteronomy and these prophetic passages, Ben Sira equates *zādhôn* in 35(32):18 with unrighteousness. He considers "the presumption of their hearts" to be the reason that the generation of the desert perished (16:10), and warns against fellowship with a "presumptuous man" (*'îsh zādhôn*), because it will lead to "involvement in his sins" (12:14). Sin is in fact "a reservoir of presumption" (*miqveh zādhôn*), from whose outlet "abominations pour forth" (10:13).

III. Qumran. At Qumran only the religious meaning is attested. No occurrence of the qal has been found (we may assume an error in 1QS 11:4[6]). The hiphil occurs in a fragmentary text in 4QpPs37 4:15; since the context immediately preceding speaks of the divine judgment, *hezîdh bᵉyādh rāmāh* can only mean "act presumptuously (against God) with premeditation." The noun *zēdhîm* appears in 11QPs[a] 18:15 in parallelism with the wicked (*rᵉshāʿîm*). In 1QH 6:35, the eschatological "wars of (or: against) the presumptuous" (*milchᵃmôth zēdhîm*) are mentioned. Here the *zēdhîm* are the enemies of the community, who "presumptuously," i.e., with premeditated defiance, oppose the will of God. In 1QS 4:10, "presumptuous zeal" (*qin'ath zādhôn*) is listed among the cardinal sins of the wicked (malice, lying, pride, deceit, cruelty, etc.). In 1QH fr 3:15 *zādhôn* stands alongside deceit (*rᵉmiyyāh*) and malice (*ʿavlāh*), and in fr 45:5 alongside faithlessness (*maʿal*). According to 4Q184 1:16, the wicked seek to seduce the devout into rebellion against God and to turn their steps aside from the path of righteousness "in order to bring presumption (upon them)" (*lᵉhābhî' zādhôn*). According to 4QpNah 3:4, the wicked will be hated and abhorred "on account of their guilty presumption" (*ʿal zᵉdhôn 'ashmāthām*). Here the presumption consists uniformly in rebellion against God and his order, which includes the order of the Qumran community.

IV. LXX. The LXX translators are very free in their treatment of *zîdh*, its derivatives, and the associated idioms. The qal in Ex. 18:11 and the hiphil in Ex. 21:14 are rendered by *epitíthestai*, the qal in Jer. 50(27):29 by *antistḗnai*. The hiphil in Dt. 1:43 is represented by *parabiázesthai*, in Dt. 17:13 and 18:20 by *asebeín*, and in Neh. 9:10,

---

[6]Cf. E. Lohse, *Die Texte aus Qumran* ([2]1971), *in loc.;* K. G. Kuhn, *Konkordanz zu den Qumrantexten* (1960), *s.v.* זוע.

16 by *hyperēphaneín*; in Neh. 9:29 it is not translated. In Sir. 3:16, the hiphil participle is represented by *blásphēmos*. Dnl. 5:20 is not translated by the LXX; in the translation ascribed to Theodotion, the Aramaic haphel infinitive is represented by *hyperēphaneúsasthai*.

For the singular of the noun *zēdh*, the LXX has *thrasýs* in Prov. 21:24; Sir. 12:4(5) is translated quite freely. For the plural, we find the translations *ánomoi* (Isa. 13:11), *paránomoi* (Ps. 86[85]:14; 119[118]:85), *allogeneís* (Mal. 3:19 [Eng. 4:1]), *allótrioi* (Mal. 3:15; Ps. 19[18]:14[13]), *hyperḗphanoi* (Ps. 119[118]:21, 51, 69, 78, 122), and *hamartōloí* (Sir. 11:9). In Jer. 43(50):2, it is not translated.

The noun *zādhôn* is represented by *hyperēphanía* (Dt. 17:12; Ob. 3; Sir. 10:13, 18), *asébeia* (Dt. 18:22), *hýbris* and its derivatives (Jer. 50:32 [= LXX 27:32]; Ezk. 7:10; Prov. 11:2; 13:10; Sir. 35:18 [= LXX 35:21]), *itamía* (Jer. 49:16 [= LXX 30:10]). For idioms involving *zādhôn* we find *sklērokardía* (Sir. 16:10) (= *zᵉdhôn lēbh*) and *anḗr hamartōlós* (Sir. 12:14; 15:7) (= *'îsh zādhôn*); sometimes a very free translation makes them hardly recognizable (Prov. 21:24; Sir. 7:6; 9:12; 16:3). The LXX omits 1 S. 17:28 along with the entire section 1 S. 17:12-31.

In general, the LXX has given additional emphasis to the religious force and reprehensibility expressed by the root *zyd*, the blasphemy of arrogantly disregarding God and his laws, through the use of *hyperḗphanos*, *hýbris*, and their derivatives to translate it. Occasionally, however, the translators had only a vague sense of the semantic content of *zyd* and its associated nouns and idioms. Their occasional perplexity in the face of derivatives of *zyd* is illustrated by their translation of *hammayim hazzēdhônîm* in Ps. 124(123):5: *hýdōr anypóstaton*, "without foundation."

The noun *nāzîdh* is uniformly translated *hépsēma*, and the hiphil of *zûdh* in Gen. 25:29 is rendered *hépsein*, reproducing the sense of the Hebrew only roughly.[7]

V. Semantic History; Theological Use. Although it is hard to date the section 1 S. 17:12-31, it probably goes back to the early period of Israelite narrative.[8] If so, we have in v. 28 evidence of great antiquity that in everyday usage *zādhôn* very early had the meaning "impudence." The hiphil of *zîdh* also occurs early in legal usage: it is used in the Covenant Code (Ex. 21:14) to describe brazen premeditated disregard for the law ("dare, venture, make bold"). The root *zyd* and its derivatives likewise found an early place in the language of Wisdom, illustrated by their occurrences in the collection Prov. 10:1-22:16, where they describe the brazen arrogance of fools who make exaggerated claims, which they press uncompromisingly even when they only succeed in making themselves ridiculous. Beginning with E (Ex. 18:11), the term was used for the arrogance of the heathen nations in claiming rights over Israel to which they were not entitled. Beginning with Deuteronomy, *zyd* and its derivative nouns served especially to characterize those within and without Israel who deliberately opposed Yahweh and his moral and religious order, thus becoming the term for blasphemous presumption, translated accurately as *hýbris* by the LXX. In Pss. 19, 86, and 119, the meanings "claim rights over someone (viz., the worshipper, to persecute him

---

[7]Cf. I.

[8]Cf. H. J. Stoebe, *KAT*, VIII/1 (1973), 312-15.

or to exploit him)'' and ''act presumptuously against God'' are interwoven, because the devout worshipper views encroachment on his rights as an attack upon God. The situation is similar in the Qumran texts, where the enemies of the community are looked upon as presumptuous antagonists of God. In Sirach, where formations based on the root *zyd* occur most often, the language of Wisdom and that of theology are interwoven.

Words based on the root *zyd* are remarkably scarce in contexts that also mention pride, haughtiness, or the like (*ga'ᵃvāh,* etc.). Such occurrences are found only in Isa. 13:11; Ob. 3; Dnl. 5:20, and some of the Qumran texts. They occur more frequently in connection with malice (*rōaʿ*), wickedness (*reshaʿ*), and terms for oppression or the like. The point is that the root does not suggest pride or haughtiness, which can be based on genuine superiority even if it should not be a matter for boasting, but rather for the most part claims that are totally unjustified—the arrogation of rights to which one is not entitled, a refusal to recognize the limits set by God and the legal or moral order. In the language of earlier Wisdom, men who act this way are subject to ridicule, because the emptiness of their claims will soon be exposed and they will be disgraced. In the religious language of the Psalms and the prophets beginning with Jeremiah, they are left to God's vengeance. Deuteronomy, Sir. 16:10, and Neh. 9:16, 29 trace God's judgment on his own people or their ancestors back to their presumptuous disobedience toward the divine commandments or the words of a man of God (Moses). In the Qumran texts, the *zādhôn* of the enemies of the community provokes the eschatological judgment of God.

The suggestion that the statements formulated with *zyd* and its nominal derivatives ''are aimed at a specific religious party, namely the Sadducees,''[9] cannot be demonstrated. The concentration of occurrences in Deuteronomy, Ps. 119, Prov. 10–22, and Sirach does show, however, that these formulations were not common to the language of Wisdom or theology as a whole, but were limited to certain circles. The repeated occurrences in Ps. 119, the prayer in Neh. 9, and in Sirach are especially striking; but it is hardly possible to argue convincingly that a specific group of the devout or of their enemies was involved.

Scharbert

---

[9] Bertram, '' 'Hochmut,' '' 36.

זָר/זוּר *zûr/zār*

Contents: I. 1. Etymology; 2. Occurrences. II. Concrete Meaning. III. Religious and Social Meanings; 1. a. The Prophetic and Political Semantic Field: Enemy, Destroyer; b. Foreign Gods; 2. The Language of the Cult: a. That Which Does Not Belong; b. Unauthorized Persons, Non-priests, Laity; 3. The Language of Wisdom: a. The Unchaste Woman; b. Becoming Surety for "Another" (Stranger); 4. Interpretation of Other Passages.

I. 1. *Etymology.* The lexicons distinguish three roots *zwr.*[1] The first, *zwr* I, "press (out)" (qal: Jgs. 6:38; Isa. 59:5; Job 39:15), is related to *zrr* II (Isa. 1:6), Syr. *zār,* and Arab. *zyr,* "press." From this root *zwr* III, "be loathsome, stink" (Job 19:17), must be distinguished; it is related to Arab. *ḏāra,* "stink, hate." *GesB* and Martin-Achard[2] connect *zwr* III with Akk. *zêru,* "hate, loathe";[3] cf. *zajāru,* "enemy,"[4] and *zā/ēʾiru,* "hostile."[5] This connection has been rightly denied by Wernberg-Møller and by Dalman,[6] who cite *zwr* II, "turn aside, go away" (qal and niphal), "be alienated" (hophal); cf. Arab. *zwr,* "be inclined toward, visit,"[7] Tigr. *zawara,* "go around, wander about," Geʿez *zōra,* "endure," Amhar. "turn, go around."[8] From this root the verbal adjective *zār* derives as a participle.[9] With respect to *zār,* cf. also Phoen. *zr,*[10] Ya'udic *zr,*[11] and Old Aram. *zr,*[12] as well as Soq. *derhi,* Meḥri *dirî,* and Šḫaurī *ḏeri,* with the meaning "alien."[13] For Middle Hebrew, cf. the name of the Mishnah tractate, *ʿᵃbhōdhāh zārāh,* "foreign cult." In medieval Hebrew philology, the terms *zr* and *mly zrh* are used for "exceptions" to a rule, and *hzrym* for "irregular" forms.[14]

---

zûr/zār. G. Boström, *Proverbiastudien: die Weisheit und das fremde Weib in Spr 1-9. LUÅ,* 30/3 (1935); P. Humbert, "La 'femme étrangère' du Livre des Proverbes," *RES,* 2 (1937), 49-64; *idem,* "Les adjectifs '*zār*' et '*nokrî*' et la 'femme étrangère' des Proverbes biblique," *Mélanges syriens offerts à M. R. Dussaud,* I (1939), 259-266 = *Opuscules d'un hébraïsant. Mémoires de l'Université de Neuchâtel,* 26 (1958), 111-18; R. Martin-Achard, "זָר *zār* fremd," *THAT,* I, 520-22; J. Milgrom, *Studies in Levitical Terminology,* I. *The Encroacher and the Levite. The Term ʿAbodah. UCPNES,* 14 (1970); L. A. Snijders, "The Meaning of *zār* in the OT," *OTS,* 10 (1954), 1-154; G. Stählin, "ξένος," *TDNT,* V, 1-36, esp. 6, 8-14; P. Wernberg-Møller, "A Note on זור 'to Stink,'" *VT,* 4 (1954), 322-25.

1 *KBL*³, 256.
2 P. 520.
3 *CAD,* XXI, 97ff.
4 *CAD,* XXI, 15.
5 *CAD,* XXI, 14.
6 *AuS,* II (1932), 144f.
7 L. Kopf, *VT,* 8 (1958), 171.
8 *TigrWb,* 502; Leslau, *Contributions,* 18f.
9 *Ble,* § 465e.
10 *KAI,* 26 A III.16, C IV.18.
11 *KAI,* 214.30, 34.
12 *KAI,* 222 B.40, context damaged.
13 *DISO,* 80.
14 Cf. L. Prijs, *Die grammatikalischen Termini des Abraham ibn Esra* (1950), 50.

2. *Occurrences.* The word *zār* occurs 70 times, 56 as a noun and 14 as an adjective. Because the letters *resh* (*r*) and *daleth* (*d*) are frequently confused, the reading *zr* (for *zd*) in several passages is disputed (e.g., Ps. 54:5 [Eng. v. 3]; 86:14[15]). In 1QIs[a] 37:25, the adjective *zārîm* is added to the word *mayim,* a divergence from the MT (cf. 2 K. 19:24). In the Hebrew fragments of Sirach, we find the word *zār* in 8:18; 11:32; 14:4; 39:24; 40:29; 45:13,18; 49:9(?).

II. Concrete Meaning. In the light of the meaning of *zwr* II, "turn aside, deviate, go away," the participle *zr* must be translated "one who distances or removes himself." Only in a few instances does this specific meaning come through clearly; usually the word has a metaphorical or abstract sense. An instance of concrete usage is the phrase *mayim zārîm,* "retreating waters," i.e., water that has seeped into the ground, especially in barren limestone areas. In this context it is very apt to speak of deceitful water or a deceitful brook: a dry wadi that disappoints the thirsty traveller (Isa. 58:11; Jer. 15:18; Mic. 1:14). By digging, one can strike underground water, "retreating water." Thus Sennacherib boasts of having exposed *mayim zārîm* in barren regions. He dug wells in which the retreating underground water collected (Jer. 18:14; 2 K. 19:24; cf. Isa. 37:25 in 1QIs[a]—here the derivation from *zûr* III, "stink," is clearly out of the question: it is hard to imagine a king being proud of having produced stinking water!). Other exploits, too, mark him as an inventive leader and a master of the environment. In Jer. 18:14, Dahood[16] correctly translates *mayim zārîm* as "flowing waters," but he is confused by his assumption that *zûr* II means "to be strange," and so postulates unnecessarily a new root *zwr,* "to flow," which he derives from *zwr* I, "to press, squeeze = to cause to flow." It is clear, however, that this derivation is forced and ignores the concrete meaning of *zwr* II, "deviate, go away."

In Job 19:13 and Ps. 78:30, also, we must understand the verb *zûr* initially in its literal sense. Job's family moved away (albeit here the metaphorical meaning also enters in). Ps. 78:30 reads: "They had not yet left their craving, they still had their food in their mouths. . . ." In other words, the people had not yet risen from their meal; and of course this also means that they were not yet full, that they had not yet pushed their food aside. Taken metaphorically, the word *zûr* in Ps. 58:4(3) and Ezk. 14:5 suggests (spiritual or intellectual) alienation from one's own milieu, a distancing from a familiar reality (e.g., a religious tradition or a generally recognized mode of life and thought). The wicked forsake the community of their own people; the apostate break with tradition. They have become aliens, and are looked upon by the devout as untrustworthy and dangerous. In the great majority of cases where *zār* is used, the association with this *zwr* II is illuminating. But the general concept takes on the coloration of each specific situation in which it is used. This confrontation between what is native and what is alien can lead to conflicts within tribes, families, religious groups, or temples with their personnel.

---

[15]Cf. Snijders, 72.

[16]M. Dahood, "Philological Notes on Jer 18, 14-15," *ZAW,* 74 (1962), 207ff.

III. Religious and Social Meanings.

1. a. *The Prophetic and Political Semantic Field: Enemy, Destroyer.* In the words addressed to Yahweh, to their own people, or to other nations, the prophets often use the term *zār* to designate the enemy, the aggressor, or the occupying power, be it the Assyrian, the Babylonian, or the Edomite. Aliens "devour" the land of Judah (Isa. 1:7), which is understood as a violent infringement on life and order. Isa. 1:7b, "it is desolate, like the overthrowing (*k^emahpēkhath*) of aliens," suggests an idiomatic usage: we are dealing with destruction like the "overthrowing" caused by *zārîm*, i.e., people of a different nature, who have nothing in common and act on entirely different principles; therefore they overthrow everything. (Since in the OT *mahpēkhath* is always followed by "Sodom and Gomorrah," *zārîm* has been read as *s^edhōm* ever since Ewald.[17]) Conversely, it is not surprising to have aliens, foreigners, or enemies assist in the reconstruction of Judah, working as herdsmen, plowmen, and vinedressers, so that the people of God can devote themselves to their priestly function (Isa. 61:5).

Important for this interpretation of *zārîm* is the fact that this word is synonymous with *ʿārîtsîm*, "usurpers, tyrants," or *ʿarîtsê gôyim*, "violent nations," and *nokhrîm*, "foreigners" in the national sense (Lam. 5:2; Isa. 25:2; Jer. 51:2, 51; Ezk. 28:7, 10; 30:12; 31:12; Joel 4:17[3:17]). The reference is to the Babylonians, Tyre, or other enemies of Judah, and occasionally to enemies of another nation (Jer. 51:2). The *zārîm* are not merely people who are different; they are the destroyers who despoil Jerusalem and its sanctuary of their splendor (Ezk. 7:21; 11:9; Ob. 11).

In Ezk. 16:32, *zārîm* has a double meaning: it refers to the other men with whom the woman commits adultery, but also to the foreign nations with which Judah makes treaties. According to Hos. 7:9, *zārîm* devour Ephraim's strength; Ephraim is described metaphorically as having let itself be stirred together with the nations and resembles a breadcake. The "aliens" are specifically the Egyptians and Assyrians, Ephraim's allies, who are despoiling the land. The people expected aid and were deceived. Cf. also 8:7.

In Hos. 5:7, the *bānîm zārîm*, "alien children," are not foreign but domestic enemies: apostasy from Yahweh (→ בגד *bāghadh*) and the practice of pagan fertility cults have created a new race that imperils the continued existence of Israel (v. 7b). This new race, like a *zār*, turns against its own people. In Isa. 28:21, Yahweh's punishment of Jerusalem is termed a *zār maʿ^aśeh*, "strange deed," and a *nokhrîyāh ʿ^abhōdhāh*, "alien work." Yahweh will act not like an ally but like an enemy, like an Assyrian or an Edomite; the consequences for the community of Israel are devastating.

b. *Foreign Gods.* Closely associated with foreign or alien nations are their gods. These embody their character and ideas. It is therefore not surprising that the term *zārîm* can be used not only for other, hostile nations but also for other, dangerous gods, who threaten and corrupt the faith of Israel and the welfare of the people. In Jer. 5:19 and 30:8, both are meant: the foreign rulers or nations and their gods. In Jer. 2:25 and

---

[17]Cf. H. Wildberger, *BK*, X (1965), 19.

3:13—as in Dt. 32:16 and Isa. 17:10—the word refers to baals. Ps. 44:21(20) and 81:10(9) speak of *'ēl zār* as an "outside" god, belonging to an alien nation. He is deceiptful, and his worship brings disaster (Jer. 3:23). Not so is Yahweh. He is not a power dangerous to men, but a deliverer.

2. *The Language of the Cult.*

a. *That Which Does Not Belong.* In the language of the cult we find the terms *qᵉṭōreth zārāh* and *'ēsh zārāh.* Ex. 30:9 contains instructions for the proper use of the incense altar. Only incense (a mixture of various ingredients) is to be burned on this altar, but *qᵉṭōreth zārāh* is explicitly excluded. Examination of Jewish religious ceremonial reveals that different kinds of incense were occasionally offered elsewhere and at other times, for instance, to put down a plague (Nu. 17:11[16:46]) and as part of the ritual of the great Day of Atonement (Lev. 16). The daily incense-offering every morning and evening, however, is entirely another matter and has its own unique place. Any incursion of alien practices into the sacred ceremony is out of place, deviant (*zār*), not a part of the salubrious order. It can be dangerous, as the tradition of the death of Nadab and Abihu shows (Lev. 10:2; Nu. 3:4; 26:61): they offered "alien fire" before Yahweh, an improper fire-offering "such as he had not commanded them." As priests, both were certainly empowered to offer the incense-offering; but now their ceremony is a violation of the sacred order because they are acting on their own initiative, disregarding the cultic regulations governing time and place. Even Aaron himself is not allowed to enter the holy place whenever he wishes (Lev. 16:2). Hos 8:12 also stands in a cultic context: Ephraim has multiplied its altars, but instead of establishing a relationship with Yahweh these alienate the people from God. The prophet recalls the many laws of Yahweh, but these are looked on as *zār,* something "strange" or "alien" in the sense of something dangerous, immoral (cf. 7:15). Instead of participating in worship of Yahweh in order to receive a blessing, the people are suspicious of him as a menacing danger.

b. *Unauthorized Persons, Non-priests, Laity.* There is another group of texts that deserves special mention: in these *zār* designates a person outside the sacred group, for whom a specific area is forbidden territory or who is not allowed to perform certain precisely defined acts. Such an outsider is a non-priest (Ex. 29:33; 30:33; Lev. 22:12; Nu. 17:5[16:40]; 18:7), someone who does not belong to a priest's house (Lev. 22:10, 13) or the tribe of the Levites (Nu. 1:51; 3:38; 18:4,7). The word "layman" is probably a good translation in these contexts, in the sense of ecclesiastical usage that distinguishes the priest from the people (*laós, laicus*). In a few passages, however, the Levite set apart from the people is himself a "layman": in these cases his office is being distinguished from that of the priest. The family of the priest must also be considered as belonging not to the people but to the clergy; in their case the term "unauthorized," which is more general in meaning, can be used. But when the matter under discussion is the relationship between the temple personnel and the congregation, the term "layman" is preferable. A layman must not cross the boundaries of the sacred precincts; neither may he participate in the priestly meal or be anointed with the sacred oil. He may not approach (→ קרב *qārabh*) to serve at the altar as a priest, to enter the inner sanctuary, or to offer incense. This does not mean that the layman does not stand in intimate relationship to the cult, where he is a "child of the family." All it means is that he is not qualified for certain functions. If, as an outsider, he were to attempt to perform these functions, he would represent a danger to the community. In such a case, he or the community may expect catastrophe (Nu. 1:53; 8:18; 16:32). It is clear that these pericopes reflect the ideas of the temple officials. The priests and the laity each have their own place and responsibilities. The priest has professional training and knowledge. He is to make halachic decisions and engage in instructing the people (Lev. 10:11; Ex. 28:30; Lev. 8:8; Ezk. 22:26).

Here, too, the term *zār* often expresses the basic meaning "deviate, depart (from the way of Yahweh)." The people murmur, they refuse instruction, they will not have faith in Yahweh, they rebel against their leaders. In Nu. 18:22, the use of the particle *ʿôdh* is striking. Previously the people had been allowed to approach the tent of meeting; in the future they are forbidden to do so. The people have alienated themselves from Yahweh through their disobedience. In this way the low status of the Levites in the postexilic sanctuary is explained: they, too, alienated themselves from God and are therefore *zārîm,* people who "run off." The *zārîm* are those who are distant in contrast to those who are near (*reḥôqîm* and *qerōbhîm,* Lev. 10:3; cf. Isa. 59:19).

3. *The Language of Wisdom.*

a. *The Unchaste Woman.* In the circle of the wise and their disciples, men are warned against associating with an *ʾishshāh zārāh* or *ʾishshāh nokhrîyāh.* She is the subject of Prov. 2:16-20; 5:1-23; 22:14. Both expressions occur side by side in 2:16; 5:20; 7:5, *ʾishshāh zārāh* alone in 5:3; 22:14. In 6:24 and 23:27, the *ʾishshāh nokhrîyāh* is called an *ʾēsheth rāʿ,* "evil woman," and a *zônāh,* "harlot." The word *nokhrîyāh* (→ נכר *nākhar*) means "unknown, unrecognizable, changed," and thus "foreign." But what does the adjective *zārāh* mean in these pericopes? Is the *ʾishshāh zārāh* an alien, foreign woman who devotes herself to sexual intercourse with men as a worshipper of Ishtar?[18] Or is she merely the wife of another man?[19] The texts do not in fact provide sufficient grounds for interpreting her as a foreigner. Neither, however, is the interpretation that she is another man's wife satisfactory. She appears as a specific type of woman, clearly described. She walks the streets and attempts to seduce young men; she is dangerous and totally untrustworthy, for instead of life and happiness she brings disgrace and death. The adjectives *zārāh* and *nokhrîyāh* designate, in my opinion, a woman who has deserted her place in society. The words "loose, unrestrained" or "unchaste" describe her true character precisely (cf. Prov. 23:27).[20] Here too, therefore, as is so often true, there is an implicit menace in the term *zār.*

---

[18]Boström.

[19]Humbert.

[20]A. Bertholet, *Die Stellung der Israeliten und der Juden zu den Fremden* (1896), 195: she is simply a harlot.

b. *Becoming Surety for "Another" (Stranger).* Various maxims in Proverbs caution against becoming surety for another person and giving a pledge (Prov. 17:18; 22:26). According to Boström,[21] the pledge (literally "handshake") is the common ceremony in commercial transactions whereby the two parties establish a covenant or contract relationship. When the guarantor and creditor exchange a handshake, this signifies that they have agreed to a "purchase contract." In 6:1, the third party for whom one becomes surety is called *zār* or *rēaʿ*, "neighbor"; according to 11:15, it will "go ill" (*raʿ-yērôaʿ*) with anyone who becomes surety for a *zār*. The "stranger" is clearly someone who does not belong to the family (members of a family regulate their affairs privately, without official transactions). This *zār* can, through insolvency, bring the creditor into the house of the guarantor, and thus represents a threat to his well-being. In 20:16 and 27:13, this aspect is emphasized by the parallel term *nokhrî*, "unknown." The guarantor is looked on as a fool whose greed has landed him in difficulties. "Beware godless commercial transactions!"[22] The curse pronounced over a wicked man in Ps. 109 calls, among other things, for the destruction of his "house": a creditor is to seize all that he has, and *zārîm*, "strangers," who are not members of his family, are to plunder the fruits of his toil. A like fate awaits the man who lets himself be seduced by the *ʾishshāh zārāh*, the loose and dangerous woman (Prov. 5:10, 17; cf. 6:31-35).

In the Wisdom of Jesus ben Sirach, the attitude toward the guarantor is more nuanced. In itself, willingness to be surety is laudable (Sir. 29:14, 20). In certain cases, however, one must be on guard, especially if the other party is a "sinner" or an ungrateful person (29:16). In Sirach, *zār* carries the same nuances as it does in the OT: it can mean the stranger, the outsider (8:18; 14:4; 40:29), the non-priest (45:13, 18), as well as the alienated apostate in the religious and moral sense (11:32; 39:24; 49:9[?]).

4. *Interpretation of Other Passages.* The term *zār*, "outsider," is fluid. Crucial for its more precise definition is the question of the immediate context in which its user is thinking and speaking. Is the milieu in question the family, the nation, the company of priests, the circle of the devout?

Thus the *zār* can be someone outside the family (Dt. 25:5), someone who neither lives in the house of the two harlots (1 K. 3:18) nor is dependent on them (who could have been a valuable witness). Job becomes a stranger, he is no longer recognizable to his family and friends (Job 19:15; cf. 19:13, 17; Ps. 31:12f.[11f.]). In days to come, however, he will no longer be an "outsider" to God, but a familiar: he will see God with his own eyes, since he will not be a "stranger," standing afar off or excluded (Job 19:27). The *zār* does not share ancestral traditions; the wisdom of the land of Teman is alien to him (Job 15:19). He is the godless man, the enemy of the faithful, the rich oppressor of the poor (Ps. 54:5[3]),[23] but also the patently unqualified compatriot. But when the word *zār* is used for such a neighbor, the emphasis is on distance. He is an

---

[21] P. 56.

[22] Boström, 100.

[23] A. Causse, *Du groupe ethnique à la communauté religieuse* (Paris, 1937), 243.

"outsider," for example, with regard to inward feelings, the whole complex world of heart and mind (Prov. 14:10). Self-praise is worthless, but when "others" outside one's family speak one's praises as independent strangers, that means something (Prov. 27:2).

In these passages the term *zār* has fewer negative overtones (in the sense of "hostile" or "menacing") than elsewhere. In such contexts, Humbert often translates *zār* as *un autre,* "another, someone else." But he, too, is aware that the person in question is not a second party, but a third ("*à autrui, à un tiers*").[24] In other words, *zār* always presupposes a primary nexus with respect to which the *zār* is the stranger, the third party. The "other" in the sense of "second party" is expressed in Hebrew by the word → אחר *'achēr.* Sometimes (e.g., under the influence of wine) a man sees "strange things" (*zārôth,* Prov. 23:33) that do not belong to his familiar everyday world, just as his mouth utters words that are torn out of context and pervert the regular world (*tahpukhôth,* Prov. 23:33b).

Snijders

---

[24]"Les adjectifs," 260.

זַיִת *zayith*

Contents: I. The Word. II. Ancient Near East. III. OT: Occurrences and General Use. IV. Religious Use. V. Personal Names.

I. The Word. The word *zait/zayith* (Ugar. *zt*) is used in the West Semitic languages for both the evergreen olive tree (*Olea europaea*) and its fruit, the olive (cf. Egyp. *ḏt,* Copt. *djoit*). Akk. *serdu* is also frequently attested in texts from Ugarit.[1] Olive oil can be called *dm zt,* "olive blood," in Ugaritic,[2] just as wine is sometimes called *dm ʿṣm.*[3]

---

zayith. W. Corswant, *Dictionary of Life in Bible Times* (Neuchâtel, Eng. tr. 1960); Dalman, *AuS,* IV (1935), 153-255; A. Drachmann, *Ancient Oil Mills and Presses* (Copenhagen, 1932); F. C. Fensham, "An Ancient Tradition of the Fertility of Palestine," *PEQ,* 98 (1966), 166f.; T. Fischer, *Der Ölbaum: seine geographische Verbreitung, seine wirtschaftliche und kulturhistorische Bedeutung* (1904); R. J. Forbes, "Food and Drink," in C. Singer, ed., *A History of Technology,* II (Oxford, 1956), 128-139; H. G. Güterbock, "Oil Plants in Hittite Anatolia," *JAOS,* 88 (1968), 66-71; H. A. Hoffner, *Alimenta Hethaeorum: Food Production in Hittite Asia Minor. AOS,* 55 (1974), 116-18; J. Hoops, *Geschichte des Ölbaums. SHAW,* 1942/43, 3 (1944); *idem,* "Die Geschichte des Ölbaumes," *FuF,* 21/23 (1947), 35-38; I. Löw, *Die Flora der Juden,* II (Vienna, 1924), 286-295; A. Neuburger, *The Technical Arts and Sciences of the Ancients* (London, 1930), 110-121.

[1]*AHw,* II, 1037.
[2]RS 24.258, vo. 6.
[3]*CTA,* 4 [II AB], III, 44; IV, 38.

II. Ancient Near East. The olive tree and its fruit are known to have existed in the eastern Mediterranean region since at least the fourth millennium B.C. Syria-Palestine, together with Greece, has been designated as the homeland of the olive tree.[4] Olive seeds have been found at Teleilat Ghassul and elsewhere.[5] Egyptian texts of the early dynastic period mention olive oil as an import from Syria and Palestine, and we know that Cyprus imported the same commodity around 2500 B.C.[6] The olive tree and its fruit were utilized extensively in everyday life: the wood was well suited for joinery and carving, while the fruit provided food, medicine, fuel for lamps, cosmetics, and oil for anointing, which could be either secular[7] or sacred. Among the Hittites, olive oil was used to attract the attention of the gods.[8] In Mesopotamia, the olive tree was occasionally associated with the tree of life. Its oil, which was frequently used in purification rituals, was thought to have healing powers.[9] Thus the anointing of a king also was intended to promote his health.

III. OT: Occurrences and General Use. The word *zayith* occurs 38 times in the OT as well as in Sir. 50:10; it usually refers to olive groves or to the tree and its fruit (as in Mic. 6:15, where the phrase *dārakh zayith,* "tread olives," occurs). In a few cases the phrase *ʿēts hazzayith* is used for the olive tree (Hag. 2:19). Olive oil is usually called → יצהר *yitshār*; the phrase *shemen zayith* appears three times (Ex. 27:20; 30:24; Lev. 24:2).

Since the olive tree does not need much water, it is well suited to the dry climate and mountainous landscape of Palestine. It grows slowly and reaches an age of several hundred years. The trunk generally grows to about 2 meters high; the crown will attain a height of 5 to 10 meters.[10] A well-developed tree can yield 110–120 kilograms of olives every second year.

As a rule, the olives were harvested at the end of the vintage. When ripe, they were shaken or knocked from the trees (*nōqeph,* Isa. 17:6; 24:13; *chābhaṭ,* Dt. 24:20). The strong east wind would also cause some to drop. According to Dt. 24:20, any left on the boughs were to be "for the sojourner, the fatherless, and the widow" (cf. Isa. 17:6). A similar commandment appears in Ex. 23:11, which states that fields, vineyards, and olive orchards shall lie fallow every seventh year.

The olives were gathered in baskets and brought to the oil presses, which were usually carved out of the bedrock underlying the orchards. Even though Mic. 6:15 uses the word *dārakh,* "tread," for the process of pressing, it is unlikely that olives—like grapes—were pressed by foot (in the Micah passage, *dārakh* is used for both *zayith* and *tîrôsh*). Normally the oil was pressed out by beating (*ktt*) the olives in a stone mortar or in bowl-shaped depressions in the rock (Ex. 27:20; 29:40; Lev. 24:2; Nu.

---

[4]Fischer, 64; cf. Hoops, 24ff.

[5]K. Kenyon, *Archaeology in the Holy Land* ([3]1971), 94; E. Anati, *Palestine Before the Hebrews* (London, 1963), 307, 314.

[6]*AuS,* IV, 201ff.

[7]*ANET*[3], 491f.

[8]Fensham, 166.

[9]G. Meier, ed., *Die assyrische Beschwörungssammlung Maqlû. AfO* sup. vol. 2 (1937), vii, 31ff.; cf. Pliny *Hist. nat.* xv.1–8.

[10]*AuS,* IV, 156.

28:5; 1 K. 5:25 [Eng. v. 11]). Oil from beaten olives was considered pure and was used in ritual contexts (→ זכה *zākhāh*). Olives could also be pressed by means of a heavy cylindrical stone, which could be rolled over them in a rectangular press hewn out of the bedrock or in a circular stone press—even indoors. It is possible that this method was used after the olives had first been crushed in a stone mortar.[11] Pressing by means of a vertical millstone rolled around a circular trough appears to have been introduced in Palestine during the Hellenistic period.[12] The oil produced was kept in jar-shaped pits sealed with clay or in large jars (1 K. 17:12ff.; 2 K. 4:2ff.); smaller quantities for immediate use were carried in oil horns (1 S. 16:1; 1 K. 1:39).

In the OT, *zayith* is mentioned from the earliest historical period in Canaan. Samson is said to have set fire to the vineyards and olive orchards of the Philistines (Jgs. 15:5). In Samuel's presentation of the royal law (1 S. 8:11ff.), we read that the king will take the best fields and vineyards and olive orchards from the people and given them to his officials (v. 14). Jotham's fable describes the olive tree as the king of trees, honored by gods and men (Jgs. 9:8f.; text uncertain). It is possible that the Israelites, like other peoples in Canaan, exported oil (cf. 1 K. 5:25[11]).

It is also clear from Hos. 14:7(6); Am. 4:9; Isa. 17:6 that *zayith* had long been grown in Canaan. According to Dt. 28:40, the olive tree was found throughout Palestine, as it is today.

The OT does not appear to distinguish the true olive from the wild olive (cf. Rom. 11:17f.); it is possible, however, that the phrase *ʿēts shemen* in Isa. 41:19; 1 K. 6:31ff.; Neh. 8:15 refers to the wild olive.

Vineyards (*kerem*) and olive trees (*zayith*) appear together 13 times as a pair of terms for fertility and food supply (Ex. 23:11; Dt. 6:11; Josh. 24:13; 1 S. 8:14; 2 K. 18:32; Neh. 9:25; Am. 4:9), along with the pair vines (*gephen*) and olive trees (Dt. 8:8; Hab. 3:17; Hag. 2:19; Ps. 128:3), and wine (*yayin*) and olive trees (Mic. 6:15). Oil is a symbol of prosperity and blessing (Dt. 32:33; 33:24; Job 29:6).

IV. Religious Use. Both the olive tree and olive oil could be used for cultic purposes. The holy oil used for anointing kings and priests was usually produced from olive oil (→ שמן *shemen*, → משח *māshach*).

The two cherubim in the *d^ebhîr* of the temple were made of olivewood (*ʿ^atsê-shemen*) overlaid with gold (1 K. 6:23). The doors of the *d^ebhîr* and the *hêkhāl* were likewise made of olivewood (1 K. 6:31-33). Ps. 52:10(8) may indicate that olive trees were planted in the vicinity of shrines. Branches of olive were sometimes used for building booths at the *sukkôth* festival (Neh. 8:15), which probably presupposes that the olives had been harvested before the festival.

The image of the olive tree and its branches and leaves appears occasionally as a symbol of life and blessing. In the Flood Narrative, the dove sent forth by Noah brings back an olive leaf as a sign that the earth can be cultivated once more (Gen. 8:11).

---

[11]Cf. J. Elgavish, "Shiqmona," *IEJ*, 22 (1972), 167 and Plate 30A.

[12]*AuS*, IV, 206ff.; Corswant, 227; R. Saidah, "Archaeology in the Lebanon 1968-1969," *Berytus*, 13 (1969), 132, Fig. b.

According to Hag. 2:19, when the temple is rebuilt Yahweh will send his blessing in the form of vines, fig trees, pomegranates, and olive trees. The temple and its cult are prerequisite for the divine blessing. In the descriptions of the promised land, the *zêthîm* and *k^erāmîm* not planted by the Israelites play an important role (Dt. 6:11; 8:8; Josh. 24:13; Neh. 9:25). Somewhat comparable is a passage in the address of Rabshakeh to the inhabitants of Jerusalem, in which he promises them a land that is like their own, including vineyards and olive trees (2 K. 18:32). Just as the promised land is to be rich in olive trees, so *zayith* appears in the words of the prophets as a sign of blessing (Hos. 2:23f.[21f.]; Joel 2:19). In Hos. 14:7(6), the ideal future of Israel is compared to the beauty of an olive tree. The children of a family can be compared to the shoots of the olive tree (Ps. 128:3). In curses and statements about the devastation of the land, we find the motif of the olive tree once again: it will be destroyed, along with grain and wine, if the commandments of Yahweh are not kept (Dt. 28:39ff.; Isa. 17:6; Am. 4:9; Mic. 6:15). This agrees with the image of Yahweh's theophany, when the produce of the *zayith* will fail (Hab. 3:17). Isa. 24:13 describes Yahweh's vengeance on the world by means of the image of an olive tree that has been beaten for its fruit so that only a few olives are left.

The metaphorical use of *zayith* is also found in connection with the righteous man, who compares himself to an olive branch (Ps. 52:10[8]), and with the godless, who resembles an olive tree that has lost its blossoms and therefore has no fruit (blessing) (Job 15:33). The two anointed of Zec. 4:14 (the king and the high priest) are compared to olive trees (Zec. 4:3). This motif can be traced back to the conception of the king as the tree of life. It reappears in Test. Levi 8:8f., where an olive branch is one of the symbols for the royal priesthood of Levi.[13]

V. Personal Names. The word *zayith* also appears as an element in several names: personal names like *zêthān* (1 Ch. 7:10) and *zēthām* (1 Ch. 23:8; 26:22), and the place name *birzayith* (1 Ch. 7:31), which has been identified with Khirbet Bir-zeit, north of Beitin.[14]

The best-known example is the Mount of Olives, *har hazzêthîm* (Zec. 14:4; cf. 2 S. 15:30). Presumably this mountain was more heavily covered with olive trees in OT times than it is now (cf. also Gethsemane, *gath shemen,* "oil press"). The Mount of Olives was probably a pre-Israelite cultic site, "where God was worshipped" (2 S. 15:32; cf. Ezk. 11:23; Zec. 14:4ff.). It was natural, therefore, for Solomon to build sanctuaries for Milkom and Chemosh "on the mountain east of Jerusalem" (1 K. 11:7; cf. 2 K. 23:13).[15] It is also possible that the Mount of Olives, called *har hammashchîth*

---

[13]G. Widengren, *The King and the Tree of Life in Ancient Near Eastern Religion. UUÅ,* 1951/4 (1951), 37f.; A. Caquot, "Le double investiture de Lévi," in *Ex orbe religionum. Festschrift G. Widengren,* I. *SNumen,* 21 (1972), 159f.

[14]Y. Aharoni, *The Land of the Bible* (trans. 1967), 223.

[15]J. B. Curtis, "An Investigation of the Mount of Olives in the Judaeo-Christian Tradition," *HUCA,* 28 (1957), 137ff., 169f.; B. Otzen, *Studien über Deuterosacharja* (Copenhagen, 1964), 202ff.

in 2 K. 23:13, played some role in the Passover festival.[16] On the day of Yahweh, the theophany will take place upon the Mount of Olives (Zec. 14:4), and in Ezekiel's vision of the last days of Jerusalem, the cherubim and Yahweh leave the city and stop upon the Mount of Olives (*ʿāmadh,* Ezk. 11:22f.). This shows that in the syncretistic religion of Judah, Yahweh, too, was connected with the Mount of Olives.[17] Jewish tradition associates the burning of the red heifer (Nu. 19) with the Mount of Olives.

Ahlström

[16]W. A. Heidel, *The Day of Yahweh* (1929), 310f.
[17]Otzen, *Studien,* 202f.

זָכָה *zākhāh;* זכך *zkk;* זַךְ *zakh*

Contents: I. Etymology. II. Occurrences and Meaning: 1. Literal; 2. Metaphorical.

I. Etymology. Corresponding to Heb. *zkh* and its by-form *zkk* we find Aram. *d^ekhî/d^ekhā'* and *z^ekhā',* "be pure, innocent, upright." Since the form with *ḏ* appears to be original, the *z* must have come about under Akkadian or Hebrew influence.[1] In Arabic, too, twin forms are found: *ḏakā* and *zakā,* "be pure, flourish"; Nöldeke considers the use of *zakā* in a moral sense in the Koran to be a borrowing.[2] The original form with *ḏ* is found in OSA *ḏky,* "be pure," II "cleanse." Akk. *zakû* can mean "be clear" (water, sky, etc.), "be pure, clean" (clothes, persons, metals), or "be free of claims."[3]

II. Occurrences and Meaning. There are two roots in Hebrew: *zky,* with 8 occurrences (4 qal, 3 piel, 1 hithpael), and the by-form *zkk,* with 4 occurrences of the verb (3 qal, 1 hiphil) and 11 of the adj. *zakh.* There is no difference in meaning between the two roots. Both can mean literally "pure, clear" and metaphorically "pure, innocent."

1. *Literal.* In the case of the adj. *zakh,* the literal meaning is used with reference to the oil intended for the golden lampstand (Ex. 27:20; Lev. 24:2 [P]) and to "pure frankincense" (*l^ebhônāh,* Ex. 30:34; Lev. 24:7 [P]). In both cases, the reference could be to pure, unadulterated material;[4] since, however, we are dealing with products used in the cult, the notion of cultic purity has probably also infiltrated.

[1]H. Zimmern, *Akkadische Fremdwörter als Beweis für babylonischen Kultureinfluss* (²1917), 25; E. Y. Kutscher in *Tarbiz,* 19 (1947-48), 125.
[2]T. Nöldeke, *Neue Beiträge zur semitischen Sprachwissenschaft* (1910), 25.
[3]*CAD,* XXI, 23-32.
[4]Cf. K. Elliger, *HAT,* 4 (1966), 328: "strained through a cloth."

Similarly, *zkk* has its literal meaning in Lam. 4:7: the princes of Zion were ''purer'' (more brilliant, whiter) than snow and whiter than milk. The sequel is noteworthy: now they have turned black.

Two passages from Job occupy an intermediate position. Job 25:5 states: ''Even the moon is not bright (*lō' ya'ᵃhîl*) and the stars are not 'clean' in his [Yahweh's] sight.'' The parallelism shows that the statement refers to the clear and bright illumination of the heavenly bodies. The author, however, uses this observation metaphorically in his argument: ''How can man be righteous (*yitsdaq*) before God? How can he who is born of woman be 'clean'?'' (v. 4). In Job 15:14f., similarly, the word is poised between literal and figurative meaning: the heavens are not ''clean'' (clear?) in the sight of Yahweh; how then could man be ''clean'' or righteous (*ṣdq*)? Here the parallel in v. 15 itself introduces a religious and ethical element: God does not even trust his holy ones (*qᵉdhōshāv*)—therefore many commentators suggest that ''heavens'' here stands for ''heavenly beings.''[5]

In these two passages, then, *zākhāh* is used in its literal sense, while the root *zkk* both times stands in parallelism with *ṣdq*.

2. *Metaphorical.* The other passages clearly exhibit a metaphorical sense, with religious and ethical force, as the parallel terms suffice to demonstrate. In three passages the adj. *zakh* is used in combination with → ישׁר *yāshar:* Job 8:6, ''If you are 'pure' and upright, God will preserve you'' (note *ṣdq* in v. 6c); Prov. 20:11, ''Even a child makes himself known by his acts, whether what he does is 'pure' and right''; and Prov. 21:8b, ''The conduct of the 'pure' is right.''

Different synonyms appear in other passages: Mic. 6:11, ''Would I [Yahweh] be pure,[6] if I tolerated wicked scales and deceitful weights?''; Ps. 51:6(4), ''. . . that thou [Yahweh] mayest be pure in thy sentence and blameless (*ṣdq*) in thy judgment''; Ps. 73:13, ''All in vain have I 'kept' my heart 'clean' (*zikkāh*) and washed my hands in innocence (*niqqāyôn* [→ נקה *nāqāh*])''; Ps. 119:9, ''How can a young man 'keep' his way 'pure' [piel]? By guarding it according to thy word''; Prov. 20:9, ''Who can say, 'I have ''made'' my heart ''clean''; I am pure [→ טהר *ṭāhar*] from my sin (*chaṭṭa'th*)?' ''; Isa. 1:16, ''Wash yourselves (*rachᵃtsû*); make yourselves clean (*hizzakkû*); remove the evil of your doings . . .''; Job 9:30, ''Were I to wash myself (*rḥṣ*) with snow, and cleanse (*hᵃzikkôthî*) my hands with lye . . .'' (I would still be guilty; note the verb *rāsha'* in v. 29).

In these passages, too, the word exhibits a certain semantic duality: on the one hand, *zkk/zākhāh* is connected with washing and ritual purification, on the other with → צדק *ṣdq*. Fisher proposes to understand the verb *zky* primarily as a legal expression, meaning ''not guilty.''[7]

In the case of the adj. *zakh,* the religious and ethical meaning predominates: Job. 11:4, ''My doctrine (*leqach*) is 'pure,' and I am clean (*bar* [→ ברר *bārar*]) in God's

---

[5]H. H. Rowley, *Job. CB,* N.S. (1970), 137, etc.

[6]The text is uncertain; most commentators read *'ᵃzakkeh* for *'ezkeh,* ''Could I declare pure, innocent. . . ?''

[7]L. R. Fisher, ''An Amarna Age Prodigal,'' *JSS,* 3 (1958), 113–122, esp. 115.

eyes''; 16:17, "There is no violence (*chāmās*) in my hands, and my prayer is 'pure' ''; 33:9, "I am 'clean,' without transgression (*pesha'*); I am pure (*chaph*), and there is no iniquity (*'āvôn*) in me''; Prov. 16:2, "All the ways of a man are 'pure' in his own eyes, but Yahweh weighs the spirit.''

Negoită-Ringgren

זָכַר *zākhar;* זֵכֶר *zēkher;* זִכָּרוֹן *zikkārôn;* אַזְכָּרָה *'azkārāh*

Contents: I. 1. Etymology; 2. Occurrences; 3. Context. II. 1. *zākhar*; 2. Man Remembering God; 3. God Remembers. III. *nizkar*. IV. *hizkîr*. V. *zēkher*, Memory. VI. *zikkārôn*, Memorial. VII. *'azkārāh*, Remembrance. VIII. Cultic Representation of the Past.

I. 1. *Etymology*. The root *zkr* occurs in all branches of Semitic: Aram. *z^ekhar, d^ekhar*, "remember''; OSA *ḏkr*, "mention, make known''; Arab. *ḏakara*, "remember, mention''; Ethiop. *zakara*, "remember, think of''; Ugar. *ḏkr*.[1] The first radical becomes *d* in Aramaic by differentiation. Akk. *zakāru(m)* means "say, name''; in all other Semitic languages the meaning is the same as that in Hebrew: "remembering.'' This becomes clear from an examination of how the root is used in the various languages. While in Akkadian it can mean "pronounce the name of a god'' or "swear

zākhar. J. Begrich, "Sōfēr und Mazkīr; ein Beitrag zur inneren Geschichte des davidisch-salomonischen Grossreiches und des Königreiches Juda,'' *ZAW*, 58 (1940/41), 1-29 = *GSAT. ThB*, 21 (1964), 67-98; H. Bietenhard, "ὄνομα,'' *TDNT*, V, 252-261; Y. Blau, "Reste des i-Imperfekts von *ZKR*, Qal; eine lexikographische Studie,'' *VT*, 11 (1961), 81-86; H. J. Boecker, "Anklagereden und Verteidigungsreden im AT; ein Beitrag zur Formgeschichte alttestamentlicher Prophetenworte,'' *EvTh*, 20 (1960), 398-412; *idem*, "Erwägungen zum Amt des Mazkir,'' *ThZ*, 17 (1961), 212-16; P. A. H. de Boer, *Gedenken und Gedächtnis in der Welt des AT. Franz Delitzsch-Vorlesungen, 1960* (1962); B. S. Childs, *Memory and Tradition in Israel. SBT*, 37 (1962); M. Dahood, "Hebrew-Ugaritic Lexicography II,'' *Bibl*, 45 (1964), 406; C. Gancho and F. Gils, "Recuerdo (heb. *zāḵar, zikkārōn;* ἀνάμνησις, μιμνήσκομαι; Vg. memorari, recordari),'' *EncBib Barc* VI, 128-132; A. Greiff, "Grundbedeutung und Entwicklungsgeschichte von Zakhar,'' *BZ*, 13 (1915), 200-214; H. Gross, "Zur Wurzel zkr,'' *BZ*, N.S. 4 (1960), 227-237; B. Jacob, "Beiträge zur Einl. in die Psalmen,'' *ZAW*, 17 (1897), 48-80; Y. Livni, "עוד לעניין זכר הזכיר,'' *Lešonenu*, 26 (1962), 279; O. Michel, "μιμνήσκομαι,'' *TDNT*, IV, 678-683; G. von Rad, *OT Theol.* (trans. 1962-65); H. Graf Reventlow, "Das Amt des Mazkir; zur Rechtsstruktur des öffentlichen Lebens in Israel,'' *ThZ*, 15 (1959), 161-175; G. Rinaldi, "זָכַר, זֵכֶר, זִכָּרוֹן,'' *BeO*, 5 (1963), 112-14; J. Scharbert, "Das Verbum PQD in der Theologie des AT,'' *BZ*, N.S. 4 (1960), 209-226; W. Schottroff, *"Gedenken" im Alten Orient und im AT. WMANT*, 15 (²1967); *idem*, *THAT*, I, 507-518; F. Schwally, "Miscellen,'' *ZAW*, 11 (1891), 176-180; J. J. Stamm, "Zum Altargesetz im Bundesbuch,'' *ThZ*, 1 (1945), 304-306; T. C. Vriezen, *An Outline of OT Theol.* (trans. 1958); H. Zirker, *Die kultische Vergegenwärtigung der Vergangenheit in den Psalmen. BBB*, 20 (1964).

[1] See Gröndahl, *PNU*, 196.

by him,'' the Amarna[2] and Lachish[3] letters contain the motif of a subject's appeal to be remembered graciously by the king. In the Hadad Inscription, invocation of the god's name is coupled with the god's remembering Panammu.[4] In the Nabatean inscriptions from Sinai, remembering ''has a clearly religious sense: it is something the deity is to do.''[5] The noun → זכר *zākhār,* ''man, male,'' does not belong to the same root, although many attempts have been made to find a common background.[6] Today this word is generally associated with a separate root.[7]

2. *Occurrences.* In studying the group of words based on *zkr* in the OT from a theological perspective, it is best to begin with the qal of the verb, occurring 168 times, to which the niphal (20 occurrences) furnishes the passive counterpart. The hiphil (31 occurrences), with the causative meaning ''bring to remembrance,'' exhibits extended usage, as does the noun *zēkher* (33 occurrences), alongside which we find *zikkārôn* (24 occurrences), which materializes remembrance as a ''memorial.'' In the Aramaic portion of Ezra we find *dikhrôn* (Ezr. 6:2) and *dokhrān* (twice in Ezr. 4:15). Finally, the cultic term *'azkārāh* derives from our root (7 occurrences).

3. *Context.* The verb *zākhār* occurs absolutely or with a verb as complement only in a few passages; in most cases it is combined with the object of the intellectual activity, with (39 times) or without (52 times) the use of *'eth*. In 24 cases the content of the remembrance is expressed by an object clause. The special relationship of the activity to a particular person is expressed 12 times by l^e-. The preposition b^e- appears in Jer. 3:16, and *ʿal* in Neh. 13:14, 29. It is therefore to be expected that the verb (whose use in the qal will be examined initially) serves primarily to express an intellectual activity that is relational and personal.

It is possible to define the verb's semantic content more precisely, because it frequently appears in combination with certain other verbs. Just as it is itself, when negated, the commonest expression for ''forget,'' we frequently find alongside statements about remembering the phrase *lō' shākhach,* ''not forget'': Gen. 40:23; Dt. 8:18f.; 9:7; 1 S. 1:11; Isa. 17:10; 54:4; Ps. 9:13 (Eng. v. 12); 74:18f., 22f.; 77:4(3); Job 11:16; 24:20 (niphal); Prov. 31:7.[8] Such parallelism shows that *zākhar* denotes the presence and acceptance of something in the mind. The latter is suggested by the parallel use of *ʿalāh* or *śûm ʿal-lēbh:* Isa. 47:7; 57:11; 65:17 (niphal); Jer. 3:16. What is remembered is ''taken to heart''—with the ''heart'' understood to be an expression for the personality as a whole (→ לב *lēbh*).[9] Similar ideas are expressed by Ps. 63:7(6); 77:7(6) (LXX), 12f.(11f.) with → הגה *hāghāh,* ''murmur over, meditate upon''; by

[2]EA 228, 19; Schottroff, 43f.

[3]Lachish Letter II, 4; Schottroff, 46.

[4]*KAI,* 214.16f.; Schottroff, 59ff.

[5]Schottroff, 73; cf. the full discussion of the etymology *ibid.,* 3-10.

[6]Cf. Schwally, 176-180; Grieff, 202.

[7]Cf. de Boer, 13f.; all the material will be found in Schottroff, 4f.

[8]According to Zirker (10), *nāshāh* is not used in this way, but cf. Isa. 44:21.

[9]De Boer, 21.

Ps. 77:4,7(3,6) with → שׂיח *śîach,* "consider"; and by Dt. 32:7 and Isa. 43:18 with → בין *bîn,* "understand." All these verbs help define *zākhar* more precisely by showing that it denotes an active cognitive occupation with a person or situation. When Jer. 14:10; 15:15 even combine *zākhar* with → פקד *pāqadh,* "act with visible results,"[10] an element of concrete performance is added; cf. Nu. 15:40: "So you shall remember and do [*ʿāśāh;* cf. also Ps. 103:18] all my commandments." There are also passages that equate God's remembering with his mercy and forgiveness (→ סלח *sālach;* → רחם *richam,* Jer. 31:20, 34). An interesting sequence of verbs appears in Nu. 15:39: look upon, remember, do. When the devout Israelite sees the tassels on his clothing, he will remember that they are connected with God's law, which imposes its obligations upon him; he will then act accordingly. Quite often, in fact, *zākhar* implies an action or appears in combination with verbs of action.[11] Observation of the context of *zākhar* reveals that the verbs used in parallel do not refer to the past only, so that the interpretation of *zākhar* as "remember" in the sense of "recall" can hardly represent its basic meaning.[12]

II. 1. *zākhar*. In six passages *zākhar* expresses the active intellectual engagement of a person with himself: Hab. 3:2 prays to God that he will remember to have mercy; in Lam. 3:20 our verb expresses the speaker's melancholy, just as it describes an attempt to come to grips with the problem of guilt in Job 4:7 and with the transitoriness of life in Job 7:7. In Job 21:6, the sufferer meditates and is dismayed, while in Ps. 22:28 the nations' coming to their senses and their turning to God are brought together in a single intellectual act.

In all these instances the subject is intellectual activity, but it would be wrong to limit this activity a priori to the religious realm. Despite the preponderance of religious statements, it must always be considered in the case of our verb that the peculiar nature of the biblical texts would lead us to expect specialization of usage in the direction of religious meanings, and that the secular use of *zākhar* may well have been common.[13] Such usage may be illustrated by the following passages, where something is to be "remembered" in the present. In Jgs. 9:2, the citizens of Shechem are to remember that Abimelech is their kinsman, which entails certain consequences. According to Job 40:32(41:8), a fight with a crocodile would be memorably perilous. Prov. 31:7 states that the enjoyment of wine helps men forget their misery. In Eccl. 9:15, it is opprobrious not to remember a poor man.

The fact that *zākhar* frequently expresses thought of the past has led to the assumption that its basic meaning is "remember" in the sense of "recall," but this is simply inappropriate in many passages.[14] It would be more accurate to say that the nuance of "recollection" springs from intellectual activity with reference to the past. The recent past is referred to when the butler at first forgets to act on Joseph's request but later

---

[10] *Ibid.,* 20; cf. also Scharbert, 209-226.
[11] Pedersen, *ILC,* I-II, 107.
[12] Cf. de Boer, 24.
[13] Cf. Childs, 50.
[14] Childs, 21; Schottroff, 4, 339.

remembers him (Gen. 40:14, 23; 41:9ff.). Shimei's plea to David (2 S. 19:20[19]) and Abigail's request that the king will remember her with favor (1 S. 25:31) likewise refer to the past experienced by the person being asked to remember or forget; cf. also Est. 2:1 and 2 K. 9:25. Not rarely a value judgment is implied, as in 2 Ch. 24:22, where the ingratitude of king Joash in killing the prophet Zechariah is exposed. It is the Israelites' lack of faith in God's guidance that leads them to remember the fish they ate in Egypt (Nu. 11:5). In Lam. 1:7,9, recollection of the glorious past is a motif accentuating the affliction of the present. And when Joseph remembers his dreams (Gen. 42:9), more is involved than intellectual recall: his understanding of God's guidance is grounded in faith.

The future can also be the subject of the intellectual activity expressed by *zākhar*. According to Isa. 47:7, Babylon should have remembered its end. A man should remember the coming "days of darkness" (Eccl. 11:8). Here we see that the intellectual objects of *zākhar* constitute a more comprehensive class than knowledge of the past. It is thus always important that recollection concerns not only past events, but also the consequences their memory entails.[15]

2. *Man Remembering God.* Our discussion so far has dealt primarily with passages that express a relationship of the intellect to persons and events. Further examination of *zākhar* in the qal shows that this holds true almost universally, and in addition that there is a predeliction for religious use of this term. The qal of *zākhar* has God as its subject 68 times; in 23 of these God is spoken of as remembering or being mindful of men; in addition there are 12 in which he remembers his covenant, i.e., his special relationship to his people. But even when something else is named as the object of God's remembering (20 times), men or God's activity on their behalf are usually involved. In many cases, too, God stands as the object of this mental activity:[16] when it is men who do the remembering (100 times), the object is usually (69 times) God, his saving acts on behalf of his people, or the like.

There are thus a few passages in which *zākhar* is used of persons remembering persons, but many more in which they remember God. Deuteronomy (with 14 occurrences of *zākhar* qal) actually provides a course of theological instruction based on the past, albeit from the fictitious perspective of Moses' recounting to the assembled Israelites their own past experience. The plagues in Egypt, ostensibly seen by the listeners with their own eyes, are to inspire confidence in God's help for the occupation of Canaan (Dt. 7:18; 24:18,22). More generally, the exodus from Egypt is the most common motif: Dt. 5:15; 15:15; 16:3, 12; 24:18,22; 1 Ch. 16:12. In addition, Dt. 8:2 interprets the years in the wilderness as a time of testing, and 9:7 understands God's wrath as a motif of his discipline. Such ideas of their religious past were thus formative for the covenant people and their faith in Yahweh in the period of Deuteronomy's origin and its associated cultic reform. The teachings of the "days of old" are authoritative for Israel's notion of God; they are to be handed down from generation to

---

[15] Gross, 231.

[16] *Ibid.*

generation (Dt. 32:7). "To speak of the past is to make it effectual, authoritative for today."[17] Specific incidents may also be entrusted to memory: in Dt. 24:9, Miriam's leprosy is recalled to illuminate the treatment of leprosy in general, and in Dt. 25:17 the actions of the Amalekites are cited as grounds for their total extermination. Quite generally, Israel's prosperity is an occasion to remember Yahweh, who has given it in fulfilment of his promise (Dt. 8:18).

Almost as frequently as in Deuteronomy, the motif of recalling God's deeds in the past occurs in Ezekiel (10 times); here, however, it is used by way of rebuke. Even in Egypt, Israel played the harlot with other "gods" (Ezk. 23:19,27). But the "days of youth" were also a time of God's mercy (16:22,43), which Israel no longer remembers. Other passages speak of recollection that leads to repentance and to Israel's sense of shame for its misconduct in days of old (16:60f.,63; 20:43; 36:31). In the end, however, the "remnant" will remember Yahweh, in other words, confess him (6:9).

Another passage rich in motifs from Israel's religious past is Isa. 63:11-14: *zākhar* appears only at the beginning to call for remembrance, but the passage goes on to speak of Moses and his call, the passage through the Red Sea, and God's guidance in the wilderness. Cf. also Isa. 46:8 and Ps. 143:5.

In the Psalms, the hymnic recollection of God's mighty acts is formulated as a command. This comprehensive theme, for example, shapes Ps. 105 in its entirety. In addition, such passages as Ps. 77:12f.(11f.) (→ הגה *hāghāh*) and 105:5 should be noted here on account of their use of *zākhar*. It is striking, however, that the passages with our verb in Ps. 106:7 and 78:42 contain verses reminiscent of Ezekiel: Israel is rebuked for not remembering the wondrous things done by God in the past, a theme that recurs in Nehemiah's prayer of confession (Neh. 9:17).

We may add a few special instances where the motif of remembering appears, for example, Josh. 1:13, with reference to the command given by Moses to the eastern tribes, and Mic. 6:5, which recalls Balaam and the entrance into Canaan.[18] In Jgs. 8:34, failure to remember Yahweh's deliverance of Israel from its enemies in the immediate past is branded apostasy. In all such cases, past events are significant for the faith and conduct of the present.

In contrast to recollection of God's acts in history, human recollection of the law is comparatively rare. Mal. 3:22(4:4) exhorts Israel to "remember" (keep) the law given at Horeb. In Nu. 15:39f., the tassels on their clothing are to remind the people of God's commandments. According to Ps. 103:18, God shows his steadfast love to all who remember his commandments. Remembrance of God's ordinances from of old is a source of comfort (Ps. 119:52). When we add the use of *zākhar* in Ex. 13:3 to enjoin the observance of Passover and in Ex. 20:8 the observance of the Sabbath (with an element of action clearly implied), we are already at the end of our list of passages in which *zākhar* has the law as its object.

The fact that remembrance of the past can also involve reference to the future may be brought out in the context of a perspective illustrated, for example, by Isa. 12:1, where

---

[17] De Boer, 37; cf. Childs, 51.

[18] Cf. T. H. Robinson and F. Horst, *HAT*, 14 (^{3}1964), 146.

we read: "You will say in that day. . . ." This perspective is also characteristic of the Apocalypse of Isaiah (Isa. 25:9; 26:1; 27:2). In Job 11:16, the future is viewed in relationship to the present and at the same time anticipated: in the future, the suffering of the present will no longer be remembered. This approach has already been noted in Ezk. 6:9; 16:60-63; 20:43; 36:31; cf. also Isa. 54:4. Isa. 43:18 is characteristic: " 'Remember not the former things, nor consider the things of old. Behold, I am doing a new thing . . . .' "

Now to passages where God himself is remembered. Dt. 8:18 cites as the motive his gift of prosperity for the sake of his covenant. Jgs. 8:34, on the other hand, rebukes the Israelites for failing to remember God even though he had just delivered them from the hand of their enemies (here remembrance is grateful fidelity to God and demonstration of *chesedh* [v. 35]). In Jonah 2:8(7), Jonah remembers Yahweh when he is in mortal danger. This goes hand in hand with the notion that men remember God as → צוּר *tsûr*, "rock," and *gō'ēl*, "redeemer" (→ גאל *gā'al*), and call on him for help (Ps. 78:35). Even when God is understood as Creator (Eccl. 12:1), the charge of Isa. 17:10 may hold true, that Israel has forgotten the God of its salvation, the Rock of its refuge.

Despite this attitude of faith that sees God solely as a source of security, it is also possible for remembrance of God to involve suffering. In Ps. 77:4(3), the worshipper remembers God and must moan and lament. According to Jer. 20:9, the prophet would like to escape from God by simply no longer thinking of him or speaking in his name, but then fire blazes up within him. Thus remembrance of God and the obedience it implies are experienced as a vitally necessary relationship, from which a man cannot and must not escape.

Deutero-Isaiah frames a theological argument along these lines (Isa. 46:8). He shows that Yahweh is the only true God, and no one like him, who declared the end from the beginning—in other words, governs history from beginning to end. These statements are introduced by the imperative: "Remember this and be strong!" This structure expresses the importance of this fundamental faith, but also the necessity of the remembrance that gives assurance. It is therefore not surprising that "memory" can be accompanied by strong emotions. Even at night the psalmist remembers Yahweh (Ps. 119:55), and the worshipper in Ps. 42:7(6) remembers with yearning God's presence in the temple. We may recall Ps. 137, where the psalmist remembers Zion with tears and invokes a curse on himself if he should forget Zion (vv. 1, 6). Although de Boer is correct to point out that v. 1 not only expresses sadness but also leads up to an eruption of wrath,[19] there is no reason to insist on the meaning "speak of" for *zākhar*.

3. *God Remembers*. The same verb *zākhar* used to denote the action of the mind that is so necessary for human existence can likewise be used of God, with an efficacy that makes it possible to speak of God's "conduct."[20] In all instances it refers to persons or to events that are important for persons. The object is frequently an indi-

---

[19]Pp. 42f.
[20]Gross, 228.

vidual; it is not necessary to draw a distinction here between God's remembering in response to prayer, or as a simple fact or promise. Because God remembers them, Rachel (Gen. 30:22) and Hannah (1 S. 1:11,19) are vouchsafed children, and Samson's strength returns (Jgs. 16:28). In the depths of despair, Jeremiah prays to God to remember him (Jer. 15:15). God does not forget to avenge the supplicant (Ps. 9:13[12]) and remembers the afflicted (Lam. 3:19). Ps. 89:51(50) beseeches God to remember how his people are scorned, and Ps. 136:23 can give thanks that God remembered the humiliation of his people—once again with a clear element of action implied (help, deliverance).

This motif of lowliness and weakness appears elsewhere as well: not only in the famous passage Ps. 8:5(4), but also in Ps. 78:39, the psalmist expresses his wonder that God should remember man, who is but flesh, just as in Ps. 89:48(47) the psalmist is impressed at the vanity for which God created all the sons of men, and prays that God will pity them. Job 10:9 sounds the same theme: " 'Remember that thou hast made me of clay; and wilt thou turn me to dust again?' " The fact that before God the worshipper can appeal to his very helplessness and distress is highly characteristic of the OT view of God.

The idea that God is just and does not let those who do good go unrewarded also helps explain the appeal to merit. Men call on God to remember both themselves and their good works. Jer. 2:2 speaks of Israel's "young love" in the wilderness, that God may remember and reward her for it—but the love is no longer there. The hardships David endured for the sanctuary are remembered in his favor (Ps. 132:1; cf. also Ps. 20:4[3]). King Hezekiah is remembered favorably because he walked in faithfulness before God (2 K. 20:3; Isa. 38:3). Jeremiah asks God to remember his intercession on behalf of his enemies (Jer. 18:20). Nehemiah's listing of his good works together with the prayer that God will remember him is very like a settling of accounts with God (Neh. 5:19; 13:14,22,31); nor does he forget the complementary prayer that God may remember the sins of the wicked, i.e., punish them (Neh. 6:14; 13:29).

The fundamental bond of mutual remembrance that unites God and man leads further to the observation that the covenant idea is obviously also important in this context.[21] Am. 1:9 speaks of a covenant between men, but in eleven instances the divine covenant is referred to. Jer. 14:21 prays: "Remember and do not break thy covenant with us." By calling the people the → עדה *ʿēdhāh,* "congregation," and → נחלה *nachᵃlāh,* "heritage," of God, Ps. 74:2 alludes clearly enough to the covenant that God is called on to remember. When God makes his covenant with Noah, he promises that he will remember it (Gen. 9:15f.). At the conclusion of the Holiness Code, too, God promises to remember his covenant for the sake of Israel (Lev. 26:45). Ezk. 16:60 makes the same promise with respect to an eternal covenant. Most of the passages presuppose the existence of the covenant and express gratitude to God for remembering it, as he does when the Israelites are oppressed in Egypt (Ex. 2:24; 6:5). This motif appears three times in the Psalms. Ps. 105:8 (= 1 Ch. 16:15) expresses the eternal duration of the covenant on the grounds of God's faithfulness. In Ps. 106:45, God's remembering his

---

[21] Schottroff, 202–211.

covenant results in mercy, and in Ps. 111:5 God shows that he remembers his covenant by feeding his people in the wilderness. In the last two passages, *zkr* implies that God acts according to the terms of the covenant.

Besides the covenant itself, God remembers the occasion of its making and the patriarchs. This is said of Noah in Gen. 8:1; 9:15f. and indirectly of Abraham in Gen. 19:29, where God remembers Lot for the sake of Abraham. In similar fashion Moses puts himself in the place of the people (Ex. 32:32), interceding and offering expiation on their behalf and invoking God's remembrance of the covenant with the patriarchs in Ex. 32:13 (cf. Dt. 9:27). In his prayer of dedication (2 Ch. 6:42), Solomon likewise mentions God's → חסד *chesedh* for David as a reason his prayer should be heard. In this context, however, it is important to note the span of time involved in the covenant relationship between God and his people. According to Ex. 2:24, the period spanned extends from Abraham to the oppression of the people in Egypt; in Ex. 32:13, it extends from the three patriarchs to Sinai; in Ps. 105:42, it extends from the patriarchs to the occupation of Canaan. Lev. 26:42,45 include the return from exile: the people had to suffer exile on account of their sin, but God remembers his covenant and brings Israel back to its land.

Although God's remembering with favor plays an important role in the OT, there are some passages in which the remembering is punitive, and still others (Hos. 7:2; 9:9; 8:13; Jer. 14:10) in which God remembers iniquities and punishes them. Such punishment can even be visited upon God's own people and sanctuary (Lam. 2:1). Just as the Israelites rage at the Edomites and pray that God may remember the "day of Jerusalem" against them (Ps. 137:7), so Nehemiah cherishes a desire for his enemies' punishment (Neh. 6:14; 13:29). The negative nature of the statement with respect to iniquity, however, can hardly reside in the word *zākhar* itself. Its sense can be either positive or negative in any given context, just as → פקד *pāqadh,* used in Hosea in the sense of "punish," really means "pay heed" to something, so that the meaning of both verbs is determined by the positive or negative circumstances of which they speak. When iniquity is threatened by God's punitive remembrance, the worshipper prays that God will not remember iniquity. Isa. 64:8(9) contains the prayer: "Remember not iniquity for ever." The fact that iniquity can continue to affect future generations (Ex. 34:7) explains the prayer that God will not remember the iniquity of the forefathers (Ps. 79:8). In Ps. 25:6f., however, the motif of divine remembrance is bipolar: "*Remember* thy mercy, Yahweh, and thy steadfast love, for they have been from of old; *remember not* the sins of my youth, or my transgressions; according to thy steadfast love *remember* me, for thy goodness' sake, Yahweh." If God does not remember sins, they are removed. Jer. 31:34 expresses this principle trenchantly: "For I will forgive their iniquity, and I will remember their sin no more"; cf. also Isa. 43:25. Jer. 44:21 is dubious.[22] The devout mentality of the worshipper in Ps. 115:12 leads him to think of God's remembering as naturally beneficent: "Yahweh remembers us, he will bless us."

Would it be correct to say that God is gracious and merciful because otherwise unbelievers could suspect him of being helpless, as Ps. 74:18,22 presuppose? Israel

[22]Cf. W. Rudolph, *HAT,* 12 (^{3}1968), 224f.

reflected more deeply on God and found a motive for his mercy within God himself, illustrated by God's self-revelation in Isa. 43:25: " 'I, I am He who blots out your transgressions for my own sake, and I will not remember your sins.' " This corresponds with the article of faith that Yahweh is " '. . . a God merciful and gracious, slow to anger, and abounding in steadfast love and faithfulness' " (Ex. 34:6). It is therefore God's own nature that explains why men can appeal to his remembrance. For there are passages in which *zākhar* takes as its object the characteristics of God mentioned in Ex. 34:6: in Ps. 98:3, God remembers his → חסד *chesedh* and *'ᵉmûnāh* (→ אמן *'āman*); alongside *chesedh*, Ps. 25:6 speaks of *ṭûbh* (→ טוב *ṭôbh*) and → רחמים *rachᵃmîm*, "that have been from old." For God to "remember" these characteristics means likewise for him to put them into practice.

Since God is thus by nature and for all eternity ready to exercise the grace incumbent upon him by virtue of the covenant, he must remember his own people. In this sense, Solomon recalls the *chᵃsādhîm* promised to David by God (2 Ch. 6:42).

The statement that God must have mercy for his own sake, on the basis of his own nature, is itself outdone by Jer. 31:20:

> "Is Ephraim my dear son? Is he my darling child? For as often as I speak against him, I do remember him still. Therefore my heart yearns for him; I must have mercy on him, says Yahweh."[23]

Here God reveals most movingly how, by virtue of his very nature, he can do nothing else than be gracious.

III. nizkar. The niphal form *nizkar* functions as a passive of the qal, but a few of its occurrences exhibit characteristic supplementary elements belonging to the meaning of *zākhar*. Childs[24] maintains that the verb must be translated "mention" in Isa. 23:16; 65:17; Ezk. 21:37(32); 25:10, and that the niphal must be taken as a passive of the hiphil; but such an interpretation is not necessary. The niphal occurs eight times in Ezekiel, specifically in the familiar discussion of the justification of sinners and the apostasy of the righteous (Ezk. 3:20; 18:22,24; 21:29[24]; 33:13,16). In these passages, of course, it is God who is the implied subject, determining whether sin or righteousness is remembered. Here, too, belongs the curse in Ps. 109:14, where the psalmist prays that the iniquity of his enemy's fathers will be remembered. In Ezekiel, it might be possible initially to accept Reventlow's thesis that *zākhar* "refers to the function of the judge."[25] But we have already found so many passages in which God's mercy, for example, is the crucial factor that legal categories can hardly comprehend the basic meaning of *zākhar* correctly.[26] When the passages cited state that iniquity or righteousness shall not be remembered, this means of course that they are no longer extant. Thus the negated niphal takes on the meaning "abolish, annihilate," as in Ezk. 21:37; 25:10, where it applies to the Maobites and Ammonites. Job 24:20 states that

---

[23]Cf. *ibid.*, 196.
[24]P. 16.
[25]P. 164.
[26]Cf. also Childs, 15.

"the sinner will not be remembered," underlining the point with a vivid image: "The womb will forget him."

The statement that someone's name will not be remembered is also an expression for bodily death. Such contexts often speak of someone's "name" (→ שֵׁם shēm). This is significant, because "name" designates "... a person's objective, outwardly visible being, which appears to others and makes its presence felt."[27] Jeremiah's enemies hope for his total annihilation, including his name (Jer. 11:19); Israel's enemies hope the same for Israel (Ps. 83:5[4]). This is the fate par excellence of idols (Hos. 2:19[17]; Zec. 13:2).

But the use of the niphal is not exclusively negative. Some passages are more interesting than significant: the forgotten harlot who seeks to be remembered by going about the city playing her harp (Isa. 23:16); the precious stones that are forgotten when compared to the value of wisdom (Job 28:18). But when God creates a new heaven and a new earth, then the former things shall not be remembered (Isa. 65:17). In these cases we are dealing with remembering on the part of men, to whom the directive always to remember the days of Purim is likewise addressed (Est. 9:28). Especially noteworthy, however, in the context of positive usage of the niphal, is Nu. 10:9, according to which the Israelites will be remembered before God at the sound of the trumpets when they go into battle. This raises the question whether we should think in terms of a signal by means of which God wishes to be reminded to remember Israel. Further passages will be discussed below. The niphal of *zākhar* in Ex. 34:19 will not be considered here; comparison with Ex. 13:12 suggests that it should be emended to *zākhār*, "male."[28]

IV. hizkîr. Up to this point we have derived the various nuances of *zākhar* from its basic meaning "remember" in the sense "be mindful of," with the meaning "recollect" when the remembered object lies in the past. On this basis, the proper causative meaning of the hiphil should be conceived as "bring to remembrance," "make someone remember or be mindful of" something. The words of Pharaoh's butler in Gen. 41:9 (in line with 40:14) should be understood in this sense: he remembers his faults before Pharaoh, thus finding a chance to speak of his imprisonment and his meeting with Joseph, whom he now recalls. Boecker is correct in rejecting the translation "remind Pharaoh of me,"[29] for a person can be reminded only of something he already knows. But this proposed basic meaning is itself incorrect,[30] so that Boecker's own translation, "denounce me to Pharaoh," appears strange: there were no grounds for denouncing Joseph. Here, at least, Boecker's thesis about forensic language is unconvincing.

The causative nature of the hiphil also appears in 1 K. 17:18, where the woman from Zarephath is afraid that the prophet's arrival will cause her sin to be remembered. Ezk. 21:28f.(23f.) and 29:16 fit well in this context. The passage dealing with the offering

---

[27]De Boer, 17.

[28]Cf. M. Noth, *Exodus. OTL* (trans. 1962), 263.

[29]P. 412; cf. de Boer, 31.

[30]Cf. also Stamm, 305.

for jealousy (Nu. 5:15) may also be noted. The point is always the remembrance of some sin. In each case, therefore, we find a theological usage in the causative mode.

Isa. 19:17 can be understood as meaning that the Egyptians will be seized by fear whenever they are reminded of Judah. The causative function of the hiphil consists in stating the effect the mention of a fact has upon the hearer: in 1 S. 4:18, for example, Eli receives word of the loss of the ark and dies. To say that here "announce" means "cause to be mentioned"[31] does not quite fit the situation. Terror is also aroused by the message of disaster in Jer. 4:16, which is introduced by the imperatives "Call to mind, announce."

The causative element in the hiphil of *zākhar* supports the translation "extol," "proclaim" in many passages. A mighty act of God is brought to remembrance and thus proclaimed, which is in itself an act praising God, but can also lead to encomium. Cf. in this sense Ex. 20:24; Isa. 26:13; 48:1; Am. 6:10; Ps. 45:18(17), in all of which the "name" to be praised appears. In Ps. 45:18(17); Isa. 12:4; 1 Ch. 16:4 (*l^ehazkîr ûl^ehôdhôth ûl^ehallēl*), the association with *hôdhāh* (→ ידה *yādhāh*), "make known,"[32] may be noted and *hizkîr* understood as "encomiastic confession." Cant. 1:4 exhibits the same usage, albeit transferred from the sacral realm to that of love poetry. Highly significant for the meaning of *hizkîr* is the sequence of verbs in Isa. 12:4, where *hôdāh,* "avow, confess," *qārā' b^eshēm,* "call on the name of God," and *hôdî'û,* "make known," are followed by *kî niśgābh sh^emô.* Thus our verb stands here in a series of words meaning "proclaim" and "extol," with the purpose of making God's mighty acts known to all nations. De Boer speaks of an "audible action."[33]

Am. 6:10 was cited above; but there is no denying that, despite the identical language, the name of Yahweh is here to be kept secret. Even in the case of the praise that is due Yahweh, it remains true that "terrible is his name" (Ps. 111:9). As Wolff says, "Undertones of magic accompany this expression, the notion being that to name Yahweh's name is necessarily to invoke the presence of Yahweh himself. Cf. 1 Sam 20:42 and 2 Kgs 2:24; and also Hans Bietenhard, 'ὄνομα' [*TDNT,* V, 255]."[34]

Since "encomiastic confession" befits God alone, other gods are excluded from it. Isa. 26:13 states expressly that Yahweh alone is acknowledged. Both Ex. 23:13 (Covenant Code) and Josh. 23:7 prohibit mentioning or praising the name of other gods, i.e., acknowledging or confessing them.

The formula "in truth and right" (Isa. 48:1) points to an oath that calls upon God as protector of the right and judge of truth. In 2 S. 14:11, the qal of *zākhar* must also be understood as requiring an oath, since David answers the woman with the formula, "As Yahweh lives." The close connection between "confessing" and swearing an oath is illustrated by Josh. 23:7, already mentioned, where both confession of other gods and swearing by them are prohibited.

Three passages require special discussion. In Ex. 20:24, God says of the (future)

---

[31] De Boer, 31.
[32] Zirker, 11.
[33] P. 23.
[34] H. W. Wolff, *Joel and Amos* (trans. 1977), 283 and n. 21.

temple that it is the place *ʾᵃsher ʾazkîr ʾeth-shᵉmî.* On the basis of the meaning established for *hizkîr* with a human subject, this would mean the place where men call upon the name of God. The substitution of the 2nd person for the 1st in the Syriac appears to be an attempt to find an easier reading. Stamm suggests "where I will make my name known,"[35] which comports well with the statement that God will "cause his name to dwell" in the temple (1 K. 8:27–30; → שֵׁם *shēm*). In addition, theophanies include God's introduction of himself by name (Gen. 15:7; 17:1; 28:13; etc.; → הוּא *hûʾ*). In Ps. 45:18(17); Isa. 12:4; 26:13, it is true, human beings are the subject of the verb; but what they are doing is more like "calling out" the name of God than "calling on" it in prayer.

The *mazkîrîm ʾeth-yhvh* in Isa. 62:6 could easily be understood as "those who confess Yahweh." But this interpretation would have no point of contact with the duty they are called on to perform: to press God for the restoration of Jerusalem. An interpretation corresponding to the frequent prayer for God to remember an important concern would therefore be more appropriate: those addressed would be men who cause Yahweh to remember, in other words, who dun him and exhort him.

In Isa. 43:26, Schottroff[36] finds the admonition: "Speak my name (to the judge)." This interpretation certainly fits the context and is possible on the basis of the root meaning of *hizkîr*. The assumption that *zākhar* stands "in the context of a forensic discourse"[37] is unnecessary.

The argument that derives the causatives in 1 S. 4:18; 1 K. 17:18; Gen. 41:9 from *zākhar,* "recollect," loses its cogency with rejection of the view that this root always deals with the past.

The nominalized hiphil participle *mazkîr* need only be mentioned in passing, since this title of a court official has no theological significance. A *mazkîr* is mentioned by name nine times: 2 S. 8:16; 20:24; 1 K. 4:3; 2 K. 18:18, 37; Isa. 36:3, 22; 1 Ch. 18:15; 2 Ch. 34:8. The passages in 2 K. 8 and Isa. 36 are identical. Since Est. 6:1 speaks of reading from the *sēpher hazzikhrōnôth,* "book of memorable deeds," and Ezr. 4:15 twice mentions the *dokhrān,* "book of records," it would be reasonable to think in terms of a chronicler, who would be the official author of these books. It must be noted, however, that all the passages except 2 Ch. 34:8 also mention a *sôphēr,* whose function might be to commit the royal decrees to writing. But Begrich has shown[38] that Egyptian prototypes have here set their stamp on court officials attested from the beginning of the monarchy at Jerusalem; the significance of these offices probably far transcended mere chancery functions.

According to Reventlow,[39] the *mazkîr* is "the highest official in the land, responsible for the legal system and the administration of justice." Reservations, however, must be raised against this interpretation, since the juridical interpretation of *zākhar*

---

35 P. 306; cf. also Schottroff, 247f.

36 P. 234.

37 Begrich, 12; cf. also Childs, 14.

38 Pp. 1–29.

39 Pp. 161–175.

will not suffice in many passages of religious content. Mettinger[40] thinks of the *mazkîr* as a "royal herald," who proclaims royal decrees and functions as chief of protocol.

V. zēkher, "Memory." The noun *zēkher,* "memory," occurs 23 times in the OT. Here, too, theological usage predominates. In a secular sense, Hos. 14:8(7) states that Israel will have a memory like the wine of Lebanon, but this fame is God's work. It is likewise God's doing that the "memory of the righteous" is a blessing (Prov. 10:7) and that the righteous are promised "eternal memory" (Ps. 112:6). Est. 9:28 decrees that the days of Purim be kept in everlasting memory, referring at least to a religious observance.

More frequently, something is being said about blotting out a memory. God cuts off the remembrance of evildoers (Ps. 34:17[16]) and enemies (Ps. 9:7[6]) from the earth. He could even blot out the memory of his own people, were it not for fear of the scorn of his enemies (Dt. 32:26). According to Ex. 17:14, the remembrance of Amalek is to be blotted out by Israel (likewise Dt. 25:19). In Ps. 109:15, the psalmist prays in his curse that God may make the memory of the wicked be cut off from the earth. In Job 18:17, too, the memory of the wicked perishes from the earth. It is clear that these passages refer to death and annihilation, just as Eccl. 9:5 says that the memory of the dead is forgotten among men. In Job 18:17 and Prov. 10:7, we read not only that the memory of the wicked is blotted out, but that they will no longer have a name (→ שֵׁם *shēm*). Denial of remembrance after physical death likewise denies the wicked any posthumous fame. His perishing as though he had never been is ascribed to God. It can be inferred conversely that remembrance means more than being recalled by name and acknowledged: it is seen as being somehow identical with existence before and through God.

God has his remembrance because of the way he reveals his name *yhvh* (Ex. 3:15): "this is my name for ever, and my *zēkher* throughout all generations." If the name Yahweh indeed signifies "the being of God, in the sense of a personal presence,"[41] then the *zēkher,* added with the conjunction v^e-, could be identical with this name,[42] or it could add an essential element in the sense of its proclamation or confession. In Hos. 12:6(5), *zēkher* is practically used as a synonym for *shēm* (cf. Akk. *zikru,* "name"): "Yahweh, the God of hosts, Yahweh is his *zēkher.*" In the same way, the worshipper in Isa. 26:8 longs for both the name and the *zēkher* of Yahweh. Both are eternal (Ps. 102:13[12]; 135:13), which is also said of Yahweh himself in the latter passage. Just as the name of God is frequently praised, so is his "memory" in Ps. 30:5(4); 97:12—probably in the sense of the name by which he is remembered. We may recall the meditation of the Deuteronomist on the problem of how God can be enthroned in heaven and yet be present in the temple, with the explanation that he causes his name to dwell there (1 K. 8:27-30). Thus theologically the name of God "takes the place which in other cults was occupied by the cultic image."[43] "Much more commonly than

[40]T. Mettinger, *Solomonic State Officials. ConBibOT,* 5 (1971), 52-62.
[41]Vriezen, 195; → היה *hāyāh.*
[42]De Boer, 32.
[43]Von Rad, I, 183.

before, שֵׁם יהוה is used after the Exile... as an alternative for Yahweh; the name stands for the person.''[44]

And yet late psalms still show that the *zēkher* of God's name involves an element of proclamation: according to Ps. 111:4, God has made a *zēkher* for his wonderful works, and Ps. 145:7 states: "They shall proclaim the memory of thy abundant goodness."[45] These passages could actually represent cultic festivals that served to celebrate this memory.[46] The fact that there is no remembrance of God in Sheol (Ps. 6:6[5]) can even be the motive for a lament in which the worshipper prays that God will remember him and let him live. Man lives because God remembers him, and is obligated to remember God's wonders with praise.

VI. zikkārôn, Memorial. In the Pentateuch, *zikkārôn* occurs only in P; to the notion of remembering it adds the element of a sign that evokes remembrance.[47] This can also be seen from the fact that it occurs several times alongside → אות *'ôth,* Josh. 4:6f.; Ex. 13:9; Nu. 17:3,5(16:38,40); Ex. 12:13f., and that it is glossed in Nu. 5:15, for example, by means of *hizkîr*. A "memorial" could be instituted by God or man; it could be intended to remind either men or God. Among the possibilities mentioned there are signs ordained by God to remind men of certain events. After the crossing of the Jordan, for example, twelve stones are set up at God's command (Josh. 4:3). They are to preserve the memory of the event for all time; therefore the questions of later generations about the meaning of the stones are taken into account (Josh. 4:7).

The words *'ôth* and *zikkārôn* are juxtaposed in Ex. 13:9f., the law concerning the eating of unleavened bread, which is explained to one's son with reference to the exodus from Egypt (Ex. 13:8). How eating unleavened bread can become a sign on the hand and forehead can hardly be explained as a metaphorical manner of speech. Phylacteries, the use of which is traced back to this passage, are intended to remind Israelites of the law and accordingly contain texts from the law (Ex. 13:1-10, 11-16; Dt. 6:4-9; 11:13-21); they are probably symbols of devotion with a different origin,[48] whose association with this passage is secondary. Two other passages with the same motif may be cited here: Nu. 15:39 (where only the verb *zākhar* occurs), which speaks of tassels on garments intended to remind the wearer to follow the commandments of the law; and Dt. 16:3, where the eating of unleavened bread is likewise intended to remind Israel of the exodus.

According to Nu. 17:3-5(16:38-40), when God intervenes against the rebels, he establishes a *zikkārôn* and *'ôth* for the stipulation that only Aaronides may offer sacrifice: the censers of the rebels are made into a bronze covering for the altar. Such a sign would be taken more logically as a mark of honor for the individuals concerned; therefore the significance of the bronze covering on the altar has all the greater need to be explained to posterity.

---

[44] Bietenhard, 257.
[45] H. Gunkel, *Die Psalmen. GHK,* II/2 (1926, ^{5}1968), 609.
[46] Zirker, 69.
[47] Schottroff, 299-328.
[48] Cf. Noth, *Exodus,* 101.

In consequence of Israel's victory over Amalek (Ex. 17:8–13), a book is written as a *zikkārôn* (v. 14), and in addition Joshua is advised orally of the requirement that the Amalekites be exterminated. According to Beer,[49] this verse does not belong to R^D; according to Eissfeldt,[50] it does not belong to L. Thus a book preserved in the sanctuary could also be a way of remembering—always assuming that there was a sense of obligation to consult it and be reminded.

The regulations governing the celebration of the first Passover (Ex. 12:1–20) include close together a *zikkārôn* for man (v. 14) and an *'ôth* for God (v. 13). The blood of the passover lamb is to be a "sign," while the day of Passover is explained as a "memorial." The verb is also used in 13:3 to command observance of the day in the future, as sons are to be instructed according to 13:8. Of the sign, we read in 12:13 that God will see it and spare the Israelites.

The covenant with Noah involves a rainbow, which God establishes as a sign of the covenant, so that when he sees it he will remember his promise never to send another deluge (Gen. 9:13). The term *zikkārôn* is not used in this context, but the verb *zākhar* appears twice (9:15f.).

Ex. 28:12, 29; 39:7, concerning the breastpiece of the high priest, likewise show clearly that the use of a sign ordained by God can effect his gracious remembrance. Since the names of the Israelite tribes are on the stones, one could go so far as to say that the juxtaposition of "name" and *zēkher* makes these names a *zikkārôn* for God.[51] Ex. 30:16 ordains that everyone numbered in the census has to pay "atonement money," which serves "as a memorial for the Israelites before Yahweh." Although the subject matter is a payment, this passage belongs in this context because God requires the tribute and promises his remembrance in return. The gold offered by the officers is also said to function as a "memorial before Yahweh" (Nu. 31:54). Nu. 10:9f. raises the question whether the sounding of the trumpets made by God's command is likewise a *zikkārôn* for God so that he will remember the Israelites. Verse 10 can be interpreted to mean that the sound of the trumpets accompanies the sacrifice, which in turn secures God's favor; but v. 9 suggests the former possibility, an interpretation also attested in Sir. 50:16.

Although no instrument is mentioned in the regulations governing celebration of the New Year Festival, Lev. 23:24 calls the day itself a *zikhrôn t^erûʿāh*. It is therefore reasonable to assume in this case, as in Nu. 10:9, that the sounding of trumpets was understood as a sign for Yahweh.

Just as the breastpiece of the high priest is a memorial before God, Neh. 2:20 could be explained as evidence that a commemoration was held for princes in the Jerusalem temple or even that they were symbolically present there in a symbol of sovereignty. When Sanballat wants to participate in rebuilding the temple, he is informed that he has neither *ts^edhāqāh* nor *zikkārôn* in Jerusalem. Here, as in Isa. 54:17 and 2 S. 19:29(28), scholars generally render the former term as "right."[52] In 2 S. 19:29(28), Mephibo-

[49] G. Beer, *HAT*, 3 (1939), 92.

[50] O. Eissfeldt, *Hexateuch synopse* (^{2}1962), 143*.

[51] De Boer (39) thinks in terms of "mentioning" the name.

[52] *KBL*^{2}, 795; de Boer, 19 ("privilege").

sheth assumes that he and Saul's house could even have expected death—in any case they have no *ts^edhāqāh* with the king. Isa. 54:17 states that the "Servant of Yahweh" is unimpeachable before the bar of justice; this is termed the *nach^alāh* of the servants and their *ts^edhāqāh*. If the *ts^edhāqāh* of Neh. 2:20 is to be understood on this basis, then the *zikkārôn* could be an outward sign of such a "right."[53]

Jer. 17:2 could also bear witness that the sins of Judah were written upon the horns of the altar "as a memento against them."[54] The crown that is placed *l^ezikkārôn* before Yahweh (Zec. 6:14) should probably be understood in the same way.[55]

Schottroff[56] distinguishes several meanings of *zikkārôn:* "record book" (Est. 6:1; Mal. 3:16; Ex. 17:14; cf. Aram. Ezr. 4:15; 6:2); "remembrance" or favorable "consideration" on the part of God (Ex. 30:16; Nu. 31:54; Zec. 6:14; also Ex. 28:12,29; 39:7; Nu. 10:10; Sir. 45:9f.); "remembrance on the part of men as a religious and cultic act" (Ex. 12:14; 13:9; Lev. 23:24; Nu. 17:5[16:40]; Josh. 4:7; Isa. 57:8; Neh. 2:20); and "miscellaneous meanings" such as "statements" (Job 13:12) and "the (lasting) remembrance among men that men seek in vain" (Eccl. 1:11; 2:16).

VII. 'azkārāh, Remembrance. Like *zikkārôn, 'azkārāh* comes from the root *zkr* and is peculiar to P. It occurs 7 times in the MT, as well as Sir. 38:11 and 45:16. While its explanation as an aphel infinitive is reasonably certain,[57] opinions differ as to its meaning. Köhler renders it as "*Erinnerung*/memory, *Duftteil*/odorous part, *Ansage*/announcement."[58] The LXX has *tó mnēmósynon,* the Vulg. *memoriale.* The Zürcher Bible translates *Duftopfer,* "sweet-smelling sacrifice," while most English versions have "memorial portion" (RSV) or something similar, two interpretations that are hard to reconcile! The word *'azkārāh* undoubtedly refers to the portion of the *minchāh*-offering consisting, according to Lev. 2:2, of a handful of flour mixed with oil, to which incense was added. These three ingredients were burned upon the altar as "an offering by fire, a pleasing odor to Yahweh" (cf. also Lev. 2:9, 16; 6:8[15]).[59]

Incense is also associated with the bread of the Presence; in Lev. 24:7 it goes with the bread as an *'azkārāh* "to be offered by fire to Yahweh." This probably is to be interpreted as meaning that the bread of the Presence was offered to God merely by being placed before him, since it could be eaten by the priests, whereas the incense, initially placed with the bread, was then burned as an *'azkārāh*. In Sir. 45:16 and 38:11, however, incense-offering and *'azkārāh* appear to be separate. It is nevertheless striking how often incense occurs alongside *'azkārāh*. When Lev. 2:2; 6:8(15); Sir. 38:11; 45:16 go on to say that such an offering is a *rêach hannîchōach,* the savor of the incense may symbolize the hope that God will be pleased with the odor of the sacrifice

---

[53]Cf. R. Kittel, *Geschichte des Volkes Israel,* III (1929), 628f.; Rudolph takes a different approach, maintaining that this interpretation goes too far (W. Rudolph, *HAT,* 20 [1949], 113).

[54]P. Volz, *KAT,* X (^{2}1928), 183; Rudolph, 97.

[55]Robinson and Horst, 231: "for a remembrance and homage."

[56]Pp. 299ff.

[57]Schottroff, 337.

[58]*KBL*^{3}, 38.

[59]Cf. R. Rendtorff, *Studien zur Geschichte des Opfers im Alten Israel. WMANT,* 24 (1967), 185f.

and thus accept it. If so, "sweet-smelling sacrifice" would not be a translation but an interpretation based on the context. In considering Ex. 30:20; Lev. 2:2; 4:35; 5:12, we might also cite Jer. 44:21, where there is no mention of *'azkārāh* or incense, although the verb *hiqṭîr* is used, which is used in connection with incense (1 S. 2:28, etc.).

There are difficulties with the interpretation "sweet-smelling sacrifice," however. In the first place, the term *'azkārāh* is used for jealousy-offering (Nu. 5:26) and sin-offering (Lev. 5:12), where the use of incense is impossible. Furthermore, the formula of the "pleasing odor" appears much more frequently elsewhere than in combination with *'azkārāh;* it is usually associated with the *'ishsheh* or fire-offering, which weakens the hypothesis that the important point is the pleasing odor as grounds for acceptance of the sacrifice.

It is therefore worth considering whether the *'azkārāh* may not be so termed because the name of Yahweh was solemnly pronounced when the sacrificial portion burned on the altar was offered, so that the term came into being on the basis of this dedication in the sense of an encomiastic remembrance of Yahweh. Jacob[60] refers to the Babylonian formula *šumka azkur,*[61] which likewise attests pronouncement of a divine name as a cultic practice. He also examines Isa. 66:3, where four kinds of sacrifice are mentioned with four verbs, including *l*e*bhônāh* with our *hizkîr*. On this basis, and taking into account the contrasts with right sacrifice described there, he comes to the conclusion: "הזכיר does not move beyond the realm of the concept: pronounce, make known, proclaim."[62]

On the basis of Akkadian parallels, Schottroff demonstrates[63] that *'azkārāh* is best rendered "invocation (by name)," because the sacrificial portion set aside for Yahweh was consecrated by having his name pronounced over it. This ritual would also account for *l*e*hazkîr* in the superscriptions to Pss. 38 and 70. Since, however, these psalms involve lament and petition, the term was later reinterpreted in this context as a prayer of petition, as can also be seen in the renderings of the LXX and Vulgate.[64]

VIII. Cultic Representation of the Past. Both when men remember the acts of God and when God remembers the covenant, the patriarchs, the exodus, and the occupation of Canaan, the common history of Israel and its God plays a very important role. This has also been illustrated by the reminiscent motifs in the Psalms. This retrospect is by no means merely information about the past. Our study of *zākhar* has shown that not only is there a personal interest, but memory deals with objects of consciousness that impinge directly on human life. "Again and again memory keeps its attention riveted on the present, even on present and future conduct."[66] Schottroff sees

[60] P. 79.

[61] *CAD,* XXI, 17f.

[62] Jacob, 52.

[63] Pp. 335ff.

[64] Cf. S. Mowinckel, *Psalmenstudien* (^{2}1961), IV, 15f.: "bring (sin) to remembrance," with reference to the purpose of the *'azkārāh* offering in Nu. 5:15.

[65] De Boer, 37.

[66] Gross, 229; cf. also Childs, 50f.

zākhar as expressing a continuous adherence to historical traditions; indeed, it means "to think of something through action."[67]

This raises the question of how something so characteristic of Israel's faith was realized in the present. At minimum there would be recollection of God's enduring election and Israel's response of faithfulness, implying the normative effect of this relationship and a mutual "yes" to its continuance. But does the process go further, so that the saving event of the past is made present for later generations through the cult? This is suggested by the frequent remembrance of the covenant and the patriarchs on the part of both God and man. God's ordinances concerning the annual celebration of Passover also deserve a special reminder.

According to Childs,[68] observance of the Sabbath is also a cultic remembrance of the exodus. It is true that the mention of servitude in Egypt (Dt. 5:15; 16:12) can be taken as a motif of the Sabbath observance (for the Feast of Weeks, cf. Dt. 15:15). In Dt. 24:18,22, however, the purpose of the reference is to motivate certain conduct toward slaves, not to account for observance of the Sabbath as a memorial of the exodus. Childs argues that what was originally a cultic realization has developed in Deuteronomy into a moral motivation from the past for observance of the law, but the earlier conception is not clearly enough attested. The fact that the Decalog uses *zākhar* in Ex. 20:8 but *shāmar* in Dt. 5:15, cited by Childs as an argument, is probably not decisive. Schottroff takes these two verbs in Ps. 103:18, for example, as being totally synonymous.[69] At least for P's understanding of the Sabbath, it is important to note Gen. 2:1-4, according to which God rested on this day and hallowed it; this theme is incorporated in Ex. 20:8.

For the Feast of Unleavened Bread, too, its annual observance is important as a remembrance of the original event (Ex. 13:8f.; Dt. 16:3). The same God who brought the event to pass also ordained its memorial. Ex. 12:24f. makes the same claim for Passover. The "historicization" of the Feast of Weeks is late; but according to Lev. 23:34-36,41-43 (P), the Feast of Booths was ordained "that your generations may know that I made the people of Israel dwell in booths when I brought them out of the land of Egypt." Despite such motifs, Schottroff does not assume any cultic realization of the past,[70] finding instead a moral motivation for obedience to the commandments based on recollection of God's blessings in the past. Gross, on the contrary, emphasizes the "feasts established by God himself."[71] When they are celebrated in fulfilment of the divine law governing the cult, the "promise of salvation associated with them" is actualized.[72] "Thanks to God's institution, such actions and conduct are followed by the gift of salvation and divine favor, by virtue of an immanent dynamic implanted by God in the memory itself." Is this understanding not supported by the

[67]Pp. 159f.
[68]Pp. 52f.
[69]P. 155.
[70]Pp. 123-26, 339.
[71]P. 235.
[72]Cf. P. Laaf, *Die Pascha-Feier Israels*. *BBB*, 36 (1970), 137: "Remembrance that actualizes the unique event of the exodus from Egypt and renders it effectual for the present in exile."

vivid actualization embodied in the urgent command to "remember" (Dt. 8:2; 7:18; 16:3; also Ex. 13:3f.)? Of course such passages have been retrojected into the Mosaic period, but the personal reference is also a sign of later and repeated present experience. Note should also be taken of passages like Ps. 111:4, which refer to "remembrance" instigated by God, and Ps. 105:5; 77:12(11). We may furthermore recall the "memorials" ordained by God himself with a promise of his grace: the breast piece of the high priest, the blood at Passover, the sounding of trumpets. Such signs indicate the reality of the relationship between God's ordinance and the corresponding activity of the persons who perform the sign, whereby the promised gift of salvation appears intimately associated with the latter.

It is not germane to object that a covenant renewal takes place only in unusual situations (e.g., under Josiah).[73] Dt. 31:10f. require a reading of the law every seven years—in other words, a periodic covenant renewal. Nor need cultic realization be limited to covenant renewal. The continuance of the covenant can also be a motif, celebrated symbolically in specific feasts so that God's salvation is realized once more in the present for the covenant people. There are analogies that bolster the probability of this interpretation. God was believed to be present in the midst of his people in the temple (Jer. 7). Pilgrimages were made to places hallowed by the history of Israel, where one could therefore be close to the place of the saving event (Sinai: 1 K. 19; Gilgal, Bethel: Am. 4:4, etc.). Such notions make it appear quite possible that on the occasion of feasts ordained by God himself for his people the worshippers had a sense of closeness in time to the event especially remembered at each feast. Moreover, the worshipper would offer sacrifices ordained by God, in which was given not only the promise of acceptance but also the experience of actual sacrificial communion with the deity. Such related notions lend credence to a cultic realization of God's saving acts, which are the great content of Israel's memory.

Eising

---

[73]Schottroff, 123.

זָכָר *zākhār*; זְכוּר *z^ekhûr*; (נְקֵבָה *n^eqēbhāh*)

Contents: I. Meaning and Etymology. II. Usage in Regard to Animals: 1. The Flood; 2. Sacrifice; 3. First-born. III. Usage in Regard to Mankind: 1. Creation; 2. Circumcision; 3. Personal Health and Conduct; 4. Social and Religious Status.

I. Meaning and Etymology. The noun *zākhār* occurs 82 times in the OT and indicates the male sex of a species of both men and animals. It is used adjectivally a

---

zākhār. H. Gunkel, *Genesis*. *GHK*, I/1 (⁷1966), 113; W. H. Schmidt, *Die Schöpfungsgeschichte der Priesterschrift*. *WMANT*, 17 (1964), 145f., 168; F. Schwally, "Miscellen," *ZAW*,

further 3 times, in each case of human beings (Nu. 3:40, 43 [P]; Jer. 20:15). We must also note 4 occurrences of the related noun *z^e^khûr,* which has the same meaning and appears in the earliest literary contexts (Ex. 23:17; 34:23; Dt. 16:16; 20:13). The most direct counterpart is *n^e^qēbhāh,* which indicates the female sex of a species and is likewise used of both humans and animals, occurring 22 times. Neither of these terms is applied to plant life, nor are they used in any metaphorical sense; contrast the cognate Akk. *zikaru,* which is used of plants and stones and also in a reference to "male" clouds.[1]

The etymology of *zākhār* is obscure; we can conjecture that the root conception is "be sharp, pointed." The evidence of Arab. *ḏakar,*[2] meaning both "male" and "penis," supports what is in any case the probable conclusion that the basic reference is "penis, phallus." In Ezk. 16:17, the phrase *tsalmê zākhār* apparently indicates images containing phallic symbols;[3] but even here the reference is to the sexual character of the image rather than to the phallus itself, which is consistent with the meaning found elsewhere.

A connection with the root *zkr,* "mention, name, remember," has often been conjectured,[4] but this remains obscure and unsupported. In Akkadian, the noun *zikaru,* "male,"[5] is kept quite distinct from the verb *zakāru,* "declare, mention, name,"[6] and the noun *zikru,* "words."[7]

The derivation of *n^e^qēbhāh* from the root *nqb,* "bore, pierce," understood in a sexual reference, is reasonably clear. That the combination *zākhār ûn^e^qēbhāh* belongs particularly to the legal sphere[8] can hardly be assured on the evidence of so few occurrences.

II. Usage in Regard to Animals.

1. *The Flood.* The division of the entire animal world into two sexes *zākhār* and *n^e^qēbhāh* is first set forth clearly in the Flood Narrative, where the preservation of each species is assured by the taking into the ark of representative members of each sex (Gen. 6:19; 7:3, 9, 16). In the J Creation Narrative, creation of the separate species of animals (Gen. 2:18f.) precedes the creation of sexuality by the creation of woman (*'ishshāh*) out of man (→ אִישׁ *'îsh*). In the P Creation Narrative, no separate mention is made of the creation of animals in two sexes, which is affirmed only of humans (Gen. 1:27 [P]).

In the Flood Narrative, J records a demand for seven pairs of clean animals and one

---

11 (1891), 176–183; C. Westermann, *Genesis. BK,* I/1 (1974), 220f.; W. Zimmerli, *I. Mose 1–11; die Urgeschichte* ([3]1967).

[1]*CAD,* XXI, 112.
[2]Wehr, 310.
[3]Cf. G. Fohrer, *HAT,* 13 ([2]1955), 89; Fohrer cites Isa. 57:8, where *yādh* is used.
[4]Cf. *BDB,* 271, and Schwally, 176f., who suggests interpreting "male" as "competent for cultic service."
[5]*CAD,* XXI, 110–12.
[6]*Ibid.,* 16–22.
[7]*Ibid.,* 112–16.
[8]Cf. Gunkel, 113.

pair of unclean (Gen. 7:3, 9 [J]), while P records a demand for one pair of each species (Gen. 6:19f. [P]). The concern with sexuality here undoubtedly arose from a desire to show that each species was preserved in its pure and original form.

2. *Sacrifice.* Distinctions between the sexes of animals are further found in the regulations for sacrifice, which may prescribe a specific sex. Thus the lamb of the Passover sacrifice (→ פסח *pesach*) is to be taken from the year-old males (Ex. 12:5 [P]). The subject of the burnt-offering (→ עולה *ʿôlāh*), too, whether taken from the cattle or the sheep, must be a male (Lev. 1:3,10). This is also the case for the sin-offering (*chaṭṭāʾth* [→ חטא *chāṭāʾ*]), whether it is a bull or a goat (Lev. 4:3,23), whereas in the case of the guilt-offering (→ אשם *ʾāshām*) a female is required, whether it is a sheep or a goat (Lev. 5:6). When the guilt-offering is a dove or a pigeon, the sex is not specified (Lev. 5:7f.; cf. Lev. 12:6, 8 in a reference to the sin-offering). In the case of the peace-offering (→ שלם *shelem*), it is explicitly stated that the animal, whether taken from the flock or the herd, may be either male or female (Lev. 3:1, 6). Animals sacrificed as a votive or freewill-offering must be males (Lev. 22:19). The reasons lying behind these varied rulings regarding the sex of the sacrificial animal are not clear, although the tendency to establish a restriction to the male in many cases suggests that at one time males must have been regarded as more valuable to God and more filled with vital energy.

3. *First-born.* The other area in which the sexuality of animals has influenced Israel's religious practices is to be found in the obligation to give to Yahweh the first-born males of flocks and herds (Ex. 13:12, 15 [J]; Dt. 15:19). The first-born foals of asses, like first-born human sons, were to be redeemed (Ex. 13:13 [J]; cf. Nu. 3:41f. [P]); it is clearly implied that this obligation applied only to male foals (cf. Ex. 13:15 [J]). This cannot, however, have been the earliest origin of the practice, which must be related to the manifestation of vital energy present in each new birth, regarded as especially prominent in males of the species.

III. Usage in Regard to Mankind.

1. *Creation.* The P narrative records that when God created humans, he created them "*zākhār* and *n*ᵉ*qēbhāh*" (Gen. 1:27), thus implying that the two sexes together form the species. This must not be taken to mean that man as originally created was bisexual, but that male and female together make up mankind, and that God stands above this sexuality. It does, however, express the view that a basic equality exists between the sexes and that they form a necessary complement to each other. In the earlier J Creation Narrative (Gen. 2:4f.), the woman's role as companion and helper to man is strongly expressed: she was created for him (Gen. 2:21-23 [J]). Her name (*ʾishshāh*) is interpreted to show that she was taken out of man (→ איש *ʾîsh*), and in marriage the man and woman become one flesh (→ בשר *bāśār,* Gen. 2:24 [J]). As a consequence of the Fall, the division into two sexes results in a curse upon woman, so that childbearing brings great pain to her; and her relationship to her husband becomes unequal, so that, although she desires him, he rules over her (Gen. 3:16 [J]). Thus the

subordinate and sometimes miserable position of women in Israelite society, which is evident in a number of ways, is interpreted as the result of a divine curse inflicted as a punishment for disobedience.

The division of mankind into two sexes finds no echo at all in Israel's conception of the divine world. Thus, despite the fact that Yahweh is frequently described anthropomorphically as a man, there is never any reference to his sexuality nor to his displaying sexual activity. The making of images of male or female creatures is explicitly prohibited (Dt. 4:16), and Ezekiel singles out the fashioning of male images (*tsalmê zākhār*) as a particularly serious offense (Ezk. 16:17). These were probably images of men on which the phallus was represented.

2. *Circumcision.* The rite of circumcision in Israel was practiced on male infants, and at one time upon young men before marriage (Ex. 4:25 [J]). When in Israel's history the performance of the rite was transferred from puberty to infancy (Gen. 17:10,12,14,23 [P]; Lev. 12:3) is not certain, but Galling thinks that it was not until the exilic era.[9] No comparable rite was performed upon young women or girls. The Deuteronomistic history recounts in Josh. 5:4 that all the males of Israel who had been born in the wilderness were circumcised at Gibeath-haaraloth after crossing the Jordan. In the treacherous action by which Simeon and Levi avenged the rape of their sister Dinah (Gen. 34 [JE]), the trick of persuading Hamor and his son Shechem that all their males should be circumcised played an important part (Gen. 34:15,22,24f. [E]). Here, as in Josh. 5:4, those who were circumcised were regarded as already grown men. The Priestly Document interprets the practice of circumcision upon infant male children as a sign of the covenant between El-Shaddai and Abram (Gen. 17:10, 14 [P]).

3. *Personal Health and Conduct.* As in the case of circumcision, a correlation between religion, health, and social acceptance is evident in a number of rules governing childbirth and sexual activity generally in ancient Israel. Thus in Lev. 12:2,7 when a woman gives birth to a male child she is to be classed as unclean for seven days, and is required to spend an additional 33 days of purification before being able to enter a sanctuary. If the child is a female, the periods specified in each case are twice as long (Lev. 12:5,7). In cases of uncontrolled emissions from the sexual organs (semen in the case of a man and blood in the case of a woman), strict precautionary rites of cleansing are demanded, consisting chiefly of bathing (Lev. 15:1f.), thereby establishing a comprehensive law for all discharges from the sexual organs, whether of male or female (Lev. 15:33). The prohibition of sodomy (Lev. 18:22; 20:13) arises from a similar awareness that human sexuality is a part of a divinely imposed order, which must not be infringed. The OT contains no explicit prohibition against lesbianism, although the prohibition against sodomy must be regarded as implying it. In cases of serious infectious illness, removal of the affected person from social contact with others is demanded whether that person is male or female (Nu. 5:3 [P]).

---

[9] *RGG*[3], I, 1091.

4. *Social and Religious Status.* In a significant range of activities, both social and religious, the superior status of the male over the female comes to the fore. Women and children in Israel generally lived in situations of dependence upon a male, as either husband or father. Hence it is only males of twenty years and upward who are counted in the great census that the Priestly Document records as taking place in the wilderness of Sinai (Nu. 1:2,20,22). In the case of the census of the Levites, however, every male from a month old and upward was counted (Nu. 3:15,22,28,34,39 [P]), and this wider basis of reckoning is then related to the number of the Israelites as a whole (Nu. 3:40, 43 [P]; 26:62 [P]). The dependent status of the female is shown throughout in that only the males are counted. For further listing of genealogies by male descendants, cf. Josh. 17:2; Ezr. 8:3-14; 2 Ch. 31:16 (where male children are counted from three years old and upward), 19.

The woman's position of dependence on men is further evidenced in a number of ways. Male children were regarded as a more important acquisition than female, and their birth was greeted with correspondingly greater rejoicing. This situation is well reflected in the words with which Jeremiah curses the day of his birth (Jer. 20:15; cf. Isa. 66:7). The superior status and authority of the male is also evident in the rules governing vows. Thus, in a late supplement to P, the valuation for votive purposes of a male aged between twenty and sixty years is set at 50 shekels, while that of a female is only 30 shekels (Lev. 27:3f.). If the male is aged between five and twenty years, the valuation is 20 shekels, while a female of this age has a valuation of 10 shekels (Lev. 27:5). If the age is between one month and five years, the valuation is 5 shekels for a male and 3 shekels for a female (Lev. 27:6), and if the age is above sixty years, then it is 15 shekels for a male and 10 for a female.

In the conduct of war, the situation of women was usually very different from that of men. Thus women were not expected to bear arms; and the instance of Jael, who slew Sisera, is clearly singled out because it was very exceptional (Jgs. 5:24-27). That it was a complete reversal of the usual situation for a woman (*n^{e}qēbhāh*) to protect a man (*gebher*) appears to be the subject of a striking affirmation of Yahweh's protection of his people in Jer. 31:22, although the text here is certainly corrupt.[10]

When a people was defeated in battle, the treatment of captured men usually differed from that of women. David's harsh treatment of Edom (2 S. 8:13f.) was particularly remembered because he had every male put to death (1 K. 11:15f.). It is not clear in this instance whether any mercy was shown to male children, which is the ruling commanded for conduct of the holy war in Israel, where every male (*z^{e}khûr*) was to be put to death, but the women, children, and cattle taken as spoil (Dt. 20:13f.). In other instances, where again ideological factors concerning the holy war are present, treatment could be even more harsh. Every male of whatever age was put to death, and also every female who was married or had had sexual relationships with a man. Only unmarried virgins were kept alive to be used as slaves. This is the practice recorded of Israel's victory over the Midianites, where every male was killed, together with every adult woman who had been sexually related to a man (Nu. 31:7,17 [P^{S}]); only the young virgins were spared (Nu. 31:18). Similar treatment was accorded the population

[10]Cf. W. Rudolph, *HAT*, 12 ([3]1968), 198f.; → חָדַשׁ *chādhash.*

of Jabesh-gilead as a punishment for their failure to participate in Israel's holy war against the tribe of Benjamin (Jgs. 21:11f.).

It is in the religious sphere that the more dominant role of the male in Israelite society becomes most fully evident, with consequent restrictions on the participation and activities of women. Thus the primary obligation to worship Yahweh by appearing before him three times in a year at the major festivals is imposed only upon the males (*zᵉkhûr,* Ex. 23:17; 34:23; Dt. 16:16). In accordance with this, it is noteworthy that early accounts of the assembly (*qāhāl*) of Israel for religious or political purposes record only the presence of males. Not until the exilic age do such assemblies note the presence of women and children (Jer. 44:15; Ezr. 10:1; Neh. 8:2, 17).[11] This prominence of the role of men in religious activities, however, certainly did not preclude the participation of women, as is shown by the example of Hannah (1 S. 1:9f.). Nevertheless only males could become priests (→ כהן *kōhēn,* Ex. 28:1f.; Lev. 8:1f.), and Hebrew has no word for priestess. In line with this superior religious status accorded males, the most holy sacrificial offerings could be eaten only by male members of the priestly families. This is the case with the cereal-offering (*minchāh,* Lev. 6:11; cf. 6:9), the sin-offering (*chaṭṭā'th,* Lev. 6:22), and the guilt-offering (*'āshām,* Lev. 7:6).

Clements

---

[11] Cf. L. Rost, *Die Vorstufen von Kirche und Synagoge im AT. BWANT,* 4/24 (1938, [2]1967), 31f.

זמם *zmm;* זְמָם *zᵉmām;* זִמָּה *zimmāh;* מְזִמָּה *mᵉzimmāh*

Contents: I. Etymology and Meaning. II. Occurrences and Use of the Verb. III. Nominal Derivatives: 1. *zᵉmām*; 2. *mᵉzimmāh*; 3. *zimmāh,* "Plan"; 4. *zimmāh,* "Wickedness, Lewdness."

I. Etymology and Meaning. Besides Hebrew, the root *zmm* is attested in various Aramaic dialects: Jewish Aram. *zam,* "think, reflect," aphel "convict (a witness) of perjury"; Syr. *zam,* "whisper, hum, sound." Compare also Arab. *zamzama,* "murmur, hum," which suggests an onomatopoetic word. Guillaume cites Arab. *zanna,* "think good or evil."[1] From the meaning "murmur," it is easy to derive the Hebrew meaning "reflect, plan."

---

zmm. P. Derchain, "A propos de deux racines sémitiques **hm* et **zm,*" *ChrÉg,* 42 (1967), 306-310.

[1] A. Guillaume, "Hebrew and Arabic Lexicography," *Abr-Nahrain,* 1 (1959/60 [1961]), 22f.

There is also a Hebrew noun *zimmāh,* "wickedness, lewdness," which may be connected with Ethiop. *zamana,* "fornicate"; but cf. Heb. → זנה *zānāh.*

II. Occurrences and Use of the Verb. There are 13 occurrences of the verb *zmm* in the OT, all in the qal. It is constructed 6 times with *l^e* + inf. (*la^{ca}śôth,* Gen. 11:6; Dt. 19:19; Zec. 1:6; *lāqachath,* Ps. 31:14 [Eng. v. 13]; *l^ehāra^c*, Zec. 8:14; *l^ehêṭîbh,* Zec. 8:15). This construction shows quite clearly that instigation to action is one of the most important semantic elements of the verb, an observation confirmed by other constructions with this verb.

The use of the verb *zmm* reveals a rather uniform picture. Semantically it is neither negative nor positive; the nature of the action is determined by the object or other words that are added.

The subject of the verb can be either Yahweh (6 times) or human beings (7 times). Depending on the context, Yahweh can plan either good or ill; human planning usually has negative overtones (Prov. 31:16 is an exception).

Jeremiah twice combines *zmm* with *dibbēr*: Yahweh will not relent from what he has spoken and "planned" (4:28); he will do to the inhabitants of Babylon what he has "planned" and spoken (51:12). In Lam. 2:17, similarly, *zmm* is combined with the noun *'emrāh:* Yahweh does what he has planned and spoken.

Ps. 37:12 speaks of a man who plots evil against the righteous. Prov. 30:32 is somewhat obscure; possibly *zmm* is meant as the opposite of *nbl,* "be foolish," in other words, "act with foresight." Prov. 31:16 is clear: the good wife acquires the field that she "plans" to buy.

The text may be corrupt in Ps. 17:3. The commentaries usually follow the LXX in reading *zimmāthî* for *zammōthî,* in other words, "thou wilt find no wickedness[2] in me." If we follow Nyberg[3] in taking *zammōthî* as an irregular infinitive, the MT could be translated: "My thoughts do not cross my lips," i.e., the psalmist utters no evil thoughts.

III. Nominal Derivatives.

1. *z^emām.* The noun *z^emām* appears only in Ps. 140:9(8), as a parallel with *ma'^avaiyê rāshā^c*, "the desires of the wicked." The psalmist prays that Yahweh will frustrate such desires and plans.

2. *m^ezimmāh.* There are 19 occurrences of *m^ezimmāh,* 5 in Psalms, 8 in Proverbs, 2 in Job, and 4 in Jeremiah.

Job 42:2 speaks of God's purpose or plan, which no man can thwart. Jer. 23:20 and 30:24 likewise speak of Yahweh's plans, which will come to pass without fail.

All the other passages refer to human plans. Job 21:27 speaks of thoughts (*mach^ashābhôth*) and *m^ezimmôth* that wrong God. Ps. 10:2 says that the wicked will be caught in the schemes that they have devised (*chāshabh*). According to v. 4, all

---

[2] M. Dahood, *Psalms,* I. *AB,* XVI (1965), 94: "idolatry."

[3] H. S. Nyberg, *Hebreisk Grammatik* (Uppsala, 1952), § 53mm.

their thoughts are: "There is no God"; their plans therefore are arrogant and godless. In Ps. 21:12(11), an oracle of salvation for the king, we read that the king's enemies will not succeed in carrying out the mischief they devise (*chāshabh*). In Ps. 37, an acrostic wisdom psalm, v. 7 warns against fretting over the man who succeeds in carrying out his (evil) devices. Ps. 139:20 speaks of those who defy God through their (evil) plans. According to Prov. 12:2, a man of evil devices (*'îsh mᵉzimmôth*) will be condemned (*yarshîaʿ*) by Yahweh, and Prov. 14:17 states that such a man is hated. In Prov. 24:8, the man who plans to do evil is called a "mischief-maker" (*baʿal-mᵉzimmôth*).

The negative meaning in these examples is not inherent in the word itself, but derives from the context. The word can likewise take on distinctly positive overtones when it is used in Wisdom Literature as one of the many synonyms for "wisdom." The purpose of Proverbs, for example, is to give prudence to the simple, knowledge and discretion (*mᵉzimmāh*) to the youth (Prov. 1:4). The man with wisdom and knowledge will be guarded by discretion (*mᵉzimmāh*) and understanding (*tᵉbhûnāh*) (Prov. 2:10f.). In Prov. 3:21 and 5:2, the reader is admonished to guard *mᵉzimmāh* and wisdom (*tushîyāh*) or knowledge (*daʿath*). Finally, personified wisdom says of herself in Prov. 8:12: "I, wisdom, possess prudence (*ʿormāh*), and I find knowledge and discretion (*daʿath mᵉzimmôth*)."

3. *zimmāh, "Plan."* Six times in the OT, the noun *zimmāh* has a meaning that corresponds to the verb *zmm*, i.e., "plans, devices." Most of the occurrences are in Wisdom Literature. The word has a positive or neutral sense only in Job 17:11, where Job laments that his days are past and his plans (*zimmōthai*) broken off. Elsewhere *zimmāh* has a negative sense. In Isa. 32:7, it stands in parallel with *'imrê-sheqer*, referring to the plans or devices conceived by the violent to oppress the poor. In Ps. 119:150, the psalmist calls his persecutors *rōdhᵉphê zimmāh*, "pursuers of deceit." In Prov. 10:23, the word constitutes the opposite of *chokhmāh*, "wisdom," and appears to refer to the fool's wilful plans. According to Prov. 21:27, the sacrifice of the wicked is an abomination (*tôʿēbhāh*), especially when it is offered with evil intent (*zimmāh*). Finally, according to Prov. 24:9, the "devising of folly" (*zimmath 'ivveleth*) is a sin.

4. *zimmāh, "Wickedness, Lewdness."* The word *zimmāh* occurs 22 times in the OT with the meaning "wickedness, lewdness." *KBL*³ derives this meaning from the common root *zmm*;[4] *GesB* postulates a different root.[5]

There are 3 occurrences of *zimmāh* in Leviticus, all of which refer to sexual offenses (lewdness). In 2 passages we find the declaratory formula *zimmāh hî'* (Lev. 18:17; 20:14).

Lev. 18 (H) contains several laws prohibiting certain sexual offenses. These prohibitions are set in a framework of 2 passages (vv. 1-5 and 24-30) in which the forbidden sexual practices are branded as Egyptian and Canaanite (v. 3) and the reader is admonished to keep the statutes of Yahweh (vv. 4,24-30). The prohibitions are impressed upon the people on the grounds that the prohibited sexual practices defile the

[4]P. 261.

[5]P. 200; see I above.

land; this is the reason the earlier inhabitants were driven out (vv. 24f.,27). The land itself takes vengeance and vomits its inhabitants out. The framework passages term these practices abominations (*tôʿēbhôth*), which stand in contrast to the commandments of Yahweh (v. 26).

In Lev. 20:14, intercourse with a woman and her daughter is called *zimmāh,* "lewdness." The punishment is death by fire. According to Lev. 19:29, it is forbidden to make one's daughter a harlot (hiphil of *zānāh*), lest the land fall into harlotry (*zānāh*) and become full of *zimmāh*. In this case no punishment is recorded.

The declaratory formula *hîʾ zimmāh* is cited in Job 31:11 with reference to marital infidelity and desire for another woman; v. 9 states the case, v. 10 determines the punishment, and then the formula appears in v. 11.

Jgs. 19–20 tell the story of a Levite whose concubine is attacked and killed by the Benjaminites at Gibeah. This outrage is called a *zimmāh* and wantonness (*nebhālāh*) (v. 6). In this case the offense is not sexual. The same is true in Ps. 26:10, which says of the bloodthirsty men (*ʾanshê dāmîm*) that their hands are full of *zimmāh* and bribes, and possibly in Hos. 6:9, where *zimmāh* stands in parallel with *rṣḥ,* "murder"; but *zenûth,* "harlotry," is mentioned in v. 10.

In Jer. 13:27, where the prophet describes Jerusalem's harlotries on the hills, *zimmāh* stands in parallel with *niʾuphîm,* "adulteries," and *mitshalôth,* "neighings," vividly describing the cultic sexual rites.

The book of Ezekiel exhibits a special predeliction for the word *zimmāh*. Of its 22 occurrences, 13 are found in this book, exclusively in discourses concerning Israel, Judah, and Jerusalem. In the allegory of chap. 16, where Jerusalem is described as a foundling, foreign cultic influences are called harlotry and "lewd behavior" (*derekh zimmāh,* 16:27). Jerusalem must pay the consequences of her lewdness (*zimmāh*) and abominations (*tôʿēbhāh*) (16:58).

Ezk. 22 contains a bitter denunciation of the city of Jerusalem, which "sheds blood" (vv. 2, 6, 9, 12). In vv. 6–12 we find a series of laws the city has transgressed. This series exhibits a striking dependence on H, and when we read (v. 9), "Men commit lewdness in your midst," there is every reason to recall the cases defined as *zimmāh* in Lev. 18–20.

Chapter 23, which depicts Israel and Judah as two lewd sisters, contains 7 occurrences of *zimmāh*. In v. 21, the sexual meaning is obvious. In several passages the word stands in parallel with words that mean lust or harlotry (vv. 27, 29, 35, 44). According to v. 48, Yahweh will put an end to the lewdness in the land, which is reminiscent of the defilement of the land by *zimmāh* in Lev. 18:24f., 27. Verse 49 shows that the lewdness is connected with idolatry, as does v. 35. According to Ezk. 24:13, Yahweh has tried in vain to cleanse the people of their lewdness, and therefore Israel must expect his wrath.

Steingrimsson

זמר *zmr;* זָמִיר *zāmîr;* זִמְרָה *zimrāh;* מִזְמוֹר *mizmôr*

Contents: I. 1. Root; 2. Etymology; 3. Meanings. II. OT Occurrences: 1. Verb; 2. Derivatives. III. Semantic Field: 1. Synonyms; 2. Person Addressed; 3. Instrumental and Vocal Performance; 4. Ancient Versions. IV. Theological Significance.

I. 1. *Root.* In addition to Hebrew, the root *zmr* I is found in Akkadian, Ugaritic, Aramaic, Syriac, Mandean, Old South Arabic, and Arabic.[1] According to Mowinckel, the root is indigenous in Akkadian, but "alien" in Arabic, Aramaic, Ethiopic, and Hebrew (Canaanite); in support of this position he cites the restricted range of meanings adopted by this root in these languages.

Besides *zmr* I (*GesB zmr* II), two and perhaps three other homonymic roots must be distinguished:

a. *zmr* II (*GesB zmr* I), "prune (grapevines)"; Gezer,[2] Middle Hebrew, Jewish Aramaic; cf. Ugar. *zbr,* Arab. dial. *zabbara.*

b. *zmr* III, according to *KBL*[2, 3] the root of *zimrāh* II, "strength, protection," and of the masculine personal names *z^emîrāh* and *zimrî;* cf. Amor. and OSA *ḏmr,* "protect," Ugar. *ḏmr,* "soldier," Arab. *ḏamir, ḏamr,* "brave."

c. *zmr* IV (*GesB zmr* III), the root of *zemer,* "antelope, gazelle"; cf. Arab. *zamara,* "jump, flee."

The existence of a root *zmr* III in OT Hebrew remains dubious; **zimrāh* in Gen. 43:11 can be derived from *zmr* II, and in Ex. 15:2; Isa. 12:2; Ps. 118:14 from *zmr* I.

2. *Etymology.* Etymologically, *zmr* I is frequently derived from *zmr* II, "prune." In this case the basic meaning would be "pluck (strings)."[3] But the root *zmr* II does not occur within the sphere of Akkadian, where *zmr* I (*zamāru,* "sing, play") appears to originate. Furthermore, "pruning" (cf. **mazmērāh,* "pruning knife") or "pinching off" (cf. **m^ezammereth,* "wick shears") does not really go well with the "plucking"

---

zmr. F. Crüsemann, *Studien zur Formgeschichte von Hymnus und Danklied in Israel. WMANT,* 32 (1969), 31-82, 126-135; G. Delling, "ὕμνος," *TDNT,* VIII, 489-503 (with bibliography); S. Mowinckel, *Psalmenstudien* (²1961), IV, 2f.; G. Rinaldi, "Alcuni termini ebraici relativi alla letteratura," *Bibl,* 40 (1959), 273f.; A. Sendrey, *Music in Ancient Israel* (1969); A. Sendrey and M. Norton, *David's Harp; the Story of Music in Biblical Times* (1964), 54-92; C. Westermann, "Musik. III. Instrumentale Musik, Gesang und Dichtung in Israel," *RGG*³, IV, 1201-1205.

[1] *KBL*³.
[2] *KAI,* 182.6.
[3] *GesB, KBL*³.

of strings (cf. *psállō*); and finally nothing in the usage of *zamāru* suggests that it was originally limited to the technical aspect of "string music."

The less common derivation from Arab. *zamara,* "cry," used of female ostriches,[4] is also to be rejected.

3. *Meanings.* a. In Akkadian, numerous occurrences (beginning with Old Babylonian) give a clear picture of the meaning. The verb *zamāru* in all stems refers to the action of singing, with or without instrumental accompaniment.[5] The G stem represents this action as casual, the D stem probably as habitual or even professional.[6] As derivatives we find the nouns *zamāru,* "song (with or without accompaniment)," *zammeru,* "(male) singer," and *zammertu,* "(female) singer." Besides ritual songs (*zamāri taknî,* "songs of praise"; *zamar ᵈIštar šarra*[*ti*], "song of Ishtar the queen"), there are ceremonial court songs (*zamār šarri akkadû,* "royal songs in Akkadian") and popular songs (e.g., in praise of Babylon). The distinctive terminology for the singers (*zammeru/zammertu* for popular songs, *nāru* for palace and temple music) makes it clear that the root *zamāru* had no "sacral" connotations. Instrumental accompaniment is often mentioned: *zamārū adapū,* "songs for the *adapu* instrument"; *ina ḫalḫallatim izammur,* "he sings to the accompaniment of the *ḫalḫallatu* drum"; *ina sammî,* "to the accompaniment of the harp" (no instances of wind instruments!). Even where it is not mentioned, accompaniment appears to have been presupposed. The word *zamāru* never refers to instrumental "music" without articulated singing.

b. Judging from the single occurrence (*'zmr . bh*),[7] the root cannot have played an important role in Ugaritic; Dhorme would like to relate *'ḏmr*[8] also to Akk. *azammur/azmur*. The usual word for "sing," as in Hittite,[9] appears to be *šyr* and its derivatives (*šr,* "singer"), borrowed from Sumerian (ideogram ŠÌR).

c. Among the later West Semitic languages, Biblical Aramaic has **zammār,* "singer, musician" (Ezr. 7:24) and **zᵉmār,* "musical instruments" (Dnl. 3:5,7,10, 15).[10] In the latter word, the meaning "sing" appears to have vanished completely. In Syriac, too, semantic shifts can be noted: the verb *zmr* (peal and pael) still means "sing, play" (cf. *zᵉmārā,* "song, revel"; *zᵉmīrā,* "singing"), but *zammārā* means primarily "flautist." The word *mazmūrā,* "psalm," is borrowed directly from Heb. *mizmôr.*

d. The development hinted at in Syriac is carried out fully in Arabic; here *zamara* (already in Old South Arabic[11]) and its derivatives refer to the action, the agent, or the

---

[4] *GesB, KBL*².

[5] *CAD,* XXI, 35-38.

[6] Cf. E. Jenni, *Das hebräische Piʿel* (1968), 12-14; but there is only one instance.

[7] *CTA,* 35, 51; *UT,* No. 823.

[8] *CTA,* 162, 3; etc.

[9] Cf. *CAD, s.v. zamāru* A.

[10] *KBL*² translates "music for strings," without evidence.

[11] ContiRossini, 129.

instrument involved in flute playing (*zamara,* "play the flute or shawm"; *zammāra* and *mazmār,* "flute"; and other derivatives). Only *zamr,* "song," and *mazmūr,* "psalm," borrowed from Syriac, recall the meaning "sing," as do Ethiop., Tigré, Amhar. *zammara,* "sing,"[12] and Tigr. *ʾazmara,* "drive (oxen to work) singing."[13] There is also Ethiop. *zamara* = *ʾazmara,* "proclaim solemnly, praise publicly, acknowledge, confess."[14]

e. The use of *zmr* I in OT Hebrew must be viewed against the background of this semantic development.

In Akkadian, the two meanings "sing" and "play" are so firmly linked that it would be more accurate to speak of two aspects of a single meaning: the single action is both "vocal" and "instrumental." This combination also appears in other ancient languages: Lat. *cano-canto, cantus*; Gk. *ádō, ōdḗ.* Only over a period of time, while *zamāru* was used as a loanword in the West and South Semitic languages, did the latter aspect achieve independence and finally supplant the former. It remains to investigate the role played by OT Hebrew in this development.

As the Akkadian evidence shows, it would be pointless to inquire into an originally secular or sacred meaning of the word. From the very beginning, the particular situation determined whether the action referred to with *zamāru* was more secular or religious. There is no need, therefore, to suggest that the word was "borrowed" by one sphere from the other.

In Akkadian usage, *zamāru* always refers to an action addressed to a person: an audible and comprehensible proclamation intended to give honor and pleasure or express gratitude to a deity, a king, or a personified city. Even when the word is used absolutely,[15] such a motive and object of favor is always presupposed.

II. OT Occurrences.

1. *Verb.* The verb *zmr* I occurs 45 times in the OT, exclusively in the piel (cf. I.3). Apart from Jgs. 5:3; 2 S. 22:50; Isa. 12:5; and 1 Ch. 16:9, all the occurrences are in the Psalter; but even the exceptions are found in contexts that could be termed "psalms."

In 15 cases, we are dealing with the "summons to praise" that is characteristic of the hymn genre, usually in the form of the impv. *zammᵉrû* (Isa. 12:5; Ps. 9:12 [Eng. v. 11]; 30:5[4]; 33:2; 47:7[6] (twice), 8[7]; 66:2; 68:5[4],33[32]; 98:4f.; 105:2; 147:7; 1 Ch. 16:9), once in the jussive (Ps. 149:3). It is usually addressed to the assembled congregation, sometimes (Ps. 68:33[32]; 98:4; cf. the jussives in Ps. 66:4) to the whole earth.

Seventeen other occurrences involve the "self-summons to praise," likewise indigenous to the hymn form (*ʾᵃzammᵉrāh,* Ps. 7:18[17]; 9:3[2]; 18:50[49]; 27:6; 57:8[7]; 59:18[17]; 61:9[8]; 71:22f.; 75:10[9]; 101:1; 104:33; 108:2,4[1,3]; 144:9; 146:2; pl. *nᵉzammᵉrāh* only Ps. 21:14[13]; Qumran: 1QS 10:9; 1QH 11:5, 23). Certain other

[12] *LexLingAeth,* 1039.
[13] *TigrWb,* 495a.
[14] *LexLingAeth,* 1039f.
[15] See *CAD,* XXI, 38.

forms may also be understood as a hymnic "self-summons": impf. *'ᵃzammēr* (Jgs. 5:3; 2 S. 22:50; cf. Ps. 18:50[49]), imperfect with suf. *'ᵃzammerkhāh* (Ps. 57:10[9]; 108:4[3]; 138:1; cf. 30:13[12]), and the formulas *ṭôbh lᵉzammēr* (Ps. 92:2[1]) and *ṭôbh zammᵉrāh* (Ps. 147:1).[16]

Where *'ᵃzammᵉrāh* comes at the end of a song, the interpretation of the cohortative as a "self-summons" is not always satisfactory (cf. 2 S. 22:50; Ps. 7:18[17]; 18:50[49]; 27:6; 57:10[9]; 59:18[17]; 61:9[8]; 71:22f.; 75:10[9]; 104:33; 144:9). In such cases it seems appropriate to interpret the form as expressing a wish, decision, or vow.

2. *Derivatives*. Of the derived substantives, *zāmîr*, plural *zᵉmîrôth*, "song," occurs 6 times (2 S. 23:1; Ps. 95:2; 119:54; Isa. 24:16; 25:5; Job 35:10). The phrase *zᵉmîrôth yiśrā'ēl* in 2 S. 23:1 means popular songs in honor of David; the late text Isa. 25:5 speaks of *zᵉmîr ʿārîtsîm*, "triumph songs of tyrants." The phrase *zᵉmîrôth ballāilāh*, "songs (of praise) in the night," in Job 35:10 is difficult; the LXX may have read *shᵉmārôth*. Ps. 119:54 does not refer to "psalm tunes," as Buber suggests, but to songs of rejoicing.

There are 4 certain occurrences of *zimrāh* I, "song" (Isa. 51:3; Am. 5:23; Ps. 81:3[2]; 98:5). It is disputed whether *zimrāth* in Ex. 15:2, as well as in Isa. 12:2 and Ps. 118:14, which depend on this text, belongs here. The more recent interpretation[17] derives it from a root *zmr* III,[18] so that it must be translated "strength, protection" or the like. This latter view is supported by the parallelism it provides between *ʿozzî* and *zimrāth* (= *zimrāthî*[19]) and the difficulty of referring to God as "my song." But *tᵉhillāthî*, "my song of praise," i.e., "object of my song of praise," in Ps. 109:1 and the uncertain existence and meaning of a Hebrew root *zmr* III mean that the traditional interpretation still has the weight of evidence on its side.

The term *mizmôr*, "song (with instrumental accompaniment)," occurs 57 times, exclusively in the Psalter and only in the superscriptions (Pss. 3-6, 8, 9, 12, 13, 15, 19-24, 29-31, 38-41, 47-51, 62-68, 73, 75-77, 79, 80, 82-85, 87, 88, 92, 98, 100, 101, 108-110, 139-141, 143). It appears 10 times alongside the term *shîr*, "song" (Pss. 30, 48, 65, 66, 68, 83, 87, 88, 92, 108). Of the 73 psalms with the superscription *lᵉdhāvidh*, 35 are termed *mizmôr;* the 12 Asaph psalms without exception bear this designation, but only 6 of the 11 Korahite psalms. In the case of the word *mizmôr*, we appear to be dealing with a late formation; it is not attested at Qumran. The precise meaning and motives for its use are unknown.

III. Semantic Field.

1. *Synonyms*. Synonyms and objective parallels to *zmr* I and its derivatives can be determined from cases of direct parallelism as well as from the larger context of their

---

16 J. Blau, "*Nāwā thillā* (Ps. cxlvii 1): Lobpreisen," *VT*, 4 (1954), 410f.

17 *KBL*^{2,3}.

18 See above, I.1.b.

19 Cf. S. Talmon, "Cases of Abbreviation Resulting in Double Readings," *VT*, 4 (1954), 206-208.

occurrences. The most important are the three verbs → שִׁיר *shîr*, "sing"; → ידה *ydh* hiphil, "praise"; and → הלל *hll* piel, "praise," together with their derivatives *shîr*, "song," *tôdhāh*, "thanksgiving song," and *tᵉhillāh*, "song of praise." Several times we also find *rnn* piel, "shout for joy," *ʿlz/ʿls*, "exult," *śmḥ*, "rejoice," *rwʿ* hiphil, "shout," *ngd* hiphil, "announce"; and occasionally *zkr* hiphil, "praise," *ydʿ* hiphil, "make known," *ngn* piel, "play," *spr* piel, "recount," *pṣḥ*, "be happy," *śyḥ*, "consider," etc.

For *zmr/šyr*, cf. Jgs. 5:3; Ps. 21:14(13); 27:6; 57:8(7); 68:5,33(4,32); 101:1; 104:33; 105:2; 108:2(1); 144:9; 1 Ch. 16:9. For *zimrāh* par. *shîr*, cf. Am. 5:23. In the larger context, cf. Ps. 33:2f.; 59:18(17) and 17(16); 149:3 and 1.

For *zmr* par. *ydh* hiphil, cf. 2 S. 22:50; Ps. 18:50(49); 30:5,13(4,12); 33:2; 57:10(9); 71:22; 92:2(1); 105:2; 108:4(3); 138:1. For *zāmîr/zimrāh* par. *tôdhāh*, cf. Isa. 51:3; Ps. 95:2; cf. 147:7. In the larger context, cf. Isa. 12:5 and 4; Ps. 9:3(2) and 2(1); 105:2 and 1; 138:1f.; 1QH 11:3 and 5.

For *zmr* par. *hll* piel, cf. Ps. 135:3; 146:2; 147:1; 149:3. In the larger context, cf. Ps. 105:2; 146:2; with *tᵉhillāh*, Ps. 33:2 and 1; 66:2.

For *zmr* par. *ngd* hiphil, cf. Ps. 9:12(11); 75:10(9). In the larger context, cf. Ps. 92:2(1) and 3(2); Ps. 71:22 and 17f.; indirectly, 30:10(9).

For *zmr* par. *ʿlz/ʿls*, cf. Ps. 9:3(2); 68:5(4). In the larger context, cf. Ps. 149:3 and 5; 68:5(4) and 4(3); indirectly, Ps. 28:7.

For *zmr* par. *rnn* piel, cf. Ps. 71:23. In the larger context, cf. Isa. 12:5 and 6; Ps. 33:2 and 1; 59:18(17) and 17(16); 81:3(2) and 2(1); 92:2(1) and 5(4); 95:2 and 1; 98:5 and 4; 149:3 and 5.

For *zmr* par. *śmḥ* (*zimrāh* par. *śimchāh*), cf. Isa. 51:3; Ps. 9:3(2). In the larger context, cf. Ps. 30:13(12) and 12(11); 68:5(4) and 4(3); 104:33 and 34; 105:2 and 3; 149:3 and 2.

For *zmr* par. *rwʿ* hiphil, cf. Ps. 98:4. In the larger context, cf. Ps. 47:7(6) and 2(1); 66:2 and 1; 81:3(2) and 2(1); 95:2 and 1.

Scattered instances of parallelism: *zkr* hiphil, Isa. 12:5 and 4; Ps. 71:22 and 16; *ydʿ* hiphil, Isa. 12:5 and 4; Ps. 105:2 and 1; *ngn* piel, Ps. 33:2 and 3; *spr* piel, Ps. 9:3(2) and 2(1); 71:22 and 15; *pṣḥ*, Ps. 98:41; *śyḥ*, Ps. 105:2; 1 Ch. 16:9; cf. 1QH 11:5.

As this survey shows, the use of *zmr* is intimately associated with the semantic field of cultic praise. Strongly represented are words that express an articulated "singing," "praising," "confessing," etc., or an unarticulated "rejoicing" or "shouting," etc. In contrast, the instrumental aspect of *zmr* scarcely appears among the synonyms (cf. *ngn*).

2. *Person Addressed.* The immediate context of the verb *zmr* includes various expressions of the object or addressee of the designated action. Although "sing" and "play" have no intrinsic need for an object, so that *zmr*, like *šyr* or *ngn*, could be used intransitively or "absolutely," no use is made of this possibility, at least in the Psalms. Singing and playing are always addressed to Yahweh. This is usually expressed by means of the preposition *lᵉ-* (*lᵉyhvh*, Ps. 27:6; 30:5[4]; 98:5; *lēʾlōhai*, Ps. 104:33; 146:2; *lēʾlōhênû*, Ps. 147:7; *lēʾlōhê yaʿᵃqōbh*, Ps. 75:10[9]; *lᵉmalkēnû*, Ps. 47:7[6]; *lᵉkhā*, Ps. 71:22f.; 144:9; *lô*, Ps. 105:2; 149:3; 1 Ch. 16:9; *lᵉshimkhā*, 2 S. 22:50; Ps. 18:50[49]; 92:2[1]; *lishmô*, Ps. 135:3). In one case the preposition *ʾel* performs an

analogous function (*'ēleykhā 'azammērāh,* Ps. 59:18; cf. v. 10), but the textual tradition is dubious.

Another possibility for expressing this relationship consists in having the person addressed follow the verb in the direct accusative as the object of the action, now understood transitively (*zammerû yhvh,* Isa. 12:5; *'elōhîm,* Ps. 47:7[6]; *'elōhênû,* Ps. 147:1; *yezammerkhā,* Ps. 30:13[12]; *'azammerkhā,* Ps. 57:10[9]; 108:4[3]; 138:1; *shēm-yhvh,* Ps. 7:18[17]; *shemô,* Ps. 68:5[4]; *shimkhā,* Ps. 9:3[2]; 61:9[8]; 66:4). In scattered instances, the divine name is replaced by a property or manifestation of the deity (*gebhûrāthekhā,* Ps. 21:14[13]; *khebhôdh-shemô,* Ps. 66:2); comparable expressions are found as early as Akkadian, for instance, *tanīdātaša lū azmur,* "let me sing songs in her [sc. Ishtar's] praise."[20] Between this transitive construction, corresponding to the hiphil of *ydh* and the piel of *hll,* "praise," and the intransitive construction with the preposition *le-*, corresponding to *šyr,* "sing," there is some vacillation in the textual tradition; cf. the variants in Ps. 47:7(6) and 68:5(4).

The verb *zmr* appears absolutely, i.e., without a direct or indirect object, in Ps. 47:7(6) (twice), 8(7); 57:8(7); 98:4; 108:2(1).[21] The context of these passages nevertheless reveals unambiguously that Yahweh is to be understood as the person addressed (Ps. 47:7[6]; 57:10[9]; 98:4f.; 108:4[3]). Ps. 47:8(7) (*zammerû maśkîl*) remains obscure.

3. *Instrumental and Vocal Performance.* Finally, the semantic field of *zmr* includes the various statements as to how the praise was performed, both instrumentally and vocally.

a. The musical instruments mentioned in this context cannot be identified precisely (*kinnôr,* "cithara"?; *nēbhel,* "harp"?; *tōph,* "tambourine"?).[22] Wind instruments are never mentioned.[23] More important is the question how the prefixed preposition *be-* is to be understood (*bekinnôr, benēbhel, benēbhel 'āśôr, bethōph,* Ps. 33:2; 71:22; 98:5; 144:9; 147:7; 149:3; *'alê-'āśôr, 'alê-nēbhel* only in Ps. 92:4[3]). The common view is that the preposition *be-* designates the instrument employed; logically, this would mean postulating a special meaning for *zmr* in the passages named, "play (an instrument)."[24] There are serious objections, however, to this view, which presupposes that the "instrumental" aspect of *zmr* has achieved independent status. In the Akk. *zamāru ina . . .,*[25] the preposition *ina* is not used to introduce the instrument "upon" which the singer "plays"; it designates rather the accompanying circumstance, the musical accompaniment to the song ("to the accompaniment of the . . . instrument"[26]). The immediate context often shows that *be-* is to be understood in this way in the psalm passages mentioned. In Ps. 33:2f., consider the phrases

[20]See *CAD,* XXI, 37.
[21]Cf. *KBL*[2,3].
[22]Cf. *BRL,* 389-394; *BHHW,* II (1964), 1258-1262; etc.
[23]Cf. I.3.
[24]Cf. *GesB, KBL*[2,3].
[25]Cf. I.3.a.
[26]*CAD.*

zamm^e rû b^e nēbhel par. *hôdhû b^e kinnôr* par. *hêṭîbhû naggēn bithrûʿāh;* the parallelism prohibits the translation "play upon the harp" every bit as clearly as it demands some such translation as "sing praises with the harp." The same consideration makes it impossible to render Ps. 71:22b "play the harp" (Jerusalem Bible), when the parallelism with v. 22a, "praise with the harp," clearly requires something like "sing praises with the harp." The translation of *zmr b^e-* as "play (an instrument)" is therefore to be rejected also in Ps. 98:5; 144:9; 147:7; 149:3. And this certainly eliminates Buber's general rendering of *zmr* as *aufspielen,* "strike up a tune."

b. The "vocal" performance of the action designated by *zmr* consists in the singing of words to honor or please Yahweh. More or less extensive summonses to articulated singing, praising, extolling, proclaiming, etc., are a familiar formal element in the hymn and thanksgiving song. But these summonses do not stand in isolation. They are followed frequently by *kî* clauses that have usually been understood as the "motivation" for the summonses in question (cf. ". . . his goodness endures for ever"). Crüsemann, however, has shown[27] that the real function of the *kî* clauses is the "execution" or accomplishment of the imperative or cohortative summons to sing, praise, etc. Such clauses thus record in direct discourse, introduced by the emphatic deictic particle *kî,* "indeed," the matter to be sung to the accompaniment of the cithara, the harp, etc. The *kî* clause in Ps. 47:8a(7a), in this interpretation, is not the motivation but the execution of the summons *zamm^e rû,* repeated four times in vv. 7f.(6f.): "God is indeed the king of all the earth!" Other examples from hymns are Ps. 33:1-4; 81:3-5(2-4); 135:3f.; and from individual laments and thanksgivings, Ps. 30:5f.(4f.); 57:8-11(7-10); 59:18(17); 71:22-24; 92:2-5(1-4); 108:2-5(1-4); 138:1f. In each case the *kî* clause comes at the end. The hymnic participles,[28] which develop the praise in a different way, are likewise an execution of the summons; cf. Ps. 33:1-4 with vv. 5, 7, 15; 9:12aα(11aα) with aβ; 144:9 with v. 10; 147:1 with vv. 2-6, and v. 7 with vv. 8f. In light of their function, these participles should not be rendered as relative clauses, but as independent statements within the framework of the required or intended song of praise.

The structural connection between the summons to praise and its execution stated in *kî* clauses and participles shows once more[29] that *zmr* without exception refers to an articulated singing and playing in which comprehensible words are uttered.

4. *Ancient Versions.* In the LXX translation of the Psalms, *zmr* is almost always rendered by *psállō.* That the translation refers exclusively to playing on a stringed instrument is shown by the observation that in Ps. 33:3 and 68:26(25) *ngn* is also translated by *psállō* (cf. *kitharízō* in Isa. 23:16). Correspondingly, *zimrāh* in Ps. 98:5 is rendered by *psalmós;* cf. *psalmós* for *n^e ghînāh* in Ps. 4:1(superscription) and everywhere for *mizmôr; psaltḗrion* for *kinnôr* and *nēbhel.* The "vocal" aspect of *zmr* is brought out only once, when *zimrāh* is translated *hýmnēsis* (Ps. 118:14).

---

[27] Pp. 32-50.
[28] Cf. Crüsemann, 126-135.
[29] Cf. III.1.

Outside the Psalms, too, the "instrumental" understanding of *zmr* predominates, although the rendering "sing praises" is somewhat commoner. In 1 Ch. 16:9, for example, *zmr* is represented by *hymnéō* (in contrast to *psállō* in Ps. 105:2), and *zimrāh* is twice rendered by *hýmnesis* (Isa. 12:2; 51:3).

In the Vulgate, the one-sided interpretation of the LXX is corrected in that Jerome, in his second version of the Psalter, gave precedence to a new interpretation. In the Psalterium Gallicanum, the rendering *cano/canto* replaces the *psállō* of the Psalterium Romanum, thus restoring the "vocal" aspect to its proper place alongside the "instrumental."[30]

IV. Theological Significance. Since *zmr* I is used in OT Hebrew solely in the sense "sing praises (accompanied by stringed instruments)," its theological significance is immediately apparent. It can be defined more precisely as follows:

1. In the long series of words for hymnic praise,[31] *zmr* occupies a middle position, being a term that covers both articulated praise that speaks in comprehensible words and unarticulated praise expressed in shouts and gestures; through it articulated praise takes on a breadth it does not otherwise exhibit, and unarticulated praise acquires a clarity it otherwise lacks.

2. One of the purposes of any hymnic praise is to create and communicate joy; this is especially true for the OT use of *zmr*. Praise expressed in words is all the more productive of joy when sung "accompanied by strings"; praise expressed in instrumental music is more effective when it is sung simultaneously in words, referring explicitly to him in whom true joy has its source.

3. The summons to sing Yahweh's praises to the accompaniment of strings is addressed primarily to the assembled congregation and its individual members, secondarily, in eschatological prolepsis, to the entire earth.[32] There is no more suggestion that this mandate be delegated to professional singers or musicians than in the case of the summons to praise, glorify, sing, etc.[33] Singing God's praises is fundamentally the function of the devout as a body; they have this joyous mandate—if we may so interpret the exclusive use of the piel[34]—not merely accidentally and occasionally, but habitually, indeed as their profession.

Barth

---

[30] Cf. I.3.
[31] Cf. III.1.
[32] Cf. II.1.
[33] III.1.
[34] Cf. I.3.a.

זָנָה zānāh; זְנוּנִים z^enûnîm; זְנוּת z^enûth; תַּזְנוּת taznûth

Contents: I. 1. Etymology and Occurrences; 2. Meaning. II. Literal Meaning. III. Figurative Meaning: 1. Apostasy; 2. Commercial Trade.

I. 1. *Etymology and Occurrences.* The root *zny/w,* which means "fornicate, be a prostitute" in Hebrew, occurs with the same meaning in Aramaic dialects (Jewish Aramaic, Samaritan, Syriac, Mandean),[1] as well as in Arabic (*zanā*) and Ethiopic (*zamawa;* cf. *zenyat,* "discharge of semen,"[2] Tigré *zannā,* "fornicate"). Akk. *zenû* means "be angry, hate";[3] Driver associates this with *zānāh* in Jgs. 19:2 (cf. LXX *ōrgísthē autṓ*).[4] According to San Nicoló, the same root is involved, since it is possible to see a semantic development from "hate" to "become apostate or faithless";[5] this is unlikely, however, since Akk. *zenû* is probably related to → זנח *zānach.*

The verb *zānāh* is the usual word for the activity of a harlot or prostitute; she is even called a *zônāh.* It is used of Tamar (Gen. 38), Rahab (Josh. 2:1; 6:17, 22, 25), the mother of Jephthah (Jgs. 11:1), etc. Harlots are mentioned in 1 K. 3:16; 22:38, and there are several warnings against them in Proverbs.

Sometimes *zānāh* is construed absolutely, sometimes with prepositions. Most frequently, *'ach^arê* is used to refer to the unrelated partner; *ʿal, 'el,* and *'ēth* are also found. The wronged man is designated by *min, mēʿal,* or *mittachath.*

Most of the occurrences of *zānāh* and its derivatives, however, have figurative meaning, referring to Israel's faithlessness toward Yahweh and worship of other gods (Lev. 17:7; 20:5f.; Nu. 14:33; 15:39; 25:1; Dt. 31:16; Jgs. 2:17; 8:27,33; 1 Ch. 5:25; 2 Ch. 21:11,13; Ps. 73:27; 106:39). This usage appears most frequently in the prophetic literature, especially Hosea, Jeremiah, and Ezekiel.[6] The noun *taznûth* appears only in Ezk. 16 and 23 (22 times), while *z^enûnîm* appears most frequently in Hosea (5 times). The noun *z^enûth* appears 3 times in Jeremiah, 3 times in Ezekiel, twice in Hosea, and once in Nu. 14:33.

---

zānāh. J. P. Asmussen, "Bemerkungen zur sakralen Prostitution im AT," *StTh,* 11 (1957 [1958]), 167-192; F. Hauck and S. Schulz, "πόρνη," *TDNT,* VI, 579-595; J. Jeremias, *Kultprophetie und Gerichtsverkündigung in der späten Königszeit Israels. WMANT,* 35 (1970), 33ff.; W. Kornfeld, "L'adultère dans l'Orient antique," *RB,* 57 (1950), 92-109; J. Kühlewein, *THAT,* I, 518-520; H. D. Preuss, *Verspottung fremder Religionen im AT. BWANT,* 92 (1971), 73, 121, 131, 176.

[1] L. Prijs, "Ergänzungen zum talmudisch-aramäischen Wörterbuch," *ZDMG,* 117 (1967), 275.

[2] Leslau, *Contributions,* 19.

[3] *CAD,* XXI, 85f.

[4] G. R. Driver, "Mistranslations in the OT," *WO,* 1 (1947), 29f.

[5] M. San Nicoló, "Vorderasiatisches Rechtsgut in den ägyptischen Eheverträgen der Perserzeit," *OLZ,* 30 (1927), 217ff.

[6] See below.

2. *Meaning*. The verb *zānāh* designates primarily a sexual relationship outside of a formal union. Because the woman is subordinate to the man, she is always the subject of *zānāh* (for a discussion of Nu. 25:1, see below). The ptcp. *zônāh* or *'ishshāh zônāh* designates a woman who has sexual intercourse with someone with whom she does not have a formal covenant relationship. Any sexual relationship of a woman outside the marriage bond or without a formal union is termed fornication. When there is already a formal union and the sexual association is formed outside this union, *zānāh* becomes synonymous with *ni'ēph*, "commit adultery" (*ni'ēph* being thus a narrower term than *zānāh*).

The term *zānāh* is used figuratively of Israel's apostasy from Yahweh and its intercourse with other gods (*'elōhîm 'achērîm;* → אחר *'āchēr*). Here Israel is compared to a woman who forsakes her husband (Yahweh) and has intercourse with other men (idols; → בעל *ba'al*, III.3). Israel acts faithlessly toward its Lord (→ בגד *bāghadh*). In Ezk. 16 and 23, the allegorical description of a harlot represents the apostasy of the people.

Occasionally *zānāh* can refer to both an extramarital sexual relationship and worship outside the covenant, for instance, Nu. 25:1; Hos. 4:13–15; 9:1; Jer. 5:7. This is because apostasy from Yahweh was frequently connected with participation in the Canaanite fertility cult with its sacral prostitution.

The verb *zānāh* can also be used for commercial contacts with pagan peoples, for any association that is not right in the eyes of Yahweh can be called harlotry.

II. Literal Meaning. Prostitution and harlotry represent a familiar phenomenon in Israel, and are often mentioned quite neutrally and without comment. Tamar disguises herself "like a harlot" and sits at the gate (Gen. 38:15); Samson has relations with a harlot at Gaza (Jgs. 16:1); 1 K. 3:16ff. tell of two harlots who live in the same house and begin to quarrel, etc.

The laws regulate sexual behavior precisely. When sexual intercourse is initiated before a marriage contract has been sealed and neither of the parties is already married, the man must marry the woman and may not divorce her (Dt. 22:28f.). If a woman has a formal partner, i.e., is betrothed or married, but nevertheless of her own free will has intercourse with another man, she must suffer capital punishment (Dt. 22:22–27). If a man has a sexual relationship with the wife of another man, he likewise must suffer capital punishment (Dt. 22:22–25).

No one born in adultery may belong to the assembly of Yahweh (Dt. 23:3). A priest may not marry an *'ishshāh zônāh* (Lev. 21:7–14). If someone makes his daughter a harlot, he makes the land faithless (*tazneh hā'ārets*), and it becomes full of wickedness (*zimmāh;* → זמם *zmm*) (Lev. 19:29).

The prophets condemn all harlotry (Am. 2:7; Jer. 5:7; etc.). To be considered a harlot is disgraceful. Dinah's brothers could not tolerate having their sister treated like a harlot (Gen. 34:31). To be married to a harlot could be viewed as a punishment from God (Am. 7:17). Wisdom Literature warns against harlots as wicked and deceitful women (Prov. 6:26; 7:10; 23:27; 29:3; in Prov. 7:10 there may be an allusion to sacral prostitution[7]). In Prov. 23:27 the harlot is called a *nokhrîyāh*, "outsider," meaning that

---

[7] See H. Ringgren, *ATD*, XVI (1962), 36f.

she is outside either the marriage bond or the covenant community. It is therefore impossible to be certain whether *'ishshāh zônāh* in Jgs. 11:1, for example, means a woman from another people (cf. Jgs. 11:2, *'ishshāh 'achereth*) or a woman who has had extramarital relationships.

In Canaanite culture, extramarital relationships in connection with the fertility cult were common. Through sacral prostitution the harlot and her lover became consecrated individuals (*qᵉdhēshah* and *qādhēsh;* → קדשׁ *qdš*). Israel tried to resist this fertility cult. According to Dt. 23:18f., there is to be no *qᵉdhēshāh* or *qādhēsh* in Israel. In reality, however, the Israelites imitated Canaanite customs, "playing the harlot after their gods" (*zānāh 'achᵃrê 'ᵉlōhêhem*), so that there were in fact *qᵉdhēshôth* and *qᵉdhēshîm* in Israel. Such individuals are mentioned, for example, during the reign of Rehoboam in connection with the cult of the high places (1 K. 14:24). Hosea attacks the existence of *qᵉdhēshôth* in the eighth century (Hos. 4:14). By the time of Josiah's reformation, the Canaanite cult had penetrated into the temple cult at Jerusalem, where there were *bāthê haqqᵉdhēshîm* (2 K. 23:7).

III. Figurative Meaning.

1. *Apostasy.* a. In the OT, the Canaanite cult is violently criticized. All sexual intercourse is to be set within a formal relationship. If this view is applied to the relationship between Israel and Yahweh, it follows that all worship of God must take place within the formal relationship of the covenant, in accordance with the covenant precepts (*mishpāṭîm, dᵉbhārîm*) of Yahweh. As God's own elect people, Israel could not worship any god other than Yahweh. Israel was to obey Yahweh's voice and keep his commandments (Ex. 19:5; Dt. 13:5 [Eng. v. 4]). "If you forget (*shākhach*) Yahweh your God and go after other gods (*hālakh 'achᵃrê 'ᵉlōhîm 'ᵃchērîm;* → הלך *hālakh*) and serve them and worship them, I solemnly warn you this day that you shall surely perish. Like the nations that Yahweh makes to perish before you, so shall you perish, because you would not obey the voice of Yahweh your God" (Dt. 8:19f.).

The terminology of the marriage contract or covenant can be applied easily to the covenant between Yahweh and Israel. As Yahweh's own people, Israel must not have intercourse with other nations, since their religion is irreconcilable with proper worship of Yahweh. If Israel associates with other nations, their "harlotry" will infect Israel (Ex. 34:14-16). This applies above all to the Canaanites. Association with them leads to worship of their gods, i.e., harlotry (*zānāh 'achᵃrê 'ᵉlōhêhem*), for their daughters will make the children of Israel play the harlot after their gods (*hiznû 'eth-bāneykhā 'achᵃrê 'ᵃlōhêhen*, v. 16). Yahweh is an *'ēl qannā'* and will not tolerate Israel's having any other lover: that is judged to be harlotry.

b. The covenant demands that Israel shall worship no other gods and not associate with those who worship them (Dt. 7:3-6; 20:16-18). If Israel does not remember all the commandments of Yahweh and follows after its own heart and its own eyes, it plays the harlot after (*zānāh 'achᵃrê*) its own desires (Nu. 15:39). Ezk. 6:9 likewise emphasizes that harlotry has its roots in the human heart (*libbām hazzôneh*). Anyone who turns to a medium (→ אוב *'ôbh*) or wizard (*yiddᵉ'ōnî*, Lev. 20:6), or to the strange gods of the land (*'ᵉlōhê nēkhar hā'ārets*), is playing the harlot after them (*zānāh ʾachᵃrê,* Dt. 31:16; Jgs. 2:17). To do so means to forsake (*ʿāzabh*) the covenant God Yahweh and break the covenant with him (*hēphēr ʾeth-bᵉrîthî,* Dt. 31:16). When the people refuse to have faith in Yahweh's promise of the land of Canaan, their faithlessness is termed harlotry (*zᵉnûth,* Nu. 14:33).[8] To trust in something else, for instance, satyrs (*śᵉʿîrîm*), is to play the harlot after them (Lev. 17:7). To sacrifice to Molech (→ מלך *mālakh*) is to play the harlot after Molech (*liznôth ʾachᵃrê hammōlekh,* Lev. 20:5). Worship of Gideon's ephod is "harlotry" (Jgs. 8:27). Worship of the *bᵉʿālîm,* especially Baal-berith, is termed *zānāh* (Jgs. 8:33). All forms of syncretism are therefore "harlotry" (cf. also 1 Ch. 5:25; 2 Ch. 21:11, 13). In Ps. 73:27, apostasy from Yahweh is termed "playing the harlot from" (*zānāh min*) him. This sets the apostate far (*rāchaq*) from Yahweh and the intimate covenant relationship with him. In Ps. 106:34–39, Israel's intercourse with the pagans is called an act of *zānāh*: they have learned their ways (v. 35) and worshipped their gods (v. 36).

When Nu. 25:1 states that Israel committed fornication with (*zānāh ʾel*) the daughters of Moab, it is because *zānāh* here refers to apostasy from the covenant, expressed in the form of intercourse with the Moabite women. Therefore *zānāh,* which everywhere else has a feminine subject, can have Israel as its subject here, because Israel plays the female role in relationship to Yahweh.

c. Hosea compares Israel to a woman of harlotry (*ʾēsheth zᵉnûnîm*) and the children of Israel to children of harlotry (*yaldhê zᵉnûnîm, bᵉnê zᵉnûnîm*) (Hos. 1:2; 2:6[4]). By its faithlessness toward Yahweh, the land has "committed great harlotry by forsaking Yahweh" (*zānōh thizneh hāʾārets mēʾachᵃrê yhvh,* 1:2). Because Yahweh chose Israel and entered into a covenant with Israel, its apostasy can be called adultery (*naʾᵃphûphîm,* 2:4[2]). Israel has forgotten (*shākhach*) its true husband (2:15[13]) and instead goes after its lovers (*hālakh ʾachᵃrê mᵉʾahᵃbhîm,* 2:7[5]), i.e., worships other gods (3:1). In 4:15, Israel's adultery is associated with the syncretistic cult at Gilgal and Beth-aven; this cult was harlotry in a double sense, since actual sexual intercourse was part of the cult (4:13f.) and its idolatry meant faithlessness toward Yahweh (4:15). Cf. also 4:18, where *hiznû* and **ʾᵃhabhhᵃbhû*[9] appear together, and 9:1, where Israel's harlotry (*hiznāh, zᵉnûth*) in forsaking Yahweh is associated with the fertility cult (*zānîthā mēʿal ʾᵉlōhêkhā . . . ʿal kol-gornôth dāghān*). In 5:3 and 6:10, the idolatry in Ephraim is called harlotry that brings defilement. A spirit of harlotry (*rûach zᵉnûnîm*) dwells within Israel (5:4); the people do not know Yahweh (*lōʾ yādhaʿ ʾeth-yhvh*), i.e., do not live in covenant community with him.[10]

d. Isaiah calls the city of Jerusalem a harlot (*zônāh,* Isa. 1:21). The people have rebelled (*pāshaʿ*, 1:2,28) against Yahweh and forsaken (*ʿāzabh,* 1:4,28) him.

e. Jeremiah, too, frequently uses the symbolism of marriage. Referring to Canaanite cult practices, he says, "Upon every high hill and under every green tree you bowed

---

[8] Cf. S. McEvenue, "Source-critical Problems in Nm 14:26–38," *Bibl,* 50 (1969), 453–465, esp. 461f.

[9] For a discussion of the text, see W. Rudolph, *KAT,* XIII/1 (1966), 108.

[10] Cf. G. J. Botterweck, *"Gott erkennen" im Sprachgebrauch des AT. BBB,* 2 (1951), 66.

down as a harlot" (Jer. 2:20).[11] Israel's careless desertion (*ʿāzabh,* 2:17,19) of Yahweh is compared to the unrestrained sexual drive of a wild ass (2:24).

In Jer. 3, apostasy is compared to adultery. Israel has not held to Yahweh as its only husband, but has "played the harlot (*zānāh*) with many lovers"; this harlotry (*zᵉnûth*) has polluted (→ חנף *chānēph*) the land (3:2). Israel is like a woman who has turned her back (*mᵉshûbhāh*) to her husband and plays the harlot under every green tree, i.e., participates in the syncretistic cult. Her sister Judah is also faithless (bāghōdhāh); her idolatry is termed "adultery with stone and tree" (*tinʾaph ʾeth-hāʾebhen vᵉʾeth-hāʿēts,* 3:9). Not to obey the voice of Yahweh (*lōʾ shāmaʿ bᵉqôl yhvh*) is to break the covenant with him; this conduct is also described by means of verbs like *pāshaʿ* (3:13) and *bāghadh* (3:20). The people have forgotten (*shākhach,* 3:21) their God.

In chap. 5, too, the desertion (*ʿāzabh*) of Yahweh by his people is termed adultery (*nʾp*). The people assemble in the house of harlots (*bêth zônāh,* 5:7), which can mean sexual wantonness in the syncretistic cult and Israel's faithlessness toward Yahweh (*bāghôdh bāghᵉdhû,* 5:11). Israel refuses to return (*mēʾᵃnû lāshûbh,* 5:3) to her true husband. In 13:27, Jerusalem's apostasy is called "your adultery" (*niʾuphayikh*) and "your lewd harlotry" (*zimmath zᵉnûthēkh*) and linked with the hated idols (*shiqqûtsîm*).

f. In the book of Ezekiel, chaps. 16 and 23 in particular use sexual terminology to depict the apostasy of the people. But 6:9 also speaks of a wanton heart (*lēbhābh hazzôneh*) in connection with the worship of idols (*gillûlîm*); and in 20:30 the verb *zānāh* is used to describe the worship of *shiqqûtsîm*. In 43:7,9, we find the promise that the *zᵉnûth* will one day be removed by the establishment of the new temple.

Ezk. 16 describes Jerusalem as a foundling that owes its life to Yahweh (v. 6), with whom Yahweh entered into a covenant (*vāʾābhôʾ bibhrîth ʾōthākh,* v. 8) and whom Yahweh adorned with gorgeous finery (vv. 13f.). But Israel repaid this kindness with terrible harlotry (*taznûth,* vv. 15ff.). It gave itself over to the worship of Canaanite gods (v. 16), worshipped images (v. 17), sacrificed its sons and daughters (v. 20), and entered into relationships with Egypt, Assyria, and Chaldea (vv. 26, 28f.). Its apostasy is compared to harlotry worse than that of the most brazen harlot. Anyone at all could have sexual intercourse with it (v. 25), even without paying the usual price (v. 31)—in fact, Israel even paid its lovers (*mᵉʾahᵃbhîm*) in order to have opportunity for harlotry (vv. 33f.). Therefore Jerusalem must suffer the penalty of women who commit adultery (*mishpᵉṭê nōʾᵃphôth*), namely, stoning (v. 40). She has had intercourse with strangers (*zārîm,* v. 32) and deserted her husband and children (v. 45); she has despised her covenant oath (*bāzîth ʾālāh*) and broken the covenant (*lᵉhāphēr bᵉrîth,* v. 59).

Ezk. 23 is an allegory describing the fate of the two sisters Oholah and Oholibah, i.e., Samaria and Jerusalem. Once again it is emphasized how the Israelites were already playing the harlot in Egypt (*zānāh,* v. 3), i.e., even before the marriage/covenant. Later Samaria bestowed her harlotries (*taznûth*) on Assyria and her idols (*gillûlîm*), as well as Egypt (vv. 7f.). This became her downfall (v. 10).

---

[11] Cf. W. L. Holladay, " 'On Every High Hill and Under Every Green Tree,' " *VT,* 11 (1961), 173.

Jerusalem went even further in her harlotry (*taznûth*) and wantonness (*z^enûnîm*) (v. 11). She doted upon the Assyrians (v. 12) as well as on the Chaldeans and their pictures (v. 15), all without shame (v. 18). She continued the lewdness of her youth (*zimmath n^{eᶜ}ûrayikh,* v. 21) and her harlotry (*taznûth*) with Egypt (vv. 19-21).

And so this lewdness (*zimmāh*) and harlotry (*z^enûth*) must be punished (vv. 27,35). In v. 29, three strong expressions are used for the apostasy and idolatry of Jerusalem: "the nakedness of your harlotry" (*ᶜervath z^enûnayikh*), "your lewdness" (*zimmāthēkh*), and "your harlotry" (*taznûthayikh*). Association with the nations is termed harlotry (*z^enôth 'ach^arê gôyim*) and pollution with their idols (*niṭmē'th b^eghillûlêhem*) (v. 30). The word *tôᶜēbhāh,* "abomination," is also used (v. 36).

Because Jerusalem has committed fornication even though Yahweh made a covenant with her, her fornication is equivalent to adultery. In v. 43, *ni'uphîm* stands in parallel with *zānāh taznûth* (cf. also Isa. 57:3). Idolatry is adultery with disgraceful idols (*'eth-gillûlîm ni'^aphû,* v. 37), and the two lewd sisters Samaria and Jerusalem can be called adulteresses (*nō'^aphôth*), who must suffer the penalty for adultery (*mishpaṭ nō'^aphôth*), i.e., stoning (v. 47).

2. *Commercial Trade.* In a few passages, commercial trade of a city is called harlotry. This is probably because Israel's commercial contacts also brought it into contact with the worship of foreign gods. Through contacts with other nations, foreign cultic practices were imported into Israel. Therefore commercial profit derived from these contacts is called the hire of a harlot (*'ethnan,* Mic. 1:7).

In Isa. 23:17, commercial contacts with various lands are termed harlotry (*zān^ethāh 'eth-kol-maml^ekhôth hā'ārets*), and the profits of trade are called the hire of a harlot. When judgment is proclaimed against Tyre, the city, laid waste by enemy armies, is compared to a forgotten harlot (*zônāh nishkāchāh,* v. 16).

In Nah. 3, an oracle of judgment against Nineveh, the "countless harlotries of the harlot" (*rōbh z^enûnê zônāh*) are mentioned (v. 4). This probably refers not only to the trade of Nineveh, but also to her idol cult and magic arts (*k^eshāphîm*).

The word *k^eshāphîm* is associated in 2 K. 9:22 with the "harlotries of Jezebel" (*z^enûnê 'îzebhel*), i.e., Phoenician idolatry.

Erlandsson

זָנַח *zānach*

Contents: I. Etymology; Occurrences. II. Use: 1. Qal; 2. Hiphil.

I. Etymology; Occurrences. The verb *zānach,* which means "reject, exclude" in the OT, occurs also in Middle Hebrew in the sense "abhor," hiphil "repudiate." It is related to Arab. *zanaḥa,* "be distant, repulse"; Yaron's suggestion that Akk. *zenû,* "hate," also belongs here is not certain, but likely.

The verb is attested 16 times in the qal, 3 times in the hiphil. It has been suggested that Lam. 3:17 be read as a niphal rather than a qal, which would be the only evidence for this form.

II. Use.

1. *Qal.* In Hos. 8:3, the verb has a human subject: Israel has "rejected" or "spurned" the good—the context suggests through idolatry. In v. 5, the form *zānach* appears a second time, which can hardly be correct; the simplest solution is to read *zānachtî,* "I [Yahweh] have spurned your calf, O Samaria," a punishment corresponding to the offense.

With God as its subject, *zānach* appears in some Psalms of Lament to describe the plight of the psalmist: God has rejected him, ignoring him and refusing to help him. Sometimes the lament takes the form of a reproachful question: "Why hast thou rejected me/us?" This is the case in the individual lament Pss. 42–43, where 43:2 asks: "Why hast thou cast me off? Why go I mourning because of the oppression of the enemy?" The problem posed by this psalm is separation from worship. The psalmist feels rejected by God and excluded from the community. In Ps. 88:15 (Eng. v. 14) we find a similar question, and the plight of the psalmist is defined by a further question: "Why dost thou hide thy face from me" (→ סתר *str;* → פנים *pānîm*). Verse 16(15) represents the psalmist as being afflicted (*ʿānî*) and suffering; v. 17(16) mentions the wrath of God.

Four communal laments make characteristic use of *zānach:* Pss. 44, 60, 74, 108. In 74:1 we find once more the question, "Why dost thou cast us off?" There is a parallel reference to the wrath of God. The psalm deals with destruction of the temple by enemies, which is taken to prove that Yahweh is angry with his people and therefore ignores his temple. Ps. 60, the last half of which (vv. 7–14[5–12]) is repeated in Ps. 108:7–14(6–13), presupposes a military defeat, which is described in v. 3(1): "O God, thou hast rejected and broken (*prṣ*) us; thou hast been angry and hast made us turn back." Verse 12(10) (= 108:13[11]) states in the form of a question that God has rejected his people and does not go forth with their armies (*lōʾ-thētsēʾ . . . bᵉtsibhʾôthênû*). The same statement is expanded in Ps. 44:10(9) by the addition of *vattaklîmēnû,* "and thou hast abased us." Verse 24(23) contains a corresponding petition: "Awake (*hāqîtsāh;*

---

zānach. R. Yaron, "The Meaning of זנח," *VT,* 13 (1963), 237-39.

→ יקץ *yāqats*)! Do not cast us off for ever!'' Verse 25(24) goes on to describe the situation by means of the expressions ''hide one's face'' and ''forget our affliction''—in other words, *zānach* means that God has totally turned his back on his people. A similar definition can be derived from Ps. 77:8-10(7-9), where *zānach* is associated with ''never be favorable (*rātsāh*),'' ''his *chesedh* has ceased,'' ''forget to be gracious (*shākhach channôth*),'' and ''shut up compassion (*qāphats rachᵃmîm*).''

Finally, in v. 39(38) of Ps. 89, a royal psalm, we find the combination *zānachtā vattimʾās,* ''thou hast cast off and rejected (→ מאס *māʾas*) (thine anointed)''; as a third verb, we find *hithʿabbar,* ''be full of wrath'' (cf. also *nēʾartāh* in v. 40[39]). The psalm speaks of the removal of the king from his office.

Lam. 2:7, like the Psalms, refers to destruction at the hands of enemies: ''The Lord has scorned (*zānach*) his altar, disowned [*niʾēr;* found only here and in Ps. 89:40 (39)] his sanctuary; he has delivered the city into the hand of the enemies.'' In Lam. 3, written in the 1st person singular, we find sometimes a lamentation, ''Thou hast excluded my *nephesh* from *shālôm*'' (v. 17), sometimes a positive statement, ''He will not cast off for ever'' (v. 31, par. *rḥm,* ''have compassion,'' in v. 32).

Zec. 10:6 is also positive: ''They shall be as though I had not rejected them.''

2. *Hiphil.* The hiphil form occurs only in Chronicles. In 2 Ch. 11:14, it refers to the exclusion of the Levites from the priesthood, and in 2 Ch. 29:19, to the desecration or better the discarding of certain temple utensils ''by faithlessness'' or by ''cutting up'' the utensils (2 Ch. 28:24). Finally, according to 1 Ch. 28:9, Yahweh will ''cast off'' forever those who forsake (*ʿāzabh*) him.

Ringgren

זָעַם *zāʿam;* זַעַם *zaʿam*

Contents: I. Etymology and Occurrences. II. With Reference to People: 1. Verb; 2. Noun. III. With Reference to God: 1. Verb; 2. Noun; 3. Theological Meaning.

I. Etymology and Occurrences. The root *zʿm* appears in the OT both as a verb (13 times) and as a noun (*zaʿam,* 22 times). In either case it can be associated with God or human beings.

---

zāʿam. → אנף *ʾānaph;* B. Albrektson, *History and the Gods. ConBibOT,* 1 (1967); H. C. Brichto, *The Problem of ''Curse'' in the Hebrew Bible. JBL Monograph Series,* 13 (1963), 20, 202f.; J. Pedersen, *Der Eid bei den Semiten* (1914); *idem, ILC,* I, 411-452; H. Ringgren, ''Einige Schilderungen des göttlichen Zorns,'' *Tradition und Situation. Festschrift A. Weiser* (1963), 107-113; G. Sauer, *Die strafende Vergeltung Gottes in den Psalmen* (1961); J. Scharbert, '' 'Fluchen' und 'Segnen' im AT,'' *Bibl,* 39 (1958), 1-26, esp. 15; W. Schottroff, *Der*

The verb, which is attested in the qal, niphal (Prov. 25:23), and hiphil (Sir. 43:16), has cognates in Syr. *za'ēm,* "attack verbally, scold," Arab. *zaġama,* "speak angrily," and OSA *z'm,* "quarrel." It may be possible to derive an element of threat from this material, but a specific basic meaning cannot be determined.

The verb also appears in the Qumran documents,[1] but only in the sense of "curse." The occurrences in later Hebrew tend in the direction of "be angry, vexed."[2]

Actual usage in the OT is not uniform. If we assume that the basic meaning is "threaten"[3] or "injure,"[4] the sense can be expressed more precisely through words ("curse"), actions ("punish, condemn"), or the implicit emotional state ("be angry"). It is hardly possible to distinguish clearly among these meanings.

What has been said here about the verb holds true for the noun as well, although the "anger" component tends to be more dominant than in the case of the verb.

II. With Reference to People.

1. *Verb.* The passages in which the verb appears with human subjects are either early or very late (Nu. 23:7f.; Prov. 24:24; 25:23; Dnl. 11:30; 1QM 13:1, 4f.; 1QS 2:7). It usually appears in the qal, with the exception of Prov. 25:23 (niphal). It is used with a preposition (*'al*) only in Dnl. 11:30. It is noteworthy that objects regarded positively (Israel, Nu. 23:7f.; "the holy covenant," Dnl. 11:30) are associated with negative subjects (Balak, Antiochus Epiphanes), while the opposite obtains in Prov. 24:24 and the Qumran documents. In Nu. 23:7f. and Prov. 24:24, the word stands in parallel with verbs of cursing: → ארר *'rr* and *nqb*/*qbb*. At Qumran there are three occurrences of a *zā'ûm* formula modelled upon the more frequent *'ārûr* formula (1QS 2:7; 1QM 13:4f.). The root *z'm* also stands in contrast to *brk* (Nu. 23:11; 1QM 13:1).

When the subject is man, the verb clearly is a curse term meaning "speak curses," "do injury to someone by cursing." In the background there hovers the magically tinged notion that words spoken as an oath, incantation, or oracle are effectually powerful and exert a direct influence on human life.[5] At least in the Balaam story we find the further conception that the effect of the curse is guided by a divine power:[6] Balaam's curses directed against Israel are ineffectual if they are not sanctioned by Yahweh (Nu. 23:8). Whether this idea is also present in Prov. 24:24 cannot be determined from the text. In Dnl. 11:30 the subject is an historical figure, Antiochus Epiphanes, who pronounces curses against (*zā'am 'al*) the Jewish cult at Jerusalem (*b^erîth qôdhesh*). The purpose of the verb is to identify the person who

---

altisraelitische Fluchspruch. WMANT, 30 (1969); W. H. Simpson, *Divine Wrath in the Eighth Century Prophets* (diss., Boston, 1968).

[1]See below.

[2]Levy, *WTM;* M. Jastrow, *Dictionary of the Targumim* . . . (1903-1950).

[3]Schottroff, 28.

[4]Pedersen, *Eid,* 81.

[5]Pedersen, *ILC,* I, 411ff.; Schottroff, 16ff.

[6]Albrektson, 16ff.

inaugurated the period of desolation or malediction that the religious policies of the Seleucids spelled for faithful Jews.

Prov. 25:23 is the only instance of a niphal form. The association with *l^eshôn sether* (cf. Hos. 7:16; Isa. 30:27) and the use of the word in Prov. 22:14; 24:24 support the translation "struck by a curse."[7]

2. *Noun*. The noun appears in clear association with a human being only in Hos. 7:16. The phrase *zaʿam l^eshônām* (cf. Isa. 30:27; Prov. 25:23) assures the meaning "curse."[8] In a judgment discourse against Ephraim, the prophet says that the princes of Ephraim have turned apostate through "the cursing of their tongue" and will therefore fall by the sword. We may assume that the cursing included an invocation of magical powers or other gods, and was directed against Yahweh and his prophets. The harsh punishment announced for the princes is probably associated with ancient Near Eastern laws against injurious magic.[9]

III. With Reference to God.

1. *Verb*. The verb occurs seven times with Yahweh as subject, plus one occurrence in the hiphil in Sir. 43:16. It appears in texts of various kinds (Nu. 23:8; Prov. 22:14; Mic. 6:10; Ps. 7:12 [Eng. v. 11]), although with a certain preponderance in postexilic prophetic texts (Isa. 66:14; Zec. 1:12; Mal. 1:4). In one case the object is a thing ("ephah," Mic. 6:10); everywhere else the object is personal: Israel (Nu. 23:8), the foolish man who is led astray by loose women (Prov. 22:14), the enemies of Yahweh (Isa. 66:14), Jerusalem and the cities of Judah (Zec. 1:12), Edom (Mal. 1:4). In some cases the verb is associated with an expression of time to indicate permanence or temporal limitation: *b^ekhol-yôm* (Ps. 7:12[11]); *shibhʿîm shānāh* (Zec. 1:12); *ʿadh-ʿôlām* (Mal. 1:4).

The synonyms suggest various nuances. The use of *nqb/qbb* in Nu. 23:8 has already been discussed. In Isa. 66:14, the word is probably associated with the fire and the flaming anger (*chēmāh ʾaph*) in the following description of a theophany (vv. 15f.). The attribute *ʾēl zōʿēm* in Ps. 7:12(11) has as its parallel the expression *ʾ^elōhîm shôphēṭ tsaddîq*, which is probably indigenous to the so-called judgment doxologies;[10] the word refers to the God who avenges and punishes. The contrasting expressions refer to the saving mercy of God: *yadh-yhvh* (Isa. 66:14), *rḥm* piel (Zec. 1:12), *môshîaʿ* (Ps. 7:11f.[10f.]).

We must probably think in terms of a certain shift of meaning. The earlier meaning, "curse," which fits well in Nu. 23:8; Prov. 22:14; Mic. 6:10, was extended by the image of Yahweh as the righteous judge (Ps. 7:12[11]) in judgment doxologies and was incorporated into the postexilic prophetic passages with their wealth of judgment and wrath terminology. In Isa. 66:14; Zec. 1:12; Mal. 1:4, it is not easy to decide between the meanings "be angry" and "curse."

---

[7]Pedersen, *Eid*, 81f.; *KBL*³.

[8]Differently W. Rudolph, *KAT*, XIII/1 (1966), 152, who understands it as the "stammering" of someone trying to speak an unfamiliar language.

[9]Schottroff, 17.

[10]H.-J. Kraus, *BK*, XV/1 (⁴1972), 60f.

In Sir. 43:16 we find a hiphil form: *b^e^khōchô yazʿîm hārîm,* "by his strength he causes the mountains to shake." Apart from the fact that the text may be corrupt (LXX: *kaí en optasía autoú saleuthḗsetai órē*), we may have here a further development of the theophany imagery (cf. Hab. 3:10–12; Nah. 1:5).

2. *Noun.* The noun appears in association with Yahweh 21 times, primarily in the prophets (14 times), but also in Psalms (4 times), Daniel (twice), and Lamentations (once). It is most common in exilic and postexilic texts.

The word almost always appears as a term for the blazing wrath of Yahweh, as its synonyms confirm: *'aph* (Isa. 10:5, 25), *ch^a^rôn 'aph* (Isa. 13:9; Nah. 1:6; Zeph. 3:8; Ps. 69:25[24]; 78:49), *chēmāh 'aph* (Isa. 66:15), *chēmāh* (Ps. 38:2ff.[1ff.]), *ʿebhrāh* (Ezk. 21:36[31]; 22:31; Ps. 78:49), *qetseph* (Jer. 10:10; Ps. 38:2ff.[1ff.]; Ps. 102:11[10]), and the construct phrase *zaʿam 'aph* (Lam. 2:6). These texts often associate *zaʿam* with the idea of blazing fire (Isa. 30:27; Ezk. 21:36[31]; 22:31; Nah. 1:6; Zeph. 3:8). As antonyms we find *yēshaʿ* (Hab. 3:12f.) and *y^e^shûʿāh* (Ps. 69:25[24]). The word appears as a kind of technical term in formulaic expressions belonging to prophetic and apocalyptic eschatology: *k^e^lî zaʿam* (Isa. 13:5; Jer. 50:25), *b^e^yôm zaʿam* (Ezk. 22:24), *ʿadh kālāh zaʿam* (Isa. 10:25; Dnl. 11:36), *b^e'^ach^a^rîth hazzaʿam* (Dnl. 8:19).

Usually the verbs associated with *zaʿam* have a clear judgment aspect. God pours out *zaʿam* (*shāphakh ʿal,* Ezk. 21:36[31]; 22:31; Zeph. 3:8; Ps. 69:25[24]) or sends *zaʿam* (*shālach b^e^,* Ps. 78:49). The *zaʿam* of God "destroys" (Isa. 13:5) or bestrides the earth (in destruction) (Hab. 3:12). Twice the verb *mālē'* is used: Yahweh's lips are full of *zaʿam* (Isa. 30:27); God has "filled" the prophet with *zaʿam* (Jer. 15:17). Two additional passages say that man cannot endure Yahweh's *zaʿam* (Jer. 10:10, *kûl;* Nah. 1:6, *ʿāmadh*).

The positive aspect is less frequent, but appears in some postexilic passages. We read that *zaʿam* comes to an end (*kālāh,* Isa. 10:25; Dnl. 11:36) or passes (*ʿābhar,* Isa. 26:20). The same idea appears characteristically in several prophetic judgment theophanies, where the noun is part of a tripartite schema: (1) account of a theophany, involving catastrophe in nature and wrath terminology, often associated with blazing fire (Isa. 30:27–28a; Nah. 1:2–6; Hab. 3:3–12; Zeph. 3:8); (2) judgment of the nations (*ʿammîm, gôyim*), who are struck by *zaʿam* (Isa. 30:28b, 30ff.; Nah. 1:8–11; Hab. 3:12, 13bff.; Zeph. 3:8b); (3) words of salvation for the prophet's own people (*ʿam, chōsê bhô*), who are promised deliverance from *zaʿam* (Isa. 30:19–26, 29; Nah. 1:7, 12f.; Hab. 3:13a; Zeph. 3:9ff.). The possibility cannot be excluded that this structure may be the result of redaction.[11] Traces of this tradition with its "selective judgment"[12] appear also in the Apocalypse of Isaiah (Isa. 26:20f.) and Trito-Isaiah (Isa. 66:14ff.).

Concretely, Yahweh's *zaʿam* is expressed in pain and suffering (Jer. 15:17; Ps. 38:4[3]; 69:25[24]; 78:49; 102:11[10]), captivity and exile (Lam. 2:6; cf. Zec. 1:12), drought (Ezk. 21:36[31]; 22:24, 31), thunder, fire, and smoke (Isa. 26:20; 30:27; 66:14ff.), earthquake (Isa. 13:5; Nah. 1:5f.; Hab. 3:12), the plagues in Egypt (Ps.

[11] O. Kaiser, *Isaiah 13–39. OTL* (trans. 1974), 300f.; K. Elliger, *ATD,* XXV ([6]1967), 51.
[12] Kaiser, *Isaiah,* 214.

78:49), and the oppression of Israel by foreign powers (Isa. 10:5,25; 13:5; Jer. 50:25; Dnl. 8:19; 11:36).

When someone is struck by God's wrath or curse, it may be possible to give the reason: the sin of an individual (Ps. 38:4[3]; 78:49); the sin of the people (Isa. 10:5; Jer. 15:17; Ezk. 21:36[31]; 22:24, 31); arrogant enmity toward God on the part of the nations, or their oppression of Israel, God's elect people (Isa. 10:5; 13:5; 26:20; 30:27; Jer. 50:25; Nah. 1:6; Hab. 3:12; Zeph. 3:8; Ps. 78:49ff.). It is also possible to face an unexpected calamity, a curse from God without apparent reason (Ps. 69:25[24]; 102:11[10]; Lam. 2:6).

As vengeance and judgment, *za'am* can strike individuals (Ps. 38:4[3]; 69:25[24]; 102:11[10]), the people of Israel (Isa. 10:5; Ezk. 21:36[31]; 22:24, 31) and their leaders (Lam. 2:6), the enemies of Yahweh (Nah. 1:6ff.; Ps. 69:25[24]), Babylon (Isa. 13:5; Jer. 50:25), Assyria (Isa. 30:27, 31), Egypt (Ps. 78:49), or the foreign nations as a group (Isa. 26:20; Jer. 10:10; Hab. 3:12; Zeph. 3:8). Jer. 15:17 is a special case: the expression "thou has filled me with *za'am*" refers formally to the suffering of the prophet as he laments; in its present context, however, the word *za'am* takes on the coloration of the judgment oracles that surround the lament, so that it also functions as a kind of symbolic action, suggesting the punishment of Jerusalem.

3. *Theological Meaning*. In 18 of its 24 occurrences, *za'am* is connected directly with an action on the part of Yahweh. Thus *za'am* forms part of the long series of expressions for divine wrath (→ אנף *'ānaph*). These words can be freely combined and are clearly more or less synonymous, without regard to any "original" meanings. This can also be seen in that *za'am*, like words belonging to the semantic field of "heat," can be associated with blazing fire. On the other hand, the fundamental meaning "curse" comes clearly to the fore in a few passages (Isa. 30:27; Mic. 6:10; Prov. 22:14). Clearly no precise distinction was drawn between wrath as a divine emotion and its expression in a curse or its realization.

In the judgment doxologies, Yahweh appears as the righteous judge, the punishing and avenging God, an *'ēl zō'ēm* (Ps. 7:12[11]). This idea lies behind the identification of *za'am* with the divine punishment itself, above all in the prophetic texts. Here the concept takes on various concrete forms: God's wrath results in all kinds of pain and suffering.[13] The attacks of enemy nations can also be construed as manifestations of divine wrath (Isa. 13:5; Jer. 50:25; Isa. 10:5 likewise belongs in this context, although the text is not totally correct).

The reason for God's wrath, curse, and punishment is usually sought in human sin and enmity toward God, although there are also cases where no reason is given for God's wrath. In such a case, whoever has fallen victim to God's wrath can appeal to God's mercy (*rach^{a}mîm*) and steadfast love (*chesedh*)—the other side of God's nature—and thus experience salvation (*y^{e}shû'āh*). Here, then, we find a tension in the nature of God, which lies behind the structure of the judgment theophany discussed above, but also appears in several other passages (e.g., Isa. 26:20f.; 66:14ff.; Jer. 15:17; Zec. 1:12; Ps. 7:12[11]; 69:25[24]; 78:49; 102:11[10]). Here God's *za'am* is

[13] See above.

directed against sinners (*lōʾ yāshûbh*), enemies (*ʾōyᵉbhîm, tsōrᵉrîm*), and foreign oppressors, while salvation is reserved to the righteous (*yishrê lēbh*), the faithful (*chōsê bhô*), or the elect people.

Occasionally this tension clearly creates difficulties. Isa. 10:24f. is very cautious about ascribing to God responsibility for oppression at the hands of Assyria; the emphasis is on the exhortation to endure until the wrath ceases. In Daniel, where *zaʿam* is used absolutely as a term for the period of persecution (8:19; 11:6), the end of this period is determined in advance by Yahweh, but the verb itself does not have a divine subject in 11:30. Here we might find one of the assumptions leading to dualism, but never totally eliminating wrath from the nature of God.

Wiklander

זָעַף *zāʿaph;* זָעֵף *zāʿēph;* זַעַף *zaʿaph*

Contents: I. Etymology and Meaning. II. Use.

I. Etymology and Meaning. The root *zʿp* is attested in several Aramaic dialects: Jewish Aram. and Syr., "be violent, angry"; Samar., "blow." Arab. *zaʿafa,* "kill on the spot," is cognate.[1] The Hebrew verb means "rage." Nominal derivatives are *zāʿēph,* "raging" (two occurrences), and *zaʿaph,* "rage, fury" (seven occurrences). Two occurrences of the verb are semantically divergent: the participle means "looking sickly, emaciated" (Gen. 40:6; Dnl. 1:10). Probably we are dealing here with another root, possibly cognate with Arab. *ḍaʿīf,* "weak,"[2] although Arab. *ḍ* does not correspond to Heb. *z.*

II. Use. In one passage (Jonah 1:15), the noun *zaʿaph* is used for the raging of the sea; elsewhere the root refers to raging anger, with either God (three times) or human beings (six times) as subject.

The first occurrence of *zaʿaph* as a term for divine wrath is in Isa. 30:30, a theophany description that uses several terms for wrath and associates God's wrath with a consuming fire. In Mic. 7:9, Zion speaks in the 1st person and says, "I will bear the 'fury' of Yahweh because I have sinned against him, until he pleads my cause and executes judgment for me." The wrath of God is thus his reaction to the sin of his people; but it will not endure forever, but will be replaced by God's restoring grace. In 2 Ch. 28:9 we read that Yahweh, in his wrath against the Judeans, gave them into the

---

zāʿaph. → אנף *ʾānaph;* זעם *zāʿam.*

[1]For a contrary view, see A. Guillaume, "Hebrew and Arabic Lexicography," *Abr-Nahrain,* 1 (1959/60 [1961]), 8; 2 (1960/61 [1962]), 13f.: *ʿazafa,* "become wretched."

[2]*KBL*[3].

hand of the northern Israelites. Here the terminology of the holy war (→ יד yādh) is applied to the sister nation of Judah.

With human subjects, *zāʿaph* appears to mean primarily "attack violently." King Uzziah attacks the priests who want to keep him from offering incense (2 Ch. 26:19). Asa is angry (*kāʿas*) with the seer who has censured him for trusting insufficiently in God, "for he was 'in a rage' with him on account of this" (2 Ch. 16:10). Ahab is twice said to be *sar vᵉzāʿēph,* "resentful and sullen," once after Elijah castigates him for releasing the Aramean king (1 K. 20:43) and again when Naboth refuses to give him his vineyard (1 K. 21:4).

Speaking in general terms, Prov. 19:12 says that the wrath of a king is like the growling of a lion; its opposite is his *rātsôn,* "favor." A special case is described in Prov. 19:3: the man whose own foolishness has brought him ruin blames Yahweh and is enraged at him. This is one of the few instances where wrath is associated with the heart (*lēbh*).

Ringgren

זָעַק *zāʿaq;* זְעָקָה *zᵉʿāqāh;* צָעַק *tsāʿaq;* צְעָקָה *tsᵉʿāqāh*

Contents: I. Ancient Near East: 1. Egyptian; 2. Akkadian; 3. West Semitic. II. 1. Etymology; 2. Statistics; 3. Distribution of Occurrences; 4. LXX; 5. Meaning. III. Secular Range of Meanings: 1. Socio-legal; 2. Politico-military. IV. Religious and Theological Range of Meanings: 1. Lament; 2. Prayer.

I. Ancient Near East.

1. *Egyptian.* The Egyptian verb *ḏʿḳ*[1] is attested in the New Kingdom (20th dynasty) with the meaning "cry, shout."[2] The crying can be directed "to (*r*) the heavens" as a cry for help. Both the verb and the substantive *ḏʿḳt,* "crying," also

---

zāʿaq. R. Albertz, "צעק *ṣāʿaq* schreien," *THAT,* II, 352-56; K. Albrecht, "Das Geschlecht der hebräischer Hauptwörter," *ZAW,* 16 (1896), 116; H. J. Boecker, *Redeformen des Rechtslebens im AT. WMANT,* 14 (²1970), 61-66; W. Fuss, *Die deuteronomistische Pentateuchredaktion in Exodus 3-17. BZAW,* 126 (1972), 38-40; E. Jenni, *Das hebräische Piʿel* (1968), 154f.; R. Marcus, "The 'Plain Meaning' of Isaiah 42:1-4," *HThR,* 30 (1937), 249-259; W. Richter, *Die Bearbeitungen des "Retterbuches" in der deuteronomischen Epoche. BBB,* 21 (1964), 18-20; I. L. Seeligmann, "Zur Terminologie für das Gerichtsverfahren im Wortschatz des biblischen Hebräisch," *Hebräische Wortforschung. Festschrift W. Baumgartner. SVT,* 16 (1967), 251-278.

[1] *WbÄS,* V, 541.
[2] *RIH,* 125, 7.

attested in the New Kingdom,[3] are Hebrew loanwords. The dictionaries refer to the Hebrew forms written *ṣ'qh/ṣ'q,* but it cannot be determined whether the Egyptian words derive from these forms or from *z'qh/z'q,* because Egyp. *ḏ* can represent Heb. *ṣ* or *z*.

2. *Akkadian*. There is no known term in Akkadian that is cognate with the Hebrew root. The verb *ragāmu(m)*[4] is used primarily for legal complaint in the sense "lodge a complaint against, accuse," etc., and thus exhibits a similarity to one of the Hebrew usages.[5] There is an even broader semantic correspondence in the use of the noun *rigmu(m),* "shout, cry, voice."[6] The phrase *rigmu(m) šakānu(m),* "lift the voice, cry," appears frequently with human subjects in reference to a dirge,[7] bewailing a defeat,[8] lamentation,[9] cries of anguish uttered by a sick man,[10] and the disturbing noise of human beings, which rises to the gods.[11]

3. *West Semitic*. Except for the place name *ṣ'q,*[12] the root is unattested in Ugaritic. A similar situation exists in Palmyrene, where we find only the personal name *z'qw,* "clamor."[13]

In Old Aramaic we find the substantives *[z']qh,* "cry,"[14] and *ṣ'[qh]*.[15] Only in the first passage does the context show that we have here the lamentation (par. to *yllh;* cf. Isa. 15:8) to be heard as a result of the curses that follow the breaking of a treaty. In Imperial Aramaic there is one occurrence in the simple stem of *z'q*[16] and one of *ṣ'q*[17]; their meanings are associated with lamentation and a legal case.

The primary forms used by Arabic are *z'q,* "cry, lament, scream," and *z'qt,* "clamor, outcry, call"; *ṣ'q*, "rumble loudly, faint on account of thunder," represents a derivative.[18]

---

[3] J. F. Champollion, *Monuments de l'Égypte et de la Nubie: Notices descriptives* (Paris, 1844-1889), 288, 6.

[4] *AHw,* II, 941f.

[5] See below, III.1.

[6] *AHw,* II, 982ff.

[7] Gilg. (Meissner Fragment) II, 7.

[8] *OECT,* 6 (1927), 38, 4.

[9] J. Nougayrol, "Aleuromancie babylonienne," *Or,* 32 (1963), 384f.

[10] R. Labat, *Traité akkadien de diagnostics et pronostics médicaux* (Paris, 1951), 66, 86.

[11] Atraḫasis Epic, I, 77, 179; III, iii.47; cf. G. Pettinato, "Die Bestrafung des Menschengeschlechts durch die Sintflut," *Or,* 37 (1968), 165-200; W. G. Lambert and A. R. Millard, *Atra-ḫasīs* (1969), vi; for a different interpretation see W. von Soden, "Der Mensch bescheidet sich nicht," *Symbolae biblicae et Mesopotamicae F. M. Th. de Liagre Böhl dedicatae. StFS,* 4 (1973), 353.

[12] *WUS,* No. 2337; *UT,* No. 2180; other occurrences in Whitaker, 541.

[13] *PNPI,* 86.

[14] Sefire I [KAI, 222] A, 29, reconstructed by C. Brekelmans, "Sefire I A 29-30," *VT,* 13 (1963), 225-28; but J. A. Fitzmyer, *The Aramaic Inscriptions of Sefîre. BietOr,* 19 (1967), 48, reconstructs as *[ṣ']qh*.

[15] Sefire II A, 8, reconstructed by Fitzmyer, *ibid.,* 86.

[16] *AP,* 71, 17; *DISO,* 79.

[17] *AP,* 52, 6; *DISO,* 246.

[18] Wehr, 377, 515.

In Syriac both *zʿq* and *zʿqh* appear.[19] Samaritan uses *zʿq* (simple stem and ithpael) as well as the forms *ṣʿq* and *ṣʿqh*.[20]

II. 1. *Etymology*. The Hebrew root *ṣʿq/zʿq* is of West Semitic origin. The dual orthography is also attested in Aramaic, Arabic, and Samaritan. The predominant use of *zʿq* and *zʿqt* in Arabic suggests that it is reasonable to consider *zʿq* the primary form. The parallel use of the verb forms *ṣʿq/zʿq* (Jgs. 10:10, 12, 14; Ps. 107:6, 13, 19, 28; Job 35:9, 12; Neh. 9:27f.), the verb and substantive *tsᵉʿāqāh/zāʿaq* (1 S. 4:13f.; Jer. 25:34, 36) or *zᵉʿāqāh/tsāʿaq* (Isa. 65:14, 19), and the substantives *tsᵉʿāqāh/zᵉʿāqāh* (Gen. 18:20f.; Jer. 48:3-5, 34; Neh. 5:1, 6), which is not limited to a single period or textual group, makes it quite clear that both spellings were actually used side by side.

In 1QIs[a], the verb *tsāʿaq* of the MT is written *zāʿaq* in five of its six occurrences (Isa. 33:7; 42:2; 46:7; 65:14), while the forms of *zāʿaq*, which appear ten times, are reproduced without change. It is not clear whether the preference for *zāʿaq* represents a copyist's error or the orthography of the original.

The hypothesis that the different spirants of the first radical represent a dialectal difference and come from different areas remains unproven.[21] It is not supported by the interchange of spirants in two texts (Gen. 18:20; Ex. 2:23) in the Samaritan Pentateuch,[22] because the Samaritan Chronicle No. 2 preserves both spellings in parallel.[23] The parallel use of different forms of the root in a wide range of OT books and their synonymy indicate that the difference between *zʿq* and *ṣʿq* in Hebrew appears to be purely orthographic.

2. *Statistics*. Derivatives of the roots *ṣʿq/zʿq* occur 168 times in the OT (including 1 Aram. pael in Dnl. 6:21 [Eng. v. 20]).[24] The Hebrew verb occurs 128 times (*zʿq* 73 times, *ṣʿq* 55 times): 107 times in the qal (*zāʿaq* 60 times, *tsāʿaq* 47 times), 12 times in the niphal (6 each), 8 times in the hiphil (*zʿq* 7 times, *ṣʿq* once), and once in the piel (*ṣʿq*). The verbal *qatal* nouns *tsᵉʿāqāh/zᵉʿāqāh* are attested 39 times (*zᵉʿāqāh* 18 times, *tsᵉʿāqāh* 21 times). The suffixed *zʿq* in Isa. 30:19; 57:13 is not an independent substantive[25] but a qal infinitive construct.[26] Giesebrecht's conjecture of *zaʿaq* in Jer. 50:46 remains problematic.[27] The only form found in the Qumran literature to date is the reconstructed verb [*z*]*ʿq* (1QpHab 1:4).

---

19 Brockelmann, *LexSyr*, 97; cf. M. H. Goshen-Gottstein, *A Syriac-English Glossary* (1970), 22.

20 See below, II.1.

21 *BLe*, § 28.

22 A. Sperber, *A Historical Grammar of Biblical Hebrew* (1966), 478, n. 4, with reservations.

23 J. MacDonald, *The Samaritan Chronicle No. II. BZAW*, 107 (1969), 43-45*, 58-60*, 80*.

24 Cf. Vogt, *LexLingAram*, 58.

25 S. Mandelkern, *Veteris Testamenti Concordantiae Hebraicae atque Chaldaicae* (1937, ²1955), I, 360.

26 Cf. E. König, *Hebräisches und aramäisches Wörterbuch zum AT* (1910), 93; Zorell, *LexHebAram*, 214; *KBL*³, 266; G. Bergsträsser, *Hebräische Grammatik* (²1962), II, 116.

27 Cf. *BHK/BHS, in loc.*; *KBL*³, 266.

3. *Distribution of Occurrences.* Thirty books of the OT contain verbs and nouns derived from *ṣ'q/z'q*. The Pentateuch contains 29 forms (*tsā'aq* 19 times, *tsᵉ'āqāh* 8 times, and one occurrence each of *zā'aq,* Ex. 2:23, and *zᵉ'āqāh,* Gen. 18:20), the writing prophets 52 (16 in Isaiah, 21 in Jeremiah, 10 in the Minor Prophets, and 5 in Ezekiel), the historical books 63 (19 each in Jgs. and 1–2 S., 10 in 1–2 K., 6 in Neh., etc.), the poetic books 13 (11 in Pss., 2 in Lam.), and Wisdom Literature 10 (8 in Job, 1 each in Prov. and Eccl.). With the exception of the Pentateuch and the Minor Prophets (where only verbal forms appear except in Zeph. 1:10), no preference for one spelling or the other can be discerned.

4. *LXX.* The LXX uses a variety of Greek words to translate the various forms of the Hebrew root. Verbal forms are translated 50 times with *boán,*[28] 46 times with *krázein,*[29] and 20 times with *anaboán*. The translations *kataboán* (Ex. 5:15; 22:26[27]), *anakrázein* (1 K. 22:32; Ezk. 21:17[12]), *kraugḗ* (Isa. 30:19; Jer. 30:15), and *parangéllein* (Jgs. 4:10; 1 S. 10:17)[30] each appear twice, while *stenázein* (Job 31:38), *kaleín* (Jgs. 4:13), and *kērýssein* (Jonah 3:7) were each selected once. The noun forms are rendered 28 times with *kraugḗ,* 4 times with *boḗ* (1 S. 4:14; 9:16; Isa. 15:5, 8), twice with *phōnḗ* (Gen. 27:34; Est. 4:1), and once each with *déēsis* (Job 27:9), *kataboán* (Ex. 22:22[23]), and *krázein* (Jer. 48[31]:3). The wealth of Greek words and compounds together with their distribution reflects the various semantic nuances of the Hebrew forms, but bears witness at the same time to the fact that the basic meaning "cry for help" is central. The LXX does not display any systematic principle of translation and shows that the derivatives of *ṣ'q/z'q* were considered synonyms.

5. *Meaning.* The major emphasis of the basic meaning of the root *ṣ'q/z'q* falls on the loud and agonized "crying" of someone in acute distress, calling for help and seeking deliverance with this emotion-laden utterance. The cry for help in distress is particularly emphasized by the use of the preposition *'el* (sometimes *lᵉ*- or the accusative object) to indicate the one to whom the cry is addressed: a human being (Gen. 27:34; 41:55; Ex. 5:15; Nu. 11:2; 1 K. 20:39; etc.) or God himself explicitly (Gen. 4:10; Ex. 14:10,15; Nu. 12:13; Dt. 26:7; Jgs. 3:9,15; etc.). This primary nuance is underscored by the use of the verb *šw'* (piel: Hab. 1:2; Job 19:7; 35:9; Lam. 3:8)[31] and the noun *shav'āh* (Ex. 2:23; 1 S. 5:12) in poetic parallelism with the derivatives of *ṣ'q/z'q*. The crying is thus a call for help in distress, which has as its goal immediate assistance in affliction and oppression.[32] Likewise significant in this context is the association of *ṣ'q/z'q* with *yš'* (hiphil: Dt. 22:27; 2 K. 6:27; Hab. 1:2)[33] and *môshîa'* (Jgs. 3:9,15; 12:2; Isa. 19:20; Neh. 9:27).

---

[28]Cf. E. Stauffer, "βοάω," *TDNT,* I, 625-28.
[29]Cf. W. Grundmann, "κράζω," *TDNT,* III, 898-903.
[30]Cf. O. Schmitz, "παραγγέλλω," *TDNT,* V, 761-65.
[31]Jenni, 248.
[32]Cf. Marcus, 251f.
[33]Cf. Boecker, 62-66; Seeligmann, 274-77.

This characteristic distinguishes the forms of *ṣʿq/zʿq* from terms that do nothing more than express pain, such as → ילל *yll* (hiphil), *yᵉlālāh,* and → בכה *bākhāh,* which likewise appear in parallelism with *ṣʿq/zʿq,*[34] as well as → הגה *hāghāh* (Jer. 48:31 par. *zʿq*), *nᵉʾāqāh* (Ex. 2:24, etc.), and several others. Other terms that mean "speak" or "utter sounds" are distinguished from *ṣʿq/zʿq* not only by the acuteness of the distress that gives rise to the crying but also by the intensity with which the cry is uttered, explicitly expressed by means of *(bᵉ)qôl gādhôl* (1 S. 28:12; 2 S. 19:5[4]; Ezk. 11:13; Neh. 9:4) or *tsᵉʿāqāh ghᵉdhōlāh* (Gen. 27:34; Est. 4:1) and *zʿq* (hiphil: Jonah 3:7; Zec. 6:8). The crying can lend expression to shock (*mar:* Ezk. 27:30; Est. 4:1), terror (the disciples of Elisha cry out, "O man of God, there is death in the pot," 2 K. 4:40), fear (1 S. 28:12), and surprise (2 K. 2:12),[35] or it can remain unarticulated (Isa. 26:17). In each case the crying is associated with a particular situation and is occasioned by acute distress.

The particular contexts define various semantic spheres in which one or another basic aspect predominates. They bear witness to the fundamental fact that crying is a basic part of human nature, and that people must rely on the aid of their fellow men and on God. Thus the root *ṣʿq/zʿq* is an important component of the biblical motif of solidarity, which binds human beings together as a group as well as binding them to God.

III. Secular Range of Meanings.

1. *Socio-legal.* The forms *ṣʿq/zʿq* appear 27 times (*zʿq* 6 times, *ṣʿq* 12 times; *zᵉʿāqāh* 4 times, *tsᵉʿāqāh* 5 times) in the socio-legal semantic sphere.

From the second millennium derive the casuistically framed prohibitions of the Covenant Code that guarantee the widow (→ אלמנה *ʾalmānāh*) and orphan protection against oppression and forced dependency (Ex. 22:22f.[23f.])[36] and give the citizen whose garment has been taken in pledge the right to reclaim it before sundown (Ex. 22:25f.[26f.]; cf. Dt. 24:12f.; Am. 2:8; Job 22:6; Prov. 27:13). If they do not receive justice through civil law and then "cry" to Yahweh (Ex. 22:22,26[23,27]) with a "cry of distress" (v. 22[23]), then he as guardian of the law will hear these weak ones and see that they have legal protection. Those who have acted contrary to the law are guilty of breaking the covenant and will experience the wrath of God (→ אנף *ʾānaph*).

Gen. 4:10 likewise speaks of crying to Yahweh in the context of a legal process modelled after the practice of private revenge.[37] When a murder goes unavenged and the perpetrator is not arrested, the spilled blood of the innocent victim "cries" from the earth, with which it is not yet covered (cf. Gen. 37:26; Isa. 26:21; Ezk. 24:7f.), to God the avenger of blood (cf. Gen. 9:5; 2 S. 4:11; 2 K. 9:7; Ps. 9:13[12]; Hos. 1:4), accusingly demanding propitiation for the deed (cf. Job 16:18; 34:28). Requital of a

---

34 See below, IV.1.

35 Cf. Jenni, 154f.

36 Cf. the Ur-Nammu law code, S. N. Kramer, *The Sumerians* (1963), 84; CH Epilogue, 24, 59-62; Aqhat Epic, *CTA,* 17 [II D], V, 7-9.

37 W. Schottroff, *Der altisraelitische Fluchspruch. WMANT,* 30 (1969), 80.

wrong by blood vengeance, which is not attested in the OT,[38] indicates the pre-Israelite nucleus of this narrative, in which the idea of blood vengeance is primarily an executive action of the deity.[39] The identification of this crying to God with the ancient Germanic *Zeterruf*[40] must be rejected.

The casuistic laws of Dt. 22:23-27 contain two ancient ordinances in which *ṣʿq* has an important function in determining criminal liability. Whether a betrothed virgin who is raped suffers the death penalty (vv. 23f.) or goes free (vv. 25-27) depends on whether the crime was committed "in the city" or "in the open country,"[41] i.e., whether the cry for help (*ṣʿq*, vv. 24, 28) is effectual or ineffectual.

From the early period of the monarchy on, we find cases in which the king exercises a legal function. A citizen guilty of lèse majesté appeals (*lizʿōq*) to the king (2 S. 19:29). The cry for legal assistance from the king, which takes place only in military situations,[42] can involve hypothetical (1 K. 20:39; cf. 2 S. 14:4) or real cases (2 K. 6:26; 8:3,5).

Normally the cry of distress serves as an accusation or appeal; someone who has been threatened or assaulted calls with utmost urgency for the intervention of the local authorities (2 S. 13:19; Isa. 5:7;[43] Jer. 20:8; Job 19:7; 31:38-40; Prov. 21:13) or their chief judge (Neh. 5:1,6; cf. Gen. 16:5[44]).

The recent suggestion that *zeʿāqāh* in Est. 4:1 is "a formal stage in the legal process, namely the bringing of an action,"[45] and is intended to move the Persian king to legal intervention, is beset with problems. On the one hand, it is to be noted that a mourning custom prevents Mordecai from entering the "king's gate," the place where the appellant initiates his action (v. 2).[46] On the other hand, the final result must not be confused with the original intended purpose.[47] The formulaic expression "wailing with a loud and bitter cry" (which appears also in Gen. 27:34) in the present context of rites of mourning and abjection is better taken as a "cry of woe" in the sense of lamentation expressing grief over the imminent destruction of the Jewish people.[48]

It must also be noted that the socio-legal semantic sphere intersects the religio-theological, since transgression of a law governing relations between people is an offense against the order ordained and guaranteed by God. It leads finally to an appeal addressed to God, which he hears and to which he responds with help.

---

38 The point is rightly stated by E. Merz, *Die Blutrache bei den Israeliten. BWAT*, 20 (1916), 70.

39 Cf. G. E. Mendenhall, *The Tenth Generation* (1973), 69ff.

40 G. von Rad, *Genesis. OTL* (trans. 1961), 102; see below.

41 Cf. the Laws of Eshnunna §26, *ANET*, 162; CH §130, *ANET*, 171; Middle Assyrian Laws §§ 55f., *ANET*, 185; Hittite Laws § 197, *ANET*, 196 = J. Friedrich, *Die hethitischen Gesetze. DMOA*, 7 (1959), § 83*.

42 Cf. G. C. Macholz, "Die Stellung des Königs in der israelitischen Gerichtsverfassung," *ZAW*, 84 (1972), 175.

43 Cf. U. Simon, "Poor Man's Ewe-Lamb," *Bibl*, 48 (1967), 207-242.

44 Von Rad, *Genesis*, 187.

45 G. Gerleman, *Esther. BK*, XXI/2 (1973), 104.

46 Herodotus *Hist*. iii.117.

47 Cf. C. A. Moore, *Esther. AB*, VIIB (1971), 47.

48 See below, IV.1.

On rare occasions, articulated crying (*ṣ'q/z'q*) appears in conjunction with the ejaculatory *chāmās* (Hab. 1:2; Job 19:7; cf. Gen. 16:5) or the double exclamation *chāmās vāshōdh* (Jer. 20:8; cf. Hab. 1:3). Contrary to the common interpretation that *chāmās* represents a specific cry of distress or appeal to the judiciary,[49] it must be emphasized that in the texts where the exclamation *chāmās* is used with *ṣ'q/z'q* the cry is directed to Yahweh, not a judiciary. In Hab. 1:2—where, it is interesting to note, the distress involves all the people—and in Job 19:7 we find the parallel term *šw'* (piel), which in these contexts certainly indicates a cry to God for help. The double cry in Jer. 20:8 appears likewise to be a cry for help, not an appeal for legal protection.[50] A cry of distress that really does ask legal protection is "Help!" (*yš'* hiphil: 2 K. 6:26; cf. 2 S. 14:4), but it is directed to the king, not the judiciary.

The current view that equates the use of the root *ṣ'q/z'q* with the ancient Germanic *Zeterruf*[51] as well as the conclusion "that in the Old Testament the Heb. root *ṣ'q* or *z'q* is the technical term for the *Zeterruf*"[52] must be met with extreme caution.[53]

The term *Zeterruf* or *Zetergeschrei* makes its first appearance in the thirteenth century in the strictly demarcated sphere of medieval east-central German legal language; it corresponds to the Low German *tiodute/jodute* (whose etymology, like that of the technical term *Zeter,* is still obscure, although it probably represents a cry of alarm summoning others to pursuit or battle). In its earliest use, the medieval legal term has two meanings. (1) Originally, the *Zeterruf* was a legally defined cry for help on the part of someone actually on the point of being ambushed, murdered, robbed, assaulted, or raped,[54] to which the citizenry was obligated to respond with assistance. (2) In the courtroom, it could be a solemn accusation at the beginning of a trial (cf. the statement of the *Sachsenspiegel* that "the cry marks the beginning of the trial") cried out three times by the plaintiff himself or by an officially appointed person called the *Zeterschreyer* or *Blutschreyer*.[55]

In contrast to the technical term *Zeter* in ancient Germanic law, which means something like "draw near" and thus expresses a summons to aid, the semantic content of the Hebrew roots does not correspond at all to the *Zeterruf.* It must be emphasized, furthermore, that, in contrast to the strictly defined legal term *Zeterruf* or *Zetergeschrei,* there is no basis in the OT for the conclusion that the cry for help was "a formal way of initiating an action in an established legal system,"[56] nor that there was a "legal institution of a cry of distress" or an "institution of a *Zetergeschrei.*"[57]

---

[49]The view of von Rad, Knierim, Boecker, and others.

[50]Cf. H. J. Stoebe, *THAT,* I, 586, with bibliography.

[51]Von Rad, *Genesis,* 102, 187; *OT Theol,* I (trans. 1962), 157, n. 34, 415, n. 65.

[52]Boecker, 62; cf. Seeligmann, 257-59; J. Jeremias, *Kultprophetie und Gerichtsverkündigung in der späten Königszeit Israels. WMANT,* 35 (1970), 72; F. Stolz, "ישׁע *jš'* hi. helfen," *THAT,* I, 786; Macholz, "Stellung," 174; etc.

[53]See especially Albertz, 354.

[54]*Sachsenspiegel* 2, 64 (*ca.* A.D. 1220).

[55]Cf. J. and W. Grimm, *Deutsches Wörterbuch* (1932), XV, 809f.; W. Mitzka, *Trübners deutsches Wörterbuch* (1957), VIII, 386; and esp. L. L. Hammerich, *Clamor, eine rechtsgeschichtliche Studie* (1941), 186ff., disputing W. Schulze, *Kleine Schriften,* II (1934), 160–189.

[56]Gerleman, *Esther,* 104.

[57]Boecker, 62 and 65, n. 6.

The cry of distress and cry for help never developed in the OT into a formal outcry establishing the expedient of self-defense (as in medieval city law).[58] Thus the hypothesis that the basic meaning of *ṣʿq/zʿq* lies in the semantic realm of the *Zeterruf,* from which all the other spheres of meaning derive,[59] turns out to be in error. We conclude that the Hebrew terms are only roughly comparable to the *Zeterruf* in a single sphere of meaning; it is out of the question to call derivatives of the root *ṣʿq/zʿq* technical terms for the *Zeterruf.*

2. *Politico-military*. The Hebrew verbs take on a specialized meaning in the politico-military sphere, where they refer to the summoning of all able-bodied men (and chariots) to muster as an army before the onset of battle (*zʿq* niphal, Jgs. 6:34f.; hiphil, Jgs. 4:10, 13; qal, Jgs. 12:2) and before its end (*zʿq* niphal, Josh. 8:16; *ṣʿq,* Jgs. 7:23), as well as the assembly of the army following the summons (*ṣʿq/zʿq* niphal [reflexive], Jgs. 7:24; 10:17; 12:1; 18:22f.; 1 S. 14:20). Here we can observe an established practice in Israel's Yahweh wars during the period of the judges. But it must also be noted that the Canaanite king of Ai likewise "calls up" his army during the wars of occupation (Josh. 8:16), just as the commander Sisera does later (Jgs. 4:13); during the monarchy, we read how the Moabite army is called up (2 K. 3:21). The terms are likewise used for the calling out of Saul's followers in the struggle with the Philistines (1 S. 13:4) and for David's calling out of Judah to suppress the Benjaminite revolt (2 S. 20:4f.).

It is characteristic that in each of these instances a concrete threat (cf. *ʿāmāl,* Jgs. 10:16f.; *yšʿ* hiphil, Jgs. 12:2) on the part of superior external or internal enemies occasions the summons, which calls on the entire nation (Moab in 2 K. 3:4ff.) or one or more tribes (Jgs. 4:10; 6:34f.; 7:23f.; 10:17; 12:1f.; 18:22f.; 2 S. 20:4f.) to lend military aid. It is inappropriate to associate this politico-military usage with the *Zeterruf.*[60] The emergency that evokes military action is of a political rather than a socio-legal nature.

IV. Religious and Theological Range of Meanings.

1. *Lament.* It is not always possible to maintain a strict distinction between the religio-theological spheres of meaning, since from a lament in a concrete situation of distress it is no long way to a prayer of petition. In some 40 texts the element of a cry for help is overlaid with or displaced by that of pain, so that it is not surprising to find terms for expression of pain in the semantic field of the root *ṣʿq/zʿq*. The cry of lament in Jer. 30:15 is occasioned by incurable "pain." Derivatives of the root → ילל *yll* (Isa. 14:31; 15:2-4, 8; 65:14; Jer. 25:34, 36; 47:2; 48:20, 31; 49:3; Hos. 7:14; Zeph. 1:10f.[61]) and → בכה *bākhāh* (Isa. 15:3, 5; 33:7; 65:14, 19; Jer. 48:4f.; Ezk. 27:30f.;

---

[58]Cf. Hammerich, *Clamor,* 194ff.

[59]Boecker, 65f.

[60]Following Boecker, 65, n. 2, disputing R. Smend, *Jahwekrieg und Stämmebund. FRLANT,* 84 (^{2}1966), 15f.

[61]Cf. L. Sabottka, *Zephanja. BietOr,* 25 (1972), 45.

Est. 4:1–3)[62] stand in parallelism with forms of *ṣʿq/zʿq*, indicating the element of pain and thus the lament itself.

The verbs are used in lament for the dead (2 S. 19:5[4]; cf. Ezk. 27:30; Ex. 11:6; 12:30). Lamentation can be raised for a national disaster that has occurred (Ex. 11:6; 1 S. 4:14; 5:10; Isa. 15:4f.,8; 33:7; Jer. 30:15; 47:2; 49:21; 50:46; 51:54; Lam. 2:18; Ezk. 27:28,30; Joel 1:14; Hab. 1:2) or is imminent (Isa. 14:31; Jer. 25:34; Ezk. 21:17[12]). An attempt has been made to identify "summons to a communal lament" as a specific genre (Isa. 14:31; Jer. 22:20; 25:34; 48:20; 49:3; Ezk. 21:17[12]; Joel 1:14; Jonah 3:7; Zeph. 1:10).[63] The manner and content of the lamentation can bear the news of a catastrophe far off (Jer. 49:21). In the face of total military defeat there is raised the "cry of destruction" (*zaʿqath-shebher*, Isa. 15:5; Jer. 48:5), which is used like the exclamation *chāmās*.

2. *Prayer*. The most profound theological significance attaches to the largest group of texts, in which forms of *ṣʿq/zʿq* are used 77 times (67 times as a verb) to address an invocation to God (or the gods). Once more it is acute distress that occasions the crying, which is a fundamental way of addressing God and thus a major term for prayer in the OT. It is characteristic of crying to God that it ascends "to heaven" (2 Ch. 32:20), is heard by God (*shāmaʿ*, Ex. 2:24; 3:7; Nu. 20:16; Isa. 30:19; Jer. 11:11; Ps. 34:18[17]; etc.; *ʾzn* hiphil, Ps. 77:2[1]), and evokes in him an inward reaction so that he gives heed (*qšb* hiphil, Ps. 142:6f.[5f.]) and grants the entreaty (*ʿtr* niphal, 1 Ch. 5:20), responding (→ ענה *ʿānāh*, 1 S. 7:9; Isa. 30:19)[64] with the outward reaction of help. In sharp contrast to the helplessness of other gods (Jgs. 10:14; Isa. 46:7; 57:13; Jer. 11:12; Jonah 1:5) are God's salvation (*yšʿ* hiphil, Jgs. 10:12,14; 1 S. 7:8; Ps. 34:18[17]; 107:13, 19; 2 Ch. 20:9) and deliverance (*nṣl* hiphil, 1 S. 12:10; Ps. 34:18[17]; Neh. 9:28), his rescuing (*mlṭ* niphal, Ps. 22:6[5]), and his sending a deliverer (*môshîaʿ*, Jgs. 3:9, 15; 12:3; Isa. 19:20; Neh. 9:27) as a demonstration of his favor of unprecedented power, sufficient to deal with any situation of distress, no matter how complex.

Theologically, it was always extraordinarily significant for Israel that its beginnings as a people were grounded in a cry for help (Ex. 2:23f.; 3:7,9; Dt. 26:7) from the social misery of Egyptian oppression. This pleading cry of lament came before God, who remembered the self-imposed obligation of the covenant with the patriarchs (cf. Gen. 15:7–18; 17:8; Ex. 6:4f.; Ps. 105:8–11; Neh. 9:6–8) and intervened to deliver Israel. These experiences of concrete deliverance brought about by God when his people cried out in lament to him were recalled repeatedly by the people in their later confessions of faith (Nu. 20:16; Dt. 26:7; Josh. 24:7; 1 S. 12:8; Ps. 22:6[5]; 34:18[17]; 107:6,13,19, 28;[65] Neh. 9:4,9; cf. Isa. 19:20). This conflicts with any derivation of the prayer of lament from the *Zeterruf*;[66] the established place of such lament in early traditions

[62]Cf. F. Stolz, "בכה *bkh* weinen," *THAT*, I, 313–16.

[63]Cf. H. W. Wolff, "Der Aufruf zur Volksklage," *ZAW*, 76 (1964), 48–56 = *GSAT*. *ThB*, 22 (²1973), 392–401.

[64]Cf. Hab. 2:11 and Jeremias, *Kultprophetie*, 72.

[65]Dating from the tenth century, according to Albright and Cross-Freedman.

[66]Boecker, 64ff.; for a different view, see Albertz, 356.

likewise contradicts a Deuteronomistic origin.[67]

The framework of the book of Judges also exhibits the sequence of a cry for help (*ṣ'q/z'q*, Jgs. 3:9, 15; 4:3; 6:6, 7; 10:10, 12, 14) followed by God's gracious deliverance. A major difference between this situation and the oppression of Israel in Egypt is that in Judges the people cry out because they have been subjugated by a foreign power as a punishment for the sin of apostasy and idolatry. Here, then, an early epoch of Israel's history has been described in terms of a theologized history based on the sequence of a prayer for help followed by Yahweh's answer (cf. 1 S. 12:10; Neh. 9:27f.). The association of a confession of sin with the cry for help (Jgs. 10:10,14f.; 1 S. 7:6,8f.; 12:8,10; cf. Jer. 14:2-9) shows that only confession and cry for help together made it possible to hope confidently for God's help. This view agrees with the message of judgment proclaimed by the prophets, according to which Yahweh will not heed Israel's cry when the people are willful (1 S. 8:18), pervert the law (Mic. 3:4), worship other gods (Jer. 11:10f.; cf. Isa. 57:13), or, in short, break the covenant (Hos. 8:1f.; Jer. 11:11). Generally speaking, when God does not hear the prayer of people who cry for help, it is because they do not cry to Yahweh "from the heart" (Hos. 7:14), i.e., they cry with their lips but without any inward commitment. He who subordinates himself in total surrender to God fulfils the fundamental condition for having his prayer of distress heard. Anything else makes it difficult or impossible for God to intervene as deliverer. In such situations the prophets can only encourage the people ironically to cry out to the powerless gods (Isa. 46:7; 57:13; Jer. 11:12; Jgs. 10:14). The poor man who cries to God in his distress is promised a hearing (Ps. 9:13[12]; cf. Job 27:9). It is a test of faith when the rightly expected help does not come at once (Job 19:7; cf. 34:28). Occasions when the cry is not heard are explicitly noted (Hab. 1:2; Lam. 3:8; cf. Ps. 77:2[1]; 88:2[1]).

In a few cases, a cry to God for help is referred to (quite correctly) as "praying" (*pll* hithpael, 2 Ch. 32:20) or "prayer" (*t^ephillāh,* Lam. 3:8).[68] But the roots *ṣ'q/z'q* differ from the typical terms for prayer (*pll* hithpael and *'tr*) in that they are always associated with a situation of acute distress, and thus specifically express the notion of a cry for help and deliverance, rather than specific petitions. A special feature of the use of *ṣ'q/z'q* is that Yahweh's actions with respect to his people move in an arc from their cry of acute distress to his saving answer. Finally the human barriers increase so enormously that God can no longer grant his aid. On the other hand, a description of future salvation promises that in the transformed circumstances of God's new creation no cry of distress will be heard (Isa. 65:19), because the living relationship between God and man will no longer be broken, so that access to the wellspring of life is open forever.

The roots *ṣ'q/z'q* have an established place in various genres. The use of the imperative of *ṣ'q/z'q* in the summons to a communal lament has already been noted.[69] In the individual laments, the petitioner cries to Yahweh for deliverance from his distress (Ps. 22:6[5]; 88:2[1]; 142:2,6[1,5]; Lam. 3:8). Only once does *z'q* appear in a penitential prayer, associated with a cultic ceremony (Neh. 9:4; cf. 1 S. 12:8, 10). The

---

[67]Fuss, 39.

[68]Cf. K. Heinen, "Das Nomen t^efillā als Gattungsbezeichnung," *BZ,* N.S. 17 (1973), 103-105.

[69]See above, IV.1.

situation is different in the case of intercession: here Moses (Ex. 8:8; 14:15), Samuel (1 S. 7:8f.; 15:11), Ezekiel (Ezk. 9:8; 11:13), and Habakkuk (Hab. 1:2) assume the prophetic function of the interceding mediator, who cries to God for help and deliverance on behalf of others.

Hasel

זער *z'r* → צער *ṣ'r*

זָקֵן *zāqēn*; זֹקֶן *zōqen*; זִקְנָה *ziqnāh*; זְקֻנִים *z^equnîm*

Contents: I. 1. Etymology; 2. Occurrences. II. Old Age: 1. As a Goal; 2. As a Limit. III. Elders: 1. Extrabiblical Evidence; 2. The Elders of Cities and of Regional Associations; 3. The "Elders of Israel."

I. 1. *Etymology*. The noun *zāqēn* is derived from the noun *zāqān*, "beard," which is attested with the equivalent radicals in most Semitic languages.[1] In its basic meaning, therefore, it refers to a man with a beard, originally perhaps an adult in general (cf. Neo-Assyr. *ša ziqni* in contrast to "eunuch"[2]). In the OT, however, it always refers to old men (once to an old woman) or elders as officials. Accordingly,

---

zāqēn. T. Ashkenazi, *Tribus semi-nomades de la Palestine du nord* (Paris, 1938); H. Berg, *Die "Ältesten Israels" im AT* (diss., Hamburg, 1961); G. Bornkamm, "πρεσβύς," *TDNT*, VI, 651-680; J. Dus, "Die 'Ältesten Israels,'" *ComViat*, 3 (1960), 232-242; G. Evans, "Ancient Mesopotamian Assemblies," *JAOS*, 78 (1958), 1-11; R. Gordis, "Democratic Origins in Ancient Israel," *Alexander Marx Jubilee Volume* (1950), 369-388, esp. 376-384; J. R. Irwin, *The Revelation of* עצה *in the OT* (diss., Drew, 1965); T. Jacobsen, "Primitive Democracy in Ancient Mesopotamia," *JNES*, 2 (1943), 159-172 = *Toward the Image of Tammuz and Other Essays on Mesopotamian History and Culture. HSS*, 21 (1960), 157-172; H. Klengel, "Zu den šībutum in altbabylonischer Zeit," *Or*, 29 (1960), 357-375; *idem*, "Die Rolle der 'Ältesten' (LÚ^{MEŠ}ŠU.GI) im Kleinasien der Hethiterzeit," *ZA*, 57 (N.S. 23) (1965), 223-236; L. Köhler, *Hebrew Man* (trans. 1956); A. R. C. Leaney, *The Rule of Qumran and its Meaning* (1966), 186-88; J. L. McKenzie, "The Elders in the OT," *Bibl*, 40 (1959), 522-540; A. Malamat, "Kingship and Council in Israel and Sumer: A Parallel," *JNES*, 22 (1963), 247-253; Pedersen, *ILC*, I-II; J. van der Ploeg, "Les anciens dans l'AT," *Lex tua veritas. Festschrift H. Junker* (1961), 175-191; L. Rost, *Die Vorstufen von Kirche und Synagoge im AT. BWANT*, 4/24 (1938, ^{2}1967); H. Schmid, *Mose. BZAW*, 110 (1968); O. Seesemann, *Die Ältesten im AT* (1895); A. Walther, *Das altbabylonische Gerichtswesen* (1917, ^{2}1968); C. U. Wolf, "Traces of Primitive Democracy in Ancient Israel," *JNES*, 6 (1947), 98-108.

[1] Cf. *KBL*^{3}, 267; *CAD*, XXI, 125f.; *WUS*, No. 782; *DISO*, 79.
[2] *CAD*, XXI, 126f.

the verb *zāqēn,* as well as the nouns *zōqen, ziqnāh,* and *z^e^qunîm,* has as its semantic content "be old, grow old." The verb *zqn* is likewise attested with this meaning in Old Aramaic.[3] Hebrew is unique, however, in using the noun *zāqēn* as a term for elders. The equivalent in Biblical Aramaic (*śābh*) and in most Aramaic dialects, as well as in Akkadian (*šību*), is derived from a common Semitic root meaning "be hoary," which has widespread derivatives with this basic meaning (Heb. *śyb*).[4] The derivatives occurring in Hebrew all reflect the basic meaning. Besides *šībūtu,* Akkadian has yet another word for great age, the frequently misunderstood word *littūtu,* which according to a Neo-Assyrian text denotes the ninth decade of life (*šībūtu* the eighth).[5] The kings wish for themselves (and others wish for them) *littūtu* even more often than *šībūtu.*

The noun **lah^a^qāh* appears to be a collective term for elders, since it corresponds to the equivalent derived from the same root in Ethiopic.[6]

2. *Occurrences.* The noun *zāqēn* is attested 178 times in the OT. A bare third of the occurrences has the meaning "old." These appear frequently in antithesis to terms for the young (→ נער *naʿar,* Dt. 28:50; *bāchûr,* Prov. 20:29; *yeledh,* Zec. 8:4f.; *ʿûl,* Isa. 65:20a; cf. Joel 2:16a), sometimes in purely formulaic usage ("young and old," Gen. 19:4). Thus *zāqēn* is the most common and most general term for someone old. Together with the verb *zāqēn* and the nouns *zōqen, ziqnāh,* and *z^e^qunîm* (with a total of 38 occurrences), it constitutes a word group represented in almost all the books of the OT. Largely synonymous is the word group formed by the root *śyb* and its derivatives. This latter group, however, has remained much more closely bound to the basic meaning of the root, sometimes merely indicating the outward sign of gray hair (Hos. 7:9; Prov. 20:29).[7] Apart from *śābh,* "elder," this word group appears a total of 22 times. Totally synonymous is the noun *yāshîsh,* attested exclusively in the book of Job (32:6 [cf. *zāqēn* in v. 9]; 12:12; 15:10; 29:8; cf. also *yāshēsh,* 2 Ch. 36:17). The basic meaning is probably "weak," but the word is never used in this sense alone. For a discussion of the expression *bāʾ baiyāmîm,* see II.2 below. In only five cases does the word group deriving from *zāqēn* apply specifically to females: Gen. 18:13; 24:36 (text uncertain); Zec. 8:4; Prov. 23:22; Ruth 1:12.

Most often by far the noun *zāqēn* is used in the specialized sense of "elder." This meaning can be recognized as a rule from determination by a dependent genitive or reference to a genitive phrase already mentioned in the context. As genitive we find terms designating specific social groups, primarily the names of cities, countries, tribes, and nations, but also general terms like *ʿîr, ʾerets,* and *ʿam,* the latter always in determined form. The elder is thus a member of a special committee representing a specific, clearly defined social community; he must be thought of primarily as the holder of an office, not the representative of a particular age group. Linguistic usage by and large makes a clear distinction between the man characterized by his age and the

---

3 *DISO,* 79; cf. Arab. *ḏiqn,* "old man."

4 Cf. *KBL*², 919, 1125, Sup. 187, 207; *WUS,* No. 2573; *DISO,* 192, 288.

5 Cf. *CAD,* IX, 220f.

6 *KBL*³, 495.

7 See I.1.

elder. In addition, the latter is frequently mentioned alongside holders of other offices.[8] The nouns **lahᵃqāh* (only in 1 S. 19:20) and Aram. *śābh* (5 occurrences in Ezr. 5f.) are always determined by a genitive (except in Ezr. 5:9, which, however, presupposes v. 5).

Conrad

In the LXX, *zāqēn* is rendered 127 times by *presbýteros,* 23 times by *presbýtēs,* 26 times by *gerousía* (principally in Deuteronomy), and 3 times each by *gérōn* and *anḗr.* In Dt. 31:28, *zᵉqan-shebheṭ* is rendered by *phýlarchos.* In Deuteronomy (except 16:18), the "elders" discussed in III.2 and 3 below are always rendered by *gerousía.* In Genesis, Leviticus, and Numbers, *presbýteros* predominates; in Exodus, *presbýteros* and *gerousía* are equally represented; in the Deuteronomistic history and that of the Chronicler, *presbýteros* is used throughout, as it is in Ezekiel. In the other scattered occurrences of *zāqēn,* it is translated *presbýteros.*

Botterweck

II. Old Age.

1. *As a Goal.* An old man is the embodiment of long experience (Dt. 32:7; cf. Ps. 37:25) and the consequent ability to give prudent counsel in political matters (1 K. 12:6-8,13; this passage does not deal with elders[9]). Therefore an old man has the best qualifications for the office of elder. To this extent old age is a sought-after goal.

In Wisdom Literature, too, the common opinion is assumed that the aged are wise (→ חכם *chākham;* → בין *bîn*) and are therefore entitled to have the last word in matters of theology as well (cf. Ps. 119:100). Those who are younger must approach them with respect (Job 32:4-7). This is in accord with the observation that in the ancient Near East wisdom teachers are often depicted as men of particularly great age.[10] There were undoubtedly similar views in Israel. It is noteworthy, however, that they have left no trace in the corpus of wisdom thought preserved in the OT. Quite the contrary—the very passages that presuppose the popular notion of the aged take vigorous issue with the assumption (Ps. 119:100; Job 12:12; 32:9 [emended]; Eccl. 4:13). According to these texts, wisdom is not the prerogative of age, nor does old age have any claim to leadership. In this respect, the tone of the OT is primarily critical.

Age, especially old age, is nevertheless an image of fulfilment. This idea finds expression in two phrases that are frequently found when death is mentioned: *bᵉśêbhāh ṭôbhāh* (Gen. 15:15; 25:8; Jgs. 8:32; 1 Ch. 29:28) and *śᵉbhaʿ yāmîm* (Gen. 35:29; Job 42:17; 1 Ch. 29:28; cf. Gen. 25:8; 1 Ch. 23:1; 2 Ch. 24:15). These phrases always refer to theologically significant figures, characterizing the age of the persons in question as the fulfilment of a life in harmony with God, to which natural death marks a

---

[8]See III.2.

[9]Cf. M. Noth, *BK,* IX/1 (1968), 273f., disputing Malamat, *passim.*

[10]H. Brunner, *Altägyptische Erziehung* (1957), 10f., 129f.; *AOT*², 454f.

meaningful conclusion. Both phrases are attested only in late strata of the OT, but they reflect a fundamental attitude that was widespread throughout the ancient Near East.[11] In wisdom thought it is the life of the righteous man that finds its fulfilment in old age (Ps. 92:15 [Eng. v. 14]; Prov. 16:31; cf. Prov. 20:29). In two late prophetic texts the age of salvation is depicted as a time when there will be innumerable old men and women or all will attain old age (Isa. 65:20; Zec. 8:4; for the contrary, cf. 1 S. 2:31f.). Of course there is also an old age without fulfilment. Unnatural death (1 K. 2:6, 9; cf. Jer. 6:11) or loss of descendants (Gen. 42:38; for the contrary, cf. Prov. 17:6) is a sign that this fulfilment is denied. Old age as the goal of human life is thus more than a temporal quantity.

2. *As a Limit.* Even more often old age appears as the limit of human potential. Formally, this notion is expressed by the phrase *bā' baiyāmîm*. It occurs primarily in contexts in which a previously responsible party must resign his position, and a new generation receives his testament (Gen. 24:1; Josh. 13:1; 23:1; 1 K. 1:1). Passages that characterize old age as a time when virility or fertility ceases make this limitation clear (Gen. 18:11f.; 1 K. 1:4; 2 K. 4:14; Ruth 1:12). At this point there is no longer any possibility of having any influence on the continuance of the family (this also explains the special love accorded the son of one's old age: Gen. 37:3; 44:20). Many passages accordingly characterize old age directly or indirectly as a time of weakness and decline, both physical and psychological (physical weakness: Gen. 27:1f.; 48:10; 1 S. 4:18; 2 S. 19:33-36[32-35]; 1 K. 1:1, 15; 14:4; 15:23; Isa. 46:4; Ps. 71:9,18; cf. Hos. 7:9; Eccl. 12:1-7 [albeit without *zāqēn* or any of its synonyms]; weakness of will: 1 K. 11:4; cf. 1 S. 2:22; 8:1,5). None of these statements—which are far from being characteristically Israelite[12]—contradicts the principle that old age is a desirable goal. They do make it clear, however, that old age represents an inexorable conclusion and that human life as a whole is finite.

But this finitude also gives rise to the obligation to honor those who are old (Lev. 19:32), i.e., maintain their rights and authority (→ הדר *hādhār;* → כבד *kbd*). More is involved here than acts of consideration or support (cf. Ruth 4:14f.) or respect for their wisdom (see II.1 above). Originally and primarily one's aged parents represent the family (the only explicit reference to their age is in Prov. 23:22, but it is presupposed in Ex. 20:12 and its parallels).[13] To honor one's parents means to maintain the order of the family as a whole and thus the fundamental structure of human life.[14] Therefore the aged are the objects of a serious religious obligation, which gives them an importance outside the family as well. Very similar notions about aged parents and old age in general are found throughout the ancient Near East.[15]

---

[11] Cf. L. Wächter, *Der Tod im AT. ArbT,* 2/8 (1967), 64-67.

[12] Cf., e.g., A. Erman, *The Literature of the Ancient Egyptians* (trans. 1927), 72.

[13] Cf. M. Noth, *Exodus. OTL* (trans. 1962), 165; cf. also Sir. 3:12f.

[14] Cf. J. Gamberoni, "Das Elterngebot im AT," *BZ,* N.S. 8 (1964), 182-84.

[15] For Egypt, cf. L. Dürr, *Das Erziehungswesen im ÄT und im antiken Orient. MVÄG,* 36/2 (1932), 32-34; for Ugarit, cf. O. Eissfeldt, "Sohnespflichten im Alten Orient," *Syr,* 43 (1966), 42-47 = *KlSchr,* IV (1968), 264-270.

III. Elders.

1. *Extrabiblical Evidence*. Elders as representatives of major social communities are well attested throughout the ancient Near East with the exception of Egypt. In the epic of Gilgamesh and Agga (preserved from the first half of the 2nd millennium B.C.), two different committees are mentioned that advise the king of Uruk: the elders of the city (sing. *abba uru*, "city father") and the "men" (*guruš*), i.e., the assembly of the free men of the city, the "assembly of the people."[16]

The texts from the Old Babylonian period are especially illuminating. In the Babylonian heartland, the elders of the city (*šībum*, pl. *šībūtum*), sometimes together with the local administrators or the "assembly of the people" (*puḫrum* or *ālum*, "city"), constituted a judicial body that functioned alongside the royal courts and decided local cases.[17] One passage clearly distinguishes the elders from the old men;[18] they clearly constitute a distinct committee, probably composed of the wealthy and respected citizens, especially the heads of the important major families. Undoubtedly the members of this committee were for the most part but not entirely of advanced years. Old Akkadian texts and the Neo-Sumerian legal documents appear to presuppose similar circumstances.[19]

According to the Mari texts, the elders in regions on the periphery of the centralized state, still dominated by an organization along tribal lines, exercised substantially greater authority, especially in the political realm.[20] They were the representatives of their cities or tribes and as such functioned more as advisers to the king than as his executive agents, knowing quite well how to preserve their autonomy to a greater or lesser degree. We also find elders of independent cities or tribes. Such evidence shows that the elders were originally an organ of nomadic tribal government; together with the leader of the tribe, they determined the internal and external affairs of their group. When there were particularly important decisions to be made, the "assembly of the people" was probably convened.

This system of government continued after the group settled permanently in one place, breaking down only gradually when it came within the sphere of influence of a strong central monarchy, so that finally the elders were responsible only for certain local legal matters (although an Old Babylonian omen text appears to indicate that the elders exercised an authority superior to that of the king[21]). Hittite texts by and large confirm these observations;[22] cf. also the largely independent council of the "great" (sing. *rabium*) in the Old Assyrian trade colony of Kanesh, at a considerable distance from the mother country.[23] Among the modern Arabic tribes, the leaders of the subdivisions of a tribe, who, like the leader of the tribe, bear the title *šēḫ* (basic meaning:

---

16 *ANET*, 44-47; Jacobsen, 165f.; Evans, 3-11; Malamat, 250f.

17 Walther, 52-63; Jacobsen, 162-65; Klengel, "Šībutum," 371-75.

18 Klengel, *ibid.*, 369.

19 Cf. *ibid.*, 357-59.

20 *Ibid.*, 360-370.

21 See K. K. Riemschneider, "Ein altbabylonischer Gallenomentext," *ZA*, N.S. 23[57] (1965), 130f.

22 Klengel, "Rolle," *passim*.

23 See Jacobsen, 161f.; Evans, 3-11.

"old man"), play a role comparable to that of the ancient Near Eastern elders.[24] There is also evidence for elders (collectively *el-iḫtiyārīye,* from *iḫtiyār,* "selection, privilege") functioning as advisers of the tribal leader and guardians of the tribal traditions.[25] But their function appears to be wholly internal.

2. *The Elders of Cities and of Regional Associations.* In Israel, too, the institution of elders undoubtedly originated in the nomadic tribal government familiar to the individual groups before their entrance into the settled territory. But direct evidence has been preserved only for the situation after settlement.

City elders exercised extensive authority well into the early period of the Israelite state. They are the guardians of the internal order of their community, and therefore exercise local jurisdiction (Ruth 4:1-12). Beyond this, they have considerable political importance as representing the community to the outside world (Jgs. 8:14,16; 1 S. 11:3; cf. 1 S. 16:4, and, for a non-Israelite city, Josh. 9:11). The body of city elders probably comprises the heads of the clans residing in the city in question. The term "men" (→ אִישׁ *'îsh;* Jgs. 8:5,15; 1 S. 11:1,9f.), after the example of the Mesopotamian sources, probably refers to the whole body of male residents capable of bearing arms (the "assembly of the people") as the highest official local authority. The "men" can therefore be mentioned in place of the elders; in reality, however, they hardly ever make an appearance, even in cases for their discussion. The number 77 in Jgs. 8:14 probably refers to this body, and has no bearing on the number of elders. The relationship to the *śārîm* remains obscure (cf. v. 6; → שׂר *śar*).

The elders play an even more important role as representatives of major tribal territories. The elders of Gilead make Jephthah the leader of their territory (Jgs. 11:5-11); the elders of the northern tribes anoint David to be king over their region (2 S. 5:3; cf. 3:17), then back the usurper Absalom (2 S. 17:4). The elders of Judah are courted by David (1 S. 30:26; 2 S. 19:12f.[11f.]). This probably refers to the elders of the cities belonging to the territory in question (cf. 1 S. 30:26-30), who would meet as the occasion demanded. Whether we are dealing here with a permanent institution cannot be determined with assurance. What has been said about the elders of the city holds true also for the role of the "men" or the "people" (Jgs. 11:11; 2 S. 16:15; 17:14; 19:15f.[16f.]; compare also 2 S. 2:4 with 5:3, and 3:19 ["Benjamin"] with 3:17).

During the course of the monarchy, the elders of the two capitals, Jerusalem and Samaria, became part of the upper stratum in the increasingly centralized government, so that they now appear alongside other dignitaries, especially royal officials (2 K. 10:1,5; Lam. 1:19; 2:9f.; 4:16; 5:12). They have thus been divested of their original autonomy; but their power has probably increased significantly, to the extent that in their new role they influence the entire body politic. Therefore when elders are mentioned in general as members of the upper class, we should probably think primarily in terms of the elders of the appropriate capital (Isa. 3:2; 9:14[15]; Ezk. 7:26). In other major cities a similar development naturally took place (for Jezreel, cf. 1 K. 21:8,11,

---

[24]McKenzie, 532-34.

[25]Ashkenazi, 55; van der Ploeg, 190f.

where the elders are likewise mentioned alongside other nobles). It is possible accordingly to speak collectively of the elders of the people (Isa. 3:14; Jer. 19:1). Concretely, their primary activity is to furnish counsel; in this respect they have the same function as the wise (cf. Ezk. 7:26 with Jer. 18:18; also Job 12:20; Ezk. 27:9).[26] As members of the upper class they are also particularly exposed to influences from outside Israel, which were favored by the monarchy, and are therefore subject to criticism on the part of the prophets. In the early prophetic tradition, however, the "elders of the land" have a more autonomous position with respect to the king (1 K. 20:7f.). They probably correspond to the elders of the tribal territories under David, who have retained their importance even in the early period of the monarchy. A certain independence of the king is probably also suggested by 2 K. 6:32.

According to Deuteronomy, the elders of the individual cities are to make decisions or effect reconciliation in local legal matters: capital offenses (Dt. 21:1-9, 18-21; 22:13-21; cf. 1 K. 21:8-14), levirate marriage (25:5-10; cf. Ruth 4:1-12), asylum (19:11f.; cf. Josh. 20:1-6). Here they exercise the function that has been theirs since time immemorial (cf. Prov. 31:23), as Mesopotamian sources attest.[27] Of course other passages in Deuteronomy speak of an official judiciary (16:18; secondarily also in 21:2), suggesting an increasing centralization in this area. In a legal case during the late monarchy, however, the "elders of the land" still play an important role (Jer. 26:17-19; it is not possible to say precisely what group of persons actually comes forward here).

During the exile, the elders constitute the leadership cadre of the Judeans, who were probably organized by clans and enjoyed limited autonomy (Jer. 29:1 [the term "rest" has not been satisfactorily explained]; Ezk. 8:1; 14:1; 20:1,3 [on the term "elders of Israel," see III.3]). For the postexilic period, an analogous function is attested in the Aramaic section Ezr. 4:8-6:18 (5:5,9; 6:7f.,14; in 6:7, Zerubbabel is mentioned before the elders). They also appear in the dispute over mixed marriages, where a distinction is made between the elders of the individual cities and their superiors, the elders of Jerusalem (Ezr. 10:8,14). Other officials, however, appear alongside the elders, and the decision is reached by a committee comprising the heads of families (→ ראשׁ *rō'sh,* 10:16). This means the elders have lost their independent significance. In the book of Nehemiah they are not even mentioned. Their place was probably taken by the heads of families (cf. Ezr. 4:2f. with 5:9). The heads of the distinguished Jerusalem families in particular may be looked on as the precursors of the later *presbýteroi.*[28] This change in terminology is undoubtedly a sign of a changed social structure, in which the clan has been replaced by small family associations with less autonomy.[29]

We find scattered references to elders of sociological groups (priests: 2 K. 19:2; Jer. 19:1; prophets: 1 S. 19:20 [**lah^a qāh*]), probably comparable to the elders of clans. The elders of the royal house (2 S. 12:17; cf. Gen. 50:7; Ps. 105:22) are court officials. In Gen. 24:2, the reference is primarily to a position of honor.

---

[26] See II.1.

[27] See III.1.

[28] Cf. Bornkamm, 658-661.

[29] Cf. Rost, 43-69.

3. *The "Elders of Israel."* In the pre-Deuteronomic period, the "elders of Israel" or the "elders of the people" (70 in Ex. 24:1,9; Nu. 11:16,24f.) constitute an entity representing the league of all twelve tribes. They appear primarily in the context of crucial events in sacred history: preparation for the exodus (Ex. 3:16,18; 4:29 [J]), the institution of Passover (Ex. 12:21 [J]), a sacrificial meal with the Midianite Jethro (Ex. 18:12 [E]), the covenant with God (Ex. 24:1,9 [E?]). But they are also mentioned in connection with disturbances during the desert period (Ex. 17:5f.* [E]; Nu. 16:25 [J]; cf. Nu. 11:14–17 [E][30]). In the present context of the Pentateuch they never play an independent role. They are silent representatives of the people, who are summoned or instructed by Moses, or appear alongside him, without ever developing any independent initiative. The same holds true for the pre-Deuteronomic complex Josh. 1:7–8:29, where they are associated with Joshua (7:6; 8:10), understood as the successor of Moses.

This overall picture can hardly be original. We may assume instead that there were traditions in which they played a more independent role and were not subordinate to Moses (this is particularly likely in Ex. 24:1,9).[31] Probably these were traditions belonging to individual groups from the early history of Israel, in which the elders accordingly represented only a limited circle.[32] Their role in the present context of the ancient Pentateuchal sources is thus the result of a traditio-historical process in which the various materials became associated with Israel as a whole and were uniformly linked with the figure of Moses. As a result, the elders, too, became a group representing all Israel, now symbolizing the unity and solidarity of the twelve-tribe league as the one true people of God. They were divested simultaneously of their original independence and now reflect instead the unique position of Moses. But this means that they symbolize the special status of Israel as a people enjoying direct divine guidance and not needing to put forward its own claims. In Gen. 50:7bβ and Nu. 22:4,7, we are probably dealing with a transference of the "elders of Israel" to other nations (quite clearly in Gen. 50:7, since the office of elder does not play any role in Egypt; Nu. 22:8, 14 speak suddenly of *śārîm*).

It is difficult to interpret the role of the 70 elders in Nu. 11:(11f.),14–17,24b–30 (E). They are to relieve Moses of the burden of dealing with the people. Usually a judicial function is understood, after the pattern of Ex. 18:13–27. But this is suggested at best by the secondary relative clause in v. 16a with its mention of *shōṭ^e^rîm* (cf. Dt. 16:18). The original text is patently concerned with something more general and fundamental. The transfer of Moses' spirit is probably meant to emphasize the importance of the elders: they are possessed of the same spirit as Moses, and thus guarantee the integrity of the people of God.[33] The addition in vv. 26–29, however, appears

[30] See below.

[31] Cf. M. Noth, *A History of Pentateuchal Traditions* (trans. 1972), 162, 179; cf. also *idem, Exodus,* 54 (on Ex. 5:3 [J]).

[32] Cf. Schmid, 40–43.

[33] Cf. *ibid.,* 68f. According to Schmid, the passage originally concerned the designation of the elders as Moses' successors; no designation of Joshua is presupposed.

intended to provide authorization for ecstatic prophets by linking them with the office of elder. But this can hardly have been the purpose of the original text.[34]

The role of the elders presented in the ancient Pentateuchal sources is continued in the Deuteronomistic sections of Deuteronomy and Joshua (including Jgs. 2), but not in Deuteronomic texts (the mention of the office in Dt. 5:23 is probably secondary). The elders appear in the following contexts: at the official recitation of the law (Dt. 31:9,28 [here *ziqnê shibhṭêkhem*]; Josh. 8:33), acceptance of the covenant obligations (Dt. 29:9[10]; cf. 27:1; Ex. 19:7), the end of the age of Joshua (Josh. 23:2; 24:1,31; Jgs. 2:7). In most of these passages it is true that other officials are mentioned, so that the elders are no longer the sole representatives of the people, but appear instead as a group belonging to the upper class, corresponding to the situation in the later monarchy.[35] Two reminiscences appear in P (Lev. 4:15 [*ziqnê hāʿēdhāh*]; 9:1), which elsewhere reflects the postexilic situation, in which the office of elder as such came to an end.[36]

Except in the Hexateuch, the elders of "all Israel" are rarely spoken of. But the usage sometimes appears in the context of events of outstanding importance in sacred history (the beginnings of the monarchy: 1 S. 8:4f.; the transfer of the ark to the temple: 1 K. 8:1-3 [of which only v. 3a is probably original[37]]) or events documenting the decline and depravity of the people of God (loss of the ark: 1 S. 4:3; judgment upon Jerusalem: Ezk. 8:11f.). In contrast to the picture painted by the Hexateuch, the elders appear here acting independently; they intervene in political matters as well. This feature is historically credible.[38] But the fact that they appear as a group representing the people as a whole emphasizes at the same time the significance of the events described for all Israel and amplifies their historical importance. This purpose is especially clear when the event described originally affected only a portion of Israel (as in 1 S. 4[39] and 1 S. 8:4-22, to the extent that the latter involves an historical tradition at all and is not merely a later interpretation of the beginnings of the monarchy[40]). But in Ezk. 8:11f., too, the recourse to the notion attested in Ex. 24:1,9 and Nu. 11:16,24 gives expression to the fact that here the one people of God is represented as a whole, so that the catastrophe whose announcement follows must be taken as total, spelling the end of God's history with his people[41] (the elders of Israel rather than Judah [as in 8:1] are mentioned accordingly in Ezk. 14:1; 20:1,3 as well[42]).

Here, too, therefore, the notion of the "elders of Israel" is an expression of the endeavor to interpret changes and events within Israel from the perspective of theology and sacred history. The same holds true for the other passages outside the Hexateuch (Jgs. 21:16: *ziqnê hāʿēdhāh*; cf. 1 S. 15:30; Joel 1:2,14; Ps. 107:32), especially in Chronicles (2 Ch. 5:2,4; 1 Ch. 15:25 and 21:16, both without parallel in 2 S.; cf. the

---

[34]For a different view, see M. Noth, *Numbers. OTL* (trans. 1968), 87-90.

[35]See III.2.

[36]Rost, 63f.; see III.2.

[37]See Noth, *BK*, IX/1, 176f.

[38]See III.2.

[39]Cf. J. Maier, *Das altisraelitische Ladeheiligtum. BZAW*, 93 (1965), 45-60.

[40]Cf. H. J. Stoebe, *KAT*, VIII/1 (1973), 178f.

[41]Cf. van der Ploeg, 182.

[42]Cf. W. Zimmerli, *BK*, XIII/2 (1969), 1258-1261.

extension to all Israel in 1 Ch. 11:3 in contrast to 2 S. 5:3[43]). Isa. 24:23 borrows directly from Ex. 24:1f., 9–11.

It is therefore unlikely that there were official "elders of all Israel" as a permanent institution within the framework of the sacral amphictyony, as maintained by Berg. In opposition to this view, it may be noted that there is frequent reference to *all* the elders without any apparent contrast with *the* elders (cf., e.g., Ex. 4:29 with 3:16). The number 70 probably likewise signifies a totality, not an institution. Only in 1 K. 8:1–3 can we assume that there was an ad hoc assembly of the elders of all the tribes. But even here the brevity of the original text shows that the point is to exhibit the involvement of the entire people of God, in other words to make a theological statement concerning sacred history. The same is true (for the southern kingdom only) in 2 K. 23:1f. (v. 2aβ is secondary).

Conrad

זָר *zār* → זור *zwr*
זָרָה *zārāh* → זרע *zāraʿ* I.1; II; → פוץ *pwṣ*

[43]See III.2.

זְרוֹעַ *zᵉrôaʿ*

Contents: I. 1. Ancient Near East; 2. LXX; 3. Qumran. II. The Human Arm: 1. Literal Usage; 2. Metaphorical Usage. III. The Arm of God: 1. The Arm of the God of War; 2. The Arm of the Creator; 3. The Arm of the Judge; 4. God's Bared Arm; 5. God's Arm as Hypostasis; 6. Locus and Origin of the Phrase "Yahweh's Arm"; 7. Conclusions.

I. 1. *Ancient Near East.* The possible Neo-Assyrian equivalent of Heb. *zᵉrôaʿ*/ Aram. *dᵉrāʿ* (cf. Dnl. 2:32), *durā'u,*[1] means "arm" or "foreleg." In the examples cited in *CAD,* it usually refers to the foreleg of an animal used for food. Ugar. *ḏrʿ*,

zᵉrôaʿ. J. Begrich, *Studien zu Deuterojesaja. ThB,* 20 (1963); T. Boman, *Hebrew Thought Compared with Greek* (trans. 1960); B. S. Childs, "Deuteronomic Formulae of the Exodus Traditions," *Hebräische Wortforschung. Festschrift W. Baumgartner. SVT,* 16 (1967), 30-39; G. W. Coats, "The Song of the Sea," *CBQ,* 31 (1969), 1–17; F. M. Cross and D. N. Freedman, "The Song of Miriam," *JNES,* 14 (1955), 237-250; K. Elliger, "Der Prophet Tritojesaja," *ZAW,* 49 (1931), 112–141; H. Fredriksson, *Jahwe als Krieger* (1945); K. Galling, *Die Erwählungstraditionen Israels. BZAW,* 48 (1928); H. L. Ginsberg, "The Arm of YHWH in Isaiah 51–63 and the Text of Isa. 53,10–11," *JBL,* 77 (1958), 152–56; O. Kaiser, *Der königliche Knecht. FRLANT,* 70 (²1962); O. Keel, "Wirkmächtige Siegeszeichen im AT," *Orbis Biblicus et orientalis,* 5 (1974), 91–109, 153–160; N. Lohfink, *The Christian Meaning of the OT* (trans. 1968), 67–86; S. Mowinckel, *Psalmenstudien,* III-IV (²1966); A. Ohler, *Mythologische*

"arm,"[2] appears in the Lament for Baal, in the course of which 'Anat lacerates her arms,[3] as does Lṭpn in the same context.[4] In *PRU,* V, 59 [445], 17 and 19 the meaning of *ḏrʿ* is disputed: Gordon[5] interprets it as "arm" in the sense of "life"; Virolleaud[6] interprets "arm of the sailors" as "*force, puissance,*" i.e., what is entrusted to the personnel, the "cargo."

Of more interest for the meaning of *z^e^rôaʿ* in the OT is the use of *zuruḫ* in the Amarna letters, if indeed *zuruḫ,* "hand," is related to *z^e^rôaʿ*.[7] The mighty hand of the king has brought Abdiḫiba of Jerusalem into the house of his (Abdiḫiba's) father,[8] given him the land of Urusalim,[9] placed him in the house of his father,[10] and was able to take cities in the past.[11] In the last passage, the word refers to military force; in the other texts it has the meaning of "power" or "favor."

2. *LXX.* In most cases the LXX renders Heb. *z^e^rôaʿ* by means of the Gk. *brachíōn.* The only exceptions are 1 S. 2:31; Isa. 33:2; 48:14; Ezk. 31:17, where the LXX has *spérma;* Ezk. 22:6, where it has *syngenḗs;* and Ps. 83:9 (Eng. v. 8), where it has *antílēmpsis.* In Dt. 3:24; 6:21; 7:8; 9:26; 29:2, the LXX adds *brachíōn hypsēlós* on the model of the familiar formula from the exodus tradition.

3. *Qumran.* At Qumran, the notion of the mighty arm has been transfered to *yādh,* "hand." The word *z^e^rôaʿ* appears only in combination with *šbr,* "dislocate," in individual laments (1QH 7:2; 8:33). The "dislocated arm" here symbolizes the weakness and helplessness of the worshipper.

II. The Human Arm.

1. *Literal Usage.* As a part of the body, the arm can be torn from its socket (Job 31:22); with the crown of the head and the right eye, it is highly vulnerable (Dt. 33:20;

Elemente im AT. KBANT (1969); K. Pauritsch, *Die neue Gemeinde. AnBibl,* 47 (1971); G. Pfeifer, *Ursprung und Wesen der Hypostasenvorstellungen im Judentum. ArbT,* 1/31 (1967); I. L. Seeligmann, "A Psalm from Pre-Regal Times," *VT,* 14 (1964), 75-92; C. Westermann, *The Praise of God in the Psalms* (trans. 1965); J. Wijngaards, "הוציא and העלה a Twofold Approach to the Exodus," *VT,* 15 (1965), 91-102; A. S. van der Woude, "זְרוֹעַ *z^e^rōaʿ* Arm," *THAT,* I, 522-24; Y. Yadin, *Hazor,* I (1958).

[1] *CAD,* III, 190f.
[2] Cf. *UT,* 733.
[3] *CTA,* 6 [I AB], I, 4.
[4] *CTA,* 5 [I* AB], VI, 20.
[5] *UT.*
[6] *PRU,* V.
[7] Cf. E. Ebeling in his glossary in J. A. Knudtzon, *Die El-Amarna-Tafeln. VAB,* II (1915, ²1964), 1545.
[8] EA 286, 12.
[9] EA 287, 27.
[10] EA 288, 14.
[11] EA 288, 34.

Zec. 11:17). In the case of animals, the word refers to the shoulder (Nu. 6:19; Dt. 18:3; cf. Sir. 7:31). Saul wears an armlet on his arm (2 S. 1:10; cf. Sir. 21:21 LXX); as Cant. 8:6 shows, such an armlet could be used as a seal.

With his arm the archer draws his bow (Gen. 49:24; 2 S. 22:35 = Ps. 18:35[34]), the reaper harvests the grain (Isa. 17:5), the shepherd gathers his lambs (Isa. 40:11), the smith fashions idols (Isa. 44:12), the potter shapes his clay (Sir. 38:30 LXX), the hunter captures and holds birds (Ezk. 13:20: *pōrchôth* [?] [cf. LXX, S]), the owner of a vineyard pulls up a vine (Ezk. 17:9). Thus warriors, shepherds, hunters, farmers, craftsmen, and housewives (cf. Prov. 31:17) find their arms indispensable.

2. *Metaphorical Usage*. The metaphorical use of *zᵉrôaʿ* appears to derive initially from the warrior's use of his arms, in which his strength resides.[12] Thus the human arm means military power: the upraised arm of Pharaoh, which Yahweh breaks, and the military might of the king of Assyria, which Yahweh strengthens (Ezk. 30:21f., 24f.);[13] military forces (Dnl. 11:15,22,31); auxiliary or mercenary troops (Ps. 83:9[8]);[14] the military might of the Assyrian infantry (Jth. 9:7); allies (Isa. 9:19[20];[15] Jer. 17:5[16]). In Ps. 37:17, the word probably refers to wealth as support for the godless. The "man of arm" (Job 22:8) is a man possessing power, which he exercises brutally.[17] In Job 35:9 the "arm" symbolizes the violence of the mighty,[18] and in Ps. 10:15 the violence of the wicked. "Horn" and "arm" (Jer. 48:25) are symbols of power (cf. also Job 40:9); whether the power is political or military cannot be determined (as also in Dnl. 11:6;[19] Ezk. 22:6; Hos. 7:15). The word *zᵉrôaʿ* stands for power or private advantage in Ezk. 22:6, and in Job 26:2 it means the person as speaker.

III. The Arm of God.

1. *The Arm of the God of War*. The characterization of the metaphor of Yahweh's arm as a "symbol of strength,"[20] or of strength, might, and effectual aid,[21] must be analyzed in greater detail if the roots of the metaphor are to be untangled.

The great majority of the texts in question involve the notion of Yahweh as a warrior (Ex. 15:16; Dt. 4:34; 33:27;[22] Isa. 30:30 [Yahweh's arm "comes smashing down like

---

[12]Fredriksson, 101f.

[13]Cf. W. Eichrodt, *Ezekiel*. *OTL* (trans. 1970), 420; W. Zimmerli, *BK*, XIII (1969), 743.

[14]Cf. H. Gunkel, *Die Psalmen*. *GHK*, II/2 (1926, ^{5}1968), 365.

[15]Contra B. Duhm, *Jesaia*. *GHK*, III/1 (^{4}1922, ^{5}1968), 95, and the usual emendation to *zeraʿ*.

[16]Cf. A. Weiser, *ATD*, XX-XXI (^{6}1969), 145.

[17]Cf. A. Weiser, *ATD*, XIII (^{5}1968), 170, 174.

[18]*Ibid.*, 229.

[19]"*Stellung*," "position," is the rendering of N. Porteous, *ATD*, XXIII (^{2}1968), 120. The English edition (*Daniel*. *OTL* [1965]) follows the RSV instead.

[20]Gunkel, *Psalmen*, on Ps. 44:4(3).

[21]Kaiser, 95.

[22]On the connection between *zᵉrōʿōth ʿôlām* in Dt. 33:27 and the original notion of a battle among the gods, cf. Seeligmann, 88.

the arm of a warrior''[23]; 33:2; 40:10; 51:9; 59:16; 62:8; Ezk. 20:33f.; Ps. 89:11, 14[10, 13]; Wisd. 5:16 [cf. 16:16]; Sir. 36:5; Bar. 2:11; 2 Macc. 15:24).

This notion has its historical ''setting'' in the exodus from Egypt and the entrance into Canaan, and the question arises whether we are really dealing with nothing more than a ''legendary view of the prophets'' to the effect that ''Israel won its victory solely through the aid of Yahweh, without any contribution of its own.''[24] Ex. 15:20f., which is generally recognized to be ancient,[25] ascribe Israel's deliverance at the sea to Yahweh, and the extension to the entrance into Canaan (Ex. 15:16) is merely a ''logical'' conclusion based on Israel's experience at the Sea of Reeds. Against this background, it is easy to understand the frequent mention of the arm of Yahweh in connection with the exodus (Dt. 4:34; 5:15; 7:19; 9:29; 11:2; 26:8; 2 K. 17:36; Jer. 32:21; Ps. 77:16[15]; 136:12; possibly also 1 K. 8:42). Since the association with the entrance into Canaan is only infrequently attested (Ex. 15:16; Ps. 44:4[3]), the idea of Yahweh as a warrior and the mention of his ''arm'' in this context appear to be derived primarily from the exodus; Kraus is probably correct in localizing this idiom in the ''cult tradition of Passover,''[26] even though it is noteworthy that the arm of Yahweh is not mentioned in this cult tradition. The frequent use in Deuteronomy of this metaphor, which accompanies and presupposes the idea of Yahweh as a warrior, suggests another approach. The polemic nature of Deuteronomy has long been recognized; it is directed primarily against the gods and their worship. In this polemic, Deuteronomy appeals above all to the experience of the exodus, in which Israel ''knew'' the power of Yahweh and not the effectuality of the gods. This ''knowledge'' then leads to the conclusion that Israel owes the blessings of field and womb as well to Yahweh and not the baals. The polemic is thus ''substitutionary'': Yahweh takes the place of Baal. If this is so, we must also reckon with the possibility that the idea of Yahweh as a warrior and the expression ''arm of Yahweh'' are likewise ''substitutionary'': the warrior Baal is replaced by the warrior Yahweh, the ''arm'' of Baal by the ''arm'' of Yahweh. Fredriksson[27] cites Egyptian representations of tutelary deities standing behind their protégés and aiding them in battle, and conjectures on this basis ''that foreign ideas contributed material to this representation of Yahweh.'' Since to my knowledge there are no parallel extrabiblical textual witnesses, we must have recourse to the relevant Canaanite iconography.[28]

2. *The Arm of the Creator*. A connection with ancient Near Eastern prototypes is also exhibited by the mention of the arm of Yahweh in the context of creation, understood as a battle with chaos (Isa. 51:9; Ps. 89:11,14[10,13]; cf. Jer. 32:17).

---

[23]G. Fohrer, *Das Buch Jesaja*, II. *ZB* (1962), 109; possibly natural phenomena are involved, as suggested by Delitzsch in Keil and Delitzsch, XVIII, 41.

[24]Gunkel, *Psalmen*, on Ps. 44:4(3).

[25]Cf. M. Noth, *Exodus*. *OTL* (trans. 1962), 121.

[26]H.-J. Kraus, *BK*, XV (^{4}1972), 901, on Ps. 136:12; cf. also Cross and Freedman, 237, n. 1. Coats (10) suggests an autumn festival.

[27]P. 103.

[28]See below, III.6.

Here, too, Yahweh appears as "the active God, creator, helper, mighty in battle,"[29] for whom nothing is impossible. Here we find echoes of ancient traditions,[30] which probably derive from mythological ideas outside of Israel,[31] but were used in Israelite prophecy and poetry as elements of historical presentation. "Myth and history are interwoven."[32] As the context makes clear, the point is not primarily "to justify God's dominion over the cosmos"[33] but to describe Yahweh's work in history.[34] This also explains why the battle with chaos is associated with what took place at the Sea of Reeds (cf. Isa. 51:10f.; Jer. 32:20).[35] In both cases (Isa. 51:9; Ps. 89:11,14[10,13]), the arm of Yahweh appears as the arm of a warrior. One of its settings is a hymn forming part of a communal lament, situated in the cult.[36]

3. *The Arm of the Judge*. The idea of Yahweh as a warrior is also in the background in passages that mention an arm of Yahweh in the context of his function as judge (establishing justice: Isa. 51:5; 59:16; Ezk. 20:33f.), since the establishment of justice involves a struggle.[37] The people are summoned as to a judicial assembly (Isa. 51:4), and Yahweh proclaims his *tôrāh* and his *mishpāṭ* (Isa. 51:4), his righteousness and support (of justice: 51:5). His arm, for which the coastlands hope, will rule or judge (*shāphaṭ*) the peoples (51:5). The subject is judgment, not grace and salvation.[38] God "will restore justice because he possesses . . . the power (arm) and will to do so."[39] In Ezk. 20:33f., we are not dealing with the "self-demonstration of the divine king,"[40] but with "the transformation of the boastful cultic invocation of God into a threat by God to come not to show his power to save but to chastize as a wrathful judge."[41] Yahweh's oath by his right hand and by his mighty arm (Isa. 62:8) probably also belongs in the legal sphere, although its use in the context is to affirm an oracle.[42]

4. *God's Bared Arm*. Isa. 52:10 and Ezk. 4:7 speak of Yahweh's bared arm; the expression is generally presumed to refer to Yahweh's intervention as a warrior.[43] But

---

[29]Fohrer, *Jesaja*, III (1964), 146, on Isa. 51:9; cf. Kaiser, 95.

[30]On Isa. 51:9, cf. Begrich, 90.

[31]Cf. Ohler, esp. 101-116.

[32]*Ibid.*, 105.

[33]The point is rightly made by Ohler, 107.

[34]Ohler, 107f., n. 21; C. Westermann, *Isaiah 40–66. OTL* (trans. 1969), 241.

[35]Ohler, 105.

[36]Cf. R. Kittel, *KAT*, XIII (^{5,6}1929), 296; H. Schmidt, *HAT*, 15 (1934), 166; Mowinckel, I, 31f.

[37]Cf. Kaiser, 95.

[38]Contra Ginsberg, 154; Delitzsch in Keil and Delitzsch, *in loc.;* P. Volz, *KAT*, IX/2 (1932), 115.

[39]Fohrer, *Jesaja*, III, 222, on Isa. 59:16; similar interpretations were already proposed by A. Knobel, *Jesaia. KEHAT*, V (^{4}1872); Delitzsch in Keil and Delitzsch, XVIII, 284; R. Kittel, *Jesaja. KEHAT*, V (^{6}1898), 438, 495.

[40]Zimmerli, *BK*, XIII, 455.

[41]Eichrodt, *Ezekiel*, 279.

[42]Pauritsch, 116, cf. 118.

[43]Knobel, *Jesaia*, 426; Delitzsch, 300; K. Marti, *Das Buch Jesaja. KHC*, 10 (1900), 344; Kittel, *Jesaja*, 446; Eichrodt, *Ezekiel*, 85.

Isa. 53:1 should caution against this interpretation, since here the bared arm of Yahweh cannot be taken exclusively as "an allusion to the hidden judgment of Yahweh . . ., carried out in the person of the Servant of Yahweh";[44] it does not refer to a warlike or (legally) punitive action on the part of Yahweh. It is rather in the entire work and fate of the Servant that there was revealed the arm of Yahweh, i.e., "his mysterious . . . governance,"[45] which is "invisible to the ordinary eye."[46] What God does, here (Isa. 53:1) ascribed metaphorically to his "arm," is not exclusively warlike. Yahweh bares his arm "like a man setting out to do a job."[47] He will be visible to the eyes of those who are capable of recognizing the "arm" of God in historical events,[48] "and all the ends of the earth shall see the salvation of our God" (Isa. 52:10). This capability is possessed above all by the figures of the prophets,[49] including Ezekiel.

In Ezk. 4:7, the prophet is called on to set his face toward the siege of Jerusalem, to bare his arm and prophesy against the city (the usual translation of *vᵉʾel-mᵉtsôr yᵉrûshālaim tākhîn pāneykhā ûzᵉrōʿᵃkhā chᵃśûphāh vᵉnibbēʾtha ʿāleyhā*). Since, however, nothing is said here of any intervention on the part of the prophet, and since elsewhere only the bared arm of Yahweh is mentioned,[50] it is doubtful whether the prophet is to stretch forth his own bared arm against Jerusalem. If the prophet is to prophesy against the city, his prophecy includes more than just the siege of Jerusalem; it also deals with Yahweh's actions expressed in the siege, i.e., Yahweh's bared arm. Ezekiel can proclaim the siege as the work of Yahweh because he sees Yahweh's bared arm. He is to turn his face to the siege of Jerusalem and to the bared arm (of Yahweh).[51]

5. *God's Arm as Hypostasis*. The image of the "glorious arm" that Yahweh caused "to go at the right hand of Moses" (Isa. 63:12) is striking. The question remains whether this choice of imagery is "rather unfortunate" or even "disastrous."[52] Since it appears only here, we must first turn to the context to explain it. Yahweh brought Moses up (*hammaʿᵃleh;* cf. *BHK*) out of the "sea" as the shepherd of his flock and placed his holy spirit within him (63:11). Here, as in vv. 13f., we are dealing with Yahweh's function as leader; v. 14 ascribes this function to the spirit of Yahweh, which gave Israel rest. Just as the spirit of Yahweh appears hypostatized, so also does his arm, which likewise performs the function of leadership. Therefore the image of the arm that goes with Moses can hardly mean the endowment of Moses with miraculous power,[53] or, more generally, Yahweh's "power which works glorious

---

[44]Kaiser, 96.

[45]Fohrer, *Jesaja,* III, 163.

[46]Duhm, *Jesaia,* 395; cf. Knobel, *Jesaia,* 439.

[47]Fohrer, *Jesaja,* III, 156, on Isa. 52:10.

[48]Cf. Delitzsch, 311.

[49]Duhm, *Jesaia,* 395, cites Nu. 24:4 in connection with Isa. 53:1.

[50]Cf. J. Herrmann, *KAT,* XI (1924), 33; Zimmerli, *BK,* XIII, 118.

[51]The interpretation suggested by Herrmann, *KAT,* XI, 33, also tends in this direction: Ezekiel's arm, bared so that it can swing freely, symbolizes the arm of Yahweh.

[52]Duhm, *Jesaia,* 468 ("da ein Arm nicht gehen Kann"); Fohrer, *Jesaja,* III, 250.

[53]*Ibid.*

things,''[54] but rather his guidance of Moses. According to the exodus traditions, however, this guidance was exercised through the *mal'ākh,* through Yahweh's *pānîm,* through the pillar of smoke and fire, and through the ark. By means of these Yahweh shows the way to Moses and his followers. What Isa. 63:12 therefore refers to is the arm that points the way and removes potential obstacles, comparable to Hobab, who is to be the ''eyes'' for Moses' band, since he is familiar with the area (Nu. 10:31).

If the image of the arm that goes with Moses is not based on an independent exodus tradition,[55] the groundwork may have been laid for it by Hos. 11:3, where, in the context of the exodus (v. 1), Yahweh points out how he taught Ephraim to walk and took them in his arms.

Isa. 51:9 and Ps. 44:4(3) have nothing to do with guidance; they refer once more to Yahweh's warlike acts. In Isa. 51:9, Yahweh's arm is addressed as an independent person and called upon to intervene, with an allusion to its warlike acts during creation and at the Sea of Reeds (51:9b, 10). Ps. 44:4(3) speaks of the arm of Yahweh and its warlike deeds in the context of the conquest of Canaan. Here, too, the arm of Yahweh appears as an independent hypostasis, in parallel with ''thy right hand'' and ''the light of thy countenance.'' This can hardly be the case in Isa. 59:16,[56] as the parallelism with righteousness shows, which Yahweh puts on like a breastplate (vv. 16f.).

The problem of the origin and date of the notion of the hypostatized arm of Yahweh[57] is rapidly solved when it is brought into conjunction with hypostatized wisdom. A late dating may also be suggested by the texts in question (Isa. 51:9; 63:12; Ps. 44:4[3]). When Pfeifer seeks for the locus of the hypostasis idea not ''in the immediate experience of God . . ., but in reflection upon it,''[58] the late dating of the idea seems to be assured. But the question may be raised whether we are not hearing echoes of ancient notions: it is sufficient to cite the relief stela at Hazor, on which two arms are depicted under the symbol of the deity—whether ''in a gesture of supplication''[59] remaining an open question.

6. *Locus and Origin of the Phrase ''Yahweh's Arm.''* Mention of Yahweh's arm is a noteworthy element of hymns and cultic confessions. Although Ex. 15:1-19 may well be ''a relatively late piece'' in comparison with 15:20f., inserted secondarily at this point,[60] v. 16 flows naturally from the characterization of Yahweh as a warrior (v. 21); there is the further point of agreement with v. 21 in that in both cases we are dealing with a hymn into which elements of a thanksgiving have been incorporated.[61] It is also possible that the recitation of history in Dt. 26:8 (with its context) is based on the schema of the thanksgiving song;[62] if so, the cult is a possible locus for the so-called

[54]Westermann, *Isaiah 40-66,* 389.
[55]*Ibid.*
[56]Contra Pauritsch, 98: ''the personified 'organ of divine efficacy.' ''
[57]On the definition of the concept of hypostasis, see Pfeifer, 15.
[58]P. 16.
[59]Yadin, 89; Plate xxix, 2.
[60]Noth, *Exodus,* 123.
[61]*Ibid.;* Lohfink, 72, 81 (cultic setting); likewise Cross and Freedman, 237; cf. Coats, 7-9.
[62]G. von Rad, *Deuteronomy. OTL* (trans. 1966), 158.

Historical Credo, even apart from the offering of firstfruits. These may well be the earliest idioms in which the arm of Yahweh is mentioned, and the locus of all of them is the cult. This is in line with the use of the expression in intercession (Dt. 9:29)[63] and in the psalmlike framework surrounding the individual sayings in the Blessing of Moses (Dt. 33:27).[64] Isa. 33 likewise exhibits the language of the Psalms,[65] and in the framework of the so-called prophetic liturgy (Isa. 33:1-6)[66] v. 2 is understood as a communal lament.[67] For Deutero-Isaiah, Begrich[68] has demonstrated its kinship with the poetry of the Psalms, especially the hymns and thanksgiving songs. Isa. 40:9-11, for example, is understood as an eschatological psalm of praise.[69] Whether Isa. 51:9 (and 10) exhibits the "features of a hymn"[70] or of a lament[71] is difficult to decide; the kinship to cultic poetry is clear in any case. Isa. 52:9f. "make up one of the hymns which form the conclusion of a section."[72] Ancient cultic poetry also stands in the background of Isa. 53:1ff.,[73] which exhibits a kinship with the "grievances of a lament or the narrative of distress in a thanksgiving song."[74] Isa. 59:15b-20 "is part of the community lament";[75] Isa. 63:7-14 can be understood as an historical psalm within a community lament.[76] Jer. 32:17,21 occur within a prayer (vv. 16-25), which, in its hymnic section, draws on familiar cultic forms.[77]

Ps. 10:15 stands in a context (vv. 12-18) that contains lament motifs;[78] the same is true of Ps. 79:11; 83:9(8); 89:22(21).[79] Ps. 44:2-4(1-3) comprises a hymnic confession,[80] 71:18-24 a "thanksgiving song using hymnic forms,"[81] and 77:11-21(10-20) a hymn,[82] as do Ps. 89:(2f.)6-19([1f.]5-18)[83] and 98:1ff.[84] Ps. 136 is a "thanksgiving

---

[63]*Ibid.*, 78.

[64]*Ibid.*, 205.

[65]Duhm, *Jesaia*, 239.

[66]Cf. Fohrer, *Jesaja*, II, 129.

[67]*Ibid.*, 130.

[68]Pp. 86f., 91f.

[69]Westermann, *Isaiah 40-66*, 44; *idem*, *Praise*, 144.

[70]Fohrer, *Jesaja*, III, 146.

[71]Westermann, *Isaiah 40-66*, 240; Begrich, 166f.

[72]Westermann, *Isaiah 40-66*, 249; Begrich, 56, terms Isa. 52:7-10 an "eschatological enthronement song."

[73]Kaiser, 96; cf. Fohrer, *Jesaja*, III, 160: "prophetic liturgy."

[74]Fohrer, *Jesaja*, III, 163; similarly Kaiser, 88; Begrich, 63, 65.

[75]Westermann, *Isaiah 40-66*, 349f.; for a different view, see Pauritsch, 103.

[76]Westermann, *Isaiah 40-66*, 386; similarly Pauritsch, 146, 169.

[77]Weiser, *ATD*, XX-XXI, 296f.

[78]Gunkel, *Psalmen*, 33; Kraus, *BK*, XV, 78.

[79]Gunkel, *Psalmen*, 392; for a different view see Kraus, *Psalmen*, 616.

[80]A. Weiser, *Psalms*. *OTL* (trans. 1962), 356; similarly Gunkel, *Psalmen*, 184f.; Kraus, *BK*, XV, 326.

[81]Gunkel, *Psalmen*, 302; similarly Kraus, *BK*, XV, 490.

[82]Gunkel, *Psalmen*, 333f.; similarly Kraus, *BK*, XV, 530.

[83]Gunkel, *Psalmen*, 386; Kraus, *BK* XV, 616.

[84]Gunkel, *Psalmen*, 427: "an eschatological hymn . . . with the motifs of a song for Yahweh's enthronement"; likewise Kraus, *BK*, XV, 677.

litany''[85] primarily in the form of a hymn.[86] It is not surprising to find such familiar cultic expressions borrowed by parenesis.[87]

In contrast to the cultic setting, the mention of the arm of Yahweh in legal contexts is of no great weight. Isa. 48:14 appears in the context of vv. 12–15, ''part of a trial speech''[88] or a disputation utterance;[89] Ezk. 20:32ff. are a disputation utterance within an historical invective;[90] Hos. 11:3 has as its context vv. 1–11, an ''historico-theological accusation,'' here ''structured in analogy to a legal complaint made by a father against his stubborn son.''[91]

The same applies to the mention of the arm of Yahweh in prophetic threats such as Hos. 7:15[92] and Zec. 11:17,[93] which, if they derive from the cry of woe,[94] exhibit cultic affinities.

It remains to inquire into how the idea of the arm of Yahweh originated. Reference to secular usage does not provide a totally satisfactory answer, since the basis is too slight. We can go further with the localization of the idea and its corresponding idiom in the cult, supported by the preceding discussion. The question remains whether the idea and idiom of the arm of God can be considered ''genuinely'' Israelite. The frequent use of this expression in the cult, in connection with war and the battle with chaos, together with the polemic stance of Deuteronomy toward the gods of Canaan, points in a different direction. Here the power of the gods (as warriors and creators) is denied and vested in Yahweh instead.[95] That the arm of the deity plays a role elsewhere in the ancient Near East is shown by a glance at the relevant non-Israelite iconography. Here a reference to the illustrations in *ANEP* will suffice:[96] the war-god Reshef with his ax raised;[97] Baal holding his raised lance, stylized in the form of a lightning bolt;[98] the weather-god of Til Barsib, likewise holding an ax in his upraised hand.[99]

7. *Conclusions.* The expression ''arm of Yahweh'' is used most frequently to represent his warlike power; this usage is reinforced by the epithets used to describe Yahweh's arm and the synonyms with which it is associated. We read of Yahweh's outstretched arm (Ex. 6:6; Dt. 4:34; 5:15; 7:19; 9:29; 11:2; 26:8; 1 K. 8:42; 2 K. 17:36;

---

[85]Gunkel, *Psalmen,* 577.

[86]Cf. Kraus, *BK,* XV, 900.

[87]Cf. Dt. 7:19, a ''war sermon'' (Von Rad, *Deuteronomy,* 69); cf. Dt. 11:2 (on the parenetic stylization, see *ibid.,* 85); on Isa. 59:16, cf. Pauritsch, 103.

[88]Westermann, *Isaiah 40–66,* 201.

[89]Begrich. 49; similarly Fohrer, *Jesaja,* III, 115.

[90]Zimmerli, *BK,* XIII, 452.

[91]H. W. Wolff, *Hosea* (trans. 1974), 193f.

[92]Cf. *ibid.,* 108.

[93]Cf. F. Horst, *HAT,* 14 (^{3}1964), 253.

[94]Cf. Hos. 7:13; Wolff, *Hosea,* 127.

[95]Cf. Coats, 15f.

[96]*ANEP,* Nos. 476, 479, 486, 490, 501, 531, 532, 651.

[97]No. 476.

[98]No. 490; similarly Nos. 501, 651.

[99]Nos. 531, 532; cf. also Lohfink, 76; Keel, 95ff., 158ff.

Jer. 27:5; etc.), i.e., his arm raised for battle; of the greatness or might of his arm (Ex. 15:16; Ps. 79:11; 89:11[10]); of his mighty arm (Isa. 62:8; Jer. 21:5; Ps. 77:16[15]). The arm of Yahweh is mentioned in such contexts as great acts of judgment (Ex. 6:6), terrors (Dt. 4:34), war (Dt. 4:34); it appears together with Yahweh's mighty hand (Dt. 4:34; 5:15; etc.). Israel experienced Yahweh's "arm" in his signs (Dt. 4:34; 7:19; etc.), wonders (Dt. 26:8; Jer. 32:21; etc.), and deeds (on Dt. 11:2, cf. vv. 3,7, etc.). Yahweh's arm spreads terror (→ אֵימָה *'ēmāh*) and dread (→ פחד *pachadh*) (Ex. 15:16), i.e., the crippling panic that stupefies those it strikes (cf. Gen. 15:12 par. *tardēmāh*).

All of this is spoken of in Israel primarily in songs of praise and of thanksgiving, in hymns, in laments—in short, in the cult. Within this framework mention of the arm of Yahweh has various functions, associated with the appropriate literary types. Frequently recollection of the arm of Yahweh prepares the way for a request that he intervene in the present; but this request can also be expressed directly, without recollection of the deeds done by God's arm in the past. Mention of the arm of Yahweh also serves as motivation for thanksgiving.

The manner in which the exodus from Egypt is announced (Ex. 6:6) is meant to engender confidence in Yahweh's promise. Recollection of how Yahweh brought Israel out "with outstretched arm" confirms the uniqueness of Yahweh (Dt. 4:34), motivates the commandment to keep the Sabbath (Dt. 5:15) or obedience in general (Dt. 11:2), and exhorts to courage in battle (Dt. 7:19).

Our possible answer to the question of how the expression "arm of Yahweh" originated has shown that the idea behind it can well be ancient and may be associated with the occupation of Canaan and the incipient conflict with the arm of Baal and the like.[100] In the context of the exodus and entrance into Canaan, "Israel" experienced the power of Yahweh and represented it by means of the image of his arm, in deliberate contrast to the "arm" of the deities worshipped in Canaan.

Helfmeyer

---

[100]Contra Boman, 103.

זָרַח zārach; מִזְרָח mizrāch

Contents: I. Etymology. II. Occurrences and Usage. III. *mizrāch.*

I. Etymology. The root *zrḥ* is found in Egyptian Aramaic, Nabatean, and Palmyrene with the meaning "rise" (cf. Syr. and Mand. *d^e naḥ*). In Arabic there is a word *ḏarīḥīy^un* found in the phrase *'aḥmar ḏarīḥī*, "brilliant red," "crimson," which may be connected with *zrḥ*;[1] cf. also OSA *ḏrḥ*.[2]

II. Occurrences and Usage. The basic meaning of the verb appears to be "light up," "shine forth"; cf. 2 Ch. 26:19, where leprosy is described as "breaking out" with reference to the bright white color associated with the skin disease. It is usually used in the literal sense of the rising of the sun: as an indication of the time or situation in narrative contexts (Gen. 32:32 [Eng. v. 31]; Jgs. 9:33; 2 K. 3:22; Jonah 4:8), in the law governing theft (Ex. 22:2[1]), and as an indication of the time in the judgment oracle against Nineveh (Nah. 3:17; when the sun rises, the princes fly away). In other cases the literal meaning has theological undertones, e.g., in such similes as 2 S. 23:4: the king is like the morning light at sunrise, i.e., he brings light and life to his land; Ps. 112:4, which states (if the text is correct) that the man who fears God "shines forth" for the upright as a light in the darkness, gracious, merciful, and righteous; or in statements about the cosmic order: Ps. 104:22, describing how the nocturnal animals retreat when the sun rises, in accordance with God's practical plan; Job 9:7, "he commands the sun not to rise," a demonstration of God's omnipotence; Eccl. 1:5, describing how the sun rises and sets in a constant cycle.

In addition, *zārach* appears in the context of theophanies—above all Dt. 33:2, where Yahweh comes from Sinai, "dawns" from Seir, and shines forth (*hôphîaʿ*; → יפע *ypʿ*) from Mt. Paran. The context suggests a comparison to thunder and lightning rather than to the sun.

Particularly impressive, albeit further removed from the initial context of theophany, is Isa. 60:1-3. Darkness covers the earth and the peoples, and then Yahweh shines forth in his *kābhôdh* upon his people. He is the light of Israel, and therefore Israel, too, can shine (*'ôrî*, v. 1). The subject of the verb is first *k^e bhôdh yhvh* (v. 1), then Yahweh himself (v. 2), but with *k^e bhôdhô yērā'eh* in parallelism. Israel will thus share in the honor and glory (brilliance) of God; the peoples will live in happiness in the light and brightness (*l^e'ôrēkh, l^e nōghāh zarchēkh*) that dawns upon them. Schnutenhaus[3] exam-

---

zārach. A. Guillaume, "Hebrew and Arabic Lexicography," *Abr-Nahrain,* 1 (1959/60[1961]), esp. 23; F. Schnutenhaus, "Das Kommen und Erscheinen Gottes im AT," *ZAW,* 76 (1964), 1-22, esp. 9.

[1] T. Nöldeke, review of M. L. Lidzbarski, *Die neu-aramäischen Handschriften der Königlichen Bibliothek zu Berlin,* in *ZDMG,* 50 (1896), 309.

[2] A. F. L. Beeston, "Notes on Some Old South Arabian Lexicography," *Mus,* 63 (1950), 265.

[3] P. 9.

ines Isa. 60:1-3 and points in particular to the concentration of verbs meaning "appear" in Dt. 33:2 (*bô'*, *zārach, hôphîaʿ*, *'āthāh*), concluding that the appearance of the sun-god was transferred to Yahweh.[4] In Isa. 58:10 we have the very common image of light as a symbol of good fortune: anyone who espouses the cause of the poor will have good fortune.

Mal. 3:20(4:2), on the contrary, strikes an almost mythological note: the sun of righteousness rises with healing in its wings. The image recalls the winged sun disk, a familiar element in Egyptian, Hittite, Akkadian, and Iranian religion.[5] Apart from this image, we have here the usual association of light with good fortune, life, and health.

The use of light terminology like *zārach* in connection with Yahweh has led to the hypothesis that Yahweh is in a certain sense a sun-god,[6] as the successor of the Canaanite El Elyon, who supposedly was a sun-god.[7] The basis of this theory is that Yahweh frequently reveals himself in light and splendor. One can walk in the light of his countenance (Isa. 60:3; Ps. 89:16[15]; cf. Isa. 2:5: *beʾôr yhvh; ʾôr pānekha* "had, in the ancient Israelite view, a very specific meaning"[8]). In Ps. 84:12(11), Yahweh is called *shemesh*. His theophany is associated with the term *nōghah*, "brightness" (Hab. 3:4; Isa. 60:3; Ezk. 10:4).[9] The verbs most commonly used to describe a theophany, *hôphîaʿ* and *zārach* (Dt. 33:2; Ps. 50:2; 94:1; Isa. 60:1f.), are also used of the sun.[10] In addition, *tiphʾereth*, which frequently appears in connection with Yahweh, is said to mean "radiance" (Isa. 28:1, 4f.; 60:19) and to suggest the solar character of Yahweh[11]—but these four occurrences stand against some fifty others, and only in Isa. 60:19 is there any association with the sun.

The association of Yahweh with radiance and light is clear beyond any doubt. But—with the exception of Ps. 84:12(11), which can also be translated differently[12]—it is never stated explicitly that this radiance has anything to do with the sun. In addition, the solar character of El Elyon is just an hypothesis; there is no clear evidence in its support. In this context the personal name *zerachyāh*, "Yahweh has shined forth," should possibly also be mentioned.[13]

III. mizrāch. The noun *mizrāch* means initially "the place where the sun rises," by extension "east." The construct phrase *mizrach (hash)shemesh* is used frequently, but in most cases only in a geographical sense without any special emphasis on the meaning "sunrise"; it means merely "east," "eastward," etc. (Nu. 21:11; Dt. 4:47;

---

4 Cf. the hymns to Shamash in *SAHG*, 240ff., 250ff.

5 See G. E. Mendenhall, *The Tenth Generation* (1973), 33ff.

6 G. W. Ahlström, *Psalm 89* (1959), 85ff., 92ff.

7 A. R. Johnson, "The Rôle of the King in the Jerusalem Cultus," in S. H. Hooke, ed., *The Labyrinth* (1935), 81ff., 96.

8 Ahlström, *Psalm 89*, 85.

9 *Ibid.*, 86.

10 *Ibid.*, 88; as was shown above, this holds true for *zārach* but not for *hôphîaʿ*, which never has the sun as its subject.

11 *Ibid.*, 92.

12 See the commentaries.

13 *IPN*, 184.

Josh. 1:15; 13:5; 2 K. 10:33; etc.). In Josh. 19:12 we find the combination *qēdhmāh mizrach hashshemesh.*

Sunrise and sunset (*mābhôʾ*) occur as terms for the uttermost ends of the earth: Yahweh summons the earth from the rising of the sun to its setting, i.e., the whole world (Ps. 50:1). From the rising of the sun to its setting the name of Yahweh is praised (Ps. 113:3) or is great among the nations (Mal. 1:11). Men shall know in the east (*mizrach shemesh*) and in the west (*maʿarābh*) that Yahweh alone is God (Isa. 45:6); his name and his glory will be feared in the west (*maʿarābh*) and at the rising of the sun (*mizrach shemesh*), i.e., throughout the world (Isa. 59:19). Similar expressions also occur without *shemesh:* from the north to the east (Am. 8:12); "your offspring will assemble from the east and from the west," i.e., from points of the compass (Isa. 43:5); people will come from the east and from the west and from the sea to give thanks to Yahweh (Ps. 107:3). As a symbol of extreme distance we find "east and west" in parallel with "heaven and earth" (Ps. 103:11f.): Yahweh removes our transgressions as far from us as the east is from the west.

Ringgren

זֶרֶם *zerem* → מטר *māṭār*

זָרַע *zāraʿ*; זֶרַע *zeraʿ*

Contents: I. Occurrences, Range of Meanings, Semantic Field: 1. Verb; 2. Noun. II. Ancient Near East. III. Literal Use: 1. Verb; 2. Noun. IV. Metaphorical Use of the Verb. V. Metaphorical Use of the Noun: 1. Primal History; 2. Promises to the Patriarchs in J and E; 3. Deuteronomy and Promises to the Moses Group; 4. P; 5. The Descendants of Aaron; 6. The Descendants of David and the Royal Line; 7. Blessings and Curses on Descendants; 8. Wisdom, Psalms, and Chronicles; 9. Judgment and Salvation in Prophecy; 10. Summary.

I. Occurrences, Range of Meanings, Semantic Field.

1. *Verb.* The verb *zāraʿ* occurs 56 times in the Hebrew OT: 46 times in the qal, 6 times in the niphal, and 3 times (Gen. 1:11f.; Lev. 12:2 [P]) in the hiphil. In addition, the form *zorāʿû* in Isa. 40:24 should probably be taken as a pual rather than a qal

---

zāraʿ. AuS, II (1932), 130ff.; cf. also I (1928), 261ff., 400ff.; J. de Fraine, *Adam and the Family of Man* (trans. 1965); P. Fronzaroli, "Studi sul lessico comune semitico," *AANLR,* 19 (1964), 259, 273; F. Hecht, *Eschatologie und Ritus bei den "Reformpropheten." PThS,* 1 (1971); L. Kopf, "Arabische Etymologien und Parallelen zum Bibelwörterbuch," *VT,* 8 (1958), 161-215, esp. 168; G. Quell, "σπέρμα," *TDNT,* VII, 536-543; J. Scharbert, *Solidarität in Segen und Fluch im AT und in seiner Umwelt. BBB,* 14 (1958); G. Wehmeier, *Der Segen im AT. Theol.Diss.,* 6 (1970), 199ff.

passive. Of the occurrences in the niphal, Nah. 1:14 should be disregarded, since *yizzākhēr* should be read (cf. Targum). The occurrences in the hiphil refer to seed-bearing plants (cf. Gen. 1:29 qal) and human offspring (Lev. 12:2; cf. Nu. 5:28 niphal); they belong in part to the group of texts that contain both verb and noun (Gen. 1:11f.,29; 47:23f.; Lev. 11:37f.; 26:16; Nu. 5:28; Dt. 11:10; 22:9; Isa. 55:10; Jer. 35:7; Eccl. 11:6). The LXX[1] usually renders the verb by means of *speírō* or *diaspeírō;* once (Nu. 5:28) it uses *ekspermatízō.*

Thus far, the verb is attested only once in the Qumran texts, and even here the text is uncertain: 1Q22 3:2, the so-called "Words of Moses," where the OT regulations governing the Sabbatical Year are actualized and it is stated that no one is to sow his field (cf. Ex. 23:10; Lev. 25:3f.; see III below).

The verb appears in the OT with the literal meaning "sow" (qal: Gen. 26:12; 47:23; Ex. 23:10; Lev. 25:11; Dt. 22:9; Jgs. 6:3; etc.); the niphal and pual furnish the corresponding passive ("be sown": Lev. 11:37; Dt. 21:4; 29:22 [Eng. v. 23]; Ezk. 36:9; "be impregnated": Nu. 5:28). The hiphil is used as a causative to emphasize the process ("yield seed": Gen. 1:11f.; "conceive a child": Lev. 12:2). Less commonly, the verb can be used in a metaphorical sense (cf. its early use in the sense of "scatter" in Jgs. 9:45; also Zec. 10:9; then Hos. 8:7; 10:12; Jer. 4:3; 31:27; Prov. 11:18; 22:8; etc.; with God as subject in Hos. 2:25[23]; cf. Jer. 31:27).

The verb has many synonyms and antonyms, most of which have analogous literal and figurative senses: *bāqa', dûsh, zārāh, chārash, māshakh hazzera', nāṭa', pûts* hiphil, *pāzar, tsāmach, qātsar,* and—occasionally (Dt. 21:4; Ezk. 36:9)—*'ābhadh,* as well as *yld* qal and hiphil in the figurative sense.

2. *Noun.* The noun is a segholate formed on the pattern qaṭl *tertiae laryngalis*; it occurs 220 times in the OT (cf. also the Aramaic in Dnl. 2:43, "offspring"). In the case of the noun, the literal meaning ("seed": Gen. 1:11f.; 8:22; 47:22ff.; Ex. 16:31; Lev. 11:37; Dt. 22:9; etc.; thence "sowing": Gen 47:19; "sown field": Isa. 17:11, thence the yield from the seed, the "harvest": Job 39:12; finally human, male "seed," "semen": Lev. 15:16; 22:4; Nu. 5:13,28) is less frequent than the figurative ("offspring": Gen. 3:15; 7:3; 12:7; 13:16; 16:10; 1 S. 2:20; etc.; "lineage, family, tribe," including, e.g., the royal line: 2 S. 4:8; 7:12; 1 K. 2:33; Ezr. 2:59; Neh. 7:61; "group, community": Isa. 1:4; Prov. 11:21; cf. also Isa. 6:13; 53:10; Jer. 2:21). We shall exclude from further consideration Mal. 2:15, which is obscure both in detail and in its general meaning, and Mal. 2:3.[2] In Ps. 97:11, *zārach* should be read, following the versions.

The LXX usually renders the noun by means of *spérma,* less often by means of *spóros* or *sporá.*

The semantic field of the noun includes both *zārûa'* and *mizrā'* as well as *'ēśebh* in the literal meaning; for the figurative meaning, it includes *'achᵃrîth, bayith, bēn, dôr,*

[1]Cf. Quell, 538-542.
[2]Cf. *BHS, in loc.*

marbîth, nekhedh, tsemach, sheʾērîth, and *perî.*[3] In 11QTgJob 20:7 both the text and interpretation of the phrase *zrʿ rwmʾh* are disputed.

II. Ancient Near East. As the common Semitic origin and meaning of the words would lead us to expect, both the verb and the noun are frequently attested elsewhere in the ancient Near East, with a similar range of meanings.

A "Proto-Semitic" *ḏrʿ*[4] became *zrʿ* in Canaanite (cf. also Phoenician), with the meanings "sow," "seed," "offspring."[5] The concrete meaning ("seed," "sow") and the figurative ("offspring," "descendants") are both found in Aramaic.[6] Ugaritic has a form *drʿ* I with the meaning "sow" or "seed,"[7] a hybrid between *zrʿ* (not found in Ugaritic) and *dry* (Heb. *zārāh*), "scatter," "winnow."[8]

In Old Akkadian, *zarʾum* is used for "seed," "descendants";[9] the later form is *zēru(m).*[10] Note also the phrases *zēr awīlūti,* "human offspring"; *zēr bît abi,* "family"; and *zēr napšāti,* "living creatures." On Lev. 15:16-18, where *zeraʿ* means "emission of semen" (cf. Jer. 31:27), note the Sumerian hymn to Martu.[11]

Egyptian, too, uses "seed" in the sense of "descendants" or "offspring."[12] This usage is of interest for the OT, especially in the Israel Stela of Merneptah,[13] which says of the foreign Israelites: "Their seed is not."[14] The context makes it clear that this expression cannot be taken literally here (and analogously in the OT), since it is far from true to historical fact.[15]

Elsewhere in the ancient Near East, statements about seed and sowing are frequently associated with statements about various deities and their actions or condition.[16] The

---

[3]Cf. also H. C. Brichto, "Kin, Cult, Land, and Afterlife," *HUCA,* 44 (1973), 24f.

[4]Cf. J. Aro, "Gemeinsemitische Ackerbauterminologie," *ZDMG,* 113 (1963/64), 475; J. Friedrich and W. Röllig, *Phönizisch-punische Grammatik*². *AnOr,* 46 (1970), 8.

[5]Cf. *KAI,* 10.15; 13.7; 14.8, 11, 22; 43.11, 15; Gezer calendar, *KAI,* 182.1f.

[6]*KAI,* 222 A.36 (Sefire I); also *DISO,* 80; then *KAI,* 214.20; 225.11; 228 A.12, 14, 22; 259.5.

[7]*WUS,* No. 793; *UT,* No. 705.

[8]*WUS,* No. 790; *UT,* No. 702; cf. now the citations in Whitaker, 189; on the subject, see also S. E. Loewenstamm, "The Ugaritic Fertility Myth—The Result of a Mistranslation," *IEJ,* 12 (1962), 87f., and *UT,* No. 702, where the question of the relationship to *zerôaʿ* is also discussed; also (with reference to Zec. 10:9) M. Dahood, *Ugaritic-Hebrew Philology. BietOr,* 17 (1965), 7; and Hecht, 144ff., 174.

[9]Cf. *zārû,* "progenitor": *CAD,* XXI, 70-72.

[10]On the change, see *GaG,* § 9a.

[11]A. Falkenstein, *SGL,* I (1959), 125, line 50.

[12]*mtw.t, WbÄS,* II, 169; *mw, WbÄS,* II, 52; cf., e.g., Ptahhotep, *ANET*³, 412ff.; Ipu-wer xii.1-6.

[13]*TGI*², No. 15.

[14]*ANET*³, 378.

[15]On the metaphorical use of "sow," "seed," etc. in Egyptian, especially from the Middle Kingdom onward, see H. Grapow, *Die bildlichen Ausdrücke des Ägyptischen* (1924), 104f., 126, 157f.

[16]Cf., e.g., *CTA,* 6 [I AB], II, 30ff.; in *WbMyth,* see the index under Adonis, Baal, Dagan, Dumuzi, Fruchtbarkeit, Getreidegottheit, Melqart, Mot, Osiris, and Vegetationsgott.

role played by "offspring" in ancient Near Eastern law, blessings and curses, oracles, and omens, is treated elsewhere.[17]

III. Literal Use.

1. *Verb.* The literal use of the verb *zāraʿ* reflects many agricultural activities. Whoever wishes to reap must have sown, since seed and harvest depend on each other (Ex. 23:16; Lev. 25:11ff.; Hos. 8:7; 10:12; Job 4:8), and seed is needed if the fields are not to lie fallow and people starve (Gen. 47:19 [J?]). The time of sowing falls at the beginning of the rainy period, in the breaks between the early rains[18]—in the OT this is the so-called winter sowing, around November/December.[19] A summer sowing (in different fields?) following the rainy period is not clearly attested in the OT.[20]

Each kind of seed has its own area (Isa. 28:25; not "portion of the field," as the Targum translates).[21] The field appears to have been plowed before sowing (Isa. 28:24; Hos. 10:11f.), but the scattered seed does not appear to have been plowed under;[22] newly broken ground therefore promises an especially good harvest (Hos. 10:11f.).[23] Seed was usually scattered broadcast (cf. Lev. 27:16);[24] it was therefore not dropped directly into the furrow, nor was there probably any seed hopper (cf. Jgs. 9:45; Zec. 10:9: "scatter").

Although Yahwism was originally not a religion associated with sedentary agriculture, and the Rechabites accordingly refused to sow seed, etc., on the grounds of fidelity to Yahweh (Jer. 35:7, 9 [with the noun]), the religion of Yahwism nevertheless influenced agriculture and sought to shape it through various legal statutes. The use of mixed seed (*kilʾayim*) is prohibited—summarily in Lev. 19:19, at greater length in Dt. 22:9, where the reason for the prohibition is necessarily added. Seed that has come in contact with an unclean animal can still be used, unless water has been poured over it (Lev. 11:37f. [with the noun]). In the seventh year both harvesting (→ קצר *qātsar*) and sowing are prohibited (Ex. 23:10f. with social justification; Lev. 25:3f. with a detailed theological justification; cf. → יובל *yôbhēl* and *shᵉmiṭṭāh;* also → שׂדה *śādheh* as object, used absolutely in Lev. 25:11, 20, 22). During the harvest festival at the close of the grain harvest, the firstfruits (→ בכור *bᵉkhôr*) of what was sowed are to be offered to Yahweh (Ex. 23:16). When an unidentified murder victim is discovered and it is not known who killed him, a young heifer is to be killed (for sacrifice?[25]) in a valley (alongside a stream?) that has been neither plowed nor sown—in other words, the very opposite of a cultic site. No evidence of any comparable ritual has been found elsewhere.

---

[17]Scharbert, 24ff.
[18]*AuS,* II, 174ff.
[19]*AuS,* II, 179ff.
[20]*AuS,* II, 136.
[21]Cf. *AuS,* II, 172.
[22]*AuS,* II, 194f.
[23]*AuS,* II, 137f.
[24]*AuS,* II, 180, 199f.
[25]Cf. G. von Rad, *Deuteronomy. OTL* (trans. 1966), 135.

Sowing and reaping are blessings bestowed by Yahweh, especially when the harvest is bounteous (Gen. 26:12 [J]; cf. 8:21f. [with the noun]; also Ps. 107:37). Because the fields lie fallow during the Sabbatical Year, Lev. 25:20–22, an addition to the jubilee-year legislation states that, since there can be no sowing or reaping, Yahweh will command his special blessing on the seed in the year preceding, so that until the new harvest from the seed of the eighth year (v. 22) the people will be able to live off the harvest of the previous year. In addition, promises of salvation—usually late—speak of a harvest that will last until the new sowing (Am. 9:13 [secondary]; Isa. 30:23 [not from Isaiah]; cf. 32:20 and Hos. 2:25[23]; on the problem of how to translate the passage in Hosea, cf. the commentaries). A similar idea appears in 2 K. 19:29 (Isa. 37:30), in the third, highly theological section of the Isaiah narratives (19:9b–35), to underscore the general promise in vv. 21–28: in the third year there will once more be seed and harvest, i.e., the famine will not be catastrophic, because the Assyrians will no longer be present. Ezk. 36:9 records a promise to the mountains of Israel that they are to be tilled and sown once more.

On the name of the plain of Jezreel, where "God himself sows" with the result that it is especially productive, cf. Hos. 2:24(22) (1 Ch. 4:3) and the commentary of Wolff.[26]

Fruitless sowing, the failure of a harvest, or its loss (e.g., to enemies) are punishments sent by Yahweh, according to Jgs. 6:3 in the Deuteronomistic introduction to 6:7ff.; in Lev. 26:16 (in contrast to 26:4f.), i.e., in the final chapter of the Holiness Code, containing threats of judgment and a list of the consequences of disobedience; and in Dt. 29:22(23) (Deuteronomistic) with reference to Yahweh's punishment of the land because Israel has forsaken the covenant of Yahweh—thus in Deuteronomistic and other exilic texts. (Cf. also Mic. 6:15; Hag. 1:6.) According to Isa. 17:9–11, judgment will be visited upon those who believe they can guarantee fertility through the worship of other gods—possibly with gardens of Adonis, cf. Ezk. 8:14 and Dnl. 11:37. They may plant, but they will not reap—just as in the gardens of Adonis! Idolatry stands under the curse and thus bears its punishment within itself. In an oracle of judgment against Babylon (Jer. 50:16 [not from Jeremiah]), we read that sower and harvester will be cut off.

A transition from concrete to figurative usage appears in Jgs. 9:45 ("sowing" or "scattering" salt [→ מלח *melach*]) and in Jer. 31:27, according to which in the coming day of salvation Yahweh will "sow" the house of Israel and the house of Judah with the seed of man and the seed of beast.

2. *Noun*. The noun, too, is used in the literal sense, in the context of the statement that grain is needed for seed (Gen. 47:19,23), which is produced by the plants themselves (Gen. 1:11f.). But the literal usage is less common than in the case of the verb, and the overtones of figurative usage are more often apparent (cf. Gen. 1:29; 7:3). Eccl. 11:6 is an exhortation to industry: "In the morning sow your seed, and at evening withhold not your hand," since no one knows what will prosper. Seed is exposed to various dangers (Am. 4:7, 9; cf. 7:1f.; Hag. 2:17; Dt. 28:22). The manna

[26] H. W. Wolff, *Hosea* (trans. 1974), 17f., 54.

was white like coriander seed (Ex. 16:31 [J]; cf. Nu. 11:7). The people complain that the desert is not a fit place for sowing (Nu. 20:5 [J?]; cf. Ex. 17:3). By contrast, Israel later sows in an abundance of water in its own land, thanks to the blessing of Yahweh (Nu. 24:7 [J]); and according to Dt. 11:10 Canaan is superior to Egypt in that there is no need for irrigation for sowing, since it receives rain. The seed sown by the Nile will come to Tyre as harvest (Isa. 23:3). The size of a field can be defined by means of the quantity of seed required to sow it (Lev. 27:16; cf. 1 K. 18:32).[27]

According to 1 S. 8:15 (Deuteronomistic), the king will take a tenth of the seed; on the tenth of the seed that constitutes Yahweh's portion and consequently cannot be offered as a freewill-offering, cf. Lev. 27:30 and Dt. 14:22.

The cry of woe in Isa. 5:10 (cf. the curse in Dt. 28:38) announces that ten measures of seed will produce only a single measure at harvest. But by virtue of Yahweh's blessing the earth brings forth seed for sowing; the word of Yahweh is similarly productive (Isa. 55:10f.). Thanks to Yahweh's blessing, the vintage will last to the time of sowing (Lev. 26:5; cf. Am. 9:13); but the curse will result in sowing in vain (Lev. 26:16; cf. Dt. 28:38). In the context of a discourse on the wild ox and its strength, couched in the style of nature wisdom, Yahweh asks in the first of God's speeches in Job (39:12) whether this wild ox will return with "your grain" (i.e., the produce of the seed, the harvest). According to Hag. 2:19, the rebuilding of the temple will bring fertility, and the seed in the barns will not decrease (cf. Am. 9:13 as a later addition to 9:11f.; on *māshakh hazzeraʿ*, cf. Ps. 126:6; the expression does not occur in Joel 4:18[3:18] and Lev. 26:5, which otherwise contain similar promises).

A distinct complex in which *zeraʿ* is mentioned frequently is the group of statutes dealing with "seed" in the sense of semen and sexual intercourse, defining the regulations governing cultic purification in these cases (Lev. 15:16–18,32 [P^S]; cf. Dt. 23:11f.[10f.]; → טמא *ṭāmēʾ*); in the Holiness Code, cf. also Lev. 18:20; v. 21 with its prohibition of child sacrifice *lᵉmōlekh* (cf. 2 K. 23:10; Jer. 7:31; 32:35) may have been appended here on account of the catchword *zeraʿ*. The same topic is dealt with more extensively in the composite passage Lev. 20:2–5, where *mōlekh* appears with the article in v. 5.[28] Cf. also Lev. 19:20; 22:4; Nu. 5:13 (all P or Holiness Code). A woman tested by ordeal and shown pure (*ṭāhôr;* → טָהַר *ṭāhar*) may conceive ("receive seed") once more (Nu. 5:28, with both noun and verb).

IV. Metaphorical Use of the Verb. One group of passages in which the verb is used metaphorically speaks in the style of Wisdom Literature, using the terms "sowing" and "reaping" to describe the connection between an action and its consequences, almost always with evil consequences in view (Hos. 8:7 [both verb and noun]; then 10:12f.; Jer. 4:3; 31:27; Job 4:8; Prov. 11:18; 22:8; cf. Gal. 6:7).[29] This group also includes the promise in Ps. 126:5f. Ritual weeping at the time of sowing may be attested in Ps. 126:5f.; Hos. 8:1–4, 7.[30]

27 *AuS*, II, 173.

28 On the general subject, see M. Noth, *Leviticus. OTL* (trans. 1965), 147–49; also → מלך *mlk*.

29 On sowing and reaping wind, cf. Hecht, 144ff.

30 See Hecht, 145f.; H. Gese, *et al.*, *Die Religionen Altsyriens, Altarabiens und der Mandäer. RdM*, 10/2 (1970), 73f.; → בכה *bākhāh*.

Job 31:8 speaks of "sowing" without "reaping" if Job's heart has strayed (cf. Jer. 12:13; Hag. 1:6). Eccl. 11:4, 6 likewise speak of the natural sequence of sowing and reaping in the context of statements about the uncertainty of human life and actions (v. 6). A man should not "sow among thorns" (Jer. 4:3f.; cf. Hos. 10:12), since a new beginning (Jer. 4:3aβb is a genuine utterance of Jeremiah in Deuteronomistic redaction) must be total (cf. Jer. 2:21 concerning pure seed; also Isa. 57:4 and Jer. 12:13 in Jeremiah's lament for his land and people: wheat was sown but thorns were reaped, on account of Yahweh's fierce anger).

Naturally statements using *zeraʿ* appear in texts that furnish a theological appraisal of the land (→ אדמה *ʾadhāmāh;* → ארץ *ʾerets*). In the consciously exaggerated description of the land in Dt. 11:10-15, the land into which Israel shall enter (→ בוא *bôʾ*, IV) is set in sharp contrast to Egypt, the land of slavery.[31] The land of Israel will not need any artificial irrigation for the seed that is sown (cf. Gen. 47:19 for the situation in Egypt), since Canaan will have more rainfall. In Jer. 2:2, Yahweh indicts Israel, recalling the period in the desert, the unsown land, when Israel was still unable to do otherwise than trust in Yahweh and follow him alone (cf. Dt. 29:22[23], describing Yahweh's punishment of the land because Israel has forsaken the covenant). In the context of Isa. 28:23-29 (cf. 41:19f.), v. 25 refers to Yahweh as a farmer. In this didactic poem of comfort—the response of the prophet to the reproach that his word will not come to pass—God's acts are presented as a meaningful sequence. He does not constantly repeat the same action; the succession of his acts is meaningful, like the actions of a farmer. Just as the plow overturns the soil, but makes a new beginning possible through sowing, this sequence is analogous to Yahweh's actions in judgment and salvation. Thus Yahweh is depicted here, in a sense, as a sower (Quell[32] maintains that this image was deliberately eschewed in the OT; Mal. 2:15 is obscure; but cf. also Ezr. 9:2; Isa. 6:13; Hos. 2:25[23]); and if Yahweh appears to be the representative of well-planned agriculture, it is possible to cite analogous myths from elsewhere in the ancient Near East.[33]

Yahweh "scatters" Israel among the nations (Zec. 10:9) as a punishment to evoke repentance; but he also desires to "sow" the house of Israel and the house of Judah with the seed of man and the seed of beast (Jer. 31:27; cf. 24:6 and 1:10), a promise from the mouth of Deutero-Jeremiah that the land will be resettled. According to Jer. 2:21, Israel was a "pure seed" (*zeraʿ ʾemeth*) planted by Yahweh (i.e., set in the land), which nevertheless became a bad vine (cf. Hos. 10:1; Ps. 80:9ff.[8ff.], albeit without the word *zeraʿ*).

Deutero-Isaiah uses the word only twice. In Isa. 55:10, the rain is said to bring forth plants giving seed to the sower (cf. Gen. 1:11f. [P], likewise exilic!); this provides a metaphor for the effectual power of the divine word (cf. once more Gen. 1). Isa. 40:24 (the only occurrence of the pual) asserts that the rulers of the earth are like plants—their seed newly sown, just beginning to take root and grow—that must soon wither and perish through the breath of Yahweh (cf. 40:7); thus Yahweh has demonstrated his

---

[31]On Egypt in Deuteronomy, see J. G. Plöger, *Literarkritische, formgeschichtliche und stilkritische Untersuchungen zum Deuteronomium. BBB,* 26 (1967), 100-115.

[32]P. 541.

[33]Cf. II above, conclusion.

incomparable (→ דמה dāmāh) superiority to these rulers and will do so again (40:12-31).

V. Metaphorical Use of the Noun.

1. *Primal History*. The metaphorical use of *zera'*, a key word for the Yahwist, makes its first appearance in Gen. 3:15.[34] At the instigation of the serpent (→ נחש *nāchāsh*) and the woman (*'ishshāh;* → איש *'îsh*), the man (→ אדם *'ādhām*) has transgressed Yahweh's command not to eat of the tree of the knowledge of good and evil (Gen. 2:16f.), overstepping the only limitation imposed on him and thereby refusing to acknowledge God's superiority ("be like God" [3:5]). Now the first of the curses (→ ארר *'rr*) spoken by Yahweh in 3:14-19 is directed at the serpent. On account of what it has done, in the future it will be cut off from the rest of the animal world: it will creep upon its belly, it will eat dust (→ עפר *'āphar*) all the days of its life, and Yahweh will put enmity between it and the woman *ûbhên zar'akhā ûbhên zar'āh*. This enmity will repeatedly spell death for the descendants of both, and it will endure as long as there are serpents and men. Any interpretation of the verse as a "protevangelium"[35] is out of the question, if only because *zera'* cannot refer here to a single person and the context is a curse. This curse is not dependent on any earlier tradition, but was framed by J himself.[36] It is of fundamental importance for his Paradise narrative and his account of the primal history;[37] here it is meant to articulate the limitations on life occasioned by human sin, both past and present. The crucial point is that this curse is meant to strike not only those to whom it was immediately addressed or those directly affected by it—which would seem more appropriate; see section 7 below and cf. also Gen. 9:25 (J)—but also their descendants, a possibility already implicit in the naming of the parents of mankind. The primal history is fundamental to all history. In this fashion, J weaves the curse (as well as the blessing; → ברך *brk*) into the totality of history, turning it into a history of disaster, and traces a fragment of postparadisal reality back to its origins.

In Gen. 4:25 (J), Adam states that God has given him other offspring in place of Abel, slain by Cain: the problem of "offspring" is to be an important motif for J.

Gen. 3:17-19 are also alluded to by 8:22 (J), in the Yahwistic epilogue to the story of the Deluge (cf. also 7:3 [J]: the animals are brought into the ark in order to preserve their *zera'*). After the Deluge, the regular progression from seedtime to harvest is assured for all time by Yahweh's promise. The verse is thus one of the Yahwist's statements about the grace of Yahweh, which endures despite all human apostasy. It is furthermore conceived in such a way as to suggest an attack—found elsewhere in J as well—on Canaanite nature religion or Baal as the supposed provider of these gifts. The way this verse is woven into J's conception of history, which is pictured as a linear

[34]For a bibliography on this verse, see C. Westermann, *BK*, I/1 (1974), 351.

[35]Westermann, 354f.; also H. Haag, *BL*², 1419-1421.

[36]Cf. O. H. Steck, *Die Paradieserzählung. BSt*, 60 (1970), 55f., 109; E. Haag, *Der Mensch am Anfang. TrThSt*, 24 (1970), 159ff.; Scharbert, 159ff.

[37]See below.

progression toward a specific goal, eliminates the possibility of reading out of it any cyclic understanding of time, which is otherwise unattested in the OT.

2. *Promises to the Patriarchs in J and E.* The substantive *zeraʿ* (usually used metaphorically) also plays an important role in the patriarchal narratives of J and E,[38] where it appears primarily in the promises made to the patriarchs.[39]

Yahweh will give the land to the descendants (!) of Abram or Abraham (first in the isolated verse Gen. 12:7 [J]; then in 15:18 [J?] in the form of an oath referring to Abram's descendants, prepared for in its present setting by 15:13 [E?], which likewise speaks only of Abram's descendants; and finally in 24:7 [J] and 28:13 [J]). This promise of the land to the descendants of Abram or Jacob is unknown to E, who likewise does not use *brk* as a key word in his patriarchal narrative. For J, on the other hand, the land is promised to the descendants of Abram and Jacob; this promise is thus the primary one from the traditio-historical point of view, since it is fundamental, for instance, for the patriarchal gods.[40] But was possession of the land promised to the patriarchs themselves[41] or to their descendants? Or is it possible that both are meant? Are their descendants not implicit in the patriarchs? Yahweh says to Abram that he will give the land "to you and to your descendants" (Gen. 13:15 [J], where the promise is even *ʿadh ʿôlām;* v. 16 picks up this wording and emphasizes it as a promise of many descendants); Lot, on the contrary, "chooses" his territory (13:11). Analogous promises are made to Isaac (albeit only in the secondary passage Gen. 26:3b–5) and Jacob (28:13 [J]; cf. also Ex. 32:13; 33:1, with Deuteronomic and Deuteronomistic elements, as well as Nu. 14:24 [J]). We need not pause to discuss the question of whether the promise of land to Abraham should be ascribed to a specific later group (Judah?), and the promises to (Isaac and) Jacob to other groups (with an oath on the part of the deity in the case of the Abraham and exodus group?[42]). The emphasis and the theological focus are never on the patriarchs alone, but always on their "descendants" as well, and thus—according to the themes of the patriarchal promises—on what is actually a second promise, albeit one that is inseparable from the first (cf. Noth; Zimmerli, too, holds that the promise of many descendants became associated at an early date with the promise of the land; according to Westermann, however, at the beginning only a single promise was made in each case).[43] Neither does it seem likely that originally there was

---

38On P, see 4 below.

39For a discussion of the promises, see Scharbert. 148ff., 168ff.; M. Noth, *A History of Pentateuchal Traditions* (trans. 1972), 54–57; C. Westermann, "Arten der Erzählung in der Genesis. 1. Teil: Verheissungserzählungen," *Forschung am AT. ThB,* 24 (1964), 11–34; J. Hoftijzer, *Die Verheissungen an die drei Erzväter* (1956); S. Herrmann, *Die prophetischen Heilserwartungen im AT. BWANT,* 85 (1965), 64–78; N. Lohfink, *Die Landverheissung als Eid. SBS,* 28 (1967); J. van Seters, "Confessional Reformulation in the Exilic Period," *VT,* 22 (1972), 448-452; H. C. White, "Divine Oath in Genesis," *JBL,* 92 (1973), 165–179.

40Von Rad and in part Noth (who also includes the promise of many descendants).

41W. Zimmerli and R. E. Clements.

42Lohfink, *Landverheissung,* 111.

43On the relationship between the promise of the land and the promise of many descendants, see now D. Vetter, *Seherspruch und Segensschilderung. CThM,* A/4 (1974), 58-65.

an isolated promise of descendants, to which there was added the promise of the land once the tribes had taken up residence in settled territory,[44] if only on account of the sociological status of those who received the promise, who were nomadic herdsmen living on the fringes of the settled territory. Because Yahweh promised the land to the descendants and to the fathers, and to the descendants in the fathers, the land (now) belongs legitimately to the descendants of these fathers, and in the gift of the land they can see the fulfilment of these promises and thus the hand of their God in history. This conclusion is underlined by the observation that only in one instance, Gen. 15:7 (J?), do we find a promise of the land to Abraham (or Isaac or Jacob) himself without simultaneous mention of his descendants (cf. also Gen. 13:17, which must, however, be read in the context of v. 15; in chap. 15, too, there are connections between vv. 1-6 and 7ff.: v. 5 contains the promise of descendants, v. 18 the promise of the land to them); this might suggest that an early text is contained in 15:7ff., if *lᵉrishtāh* in v. 7 could be considered a Deuteronomistic addition and the whole text has not undergone Deuteronomistic revision. Later texts, then, would have made the logical interpretation and spoken quite rightly of both the promise and gift of the land to descendants. In the present context, however, the promise clearly includes both descendants and the land, to which is added the promise of a "blessing"—but even this blessing, although a primary theme in J, follows naturally from the other promises, for how could the blessing of the deity be demonstrated more clearly to a nomadic herdsman than in descendants and land, with the land given to these descendants? This is underscored by the appearance of *zeraʿ* again in the promise of (many) descendants (cf. also → גָּדַל *gādhal* II, → גּוֹי *gôy,* → רבה *rābhāh,* and → פרה *pārāh*).

We may first note Gen. 15:5. The mention of descendants here may be one of the "royal motifs" (cf. 2 S. 7:12[45]—was it not in the Davidic empire that the promise of descendants "like the stars of heaven" was first realized?—and Gen. 12:3). We next find the promise of descendants in Gen. 18:10 and 46:3; descendants and a blessing are promised in Gen. 26:24; 32:13(12); 48:16. In these contexts we often read that the descendants of the person addressed will be like the dust of the earth (Gen. 13:16; cf. 15:5; 22:17 in the secondary section 22:15-18; and then 32:13[12]), the sand by the sea, or the stars of heaven—all theological similes. Gen. 22:17 states that the descendants of Abraham will possess the gates of their enemies (cf. 24:60, as a bridal blessing for Rebekah; cf. Ruth 4:11f.; the wish for descendants is also found in 1 S. 1:11; 2:20); cf. Speiser's reference to the use of this formula elsewhere in the ancient Near East.[46] With respect to Gen. 15:5, the context provided by v. 3 (both E?) should be noted (the possible reading *hûʾ lî zeraʿ* in v. 2 makes the connection even clearer); the same promise is made to Isaac in 26:4 (in the section 26:3b-5, an addition to J; cf. "for Abraham's sake" in 26:24), to Jacob in 28:14 (J); 32:13(12) (J), and to Ephraim in 48:19 (E). These descendants of Abraham will be sojourners in Egypt for four hundred years (15:13 [E?]). Two further promises of both the land and descendants (both with

[44] A. Alt.

[45] See 6 below and also R. E. Clements, *Abraham and David. SBT,* N.S. 5 (1967), 19, 55, without sharing his historical presuppositions, e.g., with respect to Hebron and Mamre.

[46] E. A. Speiser, *Genesis. AB,* I (1964), 164.

zera') occur in Ex. 32:13 (with an oath sworn to the patriarchs, and thus a Deuteronomistic addition) and later in Josh. 24:3 with reference to the descendants of Abraham (the basic stratum of Josh. 24 being E?). The promise of blessing spoken of by J (→ ברך *brk*), according to which all the families of the earth are to be blessed through Abram (Gen. 12:1-3 [J]), is interpreted in 22:18 (in the context of the secondary passage 22:15-18) in the sense that this blessing will come to the nations through the descendants of Abraham, "because you have obeyed my voice." This last expression characterizes the verse (and thus the addition) as Deuteronomistic, but also shows clearly how an ancestor and his descendants are one. Gen. 28:14 (J), however, shows that J, too, knows the statement that "by you and your descendants (!) shall all the families of the earth bless themselves." This interpretation goes beyond 12:3, but makes it clear how the various promises dovetail (cf. the juxtaposition of 15:1, 4f., 18). Whether this means that the promise of a blessing derives from the Jacob circle[47] can no longer be determined, especially since the blessing itself is naturally expected to take effect through the vertical sequence of generations.[48]

Gen. 16:10 (J) and 21:13 (E), both possibly secondary additions within the original narratives, extend the promise of many descendants (cf. 21:18) to (Hagar and) Ishmael. The reason given to Isaac is *kî zar'ᵃkhā hû'* (a kind of modified declaratory formula of adoption or acknowledgment of a child by his father?), after God has just told Abraham in 21:12 (E) that his descendants are to be named through Isaac alone; the land is likewise promised only to Isaac. P will later expressly avoid the term *zera'*, so important to him elsewhere, in the case of Ishmael (Gen. 17:20). Do these texts—especially if they are secondary additions—conceal conflicts between various groups over who should be considered legitimately the descendants of Abraham? And is this conflict to be seen as other than a conflict about disputed territory? If so, here, too, the juxtaposition of descendants and land would be intrinsic, but not secondary.

The promise of the land is also repeated to Jacob, likewise in conjunction with the promise of a blessing (Gen. 28:13 [E]); it is even joined to a promise of a blessing and many descendants to Jacob and his descendants (28:14 [E]—only in this combination in his case). The promise to Jacob of many descendants (32:13 [J]) speaks in his case, too, of descendants "like the sand of the sea." Jacob then gives thanks to God that he has been allowed to live to see Joseph's children (48:11 [E]), and repeats the promise of many descendants to Ephraim (48:19 [E]).

In contrast to the stories of the patriarchs of Israel, i.e, the true descendants of the patriarchs, we find two sharply contrasting mentions of *zera'*. Onan spilled his semen on the ground because he realized that offspring he was to beget for his brother would not be his (38:8f. [J]); he was therefore unwilling to beget offspring for his brother. In this respect, too, this story in Gen. 38 is out of context with the stories of the patriarchs. Lot's daughters likewise get *zera'* from their drunken father (19:32, 34 [J]), an

[47]A. Jepsen, "Zur Überlieferungsgeschichte der Vätergestalten," *Festschrift A. Alt. WZ* Leipzig, 3 (1953/54), 265ff.

[48]Cf. C. Westermann, *Der Segen in der Bibel und im Handeln der Kirche* (1968), 33; H.-P. Müller, *Ursprünge und Strukturen alttestamentlicher Eschatologie. BZAW*, 109 (1969), 143-47, 153.

act that merits the approbation of neither the narrator nor his listeners. Both texts, set in the context of "descendants" and the promises made to them, show who are not included among these descendants, why they cannot be included, and why their conduct is not right in the eyes of Yahweh and consequently has no share in his promises.

Finally, Caleb also receives a promise of land because he has followed (→ אחרי *'achᵃrê*) Yahweh (Nu. 14:24 [J]). Yahweh will bring (→ בוא *bô'*, IV) him into the land and his descendants will possess it.[49]

3. *Deuteronomy and Promises to the Moses Group.* In Deuteronomy and the literature leading up to it, as well as the literature influenced by it, Yahweh's oath (→ שׁבע *šb'*) plays an important role. He has sworn to the fathers (→ אב *'ābh,* III.3.c; Gen. 24:7; cf. 26:3; 50:24; in 24:7 the LXX does not include the element of the oath, which is often thought to be secondary) "to give [→ נתן *nāthan*] the land to them and to their descendants." This motif appears as early as Ex. 32:13; 33:1; it reappears in Dt. 1:8 with the addition of "after them" (cf. 4:37; 10:15; and later P); then in 11:9, followed by the exaggerated description of the land in 11:10–15; 34:4 (Deuteronomistic) has only "your descendants." Even human oaths are sometimes binding upon coming generations (1 S. 20:42). Deuteronomy mentions the promise of many descendants only in 1:10; 6:3; 7:13; 28:63; 30:5, 16; the phrase "you and your descendants" likewise does not appear (until 30:19, where it is not associated with the promise of the land[50]), although, or rather because, Deuteronomy emphasizes the solidarity of fathers and sons, the simultaneity and solidarity of generations (5:3; 30:19; etc.;[51] cf. also 26:9ff.,15; 27:3; 29:12ff.[13ff.]; 30:3,6; 31:20f.; Josh. 5:6; Jer. 11:5; 32:22). Thus promises are made in Deuteronomy to the father, to the fathers and their descendants, and to the present generation. The "descendants" are mentioned for the most part only in late passages or appendices (28:46,59; 30:6,19), where "descendants" are concerned with their participation in the history of their fathers. The fathers "and their descendants after them" were and are objects of God's election and guidance (4:37; cf. v. 40 as the purpose and goal of the historically grounded parenesis; also 10:15). According to 30:6 (Deuteronomistic), Yahweh will circumcise (→ מול *mwl*) the heart of the present generation and of their offspring.

Dt. 6:3 states that the God of the fathers (!) promised the land to the people of Israel (!), a land "flowing with milk and honey." But this description, which also appears elsewhere in Deuteronomy, does not derive from the promise of the land to the patriarchs, but rather from the promise to the Moses group (Ex. 3:8). The latter rarely appears in conjunction with "descendants" (not in Ex. 3:17; 13:5 [with an oath to the fathers]; Lev. 20:24; Nu. 13:27; 14:8; 16:14; "descendants" are mentioned only in Ex. 33:1f., together with an oath to the fathers—i.e., with Deuteronomic influence). This promise was not made to a patriarch who, as it were, included his "descendants," but to a group, so that there was not as much immediate reason to speak of "descendants."

---

[49] See W. Beltz, *Die Kaleb-Traditionen im AT. BWANT,* 98 (1974).
[50] See 7 below.
[51] See Scharbert, 187–191.

4. *P*. The word *zāra‛* is also important for P (on Gen. 1:11f., 29, see III.2 above). In Gen. 9:9 (P), God says that he will establish his (Noachic) covenant (→ ברית *b^e^rîth*) not only with Noah and his sons, but with his descendants. The promise of the land to Abraham, given special importance by P in Gen. 17, is made to "him and his descendants after him." The phrase *zar‛^a^khā 'ach^a^reykhā* is repeated frequently and emphatically (17:8f.,19; cf. 35:12 [P] and 48:4 [P]); it is a characteristic idiom of P[52] (cf. also Ex. 28:43, where it appears along with *chuqqath ‛ôlām* in a codicil to the regulation requiring the priests to wear breeches; cf. Ex. 30:21). So, too, the eternal covenant of promise between Abraham and God, here characterized as a unilateral obligation freely entered into by God,[53] begins with the emphatic statement that this promise is made to Abraham's descendants as well. The substance of the promise from generation to generation is primarily that he who gives the promise *lihyôth l^e^khā lē'lōhîm ûl^e^zar‛^a^khā 'ach^a^reykhā*, citing a portion of the covenant formula (or "solidarity formula"; Gen. 17:7,10). The promise is made to Abraham in this form only in P, but cf. Ex. 29:45 (P). In this connection, S. R. Külling points out[54] that the texts of ancient Near Eastern treaties not infrequently extend the stipulations of the treaty explicitly to the descendants of the parties involved. In the case of Gen. 17, it is not unimportant that P is the one to insert this emphasis on the promise to Abraham's descendants into this theological context (17:5f.,16; does v. 6 with its reference to future kings and the "everlasting covenant"—cf. also 35:11—exhibit the influence of the Davidic covenant theology?). Once again it is Abraham and his descendants, the generations after him, who are to accept the obligation of circumcision as a token of the covenant (17:9f.,12; vv. 9-14 probably represents a different stratum[55]); Isaac, too, and his descendants are included in this theological argumentation, while for Ishmael both the *b^e^rîth* and the idea of *zera‛*, obviously important to P, are suppressed (17:20; contrast 16:10 [J] and 21:18 [E]!). Behind all this stands the exilic situation of the basic stratum of P (cf. Isa. 41:8) and its "audience," to whom the enduring force of the covenant with Abraham, the promise of the land, and communion with God are to be forcefully demonstrated: these are theirs as the "descendants" of Abraham (cf. Deutero-Isaiah and Gen. 23 with its valuation of the land).

P also knows a repetition of the promise of the land to Jacob and his descendants (28:3f.; cf. 35:12 with its reference to the promise to Abraham; cf. 35:11 with 17:6) as well as to Isaac; the promise to Jacob is interpreted with greater emphasis on the concept of "blessing," while for Abraham the "covenant" was more important.[56] The land promised to Abraham and his descendants (17:8) God will give to Jacob and his

---

[52]For a discussion of the phrase, see F. J. Helfmeyer, *Die Nachfolge Gottes im AT. BBB,* 29 (1968), 3-6; M. Weinfeld, *Deuteronomy and the Deuteronomic School* (Oxford, 1972), 78, 181; S. E. Loewenstamm, "The Divine Grants of Land to the Patriarchs," *JAOS,* 91 (1971), 509f.

[53]Cf. E. Kutsch, *Verheissung und Gesetz. BZAW,* 131 (1973), 108-113.

[54]S. R. Külling, *Zur Datierung der "Genesis-P-Stücke"* (1964), 245f.

[55]Cf. E. Kutsch, "Ich will euer Gott sein," *ZThK,* 71 (1974), 376-79.

[56]For a discussion of the P texts concerning Jacob, see W. Gross, "Jakob, der Mann des Segens," *Bibl,* 49 (1968), 321-344.

descendants, as the new promise emphatically assures. Here, too, the exilic community is addressed: it may think of itself as the seed of Abraham or Jacob (cf. [Deutero-]Isa. 41:8; 45:19,25). In Gen. 48:4, P speaks emphatically only of the promise of the land to the descendants of Jacob forever (cf. once more 17:8), not just to Jacob himself (cf. the climactic series in 35:12). The "seed of Jacob" is also alluded to in 35:11, the first appearance in P of the promise of many descendants, which is hardly required by the context. Then Jacob came into Egypt "with all his offspring" (46:6f. [P]); we may here raise the question of the extent to which P uses "Egypt" to stand for Babylonia. This full promise to the "descendants after you," to the seed of Abraham, Jacob, and Israel, who can be confident of standing within the covenant with Abraham by virtue of the token of circumcision and of sharing the blessing given to Jacob as a member of the nation into which Jacob has grown, is a component of the kerygma of P to the exilic community, through which the community is to receive hope in an enduring communion with God and in a return to the land that is still promised to them.[57] When P omits the emphasis on descendants in Ex. 6:2ff., the explanation is clear; here the "children of Israel" are addressed directly; the exilic community is to think of itself as the "children of Israel" before its "exodus" from Babylonia (cf. P in Ex. 14 with [Deutero-]Isa. 43:16ff.). Yahweh will be their God (Ex. 6:7), just as he promised to Abraham (Gen. 17:7 [P]; cf. Ex. 29:45f.).

5. *The Descendants of Aaron.* A differently oriented priestly interest is exhibited by the texts associated with the "seed of Aaron" as the true priesthood (Ex. 30:21; Nu. 17:5[16:40]; 25:13; also 18:19 and Ex. 40:14f. without use of the word *zeraʿ;* for a discussion of the "covenant of salt" with the descendants of Aaron [Nu. 18:19] see → מלח *melach* and → ברית *beríth,* IV.1). None of the descendants of Aaron may have a physical blemish (Lev. 21:17, 21); such a man may not come near (→ קרב *qārabh*) Yahweh. The high priest must not profane his "seed"; consequently special stipulations govern his marriage (Lev. 21:15; cf. Ezk. 44:22; only a virgin of the stock of the house of Israel). Phinehas has a special promise among the Aaronides for himself and his "descendants after him" (Nu. 25:12f.). The Aaronides may not approach the holy things in a state of uncleanness (Lev. 22:3f.). The widowed daughter of a priest who has had no offspring may partake of cultic offerings (Lev. 22:13), for, as a member of the priestly family, she shares in its holiness.[58] Here, too, belongs the "Zadokite stratum" in Ezk. 40–48, from a later hand who restricts sacrificial and altar service to the descendants of Zadok (cf. Ezk. 43:19; 44:15; 48:11—sometimes with *benê* instead of *zeraʿ*, obviously with no difference in meaning).

57Cf. also K. Elliger, "Sinn und Ursprung der priesterlichen Geschichtserzählung," *ZThK,* 49 (1952), 121–143 = *KlSchr. ThB,* 32 (1966), 174–198; R. Kilian, "Die Hoffnung auf Heimkehr in der Priesterschrift," *BiLe,* 7 (1966), 39–51; H. D. Preuss, *Verspottung fremder Religionen im AT. BWANT,* 92 (1971), 178–192; W. Brueggemann, "Kerygma of the Priestly Writers," *ZAW,* 84 (1972), 397–414.

58For a discussion of the Aaronides in P, see A. H. J. Gunneweg, *Leviten und Priester. FRLANT,* 89 (1965), 138ff.; A. Cody, *A History of OT Priesthood. AnBibl,* 35 (1969), 170ff.

6. *The Descendants of David and the Royal Line.* Youths of the royal "family" are sought at the royal court (Dnl. 1:3; cf. also 9:1, "by birth a Mede," an historical inaccuracy). Persons or groups belonging to the royal family or house are mentioned similarly but more casually, and therefore with less theological relevance, in 1 K. 11:14 and 2 K. 25:25 (cf. Jer. 41:1); according to the latter passage, Gedaliah's murderer came from the royal family. Vengeance upon Saul and his descendants is mentioned in 1 S. 24:22(21) and 2 S. 4:8. Much more important are the texts associated with the tradition of Yahweh's promise to David and his descendants (cf. also the covenant with Abraham as an expression of Yahweh's favor—but more clearly meant for the people as a whole, not just the ruling dynasty). These texts take the key word *zera'* from 2 S. 7:12 (cf. 1 Ch. 17:11), according to which Yahweh will raise up a son after David, and will establish him and his kingdom (cf. the elaboration in 2 S. 7:16). Various texts in the Deuteronomistic history allude to the promise concerning descendants (1 K. 2:33; 11:39; negatively in 2 K. 11:1; cf. 2 Ch. 22:10). In the Psalms, Ps. 18:51(50) (cf. 2 S. 22:51) alludes to this promise with thanksgiving. Ps. 89:5,30, 37(4,29,36)[59] lead up to a lament (vv. 39ff.[38ff.]); v. 5(4) alludes directly, albeit with a different verb, to 2 S. 7:12, while vv. 30(29) and 37(36) cite Yahweh's promise once more. Did Yahweh not make his promise to each of David's descendants (vv. 36, 31ff., 20–28[35, 30ff., 19–27])? The lament itself (vv. 39ff.[38ff.]) makes no mention of *zera'*.

The *zera'* of David also plays a role in texts from the book of Jeremiah and in Ezekiel. On account of Jehoiachin's guilt, none of his descendants shall sit upon the throne of David (Jer. 22:28,30; secondary in v. 28 [cf. LXX]), and Yahweh will punish him and his offspring for their iniquity (36:31). In Jer. 33:14–26 (secondary) the old promises are given new force and their inviolability is emphasized; in v. 26, the election of Israel is closely linked with the endurance of the Davidic dynasty (in the period after Zerubbabel?[60]), and the promise of many descendants is transferred to the Davidic dynasty in v. 22, i.e., the latter is associated with the nation as a whole (cf. Isa. 55:3!). Ezk. 17:5 speaks allegorically of a *zera' hā'ārets* planted in fertile soil (*biśdheh zera'*) by an eagle (the king of Babylon). The text is placed here on account of 17:13 (in the interpretation of vv. 11–21), which looks back on the events of the year 587 and calls Zedekiah "one of the seed royal," placed in a vassal relationship.[61] Nowhere in the OT is it stated that the king is of divine descent, or that he is the offspring of the deity.

7. *Blessings and Curses on Descendants.* On rare occasions we find a curse (→ ארר *'rr*) that is intended to involve the descendants of the individual cursed. Within the Deuteronomistic material—albeit not in the actual curse formulas of Dt. 27–28—we find in Dt. 28:46, within the context of an interpretation of the curses, the statement

---

[59]On the use of *zera'* here, see G. W. Ahlström, *Psalm 89* (1959), 128f.

[60]Cf. W. Rudolph, *HAT,* 12 ([3]1968), *in loc.*

[61]For a discussion of the text, see K. Seybold, *Das davidische Königtum im Zeugnis der Propheten. FRLANT,* 107 (1972), 132ff.; Kutsch, *Verheissung,* 10.

that the curse will afflict Israel and its descendants if Israel does not keep the commandments of Deuteronomy (28:59; cf. v. 38). Despite the appositeness in Lev. 26:9, 29; Dt. 28:4,11,18,32,41,50,53; 30:19; 32:25, it is striking to observe that these passages never refer directly to descendants—with the exception of Dt. 30:19, where it is not the curse but life that is extended to the descendants. There are probably several reasons that brought about this evident limitation on the effects of a curse. In the first place, we have the conviction that a curse should take effect rapidly but not extend through a period of generations.[62] A curse did not have reference to a distant future; its purpose was the immediate or at least speedy extermination of the person addressed and his "descendants." In the second place, the continued efficacy of a "blessing" (→ ברך *brk*) was more desirable and of greater theological interest; blessing was historicized in the OT, but not cursing (cf. however Josh. 6:26 and 1 K. 16:34). Furthermore, the phenomenon in question goes hand in hand with the progressive religious conquest of cursing and thus of certain magical notions within Israel.[63] And by its very nature a curse formula cannot apply both to the person cursed and to his descendants (cf. → ארר *'rr*, II). In this respect, Ps. 109:6ff. are unique in their negative aspect. By contrast, Yahweh stands witness to the substance of a positive oath between Jonathan and David that extends to their descendants (1 S. 20:42).

Within the context of the actions/reward nexus, which was not truly characteristic of Yahwism but rather derived from Israel's neighbors, it can be said that the leprosy of Naaman shall cleave to Gehazi and his descendants forever as a punishment (2 K. 5:27). The blood (→ דם *dām*) of those slain by Joab shall come back upon the head of Joab and upon the head of his descendants (1 K. 2:33; → שׁוב *shûbh*), while David and his descendants shall have peace forever.[64] And on account of the sins of Jeroboam, Yahweh rejected all the descendants of Israel, i.e., both the northern and the southern kingdom (2 K. 17:20—or are vv. 19f. secondary, representing the final verdict of the Deuteronomistic historian after the fall of the northern kingdom?).

8. *Wisdom, Psalms, and Chronicles.* For the actions/reward nexus of Wisdom Literature,[65] it is an article of faith that the offspring of the righteous will be delivered (Prov. 11:21; cf. the conclusion of Eliphaz in Job 5:25, which he states with total disregard for Job and his fate). It is in line with the collapse of faith in this fundamental dogma of earlier wisdom in what befalls Job that he should here state the antithetical position: it is rather the offspring of the wicked who live secure (Job 21:8; the contrary is stated typically by Ps. 37:28). Psalms that hear the stamp of Wisdom Literature or have been influenced by it argue in the same vein with respect to the positive future that awaits the offspring of the righteous (Ps. 25:13; 37:25f.,28; 112:2).

The other psalms (apart from 126:6?) use *zera'* only in a metaphorical sense. The

---

[62] Scharbert, 47, 103, 128f., 131, 251-55.

[63] See J. Hempel, "Die israelitischen Anschauungen von Segen und Fluch im Lichte altorientalischer Parallelen," *ZDMG,* 79 (1925), 106f. = *Apoxysmata. BZAW,* 81 (1961), 110.

[64] Cf. M. Noth, *BK,* IX/1 (1968), *in loc.,* on the content of the passage.

[65] See H. D. Preuss, "Erwägungen zum theologischen Ort alttestamentlicher Weisheitsliteratur," *EvTh,* 30 (1970), 393-417, with bibliography.

seed of Jacob and the seed of Israel are to glorify Yahweh and stand in awe of him, according to the summons addressed to the congregation (gathered for a meal?) in Ps. 22:24(23). Also of interest is 22:31(30): it is part of an eschatological reinterpretation of the psalm, not just a volte-face occasioned by a favorable oracle, which depicts the subsequent thanksgiving and the deliverance that has been experienced on a gigantic scale. This interpretation is supported by the analogous passages and the analogous use of *zeraʿ* in 69:36f.(35f.) and 102:(19[18]),29(28); all these psalms are individual laments with eschatological additions.[66] Here the saving acts of Yahweh are always to be told to coming generations, so that posterity may thus praise Yahweh and serve him, as well as experiencing the same deliverance. Isa. 53:10 can also be compared to Ps. 22:30f.(29f.).

Ps. 21:11(10) contains a promise (wish?) addressed to the king, that he will destroy his enemies and their offspring. In the introduction to Ps. 105, those who are called upon to praise Yahweh are addressed (among other ways) as "offspring of Abraham his servant" (cf. also vv. 7ff.,10f. on Yahweh's actions on behalf of the patriarchs). The incorporation of this psalm in 1 Ch. 16 exhibits interesting changes of nuance (cf. 1 Ch. 16:19 with Ps. 105:12 and 1 Ch. 16:15 with Ps. 105:8). In 1 Ch. 16:13, the "seed of Abraham" becomes the "seed of Israel" (cf. Neh. 9:2;[67] but 2 Ch. 20:7)—probably because the seed of Abraham included Ishmael, i.e., non-Israelites, a circumstance out of keeping with the purpose of Chronicles[68] Ps. 106, an historical psalm, states that Yahweh punished those who murmured in the desert and raised his hand against them in order to disperse(?) their descendants among the nations and scatter them over the lands (vv. 27 and 47). This broad historical perspective interprets the exile as a punishment for the murmuring of the desert generation, who also scorned the land, which was therefore later taken from them. All of this signalizes the solidarity of all generations before Yahweh (cf. the Deuteronomistic history and also Deutero-Isaiah's treatment of the murmuring; is the exilic situation being addressed here as well?).

According to 2 Ch. 20:7, Jehoshaphat refers in his prayer of lament and petition to Yahweh's gift of the land to the "descendants of Abraham thy friend" (cf. Isa. 41:8) as grounds for having his prayer heard (cf. Neh. 9:8; vv. 7f. presuppose the combination JEP). In Neh. 9:2, "seed of Israel" designates the true community of the returnees, the cultic community that sets itself apart from all those of alien descent. Ezra likewise laments (Ezr. 9:2) that, as a result of mixed marriages, the "holy race" (cf. Isa. 6:13!—important for the way the postexilic community understands itself as a "remnant") has mixed itself with the peoples of the lands. Many of those returning could not prove their true Israelite descent and therefore named the places where they had been in exile (Ezr. 2:59; cf. Neh. 7:61). At this precise moment in history it was crucial to know whether one really belonged to the true descendants of Israel, the "seed of the Jews" (cf. Est. 6:13, from the mouth of a non-Jew!), so that nothing might prevail against such a one. What Mordecai did benefited all his people, not just his own

---

[66]Cf. J. Becker, *Israel deutet seine Psalmen. SBS,* 18 (1966).

[67]See below.

[68]But cf. also T. Willi, *Die Chronik als Auslegung. FRLANT,* 106 (1972), 163, n. 209.

descendants (Est. 10:3). Est. 9:27f. emphasize the way in which the observance and duration of Purim are to be fixed for succeeding generations.

9. *Judgment and Salvation in Prophecy.* As "offspring of evildoers" (Isa. 1:4; cf. Ps. 37:28), Israel is bewailed (→ הוי *hôy*) by Isaiah; *zera'* in the sense of "kindred" (cf. Isa. 14:20; 57:3f.; Ps. 37:28) stands in parallel to *bānîm* and is interpreted in the sense of *'am* and *gôy*. Babylon and its king are also spoken of as the descendants of evildoers, and the wicked ruler will have no descendants (Isa. 14:20). To address people as a perverse and adulterous generation (Isa. 57:3f.) itself implies an accusation. In Jer. 7:15 (probably secondary), Yahweh announces the exile of the Judahites, "as I cast out . . . all the offspring of Ephraim." Shemaiah and his descendants are to be punished and exterminated (Jer. 29:32), like the children of Esau (Jer. 49:10; cf. the promise in Ps. 21:11[10]). In Ezekiel's great sermon in which he encompasses all of Israel's history, he speaks in Ezk. 20:5 of God's oath (cf. Deuteronomy, albeit here without → שׁבע *šb'*) on the day when he chose Israel, which he swore to the seed of the house of Jacob; in other words, in his first historico-theological argumentation he refers to the generation of the exodus as the descendants of Jacob, who receive the promise that Yahweh will be their God. In the mention of the exodus and descendants as well as in the appearance of the covenant formula, we may go beyond Zimmerli[69] in noting the close connection with P here. If Israel had obeyed the commandments of Yahweh, its descendants would have been like the sand of the sea (from the secondary material in Isa. 48:19). The fact that only a few prophetic texts extend their announcements of judgment to the descendants of those addressed may underscore what was said above (v. 7) with respect to curses.

In the prophets the extensions of promises of salvation (cf. blessings) to descendants as well is much more common, beginning with the exilic situation of Deutero-Isaiah.[70] Israel, i.e., the exilic community, is the "seed of Abraham, my friend," as the legitimate heir of Abraham and the promises made to him (Isa. 41:8;[71] cf. also 51:2, where Abraham is called "your father"; 45:25, "offspring of Israel," and 45:19, "offspring of Jacob," as terms for the exilic community; cf. P and V.4 above).[72] Yahweh did not say to the offspring of Jacob that they would seek him in vain (Isa. 45:19). Yahweh will pour his spirit upon "your descendants" that they may spring up, which recalls the promise of many descendants made to the fathers (44:3). Yahweh will bring "your offspring" from the east (43:5). Israel's descendants will spread abroad and possess the nations (54:3; the promise of many descendants reappears with the promise of a blessing), and in Yahweh all the offspring of Israel shall triumph and glory (45:25), which in this context refers also to all the nations (vv. 20,22). Only in 55:10 does Deutero-Isaiah use *zera'* in the literal sense of "seed," and even there it is

---

[69]W. Zimmerli, *BK*, XIII (1969), *in loc.*

[70]On the passages in Deutero-Isaiah, see P. E. Bonnard, *Le Second Isaïe. ÉtB* (1972), 511.

[71]Not secondary; R. P. Merendino, "Literarkritisches, Gattungskritisches und Exegetisches zu Jes 41:8-16," *Bibl*, 53 (1972), 1-42.

[72]See also A. Eitz, *Studien zum Verhältnis von Priesterschrift und Deuterojesaja* (diss., Heidelberg, 1969), 72ff.; also 15f., where, however, more needs to be said.

placed in parallel with the word of Yahweh and its efficacy. In 53:10, the Servant of God is promised, when and because he makes his life an offering for sin (→ אשׁם *ʾāshām*), that he shall have *zeraʿ* and (in them?) prolong his days; v. 10b suggests that this promise be interpreted to mean that he will achieve what is pleasing to Yahweh. His fate will have a beneficial and positive effect. There is no suggestion of spiritual descendants, the devout.

Texts from the Deuteronomistic sections of Jeremiah and other later additions make similar promises: Yahweh (pictured as a sower, as in Hos. 2:25[23]?) will sow the house of Israel and the house of Judah with the seed of man and the seed of beast (Jer. 31:27), which combines the promise of many descendants and a new gift of the land with a promise of the land, using the terminology of a new creation. Renewed attention to these promises clearly played an important role in the exilic and postexilic period. In Jer. 46:27 (cf. 30:10f.; genuine?), Yahweh promises his servant Jacob/Israel together with his offspring deliverance from the land of their captivity (cf. 23:7f. [Deuteronomistic]; like 16:14f. with the addition of *zeraʿ*), and the descendants of Israel shall never cease to be Yahweh's people, nor shall they be cast off by him, just as the order of creation established by Yahweh shall never totter (cf. 31:35f.; 33:25f.; Gen. 8:21f.).

How important throughout the exile and afterward was the question of the legitimate "descendants" of Israel, the fathers, their promises (cf. Ezra, Nehemiah, Chronicles), and their salvation is also shown by texts from the postexilic prophets. The postexilic community was promised that the spirit and the word of Yahweh would never depart "out of your mouth, or out of the mouth of your children, or out of the mouth of your children's children"(!) (Isa. 59:21; possibly to be connected with 66:22-24?). Israel will be recognized by the nations as a people blessed by Yahweh, i.e., as the community of the age of salvation (61:9; cf. 65:23). In 65:9, the postexilic community receives once more the promise of the land and many descendants; the offspring of the eschatological community of the devout will remain before Yahweh in the new heaven and the new earth (66:22). This postexilic self-understanding of Israel also appears to be the best context in which to place the secondary addition to 6:13 with its "holy seed"; here, too, the "remnant" is envisaged as the delivered eschatological community. In the coming age of salvation the remnant community will sow in peace (*zeraʿ hashshālôm,* Zec. 8:12; or "I will sow salvation"?[73]).

10. *Summary*. The metaphorical use of the verb and noun *zrʿ* and related terms serves in the OT to express essential ideas. The solidarity of a patriarchal ancestor with his descendants, of the people with their descendants, in fact the question of "descendants" in general, are important to the worldly piety of the OT. The patriarch lives on in his descendants, in them his vital force is unfolded. Therefore the principal form of blessing is the gift of descendants. Whoever has descendants lives, and his life has a future. The concept of corporate personality and the solidarity of the devout individual with his descendants[74] plays a role here. Beyond that, however, the fates of an ancestor

---

[73] *BHS* and K. Elliger, *ATD,* XXV ([6]1967), *in loc.*

[74] De Fraine.

and his offspring constitute a single chain. The descendants bear the stamp of their father, both positive and negative, even—in fact especially—in their relationship to God. The sequence of generations, the notion of genealogy, is also projected into the future through *zeraʿ* and given importance. A man's name (→ שֵׁם *shēm*) also lives on in his descendants; here there enters in the idea of history, which not infrequently (*zeraʿ!*) is looked upon as a history of promise. Thus *zeraʿ* articulates more than mere blood relationship, a shared heritage and growth; it also indicates more than the intimate solidarity of the individual with the fathers and the people.[75] It expresses an organic cohesion within history under the same God, under his guidance in judgment and salvation, the unfolding into the future of the gifts given and promised to the fathers by Yahweh, and the assurance of standing in this heritage and being able to apply it to oneself. It should be emphasized in closing that, despite all the emphasis the OT places on "descendants," they play no role in any ancestor worship or cult of the dead.

Preuss

---

[75]Scharbert, 8.

זָרַק *zāraq*; מִזְרָק *mizrāq*

Contents: I. Etymology, Meaning, Occurrences. II. Sacrifice. III. Purification. IV. Mourning. V. Secular Use. VI. *mizrāq*. VII. Qumran. VIII. LXX.

I. Etymology, Meaning, Occurrences. Heb. *zāraq* corresponds to Aram. (Jewish Aram., Samar., Syr., Mand.) *zᵉraq*, "sprinkle, throw," Akk. *zarāqu*, "sprinkle (liquids)";[1] cf. also Arab. *zaraqa/ḏaraqa*, "drop excrement."

In Hebrew, *zāraq* means "pour out, sprinkle" when the object is a liquid; no instrument is ever mentioned. When the object is solid or dry, *zāraq* means "scatter." According to Ex. 9:8 and Ezk. 10:2, this is done by hand.

The verb appears 32 times in the qal and twice in the pual. It is found most often in ritual contexts, where its object can be blood (25 times), water of purification (3 times), or dust (once). It can also be used in situations where no ritual is involved. The noun *mizrāq* occurs 32 times: in one passage (Am. 6:6) it refers to a wine bowl; elsewhere it refers to a sacrificial vessel or bowl.

---

zāraq. K. Elliger, *HAT*, 4 (1966); R. Rendtorff, *Studien zur Geschichte des Opfers im alten Israel. WMANT*, 24 (1967); N. H. Snaith, "The Sprinkling of Blood," *ExpT*, 82 (1970/71), 23f.; R. de Vaux, *Studies in OT Sacrifice* (trans. 1964).

For additional bibliography, see → דם *dām*, → זבח *zābhach*.

[1]*CAD*, XXI, 65f.

II. Sacrifice. In sacrificial rituals, *zrq* designates the moment when the blood (→ דם *dām*) of the victim is placed on or poured over the altar. As subject we find Moses (Ex. 24:6,8; 29:16,20; Lev. 8:19,24), Aaron (Lev. 9:12,18; Nu. 18:17), the king (2 K. 16:13), or a priest (Lev. 7:2,14; 17:6; 2 Ch. 29:22; 30:16; 35:11). The ritual is explained on the grounds that life is in the blood (Gen. 9:4; Lev. 17:11,14; Dt. 12:23), which is therefore assigned to the altar to make atonement. The act of *zāraq dām* forms part of the ritual of the *ʿôlāh* (Ex. 29:16; Lev. 1:5,11; 8:19; 9:12; 2 K. 16:15; Ezk. 43:18; 2 Ch. 29:22), the *zebhach shᵉlāmîm* (Ex. 24:6; Lev. 3:2,8,13; 9:18; 17:6), the *shᵉlāmîm* (Lev. 7:14; 2 K. 16:13), the *ʾāshām* (Lev. 7:2), the *zebhach milluʾîm* (Ex. 29:20; Lev. 8:24), and the *bᵉkhôr* (Nu. 18:17). Both 2 Ch. 30:15ff. and 35:11ff. are problematical, in part because *zāraq* can be construed as referring to both *pesach* and *ʿôlāh,* and in part because it is not clear what the blood is sprinkled or thrown on. When the covenant between Yahweh and Israel was made, Moses threw half the blood on the altar and the other half, the "blood of the covenant," on the people (Ex. 24:6,8). It is noteworthy that this is the only instance of two *zāraq* rituals on the same occasion.

The corresponding portion of the ritual for the *chaṭṭāʾth* offering comprises three elements: (a) sprinkling (*hizzāh*; → נזה *nzh*) of blood with a finger seven times before Yahweh (Lev. 4:6,17; 5:9); (b) putting (*nāthan*) blood on the horns of the altar of incense (Lev. 4:7,18,25,30,34); and (c) pouring out (*shāphakh*) the remaining blood at the foot of the altar of burnt-offering (*ibid.*). The verb *nāthan* is also used for putting blood on various parts of the body (Ex. 29:20; Lev. 8:23; 14:14,17,25,28); *hizzāh* is used for sprinkling blood (or blood and oil) on clothing (Ex. 29:21; Lev. 8:30) during rites of consecration and purification.

III. Purification. Someone who has been made unclean by touching a dead person must be purified by having *mê niddāh* thrown upon him (Nu. 19:13,20); the verb *hizzāh* can also be used (vv. 18–21), and the sprinkling can be done with hyssop (v. 19).

When Ezekiel speaks in chap. 36 of the restoration of Israel, he says in v. 25 that Yahweh will cleanse the children of Israel from all their idols by sprinkling them with *mayim ṭᵉhôrîm*. This can be interpreted "as an introductory ritual action intended to remove the old uncleanness, especially that of the *gillulîm,*"[2] or it can be taken symbolically (cf. Ps. 51:9 [Eng. v. 7]).[3]

IV. Mourning. In Job 2:12, we find the expression *zāraq ʿāphār ʿal-roʾshêhem hashshāmāimāh* as a token of mourning. This ritual is also mentioned in Josh. 7:6; 1 S. 4:12; 2 S. 13:19; Ezk. 27:30; Lam. 2:10, but in the variant form *ʿālāh ʿāphār ʿal rōʾsh*. In Job 2:12, the two expressions (of which the former is primary) are joined together.[4] The ritual presupposes that Job's friends think that someone has maliciously brought all Job's troubles upon him and therefore throw ashes up toward heaven to call down a similar punishment (cf. Ex. 9:8,10). The ritual can also mean that Job's friends expect his imminent death.

---

[2] W. Zimmerli, *BK,* XIII (1969), 879.
[3] W. Eichrodt, *Ezekiel. OTL* (trans. 1970), 497f.
[4] G. Fohrer, *KAT,* XVI (1963), 106.

V. Secular Use. The sixth Egyptian plague is brought about by Moses' taking ashes from a kiln and throwing (*zrq*) them toward heaven, which causes a plague of boils (Ex. 9:8,10). "There may have been a popular notion that skin diseases were caused by 'dust.' "[5] In Ezk. 10:2, the man clothed in linen receives the directive to "scatter" glowing coals over Jerusalem; the point of the vision is the destruction of the city. When Josiah pulverizes the idols, he "strews" their dust (*daq*) over the graves of those who had sacrificed to them (2 Ch. 34:4). In Isa. 28:25, *zrq* is used synonymously with *hēphîts* and *śîm* as a term for sowing. The expression *gam śêbhāh zār^{e}qāh bô* in Hos. 7:9 is difficult; usually the pual is read instead of the qal: "gray hairs are sprinkled." Other suggestions cite Arab. *zaraqa,* "penetrate": "old age has crept up";[6] or Arab. *ḏariqa,* "be blue or gray."[7]

VI. mizrāq. All but one of the 32 occurrences of *mizrāq* indicate that the word refers to a cultic object. The exception is Am. 6:6, *mizr^{e}qê yayin,* where, however, the LXX reads *yayin m^{e}zuqqāq,* "filtered wine." Among the cultic occurrences, Nu. 7:13,19,25,31,37,43,49,55,61,67,73,79,84f. constitute a special group. Here the *mizrāqîm* (masc. pl.!) contain flour and oil, and are used for a cereal-offering (*minchāh*). In this case the bowls are silver.

Most of the occurrences of *mizrāq* exhibit a clear association of *mizrāq* with *mizbēach*. The plainest is Zec. 9:15: "They shall . . . be full [of blood] like a bowl, drenched like the corners of the altar." The 50 bowls in Neh. 7:69(70) are not specified more precisely, but the context suggests cultic use. There are *mizrāqôth* (fem. ending!) of copper and of gold; the former (Ex. 27:3; 38:3; 1 K. 7:40,45; Jer. 52:18; 2 Ch. 4:11) go with the copper altar of burnt-offering, but their function is obscure; the latter are mentioned in connection with the incense altar or the table for the bread of the Presence (Nu. 4:14; 1 K. 7:50; 2 K. 12:14(13); 25:15; Jer. 52:19; 1 Ch. 28:17; 2 Ch. 4:8,11, 22), but again nothing is said about their function. It is noteworthy that the verb *zāraq* never appears in combination with *mizrāq*.

VII. Qumran. Among the Dead Sea Scrolls, *zrq* (pl. *zrqwt*) appears only in the War Scroll, where it refers to a weapon (*zrqwt mlḥmh,* 1QM 6:2,3,16; 8:11), obviously a lance or the like (cf. Arab. *mizrāq,* "lance"; *zaraqat,* "lance thrust").[8]

VIII. LXX. When the object is "blood," the LXX renders *zrq* by means of *proscheín,* except in Ex. 24:8 (*kataskedánnymi*) and 2 Ch. 30:16 (*déchesthai*). *Proscheín* is also used for *shāphakh* in Dt. 12:27. When blood is not involved, the translation varies: *pássō* (Ex. 9:8,10), *perirraínō* (Nu. 19:13,20), *speírō* (Isa. 28:25), *diaskorpízō* (Ezk. 10:2), *poliaí exḗnthēsan autṓ* (Hos. 7:9), *rhaínō* (Ezk. 36:25),

---

[5] M. Noth, *Exodus. OTL* (trans. 1962), 79.

[6] J. Blau, "Etymologische Untersuchungen auf Grund des palästinischen Arabisch," *VT,* 5 (1955), 341.

[7] G. R. Driver, "Studies in the Vocabulary of the OT IV," *JTS,* 33 (1931/32), 38.

[8] Y. Yadin, *The Scroll of the War of the Sons of Light against the Sons of Darkness* (1962), 131f.

katapássō (Job 2:12), and *rhíptō* (2 Ch. 34:4). The noun *mizrāq* is usually translated *phiálē* (in Jer. 52:19, the LXX reads *mᵉzammᵉrôth;* in 2 Ch. 4:11, the word is untranslated).

André

חָבָא *chābhā'*; **חָבָה** *chābhāh;* **מַחֲבֵא** *machᵃbhē';* **מַחֲבֹאִים** *machᵃbhō'îm;* **חֶבְיוֹן** *chebhyôn*

Contents: I. Root: 1. Etymology; 2. Occurrences; 3. Meaning. II. General Use: 1. Literal; 2. Figurative. III. Theological Use. IV. Derivatives.

I. Root.

1. *Etymology*. The root *ḥb'* (by-form *ḥbh*) is widely distributed among the Semitic languages. It occurs in Akkadian (rarely), Old South Arabic, Canaanite (East Canaanite), Middle Hebrew, Syriac, Jewish Aramaic, and Ethiopic. Thus far, it does not appear to have been found in Ugaritic. Its basic meaning can be rendered in English as "hide" or "conceal," reflexively "hide or conceal oneself." In both ancient and modern Syriac the root involves the notion of "darkness," "being blacked out."

2. *Occurrences*. In the OT, *ḥb'* in its various forms occurs 34 times as a verb; the by-form *ḥbh* occurs 4 times, to judge strictly by the consonantal skeleton. Each of the three derived nouns occurs once. The verb appears in the niphal, pual, hiphil, hophal, and hithpael; *ḥbh* occurs once in the qal, with no difference in meaning from the niphal. The limited sample makes it difficult to draw conclusions about the use of the root in specific literary contexts from its distribution. It is noteworthy, however, that it is used predominantly in narrative texts. It is likewise impossible to define a specific period when the word was especially favored.

3. *Meaning*. The meaning hardly ever diverges from the basic meaning given above. The primary meaning, "hide oneself," is given by the niphal; the hiphil adds the causative and thus transitive meaning, "cause someone to hide himself, conceal." The other stems do not convey a characteristic sense; their meaning must be determined from the context.[1] Apart from the few instances of figurative use, *chābhā'* refers to persons. The action it denotes occurs in the context of pursuit and flight. The purpose is to assure safety when an opponent cannot be overcome. To "hide" means "escape the grasp of someone, vanish from someone's sight." This concept undoubtedly involves

[1] *KBL*[3] translates the hithpael as *sich versteckt halten,* "keep oneself in hiding."

not only the element of motion in escape, but also the element of being no longer perceptible to the senses. "Hiding" includes a locality, a hiding place to which it is possible to retreat unseen. Hiding is always a reaction to being taken by surprise; it provides protection and security against a real or potential threat, or at least has such protection as its purpose.

II. General Use.

1. *Literal.* In the majority of occurrences, both niphal and hiphil, the verb is used in its literal sense. In the story of the spies in Josh. 2, Rahab advises the two "men of Israel" to hide themselves (v. 16; *ḥb'* niphal) in the hills from the pursuers sent by the city-king of Jericho. According to the narrative, Rahab had earlier hidden (→ טמן *ṭāman*) them on the roof of her house. This event is referred to again later in Josh. 6:17, 25 (*ḥb'* hiphil; the archaic form in v. 17 is usually corrected after the model of v. 25). The same sequence of threat, flight, and hiding is contained in the narrative of five kings slain in a cave at Makkedah (Josh. 10:16f.,27).[2] Both passages deal with the capture of enemies, who flee (→ נוס *nûs*) and hide to escape the peril. The corresponding antonyms are "pursue" (→ רדף *rādhaph*), "find" (→ מצא *mātsā'*), "seek" (→ בקש *biqqēsh*), and "seize" (→ לכד *lākhadh*); cf. 2 Ch. 22:9. Uninhabited mountain regions, a cave, and the roof of a house piled high with flax are mentioned as potential hiding places.

The act of hiding does not in itself guarantee security. The five Canaanite kings are discovered in their cave and slain (Josh. 10); Ahaziah is likewise seized at Samaria and put to death (2 Ch. 22:9). Jotham, on the contrary, escapes by hiding (Jgs. 9:5). David, too, successfully escapes Saul's pursuit; on Jonathan's advice he stays in a secret place (*bassēther*) and hides himself (1 S. 19:2).

Successful flight demands not only mobility but also sagacity. According to 1 S. 23:23 (cf. 22), David ceases his *hithchabbē'* when Saul takes vigorous action, as expressed in the orders he gives his officers: *l^ekhû-nā' hākhînû ʿôdh ûdh^eʿû ûr^e'û 'eth-m^eqômô* (v. 22), *ûr^e'û ûdh^eʿû mikkōl hammach^abhō'îm '^asher yithchabbē' shām*—actions whose urgency is justified on the grounds of David's special cunning (*ʿārôm yaʿrim hû'*, v. 22). In the story of Absalom's revolt, too, David is depicted as cunning and experienced in his ability to elude his enemies. We read in 2 S. 17:9: *hû' nechbā' b^e'achath happ^echāthîm 'ô b^e'achadh hamm^eqômōth.* The context leaves open the possibility that this hiding is not just a defensive measure, but a military strategem aimed at the enemy, like that used by the Syrians at the time of Elisha and explicitly mentioned in 2 K. 7:12 (*ḥbh* niphal, but pointed like *ḥb'*). In military engagements, flight and hiding are often enough a mass phenomenon, as exemplified in the account of the skirmishes between Israelites and Philistines in the time of Saul (1 S. 13:6; 14:11,22). Here we also find mention of a wide range of hiding places: caves, holes, rocks, tombs, and cisterns (13:6), as well as clefts in rocks, and mountainous areas (14:11,22). In this context, the term *ḥb'* (hithpael) can be correctly rendered as "sneak away." In the eyes of the pursuer, the hiding of his quarry is contemptible. The

[2] Cf. M. Noth, *HAT*, 7 ([3]1971), *in loc.*

Philistines make ironic and disdainful comments when Jonathan and his armor-bearer crawl out of the *chōrîm* (*'ᵃsher hithchabbᵉ'û-shām*) (14:11). In 2 K. 11:3 (cf. 2 Ch. 22:12), *ḥb'* (hithpael) is to be understood as a passive. Joash, together with his aunt, was hidden (participle) in the temple from his bloodthirsty grandmother Athaliah. The state of being hidden is the result of a series of actions: the aunt of Joash (Jehosheba) takes (*lāqach*) Joash, steals (*gānabh*) him from among the king's sons who are about to be slain, and hides (→ סתר *sāthar* hiphil) him and his nurse temporarily in a bedchamber, until the temple becomes a safe hiding place (v. 2). As in Josh. 6:17, 25, we can speak of an indirect act of hiding oneself, in the one case indicated directly by the hiphil, in the other by the sequence of actions leading up to the state of being hidden. Another person undertakes the action of hiding on behalf of an endangered person, who for some reason cannot act for himself. In one instance it is an innocent child that is rescued (cf. also 2 K. 6:29), in another it is the spies who must not come to harm (law of hospitality), and in 1 K. 18:4, 13 it is the prophets of Yahweh, pursued by Jezebel the queen, whom Obadiah, the *'al-habbāyith* of Ahab, hides in a cave. The act of hiding another includes providing him with the necessities of life. Obadiah brings bread and water to the hidden prophets. This social aspect is well expressed in the hiphil passages, while the niphal and hithpael passages place more emphasis on self-preservation. Both functions presuppose the same situation: threat, pursuit, and an attempt on the life of the quarry. The endangered individual or someone acting in his behalf learns of the threat, reacts by fleeing and hiding himself or the endangered person, and, in the latter case, provides for his needs.

Two passages use *ḥb'* (niphal) in an unusual sense. In Gen. 31:27 (E, possibly with some J material), *ḥb'* is to be understood adverbially, although it appears as a finite verb form: "Why did you hide yourself to flee?" = "Why did you flee secretly?" It would be possible to think of the figurative use here, but the meaning is actually very close to the literal sense. With his intention to flee, Jacob hides himself from Laban; he sees a threat to his intended course of action, which he therefore renders invisible. It is clear, of course, that "hiding" is here used in a spiritualized sense.

The other passage is 1 S. 10:22, in the account of how the Israelites at Mizpah chose Saul by lot to be king (10:17-27); the entire section presents traditio-historical difficulties. The particular difficulty lies in the fact that, when Saul is chosen by lot, he is, unexpectedly, not found with his family. A second inquiry (in which the MT and LXX diverge) receives the divine response: "Behold, he has hidden himself among the baggage." None of the attempts to explain the passage[3] has been able to suggest a convincing reason for Saul's hiding. One common interpretation refers to Saul's modesty. Pending a new insight, the following alternatives appear possible: We may be dealing with nothing more than a retarding stylistic device intended to increase the tension.[4] In this case, other aspects in the narrative can be emphasized (Saul's bodily stature leads to his election;[5] the baggage suggests a military setting[6]), and no particular

---

[3]Hertzberg, Weiser, Eissfeldt, *et al.*
[4]Weiser.
[5]Eissfeldt.
[6]Hertzberg.

importance attaches to the statement *hû' nechbā'*. On the other hand, this feature of the account, and the corresponding passage 1 S. 9:21, may point to a stereotyped response of the elect to his election, the concrete details of which are no longer recoverable (cf. Ex. 3:11; 6:12; 1 S. 18:18; 2 S. 7:18ff.).

2. *Figurative*. There are only a few instances in which *ḥb'* (niphal and hiphil) is used figuratively. In wisdom discourse, the tongue can be considered a life-threatening force (through slander), from which one can be "hidden" by God (Job 5:21: *mishshôṭ*[7] *lāshôn tēchābhē'*, "You shall be hid from the scourge of the tongue . . ." [cf. Sir. 28:17; Ps. 12:3-5(2-4); etc.]). This maxim is spoken by Eliphaz the Temanite in his reply to Job's first lament; it is part and parcel of his uninterrupted theology of a secure world ordered by God, in which all that matters is trust in God.

In Job 29:8,10, *ḥb'* appears in a totally different context. Job is describing the power, influence, and respect he enjoyed in former days. When he appeared the young men "hid themselves" (*rā'ûnî n*^e*ʿārîm v*^e*nechbā'û*), a gesture of reverence and respect (v. 8), and the voice of the nobles "was hidden," i.e. "was hushed" (v. 10; many commentators place vv. 21-25 at this point). This metaphor, too, expresses respect for a man of honor. The verb *ḥb'* serves to describe a particular type of conduct, which comes across vividly through the technique of expression from the contrary. The one who "hides himself" gives precedence to the other. He does not take flight out of fear for his life: on the contrary, he finds the superior person most welcome with his counsel, his help, his presence. The most that one might claim is left of the basic meaning is that when the voice "hides itself" it is safe from being put in the wrong by the other's voice, and when the "young men" (defined legally or sociologically) hide themselves they are safe from being declared incompetent.

Finally, *ḥb'* is used figuratively in Job 38:30, in the context of God's poetic discourse on creation. The freezing of water is pictured as "waters hiding themselves in a [single] stone."[8]

The interpretation of 1 Ch. 21:20 is disputed.[9] The question is who is hiding from whom, and what this action denoted by *hithchabbē'* signifies. If we follow the MT, the verse describes the typical awe of those who experience a theophanic event from the divine realm. If we follow the LXX[10] and the parallel recension in 2 S. 24:20, changing *hammal'ākh* to *hammelekh,* the verb can refer to the awe of the Jebusite Ornan in the presence of king David. It is also unclear who is meant by the *bānāv ʿimmô*—the sons of David or the sons of Ornan. In the former case either interpretation would be possible; in the latter, we would merely be dealing with the general statement that the sons of David kept in the background during David's interview with Ornan,[11] although they were present.

---

[7]Following the apparatus in *BHK*³.

[8]Cf. G. Fohrer, *KAT,* XVI (1963), 488, 492, 507; he suggests reading *k*^e*bhā'ebhen*.

[9]Cf. W. Rudolph, *HAT,* 21 (1955), 146-48; K. Galling, *ATD,* XII (1954), 60, 62.

[10]Cf. the apparatus in *BHK*³.

[11]Galling.

III. Theological Use. Although there are not many passages illustrating the theological use of the root, we can nevertheless state that in the OT the action described by *ḥb'* can also have reference to God. This reference can be quite direct in oracles of disaster such as 1 K. 22:25 (using the by-form *l^ehēchābhēh,* where the par. 2 Ch. 18:24 uses the regular form *l^ehēchābhē'*), where Micaiah ben Imlah threatens the court prophet Zedekiah ben Chenaanah, saying that on the day of judgment he will flee from chamber to chamber to hide himself. Considered in isolation, the passage exhibits the same functional context of *ḥb'*: a threat to life, flight, hiding. Only now this sequence is consciously applied within the constraints of the announcement of disaster. Within this context the efforts to hide in safety are bound to fail. The disaster is intensified further by the fact that these efforts, doomed from the start, must nevertheless be undertaken.

The inexorability of disaster, the futility of all attempts to flee and hide, is announced in the last vision in Amos (9:1–4); v. 3 uses *ḥb'* in parallel with *str* (cf. Ps. 139 for content). The situation is similar in Jer. 49:10, in the context of an oracle against Edom. His hiding places will be stripped bare by Yahweh, so that Edom will not be able to conceal himself (once again the by-form, *v^enechbāh lō' yûkhāl*). The aggravation of Yahweh's judgment is expressed by the decree that the futile act of *hēchābhē'* must be performed.

A somewhat different meaning attaches to *ḥb'* in Isa. 42:22 (the only occurrence of the hophal). The entire passage 42:18–25 is difficult to interpret; beginning with v. 22, the statements clearly refer to the present situation of God's people, determined by his judgment, in the period following the catastrophe of 587 B.C. If Westermann is right, the statements (one of which is "hidden [or 'kept'] in prisons") are borrowed from the fixed terminology and imagery of the communal lament.[12] In this case, "hidden in prisons" would be the judgment actively carried out by Yahweh, and *ḥb'* would have something to do with the notion of exile or being exiled, losing historical existence. In the announcements of disaster discussed above, man is the subject who hides himself in the vain hope of deliverance, though it is God who sets the stage. Here, by contrast, God is to be seen as the sole agent of the hiding, and man as the logical object of the action.

Yet another variant of the theological sense of *ḥb'* appears in an announcement of disaster within the "Little Apocalypse" of Isaiah (Isa. 26:20; by-form *ḥbh* used in the qal). The people of God are counselled to hide in their chambers for a little while (cf. 1 K. 22:25) and shut their doors until judgment is past. Here the *ḥb'* act is the deliverance made possible and vouchsafed by God, which serves his intended purpose.

Not so easy to interpret is the expression *b^etsēl yādhô hechbî'ānî* in Isa. 49:2. The context is the account of the call and commission of the Servant of God. His mouth is made a sharp sword, and he himself is a polished arrow. Both statements are followed by an additional clause, the former by the one mentioned above, the latter by "in his quiver he hid me away (*histîrānî*)." Both the primary statements and the secondary clauses stand in strict parallelism. They are usually understood to indicate the special

[12] C. Westermann, *Isaiah 40–66. OTL* (trans. 1969), 112.

care and protection vouchsafed by Yahweh.[13] A direct development of the image is also conceivable: the Servant of God as a weapon in Yahweh's hand or panoply, a powerful force ready for use at any moment, but hidden, kept in reserve, invisible, albeit concretely present. The traditional interpretation would express the idea that the protective side of a *ḥb'* event (as observed in the common use of the hiphil stem of the verb) is most fully and effectually realized when God himself gives security and "hiddenness." The second suggested interpretation would see the verb used in a more general sense as a term for the potential of God's action through men. All initiative and responsibility reside in Yahweh, who uses his instrument when it suits him. He holds it ready in his hand and in his quiver; it is with him.

The problem of theodicy is addressed in Job 23–24 in the context of one of Job's discourses. The *ḥb'* passage (24:4, the only occurrence of the pual) is but one of a large number of instances illustrating the fact that God does not intervene against injustice and call the evildoer to account. The poor (*'ebhyônîm;* → אביון *'ebhyôn*) are thrust off the road and the wretched (*ʿanîyê-'ārets;* → עני *ʿānî*) have to hide themselves (*chubbeʿû*). The general state of injustice prohibits the economically powerless from appearing freely in public. The fact that the hiding is forced by circumstances God tolerates is expressed by the passive. The *ḥb'* reaction motivates and illustrates the indictment of God.

Flight and hiding as a reaction to a theophanic event can be explained on the basis of universal fear and awe when men come in direct contact with the sphere of the divine. This phenomenon undergoes a certain radicalization in Dnl. 10:7: it is not the one who sees the vision but his companions who flee in terror and hide (*vayyibhrechû behēchābhē'*), and what is actually involved is not a theophany but a vision (*hammarʿāh*). But it is probably legitimate to find theophanic elements worked into the notion developed here (cf. already Ezk. 1:1–2:2). A threat to life is posed by the sacredness of the divine sphere ("whoever sees God must die": Jgs. 6:22f.); for protection one may "fall with one's face to the ground" (the "visionary" loses his strength: Dnl. 10:8f.) or, as here, flee and hide. God himself is the threatening force. Note also how pregnantly the sequence of actions is formulated here: "and they fled in hiding (into hiding, by hiding)." Hiding is flight, and flight is hiding.

Finally, flight and hiding from God are mentioned in the so-called story of the Fall (Gen. 3:8, 10 [J]): the man and his wife vainly attempt to flee from God and senselessly hide from him (v. 8, hithpael; v. 10, niphal). At this point the term *ḥb'* is woven into the most profound theological anthropology of the Yahwist. It describes a fundamental stance of the man who turns away from God, the vain attempt to evade the question of God (both the question God asks him and his question about God). Man in his present state senses that he is called in question and therefore threatened. The functional range of *ḥb'* can be fully exploited.

Thus the OT exhibits a wide range of theological usage of the root *ḥb'*, which in its individual nuances paints a very vivid theological picture. It is a term of judgment in prophecies of disaster and a concept charged with proclaiming God's saving acts. It serves to illustrate the problem of theodicy and to describe a fundamental anthropologi-

[13] *Ibid.*, 208.

cal stance toward God. To put it in a nutshell, it denotes, according to the particular theological context, a prescribed human action, rational, or irrational, intended to preserve life. Performance of the action does not in itself guarantee success; but the action nevertheless is and must be carried out, according to God's will, for judgment or salvation.

IV. Derivatives. The noun *machᵃbhōʾîm,* found only in the plural, appears in the traditions of the conflicts between Saul and David. The events (1 S. 23:23) take place in southern Palestine, south and southeast of Hebron, in the "wilderness of Judah," where there are plenty of lurking places in which a fugitive can hide. The word *machᵃbhōʾîm* refers to such hiding places quite generally, without specifying concretely depressions, ledges, caves, etc.

The word *machᵃbhēʾ* appears in Isa. 32:2, in the context of a wisdom discourse describing the restored world metaphorically: man himself is described as a hiding place from the wind (*machᵃbhēʾ-rûach*), for others of course, and as a covert from the tempest (*sēther-zerem*). In the first instance, therefore, *machᵃbhēʾ* amounts to a general protection against inclement weather and suggests nothing more concrete. Here—as noted—it is used as a simile (with *kᵉ*), and can therefore be interpreted as any kind of instrument of salvation: man is himself presented as an occasion of salvation.

We come finally to *chebhyôn,* which appears in Hab. 3:4, in the context of a theophany. Unfortunately the meaning is not quite clear. The clause *vᵉshām chebhyôn ʿuzzōh* ("there is the covering of his power") fits poorly in its context.[14] Many scholars therefore emend or even transpose it. Even the possible translation "there is his mighty covering (raiment)" implies a specific interpretation of *chebhyôn,* albeit a likely one, since brightness and rays (mentioned in the parallel stichs of v. 4) are depicted frequently enough in theophanic accounts as the raiment of the deity.

By way of supplement, it should be noted that the proper name *ʾelyachbāʾ* may be compounded with a form of *ḥbʾ* (2 S. 23:32; 1 Ch. 11:33). If so, it would mean "God will hide." There are, however, other proposed derivations that have nothing to do with this root.[15] The name *chᵒbhaiyāh* (Ezr. 2:61; Neh. 7:63)[16] seems more clearly to derive from the root *ḥbh* as a by-form of *ḥbʾ*. The meaning would be similar to that given above: "Yahweh has hidden." The name would thus be a confession of the deity who bestows protection and security upon man (whether the bearer of the name or his parents); or, if *ʾelyachbāʾ* is construed as an imperfect or jussive, the name would indicate a hope or expectation, or even a wish or petition.[17]

Wagner

---

[14] Cf. comms. *in loc.*
[15] Cf. *KBL*³, 53f.
[16] *IPN,* 178.
[17] *Ibid.,* 179.

חבל ḥbl I; חֶבֶל chebhel I and II; חֹבֵל chōbhēl; חֹבְלִים chōbhᵉlîm; חִבֵּל chibbēl

Contents: I. 1. Etymology and Distribution; 2. The Concept in the Ancient Near East; 3. OT Occurrences; 4. LXX. II. Rope in Everyday Life: 1. As an Instrument; 2. In Military Contexts; 3. As a Measuring Line. III. Rope as a Metaphor: 1. For Snares and Death; 2. For Guilt; 3. For the Relationship between God and Man. IV. *chebhel,* "Region." V. *chōbhēl, chibbēl.* VI. *chebhel,* "Group," *chōbhᵉlîm.*

I. 1. *Etymology and Distribution.* The root *ḥbl* I is often connected with an Akkadian word *ḫabālu,* "tie, ensnare," *ḫābilu,* "hunter, trapper," *naḫbalu,* "snare."[1] But reference to Ugar. and Arab. *ḥbl* might sooner suggest *ḥ* than *ḫ* as the first radical, and thus Akk. *eblu,* "rope line,"[2] with its by-form *ḫi-ib-lum,* attested at Larsa.[3] From the latter derive the denominative verb *ebēlu,* "catch in a net,[4] tie, snare,"[5] and the occupational term *ēbilu,* "catcher" (par. *ḫābilu*). With this may be associated Ugar. *ḥbl,* "swarm,[6] flock/flight (of birds)."[7] This root is also attested in the Aramaic of Elephantine,[8] in Jewish Aram., Christian Palestinian Aram., and Syr. *ḥablāʾ,* "rope, snare,"[9] Mand. *habla* II, "rope,"[10] and MHeb.-Talm. *chebhel/chablāʾ/chablāh,* "string, rope," *chᵃbhîlāh,* "bundle."[11] In South Semitic the root is well attested: Arab. *ḥabl,* "rope, string, etc.," along with *uḥbūla* and *ḥibāla,* "snare, net," and the verb *ḥabala* VIII, "catch in a snare,"[12] Ethiop., Geʿez, Amhar., and Tigr. *ḥabᵉl,* "string, rope,"[13] Soq. *ḥabéhol,* "rope,"[14] and finally in some OSA personal names[15] and in the sense (also attested in Hebrew) "tract of land."[16]

2. *The Concept in the Ancient Near East.* In Akkadian, we find *eblu* as a "leather thong" in a list that includes water-skins, sandals, etc., obviously referring to a piece of equipment.[17] It also appears alongside bronze wires and chains as a part of various

---

[1] H. Zimmern, *Akkadische Fremdwörter als Beweis für babylonischen Kultureinfluss* (²1917), 15; *GesB,* 210; *KBL³,* 274f.

[2] *AHw,* I, 183; *CAD,* IV, 15.

[3] *CAD,* VI, 181.

[4] *AHw,* I, 181.

[5] *CAD,* IV, 8.

[6] *WUS,* No. 892.

[7] *UT,* No. 832.

[8] *DISO,* 81.

[9] *LexSyr,* 210.

[10] *MdD,* 115a.

[11] *WTM,* II, 5f.

[12] *Wehr,* 154f.

[13] W. Leslau, *Hebrew Cognates in Amharic* (1969), 44, 92; *TigrWb,* 78a.

[14] Leslau, *Lexique soqotri* (Paris, 1938), 159.

[15] G. Ryckmans, *Les noms propres sud-sémitiques. Bibliothèque du Muséon,* 2 (1934/35), I, 87.

[16] ContiRossini, 144; cf. Dt. 32:9; Ps. 105:11; etc.

[17] *ARM,* I, 17.31.

utensils[18] and as a tow-rope for ships navigating rivers and canals.[19] Leather and wool are mentioned as materials, but bast, hemp, and sisal were almost surely used as well. The word also can mean (par. *ginindanakku,* "measuring rod") the measuring line used to measure the site for a temple (cf. Zec. 2:5 [Eng. v. 1]; Ezk. 40:3).[20] Finally, *eblu* is used as a unit of area. In all these meanings and uses it is largely synonymous with *ašlu,* "rush, rope, measure of length."[21] "Ropes" found frequent use in war. There is literary reference to the practice of piercing the ears of prisoners of war and threading a string through them.[22] Esarhaddon similarly leads captured princes by two cords threaded through their lips.[23]

In Ugaritic, the meaning "band, flock" for *ḥbl*[24] is probably undisputed. It is attested eight times thus far,[25] and usually refers to a flock of an unspecified number of eagles.[26] In the corrupt text *CTA,* 4 [II AB], VII, 57,[27] Ginsberg suggests a "flock of clouds,"[28] while de Moor suggests the high-flying flights of birds that announce the sirocco.[29] The phrase *ḥbl-kṯrt,*[30] "band of the Kathirat,"[31] "swallows,"[32] "band of songstresses,"[33] probably implies a mythological image that cannot now be defined more precisely. In *PRU,* II, 128, 30f. (a commercial document), despite the uncertain context, *ḥblm* probably refers to some kind of implement; *PRU* suggests ropes.

In the everyday life of the Palestinian Bedouins, ropes were used primarily to stretch tent coverings between their poles.[34]

3. *OT Occurrences.* In the OT, there are 34 occurrences of *chebhel,* "rope, cord." The majority are found in the preexilic prophets and Wisdom Literature (12 each); 9 appear in the Deuteronomistic history, and there is one occurrence in Sir. 6:29. The word appears 14 times in the sense of "region" (8 times in Deuteronomy and the Deuteronomistic history, only 4 times in the prophets). The special meaning "band" appears in only one passage, 1 Sam. 10:5, 10.

The word *chōbhēl,* "sailor," appears in Jonah 1:6 and four times in a tradition recorded in Ezk. 27. The word *chibbēl,* "rigging(?)," found in Prov. 23:34, is related. The meaning of *chōbhᵉlîm* (Zec. 11:7,14) is disputed.

---

18 *OIP,* II, 110 VII 46; cf. *šummannu būrti,* "well rope."
19 *CAD,* IV, 15.
20 S. H. Langdon, *Die neubabylonischen Königsinschriften. VAB,* IV (1912), 62, 29.
21 *AHw,* I, 81; *BUA,* I, 358.
22 *KAV,* 1, V, 85.
23 *BuA,* II, 328 and Fig. 38; cf. also *ANEP,* 1, 7, 8, 9, 326, 447; similarly 1 K. 20:31f.
24 *WUS,* No. 892; *UT,* No. 832.
25 Whitaker, 255.
26 *CTA,* 19 [I D], I, 33; 18 [III D], IV, 20, 31.
27 Cf. *CTA,* 8 [II AB Var.], 10.
28 *ANET,* 135.
29 J. C. de Moor, *The Seasonal Pattern in the Ugaritic Myth of Baʿlu. AOAT,* 16 (1971), 164, 173-76.
30 *CTA,* 11 [IV AB], I, 6.
31 *CML,* 120f.
32 Virolleaud, de Moor.
33 Gordon.
34 *AuS,* VI (1939), 31.

The Qumran documents (1QH and CD) use only *chebhel,* "rope." The verb *ḥbl* is attested only in Sir. 34:6, where it has the passive sense "be ensnared (in greed for gold)." For its use in the Talmud, cf. Levy, *WTM,* II, 6.

4. *LXX.* In most cases, the LXX translates *chebhel* as *schoínos, schoiníon,* or *schoínisma* (23 times). In 5 cases, it reads *ḥbl* III (Hos. 11:4) or IV (2 S. 22:6; Ps. 18:5f.[4f.]; 116:3) or paraphrases with *rhinón* (Job 40:25) or *seirós* (Prov. 5:22). The LXX also uses *schoínisma* to translate 9 of the 14 occurrences of *chebhel,* "region," for which it elsewhere uses *períchōron* (Dt. 3) or *klḗros* (Josh. 19:9), and to render the name of the second staff in Zec. 11:7,14. *Chōbhél* is rendered *kybernḗtēs* (used also for *chibbēl*) or *prōreús.* The Vulgate translates *chebhel* as *funis* or *funiculus,* rarely as *regio.*

II. Rope in Everyday Life.

1. *As an Instrument.* Ropes are frequently mentioned in the OT as objects of everyday use,[35] without further details being supplied. Thus ropes are most often singled out for special mention when there is something out of the ordinary about them. They may be made of some valuable materials, such as silver (Eccl. 12:6) or fine linen and purple (Est. 1:6), or they may be finely crafted as gifts or items of commerce: *chᵃbhushîm,* "twisted," and *ʾᵃruzîm,* "secure" (Ezk. 27:24). For ritual use, the Talmud mentions cords of rushes, willows, and flax.[36] A *chebhel* clearly was not counted among the *mighbālôth,* "cords" (Ex. 28:14), *sharshᵉrôth,* "chains" (Ex. 28:14, etc.), and *tsavrōnîm,* "necklaces" (Cant. 4:9), etc. used as jewelry. Besides being used in the pitching of tents (Isa. 33:20)—albeit never in the context of the tabernacle—and the rigging of ships (Isa. 33:23),[37] ropes were probably used primarily to tie animals to stakes. This usage may be observed in the phrase (reconstructed on the basis of the LXX) *chabhlê hashshôr,* "ox's halter."[38] Ropes were used together with rush cords (*ʾaghmôn*) and fishhooks (*chakkāh*) in the hunting of crocodiles (Job 40:25f.[41:1f.]), and along with nets (*resheth*), snares (*pach*), and traps (*môqēsh*) for hunting in the bush (Ps. 140:6[5]; cf. Job 18:10 and Sir. 6:29).[39] Finally, ropes were used along with chains as part of the mechanism for drawing water from wells and cisterns.[40] It is possible that such ropes were used to let the prophet Jeremiah down (*shālach*) into the muddy cistern and then to lift him out (*māshakh*) secretly later (Jer. 38:6,11–13).

---

35 *Ibid.*

36 Jer. *Shab.* vii.10c.

37 For the region of Mesopotamia, cf. A. Salonen, *Die Wasserfahrzeuge in Babylonien. StOr,* 8/4 (1939); *idem, Nautica Babyloniaca. StOr,* 11/1 (1942).

38 Jerusalem Bible; similarly Dahood and Kaiser; this interpretation is rejected by H. Wildberger, *BK,* X/1 (1972), 175f.

39 On the further metaphorical use of these hunt motifs, cf. III.1 and I. Scheftelowitz, *Das Schlingen- und Netzmotiv im Glauben und Brauch der Völker. RVV,* 12/2 (1912).

40 *AuS,* II (1932), 222f.; CD 11:17.

2. *In Military Contexts.* Ropes and cords were also frequently employed in military contexts. By means of a rope (*bachebhel,* Josh. 2:15), for example, Rahab let Joshua's spies down (*yrd* hiphil) through a window in the city wall, enabling them to escape (cf. 1 S. 19:12; Acts 9:25; 2 Cor. 11:33). This rope was certainly not identical with the "scarlet cord" (*tiqvath hashshānî*) or "scarlet thread" (*chûṭ hashshānî*) mentioned in 2:18–22, which was meant to mark the house for protection when the city was taken. The interpretation proposed by Asmussen[41] is mistaken: he suggests a kind of flag designating Rahab's house as a house of prostitution. A different use of rope in military technology is apparently alluded to in 2 S. 17:13, which states that all Israel will bring ropes to drag the rebellious city into the valley. Perhaps behind the "rhetorical exaggeration"[42] here we may perceive the military technique of using ropes attached to grappling hooks to storm a wall.

The practice of binding prisoners of war with cords or chains, or even leading them by cords passed through their lips or earlobes, is well attested.[43] Conversely, it is to be taken as a sign of submission (not mourning) when Ben-hadad and his officials put *chᵃbhālîm* upon their heads (1 K. 20:31f.),[44] thus offering themselves to the Israelite king as prisoners.

3. *As a Measuring Line.* Like Akk. *eblu, chebhel* can mean both a measuring instrument and a (relative) unit of length. Both meanings occur together in 2 S. 8:2. Here David's "measuring" of the captured Moabites with a measuring line is equivalent to counting off two thirds (*shᵉnê chᵃbhālîm*) to be executed and one third (*mᵉlō' hachebhel*) to be spared.

The measuring line (*chebhel middāh*) played a special role in surveying (cf. its use in the rebuilding of a city and its wall in Zec. 2:5[1];[45] also the similar expressions *qᵉvēh hammiddāh,* "measuring line" [Jer. 31:39], and *qᵉnēh hammiddāh,* "measuring reed" [Ezk. 40:3, 5]) and the distribution of estates.[46] Here *chebhel* is often synonymous with → גורל *gôrāl,* "lot, portion." The latter plays a role primarily in the initial division of the land (Josh. 14–15); in later reminiscences it can be accompanied or replaced by *chebhel.* Ps. 78:55 extols Yahweh's great deed in apportioning (*nāphal* hiphil) his people their *nachᵃlāh* with a measuring line. It is reason for confidence on the part of the worshipper that his line has fallen (*nāphal*) on good ground (Ps. 16:6; par. terms: *chēleq, gôrāl, nachᵃlāh*); in Yahweh he has his chosen portion.[47] But when a *chebhel* is stretched upon the land, the element of chance (→ גורל *gôrāl*)

---

[41] J. P. Asmussen, "Bemerkungen zur sakralen Prostitution im AT," *StTh,* 11 (1957 [1958]), 182.

[42] Goldman.

[43] See I.2.

[44] Cf. E. Kutsch, " 'Trauerbräuche' und 'Selbstminderungsriten' im AT," *ThSt,* 78 (1965), 25–42, esp. 30.

[45] K. Seybold, "Die Bildmotive in den Visionen des Propheten Sacharja," *Studies on Prophecy. SVT,* 26 (1974), 92–110; *idem, Bilder zum Tempelbau. SBS,* 70 (1974), 54f.

[46] *B. Bath.* 103b.

[47] H.-J. Kraus, *BK,* XV/1 (⁴1972), 123; W. Dommershausen, "Das 'Los' in der alttestamentlichen Theologie," *TrThZ,* 80 (1971), 205.

vanishes and the intentions of the surveyor become important. It is therefore a sign of Yahweh's judgment when he reapportions (*chālaq*) the land with a line (Am. 7:17; cf. the similar function of the *ʼanākh,* "plumb line(?)," in Am. 7:7 and the phrase *eblum limdudušsu* in the Alalakh text Idrimi 95[48]).

The measuring line took on special significance in the Year of Release (→ דרור *d^erôr,* → יובל *yôbhel,* → שמטה *sh^emiṭṭāh*). With its aid, ancestral property was restored at regular intervals,[49] reestablishing the initial situation of the sacral division of the land.

When Yahweh threatens through his prophet (Mic. 2:4f., where *chebhel* may be a gloss[50]) that this survey will not be carried out, it means that the sinful nation has lost its claim to the heritage of Yahweh.

III. Rope as a Metaphor.

1. *For Snares and Death.* The metaphorical use of *chebhel* is concentrated for the most part in the Psalms and Wisdom Literature. From the terminology of the hunt are borrowed images and motifs that illustrate the situation of being beset by enemies. The "cords of the wicked" (*chebhlê r^eshāʻîm*) ensnare (*ʻivvēdh*) the devout (Ps. 119:61; par. "they have dug pitfalls [*shîchôth*]," v. 85; "they have laid a snare [*pach*]," v. 110), and the latter can protect themselves only by reliance on the Torah of Yahweh. With systematic cunning (*pach, ch^abhālîm, resheth,* and *mōq^eshîm*) the arrogant attempt to destroy the devout (Ps. 140:6[5]).

In a series of passages we encounter the *chebhlê māveth,* "cords of death" (Ps. 18:5[4]; 116:3), and *chebhlê sh^eʼôl,* "cords of Sheol" (2 S. 22:6; Ps. 18:6[5]; 1QH 3:9), which are meant to show the imminent mortal danger to which the worshipper is exposed. In combination with the *mōq^eshê-māveth,* "snares of death," *nach^alê bh^elîyaʻal,* "torrents of perdition," *m^etsārê sh^eʼôl,* "pangs of Sheol," etc., the *ch^abhālîm* illustrate the tight constraint exercised by the powers of the underworld. The worshipper sees himself already there, entwined in the bonds of death; only Yahweh can deliver him and save him.[52] Eccl. 12:6 characterizes the sudden end brought about by death: ". . . the silver cord is snapped, . . . the golden bowl is broken," i.e., even the most precious objects are fragile and useless when man senses the approach of death.

2. *For Guilt.* The term *chebhel* is sometimes adopted as a metaphor to illustrate the guilty state of man, especially the firm tie that binds him to the sin he has committed (Isa. 5:18; Prov. 5:22; Job 18:10; 36:8; 1QH 3:28): the sinner is "caught in the toils of his sin (*b^echabhlê chaṭṭāʼthô*)" and his iniquities ensnare (*lākhadh*) him (Prov. 5:22).

---

[48]Cf. M. Tsevat, "Alalakhiana," *HUCA,* 29 (1958), 109-134, esp. 124.

[49]Cf. A. Alt, "Micha 2, 1-5 ΓΗΣ ΑΝΑΔΑΣΜΟΣ in Juda," *Interpretationes ad Vetus Testamentum Pertinentes. Festschrift S. Mowinckel* (Oslo, 1955), 13-23 = *KlSchr,* III (1959), 373-381, esp. 377ff.

[50]Cf. H. Donner, "Die soziale Botschaft der Propheten im Lichte der Gesellschaftsordnung in Israel," *OrAnt,* 2 (1963), 239.

[51]MT, Weiser; but cf. *BHS,* Gunkel, Kraus, Gamberoni → חבל *chābhal* III, II.4, all of whom are probably correct in reading here *chōbh^elîm,* "villains," par. *gēʼîm.*

[52]Cf. C. Barth, *Die Errettung vom Tode* (1947), 106.

Bildad elaborates the image with additional motifs from the hunt (Job 18:10), which are meant to show as a logical consequence how the traps laid by the hunter finally ensnare the hunter himself. In their arrogance, men even draw *ʿāvôn* and *chaṭṭāʾth* with "cords of falsehood (*chabhlê hashshāv*)" (Isa. 5:18 MT). Whether this refers to magical rites[53] cannot be determined with certainty.[54] For Elihu, the fact that a man is caught in the "cords of affliction (*chabhlê-ʿōnî*)" resulting from sin, his "constraint," gives him a new chance to hearken to the word of God and to repent and return to him (Job 36:8).

3. *For the Relationship between God and Man.* The phrase *chabhlê ʾādhām*, parallel *ʿabhôthôth ʾahabhāh,* "bands of love," in Hos. 11:4 has long been a crux. Does *ʾādhām* here refer to some kind of material, just as the meaning "leather" has been suggested for the parallel *ʾahabhāh?*[55] Or should *ʾādhām* be emended to *ʾemeth,* "faithfulness,"[56] or *chesedh,* "mercy"?[57] Probably what is meant is "human," i.e., "humane" cords.[58] By metabole, what applies to the one who uses the cords is predicated of the cords themselves. Thus the *chabhlê ʾādhām* are a metaphor for God's wooing of his people.

IV. chebhel, "Region." In the sense "region, land," *chebhel* has basically two nuances. In the first place, in contrast to the well-defined *kāphār,* "village," *ʿîr,* "city," and *mamlekheth,* "kingdom," it can refer vaguely to a "region" that must be defined more precisely by means of additional epithets: *chebhel ʾargōbh,* "the region or Argob" (Dt. 3:4,13f.; 1 K. 4:13) in Golan,[59] an area administered by Solomonic magistrates, which was originally under the jurisdiction of Og. Then, in combination with proper names (*chabhlê-menashsheh,* Josh. 17:5; *chebhel benê yehûdhāh,* Josh. 19:9), *chebhel* comes more to designate a specific area assigned (or promised) as *nachalāh* (cf. also Josh. 17:14; Ps. 105:11; 1 Ch. 16:18) or the "territory" of Jacob allotted (i.e., elected) by Yahweh as his own heritage (Dt. 32:9, a unique expression for election not found elsewhere in the OT[60]). In Ezk. 47:13a, a gloss[61] in the schedule of land apportionment Ezk. 47:13–48:29, the *chabhlayîm,* "two portions," of Joseph are mentioned (cf. Josh. 13:33–14:5). This sense of *chebhel* as a "surveyed and allotted tract of land" exhibits the close connection with *chebhel,* "measuring line."

On the other hand, the phrase *chebhel hayyām,* "region of the sea,"[62] attested only in the secondary passage Zeph. 2:5-7, probably takes its sense primarily from the

---

53 S. Mowinckel, *Psalmenstudien,* I (1921,[2] 1961), 51f.

54 Wildberger, *BK,* X/1, 193.

55 *CML,* 133; H. H. Hirschberg, "Some Additional Arabic Etymologies in OT Lexicography," *VT,* 11 (1961), 373; H. McKeating, *The Books of Amos, Hosea, and Micah. CBC* (1971), 136.

56 Procksch.

57 Graetz, Sellin, Robinson.

58 Weiser, Jacob, Wolff, Rudolph, *et al.*

59 Cf. J. Simons, *The Geographical and Topographical Texts of the OT. StFS* (1959), § 21.

60 Noth.

61 W. Zimmerli, *BK,* XIII (1969), *in loc.*

62 Cf. the rabbinic place name Ḥabil Yamma (*Kidd.* 72a; Gen. r. s. 37).

''unit of length,'' so that reference is to a ''narrow strip of land'' along the coast, inhabited by the Philistines.[63]

V. chōbhēl, chibbēl. The crew of the magnificent ship representing Tyre includes types or categories of sailors (Ezk. 27:8f.,27–29): besides the *chōbhᵉlîm* (vv. 8,27–29), there are *shāṭîm* (vv. 8, 26), *mallāchîm* (vv. 9,27,29), *tōphᵉśê māshôṭ* (v. 29), and finally *machᵃzîqê bhedheq* (vv. 9,27), probably referring to the ''ship's carpenters'' in the extended sense, who repair small damages, leaks, seams, etc. (*bedheq*). Dalman's suggested explanations and translations have not been universally accepted: *chōbhēl,* ''rope-puller,''[64] *shāṭîm,* ''rowers,''[65] *mallāchîm,* ''mariners, 'salts,' ''[66] and *māshôṭ,* ''oar.''[67] For *mallāchîm,* Loretz[68] has noted Landsberger's derivation of *mlḥ* from *ma-,* ''ship,'' and *laḥ-,* ''guide,'' i.e., ''skipper,'' and Gelb's Akkadian parallels; he suggests that Israel borrowed Phoenician technical terminology when it came in contact with seafaring Phoenicia. For the other terms there are still no appropriate explanations.[69]

A *rabh hachōbhēl,* LXX *prōreús,* ''captain,'' is attested only in Jonah 1:6.

The meaning of *chibbēl* (a hapax legomenon) in Prov. 23:34 is uncertain. A drunkard in his drunkenness is compared to one ''who lies down in the midst of the sea, who lies *bᵉrōʾsh chibbēl.*'' LXX *hṓsper kybernḗtēs en pollṓ klýdōni* suggests *ûkhᵉchōbhēl bᵉsaʿar gādhôl,* which was either read by the LXX or paraphrased as an interpretation of the now unintelligible *bᵉrōʾsh chibbēl.* Following the LXX, several scholars have suggested a partial emendation to *ûkhᵉrōkhēbh bᵉraʿash chōbhēl,* ''and like a mariner at sea in a storm.''[70] Others translate *chibbēl* as ''mast,'' ''lookout,'' ''rigging,'' or ''rudder.'' Dahood, finally, takes *ḥbl* as a metathesis of *ḥlb,* ''mountain.''[71] This word, too, is clearly one of those Phoenician nautical terms whose nuances are still unknown.

VI. chebhel, "Group," chobhᵉlîm. Only twice in the OT do we find *chebhel* in the Ugaritic sense ''group, band,'' LXX *chóros* (= *KBL*³ *ḥbl* I). In the Talmud, the word can refer to any kind of bundle or group.[72] In contrast to *chebher* (→ חבר *chābhar* II.3) ''gang'' (Hos. 6:9), it probably refers not so much to a lawless band of brigands as to an organized band of ecstatics living in community(?) at a cultic site (Gibeah) (*chebhel nᵉbhîʾîm,* 1 S. 10:5,10). Other groups of prophets (*bᵉnê hannᵉbhîʾîm*)

63Cf. M. Noth, ''Beiträge zur Geschichte des Ostjordanlandes, I,'' *PJ,* 37 (1941), 97.

64*BDB;* Zorell, *LexHebAram:* ''sailor.''

65*BDB,* Zorell.

66*GesB;* Zorell: ''sailor.''

67*BDB;* Zorell (*LexHebAram*²).

68O. Loretz, ''Das hebräische Verbum GMR,'' *BZ,* N.F. 5 (1961), 21–24.

69For a discussion of the terminology, see S. Smith, ''The Ship Tyre,'' *PEQ,* 85 (1953), 97–110, esp. 105f.; on Ezk. 27, cf. also E. M. Good, ''Ezekiel's Ship: Some Extended Metaphors in the OT,'' *Semitics,* 1 (1970), 79–103.

70B. Gemser, *HAT,* 16 (1937), *in loc.; BHS;* etc.

71M. Dahood, ''Hebrew-Ugaritic Lexicography II,'' *Bibl,* 45 (1964), 407; *idem, Proverbs and Northwest Semitic Philology. SPIB,* 113 (1963) 49f.

72*Sukk.* 15a; *Kidd.* 65a; *Pesaḥim* 102b.

are mentioned in 1 K. 20:35-43 and 1 K. 22; there are well-known companies of prophets around Elisha at Gilgal (2 K. 4), at Ramah (1 S. 19:18ff.), and at Jericho (2 K. 2:5).[73] For Saul, the announced encounter with the band of prophets serves as a sign that God is with him and his plans; here he receives the spirit.[74]

The word *chōbᵉlîm* (no singular) is found only in Zec. 11:7,14 as the name of the second shepherd's staff, the counterpart to the first staff, *nôʿam,* "kindness,"[75] in the shepherd allegory of Deutero-Zechariah. The name is usually interpreted as meaning "union"[76] or "concord."[77] In a prophetic symbolic action, the two staffs are broken in turn (cf. Ezk. 34) to demonstrate the annulment of Yahweh's covenant with the peoples (v. 10) and of the bond of brotherhood between Judah and Israel (v. 14). As the historical background to this symbolic prophecy, besides the Samaritan schism,[78] the end of Persian hegemony marked by the advance of the Macedonians has been proposed.[79]

Fabry

---

[73]Cf. H. S. Schmitt, *Elisa* (1972), 162-172; R. Rendtorff, "Erwägungen zur Frühgeschichte des Prophetentums in Israel," *ZThK,* 59 (1962), 145-167, esp. 156ff. = *GSAT. ThB,* 57 (1975), 220-242, esp. 231ff.

[74]For a discussion of the meaning and nature of this event, see W. Beyerlin, "Das Königscharisma bei Saul," *ZAW,* 73 (1961), 186-201, esp. 187f., 190f.

[75]*KBL*².

[76]*GesB;* Sellin; Horst; I. Willi-Plein, *Prophetie am Ende. BBB,* 42 (1974), 53; etc.

[77]*KBL*³, Elliger.

[78]F. Horst, *HAT,* 14 (³1964), 253.

[79]Willi-Plein, *Prophetie,* 113-16.

חָבַל *chābhal* II; חֲבֹל *chᵃbhōl;* חֲבֹלָה *chᵃbhōlāh*

Contents: I. Etymology; Ancient Near East: 1. The Root *ḥbl*; 2. Loan Terminology: a. Sumerian and Akkadian; b. Hittite; c. Ugaritic. II. 1. OT Loan Terminology; 2. Pledge in the OT; 3. Pledge and Surety in the Mishnah; 4. Pledge and Surety in the NT.

I. Etymology; Ancient Near East.

1. *The root ḥbl.* In the Hebrew alphabet, the originally distinct Semitic phonemes *ḥ* and *ḫ* can be distinguished only through the aid of cognates in Semitic languages

---

chābhal II. J. Behm, "ἀρραβών," *TDNT,* I, 475; E. Bilgiç, "Die wichtigsten Ausdrücke über Schulden und Darlehen in den Keilschrifttexten," *Ankara Universitesi Dil ve Tarih-*

whose writing systems preserve this distinction, in particular Akkadian, Ugaritic, and Arabic. Already *GesB* distinguished four separate roots spelled *ḥbl* in Biblical Hebrew, and determined through Arabic and Akkadian cognates that *ḥbl* II, "take in pledge," and *ḥbl* III, "ruin," contained the *ḫ* phoneme, *ḥbl* IV, "give birth," contained the *ḥ* phoneme, and that the evidence was ambivalent for *ḥbl* I, "rope."

Since the 17th edition of *GesB* appeared (1915), the Akkadian evidence has multiplied many-fold, and the Ugaritic tablets found at Ras Shamra have added a new and highly important linguistic source. Since the Ugaritic cognate of Heb. *ḥbl,* "rope," is *ḥbl,* "swarm, flock of birds,"[1] and the Akkadian cognate is *eblu,* "cord, rope,"[2] the velar phoneme in *GesB*'s *ḥbl* I can now without doubt be identified as *ḥ*.

The etymological relationship of *ḥbl* II, "take in pledge," to *ḥbl* III, "ruin," is still unclear. No cognates of these Hebrew words have yet appeared in Ugaritic.[3] In Arabic, the root *ḫbl* is attested in several verbs and related nouns with the meanings, "confuse, entangle, complicate, put into disorder," but also in other verbs and related nouns with the meanings "borrow" (*istaḫbala*), "lend" (*'aḫbala*), and "loan" (*ḫabla*). In Akkadian, cognates of both Heb. *ḥbl* II, "take in pledge," and *ḥbl* III, "ruin," can be found. Akk. *ḫabālu* III, "borrow, incur a debt," is a denominative verb from *ḫubullu,* "debt, interest." Related nouns are Bab. *ḫubbulu* (Assyr. *ḫabbulu*), "debtor," and *ḫubbultu,* "debt." Cognate with Heb. *ḥbl* III are Akk. *ḫabālu* II, "oppress, wrong," *ḫibiltu,* "damage, wrong," *ḫābilu* I, "evildoer," and *ḫablu/ḫabiltu,* "unjustly treated,

Cografya Fakültesi Dergisi, 5 (1947), 419-454; H. Danby, *The Mishnah* (1933), 358, 364, 418, 435, 548f.; M. David, "Deux anciens termes bibliques pour le gage (עבוט, חבל)," *OTS,* 2 (1943), 79-86; M. Dietrich, O. Loretz, and J. Sanmartin, "Keilalphabetische Bürgschaftsdokumente aus Ugarit," *UF,* 6 (1974), 466f.; G. R. Driver and J. C. Miles, *The Assyrian Laws* (1935), 271ff.; *idem, The Babylonian Laws,* I (1952), 208ff., 216ff.; II (1955), 204ff. (on §§ 113-19, 151f.); D. O. Edzard, *Sumerische Rechtsurkunden des 3. Jahrtausends aus der Zeit vor der III. Dynastie von Ur. ABAW,* N.S. 67 (1968); G. Eisser and J. Lewy, *Die altassyrischen Rechtsurkunden von Kültepe. MVÄG,* 33 (1930) and 35/3 (1935); A. Falkenstein, *Die neusumerischen Gerichtsurkunden,* I. *ABAW,* N.S. 39 (1956), 116-19; A. Goetze, review of H. Otten, *Hethitische Rituale,* in *JCS,* 18 (1964), 92f.; *idem,* "On §§ 163, 164/5 and 176 of the Hittite Code," *JCS,* 20 (1966), 130f.; C. H. Gordon, *UT,* 461 *s.v. ʿrbn;* H. G. Güterbock, review of J. Friedrich, *Hethitische Gesetze,* in *JCS,* 15 (1961), 69; *idem,* "Bemerkungen zu den Ausdrücken *ellum, wardum,* und *asīrum* in den hethitischen Texten," Rencontre assyriologique internationale, 18th, Munich, 1970, *Gesellschaftsklassen im Alten Zweistromland und in den angrenzenden Gebieten,* ed. D. O. Edzard (1972), 94; R. Haase, "Bemerkungen zu einigen Paragraphen der hethitischen Gesetztexte," *ArOr,* 26 (1958), 28-30; H. A. Hoffner, Jr., *The Laws of the Hittites* (diss., Brandeis, 1963), 65, 101, 104, 129f., 164f., 227, 244, 247f., 285; F. Imparati, *Le leggi Ittite. Incunabula Graeca,* 7 (Rome, 1964), 261f.; J. Klíma, G. Cardascia, V. Korošec, and H. Petschow, "Gesetze," *RLA,* III, 243-297; P. Koschaker, *Babylonisch-assyrisches Bürgschaftsrecht* (1911), 36f.; B. Landsberger, "Bemerkungen zur altbabylonischen Briefliteratur," *ZDMG,* 69 (1915), 513; *idem,* review of E. Grant, *Babylonian Documents of the Classical Period,* in *OLZ,* 25 (1922), 409; H. Petschow, *Neubabylonisches Pfandrecht* (1956); M. San Nicolò, "Bürgschaft," *RLA,* II, 77-80; *idem,* "Zur Frage der Ersatzfunktion des neubabylonischen Pfandes," *ArOr,* 4 (1932), 34ff.; M. Schorr, *Urkunden des altbabylonischen Zivil-Gerichts- und Prozessrechts. VAB,* V (1913), 93-100; R. Werner, *Hethitisches Gerichtsprotokolle. StBT,* 4 (1967), 30-33; *KAI,* II, 73f., 126.

[1] *WUS,* No. 892; *UT,* No. 832.

[2] AHw, I, 183.

[3] *WUS,* No. 995 is problematic and should probably not be so divided.

wronged person." Still a third group of Akkadian nouns and verbs based on the root *ḫbl* is: *ḫabālu* IV, "tie, snare," *ḫābilu*, "trapper, hunter," and *naḫbalu*, "snare." Similarity of this last group to Heb. *ḥbl* I, "rope," must be discounted in view of Ugar. *ḥbl* and Akk. *eblu*.

2. *Loan Terminology*. a. *Sumerian and Akkadian*. In surveying loan terminology, we must take into account the different terminologies of various periods as well as the wide geographic separation of the various regions using cuneiform legal documents. The debt itself was expressed in Sumerian by the word *ur*$_5$*(-ra)*, in Akkadian mostly by *ḫubullu*, rarely by *eʾiltu* (Old Bab.) or *ḫubbultu* (Middle Bab., Nuzi). The debtor was called *ḫabbulu(m)* (Old and Middle Assyr.), *ḫubbulu* (Late Bab.), and *awīl ḫubulli* (Middle Bab., Nuzi). The creditor was called *bēl ḫubulli*, rarely *ummianu* (Middle Assyr. laws) or *rāšû* (Neo-Bab., Late Bab.). The interest was designated *máš* in Sumerian and *ṣibtu* or *ḫubullu* (Middle and Neo-Bab.) in Akkadian. The indebtedness could be described as follows: *N* (creditor) *eli N* (debtor) *šeʾam u kaspam išu*, "the creditor has so much grain or silver against the debtor."[4]

To ensure repayment of the loan, the creditor could usually require some form of guarantee, either surety or pledge. The terminology of the surety varied: Sum. (*lú-*) *šu-du*$_8$*-a*;[5] Akk. *ša qātāti* or *qātātu* (Old Assyr. and Bab., Middle Bab., Alalakh), *warkiu* (Old Assyr.), *warkû* (Old Bab.), *urkû/uškû* (Middle Bab. and later), *urkiu* (Middle and Neo-Assyr.), *arkû* (Late Bab.), *rab qātāti* (Neo-Assyr., Neo-Bab.), *bēl qātāti* (Neo-Assyr.), *mahiṣ pūti* (Middle Bab. [Nuzi], Late Bab.), *qātātum* (Old Assyr.).[6] The duty of the surety in the first instance was to ensure that the debtor would not abscond without paying his debt. He guaranteed the debtor's appearance at the time the debt came due. Only later did the practice arise of holding the surety personally responsible for payment of the debt itself. The former obligation was expressed in Neo-Babylonian by the phrase *pūt šēpi našû*, while the latter was expressed by *pūt eṭēri nasû*.

Aside from the surety, surety for the loan could be offered in the form of a pledge, for which the following terms were employed: *ma(n)zazānu* (Old Bab.), *ma(n)zāzu* (Old Bab.; rare), *erubbātum* (Old Assyr.; cf. West Semitic *ʿrbn* and Gk. *arrabṓn*), *šapartu(m)* (Assyr.: "sent pledge"), *maškanu* (Neo-Bab., Late Bab.), *maškanūtu* (Neo-Bab., Late Bab.). The debtor's offering of a pledge was described as *ana ma(n)zazāni nadānu/šuzuzzu* (Old Bab.) or *maškanu šakānu* (Neo-Bab., Late Bab.). The creditor's taking of a pledge was described as *ana ma(n)zazāni leqû* (Old Bab.) or *maškanu ṣabātu* (Neo-Bab., Late Bab.). The word *maškanu*, "pledge," is the source of the Late Heb. *māshkôn*, "pledge," and its denominative verb *mishkên*.

If the indebtedness was not discharged, the creditor could distrain (Old Bab. *nepû*, rarely *kašāšu*) someone belonging to the debtor; this person became a bondman for debt (Old Bab. *nipûtu*), and his status was termed *kiššātu*, "bondage."[7]

---

[4]Cf. CH § 113.

[5]Landsberger, "Bemerkungen," 513; *idem, OLZ*, 209; *idem, The Series lú-ša and Related Texts*. MSL, XII (1969), 166:279; Falkenstein, *Gerichtsurkunden*, I, 116ff.

[6]Cf. Eisser and Lewy, 175f.

[7]Cf. CH §§ 114–16; F. R. Kraus, *Ein Edikt des Königs Ammi-Ṣaduqa von Babylon. StDI*, 5 (1958), 176ff.; J. J. Finkelstein, "A Late Old Babylonian Copy of the Laws of Hammurapi," *JCS*, 21 (1967), 42, n. 6.

b. *Hittite.* In 1922, F. Sommer proposed[8] that the verb *appatriya-* in Hittite laws §§ 76 and 164 should be translated "take as a pledge." He was subsequently supported in this interpretation by J. Friedrich.[9] In 1964, however, A. Goetze showed[10] from an oracle text[11] that the translation "take as a pledge" for this verb was incorrect, and proposed instead the translation "appropriate, requisition under terms of feudal law." The verb also occurs in *KUB,* XIII, 8, I, 10. Thus vanishes possibly the only allusion to loans in Hittite texts. In Hittite law § 172, one man supports another with food in a year of famine, an action that might qualify as a loan. In return, when his financial situation improves, a free man must give a personal substitute (Akk. *pūḫ-šu*), whereas a slave must give ten shekels of silver.[12] The verb *wek-* in the sense of "borrow" seems to be attested only in the documents from Mesopotamia translated into Hittite.[13] In short, Hittite texts tell us nothing about indigenous practices concerning loans.

c. *Ugaritic.* For Ugaritic, Gordon maintains[14] that the verb form *wyšš3l* in *PRU,* II, 23, 5 should be translated "borrow" (but cf. Biblical Heb. *hish'îl,* "grant, lend"). He describes *PRU,* II, 23 as a "fragment of an epistle requesting a loan." But the context of this word has been destroyed, and therefore it is impossible to determine with any certainty just what the subject of the correspondence is. The only other term associated with loans in other languages is the verb *ʿrb,* "go surety," and the noun *ʿrbn,* "surety." The use of the verb *ʿrb* in *PRU,* II, 161; V, 46; V, 79 in the sense "go surety" is strongly reminiscent of *ʿrb* in Gen. 43:9; 44:32. In Phoenician texts, too, the verb *ʿrb* must be translated "go surety"[15] and the noun *ʿrb* "surety."[16]

II. 1. *OT Loan Terminology.* The following are important terms relating to loans and debts in the OT: debt: *chôbh, mashshā', mashshā'āh, mashshāh, n^eshî;* debtor: *lōveh, shō'ēl;* creditor: *nōsheh/nōshe', malveh;* interest: *neshekh, tarbîth, marbîth;* surety: *ʿōrēbh, tōq^eê-khaph;* pledge: *ch^abhōlāh, ch^abhōl, ʿ^abhōṭ, ʿērābhôn;* lend: *lāvāh, shā'al, ʿābhaṭ;* borrow: *hilvāh, nāshā', he^eʿbhîṭ, hish'îl.* In the vocabulary of Biblical Hebrew, a rather clear distinction seems to have been observed between "surety" and "pledge," both in the nouns and the related verbs. Verbs and nouns containing the roots *ḥbl* and *ʿbṭ* have to do with a pledge, i.e., they do not involve a third party. Aside from Neh. 5:3, the verb *ʿārabh* similarly denotes only "going surety," and has nothing to do with offering an animal or object as a pledge. The noun *ʿērābhôn* is exceptional: in Gen. 38 it clearly denotes a pledge, not a (human) surety. The use of *ʿērābhôn* in Gen. 38 also fails to conform to the usage of Ugar. *ʿrbn,* which

[8]F. Sommer, *Hethitisches,* II. *Boghazköi-Studien,* 7 (1922), 42, n. 1.
[9]J. Friedrich, *Hethitisches Wörterbuch* (1952), 26.
[10]Goetze, *JCS,* 18, 92f.; cf. also *idem, JCS,* 20, 130f.
[11]*KBo,* XIV, 21, I, 31f.
[12]A reference to such support in famine years is found in Werner, 30–33.
[13]E.g., *KBo,* XX, 70 obv., 12f.; *KUB,* IV, 3 obv., 16; C. Schaeffer, *Ugaritica,* V (1968), 779ff.
[14]*UT,* No. 2369.
[15]*KAI,* 119.7.
[16]*KAI,* 60.6.

in *PRU*, II, 161, 1 and 7 clearly denotes human guarantors.[17] The translation of the LXX is consistent with this overall distinction. Hebrew words in this semantic field based on the roots *ḥbl* and *ʿbṭ* were translated with Gk. *enechyrázein, enechýrasma, enechyrasmós,* and *enéchyron,* while the verb *ʿārabh,* "go surety," was translated with the Gk. *(di)engyán* and *engýasthai,* and the noun *ʿarubbāh,* "surety," was translated with *engýē* (Prov. 17:18).

The situation in 1 S. 17:18 certainly has nothing whatever to do with loans. Therefore the translation of *ʿarubbāh* as "pledge" does not constitute a real exception to the pattern established for loan terminology.

2. *Pledge in the OT.* Items commonly taken as pledges in the OT were: clothes (*beghādhîm,* Prov. 20:16; 27:13; Dt. 24:17; Am. 2:8; *śimlāh,* Ex. 22:25-27 [Eng. vv. 26-28]; Dt. 24:11-13), livestock (*shôr, chamōr,* Job 24:3), and movable property such as household utensils (*rēchayim vārākhebh,* Dt. 24:6). However, the Israelite was warned not to oppress a very poor debtor by keeping overnight the cloak (*śimlāh,* Ex. 22:25-27[26-28]) or garments (*beghedh,* Dt. 24:17) that were his only source of warmth (cf. also Job 22:6; 24:9).

Similarly, a creditor was not allowed to take in pledge an item the debtor required to make his living (Dt. 24:6: *kî nephesh hûʾ chabhōl*). On this principle, it was forbidden to take in pledge a poor person's ox (*shôr*) or ass (*chamōr*), since he needed the ox to plow and the ass as an essential beast of burden (Job 24:3).[18] It was likewise forbidden to take in pledge the mill (*rēchayim*) or upper millstone (*rekhebh*) of a debtor, since he needed it to prepare his essential food (Dt. 24:6). The rabbis understood this principle, for they wrote: "No man shall take the mill and the upper millstone in pledge. They spoke not only of the mill and the upper millstone, but of anything by means of which necessary food is prepared, as it is written, 'For he takes a man's life as pledge.' "[19] The rabbis also added to the essential means of livelihood the plow (*macharēshāh*),[20] which must be kept only at night and be returned to the debtor during the day. If one avoided taking the above objects in pledge, it was quite legal for a creditor to require a pledge of his debtor (Prov. 20:16; 27:13), although someone who waived this right was considered especially pious (Ezk. 18:16). Failure to restore a pledge was a serious sin (Ezk. 18:7,12). According to Dt. 24:11-13, the creditor was not allowed to enter the debtor's dwelling to exact the pledge, but had to wait outside for the debtor to bring it out to him. In Gen. 38, Judah, the debtor, sought to reclaim his pledge (*ʿērabhôn*) at the time when he paid in silver his debt to the harlot.

3. *Pledge and Surety in the Mishnah.* According to the Mishnah, one could take a pledge from a debtor only by consent of the court.[21] The creditor was restricted in his choice of pledges not only as in the OT,[22] but in additional ways as well. He was not

[17] Cf. also *PRU*, III, 220, *s.v. urrubānu.*

[18] Cf. Mishnah *Arakhin* vi.3.

[19] *B. Metzia* ix.13.

[20] *Ibid.*

[21] *Ibid.*

[22] See above.

allowed to take two utensils at the same time.[23] He was not permitted to take a pledge from any widow, rich or poor.[24] If the pledge was not something subject to rapid deterioration, the creditor as an ''unpaid guardian'' (*shōmēr chinnām*) was not liable for its deterioration. If, however, the pledge was subject to rapid deterioration (as in the case of produce, e.g. [Heb. *pērôth*]), the creditor was adjudged a ''paid guardian'' (*shōmēr śākhār*) and was held accountable for any decay or deterioration of the pledge. Abba Shaul maintained that the creditor, like the finder of lost property, has the right to use it until it is claimed, if the use does not produce improper wear and tear,[25] and if the profit accruing from use of the pledge is applied to reduction of the debt. Liability of the creditor for loss of the debtor's pledge depended on its value in comparison to the amount of the loan.[26] Rabban Simeon ben Gamaliel permitted a creditor to sell a pledge thirty days after the date payment was due, if he secured consent of the court.[27]

4. *Pledge and Surety in the NT*. Two terms belonging to loan terminology appear in the NT: *arrabṓn,* ''pledge,'' and *éngyos,* ''surety.'' The latter describes Jesus, who is ''surety'' for God's better covenant (*kreíttonos diathḗkēs gégonen éngyos Iēsoús,* He. 7:22). The former describes the Holy Spirit, who is the ''pledge'' given to believers to assure them that they will surely receive their inheritance (*klēronomía*), which has been promised to them (2 Cor. 1:22; 5:5; Eph. 1:14). According to this theological scheme, the Christian is the creditor to whom an eventual inheritance is due according to the terms of the will and testament of God the Father. The debtor who has promised the payment is God the Father. The surety, who has been willing to risk his life to make good the promise, is Jesus. And the pledge, whose presence is both assuring and useful to the creditor, is the Holy Spirit. Thus the ethics of a loan transaction is not the concern of the NT; the loan situation serves rather as a theological construct.

Hoffner

---

[23] *B. Metzia* ix.13; *Arakhin* vi.3ff.
[24] *B. Metzia* ix.13.
[25] *B. Metzia* vi.7.
[26] *Shebuoth* vi.7.
[27] *B. Metzia* ix.13.

חָבַל chābhal III

Contents: I. Ancient Near East, Extrabiblical and Postbiblical Literature. II. OT: 1. Lexical Problems; 2. Violence: Physical, Physiological, Political, Social; 3. Extreme Depression; 4. Sin; 5. Soteriology. III. Convergence of Homophonic Roots?: 1. Qumran; 2. OT; 3. Real or Deliberate Ambiguities?

I. Ancient Near East, Extrabiblical and Postbiblical Literature. With varying frequency, *ḥbl* with meanings in the semantic field of "violence, murder, injury" appears in East, South, and Northwest Semitic (with the exception so far of Ugaritic[1]), at Qumran, and in postbiblical Hebrew.[2]

II. OT.

1. *Lexical Problems.* The various lexicons arrange the homophonic roots *ḥbl* in different ways and with some ambiguity. We shall use the terminology of *KBL*[3].

We shall first deal with the material that can be assigned with certainty to *ḥbl* III, and then examine the possibility that other occurrences, usually assigned to other lemmas, might be associated with this root.

2. *Violence: Physical, Physiological, Political, Social.* At times we find what is probably the basic meaning, without theological overtones: agricultural damage (Cant. 2:15), destruction (rather than utilization) of a felled tree belonging to the king (Dnl. 4:20 Aram. [Eng. v. 23]), absence of bodily injury to the devout by fire (Dnl. 3:25 Aram.) or lions (Dnl. 6:23f. Aram.), political disadvantage (Ezr. 4:22 Aram.), destruction of the temple (Ezr. 6:12 Aram.). Isa 32:7b ("to ruin the poor [*ʿaniyyîm, ʾebhyônîm*]") and Mic. 2:10b ("uncleanness that destroys") are difficult; the word is probably to be taken in a social or forensic sense, as in its frequent occurrences at Elephantine.[3] In the apocalyptic context, the guarantee that the kingdom will never be destroyed (Dnl. 2:44; cf. 6:27 Aram.), nor the sovereignty given the "son of man" (Dnl. 7:14 Aram.), is also theological.

3. *Extreme Depression.* Since the proposed emendations in Job 17:1a hardly represent improvements, it is probably correct to read the pual.[4] In the two following

---

chābhal III. M. Dahood, "Hebrew-Ugaritic Lexicography II," *Bibl*, 45 (1964), 407; G. R. Driver, "Studies in the Vocabulary of the OT VI," *JTS*, 34 (1933), 375f.; S. Erlandsson, *The Burden of Babylon; a Study of Isaiah 13:2-14:23. ConBibOT*, 4 (1970); C. H. Hunzinger, "Fragmente einer älteren Fassung des Buches Milḥamā aus Höhle 4 von Qumran," *ZAW*, 69 (1957), 131-151; cf. J. L. Teicher, "A Spurious Version of the War Scroll [4QM[a]]," *ZAW*, 70 (1958), 257f., and C. H. Hunzinger, "Replik," *ibid.*, 258f.; J. Scharbert, *Der Schmerz im AT. BBB*, 8 (1955), 18-20.

[1]Cf. *UT*, No. 832.

[2]Cf. *AHw*, I, 301f.; *DISO*, 81; *KBL*[3], 274; *WTM*, II, 4-6; → חבל *chābhal* II.

[3]Cf. *LexLingAram*, 58f.

[4]Cf. *BHK*.

members of the verse, Job laments that his days are extinct, that he is "on the brink of the grave" (cf. 16:22). The idea appears frequently with similar terminology, especially in laments: Ps. 143:7; 34:19(18); 51:19(17); Isa. 57:15f.; etc. Counterparts of *chubbālāh* in Job 17:1 in these passages include the verbs *kālāh, shābhar, dākhā', shāphēl,* and *'āṭaph;* antonyms include *chāyāh* hiphil. The meaning is therefore profound emotional depression, from which the believer nevertheless reaches out to God.

4. *Sin.* In Neh. 1:7a, the 1st person pl. qal of *chābhal* with the infinitive absolute (contrary to the Masoretic vocalization) is connected with the indirect object *lākh* and with *chāṭā'* and a series of terms for sin in the formulaic style of Deuteronomy. The context is designated explicitly as a prayer (*pll,* both noun and verb) and confession of sins (*mith-vaddeh*) (1:4,6). Even the LXX seems to have had trouble finding a corresponding expression; either *diélysa dielýsamen* is used quite exceptionally without an object, or it shares an object with the following *v^e lō'-shāmarnû,* at the expense of a change in syntax (*lākh* going untranslated). Against the latter explanation, two minuscule manuscripts cited by Brooke-McLean read *kaí mataiṓsei emataiṓthēmen en soí,* and the Ethiopic version reads *et negavimus te.*[5]

In light of the meanings discussed in 2 and 3 above and the attempted renderings of the ancient versions, we may conjecture that *chābhal* means "deliberately thwart someone," in other words, an aggravation of sin.

The Wisdom expression in Job 34:31 also points in this direction. Despite all its textual difficulty, 31b is syntactically parallel to 32b (1st person sing. perf. followed by a negation and 1st person sing. impf.). What is expressed is the will to cease from iniquity (*'āvel*); cf. Dt. 32:4 and Job 34:10. Thus *lō' 'echbhōl* indicates the intention not to sin again.

In the context of "secularized" Wisdom, *yēchābhel* (niphal) appears in Prov. 13:13. Most of the versions and commentaries suggest a juridico-economic sense: "take in pledge" (→ חבל *chābhal* II),[6] primarily on the grounds that the parallel *ye shullām* (pual) means "pay back, reward," in the strictest form, in kind.[7] But this interpretation is hardly supported by the Masoretic vocalization of the two words as niphal and pual.

In the same collection there are other proverbs, framed not antithetically like the present saying but synonymously or synthetically (interpretatively), that deal in general terms with actions and their rewards. They are meant in part—and in the loose context of the book perhaps primarily—to be taken as ethico-moral maxims, not concrete instructions.

In Prov. 16:20, for example, happiness (→ טוב *ṭôbh*) depends on giving heed to the *dābhār,* and whoever trusts in God is accounted happy (cf. 17:20). According to 19:16 and 14:27 (cf. 13:14), life and death themselves depend on one's relationship to the *tôrāh* or *mitsvāh* and *yir'āh.* It is therefore highly unlikely that Prov. 13:13 is dealing with legal or economic matters, regardless of whether *dābhār* and *mitsvāh* mean in the

---

[5]Brooke-McLean, *in loc.*

[6]Cf. M. Dahood, "Congruity of Metaphors," *Hebräische Wortforschung. Festschrift W. Baumgartner. SVT,* 16 (1967), 41f.

[7]Cf. D. Daube, *Studies in Biblical Law* (1947, [2]1969), 134–147; *DISO,* 303; *AHw,* II, 1013f.

first instance merely the instructions of the wise or refer directly to the binding commandments of God.

Thus, in contrast to *y^e^shullām, yĕchābhel* means a state radically devoid of happiness, prosperity, and well-being, as a consequence of reprehensible disregard for the "word." In other words, it is associated with the extensive and complex domain of sin. Of course the saying fails to make a careful distinction between sin itself and its consequences.

This is probably also the proper context of *ch^a^bhālîm* in Job 21:17 and Ps. 140:6(5); the parallelism with *r^e^shāʿîm* and *gēʾîm,* respectively, suggests the translation "corrupt person, scoundrel, wicked man, sinner," whether the word is participle or a deverbative noun.[8]

5. *Soteriology.* Some occurrences, on the contrary, are soteriological. Isa. 10:27[9] borrows the construct phrase *ʿōl subb^o^ lô* from the beginning of 9:3(4), with its richer terminology, and expands it into two hemistichs, each with its own verb and object, in perfect chiasmus. This observation, the use of the future tense in the LXX and Theodotion, and the easy confusion of ו with י in many scripts justify the emendation of *v^e^chubbal* to *y^e^chubbāl.* In addition, the perfect chiasmus shows that the second half expresses a complete idea. Corresponding to *yāsûr* in the first half and the (wooden) yoke, *y^e^chubbal* is equivalent to "break" (*shābhar;* cf. Jer. 28:2,4,11; 30:8), "set free." Israel will be delivered from the oppression of the enemy.[10]

Isa. 13:5, like the rest of 13:2-22, is considered spurious. But within the self-contained section 2-8, it is both visually central and set apart by its nominal construction from the predominantly verbal context. The menace of Babylon is not an isolated event, but a condition; it is not contrary to God's purposes, but willed by God himself; it is not directed against a single target, but against the entire land, if not the entire earth. The word *l^e^chabbēl* means the temporary disaster that God is bringing upon Israel through invaders "from a distant land, from the end of the heavens" (*min* appears three times in 5a!).[11]

In Isa. 54:16, terminology is instructive: *mashchîth* recalls *m^e^chittāh* (54:14), and takes us by way of *hachittōthā* (Isa. 9:3) to *y^e^chubbāl* (Isa. 10:27 conj.), *yēchath* (Isa. 30:31), and *shābhar* (Isa. 14:5). The word *l^e^chabbēl* summarizes the effects of various destructive forces, all of which God has irresistibly at his disposal, like all creation. At least in Isa. 13:5 and 54:16, therefore, *chābhal* functions amid the tensions created by the paradox of the power of God, whose final purpose is salvation.

III. Convergence of Homophonic Roots? The range of possibilities and the number of homophonic roots would lead us to expect some overlapping.

---

[8]Cf. Dahood, *Bibl,* 45, 407, and *Psalms,* III. *AB,* XVIIA (1970), 302.
[9]Cf. H. Wildberger, *BK,* X/1 (1972), 421f.
[10]Cf. Driver, 375f.
[11]Cf. Erlandsson, 15, 130, 156.

1. *Qumran.* Noteworthy are the *mal'ᵃkhê chebhel* at Qumran (1QS 4:12; CD 2:6; 1QM 13:12; cf. 4QMᵃ 14:17).[12] They rule over death and destruction as the judgment decreed by God to exterminate evil.

2. *OT.* The Dead Sea Scrolls may shed new light on the sometimes uncertain hypothesis of several homophonic stems *ḥbl* (e.g., Job 21:17; Ps. 140:6[5]; Prov. 13:13, "pledge"). In Mic. 2:10b, *chebhel nimrāts* appears to refer more to social "injustice" than to a valuable pledge or undeserved distress.[13] At Qumran, the phrase appears three times in close association with the pain and distress of a woman in labor (1QH 3:8,11f.) and in connection with other OT idioms (3:8f.; 2 S. 22:5f.; Ps. 18:6[5]; 3:11: Isa. 13:8; 3:28: Ps. 18:5[4]; 116:3). Despite the punning, one may ask whether even in the OT period the noun *chebhel,* "rope" (from *ḥbl* I), was not associated by the reader or listener with our apparently ambiguous *chebhel* III (from *ḥbl* III), when it stands as *nomen regens* with negative expressions like *rᵉshāʿîm* (Ps. 119:61), *hashshāv'* (Isa. 5:18), *shᵉ'ôl* (2 S. 22:6 = Ps. 18:6[5]), or *māveth* (Ps. 116:3).

3. *Real or Deliberate Ambiguities?* In late texts *ḥbl* begins to appear more frequently, especially often in sections that may be secondary. Particularly when fragments torn out of their original context are used elsewhere, there is ample opportunity for semantic overlapping and convergence, as well as real and perhaps deliberate ambiguity.

Gamberoni

[12]See Hunzinger and Teicher.
[13]See above, II.2.

חבל *ḥbl* IV; חֵבֶל *chēbhel*

Contents: I. 1. Meaning and Definition; 2. Range and Occurrences; 3. Synonyms; 4. LXX. II. Labor in the Ancient Near East. III. OT Usage: 1. Literal; 2. Metaphorical.

I. 1. *Meaning and Definition.* Along with *chēbhel* and *chibbēl, ḥbl* IV appears to be the latest formative of the root *ḥbl,* since it appears only in Middle Hebrew, Jewish

ḥbl IV. G. Bertram, "ὠδίν," *TDNT,* IX, 667-674, esp. 668ff.; G. Binder, "Geburt II (religionsgeschichtlich)," *RAC,* IX (1976), 43-171; J. Boss, "The Character of Childbirth According to the Bible," *Journal of Obstetrics and Gynaecology of the British Commonwealth,* 69 (1962), 508-513; M. Lambert, "La signification de la naissance à travers l'histoire des religions du Proche Orient," *Vie medicale,* 44 (1964), 29-38; J. Scharbert, *Der Schmerz im AT. BBB,* 8 (1955), 18ff.; de Vaux, *AncIsr,* 42f.

Aramaic, Palestinian dialects, and Syriac.[1] Whether Mand. *hbl* II is associated with *ḥbl* IV is dubious.[3] Like Hebrew, Arabic exhibits both nominal and verbal forms. A connection with the etymon *ḫbl* (→ חבל *ḥbl* II, III; possibly → חבל *ḥbl* I) is uncertain; the connection with *ḥbl* I, "tie," "cord," etc., was already suggested by Stade, *BDB*, Mandelkern,[4] Scharbert,[5] and others. The connection between the two roots was also clearly surmised by the rabbis, since the two words are cited in mutual explanation: within the body of the pregnant woman are "ropes" that hold the unborn infant. The undoing of their knots marks the onset of labor and birth.[6]

It appears nonetheless that *ḥbl* IV does not contain any emphasis on pain such as would be expected from such an association.[7] This is expressed by adjunct terms.[8] Since it clearly signifies the state of incipient, continuing, or culminating pregnancy, its major emphasis is on the anxious uncertainty and uneasiness with which the expectant mother awaits the approaching birth (cf. esp. Isa. 13:8), then secondarily the "pangs" that mark the beginning of labor. The biblical occurrences demonstrate clearly that *ḥbl* IV refers to the state of the mother before giving birth, a state that can also be indicated with → הרה *hārāh* (Ps. 7:15 [Eng. v. 14]; Isa. 59:4f.; Job 15:35), but is clearly distinct from the painful → חיל *ḥyl* and → ילד *yāladh*. The actual pangs of labor are termed *tsîrîm*, the word used in 1 S. 4:19 for the "convulsions"[9] of a woman giving birth prematurely.

2. *Range and Occurrences*. The root *ḥbl* IV is not widespread. It appears in Arab. *ḥabila*, "be or become pregnant," II and IV "make pregnant," *ḥabal*, "pregnancy, conception,"[10] and Syr. *ḥebhal*, "conceive," and *ḥēbhlāʾ*, "pangs of birth or (metaphorically) death."[11] In the Talmud, *chibbēl* appears in the sense "feel birth pangs," par. *yāladh*,[12] while *chēbhel* is used metaphorically for the messianic woes.[13]

In the OT, the verb is attested only three times (in the Song of Solomon and Psalms), the noun eight times (all in the prophets, except for Job 39:3). The LXX also reads *ḥbl* IV in 2 S. 22:6; Ps. 18:5f.(4f.); 116:3; Hos. 11:8; but cf. → חבל *ḥbl* I. The occurrences of *ḥbl* IV in the Qumran Scrolls are disputed.[14] The major undisputed occurrences are

---

[1] *LexSyr*, 210.

[2] *MdD*, 129b.

[3] *KBL*³, 274.

[4] *Veteris Testamenti Concordantiae* (1937, ²1955), I, 367: "writhe and twist in spasms of pain," "bind-loose."

[5] P. 18.

[6] Cf. Lev. r.s. 14, 158a and 157a; *WTM*, II, 6a.

[7] Cf. also the translation of the LXX and Bertram, 669.

[8] Cf. I.2.

[9] *KBL*².

[10] Wehr, 155.

[11] *LexSyr*, 210.

[12] *Taan*. 8a.

[13] *Shab*. 118a; *Pesaḥim* 118a; Bertram, 671f.

[14] H. G. Kuhn, *Konkordanz zu den Qumrantexten* (1960), 67; Gamberoni, → חבל *chābhal* III (III.2).

1QH 3:9 (twice); 5:30 (par. *tsîrîm*); and 9:6 (par. *mishbārîm*), which exhibit clear terminological association with the idea of birth and its circumstances.[15]

3. *Synonyms*. The semantic field of birth is very highly articulated in Hebrew. In immediate proximity to *ḥbl* IV we find a series of synonymous expressions that are semantically more or less similar. Note, for example, the description of animal birth in Job 39:3: *kāraʿ*, "crouch"; *yāladh*, "bring forth"; *pillach*, "open the womb"; and *shālach chᵃbhālîm*. Parallel expressions use *chālal*, "be in labor," and *mālēʾ*, "fulfil the time." Similar terms from the animal realm include *pillēṭ*, "bring forth the fruit of the womb" (Job 21:10); *himlîṭ*, "be delivered of" (Isa. 66:7); *shābhar*, "bring to the birth" (Isa. 66:9); similarly *ʿāmadh bᵉmishbar* (Hos. 13:13); *hippîl*, more descriptively, "let fall (the fruit of the womb)" (Isa. 26:19). Less common expressions for "give birth" are *hibhkîr*, "bear a first child" (Jer. 4:31), and *chāyeh*, "giving birth easily" (Ex. 1:19).[16] The period just before delivery is expressed periphrastically: *hiqrîbh lāledheth*, "approach delivery" (Isa. 26:17). The course of human birth is depicted in 1 S. 4:19: the woman is pregnant (*hārāh*), her pains come upon her (*nehephkhû hatstsîrîm*), she bows (*kāraʿ*) and gives birth (*yāladh*). This sudden onset of the event is also referred to in other passages by expressions like *chᵃbhālîm yōʾchēzûn* (Jer. 13:21; Isa. 13:8; cf. Jer. 49:24) or *chēbhel bôʾ lᵉ* (Jer. 22:23; Isa. 66:7; Hos. 13:13). Direct synonyms of *chēbhel* are *tsîr*[17] or the verb → חיל *ḥyl*. There is one occurrence each of *hērôn*, *ʿetsebh*, and *ʿitstsābhôn* in the *locus classicus* for "pregnancy" and "pain of childbirth," Gen. 3:16. The *chᵃbhālîm* are accompanied by groans (*nḥm*, Jer. 22:23) or cries (*zʿq*, Isa. 26:17).

4. *LXX*. The LXX uniformly renders the verb by *ōdínein*, the noun by *ōdín* or (descriptively) *pónos tṓn ōdínōn* (Isa. 66:7); the word is omitted in Jer. 49:24 (LXX 30:30). The Vulgate rendering is not so uniform: it sometimes translates the verb as *parturire* (Ps. 7:5[4]), sometimes as *corrumpere* and *violare* (Job 8:5), confusing it with *ḥbl* II. The noun is usually taken in the more general sense of *dolor*, except in Isa. 66:7 (*partus*) and Job 39:3 (*fetus*).[18]

II. Labor in the Ancient Near East. In the ancient Near East and in Egypt, the events connected with birth were surrounded with numerous magical ceremonies and rituals. From early times special attention was devoted to achieving an easy delivery and reducing the associated pain. It was firmly believed that the helplessness and uncleanness (!) of the woman in labor exposed her particularly to the redoubled attack of demons.[19] Therefore the gods of childbirth came or were summoned to her aid.

---

15 For further discussion, see Bertram, 670f.

16 RSV and *KBL*³: "vigorous."

17 Scharbert, 20f.

18 Cf. G. R. Driver, "Problems of the Hebrew Text of Job," *Wisdom in Israel and in the Ancient Near East. Festschrift H. H. Rowley. SVT*, 3 (1955), 93; Bertram, 670; differently, M. Dahood, "Northwest Semitic Philology and Job," in J. L. McKenzie, ed., *The Bible in Current Catholic Thought. Saint Mary's Theology Studies*, 1; *Gruerthaner Memorial Volume* (1962), 73, "flock."

19 *RÄR*, 208f.

Akkadian rituals have been preserved that were meant for "the pregnant woman who is 'bound'" and "the woman suffering pains of labor."[20] The ceremonies surrounding delivery *ana sinništi mušapšiqti,* "for a woman in travail,"[21] were intended to promote a normal birth (*išāriš*) or quick delivery (*arḫiš*). Occasionally such ceremonies were combined with massage of the woman's body, sometimes with the administration of magical drugs. The woman in labor wore a special belt, sometimes containing a "birth-stone"; loosening it when the pains began was supposed to hasten delivery.[22] There were also herbs associated with birth, and, in the Hellenistic world, amulets against the pain of labor.[23] At times the pain was recorded in the name of the child (cf., for example, *ben-'ônî,* "son of my sorrow," Gen. 35:18). The course of labor and the form and behavior of the newborn infant were used as omens for prognostication.[24] At least in the Akkadian sphere, "birth pangs" are used in metaphors and similes.[25]

III. OT Usage.

1. *Literal.* According to Gen. 3:16, human birth has been associated with pain ever since the Fall, a familiar idea in the OT. There is no birth without travail. Even the animals have to go through *chᵃbhālîm* to bring their young into the world. In their case, however, it is considered a demonstration of divine omnipotence and of concern on the part of the Creator that animals give birth with the greatest of ease, a phenomenon almost beyond human comprehension. They crouch, they give birth, and they have already "dismissed" (*shālach,* Job 39:3) their birth pangs. If this is itself miraculous, a birth without *chᵃbhālîm* is totally unprecedented. Therefore this motif is used only with great caution as an image for the coming of the age of salvation (Isa. 66:7). Zion gives birth to her sons (i.e., the exiles return) without *chēbhel*—a statement unusual even in the context of prophecy (cf. Mic. 4:9f.). God's intervention in history can even breach the order of nature. Only later, in legendary works, do we find the motif of painless birth as a motif of the "golden age."[26]

Cant. 8:5b is undisputed: "Under the apple tree I awakened you, where your mother was in travail (*chibbēl*) with you, where she who bore you was in travail." Gerlemann renders *chibbēl* as "conceive," thinking of the motif of "love under the trees," which is common in Egyptian love poetry.[27] There is probably no allusion to the fall of Eve, as the Vulgate suggests.

2. *Metaphorical.* "Birth pangs" are a favorite metaphor for the tribulations God's judgment brings upon man. According to Hos. 13:13, the *chᵃbhālîm* stand in the first instance as a metaphor for God's judgment. Just as they mark the beginning of a birth, they should now be for Ephraim a sign that it is the right time to repent. The basis for the

---

[20]R. Labat in *RLA,* III, 178.
[21]*AMT,* 67, 1; *KAR,* 196.
[22]Binder, 46-50.
[23]*Ibid.,* 99.
[24]*BuA,* II, 260ff.; E. Ebeling in *RLA,* III, 180.
[25]For citations, see *AHw,* I, 342; cf. III.2.
[26]Apoc. Bar. 56:6; Josephus *Ant.* ii.9.4(217f.).
[27]G. Gerleman, *BK,* XVIII (1965), 214.

comparison, however, is probably even more complex, for in the background we can glimpse the mortal danger in Ephraim's situation. He is an "unwise son," since despite the *ch^{a}bhālîm* he will not[28] or cannot[29] accept the imminence of the birth and behave accordingly. Isaiah uses the motif in a threat against Babylon (Isa. 13:8). The terrible "day of Yahweh" brings terror upon those who witness it; in their *tsîrîm* and *ch^{a}bhālîm* they are like a woman in travail (cf. Mic. 4:9f.; Jer. 6:24; Isa. 21:3; Joel 2:6; etc.), standing aghast, their faces aflame (Isa. 13:8b). Here we can clearly recognize the *tsîrîm* and *ch^{a}bhālîm* as symptoms of panic in the face of a sudden overwhelming threat. Jeremiah applies the image to Jerusalem, which in its false sense of security refuses to reflect on the terror of the threatened siege. Then *ch^{a}bhālîm* will come upon the city (Jer. 22:23; cf. also 13:21, par. to the woman's sexual degradation). In Jer. 49:24 (post-Jeremiah), this metaphor for ineluctability and painful surprise serves (now somewhat less vividly) as a gloss to explain the "panic" (*reṭeṭ*) of the forsaken city of Damascus.

In Ps. 7:15(14), the statement "he conceives (*chibbēl*) evil, and is pregnant with mischief, and brings forth lies" is a Wisdom saying illuminating the connection between the actions of the wicked man and his reward (v. 10[9]). As Isa. 59:4f. and Job 15:35 show, all the members of this metaphor are interchangeable and can be assimilated to the situation at hand.

Finally, the metaphor can be applied directly to the relationship between man and God. Here the image of the woman crying out (*zāʿaq*) and writhing in her pangs (Isa. 26:17) is used for man's total impotence; it stands as a description of man's existential condition before God (v. 17b). As was true in the concrete and natural realm, the *ch^{a}bhālîm* in the metaphorical sense must not be viewed in isolation as the pain of God's judgment. In the former case they are followed by the birth of a new human being; in the latter, they are the necessary transition to a new age of salvation.

Fabry

---

[28]Rudolph.
[29]Robinson.

חָבַר chābhar; חָבֵר chābhēr

Contents: I. Roots and Etymology. II. Use in the OT: 1. The Root *ḥbr*; 2. *ḫbr*: Proper Names; 3. Prophets and Deuteronomy; 4. Exilic Texts; 5. Psalms and Wisdom. III. Late Texts and Intertestamental Literature.

I. Roots and Etymology. Heb. *ḥbr* can theoretically be associated with two different roots, depending on whether Heb. *cheth* corresponds to Proto-Semitic *ḥ* or *ḫ*. The actual situation is even more complex.

In Arabic, there are at least two if not three different roots: (1) a root *ḥbr,* which conveys the concept of color or brightness and thus joy; in South Semitic, form V means "seduce."[1] (2) A root *ḫbr,* which means "unite, be united" and is also attested in Lihyanic.[2] (3) In forms II and IV, Arab. *ḫbr* means "tell, report," which suggests some kind of audible phenomenon.

Now in Akkadian we find *ḫabāru,* "be noisy,"[3] *ebru/ibru,* "comrade, colleague,"[4] which is connected with Amor. *ḥbr,* "unite," and a different *ḫabāru,* associated by von Soden with *awāru* and *ebēru,* which means "penetrate, cross."[5] The wandering bands of *ʿpr* (Egyptian and Ugaritic) were associated with the root *ḫbr,* "unite," by the Akkadian scribes, who termed them *ḫabiru.*[6] Finkelstein connects the *bît ḫubūri,* which had been thought of as a kind of cellar or granary, with *ḫabāru,* "be noisy."[7]

At Ugarit we find *ḥbr,* "comrade,"[8] and a *bt ḫbr,* which cannot be independent of

---

chābhar. W. F. Albright, "The Eastern Mediterranean about 1060 B.C.," *Studies Presented to D. M. Robinson,* I (1951), 223-231, esp. 229f.; K. Elliger, "Ephod und Choschen," *VT,* 8 (1958), 19-35, esp. 22-24; J. J. Finkelstein, "Hebrew חבר and Semitic *Ḫ B R," *JBL,* 75 (1956), 328-331; S. B. Gurewicz, "The Problem of Lam 3," *ABR,* 8 (1960), 19-23; O. Loretz, "*ḥbr* in Jb 16, 4b," *CBQ,* 23 (1961), 293f.; A. Malamat, "Mari and the Bible: Some Patterns of Tribal Organization and Institutions," *JAOS,* 82 (1962), 143-150; B. Mazar (Maisler), "Canaan and the Canaanites," *BASOR,* 102 (1946), 7-12, esp. 9f.; R. Meyer, "φαρισαῖος," *TDNT,* IX, 16-20; M. Noth, *Die Ursprünge des alten Israel im Lichte neuer Quellen. AFNW,* 94 (1961), 35f.; H. Sauren and G. Kestemont, "Keret, Roi de *Ḫubur,*" *UF,* 3 (1971), 181-221; D. Sperber, "A Note on Hasmonean Coin-Legends; *Ḥeber* and *Rosh Ḥeber,*" *PEQ,* 97 (1965), 85-93; F. Vattioni, "Deuteronomio 18, 11 e un'iscrizione spagnola," *Or,* 36 (1967), 178-180; M. Wagner, "Beiträge zur Aramaismenfrage in alttestamentlichen Hebräisch," *Hebräische Wortforschung. Festschrift W. Baumgartner. SVT,* 16 (1967), 360f.

[1] A. Jamme, *Sabaean Inscriptions from Maḥram Bilqîs (Mârib)* (1962), 436, 442.

[2] A. J. Jaussen, *Mission archéologique en Arabie (Mars-Mai 1907)* (Paris, 1909-1922), No. 71, ed. Caskel and Jamme; the latter translates it: "conclude a treaty"; cf. F. Altheim, *Christentum am Roten Meer,* III, No. 118; also W. Leslau, *Hebrew Cognates in Amharic* (1969), 92.

[3] *AHw,* I, 302; *CAD,* VI, 7.

[4] *AHw,* I, 363f.; *CAD,* VII, 5-7.

[5] *CAD,* VI, 8; for a different analysis, see *AHw,* I, 302.

[6] Cf. J. Bottéro in *RLA,* IV, 14-27.

[7] Cf. F. Rosenthal, "Die Parallelstellen in den Texten von Ugarit," *Or,* 8 (1939), 231f., n. 2.

[8] *WUS,* No. 895; C. Virolleaud in *Ugaritica,* V (1968), 551.

Akk. *bît ḫubūri.*[9] For *ḥbr,* Ugaritic has a precursor in the Amorite from Mari, where the root with the meaning "bind" gives the noun *ḫibrum,* "clan."[10] The phrase *ḫibrum ša nawîm* refers to an encampment outside the city. The *ḫbrtnr*[11] or *ḫubur tanuri*[12] is an enigmatic figure; he brings a horse to the king of Carchemish. Perhaps there is some connection with the *bt ḫbr*[13] that stands in parallel with *qryt,* "city" (hardly "storehouse," Akk. *qarîtu*). It is not impossible that we have here a case of interchange between *ḥ* and *ḫ,* which is not uncommon in Ugaritic;[14] this could also explain Ethiop. *ḫebūr.*[15] It can be considered a proper name, and in fact *ḫbr rbt* and *ḫbr ṯrrt,* "Great/Little *ḫbr,*"[16] are two geographical terms that go together like *ʾdm rbt* and *ʾdm ṯrrt,* possibly the names of two groups of citizens that have developed into proper names.[17] Finkelstein, however, prefers to connect them with the Akk. *bît ḫubūri* from the root "be noisy." This would make it necessary to posit in Ugaritic, as in Arabic, two roots *ḫbr* I and II.

All these roots coalesce in Hebrew and West Semitic *ḥbr.* The sense "unite" appears in Egyptian[18] as a term for trade associations. The noun has the meaning "colleague" in the Marseilles sacrificial tariff[19] and probably in the Kition Inscription,[20] as well as the Aramaic Sefire Inscription.[21] In an inscription published by Solá-Solé[22] and edited by Vattioni, *ḥbr(y)* is used in parallel synonymy with *bny šʾl,* "magicians." One might ask whether the "comrades of Kothar" at Ugarit or the trade "associations" were bound together by a magical rite. The new inscription confirms this hypothesis, but we are probably dealing not so much with magical "bonds" as with magical "words" (cf. Akk. *ḫabāru*).

II. Use in the OT.

1. *The Root ḫbr.* The Arabic root *ḫbr* is represented in Hebrew by *chᵃbhûrāh,* "wound, weal" (Gen. 4:23; Ex. 21:25; Isa. 1:6; 53:5; Ps. 38:6 [Eng. v. 5]; Prov. 20:30), and *chᵃbharburôth,* "spots (of a leopard)" (Jer. 13:23). On Job 16:4, see

---

[9] *WUS,* No. 997.

[10] *AHw,* I, 344; Noth, 35; Malamat, 144f.; idem, "מארי והמקרא," *Sefer Segal. Festschrift M. H. Segal* (1964), 24ff.

[11] *CTA,* 64 [106], 34.

[12] RS 17.227, lines 32f. = *PRU,* IV, 40ff.: "*grand-écuyer,*" "Master of the Horse"; cf. *AHw,* I, 352.

[13] *CTA,* 14 [I K], 82, 173.

[14] P. R. Berger, "Zur Bedeutung des in den akkadischen Texten aus Ugarit bezeugten Ortsnamens *Ḫīlu* (*Ḫl*)," *UF,* 2 (1970), 341, n. 4; J. C. de Moor, review of *Ugaritica,* V, in *UF,* 1 (1969), 188, n. 151.

[15] Cf. Wagner, 360, n. 3.

[16] *CTA,* 15 [III K], IV, 8f., 19f.

[17] See the discussion of OT usage below.

[18] Wen-amon i.24–ii.1.

[19] *KAI,* 69.19

[20] *KAI,* 37.15, 17.

[21] *KAI,* 222 A.4 (damaged).

[22] J. M. Solá-Solé, "Nueva inscripción fenicia de España," *RSO,* 41 (1966), 97–108.

below. This root has no particular theological significance; it furnishes the climax of the lex talionis ("Eye for eye, tooth for tooth, . . . stripe for stripe," Ex. 21:24f.).

2. *ḫbr: Proper Names.* The root *ḫbr* presents a totally different situation. Perhaps on account of its magical overtones, it does not enter the biblical vocabulary until late, appearing first in proper names derived from the Amorite *ḫibrum*. Hebron could represent the "alliance" of the four clans of Kiriath-arba (Jgs. 1:20; Nu. 13:22), and *ḥebher haqqênî* (Jgs. 4:11, 17, 21; 5:24) could be a group of Kenite tribes in the plain of Jezreel.[23]

3. *Prophets and Deuteronomy.* Later the word comes to be used in a pejorative sense, both as a noun (*chebher,* "group, gang"; *chābhēr,* "companion") and as a verb ("bind, associate," attested in the qal, piel, pual, and hithpael). In Hos. 4:17, Ephraim is "joined" (passive participle) to idols (*ʿatsabbîm*), just as at Ugarit a man can become the companion of a god. Hos. 6:9 speaks of a "band" of priests who murder on the way to Shechem. According to the LXX of 1 S. 20:30, which reads *ḥbr* instead of *bḥr* (the same textual problem is found in Eccl. 9:4), Saul accuses Jonathan of having "joined himself" to the son of Jesse.

In Dt. 18:11, the meaning is not merely pejorative but magical, as in the inscription published by Solá-Solé.[24] Here there appears in parallel to the medium (*shōʾēl ʾôbh*) the *chōbhēr chebher,* i.e., "charmer of charms,"[25] who is condemned for his activity. This magical sense appears most frequently in Deutero-Isaiah, where *chebher* refers to the sorceries of the Babylonian magicians (Isa. 47:9, 12). In 44:11, with reference to those who make idols, the prophet plays on the ambiguity of *ḥbr* and *ḥrš* ("workman"/ magician"; cf. Isa. 3:3): "Behold, all his [the idol's] 'fellows' (*chābhēr*) shall be put to shame, and the craftsmen (*chārāsh*) are but men; let them all assemble . . ., they shall be terrified. . . ." Here the two roots obviously coalesce.

4. *Exilic Texts.* With Ezekiel, we find a neutral secular meaning without magical implications. Even if it is impossible to deny totally the astrological background of the *chōbhᵉrôth* that "join" the wings of the heavenly creatures (1:11[26]), in 37:16-19 Israel is "associated" with Judah. Here the word means the happy reunion of the separated brothers. This neutral sense is also present in Gen. 14:3, which speaks of the "allies" in the valley of Siddim, and in Jgs. 20:11, where the men of Israel are "united" against the outrage committed by the Benjaminites of Gibeah.

Archaizing on the basis of the sources, although later than Ezekiel in symbolism and theology, P recalls the Amorite meaning ("juncture, seam")[27] in using *chōbhereth* to designate the edges where boards or curtains are joined together in the tabernacle (Ex. 26:4, 10; 36:17), and invents the term *machbereth* for the joint ("seam," Ex. 26:4f.,

---

[23]Malamat.
[24]Cf. Vattioni.
[25]Cf. Finkelstein.
[26]But see W. Zimmerli, *BK,* XIII (1969), 5.
[27]See I.

10; 36:11f.,17). This term is then borrowed by the Chronicler in a somewhat different sense: wooden or iron binders or clamps (1 Ch. 22:3; 2 Ch. 34:11). As is well known (cf. Ex. 31:1ff.), Bezalel and his helpers who made the tabernacle inherited the wisdom and craftsmanship of the Ugaritic Kothar-and-Ḫasis, who built the palace of Baal.[28] The original religious notions, demythologized, appear with reference to the "union" of the tribes about the sanctuary: "the tabernacle shall be one whole (*'echādh*)," we read in Ex. 26:6. The qal participle appears twice (Ex. 28:7; 39:4) in connection with the ephod of the high priest as a symbol of the unity of the twelve tribes.

5. *Psalms and Wisdom.* This positive use of the root to designate the unity of the chosen people could not carry the day in all cases. In the Psalms, we find the magical sense once more (Ps. 58:6[5]: *chōbhēr chᵃbhārîm,* par. *mᵉlachᵃshîm,* as a term for "enchanters"[29]); the pejorative sense "be in league with" appears in Ps. 94:20 (alliance with the throne of the destroyer), and possibly in Ps. 45:8(7), where the king's "fellows" are surpassed by the anointed.[30] In Ps. 122:3, however, the unity of Israel is symbolized by the firmness with which the houses of Jerusalem are bound together; and in Ps. 119:63, finally, we are dealing with the company of those who fear God.

Wisdom Literature did not make much use of *ḥbr*. The meaning "companion" is appropriate in Prov. 28:24, but it is still pejorative: "He who robs his father or his mother and says, 'That is no transgression,' is the companion of a man who destroys" (*mashchîth;* cf. 18:9, with an allusion to Ezk. 21:36[31] and Ex. 12:23: "destroyer of the family"). In another proverb, which appears twice (21:9 and 25:24) with only minor variation, we find once more the ancient *bt ḫbr* of Ugarit and the cuneiform texts. Following Finkelstein, we may translate: "Better to live in a corner of the housetop than with a contentious woman and a noisy house (family)"; Gurewicz, on the contrary, takes *byt ḥbr* to mean "storeroom, granary."[31] The same pejorative meaning "noise" appears in Job 16:4.[32] In Job 34:8, however, we are dealing once more with the evil "company" of the wicked.

In Job 40:30(41:6), a difficult passage, *chabbārîm* stands in parallel with *kᵉnaᶜᵃnîm,* "merchants," a context that suggests for *ḥbr* the nuance of "agree, make a contract." This meaning suggests also the trade associations of Wen-amon, as well as Jehoshaphat's ill-starred attempt to establish seafaring trade with the Tyrians (2 Ch. 20:35-37).

III. Late Texts and Intertestamental Literature. Under the influence of Ezekiel and P, the meaning of the root becomes more positive. In Mal. 2:14, *chᵃbhērāh* is the "companion," the "wife of your youth." In the Song of Solomon,

---

[28]Cf. also *WbMyth,* I, 295f.

[29]Cf. M. Dahood, *Psalms,* II. *AB,* XVII (1968), 60.

[30]For a different view, see H.-J. Kraus, *BK,* XV/1 (^{4}1972), *in loc.*

[31]S. B. Gurewicz. "Some Examples of Modern Hebrew Exegesis of the OT," *ABR,* 11 (1963), 22f.

[32]Loretz; cf. F. Rosenthal, *A History of Muslim Historiography* (Leiden, 1952), 102, associating Heb. *ḥbr* in Job 16:4 with Arab. *ḫabar,* "information."

the *ch^a bhērîm* are the companions of the bridegroom (1:7; 8:13). In Ecclesiastes, the word refers to the companion who helps his fellow (4:10) or the man who is still joined with all the living and thus can have hope (9:4, according to some manuscripts).

The book of Sirach makes frequent use of the root. The author, whose purpose is to preserve his biblical heritage, understands its basic meaning as "join," "ally." But this human alliance is fragile in comparison to the bond of God's covenant. The *chābhēr* is the table companion who will not stand by you in the day of trouble (6:10), or the friend and companion against whom you should not devise a lie (7:12). A man who clings to one like himself runs the risk of becoming the lamb who has fellowship with the wolf (13:16f.), and whoever associates with a sinner or a proud man will become like him (12:14; 13:1). One should not forget one's associate in battle and at the division of the spoil (37:6). The meaning "marry" seems appropriate in 7:25 (A reads *ḥbr;* C and LXX read *zbd*); the selected husband should be a man of understanding. In 12:13, finally, *ḥbr* refers to the snake charmer who can be bitten by his serpent; here we find once more the ancient magical meaning.

This meaning is also attested at Qumran (1QH 5:28); there, however, as in the other Jewish sects, the predominant meaning is "companion, ally" (CD 13:15; 14:16), often with political overtones. Thus the author of Daniel uses the word in 11:6 to refer to a political alliance with evil consequences. In the Manual of Discipline, however, we read: "Their counsel is allied with the sons of heaven" (1QS 11:8). But the word is comparatively rare at Qumran; the usual term for the sectarian community is → יחד *yḥd*.

The other Jewish groups, however, prefer *ḥbr*. On Hasmonean coins, John Hyrcanus refers to himself as the head (*rō'sh*) of the Jewish league (*ḥbr*), probably after the conquest of Samaria.[33] At the same time he calls himself the "high priest." In a letter of Simon bar Kosiba to Jesus ben Galgola, a *ḥbr* is a military unit of the holy war: "The men of this *ḥbr*."[34] Among the less militant sects, *ḥbr* (as in Palmyrene[35]) refers to the members of a religious brotherhood. This holds true for the *ch^a bhērîm* of the Pharisaic groups assembled for examination, as well as for the *ch^a bhûrôth* meals.[36]

The LXX commonly renders *ḥbr* by means of *koinón, koinōnós,* or *koinōneín,* which recalls the meaning of *koinōnia* in the NT.

Cazelles

---

[33]Sperber.

[34]Cf. *RB,* 63 (1956), 48.

[35]*DISO,* 82.

[36]Cf. also J. Neusner, "*ḤBR* and *N'MN,*" *RevQ,* 5 (1964/65), 119–122.

חבש ḥbš

Contents: I. Etymology. II. Meaning and Occurrences. III. Metaphorical Use.

I. Etymology. The root *ḥbš* in the Semitic languages[1] has the basic meaning "bind up." It appears in Syr. *ḥ^e^bhaš,* "shut in, confine," Arab. *ḥabasa,* "obstruct, confine," and *ḥabs,* "prison." In this sense the root also occurs in Middle Hebrew, Jewish Aramaic,[2] Mandean,[3] and Tigré.[4]

II. Meaning and Occurrences. The verb originally meant "bind up"; it is used in various contexts:

1. It can refer to the fastening of a saddle girth around the body of an animal, and thus becomes a technical term for the saddling of asses. The saddle may be a riding saddle (Nu. 22:21; Jgs. 19:10; 2 S. 16:1; 17:23; 19:27 [Eng. v. 26]; 1 K. 2:40; 13:13, 23, 27; 2 K. 4:24) or a pack saddle (Gen. 22:3).

2. The verb *ḥbš* can be used for "binding on" a turban as a headdress, which may be made of expensive fabric (Ezk. 16:10). Removal of this turban was a sign of mourning (Ezk. 24:17). Priests also wore turbans wrapped to form a tall cone (Ex. 29:9; Lev. 8:13).[5] The image of the turban is borrowed in Jonah 2:6(5), where weeds are wrapped about the head of the drowning man.

3. In medical terminology, *ḥbš* refers to the binding up of fractures (Ezk. 30:21; 34:4,16)—an activity that is part of the shepherd's care for his flock—and other injuries (Isa. 1:6; Ps. 147:3; Job 5:18).[6] Since the purpose is always healing, the verb can also take on the more general meaning "heal" (Isa. 61:1). Thus the participle *chōbhēsh* is a term for the "healer" or "surgeon" (Isa. 3:7).

4. The use of *ḥbš* in Ezk. 27:24 is more obscure; it refers to a specific operation in the manufacture of cordage, either for handling materials or for use in clothing;[7] the context suggests the latter.

ḥbš. J. Hempel, *Heilung als Symbol und Wirklichkeit im biblischen Schrifttum* ([2]1965); P. Humbert, "Maladie et médecine dans l'AT," *RHPR,* 44 (1964), 1-29; E. F. Sutcliffe, "Notes on Job, Textual and Exegetical," *Bibl,* 30 (1949), 66-90.

[1] On the Egyptian equivalent *ḥbś,* "clothe," cf. *UT,* No. 835.
[2] *KBL*[3].
[3] *MdD,* 130b.
[4] *TigrWb,* 79a.
[5] *BRL,* 429ff.; *BHHW,* III (1966), 1491f.; K. Elliger, *HAT,* 4 (1966), 118.
[6] Cf. Hempel, 238; Humbert, 17.
[7] W. Zimmerli, *BK,* XIII (1969), 657.

5. In the technical vocabulary of mining, *ḥbš* means the "damming" of seepage (Job 28:11).[8] Since we have very little information about mining in ancient Palestine, it is impossible to determine the details of the activity designated by the verb and how it relates to the basic meaning of *ḥbš*.[9] The interpretation is therefore based less on OT evidence than on Arab. *ḥibs,* "dam, barrage."

6. The meaning "lead, govern,"[10] derived from Job 34:17, is uncertain. Isa. 3:7 cannot be cited in evidence, since *ḥbš* does not mean "govern" or "bind on a turban" there.[11] The meaning of the passage is rather that the man called to be ruler points out that he is not a healer and has no bread at his disposal. The situation of the people is depicted in such hopeless terms that "governing" can involve nothing more than healing and distributing food. Even though these features have always been part of the role of the ruler, in that, like the shepherd, he binds up the cripples (Ezk. 34:4),[12] the paradox of Isa. 3:7 consists precisely in that now only a surgeon can "govern."

In Job 34:17, too, the meaning "govern" can hardly be maintained. The translation "hold the reins"[13] derives from the image of saddling an animal, but goes far beyond the semantic range of that usage. Material considerations, too, make the meaning "govern" inappropriate in Job 34:17. The rhetorical question, "Shall one who hates justice govern?" by no means demands the desired answer, "No," because tyrants can certainly govern. But the meaning "heal" also runs up against difficulties in this passage, for the question, "Would he heal if he hated justice?"[14] must strike Job in his sufferings as cynicism. Therefore Sutcliffe suggests the translation:[15] "Can he even heal one who hates justice?" In other words, it is pointed out to Job that he is suffering because he is guilty. This interpretation accords well with the book of Job, but runs up against linguistic difficulties.

In any case, the use of *ḥbš* with the meaning "govern" cannot solve the problems of Job 34:17 and is too weakly attested to be maintained seriously.[16] Neither can *ḫapši,* which may mean "strength" in Amarna letter 147, 12,[17] support the translation "govern." In discussing the passage, Dahood connects *ḥbš* with the piel of *ḥpš* in the sense "inquire, search out."[18]

---

[8]Cf. G. Fohrer, *KAT,* XVI (1963), 389.

[9]*BRL,* 95ff.; *BHHW,* I (1962), 217ff.

[10]*KBL*^{3}.

[11]O. Kaiser, *Isaiah 1-12. OTL* (trans. 1972), 42, n.b.

[12]Cf. H. Wildberger, *BK,* X/1 (1972), 125.

[13]Fohrer, *KAT,* XVI, 462.

[14]N. H. Tur-Sinai, *The Book of Job* (Jerusalem, ^{2}1967), 480; cf. A. B. Ehrlich, *Randglossen zur hebräischen Bibel* (^{2}1968), VI, 315.

[15]P. 75.

[16]But cf. M. Löhr, "Jesaias Studien I," *ZAW,* 36 (1916), 76f.; E. R. Rowlands, "The Targum and the Peshiṭta Version of the Book of Isaiah," *VT,* 9 (1959), 183f.; *CML,* 139.

[17]EA II, 1246.

[18]M. Dahood, "The Phoenician Contribution to Biblical Wisdom Literature," in *The Role of the Phoenicians in the Interaction of Mediterranean Civilizations,* ed. W. A. Ward (Beirut, 1968), 126f.

7. The verb *ḥbš* occurs 31 times in the OT, primarily in the qal, with two occurrences in the piel (Ps. 147:3; Job 28:11) and two in the pual (Isa. 1:6; Ezk. 30:21).[19] The meaning "saddle up" is attested only in the historical books (Genesis–2 Kings), "binding up" a wound only in the prophetic books, Job, and Psalms.

III. Metaphorical Use. Israelite Wisdom Literature developed the comforting notion that Yahweh both wounds and binds up (Job 5:18), in other words, that the hand that inflicts the painful wounds is the same hand from which alone relief is to be expected.[20] This realization was open to various interpretations, which were hotly debated. If prosperity and disaster are both traced to God, disaster can have a pedagogical purpose and serve to guide men back to the right way. Wisdom itself overcame this notion, because it observed that there was no firm connection between actions and their rewards, and that the extent of the punishment was by no means always commensurate with pedagogical ends. Job, in any event, "has completely rejected such a positive interpretation of his sufferings."[21]

Hosea, too, disputes the argument cited. When the people return to Yahweh, confident that "he has stricken, and he will bind us up" (Hos. 6:1), the prophet approves the statement in principle. He denies, however, that it holds true in any naturalistic sense. For a people whose return to Yahweh is fleeting "like a morning cloud, like the dew that goes early away" (Hos. 6:4), healing can only follow judgment.

The notion that suffering has a pedagogical purpose is also addressed and refuted in Isa. 1:6. Isaiah compares Israel to a whipped slave,[22] whose entire body is covered with wounds that are not pressed out and bound up or softened with oil. This image depicts the destruction of Judah by the campaign of Sennacherib in 701. Even in this situation of almost total devastation, the prophet addresses a woe-oracle to Judah, because he knows the incurable obduracy of the people, who cannot be brought back to Yahweh even by cruel blows. Repentance is no longer a possible prospect, disaster has lost its pedagogical purpose, there can be no deliverance.

The prophets saw for Israel a time approaching when there would be only blows but no binding up of wounds, a catastrophe in which there would be none to bring healing to the people (Isa. 3:7). When Israel placed its trust in Egypt and Pharaoh Hophra, expecting—even after his defeat—that he would deliver them from the invading Babylonians, Ezekiel pointed out that Yahweh had broken the arm of Pharaoh and taken care to see that it should not be bound up and healed (Ezk. 30:21). Thus even the faint hope for a resurgence of Egyptian power was extinguished.

Despite these experiences with Yahweh's punitive actions, there still continued in Israel the living hope that he would heal and bind up after judgment. When catastrophe struck in 587, the "shepherds," the governing classes, took no thought for the fate of

---

[19]For a different view, see P. Joüon, "Notes de lexicographie hébraïque," *Bibl*, 6 (1925), 420f.

[20]F. Horst, *BK*, XVI/1 (1968), 86.

[21]G. von Rad, *Wisdom in Israel* (trans. 1972), 206ff., 226.

[22]G. Fohrer, "Jesaja 1 als Zusammenfassung der Verkündigung Jesajas," *ZAW*, 74 (1962), 257 = *Studien zur alttestamentlichen Prophetie*. *BZAW*, 99 (1967), 155.

the people (Ezk. 34:4). Against this failure is set a future in which Yahweh himself will feed his flock and bind up the crippled (Ezk. 34:16). The book of Isaiah, too, hopes for a time when Yahweh will bind up the hurt of his people, suffered during the catastrophe of 587, and heal their wounds (Isa. 30:26). A hymn extols Yahweh because he gathers the outcasts of Israel and binds up their wounds (Ps. 147:3). But not only does Yahweh himself care for his people; the prophet, too, is charged to "bind up the brokenhearted" (Isa. 61:1).

"Yahweh wounds and binds up"—this was the experience of Israel in the course of its history. But the OT did not fall into the error of seeing a necessary, naturalistic connection between the two. Yahweh's freedom was always preserved: men have no claim on his healing (Hos. 6:1); it can only be hoped for (Isa. 30:26) or received with gratitude (Ps. 147:3).

Münderlein

חָג *chagh*; חגג *ḥgg*

Contents: I. 1. Etymology; Secular Usage; 2. Ancient Versions. II. 1. Sacred Times; 2. Ancient Near East. III. 1. OT Occurrences; Synonyms and Antonyms; 2. Early Period; 3. Catalogs; 4. Theological Significance of Different Stages.

I. 1. *Etymology; Secular Usage.* Etymologically related words with similar meanings are found in other Semitic languages: Arab. *ḥağğ,* "festival, pilgrimage," *ḥiğğat,*

---

chagh. E. Auerbach, "Die Feste im alten Israel," *VT,* 8 (1958), 1-18; G. Cornfeld, *Pictorial Biblical Encyclopedia* (1964), 320-27, 637; W. Eichrodt, *Theol. OT,* I (trans. 1961), 119ff.; H. J. Elhorst, "Die deuteronomischen Jahresfeste," *ZAW,* 42 (1924), 136-145; M. Eliade, *Patterns in Comparative Religion* (trans. 1958), 353-373; G. Fohrer, *History of Israelite Religion* (trans. 1972), 190ff.; H. Frankfort, "State Festivals in Egypt and Mesopotamia," *Journal of the Warburg and Courtauld Institute,* 15 (1952), 1-12; T. H. Gaster, *Thespis* (1950); *idem,* "The Religion of the Canaanites," in V. Ferm, *Forgotten Religions* (1950), 113-143; *idem, Festivals of the Jewish Year* (^{2}1955); J. Gray, *The Legacy of Canaan. SVT,* 5 (^{2}1965), 37-76, 199-209; M. Haran, "חגים במקרא," תקופות ומוסדות (1972), 77ff.; F. Heiler, *Erscheinungsformen und Wesen der Religion. RdM,* 1 (1961), 150-161; I. Hrbek, "*ḥg* und verwandte Wurzeln in den semitischen Sprachen," *Studia orientalia in memoriam C. Brockelmann. WZ* Halle, 17 (1968), 95-104; K. Kerényi, "Vom Wesen des Festes," *Paideuma,* 1 (1938), 59-74; H.-J. Kraus, *Worship in Israel* (trans. 1966), 53-97; E. Kutsch, "Feste und Feiern. II. In Israel," *RGG*^{3}, II, 910-17; *idem,* "Von den israelitisch-jüdischen Hauptfesten," *Im Lande der Bibel,* 20 (1974), 22-26; B. Landsberger, *Der kultische Kalender der Babylonier und Assyrer. LSS,* 6/1-2 (1915), 2-14, 111-13; H. Lewy and J. Lewy, "The Origin of the Week and the Oldest West Asiatic Calendar," *HUCA,* 17 (1942/43), 1-152; R. Martin-Achard, *Essai biblique sur les fêtes d'Israël* (Geneva, 1974); M. P. Nilsson, *Griechische Feste des Jahres* (1918); *idem, Griechische Feste von religiöser Bedeutung mit Ausschluss des Attischen* (^{2}1957); E. Otto, *Das Mazzotfest in*

"pilgrimage"; OSA *ḥg, ḥgt,* "festival"; Aram. (Jewish, Syr., and Nabatean dialects) *ḥaggāʾ,* "festival." The etymology is obscure, since the root is used for the most part denominatively: Heb. *ḥgg,* "celebrate a festival" (postbiblically also "offer festival sacrifice"), South Arab. *ḥgg,* "gather for a festival, undertake a pilgrimage,"[1] Arab. *ḥağğa,* "undertake a pilgrimage," Syr. *ḥaggî,* "celebrate a festival." An exception is Ps. 107:27: the ships on the stormy seas "*yāchōggû* and stagger like drunken men." But even here it is possible to think in terms of a meaning derived from *chagh,* "sway rhythmically or ecstatically like a festal assembly." The aspect of joy has led some to suggest a connection with Egyp. *ḥ3g,* "be happy."[2] But if here the original meaning of the root is preserved, it turns out to be something like "reel, sway." In this case the relationship with *chûgh,* "go in a circle," must be noted. The root *ḥgg* could then have had the original meaning "turn in circles, become dizzy"[3] or "leap, dance,"[4] giving rise to *chagh* in the sense of "sacred round dance, cultic procession about the altar."[5]

The hapax legomenon *choggāʾ* (Isa. 19:17) would be evidence that this derivation is correct if it could be derived with assurance from the same root. On the basis of the context, the word means "terror"—a concept not far removed from "sway, reel, grow dizzy." The opposite suggestion, that the denominative *ḥgg,* "celebrate, dance," developed the secondary meaning "reel, be terrified," appears unlikely from the perspective of linguistic psychology. In his commentary on Isaiah, Jerome sees in *choggāʾ* an example of antonymy: "*in timorem pro festivitate vertitur.*" It is more reasonable, however, to associate the word with Jewish Aram. *ḥrgtʾ,* "fear, trembling,"[6] or Arab. *ḫağiʾa,* "be ashamed."[7]

Since *chagh* is closely connected with the annual cycle (Ex. 34:22; Isa. 29:1),[8] it is reasonable to hypothesize that *chagh* originally designated the solemn conclusion or beginning of this cycle.[9] In any event, the meaning "festival" must be our point of departure for OT usage.[10] Accordingly, *chāghagh* is denominative in 1 S. 30:16

Gilgal. BWANT, 107 (1975), 167-198, 351-363; H. Ringgren, *Israelite Religion* (trans. 1966), 222-240; L. Rost, "Weidewechsel und altisraelitischer Festkalender," *ZDPV,* 66 (1943), 205-215 = *Das kleine Credo und andere Studien zum AT* (1965), 101-112; H. H. Rowley, *Worship in Ancient Israel* (1967), 87ff. and *passim;* S. Schott, *Altägyptische Festdaten. AAWLM,* 1950/10 (1950); H. Speyer, *Der Festtag bei den Propheten. Jüdisch-theologisches Seminar Breslau, Bericht 1934* (1935), 9-61; F. Stolz, "Sabbat, Schöpfungswoche und Herbstfest," *WuD,* 11 (1971), 159-175; de Vaux, *AncIsr,* 484-506; H. Zimmern, *Das babylonische Neujahrsfest. AO,* 25/3 (1926).

1 Cf. G. Ryckmans, review of A. Dupont-Sommer and L. Robert, *La déese de Hiérapolis Castabala (Cilicie), Mus,* 78 (1965), 468f.

2 *WbÄS,* III, 34; cf. W. A. Ward, "Some Egypto-Semitic Roots," *Or,* 31 (1962), 405, n. 6.

3 E. König, *Hebräisches und aramäisches Wörterbuch zum AT* (1910), 98.

4 *KBL*³, 278.

5 J. Wellhausen, *Reste arabischen Heidentums* (²1897, ³1961), 106-110.

6 *GesB,* 213, 257.

7 G. R. Driver, "Studies in the Vocabulary of the OT VI," *JTS,* 34 (1933), 378.

8 See below.

9 From → חוג *chûgh,* "circle"; cf. *KAI,* 202 B.5: *mḥgt,* "ring."

10 T. Nöldeke, *ZDMG,* 41 (1887), 719.

("eating and drinking and celebrating like a *chagh*"),[11] Ps. 42:5 (Eng. v. 4) ("a multitude keeping festival"), and probably also Ps. 107:27.[12]

Kedar-Kopfstein

Hrbek takes a somewhat different etymology as his starting point.[13] According to his theory, an originally bilateral root *ḥg* with the basic meaning "(be) round, circular, crooked" (cf. Arab. *ḥağā*) developed into "form or describe a circle" (Heb., Syr., Jewish Aram. *chag* [Arab. *ḥağā* (*ḥğw*), "surround, protect"; Akk. *egū*, "include"?]) and finally "dance" (Heb. *chāghagh*). This led then secondarily to the meaning "(celebrate) a festival." Any etymological connection with Gk. *ágō*, "celebrate," Lat. *agonium*, "sacrificial festival," *agonia*, "sacrificial animal,"[14] is rejected. According to Hrbek,[15] the root **ḥg* appears in the triliteral roots *ḥgl, ḥgr, ʿgl, ʿgr,* etc.

Botterweck

In the OT, as well as in ancient Hebrew seals and Phoenician inscriptions, we find names such as *ḥgy, ḥgyh,* and *ḥgyt,* presumably given to children born on a *chagh*.

2. *Ancient Versions*. The LXX regularly renders *chagh* by means of *heortḗ* (while *môʿēdh* has a dozen different translations), a word that means "festival" and "festival procession," as well as "pleasure" or "amusement" in general. In the Vulgate we frequently find *sollemnitas*, strictly "annual festival," but also *festivitas*, "festal rejoicing." In Ezk. 46:11, for the sake of variation, there is used *nundinae*, i.e., "the ninth day," which in the Roman calendar marks the end of the week, the market day when work in the fields ceased.

II. 1. *Sacred Times*. Even in the very earliest civilizations joyous events were celebrated, such as births, marriages, or the triumphant return from a battle or hunt. The festivities bore the character of apotropaic magic, since they were meant to ward off danger and guarantee future success. Participation of the community turned these occasions into experiences that constituted and strengthened the society. The rhythm of nature, joined later with observation of the heavens, led to the notion of cyclic time.[16] Thus there arose the festival with a fixed date in the sacral calendar, i.e., the numinous point in time when one cycle ends and a new cycle begins. Precisely determined ceremonies ("rites of passage") were performed to produce a favorable change of fortunes. Finally, the occasional festival was incorporated into the sacral calendar as an

[11] Vulg.: *quasi festum;* for a different approach, see Hrbek, 95; A. Guillaume, "Hebrew and Arabic Lexicography, IV," *Abr-Nahrain,* 4 (1963/64), 5, interprets *ḥgg* as "copulated" and suggests a sexual orgy.

[12] See above.

[13] Pp. 95ff.

[14] H. Møller.

[15] Pp. 97ff.

[16] Cf. Kraus, 51ff.

historical memorial. In fact, the various motifs became increasingly intertwined: the nature festivals were given historical motivations, and historically memorable events acquired mythological overtones.

The natural phenomena that determine chronological calculation—the phases of the moon, the solstices and equinoxes, the routine of agriculture and the interplay between climate and geography—cannot be reduced to a single common denominator, and confuse the overall picture. The various festivals—their dates, motivations, and observances—are subject to constant change.

2. *Ancient Near East.* Our knowledge of festivals in the ancient Near East is based on instructions for the official rituals, often associated with a specific sanctuary, as well as descriptions and literary allusions. From this wealth of material we shall here select only a portion of what is germane to elucidating the nature of the OT *chagh.* Quite generally the coalescence of festival rituals from various cultic circles and the reinterpretation of festival motifs is noteworthy; in particular cases, comparison of individual ceremonies is possible.

In Mesopotamia, Sumerian festival traditions were transformed by the Babylonians and even more by the Assyrians in the course of time. Festivals associated with specific temples took on a variety of local forms, which were then sometimes reduced to uniformity by a powerful cultic center (such as Nippur). Calendrical calculation was associated with a belief in the magical potency of certain days, whether pernicious or beneficial. This belief produced strict regulations, which were especially numerous for the great festivals.

The most important was the New Year Festival. It was celebrated by the Sumerians at the winter solstice, while according to the later calendar of Sargon it was celebrated at the autumnal equinox. From the time of Hammurabi onward, it was shifted to the first days of Nisan, i.e., the period of the vernal equinox. In many cities, however, the earlier date was retained; in others both were observed. At Babylon, the New Year Festival was a cultic repetition of the creation of the world as described in Enuma Elish.[17] It is the festival celebrating the triumph of the creator-god over chaos and the enthronement festival of the king, but also a festival of outward and cultic purification. As early as ancient Sumer, the *hieros gamos* motif was woven into the observance.

Other festivals, too, based on agriculture, were religious in nature. At midsummer the dying of the vegetation god Tammuz was lamented, and then his resurrection was celebrated with rejoicing.[18]

In Egypt, the festival calendar was linked with the flooding of the Nile. During the period of high water, sumptuous banquets were held in honor of the god Amon, at which the corresponding cult legends were recited. At the end of the flood stage began the celebrations to guarantee the harvest, which were dedicated to the fertility-god Min (*hieros gamos*). The cutting of the first sheaf with a copper sickle was a cultic ceremony. The official coronation of a new ruler was carried out on New Year's day, often

[17]Cf. R. Frankena, *Tākultu. CO,* 2 (1954); R. Pettazzoni, "Der babylonische Ritus des Akītu und das Gedicht der Weltschöpfung," *ErJb,* 19 (1950), 403-430.

[18]Cf. *WbMyth,* I, 51ff.

in conjunction with temple consecration ceremonies. This is not the place to discuss the complex question of the date and nature of the Sed and Opet festivities.[19]

For the Syro-Canaanite region, although we know nothing about the festivals themselves, we can derive some information about cultic ceremonies from myths and liturgical texts.[20] The OT, too, provides some material (e.g., Dt. 18:9ff.; 1 K. 18:26; and similar passages). Harvest rituals are reflected in the representations of divine banquets. There were propitiatory rituals and water ceremonies intended to promote fertility.[21] Baal was a vegetation-god. He is slain by Mot ("Death"), but rises to new life, delivered by the goddess ʻAnat. He builds his house in the fall, when the rainy season begins (cf. 1 K. 8:2).

In Greece there was a whole series of festivities connected with the routine of agriculture—plowing, sowing, harvest, vintage, etc. Even though accompanied by merrymaking that sometimes reached an orgiastic level, they occasionally took on the solemn character of a day of atonement with a strict fast. Cultic actions were explained on the basis of quasi-historical etiologies: the Thargelia, for example, were associated with the Athenian tribute to Minos and Theseus' voyage of deliverance. At the Carnea, the Spartans gave thanks to Apollo for bringing them into the land as conquerors. During this festival, the people dwelt in tentlike bowers after the fashion of a military camp. The Panathenea, a harvest festival, was looked upon as a state festival instituted by Theseus.

III. 1. *OT Occurrences; Synonyms and Antonyms.* Verbal forms of the root *ḥgg* appear 16 times in the OT. The noun appears 62 times, most frequently in the Pentateuch (except for Genesis), then in the historical books (except for Joshua), in the prophets (except for Jeremiah and six of the Minor Prophets), and finally in the Psalms. The noun can be used absolutely (Isa. 30:29); more frequently it appears in the construct as the *regens* of another noun that describes more precisely the occasion of the festival: *chagh* of harvest, *chagh* of vintage, etc. (Ex. 23:16; Lev. 23:6).

Especially noteworthy is the phrase *chagh-yhvh* (found only in Ex. 10:9; Lev. 23:39; Jgs. 21:19; Hos. 9:5). This obviously ancient expression is based on the notion that the deity himself celebrates his own festival, participation in which is a favor granted to or obligation imposed upon men. It is safe to assume that *yhvh* here represents an earlier Canaanite divine name. Usually this phrase is replaced by a periphrastic dative, *chagh lᵉyhvh* (Ex. 12:14; Lev. 23:41), in which we may hear echoes of a polemic conflict: it is for Yahweh that this festival is to be celebrated (Ex. 32:5). These notions were lost to later linguistic consciousness; both expressions then designated nothing more than a *chagh* in the context of the Yahweh cult.

Only rarely is *chagh* a *nomen rectum:* after *yôm* (Hos. 9:5; Ps. 81:4[3], both used in an attempt to identify a *chagh* with the "day of Yahweh") and after *chēlebh* (Ex. 23:18) or *peresh* (Mal. 2:3), where, however, *chagh* is used by metonymy for the

[19]Cf. also *RÄR,* 158ff., 185-89.

[20]Cf. T. H. Gaster, "The Spring Festival at Ugarit," *JAOS,* 63 (1943), 222; *idem,* "A Canaanite Ritual Drama: The Spring Festival at Ugarit," *JAOS,* 66 (1946), 49-76.

[21]Cf. H. Kosmala, "Mot and the Vine," *ASTI,* 3 (1964), 147-151.

animal sacrificed on the festival (*môʿēdh* is used with a similar extension of meaning in 2 Ch. 30:22; Qimḥi also assumes such an extension in Isa. 29:1). Possessive suffixes refer to the people celebrating the festival (Dt. 16:14; Hos. 2:13[11]; Ps. 81:4[3]); in the case of *chaggî* (Ex. 23:18), the suffix refers to Yahweh (or represents a misunderstood abbreviation?), in whose honor the festal act is performed.

A *chagh* may be "held" (*ʿāśāh,* 1 K. 8:65; Neh. 8:18) or "kept" (*shāmar,* Ex. 23:15). It begins with "sanctification" (*hithqaddēsh,* Isa. 30:29). It occurs frequently as the object of *chāghagh* (Nu. 29:12; Nah. 2:1[1:15]).

In the construction *chāghagh chagh,* it would be possible to construe the noun as the object effected, in that the festival is in fact brought about by the activity described by the verb. Actually, however, the *chagh* is an existing cultic ceremony, which is merely realized by the action *chāghagh; chagh* is therefore the object affected.[22]

The expression *'isrû-chagh,* "bind the *chagh,*" in Ps. 118:27 is difficult, since the following *ʿabhōthîm* admits two possible meanings: "branches" or "cords." The *chagh* can thus be thought of as a festival procession in the course of which the altar is decked with branches or set apart with cords as a sacred area.[23] Possibly, however, *chagh* may refer here to the sacrificial animal, which is to be bound to the altar.[24]

The noun *chagh* appears in synonymous parallelism with → שיר *shîr* (Am. 8:10), → נדר *nēdher* (Nah. 2:1), → עצרה *ʿatsārāh* (Am. 5:21), and → מועד *môʿēdh* (Hos. 9:5). It is not hard, however, to distinguish the meaning of our word from that of the others. That *shîr* and *nēdher* refer merely to portions of the festival ceremony—a hymn and a thanksgiving vow—is immediately obvious. The *ʿatsārāh (ʿatsereth)* can be any community assembly, including one convoked for mourning and fasting (Joel 1:14). A *môʿēdh* is merely any "appointed time" or "season": even the animals follow their *môʿadhîm* (Jer. 8:7). It can thus be used collectively for *chagh,* new moon, and Sabbath (Ezk. 45:17), and can include the day of trumpets and the Day of Atonement (Lev. 23:2,24,27). In late usage, the word *môʿēdh* can replace *chagh* (2 Ch. 8:13); it can also, however, refer specifically to those holy days to which the name *chagh* does not apply (Ezk. 46:11). The term *chagh* is never applied to family festivals, the nomadic festival of sheepshearing, or the Sabbath and new moon, which derive from the lunar calendar (Ezk. 45:17).

In OT usage, therefore, *chagh* refers to a community festival of the Israelites, determined by the solar year, even when the festival is considered illegitimate (Ex. 32:5; 1 K. 12:32). (A festival of Baal is a *ʿatsārāh;* 2 K. 10:20.) It is marked by rejoicing and songs of thanksgiving (Dt. 16:14; Am. 8:10; Hos. 2:13[11]; Ezk. 6:22), and above all by the joyous processions that make their way to the sanctuary to offer sacrifice (Am. 5:21; Nah. 2:1[1:15]; Isa. 30:29; Zec. 14:16; Ps. 42:3,5[2,4]; 2 Ch. 5:3).

2. *Early Period.* For ancient Israel, we may assume a priori a rich variety of festivals. Diversity of origin, a geographically fragmented land, and the politico-

---

[22]For a discussion of this distinction, see H. Reckendorf, *Über die Paronomasie in den semitischen Sprachen* (1909), 120.

[23]A. Weiser, *The Psalms. OTL* (trans. 1962), 729.

[24]König, *Wörterbuch,* 98.

cultural influences of powerful neighbors must have produced a multiplicity of cultic forms and traditions, which changed constantly through coalescence and conflict. We must now examine the evidence to see whether it confirms this hypothesis. As we do so, we must keep in mind that our sources represent merely portions of reality, some preserved by accident, some tendentious. They underwent their final redaction after the postexilic normalization of the festivals was complete. This means, however, that a special importance attaches to inconsistencies, contradictions, and statements diverging from the given norm.

It is a demonstrable fact that festivals were forgotten or suppressed. The Mishnah[25] preserves mention of an important festival in the month of Ab, of which the OT sources say nothing. Recent scholarship has attempted to infer additional festivals from the texts: a festival of Yahweh's enthronement (Mowinckel), a covenant festival (von Rad), a Zion festival (Kraus). Festivities celebrated in the context of the Yahweh cult fell into disrepute after being treated like festivals of foreign gods in polemic debate (Isa. 1:29; Ezk. 8:10f.,14; Zec. 12:11). That such opprobrium was not based at all on objective criteria can be seen from the fact that even the legitimate *chaggîm* were of foreign origin and introduced foreign rites into the cult of Yahweh. Noteworthy in this regard is the term *hillûlîm* (→ הלל *hll* I and II), which designates a Canaanite festival (Jgs. 9:27) but happens also to have been retained as a technical ritual term (Lev. 19:24).

The festival catalogs list three *chaggîm.*[26] Other statements (Hos. 9:5; 1 K. 8:65) give the impression of referring only to a single *chagh.* Ezk. 45:17-25 appear to allow for two. It is methologically incorrect to rely on one of these sources and disregard the others—to begin, for example, with the statement that ancient Israel had three *chaggîm,* or to postulate a single *chagh* for the early period. Each passage, rather, is relatively accurate, in that it held true for a specific locality at a specific point in time.

Neither is there agreement among the passages describing the duration of a *chagh.* It can mark the beginning of a week's celebration (Nu. 28:17), function as the climax at the end of the week (Ex. 13:6), or encompass the entire week (Ezr. 6:22). According to Ex. 34:23, only males visit the sanctuary on a *chagh;* but the ancient festival legend Ex. 10:9 is familiar with the custom of having the entire family set forth on the pilgrimage (cf. 1 S. 1).

Above all, however, the variety of names, dates, and rituals points to a diversity of traditions. That Passover and the Feast of Unleavened Bread should be distinguished is generally recognized. Only the latter is a *chagh* (late evidence: 2 Ch. 35:17; Ezr. 6:20, 22).

In Ex. 12:14, *chagh* refers to the Feast of Unleavened Bread in the following verses. Only Ex. 34:25 speaks of *zebhach chagh happāsach.* Here, however, in a gloss on the statement taken from Ex. 23:18, *chāmēts* has been appended erroneously. On the basis of Dt. 16:1a, it might be assumed that Passover was at one time celebrated on the new moon.[27]

But in the case of the harvest festival, too, comprising the Feast of Firstfruits and the

---

[25] *Taan.* iv.8.

[26] See below.

[27] Auerbach, 10.

Feast of Weeks (Ex. 23:16,19; Nu. 28:26; Dt. 16:9), we are probably dealing with festivals that were originally distinct. Many commentators, ancient and modern, admit that the first sickle-cut and sheaf ceremony (Dt. 16:9; Lev. 23:10; cf. Old Assyr. *ṣibit nigallim,* "the grasping of the sickle"), from which the seven weeks to the Feast of Weeks are counted, is not originally identical with the Feast of Unleavened Bread. But they still maintain the close connection between the two *chaggîm,* as though they constituted the framework surrounding the period from the beginning of the barley harvest to (the end of?) the wheat harvest. This elaborate structure, however, will not stand up. In the first place, both types of grain were not planted everywhere. Second, their harvests cannot be reconciled to a schema of 50 days. Neither is the Feast of Unleavened Bread ever associated explicitly with the festival of the barley harvest. Of course the harvest festival involves the ingathering of the wheat; but Ex. 34:22, which speaks of the "firstfruits of the wheat harvest," is more likely an attempt to incorporate an additional *chagh* here. For *bikkûrîm,* "firstfruits" (→ בכור *b^ekhôr*), are the firstfruits of field and orchard (Mic. 7:1), for the presentation of which the local sanctuaries probably had different dates (Ex. 23:19; Mishnah *Bikkurim* i.3, 6).

Later in the year we encounter a festival that is meant to be celebrated precisely at the equinox as determined astronomically (*t^eqûphath hashshānāh; b^etsēʾth hashshānāh,* Ex. 34:22; 23:16). It coincided with the *chagh* of the vintage, which occurred at about the same time but on a date determined by the maturity of the grapes. The *chagh* of Booths has a different character (Gressmann compares it to the mysteries of Adonis[28]), or else it is a local adaptation of the vintage festival (Jgs. 21:19ff.), which achieved universal acceptance (Neh. 8:17).

In the traditional order of the narrative material, the word *chagh* appears for the first time in the story of the exodus (Ex. 10:9). Scholars have cited this passage in support of an early nomadic Passover. In this case the term *chagh* would not be appropriate. Instead the narrator, in order to provide the Israelites with a pretext for escape, has projected the familiar *chagh* pilgrimages into the past. It is noteworthy that here the entire family joins in the *chagh.* One could even suggest that in Moses' proposal and Pharaoh's counterproposal we can hear echoes of a dispute over the legitimacy of participants in the festival: Pharaoh limits participation to males only (Ex. 10:11; cf. 23:17).

An ancient *chagh* is described in Jgs. 21:19ff. Our hypothesis of varying *chaggîm* is confirmed by the words of the Israelites: ". . . Is there not a yearly feast at Shiloh?" The narrative transfers to the plane of history the annual custom of a vintage festival involving dancing and abduction, possibly a fertility ritual (cf. the story of the rape of the Sabine women).

The situation is similar in the case of the account of how the temple of Solomon was dedicated on a *chagh* (1 K. 8:2ff.,65f.). Here, too, much of the regular *chagh* ritual has been represented as a single unique event: the crowds gathering at the sanctuary, the procession with the ark, prayers, and sacrifices. Possibly there were annual temple dedications. In any case, a *chagh* could last twice seven days (v. 65). The temple was finished in the eighth month (1 K. 6:38) and dedicated in the seventh. Both statements

---

[28]H. Gressmann, "Wichtige Zeitschriften-Aufsätze," *ZAW,* 43 (1925), 279.

refer to the autumn festival: the former according to the calendar of the northern kingdom (1 K. 12:33), the latter according to that of Judah.

In the narrative of Ex. 32, disguised by hostile Judahite redaction, we can still discover scattered traces of the *hieros logos* of a northern Israelite sanctuary (cf. v. 4 with 1 K. 12:28). This observation also gives us clues on the observance of a *chagh*. The cry " 'Tomorrow shall be a *chagh* to Yahweh' " (v. 5) may have been the usual signal for the beginning of the festal ceremonies. We may also compare Isa. 30:29: *k*ᵉ*lêl hithqaddesh-chagh*.[29] On the *chagh* itself, sacrifices were offered, a banquet was shared, and "play" was indulged in (v. 6). This last refers to sexual rites; cf. the medieval commentaries.

Ps. 81:4(3) also mentions a *chagh*, possibly northern Israelite in nature (*y*ᵉ*hôsēph*, v. 6), that lasted two weeks, from the new moon to the full moon. Late Jewish tradition associates this psalm with the New Year Festival and the Feast of Booths. It may in fact refer to the autumn festival, but this is uncertain. We can, however, derive some information about the celebration. The beginning was marked by song and music in praise of God; then the community received admonishment, undergirded with an account of Yahweh's acts of deliverance in the past; in conclusion there followed the promise of a happy future.

Whether Hos. 9:5 refers to a specific *chagh* is uncertain (2:13[11] also uses the singular for *chagh*, new moon, and Sabbath); but here, too, the great autumn harvest festival may be intended (v. 2). In any case, sacrifice and libations of wine are involved (v. 4). The fact that the autumn festival frequently—but by no means always and everywhere—occupied a central position explains why some texts call it *hechagh*, "the feast" (1 K. 12:32; Ezk. 45:23; Neh. 8:14; etc.).

3. *Catalogs*. The repeated attempts to reduce the bewildering variety of *chaggîm* to a uniform system are expressed in various series of regulations governing the festivals. These comprise the corresponding verses in the Covenant Code (Ex. 23:14-17 [E]), the Yahwistic Decalog (Ex. 34:18,22f. [J]), Deuteronomy (16:1-17 [D]), the Holiness Code (Lev. 23:4-12,34-44 [H]), the Priestly sacrificial code (Nu. 28:16-31; 29:12-39 [P]), and the book of Ezekiel (45:21-25). The festival regulations appear in most cases not to have been an original part of the legal corpora in question, but to have been added later. The legal corpora themselves, in turn, are not organic components of the various source strata into which they have been incorporated. And finally the place and date of origin of the sources themselves are largely debatable.

These circumstances make it difficult to determine more precisely the period or locality of origin for the festival catalogs. In the following discussion, the various festival regulations will be described with an eye to their individual features that are essential to the concept of *chagh;* the whole complex of problems relating to literary history will not be examined.[30] Neither can we discuss the nature of each particular *chagh* and the regulations governing it.[31]

---

[29]Guthe (*HSAT*, I, 642) assumes that Dt. 16:6 refers to the Passover; but this interpretation is contradicted by the term *chagh*.

[30]See the various introductions to the OT.

[31]Cf. the individual articles, and especially Otto, 167-198.

Whatever relationship is posited between E and J (J dependent on E [Rost], E dependent on J [Fohrer], both dependent on one and the same prototype), it is impossible to deny their intimate connection. Their wording is all too similar; important expressions are practically identical. Both catalogs require all males to appear three times each year before Yahweh, i.e., undertake a pilgrimage to the sanctuary. The first of these festal occasions is the *chagh* of Unleavened Bread, which is to be celebrated in the month of Abib. The fact that the exodus from Egypt took place in this spring month is given as its historical motivation. Even if this comment is a later gloss,[32] it demonstrates nonetheless that the Feast of Unleavened Bread was provided with an historical explanation before the others. The second festival is the *chagh* of harvest. It is given two divergent definitions. The text in E can be taken to mean something like the statement that this harvest festival is "the first yield of the seed," just as the autumn festival signifies "the final ingathering of the yield of the field." In other words, the expression *ma*ʿ*ᵃśeykhā . . . baśśādheh,* in antithesis to *bᵉ*ʾ*ospᵉkhā* ʾ*eth-ma*ʿ*ᵃśeykhā min-haśśādheh* (Ex. 23:16), does not refer to "firstfruits" in the narrow sense (covered by the regulation in v. 19), and can therefore easily be connected with the conclusion of the wheat harvest. But J interprets the word *bikkûrîm* in this narrower sense and calls the *chagh* the feast of the "firstfruits of the wheat harvest." All of this is preceded by the term *chagh* of "weeks" (Ex. 34:22), which receives no explanation at all and thus gives the impression of being a harmonizing gloss. The third festival is the *chagh* of ingathering, to be celebrated at the end of the year.

The crucial point, therefore, is that three *chaggîm,* which clearly exhibit the character of nature and agricultural festivals, were linked in a fixed cycle. The hypothesis that a Canaanite cultic observance was here borrowed by the Israelites after the conquest[33] is convincing for each of the individual festivals, but is hardly sufficient to explain the whole cycle. Not only is an overlapping of the *chaggîm* still detectable (the second festival competes with the Feast of Unleavened Bread as a "feast of firstfruits" and with the Feast of Ingathering as a harvest festival), but the notion of three pilgrimages each year on the part of the total male population is so foreign to reality that such a requirement can hardly have come into being in an organically developed system.

It is therefore reasonable to suppose that in these festival catalogs we have a synthesis of various festival traditions. At a specific point in time, a sanctuary took over the function and thus the festival rites of other local temples and legitimized their major feasts. The politico-cultural background evokes innumerable hypotheses. One possibility is that Shechem, with its own harvest festival in the summer, replaced Shiloh with its autumn *chagh* of Yahweh, after its destruction, and Gilgal with its Feast of Unleavened Bread.[34]

The trinity of *chaggîm* gradually became the accepted norm. The original nucleus of D may have mentioned Passover only,[35] but then the Feast of Unleavened Bread was

---

[32]A. Jepsen, *Untersuchungen zum Bundesbuch. BWANT,* 3/5 (1927), 10, 49.
[33]Lods, Fohrer, and others.
[34]Cf. Otto, 351-361.
[35]Elhorst.

incorporated into the same section (Dt. 16:3,4a,8).[36] It is not, however, called a *chagh*. The motif of remembering the exodus from Egypt is emphasized. As a second festival the *chagh* of Weeks (Dt. 16:9f.) is instituted; the name is explained by reference to counting seven weeks. The cycle concludes with the *chagh* of Booths; no explanation is given for the name. The innovations are the Deuteronomic association of the *chaggîm* with the "chosen place," in practice the sanctuary at Jerusalem (Dt. 16:2, 6,11,15), and the repeated summons to rejoice on the *chagh*, as well as to share the joy of the festival not only with members of the family but also with social inferiors and the disadvantaged (vv. 11,14f.).

The Holiness Code is clearly not homogeneous. The sacrificial regulations for the Feast of Unleavened Bread are scanty in comparison with the subsequent regulations governing the sheaf and the bread of the firstfruits (Lev. 23:7,10ff.,17ff.). The *chagh* of Booths (vv. 34ff.) is mentioned and explained alongside the *chagh* of Yahweh (vv. 39ff.), although the date of both is the same. The two sections are separated by a redactional comment (vv. 37f.).

The original nucleus of H may possibly have juxtaposed only two *chaggîm* (cf. Ezekiel), the *chagh* of Unleavened Bread (Lev. 23:6-8) and the *chagh* of Booths (vv. 34-36), explaining both in almost identical words. Between the two sections were inserted regulations governing the sheaf, the counting of seven Sabbaths, and the setting apart of the fiftieth day as a feast. This feast is not named; neither is it called a *chagh*.

In this context we may ignore the regulations governing the day of trumpet blasts and the Day of Atonement (vv. 23-32), which were likewise interpolated, since neither of these is ever called a *chagh*. It should be mentioned, however, that they represent newly independent aspects of an autumn festival, namely, the beginning of the year and ceremony of propitiation.

At the end of the chapter, festival observances for the *chagh* of Yahweh are listed, as well as those for the *chagh* of Booths. As historical motivation, it is recalled that the Israelites dwelt in booths during their wandering in the desert. Apart from this statement, the interest of H focuses on the temple cult and sacrifice.

P gives the sacrificial ordinances for the various special days throughout the year. Of interest to us are the *chagh* of Unleavened Bread (Nu. 28:17), which is associated with Passover, the day of firstfruits (v. 26), and the *chagh* to Yahweh (29:12). The basis for the festivals—in nature or in history—is not mentioned. H, P, and Ezekiel give precise calendar dates for the *chaggîm*. The influence of various systems of chronology on the Israelite lunisolar calendar can be noted from the observation that the two most important *chaggîm* fall on the day of the full moon of the first month (Nisan) and the seventh month (Tishri), i.e., the two dates of the new year celebrated in the ancient Near East.

4. *Theological Significance of Different Stages*. The changes in meaning of the term *chagh* reflect changes in cultic observances and therefore also in the religious

[36]For a discussion of the festival calendar in Dt. 16, cf. esp. R. P. Merendino, *Das deuteronomische Gesetz*. *BBB*, 31 (1969), 125-170, and P. Laaf, *Die Pascha-Feier Israels*. *BBB*, 36 (1970), 69-86.

ideas of the Israelites. During their nomadic period, the Israelites borrowed primarily indigenous festivals that were associated with agriculture. These frequently exhibited a magically efficacious character, as some of the festival observances still attest.

The eating of unleavened bread was ordered because it could be prepared without admixture of leftover dough. The sheaf was to be waved before Yahweh "that you may prosper" (*lirtsōn*^e*khem,* Lev. 23:11). For the autumn festival, the Talmud is still familiar with the ceremony of pouring water upon the altar, which was intended to guarantee the rainfall of the coming year.[37]

This magical element receded into the background. The *chagh* became the festival of the deity (*chagh yhvh*), in which man may participate. When the idea of God became more refined, this notion was replaced by the explanation that the feast was celebrated not with the deity but before him and in his honor (*chagh l*^e*yhvh*). The *chagh* became a joyous festival of thanksgiving; it accompanied (without a fixed date; cf. also Jer. 5:24) the grain and fruit harvest and the vintage.

At some point in time there were attempts to bring uniformity into the multiplicity of festivals and variety of rituals. There arose the system of three *chaggîm,* in which the names and rites of the individual festivals could vary as long as the trinity was maintained. As the lunisolar calendar came to have more influence on everyday life, the *chaggîm* were associated with specific dates and lost their ties with agriculture.

The Israelites are distinguished by their sense of history. They never felt themselves to be autochthonous proprietors of Canaan. Therefore their thanksgiving for the bounty of the land was linked very early with historical observations (Dt. 26:2-10). Thus the *chaggîm* became associated with the events of sacred history—first the Feast of Unleavened Bread, associated with Passover, and then the Feast of Booths. The Talmud finally interpreted the Feast of Weeks as a memorial of the giving of the law at Sinai.[38] The agrarian character of the *chaggîm* receded more and more into the background; in the postexilic period they became commemorative festivals.

This change made it possible for the meaning to be extended: Passover, too, and in postbiblical Hebrew the day of the new moon[39] and the festivals of heretics[40] could be called *chagh.*

The religious memorial celebration was characterized by a joy born of a sacred atmosphere and a feeling of social obligation toward those without means (Neh. 8:9ff.).

The prophets criticized the *chaggîm* just as they criticized the cult in general. We find attacks on the intoxication and uproar of festivals (Am. 5:21; Isa. 1:13f.; Mal. 2:3) so harsh that they give the impression of aiming at absolute condemnation of the festivals. But the criticism is in fact directed against the improper attitude of the celebrants. Even the prophets considered the *chaggîm* signs of Yahweh's grace (Nah. 2:1[1:15]) and their absence a punishment (Hos. 2:13[11]). A noteworthy combination of the various elements is found in Zec. 14:16-18. In contrast to a belief in the magical

---

[37] *Rosh Hashanah* 16a.
[38] *Pesaḥim* 68b.
[39] Lev. r.s. 29.
[40] *Sotah* 36b.

power of festival ceremony and particularistic hostility toward the foreign nations, there is expressed here the universalistic hope that one day all nations may go on *chagh* pilgrimage to Jerusalem.

Kedar-Kopfstein

חָגַר *chāghar;* חָגוֹר *chāghôr;* חֲגוֹר *chᵃghôr;* חֲגוֹרָה *chᵃghôrāh*

Contents: 1. Etymology. II. Occurrences. III. Synonyms. IV. Literal Meaning. V. Metaphorical Meaning.

I. Etymology. In OT Hebrew, the root *ḥgr* has the meaning "gird," a primary meaning that can also be used to explain the use of the root in other Semitic languages. In mishnaic Hebrew, as well as Jewish Aramaic and Syriac, the OT meaning continues, but develops in the direction of "stumble, limp"; this corresponds to Mandean "cripple," Qumran (1QM) and Christian Palestinian Aramaic "be lame." The Ethiopic meaning "fetter" may be considered related.

A different semantic development of the root appears in Arab. *ḥağara,* "enclose, detain, block the way," Phoen. *ḥgr,* "wall," and OSA *ḥgr,* "protect," "enclosure, garden." This meaning may appear in a name found in the list of towns captured by Sheshonk: *p-ḥgr,* "the enclosure, the walled encampment" = Petra?[1]

A connection with Akk. *egēru,* "lie across,"[2] is conceivable, but by no means certain. The root is also attested in Libyan: *guggeret,* "wear a belt crossed over the breast and back."[3]

II. Occurrences. The verb *chāghar* appears 44 times in the OT, always in the qal. Other stems are found in postbiblical Hebrew. Although the occurrences are scattered through various OT writings, the majority are found in the Pentateuch, the Deuteronomistic history, and the writings of the classical prophets. The subject may gird himself or someone else, or gird his loins; in these cases, the item used in the girding is designated with b^e. In the majority of cases, however, the item girded on stands as the direct object: a belt, sackcloth, a sword, weapons, the ephod, etc. Both

---

chāghar. C. H. Gordon, "Belt-Wrestling in the Bible World," *HUCA,* 23 (1950/51), 131-36; D. Sperling, "*ḥgr* I and *ḥgr* II," *JANES,* 3 (1970/71), 121-28.

1 M. Noth, "Die Topographie Palästinas und Syriens im Licht ägyptischer Quellen, IV: Die Schoschenkliste," *ZDPV,* 61 (1938), 295ff. = *Aufsätze zur biblischen Landes- und Altertumskunde* (1971), II, 82ff.

2 *AHw,* I, 190, with a discussion of the etymology.

3 O. Rössler, "Der semitische Charakter der libyschen Sprache," *ZA,* 50 (1952), 130.

constructions occur in metaphorical usage. The good wife girds her loins with strength (Prov. 31:17), but the hills "gird themselves with joy" (Ps. 65:13 [Eng. v. 12]), and the Lord is "girded with wrath" (Ps. 76:11; in this passage,[4] however, textual emendations have been proposed).

III. Synonyms. Of the various synonyms, *'āzar* occurs 16 times in the OT. In the qal, the verb is used with various objects (loins: Jer. 1:17; Job 38:3; 40:7; strength: 1 S. 2:4; a leather girdle: 2 K. 1:8), or without an object (Job 30:18). In the niphal, we read that God is girded with might (Ps. 65:7[6]). In the piel the verb has various objects: brands (Isa. 50:11), strength (2 S. 22:40), gladness (Ps. 30:12[11]). In the hithpael, *'āzar* appears with "strength" as its object in Ps. 93:1, and absolutely without any object in Isa. 8:9.

Other synonyms are *šns,* which appears in the piel in 1 K. 18:46 (with loins as object), and → חזק *chāzaq,* which occurs twice in the piel with the meaning "gird": Isa. 22:21 with a girdle as object, and Nah. 2:2(1) with loins as object. Cf. also → **אמץ** *'āmats.*

In the LXX, both *chāghar* and *'āzar* are translated with *zōnnýnein* or *perizōnnýnai.*

IV. Literal Meaning. For both *chāghar* and its three synonyms we find the construction "gird one's loins (→ **חלצים** *chalātsayim* or → **מתנים** *mothnayim*)." As the primary situation we may assume the literal girding on of a belt or girdle (*chaghôr, chaghôrāh*). The man who girds himself is thereby ready for a task confronting him: the exodus from Egypt (Ex. 12:11) or a prophetic mission (2 K. 4:29; 9:1).

Frequently one girds on "weapons of war" (*kelê hammilchāmāh,* Dt. 1:41; Jgs. 18:11,16f.) or a sword (Jgs. 3:16; 1 S. 17:39; 25:13; Ps. 45:4[3]). It is unlikely that "girding up" for battle originated in preparation for belt-wrestling.[5] The concrete situation is more likely. An interesting passage in this respect is 2 K. 3:21, where the participial phrase *chōghēr chaghōrāh,* "whoever girds himself with a girdle," corresponds to the meaning "everyone capable of bearing arms." It is noteworthy that such a warrior is girded with a girdle rather than some weapon. A parallel that explains the expression occurs in Egyptian, where *ṯs mḏḥ,* "gird on a girdle,"[6] stands for "become sexually mature." The wearing of a girdle showed that a young man was mature and capable of bearing arms. The connection between OT usage and Egyptian in this respect is also illustrated by the correlation of a series of words in the two languages: *mēzach,* "girdle" par. *mḏḥ,* "girdle";[7] *'abhnēṭ,* "girdle" par. *bnd,* "wrap";[8] *'ēphōdh,* "ephod" par. *ỉfd*(?), "a kind of linen";[9] *'ekhes,* "anklet" par. *'gśw,* "belt, thong."[10]

The priest is girded ceremonially for his service, either with an *'abhnēṭ* (Ex. 29:9;

[4]See *BHS.*
[5]*KBL*[3], following Gordon.
[6]*WbÄS,* II, 189.
[7]*Ibid.*
[8]*WbÄS,* I, 465.
[9]*WbÄS,* I, 71.
[10]*WbÄS,* I, 236.

Lev. 8:7,13; 16:4) or the *chēshebh hā'ēphōdh* (Lev. 8:7). Lev. 16:4 is describing the vestments of the high priest on the great Day of Atonement. The other passages deal with the investiture of the priest, during which he is girded with the girdle that forms part of the priestly vestments.

We often find *chāghar* with the object → שַׂק *śaq*. The expression appears primarily in the prophets: 2 S. 3:31; Isa. 15:3; 22:12; Jer. 4:8; 6:26; 49:3; Ezk. 7:18; 27:31; Joel 1:8; Lam. 2:10. In Isa. 32:11 and Joel 1:13, no object is mentioned explicitly, but the context indicates that sackcloth is to be understood as the object. Whoever girds himself with sackcloth indicates thereby that he is in the special realm of mourning and lamentation.

In a few passages, *chāghar* comes close to the meaning of → לבשׁ *lābhēsh*. Joab was "girded" with a garment (2 S. 20:8, where, however, it is reasonable to suggest dittography). As a boy, Samuel was girded with an ephod (1 S. 2:18), as was David according to 2 S. 6:14. Apart from the question of what the ephod looked like, the girding in these cases has an element of ceremonial investiture. One can also be girded with "gold," i.e., with a golden girdle (Dnl. 10:5), and with "sweat," i.e., material that causes sweat (Ezk. 44:18).

A few passages are difficult. 2 S. 21:16 has "He was girded with a new . . ."; the context suggests some kind of equipment or weapon. In 2 S. 22:46, we find "they girded themselves out of their fastness"(?). The parallel text in Ps. 18:46 has *chāragh;* metathesis is therefore a reasonable explanation of the peculiar text.

The opposite of *chāghar* is *pāthach* (Isa. 20:2; Ps. 30:12[11]). In 1 K. 20:11, the two terms are contrasted in a proverb: "Let not him that girds on his armor boast himself as he that puts it off." This contrast was retained even when the meaning of *chāghar* developed in the direction of "be lame." Cf. Mk. 7:34, where *ephphatha,* "Be opened!" stands in contrast to the "constraint" of the sick man.

In the case of *'āzar*, passages with concrete meaning are comparatively few. The prophet is recognized by the leather girdle with which he is girded (2 K. 1:8). A man's skin can gird him like a garment (Job 30:18). In this case, too, the man who girds himself prepares himself for a task. He demonstrates that he is mature and capable of carrying out his assignment. In Jer. 1:17, the prophet at first does not dare to come forward on account of his youth, but Yahweh says to him: "Gird up your loins, arise, and preach." We find *'āzar* used in a similar way in Job 38:3 and 40:7: "Gird up your loins like a man, I will question you, and you shall declare to me." God demands that Job conduct his conversation with God as a responsible adult. Here the notion has already taken a step in the direction of metaphor.

V. Metaphorical Meaning. There are only a few examples of *chāghar* used metaphorically. The various instances can be understood on the basis of the literal meaning. In Prov. 31:17, the good wife girds her loins with strength. She is ready for her work and also capable of performing it. When the hills gird themselves with joy (Ps. 65:13[12]) or the psalmist prays that the curse will be like a belt to the wicked (Ps. 109:19), the image is best understood as deriving from the girding on or removal of sackcloth, whereby one places oneself in the realm of mourning or departs from that realm.

The metaphorical use of *'āzar* is more common; as in the case of *chāghar,* it derives from the literal use. Girding up for battle lies behind 1 S. 2:4: "The feeble gird on strength"; Isa. 8:9: "Gird yourselves and be dismayed"; and Isa. 50:11: "Gird yourselves with brands." In this use of the term, one can also be girded by another: "Thou didst gird me with strength for the battle" (2 S. 22:40; the same expression occurs in the parallel text Ps. 18:33,40[32,39]); "I gird you, though you do not know me" (Isa. 45:5). Here David and Cyrus are girded by Yahweh. The image of girding is used to show that the person in question is given an assignment by another. In Ps. 30:12(11), we find an antithesis between the realms of mourning and joy: "Thou hast loosed my sackcloth and girded me with gladness." The image of girding can also be applied to God. Yahweh is girded with might and strength (Ps. 65:7[6]; 93:1). In both passages we are dealing with God's salutary manifestations in creation.

B. Johnson

חָדַל *chādhal*

Contents: I. 1. Etymology; 2. Meaning. II. Concrete Uses in the OT. III. Usages in Theological Contexts: 1. Cessation of Human Activity; 2. Social Withdrawal; 3. Cessation of Life; 4. Yahweh's Cessation. IV. *ḥdl* II: 1. Etymology and Meaning; 2. Concrete Uses in the OT; 3. Usages in Theological Contexts.

I. 1. *Etymology.* The basic meaning of the root *ḥdl* I is "cease" or "withdraw." The Hebrew is cognate to Arab. *ḫaḏala,* "abstain from, leave, remain back," as a gazelle who remains back from following the herd.[1] The root is also found in Old South Arabic.[2] The exact meaning of Akk. *ḫadālu* is not clear.[3] The root is unknown in Ugaritic. For a discussion of *ḥdl* II, see IV below.

2. *Meaning.* In the OT, the verb occurs only in the qal. It can be translated either actively or passively, and has the following meanings:

a. It can mean "cease" or "withdraw," referring either to human withdrawal, or withdrawal from or cessation of a particular activity. This is its most common mean-

---

chādhal. P. J. Calderone, "ḤDL-II in Poetic Texts," *CBQ,* 23 (1961), 451-460; *idem,* "Supplementary Note on ḤDL-II," *CBQ,* 24 (1962), 412-19; M. Chaney, "Some Observations on חדל in Biblical Hebrew" [forthcoming]; M. Dahood, *Psalms,* I. *AB,* XVI (1965); A. Goetze, review of O. Neugebauer, *Mathematical Cuneiform Texts,* in *JCS,* 2 (1948), 35f.; M. Noth, *IPN,* 226; D. W. Thomas, "Some Observations on the Hebrew Root חדל," *Congress volume II. SVT,* 4 (1957), 8-16.

[1]Lane, 713.
[2]ContiRossini, 154.
[3]Cf. *AHw,* I, 306f.; *CAD,* VI, 22; Goetze, 35f.

ing. The term is often relational: one withdraws physically or spatially from something. Men withdraw in war (1 S. 23:13; Jer. 51:30). In Jer. 41:8, *ḥdl* means essentially the same as the English "back off": Ishmael "backed off and did not kill them" (*vayyechdal v^{e}lō' h^{e}mîthām*). To cease speaking or hearing may likewise have implied greater physical distance between people (Ruth 1:18; 2 Ch. 25:16; Ezk. 2:5,7; 3:11, 27). Sometimes a group or an individual wishes to be left alone (Ex. 14:12; Job 7:16; 10:20).

The word can also have negative overtones, as in Job 19:14, where it means "rejected" or "forsaken" (cf. par. *sh^{e}khēchûnî*). As 1 S. 9:5 and 10:2 show, *ḥdl* can be used interchangeably with *nāṭash:* Saul's father ceases (to care) about the asses. In Jotham's fable, the two trees and the vine weigh the advantages of withdrawing from their present station in life to accept the offer of another (Jgs. 9:9,11,13).

To indicate cessation of a specific activity, *ḥdl* is frequently coupled with another verb: the men of Babel ceased to build (*vayyachd^{e}lû libhnōth*) the city (Gen. 11:8); Joseph ceased to measure (*chādhal lispōr*) grain (Gen. 41:49). In Gen. 18:11, the Yahwist says periphrastically: *chādhal lihyôth l^{e}śārāh 'ōrach kannāshîm,* "It ceased to be with Sarah after the manner of women," i.e., Sarah had stopped menstruating. Sarah is old and this is to be expected, yet *ḥdl* means only that the activity stopped. Such a cessation might suggest "completion" or "fulfilment" to the modern mind, but no such idea is conveyed by this verb (cf. → תמם *tmm* and → כלה *kālāh*).

Often it is assumed that, had the activity not terminated, it would have gone on longer. The complex at Babel is left without being completed (Gen. 11:8). Warriors cease to fight before the battle is over (Jer. 51:30). And when Yahweh halts the hail and thunder (Ex. 9:29,33f.), it is presumably not because the storm is over. Yet *ḥdl* does imply a full stop; it does not mean "diminish" (*gr^{c}*).

Other Hebrew verbs meaning "cease" are → שׁבת *shābhath* and → דמה *dāmāh;* but the former means cessation of work during a period of rest (cf. Sabbath), and the latter is more active and causative than *chādhal,* usually meaning "cut off" or "destroy."

b. The verb can also mean "refrain from," in the sense of not even beginning to do something. This meaning appears in the legal texts Nu. 9:13 and Dt. 23:23 (Eng. v. 22), as well as Am. 7:5. In either/or constructions, *chādhal* is used in the second member with a main verb understood, in which case it serves primarily as a term of negation: "If it seems good for you to come to Babylon, come, . . . but if it seems wrong . . ., do not (come)" (Jer. 40:4); "If it seems right, give me my wages, but if not, do not (give them)" (Zec. 11:12). See also Jgs. 20:28; 1 K. 22:6, 15 (= 2 Ch. 18:5, 14); Ezk. 2:5,7; 3:11; Job 16:6.

The adjective *chādhēl* occurs three times in the OT; in each case the context determines the precise meaning. In Ezk. 3:27, it appears with the definite article and means "the one refraining from hearing." The context requires a passive sense in Isa. 53:3: "rejected" or "forsaken" (cf. *ḥdl* II for a possible double meaning). In Ps. 39:5f.(4f.), there is a wordplay involving *chādhēl* and *v^{e}cheldî*. With *chādhēl 'ānî* parallel to *qitstsî*, the difficult *meh-chādhēl 'ānî* must mean something like "how I withdraw (from life)," i.e., how I will die.

II. Concrete Uses in the OT. The verb *chādhal* is used for the cessation of a variety of human activities. Naomi ceased to speak (*vattechdal l^{e}dhabbēr*) when she realized that Ruth was determined to go with her (Ruth 1:18). The wise man is a man of few words, or, proverbially: "When words are many, transgression is not lacking (*lō' yechdal-pesha'*)" (Prov. 10:19). In the case of listening, the advice is just the opposite: the son is told not to cease hearing words of instruction (Prov. 19:27).

The verb appears frequently in the context of warfare. In Jgs. 15:7, *'echdāl* means "I will cease from fighting," or perhaps "I will cease from avenging myself" if *nqm* is the verb understood. In either case, it is a classic case of Hebrew understatement, for Samson will by then have killed many men (v. 8). Saul withdrew his expedition after David escaped from Keilah (1 S. 23:13). To say that a warrior has ceased fighting is a taunt from the enemy, as in the case of the Babylonian warriors described in Jer. 51:30. The killing done by Ishmael after the fall of Jerusalem was murder; only because a group had stores of hidden food did he "back off" from killing them (Jer. 41:8). Warfare also brought to a halt building projects (1 K. 15:21 [= 2 Ch. 16:5]) and caravan trade (Jgs. 5:6).

III. Usages in Theological Contexts.

1. *Cessation of Human Activity*. The prophets were messengers of the divine word, and not infrequently there was a reluctance to hear them out. A nameless prophet sent to king Amaziah was told to stop speaking (*chadhal-lekhā*)—which he did, but not before telling the king that reluctance to listen would bring about his fall (2 Ch. 25:16). Ezekiel met similar resistance, but was told by Yahweh to speak to the exiles, "Whether they hear or don't (hear) (*'im-yishme'û ve'im-yechdālû*)" (Ezk. 2:5,7; 3:11). His message is to be prefaced by the equally bold: "He that will hear let him hear, and he that won't (hear), let him not (hear) (*hashshōmēa' yishmā' vehechādhēl yechdāl*)" (3:27). The latter expression appears to be the prototype for Jesus' summons in the NT (Mk. 4:9, 23 and *passim*). Job is faced with the charge that empty speech alienates him from God, to which he replies: *'im-'adhabberāh lō'-yēchāśēkh ke'ēbhî ve'achdelāh mah-mminnî yahalōkh,* " 'If I speak, my pain is not assuaged, and if I don't, how much of it leaves me?' " (Job 16:6; cf. 15:2-16).

Whether to engage the enemy in battle or to withdraw was a question to be submitted to Yahweh. In the war against Benjamin, Phinehas the priest is asked to divine Yahweh's will: "Shall we yet again go out to battle . . . or shall we withdraw?" (Jgs. 20:28). In Ahab's time, the same question was put to the prophets (1 K. 22:6 [=2 Ch. 18:5]). It was put specifically to Micaiah, who correctly predicted Ahab's defeat (1 K. 22:15 [=2 Ch. 18:14]). Here *chādhal* must mean "refrain" rather than "withdraw," for there was no battle in progress. Syria and Israel had been at peace for three years (1 K. 22:1). In other words, it could be translated simply "not," as in the other either/or constructions: "Shall we yet again go out to battle . . . or not?"

In Josiah's abortive attempt to engage Necho, the Chronicler records a remarkable statement on the part of Necho: *chadhal-lekhā mē'elōhîm 'asher-'immî ve'al-yashchîthekhā,* "Withdraw from God, who is with me, lest he destroy you" (2 Ch. 35:21). Necho really means "withdraw from me," but his theological formulation is worth quoting verbatim, since the Chronicler takes Necho's words as coming directly from the mouth of God (cf. v. 22).

Wars also left silence in their wake. The sounds of instruments were stilled, and the joyful voices of singers ceased (Isa. 24:8). Yahweh's judgment led to the termination of the Babel building project (Gen. 11:8), and the statement "Yahweh scattered them abroad" may in fact be a theological interpretation of some unknown war.

The Pentateuch uses *chādhal* three times (with either *min* or *l*ᵉ) in the sense of refraining from some religious or moral obligation. In these legal texts, *chādhal* takes the place of the negation particles *lō'* and *'al*. If one sees the ass of someone who is unfriendly lying under its burden, one should *vᵉchādhaltā mēʿᵃzōbh lô*, "refrain from leaving him with it" (Ex. 23:5). This is an unusual construction, and perhaps *chādhal* has the rhetorical function of emphasizing the direction the action must take, counter to the normal impulse in such a situation simply to withdraw entirely. Nu. 9:13 contains legislation applying to one who is neither unclean nor on a journey, "yet refrains from keeping the Passover." Here refraining is a sin. It is also a sin to make a vow to Yahweh and not pay it. The law then states that one should rather refrain from vowing (Dt. 23:23[22]).

The other context of human activity in which *chādhal* is important is worship. Whenever men turn away from Yahweh, a crisis occurs. Samuel understood the people's request for a king in these terms. But after Samuel is reconciled to the idea of kingship, a type of covenant renewal takes place between him and the people. He promises to be a perpetual mediator between the people and Yahweh, saying he will not cease to pray (*mēchᵃdhōl lᵉhithpallēl*) to Yahweh for them (1 S. 12:23; but cf. Jer. 7:16; 15:1). In Isaiah, *chādhal* is used twice, both times as part of an antithesis. In pleading for personal cleansing in place of sustained worship, Isaiah says: *chidhlû hārēaʿ limdhû hêṭēbh*, "Cease to do evil, learn to do good" (Isa. 1:16f.). In Isa. 2:22, the plea to "withdraw from man" (*chidhlû lākhem min-hā'ādhām*) means "from man and his idols" (2:6ff.). The implied antithesis is "turn to Yahweh" (2:5). On the coming day of judgment. Yahweh alone will be exalted (2:11,17). Jeremiah, too, attacks idolatry, but he encounters a different argument: the Egyptian exiles claim that only when they "ceased" burning incense and pouring out libations to the Queen of Heaven did hard times come (Jer. 44:18).

2. *Social Withdrawal*. Prophets and other servants of Yahweh occasionally experienced social isolation. When Moses urged escape from Egypt, the people told him to leave them alone (Ex. 14:12). The Vulgate translates *chᵃdhal mimmennû* as *recede a nobis*, "withdraw from us." The Suffering Servant was also in his day rejected by men (Isa. 53:3). Job, another *ʿebhedh-yhvh* (Job 1:8), complains that his close friends have rejected him (Job 19:14), but his isolation appears at least in part to be self-imposed (Job 7:16; 10:20 *qere*).

3. *Cessation of Life*. The verb *chādhal* is also used to refer to cessation of life. The psalmist wants to know how he will withdraw from life (Ps. 39:5[4]). In Sheol there is cessation or withdrawal, but not nonexistence. The lowly see death as the great equalizer. The psalmist says ironically that the mansion of Sheol awaits the arrogant rich man: there he will cease forever (Ps. 49:9).[4] At one point Job prefers death to life, for "there the wicked cease from troubling" (Job 3:17). Ps. 49 emphasizes the con-

[4]Dahood, *in loc.*

tinuity between man and the rest of creation: man is like the beasts who perish. Job, however, argues that trees are better off than men. There is at least hope for a tree that is cut down, *vᵉyōnaqtô lōʾ thechdāl,* "that its shoots will not cease" (Job 14:7). But when a man dies, where is he (v. 10)? In v. 6, Job also engages in wordplay using *ḥdl* II: *shᵉʿēh mēʿālāv vᵉyechdāl,* "look away from him [i.e., man] that he may grow fat."[5] The complete thought, then, is: "Let man grow fat and enjoy himself, for when he dies that will be the end." This is a variation on the theme: "Eat, drink, and be merry, for tomorrow we die."

4. *Yahweh's Cessation.* On two occasions Yahweh elects to withdraw his judgment. In the plague of hail on Egypt, Moses stretches forth his hands and Yahweh causes the rain, hail, and thunder to cease (Ex. 9:29,33f.). This demonstrates that the earth belongs to Yahweh (cf. Matt. 8:23-27). In the second of Amos' three visions, Amos pleads with Yahweh to refrain from (*chᵃdhal-nāʾ*) sending fire upon Israel (Am. 7:5), and Yahweh "repents."

IV. ḥdl II.

1. *Etymology and Meaning.* Some seven occurrences of *ḥdl* meaning "grow fat" are now firmly established in the OT. This is a separate Hebrew verb, cognate to Arab. *ḫadula/ḫadila,* "become large, become plump," and the like. The proper name Hadlai in 2 Ch. 28:12 derives from this root,[6] and is perhaps equivalent to "Fats."

2. *Concrete Uses in the OT.* The teacher of wisdom warns against taking food from a wealthy man, on the grounds that it may be deceptive. Better, he says, to "grow fat from your understanding," *mibbînāthᵃkhā chᵃdhāl* (Prov. 23:4). Job's philosophy is conditioned by his own experience. Having once known great abundance and now great scarcity, he, too, scorns the rich man: *shᵉʿēh mēʿālav vᵉyechdāl ʿadh-yirtseh kᵉśākhîr yômô,* "Look away from him, that he may grow fat, even to enjoying, like a hireling, his day" (Job 14:6).

3. *Usages in Theological Contexts.* Growing fat can be equated with moral obtuseness, even sin (see Dt. 32:15 and Isa. 6:10, with the use of *šmn;* cf. also Ps. 119:70: *ṭāphash kachēlebh libbām*). The wicked man of Ps. 36 is characterized as "(too) fat to act wisely (and) do good," *chādhal lᵉhaśkîl lᵉhêṭîbh* (v. 4[3]).[7] Contrasted with him are the *bᵉnê ʾādhām* who will feast at the heavenly banquet at Yahweh's estate (vv. 8-10[7-9]).

Calderone[8] has proposed an adjective from this verb; he thinks it appears in Isa. 53:3 with the same derived meaning, viz., "dull, gross, senseless." The context certainly allows such a meaning, even to the point of suggesting that the Servant was considered

[5] For a different interpretation, see G. Fohrer, *KAT,* XVI (1963), 235, 239.
[6] *IPN,* 226.
[7] Cf. Dahood, 219.
[8] "Supplementary Note," 416ff.

sinful by his own generation. Only later is he understood to have been wounded for *our* transgressions (v. 5). There is, however, no good reason to abandon the traditional reading "rejected, forsaken" (cf. *ḥdl* I). If such an adjective did in fact exist, a context admitting both meanings suggests that the poet may have intended a double meaning.

The preacher of Deuteronomy consistently admonishes those who have to aid those who have not. In the well-known verse 15:11, the use of this root instead of *ḥdl* I gives fresh meaning.[9] The preacher is not saying, "The poor will never cease out of the land," but "The poor from the land will never grow fat." This caps a rhetorical argument that seeks to move the people to charity. After telling his audience to remember the poor (15:1ff.), he then says they need not fear that the poor will grow rich, at least not on what they give them. The poor will never grow fat on that!

These passages all reflect the viewpoint of the upper classes. They are the opinions of those who have known prosperity. The lower class view is very different: it comes to us in two of Israel's earliest songs, the Song of Deborah and the Song of Hannah. Both rejoice because a great turn of events has caused the hungry to grow fat. An early victory at Megiddo meant the end of caravan trade commissioned by the ruling elite for their own benefit. This resulted in the Israelite peasants' getting fat on booty. The Song of Deborah plays nicely on the two verbs: *bîmê yāʿēl chādhᵉlû ʾᵒrāchôth . . . chādhᵉlû phᵉrāzôn bᵉyiśrāʾēl chādhēllû ʿadh shaqqamtî dᵉbhôrāh,* "In the days of Jael, caravans ceased, . . . the peasantry grew fat, in Israel they grew fat on booty, when you arose O Deborah" (Jgs. 5:6f.).[10] The Song of Hannah celebrates a similar reversal of fortunes in a passage that has become proverbial: "Those who were full have hired themselves out for food, and those who were hungry have become fat on prey" (1 S. 2:5).[11] By attributing the poem to Hannah and putting it in its present context, the editor relates this verse to Hannah's predicament and ultimate triumph over Peninnah, the rival wife. In both the Song of Deborah and the Song of Hannah, growing fat is a mark of Yahweh's favor. He has elevated those of low estate.

Freedman, Lundbom

---

[9]Chaney.

[10]*Idem.*

[11]For a different interpretation, see H. J. Stoebe, *KAT,* VIII/1 (1973), 102: "Those who suffer hunger can celebrate forever."

חֶדֶר chedher

Contents: I. Statistics; Extrabiblical Occurrences; Basic Meaning. II. Secular Usage. III. Occurrences with Theological Implications.

I. Statistics; Extrabiblical Occurrences; Basic Meaning. The substantive *chedher* is attested a total of 38 times in the OT, and once in Sir. 4:15.[1] In addition, many have conjectured, probably correctly, that Ps. 84:11 (Eng. v. 10) originally contained *bachᵃdhārāi,* which has either been omitted by haplography or been miscopied as *bāchartî.*[2] Since the LXX translates *chedher* with *tamieíon* more than 30 times, it is safe to assume *chedher* in the Hebrew of Sir. 29:12. If we assume a Hebrew original for Tobit,[3] *tamieíon* in Tob. 7:15 and in the Sinaiticus manuscript of Tob. 7:16; 8:1,4 probably indicate Heb. *chedher.* In four instances the LXX renders *chedher* or *chedher mishkābh* as *koitṓn,* so that in Jth. 13:3f.; 14:15; 16:19 the *koitṓn* of the LXX probably corresponds to a *chedher* or *chedher mishkābh* of the Hebrew original.[4]

In Ezk. 21:19(14) we find the participle of a verb *chādhar,* which is usually taken to mean "surround, encompass."[5] In Sir. 51:19, however, the meaning "enter" seems to be demanded for the same verb, so that this meaning can also be assumed for Ezk. 21:19(14).[6] The text, however, is not intact.[7] The same is also true of the third supposed occurrence of this verb, in Sir. 50:11, where the LXX has *doxázein* = *chādhar*(?). These textually and semantically uncertain occurrences of *chādhar* I have nothing to offer for the meaning of *chedher.*

The situation changes when we turn to the verb *ḫadara,* "dwell," attested in Arabic and Ethiopic, along with the Ethiopic nouns *ḫadrat* and *maḫdar* (also with *ḥ*?), "dwelling," and the Old South Arabic noun *mḫdr,* which *KBL*[3] distinguishes as *ḥdr* II in contrast to *ḥdr* I, "penetrate deeply."[8] There is no trace of the verb *chādhar* II in Hebrew, but it certainly represents the same root as *chedher.* Nouns corresponding to the biblical *chedher* are attested in Arabic (*ḫidr,* "interior") and Old South Arabic (*ḫdrn*).[9] The noun *ḥdr* or *ḥdrh* appears in Hebrew, Phoenician, and Punic inscriptions with the meaning "(funerary) chamber."[10] In a Phoenician incantation text, the female demon being invoked is addressed as "the winged one in the chamber of darkness" (*bḥdr ḥšk*).[11] There is an exact counterpart to *chedher,* including use in parallel

[1] *KBL*[3] erroneously cites 40:15.
[2] Cf., e.g., H.-J. Kraus, *BK,* XV/2 ([4]1972), 582.
[3] E.g., L. Rost, *Judaism Outside the Hebrew Canon* (trans. 1976), 61, etc.
[4] E.g., O. Eissfeldt, *The OT* (trans. 1965), 607; Rost, *Judaism,* 53, etc.
[5] Cf. *KBL*[3], *s.v.*
[6] Following J. A. Bewer, "Beiträge zur Exegese des Buches Ezechiel," *ZAW,* 63 (1951), 198; *KBL*[3], *s.v. ḥdr* I: "*tief eindringen,*" "penetrate deeply."
[7] Cf. W. Zimmerli, *BK,* XIII/1 (1969), 472.
[8] Cf. *KBL*[3], *s.v. ḥdr* II.
[9] Cf. *KBL*[3], *s.v. chedher.*
[10] *DISO,* 82f.
[11] *KAI,* 27.19; cf. *ANEP,* No. 662.

phrases, in Ugaritic, where *ḥdr*, "chamber," is attested in both singular and plural, as well as *ḥdr mškb*, "sleeping chamber."[12]

Both the extrabiblical and the biblical occurrences of *chedher* point to the same fundamental meaning for this noun: *chedher* belongs to the world of a sedentary population, living in established cities or villages (the hypothetical occurrences in Jth. 13:3f.; 14:15; 16:19 can be understood as a transfer of the term to a commander's tent, pictured after the analogy of a solid house); it refers quite generally to the inner portion of a building, one or more of its (mostly dark) inner rooms. In the biblical occurrences, it is worth noting that the speaker or narrator is usually conceived as being outside this "interior." In the OT, *chedher* never refers to a room from which no exit can be found or in which someone could be imprisoned, in other words, a room that confines its interior. It always refers to a room that protects its interior from without, or cannot be observed from without—in other words, an interior space that is screened from without. The basic semantic component of *chedher* is thus: "inner (or dark) chamber of a solid building." The specific meaning in each case depends upon the context.

II. Secular Usage. In the meristic idiom *michûts/mēchᵃdhārîm*, "in the open/in the chambers" (Dt. 32:25), *chedher* refers to one of the two realms in which the life of a city dweller is spent: in contrast to the streets and alleys or even the commons of the city, it designates the inside of the solid houses. Instead of *mēchᵃdhārîm*, Ezk. 7:15 uses the more general expression *mibbayith* (cf. also Gen. 6:14). The contrasting pair *chûts/chᵃdhārîm* thus embraces the total living space of (sedentary) man. An alternative contrast—the house of Yahweh/the chambers of a private house—structures the statement in Ps. 84:11a(10a).[13]

With the exception of Prov. 20:27; 24:4; Job 9:9, *chedher* is used, as it is in Dt. 32:25, adverbially; it almost never appears as subject or object of an action, but as the location or goal of an event. Thus a *chedher* is the place to which Joseph withdraws to weep unseen (Gen. 43:30), the "private" chamber of David in his old age, which Bathsheba enters only when summoned by Nathan (1 K. 1:15), the "cool chamber" (Jgs. 3:24) on the roof (par. *ʿᵃlîyāh*) into which Eglon withdraws, where his servants do not wish to disturb him. When Elisha wishes to anoint Jehu out of sight of everyone, he has to lead him *chedher bᵉchādher* (2 K. 9:2), i.e., "through various chambers into the innermost."[14] One may likewise attempt to escape from his pursuers *chedher bᵉchādher*, to hide "in the innermost chamber" (1 K. 20:30; 22:25 = 2 Ch. 18:24). The phrase *chadhrî mibbayith* designates the place where one is safe and secure (Sir. 4:15).[15]

In addition, *chedher* designates the area of the house where one withdraws to sleep, the bedchamber (*chedher mishkābh*, Ex. 7:28[8:3]; cf. Ps. 105:30; 2 S. 4:7; 13:10; also 2 K. 11:2 = 2 Ch. 22:11; *chedher hammiṭṭôth* should probably also be cited here; cf. also Jth. 13:3f.; 14:15; 16:19). It is astounding and miraculous that what is said there is

---

[12] *WUS*, No. 907.

[13] See III below.

[14] *GesB*, *s.v.*

[15] On Isa. 26:20, see III below.

perceived from without (2 K. 6:12; Eccl. 10:20). A *chedher* is therefore also the place where a man can be undisturbed with a woman, a woman with her beloved (Jgs. 15:1; 16:9,12; Cant. 1:4; 3:4; Joel 2:16: par. to and identical with *chuppāh;* cf. Tob. 7:15 and (Sinaiticus) 7:16; 8:1,4; cf. also 2 S. 13:10). The plural *chᵃdhārîm* can refer to the storerooms in which possessions are stored and protected against the depredations of others (Prov. 24:4; cf. Sir. 29:12). In 1 Ch. 28:11, also, *chᵃdhārāyv happᵉnîmîm,* "its [the temple's] inner chambers," probably refers to storerooms.[16]

III. Occurrences with Theological Implications. The word *chedher* itself never becomes a theological term; it is, however, used a few times in theologically relevant contexts.

Ps. 84:11a (conj.) states that a day in the courts of the temple is better than a thousand days in the chamber of the worshipper's own house. That the contrast is not between a single day, in the sense of a brief and transitory visit to the temple, and a permanent residence in one's own house, is shown both by the parallel stich in v. 11b and by the tenor of the psalm as a whole. The point is rather that the courts of the house of Yahweh are a better habitation for the worshipper than even the innermost chamber of his own house: his dwelling place is fundamentally always with Yahweh (cf. v. 5[4]: *yšb;* Ps. 15:1: *škn/gwr;* 16:6: *nachᵃlāh;* 23:6 conj.: *yšb;* 27:4: *yšb;* 52:10[8]; 61:5[4]: *gwr;* 65:5[4]: *škn;* 92:14[13]: *shāthûl*).

The metaphor in Isa. 26:20 is based on the element of protection involved in the notion of the "interior." For the period of apocalyptic wrath and the tribulation that accompanies the final conflict, Yahweh admonishes even his own people to withdraw into their chambers, shut the doors behind them, and hide themselves for this "little while." This admonition may well be associated with the command not to leave the house during the night of Passover (Ex. 12:22).

Above all, however, there is theological significance in the transfer of notions connected with *chedher* to cosmological and anthropological situations by the language of Wisdom. In Prov. 20:27, we read that Yahweh (conj.;[17] MT: "the breath of man") searches even *chadhrê bhāṭen,* the chambers of the body. The same phrase appears again in Prov. 18:8 (=26:22) and 20:30; it refers to man in his corporeal existence, which eludes the human eye as an incomprehensible, inscrutable, and dark interior.

In Job 9:9, *chadhrê thēmān,* "chambers of the south," could be a technical term of astronomy. Undoubtedly, though, in the context of hymnic descriptions of nature couched in the language of Wisdom, there was an element of the impenetrable and overpowering suggested to human ears by the "chambers of the south." Job 37:9 speaks of the "chamber" from which the whirlwind comes. The immediate picture is probably that of a kind of storeroom in which the wind is kept. Here, too, however, *chedher* undoubtedly stresses the element of the mysterious in the natural phenomenon, its inaccessibility to human understanding (cf. Jn. 3:8).

In Prov. 7:27, finally, *chadhrê māveth,* "chambers of death," stands in parallelism

---

[16]On Job 37:9, see III below.
[17]Cf. *BHK.*

with Sheol, the Underworld. Here, too, *chedher* designates the impenetrable and incomprehensible element of the realm of death, where it impinges on the open realm of life.

In all these Wisdom expressions, *chedher* gives voices to phenomena and sectors of the human world that are indeed part of it, but are fundamentally inaccessible to human understanding (in Wisdom).[18]

Mosis

[18]On the "limits of Wisdom," cf. G. von Rad, *Wisdom in Israel* (trans. 1972), 101-114.

חָדָשׁ *chādhāsh;* חֹדֶשׁ *chōdhesh*

Contents: I. Root and Concept: 1. Akk. *edēšu, eššu*; 2. *eššešu*; 3. *arḫu*; 4. Ugaritic, Phoenician, etc.; 5. Egypt. *iʿḥ*; 6. Biblical Occurrences and Statistics. II. *chōdhesh*: 1. Never Newness but *nouménía/mēn*; 2. *yerach, yārēach, lᵉbhānāh*; 3. The Moon as a Measure of Time; 4. The Month as a Period of Time; 5. Specified Points of Time; Names of Months; 6. Sacred Months. III. New-moon Festival: 1. Moon Cult: Yerach, Sîn, Mēn; 2. Eschatological Image; 3. *eššešu* and *šapattu*; 4. Basis of New Year or Other Feasts; 5. Pejorative Use of *môʿēdh* or *chagh* like *shabbāth*; 6. Approving Use: Isa. 66:23. IV. Newness: 1. Jer. 31:31, the Inward Covenant; 2. Jer. 31:22, Eschatological Reversal and Salvation; 3. The Link with Authentic Selfhood in Ezekiel. V. "New Song": 1. In the Psalms, Redemption; 2. "New Things" in Deutero-Isaiah. VI. Trito-Isaiah: 1. More Eschatological; 2. "New Name"; 3. Use as a Verb. VII. Preexilic Hostility: 1. "New Gods"; 2. Early Ritual or Magical Overtones. VIII. Summary.

I. Root and Concept.

1. *Akk. edēšu, eššu.* The root **ḥdš* appears in Akkadian as *edēšu,* "be or become new," factitive (II) "renew," sometimes in the sense "rejuvenate," but more often

chādhash. J. Behm, "καινός," *TDNT,* III, 447-454; *idem,* "νέος," *TDNT,* IV, 896-901; L. Bushinski and J. Nelis, "Moon," *EDB,* 1554-56; *idem.,* "New Year," *ibid.,* 1633-36; A. Caquot, "Remarques sur la fête de la 'néoménie' dans l'ancien Israël," *RHR,* 158 (1970), 1-18; G. Delling, "μήν," *TDNT,* IV, 638-642; S. Gandz, "The Calendar of Ancient Israel," *Homenaje a Millás-Vallicrosa,* I (Barcelona, 1954), 623-646; M. Gruber, "The Source of the Biblical Sabbath," *JANES,* 2 (1969), 54-57; R. A. Harrisville, "The Concept of Newness in the New Testament," *JBL,* 74 (1955), 69-79; A. Jepsen, "Siehe, ich schaffe Neues! Eine kurze Betrachtung zu einem alltäglichen Wort," *TAik,* 72 (1967), 117-125; S. Kirst, "Sin, Yeraḫ und Jahweh; eine Bemerkung zum vorderasiatischen Mondkult," *FuF,* 32 (1958), 213-19; E. Koffmahn, "Sind die altisraelitischen Monatsbezeichnungen mit den kanaanäisch-phönikischen identisch?" *BZ,* 10 (1966), 197-219; J. Licht, "ראש חדש," *EMiqr,* III, 40f.; *idem,* "יָרֵחַ," *ibid.,* 837-39; I. de la Potterie, "New," *DBTh,* 386-88; R. de Vaux, *AncIsr,* 183-86, 475-77; C. Westermann, "חדש *ḥādaš neu,*" *THAT,* I, 524-530.

simply "restore," as a statue or a building by repair or reconstruction.[1] Noteworthy is the monthly "self-renewal" of the moon-god *Sîn: ina iteddušika,* "when you [Sîn] renew yourself. . . ."[2]

The adjective *eššu* I (an assimilated form of *ḥdš*), "new," is common as the opposite of *labirum,* "old,"[3] as in *bītum eššum,* a "new house."[4] In another passage,[5] *bītu eššu* stands in contrast not with *bītu labīru* but with *temen labiri,* so that *eššu* here has the sense "newfangled, new in concept."[6] The adjective can be used of new tools[7] or garments.[8] In the case of food, it has the sense "fresh, freshly harvested," with reference, for example, to barley, dates, leeks, etc.[9] It is also common in toponyms for "New City(-Quarter)" (cf. Naples and Carthage!), for instance, for Ashur.[10] The phrase "a new tablet," although sometimes explicitly contrasted to the old, means rather a revised or renegotiated contract.[11] Very seldom, chiefly at Nuzi, *eššu* alone means "new moon" or "month," like Heb. *chōdhesh.*[12]

The rare homonyms *eššu* II, "temple," *eššû* I, "cold," and *eššû* II, "door," exhibit no semantic link with *eššu* I, "new."[13]

2. *eššešu.* A closer equivalent to *chōdhesh* in its sense of "new-moon festival" would be the quite common Sumerian loanword *eššešu,* although its attestations for a "monthly" celebration[14] show no connection with "month," "new," or "moon."[15] The similarity to *eššu* is misleading; *eššešu* is a loanword from Sumerian *èš-èš.* Since *èš* (= AB) means "house," the sense is perhaps "(days for) all the different temples [for feeding the gods]."[16] Moreover, already in early texts[17] the *eššešu* festival fell not only on the 1st of each month, but also the 7th and 15th, and even the 25th.[18] Later

---

1References: *AHw,* I, 186f.; *CAD,* IV, 30-33.

2A. T. Clay, *Miscellaneous Inscriptions in the Yale Babylonian Collection. YOSBT,* 1 (1915), 45 II 42.

3*AHw,* I, 258f.; *CAD,* IV, 374–77.

4E. Chiera, *Legal and Administrative Documents from Nippur. PBS,* 8/1 (1914), 81; D. D. Luckenbill, *OIP,* 2 (1924), 153.

5S. H. Langdon, *Die neubabylonischen Königsinschriften. VAB,* IV (1912), 254, 20.

6*CAD,* IV, 375.

7*BIN,* II, 127.

8*KAJ,* 256, 2.

9CT 22, 81, 84, etc.

10E. Ebeling, *Die Inschriften der altassyrischen Könige. AOBib,* 1 (1926), 32.

11A. Poebel, *Historical and Grammatical Texts. PBS,* 5/1 (1914), Plate XCIII; CT 29, 33, 39.

12E. R. Lacheman, *Miscellaneous Texts from Nuzi, II: The Palace and Temple Archives. HSS,* 14 (1950), 106, 229; C. J. Gadd, "Tablets from Kirkuk," *RA,* 23 (1926), 145.

13*AHw,* I, 259a.

14*CAD,* IV, 372.

15*ARM,* I, 10; R. H. Pfeiffer and E. R. Lacheman, *Miscellaneous Texts from Nuzi, I. HSS,* 13 (1942), 31; R. H. Pfeiffer and E. A. Speiser, *One Hundred New Selected Nuzi Texts. AASOR,* 16 (1936), No. 12; CT 22, 191.

16Cf. A. Oppenheim, *Ancient Mesopotamia* (1964), 190; *CRRA,* 17 (1970), 60.

17Ur III; cf. E. D. Van Buren, *The Fauna of Ancient Mesopotamia as Represented in Art. AnOr,* 18 (1939), 39.

18Cf. also Chiera, *Legal and Administrative Documents,* 60, from Nippur.

hemerologies add or rather substitute the 4th, 8th, and 17th, as days of veneration for Nabû but with vigils venerating Marduk. In the latest texts, from Warka, there are eight *eššešu* days every month. It may perhaps be questioned whether these are "lucky days"[19] relating either to the "fresh start" each month brings or to a generalization of an original veneration of the new-moon day.

3. *arḫu*. In Akkadian, the word "moon" (like "sun"/Shamash) is written either with the logogram of the god Sîn[20] or, like the latter, with the sign for the number 30. According to Sjöberg,[21] *zu-en* is clearly distinct from the moon-god Nanna, while according to Jacobsen[22] the god Ensun (= "Lord Wild Bull") is identical with Nanna.

The Akkadian equivalent to *yārēach/yerach* is *warḫu* (later Bab. *arḫu*, Assyr. *urḫu*), but rarely with the meaning "moon"[23] or "new moon" as such.[24] Its frequent sense "new-moon day" corresponds rather to Heb. *chōdhesh*, and is more apt to be related to *edēšu* than *eššešu*. On the other hand, CT 46, 4, III, 20 (Atraḫasis 56f.) and *TCL* 1, 50 distinguish it from the parallel 7th and 15th. In UD-2 *warḫi* it means merely "month" ("the second day of the month"), as in 1 S. 20:34. The moon-god Sîn "appears" on the 1st day of the new moon,[25] but also on the 15th or full-moon day.[26] By far the majority of occurrences of *arḫu* have the ordinary sense of a calendar "month," often with the addition of a name.[27] An *arḫu* can also be designated by number, as can Heb. *chōdhesh* but not *yerach*. The word can be associated with pregnancy,[28] but not with menstruation like *chōdhesh* in Jer. 2:24. The Namburbi texts express the wish: "May the month bring gladness."[29] Otherwise what little religious or superstitious significance can be detected is related not to the *arḫu* itself but to its "first day."[30] Selection of an auspicious month is as important as selection of an auspicious day.[31]

---

[19]See the discussion of *šapattu* in III.3.

[20]The pronunciation *zu-en* is attested in *NFT*, 207.

[21]Å. Sjöberg, *Der Mondgott Nanna-Suen in der sumerischen Überlieferung* (Uppsala, 1960), 140.

[22]T. Jacobsen, "Mesopotamian Gods and Pantheons," *Toward the Image of Tammuz and Other Essays on Mesopotamian History and Culture*. *HSS*, 21 (1970), 25.

[23]H. Zimmern, *VAS*, 10, 215.

[24]IV R 32; Clay, *Miscellaneous Inscriptions*, 45.

[25]IV R 32.

[26]Lacheman, *Miscellaneous Texts*, II, 106.

[27]B. Landsberger, *Der kultische Kalender der Babylonier und Assyrer*. *LSS*, 6/1-2 (1915); *idem*, *The Series ḪAR-ra-ḫubullu. Tablets I-IV*. *MSL*, V (1957), 25; S. Langdon, *Babylonian Menologies and the Semitic Calendars* (1935); R. Labat, *Hémérologies et ménologies d'Assur* (Paris, 1939); for Nuzi, C. Gordon and E. R. Lacheman, "The Nuzi Menology," *RSO*, 15 (1934), 253-57, revised in *ArOr*, 10 (1938), 51-64.

[28]*CAD*, I/2, 261.

[29]R. Caplice [to whom much of this cuneiform material is due], "Namburbi Texts in the British Museum, IV," *Or*, 39 (1970), 149f.; cf. "Participants in the Namburbi Rituals," *CBQ*, 29 (1967), 40.

[30]A. T. Clay, *Epics, Hymns, Omens and Other Texts*. *BRM*, 4 (1923), 21; or the 30th: *KAR*, 177.

[31]See R. Labat, *Un calendrier babylonien des travaux des signes des mois* (Paris, 1965).

4. *Ugaritic, Phoenician, etc.* Ugar. *ḥdṯ* is attested 18 times in Whitaker.[32] Gordon, however,[33] notes 6 instances of the meaning "new," 9 of "renew" (especially *yḥdṯ yrḫ,* "renew the moon"), and 5 of "new-moon day(s)." *KBL*[3] cites Ugar. *trḫ ḥdṯ*, "new bridegroom," as a parallel to the "new wife" of Dt. 24:5.[34]

The root *ḥdš* appears as a verb meaning "restore, renew" in Phoenician and Punic, and in its Aramaic form *ḥdt* in Nabatean and Palmyrene. As an adjective meaning "new" it appears in Punic, Biblical Aramaic,[35] and Palmyrene. As a noun meaning "new moon, month" it appears in Phoenician and Punic.[36] The most interesting use is its appearance in *qrtḥdšt,* "new town," Gk. *karchēdṓn,* the name of Carthage.[37] Also to be noted is the personal name Ben Ḥodeš, which attests the religious significance of the day of the new moon in the Syrian cult.[38]

5. *Egyp. ỉʿḥ.* The normal Egyptian word for moon is *ỉʿḥ,* a cognate of *yerach.*[39] No other terms are attested until the Greek period.[40] Thoth is called the "lunar deity," but rather as protector of the moon.[41] A new-moon festival is described under the name *pśḏnṯyw.*[42] Bonnet notes that the moon, like the sun, is regarded as male.[43] A century of controversy over the two series of Egyptian names for the months[44] is summarized as follows by Gardiner: "One school of thought attributed the invention of the year to the sun-god Reʿ, another . . . to the moon-god Thoth."[45]

The root *ḥdš* does not occur in Egyptian. The word for "new" is *m3.*[46] The verb *m3wy,* "renew oneself, become new,"[47] also appears in the causative form *śm3wy,* "renew."[48] The notion of renewal, even in the sense of rejuvenation, seems to underlie the Eygptian *śd* festival: the sovereign is empowered to continue his duties after what would normally have been too long a period.[49] The term *ḥb-śd* is usually rendered "jubilee"; and despite entirely different origins, the Hebr. → יובל *yôbhēl* of Lev. 25:10 also has nuances of universal renewal or anticipation of the eschatological *apokatástasis.*[50]

---

[32] *WUS,* No. 908.
[33] *UT,* No. 843.
[34] P. 282.
[35] Cf. *KBL*[2], 1074a and Ezr. 6:4 (corrupt).
[36] *DISO,* 83.
[37] *KBL*[3], 283.
[38] Cf. F. Jeremias in P. D. Chantepie de la Saussaye, *Lehrbuch der Religionsgeschichte,* I, ([4]1925), 625; M. Höfner, "Die altsüdarabischen Monatsnamen," *Vorderasiatische Studien. Festschrift V. Christian* (Vienna, 1956), 46-54.
[39] *WbÄS,* I, 42, contra *UT,* No. 1151.
[40] *WbÄS,* VI, 106.
[41] P. Boylan, *Thoth, the Hermes of Egypt* (1922), 62, 83.
[42] *WbÄS,* I, 559; *RÄR,* 474f.
[43] *RÄR,* 472.
[44] R. A. Parker, *The Calendars of Ancient Egypt. SAOC,* 26 (1950).
[45] A. Gardiner, "The Problem of the Month-Names," *RÉg,* 10 (1955), 26.
[46] *WbÄS,* II, 26.
[47] *WbÄS,* II, 25.
[48] *WbÄS,* IV, 126.
[49] J. Vandier, *La religion égyptienne* (Paris, [2]1949), 200.
[50] R. G. North, *Sociology of the Biblical Jubilee. AnBibl,* 4 (1954), 44, 228; cf. IV.2.

6. *Biblical Occurrences and Statistics.* The verb *chādhash* is attested 10 times (9 piel, 1 hithpael); the adjective *chādhāsh,* "new," 53 times; and the noun *chōdhesh,* "month, day of the new moon," about 280 times.[51]

Not treated here are four proper names: Hodesh, a woman mentioned in 1 Ch. 8:9;[52] Hadashah, a place in Josh. 15:37; the problematical Tahtim-hodshi of 2 S. 24:6;[53] Aram. (Hazor-)hadattah in Josh. 15:25; and the corrupt *chadhath* in Ezra 6:4.

The occurrences of *chādhāsh* are distributed as follows: 10 in Isa. 40–66, 6 in Psalms, 5 in Ezekiel, and 16 in the Deuteronomistic history. There is no precise synonym for "new" in the OT; the semantic field includes *ṭārî,* "fresh" (2 occurrences); *lach,* "moist, fresh" (6 occurrences).[54] The noun *chōdhesh* appears 38 times in Numbers (9 times in connection with the minimum age to be counted in a census, otherwise mostly in the formula "on the . . . day of the . . . month"), 58 times in Chronicles and Ezra, 27 times in Ezekiel, and 24 times in Esther. As a synonym for "month," *yerach* appears 12 times (4 in Job); *yārēach* occurs 27 times, almost always in combination with *shemesh* (24 times; Ps. 72:7; in Job 25:5 and Ps. 8:4 [Eng. v. 3], the stars are mentioned as well). The noun *lebhānāh,* "moon," appears also in poetic texts, always in connection with the sun (here *chammāh,* 3 times). The noun *kese'/ keseh,* "full moon," appears twice.

II. chōdesh.

1. *Never Newness but noumēnía/mḗn.* The more superficially theological uses of the root *ḥdš* relate to the noun *chōdhesh,* "new-moon (festival)" or simply "month." The LXX renders *chōdesh* some 16 times as *noumēnía* (5 times using the uncontracted form *neomēnía*), which actually is rather the equivalent of *rō'sh (ha-)chōdhesh* (Nu. 10:10; 28:11). Once *heortḗ* stands for *chōdhesh* (1 K. 12:33, where the LXX apparently read *chagh* instead of *chōdhesh*). Elsewhere we find *mḗn,* "month" or "moon" (root *me-,* as in Lat. *metiri,* "measure," a "measure" of time; cf. Ps. 104:19; Sir. 43:6, "the moon marks the times"). There is a Phrygian deity linked with this name.[55]

Doubtless the "newness" of the reborn moon, the "fresh start" of which gives hope, accounts not only for its religious veneration but also for its secular use to denote a measure of time. Strangely, however, the segholate noun *chōdhesh* nowhere has its

---

[51] *KBL*[3]; *THAT* counts 283 occurrences, Lisowski 284.

[52] J. J. Stamm, "Hebräische Frauennamen," *Hebräische Wortforschung. Festschrift W. Baumgartner. SVT,* 16 (1967), 322; S. Yeivin, "חֹדֶשׁ," *EMiqr,* III, 35.

[53] P. Skehan, "Joab's Census: How Far North (2 Sm 24, 6)?" *CBQ,* 31 (1969), 42–49; R. North, "The Hivites," *Bibl,* 54 (1973), 54.

[54] Cf. A. van Selms, "A Forgotten God: *Laḥ,*" *Studica Biblica et Semitica. Festschrift Th. C. Vriezen* (1966), 320.

[55] Cf. Delling, 641f.; W. Fauth, "Men," in *KlPauly,* III (1969), 1194, cites U. Monneret de Villard, "Le monete dei Kushāna e l'impero romano," *Or,* 17 (1948), 227; M. Riemschneider, "Die urartäischen Gottheiten," *Or,* 32 (1963), 155f., and other updatings of A. Lesky, "Men," *PW,* XV (1931), 689–697; cf. also W. Drexler in W. H. Roscher, *Ausführliches Lexikon der griechischen und römischen Mythologie,* II/2 (1894–1897, repr. 1965), 2687–2770, and Roscher on the moon-goddess Selene, *ibid.,* IV (1900–1915, repr. 1965), 642–650.

natural and expected sense of "newness (in general)."[56] Nor does *chōdhesh* ever mean "moon" as a luminous heavenly body. As a synonym for *chōdhesh, yerach* appears 12 times (4 in Job), with the meaning "month" (Ex. 2:2; Dt. 21:13; 2 K. 15:13; Zec. 11:8; Job 7:3; 29:2; 39:2) or in conjunction with the name of a particular month (1 K. 6:37f.; 8:2); it differs from *chōdhesh* in never being specified by an ordinal numeral.

2. *yerach, yārēach, lᵉbhānāh.* The noun *yerach* itself is never used for the earth's satellite, but is a variant of *yārēach,* the usual word for the moon. The synonym *lᵉbhānāh,* "milky/white lady," occurs only in poetic texts and always in parallel with *chammāh,* "heat," i.e., the sun (Cant. 6:10; Isa. 24:23; 30:26). Both *lᵉbhānāh* and *chammāh* are feminine; the common word for sun is *shemesh,* masculine in Akkadian and sometimes also in Hebrew. But from the more usual Semitic perspective, the moon (*yārēach/qamar*), surprisingly, represents the male or dominant partner as against the sun, which is feminine in Jgs. 19:14, in Ugar. *špš,* and in the Koran, Sura 12:4, interpreting Gen. 37:9.

Unlike *lᵉbhānāh, yārēach* is often used pejoratively in the Bible. Its worship is forbidden (Dt. 4:19, par. with the sun, stars, and host of heaven; cf. Wis. 13:2), even on pain of death (Dt. 17:3, par. with the sun and the host of heaven); but the cult of the moon or the stars kept cropping up in Israel (2 K. 23:5; for Jer. 8:2, see III.1). This peril is traceable to the influence of infidel neighbors (cf. *śahᵃrôn,* "crescent amulet," Jgs. 8:21), but also to the moon's undoubted fascination (Job 31:26) as an expression of God's own creative power and rule (Ps. 136:9; Bar. 6:59; Gen. 1:16, *mā'ôr qāṭôn*).

The full moon is called *kese'* (rare: Ps. 81:4[3]; Prov. 7:20; Job 26:9[?]; Ugar. *ks'*) or perhaps *lᵉbhānāh.*[57] In Enoch 78:2, four names for the moon are mentioned, of which we can recognize *yārēach, lᵉbhānāh,* and *kese'*. The fourth name, *'ashônyebh,* which stands for *chōdhesh,* is probably corrupt (even if it is derived from *'îshôn,* "pupil" of night's eye [cf. Prov. 7:9], rather than from *'ᵉshûn,* "time," Akk. *isinnu* [a Sumerian loanword], "festival").[58]

3. *The Moon as a Measure of Time.* "The month is named for the moon," says Sir. 43:8, which is more true in Greek than appears from the rendering *mḗn katá ónoma selḗnēs.* It holds also in Hebrew if *yerach* instead of *chōdhesh* is recognized as the primitive term for month. "God made the *yārēach* for *mô'ᵃdhîm,* seasons" (Ps. 104:19), "to rule the night" (Gen. 1:16; Ps. 136:9). These passages attribute similar rule of the night to the stars, and rule of the day to the sun. But the moon makes itself visible with more exclusiveness and with more apparent caprice (Sir. 27:11) along with ultimate reliability. Hence it has always been primitively and spontaneously adopted as a measure of time, the lunar month, and therefore even merits veneration as

---

[56] I. L. Seeligmann, "Hebräische Erzählung und biblische Geschichtsschreibung," *ThZ,* 18 (1962), 313, n. 16, on 1 S. 10:27.

[57] G. Lisowsky, *Konkordanz zum hebräischen AT* (1958), 716; Licht, 838, with N. Tur-Sinai.

[58] *AHw,* I, 388a; *CAD,* VII, 195ff.

God's chosen vessel for this purpose: "In the beginning was the moon, as a measure of time, as a heavenly clock striking off the months of 30 days."[59]

Another periodicity inspiring religious awe, the month's relation to menstruation, is mentioned explicitly only with respect to an animal (Jer. 2:24). But the repeated religious strictures about *ṭum'āh*, "uncleanness" (Lev. 15:19; 2 S. 11:4), doubtless reflect belief in the influence of the moon's rebirth.[60] The hypothesis of an older Canaanite nonlunar division of the year into 7 periods of 50 days each[61] has been refuted by Landsberger.[62]

4. *The Month as a Period of Time.* Most of the 44 occurrences of *chōdhesh* (out of 280, surprisingly few), in the sense of a period of time, "lunar month, 29½ days," are devoid of religious implications: Laban stays with Jacob a month (Gen. 29:14); Judah is told of Tamar three months later (Gen. 38:24; cf. also *yerach* in II.1). Only in Job 14:5 do we have the sobering reflection that man's days are determined and the "number of his months" (*chᵒdhāshāv*) depends on Yahweh (similarly 39:2, *yᵉrāchîm*).

A special case is the insistence that a baby less than a month old is not to be included in the census (Nu. 3:15, 22, 28, 39f., 43; 26:62) nor assigned the cash value of a human life (Lev. 27:6).*

5. *Specified Points of Time; Names of Months.* Far more common is the use of *chōdhesh* to designate a point within the year or within the month itself, often both together. Rarely is it a "specific but not specified" month (Nu. 9:3; cf. *yerach,* Job 3:6; Dt. 33:14), or a month specified only as "that month" or "every month." Far more often it is specified by all or part of the formula "in the second month, on the seventeenth day of the month" (Gen. 7:11).

This formula appears 20 times (4 in Leviticus and Jeremiah, 3 in Numbers and Ezekiel), while "on the Nth day of the Nth month" occurs 5 times, chiefly in Esther. The word "month" occurs with a number identifying it 108 times, of which a third are in the Chronicler (27 times in 1-2 Chronicles, 10 times in Ezra, once in Nehemiah). Numbers (14 occurrences) and Ezekiel (13 occurrences) each account for 12 percent of these uses, and Leviticus, Esther, Kings, Jeremiah, and Haggai-Zechariah 6 percent each. In addition, Esther identifies the month by a Babylonian name 11 times (mostly Adar, for Purim), and Exodus-Deuteronomy use a Canaanite name 6 times (all Abib); 8 other texts also give a name, for a total of 25. The day of the month is given by number in 57 cases, largely overlapping the above, with or without repetition of the word *chōdhesh*. Repetition of *chōdhesh* is distributive, equivalent to "every." Only in

[59]Gandz, 623; also "The Problem of the Molad," *PAAJR,* 20 (1951), 235.

[60]L. Toombs, "Clean and Unclean," *IDB,* I, 644; M. Eliade, "Mond," *RGG*³, IV, 1095; K. Tallqvist, *Månen i myt och dikt, folktro och kult. StOr,* 12 (1948).

[61]H. Lewy and J. Lewy, "The Origin of the Week and the Oldest West Asiatic Calendar," *HUCA,* 17 (1942/43), 96.

[62]B. Landsberger, "Jahreszeiten im Sumerisch-Akkadischen," *JNES,* 8 (1949), 291.

*To what appears here in the German text, the author adds: "This may perhaps contribute a meagre historical footnote to the vexed theological discussion as to the exact moment when the life of a human individual begins and its taking becomes homicide, whether justifiable or not."

Ex. 12:2 is the concept of a month itself used as "the beginning of months . . . the first month of the year."

The month/day formula in all its banality is not without theological significance. It represents a concerted effort of the biblical compilers to suppress Canaanite names of agricultural and therefore semireligious origin. From the Bible alone we know one of these names: Abib (Ex. 13:4), usually associated semantically with the sacred firstfruits, "ears of grain" (*shibbōleth*!) of the first month, March/April.[63] Three other names are attested both inside and outside the Bible: the second month, Ziv (1 K. 6:37), "brightness" = flowers[64] or simply springtime, May; the seventh, Ethanim (1 K. 8:2), the "freshets" of September; and the eighth, Bul (1 K. 6:38), variously rendered as "torrential rain (Arab. 'urine')," "produce," or "cattle." A fifth name, Tsach, for June or the third month, was discovered in the Arad excavations.[65] Other months are named in Phoenician inscriptions: *zbḥšmš, mrpʾ*[*m*], *gibʾol, pʿlt, krr, mpʿ*. Koffmahn[66] gives a synoptic table with discussion of Ugaritic data.

Perhaps a first stage in supplanting these mythological names with more frankly secular ones is represented in the Gezer calendar (925 B.C.),[67] where four months are designated by their respective agricultural operations, but four other operations are assigned to two-month periods. Some of these names survive in Qumran chronology, alongside the "perpetual calendar" of the book of Jubilees, set in momentous relation to the NT by Jaubert.[68] The reactions have been tabulated by Carmignac.[69]

Within the Bible, the attempt to expunge the mythological element was apparently not borrowed from any Babylonian or Egyptian usage, and came in only after the reforms of Josiah (2 K. 25:1; Jer. 52:4). The month names were replaced with ordinal numbers, just as when the medieval church tried (with permanent success only in the case of Portuguese) to rename the weekdays "third," "fifth," etc., instead of "Mars' Day," "Jove/Thor's Day," etc. This trend within the Bible is accompanied by a preference for the purely secular designation of the month as *chōdhesh*, "the new," instead of the cultic term *yerach*, "belonging to the moon(god)." All this is an instructive example of what has been one of theology's major legitimate responsibilities from the beginning: to withdraw from the cultic sphere and restore to the purely secular that which rightly belonged there from the beginning.[70]

When the postexilic Hebrew community needed to utilize Babylonian month names, they seemed to feel less scruple. The Chronicler avoids them, and in 1 Ch. 27:2-15 austerely gives all 12 months only by number. The other late books often give the

---

[63]C. H. Gordon, "2. חֹדֶשׁ," *EMiqr*, III, 38.

[64]*AncIsr*, 183.

[65]Y. Aharoni and R. Amiran, "Excavations at Tel Arad," *IEJ*, 14 (1964), 143.

[66]Cf. Koffmahn, 216f.

[67]*ANET*³, 320; *KAI*, 182.

[68]A. Jaubert, *The Date of the Last Supper* (trans. 1965); *idem*, "Le Mercredi où Jésus fut livré," *NTS*, 14 (1967/68), 145-164, esp. 145.

[69]J. Carmignac, "Comment Jésus et ses contemporains pouvaient-ils célébrer la Pâque à une date non officielle?" *RevQ*, 5 (1964-66), 59.

[70]R. North, "Recent Christology and Theological Method," *Continuum*, 7 (1969), 63-77, esp. 63.

month names of great-power neighbors, usually accompanied by an explanatory numeral: the first month, Nisan (Est. 3:7); the third, Sivan (Est. 8:9); the sixth, Elul (Neh. 6:15); the ninth, Chislev (Zec. 7:1); the tenth, Tebeth (Est. 2:16); the eleventh, Shebat (Zec. 1:7); and the twelfth, Adar (Est. 3:7). The remaining five are attested at Elephantine. Macedonian names are similarly used in books like Maccabees.[71]

6. *Sacred Months.* A more genuinely doctrinal, or at least liturgical, significance attaches to the designations of the months (whether by name or by number) in their concrete biblical context as containing important religious festivals. Abib or Nisan, for example, is mentioned far more frequently and thoughtfully than any other, because of Passover. An attempt is even made to make it "the first month," as at Babylon (Ex. 12:2; also Est. 3:7) and at Qumran.[72] Various explanations are offered for the plain implication of Ex. 12:2 that previously a different month had been fixed firmly in first place, namely Tishri (Akk. *šurrû,* "begin"), which had several less important feasts, including the Jewish Rosh Hashanah, still celebrated today (see III.4).

III. New-moon Festival.

1. *Moon Cult: Yerach, Sîn, Mēn.* The cult of the moon is attested in the background of the biblical people (according to Caquot, even in the preexilic period) and of their neighbors.[73] In Jer. 19:13 and Zeph. 1:5, the "host of heaven" includes the moon, although in Jer. 7:18 "queen of heaven" refers rather to the planet Venus. Moon-worship doubtless accounts for the origin of a place name like Jericho (*y^erîchô,* Josh. 2:1), as well as the nearby Qumran (Arab. *qamar*). Nor can we exclude the possibility that the Akkadian moon-god[74] gave his name to the wilderness of Sin (Ex. 16:1), or even to Sinai. More imaginatively than convincingly, Kirst[75] enumerates biblical passages attesting a moon cult taken over from Canaan (including Hab. 3:11); he claims the Mesopotamian Sîn cult was brought to Canaan by Binu-Yamina,[76] but was replaced by a *yerach* cult ultimately related to Thoth/Taautos.[77] The important Khirbet Kerak excavation at the southwest tip of Lake Tiberias is presumably the moon-cult site Beth-yerach known from the Mishnah.[78]

The Ugaritic divinity Yeraḫ is attested in some ten texts (besides the six uses of *yrḫ*

---

71 *Idem,* "Weights and Measures," *A New Catholic Commentary on the Holy Scriptures* (1968), 106.

72 S. Talmon, "The Calendar Reckoning of the Sect from the Judaean Desert," *ScrHier,* 4 (1958), 172.

73 See II.2.

74 See I.3.

75 P. 216.

76 Cf. G. Dossin, "Benjaminites dans les textes de Mari," *Mélanges Syriens offerts à Monsieur René Dussaud* (Paris, 1939), II, 981.

77 Cf. also A. Jirku, "Der Kult des Mondgottes im altorientalischen Palästina-Syrien," *ZDMG,* 100 (1950), 202-204 = *Von Jerusalem nach Ugarit* (1966), 355-57.

78 *Bekh.* 51a; Jer. *Meg.* i.1.70a; M. Avi-Yonah and E. Oren, "Bet Yeraḥ," *EJ,* IV (1971), 778.

for "month"), especially in the poem about his marriage[79] and at Karatepe.[80] Another type of evidence for the Semitic moon cult is found in the Mari names Yantin-Eraḫ, "Moon's Gift," Zimri-Eraḫ, "Moon's Protection," and Abdu-Eraḫ, "Moon's Slave."[81] The South Arabic Saḥar, "crescent," occurs in the Aramaic inscription of Zakir of Ḥamat, alongside Baʿalšamên, Šamaš, the gods of heaven and earth, etc.[82] The South Arabic El ha-Yeraḥ is discussed by Licht.[83] In addition, the divine name *syn* also appears in Old South Arabic.

Such words as "luna-cy," generalized in many languages to include all insanity, show the primitive conviction that the moon causes madness (Ps. 121:6). But this insanity was commonly regarded more as a divine manifestation than as a mere affliction, as witness Gk. *entheosiasmós* for the frenzy of oracles (Pythian!; cf. *mḗn*, II.1) or poets. Though there is no specific invocation of the moon as God's agent, the earlier prophetism of the Bible is plainly "mantic" in the role played by frenzy or delirium (1 S. 10:11).

Dread of what the moon can do to people may be linked with menstruation,[84] but hardly with the trumpet blast of Nu. 10:10; Ps. 81:4(3) (new moon, but as a symbol of gladness) or Prov. 7:20 (full moon, here merely an indication of time).[85]

2. *Eschatological Image*. The moon's peculiar ability to make earth seem near to heaven during the darkest night accounts for the importance it gradually assumed as an eschatological image: it becomes a symbol of permanence (the *yārēach* will never wane again, Isa. 60:20) in Ps. 72:5,7; 89:38(37).[86] The moon is turned to blood (Joel 3:4[2:31], *yārēach*), or becomes "dark-skinned" (*qādhar*) rather than just "darkened," in contrast to "white lady" (Joel 2:10, *yārēach* par. the sun). Or it loses its light completely (Ezk. 32:7, par. the "beclouded" *shemesh;* Isa. 13:10, par. *chāshakh shemesh* [masculine]). Or contrariwise the moon shines by day (2 Esd. 5:4). This importance of the moon at the eschaton may well have prompted descriptions of the moon at creation (Gen. 1:16; Ps. 104:19; 136:9). On the poetic fancy of the moon's "standing still" (Josh. 10:12; Hab. 3:11), see → שֶׁמֶשׁ *shemesh*.

3. *eššešu and šapattu*. The Babylonian "monthly" festival called *eššešu* is described as a day of omen (not necessarily favorable; cf. the LXX addition of *eúsēmos* in Ps. 81:4[3]), which suggests some similarity to *šapattu*. It is impossible to prove or

---

[79] *CTA*, 24 [NK], most recently edited by W. Herrmann, *Yariḫ und Nikkal und der Preis der Kuṯarāt-Göttinen. BZAW*, 106 (1968).

[80] R. O'Callaghan, "Echoes of Canaanite Literature in the Psalms," *VT*, 4 (1954), 165; "An Approach to Some Religious Problems of Karatepe," *ArOr*, 18 (1950), 365; H. T. Bossert, "Die phönizischhethitischen Bilinguen vom Karatepe," *Oriens*, 1 (1948), 163-192; 2 (1949), 72-120.

[81] *APNM*, 43, 214f.

[82] *ANET*³, 655f.; *KAI*, 202 B.24.

[83] P. 838.

[84] See II.3.

[85] Contra T. Gaster, "Moon," *IDB*, III, 437.

[86] Cf. *CAD*, IV, 32, citing L. Messerschmidt and A. Ungnad, *Historische Texte. VAS*, 1 (1907), 33: "a life that renews itself constantly every month like the moon (god)."

disprove the origin of Babylonian *šapattu* from the moon's phases, or the influence of either on Hebrew → שׁבת *shabbāth.*[87] Undoubted parallels between new-moon feast and Sabbath in the OT are taken by Rylaarsdam[88] as a sign of lunar influence on the Hebrew week.[89] But Kutsch,[90] while admitting the new-moon day to be the most primitive of Israel's feasts, denies any influence on the Sabbath.

4. *Basis of New Year or Other Feasts.* Fiebig[91] holds that a new-moon celebration was one of the roots of Rosh Hashanah (Ezk. 40:1). He mentions instances of new-moon celebrations in preexilic Israel (1 S. 20:5, 24; 2 K. 4:23; Am. 8:5; Hos. 2:13[11]; Isa. 1:13), and notes that veneration of the moon at times degenerated into a moon cult adverse to monotheism. Later periods, however, including modern Judaism, found nothing objectionable.[92] Allegations that a new-moon feast was at the root of Passover[93] or the Feast of Booths have been refuted by Kugler[94] and others.

5. *Pejorative Use of mô*ᶜ*ēdh or chagh like shabbāth.* As a term for a day of cultic veneration of the moon, or at least a day specially named and noted, *chōdhesh* is usually a banal tag in the Bible. It is a specific instance of a *chagh* (Ps. 81:4[3]) or *mô*ᶜ*ēdh* (Ezra 3:5) or both (2 Ch. 8:13; Ezk. 45:17), often in parallel with *shabbāthôth* (1 Ch. 23:31; 2 Ch. 2:3[4]; Neh. 10:34[33]) and even without *mô*ᶜ*ēdh* or *chagh* (Am. 8:5; 2 K. 4:23; Ezk. 46:1[,6]). To us today, at least, it sounds as if all these ritualisms are "damned with faint praise" in stereotyped lists of how "Mosaic" prescriptions should be observed (Ezk. 45:17) or actually were observed: by Solomon (2 Ch. 2:3[4]; 8:13), Hezekiah (2 Ch. 31:3), Zerubbabel (Ezr. 3:5), or others (Neh. 10:34[33]).

More blatantly pejorative are Hos. 2:13(11); 5:7; Isa. 47:13 (with reference to astrology; cf. 2 K. 4:23). Isa. 1:13f. are devastating: "New moon and sabbath and the calling of assemblies—I [God] cannot endure iniquity [MT; LXX 'fasting'] and solemn assembly. Your new moons [*chodhshêkham;* others read *chaggêkhem*] and your appointed feasts [*mô*ᶜᵃ*dhêkhem*] my soul hates." This strong language is chiefly intended to reinforce the more imperative demand of social justice for the underprivileged (v. 17). Rejection of liturgy in comparison with this demand constitutes indirect praise of liturgy, or at worst a warning that there is no real liturgy that does not grow out of suitable inward disposition (v. 15).

---

87 Cf. N.-E. Andreasen, "Recent Studies of the Old Testament Sabbath: Some Observations," *ZAW,* 86 (1974), 453-469; N. Negretti, *Il Settimo giorno. AnBibl,* 55 (1973); R. North, "The Derivation of Sabbath," *Bibl,* 36 (1955), 185-201.

88 J. Rylaarsdam, "New Moon," *IDB,* III, 544.

89 Cf. also Gandz, 631, who correctly terms *šapattu* the day of the full moon.

90 E. Kutsch, "Feste und Feiern. II. In Israel," *RGG*³, II, 911.

91 P. Fiebig, *Rosch ha-schana (Neujahr). Die Mischna,* ed. G. Beer and O. Holtzmann, II/8 (1914), 13-31.

92 P. 15; cf. the new-moon liturgy in I. Elbogen, *Der jüdische Gottesdienst in seiner geschichtlichen Entwicklung* (³1931, ⁴1962), 122; N. H. Snaith, *The Jewish New Year Festival* (London, 1947); Bushinski, 1634.

93 A. Jeremias, *The OT in the Light of the Ancient East* (trans. 1911), II, 102.

94 F. Kugler, *Von Moses bis Paulus* (1922), 8.

6. *Approving Use: Isa. 66:23.* A more favorable view of the *chōdhesh* feast has been preserved from earlier times.[95] Saul's entourage took completely for granted that no one would absent himself from a *chōdhesh* ("feast" in 1 S. 20:5,18,24, but perhaps "month" in vv. 27,34). In Nu. 10:10, *rô'sh hachōdhesh* (as in 28:11) is equated with "the day of your gladness" (also in Jth. 8:6), to be hailed with trumpet blast. Philo[96] also discusses the manner and motive of venerating the day of the new moon. Ezk. 46:1,6 calls for the opening of the east temple gate on this day, together with sacrifices. The parallels cited by Blome[97] are questioned by Licht.[98] Am. 8:5 approves the prohibition of commerce on the day of the new moon. Also approved in principle is the royal ritualism noted above (2 Ch. 8:13; 2:3[4]; 31:3; Ezr. 3:5; Ezk. 45:17), despite the monotony and disgust inevitably engendered in proportion as routine diminishes the sincere spontaneity of the heart. Thus finally Isa. 66:23 can use *chōdhesh* and Sabbath, even as ordinary measures of time, to bode an eschatological newness[99] when all flesh shall constantly come to worship before God.

IV. Newness. It is not by chance that "newness" as a theological value is connected with the self-renewing moon[100] and is postexilic. "Only during the time of the exile was anything said in Israel about something new in its interaction with God—nowhere else in its whole history."[101] Less convincing is Westermann's hypothesis that Deutero-Isaiah and Trito-Isaiah preceded and influenced Jer. 31:31 and Ezk. 11:19; 18:31; 36:26 as normative examples of theological "newness."

1. *Jer. 31:31, the Inward Covenant.* Amid lyric promises of return from exile, and just after the proclamation of individual rather than clan responsibility (par. Ezk. 18:2[102]), Jer. 31:31-34 announces:

> "Behold, the days are coming, says Yahweh, when I will make a new covenant [*b^erîth*] with the house of Israel and the house of Judah, [32] not like the covenant which I made with their fathers when I took them by the hand to bring them out of the land of Egypt, my covenant which they broke, though by it I had become their *ba'al* ["senior partner" as in marriage], says Yahweh. [33] But this is the covenant which I will make with the house of Israel after those days, says Yahweh: I have [Heb. var. will] set my law (*tôrāh*) within them, and I will write it upon their hearts [par. 24:7]; and I will be their God, and they shall be my people. [34] And no longer shall each man teach his neighbor and each his brother, saying, 'Know Yahweh,' for they shall

[95]For Gen. 1:16, see II.2; Caquot; S. Aalen, *Die Begriffe 'Licht' und 'Finsternis' im AT, im Spätjudentum und im Rabbinismus. SNVAO* (1951), 29.

[96]See Philo *De spec. leg.* i.177, ii.140 (*Philo,* ed. F. Colson. *Loeb Classical Library,* VII, 201, 391).

[97]F. Blome, *Die Opfermaterie in Babylonien und Israel. SSAOI,* 4 (1934), 74, 105.

[98]P. 40.

[99]See VI.1.

[100]F. F. Bruce, "New," *IDB,* III, 542.

[101]Westermann, 526.

[102]See IV.3.

all know me, from the least of them to the greatest, says Yahweh; for I will forgive their iniquity, and I will remember their sin no more."

The massive "new thing" of this passage is the interiorization of religion. This will dictate the name adopted not only by the Qumran-related "New Covenant in the land of Damascus," but also by the "New Covenant," or "New Testament" founded upon Jesus' teaching—primarily a community, and only secondarily the designation of a book.

2. *Jer. 31:22, Eschatological Reversal and Salvation.* Jer. 31:22 speaks of a "new thing," apparently cognate to the "new thing" in Jer. 31:31, which furnishes our chief clue to the theological value of newness in the Bible. V. 22 stands as the climax to several oracles: "For Yahweh has created *chᵃdhāshāh* ["a new thing" or "a new woman"] on the earth, [namely] the female will go around [as] a male warrior." Unintelligible but suggestively modern sounding as it stands, this passage has no real Hebrew variant, even when retrotranslation attempts to reconstruct a *Vorlage* for the early versions.

Apparent parallels elsewhere in the OT have prompted innumerable attempts at interpretation. (1) "The woman [Israel] will return to [even without emending *tᵉsôbhēbh* to *tāshûbh lᵉ*[103]] her *gebher* [= Yahweh, like *gibbôr* in Isa. 9:5(6)]."[104] (2) "The accursed woman (*nᵉqabbāh*) will change into a lady [*gᵉbhîrāh* with *-h* added conjecturally[105]]." (3) "A path opens out [*niqbāh; tᵉsôbhābh* from **sbb* = *bārā'*[106]]." (4) "A woman 'woos'[107] or 'protects' [cf. Dt. 32:10: *yᵉsôbhēbh*[108]] or 'runs around like' (*tissôbh kᵉ*) or 'turns into' [as in Zec. 14:10[109]] a man."

The four attempts combined in the preceding translation probably hit the real point of *ḥdš*. "Everything will be different, all values will be reversed, even things so profoundly rooted as the psychology of the sexes will be turned upside down." This is like the Gnostic (Gospel of Thomas 22; 101; 114) eschatological *apokatástasis pántōn* (Acts 3:21; Mt. 17:11; Rev. 21:1; anticipated in the exodus: Wis. 19:6,18f.). This is also the drift of Vaccari's rendering: "The woman [Israel] will surround with her care the *gebher* [Yahweh] instead of the usual opposite."[110]

Jerome provides a tendentiously messianic rendition of Jer. 31:22: "The Lord has created a new thing upon the earth. Without the seed of a man, . . . a woman will surround a man in the recess of her womb . . . but a perfect man will be contained

---

[103] A. Condamin, "Le texte de Jérémie XXXI, 22 est-il messianique?" *RB*, 6 (1897), 396.

[104] Thus with reference to Jer. 3:12 A. Gelin, "Jérémie," *La Sainte Bible* (Paris, 1961), 1059; G. P. Couturier, "Jeremiah," *JBC*, 326.

[105] A. Bruno, *Jeremia* (Stockholm, 1954), 266; also W. Rudolph, *HAT*, 12 (^{2}1958), 182, and *idem* in *BHS*.

[106] C. Schedl, " 'Femina circumdabit virum' oder 'via salutis'?" *ZKTh*, 83 (1961), 437.

[107] *NAB*.

[108] E. Nácar, "Sobre la interpretación de 'Femina circumdabit virum' (Jer 31, 22)," *EstBib*, 1 (1942), 405-436, esp. 409; A. Penna, *Geremia* (Turin, 1952), 233.

[109] *NEB*.

[110] *Sacra Bibbia* (Florence, 1961), 1429.

within the woman's belly for the accustomed months. . . ."[111] That at least has the merit of stressing that whatever the female does to the male is presented as something supernaturally remarkable. A totally different interpretation is not without interest; the passage may be taken as a cynically[112] or noncommittally philological footnote: "Feminine here replaces (*t^eshôbhēbh*) the masculine form we would expect for either common or neuter gender."[113]

Also noteworthy, finally, is the LXX rendition of both *ch^adhāshāh* (in part) and *n^eqēbhāh* as "salvation": "The Lord has created *sōtēría* as a new (*kainḗ*) growth; men will roam about in *sōtēría*." Although this LXX rendition seems to be a pure guess or paraphrase without retrievable Hebrew *Vorlage*, we may conclude from it that there was an early conviction that the newness here proclaimed as a theological value is itself already an aspect of salvation.

3. *The Link with Authentic Selfhood in Ezekiel*. Between these two adjacent uses of "new" there comes in Jer. 31:29 the rejection of the "sour grapes" proverb in favor of individual rather than clan responsibility. This directive is not explicitly called "new," but plainly alters the previously prevailing norms and leads directly into the "new covenant" of Jer. 31:31. But the rejection of the "sour grapes" proverb appears also in Ezk. 18:2; the whole chapter then develops this rejection, stressing that a man, by his own free decisions, can unshackle himself from not only the "sins of the fathers" but also those of his own past life. This momentous liberation is summarized in Ezk. 18:31: "Cast away from you all the transgressions which you have committed against me, and get yourselves a new heart and a new spirit!"

This intensely theological "newness," almost synonymous with *metánoia*, was never developed as a value before the exilic situation. Now for the first time the salvation of the individual is plainly divorced from clan solidarity, despite the insistence of Scharbert[114] that no actual texts prior to Jeremiah's speak of condemnation on account of "sins of the fathers." In Ezk. 11:19f., too, we read that it is God himself who "will give them a 'single' [LXX: 'other'; Targ.: 'new'] heart, and put a new spirit within them; [and] take the stony heart out of their flesh and give them a heart of flesh, that they may walk in my statutes and keep my ordinances (*chuqqôthāi, mishpāṭāi*)." Here again we have a clear echo of Jer. 31:34, God's writing his law within the heart, as part of the new covenant.

This identical sentence is repeated in Ezk. 36:26; here the heart is described as "new" without any variant, and the "law" of the subsequent verse is introduced more indirectly, being preceded by an additional emphasis on the "spirit" that gives the whole passage a tone of less legalism and greater inner renewal. The context further specifies that it is God's own holiness (Lev. 17–23, related to Ezekiel!) which he is thus

[111] *CSEL*, 59/2, 1, 397 = *CChr*, LXX/1, 3, 313.

[112] Duhm.

[113] J. Paterson, "Jeremiah," *Peake*, 556, following J. A. Bewer, *The Prophets. Harper's Annotated Bible* (1954).

[114] J. Scharbert, *Solidarität in Segen und Fluch im AT und in seiner Umwelt*. *BBB*, 14 (1958), 248.

vindicating by the "renewal" of a people with whom he has permitted himself to be identified (Ezk. 36:23).

A similar "divine attribute" is echoed in Lam. 3:23, where it is God's mercy, "new every morning," rather than his holiness, that furnishes the hope of those exiles who "wait quietly for salvation" (v. 26) and have fortunately borne the yoke from early youth (v. 27).

V. "New Song."

1. *In the Psalms, Redemption.* Redemption—from exile proximately, but implicitly through a renewal and interiorization of the whole religious attitude—is prominent also in the six "new song" psalms:[115] Ps. 40:4(3), "He put a new song (*shîr*) in my mouth, a song of praise (*t^ehillāh*) to our God." The others mostly add variant motive clauses to a single acclamation, "Sing to Yahweh a new *shîr*": "his *t^ehillāh* in the assembly (*qāhāl*) of the faithful [*ch^asîdhîm,* variant *q^edhôshîm*[116]]" (Ps. 149:1); "for he has done marvelous things, . . . has made known his salvation [or 'victory,' *y^eshuʿāthô*]" (98:1f.); "sing to Yahweh, all the earth, . . . tell of his salvation" (96:1f.); "play (*ngn*) skilfully on the strings, with loud shouts" (33:3). Cf. also Ps. 144:9: "I will sing a new song to thee, O God; upon a ten-stringed harp (*nēbhel*) I will play to thee."

The contexts of these occurrences, though random and kaleidoscopic as is usual in prayer, nevertheless coalesce into a consistent image of eschatological newness: Yahweh comes to do justice upon the earth, "to wreak vengeance" (149:7), to continue and complete his work of creation (33:6,15). "Let the heavens be glad, and let the earth rejoice" (96:11), "All the ends of the earth have seen the victory of our God. . . . Let the floods clap their hands, let the hills sing for joy together" (Ps. 98:3b, 8). "What is man, that thou dost regard him?" (144:3). More pointedly the here-and-now interiorization of the "new song" is developed in 40:7-11(6-10):

> "Sacrifice and offering thou dost not desire, but an open mind [*karîthā ʾoznayim;* cf. Isa. 48:8, unless we have here an echo of the piercing of a slave's ear 'before God,' as in Ex. 21:6[117]]. Burnt offering and sin offering thou hast not required. [8(7)] Then I said, 'Take all of me (*hinnēh-bhāthî*); in the scroll of the book it is written of me: [9(8)] I delight to do thy will; thy law I have devoured (*b^ethôkh mēʿāi*). . . . [11(10)] I have spoken of thy faithfulness and thy salvation."

2. *"New Things" in Deutero-Isaiah.* A bridge from these "psalms of renewal" to other significant uses of *chādhāsh* is found in Isa. 42:10. "Sing to Yahweh a new song (*shîr*), his praise (*t^ehillāh*) from the end of the earth. Let the sea roar [reading *yirʿam* for MT *yôr^edhê;*[118] *BHS yaʾdîrēhû*[119]] and all that fills it, the coastlands and their inhabitants." This verse of the "new song" (42:10-13) was inserted as a spontaneous

---

[115]Cf. J. Gonda, " 'Ein neues Lied,' " *WZKM,* 48 (1941), 275-290.
[116]*BHS.*
[117]Cf. A. Draffkorn (A. Kilmer), "Ilāni/Elohim," *JBL,* 76 (1957), 219.
[118]Following Lowth.
[119]Volz.

echo of the declaration (42:9), "Now past (*hinnēh-bhā'û*) are the former things, and new things I now declare; before they spring forth I tell you of them."

The antithesis *ri'shōnôth/chadhāshôth,* "former things/new things," also is prominent in other passages of Deutero-Isaiah (43:19; 48:6).[120]

It must be recognized how sharply this preference for something new in God's revelation differs from any concept of religion as rigid conservatism or sentimental nostalgia. What God promises his people, and more specifically for their theology, is "renewal," a value handed down from time immemorial only in the sense that God long before warned that change was bound to come—if we can understand the questions in Isa. 44:8; 45:21 as assertions. Deutero-Isaiah does not see this notion merely as renewal or transformation of something already existing. On the contrary, God brings from nowhere a thing that previously had not existed at all (48:7): "They are created now, not long ago; before today you have never heard of them, lest you should say, 'I knew it all along.'" And yet, when new things are brought out of nowhere, we can say that "reality itself" is thus renewed. The whole of existing reality, which was already present, continues to exist but in a revitalized form. Cf. Wisd. 7:27: "Wisdom . . . remaining as before (*en haut*) renews all things (*tá pánta*)." Renewal is thus a synonym of creation (*chiddēsh,* like Arab. *'aḥdaṯa,* par. *bārā'*), but emphasizes the dynamic movement of continuity rather than replacement. Kopf[121] relates Ps. 51:12(10) to Jer. 31:31, stating that *chiddēsh* means "not a renewal of the spirit as before, but a new creation of a different, stable spirit."[122]

This phenomenon of something genuinely new—not there before yet somehow leaping forth from the midst of what was there before—can be described in the terminology of modern physics: "Continuing quantitative input issues in unpredictable qualitative change." Examples like the boiling of water, called "critical thresholds" by Teilhard de Chardin, are claimed to warrant expecting a renewal of humanity on a plane higher than any we have yet experienced. This is a legitimate modern formulation of the "renewal of theology" promised and demanded by Deutero-Isaiah's antithesis "former things/new things." We find an echo of these "innovations" of Yahweh in the metaphor of Isa. 41:15: "I have made you a threshing sledge, new, sharp, and having teeth."

These "new things" in Deutero-Isaiah are not sufficiently clarified by recourse to only those passages in which the word *chādhāsh* occurs. The larger context shows that the "new thing" is to be understood as deliverance from exile through Cyrus, a foreigner, rather than through a Jewish leader.[123] And the contrasted "former things"

---

[120]See A. Bentzen, "On the Ideas of 'The Old' and 'The New' in Deutero-Isaiah," *StTh,* 1 (1948), 183-87; C. R. North, "The 'Former Things' and the 'New Things' in Deutero-Isaiah," *Studies in OT Prophecy. Festschrift T. H. Robinson* (1950), 111-126; A. Schoors, "Les choses antérieures (ראשנות) et les choses nouvelles (חדשות) dans les oracles deutéro-isaïens," *ETL,* 40 (1964), 19-47.

[121]L. Kopf, "Arabische Etymologien und Parallelen," *VT,* 9 (1959), 254f.

[122]See VI.3.

[123]Cf. Westermann, 527.

(*rî'shônôth*) are not only God's saving acts but also his predictions of doom, which now belong to a phase that is past.[124]

VI. Trito-Isaiah.

1. *More Eschatological.* Only in Trito-Isaiah do the "new things" in contrast to the old take on a more strongly eschatological nuance. In Isa. 65:17, we read: " 'For behold, I create new heavens and a new earth; and the former things shall not be remembered or come into mind (*lēbh*).' " The idea is developed further in 66:22f.:[125] "For as the new heavens and the new earth which I will make shall remain before me, says Yahweh; so shall your descendants and your name remain. [23] From new moon to new moon and from sabbath to sabbath, all flesh shall come to worship. . . ." According to Westermann, the idea of the new heaven and the new earth is here expanded in an apocalyptic direction; only after the destruction of heaven and earth are a new heaven and a new earth to be created.[126] The continuous transformation of the world is understood as destruction and new creation (cf. Rev. 21:1). In 66:22-24, however, the new heaven and new earth only serve as an illustration of the continuance of the Jewish cultic community.[127]

2. *"New Name."* The worshipper's "name," meaning in fact his existential reality (→ שֵׁם *shēm*) continued in his descendants, is not explicitly called new or renewed in the above passage. In Isa. 62:2, however, read: "The nations shall see your vindication, and all the kings your glory; and you [Jerusalem] shall be called by a new name which the mouth of Yahweh will give." In 62:4, then, both former and new names appear: "Forsaken," "Desolate," and "My Delight," "Married." All these suggestions of eschatological and spiritual renewal foreshadow but fall far short of the emphasis on *kainós* as a Christian theological value.[128]

3. *Use as a Verb.* The eschatological *chᵃdhāshôth* seem especially cognate to most of the ten verbal occurrences of the root, especially Isa. 61:4: "They shall build up the ancient ruins, they shall raise up the former devastations; they shall repair the ruined cities, the devastations of many generations (*dôr vādhôr*)." God's universal action in past and present dominates Ps. 104:29f.: "When thou hidest thy face, they [all living things] are dismayed; when thou takest away their breath, they die and return to their dust. [30] When thou sendest forth thy Spirit (→ רוח *rûach*), they are created; and thou

---

[124]Cf. also Schoors, "Choses antérieures," and C. R. North, "Former Things," 117. We may also agree with C. Westermann, *The Praise of God in the Psalms* (trans. 1965), 145-151, and H.-J. Kraus, *BK,* XV (^{4}1972), 665, 677, that Pss. 96 and 98 are influenced by Deutero-Isaiah, without thereby extending this influence to the earlier period of Jeremiah and Ezekiel.

[125]See III.5; according to C. Westermann, *Isaiah 40-66. OTL* (trans. 1969), 408, a gloss.

[126]Westermann, *Isaiah,* 408.

[127]Westermann, *Isaiah,* 428.

[128]Behm, "καινός."

renewest (*ûth^e^chaddēsh*) the face of the ground." These words, like the rest of the psalm, echo Akhenaten's hymn to the sun:[129] "When you rise, everything comes alive; when you set, it all dies. . . . You created the whole world according to your plan while you were all alone." In Ps. 103:5, which is textually difficult, renewal means rejuvenation, *n^eʿ^ûrāikhî* (plural with singular verb; the first *yodh* is omitted in the Cairo Geniza, the second in 4QPs^b): "Your youth is renewed (*tithchaddēsh*) like the eagle's" (cf. Isa. 40:31, where *yach^a^lîphû* is a synonym of *chiddēsh*). Ps. 51:12(10) rather echoes Jeremiah and Ezekiel:[130] "Create in me a clean heart, O God, and put a new and right spirit (*rûach nākhôn,* masc.) within me." Cf. also Lam. 5:21: "Restore us to thyself, Yahweh, that we may be restored! Renew our days as of old!" Somewhat akin theologically, although more material, is the king's renewal of the altar (2 Ch. 15:8) or temple (2 Ch. 24:4,12), or the "restoring" of kingship itself (1 S. 11:14, *n^e^chaddēsh;* Kittel's conjectured *n^e^qaddēsh* is more what the situation would have led us to expect). The least religiously charged use of the verb is in Job 10:17, "Thou dost renew thy witnesses against me." In Job 29:20, "my glory ever new with me" is not a real conviction but a frustrated dream.

VII. Preexilic Hostility.

1. *"New Gods."* All the above uses of "newness" as a theological value and a characteristic of God's salvific action are from the century of the exile. Before that time, the two most important relations of "newness" to God are negative values; they illustrate, however, how the concept of divinity itself was evolving. We read in Dt. 32:17: "They sacrificed to *shēdhîm* [possibly mountain or nature forces, or, according to Bailey,[131] a lunar deity; a term for God before the revelation of the name Yahweh, Ex. 6:3 conj.], to un-god [*lô' ^e^lōah;* → **אלהים** *^e^lōhîm*], to gods (*'^e^lōhîm*) they had never known, to new gods that had come in of late, whom your fathers had never dreaded [*ś^eʿ^ārûm;* or, 'did not have as satyrs (*ś^eʿ^îrîm*)']." These "new gods" may be compared, incidentally, to the pejorative "new king who did not know Joseph" (Ex. 1:8). Cf. also Jgs. 5:8a, in the very ancient Song of Deborah: "When new gods were chosen, then there was hell to pay [text uncertain: 'war of gates,' *lāchem sh^eʿ^ārîm;* or perhaps 'satyrs' again, reading *ś^eʿ^îrîm* as in Isa. 13:21]." Here "new" implies not that these gods have just come into being, but that they have just been taken over in a community that formerly had acknowledged other gods. This vigorous and Aeschylean concept of new gods struggling to find a place is what has been agitating this century as the "death of God," our need to find better inner-worldly values in terms of which to express our concept of supreme reality and supreme good. The taunt of Qoheleth (Eccl. 1:9f.), "There is nothing new under the sun. Is there a thing of which it is said, 'See, this is new'?" has become a cynical banality; but it presupposes, according to Westermann,[132] that a higher value is set on "the new" in daily experience than had been customary in the OT.

---

[129] *ANET*^3^, 370.

[130] See IV; V.2; Kopf, "Arabische Etymologien."

[131] L. Bailey, "Israelite *'Ēl Šadday* and Amorite *Bêl Šadê,*" *JBL,* 87 (1968), 434-38.

[132] P. 529.

2. *Early Ritual or Magical Overtones.* The apparently "profane" or empirical uses of *chādhāsh* all turn out to have either ritual or faintly magical overtones. In the context of Lev. 26:10 (H), the statement "You shall clear out the old [grain] to make way for the new" is an expression of confidence and abundance, echoing in altered form the expectations of the jubilee year (Lev. 25:22). In Lev. 23:16 and Nu. 28:26, new grain is a cereal-offering (of firstfruits); perhaps echoing this, the lover in Cant. 7:14(13) boasts of an arbor stocked with "all choice fruits, new as well as old."

The "New Gate" (Jer. 26:10; 36:10; in Neh. 3:6; 12:39, we are dealing with the "renewal" or repair of the "Old Gate") and the "new court" (2 Ch. 20:5) are in the temple area, but have no further religious significance.

If all the uses of "new" with even faint overtones of orthodox religion are of late exilic vintage, conversely all the literal and purely material uses belong to the oldest parts of the Bible. They turn out, however, almost always to have the implication of some divine or supranatural power. "New things have a sacred character: the newborn (Ex. 13:12); sacrificial animals that have never borne the yoke (Nu. 19:2; Dt. 21:3)."[133] Cf. also the "new ropes" in the Samson story (Jgs. 15:13; 16:11f.); the "new cart" for the ark (1 S. 6:7; 2 S. 6:3 = 1 Ch. 13:7); David's adversary girt with a new sword (2 S. 21:16); Ahijah's "new garment" (1 K. 11:29f.);[134] Elisha's "new bowl" for purifying Jericho's water supply (2 K. 2:20). A lesser aura attaches to the Gibeonites' false claim of newness for their wineskins (Josh. 9:13; in contrast to "burst," *bāqa*ᶜ hithpael), perhaps echoed in Job 32:19. On a somewhat higher level are the new wife and new house that justify exemption from military service (Dt. 24:5; 20:5).

The normal LXX rendering of *chādhāsh* is *kainós,* in part because *néos* is usually reserved for *na*ᶜ*ar,* "youth, young man." But the translators were also apparently sensitive to the fact that the element of "noteworthiness" prominent in the classical usage of both terms has a more positive value in *kainós,* as against the pejorative nuances of *néos.*[135] Harrisville takes a different view of classical usage: *kainoí theoí* are strange or undesirable, in contrast to the noncommittal *néoi,* gods of a new generation. He nevertheless considers *kainós* and *néos* fully synonymous in the Bible. With Bruce,[136] we see no point in distinguishing "the new" in the sense of something not previously there (often adjectivally, but as a verb only in Job 10:17) from something that is new and unique in comparison to something already there.[137] Westermann[138] adds lengthy reflections on the rarity of aspects and compounds of "newness" in the OT as contrasted with modern languages. We might point out especially the absence of any concern for "new things" in the sense of information (modern Heb. *ch*ᵃ*dhāshôth* in imitation of Eng. "news"), the updating or *aggiornamento* of one's knowledge about the things that most guide one's daily life. The need

---

[133] La Potterie, 840.

[134] Cf. A. Jirku, "Zur magischen Bedeutung der Kleidung in Israel," *ZAW,* 37 (1917/18), 117; A. Caquot, "Aḥiyya de Silo et Jéroboam Iᵉʳ," *Sem,* 11 (1961), 17-27.

[135] Behm, "καινός," 447; cf. *idem,* "νέος," 897.

[136] F. F. Bruce, "New," *IDB,* III, 542.

[137] Behm, "καινός," 447.

[138] Westermann, *THAT,* I, 526.

for such "late news" is perceived under other terms in passages like Ezk. 33:4, where the sound of the trumpet gives warning of danger.

VIII. Summary. It is surprising how small a role the various kinds of newness play in the OT, especially before the exile, not only as religious values in comparison to the NT, but as an overall cultural experience. By far the commonest OT use of the root *ḥdš* is for the new moon or month (*chōdhesh*), a peripheral sense at best; the notion of newness is totally absent in the frequent cases where *chōdhesh* is applied to times of the month that are not new. The moon itself is never called *chōdesh;* the infrequent synonym *yerach* has a variant *yārēach* that does mean the luminous orb, but only in stereotyped pairing with the sun. In its assertions about the moon (mostly pejorative), the OT transmits older or more justifiable values: spontaneous veneration for the moon can be related to God or to eschatological renewal; there are moral or cultic implications of a "fresh start" in the day of the new moon. In the "new song" of Deutero-Isaiah and the related Psalms, "new" itself becomes a synonym for the recognition of God's redemption within the historical order. This newness becomes more eschatological in Trito-Isaiah, but its roots lie in the "innovation" of individual responsibility as a reappraisal of clan solidarity in Jeremiah and Ezekiel. From this premise, Jer. 31 comes to speak of a "new thing upon the earth," the "new covenant" of interior religiosity. This was plainly recognized to reach a theological level so high that from it "new testament" or "new covenant" became the chosen designation for two of the major offshoots of Judaism: Qumran and Christianity.

North

חוּג *chûgh*

Contents: I. Etymology. II. Meaning: 1. Within its Semantic Field; 2. In Translation. III. Usage: 1. Context; 2. Cosmology; 3. Creation Hymns.

I. Etymology. The root *chûgh* is attested six times in the OT: Isa. 40:22; 44:13; Job 22:14; 26:10; Prov. 8:27; Sir. 43:12 (cf. Sir. 24:5; 1QM 10:13). It appears four times as a nominal infinitive, once as a finite verb (Job 26:10; denominative?), and once (Isa. 44:13) as the derivative *m*ᵉ*chûghāh,* whence it was borrowed by the Aramaic of the Targumim and by Syriac (*hûghthāʾ*, "circle") and Middle Hebrew (*ʿûgh*).[1] Structurally, *chûgh* belongs with the words built on the basic syllable *ḥg,*

[1] E. Y. Kutscher, *Tarbiz,* 23 (1953), 47; *idem,* "Mittelhebräisch und Judisch-Aramäisch im neuen Köhler-Baumgartner," *Hebräische Wortforschung. Festschrift W. Baumgartner. SVT,* 16 (1967), 159.

such as → חָגַר *chāghar,* "bind, gird" (Phoen., OSA "enclosure, wall"); *chāghal,* "hop about"; *choggā',* "confusion" (Isa. 19:17); **ḥgh,* "hide"; Aram. **ḥgw/y,* with the fundamental meaning "describe a curve" (in order to flee or take refuge);[2] Syr. and Nab. *ḥgt'*[3] (cf. Arab. *maḥğa',* "protection, asylum"); *chāghābh,* "locust"; Aram. *mḥgt,* "ring";[4] and above all *chāghagh,* "dance, celebrate," and → חַג *chagh,* "procession, (round) dance, festival."[5] Most of these appear to incorporate the semantic element of circular movement.

The association with *chāghagh/chagh* or the *ḥg* formations in general, the fact that the word appears only in Hebrew and relatively late (exilic period, Deutero-Isaiah), and the highly specialized meaning "circle" or the like in specific contexts[6] all suggest that *chûgh/m^{e}chûghāh* are late secondary developments under the influence of Babylonian technology and cosmology, or are technical terms.

II. Meaning.

1. *Within its Semantic Field.* Within the semantic field of "circles and circular motion," the meaning of *chûgh* exhibits a highly specific profile. In contrast to the usual expressions for "turn, circle, go around, surround," *sbb* qal and niphal, *nqp* II qal and hiphil (sometimes used in technical senses, e.g., Josh. 6:3; Lev. 19:27, "round off hair," or metaphorically, e.g., Isa. 29:1, the "round" of festivals), and *chāghagh,* which designates the festival dance and procession, the verb *chûgh* in combination with *chōq* means "describe a circle," i.e., "incise a circular line."

Similarly, there are several words within the semantic field of the noun *chûgh.* The word → דּוֹר *dôr* has a wide range of meanings: "ball," "cycle, lifetime, generation" (most frequent), and (as the Akkadian loanword *dūru*) "ring, city wall, dwelling," all within the semantic field "turning, enclosure, circumvallation, ball"; *kikkār* (from *krr,* "be round, turn, dance [pilpel], roll," *kārāh, kûr,* "hollow out"), "disk, cover, loaf (of bread), region"; the Akkadian loanword and technical term *pilku/pelekh,* "district, circle"; the abstract plural *s^{e}bhîbhôth,* "circuits" (Eccl. 1:6); and the term *t^{e}qûphāh* for the "turning point" of the year (equinox) and the "circuit" of the sun (Ps. 19:7 [Eng. v. 6]) and moon (Sir. 43:7; cf. v. 12). There are also *sôdh,* "circle of friends," and finally *chagh,* "procession, festival dance."

Within this semantic field, *chûgh* is distinguished by its specifically geometrical meaning, which can be observed on the one hand from its association with spatial referents (earth, heavens, ocean) and its combination with *chōq,* "(incised) line," and on the other from its connection with *m^{e}chûghāh,* "compasses." The word thus means "circle, as drawn with compasses."

---

[2]Cf. *KAI,* 278.5; II, 333.

[3]*DISO,* 82.

[4]*KAI,* 202 B.5.

[5]*KBL*[3]; *KAI,* 278.5; see G. Levi della Vida, "Ancora sull'iscrizione aramaica di Bahadirli," *RSO,* 40 (1965), 203f.; G. Ryckmans, review of A. Dupont-Sommer and L. Robert, *La déesse de Hiérapolis Castabala (Cilicie), Mus,* 78 (1965), 467-69.

[6]See III below.

The often suggested translation "vault (of the heavens)" is therefore probably incorrect, as is the less frequent suggestion "disk (of the earth)." The notion of a "vault" derives from ancient Near Eastern cosmology with its bell-shaped heaven. For *chûgh* this translation cannot really be supported by the parallelism in Job. 22:14 ("thick clouds enwrap him"): clouds can also cover the "horizon of the heavens." Furthermore, where does the "walking" take place if not on the level ground (cf. Sir. 24:5)? Isa. 40:22b makes this meaning unlikely in v. 22a. At most, the idea of horizon circles[7] may be attenuated in Job 26:10. In Sir. 43:12, *chûgh haqqîphāh* means "describe a proper circle" (said of the rainbow); only the LXX with its circumstantial rendering introduces the "heavens."

2. *In Translation.* To render *chûgh,* the LXX strangely uses the rare word *gýros,* "ring, circle," used especially for a circular trench around a tree,[8] *gyróō,* "bend, make round, make a circular trench" (cf. *gýrōsis*). The image conveyed by this word appears to express the classic Babylonian idea of the ring of water surrounding the earth's surface[9] (cf. Sir. 24:5; 43:12 twice, used differently in Prov. 8:27).

III. Usage. The use of *chûgh* is characterized by: (1) a typical fixed context; (2) an association with cosmological ideas; and (3) hymnic style.

1. *Context.* Twice *chûgh* is found together with *chōq* (Job 26:10; Prov. 8:27); the interchangeability of the two terms (*chōq chāgh* and *b*^{e}*chûqô chûgh*) suggests a fixed idiom meaning "incise a circle," with the aid of the instrument used by the Babylonian carpenter in Isa. 44:13, together with line and *śeredh* ("pencil"?), to sketch out his work.[10] In each of its occurrences, *chûgh* is determined by a genitive (*hā'ārets,* Isa. 40:22; *shāmayim,* Job 22:14) or by the expression "upon the face of the waters/deep" (Job 26:10; Prov. 8:27). In other words, its meaning is limited to the circle of the earth or heavens (the rainbow in Sir. 43:12), i.e., the horizon, in the double sense of the coastline on either side of the primeval river that circles the entire earth and separates it from the realm of the heavens (cf. *chûgh yammîm,* 1QM 10:13).

2. *Cosmology.* This notion of two concentric circular coastlines, that of the earth disk and that of the heavenly mountain island, is directly evident in Babylonian cosmology, as reflected, for example, in the Sippar world map (6th/5th century, with earlier prototypes).[11] According to the inscription, the two circles incised about the

---

[7]See III.2 below.

[8]Plutarch.

[9]See III.2 below.

[10]On *ḥqq,* see R. Hentschke, *Satzung und Setzender. BWANT,* 83 (1963), 7ff.; the emendation *chāqaq chûgh* in Job 26:10, based on the Syriac and Targum (cf. G. Hölscher, *HAT,* 17 [^{2}1952], *in loc.*), smoothes the passage following Prov. 8:27.

[11]Reproduced in E. Unger, *Babylon* (1931), 20–24, Plate 3; cf. B. Meissner, *BuA,* II, 107ff., 374ff.; O. Keel, *The Symbolism of the Biblical World* (trans. 1978), No. 8, esp. 21ff.; for a discussion of the influence of this conception on the apocryphal literature, see P. Grelot, "La géographie mythique d'Hénoch et ses sources orientales," *RB,* 65 (1958), 33–69.

earth on the clay tablet designate the "bitter river," the ocean, in which the circular earth lies like an island and beyond which rise the "regions" of the heavenly mountains.[12] In the OT passages, *chûgh* refers to these cosmic circles. This usage presupposes the same cosmological borrowing of a geometrical model as is found in the Babylonian world map. There must be some kind of dependence, since the notion of two horizon circles—especially in mountainous Palestine—presumably does not derive from empirical observation.

3. *Creation Hymns*. In the OT, the ideas associated with the horizon circles are integrated with the belief in creation. At least four of the five occurrences are in creation hymns (Prov. 8:27; Isa. 40:22; Job 26:10; Sir. 43:12; cf. 1QM 10:13; Job 22:14 close to hymnic style). The process of creation is addressed in Job 26:10; Prov. 8:27; Sir. 43:12, the relationship between the Creator and his creation in Isa. 40:22 and Job 22:14 (cf. Sir. 24:5). The vivid technical and cosmological imagery suggested by *chûgh* stands each of the passages in good stead. The hymnic fragment recorded in Isa. 40:22ff. extols him "who sits above the circle of the earth," which he himself laid out (with compasses), over which he stretched the heavens like curtains, like a tent;[13] within this circle he set plants as in a bed (v. 24), i.e., the inhabitants of the earth, who appear to him, the Creator, like "grasshoppers" (*kach^{a}ghābhîm*, v. 22). Job 22:14 criticizes the expression of resignation that God the Creator "walks on the circle of the heavens" (cf. Sir. 24:5), i.e., stays beyond the river, in the heavenly regions, seeing but not judging (vv. 13f.).[14] Job 26:10 and Prov. 8:27 recount the creation of the world. In Prov. 8:27, *chûgh* appears in the context of "establishing the heavens" (vv. 27f.) and refers to the circular foundation of the heavenly horizon in contrast to *tēbhēl 'erets* (vv. 26,31; *chûq* in vv. 27,29). The verb *chûgh* in Job 26:10 (cf. v. 11) probably refers to the same heavenly circle, which, as the boundary of the water, serves also as the boundary between light and darkness. Finally, Sir. 43:12 links *chûgh* with the rainbow, as though drawn with compasses, and thus goes beyond the narrower limits of the other occurrences.

Seybold

---

[12]Keel; another interpretation suggests the most distant regions supposed to have been traversed by Sargon of Akkad; see E. Weidner, *Der Zug Sargons von Akkad nach Kleinasien. Boghazkoï-Studien,* 6 (1922), 85ff.

[13]K. Elliger, *BK,* XI (1970), *in loc.*

[14]Cf. Hölscher, *HAT,* 17, *in loc.*

חוה *ḥwh;* הִשְׁתַּחֲוָה *hishtachᵃvāh*

Contents: I. *ḥwy* I. II. *ḥwy* II: 1. Grammatical Form, Meaning, Semantic Field; 2. The Gesture *hishtachᵃvāh* in the OT and in the Ancient Near East; 3. Secular Greeting or Mark of Respect; 4. Cultic Act and Sign of Religious Homage to Yahweh; 5. "Thou Shalt Not Worship Other Gods."

I. ḥwy I. The root *ḥwy* I,[1] Aramaic in origin, occurs rarely in the OT and only in poetic texts. It appears only in the piel with the meaning "declare" (Ps. 19:3 [Eng. v. 2]) or "teach, instruct" (Job 15:17; 32:6,10,17); it has been conjectured in Job 13:17; Hab. 3:2; and Sir. 16:25. In Ps. 52:11(9), no emendation is necessary.[2] In Hebrew, the similar use of *higgîdh* (→ נגד *ngd*) is more common.

A possible derivative of the Aramaic loanword[3] is *'achᵃvāh* (Job 13:17? [possibly a verb form[4]]; also Dnl. 5:12?), with the meaning "declaration." The root also appears in other languages.[5]

In the early Ps. 19, where the Aramaic verb may support the hypothesis of an early date as well as that of a borrowing from outside Israel, v. 3(2) tells how one night declares knowledge to another, and they thus join in the hymn to the glory of El(!). The human hymn seeks to take part in this act of praise, which is otherwise in a language incomprehensible to man (v. 4[3]).[6] The only other place the verb appears is the second speech of Eliphaz to Job (Job 15:17: "I will instruct you, hear me") and several times with the same meaning in the introduction to the speeches of Elihu (Job 32:6,10,17; cf. also 36:2).

ḥwh. D. R. Ap-Thomas, "Notes on Some Terms Relating to Prayer," *VT,* 6 (1956), 225-241, esp. 229; J. P. Floss, *Jahwe dienen, Göttern dienen. BBB,* 45 (1975); A. Greiff, *Das Gebet im AT. ATA,* 5/3 (1915), 34-36; J. Halbe, *Das Privilegrecht Jahwes. FRLANT,* 114 (1975), 119ff.; F. Heiler, "Die Körperhaltung beim Gebet," *Orientalische Studien. Festschrift Fritz Hommel,* II. *MVÄG,* 22 (1917), 168-177; F. J. Helfmeyer, *Die Nachfolge Gottes im AT. BBB,* 29 (1968); J. Herrmann, "εὔχομαι," *TDNT,* II, 785-800; O. Keel, *The Symbolism of the Biblical World* (trans. 1978); N. Lohfink, *Das Hauptgebot. AnBibl,* 20 (1963); R. P. Merendino, *Das deuteronomische Gesetz. BBB,* 31 (1969); H. D. Preuss, *Verspottung fremder Religionen im AT. BWANT,* 92 (1971); H.-P. Stähli, "חוה," *THAT,* I, 530-33; W. Zimmerli, "Das zweite Gebot," *Festschrift für Alfred Bertholet* (1950), 550-563 = *Gottes Offenbarung: Gesammelte Aufsätze zum AT. ThB,* 19 (²1969), 234-248.

1 *KBL*³, 283b.

2 Contra *KBL*³, 283b.

3 M. Wagner, *Die lexikalischen und grammatikalischen Aramaismen im alttestamentlichen Hebräisch. BZAW,* 96 (1966), 53, Nos. 91f.

4 *KBL*³, 283b.

5 Cf. Wagner, *Aramaismen;* also *DISO,* 84; *KBL*³; *WUS,* No. 912.

6 For a discussion of the religio-historical problems, see H. Donner, "Ugaritismen in der Psalmenforschung," *ZAW,* 79 (1967), 327-331; J. van Dijk, "Sumerische Religion," in J. P. Asmussen, *Handbuch der Religionsgeschichte,* I (1971), 439, citing a Sumerian text that reads: "Heaven and earth call to each other."

II. ḥwy II.

1. *Grammatical Form, Meaning, Semantic Field.* Until quite recently, the form *histach^{a}vāh* was explained as a hithpalel from *shāchāh*[7] and seen in relationship to *šwḥ* and *šḥḥ* (cf. the juxtaposition in Isa. 2:8f.). A hithpalel from *shāchāh,* however, should actually appear as *hishtachāh,* so that there was always the problem of explaining the intrusive *vav.*

With the discovery of the Ugaritic verb *ḥwy,* it became clear that there was once a rare root *ḥwy* in Hebrew, which later vanished, from which *hishtach^{a}vāh* derives as the *t*-reflexive of the ancient causative shaphel (cf. the *št* stem or ishtaphal).[8] The Ugar. *ḥwy* likewise has the form *yštḥwy* with the meaning "he prostrates himself,"[9] "falls at someone's feet as a mark of respect," often in combination with *kbd* or *hbr,* twice with *npl.* Ugaritic does not have a hithpael or hithpolel. Also comparable is Arab. *ḥwy* V, "curl up."[10]

The verb form *hishtach^{a}vāh* appears 170 times in the OT with the following meanings: "bow (politely or respectfully)," "prostrate oneself," "make obeisance" (*proskyneín*), "bend low (in worship or as a mark of respect)." The action may be performed before persons as a greeting or as a token of respect or submission, before Yahweh in the context of prayer or sacrifice, i.e., as a cultic action, or even (usually in the context of accusation, prohibition, or ridicule) before other gods, in which case it simply stands for (cultic) "worship." Strictly speaking, therefore, the verb merely designates a gesture[11] as part of a more inclusive action; but it comes to refer also to the inward attitude thus expressed. Since the action designated by *hishtach^{a}vāh* involved falling to the ground, the verb frequently stands in combination with *'artsāh* (Gen. 18:2; 33:6; 37:10; 43:26; etc.) or with *'appayim* (Gen. 19:1, etc.), since one's "nose" touched the "ground" (both words occur in Gen. 19:1; 42:6; etc.). The range of meanings designated by *hishtach^{a}vāh* is also covered for the most part by the Aramaic loanword *sgd,*[12] which appears not only in Daniel (2:46; 3:5-28: 12 times), but also in Deutero-Isaiah (44:15,17,19; 46:6), where (except in 44:19) it always appears together with *hishtach^{a}vāh,* which in 46:6 probably expresses a stage beyond *sāghadh.*

Frequently *hishtach^{a}vāh*—since taken in isolation it merely refers to a gesture accompanying other actions or words—stands in combination with other verbs (usually in parataxis), which by and large constitute its semantic field: *hālakh 'ach^{a}rê* (→ הלך *hālakh,* → אחרי *'ach^{a}rê*), *kpp, kāra',* *nāphal, nāshaq* (Hos. 13:2; 1 K. 19:18), *'ābhadh* (esp. in Deuteronomic and Deuteronomistic texts), *'āmadh, hithpallel,*

---

7 Cf., e.g., *GK*^{28}, § 75 kk; *BLe,* § 420 k; Herrmann, 788; *KBL*^{3}, 959.

8 *KBL*^{2} *Sup.; KBL*^{3}, 283f.; S. Moscati, ed., *An Introduction to the Comparative Grammar of the Semitic Languages* (^{2}1969), 128; R. Meyer, *Hebräische Grammatik* (^{3}1966-1972), II, 126, 162f.

9 *WUS*^{4}, No. 912; *UT,* § 9.39, No. 847; citations in Whitaker, 257 (12 occurrences, always with gods).

10 Meyer, *Grammatik,* 163; Wehr, 219.

11 See II.2 below.

12 Wagner, *Aramaismen,* No. 195.

qdd (always with *histachᵃvāh*), *shāchāh, šḥḥ.*[13] The particular combinations of verbs are often mutually interpretative.

The LXX almost always uses *proskyneín* to translate the verb[14]—only in 1 K. 2:19 do we find *kataphileín* and in 1 K. 11:33 *poieín,* which significantly is also used for *ʿābhadh, kāraʿ,* and *nāshaq*.

In the Dead Sea Scrolls, 1QpHab 12:13, interpreting Hab. 2:18 (→ אליל *ʾelîl*), cites the text itself and then states that the idols (→ פסל *psl*) of the nations, which they have made to worship (→ עבד *ʿābhadh*) and "fall down before," will not save them on the day of judgment. In 1QM 12:14 (cf. the repetition in 19:6), Zion is promised that all her oppressors will pay homage to her (with a quotation from Isa. 60:14). CD 11:24 speaks of a *bêth hishtachᵃvôth;* it is not clear whether this "house of prayer" refers to the temple, a place of assembly, or a synagogue.

2. *The Gesture hishtachᵃvāh in the OT and in the Ancient Near East.* The gesture designated by *hishtachᵃvāh,* which also expresses an inward attitude, is also familiar among Israel's neighbors. It is attested both pictorially and in texts,[15] since "prostration" formed part of the cult of all deities (2 K. 5:18!).[16] Egyptian speaks of "kissing the ground" (*śn-t3*, e.g., in the Hymn to Amon),[17] and obeisance was a common part of the daily ritual before the statues of the gods.[18]

In Mesopotamia,[19] the term is *šukênu(m)* (Babylonian;[20] earlier *śuka''unum,* Assyr. *šuka''unu(m)*), which is used in the sense of "pay homage, worship."[21] Obeisance, however, was less common in Mesopotamia than in Egypt.

To describe the gesture of obeisance or prostration (cf. also Job 1:20), reference is frequently made to Islamic *suğūd,*[22] which Lane describes as follows:[23] He (i.e., the Muslim) "first goes down gently on his knees, . . . places his hands on the ground a little in front of his knees, and touches his nose and forehead likewise to the ground (the former first) between his two hands." But now one should also compare in Keel[24] the clearly distinguished stages of obeisance according to an Egyptian presentation, then the other illustrations there.[25]

---

[13]Cf. also Helfmeyer, 93ff., 152ff.; Halbe; and esp. Floss, 115, 131, 165ff.

[14]See H. Greeven, "προσκυνέω," *TDNT,* VI, 760-62.

[15]For their distribution, see Heiler, 171-73.

[16]Cf. M. Noth, *Exodus. OTL* (trans. 1962), 263.

[17]A. Erman, *The Ancient Egyptians: A Sourcebook of Their Writings* (1966), 288; for discussion, see *RÄR,* 206-208; cf. also Sinuhe, *TGI*², 10.

[18]Keel, 310f.

[19]Cf. also Heiler, 171f.; Keel, 311f.

[20]Cf. *GaG,* §109 j and m.

[21]For a discussion of the gestures, see also M. Falkner in *RLA,* III, 175-77, *s.v.* "Gebetsgebärden, Gebetsgesten," and the *labānu appa* as "make the nose flat" (*AHw,* I, 522; or "rub the nose"?).

[22]Cf. H. Wildberger, *BK,* X (1965), 103; Stähli, 531; Ap-Thomas, 229.

[23]E. W. Lane, *An Account of the Manners and Customs of the Modern Egyptians* (London, 1890); see Ap-Thomas, 229; but cf. Heiler, 172.

[24]No. 412.

[25]Pp. 287-290; see also H. J. Boecker in *BHHW,* I, 521f.; Jehu(?) before Shalmaneser III, *ANEP,* No. 355 (cf. also Nos. 45f.), and Keel, 311, Plate XXIII.

The secular gesture of greeting and respect is not primary with respect to the posture of prayer;[26] the reverse is in fact more likely (first the deity, then the king, finally a general form of greeting), since originally a line can hardly have been drawn between the sacred and the secular. What is presupposed is the sense of disparity (cf. Ps. 95:6), the overwhelming experience of the sacred;[27] the gesture is well described as an expression of panic fear, a kind of refuge in death: falling to the ground is equivalent to "the feigned death reflex familiar to behavioral psychology,"[28] a gesture of absolute submission.[29] Since the permission to rise that is hoped to follow is a part of the whole process, the dropping to the ground and touching it during prayer or sacrifice is only temporary; the actual posture of prayer is frequently kneeling or standing. Actual prostration as a posture of prayer is rare (Josh 7:6, but without *histach^{a}vāh*).[30]

3. *Secular Greeting or Mark of Respect*. If we begin by collecting the passages that exhibit *hishtach^{a}vāh* in the realm of secular greeting, respect, honor, etc., we do not mean to imply that religious usage derived from the secular. Our only purpose is thus to deal first with secular usage as the less frequent and less important. It will become clear, however, that both realms of usage (secular and religious) can merge.

One person would bow before another to greet him respectfully or to acknowledge his higher rank (Gen. 18:2; 19:1 [in both passages, however, it is ultimately Yahweh with whom Abram is dealing; cf. Nu. 22:31; Josh. 5:14, the angel of Yahweh and the commander of the army of Yahweh]; but cf. also Gen. 23:7; 24:26; 33:3,6f.; Ex. 4:31; 11:8; 18:7—common in all the pentateuchal sources). Ruth bows to Boaz (Ruth 2:10), David—out of joy!—to Jonathan (1 S. 20:41), David to Saul (24:9[8]), Abigail to David (25:23,41, a gesture of submission), Saul to "Samuel" (28:14), the Cushite to Joab (2 S. 18:21), the sons of the prophets and the Shunammite woman to Elisha (2 K. 2:15; 4:37). In blessings it may be promised or wished that others will bow to the recipient of the blessing (Gen. 27:29; 49:8[31]). One also bows when begging (1 S. 2:36). In the story of Joseph, the question of who bows or should bow to whom is a kind of leitmotif. What is dreamed in Gen. 37:7,9f. (E) later becomes reality (42:6 [E]; cf. J with the vizier: 43:26,28). Schmitt finds here what he calls a formula of acknowledgment or homage.[32] Even "Israel" bows to Joseph (47:31 [J]), but Joseph also bows to Israel (Gen. 48:12 [E]), so that according to E Joseph does not remain arrogant. It is not by accident that the tension built by E from Gen. 37:7ff. to 48:12 is brought to a climax by final statement of this sort using *hishtach^{a}vāh*.

Very often we find *hishtach^{a}vāh* in the sense of "homage to the king." Many of the occurrences belonging here make it clear that we are dealing with a gesture of submis-

[26] As argued by Heiler, 177.

[27] Keel, 308.

[28] Keel, 310, with reference to Ex. 24:11; 33:22.

[29] Boecker, *BHHW*, I, 521.

[30] Heiler, 173.

[31] On the form of the verb used here to express a future wish, see H.-J. Zobel, *Stammesspruch und Geschichte*. *BZAW*, 95 (1965), 10; the subject is discussed *ibid.*, 79f.

[32] A. Schmitt, "Die Totenerweckung in 2 Kön 4, 8-37," *BZ*, N.S. 19 (1975), 20, with citations and semantic field.

sion or surrender[33] (1 S. 24:9[8]; 2 S. 1:2; 9:6; 14:4,22; 15:5; 16:4; 18:28; 24:20 [cf. 1 Ch. 21:21]; 1 K. 1:23,53; 2 Ch. 24:17). Even Bathsheba bows to David (1 K. 1:16, 31; cf. Ps. 45:12[11], the royal bride to the king[34]). Solomon, on the other hand, bows to Bathsheba, since she is the mother of the king (1 K. 2:19). Court style requires that a new king be promised that all kings will (or should; Ps. 72:11) pay him homage. Everyone does obeisance to Haman at and in recognition of his promotion (Est. 3:2); only Mordecai refuses (v. 2), for he is a Jew (v. 4), which brings the wrath of Haman down upon him (v. 5).

4. *Cultic Act and Sign of Religious Homage to Yahweh.* There are many instances of *hishtach^{a}vāh* as a term for cultic action in general, even when it is actually only part of a larger complex (e.g., in the case of sacrifice). Not rarely, together with → בוא *bô'*, → עבד *'ābhadh,* or → זבח *zābhach,* especially in the Psalms or other texts related to the cult, the verb can not only stand for "pray," but can almost be rendered "carry out a cultic action (before Yahweh)." Such passages include Ps. 5:8(7); 95:6; 99:5,9; 132:7; 138:2; Neh. 8:6; 9:3; 1 Ch. 29:20; 2 Ch. 7:3; 20:18; 29:28-30; also Gen. 22:5; Dt. 26:10; 1 S. 1:3,19,28; 2 S. 12:20 (David before Yahweh following the death of his child); 2 S. 15:32 (David coming [→ בוא *bô'* II.1] to the high place where "God" was worshipped); finally Jer. 7:2 (cf. 26:2, with → בית *bayith*); Jgs. 7:15, with a prayer of thanksgiving.

In its regulations governing the times when the east gate of the inner court shall be open for the → נשיא *nāśî'* and the people, Ezk. 46 stipulates that during the offering of sacrifice on the Sabbath the prince shall stand by the gate and bow in worship at its threshold (v. 2), while the people (v. 3) merely assist in this act of obeisance (cf. also v. 9, with regulations governing → בוא *bô'* II.1 and → יצא *yātsā'* in the cult).

The servant of Abraham bows and worships Yahweh (Gen. 24:26; cf. vv. 48 and 52; also Gen. 18:2; 19:1; and Nu. 22:31; Josh. 5:14) out of gratitude for the choice of a bride. In Ex. 12:27, the people bow and worship after Moses tells the elders that Israel will be spared (by Yahweh, of course, although he is not mentioned explicitly). According to Ex. 24:1 (the secondary introduction to vv. 3-8,9-11; cf. also 34:8), Moses, together with Aaron, Nadab, Abihu, and the elders, is to worship Yahweh "from afar."[35] When the pillar of cloud comes down to the tent of meeting (→ אהל *'ōhel* IV.3) and stands there, the people rise up and bow in worship, each at the entrance to his tent (Ex. 33:10 [J?]). In the context of ritual legislation, Dt. 26:10 (cf. 1 S. 1:3,19,28) requires that the Israelite who offers firstfruits shall bow in worship "before Yahweh your God." Despite his sin, Saul insists on worshipping before Yahweh (1 S. 15:25,30f.). When someone is lying sick in bed, he bows likewise; the same verb *histach^{a}vāh* is used, although he obviously cannot drop to the ground (Gen. 47:31; cf. 1 K. 1:47).

That foreign nations will pay homage to Yahweh is promised by the prophets,

[33]See II above.

[34]For a discussion of the text, see H.-J. Kraus, *BK,* XV/1 (^{4}1972), 331f.

[35]See S. E. Loewenstamm, "Prostration from Afar in Ugaritic, Accadian and Hebrew," *BASOR,* 188 (1967), 41-43.

beginning with Deutero-Isaiah. According to the description of salvation in Isa. 45:14, foreign nations with their treasures will bow down in worship before Yahweh and acknowledge him the only God (cf. 60:14, where the expression is not found in the LXX; is 45:14 a displaced fragment from Isa. 60?). According to Isa. 49:7 (to follow v. 12?), kings and princes shall rise up before Israel, the servant of rulers, and prostrate themselves because of Yahweh, who is faithful and has chosen Israel. And on every Sabbath and new moon all flesh shall come "to worship before me, says Yahweh" (Isa. 66:23). The secondary addition Zeph. 2:11 promises that all the isles of the nations shall bow down to worship Yahweh, "each in its place" (cf. Zec. 14:16f., which states that they will have to make a pilgrimage to Jerusalem to do so), as a result of the great judgment that will also reveal the impotence of the gods. According to the final words of the Isaiah Apocalypse (Isa. 27:13f.; v. 13 a secondary addition to v. 12?), an eschatological promise, "on that day" the Diaspora will worship Yahweh on the holy mountain at Jerusalem.

Ps. 96:9 summons the nations (cf. 66:4, with → שׁם *shēm;* cf. 29:2) to bow before Yahweh in worship "at his holy appearing."[36] In the context of a lament, Ps. 86:9 says that all nations shall come and bow down before Yahweh, a statement that functions here as a motif suggesting that prayer has been heard or is sure to be heard. According to Ps. 22:28, 30(27, 29), all the nations and "those that are fat," the proud and the mighty, shall bow down to Yahweh[37]—in other words, we are not dealing here with praise on the part of the dead or their resurrection, although vv. 28-32(27-31) constitute an eschatological expansion of Ps. 22 (→ זרע *zāraʿ* V.8).

Even all the gods bow down before Yahweh (Ps. 97:7), although they are first disqualified in v. 7b as *ʾelîlîm* (→ אליל *ʾelîl* II)! The host of heaven worships Yahweh (Neh. 9:6), and the *benê ʾēlîm* (→ בן *bēn* IV.2.c) are to ascribe to Yahweh the glory of his name (→ שׁם *shēm;* cf. Ps. 66:4) and worship him at his appearance (Ps. 29:2).[38]

In 2 K. 18:22 (cf. Isa. 36:7; 2 Ch. 32:12), the "Assyrian" argues in typically pagan fashion, leveling the criticism that a god who has just seen most of his cultic sites removed (his interpretation of Hezekiah's cultic reform as described in 2 K. 18:4) will hardly be inclined to lend his aid.

5. *"Thou Shalt Not Worship Other Gods."* It can be reported without polemic and with remarkable toleration that Naaman was allowed to continue to worship his gods when in the company of his king, even though Yahweh had helped him through Elisha (2 K. 5:18, where *histachavāh* appears three times). Sennacherib, too, worships in the temple of his god Nisroch[39] (2 K. 19:37; Isa. 37:38), and the report of his death there does not depict it as punishment for this cultic act.

For Israel, however, the cultic worship of other gods and their images[40] is strictly

---

36. For a discussion of the text, see Kraus, XV/2, 664; also Ps. 29:2.

37. Following O. Keel-Leu, "Nochmals Psalm 22, 28-32," *Bibl*, 51 (1970), 405-413.

38. Following Kraus, *BK*, XV/1, 233; cf. the discussion of Ps. 96:6 above; on the background of this psalm in Canaanite mythology, cf. Kraus and Preuss, 107f., with bibliography.

39. For a discussion of the name "Nisroch," see Preuss, 104f.

40. See Zimmerli.

forbidden (Ex. 20:5; Dt. 5:9; cf. also Ex. 23:24; Ps. 81:10[9]; Dt. 30:17). Israel must not bow in worship before "other gods"[41] (→ אחר *'achēr* II; → אלהים *'elōhîm* IV.1) and their images, and must not serve them. Ex. 20:5(f.) is the practical expansion of v. 3; with its Deuteronomic and Deuteronomistic formulation, it probably derives from the period after Hosea.[42] The prohibition of images is thus—now!—an extended development of the first commandment and is to be so understood.[43] Ex. 34:14a formulates the prohibition in the singular ("you shall worship no other god"), which is probably closer to the original than the later Deuteronomistic plural.[44] Ex. 23:24 refers to the gods of the Canaanites, expanding on the prohibition (possibly leading up to Deuteronomy?), and Lev. 26:1 furnishes an even more extensive theological basis. The prohibition against bowing in worship before any god other than Yahweh "does not preclude certain civilities, but it does prohibit Israel from seeking the ultimate ground of its being anywhere but in Yahweh."[45]

In this context the verbs *ḥwh* and → עבד *'ābhadh* often occur together.[46] The occurrences indicate clearly that we are dealing here with a Deuteronomic/Deuteronomistic catchword; the same is true in large measure of the phrase *'elōhîm 'achērîm*. We find *'bd* before *ḥwh*[47] in Dt. 8:19; 11:16; 17:3; 29:25(26); Josh. 23:7, 16; Jgs. 2:19; 1 K. 9:6,9; 2 K. 21:21; Jer. 8:2; 13:10; 16:11; 25:6; 2 Ch. 7:19, 22. Contrariwise, *ḥwh* stands before *'bd* in Dt. 4:19; 5:9; 30:17; Ex. 20:5; 23:24; 2 K. 17:35; 21:3; 2 Ch. 7:22; 33:3; Jer. 22:9. What is forbidden is not only the cultic worship of other gods, but a way of life that departs in general from that of the people of Yahweh.

In Ex. 32:8, Yahweh says accusingly to Moses that "your people" have turned aside quickly from the commanded way, having bowed in worship before the molten calf and sacrificed to it. V. 6, however, speaks only of sacrifice, so that the *hishtachavāh* must have been a regular part of the sacrificial ritual (cf. also the interpretation of the scene in Ps. 106:19!). In Nu. 25:2, when Israel is at Shittim, the people and the Moabite women bow in worship before the god Baal-peor (v. 3; → בעל *ba'al* III.1). Because Israel worshipped other gods, gods whom they had not even known (Dt. 29:25[26]; cf. 11:28; 13:3,7,14[2,6,13]; 28:64; 32:17) and whom Yahweh had not allotted (→ חלק *chālaq;* used elsewhere in this sense only in Dt. 4:19[48]) to them, Yahweh's anger is kindled against them and the curse will take effect. This last text brings us once more into the realm of Deuteronomistic phraseology and theology, which we shall now pursue.

The prohibition against worshipping other gods and paying them homage appears with particular frequency in the OT within Deuteronomic and Deuteronomistic litera-

---

41 See Preuss, 18, with bibliography; Zimmerli, 237ff.; Floss, 169ff., 236ff.

42 Zimmerli, 237ff.; Preuss, 18, 22.

43 Zimmerli, 241; more recently Halbe, with a more nuanced analysis.

44 Halbe, 122: protodeuteronomic tradition.

45 Keel, 310.

46 According to Lohfink, 98f., the sequence *ḥwh-'bd* occurs only in the Decalog, but this is not correct.

47 See Merendino, 173, n. 16f.; Zimmerli, 237; but both lists need expansion or corrections; cf. Floss.

48 For a discussion of the problem, see Preuss, 242.

ture. Within Deuteronomy itself (where it always appears along with → עבד *ʿābhadh* except in 4:19 and 26:10, the former Deuteronomistic and the latter a fixed liturgical text), we may single out 17:3 (Deuteronomistic recension of Deuteronomy), where the worship of the heavenly bodies is forbidden, probably with reference to the Assyrian cult of the heavens[49] (cf. also Dt. 4:19 [Deuteronomistic]; also 2 K. 17:16; 21:3; Zeph. 1:5; Jer. 8:2; Ezk. 8:16). This worship of idols will destroy Israel (Dt. 8:19; 11:16f.), because no rain will come and the land will be lost (29:25[26]; 30:17).[50] In this group of texts, then, *hishtach^a vāh* is among the verbs that have their primary place in statements concerning the relationship of Israel to other gods (forbidden and provoking the judgment and anger of Yahweh), derive from the law of Yahweh (Ex. 34:14a), and undergo further theological development in the Decalog and above all in the Deuteronomistic corpus.[51]

In texts belonging to the Deuteronomistic history, this theme is once more expanded, with transparent reference both to the past in retrospect and to the present in exhortation (often in combination with → קטר *qṭr* and *hālakh ʾach^a rê*). The people turned aside to other gods and thus aroused the anger of Yahweh (Jgs. 2:12, 17), even after his saving intervention (v. 19). But worship of other gods provokes Yahweh's anger and leads to loss of the land (Josh. 23:16, which accounts for the exhortation in v. 7); it brings disaster as punishment (1 K. 9:9; 2 Ch. 7:22), because it means disregard for Yahweh's commandments and ordinances (1 K. 9:6; 2 Ch. 7:19). Solomon was guilty of such a sin (1 K. 11:33), whereupon he lost his sovereignty over the ten tribes (the passage sees Solomon against the background of an Israel belonging to a later age[52]). Ahab worshipped Baal (1 K. 16:31), as did his son Ahaziah (1 K. 22:54[53]; cf. also 2 Ch. 25:14f. with respect to Amaziah). Manasseh in particular committed this sin and worshipped the "host of heaven" (2 K. 21:3; cf. 6; v. 21 says the same of his son Amon [→ גלולים *gillûlîm*]; see also 2 Ch. 33:3; cf. also Neh. 9:6, where the host of heaven contrariwise worship Yahweh!). In the opinion of the Deuteronomistic history, this is the major reason for the coming judgment, as a review of the fate of the northern kingdom shows (2 K. 17:16b f.), where Judah's worship of the host of heaven—a typically Judahite sin?[53]—already has involved it in the destiny of the northern kingdom (according to Dietrich,[54] these texts in 2 K. 17:12-19 derive from the stratum DtrN, vv. 7-11, 20 from the Deuteronomic historian). The mixed population of the northern kingdom after 722 even worships these idols "to this day" (2 K. 17:34), although Yahweh had expressly prohibited this worship (vv. 35f., with echoes of the Decalog and expansive Deuteronomistic language that elaborates on Deuteronomy).

In the Deuteronomistic sections of the book of Jeremiah, these judgments, accusa-

---

49On the prohibition of astral worship, see Preuss, 187ff.

50See H. Breit, *Die Predigt des Deuteronomisten* (1933), 49ff.; M. Weinfeld, *Deuteronomy and the Deuteronomic School* (Oxford, 1972), 6, 321, including a treatment of Deuteronomistic terminology.

51Cf. Lohfink, 73, 75, 303f.; Halbe.

52M. Noth, *BK*, IX/1 (1968), 260.

53W. Dietrich, *Prophetie und Geschichte. FRLANT*, 108 (1972), 45.

54Dietrich, *Prophetie*, 45.

tions, and argumentations are continued; here, too, they constitute the grounds for the announced punishment (Jer. 16:11; cf. 22:9; 25:6; 44:3, with *qṭr*).[55] The Israelites have worshipped the sun, the moon, the the host of heaven (cf. Jer. 7:16–20); therefore their corpses shall litter the ground like dung (8:2; cf. 16:4; 25:33 [Deuteronomistic]). The idolatrous people will suffer the same fate as Jeremiah's waistcloth (13:10, in the interpretation of vv. 1–7; vv. 10a and 11 are clearly Deuteronomistic).

Zephaniah, too, had already spoken of the judgment that would overtake those who bow down on the roofs in worship of the host of heaven and the moon (?; Zeph. 1:5). In Ezk. 8:16, Ezekiel sees as one of the four abominations in Jerusalem how 20(?) men between the porch and the altar in the temple bow in worship toward the sun,[56] while turning their backs to Yahweh.

Finally, *hishtachᵃvāh* is properly used as a motif in ridicule of idols and their worship.[57] Here the point is to show, by way of indictment or mockery, how men can bow in worship and the like before such idols, which have been made by men, often by the very men who worship them. Isa. 2:8 initially makes this statement as an indictment; cf. the secondary addition in v. 20, which places the theme even more clearly in the context of the day of Yahweh (→ יום *yôm*), since this day will mean the end of idols. In Jer. 1:16, too, this motif appears as the grounds for judgment (nothing here suggests a Deuteronomistic interpolation, especially since the verb *hikhʿîs* [→ כעס *kāʿas*] does not appear in 25:6; 32:30; 44:8, which have undergone Deuteronomistic revision). A similar argument appears in Mic. 5:12,[58] and, following Deutero-Isaiah (Isa. 44:15,17; 46:6), Ps. 97:7 and 106:19 (v. 20!; cf. 1 Ch. 16:29). Turning away to idols is unworthy of those who worship Yahweh; it is incomprehensible, when one looks upon Yahweh, who, being incomparable (→ דמה *dāmāh;* see also → בדד *bādhādh* II.3), can only respond with anger and judgment, which the first and second commandments (Ex. 20:3ff. par.) indicate will and must be the necessary consequence for those who transgress them.

Preuss

---

[55]On the texts, cf. W. Thiel, *Die deuteronomistische Redaktion von Jeremia 1–25. WMANT,* 41 (1973).

[56]On the text, see W. Zimmerli, *BK,* XIII (1969), 195.

[57]On these passages and their function, see Preuss, 18, 108, 132f., 158, 211, 250, 281.

[58]On this passage, see Preuss, 132f., and J. Jeremias, "Die Deutung der Gerichtsworte Michas in der Exilszeit," *ZAW,* 83 (1971), 343–46.

חַוָּה chavvāh

Contents: I. Etymology; Ancient Near East. II. Occurrences. III. Religious Significance.

I. Etymology; Ancient Near East. The origin and etymology of the name *chavvāh* have been the subject of much discussion. Many attempts have been made to solve the problem. The narrative in Gen. 3 offers its own explanation: "The man called his wife's name *chavvāh,* because she was the mother of all living (*chai*)" (v. 20). Here the name is obviously associated with *chāyāh,* "live," an association many scholars consider a popular etymology and therefore reject. There are two reasons for this quick rejection of the Yahwist's theory: first, the different forms of the two words appear unnecessary and inexplicable; second, there was early acceptance of a theory proposed by the medieval rabbis, who saw in the name *chavvāh* the term *chēvyā',* "serpent." This theory was taken up once more by Nöldeke[1] and Gressmann, who developed it in a new direction. Behind the present narrative an earlier narrative was conjectured, in which only God, man, and a serpent deity played a role. There is no known trace of such a narrative; it is merely inferred on the basis of the Aramaic word *chēvyā'*. Even Gressmann sensed the weakness of his position. Following some leads

---

chavvāh. W. F. Albright, "The Goddess of Life and Wisdom," *AJSL,* 36 (1919/20), 258-294, esp. 284; *idem,* "The Location of the Garden of Eden," *AJSL,* 39 (1922/23), 15-31, esp. 27; L. Arnaldich, "La création de Eva; Gen., I, 26-27; II, 18-25," *Sacra Pagina I. BETL,* 12 (1959), 346-357; H. Bauer, "Kanaanäische Miszellen. 10. Eva," *ZDMG,* 71 (1917), 413; J. Boehmer, "Die geschlechtliche Stellung des Weibes in Genesis 2 und 3," *MGWJ,* 79 (1935), 281-302; W. Eichrodt, *Man in the OT. SBT,* 4 (trans. 1951); K. Galling, *Das Bild vom Menschen in biblischer Sicht. Mainzer Universitätsreden,* 3 (1947); A. Gelin, *The Concept of Man in the Bible* (trans. 1968); H. Gressmann, "Mythische Reste in der Paradieserzählung," *ARW,* 10 (1907), 345-367; J. Heller, "Der Name Eva," *ArOr,* 26 (1958), 636-656; J. Hempel, *Gott und Mensch im AT. BWANT,* 3/2 (²1936); I. M. Kikawada, "Two Notes on Eve," *JBL,* 91 (1972), 33-37; L. Köhler, *Hebrew Man* (trans. 1956); S. N. Kramer, *The Sumerians* (1963); H. Lamparter, *Das biblische Menschenbild* (1956); M. Löhr, *Die Stellung des Weibes zu Jahwe-Religion und Jahwe-Kult. BWANT,* 1/4 (1908); J. Meinhold, "Die Erzählungen vom Paradies und Sündenfall," *Festschrift K. Budde. BZAW,* 34 (1920), 122-131; J. Morgenstern, "Beena Marriage (Matriarchat) in Ancient Israel and its Historical Implications," *ZAW,* 47 (1929), 91-110, esp. 95; J. Pedersen, *ILC,* I-II (1926, ³1954); G. Pidoux, *L'homme dans l'AT* (Neuchâtel, Paris, 1953); W. Plautz, "Zur Frage des Mutterrechts im AT," *ZAW,* 74 (1962), 9-30; *idem,* "Monogamie und Polygynie im AT," *ZAW,* 75 (1963), 3-27; S. Reinach, "La naissance d'Ève," *RHR,* 78 (1918), 185-206; O. Schilling, *Das Mysterium Lunae und die Erschaffung der Frau* (1963); W. R. Smith, *Kinship and Marriage in Early Arabia* (Cambridge, ²1903); F. J. Stendebach, *Theologische Anthropologie des Jahwisten* (diss., Bonn, 1970); St.-B., IV, 1125; H. Tuerck, *Pandora und Eva* (1931); T. C. Vriezen, *Onderzoek naar de paradijsvoorstelling bij de oude semietische Volken* (Wageningen, 1937), 192f.; C. Westermann, *BK,* I/1 (1974), 312-321; G. Whitfield, *God and Man in the OT* (London, 1949); W. Zimmerli, *Man and His Hope in the OT. SBT,* 20 (trans. 1971); *idem, Das Menschenbild des ATs. ThEH,* N.S. 14 (1949).

[1] T. Nöldeke, *ZDMG,* 42 (1888), 487.

suggested by Lidzbarski,[2] he suggested that there may have been a connection with the Phoenician goddess Ḥavat, whom Lidzbarski considered a serpent-goddess and a goddess of the Underworld. The form of the name *ḥwt* explains the Hebrew form *chavvāh* more easily than does *chēvyāʾ*, although it followed the old suggestion of the rabbis.

But this was not the end of the matter; there were other possibilities. H. Bauer contended that there was also another word *ḥwh* in Hebrew, which appeared only in the plural: *chavvôth*, "encampment, tent village" (Nu. 32:41; Dt. 3:14; Josh. 13:30; etc.). Following analogies in Arabic (*ʾahl*, "family," "wife"),[3] Bauer saw here a possibility that "tent" could also mean, "mother, motherly origin." Bauer himself, however, felt it necessary to concede that this meaning is not (or no longer) attested in the known vocabulary of Hebrew.[4]

Even before Bauer, scholars claimed to find in the name *chavvāh* remnants of a matriarchal tribal organization. Smith[5] suggested that the Hebrew counterpart to Arab. *ḥawwat* was *chaiyath*, the mother of the matriarchal group. Another attempt to connect the word and its referent with tribal life was made by Meinhold.[6] He proposed *chivvāh* as the original vocalization of *ḥwh*, and identified this *chivvāh* with the tribal mother of the Hivites (Gen. 10:17; Ex. 3:17; Dt. 7:1).

The word nevertheless gives the impression of being so closely related to *chāyāh* that many attempts have been made to interpret it as "bearer, lifegiver," etc. The form *chavvāh* has been understood as an evasive alternate for *chaiyāh*, used to avoid a form that can also mean "animal." The meaning of the word, which in this case would have to be purely Hebrew, would be something like "the living woman." This solution would then be in good agreement with that of the ancient narrator.

But the question remains whether the word is really an evasive form selected deliberately, or whether it is a form that was in actual usage, at least during the period of oral transmission. Ugaritic can probably furnish the answer to this question. The word *ḥyt* for "life" is used only rarely; more often we find *ḥwt*. The latter, which sometimes is also used for "animal" (i.e., something "living"), is not only a parallel to Heb. *chavvāh* but is absolutely identical with it, and thus supports the ancient narrator in his interpretation. The word is thus of Canaanite/Phoenician origin, and was borrowed into Hebrew as it was spoken in the ancient language of the indigenous population.

This theory, which arises quite naturally, is also supported by another argument. Much has been written about the man's rib. Kramer has sought to find the background for this narrative in Sumerian ideas. When the god Enki was sick, several goddesses were created to heal his various ills. The goddess Nin-ti was called to life to heal his rib (Sum. *ti*). Her name thus means "lady of the rib." In Sumerian, however, a syllable could have several meanings. This is true of *ti*, which meant not only "rib" but also "make alive." Nin-ti was accordingly not only the "lady of the rib," but also the "lady who makes alive." According to Kramer, this is "the oldest pun in world literature."

---

[2] *LidzEph*.
[3] Wehr, 33.
[4] P. 413.
[5] P. 208.
[6] P. 128.

Of course it could not be reproduced in Canaanite or Hebrew, where the words for "rib" and "live" (or "make alive") were not homophones.[7] Nevertheless, the first woman in the ancient narratives was associated with both the rib and with making alive, and her name, *chavvāh,* actually meant "alive" in the ancient Canaanite dialect.

II. Occurrences. The name *chavvāh,* "Eve," is attested only twice in the OT, in both cases under questionable circumstances. In the first passage, Gen. 3:20, the statement: "The man called his wife's name *chavvāh,* because she was the mother of all living," comes between the expulsion of the man and the woman from the garden of God and the statement that Yahweh made garments of skin for them. The information about the naming of the woman and the interpretation of her name appear quite unexpectedly and inappropriately here, as Gunkel already noted.[8] Von Rad[9] finds a "fracture" here, and thinks that the verse probably derived originally from another context.

In the second passage, Gen. 4:1, we read, "The man knew his wife *chavvāh,* and she conceived and bore Cain." To Gunkel, the name *chavvāh* here appears totally superfluous, since the rest of the narrative deals with the man and his wife without mentioning names. He therefore suggests that *chavvāh* was inserted here from Gen. 3:20. However that may be, the name is present in both cases and is mentioned deliberately in each, which is naturally important for the understanding of the present text.

III. Religious Significance. The first man had a name, Adam (→ אדם *'ādhām*), that associated him with the earth from which he was formed. His name was always a reminder that he belonged to the earth and must return to the earth when his life was at an end. But even after the departure of the individual, life continued, for alongside the man stood the woman, and the name of the first woman was *chavvāh,* "life," because she was "the mother of all living." Through her life continued; from her the new generation was born. The man was unable to continue life. He stood alone until he had a helper who was herself "life" and could continue life. Both had their life from Yahweh; that they had in common. They were God's creatures, but with their individual characteristics. The man was formed from the earth and had to labor with the earth. The fact that this labor was so hard was connected with the fact that the man had sinned and thus drawn God's curse down upon himself (Gen. 3:1-19). For the woman the situation was the same; she, too, had sinned. The continuation of life, which should have been a joy to her—probably the deepest meaning of her life—became a burden and a hardship on account of her transgression (Gen. 3:16). She and the man stood together under the curse, as they had acted together in their transgression; therefore they were both expelled from the garden of God. The man had been informed explicitly that he must not eat of the fruit of the tree of knowledge, lest he die (Gen. 2:17). But the man, though himself created through the will of God, defied this will and consequently brought it about that death entered the world as a powerful reality. For the

---

[7]Kramer, 149.

[8]H. Gunkel, *HAT,* 1 (^{8}1969), 23.

[9]G. von Rad, *Genesis. OTL* (trans. 1961, ^{2}1972), 93.

woman the situation was equally bad; it was a divine irony that the very one who was to continue life in a special way contributed through what she did to the fact that death came into the world as the enemy and opponent of life.

But hardly had the man and the woman been expelled from the garden of God, hardly had the curse taken effect, when they came together and created the very life that was already implicit in the woman's name. What had been spoken in her name now became reality. There was probably no lack of pain and hardship, but of them nothing is said. The important thing was that the woman conceived and bore a son (Gen. 4:1). Although the narrator undoubtedly knew and emphasized that the man shared in the creation of new life, he has *chavvāh* declare at once that Yahweh was the author of the whole thing. The full meaning of the last clause in Gen. 4:1 is not clear: *qānîthî 'îsh 'eth-yhvh*. But the mention of Yahweh's name suggests that to him was given the honor for the new life, in one way or another. From him, ultimately, came life. That is the primary experience and essential message of the ancient narrator, and the meaning of the name *chavvāh* pales in the light of this knowledge. As already suggested, the name appears to derive from Canaanite sources, and it was unable to strike root in ancient Israel. This fact is illustrated by the use—or rather the nonuse—of the name *chavvāh*. Outside of the creation and Paradise narrative it does not appear in the OT, which makes it clear that *chavvāh* was a foreign element in ancient Israel.

Kapelrud

חוּל *chûl;* מָחוֹל *māchôl;* מְחֹלָה *m^echōlāh*

Contents: I. Occurrences and Parallels. II. Etymology. III. Metaphorical Use. IV. Cultic Dance. V. Victory Dance and Festal Dance. VI. Forms of Dance.

I. Occurrences and Parallels. The root *chûl,* meaning "dance," is of particular interest to us here as evidence for cultic dance. Determination of the number of occurrences depends on how much weight is attached to the phonetic similarity to → חיל *ḥyl,* "writhe," "be in labor," which Mandelkern even lumps together with *chûl,* giving a range of meanings that extends from "dance" through "cut into" to "be in

---

chûl. E. L. Backman, *Religious Dances in the Christian Church and in Popular Medicine* (trans. London, 1952); E. Brunner-Traut, *Der Tanz im Alten Ägypten. Äf,* 6 (1938); E. Erman and H. Ranke, *Ägypten und ägyptisches Leben im Altertum* (1923), 280–83; F. Humborg, "Labyrinthos," *PW,* XII (1924), 312–321; O. Keel, *Die Weisheit spielt vor Gott* (1974); G. van der Leeuw, *In den hemel is eenen Dans* (Amsterdam, 1930) = *In dem Himmel ist ein Tanz* (trans. 1930); W. O. E. Oesterley, *The Sacred Dance: A Study in Comparative Folklore* (Cambridge, 1923); R. Torniai, *La danza sacra* (Rome, 1951); G. Warnecke, "Tanzkunst," *PW,* ser. 2, IV (1932), 2233–2247; F. Weege, *Der Tanz in der Antike* (1926).

labor."[1] *GesB* distinguishes three spheres of meaning: (1) "move in a circle, dance" (4 occurrences); (2) "strike, fall upon" (6 occurrences); and (3) 4 passages that belong semantically with *ḥyl*.[2] *KBL*[3] lists 45 passages for *ḥyl*, leaving 8 for our *chûl,* with 2 additional occurrences based on conjecture (1 S. 18:6; 1 K. 1:40).[3]

With *chûl* belong the nouns *māchôl* and *m*ᵉ*chōlāh*. We must also take into account statements about dancing that use other verbs: *rqd* (9 times), *śḥq* (9 times), *krr* (3 times), and one occurrence each of *pzz* and *psḥ*. In addition, the noun → חג *chagh,* which stands for a pilgrimage festival, could have the original meaning "dance."[4] This would better explain the expression *'āsar chagh* in Ps. 118:27. *KBL*[3] assumes that the most frequent sense is "celebrate a festival," but follows Oesterley in seeing "leap, dance" as the basic meaning.[5]

II. Etymology. The root *ḥwl* does not appear in Canaanite or Old Aramaic inscriptions, but is attested in Ugaritic[6] with the meaning "dance." The root *ḥyl* for "be in labor" also appears.[7] Our root also appears with the same meaning as in Hebrew in Middle Hebrew, Jewish Aramaic, and Samaritan texts, as is confirmed by Arab. *ḥwl,* "turn."

For Akkadian, Landsberger[8] connects *māchôl* and *m*ᵉ*chōlāh* with *mēlultu,* "game,"[9] which he takes as deriving from a verb *ḥll,* maintaining that *chûl* is poorly attested in the OT. But his hypothetical *ḥll* with the meaning "play" does not appear at all in the OT. Landsberger asserts that in Akkadian, "dance" was expressed by *raqādu* (our *rqd*) or *sâru,* but is unwilling to exclude "dancing" as part of the *mēlultu* game. It is questionable whether the meaning suggested by Akkadian does justice to the OT nouns and the occurrences of *chûl.* The statement that *mēlultu* is "practically a synonym of *zamāru*" hardly leads to a better understanding of *māchôl* in Ps. 149:3 and 150:4 in place of "dance."

III. Metaphorical Use. There are four passages where the meaning of *chûl* is only remotely related to the notion of joyous dancing; the effect of its metaphorical use is even harsher. In Hos. 11:6, the raging of the sword against the cities of Israel is conceived as a dance. In Jer. 23:19 and 30:23, likewise, the whirlwind dances through the people as an affliction. Especially harsh is the vivid imagery in 2 S. 3:28f., where the blood of Abner is to fall upon the head of his murderer.

---

[1] S. Mandelkern, *Veteris Testamenti Concordantiae Hebraicae atque Chaldaicae* ([2]1955), I, 374.

[2] Pp. 217f.

[3] P. 285.

[4] Cf. Syr. *ḥag,* "go around"; A. Jeremias, *The OT in the Light of the Ancient Past* (trans. 1911), II, 102.

[5] P. 278.

[6] *WUS,* No. 1026.

[7] *WUS,* No. 1025.

[8] B. Landsberger, "Einige unerkannt gebliebene oder verkannte Nomina des Akkadischen," *WZKM,* 56 (1960), 119f.; 57 (1961), 22.

[9] Cf. also *AHw,* I, 644: *mēlulu(m).*

IV. Cultic Dance. Although the evidence for dancing as part of worship is not abundant,[10] such dancing was a matter of fact in Israel and the ancient Near East. Heliodorus[11] records how merchants from Tyre performed dances at a sacrifice in honor of Melkart.[12] On Delos, sacrifice was always associated with dancing.[13] Within the OT, dancing in the sanctuary is attested in Ps. 87:7. Both the psalm and this particular verse have been the subject of much discussion.[14] Usually *chōlᵉlîm* in v. 7 is taken as an abbreviated pilpel of *chûl* or (also contrary to the LXX) *kᵉ-* is emended to *mᵉ-:* "they sing like dancers." Buber takes a different approach: "They sing like playing the flute," corresponding to *ḥll.*[15] Almost all other interpreters find a reference to dancing, for we are dealing with a "hymn to Zion" sung "during a processional dance."[16] Ps. 149 also mentions dancing; its setting is Zion on the occasion of a "victory festival of the future."[17] In Ps. 150, all kinds of musical instruments are heard in the temple of Yahweh (v. 1); the *tōph* gives the beat for the *māchôl* (v. 4). Because this instrument is associated with the dance, we may also cite Ps. 68:26 (Eng. v. 25), where *ʿᵃlāmôth tôphēphôth* take part in the procession. In Ex. 32:5, a *chagh* for Yahweh is celebrated with dancing around a golden calf.[18] A round dance was performed around the altar (cf. Ps. 26:6 and *chêl,* "[surrounding] ramparts," in Ps. 48:14[13]). The verb *pāsach* is used uniquely for "dance" in 1 K. 18:26; according to v. 21 it must mean "limp," and so the passage may refer mockingly to a kind of limping dance around the altar. The festal procession "up to the horns of the altar" in Ps. 118:27 refers likewise to a cultic dance in the sanctuary.[19]

But dances were also performed in processions outside the temple, as when the ark was brought in under the leadership of David (2 S. 6:5). The dancing is already implicit in the statement that all the Israelites are *mᵉśachᵃqîm liphnê yhvh,* accompanied by *tuppîm.* It is clearer in the continuation of the procession (2 S. 6:14: *mᵉkharkēr*), but most explicit in the mockery of Michal (2 S. 6:16, 20). Here the dancing is described by the words *mᵉphazzēz ûmᵉkharkēr,* but in 1 Ch. 13:8 by *mᵉśachᵃqîm,* and in 15:29 by *mᵉraqqēdh ûmᵉśachēq.*

Ancient Near Eastern usage raises the question whether dancing also appears in the realm of the divine. At Ugarit, it is reported that the goddess ʿAnat danced;[20] dancing is also attested in the case of the Greco-Roman deities.[21] An inscription discovered near Beirut mentions a Baal-markod, a god of the dance.[22] For Egypt, the dwarfish deity Bes is "the god of dance and joy"; a statuette of him was found at Tell Taanach.[23] The

---

[10] A. Jeremias, *Handbuch der altorientalischen Geisteskultur* (²1929), 406.
[11] *Aethiopica* iv.17.
[12] A. Šanda, *Die Bücher der Könige. EHAT,* 9 (1911), I, 433.
[13] Weege, 61.
[14] Cf. the commentaries.
[15] M. Buber, *Das Buch der Preisungen* (1962), 131; cf. *KBL*³, 307.
[16] H. Gunkel, *GHK,* II/2 (1926; ⁵1968), 378ff.; H.-J. Kraus, *BK,* XV (⁴1972), 603.
[17] Gunkel, *GHK,* II/2, 620.
[18] Cf. Weege, 61; G. Bertram, "παίζω," *TDNT,* V, 628.
[19] Cf. Kraus, *BK,* XV, 809.
[20] *CTA,* 10 [IV AB], II, 29.
[21] Weege, 56, 147; Oesterley, 63f.
[22] Šanda, *EHAT,* 9, I, 433.
[23] *AOB,* No. 558.

only thing in the OT that resembles such motifs is the notion of Wisdom dancing before God (*śḥq,* Prov. 8:30).

V. Victory Dance and Festal Dance. When David's victory over Goliath is celebrated, dancing is mentioned by means of the term *m^e^chōlāh* and confirmed by *b^e^thuppîm* (1 S. 18:6). The term *m^e^chōlāh* also appears when this triumph is recalled later (1 S. 21:12[11]; 29:5). In like fashion, Jephthah's daughter greets her father on his victorious return with timbrels and dances (*m^e^chōlôth,* Jgs. 11:34; cf. also Ps. 68:26[25]). The same thing is attested in the Song of the Sea (Ex. 15:20). The harvest rejoicing in the vineyards at Shiloh includes dancing (Jgs. 21:19; *lāchûl bam-m^e^chōlôth,* v. 21; *hamm^e^chōl^e^lôth,* v. 23). Naturally such celebrations also have religious character in Israel, for the ark of God can be brought upon the field (1 S. 4:4; Ps. 24:7-10), just as the dancing at Shiloh takes place on a festival of Yahweh. The custom of dancing at marriages is attested by Cant. 7:1(6:13). That there were probably also sword dances performed by the soldiers can be concluded from the use of *śḥq* in 2 S. 2:14.

The dance as an expression of great rejoicing plays its role in Israel's idea of the eschaton. Just as God will then turn mourning into dancing (Ps. 30:12[11]), so the nations will go up to Jerusalem to keep the Feast of Booths (*lāchōgh ʾeth-chagh hassukkôth,* Zec. 14:16); we may compare Jer. 31:4 (*bimchôl m^e^śach^a^qîm*) and 31:13 (*b^e^māchôl*), for joyous dancing with timbrels accompanies the procession.

Because our Hebrew words are rendered by *choreúō* and *chorós* in the LXX, parallels may be cited from Judith. On one occasion, Holofernes is received with dancing (3:7); dancing likewise celebrates Judith's victory (15:12f.). In 3 Macc. 6:32, 35, the Jews celebrate their deliverance from mortal danger by dancing. In this late literature we may see a figurative notion of dancing, as an expression of harmonious social cohesion. In 4 Macc. 8:4, the Maccabean martyrs stand "in chorus" around their mother; in 13:8, they constitute a "sublime chorus of devotion." Since, according to 18:23, they are joined with "the chorus of the fathers," the community of the departed is likewise envisioned as a solemn dance.

VI. Forms of Dance. In discussing the question of how the dancing was performed, we may cite the dual in *m^e^chōlath hammach^a^nāyim* (Cant. 7:1[6:13]), which should probably be rendered as a double row dance.[24] Additional detail may possibly be derived from the verbs *krr* and *rqd,* if they may be understood as referring specifically to forms of turning and skipping in addition to ceremonious pacing. For the clothing worn while dancing, Michal's mockery of David (2 S. 6:20) is descriptive for the instance in question; *gālāh* probably presupposes that he was clothed indecorously.[25] In 3 Macc. 7:16, we read that the dancers were "wreathed with sweet-smelling flowers."

In 2 Macc. 10:7, those celebrating "in the manner of the Feast of Booths" carry ivy-wreathed wands, beautiful branches, and palm fronds. Those who interpret the *ʿ^a^bhōthîm* of Ps. 118:27 as referring to "branches" can cite in support Ezk. 19:11; 6:13;

[24]W. Rudolph, *KAT,* XVII/1-3 (1962), 168; otherwise G. Gerleman, *BK,* XVIII (1965), 188.
[25]For a discussion of partial nudity, see Erman-Ranke, 280-83.

Lev. 23:40; etc.[26] Gunkel[27] and Kraus[28] think instead of *ʿăbhōth,* "cord," held by the dancers to form an advancing row. This custom is well attested among both the Greeks and the Romans.[29] This would explain the idiom of "binding" (*ʿāsar*) a "dance" (*chagh*), and Ps. 118:27b would be translated: "Bind the festal dance with cords."

Of course the dancing was accompanied by singing. In Ps. 87:7, "All my springs are in you" is probably the torso of a dancing song. In 1 S. 18:6f. a song glorifying a victor is preserved; Ex. 15:20 constitutes the refrain to the Song of the Sea. In Ps. 118, vv. 27 or 28 may be taken as verse of the song accompanying the dance.

Eising

---

[26]Cf. R. Kittel, *KAT,* XIII ([5,6]1929), 371, 375; B. Duhm, *KHC,* XIV ([2]1922), 414.
[27]*GHK,* II/2, 510f.
[28]*BK,* XV, 801, 809.
[29]Weege, 61, 149; cf. also Humborg, 320f., and Warnecke, 2239; *AOB,* No. 554.

חול *chôl*

Contents: I. Etymology. II. Occurrences and Meaning: 1. Secular Use; 2. Religious Meaning.

I. Etymology. The word appears in Jewish Aramaic in the forms *ḥôlāʾ* and *ḥālāʾ;* the latter appears also in Syriac. The Arab. *ḫālun* is probably also related. The root *ḥwl* does not appear in all the Semitic languages; with the meaning "sand," it is not attested in either Ugaritic[1] or Akkadian. The origin of the root has been sought in the verb *ḥwl,* "dance, whirl" (Jgs. 21:21,23; Jer. 23:19). What started as a term for the grains of sand dancing in the winds was later extended to the grains themselves and finally to the general concept "sand." The use of *chôl* frequently illustrates that the word refers especially to the enormous multitude of the grains of sand.

II. Occurrences and Meaning.

1. *Secular Use.* Many occurrences exhibit the notion of multitudinous grains of sand. The word *chôl* can be used in combination with the stars of heaven to indicate a great multitude (Gen. 22:17). In Gen. 41:49, we read how Joseph stored up grain in

---

chôl. M. Dahood, "Nest and Phoenix in Job 29, 18," *Bibl,* 48 (1967), 542-44; G. Dalman, *AuS,* II (1932); J. L. Kelso, *The Ceramic Vocabulary of the OT. BASORSup,* 5/6 (1948); M. Rim, "Sand and Soil in the Coastal Plain of Israel," *IEJ,* 1 (1951), 33-48; A. W. Schwarzenbach, *Die geographische Terminologie im Hebräischen des ATs* (Leiden, 1954).

[1]Cf. however C. Kühne, "Mit Glossenkeilen markierte fremde Wörter in akkadischen Ugarittexten," *UF,* 6 (1974), 166f., discussing two toponymns.

abundance like the sand of the sea. Here the comparison involves not only the quantities but the granular form of the two substances. In Isa. 48:19, *chôl* and its grains are used in parallel to suggest an enormous multitude. Hab. 1:9, too, probably refers to the multitude of grains of sand, but the emphasis may also be on the loose texture of sand: the Chaldeans, in other words, will scoop up captives like sand. Hard earth could not be scooped up, whereas sand could; water, of course, can also be scooped up, but the grains of sand provided a better image.

In Ex. 2:12 and Dt. 33:19, *chôl* is used more neutrally, without any notion of quantity or consistency. Both passages speak of objects buried in the ground. The former tells how Moses slays the Egyptian and immediately buries the dead body in the sand, probably because it was easier to dig in the sand than in ordinary earth. In this case, Ex. 2:12 belongs with the previously mentioned passages. In Dt. 33:19, on the contrary, we read of the rich treasures of the earth (sand). Here *chôl* appears to be used in the sense of "earth."

Prov. 27:3 and Job 6:3 are in the same vein. Here the heaviness of sand is particularly underlined: "A stone is heavy, and sand weighty." In Job 6:3, Job states that his vexation weighs more than the sand of the sea.

The word could also suggest the broad stretches of sand along the sea, which were also used as images. It was said of king Solomon that the largeness of his heart was like the sand on the shore of the sea (1 K. 5:9 [Eng. 4:29]). By the sea the sand also had a special function appointed by God himself: "Do you not fear me? says Yahweh. . . . I placed the sand as a bound for the sea, a perpetual barrier which it cannot pass" (Jer. 5:22).

Almost all the passages cited yield the startling conclusion that in ancient Israel and Judah *chôl* was thought of as referring only to the sand of the seashore. The great sandy areas of the Syrian and Arabian desert seem to have been unknown to the old poets and storytellers. The great sandy deserts were very difficult to cross, and were therefore probably little known. The sand by the sea, on the other hand, was obviously familiar to most of the inhabitants of ancient Israel, for the most part on the basis of firsthand experience. These experiences find expression in the very earliest traditions, and suggest that the Israelites migrating into Canaan were never true Bedouins. Had they been such, they would surely have spoken of the sand of the great deserts, which remain strikingly unmentioned in the OT.

The multitude of sand usually stands as a term of comparison in the images that are used so frequently in narratives: "Judah and Israel were as many as the sand of the sea" (1 K. 4:20). When the enemies gathered against the invading Israelites, we are told that they were a great host, countless as the sand of the sea, with innumerable horses and chariots (Josh. 11:4). Another time the camels of the enemy were countless as the sand upon the seashore (Jgs. 7:12). The Philistines mustered an army in multitude like the sand on the seashore (1 S. 13:5). When Hushai gave his counsel to rebellious Absalom, he suggested that all Israel should be called to arms, as the sand by the sea for multitude (2 S. 17:11).

2. *Religious Meaning*. The image of sand is used often to depict the future multitude of Israel. An image especially adapted to painting the picture of an enormous

host was particularly apropos when the ancient storytellers or poets spoke of the blessing that Yahweh would bestow upon his people. Thus great fertility was counted a blessing, in consequence of which the ancestors of Israel would have ever-increasing descendants. Without such an ever-increasing multitude, Israel would have small chance to survive, especially since it was constantly threatened and oppressed by enemies or competitors. God's blessing meant fertility and many offspring, while judgment and curse meant extermination and downfall.

This is clear in God's promise to Abraham when the latter showed that he was willing to sacrifice his son at God's command: "By myself I have sworn, says Yahweh, because you have done this, and have not withheld your son, your only son, I will indeed bless you, and I will multiply your descendants as the stars of heaven and as the sand which is on the seashore" (Gen. 22:16–17a). When Jacob was afraid to meet his brother Esau, he reminded God in his prayer of the ancient blessing: "But thou didst say, 'I will do you good, and make your descendants as the sand of the sea, which cannot be numbered for multitude'" (Gen. 32:13[12]).

Hos. 2:1(1:10), too, recalls the same blessing immediately after the harsh words of the prophet in 1:9: "Call his name Not my people, for you are not my people and I am not your God." It is probably a glossator or a disciple of the prophet who added: "Yet the number of the people of Israel shall be like the sand of the sea, which can be neither measured nor numbered" (Hos. 2:1[1:10]). The same idea likewise appears in Jer. 33:22: "As the host of heaven cannot be numbered and the sands of the sea cannot be measured, so I will multiply the descendants of David my servant, and the Levitical priests who minister to me."

The harsh verdict of the prophet Jeremiah in chap. 15 is set in contrast to the same oath: "I have winnowed them with a winnowing fork in the gates of the land; I have bereaved them, I have destroyed my people, since they did not turn from their ways. I have made their widows more in number than the sand of the seas" (Jer. 15:7f.).

In the Psalms, *chôl* is used twice as an image representing God's plenty. The first image applies to the abundant food bestowed upon Israel by Yahweh in the desert after the exodus from Egypt: "He rained flesh upon them like dust, winged birds like the sand of the seas" (Ps. 78:27). In Ps. 139, the poet likens the multitude of God's thoughts to the multitude of sand: "How precious to me are thy thoughts, O God! How vast is the sum of them! If I would count them, they are more than the sand" (Ps. 139:17–18a).

In Job 29:18, *chôl* is commonly understood to mean "phoenix."[2] If it is taken as "sand" in this passage, too, we are dealing once more with a great multitude, this time with the days of a man's life.

Kapelrud

---

[2]Cf. M. Dahood, "Ḥôl 'Phoenix' in Job 29:18 and in Ugaritic," *CBQ*, 36 (1974), 85–88.

חוֹמָה chômāh

Contents: I. Philology. II. 1. Walls as Fortifications; 2. Walls of Houses and Vineyards; 3. Walls in Metaphorical Usage.

I. Philology. The word *chômāh,* "wall, city wall" (LXX [*peri*]*teíchos, phragmós*), is attested 120 times in the OT, 8 times with the defective spelling *ḥmh.*[1] It does not occur in Akkadian, although in *ḫamātu,* "help," we obviously have a derivative.[2] As a rule, the concepts "city wall, fortified wall, house wall" are represented in Akkadian by *dūru*/*durāni.*[3] The etymology of *chômāh* points to Old South Arabic, where *ḥmy,* "protect" (cf. Arab. *ḥamā,* "defend"), *ḥmh,* "sacred precinct, protective association," are well attested. As a West Semitic loanword, *ḫmy* found its way into Akkadian.[4] In Ugaritic, *ḥmt* is attested only scantily.[5] We find there the parallelism *mgdl*/*ḥmt,* as in Isa. 2:15.[6] Knudtzon[7] gives *ḫu-mi-tu* as a synonym of *dūru.*[8] Egyptian, too, appears to exhibit the use of *ḥmy* in the sense "protector against . . ." during the 18th dynasty (16th–14th centuries B.C.).[9] Besides *chômāh,* the nominal derivative of *ḥmh,* Hebrew has several other terms that can mean "wall": *sābhîbh* (2 S. 5:9; Ezk. 46:23; Nah. 3:8); *shûr* II (Gen. 49:22; 2 S. 22:30; Ps. 18:30 [Eng. v. 29]); *qîr* (1 S. 18:11; 2 K. 9:33; Isa. 22:5; Hab. 2:11), and *gādhēr* (17 occurrences in the OT).[10]

---

chômāh. Y. Aharoni, "The Date of Casemate Walls in Judah and Israel and their Purpose," *BASOR,* 154 (1959), 35-39; A. Alt, "Hic murus aheneus esto," *ZDMG,* 86 (1932), 33-48; W. Andrae, "Städtebau; im Orient," *PW,* ser. 2, II/3 (1929), 1974–1982; H. Cazelles, "Befestigung," *BL*², 179–182; G. Cornfeld, *Pictorial Biblical Encyclopedia* (1964), *s.v.* "Ancient Cities: Jerusalem, Lachish," "Warfare," "Conquest"; G. Dalman, *AuS,* VII (1942), 1-175, *passim;* R. P. Dougherty, "Sennacherib and the Walled Cities of Judah," *JBL,* 49 (1930), 160–171; K. Galling, "Mauer und Mauertechnik," *BRL,* 371–74; E. Hora, *Die hebräische Bauweise im AT* (Karlsbad, 1903); K. Jäger, *Das Bauernhaus in Palästina* (1912); K. M. Kenyon, *Jerusalem: Excavating 3000 Years of History* (1968); H. Lesêtre, "Mur," *DB,* IV (1908), 1340–43; F. Nötscher, *Biblische Altertumskunde. HSAT,* III (1940), 156-163, 239-250; P. J. Parr, "The Origin of the Rampart Fortifications of Middle Bronze Age Palestine and Syria," *ZDPV,* 84 (1968), 18–45; A. Salonen, "šahāṭu = 'glasieren' (d.h. Ziegel)," *BiOr,* 28 (1971), 24f.; R. de Vaux, *AncIsr,* 232–38; Y. Yadin, *The Art of Warfare in Biblical Lands* (1963), *passim.* See also → בית *bayith* and → בנה *bānāh.* For archeology, see *ZAW,* 88 (1976), 124f.

[1] *KBL*³, 285f.

[2] *AHw,* I, 316.

[3] BÀD[ki]; *CAD,* III, 192-97; cf. דור *GesB,* 159, with additional citations, and also Akk. *dūr appi,* "cheek."

[4] R. de Langhe, *Les Textes de Ras Shamra-Ugarit et leur Rapports avec le Milieu Biblique de l'AT* (Paris, 1945), II, 82.

[5] *WUS,* No. 944.

[6] L. R. Fisher, *Ras Shamra Parallels I. AnOr,* 49 (1972), No. 343, 255f.

[7] EA 141, 44.

[8] *Die El-Amarna-Tafeln. VAB,* II (1915, ²1964), I; cf. *DISO,* 90.

[9] *WbÄS,* III, 80.

[10] *KBL*³, 173.

The root *gdr* in the sense "enclose (with a wall)" is amply attested: besides Canaanite and Punic,[11] there is above all Arab. *ğaddara, ğadr.*[12] Ugar. *gdrt,* "enclosure?"[13] has not been explained satisfactorily; a personal name Gudarana(?) is also attested.[14] Arab. *ğadīr,* "circumvallated place," is used as a toponym, especially for the city of Cadiz. Among the Berber tribes, *agadir* took on the meaning "acropolis, fortress." In Tigré, *gedā/ōr,* "within the circle of," often occurs in a context dealing with the maintenance of totality and integrity.[15]

II. 1. *Walls as Fortifications.* As early as the Bronze Age there is evidence in Palestine for the existence of fortified settlements for protection of the fellahin against incursions of the Bedouin hordes (Jericho, Megiddo, Ai); it is in fact an open question whether in this period there were any permanently established dwelling places that were not fortified. The early casemate walls appear as a rule to have consisted of two parallel vertical outer walls made of medium-size stones, initially unhewn (Ex. 20:25?), each some three to six feet thick. The enclosed space was filled with rubble, gravel, and earth, so that such walls, following the contours of the land, could exhibit a total width of 17 to 23 feet or more (Jericho D: Late Bronze period). These casemate walls contained windowless chambers that could be used as storerooms for military purposes. Sometimes the city wall served also as the wall of a private house (Josh. 2:15). From the period of the conquest (13th century) at the latest, fortified cities were probably considered common (Dt. 3:5). The city walls, frequently battered, might be as much as 33 feet thick at their foundations, which reached bedrock whenever possible; their height was about the same. The statements in Dt. 1:28; 3:5; etc., according to which the semi-nomadic Israelite tribes in the process of becoming settled were confronted with unfamiliar cities, effectively untakable, make it only too easy to understand their fear and, on the other hand, the pride of many a city in its high and fortified walls (Dt. 28:52; Isa. 25:12; 1 QH 6:25). Thus the city of David can boast of having such a strong wall that even the blind and lame can defend it (2 S. 5:6).

In Israel two basic types of wall became standard. On the one hand, the ancient Canaanite city walls already encountered during the occupation were utilized (Nu. 32:17; 1 K. 4:13); on the other, casemate walls and squamiform walls with redans were built from scratch. To make them easier to defend, the latter were comprised of salients and reentrants interspersed with especially strong towers (Lachish, Megiddo, Mizpah). After frequent unfortunate experiences during sieges when enemy troops undermined such city walls and thus penetrated into the fortified settlements, a different technique came into use: the foundations were sunk several feet into the earth and a deep trench was dug in front of the walls. Frequently an outer wall (*chēl/chêl*) is found in front of this trench (Isa. 26:1; Lam. 2:8; Nah. 3:8; Gezer, Jericho, Shechem). The empty space

---

[11] *LidzNE,* 249.

[12] Wehr, 114.

[13] *WUS,* No. 634.

[14] *PRU,* III, 520.

[15] *TigrWb,* 600; cf. Heb. *g^e^dhērāh,* "fold, pen"; Palmyrene-Nab. *gdr(')* in G. R. Driver, "Hebrew Roots and Words," *WO,* 1 (1947–1952), 415.

between the *chômāh* and *chēl* could be used for military patrols and other defensive purposes. Numerous reliefs show that the tops of the walls were often wide enough for soldiers or sentries (2 K. 6:30; 2 Ch. 32:18; Isa. 62:6; Cant. 5:7), especially archers (2 S. 11:20,24). Such walls marked the distinction between a city (*ʿîr*) and an open village (*chātsēr*) (Lev. 25:31), so that Prov. 25:28 can liken the abnormal situation of an *ʾîr ʾên chômāh* to a foolish man without self-control. At the end of the eighth century, the Assyrian king Sennacherib can boast of having besieged and taken 46 fortified cities of Judah (Annals of Sennacherib, III, 19; cf. 2 K. 18:13). A mural relief from the palace at Nineveh[16] (cf. 2 K. 18:17) shows Sennacherib's siege of the city of Lachish. Together with his account of the capture of the city,[17] it gives a vivid impression of how siege troops dealt with the obstacle of a city wall.

The inhabitants were first called on to open their gates (cf. Dt. 20:10ff.). If they refused, the city was attacked. Such sieges could last months and even years. As early as the second millennium, battering-rams came into use, initially in the form of simple beams with a strong metal point like that of a lance. At Mari and in the armies of the Assyrian kings, such rams were soon attached to towers, thus becoming even more effective. Later it became the general practice to provide battering rams with poles. The attackers would try to fill the trenches between *chēl* and *chômāh,* or at least to build embankments at several points (2 S. 20:15; Ezk. 4:2). Frequently simultaneous attempts were made to breach and undermine the wall. Especially courageous fighters would try to climb the wall with the help of ladders (2 S. 22:30: *shûr*). To make the climbing more difficult, the lower outside portion of the wall was therefore often covered with plaster to make it smooth. At the same time, such a coat of plaster gave the appearance, frequently deceptive, of great stability (1 K. 20:30; Isa. 30:13; Ezk. 13:10–16). When the city was taken, the few city gates were set on fire, smashed in, and battered into ruins (Isa. 24:12), and the body of the defeated commandant was fastened to the city wall (1 S. 31:10; cf. Jth. 14:1).

2. *Walls of Houses and Vineyards.* Most houses in ancient Israel were rectangular; their walls often consisted merely of clay and poor quality brick, whereas the remains of house walls found in Babylonia suggest a preference for the use of either fired or merely sun-dried bricks held together with reeds and wattle. Only a few structures were executed entirely in stone. They are mentioned as a luxury in Am. 5:11 and Isa. 9:9(10). Only under the influence of Phoenician architects did the use of ashlar gradually make its appearance in the Solomonic empire. Sometimes the walls of houses were plastered with clay or lime (Lev. 14:41f.; Dt. 27:2; Ezk. 13:10). Glazing and kiln firing were rare. Walls were mortared poorly if at all, so that a *qîr* could be dug through with one's bare hands (Ezk. 12:7). Potter's clay mixed with mussel shells or potsherds served as mortar; bitumen, commonly employed in Mesopotamia (Gen. 11:3[18]), was scarcely used. As Nah. 3:14 shows, clay bricks were made in wooden molds and dried in the sun; the wet clay was mixed with chopped straw (Ex. 5:7). Dt.

---

[16] *AOB,* 134, 141.
[17] Annals of Sennacherib, III, 18–23.
[18] Diodorus Siculus ii.7, 12.

22:8 requires that a flat roof be provided with a parapet (*maʿaqeh*), lest blood guilt come upon the house if someone should fall from an unprotected roof. In Lev. 14:33-53, finally, we find regulations governing leprosy in houses. It was rare to find an interior wall (*chayits*) inside a house (Ezk. 13:10); multiple stories appear to have existed only in the buildings constituting the palace of the royal family.

The vineyards and gardens of the Israelites usually were surrounded by walls (*gādhēr*, Isa. 5:5; Ps. 80:13[12]). Prov. 24:31 speaks of the collapse of the *gādhēr* of an untended field.

3. *Walls in Metaphorical Usage*. Metaphorical usage appears in the idiom *hāyāh chômāh (ʿal-)PN*, "effectually protect someone," used with personal subjects. It is used in 1 S. 25:16 of the conduct of David's followers toward the servants of Nabal; in Ezk. 13:5 (with *gādhēr*) it characterizes the function of the prophet with respect to the people of Israel (cf. Ezk. 22:30; Jer. 1:18; 15:20, and Alt's essay). A triumph song in the Apocalypse of Isaiah (Isa. 26:1) compares the *yeshûʿāh* of Yahweh graphically to the mighty fortifications of a city: *chômôth vāchēl;* similarly a chiasmus in Isa. 60:18 calls the walls of the new Jerusalem "Salvation" (*yeshûʿāh*) and her gates "Praise" (*tehillāh*). In the context of Wisdom Literature, Prov. 18:11 uses the same idiom with the preposition *ke*- to characterize inanimate objects: "A rich man's wealth is his strong city and his high wall—as he wrongly imagines."[19] In Ex. 14:22 (P), *ham-mayim lāhem chômāh* may be an image of security and protection (cf. Nah. 3:8), just as Ps. 122:7 ascribes to the *chēl* the preservation of *shālôm*. In 1QH 3:37, the worshipper praises the Lord, who has proved to be his strong wall (*lechômath ʿôz*). In Cant. 8:9f., a humorous dispute between some brothers and their enamored sister, *chômāh* appears as an image for a virgin (cf. Egyp. *ḥm.t*, "immature girl"[20]), while *deleth*, "door," designates a young woman who has a man.[21] Ringgren,[22] however, prefers to interpret "wall" and "door" in this passage (as in Ezk. 38:11) as being synonymous.

The helpless individual is increasingly hard pressed by his enemies; they set upon him like a *gādhēr* or *qîr* on the point of collapse (Ps. 62:4[3]—cf. "defenseless"). If the function of a wall is effectually to protect the city, Israel nevertheless realizes that it is Yahweh who ultimately guarantees the security of the people. Only walls that have permanence in the eyes of Yahweh can protect against assaults (Josh. 6:5, 20; Isa. 49:16; Ps. 18:30[29] [*shûr*]; 48:14f.[13f.] [*chēl*]; 89:41[40] [*gādhēr*]). Occasionally the community refers to Yahweh himself as a *chômāh* (1QS 8:7; 1QH 7:8f.). A Qumran blessing formula compares the prince of the community (*neśîʾ hāʿēdhāh*) to a strong tower on a high wall (1QSb 5:23). It is Yahweh who lays his plumb line critically against the wall of Israel (Am. 7:7-9), no longer ready to forgive. The decision of the builder is, "Tear it down!" (Lam. 2:8). The ruined city wall (Jer. 52:14) is an occasion of lament to Yahweh (Neh. 1:3ff.). The God of Israel himself is a

[19]Following Hamp.

[20]*WbÄS*, III, 76.

[21]O. Loretz, *Studien zur althebräischen Poesie, I. Das althebräische Liebeslied. AOAT*, 14/1 (1971).

[22]H. Ringgren, *ATD*, XVI/2 (²1967), 291f.

gādhēr to his people in Judah (Ezr. 9:9) and a *chōmath ʾēsh sābîbîbh* in Jerusalem (Zec. 2:9[5]).

In der Smitten

חוס *chûs*

Contents: I. Root: 1. Etymology; 2. OT Occurrences; 3. Meaning. II. Theological Usage. III. General Usage.

I. Root.

1. *Etymology*. The root *ḥws* apparently does not occur in the earlier Semitic literary monuments. It is not found in Akkadian or Ugaritic, but is attested in Middle Hebrew, Jewish Aramaic, Samaritan, Christian Palestinian, Syriac, Mandean, Arabic, and Ethiopic. The meaning found in Hebrew ("have pity, compassion") is itself probably a secondary development. The construction with *ʿayin* ("eye") may preserve a more original sense: "the eye overflows [undoubtedly with tears] concerning (*ʿal*) a person or thing," i.e., the actual subject weeps or suffers on account of something or some situation. It is easy to see how this earlier meaning could be used to express emotions thought of in less concrete terms, especially pity.

2. *OT Occurrences*. In the OT, *chûs* appears only as a verb in the qal (24 times). Despite the narrow range of use, it can be stated that usage is clearly concentrated in later literary contexts. Its relatively frequent appearance in Ezekiel is striking (9 occurrences, more than a third of the total). Next comes Deuteronomy, with 5 passages. Including the 6 other prophetical passages, *chûs* appears 15 times in prophetical texts (once each in Isaiah and Joel, twice each in Jeremiah and Jonah). There are single occurrences of the root in the story of Joseph and in 1 Samuel, Nehemiah, and Psalms. In the prophetical texts, *chûs* is used almost exclusively in prophecies of disaster; in Deuteronomy, it always appears in prohibitions within legal stipulations. In the overwhelming majority of instances, the form of *chûs* is constructed with a negation. The number of passages illustrating a general usage of the root is very small. It would almost be possible to assume that *chûs* functions only in theological contexts. It is debatable whether the original locus of usage is to be found in the realm of priestly law or in prophecies of disaster. Taking into account the likelihood that Ezekiel was himself a priest, one could assume that his (frequently metrical) prophecies of disaster in passages using *chûs* derive from (priestly) legal formulas of prohibition.[1] For the

[1] Cf. W. Zimmerli, *BK*, XIII (1969), 70.

time being, however, we are limited to conjectures, which will need the support of further detailed studies.

3. *Meaning*. To amplify what was said above (see I.1) concerning the range of meanings of *chûs,* it should be stressed that *chûs* belongs to the class of verbs that describe emotions. Specifically, *chûs* refers to the emotion of sympathy, i.e., the shared suffering due to the misfortune or disaster that befalls another. Its reference is therefore primarily personal. The fact that the object of the emotion can also be impersonal probably represents an extension of what was originally a personal relationship (Gen. 45:20; Jonah 4:10). The object is frequently introduced by *ʿal*. The concept "have pity/sympathy" does not refer to a state or attitude based on the perspective of an outside observer, but to a stance that motivates and initiates action on behalf of the one pitied. Sympathy or pity is the antecedent of action. Therefore the meaning can be extended to the English equivalent "spare." The reference is always to a positive attitude toward the object, with the intention of performing a helping act. A soteriological activity can be understood in the action of *chûs* (cf. Ps. 72:13).

In most of the biblical passages, however, this nexus of attitude and action described by *chûs* is transformed by a negation into its opposite. Refusal to have pity and consequently come to someone's aid means intensified alienation from the one on whom punishment, or disaster, or distress, has fallen. This alienation itself is not to be understood as an introverted fundamental attitude, but as an action.

II. Theological Usage. As already noted, the predominant usage of *chûs* is theological. In the five Deuteronomy passages we find a striking stereotyped formula, whose construction is clear: *lōʾ thāchōs ʿênᵉkhā ʿal,* a negated indicative as the predicate, *ʿayin* with the 2nd masc. sing. suffix as the subject, and *ʿal* introducing the semantic object (7:16; 13:9 [Eng. v. 8]; 19:13,21; 25:12—in the latter two instances without *ʿal,* although the reference is clear from the context). All five instances presuppose a situation involving sacral law with stipulated punishment, which is to be executed without pity. We shall now examine the individual passages in detail.

Dt. 7:16 refers to the ban;[2] its execution is required apodictically, without mitigation or qualification.[3] In the context of 13:7-12(6-11), 13:9(8) deals with the case in which someone entices a member of his own family into apostasy. The law provides for ruthless execution of the penalty (stoning of the transgressor), which is especially hard because the enticer is a member of the family (alongside *chûs* we find → חמל *chāmal* and, remarkably, *kāsāh* in the piel plus *ʿal,* "cover, conceal" in the sense of solidarity with the criminal and downgrading of his crime). The theme of cities of refuge[4] is broached in the first half of chap. 19; vv. 11-13 deal with the special case of

---

[2]Cf. G. LindesKog, "Bann," *BHHW,* I, 194; C. Brekelmans, "Le Ḥerem chez les prophètes du royaume du Nord et dans le Deutèronome. *Sacra Pagina,* I. *BETL,* 12-13 (1959), 377-383.

[3]But cf. H. Cazelles, "ʿal tḥws ʿn ʿl," *GLECS,* 12-13 (1967ff.), 132-34, who translates the expression in Dt. 7:16 as "*se soucier de . . . ,*" "be worried about."

[4]Cf. L. Delekat, "Asylie," *BHHW,* I, 143f.; *idem, Asylie und Schutzorakel am Zionheiligtum* (Leiden, 1967); de Vaux, *AncIsr,* 160-63.

an illegitimate claim for asylum. In a case of premeditated murder, the murderer is to be handed over without mercy to the avenger of blood (*gō'ēl haddām*); the elders of his city are obligated to fetch him even from a city of refuge and see that he dies. This is to be done without pity (v. 13). The second half of chap. 19 deals with (among other things) the case of a trial in which a false witness has demonstrably accused someone falsely (vv. 16–21). The accuser must then suffer the punishment he intended to see inflicted on the accused through his false testimony. Here, too, pity is forbidden (v. 21). The severity of the law is given its motivation through an abbreviated form of the lex talionis.

Chap. 25 contains a series of legal norms, among which that contained in vv. 11f. is unique in the OT: if a woman comes to the aid of her husband when he is being beaten by another and seizes her husband's opponent by his private parts, her hand shall be cut off. Here, too, pity is forbidden (v. 11). The word *hech^e zîqāh* undoubtedly refers to an injury to the male sex organs (tearing or crushing) intended to disable the victim so that he will withdraw from the fight.

In the case of some of these ordinances, which are clearly communicated in parenetic form involving some degree of revision, an earlier recension can be found in the Covenant Code (cf. Dt. 19:13 with Ex. 21:12–14, Dt. 19:21 with Ex. 23:1). Comparison reveals the new historical setting in Deuteronomy and attests to the fact that the transmission of these passages has a history. In the case of Dt. 7:16 and 13:9(8), it is not impossible that a Deuteronomistic redaction has continued the process a transmission yet further.

In four of the five Deuteronomy passages (all but 7:16), the appearance of the juristic formulation stands out in its context. The case is typically introduced by *kî*, "when, if." Then the modes of conduct and punishments are named. No matter how the complex history of the legal material in Deuteronomy may have taken place and in whatever form it has come down to us, its background in casuistic law is clearly discernible. The use of *chûs* in the typical constructions cited above, together with the use of *lō'* and the indicative, is reminiscent of apodictic legal formulation. The restricted range of the evidence makes it impossible to determine whether *chûs* referred to a specific form of mitigation of punishment in the legal system. It is of course also conceivable that this idiom belongs to Deuteronomic homiletic, parenesis, and catechesis. If so, these latter were drawing upon typical legal formulas. The explicit emphasis on the elimination of pity might suggest that, when punishment was inflicted, there was room for discrimination among fixed regulations.[5]

The second complex in which *chûs* appears in this typically negative idiom comprises the prophecies of doom in the book of Ezekiel. In 5:11, Zimmerli[6] finds a portion of an explanatory section (vv. 11–13) appended to the original saying (5:5–6a,8f.,14f.), in which the announcement of judgment is lent concrete form.[7] In the first-person style

---

[5]Cf. G. von Rad, *Deuteronomy*. *OTL* (trans. 1966), 129; on the form *tāchôs* as an indicative, see R. Meyer, *Hebräische Grammatik*, II ([3]1969), 149; G. Bergsträsser, *Hebräische Grammatik* (1929, repr. 1962), II, § 28d.

[6]*BK*, XIII, 132–35.

[7]Similarly G. Fohrer, *HAT*, 13 ([2]1955), 33f.

of a divine oracle of doom, destruction is proclaimed upon Jerusalem (as the focus of sin in the house of Israel)—without pity (*v^elō' thāchôs 'ênî v^eghām 'anî lō' 'echmôl*). The two occurrences in 7:4,9 likewise appear in a context that is traditio-historically obscure.[8] The two oracles in 7:2-4 and 7:5-9 are variations on the theme of an imminent end. The two variants may go back to Ezekiel himself.[9] Beginning with v. 5, ideas deriving from prophecy of the disastrous *yôm yhvh* are incorporated. Once again, of central importance for the understanding of the passage is the intensification in the statement that Yahweh will have no pity when he judges, expressed by means of the stereotyped expression cited above (in v. 4 constructed with *'al,* and in both verses—4 and 9—with the verb *chāmal* in parallelism).

The situation is not basically different in 8:18 (where 18b is probably a secondary expansion; cf. LXX) and 9:10,[10] both times with the same fixed formula. The formula is altered in 9:5 (reading *'ên^ekhem* and *'al* with the *qere*) to the extent that the verbs *chûs* and *chāmal* refer to the agents appointed by Yahweh to carry out his punishment. They are to execute judgment without mercy and without pity. The construction used here is *'al* plus the jussive, i.e., a negative imperative, tantamount to an explicit order to act without pity, an order for which the one who issues it—Yahweh—takes final responsibility.

In Ezk. 24:14, too, one of the interpretative passages in 1-14, the common form of expression is abandoned. Here *chûs* is used in the 1st person singular (*v^elō' 'āchûs*), and in parallelism with *nḥm* and *pāra'*. The verb *chûs* has been separated from its referent (*'ayin*) and now conveys its meaning alone, probably a secondary development. The meaning is the same: the harsh judgment of Yahweh's wrath upon Jerusalem.

Whether the individual passages go back to Ezekiel himself, whether sayings of Ezekiel were used by a circle of his disciples, or finally whether in the period after Ezekiel certain fixed formulas came to be used to characterize and define God's judgment, the formulaic nature of the *chûs* idiom can be observed everywhere. The slight variants exhibited by the exceptions appear to confirm the rule. The striking similarity to the use of *chûs* in Deuteronomy cries out for an explanation, possibly suggesting that the formula did indeed have its original setting in the procedures of sentence and execution.

The verb *chûs* appears with a positive sense in Ezk. 20:17, in the context of an extended passage in which the prophet finds the reason for the imminent disaster in the history of the people of Israel, a history of continued unfaithfulness toward Yahweh. The chain of Israel's repeated apostasies is contrasted with the history of Yahweh's faithfulness toward his people. V. 17 uses *chûs* to describe Yahweh's favor toward his people: *vattāch^os 'ênî 'alêhem mishshach^athām.* Here *chûs* is a term for the neutralization of the deserved punishment, destruction. Only in the benevolence of pity (the pity of a tearful eye) was there not merely a mitigation or discrimination in executing the punishment, but suspension of the sentence, setting aside of the verdict, suppres-

---

[8]Cf. Zimmerli, *BK,* XIII, 158-173.

[9]Cf. Fohrer, *HAT,* 13, 42.

[10]For details see the commentaries.

sion of the proceedings, deliverance. The stereotyped construction with *ʿayin* and *ʿal* (this time without negation) is striking here, recalling the association just mentioned with the execution of a sentence. Such a background, which could have involved a fixed formula, was drawn upon to illustrate God's kindness (cf. also Jonah 4:11, where *ʿal* is used without *ʿayin,* the affirmation being expressed through formulation as a rhetorical question).

Quite similar to this passage is Ezk. 16:5, although formulated negatively. Here, too, a prophecy of disaster is grounded on history. Again the addressee is Jerusalem, representing the chosen people. The account compares Jerusalem to a bride married by Yahweh. The beginnings of this "marriage account" are traced back to the birth of the "bride." The present faithlessness of "Jerusalem" is contrasted to the constant faithfulness and mercy of Yahweh. The child had been exposed on the day of her birth, and on that very day Yahweh had taken pity on her, so that she owed her very life to him. Ezk. 16:5 (together with v. 4) describes the potential death awaiting the exposed child, uncared for: *lōʾ chāsāh ʿālayikh ʿayin,* "no one pitied you" to perform any of the necessary care ("no one's eye overflowed with tears on your behalf . . ."). Deliverance through Yahweh rested in the *chāsāh* of his eye, not mentioned explicitly but clear from the context (the parallel term *chāmal* appears in the nominal form *chumlāh*). Here, too, *chûs* is a key concept. We may well ask whether it merely refers to feelings or emotions, or whether it has not been used instead to express more concrete legal regulations, even though the actual juristic formula has not been preserved. The death sentence upon the exposed newborn child stands in contrast to the judgment of Yahweh, which vouchsafes life.[11]

The other prophetic passages do not take us beyond the limits of the interpretation sketched by Ezekiel. As in Ezk. 24:14, the formulaic idiom is abandoned in Jer. 13:14, where God speaks in the 1st person. Here *chûs* (without *ʿayin* and *ʿal*), together with the parallel terms *chāmal* and *rḥm,* conveys the idea of the pitilessness of God's judgment, which is proclaimed in vv. 12–14 (all three forms relate to the expression *mēhashchîthām*).

Just as in "juridical" regulations of Deuteronomy the execution of the sentence in its various forms is assigned to the community, so in Jer. 21:1–10 v. 7, which concerns us here, delegates the execution of God's sentence to Nebuchadrezzar. He will smite Jerusalem and king Zedekiah without pity (*lōʾ yāchûs ʿalêhem,* without *ʿayin,* but with the parallel terms already mentioned in 13:14). Yahweh himself takes responsibility for these events (v. 5, a 1st-person proclamation of a "holy war" against Yahweh's own people).

The same notion is developed in Isa. 13:18, a prophecy of disaster directed against Babylon. Yahweh delegates the punishment of Babylon to the Medes (v. 17), who, in a war without mercy, will destroy the very biological foundation of Babylon (the fruit of the womb/children) (v. 18). Here the full formula is used; *chûs* stands in parallel with *rḥm.* One may ask whether here, as in Jer. 21:7, the negated indicatives are not to be understood as prohibitions, a prescribed mercilessness that increases the severity of the judgment.

---

[11]On all the Ezekiel passages see the commentaries of Zimmerli and Fohrer.

The fact that *chûs* can be used in other than negative contexts is illustrated by such passages as Ezk. 20:17; 16:5; Jonah 4:11. It is true that only in Ezk. 20:17 do we find *chûs* without *lō';* in the other two passages only the construction (a rhetorical question in Jonah 4:11), or the specific meaning (Ezk. 16:5), makes the position clear.

Two passages can be set alongside Ezk. 20:17: Joel 2:17 and Neh. 13:22. Both derive from the realm of prayer formularies. The worshipper appeals to Yahweh using the imperative (with the cohortative suffix *-āh*) *chûsāh* + *ʿal* with suffix or object (*ʿayin* is not used). In Joel, the name Yahweh also appears (in the vocative). The context of Joel 2:17 is a cry of lament within a penitential liturgy (vv. 12-14,15-17), in which Yahweh is entreated to have mercy on his people (cf. Ps. 42:4,11[3,10]; 79:10; 115:2; Ex. 32:11f.; Dt. 9:26-29): "Have mercy, O Yahweh, upon your people!"[12]

In Neh. 13:22, "Spare me according to the greatness of thy steadfast love," the prayer for mercy appears in the context of Nehemiah's accounting, which the memoirs can be taken to be. In them Nehemiah takes responsibility for all his actions before God. The plea for mercy appears to follow set liturgical style. Even though *chûs* is not used explicitly, an analogous petition can be found in Ps. 25:6f.; 51:3(1); 69:17(16); 106:45; etc. The parallel stich to the passage with *chûs* reads *zokhrāh-lî* with vocative and object; it has direct parallels in Neh. 5:19; 13:14, 31, so that it, too, gives the impression of being a set formula. Following certain reflections by Galling, many scholars today think of these *zkr* petitions in Nehemiah as "blessing petitions" in a "founder formula."[13] Thus the stich with *chûs* may be used here secondarily to stand for this formula.

In the Joel passage, the context is still that of announced judgment and disaster, in the face of which the penitential lament hopes for revocation of the punishment—not merely leniency in execution, but total forbearance, grounded solely in Yahweh's change of heart. In Nehemiah, the association with this conceptual realm is very loose. There is much to suggest, however, that the *chûs* formula does not belong to the *zkr* petitions and that its secondary interpolation in 13:22 (it does not appear in the parallel passages) demands a special interpretation. Nehemiah adds a petition that his actions will be judged with mercy should he be accused. Calling on God to be his judge, he hopes—though there is every reason for condemnation—for mercy, for pity, for an act of favor. Accordingly, *chûs* would have served its function not only in the lament of a penitential liturgy, but also in the prayer of the accused.

III. General Usage. In comparison to the overwhelming majority of instances where *chûs* is used in a theological sense, the few passages attesting the general usage of the root are of minor importance. In Gen. 45:16-20, in the story of Joseph, Pharaoh invites the brothers and father of Joseph to come to Egypt. They are to give no thought to their goods (v. 20), for the best of all the land of Egypt will be theirs. The literal

[12]Cf. H. W. Wolff, *Joel and Amos* (trans. 1977), 51.

[13]K. Galling, "Königliche und nichtkönigliche Stifter beim Tempel von Jerusalem," *BBLAK* (=*ZDPV*), 68 (1949/51), 134-142; cf. W. Schottroff, "*Gedenken" im Alten Orient und im AT. WMANT,* 15 (^{2}1967), 218-222.

translation would be: "your eye shall not overflow (*'al tāchōs*) on account of your goods." The familiar formula is used in full, applied to inanimate objects. The meaning is this: the members of Joseph's family are not to be saddened or worried because they have to leave their possessions behind, for in Egypt they will receive something better in their place. The verb *chûs* has been reduced to the meaning "be concerned, be worried." The allusion to the more specific meaning can still be perceived.

In Jonah 4:10, the object of pity is once more inanimate, a plant (*chastā ʿal-haqqîqāyôn*); but now the verb is used in its strict sense. The argument demonstrating Yahweh's pity toward Nineveh proceeds from the lesser to the greater: if Jonah pities even a withering castor oil plant, how can Yahweh help having pity on Nineveh (vv. 10f.)!?

We come to personal references in 1 S. 24:11(10) and Ps. 72:13. In 1 S. 24:11, we read how David spared Saul although he had him in his power. This action is explained on the grounds that Saul holds the office of *māshîach*. The MT uses the expression *vattāchos ʿālekhā*, even though the context is in the first person. Presumably the word *ʿênî* has been omitted. The LXX, Targum, and Syriac sensed the difficulty and changed the reading to *vā'āchus*. The MT is of course closer to the original. About the meaning in this human context there is nothing more to be said than in the theological usage of the root. Saul's life would have been forfeit had David not restrained himself. Here, too, *chûs* means total renunciation of what one is legally empowered to do, not a mitigation of a punishment.

In the royal expectation of Ps. 72, the king's function as deliverer plays a role (v. 13: *yāchos ʿal dal*): he will have pity on the weak and needy, and save the lives (*yôshîaʿ*) of the humble. The construction of *chûs* without *ʿayin* corresponds to Ezk. 24:14 and Jer. 13:14. The meaning remains within the sphere we have been examining. The reference to the realm of law is unmistakable. Since the king's actions are considered to be authorized and brought about by God, this passage bears indirectly on the theological usage of *chûs*.

The same notion may appear in 1 S. 24:11(10). David's mercy is occasioned by the sacral nature of King Saul as *m^eshîach yhvh*. There is thus in the general usage of *chûs* nothing to record that has not already been discussed in the context of its theological usage. We merely see once more that *chûs* with its range of meanings finds employment primarily in theological contexts. The few instances of general usage are exceptions confirming this rule.

That *chûs* was originally a term in the vocabulary of law and was drafted for service in theological statements appears very probable. Certain formulaic constraints support this hypothesis. The paucity of source material, however, unfortunately makes it impossible to state the thesis with more precision.

Wagner

חוּשׁ *chûsh*; חִישׁ *chîsh*

Contents: I. 1. Occurrences; 2. Meaning; 3. The Root *ḥwš* II. II. 1. Secular Usage; 2. Theological Usage.

I. 1. *Occurrences*. The root *ḥwš* appears 22 times in the OT: once as a noun, otherwise as a verb (14 times in the qal, 7 in the hiphil). The verb appears also in the texts from Ugarit[1] and in the Dead Sea Scrolls (1QS 8:8; 1QM 1:12; 1QH 3:10; 6:29).

2. *Meaning*. The basic meaning of *chûsh* is "hasten"; → מהר *mhr* is used as a synonym (1 S. 20:38), *mhh* as an antonym (Ps. 119:60). For the hiphil, the meanings "hasten," "take flight"[2] are given. This agrees with the usage of *chûsh* at Qumran. In the Ugaritic texts, *ḥš* has the meaning "hurry, flee"; like Heb. *mhr*, it also appears as the adverb "hastily, quickly."[3] In Akkadian, a verb *ḫiāšum/ḫâšu* is also attested.[4]

3. *The Root ḥwš II*. Frequently Eccl. 2:25 is suggested as evidence for a root *chûsh* II, whose meaning, however, is disputed. *GesB* translates *chûsh* in this passage as "*geniessen,*" "enjoy." Citing Akk. *ḫâšu(m),* Ellermeier assumes a root *chûsh* II with the meaning "be worried."[5] In Isa. 28:16, Driver translates *chûsh* as "be agitated" or "be disturbed," also postulating a root *chûsh* II in Hebrew. Lindblom, on the contrary, considers the hiphil of *chûsh* merely a modification of the qal, "hasten," and translates "*wegeilen,*" "hasten away." It is difficult to determine whether there were always two different roots *chûsh* with distinct ranges of use, or whether we are dealing only with a change of meaning from describing a spatially verifiable movement to rendering inward agitation. It is worth noting, however, that the use of *chûsh* within

---

chûsh. J. Aistleitner, "Ein Opfertext aus Ugarit (No. 53)," *AcOrASH,* 5 (1955), 1-7; R. Braun, *Kohelet und die früh-hellenistische Popularphilosophie. BZAW,* 130 (1975), 110f.; G. R. Driver, "Studies in the Vocabulary of the OT, II," *JTS,* 32 (1931), 250-57; F. Ellermeier, "Das Verbum חוּשׁ in Koh 2[25]: eine exegetische, auslegungsgeschichtliche und semasiologische Untersuchung," *ZAW,* 75 (1963), 197-217; *idem,* "Das Verbum חוּשׁ von Qoh 2[25] in der Forschung," "Akkadisch *ḫâšu(m)* 'sich sorgen,'" in his *Qohelet,* I, § 2, excursus 7 ([2]1970); J. Lindblom, "Der Eckstein in Jes 28, 16," *Interpretationes ad Vetus Testamentum Pertinentes. Festschrift S. Mowinckel* (Oslo, 1955), 123-132; J. Reider, "Etymological Studies in Biblical Hebrew," *VT,* 2 (1952), 113-130; W. von Soden, "Akkadisch *ḫâšum* I 'sich sorgen' und hebräisch *ḫūš* II," *UF,* 1 (1969), 197; E. Vogt, "'Eilig tun' als adverbielles Verb und der Name des Sohnes Isaias in Is. 8, 1," *Bibl,* 48 (1967), 63-69; H. Wildberger, "'Glauben'. Erwägungen zu האמין," *Hebräische Wortforschung. Festschrift W. Baumgartner. SVT,* 16 (1967), 372-386.

[1] *WUS,* No. 1093.
[2] *GesB, KBL*[3].
[3] *CTA,* 4 [II AB], IV-V, 113-16.
[4] *AHw,* I, 343.
[5] Cf. *KBL*[3].

the OT demonstrates such a tendency, and that Aramaic and Modern Hebrew[6] use *chûsh* in the sense "reflect on, feel, take care of."

II. 1. *Secular Usage*. In the OT, *chûsh* is used to describe rapid military action of a group in Nu. 32:17 (*chāshîm* instead of the passive participle?) and Jgs. 20:37. Hab. 1:8 depicts the advance of the Assyrian armies with the simile: "They fly as eagles hasten to their prey." In Isa. 8:1,3, Isaiah gives his son the name *mahēr shālāl chāsh baz* to say that the might of Damascus and Samaria symbolized by this name is on the verge of conquering and plundering (→ בזז *bzz*).

A single individual is involved in 1 S. 20:38, where Jonathan calls on his servant to make haste (*m^e hērāh chûshāh*) and not stand still, to gather up the arrows he has shot. Job 31:5 also speaks of the rapid movement of an individual, but here the event is not to be taken absolutely in a spatial sense. This is even clearer in Job 20:2: *chûshî* describes the inward state of Job's friend Zophar, who is protesting against Job's charges.[7]

Thus we arrive at a further realm of usage of *chûsh:* it comprehends not only observable spatial movement but also the inward stirring and agitation of a person. This makes it possible for the word to be used in religious language as well as secular. This is also illustrated by Ps. 90:10, where the noun *chîsh,* derived from *chûsh,* is used adverbially; for the general statement that the years of a man's life pass "hastily"[8] has theological relevance in this context.

2. *Theological Usage*. In any case, we are dealing with a specifically theological use of *chûsh* in the following psalms, in which Yahweh is the subject of the verb *chûsh*. Yahweh is called on to hasten to the aid of the worshipper: *l^eʿezrāthî chûshāh* (Ps. 22:20 [Eng. v. 19]; 40:14[13]; 70:2[1]; 71:12) or *chûshāh l^eʿezrāthî* (Ps. 38:23[22]; similarly 70:6[5], after which 40:18[17] should be corrected, and 141:1). It is noteworthy that the synonymous root *mhr* (cf. 1 S. 20:38) is never used in this idiom. The use of *chûsh* in the worshipper's plea for help must have been a fixed usage when these psalms were composed. It is probably of great antiquity, since in the Ras Shamra texts we find the same idiom in a petition to El:[9] "El, hasten! El, come quickly (*3l ḥš 3l ndd*) to the aid of *Ṣpn-s,* to the aid of Ugarit, with your lance, O El, with your raised lance, O El!"

Besides this fixed formula, we also find Yahweh or his deeds associated with the root *chûsh* as subject. Yahweh's promises of salvation for Jerusalem conclude with the words: "I am Yahweh, in its time I will hasten it" (Isa. 60:22). Dt. 32:35 speaks of Yahweh's judgment approaching his people: "For the day of their calamity is at hand, and their doom hastens." Isa. 5:19 describes the mockery of Isaiah's contemporaries,

---

[6] *WTM,* II, 27.

[7] *BDB:* "my inner excitement"; K. Budde, *GHK,* II/1 (²1913), 110: "mein Ungestüm," "my turbulence."

[8] See the commentaries.

[9] *CTA,* 30, 9ff.

who provocatively call for Yahweh's act of judgment: " 'Let him make haste, let him speed his work that we may see it. . . .' "

As suggested above,[10] the use of *chûsh* to describe inward agitation lends it theological relevance. This is clear when Job swears his innocence before Yahweh (Job 31:5) or in the confession of Ps. 119:60. The attitude of the faithful believer is described in Isa. 28:16: "He who believes will not be in haste." Here, as in Ps. 55:9(8), *chûsh* refers less to literal flight than to inward agitation.

Beyse

חוֹתָם *chôthām* → חתם *ḥtm*

---

[10]II.1.

חָזָה *chāzāh;* חֹזֶה *chōzeh;* חָזוֹן *chāzôn;* חֲזוֹת *ch^a zôth;* חָזוּת *chāzûth;* חִזָּיוֹן *chizzāyôn;* מַחֲזֶה *mach^a zeh;* מֶחֱזָה *mech^e zāh*

Contents: I. Distribution. II. 1. Statistics; 2. *Sitz im Leben*. III. *ḥzh* as a Technical Term for a Nabi's Revelation: 1. What Is Received? 2. How Was the Word of God Received? IV. Origin. V. History: Acceptance and Criticism. VI. Extended Use: 1. Seeing God; 2. Inspecting; 3. Individual Passages. VII. Summary and Evaluation.

I. Distribution. As starting-point for the history of the root *chāzāh* and its derivatives in Hebrew we must first of all observe that we are dealing with an Aramaic loanword.[1]

---

chāzāh. W. W. Graf Baudissin, " 'Gott schauen' in der alttestamentlichen Religion," *ARW,* 18 (1915), 173-239, esp. 185ff. (repr. in the work by Nötscher cited below, 195-261, esp. 207ff.); J. Blau, "הערות לאוצר המלים שבמקרא," *Sefer Yosef Braslavi* (Jerusalem, 1971), 439-443; K. Budde, "Amos I2," *ZAW,* 30 (1910), 40; M. Dahood, "Ugaritic-Hebrew Lexicography, II," *Bibl,* 45 (1964), 407f.; R. Degen, *Altaramäische Grammatik der Inschriften des 10. bis 8. Jh. v. Chr. AKM,* 38/3 (1969), esp. 77f.; J. H. Eaton, "Some Misunderstood Hebrew Words for God's Self-Revelation," *BT,* 25 (1974), 331-38; H. L. Ginsberg, "Lexicographical Notes," *Hebräische Wortforschung. Festschrift W. Baumgartner.*
continued on p. 281

[1]F. Altheim and R. Stiehl, *Die aramäische Sprache unter den Achaimeniden,* I/3 (1963), 270; *KBL*², 1074, Sup. 201; Wagner, Nos. 93-98; denied by Ginsberg, 71f.; Dahood, 407f.; with caution *KBL*³, 228; Blau, 440, undecided.

The root can hardly be attested with certainty in other Semitic languages; cf., however, Egyp. *ḥs3*, "look wildly,"[2] Arab. *ḥazā*, "prophesy as an augur," *ḥāzin*, "seer,"[3] and Tigré *ḥaza*, cf. Amhar. *ayyä*.[4] For Phoenician, two occurrences in the Kilamuwa Inscription[5] may be cited; but this inscription is one of the Zenjirli inscriptions, which exhibit unmistakable Aramaic influence. Kilamuwa himself provides the aramaism *bar;* should he not be capable of another? In any case, this single passage hardly suffices to show the presence of this root in Phoenician. The rare occurrence of *ḥd(w)* in Ugaritic is likewise insufficient to demonstrate a further extension of the root *chāzāh* in Semitic. For the present, it is hard to decide with certainty whether we are dealing with the same word,[6] with a word corresponding to Arab. *ḥaḏa*, "guard," or *ḥaḏā*, "sit opposite,"[7] or with another root entirely. However the case may be, even an actual occurrence in Ugaritic would not prove that the word was also found in ancient Hebrew.[8] Brockelmann's observations[9] do more to conceal the problem than to solve it. Even aside from the problem of hybrid language, there remains the question of why Hebrew should have alongside → ראה *rā'āh* a second word largely similar in meaning, and that not just in poetry.

The root *ḥzh* is the usual word for "see" in the various dialects of Aramaic. It has a

---

SVT, 16 (1967), 71-82, esp. 71f.; J. Hänel, *Das Erkennen Gottes bei den Schriftpropheten. BWANT*, 2/4 (1923), esp. 7ff., 105ff.; F. Häussermann, *Wortempfang und Symbol in der alttestamentlichen Prophetie. BZAW*, 58 (1932), esp. 5ff.; R. Hentschke, *Die Stellung der vorexilischen Schriftpropheten zum Kultus. BZAW*, 75 (1957), esp. 150-172; G. Hölscher, *Die Profeten* (1914), esp. 83ff.; A. Jepsen, *Nabi* (1934), esp. 43ff.; A. R. Johnson, *The Cultic Prophet in Ancient Israel* (²1962); H. Junker, *Prophet und Seher in Israel* (1927); W. Käser, "Beobachtungen zum alttestamentlichen Makarismus," *ZAW*, 82 (1970), 225-250, esp. 244f.; R. Knierim, "Offenbarung im AT," *Probleme biblischer Theologie. Festschrift G. von Rad* (1971), 206-235; E. König, *Der Offenbarungsbegriff des ATs* (1882), esp. II, 29ff.; E. Kutsch, *Verheissung und Gesetz. BZAW*, 131 (1973), esp. 34-38; J. Lindblom, *Prophecy in Ancient Israel* (1962), esp. 89ff.; W. Michaelis, "ὁράω," *TDNT*, V, 315-382, esp. 324-334; S. Mowinckel, *Psalmenstudien* (Amsterdam, ²1966), esp. III, 9ff.; F. Nötscher, *"Das Angesicht Gottes schauen" nach biblischer und babylonischer Auffassung* (1924, ²1969); C. von Orelli, "Prophetentum des ATs," *RE*³, XVI (1905), 81-105, with bibliography of earlier literature; H. M. Orlinsky, "The Seer in Ancient Israel," *OrAnt*, 4 (1965), 153-174; M. A. van den Oudenrijn, "De vocabulis quibusdam, termino נָבִיא synonymis," *Bibl*, 6 (1925), 294-311; O. Plöger, "Priester und Prophet," *ZAW*, 63 (1951), 165ff.; J. F. A. Sawyer, *Semantics in Biblical Research. SBT*, N.S. 24 (1972); E. Schütz, *Formgeschichte des vorklassischen Prophetenspruchs* (diss., Bonn, 1958); E. Sellin, *Der alttestamentliche Prophetismus: Drei Studien* (1912), esp. 243f.; D. Vetter, "חזה *ḥzh* schauen," *THAT*, I, 533-37; *idem, Seherspruch und Segensschilderung. CThM*, A/4 (1974); M. Wagner, *Die lexikalischen und grammatikalischen Aramaismen im alttestamentlichen Hebräisch. BZAW*, 96 (1966), Nos. 93-98.

[2] F. Behnk, "Lexikalische Beiträge zur ägyptisch-semitischen Sprachvergleichung," *ZÄS*, 62 (1926), 80-83; cf. *WbÄS*, III, 11.

[3] *CML*, 138, n. 18; Degen, 59; *KBL*³, 288.

[4] Leslau, *Contributions*, 20; *idem, Hebrew Cognates in Amharic* (1969), 32.

[5] *KAI*, 24.11-12.

[6] Dahood, 407f.; Ginsberg, 72; Degen, 59 consider it possible.

[7] Cf. *WUS*, No. 905.

[8] Contra Wagner, 54.

[9] C. Brockelmann, "Das Hebräische," *HO*, I/III (Leiden, 1964), 61.

wide range of meanings, referring both to the natural vision of the eyes and to supernatural visions of various kinds. Heb. *rā'āh* occupies an analogous position; it, too, is used for vision in general as well as for unusual experiences, as, for instance, at the beginning of Isaiah's vision: *vā'er'eh 'eth-'adhōnî*. This holds true also for the root's derivatives such as *mar'eh* and *rō'eh*.

If Hebrew could use *rā'āh* for all kinds of sight and vision, the word *chāzāh* appearing alongside it must be considered an Aramaic loanword.[10] The question is then: what led to the introduction of this loanword and with what meaning was it used?

II. 1. *Statistics*. Besides 45 occurrences in Aramaic and various proper names, the concordance lists 129 occurrences of *chāzāh* and its derivatives: *chāzāh,* 55; *chōzeh,* 17; *chāzôn,* 35; *chazôth,* 1; *chāzûth,* 5; *chizzāyôn,* 9; *machazeh,* 4; and *mechezāh,* 3. In 5 passages (Job 8:17; 34:32; Dnl. 8:8; probably also Isa. 28:15,18), the text is so uncertain that it is impossible to use them for the meaning of the root and its history. The noun *mechezāh* has a specialized meaning, "something to see through," i.e., "window."

In 6 passages the verb and noun are associated so closely that they must be counted together: Isa. 1:1; Nu. 24:4,16; Ezk. 12:27; 13:7,16. We are left, then, with 115 passages in which the root is attested: 9 in the historical books, 10 in the Psalms, 4 in Proverbs, 11 in Job, 2 in Song of Songs, 3 in Lamentations, 19 in Isaiah, 14 in Ezekiel, 17 in other prophets, 13 in Daniel, and 13 in Chronicles. We may note that the prophetic books with 63 passages have the major share; in addition, 7 passages from the historical books, the 3 from Lamentations, and the 13 from Chronicles all deal with prophecy. By far the largest number of passages, at least 86 out of 115, are associated with prophecy. Why this particular association?

2. *Sitz im Leben*. An initial answer comes from the observation that the derivatives of the root frequently are associated with *nābhî'*. Lam. 2:9, for example, states that Zion's nabis obtain no *chāzôn* from Yahweh; 2:14 twice ascribes a deceptive *chāzāh* to the nabis. In Mic. 3:6, they are threatened with a night without *chāzôn;* Jer. 14:14 accuses them of prophesying *chazôn sheqer,* and a similar accusation appears in Jer. 23:16. According to Ezk. 7:26, the people seek *chāzôn* from the nabi; according to 13:6-9, *chāzāh* and *machazeh* form part of the nabis' activity (cf. also 13:16, 23; 22:28). In Hab. 1:1, the nabi Habakkuk is the subject of the verb *chāzāh,* and in Zec. 13:4 the nabis have a *chizzāyôn*. According to 2 S. 7:15 (1 Ch. 17:15), the nabi Nathan received a *chizzāyôn;* 2 Ch. 32:32 speaks of the *chāzôn* of the prophet Isaiah. In 17 passages, then, derivatives of the root are associated with the activity of nabis. In addition, we may observe that *chōzeh* and *chāzôn* also appear in parallelism or association with *nābhî'*. In Am. 7:12, for example, the prophet is first addressed as *chōzeh* and then as *nābî'*. In Hos. 12:11 (Eng. v. 10), *chāzôn* stands in parallelism with *nebhî'îm*. The two words *nebhî'îm* and *chōzîm* appear in parallel in Isa. 29:10; Mic. 3:6f., and are juxtaposed in 2 S. 24:11; 2 K. 17:13. On the basis of this evidence, we may ask whether a connection with nabis and their activity should not be assumed in other passages as well.

---

[10]This point is also made by Wagner, 54, although his historical sequence is not totally clear.

III. ḥzh as a Technical Term for a Nabi's Revelation. What is meant when *chāzāh, chāzôn,* or *chizzāyôn* is used in connection with a nabi?

1. *What Is Received?* The answer is unambiguous: not a visual image but a word from God. In Gen. 15:1, God's word comes to Abram in a *machªzeh*. According to 1 S. 3:1, the word of God was rare, there was no *chāzôn*. In a *chizzāyôn* Nathan receives his commission from Yahweh, his words (2 S. 7:4,17). According to Ps. 89:20(19), God spoke in a *chāzôn*; a *chāzôn* is thus an event in which words are received. In *chezyônôth* of the night Eliphaz receives the words that his ear perceives from God (Job 4:13; similarly 33:14–16). In Hos. 12:11(10), *chāzôn* is the means through which God speaks to the nabis. Cf. also Jer. 14:14; 23:16; Ezk. 12:23; also the (secondary) superscription Isa. 2:1, in which *dābhār* is the object of *chāzāh;* and Ob. 1, where God's words follow.

In many passages, the word that the nabi "sees" is called *maśśā'* (e.g., Lam. 2:14; Nah. 1:1; Hab. 1:1). In these cases, *maśśā'*, whatever its etymology, is "a technical term for a prophetic oracle of a particular kind,"[11] i.e., a threat that the nabi has "seen" against foreign nations.[12] This usage can hardly be traced back to Isaiah or his disciples; it should probably be assigned to the same redactors that ascribed *chāzāh* and *chāzôn* to the "nabi" Isaiah and gave the name *maśśā'* to the threats against the nations incorporated into his book.

2. *How Was the Word of God Received?* The paucity of evidence makes this question difficult to answer. It is at least possible to say that *chāzôn,* etc., were clearly distinguished from dreams. It is true that *chāzôn* is used a few times in combination or in parallel with *chªlôm* (→ חלם *chālam*) (Isa. 29:7; Job 20:8; 7:14; 33:15; Zec. 10:2; Joel 3:1[2:28]), but a theophany or visual image to be interpreted is never mentioned in connection with *chāzôn*. Undoubtedly such a "perception" usually takes place at night; this is suggested by Mic. 3:6; 2 S. 7:4,17, as well as Gen. 15:1 and 1 S. 3, if the context can be understood to mean that Samuel receives a *chāzôn,* a nocturnal experience of the divine word. Cf. also Job 4:13; 33:15; 20:8. The essential element is therefore a noctural audition, albeit under special circumstances. The most vivid description of such an event is probably that in the speech of Eliphaz (Job 4:12–16). The revelation of a word is involved, but under mysterious circumstances: trembling and dream come upon him while he is sound asleep, he feels a hand, he sees something that he cannot recognize, and in the silence he hears a voice. (The key word *tardēmāh* appears a few other times in similar contexts: Job 33:15; Isa. 29:10; and probably also Gen. 15:12: "deep sleep" is the time of divine revelation.) One may ask whether a late description taken from a wisdom book may be utilized for an understanding of the earlier nabis. But the passage agrees that *chāzôn* takes place at night, that it is distinct from dreaming, and that the revelation of a word is involved.

Finally, what is probably the earliest passage where *chāzāh* and *machªzeh* appear in

---

[11]M. Saebø, *Sacharja 9-14. WMANT,* 34 (1969), 139.

[12]For a more detailed classification, see B. B. Margulis, *Studies in the Oracles against the Nations* (diss., Brandeis, 1967).

Israelite literature, Nu. 24:3f.,14f., appears to point in the same direction; here, too, we are dealing with revelation of the divine word under mysterious circumstances.[13]

Thus for *chāzāh,* etc., in the context of the nabis, we may conclude that it refers to a revelation of the divine word, usually at night during a (deep) sleep and sometimes associated with emotional agitation. Visual manifestation, however, plays no role, or at most a minor one.[14] This understanding of *chāzāh* in relationship to the nabis' experience is probably in better agreement with the tradition than the attempt to distinguish *chāzāh* from *rā'āh* as meaning "the internal appropriation of what is seen."[15]

IV. Origin. König was probably the first to raise the question of how this revelation is to be evaluated. He observed correctly that *chāzāh* and its derivatives are primarily associated with the nabis, but then felt justified in concluding from the fact that the literary prophets do not use the term for their own experiences that *chāzāh* is used to designate a false "vision," in contrast to the real seeing of a transcendent reality on the part of the literary prophets, termed *rā'āh*. In this extreme form, which is connected with König's attempt to demonstrate the concrete reality of prophetic revelation, his interpretation has been generally rejected.[16] Apart from König's theological presuppositions, which might still be a matter of debate, this thesis is contradicted by the fact that *chāzāh* and its derivatives are often used in the positive sense of a Yahweh revelation, as in Gen. 15:1; Nu. 24:4,16; 2 S. 7:17; Hos. 12:11(10). But the observation itself is undoubtedly correct; what is dubious is how it should be evaluated.

There is also the further observation that, while *chāzāh,* etc., appear as a function of the nabis, *chōzeh* and *chōzîm* are found alongside the *nᵉbhî'îm*. To put the problem in different terms: was there a particular class of *chōzîm,* or is *chōzeh* only another term for *nābhî'*, intended to bring out the unique mode of revelation of the nabis? It is hard to give an answer because there are few very relevant passages for the early period. There is no unambiguous evidence for either the nabis or the "seers." The missing evidence cannot be replaced by the suggestion that there must have been seers at an early date in Israel because they are found throughout the ancient Near East. The ways of seeing the future were quite varied, and although it is probably safe to assume that such a phenomenon was known in Israel, this does not indicate its nature or whether it corresponded to what was suggested by *chāzāh*.

A few observations may be combined with great caution:

a) The word *chāzāh* is Aramaic; if it was borrowed into Hebrew, there must have been a special reason.

---

[13]Cf. Vetter, *Seherspruch,* 32f.; Johnson, 12, n. 2; similar approach: Jepsen, 48f.; H. Wildberger, *BK,* X (1965), 5.

[14]But cf. H. W. Wolff, *Joel and Amos* (trans. 1977), 310f.

[15]Baudissin, 217.

[16]Cf., e.g., Sellin, 244f.; Hänel, 7ff.

b) In Aramaic, there is at least one occurrence of *ḥzyn* in the sense "interpreter of the future."[17]

c) The first figure in OT tradition to whom *chāzāh, machᵃzeh* are ascribed is the Aramean Balaam.[18]

d) For the period of Samuel, we are told that there was no *chāzôn;* in other words, the revelation to Samuel is probably represented as the first example of such a revelation in Israel.

These observations would yield the following historical picture: In the Aramaic area there were *ḥzyn;* the hypothesis that their mode of revelation corresponded to that of the later *chōzîm* in Israel is possible, but is still conjecture. It is supported to the extent that the Aramean Balaam speaks of receiving the word in terms corresponding to those used later.

The description of how revelation was received is unfortunately not wholly unambiguous. It is clear that we are dealing with the hearing of divine words and a perception of what the "Almighty" causes to be perceived. The eyes are somehow involved; whether open or shut is debated. In any case, something is also unveiled to the ears. The words of Balaam are thus undoubtedly to be understood as depicting his reception of the word, which is associated with mysterious perceptions. The term "ecstasy" is hardly appropriate here.[19]

One could then assume that in the premonarchic period (Samuel), at about the same time the ecstatic prophecy of the nabis was borrowed from the Canaanite realm, the practices of the "seers" were borrowed from the Arameans. At least from the time of David onward the two phenomena were intimately associated: *chāzāh* and *chāzôn* became a means of receiving a revelation among the nabis. The Aramaic word was retained because it was a technical term for a particular noctural experience of the divine word, distinct from dreams.

These assumptions would help explain why *chāzāh* is used so often of the nabis, whereas they themselves can be called *chōzîm*. It is most unlikely that during the monarchy there was a class of *chōzîm* distinct from the *nᵉbîʾîm*.

V. History: Acceptance and Criticism. It may be an accurate reminiscence when 1 S. 3:1 states that in the early period of Samuel there was no *chāzôn* and therefore no word of God. What is granted to Samuel is such a *chāzôn;* he is summoned during the night and receives a message from God. This, however, makes him a nabi (v. 20).[20] It appears therefore that in this period, when the tribes of Israel borrowed so much from their neighbors, the nabis also adopted the "method" of

---

[17] *KAI,* 202A.12.

[18] On the origins of this section, see M. Noth, *Numbers. OTL* (trans. 1968), 172; W. Gross, *Bileam. StANT,* 38 (1974), 96ff.; the significance of Balaam for the understanding of "seers" has also been pointed out by Junker, 79ff., Lindblom, 90ff., and others; most recently, G. W. Coats, "Balaam: Sinner or Saint?" *BiblRes,* 18 (1973), 21-29; Gross, 274ff.

[19] Contra Noth, *in loc.*

[20] Now also H. J. Stoebe, *KAT,* VIII/1 (1973), 120ff.: the call of Samuel to be a prophet.

chāzôn as a means of revelation. In like manner, the absence of *chāzôn,* i.e., the absence of divine revelation, is later interpreted as the ruin of the people (Prov. 29:18).

It is therefore also appropriate for a *chizzāyôn,* a nocturnal word from God, to be ascribed to the nabi Nathan (2 S. 7:4,17). It is possible that 2 S. 24:11, where the nabi Gad is called *chōzēh dhāvīdh,* also points in the same direction.

It would hardly be advisable, however, to deduce too much from this mention of the *chōzēh dhāvīdh*—to see in it, for instance, a court title of the Davidic period. It is possible that these words represent a secondary addition from Chronicles, specifically 1 Ch. 21:9. The Chronicler changed the text of 2 S. 24:11b slightly, calling Gad a *chōzeh,* as he does also in 1 Ch. 29:29; 2 Ch. 29:25. It is therefore dubious whether *chōzeh* can really be considered a "solemn term of address for extraordinary charismatics," as Wolff assumes in the context of Am. 7:14.

Gen. 15:1 may also belong to the preprophetic period; if God's word (during the night [v. 5]?) comes to Abram in a *mach^{a}zeh,* he may be represented as a nabi both here and in chap. 20. And in fact chap. 15 is usually thought to belong in part to the same stratum of tradition as chap. 20.

Occurrences of the term in the literary prophets also exhibit this outward association with the nabis. A positive evaluation of the nabis is often involved.

In Hos. 12:11(10), a *chāzôn* is traced back to Yahweh, clearly as an event through which he himself spoke to the nabis. In Isa. 30:10, too, the *chōzîm* and *rō'îm* are taken seriously; the rebellious people are accused of refusing to hear the truth proclaimed by the seers and prophets (*chōzîm*) on the basis of what they see. Hab. 1:1 speaks of the oracle which Habakkuk the nabi "saw," i.e., perceived or heard as divine revelation; and according to 2:2f. he is to write down the *chāzôn,* the divine oracle he has received, for it awaits its time, which is surely coming. Also positive is the evaluation of *chāzôn* in Ps. 89:20(19), where again God himself speaks in a *chāzôn* to his "faithful ones,"[21] and of *chāzûth* in Isa. 21:2, where the speaker appeals for his words to a *chāzûth qāshāh* that has been told him.

It is therefore not surprising that the retrospective statement in 2 K. 17:13 says that Yahweh spoke in Israel and Judah *b^{e}yadh kol-nābhî' v^{e}kol-chōzeh,* and it is expected for the future that the young men will receive revelation by seeing a *chāzôn*. A *chāzôn* is therefore an event through which Yahweh speaks to a nabi, who therefore is also called *chōzeh*.

The evaluation of *chōzeh* in the case of Amos is not totally clear. When addressed as *chōzeh,* he responds with *lō'-nābhî' 'ānōkhî* (Am. 7:14). For him, then, the two are the same. Why Amaziah choses the term *chōzeh* to address him is unclear; was it really intended to show respect to the one addressed? But fundamental criticism of the institution of the nabis is probably not intended. What Amos wishes to emphasize is that he does not belong to this circle. Wolff's commentary[22] contains the most recent discussion of the question whether *lō'-nābhî'* is to be translated as a present or preterite; he decides—correctly, in my opinion—in favor of a present interpretation.

---

[21]Cf. the commentaries.

[22]*Joel and Amos,* 312f.

In other contexts, of course, criticism of the nabis also casts doubts on their "visions." An example is Isa. 29:10f. The text is difficult; *hachōzîm* and *hann^e^bhî'îm* are usually taken as epithets for eyes and heads. But were the "prophets" really to be looked upon as such? Some eliminate both words as a gloss. In that case, however, the passage would speak of revelations to the people, to whom "visions" are never ascribed elsewhere. The sense becomes clear if (with *'ēth* removed) *hann^e^bhî'îm* and *hachōzîm* are taken as vocatives, despite Quell's objection that a vocative is syntactically impossible (cf. Prov. 8:4; also Isa. 40:9; Hos. 13:4; Eccl. 10:17). Then the nabis are addressed, who are to be drunk without wine: "For Yahweh has poured out upon you a spirit of deep sleep, and has closed your eyes, you *n^e^bhî'îm,* and covered your heads, you *chōzîm.* Thus the vision of all this has become to you like the words of a book that is sealed." The point is therefore that the nabis with their message are represented as having been blinded by Yahweh.

In Mic. 3:5-8, an oracle against the nabis, Micah accuses them of corruption; as punishment, they shall receive neither *chāzôn* nor *qesem.* Thus they will cease to be *chōzîm* and *qōs^e^mîm,* and will be disgraced; for only so could they proclaim words of God.

Even sharper is Jeremiah's criticism of the nabis (14:14; 23:16): they offer lying "visions," visions that come from their own hearts and not from God. This is connected with the lament in Lam. 2:9,14 that the nabis receive no "vision" from Yahweh, which is the basis of their very existence, but instead see false and deceptive visions.

In Ezekiel, God himself charges the "prophets" and "prophetesses" with having "seen" falsehood and lies, with having seen peace where there is no peace: 13:6-9, 16,23. The same idea appears in the oracle against Ammon (21:34[29]) and in 23:28. It is understandable, therefore, that the people should despair of any "vision" and rejected even the vision of Ezekiel (12:22,27). But God acknowledges every true vision and word (12:23,28), whereas false visions will not endure.

One senses clearly how the problem of prophecy makes its appearance in these critical passages, just as in Jer. 28 and Dt. 19: how can true vision be recognized and distinguished from false? Also critical of vision, finally, are Zec. 10:2; 13:4.

On the other side, *nabhî'* and *chōzeh/chāzôn* are felt to be so closely associated that the redactors frequently ascribe a *chāzāh* or *chāzôn* to the literary prophets as the means by which the word is revealed to them, although the prophets themselves do not appeal to it. This is true in the relative clauses Isa. 1:1; 13:1; Am. 1:1; Mic. 1:1, all of which are probably the work of the redactors.[23] The object of the *chāzāh* or *chāzôn* is usually a *dābhār* or *maśśā',* which is thus "seen." In the case of Nahum and Obadiah, there is some doubt whether the use of *chāzôn* characterizes them as nabis; it is certainly possible, however. In Isa. 1:1, *chāzôn* refers simply to the receiving of the word. Isa. 2:1 is probably a later superscription to 2:2-4, tracing this message back to Isaiah.

---

[23]Cf. I. Willi-Plein, *Vorformen der Schriftexegese innerhalb des ATs. BZAW,* 123 (1971), 15, 70; T. Lescow, "Redaktionsgeschichtliche Analyse von Micha 1-5," *ZAW,* 84 (1972), 46-85, esp. 61-64.

In line with this later usage, Chronicles also uses *chōzeh* and *chōzîm* in parallel with *nābhî'* and *rō'eh*. Thus the *chōzîm* Gad and Iddo are mentioned as sources (1 Ch. 29:29; 2 Ch. 9:29; 12:15). Gad, Heman, Asaph, and Jeduthun are called *chōzeh hammelekh* (1 Ch. 21:9; 25:5; 2 Ch. 29:25,30; 35:15). Jehu ben Hanani is a *chōzeh* (2 Ch. 19:2), and the *chōzîm* speak to Manasseh in the name of Yahweh. A "vision" is mentioned in connection with the prophets Nathan (1 Ch. 17:15) and Isaiah (2 Ch. 32:32). Thus *chōzeh* becomes a term for someone called by Yahweh to speak, without any particular emphasis on the originally observable mode of revelation.

An echo of this usage appears in several passages in the book of Daniel. In the Aramaic chapters (2–6), *chᵃzāh* has only the usual Amaraic sense of "see." This is obviously true in chaps. 3 (vv. 19,25,27) and 5 (vv. 5,23). But in chaps. 2 and 4, too, *chᵃzāh*, "see," refers only to the images seen in the dream (2:26; 4:2[5], 23[26], as in 2:31,34,41,43,45; 4:2(5),6(9),7(10),10(13),15(18),17(20),20(23). When 2:28; 4:2(5), 6(9),7(10),10(13) speak of *chezvê rê'sh,* these "visions" are so intimately associated with the dream images that they cannot be separated from them. (We ignore the question of how well the text has been preserved in these passages.) Only in 2:19 do we hear echoes of the old association with the nabis. The subject is Daniel's experience of the mystery: "Then the mystery was revealed to Daniel in a vision of the night." God speaks to Daniel during the night as he once spoke to Nathan.

Chap. 7 occupies a special position. V. 1 speaks of a dream Daniel had, which he wrote down. But the text that follows speaks only of *chezvê lêlyā'* (vv. 2,7,13) or *chezvê rê'sh* (v. 15), so that the intent is probably to suggest a noctural revelation from God. The images beheld, however, are so reminiscent of dream images in their clarity that the introductory statement in v. 1 is understandable. In any case, this style of expression is intended to make Daniel resemble the prophets of an earlier age. He is more than a wise man who can understand and interpret dreams with God's help (2:19); he himself receives "visions" that illuminate the future.

This notion is also taken up in the Hebrew section of the book of Daniel. In chap. 8, a *chāzôn* appears to Daniel, a clear image, which is called a *mar'eh* in v. 16. In chap. 10, too, the *mar'eh* described in vv. 5ff. is called a *chāzôn* in v. 14. The special associations of *chāzôn* seem to have vanished almost totally in the later period.

VI. Extended Use. The verb *chāzāh* together with its derivatives is thus predominantly a technical term for a specific type of divine revelation to the nabis. Its use in other contexts is comparatively rare.

1. *Seeing God.* Closest to prophetic vision are probably the passages that speak in some sense of "seeing God," i.e., a theophany. An example is Ex. 24:11, where the elders of Israel "behold God."[24] Several passages in the Psalms speak of "beholding" God in a special way: 63:3(2) ("thee"); 17:15 ("thy face"); 11:7 ("his face");

[24]For an explanation of the incident, see T. C. Vriezen, "The Exegesis of Exodus XXIV, 9–11," *OTS,* 17 (1972), 100–133; E. W. Nicholson, "The Interpretation of Exodus XXIV, 9–11," *VT,* 24 (1974), 77–97; *idem,* "The Antiquity of the Tradition in Exodus XXIV, 9–11," *VT,* 25 (1975), 69–79.

27:4 ("the beauty of Yahweh"); 46:9(8) ("the works of Yahweh"). It is probably intentional, therefore, when Job is made to wish (Job 19:26f.) that he may "see God," an expression which should probably be understood as meaning a hoped-for theophany.[25] Job 36:35 likewise speaks of beholding God's works; cf. v. 24 (as in Isa. 48:6, if the text is correct[26]).

Some kind of reference to God is involved in Job 23:9; 24:1; Isa. 26:11 (where the text is very difficult; in any case, it is God's lifted hand that is seen or not seen); and Job 27:12, where God's power is seen. In Isa. 33:17, "the king" may also refer to God.[27]

Of course the Hebrew verb *rā'āh* is also used to express the notion of seeing God; but it can hardly be accidental that in the late period the verb *chāzāh,* known from Aramaic, was introduced in passages dealing with a special vision of God similar to that of the nabis.

2. *Inspecting.* Other overtones of *chāzāh* can be detected in the two Psalms passages where the word is used with Yahweh himself as subject: Ps. 11:4, "His eyes behold, his eyelids test, the children of men"; Ps. 17:2, "Let thy eyes see the right, if thou triest my heart." In each case, God's seeing—expressed in terms of his eyes—involves testing: God "sees through" men, knowing what is within them. This sense of "seeing through" also appears in Ex. 18:21, where Jethro advises Moses: "Choose (*'attāh thech^e^zeh*) able men from all the people." The process of selection includes a searching inspection of the heart. Such inspection is probably meant in Prov. 22:29 and 29:20, where someone is seen to be "skillful" or "hasty in his words," as well as in 24:32, where the "seeing" probably involves "testing." In Cant. 7:1 (8:13), the use of *chāzāh* could be explained as meaning such a "close observation" by the dancing Shulammite. The same overtones would explain Isa. 47:13: the work of those who "gaze at stars" is just such "inspection." Eliphaz, too, means to declare the results of his "inspection" (Job 15:17).

3. *Individual Passages.* In the few remaining passages, mostly from the later period, *chāzāh* can hardly be distinguished from *rā'āh:* Ps. 58:9(8); cf. Eccl. 7:1; 58:11(10); cf. Jer. 20:12; Mic. 4:11; Isa. 33:20. The choice of *chāzāh* in Isa. 57:8 may be connected with the object (*yādh* = phallus?). In connection with *ch^a^lôm, ch^a^zôn lailāh* is a sign of perishableness (Isa. 29:7; Job 20:8). The same parallelism is used in Job 7:14 for the period of terror brought by God. In Isa. 28:15,18, *chāzah* and *chāzûth* are used in parallelism with *b^e^rîth.* Whether they have here a special meaning, something like "agreement,"[28] or the text is corrupt is disputed. In any case, these verses have no bearing on the meaning and usage of the root in general. The reason for calling a valley *gê' chizzāyôn,* "valley of vision," in Isa 22:5 can be conjectured but not explained.

---

[25]Cf. now G. Fohrer, *KAT,* XVI (1963), 322.

[26]*BHS;* cf., however, C. Westermann, *Isaiah 40-66. OTL* (1969), 194, who reads *hazzō'th.*

[27]Cf. O. Procksch, *KAT,* IX/1 (1930), *in loc.*

[28]Cf. Kutsch, 34-39.

VII. Summary and Evaluation. While the Heb. *rā'āh* has a wide range of meanings, beginning with the natural sight of the eyes, the usage of *chāzāh,* a borrowing from Aramaic, is sharply restricted. Its primary meaning is a form of revelation (borrowed from the Arameans?), consisting in noctural perception of a divine voice during a deep sleep. This type of revelation was adopted by the nabis of Israel and was looked upon well into the late period as a characteristic of the prophets, with the result that even the words of the literary prophets were traced back to an instance of *chāzāh,* although the prophets themselves never appealed to such a *chāzôn*. The verb was also used in the sense of perceiving God and his works, undoubtedly from the realization that in the prophetic experience the word refers to a kind of perception, i.e., hearing God. A third meaning of *chāzāh* is an inspection that "sees through" men, something more than outward observation. Only rarely is seeing with the eyes meant. It is also rare for the meaning to be determined through use in parallel with *rā'āh*.

How are we now to understand the reality designated by *chāzāh?* We might attempt to interpret it on the basis of modern psychological discoveries, as do Hölscher, Ehrlich, and others. But the question always remains whether what we observe today corresponds to what was experienced then. It might be more appropriate to cite by way of comparison certain experiences of modern medicine men among so-called "primitive" peoples.[29]

It is more important to note that *chāzāh,* etc., refers to a special type of divine revelation, probably during the night but distinct from a dream. In any case, it is assumed that the God of Israel makes use of this method to reveal his word, just as he uses dreams and Urim (1 S. 28:6). Above all, the word of God was revealed to the nabis through *chāzôn*.

But *chāzāh* also shares in the crisis of the nabis. When their function becomes involved in specific political developments, they are exposed to the danger that they will claim a *chāzôn* in support of a divine word in line with the hopes of the populace and thus declare "the imagination of their own heart," i.e., a "lie."

But this very criticism of the nabis in the period from Isaiah to Ezekiel makes it clear that *chāzāh* and its derivatives should actually be reserved for a genuine encounter with God and his word: speak, Lord, for your servant hears.

Jepsen

[29]Cf., e.g., the references in Lindblom, 83ff.

חֲזִיר *chᵃzîr*

Contents: I. 1. Etymology; 2. Occurrences; 3. LXX. II. Swine in Near Eastern and Greek Religion and Magic: 1. Egypt; 2. Babylonia and Assyria; 3. Hittites; 4. Ugarit; 5. Palestine; 6. Syria; 7. Phoenicia; 8. Greece; 9. Maccabeans and Seleucids. III. Old Testament: 1. Everyday Life; 2. Uncleanness; 3. Cultic and Magical Use; 4. Uncleanness and Cultic Use in the Light of Israel's Environment.

I. 1. *Etymology.* The Hebrew word *chᵃzîr* means "swine" (*sus scrofa*), both the wild boar and the domesticated pig. There is evidence for the existence of swine in the

---

chᵃzîr. W. W. Graf Baudissin, *Adonis und Esmun* (1911), 142-160; F. Blome, *Die Opfermaterie in Babylonien und Israel, I. SSAOI,* 4 (1934); F. S. Bodenheimer, *Animal Life in Palestine* (Jerusalem, 1935), see index under *sus scrofa; idem, Animal and Man in Bible Lands,* I (trans. 1960), see index under *sus;* H. Bonnet, *RÄR,* 690f.; R. J. Braidwood and B. Howe, *Prehistoric Investigations in Iraqi Kurdistan. SAOC,* 31 (1960), 138-141; B. Brentjes, "Das Schwein als Haustier des Alten Orients," *Ethnographisch-Archäologische Zeitschrift,* 3 (1962), 125-138; *idem, Die Haustierwerdung im Orient* (1965), see index under "Schwein"; E. D. Van Buren, *The Fauna of Ancient Mesopotamia as Represented in Art. AnOr,* 18 (1939), 78-81; *idem, Symbols of the Gods in Mesopotamian Art. AnOr,* 23 (1945); G. S. Cansdale, *Animals of Bible Lands* (1970), 96-100; I. M. Casanowicz, "Swine," *JE,* XI (1905), 609f.; T. Chary, *Les prophètes et le culte à partir de l'exil* (Tournai, 1955), 100-103; M. J. Dahood, "Textual Problems in Isaiah," *CBQ,* 22 (1960), 400-409; J. Döller, *Die Reinheits- und Speisegesetze des ATs in religionsgeschichtlicher Beleuchtung. ATA,* 7/2-3 (1917); E. Ebeling, *Die babylonische Fabel und ihre Bedeutung für die Literaturgeschichte. MAOG,* 2/3 (1927), 41f.; K. Elliger, *Die Einheit des Tritojesaia (Jesaia 56-66). BWANT,* 3/9 (1929), 99-109; *idem,* "Der Prophet Tritojesaja," *ZAW,* 49 (1931), 112-141; *idem, HAT,* 4 (1966), 140-44, 148, 150f.; W. H. Gispen, "The Distinction between Clean and Unclean," *OTS,* 5 (1948), 190-96; W. Kessler, "Zur Auslegung von Jesaja 56-66," *ThLZ,* 81 (1956), 335-38; *idem,* "Studie zur religiösen Situation im ersten nachexilischen Jahrhundert und zur Auslegung von Jesaja 56-66," *WZ* Halle, VI/1 (1956/57), 41-73; *idem, Gott geht es um das Ganze. BAT,* 19 (1960); K. Koch, *Die Priesterschrift von Exodus 25 bis Leviticus 16. FRLANT,* 71 (1959), 74-79, 100f.; W. Kornfeld, "Reine und unreine Tiere im *AT,*" *Kairos,* 7 (1965), 134-147; V. Korošec, "Das Eigentum an Haustieren nach dem hethitischen Gesetzbuch," *Symbolae ad Iura Orientis Antiqui pertinentes. Festschrift P. Koschaker* (Leiden, 1939), 37-49; B. Landsberger, *Die Fauna des alten Mesopotamien. ASAW,* 42/6 (1934), 100-103; S. E. Loewenstamm, "חֲזִיר," *EMiqr,* III, 90-94; B. Meissner, *BuA,* I, see index under "Schwein" and "Wildschwein," II, see index under "Schwein"; P. E. Newberry, "The Pig and the Cult-Animal of Set," *JEA,* 14 (1928), 211-225; H. Odeberg, *Trito-Isaiah (Isaiah 56-66). UUÅ* (1931); F. Orth, "Schwein," *PW,* ser. 2, II/2 (1923), 801-815; W. Pangritz, *Das Tier in der Bibel* (1963), 25; W. Paschen, *Rein und Unrein. StANT,* 24 (1970), 57ff.; K. Pauritsch, *Die neue Gemeinde: Gott sammelte Ausgestossene und Arme (Jesaia 56-66). AnBibl,* 47 (1971); M. H. Pope-W. Röllig, *WbMyth,* I (1965), 267; M. Radin, *The Jews Among the Greeks and Romans* (1915), 204ff.; R. Rendtorff, *Die Gesetze in der Priesterschrift. FRLANT,* 62 (1953, ²1963), 38-45; A. Salonen, *Beiträge zur Geschichte des Schweines im Zweistromlande. StOr,* 43/9 (1974), *passim;* G. Sauer, "Schwein," *BHHW,* III, 1748f.; W. R. Smith, *Lectures on the Religion of the Semites* (London, ³1927, repr. 1969); F. J. Stendebach, "Das Schweineopfer im Alten Orient," *BZ,* N.S. 18 (1974), 263-271; R. de Vaux, "The Sacrifice of Pigs in Palestine and in the Ancient East," in his *The Bible and the Ancient Near East* (trans. 1971), 252-269 = *BZAW,* 77 (²1961), 250-265; N. Walker, "'Adam' and 'Eve' and 'Adon,'" *ZAW,* 74 (1962), 66-68; K. Wigand, "Die

ancient Near East since the Neolithic Age.[1] Alongside Heb. *chᵃzîr*, we find Samar. *'āzzēr*, Babylonian Jewish *hu/ozîr*,[2] *ḥwzyr* (1QIs[a]), and Middle Heb. *chôzîr*. These u/o forms have their counterpart and basis in Akk. *ḫuziru, ḫuzirtu*,[3] which Landsberger prefers to consider an Aramaic loanword,[4] since he finds the etymological equivalent to the West and South Semitic words for "swine" in Akk. *ḫamaṣīru, ḫumṣīru*, "rat," "mouse."[5] There are also forms with n, such as Ugar. *ḫnzr*, "swine,"[6] "(wild) boar,"[7] Arab. *hinzīr*, an Aramaic loanword,[8] Ethiop. *ḥenzîr, ḥanzar*,[9] etc. We may be dealing with an onomatopoetic etymology **ḥu/ozîr*.

2. *Occurrences*. There are 7 occurrences of Heb. *chᵃzîr*, "swine," in the OT, sometimes alone, sometimes further defined by *bᵉśar* (Isa. 65:4; 66:17), *dam* (Isa. 66:3); *mîyā'ar* (Ps. 80:14 [Eng. v. 13]); and *'aph* (Prov. 11:22). As a personal name, we find *chēzîr* in 1 Chr. 24:15 and Neh. 10:21 (20). Cf. the Akkadian names *Ḫuzira, Ḫuziranu*;[10] *Ḫiziri*;[11] Ugar. *ḫzr, bn ḫzr* as a term for a person (swineherd?) alongside craftsmen (*'śr ḥrś*);[12] personal names *ḫnzr, bn ḫnzr*;[13] OSA *ḥnzr*;[14] etc.

3. *LXX*. The LXX translates *chᵃzîr* 3 times as ὗς, 3 times as ὕειος (υἵος), and once as σῦς.

II. Swine in Near Eastern and Greek Religion and Magic.

1. *Egypt*. Swine are known in Egypt from the Neolithic period on.[15] As a Typhonian animal it became a form of Seth,[16] who changes himself into a black swine during

altisraelitische Vorstellung von unreinen Tieren," *ARW*, 17 (1914), 413-436; J. G. Wood, *Bible Animals* (1870), 292; R. K. Yerkes, "The Unclean Animals of Leviticus 11 and Deuteronomy 14," *JQR*, N.S. 14 (1923/24), 1-29; J. K. Zink, "Uncleanness and Sin: A Study of Job XIV 4 and Psalm LI 7," *VT*, 17 (1967), 354-361.

[1]On the paleontology and domestication of swine in the ancient Near East, see Bodenheimer, *Animal Life*, 36f.; *idem*, *Animal and Man*, 15, 18, 22ff., 51, 110, 128; Brentjes, 126-131.

[2]P. Kahle, *Der masoretische Text des ATs nach der Überlieferung der babylonischen Juden* (1962, repr. 1966), 72.

[3]*AHw*, I, 362; *CAD*, VI, 266.

[4]*Fauna*, 101.

[5]For a different view, see E. Ebeling, *Kritische Beiträge zu neuen asyriologischen Veröffentlichungen. MAOG*, 10/2 (1937), 51; G. Widengren, review of S. Moscati, ed., *Le antiche divinità semitiche, JSS*, 5 (1960), 397f.

[6]*UT*, No. 977.

[7]*WUS*, No. 1048.

[8]According to S. I. Fraenkel, *Die aramäischen Fremdwörter im Arabischen* (Leiden, 1886), 110f.

[9]*LexLingAeth*, 109.

[10]*AHw*, I, 362; *CAD*, VI, 266.

[11]EA 336.3; 337.4.

[12]*UT*, No. 948; *WUS*, Nos. 1013f.; *PRU*, II, 24 III 4-9; P. D. Miller, "Animal Names as Designations in Ugaritic and Hebrew," *UF*, 2 (1970), 179.

[13]*UT*, No. 977; *WUS*, No. 1049.

[14]W. Müller, "Altsüdarabische Beiträge zum hebräischen Lexikon," *ZAW*, 75 (1963), 309.

[15]Newberry, 211.

[16]Cf. *RÄR*, 690f.; de Vaux, 256f.

the Middle Kingdom.[17] The swine has a special relationship with the moon and the lunar deities: swine were sacrificed and offered to Horus, the lord of the lunar eye. This is already the case in the festival calendar of Medinet Habu; at Edfu these sacrifices were performed on the 15th of Pakhon, the day of the full moon.

According to Herodotus,[18] the worshipper "lays the tip of the tail together with the spleen and covers them with fat from the belly, then burns them all in the fire." The rest of the flesh, strangely, was eaten during the period of the full moon, as the swine was supposedly considered taboo and unclean. The enmity between the swine and the lunar deity is explained as assimilation to the myth of Nut, who daily devours her children (the stars) and gives birth to them once more; Nut is thus represented as a sow with her sucklings. Finally Isis took the place of Nut, as is shown by sow amulets inscribed with the name of Isis.

The sacrifice of swine is attested in Egypt only within narrow and well defined limits. The "uncleanness" of the swine is not universally attested; most of the evidence comes from the New Kingdom.

2. *Babylonia and Assyria*. From Mesopotamia, there are preserved numerous seals, amulets, figurines, and reliefs depicting either the wild boar or the domestic pig.[19] The normal Akkadian word for swine is *šaḫû*.[20]

While the boar appears as game,[21] the domesticated pig, kept in a sty or rummaging through the streets with dogs, hawks, etc., is used for food, commerce, production of drugs, and magic. During the period of Hammurabi, pigs were fantastically cheap,[22] because, according to Meissner, they were considered unclean and because certain illnesses were ascribed to the enjoyment of pork.[23]

According to the Babylonian hemerology, the eating of pork was prohibited on certain days. Roast pork was nevertheless furnished to the priestesses, and the fat of pigs was offered during incantations.[24] The head and fat of swine in particular were used for the manufacture of medicaments.[25] In incantations against the female demon Lamaštu, who robbed mothers of their children in order to drink their blood or devour their flesh, the pig plays a special role. In other incantations against demons, too, the pig was used as a substitute for the sick person in order to entice the demon away from the sufferer.

We may mention the faience head of a boar from the temple of Ishtar at Nuzi, dating from the fifteenth century B.C.[26]

From the Neo-Babylonian period we have animal fables and proverbs in which the

---

[17]Book of the Dead, chap. 112.
[18]*Hist.* ii.47.
[19]Van Buren, *Faune,* 78-81.
[20]For citations, see *AHw,* I, 1133.
[21]*BuA*, I, 212f., 224f.
[22]*Ibid.*, 364f.
[23]*Ibid.*, 416.
[24]*Ibid.*, 220f.
[25]*BuA*, II, 307f.
[26]R. F. S. Starr, *Nuzi,* II (1939), 435ff. and Plate 112B.

swine is characterized as dirty, stupid, or an abomination.[27] Esarhaddon inscription § 27 III 42 speaks of a wild boar guarding a city gate.

3. *Hittites*. Among the Hittites, too, the sacrifice of swine was unusual, but swine did play a special role in incantation and purification rituals. For example, in an incantation ritual from Boghazköy against a plague, an old goat, a ram, and a swine are sacrificed together with the offering of three loaves and intoxicating drink in order to appease the angry god.[28] A young swine is also sacrificed in a ritual against sterility and impotence[29] and in a ritual against domestic quarrel.[30] The Hittite law code imposed capital punishment for sodomy with a swine,[31] while sodomy with a horse, for example, carried no punishment.

4. *Ugarit*. At Ugarit, *ẖzr/ẖnzr* is attested as the name of an animal and as a personal name or the name of a group of persons.[32]

In the badly damaged Baal text CTA 5 [I* AB] V, 7ff., the words *mdl* and *ḥnzrk* are uncertain: *mdl* is variously translated "carriage,"[33] "cloud-chariot,"[34] "bucket,"[35] "weather phenomenon";[36] *ḥnzrk*, "swine," is interpreted differently by various scholars: Gray thinks of "boar-hunters,"[37] whereas de Moor suggests "boar" as a term for the Pleiades, which would be appropriate in the context of "clouds," "wind," a weather phenomenon(?), and rain. Gray finds an association with Adonis: "And thou, take thy clouds, thy wind, thy *mdl*, thy rain. With thee thy seven lads (*ġlmk*), thine eight swine (*ẖnzrk*). . . ." With these (as retinue?) he is to seek out a mountain and then descend into the underworld, to become like the powerless dead. Thus the notion of a "carriage" drawn by eight boars is uncertain, as is the astronomical interpretation of *ẖnzr* as the Pleiades. Neither the figure of a swine on the back of a ceremonial axe nor the two boars' heads on a hunting weapon[38] can count as evidence for any religious significance.

5. *Palestine*. At Tell el-Far'ah, identified since Albright with Tirzah, in a room connected with a vanished temple, there were discovered the bones of a pig several months old and the bones of an embryo; these can only be the remains of a sacrifice. At

---

[27]Ebeling, 3, 41f.

[28]J. Friedrich, *Aus dem hethitischen Schrifttum, 2. AO*, 25/2 (1925), 12.

[29]A. Goetze and E. H. Sturtevant, *The Hittite Ritual of Tunnawi. AOS*, 14 (1938), §§ 3, 12.

[30]*ANET*³, 351.

[31]*HG*, II, §§ 85f.

[32]See I.2 above; citations in Whitaker, 269f., 277; cf. also *WUS*, No. 1013/1049; *UT*, No. 948/977.

[33]*WUS*, No. 744a.

[34]U. Oldenburg, *The Conflict between El and Baʿal in Canaanite Religion. DHRP*, 3 (1969), 76; cf. J. C. Greenfield, "Ugaritic mdl and its Cognates," *Bibl*, 45 (1964), 527-534.

[35]*CML*, 17, 107.

[36]*UT*, No. 1430; similarly J. C. de Moor, *The Seasonal Pattern in the Ugaritic Myth of Baʿlu. AOAT*, 16 (1971), 183.

[37]J. Gray, *The Legacy of Canaan. SVT*, 5 (²1965), 59.

[38]C. F.-A. Schaeffer, *Ugaritica*, I (Paris, 1939), Plate XXII, Figs. 100f.; Plate XXIII, Fig. 104.

Gezer, bones of pigs were discovered in a grotto. More significant is the fragment of an alabaster statuette (*ca.* 2000 B.C.) representing a naked man holding a young pig to his chest and grasping its genitals in his hand; one of the pig's feet is standing on the man's phallus. The hollow statue obviously served as a libation vessel for fertility rites.

Alabaster fragments from the Early Bronze period from et-Tell (Ai) exhibit the tail end of an animal bound up for sacrifice, very probably a pig.[39] A bronze figurine from Megiddo IX (16th century B.C.) appears to represent a wild boar; it is impossible to say more than that it had a religious purpose. Brentjes has also pointed out the statuette of a swine from the megaron temple at Jericho (fourth millennium), a cultic pedestal with the head of a swine from the holy of holies of the temple at Beth-shan, and a rhyton with a swine's head from Jericho (Bronze II).

6. *Syria.* The old Syrian calendar still preserves the Aramaic name of the month Heziran, but we have no details about any religious, cultic, or astronomical connection with the wild boar. On the other hand, with respect to the month of Heziran in the Sabian calendar of Harran (10th century), we are told by al-Nadim that the Sabians every year on a specified day sacrificed a pig to their gods, and ate any pig meat that came into their hands.[40] Nothing more is known of this practice.

7. *Phoenicia.* For information on the Phoenicians, we must rely on Greek authors.[41]

First Renan, then Smith and Baudissin, and most recently Stendebach[42] have cited a rock carving from Jrapte, east of Byblos, purported to represent a pig being led, "undoubtedly as a sacrifice,"[43] to an altar with the medallion of a deity. According to a recent study,[44] the carving does not represent the sacrifice of a pig: the animal depicted is a sheep, and the medallion represents not a deity, but a veiled woman!

According to Porphyry and Herodian, the Phoenicians neither ate nor sacrificed swine. According to Lucian, the Syrians of Hierapolis considered the swine unclean and therefore did not sacrifice it, while others considered it sacred. In the cult of Astarte/Aphrodite on Cyprus, the swine was considered sacred. According to Joannes Lydus, wild boars were sacrificed to Aphrodite on Cyprus on April 2, supposedly in memory of Adonis, who had been killed by a wild boar. In the cult of Aphrodite the swine was generally forbidden, but swine were sacrificed at the sanctuaries of Argos and Samos, as well as in Pamphylia.

8. *Greece.* Among the Greeks,[45] swine were sacrificed primarily to the chthonic deities, especially Demeter and Dionysus. A unique propitiatory sacrifice was offered by the women of Athens at the Thesmophoria, celebrated in honor of Demeter and

[39] Cf. de Vaux, 254.
[40] Citations in de Vaux, 260, n. 50, 261, n. 51.
[41] Cf. the citations in *ibid.,* 261f.
[42] P. 267.
[43] *Ibid.*
[44] H. Seyrig, "Antiquités syriennes," *Syr,* 21 (1940), 116f.
[45] Cf. Orth, 811-13; de Vaux, 261f.

Persephone: they threw live piglets into ditches (*chásmata, mégara, ádyta*), so that the decomposing remains could later be removed and sacrificed upon the altar.[46] Noteworthy is the similarity of *mégara* to Heb. *mᵉʿārāh,* "cave," which recalls the pits (*favissae*) of Tell el-Far'ah and Gezer.[47]

The pig or boar also plays a role in oath sacrifices; in sacrifices of purification, a young pig is preferred.

9. *Maccabeans and Seleucids*. The traditions recorded in Maccabees, Josephus, etc. concerning the religious persecution of the Jews under Antiochus Epiphanes report that the Seleucid ruler ordered the Jerusalem temple dedicated to Zeus Olympios and the offering of forbidden sacrifices there (2 Macc. 6:2,5). He forbade the Jews, under penalty of death, to circumcise their males, observe the Sabbath, or offer sacrifice (1 Macc. 1:44–50); at the same time, however, he commanded them to sacrifice "swine and other unclean animals" to Zeus and the other gods (1:47). According to Josephus,[48] Antiochus himself sacrificed swine. Eleazer, the seven Maccabees, and their mother suffered martyrdom because they refused to eat the flesh of swine from the sacrificial meals (2 Macc. 6–7). This imposition of the sacrifice of swine to Zeus Olympios and the requirement that the Jews eat the flesh of pigs were actually in conflict with Seleucid religious policies, according to which bulls rather than swine were sacrificed to Zeus. By means of his religious interdict, the cult of Zeus, and the compulsory sacrifice of swine, Antiochus sought to destroy the Maccabean opposition in its monotheistic and cultic substance and to integrate it into the state religion.

III. Old Testament.

1. *Everyday Life*. The wild boar appears in the OT in Ps. 80:14(13): "The boar from the forest (*chᵃzîr mîyāʿar*) ravages it [the vineyard], and all that move in the field (*zîz śādhai*) feed on it." Other passages, too, liken the depredations of war to the depredations of wild beasts (cf. Isa. 56:9; Hos. 2:20). Several scholars prefer to read *yaʿar* as *yᵉʾōr* (*ʿayin suspensum*), seeing in the boar (*chᵃzîr*) the invasion of Pharaoh Necho from the (land of the) Nile during the reign of Josiah.

Little sympathy for the swine is displayed by the coarse and ironic simile in Prov. 11:22: "Like a golden ring in a swine's snout is a beautiful woman without discretion." A golden nose ring, usually worn by a woman as an ornament (Gen. 24:47; Isa. 3:21; Ezk. 16:12), in the snout of a swine as it roots about is an absurd image, as inappropriate and contradictory as a beautiful woman (*ʾishshāh yāphāh*) without tact and consideration (*ṭaʿam;* cf. Prov. 26:16; 1 S. 25:33; Job 12:20; Ps. 119:66). The contempt expressed here is especially clear when contrasted with the general OT praise of feminine beauty (Sarah, Rebecca, Rachel, Judith, Esther, etc.) and high opinion of women (Prov. 11:16; 12:4; 18:22; 31:10ff.).

---

[46] Cf. S. Eitrem, "Les Thesmophoria, les Skirophoria, et les Arrhétophoria," *Symbolae Osloenses,* 23 (1944), 32–45.

[47] De Vaux, 263.

[48] *Ant.* xi.253.

2. *Uncleanness.* In the regulations governing what is clean and unclean, the wild boar is listed among the animals that may not be eaten (Lev. 11:7 par. Dt. 14:8). The instructions about what animals are not to be eaten (Lev. 11:2b–23 par. Dt. 14:4–20) comprise various lists formulated positively (Lev. 11:2b f., 9) and negatively (4a, 11f.) in the style of priestly torah, from the perspective of what may and may not be eaten and the danger of rendering Israel unclean.[49] Despite the late redaction of Lev. 11 and Dt. 14, we are dealing with "old, perhaps even primitive regulations."[50] The distinction between clean and unclean animals is used by the Yahwist (Gen. 7:2; 8:20), and surely antedates his work.

Together with the camel, the rock badger, and the hare, the boar belongs to a group of animals that are clearly set apart from those that may be eaten (Lev. 11:3 par. Dt. 14:6) on the grounds that they meet only one of the two criteria (cloven-footed and ruminant) and may therefore not be eaten (Lev. 11:4–8a par. Dt. 14:7f.). They are disqualified for the cult by the priestly declaratory formula, ". . . is unclean to you." The boar must not be eaten "because it parts the hoof [and is cloven-footed] but does not chew the cud," and is therefore unclean (Lev. 11:7 par. Dt. 14:8). The few intelligible and only partially accurate motivations for the four exceptions to the animals that may be eaten (Lev. 11:3 par. Dt. 14:6) show clearly that the external classification into edible and nonedible, clean and unclean was not based on scientific criteria; the motivations were added secondarily to account for a distinction already made. The list of animals is far from complete—why should precisely these four be named? Then there is added a new version of the prohibition against touching their carcasses (Lev. 11:8 par. Dt. 14:8), perhaps anticipating Lev. 11:24ff. par. Dt. 14:21a.

The boar, like the camel, the rock badger, and the hare, is "unclean" (→ טָמֵא (*ṭāmē'*) (Lev. 11:4–8,26f.), but it is not categorized as an "abomination" (→ שֶׁקֶץ *sheqets*), which appears to represent a more extreme cultic disqualification.

In Dt. 14:3, the redactor precedes the two lists of permitted and forbidden animals with a general prohibition: " 'You shall not eat any abominable thing' " (→ תּוֹעֵבָה *tôʿēbhāh*), which may suggest an independent list of *tôʿēbhāh* animals.

3. *Cultic and Magical Use.* In Trito-Isaiah (Isa. 65:4; 66:3,17), the eating of swine's flesh appears in the context of pagan or superstitious cults. Thus the announcement of judgment in 65:1–7 is addressed to a "rebellious" people (v. 2a), people who "provoke" Yahweh (v. 3a), "sacrificing (*zbḥ*) in gardens and burning incense (*qṭr* piel) upon bricks (*lᵉbhēnîm,* possibly better translated 'incense altars'[51])" (v. 3b). In addition to these garden cults (cf. the high places in v. 7), they "sit in tombs and spend the night in secret places [perhaps *ûbhên tsûrîm,* 'among (fissures in the) rocks'[52]]." In these tombs and fissures they seek contact with the spirits of the dead (cf. 8:19; 29:4) in order to obtain information through incubations or dreams (cf. LXX *di' enýpnia*) (cf. Gen. 28:11ff.; 1 K. 3:4ff.). The prophet goes on to castigate the sacral

---

49Cf. Rendtorff, 38ff.; Koch, 77; Elliger, *HAT,* 4, 148f.

50M. Noth, *Leviticus. OTL* (^{2}1977), 91.

51Dahood, 400–409.

52A. B. Ehrlich, *Randglossen zur hebräischen Bibel* (^{2}1968), IV, 227; *et al.*

meals (v. 4b): "... who eat swine's flesh, and broth (*m^eraq*) of abominable things (*piggulîm* [possibly unclean decayed sacrificial flesh, on the basis of Lev. 7:18; 19:7, or the flesh of unclean animals, on the basis of Isa. 66:17; Ezk. 4:14])." After participation in these meals and cultic ceremonies, they consider themselves holy, like initiates or mystae, and warn the unitiated (v. 5a): "Keep to yourself, do not come near me, or 'I will make you holy' [reading *qiddashtîkhā* for *q^edashtîkhā*, i.e., unclean as a result of contact with the apostate who has become 'holy' = taboo, unclean in these alien cults; cf. Ezk. 44:19; 46:20; Mk. 5:27ff.; → קדשׁ *qdš*]." Finally, the prophet relates the activities of his contemporaries to the deeds of their fathers (vv. 6–7a): "They burn incense (*qṭr* piel) upon the mountains and revile me (*ḥrp* piel) upon the hills." Both are requited together (cf. Ezk. 20:5; Jer. 32:18; a different position is taken by the casuistic argument of Ezk. 18).

Isa. 66:17 is unfortunately highly obscure: "Those who sanctify and purify themselves for the gardens, following one [K: masculine; Q, 1QIs[a], mss.: feminine] in the midst (*battāvekh*), eating swine's flesh and 'vermin' [reading *sherets* for *sheqets*] and mice, shall all come to an end together (*y^achdav yāsuphû* [many follow Duhm in taking 'their works and their thoughts' in v. 18aα as the subject of 17bβ]), says Yahweh." In the Hebrew context, v. 17 is not linked with either v. 16 or vv. 18–24,[53] and is probably an editorial addition[54] whose subject matter is more appropriate to 65:3b–5.[55] The act of sanctification and purification "following one in the midst" performed in the gardens has long been explained as a mystery cult; the "one" in the middle has been identified with the mystagogue or hierophant behind (*'achar*) whom the participants in the cult followed.[56] Volz[57] recalls "the mystagogue of the Eleusinian mysteries or the *pater patrum* of the Mitraic circle,"[58] and therefore dates Isa. 65; 66:3f., 5f., 17; 66:7–24 to the Hellenistic period.[59] There is no other evidence for the cultic eating of mice (→ עכבר *'akhrābh*).

Reminiscent of Isa. 65:3–5, 7; 66:3; and especially 66:17 is the description of the forbidden cults in Ezk. 8:5–15, especially vv. 10f.: "There, portrayed upon the wall round about, were all kinds of creeping things and loathsome beasts ... and before them stood seventy men of the elders of the house of Israel, with Jaazaniah the son of Shaphan standing among them. Each had his censer in his hand, and the smoke of the cloud of incense went up." In this offering of incense before the carved representation of animals (creeping things, loathsome beasts, or, giving *sheqets* its usual meaning, idols), we may have a "syncretistic cult of Egyptian origin, probably containing strong magical elements."[60]

---

[53] A different view is held by Feldmann, Muilenburg, *et al.*

[54] Elliger, Volz, Kessler, Leslie, Fohrer, Westermann.

[55] Volz places it after 4a; Kessler, Westermann after 5a; Fohrer after 5b.

[56] Duhm, Feldmann, Volz, Muilenburg, *et al.*

[57] P. Volz, *KAT*, IX/2 (1932), 292.

[58] Cf. F. Cumont, *The Mysteries of Mithra* (^{2}1910, trans. 1956), 155.

[59] For other interpretations see F. Feldmann, *Das Buch Isaias. EHAT*, 14 (1925), 293; J. Muilenburg in *IB*, V, 770.

[60] W. F. Albright, *Archaeology and the Religion of Israel* (^{4}1956), 166f.; G. Fohrer, *HAT*, 13 (1955), 51; W. Eichrodt, *Ezekiel. OTL* (trans. 1970), 124; and, with slight modifications, W. Zimmerli, *BK*, XIII/1 (1969), 217f.

In Isa. 66:3, the sacrifice of swine appears among four forbidden pagan cultic acts that are contrasted with four legitimate sacrificial acts: "He who slaughters (*shōchēṭ*) an ox—he who kills (*makkēh*) a man; he who sacrifices (*zôbhēach*) a lamb—he who breaks (*ʿôrēph*) a dog's neck; he who presents (*maʿᵃlēh*) a cereal offering—he who offers [supplying *nôsēkh;* others[61] read *chômēdh* for *dam,* 'is greedy for swine'] swine's blood; he who makes a memorial offering (*mazkîr* denominatively from *'azkārāh*) of frankincense—he who blesses an idol (*'āven*)." On the valuation of dogs, see → כלב *kelebh.*

The mutual relationship between the four proper and improper cultic acts has been interpreted variously.[62] Following the LXX (*hōs*), 1QS (*kᵉ*), and Vulgate (*quasi*), many read "He who slaughters an ox is *like* him who kills a man; he who sacrifices a lamb is *like* him who breaks a dog's neck," etc. In this cultic polemic, accordingly, the legal cultic acts would be equated with the loathsome false cults. In this case, Trito-Isaiah with his total identification of the legitimate cult with the pagan cults would be going far beyond any previous cult polemic. In connection with the polemic against an unspecified temple (probably an allusion to the rebuilding of the Jerusalem temple between 520 and 515 B.C. and the associated expectations [cf. Hag. 2:19]),[63] this interpretation calls into question or totally rejects the significance of temple and cult.

More likely, however, is a different interpretation of the double phrases without connecting particles: "the antithetical actions are combined in each instance in one and the same subject: he who slaughters an ox is *also* he who kills a man. . . ."[64] In other words, legitimate sacrifices are being offered alongside superstitious and pagan sacrifices. In this case, the cultic polemic would be directed against any juxtaposition of legitimate and pagan cults, and against all syncretistic forms of the cult. Then if 66:1f. was in fact originally associated with v. 3, the temple in this phase of syncretism is being called into question in favor of a new form of worship on the part of those who are "humble and contrite in spirit" and tremble at Yahweh's word (66:2).

4. *Uncleanness and Cultic Use in the Light of Israel's Environment.* The cultic declaration of the *chᵃzîr* as unclean and its disqualification for human consumption on the basis of unconvincing and zoologically inaccurate criteria (Lev. 11:7 par. Dt. 14:8) clearly arose more from the need to avert alien phenomena that were suspect or injurious to Yahwism and exclude them from the religious and cultic life of the community. Trito-Isaiah describes illegal cultic and magical practices involving swine (Isa. 65:4; 66:3,17). Is it possible to illustrate and account for the cultic and magical significance of the swine on the basis of Israel's environment? There is a broad spectrum of evidence from the ancient Near East and from Greece. In Egypt, the swine is associated with Seth and the lunar deities; at Medinet Habu and Edfu, swine were sacrificed to Horus. Among the Assyro-Babylonians and Hittites, the swine (or piglet) was used in incantations against Lamashtu and as a substitutionary sacrifice against demons for someone who is sick. At Tirzah and Ai, bones of piglets have been

---

61 Volz, Fohrer, *BHS,* etc.

62 Cf. the commentaries of Volz, Feldmann, Muilenburg, Kessler, and Westermann.

63 Other suggestions in J. Muilenburg, *IB,* V, 758ff.

64 Feldmann, 288.

discovered as sacrificial remains, and the libation vessel in the form of a man with a swine seems to have been used in a fertility cult. On Cyprus, the swine is associated with the cult of Aphrodite/Astarte. During the Thesmophoria, dedicated to Demeter and Dionysus, the Greeks offered sacrifices of swine; swine were also offered in purification and oath sacrifices, and in propitiatory sacrifices living piglets were thrown into ditches and their decayed remains offered as sacrifice.

The evidence bearing on the question of whether the swine was clean or unclean and whether its flesh might be consumed is equally varied. In Egypt, Mesopotamia, and Harran, the consumption of swine's flesh is explicitly permitted or forbidden on specific days or in specific regions; there is no evidence for a general prohibition. The radical disqualification of the swine through its declaration as unclean and unfit to be eaten (Lev. 11:7 par.) as well as Trito-Isaiah's polemic against cultic and magical practices involving the sacrifice of swine and consumption of swine's flesh appear to be based on a variety of factors and motives: (a) Brentjes has shown[65] that the importance and valuation of the swine in the ancient Near East after the late Neolithic period declined with the decline of pig keeping and turned into proscription. With the decline of forest pasturage in Palestine, the swine was eliminated from the spatially restricted mixed economy of cattle raising and agriculture. (b) For reasons of political and religious self-preservation, Israel was forced at various periods in its history to defend itself against the cultural and religious ideas and influences of its neighbors and to put a stop to syncretism in religion, cult, and magic. Thus the sacrifice of swine and magical ritual practices involving swine, of whatever provenance, were banned. (c) Despite various prophetic and royal reformers, alien and superstitious abuses continued to recur. Thus it became necessary, for example, to codify lists of "clean" and "unclean" animals, whose consumption was permitted or forbidden. The real reasons for the distinction were obviously replaced by formalistic criteria. (d) During the exilic and early postexilic period, alien cults exerted a great influence, as Isa. 65:1-7; 66:3,17; Ezk. 8:5-15 and other passages show. Even though the illegal cults in Trito-Isaiah have not been identified satisfactorily with concrete forms found in the ancient Near East, the OT proscription of the swine is connected with the cultic and magical role it played in Israel's environment, as it is also attested for the fifth or fourth century B.C. Later, Antiochus Epiphanes singled out the sacrifice of swine as a way to destroy the Jews' sense of identity and exceptional position. For further discussion of "uncleanness," see → **טמא** *ṭāmēʾ*.

Botterweck

---

[65] Pp. 132ff.

חָזַק chāzaq; חָזָק chāzāq; חָזֵק chāzēq; חֵזֶק chezeq; חֹזֶק chōzeq; חֶזְקָה chezqāh; חָזְקָה chozqāh

Contents: I. Occurrences: 1. Basic Meaning; 2. Ancient Near East; 3. Frequency; 4. Proper Names; 5. LXX. II. Secular Usage: 1. Individuals; 2. Nations and Their Representatives; 3. Things; 4. Special Meaning; 5. Hiphil, "Grasp." III. Religious Usage: 1. Yahweh; 2. Temple; 3. Hiphil; 4. Imperative; 5. Hardness of Heart.

I. Occurrences.

1. *Basic Meaning.* We take as our starting-point the basic meaning "be/become strong," from which all other meanings that are found can be derived. We can be content with the statement of this basic meaning; the search for an "original meaning"—often taken to be "tie firmly, gird"[1]—contributes nothing, even if it can be supported by Isa. 22:21 and Nah. 2:2.

2. *Ancient Near East.* In the case of the Aramaic and Arabic equivalents, *chᵉzaq* and *ḫazaqa,* it is likewise reasonable to assume the original meaning given above. The root is not attested in other Semitic languages. The connection with Akk. *ešqu,* "massive," is more than uncertain.[2]

3. *Frequency.* The verb *ḥzq* is attested 81 times in the qal, 64 in the piel, 118 in the hiphil, and 127 in the hithpael. It occurs with striking frequency in the later literature, especially the Chronicler's history (98 occurrences), but is present also in the earlier documents. An analogous distribution appears for the adjectives *chāzāq* (56 occurrences) and *chāzēq* (2 occurrences), as well as the substantives *chōzeq* (5 occurrences), *chēzeq* (1 occurrence), *chezqāh* (4 occurrences), and *chozqāh* (6 occurrences; but the form in 2 K. 12:13 [Eng. v. 12] should probably be replaced with the piel infinitive).

4. *Proper Names.* The root *ḥzq* enters into the proper names "Hezekiah" and "Ezekiel." "Hezekiah" appears in five different forms: *yᵉchizqîyāhû* (40 times), *yᵉchizqîyāh* (3), *chizqîyāhû* (74), *chizqîyāh* (13), and *chizqî* (1). "Ezekiel" = *yᵉchezqēʾl* is attested 3 times, plus once in Sir. 49:8. In 4 cases (Ezr. 2:16; Neh. 7:21; 10:18[17]; 1 Ch. 3:23), "Hezekiah" refers to someone other than the Judahite king of this name; in 1 case (1 Ch. 24:16), *yᵉchezqēʾl* does not refer to the exilic prophet Ezekiel. In Zeph. 1:1, it is unclear whether king Hezekiah or someone else by the same name is meant.

---

chāzaq. F. Hesse, *Das Verstockungsproblem im AT. BZAW,* 74 (1955), 7-12; S. Lieberman, "התחזק," *Lešonenu,* 33 (1968/69), 77; A. S. van der Woude, "חזק *ḥzq* fest sein," *THAT,* I, 538-541; D. Yellin, "חסר, אמץ, חזק," *Sinai,* 65 (1969), 139f.

[1] E.g., J. L. Palache, *Semantic Notes on the Hebrew Lexicon* (Leiden, 1959), 29.

[2] *AHw,* I, 257; on Akk. *izaqtu/išqatu,* cf. W. von Soden, *AfO,* 20 (1963), 155; *AHw,* I, 408 (Aramaic loanword).

5. *LXX*. When *ḥzq* appears in any of its four usual stems, the LXX renders it as *enischýein, katischýein, krateín,* or *krataioún*. For the qal, piel, and hithpael, the translation *krataioún* clearly predominates over *krateín,* while in the rendering of the hiphil 18 instances of *krateín* contrast with a single instance of *krataioún*. The translation *ischýein* is used for the qal, piel, and hithpael. In the qal and piel, the LXX can render *ḥzq* as *stereoún* or *sklērýnein;* the piel and hiphil are rendered as *katakrateín* or *antilambánesthai*. For the qal alone we also find *andrízesthai, barýnein, katabiázesthai, anistánai, hyperischýein, epikrateín,* and *hyperkrateín,* with *andrízesthai* by far the most common. The piel is rendered as *parakaleín, ochyroún,* or *episkeuázein,* the hithpael as *boētheín, anthistánai,* or *proskartereín*. For the hiphil *epilambánein* and *katéchein* are common, and there are occasional occurrences of *eiságein, cheiragōgeín, biázesthai, katadynasteúein, échein, antéchein, proséchein, synéchein, enkrateín, lambánein,* and *chōreín*.

II. Secular Usage. The secular usage of the verb *chāzaq* in the sense "be or become strong," piel and hiphil "make strong," predominates in biblical usage. The possible distinction of an "inchoative" usage ("become strong") from a "durative" usage ("be strong") turns out to be meaningless in practice.

1. *Individuals*. In the most immediate meaning of the word, it is living beings, persons, who are or become strong. The reference is primarily to bodily strength. With the exception of Ezk. 34:16, where the adjective is used, this usage is limited to human beings and is also relatively uncommon. Someone who has recovered from illness is "strong" again (Isa. 39:1). According to a gloss in Ezk. 30:22, Pharaoh has a sound ("strong") arm and a broken arm, symbolizing his power and his impotence. Despite his advanced age, Joshua still feels "strong" (Josh. 14:11). To be stronger than someone, even with the help of "technology," is to prevail over him (1 S. 17:50). When a man abuses his physical superiority over a woman, the verb can have the precise meaning "rape, violate" (2 S. 13:14). The piel *chizzēq* used in this sense means "strengthen the physical powers of someone" (Jgs. 16:28). Someone who is not or is no longer strong can still make the effort to summon up what strength he has (*hithchazzēq,* Gen. 48:2). "Being strong," however, concerns more than just bodily strength: it involves securing one's position in a comprehensive sense. The poor (Lev. 25:35; Ezk. 16:49), for example, or captives (2 Ch. 28:15) need strengthening in this sense. In these three passages the hiphil is used.

2. *Nations and Their Representatives*. It is not merely individuals who can be made strong and be strong; but also nations and their representatives—as a rule their kings—can "grow strong" and then exercise political power, usually military. This usage, which uses all of the stems in which *ḥzq* appears, can be found throughout the entire history of Israel down to the late postexilic period. In this case the qal has the meaning "grow strong militarily," and can also refer to the result of such increased strength, namely superiority over someone else and the ability to subjugate him (Josh. 17:13; Jgs. 1:28; 2 S. 10:11 = 1 Ch. 19:12; 1 K. 16:22; 20:23, 25; Ezk. 30:21—where

the piel should probably be read; Dnl. 11:5; 2 Ch. 8:3; 26:15; 27:5). In a more general sense, the superior nation is capable of exerting pressure on the weaker to get them to do some particular act (Ex. 12:33; 2 Ch. 28:20 [read as piel]). When the piel and hiphil of *ḥzq* are used in the politico-military sense, it is common to speak of making someone's arms strong (Ezk. 30:21 [read piel instead of qal], 24f.). More generally, the piel of *ḥzq* can be used to describe the strengthening of a kingdom and its king (2 Ch. 11:17), or the strengthening of his official power (Isa. 22:21). The hiphil can also mean "exhibit strength," and thus can be used intransitively, though only in late usage: "show oneself strong, superior, victorious" (Dnl. 11:7,32; 2 Ch. 26:8) or even "seize power" (Dnl. 11:21). A weakened nation gathers its strength (*hithchazzēq;* Jgs. 20:22); but a victorious king can be called upon to do the same (1 K. 20:22). The hithpael can also mean that someone has strengthened his position as king (2 Ch. 1:11; 12:13; 13:21; 21:4; 27:6) or has prevailed over someone else (2 Ch. 13:7; 17:1). An adjective or substantive from the root *ḥzq* is used in this sense in Nu. 13:18,31; Josh. 17:18; Jgs. 18:26; 2 S. 3:1; Isa. 28:2; Jer. 31:11; Ezk. 26:17; Am. 2:14; 6:13; Hag. 2:22; Dnl. 11:2; 2 Ch. 12:1; 26:15f. By synecdoche, the phrase "strong hand" is used for the military might of a nation (Nu. 20:20).

3. *Things.* Now it is also possible to describe certain things as "being (made) strong." This can have favorable consequences for those affected, as when we are dealing with the strengthening of the power of a king or other official (qal: 2 K. 14:5 = 2 Ch. 25:3 [read *bydw* for *ʿlyw*]; piel: Isa. 22:21; 2 Ch. 11:17)—here there is no fundamental difference from the citations in II.1 above—, or when the strengthening of fortified cities or fortifications is described (piel: Nah. 3:14; Ps. 147:13; 2 Ch. 11:11f.; 26:9; 32:5). But it can have unfortunate consequences when, for example, the battle "grows stronger" than the king involved in it, meaning indirectly that he is not up to facing his opponent (qal: 2 K. 3:26 [read *ḥzqh* for *ḥzq*]; a battle is also described as "strong" in 1 S. 14:52; 2 S. 11:15 [adj.]). The disastrous consequences for those affected are obvious in the case of a "strong" famine (qal: Gen. 41:56f.; 47:20; 2 K. 25:3; Jer. 52:6; adj.: 1 K. 18:2) or a "strong" sickness (adj.: 1 K. 17:17). Bonds or chains that are "made stronger," i.e., tighter and therefore more painful, are anything but pleasant for those affected; therefore the prophet can use such a measure as a threat (qal: Isa. 28:22). The strengthening of foreign domination can also prove disastrous (hiphil: 2 K. 15:19). The other things that are "made strong" are quite diverse: tent stakes that are driven deeper into the ground (piel: Isa. 54:2); an idol fastened more securely (piel: Isa. 41:7; Jer. 10:4); a mast held upright by its rigging (piel: Isa. 33:23). Things exhibiting damage such as holes or leaks are repaired by being "strengthened" (hiphil: Ezk. 27:9; Neh. 3:4-32 [in v. 19 the hiphil should probably be read for the piel]). Making a watch "strong" is equivalent to intensifying it (Jer. 51:12). Other things of which "strength" is predicated by means of the adjective *chāzāq/chāzēq* include the wind (Ex. 10:19; 1 K. 19:11 [text unclear]), a trumpet blast (Ex. 19:16, 19 [*chāzēq* in v. 19]), and the sky (Job 37:18). Words, too, especially commands, can be "strong," which in this context means "harsh, almost unbearable" (2 S. 24:4 = 1 Ch. 21:4).

4. *Special Meaning.* In a few passages, *ḥzq* develops a specialized meaning. It is possible—in the literal sense!—to be "hung up" on something (qal: 2 S. 18:9). The meaning of the phrase *chazzēq 'eth-yādhāi* in Neh. 6:9 is obscure; the imperative *chazzēq* is out of place here. Probably we should read *chizzaqtî*, and interpret the phrase as part of Nehemiah's report: "But I strengthened my hands [i.e., 'set to work'] all the more." When parts of the body appear as the object, we find *yādhayim* (→ יד *yadh;* esp. common) and *z^erō^ʿôth* (→ זרוע *z^erôaʿ*), as well as one occurrence of *mothnayim* (with the piel: Nah. 2:2[1]); in this case, however, we are dealing with a metaphor in which the city is called upon to take specific defensive measures. "Summoning up strength" can also serve to support someone as a firm ally (hithpael: 2 S. 3:6; Dnl. 10:21; 1 Ch. 11:10; 2 Ch. 16:9).

5. *Hiphil, "Grasp."* Only the hiphil of *ḥzq* develops the specialized meaning "grasp"; it is not found in the other stems. The semantic shift from "make strong" to "grasp" is not easy to explain. Probably the ritual of appointment to office plays an important role: when a person in power appoints someone else to a specific office, he grasps him by the hand. Through this act, "power" flows from the hand—itself a symbol of power—of the stronger into the hand of the new official, in other words, the one appointed to office is made strong through the ritual gesture of "grasping the hand" (cf. Isa. 41:13; 42:6; 45:1). Then the gesture and its effect become identified and interchangeable: *hech^ezîq* can now mean both "make strong" and "grasp the hand of." The latter meaning soon becomes independent of its ritual background, taking on the general meaning "grasp" in both punctiliar and durative sense.

a. The old association is most perceptible in those cases where persons are grasped, and particularly their hands, in order to "strengthen" them (cf. the Deutero-Isaiah passages mentioned above; also Jer. 31:32; Job 8:20).

b. At a relatively early date the independent usage arose, whereby *hech^ezîq* means merely "grasp," without any overtones of "strengthening." Persons may grasp objects (Jgs. 7:20; 2 S. 3:29; 1 K. 1:50; 2:28; Jer. 6:23; 50:42; Zec. 8:23; Ps. 35:2; Neh. 4:10f.,15[16f.,21]) or other persons (2 S. 15:5; Isa. 4:1; Prov. 7:13; Dnl. 11:6), by their hands (Gen. 21:18; Jgs. 16:26) or their feet (2 K. 4:27). A snake may be grasped by the tail (Ex. 4:4), a dog by the ears (Prov. 26:17). The purpose is not always to hold fast that which is grasped; various purposes are possible. The meaning of *hech^ezîq* is intensified when it expresses "solidarity" with other persons (Neh. 10:30[29]) or "holding fast" to an object (Job 8:15).

c. Conversely, a physical or mental state—usually anguish—can "seize" a person (Jer. 6:24; 8:21; 49:24; 50:43; Mic. 4:9).

d. When a living creature or one of its members is "seized" or "grasped," we are often dealing with an act of violence (Gen. 19:16; Ex. 9:2; Dt. 22:25; 25:11; Jgs. 19:25, 29; 1 S. 15:27; 17:35; 2 S. 1:11; 2:16; 13:11; 2 K. 2:12; Jer. 50:33; Zec. 14:13;

Job 18:9; Prov. 26:17). "Holding fast" to an attack (2 S. 11:25) means the use of violence against the object of the attack.

e. There are various specialized uses of *hech^{e}zîq:* one may retain a specified number of qualified persons (Jgs. 7:8), keep people with one through hospitality (Jgs. 19:4; 2 K. 4:8), or "hold" to work (Neh. 5:16); finally, a hollow object can "hold" a specific quantity (2 Ch. 4:5).

III. Religious Usage.

1. *Yahweh.* Most of what *chāzaq* can predicate of human beings can also be predicated of Yahweh, for Yahweh is conceived anthropomorphically as a human being: he has human form and is endowed with physical strength, mental powers, and emotional impulses like those of a human being, but as it were on a gigantic scale. This very fact makes Yahweh infinitely superior to mankind. In one of Jeremiah's confessions (Jer. 20:7), he speaks of such divine superiority over mankind in general and the prophet in particular; this superiority naturally consists not merely or only minimally in physical attributes, but in every respect. The superiority of the personal God Yahweh is often concentrated in the strength of his hand; the prophet Ezekiel, for example, suffers in his ecstasy under the weight of Yahweh's hand (Ezk. 3:14; the form *ḥzqh* is not clearly identifiable). We often read of the "strong" or "mighty" hand (→ יד *yadh*) of Yahweh, or of the "strength" of his hand, often in combinations with such other idioms as "great power" (Ex. 32:11; Neh. 1:10), "greatness" (Dt. 3:24), "outstretched arm" (Dt. 4:34; 5:15; 7:19; 11:2; 26:8; 1 K. 8:42 = 2 Ch. 6:32 [here in combination with "great name"]; Jer. 21:5 ["hand" and "arm" interchanged]; 32:21; Ezk. 20:33f.; Ps. 136:12), or "great deeds" (Dt. 34:12). Without such an associated expression we read of the "mighty hand" of Yahweh in Ex. 3:19; 6:1 (twice); 13:3,9, 14,16; Dt. 6:21; 7:8; 9:26; Josh. 4:24; Dnl. 9:15. In Ex. 3:19 and 6:1, it is not stated explicitly that the "mighty hand" belongs to Yahweh. Moses, the man of God, has a "mighty hand" in consequence of the power granted him (Dt. 34:12). Yahweh likewise has a (hard and great and) "strong" sword (Isa. 27:1); quite generally he is described as strong, sometimes by means of the adjective, sometimes by means of one of the available substantives (Isa. 40:10; Jer. 50:34; Ps. 18:2[1]; Prov. 23:11).

In many cases, Yahweh's strength is the presupposition behind his ability to make men strong as well (cf. Dt. 34:12, mentioned above). The Arameans fear him as a mountain God, because his strength makes the Israelites superior to them in the mountains (1 K. 20:23). Yahweh can lend an individual unbelievable physical strength (Jgs. 16:28), but he can also lend nations and kings political and military strength, whether we are dealing with Israel (Hos. 7:15), an official of Judah (Isa. 22:21), or foreign kings (Jgs. 3:12; Ezk. 30:21, 24f.). Yahweh lends strength when those whose office it is to do so fail (Ezk. 34:4,16). Finally, the Chronicler can state sonorously that Yahweh can make great and give strength to all (1 Ch. 29:12). Yahweh can also strengthen objects such as the bars of gates, in consequence of his strength that surpasses every human measure (Ps. 147:13). Because Yahweh shares his strength with those to whom he lends authority, they are themselves able to strengthen others in like manner (Dnl. 10:18; 11:1 [the latter passage being textually and literarily very unclear; MT thinks of "assistance for Michael through the messenger who is speaking[3]]). Whoever Yahweh has made strong, in whatever manner, feels strong (hithpael: Dnl. 10:19). If Yahweh is thus conceived in human terms, albeit surpassing every human measure, it is not surprising that men in turn should speak to him in "strong," i.e., harsh words (Mal. 3:13), that they should try to withstand his kingdom (2 Ch. 13:8).

The hiphil of *ḥzq* in the sense of "grasp" can likewise be used of Yahweh, usually with him as subject. He grasps men by the hand to appoint them to office (Isa. 42:6; 45:1), or to vouchsafe them salvation (Isa. 41:9,13; Jer. 31:32), which he then logically refuses to do in the case of evildoers (Job 8:20). Yahweh the warrior is called on to take hold of his shield in order to be ready to come to the aid of the worshipper (Ps. 35:2). He is praised as one who does not hold fast to his anger, an emotion (Mic. 7:18). On the other hand, he can expect men to take hold of him (Isa. 64:6[7]) or of his protection (Isa. 27:5).

2. *Temple.* Just as objects, furnishings, and above all buildings that exhibit defects can be "strengthened" by repairs, so, too, can the house of Yahweh (2 K. 12:13[12], twice; the piel should probably be read for the qal). The sources of Kings associate *chizzēq* almost as a rule with the object *bedheq,* "damage" (2 K. 12:7-9, 13 [6-8, 12]; 22:5; without *bedheq:* 2 K. 12:15[14]; 22:6), which the Chronicler systematically avoids. He speaks of "strengthening" or repairing the house of Yahweh, using the construction that appears already in 2 K. 12:15[14]; 22:6 (2 Ch. 24:5, 12; 34:8,10), and also its doors (2 Ch. 29:3). The use of dedicated battle spoil to maintain the temple he also refers to as "strengthening" (1 Ch. 26:27).

3. *Hiphil.* a. The hiphil of *ḥzq* can also be used with reference to what the devout man does or the wicked fool refuses to do: it is important to "hold fast" to devotion, to the commandments, to the covenant, but not to deceit (Isa. 27:5; 56:2,4,6; Jer. 8:5; Job 2:3,9; 27:6; Prov. 3:18; 4:13), and men must be warned against "laying hold" on other gods instead of Yahweh (1 K. 9:9 = 2 Ch. 7:22). Assimilation of the qal to this usage, probably secondary (Deuteronomistic/Chronistic), is found in Dt. 12:23; Josh. 23:6; 1 Ch. 28:7; 2 Ch. 31:4.

b. The use of *hech^ezîq* in this sense also plays a role in the sacral act of catching hold of the horns of the altar (1 K. 1:50; 2:28), whereby one may escape human vengeance. In another passage, the prophet laments that the "children of Jerusalem" have failed to take the city—conceived of as a person—by the hand and thus make her "strong" (Isa. 51:18).

4. *Imperative.* "Strength" can also be evidenced by inward superiority: a task can be undertaken calmly, confidently, courageously. The imperative "be strong" is there-

[3]O. Plöger, *Das Buch Daniel. KAT,* XVIII/1 (1965), 146.

fore frequently used as a formula of encouragement. As the *Sitz im Leben* for this imperative, which is frequently combined with the imperative of → אמץ *'āmats,* we may postulate the rituals of the Yahweh war. (Schreiner, who has coined the term "formula for encouragement" for these imperatives,[4] suggests—with less likelihood—the "royal ideology" as the *Sitz im Leben.*) But the formula continues to be used even in the latest period. Although the heart is generally considered the center of all intellectual, psychological, moral, and religious powers, the word → לב *lēbh* is never used in this context. For the use of *ḥzq* with *lēbh,* see III.5 below; with this meaning, *ḥzq* appears only in the qal and hithpael.

a. The imperative *chᵃzaq* rarely appears by itself (3 times in Hag. 2:4, each addressed to a different person; 2 Ch. 25:8 is texually uncertain). Most often it is used together with the imperative of *'āmats* (Dt. 31:6f.,23; Josh. 1:6,9,18; 10:25; Ps. 27:14; 31:25[24]; 1 Ch. 22:13; 28:20; 2 Ch. 32:7; Dnl. 10:19 [emended]). Additional calls to fearlessness can follow, using such verbs as *yārē'*, *'ārats, ḥtt,* etc. (Dt. 31:6; Josh. 1:9; 10:25; 2 S. 2:7; 13:28; 1 K. 2:2; Isa. 35:4; Zec. 8:13; Dnl. 10:19; 1 Ch. 22:13; 28:20; 2 Ch. 32:7). In such series, *ḥzq* usually comes first. On the basis of the qal imperative, "show courage," the hithpael of *ḥzq* can have the meaning "take courage, exhibit bravery" (Nu. 13:20; 1 S. 4:9; 2 S. 10:12 = 1 Ch. 19:13 [qal and hithpael in juxtaposition]; Dnl. 10:19; Ezr. 7:28; 2 Ch. 15:8; 23:1; 25:11; 32:5) and in one instance "have confidence in someone" (1 S. 30:6).

b. In the later period, the direct consequence of taking courage, namely, the act that follows, is added in the form of a second imperative to the imperative of *ḥzq* (Ezr. 10:4; 1 Ch. 28:10,20; 2 Ch. 19:11). The call to take courage can be made more precise by urging the person addressed to have "strong hands" (2 S. 2:7; 16:21; Ezk. 22:14; Zec. 8:9,13) or not to let his hands be weak (2 Ch. 15:7).

c. The person who encourages another usually adds the reason for his ability. Commonly this is an assurance of Yahweh's presence and aid. In its simplest and probably most primitive form, this assurance states "Yahweh is with you" (Dt. 31:6, 23; Josh. 1:9; Hag. 2:4; 1 Ch. 28:20; 2 Ch. 32:7).[5] In later periods it can be altered: Yahweh, we now read explicitly—and restrictively!—, is with the upright (2 Ch. 19:11). Yahweh's presence means that he will not forsake the person in question (Josh. 1:5f.); it brings prosperity and blessing (Zec. 8:9,13), i.e., *shālôm* (Dnl. 10:19), and guarantees entrance into the promised land (Dt. 31:7) through Yahweh's annihilation of the enemy (Josh. 10:25). The assurance can also consist in the promise of competence to act in a qualified manner (1 Ch. 28:10). Encouragement can also be motivated simply by the promise of a reward (2 Ch. 15:7). In one passage, the imperative to take courage is altered into an indicative assurance that the hands of the person addressed will be "strengthened" (Jgs. 7:11). In Isa. 35:4, the statement that Yahweh will come with

---

[4]Cf. → I, 325f.

[5]For a discussion of this formula, see H. D. Preuss, ". . . ich will mit dir sein!" *ZAW,* 80 (1968), 139-173; → את *'ēth.*

vengeance and salvation takes the place of the motivating assurance. The alternative, namely, that refusal to take courage spells defeat by the enemy, is grounded in God's power to bring victory or to cast down (2 Ch. 25:8). The almost fatalistic understanding of God in the court history of David eschews the motivating assurance; the author can only have Joab express the wish that Yahweh may do what seems good to him (2 S. 10:12). In some cases the motivation of the encouragement formula has no reference to anything done by Yahweh (2 S. 2:7; 13:28; 16:21; Ezr. 10:4).

d. The later period cannot help associating the encouragement formula with the keeping of God's commandments. The logical relationship between the two can take on various forms: strength can be presented as a consequence of obedience to the commandments (Dt. 11:8; Ezr. 9:12); on the other hand, *chāzaq* can be a prerequisite for keeping the commandments (Josh. 1:7; the author of this verse is probably not the same as the author of the context, although both are to be reckoned among the "Deuteronomists"). Sometimes the two are juxtaposed without any causal or conditional linkage (1 K. 2:2f.; 1 Ch. 22:13). In some passages, especially where a kind of concluding summary is being given, there is no further explanation (Josh. 1:18; Ps. 27:14; 31:25[24]); this is obviously the case when we are dealing not with an assurance but with a statement in a different context (Ezk. 22:14).

e. The imperative *ch^{a}zaq* can lose most of its meaning and turn into a general auxiliary imperative like *lēkh* or *habh, hābhāh* (Isa. 41:6).

5. *Hardness of Heart.* When it appears with *lēbh* as its subject (or in the piel with *lēbh* as object), *ḥzq* has a specialized meaning. Here is no trace of any positive significance; in this case, the fundamental meaning "be or become strong" is not the point of departure, but the derived meaning "be or become hard." A heart that has grown hard is unreceptive to outside influences. In other words, the entire person whose heart has grown "hard" shows himself intractable, obdurate, hardened. The Pharaoh of the Mosaic period is so described several times, by E (Ex. 9:35, where the piel should be read for the qal) and especially by P (Ex. 7:13,22; 8:15), whereas J prefers the verb → כבד *kābhēdh*. The piel *chizzēq* has the corresponding active meaning "harden," always with Yahweh as subject (Ex. 10:20, 27 [E]; 9:12; 11:10; 14:4,8,17 [P]; 4:21 [R]; Josh. 11:20 [D]). As a rule, the heart is the object. In one case, the object is the face; here, however, the hardening is self-imposed (Jer. 5:3). When the adjective is used in this sense, not only the heart (Ezk. 2:4), but also the forehead (Ezk. 3:7-9), which is "harder" than flint (3:9), and the face (3:8) can be described as hard.

Hesse

חָטָא *chāṭā'*; חֵטְא *chēṭ'*; חֶטְאָה *cheṭ'āh*; חֲטָאָה *chaṭā'āh*; חַטָּאָה *chaṭṭā'āh*; חַטָּאת *chaṭṭā'th*; חַטָּא *chaṭṭā'*

Contents: I. General: 1. Sin in the Ancient Near East; 2. The Root *ḫ/ḥṭ'*; 3. Distribution and Derivatives; Semantic Field; 4. Concrete Basic Meaning? II. Early Historical Books: 1. Communal Background; 2. Reward-Punishment Nexus; 3. *chaṭā'āh* and *chaṭṭā'th*; 4. Connection with *nś'*; 5. Cultic Associations. III. Psalms. IV. Prophets: 1. *chaṭṭā'th* as History of Sin; 2. Objects of Criticism; 3. Future Elimination of Sin. V. *chēṭ'*. VI. P and Ezk. 40–48: 1. Occurrences; 2. Ritual, not Sacrifice; 3. Connection with *nephesh, 'āshām, qōdhesh*; 4. Legislation and Individualization; 5. Removal through Substitutionary Death; 6. *'āshām* Ritual; 7. Cleansing of the Sanctuary; 8. Annual Festivals; 9. Usage before P? VII. Apocalyptic. VIII. Qumran.

I. General.

1. *Sin in the Ancient Near East.* Sin as the religious disqualification of specific modes of human behavior plays varying roles in the individual civilizations of the

---

chāṭā'. V. J. Almiñana Lloret, "El pecado en el Deuteronomio," *EstBib*, 29 (1970), 267-285; J. Z. Baruch, "The Relation between Sin and Disease in the OT," *Janus*, 51 (1964), 295-302; A. Barucq, "Péché et innocence dans les psaumes bibliques et les textes religieux de l'Égypte du Nouvel Empire," in *Études de critique et d'histoire religieuses. Festschrift L. Vaganay* (Lyon, 1948), 111-137; E. Beaucamp, *Données bibliques pour une réflexion théologique sur le péché* (1963); *idem*, "Le problème du péché dans la Bible," *LTP*, 25 (1969), 88-114; *idem*, "Péché, I. Dans l'A.T.," *DBS*, 7 (1966), 407-471; *idem*, "Sin and the Bible," *Review for Religious*, 22 (1963), 129-147; K. H. Fahlgren, *Ṣ^e^dāḵā* (Uppsala, 1932), repr. in *Um das Prinzip der Vergeltung in Religion und Recht des AT*, ed. K. Koch. *Wege der Forschung*, 125 (1972), 93-106; J. J. Ferrero Blanco, "El pecado en la Biblia," *Sinite*, 8 (1967), 181-212; M. Garcia Cordero, *Teología de la Biblia*, I: *AT* (Madrid, 1970); A. Gélin, "Sin in the O.T.," in his *Sin in the Bible* (trans. 1965), 7-39; A. George, "Le sens du péché dans l'AT," *Lumière et Vie*, 5 (1952), 21-40; R. Knierim, *Die Hauptbegriffe für Sünde im AT* ([2]1967); *idem*, "חטא *ḥṭ'* sich verfehlen," *THAT*, I, 541-550; K. Koch, "Gibt es ein Vergeltungsdogma in AT?" *ZThK*, 52 (1955), 1-42, repr. in *Um das Prinzip der Vergeltung*, 130-180; *idem*, "Sünde und Sündenvergebung um die Wende von der exilischen zur nachexilischen Zeit," *EvTh*, 26 (1966), 217-239; N. Lade, "The Concept of Sin in the Law," *ABR*, 7 (1959), 54-57; B. A. Levine, *In the Presence of the Lord. StJLA*, 5 (1974); L. Ligier, *Péché d'Adam et péché du monde* (Paris, 1960/61); N. Lohfink, "Die Ursünden in der priesterlichen Geschichtserzählung," in *Die Zeit Jesu. Festschrift H. Schlier* (1970), 38-57; F. Maass, "אָדָם *'ādhām*," *TDOT*, I, 86f.; R. Mayer, "Sünde und Gericht in der Bildersprache der vorexilischen Prophetie," *BZ*, N.S. 8 (1964), 22-44; J. Milgrom, "החטאת הפקיד קרבן; The Function of the *haṭṭā't* Sacrifice," *Tarbiz*, 40 (1970/71), 1-8, I; L. Morris, "The Punishment of Sin in the OT," *ABR*, 6 (1958), 61-86; J. Pedersen, *ILC*, I-II (1926), 411-452; Š. Porúbčan, *Sin in the OT. Aloisiana*, 3 (1963); G. von Rad, *OT Theol.*, I (trans. 1962), 262-272; R. Rendtorff, *Studien zur Geschichte des Opfers im Alten Israel. WMANT*, 24 (1967), 199-234; G. Robinson, "A Terminological Study of the Idea of Sin in the OT," *Indian Journal of Theology*, 18 (1969), 112-123; J. Scharbert, "Unsere Sünden und die Sünden unserer Väter," *BZ*, N.S. 2 (1958), 14-26; *idem*, *Prolegomena eines Alttestamentlers zur Erbsündenlehre. Quaest Disp*, 37 (1968); P. Schoonenberg, "Der Mensch in der Sünde," in *Die Heilsgeschichte vor Christus. Mysterium Salutis*, II (Einsiedeln, 1967), 845-941; L. van den Wijngaert, "Die Sünde in der priesterschriftlichen Urgeschichte," *ThPh*, 43 (1968), 35-50.

ancient Near East. The Egyptians, who recognized cosmically determined *ma'at* (justice, righteousness) as the ideal that rules the totality of life, speak above all of *isf.t*[1] as behavior contrary to *ma'at,* which brings misfortune upon the doer. The occurrence of series of declarations of innocence, especially in a funerary context,[2] where we may possibly be dealing with magical denial of one's own misdeeds, casts a special light on the Egyptian ideas of sin, how it is made possible, and how it can be prevented.

The Sumerians are more inclined to refer calamity to malicious caprice on the part of the gods than to one's own evil deeds. This probably changes in the Akkadian realm, where sin (*arnu, ḫīṭu, šertu,* etc.) and atonement (*šuluḫḫu, kuppuru*) become central religious issues.[3] Nowhere else, however, does sin achieve such anthropological and theological importance as in the OT, under the influence of the reforming prophets and the cultic institutions of the postexilic period. For a discussion of the concept of sin in the ancient Near East, see → עון *'āvōn.*

2. *The root ḫ/ḥṭ'.* All the Semitic languages share the root *ḥṭ'*—strictly speaking *ḫṭ'*, later occasionally *ḥṭy.* It designates negative conditions and conduct, especially with reference to human agents in a religious context. The significance of the root in the religious conceptual system varies, however. Arabic (*ḫaṭi'a,* "make a mistake")[4] and Ethiopic (*ḫaṭa'a,* "fail to find")[5] exhibit a degraded usage. In Ugaritic only the verb *ḫṭ'* is definitely attested ("sin"? "free from sin"?);[6] other modes of usage are disputed.[7] In many Aramaic dialects such as Biblical and Jewish Palestinian Aramaic, the root *ḥwb* takes the place of Heb. *ḥṭ'*. But wherever *ḫ/ḥ/hṭ'* plays an important religious role, not only are the various stems of the verb used, but both masculine and feminine nouns are found, derived from both the basic stem and the intensive stems. This is true for both Mandean (the nouns *haṭia, hṭata, hṭita,* and *haṭaiia,* in addition to the verb)[8] and Syriac.[9] Even in Akkadian we find not only the verb *ḫaṭû* II in the G, Gtn, D, Dtn, and Š stems, but also the derivatives *ḫaṭû* I and *ḫaṭṭû,* "faulty, guilty," *ḫaṭṭa/i'u* and *ḫaṭṭû,* "sinner," *ḫīṭu* and later *ḫiṭṭu,* "fault, damage, guilt, sin," as well as *ḫiṭitu,* "damage."[10]

3. *Distribution and Derivatives; Semantic Field.* In the OT, *ḥṭ'* and its derivatives, from the earliest to the latest strata, provide the most common means of expressing religious disqualification of specific human acts and modes of conduct. Only in a few of the prophets, for instance, Amos, do other words such as → פשע *pš'* come to the fore.

---

1 *WbÄS,* I, 129.
2 Book of the Dead, chap. 125; *ANET*³, 34-36.
3 W. von Soden, "Religion und Sittlichkeit nach der Anschauungen der Babylonier," *ZDMG,* 89 (1935), 143-169.
4 Wehr, 245.
5 *LexLingAeth,* 619f.
6 *CTA,* 32, 11, 14f.
7 *WUS,* No. 1019; *UT,* No. 951.
8 *MdD,* 118, 140.
9 *LexSyr,* 226f.
10 *AHw,* I, 337f., 350.

The verb appears about 175 times in the qal, 15 in the piel, 32 in the hiphil, and 9 in the hithpael.

In addition, there are six nominal forms. From the simple stem we have the segholate form *chēṭ'* (33 occurrences),[11] with a possible feminine variant *cheṭ'āh* (Nu. 15:28), as well as the substantive *chᵃṭā'āh* (9 occurrences).

The following intensive forms appear: the adjective *chaṭṭā'* (19 occurrences), a feminine substantive with an open ending *chaṭṭā'āh* (only Ex. 34:7; Isa. 5:18), and one with a closed ending *chaṭṭā'th* (about 290 occurrences). There are probably semantic differences between the individual forms, but this problem has not been explored. The substantives are all uniformly rendered as "sin" or the corresponding word in another modern language. We shall attempt below provisionally to determine variant connotations.

The semantic field includes above all → עוֹן *'āvōn* and → פֶּשַׁע *pesha'*, also → רַע *ra'*, "evil, wicked," → טָמֵא *ṭāmē'*, "unclean," etc.

4. *Concrete Basic Meaning?* Scholars commonly postulate a "concrete" basic meaning "miss (a mark)," citing Jgs. 20:16; Prov. 8:35f.; 19:2; Job 5:24. But this is scanty evidence in view of the religious usage attested centuries earlier among the Semites. Was there ever a concrete basic meaning? Is it not more likely that the four passages cited contain a "metaphorical" usage (cf. "sinfully delicious")?

II. Early Historical Books.

1. *Communal Background.* In the early historical books, *chāṭā'* means to commit an offense against someone with whom one stands in an institutionalized community relationship. The substantives refer to antisocial conduct directed against a person (in contrast to other terms for guilt such as → אָשָׁם *'āshām* or → עוֹן *'āvōn*). Such conduct includes offenses against one's own brother (Gen. 42:22; 50:17) and murder of a compatriot (2 K. 21:17), rebellion against one's king (Gen. 40:1; 1 S. 24:12 [Eng. v. 11]; 26:21), and rebellion of a vassal against an overlord (2 K. 18:14). But the term *ḥṭ'* can also be used for mistreatment of a subject by the king (1 S. 19:4f.), of Israel by Pharaoh (Ex. 5:16), of the sojourner's wife by Abimelech (Gen. 20:9), or of a servant by his master (Gen. 31:36). When someone commits an offense against a superior, → פשׁע *pš'* can be added interpretatively (Gen. 31:36; 50:17). The victim of the offense is introduced by the particle *lᵉ*-. It is noteworthy that God himself is usually the victim (52 times, as against 14 instances of *lᵉ*- with human victims). Did *ḥṭ'* originally mean the breaking of a taboo? This would explain the predominance of offenses directed against God. It is a sin against Yahweh to transgress his commandment (1 S. 15:24), to mistreat his people (Ex. 10:17), or to infringe on his divine power over life by consuming blood (1 S. 14:33f.). Above all it is a sin to practice divination (1 S. 15:23) or idolatry (Ex. 32:30–34; Dt. 9:16–18). In the preexilic period, however, no reference is ever made to any explicit law or commandment of God as a norm. It appears that what is sinful is not yet determined by law.

---

[11] *BLe,* § 580t'.

2. *Reward-Punishment Nexus.* For the Hebrew, there was an obvious connection between an action and its consequences. Therefore *chaṭṭā'th* means not only the evil deed, but also the associated consequences. The deed itself is conceived of as a sphere surrounding the sinner, bringing calamity upon him in the course of time. It is also possible to conceive of *chaṭṭā'th* as an independent agent prior to human action, a *rōbhēts,* "demon," crouching at a man's door, waiting to lead him astray; but this conception appears in only a single early passage (Gen. 4:7 [J]). It is likewise possible for someone deliberately to bring *ch^{a}ṭā'āh* upon someone else (*hēbhî,* Gen. 20:9; Ex. 32:21). It is clear in any case that *chaṭṭā'th* and *māveth* go together (Ex. 10:17). Whoever surrounds himself with *chaṭṭā'th* must necessarily die. The sphere of calamity has collective effects. In the long run it destroys not only the sinner but his entire house, for generations (1 K. 13:34).

Such a sin not only remains invisibly associated with the sinner on earth, pregnant with disaster; it is also—in every case of *ḥṭ'* or only in the case of sacral transgressions?—visible in the sight of Yahweh (1 S. 2:17), arousing his anger (1 K. 8:46) and provoking Yahweh's personal reaction against the sinner, called *pāqadh,* "visit, punish" (Ex. 32:34; Hos. 8:13; 9:9). Whenever *chaṭṭā'th* is used, there is always more involved than the consequences of the deed upon the doer; a further divine intervention is always expected.

3. *ch^{a}ṭā'āh and chaṭṭā'th.* The various nominal derivatives of the root appear to possess semantic distinctions, which, however, are difficult to bring to light because the textual evidence is so fragmentary. Thus it appears that the feminine form derived from the simple stem with the open ending, *ch^{a}ṭā'āh,* refers to the individual deed, whereas the feminine form based on the intensive with closed ending, *chaṭṭā'th,* refers to the enduring sphere of conduct observed by Yahweh, which he will one day punish or which must be atoned for. The double alternation between the two substantives in Ex. 32:30-32 can be explained in this way:

Moses to the people:

'attem ch^{a}ṭā'them ch^{a}ṭā'āh gh^{e}dhōlāh . . .
'ûlai '^{a}khapp^{e}rāh b^e'adh chaṭṭa'thkhem.

Moses to Yahweh:

'ānnā' chāṭā' hā'ām hazzeh ch^{a}ṭā'āh gh^{e}dhōlāh . . .
v^e'attāh 'im-tiśśā' chaṭṭā'thām.

In this case, *ch^{a}ṭā'āh* means the people's deliberate rebellion, *chaṭṭā'th* the corresponding circumstance of guilt in the eyes of God. In general, nouns derived from the root *ḥṭ'* can refer to objective transgressions of a communal relationship, whether committed consciously and deliberately or unconsciously (Gen. 20:9; Ps. 38:4,19[3, 18]; cf. the verb in Ps. 41:5[4]). In the course of time, however, we can observe an increasing concern with individual responsibility (see the discussion of P below).

4. *Connection with nś'*. Part of the conception of *ḥṭ'*, "sin," is that it must be borne by the sinner and his circle (cf. Old Bab. *ḫiṭīṭam našūm* and Assyr. *ḫīṭa našū*).[12] Of course the verb *nāśā'* has this sense of bearing the sphere of sin only when it is associated with the masculine noun *chēṭ'* (8 times; see below) or with *'āvōn,* which is related to the derivatives of *ḥṭ'* (13 times).[13] The idiom *nāśā' chaṭṭā'th,* i.e., the verb with feminine object, always means the carrying away of the sphere of guilt from the sinner by a third party, who intervenes vicariously, intercedes, and averts the consequence of death (Ex. 10:17; 1 S. 15:25). It can also mean the removal of the sphere of guilt from the sinner by the injured party himself, if he is willing and able to do so (Gen. 50:17; Ex. 32:32, cf. 34:7; *nāśā'* with *l^e-:* Josh. 24:19; Ps. 25:18).

5. *Cultic Associations*. The root *ḥṭ'* belongs to the language of the cult and has its *Sitz im Leben* in specific ceremonies. In the case of a serious misdeed, the sinner is convicted according to sacral law or prophetically in the name of Yahweh and compelled to confess his sin. In the case of an individual, the form is *chāṭā'thî l^eyhvh* (Josh. 7:20; 2 S. 12:13; etc.).[14] This is followed either by remission of the punishment (through an act of atonement) or by execution. The people confess *chāṭā'nû;* in later texts, *'āvînû* is added (Dnl. 9:5; cf. 2 Ch. 6:37); the confession appears to have been recited in the context of communal laments (1 S. 7:5f.).[15]

Yahweh's conduct toward the sinner is primarily motivated by the desire to remove the sphere of calamity from the sinner. God's will for the Israelite is salvation and well-being. This purpose is accomplished through rites meant to → כפר *kpr* or → סלח *slḥ* (Ex. 32:30; 34:9; 1 K. 8:34,36,50; Jer. 36:3; 2 Ch. 6:25,27). By their means, he causes *chaṭṭā'th* to pass by the sinner (*'ābhar,* 2 S. 12:13; 24:10) or to turn aside from him (*sûr,* Ex. 10:17); a child, for example, can die as a means of atonement for his father (2 S. 12:14). In the case of human beings, repentance is (later?) presupposed (→ שׁוּב *shûbh,* 1 K. 8:46). In addition, an intercessor is needed, i.e., a specially gifted man of God (*pll,* Nu. 21:7; 1 S. 2:25; 1 K. 8:45-49).

III. Psalms. In the Psalter, *ḥṭ'* appears almost exclusively in laments. The singers acknowledge the connection between acts and their consequences in their suffering. On account of the worshipper's *chaṭṭā'th,* there is no health in his bones (38:4[3]). Ps. 51:5(3) should perhaps be understood in the same sense: *chaṭṭā'th* stands constantly before the worshipper. Those who lament cry out to Yahweh, praying him to hide his face from human *ch^aṭā'îm* (51:11[9]), to forgive their *chaṭṭō'th* (25:18; 32:5) or to cover them (32:1; 85:3[2]), blot them out (109:14), wash them (51:4,9[2,7]), not to remember them (25:7), to purge them (*ḥṭ'* piel, 51:9), and to atone for them (79:9). Concrete cultic acts of atonement are probably intended.

---

[12] W. Zimmerli, *BK,* XIII/1 (1969), 306.

[13] W. Zimmerli, "Die Eigenart der prophetischen Rede des Ezechiel," *ZAW,* 66 (1954), 10f. = his *Gottes Offenbarung. ThB,* 19 ([2]1969), 159f.

[14] Knierim, 21.

[15] *Ibid.,* 35-37.

A few psalms exhibit a truly genuine and profound consciousness of sin, particularly 32:1-5 and 51:3-11(1-9), a conviction that "against thee, thee only, have I sinned," as well as a sense of being entangled in a sphere of sin even before birth, through family solidarity (51:6f.[4f.]). The careful distinctions made by the psalmists are illustrated by the difference between *chᵃṭā'āh* (an individual act?) and *chaṭṭā'th;* the latter must be confessed and borne as a single whole (32:1,5; cf. also 109:7 and 14). A distinction is also made between *chaṭṭā'th* of an individual, which requires atonement, and *chēṭ'* extending over generations, for which, of course, no atonement can be expected (51:4-7[2-5]). Terms derived from the root *ḥṭ'* can be preceded by *'āvōn* as the comprehensive guilt of sin (32:5; 51:7[5]; 38:19[18]; 109:14). In its place or in addition we also find *pesha'* (51:3f.[1f.]; 59:4[3]).

IV. Prophets.

1. *chaṭṭā'th as History of Sin.* The reforming (writing) prophets are so convinced that the situation of their nation is untenable that they consider its destruction inescapable. It therefore becomes their primary task to proclaim to Israel its *chaṭṭā'th* (Mic. 3:8). To them *chaṭṭā'th* appears as a force that transcends the course of history and therefore determines the immediate future negatively. From the days of Gibeah Israel has sinned; now the time is finally at hand when Yahweh *yiphqōdh chaṭṭôthām* and reverses the course of sacred history by making Israel return to Egypt (Hos. 10:9; cf. 8:13; 9:9; cf. Jer. 14:10). With the fathers *chaṭṭā'th* began, and it continues to the present day (Jer. 3:25; 14:20). The entire land, not just its inhabitants, is polluted (Jer. 16:18; 17:3). Rain and harvest are prevented by an immense sphere of *chaṭṭā'th* (Jer. 5:25), and enemies are justified in what they do to an Israel weakened by its *chaṭṭā'th* (50:7). Both Samaria and Jerusalem had their own *chaṭṭō'th,* on which each has foundered or will founder (Ezk. 16:51f.). As a logical consequence of this history of sin, the state was destroyed in 585/586, as Jer. 40:3 has a Babylonian officer say.

In the face of such historical burdens imposed by the ancient heritage and recent activation of *chaṭṭā'th,* rituals of atonement are useless. Hos. 4:8 and Mic. 6:7 clearly presuppose such rites, in which a son or a domestic animal is given over to die vicariously for the head of the house. Here *chaṭṭā'th* already takes on the meaning of a means of atonement (see the discussion of P below). It is no surprise that the prophets expect nothing positive of such actions.

2. *Objects of Criticism.* What gives the conduct of Israel its *ḥṭ'* character can for the most part be determined only indirectly from the prophets' criticism of their own generation. For Hosea, the high places with their cultic practices are the locus of Israel's *chaṭṭā'th* (Hos. 10:8); for Jeremiah, too, idolatry above all is a personal insult to Yahweh, and is termed apostasy (*mᵉshûbhāh,* Jer. 14:7; 16:10f.; 17:1,3; 32:35; 44:23). Refusal to obey God's voice has the same dire consequences (Jer. 2:35; 40:3; 44:23). For Isaiah, on the contrary, *chaṭṭā'th* is arrogant alliance with human powers (Isa. 30:1) or mockery of Yahweh's supposedly delayed plan (5:18f.). For Micah, the mighty garrison city of Lachish is the beginning of all *chaṭṭā'th* (Mic. 1:13). Whatever the criticism may be in detail, one result in each case is always the fact that

the calamitous connection between deeds and their consequences can no longer be evaded. The sinners have inscribed their *chaṭṭā'th* on the tablet of their heart (Jer. 17:1); they have brought evil upon their own *nephesh* (Isa. 3:9); they lie down in their shame (Jer. 3:25) and can only await the end. The coming day of Yahweh will destroy all *chaṭṭā'îm* from the earth, and the burden of sin will finally be atoned for when altars and cities are destroyed (Isa. 27:9).

3. *Future Elimination of Sin.* The prophets nevertheless think in terms of a final turn to the positive. With Jeremiah (deuteronomistically edited?) we begin to hear encouragement to turn and repent, which will be followed by *slḥ* and *ṭhr* on the part of Yahweh (Jer. 36:3; cf. 31:34; 33:8; 50:20). And Ezekiel never tires of calling on the individual to turn away from his wicked way and *chaṭṭā'th* (18:21; 33:10,14), lest he die in his sphere of calamity brought on by sin (*b^echaṭṭa'thô yāmûth,* 3:20; 18:24). Yahweh himself will help men renew their lives by giving them new minds (→ לֵב *lēbh*), to which the evil bent toward sin is unknown (Jer. 31:31-34; Ezk. 37:23f.).

V. chēṭ'. The most momentous of the derivatives of *ḥṭ'* is *chēṭ'*. It occurs only 33 times, but particularly in the realm of D and P (8 times each) it refers to an unforgivable burden of sin transcending individual acts, leading ineluctably to death through the connections between acts and their consequences. Outside of cultic language, *chēṭ'* appears only twice, referring each time to a (capital) offence against an earthly king, characteristically never against ordinary men (Gen. 41:9; Eccl. 10:4). Frequently *chēṭ'* is accompanied by the substantive *'āvōn,* but always precedes it, just as *'āvōn* in turn precedes the feminine form *chaṭṭā'th,* so that we may postulate a conceptual hierarchy *chēṭ'—'āvōn—chaṭṭā'th* (Dt. 19:15; Nu. 18:22f.; Hos. 12:9[8]; Ps. 51:11[9]; 103:10; Dnl. 9:16).

An earlier period (or noncultic circles?) reckons with the possibility that Yahweh can deliver a man from his sphere of *chēṭ'* through an atoning judgment (Isa. 1:18), effectively ignoring the sinful man (Isa. 38:17; Ps. 51:11[9]; 103:10), or the mediation of the atoning Servant of God (Isa. 53:12). For Deuteronomy and P, however, *chēṭ'* (not *chaṭṭā'th!*) necessarily leads to the destruction of the one who bears it. When *chēṭ'* comes into being in (*hāyāh b^e-*) a man through a terrible social and cultic crime (Dt. 15:9; 21:22; 23:22[21]; 24:15), death is inescapable (Lev. 22:9; Nu. 18:22; cf. Lam. 1:8). For *chēṭ'* impinges on the *nephesh,* the center of life (Nu. 9:13; Isa. 38:17; 53:12). Death therefore threatens *hannephesh hachōṭē'th* (Ezk. 18:4,20).[16] The responsible party—but he alone as an individual—must die in his *chēṭ'* sphere (*b^echeṭ'ô yāmûth,* Nu. 27:3; Dt. 24:16; 2 K. 14:6 = 2 Ch. 25:4). The psalmist and Deutero-Isaiah, by contrast, can see *chēṭ'* as an entity encompassing generations or many people (Ps. 51:7[5]; Isa. 53:12). Idolatry is a frequent source of *chēṭ'*. The *'^elîlîm* (→ אֱלִיל *'^elîl*) or images, fashioned by human hands as objects of worship, secretly take on a life of their own and are followed by men as though in an hypnotic trance (2 K. 10:29; Isa. 31:7; Ezk. 23:49).

---

[16] *Ibid.*, 48f.

When a *chēṭ'* sphere comes into being, the evildoer must bear its invisible presence until it brings him to an end through death. The common expression is *nāśā' chēṭ'* or *cheṭ'ô* (Lev. 19:17; 20:20; 22:9; 24:15; Nu. 9:13; 18:22, 32; Ezk. 23:49), different in meaning from *nāśā' chaṭṭā'th*. Deutero-Isaiah still considers the possibility that another might vicariously bear *chēṭ'* for an evildoer (Isa. 53:12), which is true only of *chaṭṭā'th* in the realm of P (see below).

VI. P and Ezk. 40–48.

1. *Occurrences*. On the 293 occurrences of *chaṭṭā'th,* 126 or 43 percent are found in the P sections of the Pentateuch. Lexicographers are wont to recognize the meaning "sin" for only a minority of these, translating the majority as "sin offering."[17] The next greatest number of occurrences is in the book of Ezekiel, where *chaṭṭā'th* appears 24 times; in the majority of occurrences, once again, it is translated "sin offering" (14 times). The assignment to one or the other meaning varies from exegete to exegete. Should we really postulate a double usage of the word, a technical meaning alongside the common meaning? Or are the two meanings really more closely related than they seem to the modern western observer? In any case, in the exilic/postexilic period the word *chaṭṭā'th* takes on a special religious significance. This change is undoubtedly connected with the large-scale reinterpretation of the Israelite cult in Ex. 25–Lev. 16, where P makes practically all the cultic acts around the tent of meeting serve the purpose of atonement and the removal of sins. The same purpose is suggested by some derived stems of the verb *chāṭā'* that make their first appearance in this period. The piel is used 15 times (7 in P and 4 in Ezekiel), meaning "perform a ritual of purification." Of 9 hithpael forms, 8 belong to P with the meaning "purify oneself."

2. *Ritual, not Sacrifice*. The translation "sin offering" for the ritual referred to by *chaṭṭā'th,* however firmly established, nevertheless appears to be a serious blunder, dating from a time when every non-Christian ritual act was conceived of in the sense of the Latin *do ut des* as a sacrifice to the deity. But Yahweh is not the recipient of the *chaṭṭā'th*. The ritual is admittedly termed *qorbān* (Lev. 4:32), an offering at the sanctuary, but solely because only there can it take effect—to the benefit of the one offering it! The purpose of performing *chaṭṭā'th* is the destruction of sin, *kipper* and *sālach* for the worshipper (Lev. 4:20, 26, 31, 35, etc.).

Yahweh does not receive, he gives; he is not the object but the subject of an act that is performed in his name by the priest. In a single passage, Lev. 4:31, the fat of the *chaṭṭā'th* is described as *l^ereach nîchōach l^eyhvh,* but this is the result of textual corruption.[18]

3. *Connection with nephesh, 'āshām, qōdhesh*. The ritual in P derives its meaning from the Hebrew idea of a sphere of consequences arising from an act. Sin has its locus in the *nephesh* (Lev. 4:2,23f., 27f.; Nu. 15:27), which seals its own doom thereby.

---

[17]According to Lisowski-Rost, *Konkordanz zum hebräischen AT,* 89 passages.

[18]See *BHS* and v. 35; J. Herrmann, *TDNT,* III, 305, n. 22.

Similarly, the verb *chāṭā'* means both "sin" and "bring calamity upon oneself," "punish oneself" (Lev. 5:7,11; Nu. 27:3). The consequence of sin is called *chēṭ'* (Nu. 9:13; 18:22). Usually, however, a *chaṭṭā'th* done against the will of Yahweh imposes its burden on the doer as an *'āshām* sphere. Not *'āvōn*, as in the preexilic texts, but *'āshām* is the usual consequence of *chaṭṭā'th* and the corresponding burden for the doer (Lev. 4:2,13,22, etc.). The term *'āvōn* appears relatively infrequently and represents something more than *'āshām* (Lev. 5:1,17; 16:21). To bear one's *'āvōn* means to perish (Nu. 5:31).

Whenever sinners approach the sanctuary of Yahweh, divine holiness will prove deadly to them. For everyone who enters into a close relationship with Yahweh, it is therefore necessary to remove the sphere of *chaṭṭā'th*. This is especially true of priests at their ordination (Ex. 29:14; cf. Ezk. 44:27) and of Levites (Nu. 8:7f.).

4. *Legislation and Individualization.* Of course the word *chaṭṭā'th* itself no longer means—as formerly—both the act and its consequences; the root *ḥṭ'* has also lost its communal facet, probably on account of the collapse of the old social institutions during the exilic period. Henceforth the criterion for what counts as sin is provided by the law of Yahweh, his *mitsvōth* (Lev. 4:2,13,22, etc.; cf. already Jer. 16:10–12). There is a corresponding thorough individualization of the concept of sin (Nu. 16:22: "Shall one man sin, and wilt thou be angry with all the congregation?"), broken only by the corporative responsibility of the messiah-priest (Lev. 4:3; 16:21f.).

5. *Removal through Substitutionary Death.* Through his instructions promulgated at Sinai, Yahweh in his wise providence took account of human sinfulness by making it possible for an Israelite sinner to be freed from his sphere of sin at the sanctuary (*v^ehēbhî eth-'^ashāmô '^asher chāṭā'*, Lev. 5:7). The person in question comes to the sanctuary with one of his domestic animals, a bull, sheep, goat, or dove. There, by being sacrificed in the effectual presence of Yahweh, the animal becomes sin in the literal sense, i.e., the sphere of *chaṭṭā'th* becomes concentrated in the animal, as it were becoming flesh in an animal body (*'al chaṭṭā'th* the animal becomes *l^echaṭṭā'th;* cf. Lev. 4:28 with v. 3). Through the imposition of hands, sometimes accompanied by a confession of sin (Lev. 5:5; Nu. 5:6f.), the act of transfer is made manifest (Lev. 16:21). In the name of Yahweh the priest slaughters the animal. The blood is disposed of in part by sprinkling (*nāzāh* hiphil) on sacred objects (usually the horns of the altar, but the more serious the transgression, the closer the blood must be brought to the ark in the holy of holies; cf. Lev. 4:6,16), and by pouring (*shāphakh*) at the base of the altar. Thus the death of the sin animal takes place vicariously for its human owner. The sinner is now forgiven (*sālach*). His vital center (*nephesh*) has been atoned (*kpr*) "from its previous *chaṭṭā'th* sphere" (*mēchaṭṭā'thô*, Lev. 4:26; 5:6,10). Atonement has been made "upon" ("on account of"?) his *chaṭṭā'th* in which he had sinned (*'al chaṭṭa'thô '^asher chāṭā'*, Lev. 4:35; 5:13); for the sinning took place "upon the *nephesh*" (Nu. 6:11). In the atonement ritual for an individual, the flesh of the animal is consumed by the priests (Lev. 7:35–37; Ezk. 42:13; 44:29). For sins of the community or the priest himself, it is burned in front of the camp (Lev. 4:12–21).

6. *'āshām Ritual.* In Lev. 5, the priestly cultic legislation distinguishes a similar (later?) *'āshām* ritual from the *chaṭṭā'th* ritual. It appears as though the *chaṭṭā'th* animal is used only for unintentional sins (*sh^e ghāghāh*) that are later made known (by lot or prophetic oracle? Lev. 4:14, 23) or for kinds of impurity that come unavoidably (Lev. 12:6,8; 14:13,19,22,31). The *'āshām* animal (or *'āshām* flour), which as a rule is an addition to the *chaṭṭā'th* ritual, would then atone primarily for deliberate transgressions.[19] The underlying concept, however, remains the same. The *'āshām* ritual, too, grows out of a *chaṭṭā'th* act that has been "sinned" (Lev. 5:6, 15).

7. *Cleansing of the Sanctuary.* Since a sphere of sin infects not only the sinner but also his surroundings and above all the sacred objects on earth, *chaṭṭā'th* blood must regularly atone for the altar and sanctuary (Ex. 30:10; Lev. 16:16-20,33; Ezk. 43:19-26), so that they may be consecrated again by subsequent anointing (Ex. 29:36; Lev. 8:15).

8. *Annual Festivals.* The ordinances of P are permeated with the conviction that men will repeatedly fall into sin, and are motivated by the concern that a future Israel, united with its God around the tent of meeting (Ex. 29:43-45), might slide once more into a history of decay as experienced by the preexilic nation. Protection against sin therefore becomes a determining element of every major cultic act. Appropriate rituals are therefore incorporated into the annual festivals—not yet the Sabbath, but the beginning of the month, Passover, the Feast of Weeks, the New Year Festival, the Feast of Booths (Nu. 28:15,22,30; 29:5,16,19,25; Ezk. 45:18-25). The cultic year culminates in the Day of Atonement for all the sins of Israel, the regulations for which are therefore placed at the conclusion of the cultic legislation in Lev. 1-16.

Even apart from these ceremonies it may be possible and necessary to be freed from a *chaṭṭā'th* sphere. Whoever becomes unclean through contact with a corpse uses the water of the red *chaṭṭā'th* heifer to cleanse himself (Nu. 19:9-13). And as long as priests are in service, they "bear" the *'āvōn* that otherwise would be upon the sanctuary (Nu. 18:1; cf. Ex. 28:38), as they do particularly by eating the remains of the *chaṭṭā'th* animal (Lev. 10:17).

9. *Usage before P?* It has often been suggested by OT scholars that even before P the word *chaṭṭā'th* was used with the technical meaning "sin offering," specifically in Hos. 4:8; Mic. 6:7 (the first-born offered as *chaṭṭā'th nephesh*); Ps. 40:7(6) (*ch^a ṭā'āh,* with an open ending); and finally 2 K. 12:17(16) (the priests are given money for *'āshām* and *chaṭṭā'th,* presumably for performing the corresponding rituals). The debate over whether or not technical usage is exhibited is otiose if the conclusion presented above is correct, namely, that even in P *chaṭṭā'th* as an atonement ritual and as an embodied sphere of sin are intimately related. It is then only necessary to assume that the idea of being able to remove a *chaṭṭā'th* sphere at the sanctuary of Yahweh through the substitutionary death of another living creature was familiar in the preexilic

[19] For a discussion, see → אשׁם *'āshām,* I, 431-35.

period. It can then remain an open question to what extent *chaṭṭā'th* was already a standard term for a very specific ritual.

VII. Apocalyptic. It is unfortunately no longer possible to tell to what extent the talk of human in apocalyptic literature involves the root *ḥṭ'*. But in this literature sin becomes a negative force encompassing all mankind, brought into being by men of their own accord (1 En. 98:4). "All that are born are corrupted with wickedness, full of sins, burdened with guilt" (2 Esdr. 7:68f.; cf. v. 46; 8:35). For the origin of these sins, two explanations are possible. On the one hand, the fallen angels are accounted as those who brought sin to the earth (1 En. 10:4ff.; 64:1ff.); on the other, Adam (or Eve, Sir. 25:24) is held accountable for the sins of all his descendants (2 Esdr. 3:21ff.; 7:11f.,48ff.; 2 Bar. 23:4; 48:42; 54:15). Eschatological hope, by contrast, looks forward to a time when the earth will be free of sin and the elect will no longer sin, either through carelessness or through pride (1 En. 10:22; 5:8f.).

VIII. Qumran. The ideas of the Qumran community are a logical extension of what the late portions of the OT say about the role of sin in the history of mankind. The origin of sin is now ascribed to the sovereignty of Belial, which brings about *ʿavōnôth, pishʿê 'ashmāh/maʿᵃśîm,* and *chattô'th*. Thereby the human side of Israel's history is determined, just as the salutary *ṣdq* side was created by God himself (1 QS 1:21-23; cf. 4QFlor 1:6). The angel of darkness leads even the Israelites as *bᵉnê tsedheq* astray into the nexus of sin and calamity (1QS 3:22). The human individual thus becomes an edifice of *chᵃṭā'āh,* and is therefore consigned to dust and vermin (1QH 1:22; 11:20; 1QS 11:9).

There is hope for the sinner, however, if he repents and leaves the *chᵃṭā'āh* sphere (1QH 6:6). For Qumran, too, sin remains an almost concrete, spatial sphere; therefore no one can free himself from it by his own power. Atonement is necessary, which is vouchsafed by divine agency. Entities like the divine *rûach* or *tsᵉdhāqāh* make atonement for (*ʿal*) man by removing and destroying his sphere of sinfulness, as was promised by Moses (1QS 3:8; 11:15; 1QH 17:12). Thus *rātsôn* will flourish once more in the land (1QS 9:4).

Such atonement takes place within the bounds of the *yachadh*. Entrance into the covenant is marked by a confession of sin, *nʿwynw [pšʿnw ḥṭ]'nw hršʿnw* (1QS 1:25), which identifies the beginning of liberation from the nexus of sin and calamity. Whoever experiences this divine atonement thereupon swears (in a liturgical act?) never to sin again (1QH 14:17). The elect hopes for divine aid to keep him from stumbling in the future (1QH 17:22f.).

Koch

חֹטֶר chōṭer → נֵצֶר nētser

חִידָה chîdhāh

Contents: I. Philological Discussion. II. True Riddles in the OT. III. Riddles in the Extended Sense: 1. In Wisdom Texts; 2. In Prophecy. IV. Theological Significance.

I. Philological Discussion. The substantive *chîdhāh* occurs 17 times in the Hebrew OT (excluding Sirach), 8 of which are in Jgs. 14:12-19. The denominative verb *ḥwd* (qal) appears only in Jgs. 14:12f.,16; Ezk. 17:2, in each case in the etymological figure *chûdh chîdāh,* "put a riddle." In Aramaic, the noun has the form *'ᵃchîdhāh* (Dnl. 5:12 pl. *'ᵃchîdhān;* Ahikar 99 *'ḥdy*), in the Targumim and in Syriac, *'ûchadhtā'* or *'achᵃdhûtā'*.[1] The short form *chûdhtā'* or *chîdhtā'*,[2] more frequent in the Targumim, is most likely not ancient, but an imitation of the Hebrew form. It is commonly assumed that the short Hebrew form was derived from the Aramaic, and that both are based on the common Semitic root *'ḥd* (*'ḥz*). This usually means "grasp" or "seize," but in Aramaic it means also "include, shut" (like Heb. *'āchaz* in Neh. 7:3). The semantic development would thus be: grasp > include > shut, with the passive participle developing the meaning "secret, riddle."[3] Rinaldi[4] prefers the development "grasp > comprehend," and notes Akk. *aḫāzu,* the causative of which means "teach someone." But this specialized meaning is not present in Northwest Semitic, and is rather remote from the meaning of "riddle." In fact the derivation from *'ḥd/'ḥz* creates substantial problems, and the dropping of a radical *aleph* in Hebrew during or after the borrowing is not supported by convincing parallels. On the contrary, there are many examples in later Aramaic for *nomina actionis* to acquire a preformative *aleph.*[5] Without reference to any Aramaic intermediary, Müller, following a suggestion by von Soden, cites an Akkadian verb *ḫiādu,* 'utter" (cf. Arab. *ḫāta*[*i*]) and its derivative *ḫittu* II, "utterance." Less likely is a basic meaning "knot," from Arab. *ḥāda(ī),* "tied a knot."[6]

II. True Riddles in the OT. In the OT—as elsewhere—a riddle is in the strict sense a riddling question, usually popular, often cast in the form of verse; a riddle can

chîdhāh. O. Eissfeldt, "Die Rätsel in Jdc 14," *ZAW,* 30 (1910), 132-35; A. Jolles, "Rätsel," in his *Einfache Formen* (1930, ²1956), 104-123; G. Kittel, "αἴνιγμα," *TDNT,* I, 178-180; H.-P. Müller, "Der Begriff 'Rätsel' im AT," *VT,* 20 (1970), 465-489; K. von Rabenau, "Die Form des Rätsels im Buche Hesekiel," *WZ Halle-Wittenberg,* 7/5 (1957/58), 1055-57; G. Rinaldi, "Alcuni termini ebraici relativi alla letteratura," *Bibl,* 40 (1959), 274-76; W. Schultz, "Rätsel," *PW,* II/1, 62-125; H. Torczyner, "The Riddle in the Bible," *HUCA,* 1 (1924), 125-149; M. Wagner, *Die lexikalischen und grammatikalischen Aramaismen im alttestamentlichen Hebräisch. BZAW,* 96 (1966), 55f.

[1] *WTM,* I, 53; *LexSyr,* 12.
[2] *WTM,* II, 21.
[3] *GesB, KBL³*, Wagner, and others.
[4] P. 275.
[5] Citations in Müller, 485f.
[6] *LexHebAram,* 226.

also appear in declarative form. In the broader sense, a riddle can be an obscure and metaphorical mode of expression, the real meaning of which must be guessed. The literary genre of "riddle" plays an important role even in Indo-Iranian literature, then particularly in classical and Germanic literature.[7] By contrast, few examples are known from the non-Indo-European ancient Near East.[8]

The earliest biblical example of a popular riddle is in Jgs. 14, the riddle put to the thirty Philistines by Samson. According to the present text, the riddle derives from a personal experience on the part of Samson and is therefore impossible for anyone else to guess. The whole passage is somewhat illogical as well as scientifically unrealistic (bees in a carcass!). But the very primitiveness of the account argues for an early date, even if the original form has not been preserved. That the guessing of riddles to win prizes was a popular form of entertainment at banquets and wedding feasts[9] is well attested.[10] The answers to wedding riddles were often deliberately erotic. Therefore Eissfeldt and others have proposed that the questions in this passage, too, originally had an erotic sense, obscured in their present form.[11] A riddle can often have several correct answers.

Another example is provided by 1 K. 10:1 = 2 Ch. 9:1, where the queen of Sheba tests Solomon by means of riddles and he is able to answer all her questions. Perhaps the account is based on the custom of contests between kings, with a "tournament of wisdom" replacing armed combat.[12] The point of the biblical text is to parade the incomparable sagacity of Solomon. In early Israel and even more so in Egypt, wisdom was especially cultivated at the royal court. Although no riddle is quoted, we may think primarily of questions from the realm of natural history (cf. 1 K. 5:13 [Eng. 4:33]). Later legend sought to supply the omission.[13]

A formal riddle belonging to the genre of the comparative riddle appears in Sir. 22:14: "What is heavier than lead?" The answer follows. The following verse (15) should also be noted, as well as Prov. 27:3, although these are not true riddles, but only declarative comparisons. It is also questionable whether the so-called numerical proverbs are based originally on numerical riddles.[14]

III. Riddles in the Extended Sense.

1. *In Wisdom Texts.* In the OT, court wisdom became increasingly democratized and thus came to its greatest flowering in the postexilic era. The term *chîdhāh* became one of the many almost synonymous terms for wisdom maxims. Symbolic utterances

---

[7]Cf. Schultz, 72-125; W. Porzig, "Das Rätsel im Rigveda," in *Germanica. Festschrift E. Sievers* (1925), 646-660; W. Schultz, *Rätsel aus dem hellenischen Kulturkreise. Mythologische Bibliothek,* III/1 (1909), V/1 (1912); R. Petsch, *Das deutsche Volksrätsel* (1917).

[8]Schultz, *PW,* 122-24.

[9]Cf. "Brautwerbe-Rätsel," *ibid.,* 69f., 124.

[10]*Ibid.,* 89; Petsch, 13; Müller, 470.

[11]Cf. the commentaries and the thorough discussion in Müller, 465-471.

[12]Müller, 477.

[13]*Ibid.,* 478f.

[14]Cf. Torczyner, 135f.; contrariwise Müller, 486f.

and similes, paradoxes and profound psalms could all be called riddles. The special cryptic language of wisdom always had to be deciphered by someone knowledgeable. Most closely related is the flexible term → מָשָׁל *māshāl*. In Hab. 2:6, the context suggests that *māshāl* has the meaning "taunt song," and *m^e^lîtsê chîdhôth* are "riddling taunts."[15] Again we find *chîdhāh* alongside other wisdom terms in Ps. 49:5(4) (the alteration of *chîdhāh* proposed by Müller[16] is not sufficiently justified), where the difficult problem of theodicy is explored, and in Ps. 78:2, which sings of the unfathomable wonders performed by God in the sacred history of Israel. The word also appears in Prov. 1:6; Sir. 8:8; 39:3 (Greek: *en ainígmasi parabolṓn*); 47:17, all of which deal with the clever sayings of wise men. According to Wisd. 8:8, personified Wisdom is skilled in *strophás lógōn kaí lýseis ainigmátōn*.

Even where the word *chîdhāh* does not appear in the OT, allegorical descriptive poems can be understood as riddles in the extended sense. Torczyner, for example, includes Eccl. 12:2-6; Cant. 8:8f.; Ps. 19:2-7(1-6) in this genre.[17] The same can be said in general of the prophetic allegories (see below).

2. *In Prophecy*. The wisdom mode of thought and expression also influenced narrative and prophetic literature. "Riddles" are already mentioned in a derogatory sense in Nu. 12:8: only with Moses does Yahweh speak directly, mouth to mouth, rather than in *chîdhôth*. The passage is ascribed to J and presupposes a familiarity with the more "riddling" symbolic dreams and visions (v. 6) that commonly come to the prophets.[18] The poetic metaphors beloved by the writing prophets as well as their symbolic visions—Jer. 1:11-14; 24:1-10, for instance—also demand interpretation and can therefore be called riddles in the extended sense. The fact that despite Nu. 12:8 the term *chîdāh* almost never appears in the classical prophets (in Hab. 2:6 it has a secondary meaning, strictly associated with wisdom) is probably due to the comparative ease with which the symbolic discourses of the prophets can be penetrated and interpreted. They are not meant to propound obscure riddles but to be understood by their hearers. This distinguishes the discourses of the prophets sharply from such oracles as those of Pythia, the sphinx, or the Sibyllines, which are often deliberately obscure or even impenetrable.

The word *chîdhāh* does appear in Ezk. 17:2. It is followed by the obscure allegorical discourse about the eagle and its interpretation. Here, then, *chîdhāh* means more "parable" than "riddle."[19] It is unconvincing to speak of a "special casuistic form of riddle."[20] Here, too, *māshāl* stands in parallelism with *chîdhāh;* in Ezekiel, the former can refer to an obscure and allegorical sermon (Ezk. 21:5[20:49]; 24:3).[21]

A special case, likewise associated more with wisdom than with prophecy, is the interpretating of riddling dreams or phenomena (cf. the discussion of Nu. 12:6-8 above

---

15 Müller, 480; O. Eissfeldt, *Der Maschal im AT. BZAW*, 24 (1913), 11.

16 Pp. 481f.

17 Pp. 136-149.

18 Cf. Müller, 471f.

19 Schultz, 124.

20 Graf Rabenau, 1057.

21 Cf. Eissfeldt, *Maschal*, 14-16; A. R. Johnson, "מָשָׁל," in *Wisdom in Israel and in the Ancient Near East. Festschrift H. H. Rowley. SVT*, 3 (1955), 168f.

and → חלם *chālam*). To decipher these, "mantic wisdom" was needed.[22] The earliest example is Joseph in Egypt, who both had symbolic dreams himself and understood how to interpret them for others. In the late period, Daniel similarly possesses the mantic wisdom to explain riddling phenomena. According to Dnl. 5:12 (Aramaic), he has "an excellent spirit, knowledge, and understanding to interpret dreams, to explain riddles (*'achavāyath 'achîdhān*), and to solve problems." The task at hand is the deciphering of the mysterious inscription. Similar wisdom-related qualities are predicated of Daniel in 5:11 and 1:17. On the other hand, in Dnl. 8:23 *mēbhîn chîdhôth* must be taken in a pejorative sense as "wily, tricky"; even so, a kind of intellectual superiority on the part of the upstart king is expressed. Without using the word *chîdhāh,* Dnl. 2 and 4 describe how the wise prophet interprets the symbolic images of the image and the world tree.

IV. Theological Significance. The concept of "riddle" is philosophically and theologically relevant in that it is used especially in Wisdom Literature for the mysteries of how the world is ordered and takes account of the paradoxes and analogies of being.[23] In addition, cryptic vision and speech express the separation between God and man. God himself and his actions are often impenetrable, not to mention unmanipulable, and are not accessible to man except by revelation. On the other hand, for God there can be nothing unknown. The extent to which he allows his elect to share in his knowledge of the present and future is his personal decision, based on his grace. In general, it holds true for men that we see in this life only "in a mirror, and riddles" (1 Cor. 13:2, the only passage in the NT with the word *aínigma*).

Hamp

---

[22]Müller, 472f.
[23]*Ibid.*, 488f.

חָיָה *chāyāh;* חַי *chai;* חַיִּים *chaiyîm;* חַיָּה *chaiyāh;* מִחְיָה *michyāh*

Contents: I. Ancient Near East: 1. Egypt; 2. Mesopotamia; 3. West Semites. II. 1. Etymology; 2. Occurrences. III. "Life" in the OT: 1. Life-span; 2. Life and Death; Survival; 3. Life as Activity or Well-being; 4. Life as Health; Life to the Full; 5. Life through Keeping the Commandments; 6. Life and the King; 7. The Life of the Nation in the Prophets; 8. God Gives Life; 9. The Living God; 10. The Tree of Life, Book of Life, Land of the Living; 11. Man's Mortality; Eternal Life. IV. 1. "Every Living Thing"; 2. *chaiyāh,* "Animal"; 3. *ʿēth chaiyāh;* 4. *michyāh.*

I. Ancient Near East.

1. *Egypt.* a. The Egyptian word *ʿnḫ,* meaning "life" and "live,"[1] is written from the earliest period with the crux ansata or ankh. This sign, which is also found as

---

chāyāh. C. Barth, *Die Errettung vom Tode in den individuellen Klage- und Dankliedern des AT* (Zollikon, 1947); W. W. Graf Baudissin, *Adonis und Esmun* (1911), 390-426, 450-510; G. J. Botterweck, "Marginalien zum atl. Auferstehungsglauben," *WZKM,* 54 (1957), 1-8; M. M. Bravmann, "North Semitic *Ḥayyîm/n* 'Life' in the Light of Arabic," *Mus,* 83 (1970), 551-57; E. A. S. Butterworth, *The Tree at the Navel of the Earth* (1970); B. Couroyer, "Le chemin de vie en Égypte et en Israël," *RB,* 56 (1949), 412-432; L. Dürr, *Die Wertung des Lebens im AT und im antiken Orient* (1926); O. Eissfeldt, *Der Beutel der Lebendigen. BSAW,* 105/6 (1960); G. Gerleman, "חיה *ḥjh* leben," *THAT,* I, 549-557; M. Greenberg, "The Hebrew Oath Particle, *Ḥay/Ḥē,*" *JBL,* 76 (1957), 34-39; W. Herrmann, "Das Buch des Lebens," *Altertum,* 20 (1974), 1-10; E. O. James, *The Tree of Life. SNumen,* 11 (1966); E. Jenni, *Das hebräische Piʿel* (Zurich, 1968), 61-64; A. R. Johnson, *The Vitality of the Individual in the Thought of Ancient Israel* (Cardiff, ²1964); L. Koep, *Das himmlische Buch in Antike und Christentum. Theophaneia,* 8 (1952); H.-J. Kraus, "Der lebendige Gott," *EvTh,* 27 (1967), 169-200 = his *Biblisch-theologische Aufsätze* (1972), 1-36; M. R. Lehmann, "Biblical Oaths," *ZAW,* 81 (1969), 74-92; O. Loretz, "*kʿt ḥyh*—'wie jetzt ums Jahr' Gen. 18, 10," *Bibl,* 43 (1962), 75-78; R. Marcus, "The Tree of Life in Proverbs," *JBL,* 62 (1943), 117-120; R. Martin-Achard, *From Death to Life* (Edinburgh, trans. 1960); A. T. Nikolainen, *Der Auferstehungsglauben in der Bibel und ihrer Umwelt; 1: Religionsgeschichtlicher Teil. AnAcScFen,* B, 49/3 (1944); F. Nötscher, *Altorientalischer und alttestamentlicher Auferstehungsglauben* (1926, repr. 1970 with sup. by J. Scharbert); G. Pidoux, "Encore les deux arbres de Genèse 3," *ZAW,* 66 (1954), 37-43; G. von Rad, "'Righteousness' and 'Life' in the Cultic Language of the Psalms," in his *The Problem of the Hexateuch and Other Essays* (trans. 1966), 243-266; G. Stemberger, *Der Leib der Auferstehung. AnBibl,* 56 (1972); R. Taylor, "The Eschatological Meaning of Life and Death in the Book of Wisdom I-IV," *ETL,* 42 (1966), 72-137; F. Vattioni, "L'albero della vita," *Aug,* 7 (1967), 133-144; J. Vergote, *Joseph en Égypte. OrBibLov,* 3 (1959), xi, 1-219; G. Widengren, *Sakrales Königtum im AT und im Judentum* (1955); *idem, The King and the Tree of Life in Ancient Near Eastern Religion. UUÅ,* I (1951), 1-80; J. A. Wilson, "The Oath in Ancient Egypt," *JNES,* 7 (1948), 129-156; R. Yaron, "*Kaʿeth ḥayyah* and *koh leḥay,*" *VT,* 12 (1962), 500f.; W. Zimmerli, "'Leben' und 'Tod' im Buche des Propheten Ezechiel," *ThZ,* 13 (1957), 494-508 = his *Gottes Offenbarung. ThB,* 19 (²1969), 178-191.

[1] *WbÄS,* I, 193ff.

a symbol outside Egypt, probably represents a "magic knot."[2] The ankh sign is an attribute shared by all the gods, for possession of life is fundamental to the nature of every deity. In pictures, accordingly, nearly every deity is represented holding an ankh before him. One common scene shows the deity extending "life" toward the nose of the king, bestowing on him the breath of life. In the Amarna period, the rays of the sun disk terminate in arms, each bearing an ankh. Also worth mentioning is the use of the ankh at the beginning of inscriptions and before the names of kings and gods, normally rendered "Long live . . ." for the earlier periods, later taken as ornamental and left untranslated.[3] The ankh survived actively in Coptic civilization.[4]

b. The word *ʿnḫ,* "life," represents both the absolute precondition and culmination of all existence. It can refer to both the sum of all the vital forces and to various concrete forms of provision (grain, food, milk, water, etc.), especially in sacrificial scenes. Horus, for example, is called "Lord of Nourishment, Rich in Food, Creator of Life for All";[5] and of Hathor we are told: "One lives when one sees her, who guides the life of the living, the Lady of Foodstuffs."[6] Otto, who has assembled a wealth of textual material illustrating a complex "light-breath of life-air theology,"[7] emphasizes that "life" stands as the more general concept, inclusive of the other three terms. "For the Egyptian, life is not something abstract, to be defined, but the concrete existence of all creatures, in all their variety of manifestations and needs."[8] In fixed formulas listing the highest goods,[9] *ʿnḫ,* almost always comes first, for instance, *ʿnḫ wḏ3 śnb* (a greeting), "may he live, may he be healthy and well"; *ʿnḫ ḏd w3ś* (a term for a sacrifice), "life, endurance, power."[10]

It is noteworthy that *ʿnḫ* also means "oath,"[11] on the basis of the oath formula *ʿnḫ n.y NN,* "as NN [king, god] lives for me."[12]

c. Life is intimately associated with the creation and ordering of the world. The flooding of the Nile, which in a sense represents the waters of the primal ocean, pregnant with life, can be called "living water," "the cool water that begets every

[2]H. Schäfer, "Djed-pfeiler, Lebenszeichen, Osiris, Isis," *Studies Presented to F. Ll. Griffith* (London, 1932), 424-431; M. Cramer, *Das altägyptische Lebenszeichen im christlichen (Koptischen) Ägypten* (1955), 1ff.

[3]*WbÄS,* I, 193, 4-7.

[4]Cramer, 7ff.

[5]Edfu, II, 162.

[6]E. Chassinat, *Le temple de Dendara,* IV (Cairo, 1935), 191.

[7]E. Otto, *Gott und Mensch nach den ägyptischen Tempelinschriften der griechisch-römischen Zeit. AHAW,* Phil.-Hist. Kl. (1964), 47ff.

[8]Otto, 55.

[9]*WbÄS,* I, 196.10-197.10.

[10]Cf. E. Winter, *Untersuchungen zu den ägyptischen Tempelreliefs der griechisch-römischen Zeit. DÖAW,* 98 (1968), 69-76.

[11]*WbÄS,* I, 202f.

[12]Cf. Wilson; Vergote, 162ff.; A. Gardiner, *Egyptian Grammar* (London, [3]1957), § 218.

living creature."[13] This notion was especially enshrined in the myth of Osiris. In the cosmogonies, the relationship of life to light and to air is especially prominent.[14] Life is associated most closely with the creator-god, who is called simply "the Living One."[15] Several deities appear in personal names as "possessors of life."

Thus the gods appear as creators, bestowers, and preservers of life; by nature they are "the living ones." Shu, the god of the air, is even called "Life."[16] Through him the primal god Atum has life—since one lives by breathing air.[17] The vivifying sun is also considered the source of life. The sunrise brings life to all creatures. Gods and men have life through its appearance.[18]

d. The king is the primary recipient and steward of god-given life.[19] The official style of the titulary of the pharaoh regularly includes *dy(w) ʿnḫ,* which can mean either "given life" or "giving life."[20] For the Egyptian, he is the visible bestower of life and is therefore placed alongside the gods (at length in the great dedicatory inscription to Rameses II at Abydus,[21] where we read: "We are here before Your Majesty that you may decree for us life out of that which you give, O Pharaoh, may he live, may he be healthy and well, the breath of life for our noses [as at Amarna], which brings life to all men through its rising" [lines 39f.]). The king is also considered the "living image" (*ḫnty ʿnḫ, twt ʿnḫ*)[22] of the gods (cf. → דמה *dāmāh* III, → צלם *tselem*).

e. Thanks to the gods, the vital force of creation is bestowed on individual creatures. Even before birth "Amun vivifies the young in the egg and fastens the seed in the bone."[23] Similar statements are often made of Aton at Amarna.[24] At the very moment of birth the span of one's life is determined by the gods, but as gods of destiny they can mercifully extend it.[25] The ideal life-span was considered 110 years.[26] In the context of oracles, we frequently find the formula that "life and death depend on the utterance" of a god or gods.[27]

---

[13]H. Grapow, *Die bildlichen Ausdrücke des Ägyptischen* (1924), 135ff.

[14]Otto, 47ff.; J. Bergman, "Mystische Anklänge in den altägyptischen Vorstellungen von Gott und Welt," *Mysticism. SIDA,* 5 (1970), 70-76.

[15]Hermann Junker, " 'Der Lebendige' als Gottesbeiname im Alten Reich," *AÖAW,* 91 (1954), 169-191.

[16]*CT,* II, 32bff.

[17]Winter, 76ff.

[18]Otto, 47ff.

[19]E. Blumenthal, *Untersuchungen zum ägyptischen Königtum des Mittleren Reichs. ASAW* 61/1 (1970), 82-84.

[20]K. Martin in *Studia aegyptiaca. Festschrift V. Wessetzky* (Budapest, 1974), 82-84.

[21]See G. Roeder, *Kulte, Orakel, und Naturverehrung im alten Agypten* (Zurich, 1960), 43-71.

[22]*WbÄS,* I, 196, 6f.

[23]E.g., F. Daumas, *Les mammisis de Dendara* (Cairo, 1959), 31.

[24]S. Sauneron, "Le germe dans les os," *BIFAO,* 60 (1960), 19-27.

[25]S. Morenz and D. Müller, *Untersuchungen zur Rolle des Schicksals in der ägyptischen Religion. ASAW,* Phil.-Hist. Kl., 52/1 (1960), 18f.

[26]J. M. A. Janssen, "On the Ideal Lifetime of the Egyptians," *OMRO,* 31 (1950), 33-43.

[27]Otto, *Gott,* 16-18.

f. For the Egyptian, life and death represent the two sides of existence, just as the world of day and the world of night together constitute the ordered universe.[28] The cycle of life, which includes both the diurnal and the nocturnal journey of the sun, is secured by the union of Re and Osiris. The death of Re at the western horizon coincides with the conception of new life in the body of Nut, the goddess of the heavens. Thus life arises out of death.[29] The extreme interest in the world of the dead indicates a conscious concentration on potential life, life at its critical stage. Thus the tomb is considered a "place of rejuvenated life," and the world of the dead is accounted "the world of the living." In utterances concerning the dead, restoration to life with the sun-god is often emphasized.[30] Survival in the tomb and survival of the father in the son are other frequent themes.

g. Special idioms: *ʿnḫ ḏ.t,* "live eternally, eternal life,"[31] is a common expression, often followed by "with Re," the sun-god. The "house of life" is a central chamber in the temple, where books, images of the gods, and other cultic paraphernalia are "revived." The doctrine of Amarna is termed *śb3y.t n ʿnḫ,* "doctrine of life."[32] For a discussion of the "way of life," see → דֶּרֶךְ *derekh*. The "tree of life" (*ḫt n ʿnḫ*) is a particular kind of fruit tree.

2. *Mesopotamia*. Akk. *balāṭu,*[33] etymologically associated with Heb. and Aram. *plṭ* (→ פלט *pālaṭ*), is both a verb and a noun. The corresponding Sumerian word is *ti (-la)* or *nam-ti.la; zi* is also found.[34] The Akkadian (and in part the Sumerian) term for life agrees in its essentials with its Hebrew counterpart.[35] Another word for "life" is *napištu* (→ נפש *nephesh*).

a. The noun *balāṭu* can refer to the length or span of life, as in *mādātim šanāt balāṭim,* "many years of life";[36] with *arāku* Š, it means "lengthen life," i.e., "grant long life"; with *arāku* D, "lengthen life" in the sense of "live long." Long life is considered a gift of the gods.[37] The long life of the king is especially important.[38] An "enduring long life" was asked of Anu; "many years of life" were granted by Ishtar to Ammiditana.[39] There is a prayer to Ningal on behalf of Sargon for "enjoyment of life

---

[28] E. Hornung, *Die ägyptische Unterweltsbücher* (Zurich, 1972), 37ff.
[29] W. B. Kristensen, *Het Leven uit de Dood* (Haarlem, trans. 1926, ^{2}1949).
[30] See *WbÄS,* I, 193, 11-13.
[31] *WbÄS,* I, 197, 12-198, 2, 9.
[32] *WbÄS,* I, 199, 6.
[33] *AHw,* I, 98f.
[34] On the distinction, see *SGL,* I, 26^5.
[35] For citations, see *CAD,* II, 46ff., 52ff.
[36] F. Thureau-Dangin, "Un Hymne à Ištar de la haute époque babylonienne," *RA,* 22 (1906), 173, r. 47.
[37] *SAHG,* 60, 186 (Sumerian).
[38] *SAHG,* 102, 103, 109 (Sumerian); 237 (Akkadian).
[39] Note 36 above; cf. *SAHG,* 239.

through distant days.''[40] Nebuchadnezzar prays for ''life until the most distant days,''[41] ''everlasting life and progeny,''[42] a long life and progeny,[43] and ''life for long days.''[44] Nabu says to Ashurbanipal: ''I will vouchsafe you a long life.''[45] Especially interesting in this regard is the hymn to Shamash: he who deals justly ''pleases Shamash well and earns a longer life.''[46] In other words, a long life is promised as a reward for proper ethical and religious conduct. The meaning ''life-span'' is also illustrated by such expressions as ''enjoy something *adi balāṭišu* [during one's lifetime, as long as one lives]'' or *ina balāṭi ša šarri,* ''as long as the king lives.''[47] The verb is also used in similar contexts: ''He shall provide for her *adi balṭat* [as long as she lives]'';[48] ''*adi ūm balṭāku* [as long as I live] I will praise you.''[49]

b. ''Live'' and ''die'' are linked as opposites: ''I do not know whether NN is alive or dead'';[50] ''he who was alive yesterday is dead today.''[51] The negative *lā balāṭu,* ''not to live,'' is ''death'': ''He commanded *lā balāṭsu,*'' i.e., condemned him to death.[52] The verb often means ''stay alive, survive'': ''I do not know whether he will die (of his sickness) or survive.''[53] It can also mean ''escape alive'': ''Did anyone escape? Did anyone survive destruction?''[54] The D stem similarly means ''keep alive, preserve,'' often with the gods as subject, for instance, ''May Shamash preserve you.''[55]

c. In addition, ''live'' can be tantamount to ''be healthy and vigorous'': *lū šalmāta lū balṭāta,* ''may you be safe and healthy'' (an epistolary greeting).[56] Similarly, the noun often occurs together with *šulmu,* ''well-being.''[57] Here belongs the common divine epithet *muballiṭ mīti,* ''giver of life to the dead,'' i.e., ''healer of the sick'';[58] cf. ''it is within your power to make them living (healthy),''[59] (Marduk) ''who loves to bring to life.''[60]

---

[40] *SAHG,* 280.
[41] *SAHG,* 285; cf. 288.
[42] *SAHG,* 286.
[43] *SAHG,* 287.
[44] *SAHG,* 288.
[45] *SAHG,* 293.
[46] *SAHG,* 244.
[47] *CAD,* II, 51.
[48] CH § 148, etc.
[49] *KAR,* 228, 10.
[50] J. Levy, *Tablettes Cappadociennes,* ser. 3, 1, *TCL,* 19, Plate LXXIII, 7.
[51] *BWL,* 40, 33 [Ludlul II]; additional citations in *CAD,* II, 56.
[52] E. Weidner, ''Hochverrat gegen Nebukadnezar II,'' *AfO* 17 (1954/56), 1, 19; *CAD,* II, 51.
[53] CT, 22, 114, 15.
[54] Gilg. XI, 173.
[55] *CAD,* II, 59f.
[56] *CAD,* II, 55.
[57] *CAD,* II, 48; *SAHG,* 238: ''health and life.''
[58] K. Tallqvist, *Akkadische Götterepitheta. StOr,* 7 (1938), 67f.; *CAD,* II, 58f.
[59] R. Borger, ''Das dritte 'Haus' der Serie *bīt rimki* (VR 50–51, Schollmeyer HBŠ, NR. 1),'' *JCS,* 21 (1967), 5, 39.
[60] *SAHG,* 307.

d. Life is often associated with the king (cf. what was said in I.2.a about long life). Examples are especially common in the Amarna letters,[61] but elsewhere, too, we find expressions like "We 'live' in the shadow of the king our lord"[62] and "When I saw the face of the king, my lord, I felt fine."[63] The king transmits life and prosperity to his land: "The lord who preserves the life of Uruk by bestowing abundant water upon his people. . . ."[64] This holds true even more for the deified Sumerian kings. Of Iddin-dagan, we read: "According to the word of Enlil, your gaze gives life to men, your word heals men."[65] Lipit-ishtar says: "I am the life of the land of Sumer."[66] Occasionally we also find the optative "may he live" (*libluṭ*) with reference to the king.[67]

e. Life comes from the gods. Of various deities it is said that their gaze, their face, or their command gives life.[68] We find the prayer: "Give me life, then shall I do you homage," and also: "Through your breath may I live."[69] The gods give life or long life;[70] in many cases, the context shows that what is meant is a happy or successful life.[71] Incantations speak of the life-giving formula that heals the sick;[72] similarly, we often find a prayer for life: "Give me life, that I may be joyful forever";[73] "Decree for me a destiny of life";[74] "May I live and be healthy";[75] "Preserve my life, then shall I do you homage";[76] "Give the command to live."[77]

Eternal life is the privilege of the gods. The only exception was Utnapishtim, the hero of the deluge in the Gilgamesh Epic, together with his wife. The point is made programmatically in the Old Babylonian Gilgamesh Epic: "When the gods created mankind, they apportioned death to mankind and claimed life for themselves."[78] Therefore "the life you are seeking you will not find."[79] As is well known, Gilgamesh nevertheless does find the plant of life and would have been able to enjoy eternal life; but the plant is snatched away by a serpent and Gilgamesh remains mortal. The same theme dominates the Adapa Myth: Adapa is offered the food and drink of life, but, warned by Ea, rejects them and loses the chance for eternal life. Etana, too, despite his flight into the heavens, fails to gain eternal life, as the Etana Myth relates.

---

[61] *CAD,* II, 55.
[62] *ABL,* 886, vo. 4.
[63] *ABL,* 880, 10; *CAD,* II, 56.
[64] CH, II, 37; Seux, 47; many Amarna citations, *CAD,* II, 60.
[65] *SAHG,* 121.
[66] *SAHG,* 127; W. H. P. Römer, *Sumerische Königshymnen der Isin-Zeit* (1965), 34.
[67] *SAHG,* 237; *CAD,* II, 55.
[68] Citations in *CAD,* II, 46f.; cf. *SAHG,* 235: "Their mouth is life."
[69] *SAHG,* 253.
[70] *CAD,* II, 47f.; Sumerian: *SAHG,* 72, 114.
[71] *CAD,* II, 48.
[72] *SAHG,* 295.
[73] *Ibid.*
[74] *SAHG,* 297.
[75] *SAHG,* 298.
[76] *SAHG,* 300.
[77] *SAHG,* 305.
[78] A. Schott and W. von Soden, *Das Gilgamesch-Epos* (1958), 75; III. 3-5.
[79] Schott and von Soden, 2.

f. At Mari and Amarna, we find instances where *balāṭu* means "provisions."[80]

g. There is a specialized use of *balāṭu* in the idiom *ina/ana/adi balāṭ,* "in the coming year, until next year."[81] Cf. the discussion of *ʿēth chaiyāh* in IV.3 below.

3. *West Semites.* Ugaritic has the verb *ḥwy/ḥyy* and the nouns *ḥyt* and *ḥym,* both meaning "life." The occurrences are not especially numerous, but relate to important ideas.

In the myth of Baal, the transformation of sorrow into joy at Baal's return to life is signaled by the words *ḥy ʾl3yn bʿl 3ṯ zbl bʿl ʾrṣ,* "Aliyan Baal lives, the prince, the lord of the earth exists."[82] The context describes the revitalization of nature: "The heavens rained oil, the rivers flowed with honey." The life of nature is thus concentrated in the god Baal.

This mythological event is alluded to in the Aqhat Epic, in a scene where the goddess ʿAnat offers Aqhat eternal life in exchange for his beautiful bow:[83] "Ask for life (*ḥym*), O mighty Aqhat, ask for life and I will give you immortality (*blmt*); I will let you count the years with Baal, and you shall count the months with the son of El," i.e., you will live eternally, like the gods. "When Baal comes to live, men rejoice and offer him drink, they sing and praise him; so I will bring mighty Aqhat to life." But Aqhat rejects the offer of the goddess; he knows that he must die like all men.

The epic of Keret twice refers to a conversation about the life of the king. Keret is sick, and his son is worried by his condition. Usually, he says, we rejoice over your life (*ḥyk*) and your immortality (*blmt*); now you look so wretched—will you die like other men?[84] The disquieting question is: How can Keret be the son of El and still die? "The offspring of Lutpan will surely live."[85] The king, in other words, is considered the son of a god and should be immortal like the gods, but now his life is in danger.

The other occurrences are less significant. Baal greets ʿAnat with the words: "May you live, O sister" (*ḥwt ʾḫt*).[86] Other uses are "I will revive him"[87] and "He revived the soul (*npš*) of Danil."[88] Twice we find the phrase *ḥyt ḥẓt,* "life of happiness."[89]

Phoenician and Punic funerary inscriptions use the verb *ḥyh* to indicate life-span: "He lived so-and-so many years."[90] The verb is often written *ʾwḥ, hwʾ, ʿwʾ, ʿwh,* or *ʿwʿ*, which testifies to a degree of uncertainty in the use of laryngeals.[91]

The adjective *ḥy,* "living," is used in various contexts. In curse formulas, "no

---

[80] *CAD,* II, 52.
[81] *CAD,* II, 51f.
[82] *CTA,* 6 [I AB], III, 3, 8.
[83] *CTA,* 17 [II D], VI, 25ff.
[84] *CTA,* 16 [II K], I, 14ff.; II, 36ff.
[85] *CTA,* 16, I, 23; II, 44.
[86] *CTA,* 10 [II AB], II, 20.
[87] *CTA,* 19 [I D], I, 16.
[88] *CTA,* 17 [II D], I, 37.
[89] *CTA,* 1 [II AB], IV, 42; 3 [V AB], V, 31.
[90] *KAI,* 128.3; 134.2; 135.3; 140.7; 142.2f.; 144.2; 171.3; etc.
[91] Cf. *KAI,* commentary on 135.3.

offspring among the living'' is given as a punishment.[92] A tombstone is a ''memorial stela among the living.''[93] ʿAnat is the ''refuge of the living.''[94] Especially interesting is the phrase *ḥy ḥym,* probably meaning ''preeminent among the living,'' as a royal title.[95]

The noun *ḥym,* ''life,'' often appears in the expression ''during my [his, etc.] lifetime''[96] and in mortuary inscriptions in the phrase ''upright in life'' (*tm bḥym*).[97] ''Length of life'' is wished for Rkb-El,[98] and the donor of a votive offering at Memphis states the wish: ''May [the gods] bless me and my sons and may they give them grace (*ḥn*) and life.''[99] In the Karatepe Inscription, Azitawadda states that Baal has given him life, well-being, and powerful strength (*ḥym wšlm wʿz ʾdr*).[100] A governor built an altar ''for my life and the life of my progeny.''[101] In Aramaic mortuary inscriptions we often find the statement that the monument was set up ''for the life of NN.''[102]

Finally, we may note the proper names, already discussed by Baudissin,[103] which describe the deity as ''living'': *ḥyʾl, kmš-yḥy, Iaḫi-milki.*[104]

II. 1. *Etymology.* The root *ḥyy* (or *ḥwy*), which appears in Hebrew as both *chāyāh* (ל״ה) and *chai* (ע״ע), occurs with a similar meaning in most other Semitic languages: Ugar. *ḥwy;*[105] Phoen. *ḥwʾ;* Aram. *ḥyʾ;*[106] OSA *ḥy, ḥyw, ḥwy;*[107] Arab. *ḥayya* (impf. *yaḥyā*—but another word for ''live'' is *ʿarm;* cf. *ʿamara,* ''live long,'' ''dwell,'' *ʿamura,* ''flourish''[108]); Ethiop. *ḥaywa.*[109] The root is not, however, found in Akkadian, where ''live/life'' is represented by *balāṭu.*[110]

2. *Occurrences.* The verb is attested in Hebrew in the qal (199 times according to Mandelkern), traditionally translated ''live,'' the piel (56 times), ''keep alive, make alive,'' and the hiphil (23 times), ''keep alive,'' and in a single instance (Isa. 57:15) ''restore to life.'' In addition, we find the adjective *chai,* ''living'' (224 times according to Lisowski and Mandelkern, including 68 occurrences of the oath formula *chai*

---

[92] *KAI,* 13.7.
[93] *KAI,* 53.1.
[94] *KAI,* 42.1.
[95] *KAI,* 161.1 (Punic).
[96] *KAI,* 35.2; 40.5; 43.7f.
[97] *KAI,* 152.3; 134.3.
[98] *KAI,* 25.7.
[99] *KAI,* 48.
[100] *KAI,* 26A iii.3 = 26C iii.17f.
[101] *KAI,* 43.11.
[102] *KAI,* 229.4; 238.5; 242.3; 249.5; 253.2f.; 257.4.
[103] Pp. 466ff.
[104] See D. Marcus, ''The Verb 'To Live' in Ugaritic,'' *JSS,* 17 (1972), 76-82.
[105] See I.3 above.
[106] *DISO,* 87; *MdD,* 140.
[107] ContiRossini, 147f.
[108] Wehr, 643.
[109] Baudissin, 480ff.
[110] See I.2 above.

yhvh, etc.); the noun *chaiyîm,* "life" (147 times, plus a single occurrence with the meaning "provisions" according to Lisowsky), often difficult to distinguish from the plural of the adjective *chai;* the noun *chāiyāh,* "living creature, animal," occasionally "life" (12 times); the noun *chaiyûth,* "lifetime" (2 S. 20:3); and the noun *michyāh,* which has several meanings: "preservation of life" (Gen. 45:5; Sir. 38:14), "sustenance" (Jgs. 6:4; 17:10), "reviving" (Ezr. 9:8f.), "living thing" (2 Ch. 14:12 [Eng. v. 13]), "formation of new flesh" (Lev. 13:10,24).

III. "Life" in the OT.

1. *Life-span.* The verb *chāyāh* refers initially to the length of time one lives, usually a certain number of years (15 times in the list of generations in Gen. 5, 16 times in the list in Gen. 11:11ff.; also Gen. 9:28; 47:28; 50:22; 2 K. 14:17; 2 Ch. 25:25; cf. also Gen. 25:7: *y^emê chaiyê ʾabhrāhām ʾ^ašer chai;* Jer. 35:7: *yāmîm rabbîm;* Eccl. 6:3,6; 11:8). A similar usage is found in Phoenician mortuary inscriptions.[111] There is a comparable use of *chaiyîm* to designate the life-span in such expressions as "the life-years of NN" (Gen. 23:1; 25:7,17; 47:8,28; Ex. 6:16,18,20) and "all the days of your [or: 'his,' etc.] life" (primarily Deuteronomic and Deuteronomistic: Gen. 3:14, 17; Dt. 4:9; 6:2; 16:3; 17:19; 28:66; Josh. 1:5; 4:14; 1 S. 1:11; 7:15; 1 K. 5:1[4:21]; 11:34; 15:5f.; 2 K. 25:29f.; Isa. 38:20; Jer. 52:33f.; Ps. 23:6; 27:4; 128:5; Prov. 31:12; cf. 2 S. 19:35; Eccl. 9:9); cf. also the simple phrase *y^emê chaiyāv* (etc.) in Eccl. 2:3; 5:17(18),19(20); 6:12; 8:15. In this context also belongs the expression *b^echaiyai* (etc.), "in my [or: 'your,' etc.] life," i.e., "as long as I live" (Ps. 49:19[18]; 63:5[4]; 104:33; 146:2; cf. also Gen. 7:11; Lev. 18:18; Jgs. 16:30; 2 S. 18:18), as well as the phrase *ʿôdh chai,* "be still alive" (Gen. 43:7,27f.; 45:3,26,28; 46:30; Ex. 4:18; 2 S. 12:22; 18:14; 1 K. 20:32).

2. *Life and Death; Survival.* "Live" and "die" are often juxtaposed; most frequently we find the combination "live and not die" (Gen. 42:2, Jacob; 43:8, Judah; 47:19, Joseph's brothers; Dt. 33:6, Reuben; 2 K. 18:32, in the speech of the Rabshakeh; Nu. 4:19, after contact with certain objects; Ps. 118:17, "not die but live," an expression of confidence in God's help). The opposite, "not live but die," appears in Isaiah's threat to Hezekiah (2 K. 20:1 = Isa. 38:1). The juxtaposition most often serves for emphasis; occasionally an alternative is offered (2 K. 7:4), a promise or hope is expressed (2 K. 18:32; Ps. 118:17), or a judgment is proclaimed (Isa. 38:1). Ps. 89:49(48) states that no one can escape death ("live and never see death"; cf. 49:10[9]).

Rather rarely, the substantives "life" (*chaiyîm*) and "death" (→ מות *māveth*) are juxtaposed: Dt. 30:19 (see below); 2 S. 15:21, "whether for death or for life"; Jer. 8:3, "death shall be preferred to life"; 21:8, "I set before you the way of life and the way of death"; Jonah 4:3,8, "it is better for me to die than to live"; Prov. 18:21. "Living" (*chai*) and "dead" (*mēth*) are also juxtaposed: Nu. 17:13(16:48); 1 K. 3:22f.; 21:15; Ruth 2:20; Isa. 8:19; Eccl. 9:5.

---

[111] See I.3 above.

"Not live," i.e., "die," can also appear as a punishment: Gen. 31:32, theft of the *t^erāphîm*; Ex. 19:13, whoever touches the mountain shall be put to death; 2 K. 10:19, the missing prophets of Baal shall die; Zec. 13:3, whoever appears as a prophet.

In contrast, there are several instances where *chāyāh* means "remain alive, survive": Gen. 20:7, Abraham prays for Abimelech to remain alive (opposite *môth tāmûth*); 42:18, Joseph says to his brothers, "Do this and you will live"; Ex. 1:16, the daughters born in Egypt; Nu. 14:38, only Joshua and Caleb among the spies; 24:23, "Who shall live when God does this?"; Dt. 4:42; 19:4f., law of asylum; Josh. 6:17, Rahab; 9:21, the Gibeonites; 2 S. 12:22, perhaps the child may live; Jer. 21:9; 27:12, 17; 38:2,17,20, whoever surrenders to the Babylonians will save his life; Ezk. 16:6, Yahweh says to the foundling, "Live!"; Est. 4:11, the king gives a sign that someone may live; Neh. 5:2, "Let us get grain, that we may eat and keep alive." A special nuance appears in the passages that speak of someone seeing or hearing God and nevertheless remaining alive: Ex. 33:20; Dt. 4:33; 5:24f.; cf. Nu. 4:19, touching the most holy things; Neh. 6:11, entering the temple and nevertheless living; Ex. 19:13, touching the mountain. Holiness is dangerous and can cause death.

3. *Life as Activity or Well-being.* In Hebrew, "life" has nuances besides purely physical life. A few examples will illustrate the point and lead us to other interesting aspects. In two late passages, the piel is used for the restoration of walls or a city (Neh. 3:34[4:2]; 1 Ch. 11:8): the ruins are "revived," made functional once more. In Hos. 14:8(7), we find the expression *chîyāh dhāghān,* i.e., "grow grain" (although the text is frequently emended). "Living water," *mayim chaiyîm,* is fresh running water or spring water, in contrast to the still water in cisterns (Lev. 14:5f.,50–52; 15:13; Nu. 19:17 [all P]).[112] As the passages cited show, such water is to be used for certain purification rituals. The concept is also used figuratively. Jeremiah likens Yahweh, whom Israel has deserted, to a spring with fresh water, in contrast to the idols, which are likened to "broken cisterns" (Jer. 2:13; 17:13). Deutero-Zechariah speaks of the living waters that will flow from Jerusalem at the eschaton, waters that also bestow life (Zec. 14:8; → גיחון *gîchôn*). The phrase *bāśār chai* means skin that is "growing wild," as it were with a life of its own (Lev. 13:10,14–16); it is termed a symptom of leprosy.[113]

It appears that these usages are based on a concept of movement, activity, or functioning. This impression is reinforced by the observation that *chāyāh* is combined occasionally with → שׁלום *shālôm*. It is said of Wisdom, for example, that all her ways are *shālôm* and that she is a tree of life[114] to all those who lay hold on her (Prov. 3:17f.); the context speaks of long life, riches, honor, and happiness. Mal. 2:5 states that Yahweh's covenant with the Levites is a covenant of "life and peace." There are also associations with *b^erākhāh* (→ ברך *brk*). Thus we read in Dt. 30:16, "You will live and multiply, and Yahweh your God will bless you," and in 30:19, "I have set before you life and death, blessing and curse"—in other words, life means blessing

---

[112]Cf. K. Elliger, *HAT,* 4, 187.
[113]Elliger, 182.
[114]III.9. See below.

and death is a curse. It follows, then, that the description of the blessing in Dt. 28:3ff. is also applicable to the concept of "life."

4. *Life as Health; Life to the Full.* The word *chāyāh* thus means not merely "be or stay alive," but also to enjoy a full, rich, and happy life. Often it simply means "be strong and healthy." The Israelites bitten by the serpents in the desert looked on the brazen serpent and "lived," i.e., were healed (Nu. 21:8f.). The men circumcised by Joshua remained in the camp until they were "healed" (Josh. 5:8). Samson, almost dying of thirst, "revives" and his spirit returns (*shûbh*), i.e., his strength is restored (Jgs. 15:19; cf. Gen. 45:27, where joy "revives" Jacob's spirit). Ahaziah sends to find out whether he will "recover" from his sickness (2 K. 1:2; similarly 2 K. 8:8–10, 14, of Ben-hadad, king of Damascus; 2 K. 20:1,7 = Isa. 38:1,9,21, of Hezekiah). Job 7:16 is not entirely clear, but probably the passage means that Job has given up hope of recovering and being able to lead a full life. In contrast, in 1 K. 17:22; 2 K. 13:21 a dead man is restored to life. For a discussion of Isa. 26:14,19, see below.

This constellation of meanings must also provide the starting-point for our analysis of the use of the piel in many of the psalms. Here other words occurring in the context of *chāyāh* furnish valuable insight into the definition of the concept "life." In Ps. 143:11, parallel to the plea "Yahweh, preserve my life" we find "Bring my → נפש *nephesh* out of trouble (*tsārāh*)." In Ps. 33:19, we read: "He may deliver their *nephesh* from death, and 'keep them alive' in famine." In Ps. 41:3(2), we have: "Yahweh protects (*shāmar*) him and 'keeps him alive' "; the continuation speaks of deliverance from enemies. In such contexts there is often a reference to the grave, the pit, or the realm of the dead, for instance, Ps. 71:20: "Thou . . . wilt revive me again, from the depths (*t^ehōmôth*) of the earth thou wilt bring me up again," or Ps. 30:4(3): "Thou hast brought up my *nephesh* from Sheol, restored my life from among those gone down to the Pit (*bôr*)." With this group of passages belongs Isa. 38:16, from the thanksgiving psalm of Hezekiah. Here the hiphil of *ḥlm,* "make strong, restore to health," is used alongside the hiphil of *chāyāh* (only here in this sense, which is elsewhere rendered by the piel), i.e., "make me strong, let me live." This usage is obviously based on the idea that sickness and distress impair the forces of life and represent, as it were, a potential death; deliverance is therefore appropriately termed "life."

The psalms that are communal laments use similar expressions with reference to happiness and prosperity: Ps. 85:7(6), "Wilt thou not 'revive' us again, that thy people may rejoice in thee" (cf. v. 8[7]: *chesedh* and salvation [*yeshaʿ*]); Ps. 80:19f. (18f.), "Give us life . . . , let thy face shine, that we may be saved (*yšʿ*)." In this last example, note the association of life with light; cf. Ps. 56:14(13): ". . . that I may walk before God in the light of life (*ʾôr chaiyîm*)."

5. *Life through Keeping the Commandments.* A special case comprises the passages that speak of life as the consequence of keeping the commandments. This notion is expressed most clearly in Deuteronomy. Here "life" is associated with "possession of the land" (4:1; 5:33; 8:1); in 5:33, it is also associated with → טוב *ṭôbh* ("that it may go well with you"; cf. the same combination in the Decalog [5:16], albeit with *yaʾ^arikhun yāmeykhā* rather than *chāyāh*), and in 8:1 with → רבה *rābhāh,* "multiply." In 16:20, "live" and "inherit the land" are associated with the precondition of

"justice." In 30:16,19, life is associated with blessing (see above). The same idea appears in Lev. 18:5 (H): "You shall therefore keep my statutes and ordinances, by doing which a man shall live (. . . *'ᵃsher yaʿᵃśeh 'ōthām hā'ādhām vāchai bāhem*)." Ezk. 20:11,13,21 repeat the same clause three times; it probably derives from the legal tradition of the cult.[115] Ezk. 20:25 inverts the statement: *chuqqîm lō' ṭôbhîm* by which they could not have life. Finally, Neh. 9:29 states that Israel did not keep the commandments through which a man shall live.

Similar ideas appear in Wisdom Literature with reference to the instruction of the teacher: "Keep my commandments, and live" (Prov. 4:4; 7:2; cf. also 9:6, "Leave simpleness [*pᵉthā'îm*], and live"; 15:27, "He who hates bribes will live"). The meaning of "live" is not apparent in these passages. Neither do the many occurrences of *chaiyîm* provide exact information; but the context is occasionally suggestive.

In Prov. 8:35, for example, we read: "He who finds me [Wisdom] finds life and obtains favor (→ רצון *rātsôn*) from Yahweh"; and in Prov. 21:21: "He who pursues *tsᵉdhāqāh* and *chesedh* will find life and honor [*kābhôdh;* omitting *tsᵉdhāqāh* in v. 21b]." Life is represented as the result of wisdom (Prov. 3:22) or of the words of the wise (4:22), of righteousness (*tsᵉdhāqāh,* 11:19; 12:28; cf. 10:16), and of instruction (*mûsār,* 4:13). The phrase *mᵉqôr chaiyîm,* "fountain of life," appears four times, referring to the mouth of the righteous (10:11), the teaching (*tôrāh*) of the wise (13:14), the fear of God (14:27), and insight (*śēkhel,* 16:22). The expression *'ōrach chaiyîm,* "path of life," appears three times, with an additional occurrence in the plural (2:19); once we find *derekh chaiyîm* (6:23). This path is contrasted to Sheol (2:19; 5:6, with reference to the loose woman; 15:24) or paths that go astray (*tāʿāh* hiphil, 5:6; 10:17). The commandments, instruction (*tôrāh*), and discipline (*mûsār,* 6:23; 10:17) guide along the path of life. In 6:23, the parallel line speaks also of light; only 2:19 offers more detail: the context speaks of the paths of the righteous and of inhabiting the land (cf. Deuteronomy above). In view of the general attitude of Wisdom Literature, it is likely that "life" is equivalent here to a happy and successful life. In 3:2 and 9:11, the reference is to a long life (*shᵉnôth chaiyîm*).

It is also noteworthy that here, too, the figurative language of the Psalms is used, with death and Sheol as contrasts to life.

Another figurative expression, "tree of life," appears four times, but in a weakened sense that has nothing to do with the tree of life in Paradise (see below). The expression is used for wisdom (3:18), the fruit of the righteous (11:30), a desire fulfilled (13:12), and a gentle tongue (15:4). In the first case, the reference is to long life (3:16) and happiness (*shālôm,* etc., vv. 16–18b). In 13:12, the opposite is "sickness of heart" (*machᵃlāh lēbh*), in 15:4, a broken spirit (*shebher bᵉrûach,* MT). In short, "tree of life" has here become simply a symbol of happiness.[116]

6. *Life and the King.* The acclamation *yᵉchî hammelekh,* "May the king live,"[117] deserves special attention. It appears only eight times (1 S. 10:24; 2 S. 16:16; 1 K.

[115] Von Rad, 252; W. Zimmerli, *BK,* XIII/1, 396ff.; Elliger, *HAT,* 4, 238.

[116] Cf. Johnson, 102f.

[117] See de Boer, "Vive le roi," *VT,* 5 (1955), 225ff.; cf. D. Michel, "Studien zu den sogenannten Thronbesteigungspsalmen," *VT,* 6 (1956), 45ff.

1:25,31,34,39; 2 K. 11:12; 2 Ch. 23:11). In its context it is used as an acclamation and expresses recognition of the kingship of the individual acclaimed; originally, however, it must have meant a wish for "life" in the sense of life as a true king, with power and success.

Ps. 21:5(4) provides an illustration: the king asked for and received life or a long life (*ʾōrekh yāmîm ʿôlām vāʿedh*; cf. Ps. 61:7[6]: *yāmîm, shānôth*). The king can also "bestow life" upon his people: "In the light of a king's face there is life" (Prov. 16:15); the parallel line speaks of the king's favor (*rātsôn*), which is like life-giving rain. The high point of such statements is Lam. 4:20: "The anointed of Yahweh was the breath of our nostrils (*rûach ʾappēnû*) . . . we said, 'Under his shadow we shall "live" among the nations.' " The king thus transmits to his people the life vouchsafed by God.[118]

7. *The Life of the Nation in the Prophets.* Much more difficult to evaluate are the numerous passages in Ezekiel where life is placed in prospect for those who turn and act righteously. The primary passages in question are Ezk. 33:10-20 and chap. 18, where the expression occurs repeatedly.[119] The first of these is introduced by a discouraged question: "Our transgressions and our sins are upon us, . . . how then can we 'live' [or: 'survive']?" The prophet replies with an oracle from God: "I have no pleasure in the death of the wicked, but that the wicked turn from his way and live." The prophet goes on to develop the idea that when a righteous man sins, his former righteousness does not suffice to secure him life: he must die. Obversely, when the wicked man turns and acts righteously, "he shall surely live (*chāyô yichyeh*), he shall not die" (v. 15). God will judge each according to his ways. In chap. 18, the same idea is applied systematically to a series of examples; each section concludes with a version of the declaratory formula *tsaddîq hûʾ* (→ הוא *hûʾ*) *chāyōh yichyeh* or *môth yāmûth*. The form is obviously borrowed from priestly jurisprudence. The conclusion reads: "Turn, and live" (18:32).

Other scattered passages point in the same direction: 3:21, whoever takes warning will save his life; 20:11,13,21, whoever keeps the commandments will live (see above).

The question is, what do "live" and "die" mean in this context? A third section (chap. 27) might suggest that what is at stake is the national life of the people of God when it speaks of the dead bones that come to life again. The dry bones are Israel, whose existence as a nation has apparently ended. By human standards, there is no hope for revival. But with the help of God's *rûach,* the bones nevertheless come to life—in other words, Israel is restored as the people of God and can continue to live so.

The two other passages appear at first glance to have a different, more individualistic character. But the "we" that speaks and says, "How can we live?" or "We are suffering for the sins of our fathers" is none other than the nation in exile, thinking that return is hopeless. The prophet rejects this conclusion, on the grounds that God wishes repentance and return, with the life that results; the repentance and return of the present

[118]Cf. I.1 above.
[119]Zimmerli.

generation will result in life, independently of the guilt of earlier generations. The impression of individualism stems from the literary form and the theoretical argument.

Other prophetic texts also illuminate this theme, especially Am. 5. There we read (v. 4): "Seek me and live"—with the continuation, "Do not seek Bethel, and do not enter into Gilgal or cross over into Beer-sheba," obviously a polemic against the priesthood of the northern kingdom, which encouraged such pilgrimages with promises of life.[120] The same idea appears also in v. 6: "Seek Yahweh and live, lest he break out like fire in the house of Joseph and devour it": the opposite of "life" is here national destruction. In v. 14, we read: "Seek good, and not evil, that you may live, and so Yahweh, the God of hosts, will be with you, as you have said." Here "live" is synonymous with "God is with you." This verse, too, can refer only to the national existence of the people of God; the opposite is the destruction and devastation of the land. But, as Zimmerli emphasizes, the promise of life is conditional: life is possible only as the consequence of repentance and return.

The statement in Hab. 2:4, "The righteous shall live by his *ʾemûnāh,*" is much more vague. However the preceding clause is understood (it is possible to make sense of the MT: "Behold, his soul is puffed up, dishonest within him"; the commentaries propose various emendations), it must refer to the hostile powers of the world; the "puffed up" man is contrasted with the "righteous" man. The enemy will perish, the righteous (Judah? Israel?) will live through his faithfulness. "Life," as Elliger says,[121] is "political existence . . . in the saving presence of God."

Hos. 6:2 is totally unique. The nation wishes to return (*shûbh*) to Yahweh; "for he has torn that he may heal [→ רפא *rāphāʾ*] us. . . . After two days he will revive us (piel of *chāyāh*), on the third day he will raise us up (*yᵉqimēnû*), that we may 'live' before him." It is generally recognized that lurking behind this statement are Canaanite ideas of the resurrection of a dead god. It will be noted, however, that the prophet does not approve of these notions. What is expressed here is the false hope of the people. The prophet's verdict in v. 4 is negative: the willingness of the people to return is fleeting.

8. *God Gives Life*. That Yahweh is lord of life and death is obvious. When Naaman sent messengers to the king of Israel with a request for help, the latter replied: "Am I God, to kill and to make alive?" (2 K. 5:7). The reply presupposes that only God can "make alive." In addition, we have here a typical illustration of the fact that "make alive" is practically synonymous with "cure disease." The same idea is expressed positively in Dt. 32:39 and 1 S. 2:6. In the first passage, we have the parallelism: "I wound (*māchatstî*) but I also heal (*ʾerpāʾ*)"; the point of the verse is: I alone am God. The second passage involves a series of antitheses: Yahweh brings down to Sheol and raises up, makes poor and makes rich, brings low and exalts—a typical way of expressing the monistic view of the OT.[122]

Positively, human life is traced back to the creative act of God: God makes man out of earth and breathes the breath of life (*nishmath chaiyîm;* → נשמה *nᵉshāmāh*); thus

---

[120]Zimmerli, 185.

[121]K. Elliger, *ATD,* XXV (^{6}1967), 41.

[122]H. Ringgren, *Israelite Religion* (trans. 1966), 72.

man becomes a *nephesh chaiyāh* (Gen. 2:7). Life (including the life of animals; cf. *rûach chaiyîm,* Gen. 6:17; 7:15,22) therefore comes from God; thus man becomes "living."[123] It is noteworthy that *nephesh,* which itself can also mean "life," here has joined to it the attribute *chaiyîm*. (In addition, the verb *chāyāh* often appears with *nephesh* as its subject: Gen. 12:13; 19:20; 1 K. 20:32; Isa. 55:3; Jer. 38:20.)

Many passages speak of life as the gift of God, for instance, Job 10:12: "Thou hast granted me life and *chesedh,* and thy care (*p^{e}quddāh*) has preserved my *rûach*"; Ps. 36:10(9): "With thee is the fountain of life (*m^{e}qôr chaiyîm*); in thy light do we see light" (the context speaks of God's protection in association with the temple; note the combination life/light; the text may be corrupt: *ʾôr/ʾôr* appears tautological); Ps. 66:9: "(God) has kept our *nephesh* alive" (though the reference here may be to deliverance from distress). Here, too, belong all the psalms that speak of God as giving or preserving life (usually piel), for instance, Ps. 143:11: "For thy name's sake, O Yahweh, preserve my life [piel]," parallel to "Bring my *nephesh* out of trouble (*tsārāh*)." Cf. Ps. 30:4(3): "Thou hast brought up my *nephesh* from Sheol, restored me to life from among those gone down to the Pit (*bôr*)." Other passages include Ps. 41:3(2): "Yahweh protects him and keeps him alive [piel]," parallel to "Thou dost not give his *nephesh* up to the will of his enemies"; Ps. 71:20: "Thou who hast made me see many sore troubles (*tsārôth rabbôth v^{e}raʿôth*) wilt revive me again; from the depths of the earth thou wilt bring me up again" (cf. also Ps. 119:25,37,40,88,93,107,149,154,156,159); Ps. 85:7(6): "Wilt thou not 'revive' us again, that thy people may rejoice in thee?" (cf. Ps. 80:19[18]). In most cases, the verb probably refers to deliverance from danger or distress, i.e., from a wretched existence in the power of death into rich and full life ("joy" in Ps. 85:7[6]).

Ps. 30:6(5) probably also belongs in this context: "For *reghaʿ* is in his wrath, but life in his *rātsôn*." Whatever *reghaʿ* may mean here, the antithesis "moment/lifetime" can hardly be intended.

9. *The Living God*. Yahweh is the living God (*ʾ^{e}lōhîm chaiyîm,* 1 S. 17:26; Dt. 5:26; Jer. 10:10; 23:36; Dnl. 6:21,27[20,26] [Aramaic]; *ʾ^{e}lōhîm chai,* 2 K. 19:4,16; *ʾēl chai,* Josh. 3:10; Hos. 2:1[1:10]; Ps. 42:3[2]; 84:3[2]). What this expression is intended to mean is not entirely clear. It is dubious whether Ps. 18:47(46) (*chai yhvh*) points the way to the solution. Widengren[124] compares this expression to Ugar. *ḥy ʾl3yn bʿl,*[125] the shout of triumph that greets the dead god as he returns to life.[126] In an OT context, however, it seems highly unlikely that Yahweh could be dead and return to life. Widengren[127] points out that there are also passages that speak of Yahweh's sleeping or rising from sleep. This obviously means that he is apparently inactive or intervenes actively. The latter would also be appropriate in the context of Ps. 18: Yahweh is the active God, who intervenes and delivers men from their adversaries (v.

---

[123]Cf. C. Westermann, *BK,* I/1 (1974), 282f.
[124]*Sakrales Königtum,* 69.
[125]*CTA,* 6 [I AB], III, 8f.
[126]See I.3 above.
[127]Pp. 67f.

49[48]). Furthermore, we find "the God of my salvation" (*'ᵉlōhê yišʿî*) in parallelism with *chai yhvh*.

Does this interpretation work in the *'ēl chai* passages? Dt. 5:26 speaks of the unprecedented fact that someone hears the voice of the living God and still remains alive. Josh. 3:10 says that the ark will go before through the Jordan and thus show "that the living God is among you," who will drive out the enemy nations. In 1 S. 17:26, we read: "Who is this [Goliath], that he should defy the armies of the living God?" In 2 K. 19:4, we are told how Rabshakeh mocks the living God; the passage expresses the conviction that Yahweh will avenge the insult. In Jer. 10:10, Yahweh is called "the true God (*'ᵉlōhîm 'ᵉmeth*), the living God and the everlasting king," and we learn that the earth quakes at his wrath—possibly in contrast to the powerless idols (vv. 11ff.). Hos. 2:1(1:10) states that Israel is no longer to be called "Not my people," but rather "Sons of the Living God"—in other words, Yahweh has once more actively taken them into his charge. Ps. 42:3(2) speaks of thirsting for *'ēl chai* as the God who is present in the temple; the same is true of 84:3(2). This survey appears to confirm the interpretation of the phrase as meaning "intervening actively" or "obviously present." There is no trace in any of the passages of a contrast with a dying god of the Canaanite type.

The expression *gō'ᵃlî chai* (Job 19:25) probably belongs here also. Job knows that he has an active advocate to take his side. Logically, that would mean that Yahweh is siding with Job against himself, but hardly any other solution seems satisfactory. Cf. also the expression "redeemer of my soul" in Ps. 103:4 and Lam. 3:58, in which *gā'al* and *chaiyîm* also appear together.

We must also discuss the oath formula *chai yhvh*, which occurs 43 times (and twice in the Lachish letters: III, 9; XII, 3). Related formulas include: *chai 'ēl* (Job 27:2); *chai hā'ᵉlōhîm* (2 S. 2:27); *chai 'ānî*, always with God speaking in the 1st person (23 times). With reference to other gods, we find *chê 'ᵉlōheykhā dān* and *chê derekh bᵉ'ēr-shebhaʿ* (Am. 8:14).[128] Finally, *chê pharʿōh* appears in Gen. 42:15f.[129] The question is whether *chai* is to be understood as a verb, i.e., "as Yahweh lives," or as the noun "life," i.e., "by the life of NN" (cf. Arab. *laʿamraka, biḥayātika*, "by your life," and Akk. *nīš ilim* or *nīš šarrim tamū/zakāru*,[130] as well as the Egyptian oath formulas discussed by Wilson and Vergote).

The construct form *chê* supports the latter view, as do the Akkadian and Egyptian parallels.[131] We may follow Kraus in concluding that the God so invoked becomes a witness to the oath and keeps watch over it (cf. 1 S. 20:23: "Yahweh is between you and me forever"). The nature of the ideas associated with the oath can be observed from several passages cited by Kraus,[132] in which the formula is expanded: Jer. 16:14f.; 23:7f.: ". . . who brought up the people of Israel out of the land of Egypt"; 1 K. 2:24: ". . . who has established me and placed me on the throne of David my

[128]On the text, see *BHS* and the commentaries.
[129]Cf. Vergote, 162ff.
[130]Greenberg, 37.
[131]Greenberg, 37f.
[132]Pp. 177f.

father''; 2 K. 3:14; 5:16: ''. . . whom I serve''; 2 S. 4:9; 1 K. 1:29: ''. . . who has redeemed my life out of every adversity''; Jer. 38:16: ''. . . who made our souls.'' In these cases, then, we are dealing with the God who acts effectually.

10. *The Tree of Life, Book of Life, Land of the Living*. As was suggested above,[133] the idea of life in the ancient Near East was often connected with the notion of an object, possession of which as it were guaranteed life. In the Gilgamesh Epic it is the plant of life, in the myth of Adapa it is the food and water of life, and in Gen. 2:9; 3:22, 24 it is the tree of life (*ʿēts chaiyîm*). In the Paradise story, the tree of life is remarkably peripheral to the narrative, which centers on the tree of knowledge. In 2:9, the mention of the tree of life seems most likely to be an afterthought; only 3:22,24 make it clear that the tree of life could have secured mankind the possibility of living *leʿôlām,* but that the Fall cost mankind access to this tree. In the Gilgamesh Epic, the hero finds the plant of life but loses it again, meaning that he does not find eternal life—it is the privilege of the gods. In the myth of Adapa, Adapa refuses the proffered symbols of life and remains mortal.[134] Although much has been written about the notion of the tree of life and its Mesopotamian prototypes,[135] the expression itself has not yet been found in Akkadian literature.[136] The occurrences in Proverbs mentioned above[137] are purely figurative; it is most unlikely that they have anything to do with the tree of life in Paradise.

Here we may also mention the notion of the ''book of life'' (or ''book of the living,'' *sēpher chaiyîm* [→ ספר *sēpher*], Ps. 69:29[28]). The context expresses the wish that the enemies of the psalmist be blotted out of the book of life or not enrolled among the righteous; in other words, they are consigned to death. Similar ideas are expressed in other passages, albeit without the use of this particular term: Ex. 32:32: ''Blot me out of thy book which thou has written''; Ps. 139:16: ''My days are written in thy book''; Isa. 4:3: ''Everyone who has been recorded for life [i.e., continued existence] in Jerusalem''; Mal. 3:16, a book of remembrance with the names of those who fear Yahweh; Dnl. 12:1, those whose names are found written in the book will be delivered (cf. v. 2, rising to eternal life).

It has been suggested that these passages are based on the notion of a heavenly book or the tablets of destiny found in Babylonian religion.[138] But the prototype might equally well have been the lists of particular groups in the population found in the Ugaritic texts or registers of Israelite citizens (cf. Ezk. 13:9a).[139]

Another possible source is suggested by 1 S. 25:29. There Abigail expresses the wish that David may be ''bound in the bundle of the living [or: 'of life'; *tseṛôr hachaiyîm*],'' i.e., that he will be kept alive by God. According to Eissfeldt, this idiom

---

[133] I.2.

[134] Cf. H. Ringgren, ''Israel's Place Among the Religions of the Ancient Near East,'' *Studies in the Religion of Ancient Israel. SVT,* 23 (1972), 4f.

[135] E.g., Widengren, *Tree of Life*.

[136] H. Genge, ''Zum 'Lebensbaum' in den Keilschriftkulturen,'' *AcOr,* 33 (1971), 321-334.

[137] II.5.

[138] Koep; G. Widengren, *The Ascension of the Apostle and the Heavenly Book. UUÅ,* 1950/7 (1950), 7ff.

[139] Herrmann, 7f.

derives from the shepherd's custom of keeping a small bundle containing as many pebbles as there are animals in the flock.[140]

The expression *ʾerets chaiyîm,* "land of the living" (or "land of life"?), occurs 14 times. It refers to the earth as the place of living creatures. Among its occurrences, Ezk. 32:23-25,27,32 occupy a special position. Here we read that hostile nations have spread terror in the land of the living, i.e., the human world. Since, however, these nations are depicted as the dead dwelling in the Underworld, we have a contrast between their present impotent condition and their former power when they were still alive. This contrast is even more marked in the other occurrences. In Hezekiah's psalm of thanksgiving, for example, we read: "I said, I shall not see Yahweh in the land of the living," i.e., I shall no longer live but die (Isa. 38:11). In the fourth of the Servant Songs, we read that the servant was cut off (*nighzar*) from the land of the living, i.e., died (Isa. 53:8). Ps. 52:7(5) expresses the wish that God will destroy the enemy, sweep him out of the tent, and uproot (*sheresh*) him from the land of the living—in other words, totally annihilate him. In a similar vein, Jer. 11:19 has the enemies of the prophet say: " 'Let us cut him off (*kārath*) from the land of the living, that his name be remembered no more' "—once again total annihilation. In a threat discourse against Tyre, Ezekiel has Yahweh say that he will cast the city into the Underworld, while he himself will do glorious things in the land of the living (Ezk. 26:20). In other words, God will carry out his work among mankind on earth, while the unrighteous city lies powerless in the Underworld.

In other cases, the expression is used in positive contexts. Twice a grateful psalmist expresses the conviction that he will see the goodness of Yahweh or walk before Yahweh in the land of the living (Ps. 27:13; 116:9). Here deliverance from death is expressed in terms of divine intervention; the result is life to the full in the communion of God. The same sense is probably intended in Ps. 142:6(5): "Thou art my refuge, my portion in the land of the living." Finally, the expression appears in a weakened sense in Job 28:13: there is no wisdom in the land of the living, i.e., among mankind.

11. *Man's Mortality; Eternal Life*. The narrative of the tree of life explains why human beings are mortal. No one can ransom his life and live forever, says Ps. 49:9f.(8f.), even though the text may be somewhat corrupt.[141] Eccl. 9:5 states that the living know that they must die. Two well-known passages in the Apocalypse of Isaiah, Isa. 26:14, 19, belong in a way in this context. "They are dead, they will not live; they are shades (*r^{e}phāʾîm*), they will not arise" states the lament section. This can easily be a general statement, but in the historical situation it probably refers to national existence. When v. 19 then states: "Thy dead shall live, my bodies shall rise," the context speaks of those who lie in the dust, but here, too, national existence can be meant.

On the other hand, Dnl. 12:2 is totally clear and unambiguous: "Many of those who sleep in the dust of the earth shall awake, some to everlasting life (*chaiyê ʿôlām*), and

---

[140]Cf. Herrmann, 5f.

[141]See the commentaries.

some to shame and everlasting contempt." Note here the antithesis life/shame (*chᵃrāphôth* [→ חרף *ḥrp* II], *dirʾôn ʿôlām*).

IV. 1. *"Every Living Thing."* The expression *kol-chai,* "every living thing," occurs 6 times in the OT, plus 2 occurrences in the plural, *kol-hachaiyîm,* "all living things" (Eccl. 4:15; 9:4). In its broadest sense it refers to all living creatures, including the animals. This is the case in the narrative of the Deluge, where according to Gen. 6:19 (P) two of "every living thing" are to be brought into the ark in order to preserve the various species of animals, and according to Gen. 8:21 (J) Yahweh promises never again to destroy "every living thing." In a similar context, P uses *kol-bāśār,* "all flesh" (Gen. 9:11), and *kol-nephesh chaiyāh,* "every living creature" (9:12,15f.): God makes a covenant with all living creatures that he will never again destroy them. In the latter passage the two expressions are combined. The phrase *kol-nephesh hachāyyāh* appears also in Gen. 1:21; 9:10; Lev. 11:10,46 (all P).

Elsewhere, *kol-chai* seems to refer primarily to human beings: Eve is called "the mother of all living" (*ʾēm kol-chai,* Gen. 3:20), clearly an illusion to her name (→ חוה *chavvāh*); the realm of the dead is the place where all living, i.e., all men, assemble (Job 30:23); no man living (*lōʾ . . . kol-chai*) is righteous (→צדק *ṣdq*) before God (Ps. 143:2). When Job (28:21) states that wisdom is hid from the eyes of all living, one thinks immediately only of mankind; but the second half verse adds that it is also concealed from the birds of the air, which could suggest the broader meaning of the term.

2. *chāiyāh, "Animal."* The noun *chaiyāh* means "animal,"[142] in the first instance animals of any kind (e.g., *kol-(ha)chaiyāh:* Gen. 1:18; 7:14; 8:1,17; 9:5; plural, Ps. 104:25). It can also refer more specifically to wild animals when qualified by such words as *hāʾārets* (Gen. 1:25; 1 S. 17:46; Ezk. 29:5; variant *chaithô-ʾerets,* Gen. 1:24; Ps. 79:2), *haśśādheh* (Gen. 2:19; 3:1; Ex. 23:11; Isa. 43:20; Hos. 2:14[12]; Job 40:20; variant *śādhāi,* Isa. 56:9; Ps. 104:11), or *yaʿar* (*chaithô,* Ps. 50:10; 104:20; cf. *baiyāʿar,* Isa. 56:9). When contrasted with *ʿôph* and *dāghāh,* it refers to land animals (Gen. 1:28; 8:19; Lev. 11:2). In Isa. 46:1 it means beasts of burden, in Ps. 104:25 creatures of the sea. In addition, *chaiyāh* alone can designate wild animals or predators, in contrast to → בהמה *bᵉhēmāh* (Ezk. 14:15; 33:27; Zeph. 2:15; Ps. 148:10; Job 37:8). The phrase *chaiyāh rāʿāh* means "beast of prey" (Gen. 37:20,33; Lev. 26:6; Ezk. 5:17; 14:15,21; 34:25). Finally, *chaiyāh* is used as a term for the animal-like creatures in Ezekiel's call vision (see below).

In the creation account of P, we read in Gen. 1:24f. how the *nephesh chaiyāh,* namely, *chaiyath hāʾārets,* birds, and fish, were created on the sixth day. In 1:28, mankind is given authority to rule over all of them, and in 1:30 they all receive permission to live off the plants of the earth. J has the same categories as the object of God's → יצר *yātsar* (2:19); then the man gives them names (2:20).

In the story of the Fall, the serpent is more subtle than all *chaiyath haśśādheh* (Gen. 3:1), and is cursed by God *mikkol-chaiyath haśśādheh,* either "more than" or "away

[142]On the meaning "life" in 18 passages, see *KBL*³, 297.

from'' the other animals. In the account of the Deluge, all the animals appear once more: all the categories enter the ark (7:14), all die (*gāvaʿ*) in the Flood (7:21), God remembers them (8:1), and they go forth when the Flood is past (8:17, 19). It is significant that all the categories are represented among those spared. According to Gen. 9:2, furthermore, all animals are to fear man, and according to 9:5, God will avenge man's life against every animal. In 9:10, God makes a covenant with mankind and the animals never again to send a flood.

Lev. 11:47 speaks of animals that may be eaten and animals that may not be eaten (cf. also 11:2,27).

The vanquished foe is left to the birds and the wild animals: the Philistines (1 S. 17:46), Pharaoh and the Egyptians (Ezk. 29:5), Gog and his army (Ezk. 39:4). But the same fate awaits Israel: Ezekiel lists sword, pestilence, and wild animals (5:17; 14:15, 21; 33:27; 34:5,8). Wild animals dwell in the desolated land (Zeph. 2:14; cf. Hos. 2:14[12]). In Isa. 56:9, the beasts of the field and of the forest are summoned to come and devour because the leaders of the land are blind (cf. also Jer. 12:9). Ps. 79:2 laments that the enemy has given ''the bodies of thy servants'' to the birds and the wild animals; in Ezk. 32:4, Pharaoh is similarly left to the birds and the animals. On the other hand, it is a sign of peace and well-being when the wild beasts make no disturbance (Isa. 35:9; Ezk. 34:25,28). Hosea even speaks of a covenant between God and the beasts of the field, the birds, and the creeping things of the ground for the benefit of Israel (Hos. 2:20[18]). In like manner, Eliphaz speaks optimistically of the security of the righteous man against wild animals, on the grounds that he lives in harmony with stones and beasts (*bᵉrîth . . . hoshlᵉmāh-lākh,* Job 5:23).

The animals are a part of Yahweh's creation. Every beast of the forest belongs to Yahweh (Ps. 50:10: therefore he needs no sacrifice; cf. Isa. 40:16: the animals of Lebanon would not suffice for sacrifice). Ps. 104 in particular describes the care of the Creator for the animals: he gives them drink (v. 11), he gives the wild animals night so that they can find food (vv. 20f.), animals large and small live in the sea (v. 25). Similar ideas appear in God's answer to Job (Job 37:8; 40:20). In Ps. 148, a hymn, v. 10 lists wild and domestic animals, creeping things and birds among those called on to praise Yahweh. But when, as a consequence of the nation's sin, Yahweh withdraws his care for the land, animals, birds, and vermin languish (Hos. 4:3).

Finally, *chaiyāh* is used analogously for the angelic beings in Ezekiel's call vision, which share many features of animals (Ezk. 1:5f.,11,13-15,19,21-23). They appear again in the vision in chap. 10, where they are called *kᵉrûbhîm* (→ כרוב *kᵉrûbh*); a special point is made of the fact that they are identical with the *chaiyôth* of chap. 1 (10:15,20).

3. *ʿēth chaiyāh*. In Gen. 18:10,14, the expression *kāʿeth chaiyāh* designates the time when Sarah will bear a son. Gunkel[143] paraphases this with : ''about this time, when it revives once more, i.e., a year hence.'' Speiser[144] interprets it as referring to the term of pregnancy. This interpretation fits the context but is less likely, since, as

[143]H. Gunkel, *HAT,* 1 (^{7}1966), 179.

[144]E. Speiser, *Genesis. AB,* I (1964), 130.

Yaron and Loretz have shown independently,[145] Akk. *ana balāṭ* is used in the sense "a year from now, next year."[146] The expression also appears in a similar context in 2 K. 4:16.

4. *michyāh.* The word *michyāh* has several meanings. It can mean the preservation of life: God sent Joseph to Egypt before his brothers *l^e michyāh* (Gen. 45:5); according to Sir. 38:14, *michyāh* is the purpose of a physician's work. It can also mean the formation of new flesh in wounds: raw flesh or scar tissue (Lev. 13:10,24). The third meaning is "provisions" (Jgs. 6:4; 17:10). A fourth meaning is found in Ezra 9:8f., where it is used for the "reviving" vouchsafed to the people by God after their captivity. Finally, in 2 Ch. 14:12(13) it is used for the (non)survival of the Ethiopians attempting to escape. It appears twice with this last meaning in the Qumran texts, with reference to those remaining alive for the new covenant (1QM 13:8; 1QH 6:8), in each case parallel with *sh^eʾērîth,* "remnant."

Ringgren

---

[145]Yaron, *VT,* 12 (1962), 500f.; Loretz, *Bibl,* 43 (1962), 75–78.
[146]*AHw,* I, 99.

חיל *ḥyl;* חִיל *chîl;* חִילָה *chîlāh;* חַלְחָלָה *chalchālāh*

Contents: I. 1. Etymology; 2. Meaning and Occurrences. II. Secular Usage: 1. Birth, Labor; 2. Fear, Trembling. III. Religious Usage: 1. Creation, Awe; 2. Birth Pangs of the Messianic Age.

I. 1. *Etymology.* The root *ḥyl* cannot always be easily distinguished from words derived from the roots *ḥwl, ḥll, ḥālāh,* and *yḥl*, all of which likewise contain the radicals *ḥ* and *l.* There has therefore been no lack of attempts to find etymological connections.[1] These seem most likely in the case of → חול *chûl.*[2]

In the few Canaanite, Ugaritic, and Phoenician occurrences, however, the root is always connected with → ילד *yāladh,* "give birth." In Akkadian, too, the meaning

---

ḥyl. P. R. Berger, "Zur Bedeutung des in den akkadischen Texten aus Ugarit bezeugten Ortsnamens *Ḫīlu (Ḥl),*" *UF,* 2 (1970), 340–46; D. R. Hillers, "A Convention in Hebrew Literature: The Reaction to Bad News," *ZAW,* 77 (1965), 86–90; T. Nöldeke, *Beiträge zur semitischen Sprachwissenschaft* (1904), 42; J. Scharbert, *Der Schmerz im AT. BBB,* 8 (1955), 21–26; J. van der Ploeg, "Prov. XXV 23," *VT,* 3 (1953), 189–192; R. de Vaux, *AncIsr,* 52.

[1]Cf. Scharbert, 21f.
[2]Scharbert.

"be in labor" predominates; it can also be applied figuratively to males, lands, etc.[3] Since the LXX does not exhibit a uniform interpretation of the meaning of *chîl,* translating it contextually, the best course in Hebrew seems to be to begin with the meaning of the root in the other Semitic languages. Akk. *ḫalḫallatu(m),* "a kind of drum,"[4] and Aram. *'ᵃchîlû,* "a kind of fever" (chills?), may cast light on the semantic range of the root.

2. *Meaning and Occurrences.* Contrary to Scharbert and Gerleman,[5] when *chîl* means "be in labor" it does not refer primarily to screaming and groaning, an interpretation that may have been suggested by the German translation *kreissen,* "be in labor," which is etymologically connected with *kreischen,* "groan." The Hebrew word is in fact a comprehensive term for everything from the initial contractions to the birth itself. This state is characterized by recurring spasms of pain which are not subject to conscious control, during which the woman in labor writhes—a process that can be accompanied by a sense of fear or anxiety, screams, and groans. That *chîl* is the inclusive term is also shown by the fact that the words for labor pains (→ חבל *ḥbl* IV) and birth pangs (*tsîrîm*) always occur in the plural, while *chîl, chîlāh,* and *chalchālāh* always appear in the singular.

It is easy to see how *chîl* could be applied figuratively to situations in which the subject feels a similar helplessness, expressed in uncontrollable rhythmic movements—above all shuddering or trembling in fear or awe.

The verb appears 47 times in the OT, including Ps. 109:22 and 110:3,[6] in a variety of forms. The noun *chîl* appears 6 times, *chîlāh* once, and the by-form *chalchālāh* 4 times. Most of the occurrences are in the prophetic books (esp. Isaiah and Jeremiah) and the Psalms; the root hardly appears at all in the historical books.

II. Secular Usage.

1. *Birth, Labor.* The OT contains hardly any descriptions of childbirth; from Isa. 26:17f.; 66:7f., however, we can determine that *chîl* begins with the first contractions and ceases with actual *yāladh* (cf. Jn. 16:21). The verb appears several times in the context of statements about parents, where it describes the role of the mother in contrast to that of the father (Isa. 45:10; 51:2; cf. Dt. 32:18) or serves to emphasize the very beginning of human life (Ps. 51:7 [Eng. v. 5]). It appears frequently in parallel with → ילד *yāladh* to describe the entire process of birth (Isa. 54:1; Ps. 110:3[?]; of animals: Job 39:1; figuratively: Isa. 23:4; 66:7f.; Ps. 90:2; Job 15:7). Occasionally *chîl* is used in the polel and polal in the sense "bring forth" (Prov. 25:23;[7] 26:10), but this sense is still associated with the origins of the word in the realm of birth.

2. *Fear, Trembling.* Much more common than direct reference to actual birth is the figurative use of the verb in situations of anxiety or fear, which outwardly recall the

---

[3]Cf. *ḫ(i)ālu, AHw,* I, 342b.
[4]*AHw,* I, 311b.
[5]Contra Scharbert and G. Gerleman, *BK,* XXI/2 (1973), 105.
[6]Cf. *KBL*[3].
[7]Cf. van der Ploeg.

manifestations of labor. That this usage is secondary can be seen from the very fact that the metaphorical nature of the statement is often emphasized (Isa. 26:17: "like a woman with child . . . when she is near her time"; cf. Jer. 4:31: "as of a woman in travail [*k*ᵉ*chôlāh*]"). Most frequently *chîl* is explained by the addition of "like a woman in travail" (*kaiyôlēdhāh*): Isa. 13:8; Mic. 4:10; and all occurrences of the noun *chîl* except Ex. 15:14. The other expressions referring to the process of birth that appear in conjunction with *chîl* point in the same direction. The application of this metaphor to males is anything but flattering; it is tantamount to saying that men in panic have become "like women."[8]

In many such passages, the point is primarily to describe the situation in which these men find themselves. The sudden seizure is depicted by such verbs as → בוא *bô'*, → חזק *chāzaq,* and *'āchaz,* which are also used for the onset of birth pangs (*ch*ᵃ*bhālîm, tsîrîm*). The physical effects are described: the loins are filled with *chîl* (Isa. 21:3; cf. Nah. 2:11[10]), the knees tremble (Nah. 2:11[10]), the hands fall helpless (Jer. 6:24; Mic. 4:9), faces pale (Joel 2:6; Nah. 2:11[10]; cf. Isa. 13:8), groans (Jer. 4:31; 22:23; Mic. 4:10) and cries (Isa. 26:17; Jer. 4:31) are heard. These details give us a clear picture of what is meant by *chîl:* involuntary and uncontrolled spasmodic movement, to which the body is surrendered, accompanied by a sense of weakness and heat. The symptoms described are almost exclusively external. At the same time, however, it is clear that the verb refers also to the inward state of the person in question: a state of trembling, panic fear.

Such a state can occur in the face of battle, in times of judgment, on the "day of Yahweh." It is therefore often stressed that *chîl* comes in reaction to disastrous news.[9] This is most readily apparent in Est. 4:4.[10] The same point is implied by the frequent instances when *chîl* is evoked by hearing (→ שמע *shāma'*: Ex. 15:14; Dt. 2:25; Isa. 21:3; 23:5; Jer. 4:19; 6:24; 50:43) or seeing (→ ראה *rā'āh*: Isa. 21:3; Zec. 9:5; Ps. 97:4). Usually the nature of *chîl* as a reaction is implied simply by the temporal sequence. The agent causing the terrifying impression is identified by means of *min:* it can be enemy archers (1 S. 31:3 = 1 Ch. 10:3) or other foes; in theophanies it is God himself (e.g., Isa. 26:17; cf. Jer. 51:29). In the context of a theophany, *chîl* can also appear in parallel with "tremble" (→ רעש *rā'ash,* Dt. 2:25; Jer. 51:29; → רגז *rāghaz,* Ex. 15:14; Ps. 77:17[16]).

Primarily in later usage, we also find a use of *chîl* that says more about the inner state of the person in question. It can apparently take on the weakened meaning "be afraid, be upset" (Zec. 9:5). Occasionally it seems to be tantamount to the fear of death (Ps. 55:5[4]; Job 6:10; 15:20). That the inner state is more important in this context is shown by the absence of the usual description of symptoms or the localization of *chîl* in the heart (Jer. 4:19; Ps. 55:5[4]; 109:22).

III. Religious Usage.

1. *Creation, Awe.* In a series of passages, *chîl* is used in statements about the process of creation. In Dt. 32:18, the usage described in II.1 is applied to Yahweh: he

[8]→ איש *'îsh* II.2.c.

[9]Cf. Hillers.

[10]See Gerleman, 105.

is both father and mother to Israel, i.e., he is responsible in every respect for Israel's existence. In Isa. 66:7f., the new creation of the nation in the future is depicted as a birth.

But *chîl* is also used in statements about creation in the narrower sense. Statements about the age of certain phenomena serve to determine their relative status. Since Job was not yet present when the mountains were in labor and when the first man was born (Job 15:7), his status is low and he should keep silent. Since Wisdom, contrariwise, was already present before the depths and the springs, before the mountains and the hills (Prov. 8:24f.), she ranks above the rest of creation and is close to God. Only of God, however, can it be said that he was present before the mountains were brought forth and the earth and the world were made (Ps. 90:2). This form of expression is probably based on mythological prototypes,[11] but without any specific allusion; in the present version, incomparably great age or its opposite is symbolized vividly by such undoubtedly primeval phenomena as mountains, springs, depths, and the first human beings.

Mythological ideas can be recognized more clearly where allusions to creation occur in the context of theophanies. Before the appearance of Yahweh, the mountains writhe and raging waters sweep down from the clouds (Hab. 3:10). Allusions to the battle with the forces of chaos are found also in Ps. 29:8f.; 97:4; 110:3(?); 114:7; Job 26:5; Jer. 5:3,22; 1 Ch. 16:30. Here, too, though, the mythological element is much attenuated. In Ps. 77:17(16), the battle with chaos has been historicized into the miracle at the Sea of Reeds. In most of the passages mentioned, furthermore, *chîl* refers not so much to a reaction of fear—panic terror—as to trembling in awe and wonder before the majesty of Yahweh. This is quite clear in Ps. 96:9, where *chîlû* stands alongside *hishtachavû* (→ חוה *ḥwh*). Here are no longer any overtones of rebellion, only the subordination of the forces of nature to Yahweh.

2. *Birth Pangs of the Messianic Age.* The metaphorical use of birth imagery to describe situations of fear and anxiety as outlined in II.2 sometimes acquired apocalyptic overtones—especially from the perspective of late postexilic readers, who found here premonitions of *the* judgment and its terrors. In Isa. 66:7ff., the subject is the new creation of the nation after the period of dispersion, but v. 7 could be understood as an allusion to the birth of an individual child. Perhaps on the basis of this passage, rabbinic literature came to speak of the "birth pangs of the Messiah" (*chebhlô shel māshîach*).[12] The usual term employed, however, was *chabhālîm*. There is but one further occurrence of *chîl* in the Dead Sea Scrolls, in the context of a detailed description of the terrors of the eschaton in 1QH 3:8.

Bauman

---

[11]H. Ringgren, *ATD*, XVI/2 (²1962), 40.

[12]Cf. St.-B., I, 950, and *ōdínes* in the NT.

חַיִל chayil

Contents: I. 1. Occurrences; 2. Etymology; 3. LXX. II. Basic Meaning. III. Persons with "Power": 1. With *ben*; 2. With *'îsh*; 3. With *gibbôr*; 4. With *śārîm, pᵉqûdhîm*. IV. Term for "Army." V. Wealth. VI. 1. God Gives *chayil*; 2. From *chayil* to *chayil*: Ps. 84:8(7); 3. God Gives Strength. VII. Divine Attribute?

I. 1. *Occurrences*. The verb *yāchîl,* associated with the noun *chayil,* is found only in Job 20:21, where it means "endure." Berger claims to find an additional verbal form in Ps. 10:5.[1] The verb is probably a denominative derived from the noun, corresponding to its basic meaning, "strength." The noun itself often has the more concrete meaning "wealth" or "army."

The noun *chayil* is used 240 times in the Hebrew OT, with an additional 6 occurrences in the Aramaic sections. It appears with surprising frequency in Jeremiah (29 times), but also in 1 and 2 Chronicles (28 and 27 times respectively). The subject matter may account for its frequency in Jeremiah, since armies and commanders of armies appear in the narrative sections. Accounts of battles can also account for the large number in 2 Chronicles, while in 1 Chronicles the long lists accentuate the use of *chayil*. Even so, the contrast is striking with 1 and 2 Samuel (22 occurrences) and 1 and 2 Kings (25 occurrences). Since our word also appears in earlier passages, however, it is reasonable to assume that usage of the word increased in the later period, but it did not originate then.

2. *Etymology*. The root *chayil* has always had a great range of meanings in the Semitic languages. In Akkadian, the meaning "kindred, tribe," in a negative sense "enemy troops," is cited for *illatu(m)*.[2] It is also used for "animals," for instance, dogs, and can mean "caravan." (It is doubtful, however, whether this word is connected with *chayil*.) The Aramaic loanword *ḫi'ālu; ḫilayālu* is cited with the meaning "a kind of troops."[3] For Ugaritic, the meaning "military forces" is attested,[4] as well as "army of the sun- and the sea-god."

---

chayil. P. R. Berger, "Zur Bedeutung des in den akkadischen Texten aus Ugarit bezeugten Ortsnamens *Ḫīlu (Ḫl)*," *UF*, 2 (1970), 340-46; A. Bertholet, *Das Dynamistische im AT*. *SgV*, 121 (1926); *idem, Dynamismus und Personalismus in der Seelenauffassung*. *SgV*, 142 (1930); W. Grundmann, *Der Begriff der Kraft in der neutestamentlichen Gedankenwelt*. *BWANT*, 4/8 (1932); *idem,* "δύναμαι," *TDNT*, II, 284-317; *idem,* "ἰσχύω," *TDNT*, III, 397-402; L. Kopf, "Arabische Etymologien und Parallelen zum Bibelwörterbuch," *VT*, 8 (1958), 161-215, esp. 176f.; J. van der Ploeg, "Le sens de *gibbôr ḥail*," *Vivre et Penser*, 1. *RB*, 50 (1941), 120-25; *idem,* "Les chefs du peuple d'Israël et leurs titres," *RB*, 57 (1950), 40-61; *idem,* "Les 'nobles' israélites," *OTS*, 9 (1951), 49-64, esp. 58f.; W. Spiegelberg, "Die ägyptische Gottheit 'der Gotteskraft,'" *ZÄS*, 57 (1922), 145f.

1 P. 343.

2 *AHw*, I, 372.

3 *Ibid.*, 342.

4 *WUS*, No. 927.

In Old Aramaic and Punic, we find the meanings "strength," "troops," "wealth."[5] In Syriac,[6] *ḥailā* means "strength," "army," "means"; the Mandaic verb *hil* means "strengthen," "lend courage," "overcome,"[7] while the meaning "army" is attested for the noun.[8]

3. *LXX*. The LXX translates *chayil* with *dýnamis* 165 times, with *ischýs* 27 times, and with *dynatós* 18 times; they cover the whole semantic range of *chayil*.[9] There are also cases of interpretative variation, where the LXX renders *chayil* as *ploútos* (9 times) or *stratiá* (3 times).

II. Basic Meaning. Despite the frequent occurrence of *chayil* in the sense of "army," its basic meaning must be given as "strength, power." The concept of "army" or "wealth" can hardly be made to fit the statement in Eccl. 10:10 that someone who wants to cut with a dull knife must use more strength. "Men of strength" (*'anshêchāyil*) in Eccl. 12:3 is an image for legs that grow weak in old age. Strength is also ascribed to the horse, though according to Ps. 33:17 it cannot save its rider. In Ezr. 4:23 (Aramaic), a case is stated "by force and power" (*b^{e}'edhrā' v^{e}chāyil*). The only other occurrences in Aramaic are in Dnl. 3:4; 4:11 (Eng. v. 14); 5:7, where *b^{e}chayil* is merely used adverbially, but in the sense of crying "strongly," i.e., "aloud."

In the natural realm, *chayil* can refer not only to the fertility of trees (Joel 2:22) but also to sexual potency. Thus Prov. 31:3 cautions against wasting it on prostitutes. In Ruth 4:11, *chayil* could also be understood as meaning the blessing of many offspring;[10] at the same time, however, there are overtones of the related notion of military might, since the verse is speaking of David's forbears. Cf. Gen. 24:60, in the context of an individual blessing: "May your descendants possess the gate of those who hate them!" The statement in 1 S. 2:4 that "the feeble gird on strength" also has military overtones, since the antithesis speaks of "the mighty whose bows are broken." Ps. 60:14(12) (=108:14[13]), "With God we shall do valiantly," belongs in the same context, as do Ps. 18:33,40(32,39) (=2 S. 22:33,40), where God girds the king with strength, that his feet may not slip (v. 37[36]). For the "day of your power" as the day of the king's birth and enthronement, God promises him victory over his enemies (Ps. 110:3). All these passages illustrate the basic meaning "strength and power," but with a strong tendency for the concept of strength to mean military strength, involving the holy war, in which it is frequently God who vouchsafes *chayil*.

III. Persons with "Power."

1. *With ben*. The military overtones can also be observed in the passages where *chayil* is combined with individualizing words. First we may note its use with *ben* to

---

[5] *DISO*, 87.

[6] Cf. *LexSyr*, 229.

[7] *MdD*, 143.

[8] Cf. W. von Soden, "Aramäische Wörter in neuassyrischen und neu- und spätbabylonischen Texten. Ein Vorbericht, I (*agâ-*mūs*)," *Or*, 35 (1966), 11.

[9] Cf. Grundmann, "δύναμαι," 286-88.

[10] Cf. C. J. Labuschagne, "The Crux in Ruth 4[11]," *ZAW*, 79 (1967), 364-67.

represent the concept "possessor of power." This phrase appears 16 times, including 9 passages that refer to military prowess (e.g., Dt. 3:18; Jgs. 21:10; 2 S. 2:7), including such individuals as David (1 S. 18:17; cf. 1 S. 14:52). But there is also significant use of *ben-chayil* in a peaceful sense; in 1 K. 1:52 it characterizes a man who is faithful and reliable. If Adonijah shows himself to be such, Solomon will protect him. This usage is especially common in Chronicles. In 1 Ch. 26:7,9,30, the gatekeepers are described as "able" men;[11] overseers are described in the same way in v. 32, and priests in 2 Ch. 26:17.

2. *With 'îsh.* Similar observations apply to the use of *chayil* with *'îsh* or *'ᵃnāshîm*. In 17 of the 23 occurrences, the reference is to warriors; this is further emphasized in Nah. 2:4(3); 1 Ch. 5:24; 8:40; etc. by the addition of *gibbôr* (→ גבר *gābhar* V), and in 2 S. 24:9 by the addition of "who drew the sword." Besides frequent occurrences of the plural (2 S. 11:16, etc.), an individual warrior can be called a man of strength or might (or: "of the army"[?]), for instance, David (1 S. 16:18) and Jehoiada the father of Benaiah (1 Ch. 11:22) (cf. 1 S. 14:52; 2 S. 23:20). Here, too, however, there are noteworthy passages without military overtones: neither the Israelites put in charge of Pharaoh's cattle in Gen. 47:6, nor the judges in Ex. 18:21,25, nor the gatekeepers in 1 Ch. 26:8 are referred to as *'îsh-chayil* because of some association with battle. The followers of the prophets who want to visit Elisha also call themselves *'ᵃnāshîm bᵉnê-chayil* (2 K. 2:16). The priest's son Jonathan is a "worthy man" (1 K. 1:42); and in the hymn glorifying the fathers in Sir. 44:6, the context suggests men who are peaceful, rich, and respected, but hardly soldiers. Similarly, the LXX speaks of rich men in Ps. 75:6 (Heb. 76:6[5]), although the passage probably refers to defeated warriors.

Above all, a more general and peaceful sense of *chayil* must be assumed when it appears in the phrase *'ēsheth chayil,* as in Ruth 3:11 (describing Ruth) and Prov. 12:4; 31:10. In Prov. 31:29, too, it might mean the general ability of the housewife, if so much had not been said already about her efficiency and of "making" *chayil* (see below).

3. *With gibbôr.* Another characteristic compound, occurring 41 times, is *gibbôr chayil,* whose meaning is further emphasized when the same context speaks of "war" (*milchāmāh,* Josh. 8:31; 1 S. 16:18; 2 Ch. 17:13) or the "army" (→ צבא *tsābhā'*, 1 Ch. 12:9,22,26, etc.). Those called *gibbôr hechāyil* include Gideon (Jgs. 6:12), Jephthah (Jgs. 11:1), Jeroboam (1 K. 11:28), Naaman (2 K. 5:1), etc. The term is applied to a host of warriors in Josh. 1:14 (the Israelites) and 6:2 (the warriors of Jericho). Our compound term appears most frequently in Chronicles, 16 times in 1 Chronicles and 9 in 2 Chronicles, or 25 occurrences out of a total of 41.

Although *gibbôr* appears to underline the military element of *chayil,* even here are passages referring to other types of people: Neh. 11:14; 1 Ch. 9:13 refer to priests, 1 Ch. 12:29 refers to Zadok, and 1 Ch. 26:6 refers to gatekeepers. Probably they are just being called "able" men. Although in Ruth 2:1 Boaz does not really appear as a

[11] W. Rudolph, *HAT,* 21 (³1968), 170, 176.

warrior, he, too, is called *'îsh gibbôr chayil*. If this term is used not only for warriors but also for able men in general, and especially men of wealth, the explanation may be found in 2 K. 15:20. Here we read of a tax imposed by Menahem on all *gibbôrê hachayil,* presumably those able to pay it.[12] What is true of Boaz could also be true of Saul's father (1 S. 9:1): military ability and wealth go together, because the warrior had to arm and maintain himself. Such citizens could well be meant by the rather high number of people taxed as well as the ten thousand (2 K. 24:14) carried into exile from Jerusalem, while "the poorest people of the land" were let stay behind. This suggested explanation stops short of meaning that *chayil* can be translated "wealth" or "means" here. As is true of *gibbôr,* the primary aspect of *chayil* is military: it would be hard to characterize the 30,000 men led by Joshua against Ai (Josh. 8:3) or Jephthah (Jgs. 11:1) as wealthy property owners.

4. *śārîm, p^eqûdhîm.* In 2 K. 24:14, *śārîm,* "military commanders" (RSV: "princes"), are mentioned alongside the *gibbôrê hachayil* among those carried away into exile. Such *śārîm* are mentioned in 19 other passages, all referring to the military. There are commanders under Joab (2 S. 24:2,4) and Jehu (2 K. 9:5), as well as in the revolution against Athaliah (2 K. 11:15). Commanders are also mentioned in the Syrian army (1 K. 15:20; cf. 2 Ch. 16:4). The same officers appear in Nu. 31:14; 2 K. 11:15; 2 Ch. 23:14 as *p^eqûdhê hachayil,* "officers of the army," rather than *śārîm*. After the fall of Jerusalem, commanders appear as national leaders, especially in Jeremiah (Jer. 40:7,13; 41:11,13,16; cf. 2 K. 25:23; Jer. 42:1,8). Contrary to the implication of Jer. 39:10, they obviously stayed in the land even after the capture of Jerusalem. Are they comparable to the commandants placed in the cities by Manasseh (2 Ch. 33:14; cf. 1 K. 20:19; Est. 1:3)? They recognized Gedaliah, and fled to Egypt with the rest of the people after his murder (Jer. 43:4f.; 2 K. 25:26). Later, when Nehemiah is sent to Jerusalem (Neh. 2:9), he is accompanied by *śārê chayil* at the head of the cavalry.

IV. Term for "Army." As the foregoing discussion has indicated, the concept of "army" is the most important meaning of *chayil,* with 71 additional occurrences. It is noteworthy that in 1 Ch. 12:26; 20:1; 2 Ch. 26:13 *chayil* is amplified by the addition of → **צבא** *tsābhā'*, which shows that behind the concrete army stands the determinative conception of its "strength" or "power." The many wars of Israel lead to such use of the term for Saul's army (1 S. 10:26; 14:48; 17:20). David's army is referred to in 1 Ch. 20:1 and the lists in 1 Ch. 12:22,26,29,31. The army of Judah is mentioned under Asa (2 Ch. 14:7[8]), under Jehoshaphat (2 Ch. 17:2), and under Uzziah (2 Ch. 26:11, 13). During the wars between the northern kingdom and Syria, *chayil* in the sense of "army" appears only in 1 K. 20:19, with a reference to the "sound of a great army" in 2 K. 7:6. The army of Judah under Zedekiah is mentioned in 2 K. 25:5 and Jer. 52:8. The word is used in a less military sense for the retinue of the queen of Sheba on her visit (1 K. 10:2; 2 Ch. 9:1) and the band accompanying Ezra (Ezr. 8:22). It is

---

[12] Cf. *AncIsr,* 70.

used for pharaoh's army in Ex. 14:4,9,17,28; 15:4; Dt. 11:4. In the period of Asa, 2 Ch. 14:8(9) and 16:8 speak of an Ethiopian army. Finally, the Egyptian army plans a role as a treacherous relief force for Jerusalem in Jer. 37:5,7,11; 46:2; Ezk. 17:17; 32:31. It is strange that nothing is said about any *chayil* during the Assyrian campaigns. It is mentioned frequently during the wars with the Syrians, during the time of David (2 S. 8:9; 1 Ch. 18:9) and in the later period (2 Ch. 16:7; 24:23f.); Isa. 8:4 and Jer. 35:11 also belong in this context. The wars between the northern kingdom and Syria are the subject of 1 K. 20:1,25; 2 K. 6:14f. In these three passages, together with Ezr. 8:22; Ex. 14:9; Isa. 43:17, it is important to note that horsemen are mentioned together with *chayil,* from which we can conclude that *chayil* is to be understood as referring primarily to the infantry and camp followers. The most frequent usage of *chayil* for a foreign army is for "all the army of the Chaldeans," in 2 K. 25:1, 5,10 and especially in Jeremiah (32:2; 34:1,7,21; 35:11; 37:10f.; 38:3; 39:1,5; 52:8,14), as well as Ezk. 29:18f. According to Dnl. 3:20, the men who cast the three youths into the furnace belong to the army. It is interesting that in Jer. 46:22 the army of the Chaldeans is compared to a hissing serpent.

For the later period, we find in Daniel the Jews doubly threatened by the *chayil* of the Ptolemies (11:7,[13] 10,25) and of the "kings of the north" (11:13). In Est. 1:3, the army of Persia and Media is invited to a feast.

Neh. 3:34(4:2) presents a special problem. The "army of Samaria" (*chêl shōm^{e}rôn*) is addressed by Sanballat in the presence of his "brethren." Alt finds here what is probably "an official term for the 'upper classes of the city.' "[14] This would be in accord with the observation that *chayil* can also be used with reference to able and wealthy persons and to officeholders.

V. Wealth. As in the characterization of persons possessing *chayil,* there are besides the great number of occurrences in the sense of "army" 34 cases where the meaning is "wealth" or "riches." This sense is frequently indicated by a corresponding parallel term. In Job 20:18 and Ezk. 28:5, *chayil* is associated with trade and commerce. In Dnl. 11:10, *ch^{a}yālîm* is combined with *h^{a}môn,* which also means "army" in Jgs. 4:7; Dnl. 11:11-13, but "wealth" in Ezk. 29:19; 30:4; Eccl. 5:9(10); 1 Ch. 29:16. The action involved can also require the concept of "wealth." In Isa. 30:6; Jer. 15:13; Mic. 4:13, *chayil* is given up to pillage. In Gen. 34:29; Isa. 8:4; 10:14, we are dealing with spoil. In Dt. 8:18, *ʿāśah* refers to the acquisition of wealth, and in Job 5:5, *shāʾaph* means a thirst for possessions. In Isa. 61:6, the priests are promised that they will eat (*ʾākhal*) the wealth of the nations. In such cases, possessions are desirable. But it is frequently clear that there is a certain reserve shown toward wealth. It is easy to set your heart on riches (Ps. 62:11[10]; 73:12; Job. 21:7). In Job 31:25, the patient sufferer denies any alleged attachment to his wealth. Riches lead to pride (Ezk. 28:5). At death, wealth must be left behind (Ps. 49:11[10]).

---

[13] But cf. *BHK: chêl;* and the commentaries *in loc.*

[14] A. Alt, "Die Rolle Samarias bei der Entstehung des Judentums," *Festschrift für Otto Procksch* (1934), 12 = *KlSchr,* II ([3]1964), 323.

Because wealth is understood to be a gift of God (see below), the frequently observed wealth of the wicked becomes a test of faith (Ps. 73:12[11]; Job 21:7). But they get no enjoyment from their wealth (Job 15:29; 20:18), because they squander it and must lose it (Job 20:15). The riches of the sinner dry up like a brook (Sir. 10:13); they are given over to pillage (Jer. 15:13; Zeph. 1:13) or left to the righteous (Ps. 49:11[10]; Prov. 13:22).

Nu. 31:9 and Zec. 14:14 are informative with respect to the precise meaning of *chayil* in this context. In the first passage, women, children, and cattle are listed as booty in addition to *chayil* and are therefore not included in the concept, which could accordingly comprise money, food, and household goods. Zec. 14:14 confirms this conjecture through its listing of gold, silver, and garments as constituting *chayil*, indicating that the term refers primarily to money and possessions.

VI. In determining the meaning of *chayil*, we have already mentioned passages containing a motif of primary interest: the fact that the OT frequently associates *chayil*—whether in the sense of "strength," "wealth," or "military forces"—with God. This holds true of riches, which are a gift of God. In the Blessing of Moses, we find this wish for Levi: "Bless, O Yahweh, his substance" (Dt. 33:11; cf. Dt. 8:17f.; Isa. 61:6; Ezk. 22:12[?]; 28:4f.; Prov. 13:22). Even the spoil of war is considered the gift of God (Nu. 31:9), although it should be offered to God (Mic. 4:13).

But God can do more than give wealth: he also has the right to take it away. In Jer. 15:13, God threatens to take Israel's wealth and give it as spoil. In Ob. 13, Edom is censured for having looted the goods of Judah. Isa. 10:14 likens God's taking away of the wealth of the nations to the emptying of a nest. Although it is clear that human wealth is dependent on God, Dt. 8:17 speaks explicitly of human efforts. Israel is not to think that it has prospered through its own power. God has given Israel the *kōach* that leads to *chayil*. Thus with the strength given by God, man has the possibility of achieving prosperity, which is accordingly an indirect gift of God. Thus *kōach*, which "in the book of Job represents almost thematically God's omnipotence,"[15] can also be a power in man, itself of course the gift of God. God thus gives both *chayil* and *kōach*, the latter being understood as intellectual and physical power the use of which is blessed with success.

1. *God Gives chayil*. OT man knows that he is dependent on God and in need of *chayil*. God girds the worshipper with *chayil* (Ps. 18:33,40[32,39] = 2 S. 22:33,40). Ps. 60:14(12); 108:14(13) say practically the same thing: human help is in vain against the enemy, but the worshippers will "do valiantly" with God. In Hab. 3:19, God is the "strength" of the worshipper, just as in the Song of Hannah (1 S. 2:4) he is extolled as girding the feeble with strength. According to Nu. 24:18, Edom will be dispossesed, while Israel is promised an increase of strength. In such passages, *chayil* comes through an act of God that gives men a quality enabling them to stand firm in time of trouble and vouchsafing them deliverance and victory.

---

[15]A. S. van der Woude, *THAT*, I, 824.

2. *From chayil to chayil: Ps. 84:8(7).* Before we pursue this line of thought further, Ps. 84:8(7) demands special attention. It speaks of a pilgrimage to Zion, in the course of which the people go *mēchayil ʾel-chāyil,* almost universally translated "from strength to strength." Kittel, however, translates "from wall to wall,"[16] assuming *chēl,* "outer wall," from the root → חול *chûl,* "dance (around)." Appropriate as this is to a pilgrimage, especially when coupled with the use of the verb → הלך *hālakh,* there is much to be said for advancing with increasing strength, as lent by God. The notion is introduced in v. 6(5); in v. 7(6) a motif of local geography is elevated to the symbolic and spiritual level, so that v. 8(7) should be understood in the same sense rather than from the assumption that we have left the realm of poetry and are dealing with way stations. That spiritual growth can be expressed in terms of advancing from *chayil* to *chayil* is shown analogously by the advance from evil to evil (*mērāʿāh ʾel-rāʿāh yātsāʾû*) in Jer. 9:2(3). In our interpretation of v. 8(7), *chayil* is understood as the spiritual strength given by God, in which the pilgrims advance with enthusiasm toward Zion (cf. LXX: *ek dynámeōs eis dýnamin;* Vulg. even reads: *De virtute in virtutem*).

3. *God Gives Strength.* With such a high estimate of the spiritual strength given by God, men frequently wish for strength from him that will bring deliverance and victory. God's power is mightier than enemy armies (Ex. 14:4; 2 Ch. 24:24). The significance of God as giver of *chayil* in battle is underlined by the denigration of other aid: according to Ps. 33:17, a horse cannot save despite its speed, and according to v. 16, "a king is not saved by his great army (*robh-chāyil*), a warrior is not delivered by his great strength (*beʳrobh-kōach*)." However important an army is, and however much one may pray to God for strength, it is more important that God himself takes the side of his own people. Similarly, Zec. 4:6 ascribes the demonstration of God's power to God himself. It almost looks like a negation of common promises and prayers when the prophet states: "Not by (military) might (*chayil*), nor by power (*kōach*), but by my Spirit, says Yahweh of hosts." Although *chayil* is denigrated, the absolute necessity for God's help is emphasized even here, the only difference being that the help comes through his "Spirit." God's help is comparable to the power of the spirit that comes upon judges and prophets (Jgs. 6:34; 1 S. 11:6; 2 K. 2:9,15). This spirit of God also dominates the vision of Ezekiel (Ezk. 37). God puts "spirit" or "breath" into the dead bones by means of the prophetic word (vv. 6,9), thus creating Israel afresh as an "exceedingly great host" (v. 10). Just as God creates the army of a new Israel, he is also seen as Lord over an enemy army, which he brings to destruction in order to deliver his people (Isa. 43:17). Through his power, God has at his disposal all the powers of this world, even the terrible army of Ezekiel's eschatological vision, "a great host (*qāhāl gādhôl*)," "a mighty army (*chayil rābh*)" (Ezk. 38:4,15), which he summons to destroy in the midst of the land of Israel (38:21–23).

God's power is expressed in even more comprehensive terms in Dnl. 4:32(35) (Aramaic), where Nebuchadnezzar's proclamation states that God "does according to

---

[16] R. Kittel, *KAT,* XIII (^{5,6}1929), 279.

his will in the host (*chayil*) of heaven and among the inhabitants of the earth." The parallel phrase "inhabitants of the earth" suggests that "host of heaven" refers to the angels, which were probably closely associated with the stars in the period of Daniel.[17] A similar statement appears in Dnl. 8:10f., where the word for "host of heaven" is *tsābhā'*.

VII. Divine Attribute? Since God is also Lord of the host of heaven, the question arises whether power can be attributed to God himself, who has powers at his command and gives power. *KBL*³ emphasizes that only *kōach*, not *chayil*, can be used of God in this sense.[18] This question cannot be decided by the statement of Ps. 118:15f. that God does *chayil*, since this is not a personal attribute but rather an attribute of his acting. The analogous experience of the psalmist in v. 10, "All nations surrounded me; in the name of Yahweh I cut them off!" says little more in its final clause. But when a worshipper in similar straits prays in Ps. 59:12(11), "Make them totter by thy [Yahweh's] power," *chayil* is associated with the possessive pronoun referring to Yahweh.

With regard to the conclusion of *KBL*³, it should be noted that the statement of Ps. 59:12(11) can be evaded only by a textual emendation such as proposed by Gunkel[19] and Kraus.[20] This emendation is no longer noted in *BHS*, however, and there are really no grounds for it. Thus this one passage indicates that *chayil* is not only effected by God, but is also one of his attributes. This conclusion is supported by the common use of *kōach* and *chayil* in parallel, whether in the human realm or as the gift of God (cf. Ps. 33:16; Dt. 8:17). Nevertheless, our passage remains an exception, contrasting with the standard use of *kōach* as a divine attribute.

Eising

---

17. P. Volz, *Die Eschatologie der jüdischen Gemeinde im neutestamentlichen Zeitalter* (²1966), 400.

18. P. 298; cf. also van der Woude, 823.

19. H. Gunkel, *GHK*, II/2 (1926; ⁵1968), 255.

20. H.-J. Kraus, *BK*, XV/1 (⁴1972), 420f.

חֵיק *chêq*

Contents: I. Etymology, Occurrences. II. Usage: 1. Part of Chariot or Altar; 2. Bulge of a Garment; 3. Bosom, Lap; 4. Innermost Part of Man; 5. Qumran. III. LXX.

I. Etymology, Occurrences. Heb. *chêq,* "bosom," has been associated with Arab. *ḥāqa(u),* "include," and Akk. *ḫiāqu,* "mix."[1] It is unclear, however, whether the word really derives from a verbal root. More likely cognates are Arab. *ḥaqw,* Ethiop. *ḥaqwe, ḥawqe,* Tigr. *ḥ^e qaq,* "loins."[2]

Of the 36 occurrences in the OT, 4 refer to a chariot or altar, 10 to a garment, and 22 to human beings. The word occurs only in the singular.

II. Usage.

1. *Part of Chariot or Altar.* The word *chêq* is used for the interior of a chariot (1 K. 22:35) and for the bottom of the altar in Ezekiel (Ezk. 43:13f.,17). In both cases, Halper derives *chêq* from *ḥqq,* "hollow out."[3] Albright compares *chêq hāʾārets* in Ezk. 43:14 to Akk. *irat erṣeti* and *irat kigalli,* "edge [literally: 'breast'] of the earth" or "underworld," in the inscriptions of Nebuchadnezzar, referring to the foundation platform of the palace and of the temple tower Etemenanki. According to this interpretation, *chêq* would be a foundation for the altar, set into the ground. The surface of the foundation was separated from the surrounding stone by a "boundary" (*g^e bhûl*).[4] Zimmerli, on the contrary, argues that the usage of *chêq* elsewhere in the OT contradicts this interpretation, and thinks instead of a depression in the earth, forming at the same time a drainage ditch alongside the altar for blood and water.[5] The enclosure (*g^e bhûl*) alongside the *chêq* prevented the blood from escaping onto the surrounding area and kept people approaching the altar from falling into the trench.

2. *Bulge of a Garment.* The noun also refers to the bulge of a garment above the belt, into which the hands or objects can be placed. Yahweh has Moses place his hand

---

chêq. W. F. Albright, "The Babylonian Temple-Tower and the Altar of Burnt-offering," *JBL,* 39 (1920), 137-142; *idem, Archaeology and the Religion of Israel* (1942), 150-52; B. Halper, "The Participial Formations of the Geminate Verbs," *ZAW,* 30 (1910), 99-126; L. Koehler, "Die Adoptionsform von Rt 4[16]," *ZAW,* 29 (1909), 312-14; A. Marmorstein, "Comparisons between Greek and Jewish Religious Customs and Popular Usages," *Occident and Orient. Festschrift M. Gaster* (1936), 409-423; R. de Vaux, *AncIsr,* 350-53; W. A. van der Weiden, *Le Livre des Proverbes: Notes philologiques. BietOr,* 23 (1970), 124f.

[1] *KBL*[3].

[2] W. Leslau, "The Expressions 'Under, After' in the Ethiopic Languages," *JNES,* 15 (1956), 241f.

[3] P. 122.

[4] Albright, *JBL,* 139f.; *Archaeology,* 150-52.

[5] W. Zimmerli, *BK,* XIII/2 (1969), 1090, 1092.

inside his garment and makes it leprous; when Moses places his hand back in his garment, Yahweh restores it (Ex. 4:6f.), in order to arouse the faith of the people. To keep one's hand in the bosom of one's garment means to be passive (Ps. 74:11 par. *tāshîbh yādhᵉkhā*). A bribe can be hidden in one's bosom (Prov. 17:23; 21:14), but not fire, for the garment would burn (Prov. 6:27). Prov. 16:33 speaks of the *chêq* in connection with the casting of lots. Halper equates *chêq* with *chāqîq,* "something hollowed out,"[6] citing Arab. *ḥuqqat,* which refers to a container made of a material that can be carved, and Gk. *kólpos,* "urn." The translation would then be: "The lot is cast [*ṭûl* hophal; only here for casting lots] into the urn." But the translation "pocket" or "bulge" deserves serious consideration.[7] In this case, there is probably in the background the idea of the "breastpiece of judgment" (*chōshen mishpāṭ*) of the high priest, in which the Urim and Thummin were kept (Ex. 28:15-30). The point of the proverb is the same as 16:1,3,9; 19:21,24: every decision is in God's hands.

3. *Bosom, Lap.* In the sense of "bosom" or "lap," *chêq* is used to refer to sexual relationship. The phrase *'ēsheth chêq* means "wife" (Dt. 13:7 [Eng. v. 6]; 28:54), and *'îsh chêq* means "husband" (Dt. 28:56). Hagar lay in Abraham's *chêq* and became pregnant (Gen. 16:5). "She lay (*shākhᵉbhāh*) in the *chêq,*" we are told of the girl brought to warm David in his old age (1 K. 1:2; but *lō' yᵉdhāʿāh*!); the same verb, without *bᵉ-*, is used of a married woman in Mic. 7:5. The phrase *chabbēq chêq nokhrîyāh* means to be infatuated with the alien woman (Prov. 5:20).

The word is also used to describe an intimate but nonsexual relationship, especially between mother and child (1 K. 3:20; 17:19; Lam. 2:12). When Naomi lays the child in her *chêq* (Ruth 4:16f.), we may be dealing with an adoption ceremony.[8] In Nathan's parable in 2 S. 12, the poor man's lamb lay (*tishkabh*) in his *chêq* and was like a daughter to him (v. 3; cf. v. 8). The parental image appears again in Nu. 11:12, where Yahweh commands Moses to carry the people in his *chêq* as a nurse carries a sucking child. The image of Yahweh as a shepherd, carrying the lambs in his *chêq,* in the bulge of his garment at his chest, both expresses the notion of solicitude and says that the return from exile is meant for every single individual (Isa. 40:11; cf. 40:26; 43:7).

4. *Innermost Part of Man.* The word *chêq* can, finally, refer to the innermost part of man, the seat of the passions. Job, having just spoken of the intervention of his *gō'ēl,* says that his kidneys in his *chêq* are devoured with a longing for him (Job 19:27). The fool is characterized by anger *bᵉchêq* (Eccl. 7:9). The fallen king bears the scorn of the enemy nations in his *chêq* (Ps. 89:51[50]).

In Ps. 35:13, the clause *tᵉphillāthî ʿal-chêqî thāshûbh* is obscure. According to one ancient theory, the expression means that the psalmist is standing bowed (cf. 1 K. 18:42), so that his prayer returns, as it were, to his own bosom. Gunkel and others read *chikkî,* "my gums," and translate: "My prayer keeps returning to my mouth," i.e., I pray continually for them. Marmorstein suggests that the expression is based on the

---

[6]Pp. 121f.

[7]*AncIsr,* 352; van der Weiden, 124.

[8]Cf. Koehler; *AncIsr,* 51; E. Würthwein, *HAT,* 18 (²1969), 23f.

belief of the psalmist's enemies that he has been fasting to cause their death by disease; he demonstrates that his prayer is genuine by wishing upon himself what he has wished upon them.[9] Others suggest that the psalmist is, at it were, taking back his prayer for his enemies, wishing that it may go unanswered (cf. Isa. 55:11; Mt. 10:13).[10] Dahood derives *tāshûbh* from *shûbh* as a by-form of *yšb,* and translates: "My prayer rested on my bosom = my prayer was like a close friend."[11]

Four passages speak of Yahweh's vengeance *'el/ʿal chêq,* emphasizing that sin against Yahweh is punished in man's inmost depths. Ps. 79:12 states that the taunts of the neighbors against Yahweh are to be returned (*hēshîbh*) "sevenfold *'el chêqām.*" The cultic sins of the present generation and their fathers Yahweh will repay (*shillam*) and measure (*mdd*) into their bosom (*'al chêqām*) (Isa. 65:6f.). Jer. 32:18f. state that God will requite (*shillam*) the guilt of the fathers *'el-chêq b^{e}nêhem,* i.e., upon their children.

5. *Qumran.* In the Dead Sea Scrolls, *chêq* occurs only in 1QH, where it always means "bosom" in the literal sense. A suckling can take pleasure (*šʿšʿ*) in the bosom of its nurse (7:21f.). According to the list in 9:31, *b^{e}chêq 'ômantî* refers to the same time as the nursing period indicated by *mishsh^{e}dhê hôrîyāthî.* The text of 9:31 is damaged, but can be compared with 9:36, where the care of a foster-father *b^{e}chêq* is compared to the joy of a mother over her child.

III. LXX. The LXX usually translates *chêq* as *kólpos,* using the plural in Jer. 32:18. In three of the cases discussed in II.3 above, the expression is paraphrased: *koimēthḗsetai met' autoú* (1 K. 1:12); *apó tēs synkoítou sou phýlaxai* (Mic. 7:5); *mēdé synéchou ankálais tḗs mḗ idías* (Prov. 5:20). In Isa. 40:11, Yahweh does not carry the lambs in his bosom; the MT is reinterpreted: *kaí en gastrí echoúsas parakalései.* In Prov. 21:14, the LXX inverts the sense of the MT: *dṓrōn dé ho pheidómenos thymón egeírei (yikhpeh) ischyrón.* In Ezk. 43:13, *chêq* is translated *kólpōma,* in 43:17, *kýklōma,* while *ûmēchêq hā'ārets* in v. 14 is rendered freely: *ek báthous tḗs archḗs toú koilṓmatos.*

André

---

[9] P. 417.
[10] H.-J. Kraus, *BK,* XV/1 (⁴1972), 277.
[11] M. Dahood, *Psalms,* I. *AB,* XVI (1965), 213.

חָכָה *chākhāh*

Contents: I. 1. Root; 2. Basic Meaning; 3. Versions. II. 1. Occurrences; 2. Date; 3. Forms; 4. Objects; 5. Semantic Field. III. 1. Waiting for Yahweh; 2. Affirmation of Trust; 3. History.

I. 1. *Root.* The root *ḥkh* is poorly attested outside Biblical Hebrew. It appears in the Mari texts as the hapax legomenon *ḫakū(m),* "wait."[1] The same root is probably present in Pun. *aocca* (1st person sing. qal impf.),[2] and definitely in Jewish Aram. *ch^{a}khā'* and Middle Heb. *chikkāh,* "wait."

Highly dubious is the association with Arab. *ḥakā,* "tell,"[3] or *ḥağā,* "stay."[4]

2. *Basic Meaning.* The problem of the basic meaning has still not been solved convincingly. The following possibilities must be considered.

a. Arab. *ḥakā* and Tigr. *ḥāka,* "tell, imitate," in the causative stem (IV) mean "make something secure." From this observation, an original meaning "be strong or secure" might be derived for *chākhāh,*[5] such as postulated by Kopf for other verbs of waiting and hoping as well (e.g., *qivvāh* and *yḥl*).

b. Arab. *ḥağā,* "stay," could lead to an original meaning "stay, persist" for *chākhāh,*[6] but it is unlikely that the two verbs are cognate (alternation *k/ğ*).

c. If the difficult *ûkh^{e}chakkê* of Hos. 6:9 is to be explained as a form of *chākhāh* (inf. const.[7] or conj. *m^{e}chakkê*[8]), a meaning "lie in wait" may be assumed, and the basic meaning could be sought in this area.

OT usage exhibits the general meaning "wait." Depending on the context, the waiting can have the sense "stay, persist," or the more future-oriented "await."

---

chākhāh. F. Hauck, "μένω," *TDNT,* IV, 574-588; E. Jenni, *Das hebräische Pi'el* (Zurich, 1968), 171-73; L. Kopf, "Arabische Etymologien und Parallelen zum Bibelwörterbuch," *VT,* 8 (1958), 176f.; 9 (1959), 255; J. van der Ploeg, "L'espérance dans l'AT," *RB,* 61 (1954), 481-507; M. Wagner, "Beiträge zur Aramaismenfrage im alttestamentlichen Hebräisch," *Hebräische Wortforschung. Festschrift W. Baumgartner. SVT,* 16 (1967), 355-371, esp. 361f.; C. Westermann, "Das Hoffen im AT," *ThViat,* 4 (1952/53), 19-70 = his *Forschung am AT. ThB,* 24 (1964), 219-265; W. Zimmerli, *Man and His Hope in the OT. SBT,* ser. 2, 20 (trans. 1971), 1-10 and *passim;* → קוה *qwh.*

[1] *AHw,* I, 309b; a West Semitic loanword according to *CAD,* VI, 33.

[2] *DISO,* 87; cf. Wagner.

[3] *GesB, KBL*^{3}, Kopf.

[4] Wagner; cf. *KBL*^{3}, *s.v. ḥgh.*

[5] Kopf.

[6] Wagner.

[7] Cf. *GK,* § 75aa; H. S. Nyberg, *Studien zum Hoseabuche, UUÅ,* 1935/6 (1935), 43.

[8] Cf. *KBL*^{3}.

3. *Versions.* The LXX translates *chākhāh* by means of *ménein* (4 times), *hypoménein* (6 times), and *emménein* (twice); Vulg. usually uses *expectare,* less often *sustinere* (twice) or *subsistere* (once). It appears that this usage reflects a difference between the two translations with respect to interest in the present as opposed to the future aspect of the word.

II. 1. *Occurrences.* The 14 occurrences in the OT are found primarily in the prophetic (Hos. 6:9[?]; Isa. 8:17; 30:18[twice]; 64:3[Eng. v. 4]; Hab. 2:3; Zeph. 3:8; Dnl. 12:2) and poetic books (Ps. 33:20; 106:13; Job 3:21; 32:4), only rarely in the historical books (2 K. 7:9; 9:3).

2. *Date.* The use of the verb in 2 K. 7:9 and 9:3 could go back to the ninth century. Isa. 8:17 and Hos. 6:9 are from the eighth century, Hab. 2:3 and Zeph. 3:8 from the seventh. Ps. 33:20; 106:13; Job 3:21; 32:4; Isa. 64:3(4) must be dated between the fifth and third centuries. Isa. 30:18 is hard to date. The latest occurrence is Dnl. 12:12. Surprisingly, the word does not appear in the Dead Sea Scrolls.

3. *Forms.* No derivatives are attested for the verb *chākhāh,* nor was it used in personal names. The piel is the predominant stem (perf.: Isa. 8:17; Ps. 33:20; 106:13; Job 32:4; impf.: Isa. 30:18a; 2 K. 9:3; impv.: Hab. 2:3; Zeph. 3:8; ptcp.: Isa. 64:3; Job 3:21; Dnl. 12:12; Hos. 6:9 [conj.]); the qal appears only once (ptcp.: Isa. 30:18b).

Like *chākhāh,* other verbs of waiting and hoping (*qivvāh, yḥl,* and *śbr*) exhibit a clear preponderance of piel forms over qal forms. Jenni attempts to explain the affinity of these verbs for the piel on the basis of an inherent "focus on a specific goal"; in his view, this "goal-directedness" is best expressed by the piel as a "resultative" (the result of an action upon its object!).[9] According to Jenni, the piel forms always involve a new act of hope with a specific object, whereas the less common qal forms focus on something that is permanent and absolute. It remains to be seen, however, whether an inner "goal-directedness" can be postulated for verbs of waiting.

4. *Objects.* In fact, an object of expectation is frequently mentioned; the usual construction is *chikkāh lᵉ-* (9 times). One may wait for "Yahweh" (Isa. 8:17; Ps. 33:20; cf. Isa. 30:18b; 64:3[4]; Zeph. 3:8), "his counsel" (Ps. 106:13), "death" (Job 3:21), or the final revelation (Hab. 2:3; *chakkēh lô* appears to refer to *chāzôn*). Yahweh himself waits "to be gracious to you" (*lachᵃnankhem,* Isa. 30:18a).

In the other occurrences—including the earliest[10]—there is no reference to any object of the waiting, although such an object might of course be intended.

In 2 K. 9:3, a disciple of the prophets is ordered to flee and not to tarry (*vᵉlōʾ thᵉchakkeh*) after delivering his message. The command means merely not to linger or delay.[11] The four lepers in 2 K. 7:9 are afraid to be silent on "a day of good news" and "wait (*vᵉchikkînû*) until the morning light." This point in time is the limit set by the

---

[9] P. 171.

[10] See above, 2.

[11] Jenni, p. 172: "not wait for any reaction."

situation, by no means the "goal" of the lepers' waiting.[12] In Job 32:4, Elihu "waits" in silence while Job's friends are speaking with him (reading *bdbrm* for *bdbrym*[13]); once again, what is involved is "waiting" for a specified period, not "awaiting" some desired goal.[14] Even the patient "waiting" or "enduring" in Dnl. 12:12 (*'ashrê ham^echakkeh*) refers only indirectly to the approaching end: blessed is he who "waits" in the "not yet" of the delayed end and with this attitude "comes to the 1335 days."[15] The difficult text Hos. 6:9 will not be discussed here.

In these passages, then, we are dealing with a "waiting" whose interest is in "staying" and "enduring"; its opposite is "change," "become active," or the like. As this usage shows, a "focus on a specific goal" is far from being "inherent" in the word.[16] Only with explicit reference to an object of hope does *chikkāh* take on the meaning "wait *for,*" "*a*wait," "hope *for.*"

There is nothing to the statement that *ḥkh* means "eager hope in a desperate situation for help from without, hope for an utter miracle."[17]

5. *Semantic Field.* a. OT usage of *chākhāh* is relatively poor in contextual synonyms and parallels. A clear parallelism occurs in Isa. 8:17: "I will wait for Yahweh (*v^echikkîthî l^eyhvh*) . . . and I will hope in him (*v^eqivvêthî lô*)"; but it remains to be seen whether *chikkāh* and *qivvāh* (→ קוה *qwh*) are fully synonymous here. It is certainly not true that the two words "really signify a condition of acute tension."[18] The literarily late proclamation of salvation in Isa. 30:18 concludes by praising all who wait for Yahweh (*'ashrê kol-chôkhê lô*). It is possible that the sense of *chākhāh* here has been influenced by the condition for God's help stated by Isaiah in 30:15:[19] "those who wait for Yahweh" are those who heed the prophetic call for return and rest, for quietness and trust (*biṭchāh*).

The verb → בטח *bāṭach,* "trust," also appears in the context of *chākhāh*. In Zeph. 3:1-4, 6-8bα, an oracle of judgment upon Jerusalem, the concluding call to wait for Yahweh (*lākhēn chakkû-lî,* v. 8) corresponds to the introductory accusation that the city does not trust in Yahweh (*b^ayhvh lō' bhāṭāchāh,* v. 2). Similarly, in Ps. 33:20 the confession *naphshēnû chikk^ethāh l^eyhvh* is followed closely by the elaboration *b^eshēm qodhshô bhāṭāch^enû* (v. 21). In the same context, → יחל *yḥl* piel, "hope," appears twice in semantic equivalence to *ḥkh* (vv. 18, 22).

There is also a semantic link between *ḥkh* and → אמן *'āman,* "be secure," hiphil "trust." In Hab. 2, for example, the summons to the devout to wait for Yahweh (*chakkû-lô,* v. 3) is followed by the famous promise of v. 4, according to which the righteous will live "by his faith" (*be'^emûnāthô*). In Ps. 106, "they did not wait for his

[12]Interpreted differently by Jenni, 172.

[13]Cf. *GesB, BHK*³.

[14]Jenni takes a different position, 172.

[15]Jenni takes a different position, 172.

[16]Jenni, 171.

[17]W. Käser, "Beobachtungen zum alttestamentlichen Makarismus," *ZAW,* 82 (1970), 225-250, esp. 247, n. 53.

[18]O. Kaiser, *Isaiah 1-12. OTL* (trans. 1972), 121.

[19]O. Kaiser, *Isaiah 13-39. OTL* (trans. 1974), 298.

counsel'' (*lō' chikkû la'atsāthô,* v. 13) has a formal and semantic counterpart in ''they did not trust in his word'' (*lō' he'emînû lidhbhārô,* v. 24).

b. To the series of verbs closely associated with *chākhāh* (*qwh, yl, bṭḥ, 'mn*) should be added the piel of *śbr,* ''wait'' (only in late texts). On account of the etymology of *śbr,* we can also include here *tsāphāh,* ''keep lookout,'' and the hiphil of *nbṭ,* ''look at,''[20] both often used in the sense ''await.'' The ''classic'' verbs of waiting and hoping are *ḥkh, yḥl,* and *qwh.* Their semantic development has so converged through centuries of analogous use that distinct translation has little more than stylistic significance.

A distinction between the words for hope (*qwh* and its derivatives) and the words for waiting (e.g., *ḥkh, yḥl, śbr*) is undesirable, if only because *qwh* often has the meaning ''wait,'' while *ḥkh, yḥl, śbr,* etc. have the meaning ''hope.''[21]

III. 1. *Waiting for Yahweh.* The use of *chākhāh* is theologically significant primarily where the waiting and hoping is somehow concerned with the preservation or restoration of the historical solidarity between Yahweh and ''Israel.'' It is in this sense that the devout wait ''for Yahweh,'' i.e., for a demonstration of his help (Ps. 33:20; Isa. 30:18b; 64:3[4]) or judgment (Zeph. 3:8), for his counsel (Ps. 106:13) or the fulfilment of his word (Isa. 8:17; Hab. 2:3; Dnl. 12:12), or are called upon to wait (Hab. 2:3; Zeph. 3:8). In one case it is Yahweh who waits for the moment of his own intervention (Isa. 30:18a). A contrast with ''waiting for Yahweh'' appears in Job 3:21: ''who wait for death, but it comes not.''

In narrative texts, the word is used only in a neutral sense (2 K. 7:9; 9:3; Job 32:4).[22] This raises the question of the relationship between form and content in the phrase ''waiting for Yahweh.''

2. *Affirmation of Trust.* The phrase ''wait for Yahweh'' appears almost exclusively in the Psalms and the prophetic books; the same is true of ''trust in Yahweh'' and ''hope in Yahweh'' (exception: *'ôchîl l'yhvh,* 2 K. 6:33; Gen. 49:18 uses the language of the Psalms). When one considers that the majority of the prophetic passages really belong to the language of the Psalms (for *ḥkh:* Isa. 8:17; 30:18b; 64:3[4]; Dnl. 12:12), the form-critical origin for the phrase becomes clear: it derives from an idiom of the Psalms, more particularly from the ''confession of confidence,''[23] an ''expression of trust,'' which has its focus as the ''real basis of petition''[24] in the Psalms of Lament of the individual and of the people, and thence in the thanksgiving and the so-called song of trust.[25]

---

[20]Following Westermann, 36f. (234f.).

[21]Contra Westermann, 33ff. (232ff.).

[22]See above, II.4.

[23]Westermann.

[24]Gunkel.

[25]Cf. H. Gunkel and J. Begrich, *Einl. in die Psalmen. GHK,* sup. vol. (1933), 232-36; J. Begrich, ''Die Vertrauensäusserungen im israelitischen Klageliede des Einzelnen und in seinem

Both Gunkel and Begrich espouse the view that the expression of confidence in the Babylonian lament serves primarily the introductory function of glorifying the deity, and therefore in this context does not express a personal relationship with God. Words for hope or trust are infrequent in the "prayers with raised hands"; but cf. the phrase, attested with several variants, *bēltu/bēlti kāši atkalki,* "Lady, I trust in you."[26]

3. *History*. Because of the paucity of the evidence, the history of the word can only be sketched in outline. The verb *chākhāh,* used in narrative texts as a neutral term for "wait," entered into the language of sacral poetry at a date that cannot now be determined. Here, together with *yḥl, qwh, bāṭach,* and other words for waiting, trusting, and hoping, it was used initially in the expression of confidence addressed to God in the Psalms of Lament ("I/we wait for you"); later it was used in communal confession of confidence ("I waited for Yahweh" in thanksgivings), in exhortation ("wait for Yahweh"), and in macarism ("blessed is he who waits for Yahweh"). Referring to the devout as "those who wait for Yahweh" also derives from the language of the Psalms. The prophets beginning with Isaiah made use of the expression; here "waiting for Yahweh" often means waiting for the fulfilment of the prophetic message. What distinguishes *chākhāh* from other words for waiting and hoping is just this prophetic use of the idiom: what is needed is patient "waiting" and "endurance" with Yahweh.

Barth

---

babylonischen Gegenstück," *ZAW,* 46 (1928), 221-260 = *GSAT. ThB,* 21 (1964), 168-216.

[26]C. J. Mullo Weir, *A Lexicon of Accadian Prayers in the Rituals of Expiation* (Oxford, 1934), *s.v. takālu.*

חָכַם chākham; חָכָם chākhām; חָכְמָה chokhmāh; חָכְמוֹת chokhmôth

Contents: I. Ancient Near East: 1. The Root *ḥkm* outside the Bible; 2. Akkadian; 3. Egyptian. II. Forms and Basic Meanings: 1. Verb; 2. Nouns. III. Semantic Field: 1. Synonyms; 2. Antonyms. IV. Types of "Wisdom": 1. Nonspecific Usage; 2. Court Wisdom: a. Aphorisms with *ḥkm*; b. Narratives; 3. Mantic Wisdom; 4. Magical Wisdom; 5. Artisans. V. Theological Usage: 1. Hebrew Wisdom's Understanding of Reality; 2. Synthesis with Historical and Nomistic Piety; 3. Hebrew Wisdom's Understanding of God. VI. Criticism of Wisdom: 1. Prophetic; 2. Skeptical.

I. Ancient Near East.

1. *The Root ḥkm outside the Bible.* The Akkadian verb *ḫakāmu(m),* relatively common only in Neo-Assyrian, was thought by Zimmern to be of West Semitic

---

chākham. W. Baumgartner, "Die israelitische Weisheitsliteratur," *ThR,* 5 (1933), 259–288; *idem, Israelitische und altorientalische Weisheit. SgV,* 166 (1933); E. Cantore, "La sapienza biblica, ideale religioso del credente," *RivBibl,* 8 (1960), 1–9, 129–143, 193–205; J. Fichtner, *Die altorientalische Weisheit in ihrer israelitisch-jüdischen Ausprägung. BZAW,* 62 (1933); G. Fohrer, "σοφία," *TDNT,* VII, 476–496; E. Gerstenberger, "Zur alttestamentlichen Weisheit," *Verkündigung und Forschung,* 14 (1969), 28–44; H. Gese, *Lehre und Wirklichkeit in der alten Weisheit* (1958); *idem,* "Weisheit," *RGG*³, VI (1962), 1574–77; H. J. Hermisson, *Studien zur israelitischen Spruchweisheit. WMANT,* 28 (1968); P. Humbert, "Weisheit," *RGG*², V (1931), 1800–1803; P. van Imschoot, "Weisheit," *BL,* 1877–1881; J. Malfroy, "Sagesse et Loi dans le Deutéronome," *VT,* 15 (1965), 49–65; R. E. Murphy, "Assumptions and Problems in OT Wisdom Research," *CBQ,* 29 (1967), 407–418; M. Noth and D. W. Thomas, eds., *Wisdom in Israel and in the Ancient Near East. Festschrift H. H. Rowley. SVT,* 3 (1955); F. Nötscher, "Biblische und babylonische Weisheit," *BZ,* N.S. 6 (1962), 120–26; G. von Rad, *OT Theol.* I (trans. 1962), 418–459; *idem, Wisdom in Israel* (trans. 1972); M. Saebø, *THAT,* I, 557–567; H. H. Schmid, *Wesen und Geschichte der Weisheit. BZAW,* 101 (1966); N. H. Tur-Sinai, "חָכְמָה, חָכָם," *EMiqr,* III, 127–133; R. N. Whybray, *The Intellectual Tradition in the OT. BZAW,* 135 (1974); J. Ziegler, *Chokma, Sophia, Sapientia. Würzburger Universitätsreden,* 32 (1961); G. Ziener, "Die altorientalische Weisheit als Lebenskunde," *Wort und Botschaft,* ed. J. Schreiner (1967), 258–271; W. Zimmerli, "Zur Struktur der alttestamentlichen Weisheit," *ZAW,* 51 (1933), 177–204; *idem,* "Ort und Grenze der Weisheit im Rahmen der alttestamentlichen Theologie," *Les sagesses du Proche-Orient ancien* (Paris, 1963), 121–137 = *Gottes Offenbarung. ThB,* 19 (1963), 300–315; *idem,* "Die Weisheit Israels," *EvTh,* 31 (1971), 680–695; *Les sagesses du Proche-Orient ancien,* Colloque de Strasbourg 17–19 Mai 1962 (Paris, 1963).

On I.2: J. J. A. van Dijk, *La sagesse suméro-accadienne. CO,* 1 (Leiden, 1953), with discussion of Sumerian wisdom terminology on pp. 17–21.

On I.3: H. Brunner, "Die Lehren," *Ägyptologie. HO,* I:1:2 (²1970), 113–139; E. Edel, *Altägyptische Grammatik,* I. *AnOr,* 34 (1955); A. Gardiner, "The Coronation of King Ḥaremḥab," *JEA,* 39 (1953), 13–31; R. Grieshammer, "Altes Testament," *LexÄg,* I (1975), 159–169; W. Helck, ed., *Die Prophezeihung des Nfr.tj. Kleine ägyptische Texte* (1970); J. M. A. Janssen, *De traditioneele egyptische Autobiografie voor het Nieuwe Rijk* (Leiden, 1946); S. Morenz, "Die ägyptische Literatur und die Umwelt," *Ägyptologie. HO,* I/1/2 (²1970), 226–239; *idem, Egyptian Religion* (trans. 1973); K. Sethe, *Dramatische Texte zu altägyptischen Mysterienspielen. Untersuchungen zur Geschichte und Altertumskunde Ägyptens,* 10 (1928); Z.

origin,[1] contrary to the opinion of von Soden[2] and *CAD*. In the G and D stem it means "know, understand" in the most general sense, while the Š stem can mean "inform" (about a situation[3]), "explain" (medical symptoms,[4] written characters,[5] a constella-

Žába, *Les maximes de Ptaḥḥotep* (Prague, 1956); J. Zandee, "Das AT im Lichte der Ägyptologie," *Vruchten van de Uithof. Festschrift H. Brongers* (Utrecht, 1974), 145-157; *idem*, "Egyptological Commentary on the OT," *Travels in the World of the OT. Festschrift M. A. Beek* (Leiden, 1974), 269-281.

On III: W. Caspari. "Über den biblischen Begriff der Torheit," *NKZ*, 39 (1928), 668-695; R. B. Y. Scott, "Wise and Foolish, Righteous and Wicked," *Studies in the Religion of Ancient Israel. SVT*, 23 (1972), 146-165.

On IV.2; A. Alt, "Die Weisheit Salomos," *ThLZ*, 76 (1951), 139-144 = *KlSchr*, II ([3]1964), 90-99; M. Noth, "Die Bewährung von Salomos 'göttlicher Weisheit,'" *Wisdom in Israel and in the Ancient Near East. Festschrift H. H. Rowley. SVT*, 3 (1955), 225-237 = *GSAT*, II. *ThB*, 39 (1969), 99-112; N. W. Porteous, "Royal Wisdom," *Wisdom in Israel and in the Ancient Near East. Festschrift H. H. Rowley. SVT*, 3 (1955), 247-261 = his *Living the Mystery* (1967), 93-112; G. von Rad, "The Joseph Narrative and Ancient Wisdom," in his *The Problem of the Hexateuch and Other Essays* (trans. 1966), 292-300; R. B. Y. Scott, "Solomon and the Beginnings of Wisdom in Israel," *Wisdom in Israel and in the Ancient Near East. Festschrift H. H. Rowley. SVT*, 3 (1955), 262-279.

On IV.3-4: H.-P. Müller, "Magisch-mantische Weisheit und die Gestalt Daniels," *UF*, 1 (1969), 79-94; *idem*, "Der Begriff 'Rätsel' im AT," *VT*, 20 (1970), 465-489; *idem*, "Mantische Weisheit und Apokalyptik," *Congress Volume. SVT*, 22 (1972), 268-293.

On V: H. D. Preuss, "Das Gottesbild der älteren Weisheit Israels," *Studies in the Religion of Israel. SVT*, 23 (1972), 117-145.

On "Wisdom" as a mythological figure: W. F. Albright, "The Goddess of Life and Wisdom," *AJSL*, 36 (1919/20), 258-294; G. Boström, *Proverbiastudien: die Weisheit und das fremde Weib in Spr 1-9. LUÅ*, 30/3 (1935); H. Conzelmann, "Die Mutter der Weisheit," *Zeit und Geschichte. Festschrift R. Bultmann* (1964), 225-234 = his *Theologie als Schriftauslegung. BEvTh*, 65 (1974), 167-176; H. Donner, "Die religionsgeschichtlichen Ursprünge von Prov. Sal. 8," *ZÄS*, 82 (1957), 8-18; M. Hengel, *Judaism and Hellenism* (trans. 1974), I, 153-175; C. Kayatz, *Studien zu Proverbien 1-9. WMANT*, 22 (1966), 76-134; O. Keel, *Die Weisheit spielt vor Gott* (1974); W. L. Knox, "The Divine Wisdom," *JTS*, 38 (1937), 230-37; B. Lang, *Frau Weisheit: Deutung einer biblischen Gestalt* (1975); B. L. Mack, "Wisdom Myth and Mythology," *In*, 24 (1970), 46-60; *idem, Logos und Sophia. StUNT*, 10 (1973); J. Marböck, *Weisheit im Wandel. BBB*, 37 (1971); G. Pfeifer, *Ursprung und Wesen der Hypostasenverstellung im Judentum. ArbT*, 1/31 (1967); H. Ringgren, *Word and Wisdom* (Lund, 1947); J. de Savignac, "La sagesse en Proverbes VIII 22-31," *VT*, 12 (1962), 211-15; R. B. Y. Scott, "Wisdom in Creation: The 'Āmôn of Proverbs VIII 30," *VT*, 10 (1960), 213-223; R. N. Whybray, *Wisdom in Proverbs. SBT*, 45 (1965, [2]1967); U. Wilckens, *Weisheit und Torheit. BHTh*, 26 (1959), 160-196; P. Zerafa, *Wisdom in Pr. 1,20-33; 8,1-31* (diss., Pont. Univ. S. Thomae de Urbe, Rome, 1967).

On VI: J. Fichtner, "Jesaja unter den Weisen," *ThLZ*, 74 (1949), 75-80 = *Gottes Weisheit. ArbT*, 2/3 (1964), 18-26; J. Lindblom, "Wisdom in the OT Prophets," *Wisdom in Israel and in the Ancient Near East. Festschrift H. H. Rowley. SVT*, 3 (1955), 192-204; W. McKane, *Prophets and Wise Men. SBT*, 44 (1965).

Since the manuscript of this article was finished in the summer of 1973, works published after that date could not be taken into consideration.

[1]H. Zimmern, *Akkadische Fremdwörter als Beweis für babylonischen Kultureinfluss* ([2]1917), 29.

[2]*AHw*.

[3]*LAS*, 163, 11; 310, vo. 3.

[4]*LAS*, 246, 10.

[5]*LAS*, 320, 7.

tion[6]), or "prescribe" (a medical treatment,[7] rituals[8]); the passive Št stem is also attested (*ú-saḫ-ka-mu-ni*).[9] The N stem is used in the sense "be understood"[10] and "be recognizable."[11] The only attested nominal derivative of *ḫakāmu* is the adjectival form *ḫa-ka-a*[*m!-m*]*a!-am*.[12]

The Ugaritic root *ḥkm,* which does not appear in the preformative conjugations, is associated with the high god El in all its occurrences. In a flattering address on the part of the goddess Athirat,[13] *lḥkmt,* "you are wise indeed," follows *rbt,* "you are old"; the idea is pursued in line 66: *šbt dqnk ltsrk,* "the gray of your beard has truly instructed you." In another passage,[14] the same predicate is applied to El's decision, which Athirat attempts to influence in Baal's favor: the equivalent expression in lines 41f. is *ḥkmt*/*ʿm ʿlm,* "you are wise for eternity."[15] Elsewhere[16] *ḥkmt* is addressed to someone else, but the exemplary wisdom of El is cited by way of comparison: *k3l . . . kṯr ltpn,* "like El . . . like the bull, the gracious."

In the Phoenician-Hieroglyphic Luwian bilingual inscription from Karatepe, dating from *ca.* 720 B.C.,[17] Azitawadda, "king of Danuna," boasts that every king has chosen him as overlord on account of his righteousness, wisdom (*bḥkmty*), and graciousness.[18] His contemporary Barrakib[19] says of his father, Panammuwa II of Jaudi, that in his wisdom (*bḥkmth*) and righteousness he grasped the hem of his Assyrian overlord's garment. In the former case, *ḥkmt,* etc. refer to genuine virtues of a sovereign, but in the latter case we should think less specifically in terms of mere tactical sagacity.

In the Imperial Aramaic of Ahikar, the pael of the verb appears in line 9 with the meaning "instruct" and in line 10 with the meaning "give answer" (in a test of wisdom). In line 1, Ahikar is called "a wise and skillful scribe" (*spr ḥkym vmhyr*), and in line 12, "the wise scribe" (*sprʾ ḥkym*) and counselor of all Assyria (cf. lines 7, 17f., 36f., 42). The fragmentary statement in line 178 gives as the function of a wise man at court "instructive speech" ([*mll*]. *ḥkmh*). In line 19, *ḥkmh* designates the content of *ʿṭh,* "counsel," and in lines 92, 94, 146f., the ethical ideal of courtly education represented to Shamash.

The person who is "knowledgeable about (painful) worms" (*ḫa-ki-mi tum-li-e-ia*[20])

---

6 *LAS,* 40, vo. 7.

7 *LAS,* 246, vo. 13; 252, vo. 19.

8 *LAS,* 172, vo. 18; 205, vo. 5; 223, vo. 9.

9 *LAS,* 179, vo. 8 (oral communication from von Soden).

10 *LAS,* 312, 8; I6, vo. 8.

11 Of stars, *LAS,* 290, vo. 3, 8.

12 A. Finet, "Les médicins au royaume de Mari," *Annuaire de l'Institut de Philologie et d'Histoire Orientales et Slaves,* 14 (Brussels, 1954/57), 132, 15.

13 *CTA,* 4 [II AB], V, 65.

14 *CTA,* 4 [II AB], IV, 41.

15 C. H. Gordon, *Ugaritic Literature. SPIB,* 98 (1949), 32; a different interpretation is given by Aistleitner, *WUS,* No. 924; cf. *CTA,* 3 [V AB], V, 38f.

16 *CTA,* 16 [II K], IV, 3.

17 *KAI,* 26 A, I, 13.

18 For a different interpretation, see *DISO,* 232, *s.v.* פעל 10.

19 *KAI,* 215, 11.

20 Reading from von Soden, orally.

in line 26 of the Aramaic cuneiform tablet AO 6489 from Uruk (Seleucid period)[21] is probably someone skilled in medicine (dentistry). An Aramaic inscription from Arebsum in Cappadocia (*RES* 1785 A 1; 2nd century B.C.)[22] speaks of someone who is "wise" before Bel (=Ahura Mazda?) and the gods, whose function it is to hide the sacred fire. In *RES* 1785 E 5, which presupposes the marriage of Bel with an hypostasis of Mazdaism(?), the latter appears to be addressed by Bel as "very wise" (*śgy' ḥkym*[. . .]).

OSA *ḥwkm* is the name (epithet?), often identical with *'nby,* "speaker (of justice)," of a god, probably 'Amm. Mukarrib of Qataban calls himself *bkr 'nby wḥwkm ḏ'mr wšmr,* "first-born of 'nby and Ḥwkm, of the lord of (oracular) command and decision."[23] The wisdom of God is thus mantic in nature:[24] he obviously provides judicial oracles.

In classical and modern Arabic, the root acquired two specialized senses, one judicial (*ḥakama* I, "pronounce judgment," *ḥukm,* "judgment"), the other medical (*ḥakīm,* "wise man, philosopher," esp. "physician"). Corresponding to Heb. *chokhmāh* we find *ḥikmat,* with the meaning "knowledge, theologico-ethical lore, maxims," derived from the stative verb *ḥakuma,* "be wise." The verb *ḥakama* II, "bridle," probably involves a different root; from it comes *ḥikmat* in the sense "what prevails, or restrains from ignorant behaviour."[25]

In Ethiopic, the root is hardly attested. Geez and Amhar. *ḥakīm,* "physician," and Amhar. *akkämä,* "treat (medically)," are due to Arabic influence.[26]

2. *Akkadian.* Within the Semitic languages, Akkadian developed the richest terminology for the semantic domain of wisdom. Closest to the range of meanings of Heb. *ḥkm* is the stative verb *emēqu(m),* "be wise," and its cognates. The adjective *emqu(m)* means "clever, cunning" in a general sense,[27] as well as "wise" in the sense of the higher faculties when applied to gods and kings, elders and scribes, mantic experts (such as diviners), and above all craftsmen and technicians.[28] One admonition suggests an ethical ideal.[29] In one passage, the abstract noun *nēmequ(m)* means the "cunning" of a woman;[30] elsewhere it means the manifold wisdom of men and gods (e.g., Marduk in the familiar opening verse of *Ludlul bēl nēmeqi*[31]).

Like Sum. *geštu,* "ear," "hearing," "intellect," the derivatives of the root *ḫss* associate understanding and intelligence with the functions of hearing: *ḫasīsu(m),*

---

21 A. Dupont-Sommer, "La tablette cunéiforme araméene de Warka," *RA,* 39 (1942/44), 35-62.

22 *LidzEph,* I, 66.

23 *RES* 3540, 2/3; 3880, 2/3; 3881, 1; for a different interpretation, see G. Ryckmans, "Mélanges," *ETL,* 39 (1963), 467f.

24 See IV.3.

25 Lane, 617.

26 W. Leslau, *Hebrew Cognates in Amharic* (1969), 23, 45.

27 Used of a fox in a fable, *BWL,* 200, 18; 204, 6.

28 See IV.3, 5.

29 *BWL,* 99, 25.

30 *KAV,* 197, 51.

31 *BWL,* 32, 1; Lambert thinks in terms of the arts of the exorcists.

"ear," "hearing," "understanding," "intelligence";[32] *pīt ḫasīssi,* "opening of the ear," hence "wisdom";[33] *palkû uzni,* "of broad (hearing >) understanding." The phrase *ḫāsis kal šipri,* "expert in every craft," refers to the "wisdom" of craftsmen.[34]

The notion of skillful "making" (*epēšu*[*m*]) gives rise to the adjectives *itpēšu(m),* "experienced, able," *eppešu* (of gods like Ninurta as *eppeš tāḫāzi,* "experienced in battle,"[35] and Ea), and *etpušu* (same meaning).

Loanwords from Sumerian include *apkallu(m),* "wise man" (< *ab gal,* "master"), *igigallu(m),* "wisdom," "wise" (< *igi gál,* "let the eye be" > "make effectual"), and *ummânu(m),* "craftsman (scribe >), scholar" (< *ummea*). Several words such as *eršu(m),* "wise," *itpēšu(m), apkallu(m), igigallu(m),* and *muštālu(m),* "circumspect," are used primarily of gods and kings. Marduk and Ea are called *apkal ilī/ ilāni;* Ea is also called *apkal nēmeqi.*[36] The word *apkallu(m)* is also used especially for wise mythological figures such as Adapa and Enmerkar and the famous seven sages of the Primeval Age.[37] The latter may be compared to the inventors of various cultural activities in Gen. 4:17-22.[38] The *apkal šamni,* "oil expert," represents once again the type of the mantic wise man.[39]

Müller

3. *Egyptian.* a. In Egyptian, the root *ś33*[40] means "be wise," "understand," "wise man,"[41] "wisdom."[42] The citations[43] extend from the Pyramid texts to the eighteenth dynasty. In the Middle Kingdom, the noun *ś3t,* "wisdom," is attested in the phrase *nb ś3.t,* "lord of wisdom."[44]

b. The synonymous root *ś3r,* attested from the Middle Kingdom through the Greek period,[45] and the noun *ś3r.t,* "wisdom," attested from the eighteenth dynasty on,[46] are

---

[32]*AHw.*

[33]Sargon, II, 8, 23, 113.

[34]See IV.5.

[35]*KAR,* 76, vo. 22.

[36]*CAD,* I/2, 171.

[37]See E. Reiner, "The Etiological Myth of the 'Seven Sages,'" *Or,* 30 (1961), 1-11; J. J. A. van Dijk in H. J. Lenzen, *XVIII. vorläufiger Bericht über die . . . Ausgrabungen in Uruk-Warka. ADOG,* 7 (1962), 44-61.

[38]Cf. C. Westermann, *BK,* I/1 (1974), 441.

[39]H. Zimmern, *Beiträge zur Kenntnis der babylonischen Religion* (1901), 1-20, 120; 24, 23; see IV.3.

[40]II geminate according to *WbÄS,* IV, 16; Sethe, 68; Edel, §§ 601 and 630bb. The reading *ś3ỉ* (III weak) is preferred by Gardiner, 16; Žába, 112; R. Faulkner, *A Concise Dictionary of Middle Egyptian* (Oxford, 1962), 208. Gardiner explains the form *ś3.t* as an infinitive, *ś33* as a participle.

[41]Merikare, 33; Neferti, 6.

[42]Papyrus Prisse, XII, 10; XV, 12.

[43]*WbÄS,* IV, 4-16.

[44]*Ibid.,* 16.

[45]*Ibid.,* 18.

[46]*Ibid.*

related to if not identical with the root discussed above.[47] The verb *š33*, "be wise," is used of gods,[48] kings who are wise as gods, more specifically as wise as Thoth, the god of wisdom,[49] princes,[50] and persons in general, especially in autobiographies.[51] In the twelfth dynasty, owners of tombs even describe themselves as having been born wise;[52] the same had been said of the king in the Instruction of Merikare.[53] More realistic is the statement in the Instruction of Ptahhotep[54] that no one is born wise. This latter statement agrees with several passages saying that children are without understanding or wisdom (*nn š3rt.f*).[55] This holds true even for the young Haremhab,[56] who later, as king, is described as being "of exceptional understanding" (*ikr.t š3r.t*).[57] High officials of the New Kingdom make the same claim.[58] Sinuhe calls the new king "lord of wisdom" (*nb š3.t*),[59] and a local prince in the Middle Kingdom says the same of himself.[60] Thutmose III calls himself "shrewd in wisdom."[61]

In the narrative framework of the Prophecy of Neferti,[62] a wise son of the college of officials attached to the palace should be able to speak perfect words or select statements to the king, rejoicing his heart. The high esteem in which the wise man was held is also illustrated by the statement in the Instruction of Merikare[63] that the wise man is a school for the great.

c. The verbs *š33* and *š3r* are often used in autobiographies in association with other verbs of similar meaning, for instance, *š33* with *šbḳ*, "be intelligent, prudent,"[64] and *š3r* with *rḫ*, whose basic meaning is "know."[65] The verb *rḫ* without an object, "be knowledgeable, learned,"[66] is also used of craftsmen in the sense "skillful, experi-

---

[47]Gardiner, 16.

[48]Pyr., 997; cf. also 854.

[49]*Mem. Miss.*, XV, 10, 3, where Amenhotep III calls himself wise as Thoth.

[50]Hatnub, Graf. 24, 1.

[51]For the eleventh and twelfth dynasties, cf. Janssen, I, 31f.; II, 49f.

[52]Leiden V, 4, 6; Berlin 1204, 8; cf. the parallels in *Urk.*, VII, 6, 6, with *rḫ*, "know," instead of *š33*.

[53]115f.

[54]Papyrus Prisse V, 6.

[55]Admonitions of an Egyptian sage, 16, 1.

[56]Turin statue, line 3; cf. Gardiner, 14 and 16, with citations.

[57]Line 11.

[58]E.g., *Urk.*, IV, 481, 13: *ikr š3r.t;* cf. also the phrase *nfr š3r.t*, *Urk.* IV, 993, 4, and *nb š3r.t*, "lord of wisdom," *Urk.*, IV, 67, 10; 513; 6.

[59]48.

[60]*Urk.*, VII, 64, 10.

[61]*Urk.*, IV, 160, 6.

[62]6; Helck, 7 (Text Ik).

[63]33.

[64]*WbÄS*, IV, 94; citations also in Janssen, I, 32.

[65]*WbÄS*, II, 442; citations from the biographies of the Middle Kingdom in Janssen, I, 73ff.; II, 108ff.; further citations in Zandee, *Festschrift Brongers*, 148. Zandee considers *rḫ* the equivalent of Heb. *yādhaʿ*.

[66]*WbÄS*, II, 445, 1.

enced.''[67] The phrase *rḫ ỉh.t,* ''he who knows,''[68] can also mean ''skilled in magic.''[69] The substantive *rḫ,* ''he who knows,''[70] attested from the Middle Kingdom on, is frequently used in contrast with *ḫm,* ''he who is ignorant.''[71]

The form *śỉ3* is attested from the Pyramid texts on; as a verb, it means ''recognize, have knowledge of,''[72] as a noun, ''knowledge, insight, understanding.''[73] In the phrase *śỉ3 ḫt,* it means ''wisdom.''[74] It also appears as an hypostasis and as the personification of knowledge and understanding,[75] often in association with Hu, the embodiment of the word; it is Hu who calls to life that which is devised by Sia.[76] The heart is the seat of Sia;[77] cf. *chᵃkham-lēbh.*[78] Sia and Hu also appear in association with Maat. Maat—like *ḥkm* in Israelite and Aramaic Wisdom Literature—is the great theme of the Egyptian Instructions or Teachings, formerly erroneously called ''Wisdom Instructions'' through the influence of OT Wisdom Literature.[80] These Instructions influenced OT Wisdom Literature both as a genre and in individual ideas.[81] Whether the personification of Maat also falls in this category is disputed.[82]

Krause

II. Forms and Basic Meanings.

1. *Verb.* The Hebrew verb *chākham* in the qal usually refers to the state of being wise. As in Ugaritic, therefore, the perfect usually functions as a stative (Zec. 9:2; Prov. 9:12; 23:15; Eccl. 2:15; with *lû* as in Akkadian,[83] Dt. 32:29). Only in Eccl. 2:19 is it used as a preterite in the sense ''to have conducted oneself wisely.'' The imperfect and imperative are ingressive (''become wise''); in Job 32:9, *lō᾿ . . . yechkāmû,* like the parallel (*lō᾿ . . .*) *yābhînû,* designates a state or condition.

The consecutive imperfects *vattērebh . . . vaiyechkam* in 1 K. 5:10f. are difficult. The fientic character of *vaiyittēn* (v. 9), which introduces the sequence, would suggest

---

[67] *Ibid.,* 4; cf. IV.5.

[68] Merikare, 115.

[69] *WbÄS,* II, 443, 30; cf. IV.4.

[70] *WbÄS,* II, 445.

[71] *WbÄS,* III, 280; e.g., Papyrus Prisse V, 7ff.; cf. III.2.

[72] *WbÄS,* IV, 30.

[73] *Ibid.,* 31.

[74] *Urk.,* I, 39, 15.

[75] Cf. Ringgren, *Word and Wisdom,* 9ff.; *RÄR,* 318ff.

[76] See V.1.

[77] See III.1; cf. Leiden Papyrus I, 350, 5, 16; 347, 12, 1-2; Sethe, 53-54; Kuban Stele, line 18.

[78] See III.1; Zandee, *Festschrift Beek,* 272f.

[79] Cf. Ringgren, *Word and Wisdom,* 51 and n. 1; on the definition of Maat see Morenz, *Egyptian Religion,* 147ff.

[80] Cf. Brunner, 113ff.

[81] Cf. Morenz, *HO,* I/1:2, 229–230; Grieshammer, 163f., with bibliography.

[82] H. Donner, *ZÄS,* 82 (1957), 17f.; cf. V.3.

[83] *GaG,* § 81b.

the ingressive translation "it grew greater . . . he grew wiser"; but the affirming statements in vv. 10f. suggest an interpretation after the analogy of the stative perfect.[84]

The piel refers to the causation of the state indicated by the qal, i.e., "make wise," "instruct."[85] We also find the passive participle (pual) *m^e^chukkām*, "instructed," in Ps. 58:6 (Eng. v. 5). The hiphil in Ps. 19:8(7) is probably also factitive.[86] In Ex. 1:10, the hithpael is factitive reflexive, referring to the self-realization of being wise.[87] In Eccl. 7:16 and Sir. 10:26, there is an additional element of exaggeration or hypocrisy: "Don't play wise."

The niphal in Sir. 37:19,22(23D) is obviously equivalent in meaning to the qal, as in the case of → בִּין *bîn* and several comparable stative verbs.[88]

2. *Nouns*. The noun *chākhām,* whether used adjectivally or as a substantive, refers to a living being in the state of *chokhmāh,* as designated by the qal perfect.

The forms *chokhmôth/chakhmôth* (Prov. 1:20; 9:1; 14:1; Sir. 4:11) are feminine singular, like *chakhmôth śārôtheyhā,* "the wisest one of her ladies," in Jgs. 5:29. We are obviously dealing with a by-form of **chakamath,* with changes of *-ath* to *-ôth* as in Phoen. *^I^Ab-di-mil-ku-ut-ti* for *ʿbd-mlkt* in Esarhaddon 48, 65.[89] In the passages cited, however, unlike Jgs. 5:29, *chokhmôth/chakhmôth* designates the personified "Lady Wisdom," obviously distinguished deliberately from *chokhmāh;* it is not so clear that this holds true for the antonym *hôlēlôth* in Eccl. 1:17; 2:12; 7:25; 9:3; 10:13.[90] Later, in Gnostic circles, the Gk. *achamōth* became the name of a Sophia figure.[91]

On the other hand, *chokhmôth* in Ps. 49:4(3); Prov. 24:7; Sir. 4:11; 32:16 (like the par. *t^e^bhûnôth* in Ps. 49:4[3]) is an abstract plural[92] and thus identical in meaning with *chokhmāh*.

III. Semantic Field.

1. *Synonyms*. The roots → בִּין *bîn* and → יָדַע *yādhaʿ* are substantially similar in meaning to *ḥkm*. In Dt. 32:29 and Job 32:9, *chākham* and *bîn* stand in parallel; *nābhôn* appears as a synonym of the adjective *chākhām* in Gen. 41:33,39; Dt. 1:13; 1 K. 3:12; Isa. 5:21; Jer. 4:22; Hos. 14:10(9); Prov. 1:5; 16:21; 17:28; 18:15 (cf. *bānîm,* Jer. 49:7; *m^e^bhînîm,* Sir. 4:11). Also frequent is the synonymous use of *chokhmāh* and *bînāh* or *t^e^bhûnāh*[93] (cf. also *b^e^chokhmāthî kî n^e^bhunôthî,* Isa. 10:13). We find *yābhēn* as a verb with *chākhām* as its subject in Jer. 9:11 and Hos. 14:10(9).

---

84 Cf. E. Jenni, *Das hebräische Piʿel* (Zurich, 1968), 27.

85 A different interpretation: *ibid.,* 73.

86 A different interpretation: *ibid.,* 85.

87 Saebø, 559.

88 G. Bergsträsser, *Hebräische Grammatik,* II (1929, repr. 1962), § 16c.

89 J. Friedrich and W. Röllig, *Phönizisch-punische Grammatik*^{2}. *AnOr,* 46 (1970), § 228.

90 Cf. M. Dahood, "Qoheleth and Northwest Semitic Philology," *Bibl,* 43 (1962), 350; Dahood cites other Hebrew forms in *-ôth* in his review of A. Barucq, *Le livre des Proverbes* (1964), in *Bibl,* 46 (1965), 233, with the addition of *'āchôth,* "sister!"

91 R. Köbert, "Achamoth," *Bibl.,* 45 (1964), 254f.

92 C. Brockelmann, *VG* (^{2}1961), II, 59.

93 Saebø, 564.

With subjects derived from the root *ḥkm* there appear predicates derived from *yd*ᶜ in Eccl. 8:5,17; 2 Ch. 2:11(12) and objects derived from *yd*ᶜ in Job 15:2; Prov. 15:2; 18:15 (similar combinations are found in 2 S. 14:20; 1 K. 2:9; Eccl. 8:1,7). Forms of *yd*ᶜ appear with *chokhmāh* as object in Job 32:7; Prov. 1:2; 24:14(?); Eccl. 1:17; (7:25); 8:16. As synonyms for *chokhmāh,* besides the common *daᶜath,*[94] we find the late *maddā*ᶜ (2 Ch. 1:10–12; Dnl. 1:4,17) and Aram. *manda*ᶜ (Dnl. 2:21). In Ex. 31:3; 1 K. 7:14; Prov. 2:6; 3:19f., *chokhmāh, tᵉbhûnāh,* and *daᶜath* appear together.

In Prov. 21:11, *yechkam* stands in synonymous parallelism with *yiqqach daᶜath;* cf. 9:9, *yechkam ᶜôdh* par. *yôseph leqach,* and 1:2f., *lādhaᶜath* par. *lᵉhābhîn* par. *laqachath mûsār,* etc.

Thus *leqach* by ellipsis becomes a technical term for "instruction" or "education": for example, *lāmadh leqach,* "accept instruction," Isa. 29:24; Sir. 8:8; *hôsîph leqach,* "teach instruction," Prov. 16:21,23. Finally, *leqach,* "instruction," occurs in Dt. 32:2; Job 11:4; Prov. 4:2; 7:21.

We often find *ḥkm* associated semantically with → זקן *zāqēn* and → צדק *tsādhaq.* Ezk. 27:8f. use the nouns *chākhām* and *zāqēn* synonymously; a corresponding adversative sequence appears in Eccl. 4:13. The superior wisdom of the "old" (*rabbîm* par. *zᵉqēnîm;* cf. Ugar. *rb*[*b*]) is disputed in Job 32:9 (contradicting v. 7); according to Ps. 105:22, Joseph taught Pharaoh's *zᵉqēnîm* wisdom. Ugar. *rb*[*b*] par. *ḥkm* is associated with *dqn,* "beard."[95] The nouns *chākhām* and *tsaddîq* appear in parallel in Prov. 9:9; 23:24 and additively in Dt. 16:19; Eccl. 9:1. On the relationship between *tsaddîq* and *chokhmāh,* cf. also Ps. 37:30; Prov. 10:31.[96] In Eccl. 7:16, the hithpael of *ḥkm* stands in parallel with *hāyāh tsaddîq.*

The heart (→ לב *lēbh*) is the seat of wisdom. The wise are therefore called *chᵃkham lēbh* (Job 9:4; 37:24; Prov. 10:8; 16:21; cf. the statements about the heart of the wise in Prov. 16:23; 18:15; Eccl. 8:5). The phrase is applied in a more specialized sense to sacral craftsmen[97] in Ex. 28:3; 31:6; 35:10; 35:25 (feminine); 36:1, 8; cf. *chokhmath lēbh,* "ability," 35:35. God accordingly gives a wise and discerning "heart" (1 K. 3:12; cf. Sir. 6:37b), or gives "ability" to the "heart" (Ex. 31:6; 36:2). According to 1 K. 5:9(4:29), *chokhmāh* is identical with *rōchabh lēbh,* "breadth of (heart >) knowledge"; cf. Akk. *palkû uzni.*[98] The "fool" is referred to as *chᵃsar lēbh,* "without sense," in Prov. 9:4, 16, *ʾên lēbh* in Jer. 5:21. The niphal of *lbb,* "get understanding," in Job 11:12 is denominative.

2. *Antonyms.* As antonyms to *ḥkm* we find the nouns *kᵉsîl,* "(fat > clumsy >) stupid," *ʾᵉvîl,* "foolish, fool" (cf. *chokhmāh* in contrast to *ʾivveleth,* Prov. 14:1), *sākhāl,* "foolish" (along with the abstract *ś/sikhlûth,* Eccl. 1:17; 2:12f.; 7:25, and the piel *śikkēl,* referring to the wise men of Babylon in Isa. 44:25), and *nābhal.* Possibly more concrete is the root *lîts* with its conjectured basic meaning "dominate conversa-

---

[94] *Ibid.*

[95] See I.1; L. R. Fisher, *Ras Shamra Parallels,* I. *AnOr,* 49 (1972), No. II, 187, 515.

[96] *Ibid.,* No. III, 80.

[97] See IV.5.

[98] See I.2.

tion'';[99] thus *lēts* in contrast with *chākhām*(Prov. 13:1; 15:12; 21:11)means''babbler'' (Isa. 28:14[100]), corresponding to *latstā,* ''you are a babbler'' (Prov. 9:12).

IV. Types of "Wisdom."

1. *Nonspecific Usage.* The earliest occurrences of the root *ḥkm* attest to a usage that is still nonspecific. The *chakhmôth śārôtheyhā* of Jgs. 5:29 is simply ''the wisest of her princesses''; the *'ishshāh chᵃkhāmāh* of 2 S. 14:2; 20:16,22 is not much more than a ''clever woman.'' In 2 S. 13:3, Jonadab is called an *'îsh chākhām* on account of his more or less criminal advice; tactical ability of the same ambiguous nature is imputed by David to his son Solomon when he addresses him in 1 K. 2:6,9 (cf. Pharaoh's self-exhortation in Ex. 1:10). Such ''skill'' is also the subject of the accusation in Jer. 4:22.

In Hos. 13:13, *bēn lō' chākhām* is a term for a fetus that does not appear at the proper time at the mouth of the womb. The lament over the transitoriness of life in Job 4:21 says of men that *yāmûthû vᵉlō' bhᵉchokhmāh,* ''they die, they know not how.'' Animal species with unusual abilities are referred to in Prov. 30:24 as *chᵃkhāmîm mēchᵃkhāmîm,* ''wiser than the wise'' (pointing based on the LXX; cf. Syriac and Vulg.); the ''wisdom'' of the ibis (Job 38:36) probably consists concretely in its supposed ability to sense the imminent flooding of the Nile. In Ezk. 28:4 and Eccl. 2:19, the root *ḥkm* means a good head for trade; in Ezk. 28:3f., expertise in navigation and shipbuilding; in Prov. 21:22, the art of military tactics. In Jer. 9:22(23), alongside ''might'' and ''riches,'' *chokhmāh* simply means ''intelligence.''

In Deuteronomy, *ḥkm* is associated with the institutions of nomadic society: according to 1:13-15, Moses ordered that leadership be placed in the hands of *'ᵃnāshîm chᵃkhāmîm ûnᵉbhōnîm vîdhuʿîm;* 16:19 presupposes that ''wise men'' hold judicial office. Here, however, we are dealing merely with retrospective statements. The terms deriving from the root *ḥkm* do not furnish any basis for speaking of ''clan wisdom.'' Neither is Ezk. 7:26 relevant in this regard: unlike Jer. 18:18, this verse associates *ʿetsāh* not with the wise but with the ''elders,'' a class of the exilic community.

2. *Court Wisdom.* After the beginning of the monarchy, it is commonly understood that the root *ḥkm* refers above all to the academic wisdom of the court and the ideals of the class entrusted with it.

a. *Aphorisms with ḥkm.* Proverbial wisdom contains definitions of the qualities of a wise man. According to Prov. 12:15, he listens to advice, whereas the fool's inflated opinion of himself prevents him from doing so. According to 13:1, a wise son loves instruction (reading *mûsār 'ōhēbh*), in contrast to the scoffer or babbler, who ''does not listen to rebuke.'' The wise man knows how to answer discreetly (26:16); in line with the Egyptian ideal of silence, he allays or holds back his wrath (29:8,11; cf. the phrase *qar-rûach* [17:27] and above all *'erekh 'appayim* [14:29; 15:18]). Prov. 20:26

---

[99] *KBL*³.

[100] H. N. Richardson, ''Some Notes on ליץ and Its Derivatives,'' *VT*, 5 (1955), 166.

recognizes a wise king by the judgment he brings upon the wicked. But the empty boast of wisdom is even more hopeless than naive folly.

The profit gained from the "teaching" (Prov. 13:14) or "words" (Eccl. 10:12; cf. 12:11) of the wise is accordingly esteemed, in contrast to the shouting of foolish braggarts (Eccl. 9:17). Prov. 16:21 (23f.) appears to have recognized the mysterious persuasiveness lent by the aesthetic form of wisdom sayings. Cf. what is said about the tongue (Prov. 12:18; 15:2), the lips (15:7), the heart,[101] and the ear (18:15) of the wise man.

The ideal of the *ḥkm* concept finds expression in the calls to be wise, which make exhortation a dominant concept: "Hear, my son, and be wise, and direct your mind in the (right) way" (Prov. 23:19; similar exhortations include 19:20; 8:33; and the so-called introductory formulas in 1:5; 22:17f.; Job 15:17–19). Prov. 13:20 admonishes its hearers to associate with the wise in order to become wise, while the company of fools is harmful (cf. 15:31); 6:6 holds out the prospect of becoming wise to the sluggard through observation of the ant. Eccl. 7:5 sets a higher value on the rebuke of the wise than on praises sung by fools. In Prov. 27:11, the call to be wise is grounded on the satisfaction the educator will receive (cf. 10:1; 15:20; 23:15).

There are also exhortations to teach wisdom, which promises particular success when the wise are involved (Prov. 22:11; 9:9); but even "the simple becomes wise when a scoffer is punished" (21:11; cf. 1:4). Sir. 32:4 cautions against making pronouncements of a wisdom nature in the wrong situation, as at a revel. Parents should not withhold discipline, because it produces wisdom (Prov. 29:15). In Job 15:2f., we catch a glimpse of the wise man's ethics of truthfulness.

Little is added to the picture of the wise man at court by occurrences of the root *ḥkm* apart from aphorisms and exhortations. Jer. 18:18 distributes the functions of the Jerusalem leadership in such a way that the priest is responsible for → תורה *tôrāh,* "instruction" (cf. Ezk. 7:26; assigned differently in Prov. 13:14; 31:26), the wise man for *ʿētsāh* (→ יעץ *yāʿats*), "counsel," and the prophet for *dābhār* (→ דבר *dābhar*), "the word." According to the superscriptions Prov. 22:17; 24:23, the wise man is accounted to be an author of proverbs; 1:6 divides his output into four genres: *māshāl* (→ משל *māshal*), "proverb," *mᵉlîtsāh* (→ ליץ *lîts*), "taunt," *dibhrê chᵃkhāmîm* (→ דבר *dābhar*), "words of wisdom," and *chîdhāh* (→ חידה *chîdhāh*), "riddle" (cf. also Hab. 2:6; Sir. 47:17); it is likely, however, that the terms are used more to express the total confidence of the speakers than to convey terminological precision. According to Eccl. 12:9, the activity of a late postexilic sage seems to be divided into teaching (*limmadh daʿath ʾeth-hāʿām*), research (*vᵉʾizzēn vᵉchiqqēr*), and writing (*tiqqēn mᵉshalîm harbēh,* further developed in v. 10).

Whybray disputes the professional nature of the skills and abilities designated by *ḥkm,* as well as the technical use of the noun to refer to the class of scholars within the complex institution of the Israelite court. He traces the intellectual pursuits of wisdom back to a small educated class of prosperous citizens, who read and wrote for their own edification and pleasure, and occasionally produced literary talents. "In so far as there were in every generation men who . . . made their thoughts known to others, there may

[101] See III.1.

be said to have been an 'intellectual tradition' in Israel which was distinct from other traditions such as the historical, legal, cultic, and prophetic. But there is no evidence of an *institution* existing through the centuries which acted as the vehicle of this 'tradition.' "[102]

b. *Narratives*. The ideal of the wise king was lent narrative form in the figure of Solomon.

According to the list in 1 K. 5:9-12(4:29-34), Solomon's wisdom was demonstrated in the "literary" field: v. 12(32) represents the king as the author of 3000 proverbs and 1005 songs; v. 13(33), by contrast,[103] suggests encyclopedic scholarship in prose, involving lists introducing an organization of natural phenomena.

The narrative tradition in 1 K. 3:4-15,16-28, on the contrary, presents a vivid portrait of Solomon as a wise judge. The fact that he receives his inspiration during an incubation at the high place of Gibeon may be due in general to the preeminent position of the king in sacrifice and revelation, and more specifically to the influence of the genre of the Egyptian royal novella.[104] The opportunity for the king to express a wish at his enthronement is also presupposed by Ps. 2:8. Now if wisdom is the result of inspiration (cf. 1 K. 5:9[4:29],26[12]; 10:24), what we have is most likely the narrative precipitate of the notion of a superhuman wisdom like that of *'ᵉlōhîm,* as suggested by the expression *chokhmath 'ᵉlōhîm bᵉqirbô* (3:28). In the two elements of the phrase *lēbh shōmēaʿ* (3:9), Brunner claims to find reminiscences of Egyptian wisdom literature;[105] but the aphorisms and exhortations discussed above show that the concept of hearing had constitutive significance for the Israelite ideal of wisdom as well.

The first passage in which Solomon's wisdom is truly put to the test is 1 K. 10:1-10, 13. According to vv. 2f., Solomon must admit to being questioned by the queen of Sheba, who determines thereby whether this potentate newcomer is her equal. The narrator's purpose is to demonstrate that his own kingdom is every bit as good as those established earlier; the expansive aretalogy in vv. 6-9 serves the same purpose. What is to be demonstrated therefore is not just the "wisdom" illustrated by the ability to answer riddles, but the royal "quality" (*ṭôbh,* v. 7) exemplified by the narrative in the existence of the palace (v. 4), its luxury and sacrifices (v. 5), and not least the offering of gifts (v. 13).[106]

Joseph represents the ideal of the wise courtier.[107] The Genesis narrative portrays him on the basis of an educational ideal comprising, among other elements, the art of public speaking and counsel, "upbringing, modesty, learning, courtesy, and self-discipline," the last being grounded in a "godly fear" such as is acquired in the school of humility (*ʿᵃnāvāh*). It is characteristic of the interpenetration of rationalistic and occult elements

[102]Whybray, 70.

[103]Alt interprets the passages differently.

[104]S. Herrmann, "Die Königsnovelle in Ägypten und in Israel," *Festschrift A. Alt. WZ Leipzig,* 3 (1953/54), 51-62.

[105]H. Brunner, "Das hörende Herz," *ThLZ,* 79 (1954), 697-700.

[106]Cf. Müller, *VT,* 20 (1970), 478f.

[107]Von Rad, "Joseph Narrative," 294f.

that the wise courtier also has mastered the mantic "science" of dream interpretation, toward which his own predictive dreams have disposed him.[108]

It may be of sociological interest that the hero is the product of a nomadic culture seen retrospectively as being already enlightened, which allows the didactic Wisdom narrative to be incorporated into the patriarchal stories. The moving force of the second part of the narrative is accordingly the conflict that Joseph, as a parvenu at court, must go through with his clan: in his figure is reflected the deracination that has probably always been the lot of a courtier when he leaves the society of his family.

The influence of the literary figure of Joseph is found only in Ps. 105:16–22 and possibly Eccl. 4:13f., an observation that is unfavorable to the commonly espoused early dating of the Joseph narrative, and especially to its assignment to the sources J and E. Furthermore, it would have been difficult for the figure of the mantic sage, whose art had flourished at the great courts of the ancient Near East, becoming a specialty with pseudo-scientific methodology, to survive the rigor of earlier Israelite religion.[109]

3. *Mantic Wisdom.* Deutero-Isaiah still adopts an avowedly polemic attitude toward all of Babylonian magic and the study of prodigies. In 44:25f., he establishes a contrast between the "omens" of the *baddîm* and the *qos^{e}mîm* (both oracle priests), who are described as *ch^{a}khāmîm* possessed of *da'ath* in v. 25b, and "the word of his servants" and "the counsel of his messengers," the prophets. The aretalogically formulated passage states that Yahweh "frustrates" and "makes fools of" the former, while the message and warning of the latter are confirmed and established. In 47:10, the *chokmāh* and *da'ath* of Babylon are wholly the object of prophetic attack, which is directed (v. 13) against three groups of mantic experts: the *hōbh^{e}rê shāmayim,* "those who worship the heavens" (on *hōbhēr,* cf. Ugar. *hbr,* "bow down"[110]), the *chōzîm bakkôkhābhîm,* "those who gaze at the stars," and the *môdhî'îm lech^{o}dhāshîm mē'^{a}sher yābhō'û 'alāyikh,* "those who foretell the months in which [evil] will overtake you." The (magico-) mantic and foreign nature of this wisdom is indicated by such contextual words as *kesheph,* "sorcery" (vv. 9, 12; < Akk. *kišpu*), *chebher,* "enchantment" (vv. 9,12), *shachar,* "magic" (v. 11), *sōchēr,* "magician" (v. 15; < Akk. *saḫāru* in the technical sense "enchant"[111]), and *kippēr hōvāh,* "expiate disaster" (v. 11). The prophet has a double motive for his attack: the inefficacy of mantic practice, and its concomitant attitude of self-assurance (vv. 8, 10). Jer. 50:35f. attack the manticism of Babylon in like fashion: among other dignitaries, the *baddîm* (read *baddeyhā?*) are listed immediately after *ch^{a}khāmeyhā*. Isa.

---

[108]See IV.3.

[109]Cf. R. N. Whybray, "The Joseph Story and Pentateuchal Criticism," *VT,* 18 (1968), 522–28; D. B. Redford, *A Study of the Biblical Story of Joseph. SVT,* 20 (1970), 244ff.; also A. Meinhold, "Die Gattung der Josephsgeschichte und des Estherbuches: Diasporanovelle I," *ZAW,* 87 (1975), 306–324; 88 (1976), 72–93.

[110]*UT,* No. 745; *WUS,* No. 812; J. Blau, "hōḇ^{e}rē šāmājim (Jes xlvii 13) = Himmelsanbeter?" *VT,* 7 (1957), 183.

[111]*AHw.*

19:1-15 is a postexilic oracle of disaster against the manticism of Egypt: the taunt in vv. 11-13 demands of the "wisest counselors of Pharaoh" and the "wise men of Egypt" that they tell what Yahweh has decreed concerning Egypt; the subjects of this mockery obviously try to demonstrate their art by issuing oracles.

The mention of *ch^{a}khāmîm* at the court of the Persian king (Est. 1:13a) is merely made in passing and has no polemic overtones. The added phrase *yōdh^{e}ʿê hāʿittîm,* "who knew the times," may indicate more specifically that astrologers are meant, as the Targum assumes in the case of the other passage where the expression occurs, 1 Ch. 12:33(32). V. 13b, lessening the pagan element, adds that they were *yodh^{e}ʿê dāṯ vādhîn,* "versed in religion and law." For *yādhaʿ* as a term for mantic knowledge, cf. Nu. 24:16 (with *daʿath ʿelyôn* as its object) and *yidd^{e}ʿōnî,* "knowing one," as an epithet for the shades.

The mantic sage became a literary type in the figure of Daniel as it appears in Dnl. 4-5, a fairy tale whose theme, status, is given apocalyptic treatment in chap. 2, and in the expository chap. 1.[112] Behind the biblical Daniel stands the legendary Canaanite figure of Dan'el, to whose wisdom that of the prince of Tyre is likened in Ezk. 28:3 (cf. also Ezk. 14:14, 20; 1 En. 6:7; 69:2; Jub. 4:20). Dan'el is ultimately identical with the Ugar. *dn3l.*[113] In Dnl. 4-5 (1-2), Daniel appears as the archetypal Jewish mantic, who, like Joseph, outdoes his pagan colleagues and competitors in their own field; thus he is introduced in 5:11 (2:48) as chief of the foreign occultists. These latter are called *chakkîmê bhābhel,* "the wise men of Babylon," in 2:12-14,18,24,27,48; 4:3(6), 15(18); 5:7f.,15; *ʾashshāphîm/ʾash^{e}phîn* (<Akk. [*w*]*āšipu*), "enchanters," in 1:20; 2:27; 4:3f.(6f.); 5:7f.,11; *charṭummîm/n* (< Demotic *ḥr-ty*[*y*] < *ḥr-tp* < Egyp. [*ḫry-hb.(t)*] *ḥry-tp,* "chief ritual book bearer" > "(religious) lector"; cf. Neo-Assyr. *ḫarṭibi*)[114] in 1:20; 2:2,10,27; 4:4(7),6(9); 5:11; and *gāz^{e}rîn,* "determiners of destiny" > "seers," in 2:27; 4:4(7); 5:7,11 (cf. 4QOrNab A 4). Their function is reduced to a formula in 2:27 in the expression *rāzāh . . . l^{e}hach^{a}vāyāh,* "make known the mystery." Daniel, however, is able not only to *pishrîn l^{e}miphshar,* "give interpretations," and *qiṭrîn l^{e}mishrê,* "solve problems," but also to "interpret dreams" and "explain (oracular) riddles" (5:12). The exposition of chap. 1, obviously following the model of the Joseph narrative, combines the idea of such mantic wisdom with that of court education. Unlike Joseph, Daniel and his friends are cultivated in both, as is proper for aristocrats at the pagan court.

According to Dnl. 2:19, however, because Nebuchadnezzar wants to have his apocalyptic dream not only interpreted but also guessed, Daniel receives a night vision that reveals the secret to him. Thus he becomes the prototype of the apocalyptic seer; this is the role in which the author of the book of Daniel uses him in chaps. 7-12. In other respects, too, there is both a phenomenological and a genetic connection between mantic wisdom and apocalyptic. This connection helps explain a series of features in which apocalyptic is at odds with classical prophecy (though not with the epigonic prophetism of the postexilic period): its determinism, its claim to inspiration,

---

[112]Cf. H.-P. Müller, "Märchen, Legende, und Enderwartung," *VT,* 26 (1976), 338-350.
[113]Müller, *UF,* 1 (1969).
[114]*CAD,* VI, 116.

its use of symbolic imagery to cloak reality, and its penchant for pseudonymity.[115] In the mantic features of apocalyptic there surfaces an undercurrent that lent new strength to the period's propensity for religious atavisms. When the great Semitic religions and the particular cults of Syria and Palestine became enervated, a "second religiosity" began to take hold in the recesses of historico-political life, bringing together ancient elements of diverse traditions and breathing new life into them with helpless enthusiasm.

4. *Magical Wisdom.* The archaic forms of "wisdom" include magic, although terms derived from the root *ḥkm* are found only rarely with this meaning. Ps. 58:6(5) speaks in passing of the "cunning enchanter [snake charmer]" (*chôbher chᵃbhārîm mᵉchukkām*) along with the "voice of charmers." In Jer. 9:16(17), the feminine substantive appears as a synonym of *mᵉqônᵉnôth:* the "mourning women" are "wise women" because there is a magical aspect to lament for the dead. The magic terminology in Isa. 47:9-13 is discussed above.

In practice, magic and manticism are closely related: the mantic seeks not only to know the future in advance, but to influence it. According to Ex. 7:11 (P), Pharaoh summons the *chᵃkhāmîm* and *mᵉkhashshᵉphîm* ("sorcerers") to turn their rods into serpents, as Aaron did; the métier of the *charṭummê mitsrayim,* "magicians of Egypt," is indicated as being "secret arts" (*lahᵃṭîm/lāṭîm,* Ex. 7:11,22; 8:3[7], 14[18] [P]). In the exodus narrative, especially in P, Moses and Aaron are well on their way to becoming archetypes of the Jewish magicians, just as Solomon was in later Jewish (cf. already Wis. 7:17ff.) and Islamic legend.

5. *Artisans.* Finally, the root *ḥkm* is associated with the skills of religious craftsmanship. The earliest occurrence is probably the mention of the "experienced craftsman" (*chᵃkham chᵃrāshîm*) in Isa. 3:3; the mention of the "expert in charms" (*nᵉbhôn lāchash*) that follows and the magical overtones of the root *ḥrš* III (Prov. 3:29; 6:14 seem to have black magic in mind)[116] show that craftsmanship was still associated with the manipulation of the appropriate powers. The maker of idols is both craftsman and magician; in Isa. 40:20, he is called *chārāsh chākhām* (cf. the term *maʿᵃśēh chᵃkhāmîm* for idols in Jer. 10:9). According to 1 K. 7:13f. (late), Hiram of Tyre, a bronzeworker brought to work on the temple, was full of *chokhmāh, tᵉbhûnāh,* and *daʿath.* This holds true in the strict sense of inspiration for the sacral craftsmen in Ex. 28-36 (P) who are entrusted with the making of the tabernacle (derivatives of *ḥkm* appear in 28:3; 31:2f.,6; 35:30f.; 36:1f.); 35:34 associates the ability to teach such craftsmanship with divine inspiration.

Besides Solomon, Joseph, and Daniel, as well as "the men of Hezekiah" (Prov. 25:1), postexilic prototypes of wisdom included the Phoenicians (Ezk. 27:8; 28:3-5;

---

[115]For details, see Müller, *UF,* 1 (1969).

[116]On Ugar. *ḥrš,* cf. *UT,* No. 903; *WUS,* No. 976.

Zec. 9:2; 2 Ch. 2:6[7],12f.[13f.])[117] and the Edomites (Jer. 49:7; Ob. 8; Bar. 3:23).[118] The wisdom of Babylon is always a negative paradigm (Isa. 44:25; 47:1-15; Jer. 50:35; 51:57).

V. Theological Usage.

1. *Hebrew Wisdom's Understanding of Reality*. To begin with, the root *ḥkm* reflects the understanding of reality inherent in ancient Hebrew Wisdom when it is used in aphorisms and didactic discourses about how wisdom is acquired.

The saying in Prov. 21:22 about the superiority of the wise over mere physical strength gives expression to a simple experience that is still based on the nonspecific concept of being clever or knowledgeable; Eccl. 7:19 says much the same thing of the wise individual in conflict with rulers. The milieu of court wisdom furnishes the background for Prov. 16:14, according to which the *'îsh chākhām* knows how to appease the deadly wrath of a king. In society, the wise man enjoys the respect due a *nābhôn* (Prov. 16:21); his words win him favor (*chēn*, Eccl. 10:12). Also in the realm of concrete observation is Eccl. 8:1, according to which a man's wisdom makes his face shine, whereas insolence (*ʿōz*) disfigures his features. Prov. 24:14 deals with the concept of time: whoever finds wisdom has hope and a future.

Within the didactic discourses of Prov. 1-9 (especially in chap. 2), there are several passages that treat the theme of how wisdom is come by. Wisdom may consist in a good head for business,[119] which brings riches (3:16; cf. Ezk. 28:4; Eccl. 2:19). Wisdom (in the more comprehensive sense) also brings honor (3:16f.; cf. 3:35) and long life (cf. 3:22; 13:14), as well as its benefits, *nōʿam* and *shālôm;* 3:18 therefore calls it "a tree of life," so that those who hold it fast are happy. According to 2:12,16, the knowledge that comes through wisdom can "save" or "deliver," both "from the way of evil, from men of perverted speech," and above all "from the foreign woman." Whoever listens to wisdom dwells secure (1:33). In short, whoever is wise is wise to his own benefit (9:12). Therefore wisdom should be sought like silver or treasure (2:4); its gain and profit are better than silver and gold, better than corals and gems (3:14f.; cf. Job 28:15-20; Prov. 8:11, 19; Wisd. 7:9). Such statements do not depreciate material values in favor of spiritual or intellectual: Prov. 8:18 and Wisd. 7:11 still depict wisdom as being profitable. The mechanism of an order that is both natural and social and guarantees success does not differ from that which justly rewards religious virtues, so obvious does the unity of reality appear. Nevertheless, Eccl. 2:9 finds it worthy of comment that someone should retain his wisdom despite

[117]See W. F. Albright, "Some Canaanite-Phoenician Sources of Hebrew Wisdom," *Wisdom in Israel and in the Ancient Near East. Festschrift H. H. Rowley. SVT,* 3 (1955), 1-15; M. Dahood, "The Phoenician Contribution to Biblical Wisdom Literature," *The Role of the Phoenicians in the Interaction of Mediterranean Civilizations,* ed. W. A. Ward (Beirut, 1968), 123-152.

[118]See R. H. Pfeiffer, "Edomitic Wisdom," *ZAW,* 44 (1926), 13-25; B. G. Boschi, "Saggezza di Edom, mito o realtà?" *RivBibl,* 15 (1967), 357-368.

[119]See III.1.

his incomparable wealth (*chokhmāthî ʿām^edhāh-llî;* opposite: *ḥkmth ʾbdh,* Ahikar 94; cf. 147).

In Prov. 1:20; 9:1; 14:1 (deleting *nāshîm*), "Lady Wisdom" (*chokhmôth/chakhmôth*) becomes a soteriological figure, as does "Wisdom" (*chokhmāh*) in 8:12 and elsewhere. Thus personified she cries aloud in the streets and marketplaces (1:20; but cf. also 11QPs^a 2 [=Syr. Ps. 154], v. 12[120]). Like a mother she comes to the neophyte and welcomes him like a young wife (Sir. 15:2). She builds a house and invites men to a generous banquet (Prov. 9:1, 4); she speaks of her creation before the world as the basis for her claims (8:22-31). The benefit of wisdom is therefore described in 4:6 as personal protection (cf. 6:22; Sir. 15:4f.). Indeed, Wisdom loves those who love her (Prov. 8:17), and is deified as the giver of life (8:35; Sir. 4:12). Therefore personified Wisdom must not be forsaken (Prov. 4:6), but loved like a feminine numen (4:6; 8:17; Sir. 4:14) and embraced (Prov. 4:8), addressed as a sister and intimate friend (7:4), and watched for daily at her gate (8:34; cf. 11QPs^a 2:8) as at a sanctuary (cf. Prov. 9:1). The "Solomon" of Wisd. 8:2 wished to bring her home as his bride. Anyone who refuses to listen to her brings upon himself calamity, panic, and death (Prov. 1:24-32; 8:36; Sir. 4:19). According to Sir. 4:17f., she is a careful pedagogue.

Sometimes the theological background of such an understanding of reality is explicated in more detail. Prov. 28:26 contrasts the *bôṭēach b^elibbô,* who is a fool, with the *hôlēkh b^echokhmāh,* who can count on deliverance. In the didactic introduction to the collection that incorporates some of the Instruction of Amenemope, 22:19 calls the "goal" of wisdom instruction *lihyôth b^eyhvh mibhṭachekha,* "that your trust may be in Yahweh." According to Isa. 33:6, *chokhmath vādhaʿath* (par. *yirʾath yhvh*) are an abundance of salvation.

Prov. 15:33 interprets the fear of Yahweh, corresponding to humility (*ʿ^anāvāh*) in the parallel verse, as *mûsar chokhmāh,* i.e., "the teacher who leads to wisdom."[121] What evokes this humility is shown by the appearance of *yirʾath yhvh* in parallelism with *daʿath q^edhōshîm,* "knowledge of the Holy One," in 9:10 and 30:3, with *yirʾath yhvh* being termed the "beginning of wisdom" in 9:10 (on *yirʾath yhvh* as *daʿath* [*ʾ^elōhîm*], cf. 1:29; 2:5). In 1:7, too, the fear of Yahweh is the "beginning" (*rēʾshîth* in the sense of *principium*) of *daʿath*. In Ps. 111:10, *yirʾath yhvh* as *rēʾshîth chokhmāh* is more concretely the object of an action (reading *ʿośeyhā*!). Prov. 2 likewise identifies the fear of Yahweh or knowledge of God gained through attentiveness to wisdom (vv. 2,5) with concepts like *tsedheq, mishpāṭ,* and *mēshārîm* from the realm of social ethics (v. 9; cf. 1:3b). In Job 28:28, too, the fear of Yahweh identified with *chokhmāh* has an explicitly ethical dimension (par. *sûr mērāʿ*); here, in an appendix to vv. 1-27 (cf. Prov. 3:7; Job 37:24),[122] it appears as an alternative to the devalued seeking after

[120] Most recently discussed by A. S. van der Woude, "Die fünf syrische Psalmen (einschliesslich Psalm 151)," in W. Kümmel, ed., *Jüdische Schriften aus hellenistisch-römischer Zeit,* IV/1 (1974), 43f.

[121] B. Gemser, *HAT,* 16 (^{2}1963), 69.

[122] See VI.2.

"truth" (the meaning of *chokhmāh* in v. 12 [see VI.3]) that springs from scrupulosity. It has a similar function in Eccl. 12:13f.

2. *Synthesis with Historical and Nomistic Piety.* More productive was the synthesis, beginning in the exilic period, in which the earlier wisdom theology, which for the most part had not advanced beyond the stage of implications, was combined with theological schemata based on law and history.

Ps. 107:43 probably reflects a relatively late wisdom occupation with the history of the people of God when it answers the rhetorical question of who is wise with a reference to consideration of the *chasdhê yhvh,* Yahweh's deeds that proclaim his favor toward Israel. Contrariwise, Dt. 32:6 calls Israel a "foolish and senseless people" because they have failed to see Yahweh at work in creation (v. 6b) and in the history of Israel (vv. 7ff.), thus refusing to take the end of their enemies as a warning example for themselves (v. 29). According to 11QPs^a 2 (=Syr. Ps. 154) vv. 5-8, wisdom is given or made known to man that he may proclaim the glory or the multitude of the deeds of Yahweh (cf. Sir. 5:10).

In Jer. 9:11(12), the Deuteronomist asks for someone wise enough to act as an inspired interpreter of the catastrophe of Judah; cf. the question of the "wise" reader of the book of Hosea in Hos. 14:10(9) (and *chākhām* par. *yôdhēaʿ pēsher dābhār,* Eccl. 8:1). Finally, the mantic sage and apocalyptic visionary Daniel becomes a divinely inspired interpreter of scripture in Dnl. 9.

Jer. 8:8f. may represent a polemic against a nascent identification of the (written) commandment of Yahweh with the ethos of Wisdom: the priests boast that they are "wise" because they have "the law of Yahweh" (*tôrath yhvh;* cf. 18:18). Dt. 4:6 depicts Deuteronomy as a demonstration of Israel's *chokhmāh* in comparison to the nations. The identification is complete in Ezr. 7:25, which uses *chokhmāh* as a synonym for "law code," and in Ps. 19:8(7); 119:98, where the *ʿēdhûth* and *mitsvōth* of Yahweh "make wise" the simple and the devout psalmist, respectively.

In Sir. 24, *chokhmāh* is once again a soteriological figure, mythologized according to the prototype of Isis(?)[123] and identified with the law; she commends herself to the community of Israel. Having come forth from the mouth of God (v. 3), starting from her heavenly dwelling place (cf. 1 En. 42:1) where she is enthroned upon a pillar of cloud (cf. Ahikar 95 conj.), alone she makes the circuit of the firmament and the depths of the abyss, the sea and the earth (vv. 4-6). Thus she seeks a resting place on earth (v. 7), until she is firmly established in Zion (vv. 10f.). There she exercises dominion (v. 11b), spreading like rivers or plants (vv. 12-17,26f.,29) and giving of herself like sacramental food and drink (vv. 19-21; cf. Sir. 15:3; 11QPs^a 2:13). In Sir. 43:33 and Bar. 3:37, too, wisdom is limited to Israel with its devotion to the law. In Wisd. 7:28 the opposite image appears: God loves only *tón sophía synoikoúnta.*

3. *Hebrew Wisdom's Understanding of God.* Little that is uniquely Israelite is exhibited by the understanding of God inherent in earlier wisdom, before its identifica-

[123] Conzelmann, 228-231.

tion with torah-centered piety.[124] In the narrative of 1 K. 3:4–15, we may assume that we have a narrative embodying the idea implied in the phrase *chokmath ʾelōhîm beqirbô* (3:28); the motif of the divine nature of the king's wisdom is in the first instance probably just a reflex of the numinous impression made by the king as the exemplary sage. Neither do we sense much that is Yahwistic when the "wise" or "clever" woman of 2 S. 14:20 compares David's wisdom to the *chokhmath malʾakh hāʾelōhîm;* we are reminded rather that in Ugaritic, too, the wisdom designated by *ḥkm* is exemplified by the high god El.[125] In Prov. 30:3, if we follow the LXX in reading *(ve)ʾēl limmadh ʾôthî,* then El has "taught wisdom" to the speaker. The Joseph narrative stresses that the art of dream interpretation comes from *ʾelōhîm* (Gen. 40:8; 41:16, 25,28,38f., all usually assigned to E). But even in Isa. 28:26 the farmer is instructed not by Yahweh but by "his Elohim." And according to Ex. 31:3 (P), spoken by Yahweh, the skills of sacral craftsmanship necessary for building the tabernacle depend on inspiration by the *rûach ʾelōhîm* (but cf. 31:6; 36:1f.). Most striking is the way the earlier tale of Daniel as mantic sage (chaps. 4–5) describes the origin of his atavistic skills: from the mouths of pagans we hear that his enlightenment is due to "wisdom like the wisdom of the gods (*chokhmāh kechokhmath-ʾelāhîn,* 5:11), in fact to the "spirit of the (holy) gods" (*rûach ʾelāhîn* [*qaddîshîn*], 4:5f.[8f.], 15[18]; 5:11,14). The only reason the strictly monotheistic narrator does not correct these expressions is probably the ambiguity of the plural *ʾelāhîn.* Only chap. 2, which prepares for the role of Daniel as an apocalypticist, ascribes the revelation of the "mystery" to a saving inspiration of *ʾelāh shemaiyāʾ*, identified with the God of Israel (vv. 19,23; cf. 3 Esdr. 4:59f.).

There may also be echoes in the book of Job of the non-Yahwistic and mythological way of calling God the giver of wisdom. Someone like Eliphaz in Job 15:7f., who wants to disallow a pretentious claim to theological knowledge, can insinuate ironically that his opponent blasphemously got his *chokhmāh* at the divine council, as can truly be said only of the primal man, born before the hills. Job 11:5f., on the contrary, speak of "secrets of wisdom" (*taʿalumôth chokhmāh*) being communicated through the mouth of God. Job 4:12–21 is a grandiloquent description of how a wisdom doctrine comes by inspiration.

Prov. 20:12 nevertheless states that it is Yahweh who makes the hearing ear and the seeing eye. And in Isa. 11:2 the *rûach chokhmāh* of the Messiah is derived specifically from the *rûach yhvh.* According to Ps. 90:12, he whom Yahweh teaches to number his days will acquire a wise heart. We also find the ascription of wisdom to Yahweh in Jer. 9:11(12), in the parallelism between *hāʾîsh hechākhām* and *ʾasher dibber pî-yhvh ʾēlāv,* and in the petition of Ps. 51:8(6). In Prov. 2:6, this idea has hardened into a colorless dogma (cf. Sir. 1:1).

The unusual character of the notions of creation expressed with the aid of the root *ḥkm* also suggests that it would be wrong simply to include the other biblical myths of creation in the idea of God found in Wisdom. It is without parallel, for example, that according to Job 35:10f. the Creator instructs the beasts of the earth and the birds of

[124] Preuss.

[125] See I.1.

the air (*'lp* piel[?] par. *ḥkm* piel), but man even more, giving him songs in the night, as Elihu points out to Job. Insight into the order of nature that is hidden from man is the content of the *chokhmāh* given to the ibis and the *bînāh* given to the cock (Job 38:36). According to Eccl. 1:13; 7:23f.; 8:16f., the search for such order in the most comprehensive sense is the task of the human mind, without prospect of success. The inherent order of all reality as its "truth" is a *chokhmāh,* access to which, according to Job 28, the Creator has reserved to himself.[126] As the hypostasis of the "truth" inherent in the ordered world, in Prov. 8:22(-31) *chokhmāh* becomes the beginning of Yahweh's work, "the first of his acts of old" (cf. Sir. 24:3,9). Her form, obviously pictured as perfect in beauty, makes her the delight (*sha'ashû'îm,* v. 30) of God, beside whom she plays like a girl on the ground (v. 31a),[127] afterwards showing her own favor (*sha'ashû'ai*) to the sons of men (v. 31b). In Wisd. (8:3) 9:4, *sophía* becomes the *páredos* of God.

In Sir. 1:9, by contrast, the notion is divested of this extremely mythologized form: the Lord pours out wisdom, his creation, upon all his works, albeit with the limitation put by v. 10 *katá tḗn dósin autoú,* "he supplied her to those who love him."

But in the context of creation, *chokhmāh* is more than just God's gift and (unattainable) goal: according to Prov. 3:19f., Yahweh himself founded the earth *bechokhmāh,* which, like *tebhûnāh* and *da'ath* in the parallel stichs, probably refers in the first instance merely to skill that is similar to expert craftsmanship (cf. *bithbhûnāthô* par. *bekhōchô,* Job 26:12). In the similar aretalogy Jer. 10:12 (=51:15), *bechokhmāthô* appears in parallelism with *bekhōchô,* "by his power" (cf. the same nouns used adverbially with *'āśāh* to describe hubris in Isa. 10:13). Ps. 104:24 also describes Yahweh's creation as a "making" *bechokhmāh,* while according to Job 38:37 man must confront the question of whether he can number the clouds *bechokmāh.*

In Wisd. 7:12,22; 8:1, the Wisdom with which God created the world has become a demiurge through hypostatization: here she is called *genétis* (7:12) and *hē pántōn technítis* (7:22), terms that are then developed mythologically in the hymn that follows (vv. 22ff.). A comparable phenomenon appears in Aboth iii.14, where the torah is the instrument through which the world was created.

The hypostatization of "wisdom" seems to be explainable through the figurative use of statements that were originally neither mythic or mythological, having quite diverse functions in their original contexts. It belongs to the stage of deliberate myth*olog*ical reflection,[128] not to the virulent domain of naive myth and its effects. Mythological hypostatization thus merely gives concrete form to earlier linguistic hypostatization, which treated the abstract term *chokhmāh* as an independent factor. Its realm is poetic personification; its content derives from the elaboration of a poetic mythologema.[129] It may well be asked, therefore, whether a motive of aesthetic enjoyment does not also lie behind the intellectual need to systematize that sought to embody

---

[126]See VI.2.
[127]On the iconography of *meśacheqeth,* cf. Keel.
[128]Conzelmann, 227, 234.
[129]Cf. Lang, 170f.

in a single figure the profit brought by wisdom (see V.1), her demanding authority (see V.2), and the "truth" of an ordered world and intermediary in creation.

It is also possible that personified *chokhmāh* may have as her prototype or antitype earlier mythic or mythological figures, such as hypostatized Maat,[130] or actual goddesses such as Isis[131] or a Semitic goddess of love,[132] or, less probably, the Iranian Spenta Ar(a)maiti[133] or the primal man.[134] It must be noted, however, that the transmutation of speculative concepts into "deities of the moment"[135] has always been widespread,[136] especially in the syncretistic world of Hellenism.[137]

Apart from polemic statements like Isa. 31:2 and Job 9:4, the predicate "wise" as applied to God is both rare and late. Hymnic passages such as Jer. 10:6f.; Job 12:13 (both probably secondary[138]) and Dnl. 2:20b praise the *chokhmāh* and *g^ebhûrāh* of God. Dnl. 2:22 bases the ascription on the inspiration Daniel has just received, through which God has shown himself to be the revealer of "deep and mysterious things," in this case an apocalyptic secret.

VI. Criticism of Wisdom.

1. *Prophetic*. The first criticism of Wisdom—from a perspective external to its axioms—comes from the prophets. It is true that Isa. 28:23-29 draw an analogy between the "counsel" of Yahweh he is proclaiming, which will surely come to pass, and the expertise of the farmer taught by his God. But arrogant court wisdom is clearly already the object of attack in 5:21, which proclaims disaster for the *ch^akhāmîm b^e'ênêhem* (cf. 3:2f.; 10:12f.). Above all, the reference to Yahweh's wisdom in 31:2 treats with irony the claim to wisdom of the Jerusalem leadership: the tactical shrewdness of those "who go down to Egypt for help" and "rely on horses" instead of on Yahweh (v. 1) overlooks the difference between "man" and "deity," between "flesh" and "spirit" (v. 3). "Deity" and "spirit" are manifested in the intervention of Yahweh's outstretched hand (v. 3b), for which Wisdom has no categories. According to 29:14, the wisdom of the wise will perish when Yahweh acts; v. 13 accuses "this people" of having reduced fear of Yahweh to a rote precept.

In Jer. 8:8f., it is the priests whose claim to possess wisdom is rejected: their lying pens have turned the torah, to which they appeal, into a lie. The vitality of God's instructions seems called into question by written codification and pedantic manipulation. Thus those who claim to be wise will be destroyed by Yahweh's prophetic

---

130 Donner; Kayatz, 97ff.

131 Knox; Conzelmann on Sir. 24.

132 Albright, Boström.

133 W. Bousset and H. Gressmann, *Die Religion des Judentums im späthellenistischen Zeitalter. HNT,* 21 (³1926, repr. 1966), 520; cf. R. Reitzenstein, *Das mandäische Buch des Herrn der Grösse und die Evangelienüberlieferung. SHAW,* 10/12 (1919), 46ff.

134 G. Fohrer, *TDNT,* VII, 491.

135 Lang.

136 Ringgren.

137 R. Kittel, *Geschichte des Volkes Israel,* III/2 (1929), 731f.; Hengel.

138 W. Rudolph, *HAT,* 12 (³1968), 72f.; G. Fohrer, *KAT,* XVI (1963), 245f.

"word," whose proclamation of disaster is closer to casuistic (priestly) "instruction" than to the first attempts to establish a book religion.

2. *Skeptical.* Of course Wisdom itself can recognize the limits of the intellectual horizon bounded by its axioms. The condemnation of the *chᵃkhāmîm beʿênêhem* in Isa. 5:21 has its parallel in Prov. 26:12.[139] More religiously motivated is the statement that no *chokhmāh, tᵉbhûnāh,* or *ʿētsāh* can prevail against Yahweh, who alone gives victory on the day of battle, however prepared the horses (21:30f.). Eccl. 7:16 warns against the self-destructive attempt to carry out the maxims of wisdom, and Sir. 10:26 cautions against the hypocritical pretense of being motivated by wisdom. "Wisdom will die with you," retorts Job sarcastically to his friends (Job 12:2), and Elihu rejects the position that wisdom should always be sought uncritically among the old (32:9).[140] According to Job 28, access to "truth," which seems to be thought of here almost like a numinous material object, is barred not only to *homo faber* (vv. 1-13), but to the primeval deep (v. 14), the Underworld, and death (v. 22); God alone knows the place where it is found and the way to it (vv. 23,27); he alone, as lord of creation, makes use of it (vv. 25f.).

Ecclesiastes, moreover, deplores the arbitrary way in which God bestows *chokhmāh vᵉdaʿath* and the joy they bring only upon those who please him (2:26). He himself, according to 1:13, vainly "applied his mind to seek and to search out wisdom [prepositional object!] concerning all that is done under heaven."[141] This skeptical questioning of whether following the dictates of wisdom has any meaning in view of the equality of men's fates, which contradicts what is said of the profit brought by wisdom, leads in 2:14-17 to a profound diastasis separating the world from the self,[142] and thus to the brink of libertine conclusions. According to 7:23f., the test by wisdom merely makes it clear how "far off" and unfathomably "deep" is everything that takes place (*mahshshehāyāh*), whose order should demonstrate its truth. According to 8:17a, moreover, it is the sight of "all the work of God" that convinces man that he "cannot find out the work that is done under the sun": the intertwining of natural events with divine activity prevents man from carrying out a task imposed on him by God. Thus the divine author of the human condition enters into self-contradiction. When knowledge fails, the *ultima ratio* of such a theonomic skepticism is hedonism (2:24-26; 3:12; 5:17[18]; 8:15; 9:7-9; 11:9f.), but at the same time a fear of God consisting solely in an acceptance of the existential condition of man (3:14; 5:6[7]; 7:18), without rebellion and without expectation. Only in 12:1 does this fear of God afford a kind of affirmation of the world in the manner of Gen. 1.

Müller

---

[139]See IV.2.a.

[140]See III.1.

[141] For the translation, see F. Ellermeier, *Qohelet,* I/1 (1967), 178.

[142]H. Gese, "Die Krisis der Weisheit bei Koheleth," *Les sagesses du Proche-Orient ancien,* Colloquede Strasbourg 17-19 Mai, 1962 (Paris, 1963), 139-151 = his *Vom Sinai zum Zion. BEvTh,* 64 (1974), 168-179.

חָלָב *chālābh;* גְּבִינָה *g^e^bhînāh;* חֶמְאָה *chem'āh*

Contents: I. "Milk" in the Semitic Languages. II. Usage: 1. Secular; 2. "The Kid in its Mother's Milk." III. Metaphorical and Symbolic Meaning. IV. Foods from Milk: 1. Cheese; 2. *chem'āh.*

I. "Milk" in the Semitic Languages. The root *ḥlb* (to be distinguished from the root from which → חלב *chēlebh,* "fat," derives) is attested in all the West Semitic languages; it is the most comprehensive term for milk. It appears in Ugaritic and possibly also in Phoenician. The word *ḥlb* appearing twice in line 14 of the Punic) sacrificial tariff from Marseilles[1] means "milk" in one case and "fat" in the other, if we do not in fact have a case of dittography here. The other Punic occurrences of *ḥlb* are ambiguous. The term appears in all dialects of Aramaic as *chalbā'*. It also appears in Arabic (*ḥalab*) and in modern South Arabic (Soq. *ḥelob*). The Arabic form *ḥalīb,* which has become established in the dialects, and Ge'ez *ḥalīb* are probably secondary constructions, based on the schema of the passive noun, from the denominative verb *ḥlb,* "milk," "give milk," attested in Arabic, Aramaic, and Mishnaic Hebrew. Of the Akkadian dialects, only Neo-Assyrian has the rare verb *ḫalāb/pu,* "milk," and the equally rare substantive *ḫilpu,* "milk."[2] Here we probably have a borrowing from West Semitic: the Akkadian word for milk remained *šizbu*. The other languages of the Hamito-Semitic family use other terms.

The only derivative attested in Biblical Hebrew is the name of a plant used in making sacral incense, *chelb^e^nāh,* translated "galbanum" in Ex. 30:34. The name probably derives from its milky sap; in Akkadian it is likewise called *ḫilabānu* or *šizbānu*.

The biblical vocabulary for milk seems to lack precision in comparison to Arabic. In particular, no distinction seems to have been made between fresh milk and curdled milk (Arab. *ḥalīb/laban*).

II. Usage.

1. *Secular.* To determine the way the ancient Israelites used milk, we must draw on the scanty literary evidence in the usage of the Arabs, both settled and nomadic.[3] We

---

chālābh. G. Barrois, *Manuel d'archéologie biblique,* I (Paris, 1939), 336; H. Beinart, "חָלָב חָלָב וּמוֹצְרָיו," *EMiqr,* III (1958), 135–39; I. Benzinger, *Hebräische Archäologie* (³1927), 66–68; A. van den Born, "Milch," *BL*², 1154; *idem,* "Milch und Honig," *BL*², 1154f.; A. Dalman, *AuS,* VI (1939), 288-313; F. C. Fensham, "An Ancient Tradition of the Fertility of Palestine," *PEQ,* 98 (1966), 166f.; H. Gross, *Die Idee des ewigen und allgemeinen Weltfriedens im alten Orient und im AT. TrThSt,* 7 (1956, ²1967), 71-78: "Land, da Milch und Honig fliesst"; I. Guidi, "Une terre coulant du lait avec du miel," *RB,* 12 (1903), 241-44; S. Krauss, *Talmudische Archäologie* (1910-1912, repr. ²1966), II, 134-36; H. Lesêtre, "Lait," *DB,* IV (1908), 37-39; E. Power, "Terra lac et mel manans," *VD,* 2 (1922), 52-58.

[1] *KAI,* 69.
[2] *CAD,* VI, 33, 36, 187.
[3] Cf. Dalman.

know that they prefer the milk of sheep and goats to that of cows.[4] According to Dt. 32:14, milk is primarily the product of sheep and goats (*tsō'n*). Goat's milk and sheep's wool are the major source of income for the herdsman addressed in Prov. 27:26f. Since the patriarchs are depicted living as herdsmen, it is no surprise to find Abraham preparing a meal of milk and meat (Gen. 18:8). The obvious transgression of Jewish dietary laws (*kashrûth*) illustrated by this episode bothered the rabbis. It was therefore proposed that the angels ate the dairy products and the meat separately, or that they did not really eat,[5] or else it was recognized that they committed a sin at which God took offense.[6]

Indispensable as milk is as a source of nutrition for herdsmen, it is no less esteemed by those living in settled towns, and the value ascribed to it by the Bible should not be called a "remnant of nomadism." The farmers of Palestine also raised animals that gave milk. Thus in Isa. 55:1 milk can be counted among the basic foods, along with water, grain, and wine. Sir. 39:26 lists it among the products that are absolutely necessary for human life. There is nothing to indicate more precisely whether milk was valued so because it was the raw material of dairy products or because it was used directly as a beverage. Only Jgs. 4:19 states that milk is considered a beverage, even more refreshing than water. In this verse, *chālābh* undoubtedly means not fresh milk but the slightly fermented and somewhat curdled milk that is a good thirst-quencher, called *laban* by the Arabs.

Milk played a certain role in the cults of ancient Egypt (being the typical sacrifice to the gods and the dead), of the Greeks (mixed with honey and water to form *nēphalía*), and in Mesopotamia.[7] The Phoenicians in Carthage seem to have made milk-offerings.[8] According to Jaussen,[9] the first milk is never drunk without a preceding sacrifice of firstfruits.

In Israel, there are no milk-offerings; neither tithes nor firstfruits are taken from it. In Josephus' account of the sacrifice of Abel,[10] he does state that Abel offered to God milk and the firstlings of his flock, but he is interpreting *chēlebh* here as though it were *chālābh,* thus diverging both from the LXX and from the Hebrew text of Gen. 4:4. In order to explain this exclusion of milk from cultic life, which seems to limit it to a purely secular foodstuff, Lagrange[11] and Blome[12] point out that milk, like honey, is subject to fermentation. Another possible reason is that milk is a food that man acquires without contributing his own labor, in contrast to such products as grain, oil, and wine, which are presented as offerings. On the other hand, it is also possible that the offering of the firstlings of the flocks makes superfluous an additional offering of what the flock produces.

---

[4]Cf. also A. Jaussen, *Coutumes des Arabes au pays de Moab* (Paris, 1908, repr. 1948), 67.

[5]*Gen.r.* 48:14.

[6]*PesiqR* 25:3.

[7]Cf. F. Blome, *Die Opfermaterie in Babylonien und Israel. SSAOI,* 4 (Rome, 1934), §§166, 286.

[8]*KAI*, 69, 14.

[9]P. 364.

[10]*Ant.* i.2.1.

[11]M. J. Lagrange, *Études sur les religions sémitiques. ÉtB* (Paris, ²1905), 203.

[12]*Opfermaterie,* § 289.

2. *"The Kid in its Mother's Milk."* The only ritual regulation referring to milk is negative. It is Ex. 23:19, a section of the Covenant Code, which is repeated in the Yahwistic law (Ex. 34:26) and the Deuteronomic law (Dt. 14:21): "You shall not boil a kid in its mother's milk." This regulation serves as the scriptural justification for a characteristic feature of Jewish life, the prohibition against eating meat and dairy products at the same time;[13] the targumim therefore substitute "meat" for "a kid" and eliminate "its mother's." This requirement, whose strangeness was recognized by rabbinic tradition,[14] has been variously explained.

Since time immemorial the forbidden action has been seen as an act of cruelty.[15] Robertson Smith[16] thought that milk, like blood, was considered a "vital fluid," and that therefore cooking meat in milk is analogous to "eating with blood." Frazer[17] seeks the origin of the prohibition in the magical mentality and in the nomadic past of Israel; some African herdsmen, for example, prohibit cooking with milk since they believe that doing so spoils the milk of their cows or causes them to dry up. More recently, this explanation has been proposed again in Beer's commentary.[18] It runs afoul of the fact that the herdsmen closer to Israel made a practice of cooking meat in milk. Ibn Ezra even sees in it a custom of the "Ishmaelites," and it has been observed by various travellers.[19] One popular theory has been that this practice represents a deliberate reaction against a pagan custom; according to a Karaite commentary cited by Borchart,[20] the Bible wanted to illustrate fertility magic. The discoveries at Ugarit have confirmed this hypothesis, as is generally conceded today. In fact one text has been read as: "Boil a kid in the milk, a lamb in the butter."[21] It must be noted, however, that neither the text nor the translation of this liturgical rubric is certain: *gd,* which immediately calls to mind Heb. *g^edhî,* "kid," is a dubious reading and is not otherwise attested at Ugarit, where *ll3* is the word for "kid." The parallel term *'nnḫ* more likely refers to a plant (cf. Akk. *ananiḫu,* "mint") than an animal. Likewise *gd,* if this reading is correct, would be explained better by Heb. *gadh,* "coriander." For other interpretations, see → גדי *g^edhî* II.5. The interpretation of Ex. 23:19 as a rejection of a religious or secular practice of Israel's neighbors nevertheless is still the most likely explanation.

III. Metaphorical and Symbolic Meaning. The lack of significance attached to milk in the religious practice of Israel is to be sought in its relatively meager symbolic content. The Bible comes nowhere near using the full range of milk's metaphorical potential.

It is first of all a symbol of whiteness, a color of beauty and splendor, especially

[13] Mishnah *Ḥullin* viii.14.
[14] *Pesaḥim* 44b.
[15] Philo *De virtutibus* xxvi.142–44; Ibn Ezra.
[16] W. Robertson Smith, *Lectures on the Religion of the Semites* (²1894), 221.
[17] Cf. T. Gaster, *Myth, Legend, and Custom in the OT* (1969), 250–262.
[18] G. Beer, *HAT,* 3 (1939), *in loc.*
[19] A. Musil, *Arabia Petraea,* III (Vienna, 1908), 149; Jaussen, *Coutumes,* 65.
[20] S. Borchart, *Hierozoicon,* 731.
[21] *CTA,* 23 [SS], 14.

when contrasted with red or black.[22] Lam. 4:7 describes the beauty of the "youths" (*n*ᵉ*ʿāreyhā*) of Jerusalem by means of the hyperbole "much whiter than milk," expressed through the reinforcement "snow" and the contrast with red (cf. Cant. 5:10). The portrait of "Shiloh" in Gen. 49:12, which comes very close to the lyric descriptions of the Song of Songs, contrasts the whiteness of teeth ("much whiter than milk") with the dark glow of eyes. The imagery of Cant. 5:12 is hard to understand, but it can probably be traced back to the same symbolism, contrasting black eyes (like doves) with whiteness of face ("bathed in milk"). In the Song of Songs, milk is a symbol of charm. In combination with aromatics, with wine and honey, it represents the pleasures of love (Cant. 5:1; with honey alone, 4:11). It should be noted that milk is not called "sweet" (*māthôq*) here, suggesting that in this passage, too, *chālābh* can have the sense of Arab. *laban*.

Finally, milk is a symbol of wealth. To describe the wealth of the wicked, Job appears to use the image of a superabundance of milk (Job 21:24a). The obscure hapax legomenon *ʿaṭîn* makes the first half of the verse hard to understand. It is often taken to mean "his intestines [or 'loins'; RSV: 'body'] are full of fat," reading *chēlebh* for *chālābh*. The emendation would be unnecessary if we knew the meaning of *ʿaṭîn*. The translation "intestines" (LXX, Vulg.) comes from an etymology that associates *ʿaṭîn* with *ʿāṭāh*, "hide." The translation "loins" attempts to explain *ʿaṭîn* by means of Aram. *ʿaṭmā*, "thigh," "rib." Rashi conjectured that the rare word might refer to a kind of jar. In this obscure passage, milk may symbolize individual wealth.

Much more frequently it is used as an image of collective wealth. The natural fertility of Palestine is suggested by the cliché "a land flowing with milk and honey" (Ex. 3:8,17; 13:5; 33:3; Lev. 20:24; Nu. 13:27; 14:8; 16:13f.; Dt. 6:3; 11:9; 26:9, 15; 27:3; 31:20; Josh. 5:6; Jer. 11:5; 32:22; Ezk. 20:6,15; Sir. 46:8), an expression that does not require any "mythological" interpretation.[23] In the eschatological context of Joel 4:18 (Eng. 3:18), we find a variant that associates milk with *ʿāsîs*, "sweet (unfermented) wine," rather than honey. In a satirical context, Ezekiel uses milk and "fruit" to symbolize the possessions of the Ammonites, which will be left for plunder (Ezk. 25:4). In a similar vein, the "milk of nations" in Isa. 60:16 refers to the riches of the world, which a restored and exalted Israel will take into its possession.

It is striking that the Bible has so little to say about milk as the food of sucklings. The Israelites appear not to have associated the symbolism of "earliness" with milk, as late antiquity did.[24] The image of the king nursed by goddesses is familiar from Egypt[25] and Ugarit.[26] This motif necessarily remained alien to Israelite religion, since it has no female deity. We may note, however, that the archetype of the mother goddess is applied to Jerusalem in Isa. 66:5-13: the city is described "like a mother" (cf. Ps. 87),

---

[22]For a discussion of this motif, see R. Mach, *Der Zaddik in Talmud und Midrasch* (Leiden, 1957), 65-74.

[23]→ דבשׁ *d*ᵉ*bhash*.

[24]Cf. H. Schlier, "γάλα," TDNT, I, 645-47.

[25]Cf. J. Leclant, "Le rôle du lait et de l'allaitement d'après les textes des Pyramides," *JNES*, 10 (1951), 123-27.

[26]*CTA*, 15 [III K], II, 26f.; cf. also W. A. Ward, "La déesse nourricière d'Ugarit," *Syr*, 46 (1969), 225-239.

but is also represented as a nurse to her inhabitants (v. 11). Yahweh himself occasionally takes on the characteristics of a mother; in Dt. 32:18, for example, he is called the God "who gave you birth" (*m^echōlēl*); therefore the same poem can use the verb *hênîq*, "suckle," to describe the riches of the earth as the gracious gift of God (v. 13).

IV. Foods from Milk.

1. *Cheese*. The actual word for cheese, *g^ebhînāh*, corresponding to Aram. *gûbhnîn*, Arab. *ǧubn*, Ge'ez *gĕbnat*, Akk. *gubnatu* (Aramaic loanword), occurs only in Job 10:10, where the formation of the human embryo is explained after the analogy of the production of cheese: the human being is like milk (an image of sperm?) that God curdles into cheese. The verb *qp'*, which means "turn to ice" in Zec. 14:6, can also refer to curdling. It is generally agreed that the *ch^aritsê hechālābh*, literally "slices of milk," sent to Saul by Jesse (1 S. 17:18) are to be understood as cheeses. The phrase recalls Ethiop. *ḫĕbĕsta ḥalîb*, "milk-loaves," corresponding to Lat. *caseum* in Jub. 29:15. It is highly unlikely, however, that *sh^ephôth bāqār*, mentioned in 2 S. 17:29 along with other provisions, refer to dairy products, as the Aramaic versions and the rabbinic commentaries show (while Theodotion and Jerome think calves are involved). The term *sh^ephôth* remains a mystery.

2. *chem'āh*. It is erroneous to confuse the products resulting when milk protein coagulates (sour milk, cottage cheese) with butter, the result of churning, which separates the fat particles and then combines them. The meaning of *chem'āh* has been debated, but the term cannot be ambiguous and refer to the results of two very different processes. The word *chem'āh* cannot refer in one place to coagulated milk and in another place to butter, but only to one and the same product. The etymology is unknown (it appears in Ugar. *ḫm't*, Akk. *ḫimētu*, Jewish Aram. *chem'^atā*, and Syr. *ḥewtā'*), but several pieces of evidence suggest the meaning "butter."

a. The Greek and Latin versions translate "butter"; Arab. *zubd*, "sweet butter," or *samn*, "butterfat," are glosses on *ḥewtā'* of the Peshitta. The *sh^eman* of the targumim corresponds to Arab. *samn*.

b. The identification of *chem'āh* with "cream," proposed by Rashi for Gen. 18:8, appears to be excluded by Prov. 30:33aα, the only biblical reference to the production of *chem'āh*. It is produced by a vigorous treatment of milk. The term *mîts* that designates this process corresponds to Akk. *mâṣu*, "churn";[27] the *myṣm* of the Ugaritic text *PRU*, II, 99 [265], 8 might be makers of butter.

c. The product *chem'āh* comes from cattle (*bāqār*), *chālābh* from sheep and goats (Dt. 32:14). It is therefore not a characteristic product of a nomadic economy but of peasant life. The modern fellahin also prefer to use their milk for making butter.

---

[27] *AHw*, II, 621.

d. *chem'āh* is more valuable than milk, which is not identical with curdled milk. Jgs. 5:25, a poetic elaboration of 4:19, uses the series water-milk-*chem'āh*.

e. Ps. 55:22(21) uses *chem'āh* as an example of smooth unctuousness, in the same sense as oil. This metaphorical usage excludes the possibility of identifying *chem'āh* with curdled milk.

Because sweet butter is difficult to keep, it is quite likely that *chem'āh* actually means refined butterfat, like Arab. *samn,* Indic *ghee,* and the *butyrum* whose production is described by Pliny.[28] It is a costly foodstuff, because its manufacture requires large quantities of milk (cf. Isa. 7:22). Thus *chem'āh,* like milk, is a symbol of wealth, but in the context of a more advanced civilization whose characteristics are more agricultural than nomadic. Job 20:17 and 29:6 point to enormous prosperity when they associate *chem'āh* with oil, the typical product of agriculture. Even though the former text still speaks of honey, this may be because the author had in mind a food worthy of the gods, like *dišpu ŭ ḫimētu* in Mesopotamia and *chem'āh* and honey (→ דבש *d^e bhash*) for Immanuel (Isa. 7:15).

Caquot

[28]*Hist. nat.* xxviii.133-34.

חֵלֶב *chēlebh*

Contents: I. Etymology, Occurrences. II. Sacrificial Fat: 1. Yahweh's Portion; 2. Ritual; 3. Significance; 4. "Food for Yahweh"; 5. Metaphorical Meaning. III. The Best. IV. Human.

I. Etymology, Occurrences. The root *ḥlb* appears originally to have been a technical term for the diaphragm or midriff, like Arab. *ḫilb* and Syr. *ḥelbā'*.[1] It appears

chēlebh. F. Blome, *Die Opfermaterie in Babylonien und Israel. SSAOI,* 4 (Rome, 1934); K. Elliger, *Leviticus. HAT,* 4 (1966); J. Heller, "Die Symbolik des Fettes im AT," *VT,* 20 (1970), 106-108; R. Rendtorff, *Studien zur Geschichte des Opfers im Alten Israel. WMANT,* 24 (1967); H. H. Rowley, *Worship in Ancient Israel* (1967); R. Schmid, *Das Bundesopfer in Israel. StANT,* 9 (1964); W. R. Smith, *Lectures on the Religion of the Semites* ([3]1927, repr. 1969), 379-385; N. H. Snaith, "Sacrifices in the OT," *VT,* 7 (1957), 308-317; R. de Vaux, *AncIsr,* 271-517; *idem, Studies in OT Sacrifice* (trans. 1964); A. Wendel, *Das Opfer in der altisraelitischen Religion* (1927).

[1]Smith, 379, n. 4; C. R. North, "The Religious Aspects of Hebrew Kingship," *ZAW,* 50 (1932), 15.

in Punic with the meaning "fat."[2] The suggested association of Ugar. *ḫlb,* "fat covering the skin and intestines,"[3] with Heb. *chēlebh* does not merit support.[4]

Apart from the OT, the word may appear in the sacrificial tariff from Marseilles, if dittography is not involved.[5] The Punic occurrences nevertheless are ambiguous, since an offering of milk is also possible.[6] Hittite texts appear to speak of "fat and bread as the food of the gods."[7] In Mesopotamia, *ḫimṣu* can be offered, a term that is translated "loins,"[8] but also "fatty tissue,"[9] so that one might think in terms of the kidneys with their surrounding fat.[10] This interpretation, however, is probably inspired by the OT ritual. The closest analogy to the latter is the form of sacrifice known from ancient Greece, in which a piece of flesh wrapped in kidney fat could be offered.[11]

There are 90 occurrences of *chēlebh* in the OT, most of them in the description of sacrificial offerings in Leviticus and Numbers (54). There are 6 occurrences in the Psalms and 9 in the prophetic books; the rest are scattered throughout the OT.

II. Sacrificial Fat.

1. *Yahweh's Portion.* The OT reveals a process of development during which fat became increasingly the property of Yahweh, so that finally it was completely excluded from human consumption. In the early period, there was no hesitation about using the fat for food; it is in fact a sign of Yahweh's favor that he gives Israel fat and marrow (Ps. 63:6 [Eng. v. 5]) and the fat tail of lambs (Dt. 32:14) to eat. The psalmist likens the "refreshing power of God's presence" to feasting on marrow and fat (Ps. 63:6[5]), and the fat tail of sheep seems at one time (as it still is among the Arabs) to have been a special delicacy, a portion of honor reserved for an important personality (1 S. 9:24 conj., reading *vᵉhā'alyāh* for *vᵉheʿāleyhā*[12]).

Then, in the sacrificial instructions primarily found in the P tradition *chēlebh* refers to the sacrificial fat, i.e., the portion of the sacrificial animal to be burned. The formularies further reveal that it was not simply "all the fat" that was offered, but precisely defined pieces: "the fat covering the entrails and all the fat that is on the entrails, and the two kidneys with the fat that is on them at the loins, and the appendage of the liver" (Lev. 3:3f.,9f.,14f.; 4:8f.; 7:3f.; described differently: 8:16,25; 9:10,19; Ex. 29:13,22). The following, therefore, are to be offered: (1) the fat covering the

---

2 *DISO,* 88; cf. *KAI,* 69.

3 *WUS,* No. 1029.

4 Cf. *UM,* 708; *UT,* No. 963; *PRU,* II, 1, 4.

5 *KAI,* 69, 14.

6 Cf. *KAI,* 74, 10; *CIS,* I/III, 3916, 1.

7 M. Witzel, *Hethitische Keilschrift-urkunden* (1924), 65, vo. III, 7.

8 *BuA,* II, 87.

9 *AHw,* I, 346; *CAD,* VI, 192.

10 Blome, 165.

11 L. Rost, "Erwägungen zum israelitischen Brandopfer," *Von Ugarit nach Qumran. Festschrift O. Eissfeldt. BZAW,* 77 (²1961), 180 = his *Das kleine Credo und andere Studien zum AT* (1965), 115; cf. R. K. Yerkes, *Sacrifice in Greek and Roman Religions and Early Judaism* (1952), 97-112; and Schmid, 73f.

12 Cf. Schmid, 38; a different interpretation is given by H. J. Stoebe, *KAT,* VIII/1 (1973), 196.

entrails; (b) the fat on the individual entrail; (c) the fat on the kidneys; (d) the kidneys; (e) the appendage of the liver.[13] In other words: "the greater omentum, the mesentery, and the fat in which the kidneys are embedded,"[14] as well as the visceral fat. The sheep is discussed separately in the sacrificial regulations, because in its case the fat tail is also to be offered (Ex. 29:22; Lev. 3:9; etc.).

At first, then, only specific pieces of fat are to be burned as Yahweh's portion—although what is named is the major portion of the fat that comes to light when an animal is butchered. Later, however, a different principle is established: "All fat is Yahweh's" (Lev. 3:16); it is made a "perpetual statute" that neither fat nor blood shall be eaten (v. 17). Thus the specialized sacrificial regulations are dropped and general dietary laws are formulated; these applied in Lev. 7:22-25 to the case when a sacrificial animal dies or is torn by beasts. Its fat may then be utilized for commercial purposes, but not eaten (vv. 23f.); whoever eats the fat of an animal suitable for sacrifice "shall be cut off from his people" (v. 25).

Elliger raises the question of why Lev. 7:22ff. deal with the fat of animals that die a natural death or are killed by other animals, but not with the nonreligious slaughtering of animals.[15] Since we must assume on the basis of the words "in any of your dwellings" (v. 26) that nonreligious slaughtering was practised (Dt. 12:20-22), Elliger argues that we can only conjecture that the treatment of meat slaughtered in this way was still unclear and is therefore not discussed. This conjecture is contradicted, however, by the observation that apparently only the use of animals dying a natural death or killed by other animals created a problem, which was solved by reference to the fundamental prohibition against eating fat. In other words, nonreligious slaughtering was probably still unknown or totally rejected when the regulation in question came into being, so that the nucleus of Lev. 7:22-25 is earlier than Dt. 12:20-22. Lev. 7:26f. with their absolute prohibition against eating blood, even of animals not suitable for sacrifice, cannot prove anything in this context: these verses appear to be a later addition, especially since they do not deal with a concrete case but rather attempt to establish a general dietary law—now also applicable to animals slaughtered nonreligiously—to be observed in every dwelling, including the Diaspora.[16]

When an animal was sacrificed, the blood and fat were considered Yahweh's portion and were thus withdrawn from human use. During the course of history this practice evolved into a dietary law prohibiting the eating of blood and fat long after the sacrificial system in which this regulation originated had lost its meaning (cf. Lev. 3:17, where the prohibition is extended not only to "all your dwelling places" but to "all your generations").

The absolute prohibition against eating fat stands at the end of a long development. P still betrays the fact that only a precisely defined portion of the fat was to be given to Yahweh, while in the early period fat was freely praised as a special delicacy for human consumption.

---

[13]Elliger, 52.

[14]J. Preuss, *Biblisch-talmudische Medizin* (1911, repr. 1971), 592.

[15]P. 101.

[16]Cf. P. Grelot, "La dernière étape de la rédaction sacerdotale," *VT*, 6 (1956), 179; Elliger, 53.

2. *Ritual.* The OT provides almost no details of the fat ritual reserved to the priests, while slaughtering and butchering could be performed by laymen (cf. Lev. 3:2,8,13, etc.). It would be reasonable to suppose that the fat was burned at the beginning of the sacrificial ritual, so that Yahweh would received his portion at once, before the participants devoured their allotted pieces. But 1 S. 2:15f. seem to presuppose that at the sacrifice at Shiloh the meat was prepared first but not eaten until after the burning of the fat,[17] so that the offering of Yahweh's portion represented a climax in the course of the sacrificial ritual. But it is difficult to reconstruct the original ritual from this text, since three different charges are levelled simultaneously against the sons of Eli: (a) they took more than their portion (vv. 13f.); (b) they demanded raw meat to roast (v. 15); and (c) they asked for their portion before the fat had gone up in smoke (vv. 15f.).[18] We may therefore suppose that only a relatively late period felt that the transgression of Eli's sons consisted in their eating the meat before the fat was burned, thus wrongly taking Yahweh's portion. This interpretation at least accounts for the request, "Let them burn the fat first, and then take" (v. 16). Thus even here we find the beginnings of a development that later leads to the principle: "all fat belongs to Yahweh."

On the other hand, the burning of the fat seems to constitute the conclusion of the sacrificial feast when it is required that none of the fat remain until morning (Ex. 23:18), in other words, that the fat be offered on the day of the festival itself[19]—if the text does not in fact presuppose that the fat, too, is eaten, and prohibit merely the keeping of leftover fat (cf. Lev. 7:15-18).

3. *Significance.* It is hardly possible to determine why the fat became the material of the sacrifice. Many authors therefore do not even venture an answer. God receives the fat "because it is the fat,"[20] or fat and blood "must not be eaten by man because they are too sacred."[21] Heller, however, conjectures that eating of fat was prohibited because it was a way of trying to acquire strength and power by magical means.[22] The explanation can account for the prohibition, but does not make it sufficiently clear why fat became the material of the sacrifice. Neither is it possible to maintain the hypothesis on which this theory rests, namely, that the "prohibition against eating fat is observed throughout the entire OT."[23] Any attempt to answer the question must rather take into account the changing interpretation of the sacrifice of fat in the course of history. The P texts show that originally the fat was not treated separately; together with the kidneys, which are also considered especially valuable in Babylonian sacrifices,[24] it constitutes the actual material to be burned, "and the kidneys, so to speak, represent concretely

---

[17]Rendtorff, 147; but cf. L. Moraldi, *Espiazione sacrificale e riti espiatori nell'ambiente biblico e nell'AT. AnBibl,* 5 (1956), 131.

[18]Stoebe, *KAT,* VIII/1, 112.

[19]M. Noth, *Leviticus. OTL* (trans. 1965, ^{2}1977), 172.

[20]Snaith, 312.

[21]Rowley, 124; cf. de Vaux, *Studies,* 42.

[22]P. 107.

[23]P. 108.

[24]Schmid, 53.

the point of reference relative to which the locations of the fat are described."[25] Since in antiquity the kidneys were erroneously associated with the reproductive organs, they and the fat surrounding them—the only burnable portion of the animal, especially suited to "go up in smoke"—were considered the "seat of life" (cf. Ps. 139:13)[26] and were probably therefore offered in sacrifice.[27] The OT, it is true, deviates from this idea: although even in the late formularies the sacrificial regulations retain the important traditional sacrificial portions,[28] even referring expressly to the familiar procedure when detailing a ritual (Lev. 4:19f.,26,31,35, etc.), they dissolve the organic connection between the fat and the kidneys (and thus the sex organs), making it, like the blood, the independent vehicle of life.[29] It is probably in the course of this process that the fat tail was included in the sacrificial portions. Apart from the regulations governing sacrifice, there is no mention of fat as the vehicle of life;[30] neither does it represent the seat of "the soul, the disposition, [or] life."[31]

When the OT speaks of sacrifice apart from the specific description of the portions assigned to Yahweh, only blood and fat are mentioned; the same combination is attested in Babylonia as a summary expression for sacrificial material.[32] The portions to be burned are all included in the term *chēlebh* (Lev. 4:18ff.; 7:3,30f.,33; 9:18ff.; Nu. 18:17; etc.), even when the kidneys are explicitly mentioned. In fact, the word *chēlebh* can become a term for the sacrifice itself (Lev. 9:24; 1 S. 15:22; Isa. 1:11; cf. 1 K. 8:64). The sacrificial portions are frequently subsumed under the term *chēlebh* in passages that give evidence of being secondary (cf. Lev. 6:5[12]; 8:26; 9:20,24; 10:15; 16:25;[33] Gen. 4:4 also speaks of the firstlings and their fat to explain *minchāh*;[34] see also 2 Ch. 7:7; 29:35; 35:14). We may therefore assume that Israel came increasingly to understand sacrifice as the offering of (blood and) fat, while the kidneys, although remaining part of the traditional sacrificial material, ceased to have any special significance for the practice. Finally, *chēlebh* as a technical term for sacrifice became so prevalent that the meaning of sacrifice could be identified with the avoidance of eating fat (Lev. 3:16f.; 7:22ff.).

4. *"Food for Yahweh."* A further change goes hand in hand with this development. The fat and kidneys together were originally offered to the deity because in this way "life" was, as it were, returned to its origin. The isolation of the fat as the material to be sacrificed led increasingly to its being considered food for the deity.

---

25 Blome, 164.
26 H. W. Wolff, *Anthropology of the OT* (trans. 1975), 65f.
27 Wendel, 43; Rost, "Opfer," *BHHW,* II, 1350.
28 Rendtorff, 221.
29 W. O. E. Oesterley, *Sacrifices in Ancient Israel* (1937), 183; *AncIsr,* 418; Snaith, 312; *BL,* 477f.
30 Cf. IV below.
31 Cf. Schmid, 34.
32 D. J. McCarthy, "The Symbolism of Blood and Sacrifice," *JBL,* 88 (1969), 171.
33 Cf. also Elliger, 84, 119, 121, 128, 135, 206; Rendtorff, 221.
34 Also C. Westermann, *BK,* I/1 (1974), 404.

According to de Vaux, this development took place during the exile, under Babylonian influence (but cf. Isa. 1:11).[35] Thus Yahweh can say that he is full of the fat of fed beasts (Isa. 1:11), or accuse his people of having failed to satisfy him with the fat of his sacrifices (43:24), while other gods ate the fat of the sacrifices (Dt. 32:38). While 1 S. 15:22 states that hearkening to Yahweh is better than the fat of rams, a disciple of Ezekiel looks forward to the time when the Levitical priests will once again offer fat and blood (44:15), the food of Yahweh (44:7 conj.), while the prophet himself as much as prophesies the end of the cultic personnel.[36]

It can be seen, therefore, that in the course of time blood and fat became the essential material to be sacrificed, with the fat, as a special delicacy, being reserved to God as his food. Anthropomorphic misunderstandings were countered by the notion of the "burnt-offering"[37] and by interpreting the sacrifice as a "pleasing odor" to Yahweh (Lev. 4:31; 17:6; Nu. 18:17). It was also expressly denied that Yahweh is dependent on food (Ps. 50:12ff.). Finally, a law was formulated stating that all fat, even that of animals not suitable for sacrifice, was the property of Yahweh, thus causing it to lose its character as a food of God (Lev. 3:16f.).

5. *Metaphorical Meaning*. Sacrificial terminology can be used metaphorically of military exploits. The enemies of Israel, especially the Edomites, can be likened to sacrificial animals: Yahweh's sword drips with their blood and fat, which fill the whole land (Isa. 34:6f.). God can even give the blood and fat of the enemy to the animals as food (Ezk. 39:19). This image may also lie behind 2 S. 1:22, where we read that the sword of Saul never returned empty of the blood of the slain and the fat of the mighty (if the phrase does not mean the outstanding warriors;[38] but the juxtaposition of blood and fat is more suggestive of sacrificial terminology).

III. The Best. Since fat is considered a special delicacy (Ps. 63:6[5]), *chēlebh* can also be used metaphorically to mean simply the "best." Of all that they have received, the Levites are to give a sacred offering from the *chēlebh,* the best (the fat having already been burned; Nu. 18:29f.). The gifts to be offered to Yahweh can be termed the *chēlebh* of wine, grain, and oil. Just as Joseph cares for his brothers by giving them the *chēlebh* of the land to eat (Gen. 45:18), so Yahweh once fed Israel with the *chēlebh* of lambs, but also with the kidney fat of wheat (Dt. 32:14). Indeed, he cares for the faithful and fills them with the *chēlebh* of wheat, the "precious gift of the harvest" (Ps. 147:14; cf. 81:17[16]).

IV. Human. In the human context, *chēlebh* has negative overtones, for fatness goes hand in hand with arrogance (Dt. 32:15; Ps. 73:3ff.; Neh. 9:25; Jer. 5:28), a view that appears to invert the action/consequences nexus. The heart of the wicked is gross with fat (Ps. 17:10; 119:70; cf. Isa. 6:10), i.e., incapable of knowing God and caring

---

35 *Studies,* 40.

36 W. Zimmerli, *BK,* XIII/2 (1969), 1140.

37 Elliger, 53.

38 Cf. III below and Heller, 108.

for his fellow man. This is probably also the sense of the difficult passages that say of the wicked that their eyes[39] swell out "with fatness" (Ps. 73:7; Luther: they preen themselves like a fat belly) or that their faces are covered with fat (Job 15:27). It is also possible that Jgs. 3:22 is describing the death of a sinner by calling Eglon, the Moabite king, a fat man, whose fat closed over the sword of his slayer Ehud.

Münderlein

[39]H.-J. Kraus, *BK*, XV/2 (⁴1972), 502: "their guilt."

חֶלֶד *cheledh;* חֹלֶד *chōledh;* חֻלְדָּה *chuldāh;* חֵלֶד *chēledh;* חֶלְדַּי *cheldai*

Contents: I. Occurrences, Etymology, Meaning. II. 1. Theological Usage; 2. Conjectures. III. The Root *ḥld* II and its Derivatives in the OT.

I. Occurrences, Etymology, Meaning. In 5 OT passages, all poetic (Psalms and Job), we find the noun *cheledh,* derived from a root *ḥld* (I), which is rendered "be permanent, eternal" on the basis of Arabic (for *ḥld* II, see III below). Therefore *cheledh* can refer to something lasting for a considerable time; in Ps. 39:6 (Eng. v. 5) it takes on the meaning "lifetime" in parallelism with *yôm*. In Ps. 49:2(1), however, the phrase *yōshᵉbhê chāledh* stands in parallelism with *ʿammîm,* and *cheledh* must have the meaning "world," something that is also characterized by endurance.

II. 1. *Theological Usage*. The occurrence of *cheledh* in religious poetry justifies our speaking of its theological usage; ideas about life and the world belong in the realm of theology. In Ps. 39:6(5), the psalmist laments the brevity of life: "Behold, thou hast made my days a few handbreadths, and my lifetime (*cheledh*) is as nothing in thy sight." The term *cheledh,* however, probably refers not just to the temporal duration of life, but to its character and content (cf. Ps. 89:48[47], where *cheledh* corresponds to

cheledh. F. S. Bodenheimer, *Animal Life in Palestine* (Jerusalem, 1935), 99, 102, 108; E. Briliq, "חֹלֶד," *EMiqr,* III (1958), 140-42; G. Cansdale, *Animals of Bible Lands* (1970), 27, 135; M. J. Dahood, "Hebrew-Ugaritic Lexicography IV," *Bibl,* 47 (1966), 403-419; G. Dalman, *AuS,* II (1932), 342; J. Feliks, "Maulwurf," *BHHW,* II, 1178; *idem,* "Maus und Ratte," *ibid.; idem,* "Wiesel," *BHHW,* III, 2172-73; *idem, The Animal World of the Bible* (trans. Tel Aviv, 1962); G. B. Gray, *Studies in Hebrew Proper Names* (London, 1896); S. E. Loewenstamm, "חֶלֶד," *EMiqr,* III, 140; *idem,* "חֻלְדָּה," *ibid.,* 142; T. Nöldeke, *Beiträge zur semitischen Sprachwissenschaft* (1904); M. Noth, *IPN*; H. B. Tristram, *The Survey of Western Palestine: The Fauna and Flora of Palestine* (London, 1884), 12, 14; *idem, The Natural History of the Bible* (London, 1867, ³1873); F. Wutz, *Die Psalmen textkritisch untersucht* (1925).

the term *shāv*'). Job 11:17 is similar in nature: the nouns *tsoh^orayim* and *bōqer,* together with the verb *'ûph* II, "grow dark,"[1] symbolize specific states of life. Fohrer translates: "Brighter than noonday your life will rise; if it grows dark, it will be [bright] like morning."[2] In Ps. 17:14—a corrupt text that has given rise to many conjectural emendations—the psalmist prays that Yahweh will remove the wicked from their sphere of life through death (*bachaiyîm* par. *mēcheledh*[3]).

2. *Conjectures.* In some poetic passages of the OT, *cheledh* has been proposed as a conjectural emendation. This is in accord with the fact that *cheledh* belongs to elevated discourse. In Isa. 38:11 ("I said, I shall not see Yahweh in the land of the living [*'erets hachaiyîm*]; I shall look upon man no more among the inhabitants of the realm of the dead [*yôsh^ebhê chādhel*]"), the parallelism becomes more appropriate through the emendation *yôsh^ebhê chāledh,* "inhabitants of the world." The meaning "inhabited world" (LXX: *oikouménē*) likewise occurs in the emendation proposed for Ps. 11:4. In Ps. 49:9(8)—assuming that the verse is not taken as a gloss on what precedes it—instead of *ḥdl* some have proposed the verb *ḥld,* not otherwise attested in the OT, but undoubtedly the root from which *cheledh* derives,[4] or the noun itself,[5] used as a synonym for *ḥyh,* "life." While it is hardly possible to avoid emendation in Job 10:20 (reading *h^alō' m^e'aṭ y^emê cheldî shîth mimmennî*), Job 10:12 is sufficiently clear without emendation of *chesedh* to *cheledh.*[6] All these passages presuppose the double meaning of *cheledh:* "life, lifetime" and "(inhabited) world."

III. The Root ḥld II and its Derivatives in the OT. In the Middle Hebrew of the Talmud, as well as in Christian Palestinian Aramaic and Syriac, although not in Biblical Hebrew, we find the root *ḥld* with the meanings "dig" and "creep."[7] This is undoubtedly the etymology of the animal name *chōledh* in Lev. 11:29. It is difficult to define the meaning of *chōledh* with zoological precision. It is usually translated "mole,"[8] probably referring not to the mole belonging to the family Talpidae, but rather *Spalax Ehrenbergi,* belonging to the family Spalacidae. The LXX, Targum Jonathan, the Peshitta, and the Talmud, however, interpret *chōledh* as "weasel" (*Mustela nivalis*). Feliks conjectures that *chōledh* refers to a kind of rat. The problem might be considered almost wholly irrelevant were it not for a series of proper names in the OT that may derive from *ḥld* II and thus be connected with *chōledh.* Nöldeke emphasizes, however, that these names can be derived just as probably from *ḥld* I.

The name of the prophetess *chuldāh* in 2 K. 22:14 and 2 Ch. 34:22 is generally derived from *chōledh.* According to Noth, personal names based on the names of

---

[1] *KBL*², 689.

[2] G. Fohrer, *KAT,* XVI (1963), 221f.

[3] M. J. Dahood, *Psalms I. AB,* XVI (1966), *in loc.;* cf. also D. D. Gualandi, "Salmo 17 (16), 13-14," *Bibl,* 37 (1956), 199-208, esp. 201-204.

[4] H. Schmidt, *HAT,* 15 (1934), 93f.; *KBL*³, 303.

[5] H. Gunkel, *GHK,* II/2 (⁵1968), 211f.

[6] Cf. Fohrer, *KAT,* XVI, *in loc.*

[7] *WTM.*

[8] *GesB, KBL.*

animals may either be desiderative in nature or express a characteristic that appears at birth (or during the person's lifetime in the case of names adopted later). In the former case, "weasel" would make sense as a desiderative name; in the latter, the feminine form of *chōledh* could describe the child's unattractive appearance at birth. Since, however, the use of animal names as personal undoubtedly had its origin early in the history of Israel, it is possible that that such names were used later without particular reference to their original meaning. As to the other personal names deriving from *ḥld* found in the OT, we are dealing with two individuals: one of David's warriors, called *chēledh* in 1 Ch. 11:30 and *cheldai* in 1 Ch. 27:15 (undoubtedly identical with the *chēlebh* of 2 S. 23:29); and one of the exiles in Zec. 6:10,14 conj. These names may appropriately be derived from *ḥld* I.

Beyse

חָלָה *chālāh;* חֳלִי *chᵒlî;* חִלָּה פָנִים *chillāh phānîm*

Contents: I. 1. Occurrences; 2. Distribution; 3. Identification; 4. Semantic Field; 5. Translations; 6. Range of Meaning. II. 1. Verbs and Nouns; 2. More Precise Definitions; 3. Negations. III. 1. With God as Subject; 2. Theological Contexts; 3. Isa. 53; 4. Metaphorical Usage; 5. *chillāh phānîm*.

I. 1. *Occurrences.* Because the phoneme sequence *ḥl* appears so frequently, the group of Hebrew words *chālāh* I with the common root *ḥly* (in contrast to *chālāh* II and III(?), *ḥyl/ḥwl* I and II, *ḥll* I, II, and III, *ḥly* I, II, and III, *ḥl'h* I and II, *mḥlh* II[1]) is hard to identify precisely. The group in question comprises the verb *chālāh,* its rarer by-form *chālā',* and a series of regularly formed nouns: *chᵒlî, machᵃleh, machᵃlāh, machᵃluyîm, tachᵃlu'îm, machlôn*(?). There is a striking tendency in the case of the verb (which is attested in all stems) for nominal forms to be used: 24 of the 74

---

chālāh. G. R. Driver, "Ancient Lore and Modern Knowledge," *Hommages à André Dupont-Sommer* (Paris, 1971), 277-286, esp. 283f.; *idem,* "Isaiah 52[13]-53[12]: the Servant of the Lord." *Festschrift P. Kahle. BZAW,* 103 (1968), 90-105, esp. 98-101; *idem,* "Linguistic and Textual Problems: Ezekiel," *Bibl,* 19 (1938), 175-187, esp. 176; *idem,* "Linguistic and Textual Problems: Jeremiah," *JQR,* 28 (1937/38), 97-129, esp. 101; *idem,* "Some Hebrew Words," *JTS,* 29 (1927/28), 390-96, esp. 392; P. Fronzaroli, "Studi sul lessico commune semitico," *AANLR,* 19 (1964), 251-265; J. Hempel, *Heilung als Symbol und Wirklichkeit im biblischen Schrifttum. NAWG,* I, 1958/3 ([2]1965), 237-314; P. Humbert, "Maladie et médecine dans l'AT," *RHPR,* 44 (1964), 1-29; J. Scharbert, *Der Schmerz im AT. BBB,* 8 (1955), 36-40; K. Seybold, *Das Gebet des Kranken im AT. BWANT,* 99 (1973), 19-31; F. Stolz, "חלה *ḥlh* krank sein," *THAT,* I, 567-570; T. Struys, *Ziekte en Genezing in het OT* (Kampen, 1968), 386-393.

[1] See I.2.

occurrences, about a third, are participles, including 16 in the qal. The preponderance of nominal forms in this group of words is shown in the distribution of the roughly 110 occurrences: 64 are nouns, participles, or infinitives.[2]

2. *Distribution.* The root *ḥlh* I is attested in Hebrew and—probably through Hebrew influence—more rarely in Jewish Aramaic (*ḥlʾ*, *ḥlyʾ*) and Mandean. In Akkadian, there is a unique occurrence at Mari (Old Babylonian) of the verb *ḫalû,* "be sick," in the stative, applied to a lion: *ši-ba-at u ḫa-la-at,* "old and sick,"[3] probably as a Canaanite loanword. Otherwise the root phonemes serve other functions in Aramaic[4] and Akkadian.[5] The following South Semitic parallels have been suggested: OSA *ḥlʾ*, "do penance," *yḥln,* "be contrite";[6] Arab. *ḫalā,* "be empty," *ḥalala,* "be weak in the knees,"[7] *ḥalaʾa,* "be covered with dust or powder";[8] Tigr. *ḥll,* "be unfit, weak, tired," *ḥlt,* "a disease (of the hair?)."[9]

3. *Identification.* The etymological situation is opaque. The problem of homonyms interferes with all attempts to identify the various roots.[10]

a. *ḥlh,* Indo-European **al-*, "be sweet," alongside **al-*, "be loose, weak,"[11] is attested in Hebrew only in the nouns *chᵃlî* and *chelyāh,* "jewelry." Arabic equivalents *ḥaluwa, ḥaliya, ḥalā,* "be sweet, pleasing," as well as *ḥalā,* "bedeck,"[12] have occasioned various attempts to derive the piel formula *chillāh phānîm* from this root. Although this derivation might account for the apparent peculiarity of the formula in the semantic field of *ḥlh* I, lack of sufficient evidence has generally kept lexicographers from accepting it.[13]

b. *ḥlh,* related to Arab. *ḫly,* "make bright, calm," possibly in Prov. 19:6.[14]

---

[2]For statistics, see Stolz, 567f.

[3]G. Dossin, "Les archives épistolaires du palais de Mari," *Syr,* 19 (1938), 125: "*tremblotante*"; cf. *CAD,* VI, 54; *AHw,* I, 314b.

[4]*DISO,* 88.

[5]*CAD, AHw.*

[6]*KBL*³, 302f.

[7]Driver, *JTS,* 29 (1927/28), 392; *idem, BZAW,* 103 (1968), 98-202; A. Guillaume, "Hebrew and Arabic Lexicography: A Comparative Study, II," *Abr-Nahrain,* 2 (1960/61 [1962]), 14; D. R. Ap-Thomas, "Notes on Some Terms Relating to Prayer," *VT,* 6 (1956), 239f.; *KBL*³, 302f.; cf. J. Barr, *Comparative Philology and the Text of the OT* (Oxford, 1968), 326.

[8]Driver, "Ancient Lore," 283f.; *idem, Bibl,* 19 (1938), 176; see I.3.

[9]*TigrWb,* 52bf., 55b.

[10]Cf. Barr, *Comparative Philology,* 326f.

[11]H. Möller, *Vergleichendes indogermanisch-semitisches Wörterbuch* (1911, ²1970), 6f.

[12]Wehr, 203.

[13]With the exception of E. König, *Hebräisches und aramäisches Wörterbuch zum AT* (⁵1931), *BDB, LexHebAram;* cf. Ap-Thomas, *VT,* 6 (1956), 239f.; E. Jenni, *Das hebräische Piʿel* (Zurich, 1968), 64f.; Stolz, 570; see III.5.

[14]D. S. Margoliouth in J. Hastings, *A Dictionary of the Bible,* III (1906), 29, cited in B. Gemser, *HAT,* 16 (²1963), 112.

c. A root *ḥlh,* attested by the Ethiopic verb *ḫly,* "think, meditate, consider,"[15] is postulated especially for 1 S. 22:8,[16] as well as Jer. 5:3 and Am. 6:6 ("take to heart," "be concerned for"). These particular passages, however, stand out syntagmatically by their use of negations (or the niphal with the preposition *ʿal,* in the case of Amos). The etymology remains necessarily hypothetical.[17]

d. For Eccl. 5:12, a root *ḫlh* with the meaning "be alone," after Arab. *ḫalā,* has been suggested.[18] The same proposal has been made for the occurrences of the piel with *pānîm.*

e. A root *ḥlh,* Arab. *ḥalaʾa,* "rub, stroke," is occasionally proposed.[19]

f. *ḥlʾ* (2 Ch. 16:12; Isa. 53:10) appears in the hiphil in Middle Hebrew, deriving from **ḥlʾh* I, "rust," with the meaning "become rusty," OSA *ḥlʾ,* Arab. *ḥaliʾa.*[20] The latter meaning has also been proposed for 2 Ch. 16:12; 21:15ff.; Isa. 1:5 (Dt. 29:21 [Eng. v. 22]; Jer. 14:18; Ps. 103:3).[21]

4. *Semantic Field.* a. In OT usage, of the various expressions available for referring to general conditions of bodily malaise and disease, the group of words based on *ḥlh* is drawn on by far the most frequently. Their use was obviously based on the notion of a normal state of health, for which *shālôm* furnished the broadest term. The direct antonyms of *ḥlh* (and other terms for sickness) are forms of the verb *rāphāʾ,* "heal," and *chālam* I, "recover"(?),[22] together with forms of *chāyāh,* "live" (piel and hiphil).

Besides the *ḥlh* group, various other resources are available to the language: (1) the group of words deriving from the common Semitic root *dwh,* referring to an indisposition, specifically to menstruation,[23] in most cases used metaphorically in a general sense in combination with *lēbh;*[24] (2) the equally large group based on → **כאב** *kāʾabh,* which also accents the objective situation,[25] but on the whole with a more marked subjective component than *ḥlh* ("feel pain," "pain"), thus coming close to representing one facet of *ḥlh;* (3) a series of rare verbs that are much harder to categorize: *ʾnš* niphal (2 S. 12:15), *nss* I participle (Isa. 10:18, highly problematical), and *mrṣ* niphal (Mic. 2:10; 1 K. 2:8; Job 6:25) and hiphil (Job 16:3). The meaning of *mrṣ* can only be approximated as "be sick, weak, unwell," "be vexed" on the basis of Job 16:3 and Semitic equivalents.

---

15 *LexLingAeth,* 577ff.
16 Driver, *JTS,* 29 (1927/28), 392; *idem, BZAW,* 103 (1968), 98ff.
17 *KBL*³.
18 I. Eitan, "A Contribution to Isaiah Exegesis," *HUCA,* 12–13 (1937–38), 62.
19 König, *Wörterbuch.*
20 *KBL*³.
21 Driver, "Ancient Lore," 283f.: "to be gangrenous."
22 Cf. Seybold, 30.
23 Cf. *KBL*³; cf. "Bücherschau," *ZAW,* 80 (1968), 435.
24 Used colloquially in Lachish Letter III, 7; cf. Hempel, 238.
25 Scharbert, 41ff.

b. Forms of this last root provided the usual terminology for sickness in the Semitic languages: Akk. *marāṣu, murṣu,*[26] Aram. *mrʿ*,[27] Ugar. *mrṣ,*[28] OSA *mrʿ*, Arab. *mariḍa, maraḍ.*[29] This raises the question of what factors led to the obvious replacement of *mrṣ* by *ḥlh* in Hebrew. The use of *mrṣ* in combination with the obscure phenomenon *chebhel,* "destruction" (Mic. 2:10; cf. Eccl. 5:12,15[13,16]), and *qᵉlālāh,* "curse" (1 K. 2:8; Job 6:25 [obscure]), with the similar causative use in Job 16:3,[30] as well as the magical and demonic associations of the verb and its derivatives in the other Semitic languages suggest the conjecture that in the linguistic domain of the OT texts this word with its overtones was repressed for religious and theological reasons[31] and replaced with the more neutral *chālāh,* "be weak," which may be etymologically connected with *ḥlʾ*, "roast."[32]

5. *Translations.* The Targumim render forms of *chālāh* with forms of *mᵉraʿ: mᵉraʿ*, "be or become sick, weak"; *mᵉrîaʿ*, "sick, unhealthy, ailing"; *marʿāʾ*, "disease, pain, weakness"; *mᵉrôʿāʾ*, "disease"; *marʿîthāʾ*, "disease, pain."[33] For the piel formula they use the pael *tsallî qᵒdhām,* "pray or plead before" (peal "bow").

The LXX does not translate uniformly. In order of frequency, *ḥlh* is rendered as *arrōsteín, poneín, astheneín, malakízesthai, enochleín (metriázein,* Neh. 2:2; *páschein,* Am. 6:6; *phlegmaínein,* Nah. 3:19), etc. The piel formula is usually rendered *deísthai.* The derived nouns are variously rendered as *arrōstía, malakía, nósos, pónos* (*hamartía,* Isa. 53:4; *traúma,* Jer. 10:19), confirming the semantic range of the Hebrew expression. The name *machlôn* (Ruth 1:2,5; 4:9f.) is transcribed as *Maalṓn* (Josephus *Malaṓn, Mállōn, Málaos*).

6. *Range of Meaning.* The semantic potential of both the verb and the nouns may be characterized by calling them general terms for a "state of bodily weakness,"[34] to be translated "be or become weak," "weakness." This broad range can be limited through contextual determinatives to instances of physical or mental impotence, organic diseases, and injuries, so that in most cases "be or become sick," "sickness" are accurate translations. Besides "bodily debility," the context can shift the accent to mean "be in pain, suffer"[35] (cf. Prov. 23:35; Jer. 5:3). The same holds true for "fatigue" or "exhaustion." The semantic skeleton "state of weakness" (with or without pain) can be fleshed out in a variety of ways, many of them metaphorical, allowing the integration of the piel *pānîm* formula (which may have another derivation) alongside the obvious use of the piel in Dt. 29:21(22) and the pual in Isa. 14:10

[26] *AHw,* I, 609f., 676f.
[27] *DISO,* 168.
[28] *WUS,* No. 1683.
[29] Wehr, 903f.; cf. Fronzaroli, 263, 2, 12.
[30] Cf. *BDB,* 599.
[31] See Seybold, 39ff.
[32] Cf. Driver, "Ancient Lore," 283f.
[33] Cf. Levy, *WTM,* III, 256f.
[34] Scharbert.
[35] *GesB,* No. 3; *KBL*[3], No. 3; Scharbert (limited to outward symptoms).

(MT). Besides this formula and the abstract plurals as terms for a disease or its symptoms, we find the proper name *machlôn*, "weakness" (Ruth 1:2,5; 4:9), alongside *kilyôn*, "consumption," both probably to be taken as "meaningful names devised ad hoc"[36] rather than true personal names.[37]

II. 1. *Verbs and Nouns.* In the everyday language of the OT, the group of words based on *ḥlh* serves to express a state of weakness or disease. A man injured in a fall from an upper story becomes sick (*vaiyāchal*, 2 K. 1:2). He is a *chôleh*, in a state of *chᵒlî*, from which he may return "to life" once more (2 K. 1:2; 8:7f.,29; Isa. 38:9). In this usage the qal participle appears frequently as an adjective. Used absolutely, it evokes a general sense of debility that causes concern (Gen. 48:1), which can be used as an excuse to protect someone from attack (1 S. 19:14), as an occasion for the king to visit (2 K. 8:29), and as grounds for constituting a special group in liturgical worship (Ps. 107:17 conj.). In the case of animals, such a state makes them unfit for use as offering or sacrifice (Mal. 1:8,13; cf. Ezk. 34:4,16,21; see I.2). When someone looks poorly, he can be asked whether he is *chôleh* or "sad of heart" (*rōaʿ lēbh*) (Neh. 2:2). The seven stems of the verb indicate nuances of meaning that are confirmed by the basic meaning of a state of deficiency predicated of a subject: niphal, reflexive and tolerative (Jer. 12:13, "be tired out"; Ezk. 34:4, 21, "exhausted"; Dnl. 8:27, "be overcome by weakness"); piel, factitive and resultative (Dt. 29:21[22], "make sick," redundant); pual, passive (Isa. 14:10[MT], "become [deathly] weak"); hithpael, demonstrative (2 S. 13:2, 5f., "act sick"); hiphil, indirectly causative with subordinate subject (Prov. 13:12; Isa. 53:4 [MT]; Hos. 7:5; Mic. 6:13; cf. 4Q 160 3f., III, 1, "cause to be sick," see III.3); hophal, passive of the hiphil (1 K. 22:34 par. "be [seriously] wounded").

The state with its various aspects indicated by the verb is designated nominally (following the participle and infinitive) primarily by the noun *chᵒlî*. Prepositional constructions give to *chᵒlî*, too, the semantic dimensions of space and time (Isa. 38:9). Among the derivatives, the abstract plurals *machᵃluyîm* and *tachᵃluʾîm* emphasize visible symptoms (cf. Dt. 29:21[22])[38] and summarize conceptually individual manifestations (cf. Jer. 16:4; 14:18; 2 Ch. 21:19),[39] suggesting a particular rhetorical purpose. The name *machlôn*, an ad hoc formation as a verbal adjective, derives its special force from the parallel *kilyôn*. Somewhat obscure is the semantic contribution of the niphal participle in the stereotyped phrase *makkāh nachlāh*, probably "blow or injury that makes sick," "incurable injury" (by metonymy), in Jer. 10:19; 14:17; 30:12; Nah. 3:19 (cf. Isa. 17:11; Mic. 2:10; 1 K. 2:8).

2. *More Precise Definitions.* Our observation that this group of words serves a primarily denominative function, characterizing in general terms a state of physical weakness, is confirmed by the recognizable OT tendency to describe and define the situa-

[36] *IPN*, 10f.; E. Würthwein, *HAT*, 18 (²1969), 10.
[37] W. Rudolph, *KAT*, XVII/1 (1962), 38; G. Gerleman, *BK*, XVIII (1965), 14.
[38] Driver, "Ancient Lore," 283f.: "sores," from *ḥlʾ*; cf. I.3.f.
[39] Scharbert, 37.

tion more precisely. On the one hand, the *chālāh* statement can be limited by further attributes. The weakness can be localized by the mention of specific parts of the body: the feet (1 K. 15:23 par.), the head (Isa. 1:5), the bowels (2 Ch. 21:15ff.). Its seriousness can be specified by the diagnostic alternative of life or death (e.g., Isa. 38:1,9; 2 K. 13:14). It can be ranked in series (Mal. 1:8,13) or be specified by a genitive: *chôlath 'ahᵃbhāh* (Cant. 2:5; 5:8). On the other hand, the statement can be broadened and extended to other subjects. It can be applied, for example, to the Herculean weakness of a Samson (Jgs. 16:7,11,17), the weakness of Jacob's old age (Gen. 48:1), even to the condition of animals (Mal. 1:8,13; Ezk. 34:4,21),[40] and finally to general situations: an incurable evil (Eccl. 5:12,15[13,16]) and general suffering (Jer. 6:7; 10:19). It can occasionally even be applied to the cause of a corresponding state (Jer. 10:19; 14:17; 30:12; Nah. 3:19).[41]

3. *Negations*. Etymologically obscure is the use of *chālāh* in various passages in the sense of "feel pain, grieve" (1 S. 22:8; Jer. 5:3; 4:31 conj. [from *ḥyl*?]; Prov. 23:35; Isa. 57:10; Am. 6:6 niphal).[42] Both homonymy and polysemy appear possible. What is striking is the negative formulation (except for Jer. 4:31) and the construction with *'al,* which appears twice (1 S. 22:8; Am. 6:6). It is therefore reasonable to hypothesize an idiom developing out of the semantic system of *chālāh* or incorporated into it, which negates the expectation expressed by the context and exaggerates it ironically: in agitated rebuke (1 S. 22:8; Am. 6:6; Jer. 5:3; Isa. 57:10) or the speech of a drunkard (Prov. 23:35). The preposition *'al* would then indicate the "reason, occasion, or condition" for the expected reaction.[43]

III. 1. *With God as Subject*. As one would expect, God appears as the subject of the verb only in the modified stems: piel (Dt. 29:21[22]) and hiphil (Isa. 53:10; Mic. 6:13). The Micah passage could possibly be taken as an example of metonymy, like the *makkāh nachlāh* formula,[44] but should probably be emended on the basis of the versions to *hᵃchillôthî*.[45] In the first passage, the factitive element of the piel receives full expression. The proleptic description of the effects of the covenant curse, introduced for homiletic reasons (v. 19[20]), vividly depicts the "the afflictions of that land and the sicknesses with which Yahweh has made it sick." The OT belief in Yahweh as the bringer of sickness (and healing) finds here its tersest and bluntest statement, reinforced by the effect of the plural noun and the prepositional construction (*bāh*).

The hiphil construction in Isa. 53:10, with the person of the Servant as its object, is another matter. Despite the use in this context of the verb *dk'* (piel), the causation is conceived indirectly, medially, involving an intermediate subject. The verse thus

---

[40]Cf. the Mari text cited in I.2 above.
[41]See III.4.
[42]Cf. I.3.c.
[43]*Synt,* §110e.
[44]II.1.
[45]*BHS*.

achieves a perceptible distance between Yahweh and the suffering of the Servant: "he caused him to become sick" (MT: *hech^{e}lî*; 1QIs^a: *wyḥllhw,* from *ḥll* II).[46]

2. *Theological Contexts.* The group of words deriving from *ḥlh* appears with particular frequency in the parenetic strand of tradition defined by Ex. 15:26; 23:25, then 1 K. 8:37 and Dt. 7:15; 28:59,61; 29:21(22). Common to these passages are an association with the theologoumenon setting forth the alternatives of blessing or curse (or the relationship between sin and punishment), the use of *kōl* to evoke the idea of totality (Ex. 23:25 substitutes the indeterminate collective *mach^{a}lāh,* Dt. 29:21[22] and 28:59 the plural), and finally an allusion to the theme of the Egyptian plagues (except for Ex. 23:25 and 1 K. 8:37), as a concrete instance of the general and abstract statement. The context shows that this group of words can refer both to epidemics and to individual cases of sickness (cf. 1 K. 8:37ff.).

3. *Isa. 53.* The group of words is represented 3 times in Isa. 52:13–53:12, the last of the Servant texts.[47] In the description of the Servant's suffering (vv. 2ff.), there appears as one of the many terms describing him the double expression *'îsh makh'ōbhôth vîdhûaʿ chōlî* (v. 3a), characterizing the Servant with respect to his physical state as a person afflicted with pain and sickness. Like the first phrase, "man of pains," which has both physical condition and psychological suffering in view, the second has a double aspect. If it is true that *vîdûaʿ* derives not from *yādhaʿ*, "know," but from *yādhaʿ* II, "bring low, humiliate,"[48] the phrase should be rendered "brought low by sickness" rather than the difficult "acquainted with sickness" or "known for his sickness." It exposes the depths of the effects of sickness—in the psychological realm, in the religious and ritual realm, and in the social realm, explicitly mentioned in the context. Thus *ch^{o}lî* becomes the term for the innermost core of ideas concerning the physical and psychological constitution of the sufferer. About it, deriving by association from the typical picture of sickness, grow concentric circles of ideas constituting the paradigm found here as well as in Job 33:19ff. or Ps. 38: from penance (v. 7) through the degraded existence of the realm of the dead (vv. 8f.) to restoration (vv. 10f.).

In v. 10 we find once more the summary statement, using the hiphil, of Yahweh's indirect causation of sickness, if MT *hech^{e}lî* is not to be emended to *vyḥllhw* (following 1QIs^a)[49] or in some other way, for instance, to *hech^{e}lîm* (cf. Isa. 38:16).[50]

The third occurrence in Isa. 53 brings us to the climax of the passage: "Surely it was our sicknesses he bore, and our pains he carried" (v. 4). Against the background of the idea of vicarious suffering, the plural formulation makes it clear that, however stylized

---

[46]For further discussion, see III.3.

[47]See III.1.

[48]D. W. Thomas, "The Root ידע in Hebrew," *JTS,* 35 (1934), 298-306; *idem,* "More Notes on the Root ידע in Hebrew," *JTS,* 38 (1937), 404f.; Barr, *Comparative Philology,* 19ff.

[49]See III.1.

[50]E.g., *hech^{e}lîm* (Begrich); cf. Isa. 38:16.

it may be, the account of the sickness initiated and permitted by Yahweh, fraught with all its consequences, describes the suffering of an individual, the man of pains, who nevertheless takes on an exemplary and fundamental significance transcending individuality.

4. *Metaphorical Usage*. Despite a tendency toward standardization of usage, it is clear that the group of words is not used metaphorically in the Psalms: 35:13, with a reference to sympathetic conduct, "when they were sick"; 41:4(3), where the context speaks of "bed" and "sickbed" (cf. also vv. 5ff.[6ff.]); or even 103:3, where vv. 3-5 constitute a homogeneous structure in which the abstract plural means "manifestations of sickness," generalized from a perspective of distance (*kōl*, ptcp.). The same is true of the conjectural *chôlîm*, "sick," in 107:17 (for MT *'ᵉvilîm*, "fools")—"through their sinful ways," cf. vv. 18f. Ps. 77:11 is obscure: The MT reads *challôthî*, piel infinitive of *chālāh* or qal infinitive of *chālal;* conjectures include such suggestions as *chᵃlôthî*, possibly with the limited sense "my suffering."[51]

Neither can we recognize metaphorical usage in the statements concerning the Servant in Isa. 53, whose language is closely related to that of the Psalms of Lament and praise. Here, as in the psalms, despite the paradigmatic language, we are dealing with the concrete situation of an individual person (*chᵒlî*), the Servant, and that of the confessional community he represents (*chᵒlāyēnû*).

We do, however, encounter metaphorical usage in prophetic and parenetic texts where the fate designated by *chālāh/chᵒlî* is predicated of a collective entity. A political crisis is referred to in Hos. 5:13 as "Ephraim's sickness" (par. to *māzôr*, "wound"), in Isa. 1:5 as a "sickness" (*chᵒlî*, conj. **chulai*, "wounds, ulcers"[52]) afflicting the entire head (of the people). An analogous idea is found in Isa. 57:10. The catastrophe described in Dt. 29:21(22) is couched in the imagery of a sickness of the devastated land.

This metaphorical transfer of the term to the corporate personality is motivated by the implications associated with saying that someone is sick. These implications extend both backwards through the nexus of reward and punishment to origins and causes (cf. Hos. 5:8ff.; Isa. 1:4; 57:11; Dt. 29:21ff.[22ff.]) and forwards to reactions and consequences (Hos. 5:14f.; 6:1ff.; Isa. 1:5a,9; 57:10; Dt. 29:21ff.[22ff.]), thus evoking the *status confessionis* that the crisis of sickness means for the person afflicted.

Ecclesiastes makes strikingly frequent use of the group of words (5:12,15,16[13, 16,17]; 6:[1],2) in its aphorisms on the value and worthlessness of riches (5:9-19[10-20]; 6:1-6[53]), sometimes in participial-adjectival association with *rāʿāh*, "evil" (5:12,15[13,16]; 6:1 conj.), resulting in intensification by metonymy (like the use of the niphal participles),[54] sometimes in a series of nouns that shape the meaning of the discourse: 5:16(17) *vᵉcholyô vāqātseph* MT, "(vexation) and sickness and resentment"; 6:2 *chebhel vāchᵒlî rāʿ*, "vanity (*chebhel*, → חבל *ḥbl* I), a sore affliction."

[51]See Seybold, *in loc.*

[52]Driver, "Ancient Lore," 284.

[53]K. Galling in E. Würthwein and K. Galling, *HAT*, 18 ([2]1969).

[54]See II.2.

This latter combination and the striking association of the *chālāh* group with the theme of "worthlessness of riches" raises the question whether in this particular section of the text Ecclesiastes did not deliberately use the etymological or at least phonological connection with the group *ḥl'*, "rust," to produce certain overtones.

5. *chillāh phānîm*. The idiom *chillāh phānîm,* as distinct from the nonformulaic use of the piel (Dt. 29:21[22]), occurs 16 times in the OT. Thus far there has been no convincing account of its derivation.[55]

There are two possibilities: (a) The idiom owes its meaning to a specialized development of the verb *chālāh,* "be weak, sick," in combination with *pānîm,* "face, countenance," by virtue of a specialized usage, primarily cultic, contrasting with *ʿaz pānîm,* "hard, stern of countenance" (Dt. 28:50; Dnl. 8:23; Eccl. 8:1) and *hēʿēz pānāv* (hiphil), "make one's face hard" (Prov. 7:13; 21:29).[56] (b) The idiom derives from the root *ḥlh,* "be sweet, pleasant," piel "adorn, bedeck" (attested in Hebrew only in nominal forms), or the homonymous root "be free, empty" (or "calm"),[57] and has been integrated by affinity into the system of the root *ḥlh,* "be weak, sick," within which it constitutes a separate domain.[58] Despite the lack of evidence for the intermediate stages, several considerations favor the latter derivation: the occurrence of the idiom alongside the normal form of the piel; the distribution of the occurrences in the verbal sector (imperfect consecutive, imperative); the association with *pānîm,* not otherwise attested for the entire *ḥlh* group; the difficult semantic derivation of *ḥlh* in the formula ("make weak," i.e., "make soft, gentle," or even "stroke"[59]); and above all the scarcely conceivable application of the factitive piel to the *pᵉnê yhvh* (despite the calm and neutral use of the idiom), which is subject to all kinds of misinterpretation. In any case, both the formulaic usage and the homonymous ambivalence appear to have clouded the concrete notions behind the idiom—albeit not to such a degree to prevent their being recognized in the substructures.

The function of the idiom is determined by the following factors.

a. Ceremonial reference. The secular passages, like those referring to the countenance of Yahweh, all show that the action designated by *chillāh phānîm* has ceremonial associations and is rooted in the ideology and ceremonial of the court. This appears most clearly in Ps. 45:13(12) (in par. with bowing in obeisance, in the context of homage to the queen on the part of the wealthy), as well as Prov. 19:6; Mal. 1:9 (cf. the

---

[55]I.3.

chillāh phānîm. D. R. Ap-Thomas, *VT,* 6 (1956), 225-241, esp. 239f.; E. Dhorme, *L'emploi métaphorique des noms de parties du corps en hébreu et en akkadien* (Paris, 1923, ²1963), 59; F. Nötscher, "*Das Angesicht Gottes schauen" nach biblischer und babylonischer Auffassung* (1924, ²1969), 96-98; J. Reindl, *Das Angesicht Gottes im Sprachgebrauch des ATs. ErfThSt,* 25 (1970), 175-185; K. Seybold, "Reverenz und Gebet: Erwägungen zu der Wendung *ḥillā panîm,*" *ZAW,* 88 (1976), 2-16.

[56]Dhorme, Nötscher, Ap-Thomas, Stolz, Reindl, and others.

[57]For Arabic equivalents, see I.3.

[58]Cf. Ap-Thomas, Driver, Seybold, and others.

[59]Nötscher, *Angesicht,* 97; see I.3.e.

"governor" metaphor in v. 8); Zec. 7:2. This observation is confirmed by an analogous idiom in Arabic, cited by Ap-Thomas: *ḫalā wağhuhu,* which in the basic stem of the verb obviously means "grant a private audience."[60] The possible associations with "bedeck" can be understood easily within the framework of this setting (cf. the formula *hādhar pānîm,* Lev. 19:15,32; Lam. 5:12; Prov. 25:6), in which, moreover, we read of gifts and homage (Ps. 45:12f.[11f.]), tribute (Mal. 1:8), favor and honor (Job 11:19; Prov. 19:6), petition and response.

b. Subject. In the secular domain, the subject of the ceremonial actions called *chillāh phānîm* belongs to a group subordinate to the individual concerned or at least declaring its subordinate status (cf. Ps. 45:13[12]: the queen and the wealthy citizens; Mal. 1:8f.: governor and priests; Lev. 19:15: the great [*gādhôl*] and the lay judge), but nevertheless privileged, allegedly or in reality. In the religious realm, the subjects function primarily as "official representatives" of the people of Yahweh: Moses (Ex. 32:11), the man of God (1 K. 13:6), priests (Mal. 1:9), kings (1 S. 13:12 [before a conflict]; 2 K. 13:4; Jer. 26:19; 2 Ch. 33:12), official emissaries (Zec. 7:2), but also the "we" of the Yahweh community (Dnl. 9:13) and of non-Jewish worshippers of Yahweh (Zec. 8:21f.), and in one instance (Ps. 119:58) the individual worshipper. All these clearly have the right to present their case before the deity (*'ēl,* Mal. 1:9) in some ritual manner that cannot be visualized in greater detail. In Zec. 8:21f., we find twice in parallel the presumably less specific phrase *biqqēsh 'eth yhvh.*[61] Yahweh never appears as the subject of *chillāh phānîm.*

c. Introductory position. Once the scene has been set, the position of the idiom in the structure of the passage shows that the action referred to constitutes one part of a larger context. In many passages it signals an action that marks the beginning of a narrative sequence, in each case preceding the spoken word: Ex. 32:11 (*vay^{e}chal–vayyō'mer,* v. 14); 1 K. 13:4ff.; 2 Ch. 33:10ff. (albeit in the dependent perfect); Ps. 119:58; Zec. 7:2 (continued by a statement of purpose). We may therefore assume that we are dealing with an introductory ceremony of fundamental significance for the discourse to follow, probably giving it a special character. The phrase, then, refers to the introductory act of a ceremony defining the fundamental relationship that commonly issues in a petition.

d. Language used by laymen. In the majority of passages speaking of the *p^{e}nê yhvh,* the phrase refers to cultic acts but does not belong to the technical language of the cult.[62] There is no evidence, of course, for a ritual stroking of a divine image or the like as a basis for the concept.[63] But in 1 S. 13:12, probably the earliest reference, *chillāh phānîm* takes place with the help of a sacrifice offered prematurely on the initiative of Saul. Offerings are probably also involved in Mal. 1:9 (gifts in Ps.

60 Pp. 239f.
61 Nötscher, *Angesicht,* 135ff.
62 Stolz, 570.
63 Reindl, 183f.

45:13[12]). The setting of 1 K. 13:6 is the sanctuary at Bethel, of Zec. 7:2; 8:21f. the sanctuary of Zion. Liturgical ceremonies may also be assumed in the case of 2 Ch. 33:12 (the context being a ritual of penitence; cf. Ps. 119:58), Jer. 26:19, and Dnl. 9:13. But none of the speakers who employ the phrase is a cultic expert: Saul (1 S. 13:12), the king (1 K. 13:6), the elders (Jer. 26:19), legates and pilgrims (Zec. 7:2; 8:21f.), the lay community (Mal. 1:9), Daniel (Dnl. 9:13), the psalmist (Ps. 119:58), and the anonymous authors of Ex. 32:11; 1 K. 13:6; 2 K. 13:4; 2 Ch. 33:12. The formulaic nature of the usage here betrays a certain lack of interest in ritual detail. The idiom belongs to the religious language of the laity.

In the religious realm, the expression always refers to an initiatory act with introductory function. It sets the stage for prayer to Yahweh, and lends to this prayer special weight. Even in Ps. 119:58, which clearly emphasizes the inward attitude ("with all my heart"), ritual actions are still involved; cf. also Zec. 7:2; 8:21f. The expression designates a gesture of respect, of worship, and of submission, performed with the purpose of seeking favor. It appears very dubious, therefore, that the usage of the phrase carries overtones associated with the semantic field of *chālāh,* "be weak, sick."

Seybold

חֵלְכָּאִים → דָּכָא *dākhā'*

חלל *ḥll* I; חֹל *chōl;* חָלִיל *chālîl*

Contents: I. Etymology. II. Use and Theological Meaning in the OT: 1. Profaning the Name of Yahweh; 2. Profaning the Sanctuary; 3. Profaning of Other Persons and Things; 4. Sacred and Profane.

I. Etymology. The root *ḥll* appears throughout the entire range of the Semitic languages, albeit only as an Aramaic loanword in Akkadian.[1] According to Palache,[2] the original meaning was "untie, loosen." Akk. *elēlu,* alongside the meaning "be

---

ḥll. J. Begrich, "Die priesterliche Tora," *Werden und Wesen des ATs,* ed. P. Volz. *BZAW,* 66 (1936), 63-88, esp. 85-87 = *GSAT. ThB,* 21 (1964), 232-260; J. Blau, "חֵחֵל בוראת 'תחיל' בדבר המשיך בו," *Lešonénu,* 31 (1968), 53-58; W. C. H. Feucht, *Untersuchungen zum Heiligkeitsgesetz. ThArb,* 20 (1964); M. Held, "A Faithful Lover in an Old Babylonian Dialogue," *JCS,* 15 (1961), 21; P. van Imschoot, "Entweihen," *BL*², 398f.; R. Kilian, *Literarkritische und formgeschichtliche Untersuchung des Heiligkeitsgesetz. BBB,* 19 (1963), esp. 84-103; M. R. Lehmann, "Biblical Oaths," *ZAW,* 81 (1969), 74-92, esp. IV חלילה, 82f.; F. Maass, "חלל *ḥll* pi entweihen," *THAT,* I, 570-75; H. Graf Reventlow, *Das Heiligkeitsgesetz formgeschichtlich untersucht. WMANT,* 6 (1961), esp. 92-103; P. S. Saydon, "The Inceptive Imperfect in Hebrew and the Verb הֵחֵל 'to Begin,'" *Bibl,* 35 (1954), 43-50; J. A. Soggin, "Entweihen," *BHHW,* I, 415.

1 *AHw,* I, 309.

2 J. Palache, *Semantic Notes on the Hebrew Lexicon* (Leiden, 1959), 31.

free, set free'' (of claims, slaves), often has the meaning ''be pure, purify'' (for the cult).[3] In Arabic, the predominant sense of *ḥalla* is ''loosen, be permitted.'' In the OT, *ḥll* in the piel (and twice in the hiphil) always means ''profane, desecrate.'' We also find *chōl,* ''profane,'' and *chālîl,* ''far be it from,'' said of something profane or reprehensible. There is no change in meaning in the Dead Sea Scrolls. In post-biblical Hebrew, the meaning ''profane,'' both verb and adjective, continues to predominate. The term *chālûl,* for example, is applied to the redemption of the second tithe.[4] In the hiphil, *ḥll* also very often means ''begin,'' *t^echillāh* means ''beginning.'' The connection of this group with *ḥll* in the sense of ''profane'' probably is to be found where *ḥll* means ''take for profane use after a period of consecration'' (cf. Jer. 31:5).

II. Use and Theological Meaning in the OT.

1. *Profaning the Name of Yahweh.* Most numerous are the passages that speak of profaning the name of Yahweh. The earliest reference is Am. 2:7b; we follow Rudolph[5] rather than Wolff,[6] who considers the statement secondary. Israel is pilloried for making slaves of free citizens on account of minor debts, for abusing the humble, and for sexually mistreating helpless female slaves. Such conduct shows disrespect for Yahweh, it profanes Yahweh himself, because it is a conscious transgression of his commandments. The name of Yahweh stands here for the person of Yahweh; there may be overtones of the idea that Israel's inhuman conduct implicates the name of Israel's God, so that other nations cease to respect it.

Jer. 34:16 castigates similar behavior as profanation of the divine name: during the emergency of the Babylonian siege, the upper classes undertook ''before Yahweh'' to release all Hebrew slaves; but when the acute danger was removed by the approach of the Egyptian army, the release was rescinded.

Ezekiel's great concern—in positive terms—is the sanctification of the divine name. He stands totally within the prophetic tradition when he sees this name being profaned by the conduct of men. In the situation of the exile, with its resigned adaptation to many pagan customs, he speaks out: let everyone discard his idols—cease profaning God's holy name with your gifts and your idols (Ezk. 20:39)![7] Anyone who worships other gods or offers gifts to Yahweh the way gifts are offered to other gods profanes the holy name; as a sanction, he must count on being excluded from the new community of those returning.

But Ezekiel also gives the expression ''profane the name of Yahweh'' a new meaning. At three stages of history (Ezk. 20:5-24)—once in Egypt and twice in the desert—Yahweh had reason to proceed against Israel, because Israel had defiled itself (→ טמא *ṭāmē'*) through idols (vv. 7, 18), rejected (→ מאס *mā'as*) Yahweh's ordinances (vv. 13,16,24), and profaned (*ḥll,* vv. 13,16,21,24) or failed to hallow

---

[3]*AHw,* I, 197f.
[4]*WTM,* II, 60.
[5]W. Rudolph, *KAT,* XIII/2 (1971), 143f.
[6]H. W. Wolff, *Joel and Amos* (trans. 1977), 181.
[7]Cf. the emendation proposed by W. Zimmerli, *BK,* XIII (1969), 437.

(→ קדשׁ *qdš,* v. 20) his Sabbaths. But destruction of Israel would have resulted in a profanation of the divine name "in the sight of the nations" that had also experienced the exodus (vv. 9,14,22). God's recognition and respect among the other nations would have been impugned if he had punished Israel: they would have seen therein not the result of Yahweh's righteousness but rather the weakness of a God unable to save his people from destruction. Babylon now, like Egypt and the desert then, is the occasion for the profanation of the divine name (36:20–23). The Babylonians see Yahweh's people driven out of Yahweh's land, and they mock and belittle this impotent and destroying God. Out of concern (→ חמל *chāmal*) for his holy name (v. 21) Yahweh will now act. He will put an end to the misunderstanding of the Babylonians and demonstrate his absolute holiness: he will bring his people back into their own land. It is striking that Ezekiel here stresses the honor and holiness of Yahweh rather than his mercy and love toward the exiles. It is obviously the prophet's purpose to provide the exiles, who have gone astray with their talk of God's mercy, with a new basis for their hope for deliverance. He also wishes to emphasize "how great the guilt of Israel is, and how totally undeserved their new salvation."[8] The holiness of Yahweh's name—the word *qdš* appears three times—is also the concern of 39:7, a secondary verse appended to the Gog prophecy. The time of profanation of this name by the exiles is past. Through the destruction of Gog and his land, the other nations will know that Yahweh is the almighty and holy God of Israel.

According to Deutero-Isaiah (Isa. 48:11), Yahweh will bring his people back to Palestine from Babylon because the end of Israel would also have meant the end of Israel's God in the eyes of the world.

In the Holiness Code, the profanation of the divine name is twice associated with the sacrifice of children to Moloch. In the context of commandments dealing with unchastity, Lev. 18:21 appears a bit strange, with its prohibition against giving "any of your children to devote them (by fire) to Molech." It is hard to determine whether we have here merely an echo of the catchword *zeraʿ* from v. 20, or whether the reference is to children born out of certain sexual rites. The prohibition is reinforced by the brief formula "I am Yahweh," undoubtedly intended to arouse a sense of the holiness of the bearer of this name and threaten punishment for offending it. Lev. 20:3 complements 18:21: the apodictic prohibition of Moloch worship is stylized by having Yahweh speak in the first person, and the profanation of his holy name is equated with defilement of the sanctuary. Lev. 19:11f. begin with four prohibitions couched in the plural: you shall not steal, nor deal falsely, nor lie, nor swear falsely. The reason is stated in a *ḥll* clause couched in the singular (*vᵉchillaltā ʾeth-shēm ʾᵉloheykhā*) in combination with the brief formula of Yahweh's self-introduction (*ʾᵃnî yhvh*). The change from plural to singular may be due to the telescoping of two series, one originally in the plural, the other in the singular.

In Lev. 21:6 and 22:2, the *ḥll* stipulation is associated with the special holiness of the priests. They offer Yahweh the "fire-offerings," referred to also by the archaic expression "the bread of Yahweh." They must therefore not expose themselves to any

---

[8] G. Fohrer, *HAT,* 13 (²1955), 204.

defilement through contact with a corpse or engage in superstitious mourning customs such as lacerating the skin, shaving a bald spot on the head, or disfiguring the edge of the beard. They must also not violate the "holy things" (*q^e dhōshîm*). This prohibition probably refers primarily to the portion reserved to the priests when animals were sacrificed or food was offered, for the consumption of which cultic purity is prescribed.

Lev. 22:31ff., a concluding parenesis couched in the plural, summarize the preceding stipulations of the Holiness Code: you shall keep my commandments, and you shall not profane my holy name. The motivation is stated with particular emphasis by means of the self-introduction formula coupled with a reference to holiness: I am Yahweh who sanctifies you.

The prophet Malachi chastises the priests for despising (→ בזה *bāzāh*) the divine name by sacrificing blind, lame, or otherwise sick animals to Yahweh (Mal. 1:8-10). V. 12 contrasts the ideal of divine worship with the present disgraceful practice. The priests are castigated as "profaners" (of the name of Yahweh); what they are in fact only thinking is stated with pitiless clarity by the prophet: the table of the Lord may be polluted and its food despised.

To the group of passages that speak of "profaning the holy name of Yahweh" we may add two Ezekiel passages that speak of profaning Yahweh himself. Ezk. 13:19 is an invective against female magicians who have been gaining power over the exiles by means of Babylonian magic, intending to lead them into apostasy from Yahweh. But in Israel all power belongs to Yahweh, especially power over life and death. He has promised life to the righteous, death to the sinner who transgresses his commandments. The magicians disregard this divine law of retribution, for example, by using their arts to heal the sick who deserve to die. Their blasphemous conduct is further increased by the fact that they perform their services in return for payment in kind. Not only is this a profanation of the people of God, it is ultimately a profanation of the holy and righteous one himself.

Finally, we come to Ezk. 22:16, in an oracle of judgment against Jerusalem. Yahweh will scatter the inhabitants of the city among the nations, through this punishment mercilessly destroying all filthiness. Yahweh knows that in the forum of the nations this action will make him "profaned" and dishonored, because they will see only the destruction from which he could not deliver his people. His righteousness, however, is of more value to him than his reputation among the pagans.[9]

2. *Profaning the Sanctuary.* In Ezk. 7:21-24, Israel is threatened with Yahweh's judgment, probably with reference to the events of the year 587. The most terrible blow is the profanation of Yahweh's "precious place" (*chill^e lû 'eth-ts^e phûnî*), probably referring to the temple rather than the entire land. It is the Babylonians who will execute God's judgment, the "worst" idolators among the nations. They will rob the temple of its holiness by invading and despoiling it. But also profaned—and in this

---

[9]For a discussion of the whole subject, see Feucht, 162f.; H. Brongers, "Die Wendung *b^e šēm jhwh* im AT," *ZAW*, 77 (1965), 11f.

case that means destroyed—will be the idols Israel had fashioned from its golden jewelry, and the high places and private sanctuaries built in a spirit of religious self-assurance.

In a symbolic action, Ezekiel interprets the death of his wife to the exiles in Babylon in terms of the profanation of the temple (*miqdāsh,* 24:21). Here the sanctuary is given predicates that truly lay bare the enormity of the profanation. This temple, like Ezekiel's wife, was a delight to the eyes (24:16), a joy to the heart, and Israel considered it an impregnable bulwark ("the pride of your power"). Its profanation will hit the exiles so hard that they, like the prophet, will be incapable of any mourning rites. The profanation of the temple also provides occasion for the Ammonites to gloat. They have cried out "Aha!" over the sanctuary of Yahweh, thus casting scorn on the holy God himself. In a threat (25:3), the prophet proclaims their own destruction at the hands of Bedouin tribes invading from the east.

According to a communal lament (Ps. 74:7), the sanctuary is profaned by the blood-stained pagan soldiers of Nebuchadnezzar. They smash the artful carvings with their axes and set fire to the walls. They destroy the place of the presence of the name of Yahweh down to the very ground, so that the sacrificial cult can no longer be carried out in Israel.

Besides Babylon, there are other agents responsible for profanation of the temple. Among the cultic transgressions of the two sisters Oholah (Samaria) and Oholibah (Jerusalem), Ezk. 23:39 singles out their entering the sanctuary with blood-stained hands. The stains are a kind of sacrifice performed in dire emergencies: the sacrifice of children to Moloch. "The complete disregard for bringing defilement upon the sanctuary shown here is evidently regarded as adding further to the sin."[10]

In Ezk. 44:7 (in the words of a P redactor), the priests are instructed not to repeat past mistakes in the new temple. This includes the use of non-Israelite slaves to perform minor duties when sacrifice is offered, a practice apparently borrowed from the Canaanites. Since these temple slaves are "uncircumcised in heart and flesh," i.e., are pagans both inwardly and outwardly, they profane the sanctuary of Yahweh. The specifics cannot be determined with certainty. But in Ezr. 2:43,55 the descendants of the temple servants (*n*ᵉ*thînîm*) and of the slaves of Solomon are listed among the returning exiles.

In addition, priests who have physical imperfections may not enter the "sanctuaries" (temple and altar: Lev. 21:23). Every member of a priestly family is a priest. He possesses a certain degree of holiness and has a legitimate claim to share in the sacrificial offerings and other income. But the actual exercise of priestly functions is denied those who are blind or lame, to hunchbacks, to those with skin diseases, etc. Possibly this prohibition was based originally on the idea that these infirmities were caused by demons. There is no reconciling demons with the sanctuary. The anointed high priest is subject to especially strict regulations governing his holiness. In order to avoid all contact with anything unclean he must have his dwelling place within the

---

[10]W. Eichrodt, *Ezekiel. OTL* (trans. 1970), 333.

temple precincts, which he must not leave, to take part, for instance, in mourning ceremonies (Lev. 21:12). If he were to become unclean, the temple itself would be profaned.

In Mal. 2:11, the prophet states that Judah has been faithless and committed an abomination, in which he sees a profanation of the temple. Very probably he means that every crime that disturbs the brotherhood of the covenant community also affects the covenant sanctuary, the common ancestral house of the community. Above all, of course, such "abominations" as idolatry, uncleanness, and disregard for ritual regulations profane the temple. V. 11b proves to be a later addition: marriage with a pagan woman, who does not know and understand the God of Israel, impugns the holiness of the temple.

Ezk. 28:18 is the only passage in the OT that speaks of profaning pagan sanctuaries. The fall of the king of Tyre from the mountain of God is prophesied in mythological imagery, on the grounds that he has "profaned" the sanctuaries on this mountain through his commercial dishonesty. It is possible that Ezekiel has in mind goods deposited in the temple treasury that were obtained by fraud and other kinds of deception.

Finally, Dnl. 11:31 calls the transformation of the Second Temple into a pagan sanctuary a profanation. In the year 167, the troops of the Seleucid Antiochus Epiphanes not only rendered the fortresslike temple precincts unclean through their presence, but also did away with the daily sacrifice and set up an altar of Zeus Olympios on the altar of burnt-offering as the "abomination of desolation" (cf. 1 Macc. 1:54).

3. *Profaning of Other Persons and Things.* According to Isa. 47:6, Yahweh's covenant love was transformed into wrath on account of Israel's faithlessness. By way of punishment he handed over his people, his sacred heritage, to the power of the pagan Babylonians, thus profaning it. Indeed, the whole kingdom is profaned, for the anointed king, his princes, and the leaders of the priesthood have been carried off into Babylonian captivity, where they can no longer carry out their functions (Lam. 2:2; Isa. 43:28). In neither passage should *ḥll* be read as "slain" or "pierced."[11] Cf. also Ps. 89:40 (Eng. v. 39), where the poet describes the desolation that God's wrath has brought upon king and people: "You have 'profaned' his crown in the dust."

In an oracle of judgment, Ezekiel proclaims that the splendor of the prince of Tyre will be "profaned" by the troops of Nebuchadnezzar. This prince, who has gained enormous wealth through his wily commercial policies, sits enthroned on his island fortress as on a mountain of God. With blasphemous arrogance he compares himself to the deity, and therefore his destruction can be called a "profanation" (Ezk. 28:7,16).

Lev. 21 discusses the holiness of the priests. V. 4 has been corrupted in the course of transmission, but in all probability means that a priest should not come near the dead relatives of his wife, because he would be defiled or profaned (*l^e^hēchallô*). A priest's unmarried daughter who commits fornication profanes not only herself but also her

[11] T. McDaniel, "Philological Studies in Lamentations, I," *Bibl,* 49 (1968), 35f.; J. McKenzie, *Second Isaiah. AB,* 20 (1968), 58.

father (v. 9). "That the daughter in a sense shares the objective holiness of her father and consequently can 'profane' herself not only morally but also cultically is a notion that may already be implicit in the marriage regulations for priests, but can also be derived from the stipulations determining how the members of the family share in the sacred offerings."[12] The high priest can only marry a virgin belonging to a priestly family; otherwise he would profane his own offspring (Lev. 21:15). In other words, the prospective high priest can be born only of a mother worthy of his office. Commercial fornication and cultic prostitution are forbidden in Israel. According to Lev. 19:29, a father who encouraged his daughter to become a harlot would be "profaning" her.

Of the various things that must not be profaned, the most important is the Sabbath. Eleven times the OT warns against profaning the Sabbath, six of them in Ezekiel. The Sabbath is undoubtedly a preexilic day of rest, established for religious and social reasons. During the exile it became an important confessional symbol distinguishing Jews from pagans. In a brief historical survey (Ezk. 20:13,16,21,24), Ezekiel accuses the first and second wilderness generations of having profaned the Sabbaths. Possibly he has in mind the facts recounted in Ex. 16:27ff. and Nu. 15:32-36 (gathering of manna and sticks on the Sabbath). He likewise chastizes the inhabitants of Jerusalem and Samaria for profaning the Sabbath (22:8; 23:38). Noteworthy is Ex. 31:14f. (P), with its thrice-repeated declaration that work done on the Sabbath will be punished with death. The orthodoxy and devotion of a member of the postexilic community can be judged most clearly from his observance (nonprofanation) of the Sabbath. The Sabbath commandment is also binding on the foreigner (proselyte) without exception (Isa. 56:2,6). Neh. 13:15-22 graphically depict the activity of those who profane the Sabbath day (*m^echall^elîm ʾeth-yôm hashshabbāth*). On his inspection of the countryside Nehemiah finds vintners and farmers who are treading the wine press and loading grain despite the Sabbath. Even in Jerusalem itself the market place is busy, and Nehemiah remonstrates with the nobles of Judah: "Did not your fathers act in this way, and did not our God bring all this evil on us and on this city?" He therefore gives orders that the gates be shut and guarded by Levites, to keep the Sabbath day holy (*l^eqaddēsh ʾesh-yôm hashshabbāth*).

Moreover, the holy offerings of the Israelites must not be profaned. This includes all the tribute Israel devotes to the support of its priests. In Lev. 22:9,15, the priests are admonished conscientiously to observe all the regulations governing their enjoyment of the sacrificial offerings, eating them only in a state of purity. Otherwise Yahweh himself will punish them with premature death. The same sanction applies to anyone who still eats the flesh of the community sacrifice on the third day (Lev. 19:8); such behavior shows that he does not distinguish holy food from ordinary food.

The prophets Zephaniah and Ezekiel are referring to these regulations when they accuse the Jerusalem priesthood of profaning what is sacred and not distinguishing what is holy from what is common (Zeph. 3:4; Ezk. 22:26). Nu. 18:32 demands that the Levites not profane the tithe received from the people by forgetting to give a tithe of this tithe to the priests.

The altar on which the sacrifices are burned is also accounted a sacred object. It is

[12] K. Elliger, *HAT*, 4 (1966), 289.

profaned if it is not built out of unhewn stones (Ex. 20:25). This restriction is probably based on the belief that only untouched objects are sacred and can be used in the presence of the deity.

In addition, a vow of abstinence that has been sworn before Yahweh must not be broken (*lō' yachēl*); one must do precisely what has been said (Nu. 30:3[2]). This holds true for any solemnly established covenant. Ps. 55:21(20) may refer to a covenant of friendship that has been broken by faithlessness. Ps. 89:32-35(31-34) speaks clearly of the covenant made by Yahweh with David and his descendants, which he will not "profane" or violate even though the other party may be guilty of "profaning" the statutes. For Malachi, Israel's common sonship and the covenant at Sinai impose a special obligation to mutual solidarity. He can therefore ask: "Why then are we faithless to one another, profaning the covenant of our fathers?" (2:10).

Yahweh's land is profaned by the unclean carcasses of the idols worshipped there (Jer. 16:18). Isaiah proclaims the downfall of the wealthy commercial center of Tyre and speaks metaphorically of "profaning the pride of all glory" (Isa. 23:9). Finally, Gen. 49:4 and 1 Ch. 5:1 speak of Reuben's profaning the couch of his father Jacob and thus losing the right of primogeniture. The authors clearly see Reuben's sleeping with Bilah, his father's concubine (Gen 35:22), a profanation of Jacob or of his intimate marriage relationship.

4. *Sacred and Profane*. *ḥōl* is the opposite of → קדשׁ *qdš;* both terms are frequently used in parallelism with → טמא *ṭāmē'* and (→ טהר *ṭāhar*). In Lev. 10:10, the priests are required to abstain from wine and strong drinks. While v. 9 bases this demand on the dangerous proximity of the deity in the sanctuary,[13] the author of v. 10 has purely practical ends in view: only in this way will the priests be protected against mistakes when carrying out their duties, which include instructing the people concerning the laws of purity and the conduct of a holy life. Cf. Ezk. 22:26, where sins in these matters are castigated, and Ezk. 44:23, where the priestly duties of the new cultic law are set forth.

The new temple area constitutes a square 500 cubits on a side, surrounded by a wall separating the holy (the temple building and its courts) from the common (Ezk. 42:20). "In its new, pure dimensions the plan of the temple area is understood as a clear separation of the sacred precincts from the realm of the profane, through which in the future all profanation through 'abominations' will be prevented."[14] But the city itself together with the surrounding pasturage is profane (48:15). Zimmerli finds in the formula *chōl hû'* the linguistic form of the priest's declaratory judgment.[15]

In the OT narrative 1 S. 21:5f.(4f.), *chōl* occurs twice. The priest Ahimelech has no common bread (*lechem chōl*) at his disposal to offer to David and his followers. But the bread of the Presence can be eaten only by the priests, and only in a state of purity. Ahimelech will make an exception in the case of David if the condition of purity (abstinence from sexual intercourse) has been fulfilled. David assures him that his

---

[13] *Ibid.*, 134.

[14] Zimmerli, *BK*, XIII, 1069.

[15] *Ibid.*, 1223.

followers are pure, even though what is involved is not a "holy" but only an "ordinary" undertaking (*derekh chōl*).

Finally, the interjection *chālîl* and its emphatic form *chālîlāh,* which occur 21 times, are to be understood on the basis of the OT *qdš* notion. The expression is usually translated "far be it from me," *chālîlāh lî mîyhvh* (1 S. 24:7[6], etc.) as "Yahweh forbid." The original meaning is probably expressed in some such wording as "May it be (my) profanation (in the eyes of God) if I break my oath."[16]

Dommershausen

[16]Cf. Lehmann, 82f.

חָלַל *chālal* II

Contents: I. Etymology and Occurrences. II. Secular Usage. III. Theological Usage: 1. Slain in Battle; 2. Murdered or Executed; 3. Wounded; 4. "Wounded for Our Transgressions." IV. Metaphorical Usage.

I. Etymology and Occurrences. The root *ḫll* is found throughout the entire range of the Semitic languages, always with the meaning "hollow out, pierce." Akk. *ḫālilu* is an iron tool for digging; in Neo-Babylonian it means "canal."[1] In Arabic, too, in spite of a few points of contact, it is not necessary to assume a connection between *ḫalla,* "pierce, wound," and *ḥll* I. Cf. also Arab. *ḫillat,* "stone coffin," and *ḫallat,* "fissure."

Of the derivatives, the adjective *chālāl,* "pierced, slain," appears most frequently in the OT, with 94 occurrences in 21 books. There are also the words *challôn, challônî,* "window," "having many windows," *challāh,* "ring-shaped bread," and *m^echillāh,* "cave." An independent group is formed by *ḥll* III, "play the flute," which, however, derives undeniably from *ḥll* II. Cf. Ethiop. *ḫel(l)at,* "hollow stick," with *chālîl,* "flute." In post-biblical Hebrew we also find *chôlēlā'*, "drill," and *ch^alîlā'*, "round about." Also worth mentioning are the metaphorical meanings: *chālāl,* "interior," "thoughts," and *ch^alālā'*, "wealth."[2]

chālal. O. Eissfeldt, "Schwerterschlagene bei Hesekiel," *Studies in OT Prophecy. Festschrift T. H. Robinson* (1950), 73-81 = *KlSchr,* III (1966), 1-8; J. J. Glück, "Ḥalālîm (Ḥālāl) 'carnage, massacre,'" *RevQ,* 7 (1969/71), 417-19; M. Z. Kaddary, "חלל = 'BORE', 'PIERCE'?" *VT,* 13 (1963), 486-89.

[1]*AHw,* I, 311.
[2]*WTM,* II, 59f.

II. Secular Usage. The primary use of *chālāl* is as a technical term in military language: the *chᵃlālîm* are those "pierced" in battle, the slain of one's own forces or of the enemy (1 K. 11:15; 1 S. 17:52), the corpses that are stripped and then buried (1 S. 31:8). Sometimes the weapons that inflict the wounds are also mentioned. Jeremiah (14:18) has a vision of the coming disaster: the war lost, and the battlefield full of those slain by the sword (*chalᵉlê-cherebh*). Of David's mighty men we are told that they wielded their spears against three hundred slain (2 S. 23:8,18). Frequently *chālāl* is found in combination with *nāphal*. Cf. *vaiyippᵉlû chᵃlālîm* in Jgs. 9:40 and 1 S. 31:1. But *chᵃlālîm* can also refer to the victims of murder. At Mizpah, after the gruesome slaying of Gedaliah, Ishmael has defenseless pilgrims slaughtered without apparent reason and the "slain" cast into a cistern (Jer. 41:9). The teacher of wisdom warns against adultery, which has claimed many victims (*chᵃlālîm,* Prov. 7:26).

III. Theological Usage.

1. *Slain in Battle.* According to the Song of Moses (Dt. 32:42), Yahweh swears that he will intervene as a warrior on behalf of his people, "slaying" with his sword the heads of the enemy leaders. That in the past wars fought by Israel were actually "wars of God" is clearly stated in 1 Ch. 5:22; for this reasons many "fell pierced" (*chᵃlālîm rabbîm nāphālû*) in the war between the transjordanian tribes and their neighbors. In his war against a coalition of kings, Joshua receives a comforting message from Yahweh: "Do not be afraid . . . for I will give over all of them slain to Israel" (Josh. 11:6). The Chronicler uses a similar formula from the holy war (2 Ch. 13:16f.): God gave Jeroboam and Israel into the hand of Abijah of Judah, so that many choice men fell "slain."

This ancient usage is also incorporated into the prophetic oracles against the nations, and it is therefore fundamentally Yahweh who cuts down the slain: " 'I will cast down your "slain" before your idols' " with the help of the Babylonians (Ezk. 6:4,7,13), " 'I will fill [Edom's] mountains with the "slain," . . . in all your ravines those "slain with the sword" shall fall' " (Ezk. 35:8), " 'I will send . . . blood into the streets (of Sidon),' " where the "slain" will fall (Ezk. 28:23). And on the day of Yahweh the sword of the Babylonians will come upon Egypt so that the "slain" will fall (Ezk. 30:4). But in Jer. 51:3f.,47-52, Yahweh himself orders the Babylonians to give up their hopeless battle for their own land and city, while at the same time he summons the attackers to carry out the ban: all of Chaldea will be full of "slain" and pierced. Here *mᵉdhuqqārîm* stands as a synonym for *chᵃlālîm*. In the bloody downfall of the world power God's righteousness is revealed: Babylon must fall for the "slain" of Israel, just as the "slain" of all the earth have fallen for Babylon (v. 49). In an oracle of Yahweh against the Assyrian Empire, Nahum draws a sharply etched picture contrasting the tumultuous battle with the deathly stillness of the petrified battlefield (Nah. 3:3). "The effect of the various terms for the dead . . . is ghastly":[3] *chālāl, pegher, gᵉvîyāh*. Such a battlefield with the corpses of the slain, with the birds of prey feeding on decaying flesh, is also envisioned in Job 39:30.

---

[3] K. Elliger, *ATD*, XXV (⁶1967), 18.

2. *Murdered or Executed.* The allegory of Pharaoh as a mighty tree (Ezk. 31:17f.) and the dirge on his descent into the Underworld (Ezk. 32:20-32) several times associate those "slain by the sword" with the uncircumcised. To them—according to the word of Yahweh—the king must descend. This represents his utmost disgrace: he will not lie in honor among the mighty men with their swords laid beneath their heads (v. 27), but among unclean pagans and those executed or murdered by the sword.

The psalmist lamenting in Ps. 88:6f. (Eng. vv. 5f.) feels that Yahweh has put him among the *chalālîm* "in the depths of the Pit"; here, too, we probably have an allusion to the place of those who have been murdered or executed. According to Ezk. 9:6f., Yahweh orders the murderers to institute a bloodbath in the very precincts of the temple, and "slay" all who do not bear the mark put on their foreheads. Those who remained behind in Jerusalem after 597 have a multitude of murdered compatriots on their consciences (probably killed for nationalistic reasons), and Yahweh will call them to account (Ezk. 11:6f.).

In Jeremiah's vision, Yahweh's judgment upon the nations transforms the earth into an enormous field of corpses. The poet pictures God himself going forth, delivering the wicked to his avenging sword by his own hand (Jer. 25:33, "those slain by Yahweh"). An equally grim picture of the final judgment is painted by Isa. 34:3. Yahweh has put the nations under his ban, and therefore they must be slain. The "slain" are not granted burial, because as sinners they do not deserve it. Instead "the stench of their corpses shall rise; the mountains shall flow with their blood." The devout will find mercy in God's judgment, but those who worship idols will be slain by fire and the sword, and "those slain by Yahweh" will be many (Isa. 66:16). In Zeph. 2:12 likewise, in an oracle against the Cushites (Egyptians), the sword of Yahweh "is better visualized as a sword of judgment than as a sword of war, so that here, too, the *chalelê cherebh* are more likely the victims of execution or murder than battle casualties."[4]

In the religious sphere are two rituals described in the Pentateuch. Whoever touches someone who has been "murdered" or has died through disease or accident, or even touches human bones or a grave, becomes unclean for seven days and must be sprinkled with a special water of purification on the third and seventh days (Nu. 19:16-19). Here *chalal cherebh* stands in parallelism with *mēth,* i.e., someone whose death was not violent. The word *chālāl* in Dt. 21:1-3, 6 is to be understood in the same sense: someone is found "slain" in the open country, and the murderer is unknown. The community, in this case the inhabitants of the village nearest the scene of the crime, must make propitiation; for, in the eyes of ancient Israel, blood wrongly spilled cries out for vengeance. The act of propitiation consists in the slaying of a heifer by a stream. The blood swept away by the water symbolizes the removal of the blood of the murder victim.

Finally, three passages should be mentioned which describe Yahweh (Ps. 89:11[10]), his arm (Isa. 51:9), or his hand (Job 26:13) as "piercing" (*mechôleleth, chōlalāh*). In each case Yahweh's act of creation is being depicted, using mythological language, as the slaying of the dragon or the monster Rahab.

---

[4]Eissfeldt, *KlSchr,* 5.

3. *Wounded.* Four passages in the OT speak of the *ch*ᵃ*lālîm* as groaning or crying for help. Jeremiah tries to disperse the hopeless gloom of the exiles by means of an oracle: Yahweh will carry out his judgment upon Babylon, and the battlefield will be strewn with the destroyed images and the "groaning wounded" who worshipped them (Jer. 51:52). Ezk. 26:15 paints a similar picture of the fall of Tyre. The sound of her fall and "the groans of the wounded"—in true Semitic hyperbole—shake the isles, i.e., the inhabitants of the coastlands must fear that the same fate awaits them. According to Ezk. 30:24, it is Yahweh's intention to see Jerusalem destroyed by the king of Babylon. The prophet has the concrete historical situation before his eyes: Nebuchadnezzar destroys the Egyptian army sent to help lift the siege of Jerusalem, so that Pharaoh groans like a man mortally wounded. Job (24:12) lists examples of injustice that provoke divine judgment, but God remains silent when murderers commit their crimes in the city and the "abused" cry for help.

4. *"Wounded for Our Transgressions."* Ps. 69 is the lament of a "servant of Yahweh" (v. 18[17]), who, despite his zeal for the temple and God's cause, is unaccountably smitten by Yahweh and "wounded" (v. 27[26]). The reference is to a serious disease with which he is afflicted. His enemies—in accordance with the old belief that sickness is a punishment for sin—attempt to ferret out the sins of the servant, thus adding to the pain of "him whom Yahweh has wounded" (*ch*ᵃ*lāleykhā*).

The Servant of Yahweh in Isa. 53:5 is also "wounded" (*m*ᵉ*chōlāl*) in his body: he bears the stripes of punishment and is familiar with sickness. He is a prophetic servant of God, for whom the suffering Jeremiah may have furnished a model. But in his case salvation for Israel and the nations comes not from what he preaches, but from his offering of his life as a propitiation for many, his innocent and vicarious suffering on behalf of others. The healing gained for others through his wounds comprises the forgiveness of sins and the removal of their punishment, in other words, the alleviation of suffering.[5] Cf. also Isa. 53:10 with the reading attested in 1QIsᵃ "and he caused him to be wounded" (*vaichall*ᵉ*lēhû*).[6]

IV. Metaphorical Usage. In Lam. 4:9, "those pierced by the sword" are contrasted with "those pierced by hunger"; the death of the victims of the sword is considered preferable. The poet is obviously thinking of slow starvation.[7] Hungry infants are also described as *kechālāl* (Lam. 2:12). And when Isaiah cries to the city of Jerusalem, "Your 'slain' are not 'slain' with the sword" (22:2), he likewise means that they will be "pierced" by plague or starvation. Cf. also Jer. 8:20,23(9:1).

Ezekiel uses *chālāl rāshā*ᶜ in the sense "mortal sinner" as a term of condemnation for king Zedekiah and the inhabitants of Jerusalem (Ezk. 21:30[25],34[29]). Also metaphorical is Ps. 77:11(10), "I am pierced, that the right hand of the Most High has changed," if *challôthî* is not to be read as the qal infinitive construct of *chālāh,* "be

---

[5] C. Westermann, *Isaiah 40–66. OTL* (trans. 1969), 269.

[6] J. Morgenstern, "The Suffering Servant—a New Solution," *VT,* 11 (1961), 318.

[7] A. Guillaume, "A Note on Lamentations IV 9," *ALUOS,* 4 (1962/63), 47f.

sick.''[8] A similar expression is possible in Ps. 109:22, if we are not dealing with a pual of *chîl,* ''writhe.''

Only in Lev. 21:7,14 do we find *chᵃlālāh* (a ''pierced'' woman). The priests are required not to marry a woman who has already been deflowered, ''neither a prostitute nor a woman who has been dishonored against her will or in a moment of indiscretion.''[9]

Dommershausen

[8]M. Dahood, *Psalms II, AB,* XVII (1968), 229.
[9]K. Elliger, *HAT,* 4 (1966), 289.

חָלַם *chālam;* חֲלוֹם *chᵃlôm*

Contents: I. Ancient Near East: 1. Egypt; 2. Mesopotamia, Hittites, Mari; 3. West Semites. II. 1. Etymology; 2. Occurrences; 3. Form of Dream Narratives. III. Significance of Dreams in the OT: 1. Incubation; 2. Valuation of Dreams; 3. Nonsymbolic Dreams; 4. Symbolic Dreams; 5. Interpretation of Dreams; 6. Dreams in Similes.

I. Ancient Near East.

1. *Egypt.* The Egyptian word for ''dream'' is *rśw.t.*[1] It is common in such expressions as ''see a dream,'' ''see something in a dream,'' etc. The word, which also

chālam. F. Alexander, ''Dreams in Pairs and Series,'' *International Journal of Psycho-Analysis,* 6 (1925, repr. 1953), 446-452; H. Bonnet, ''Traum,'' *RÄR,* 835-38; A. de Buck, *De godsdienstige Opvatting van den Slaap inzonderheid in het oude Egypte. MEOL,* 4 (Leiden, 1939); A. Caquot, ''Les songes et leur interpretation selon Canaan et Israel,'' in *Les songes et leur interprétation. Sources Orientales,* 2 (Paris, 1959), 99-124; E. L. Ehrlich, *Der Traum im AT. BZAW,* 73 (1953); *idem,* ''Der Traum im Talmud,'' *ZNW,* 47 (1956), 133-145; *idem,* ''Traum,'' *BHHW,* III, 2023-25; T. Höpfner, ''Traumdeutung,'' *PW,* ser. 2, VI 2 (1937), 2233-2245; J. Obermann, *How Daniel Was Blessed with a Son. JAOSSup,* 6 (1946); A. Oepke, ''ὄναρ,'' *TDNT,* V, 220-238; A. L. Oppenheim, *The Interpretation of Dreams in the Ancient Near East, with a Translation of an Assyrian Dream-Book. TAPhS,* N.S. 46/3 (1956); I. Rabinowitz, '' 'Pēsher/Pittārōn': Its Biblical Meaning and its Significance in the Qumran Literature,'' *RevQ,* 8 (1972/75), 219-232; A. Resch, *Der Traum im Heilsplan Gottes* (1964); W. Richter, ''Traum und Traumdeutung im AT,'' *BZ,* N.S. 7 (1963), 202-220; S. Sauneron, *et al., Les songes et leur interprétation. Sources Orientales,* 2 (Paris, 1959); F. Schmidtke, ''Träume, Orakel und Totengeister als Künder der Zukunft in Israel und in Babylonien,'' *BZ,* N.S. 11 (1967), 240-46; J. Vergote, *Joseph en Égypte. OrBibLov,* 3 (1959); A. P. F. Volten, *Demotische Traumdeutung. Analecta Aegyptiaca,* 3 (1942); A. Wikenhauser, ''Doppelträume,'' *Bibl,* 29 (1948), 100-111; → חָזָה *chāzāh.*

[1]*WbÄS,* II, 452.

means "awaken" (both transitive and intransitive), has an open eye as its determinative, apparently representing dreaming as a special state of consciousness, something like "watching during sleep."[2] According to Gunn,[3] *wp.t m3ᶜ.t,* "message of truth," also refers to a dream revelation. Dreams do not belong solely to the night, which is considered a temporary death;[4] the dream of Thutmose IV[5] takes place at noon, and the Instruction for Merikare[6] speaks of "dreams by day and night."

The Egyptians are familiar with both pleasant dreams and nightmares;[7] the latter are associated with Seth. In addition, "dream" can stand metaphorically for something without substance, for instance, "The time of that which is done upon earth is like a kind of dream."[8]

The Egyptian accounts of dreams have been collected by Oppenheim[9] and Sauneron. Among them royal dreams, both historical and literary, play an especially important role, even though Volten's thesis[10] that all other dream narratives should be taken as "popularizations" of this genre is not convincing. The earliest attested example is the dream in which Amon reveals himself to king Amenhotep II to give him strength and protection in battle. The most famous is the detailed account of a dream on the sphinx stela of Thutmose IV,[11] a fully developed "princely novella" whose significance for 1 K. 3:1–15 has been emphasized by M. Görg.[12] An announcement of the future kingship and a formula promising assistance here frame the commission to free the colossal statue of the sphinx from the sands of the desert. The vision of a huge statue of Ptah in a dream of Merneptah,[13] in which a sword is handed to him, also promises support in battle. The symbolic dreams of the two Ethiopian pharaohs Shabaka[14] and Tanutamon[15] refer to the losing and gaining of hegemony. The late so-called Famine Stela, where Khnum promises Zoser blessing and fruitful years after seven years of famine, has long been associated with the biblical account of Pharaoh's dreams (Gen. 41:1ff.).[16]

But the Joseph traditions themselves remind us that it is not just kings to whom the gods give instruction in dreams. This circumstance is also attested by the Egyptian dream books,[17] which illustrate more than two thousand continuous years of oneiro-

---

[2]Cf. Oppenheim, 226.

[3]B. Gunn, "Notes on Ammenemes I," *JEA,* 27 (1941), 2–6.

[4]De Buck; Sauneron, 19f.

[5]Sphinx stela, see below.

[6]Lines 136–37.

[7]Sauneron, 55, n. 9.

[8]Song of the Harpist; see H. Grapow, *Die bildlichen Ausdrücke des Ägyptischen* (1924), 140, with additional references.

[9]Pp. 251–54.

[10]P. 41.

[11]*Urk.*, IV, 1539–1544.

[12]M. Görg, *Gott-König-Reden in Israel und Ägypten. BWANT,* 105 (1975), 54ff.

[13]Sauneron, 24f.

[14]Herodotus *Hist.* ii.139.

[15]*Urk.*, III, 61f.

[16]Vergote, 43ff.

[17]Sauneron, 32ff.

mancy. The hieratic Book of Dreams (Papyrus Chester Beatty III, dating from the Ramesside period), whose content appears to go back to the Middle Kingdom, lists formulaically a host of situations ("When a man sees in a dream how he . . . ") and then states whether the dream is to be interpreted "favorably" or "unfavorably." In the interpretation, the personality of the dreamer is also taken into account, viz., whether he is dominated by Horus (good) or Seth (bad). The widespread use of such dream books in the late period is attested by much demotic evidence.[18] The demotic Book of Dreams published by Volten (Papyrus Carlsberg XIII and XIV vo.) is the best preserved. There were also special interpreters of dreams, usually associated with the "house of life" of the temple complex. Vergote[19] derives the Heb. *chartummîm* (→ חרטם *charṭōm*) from an Egyptian title *ḥry-tp*.

The practice of incubation with the purpose of receiving a dream oracle is attested in the late New Kingdom for the sanctuary of Meretseger at Deir el-Medineh, but the bulk of the evidence dates from the later period.[20] At the "sanatoria" in the late temple complexes, too, especially at Dendera, the practice probably developed out of dream oracles.[21] Greek papyri speak of healing dreams, in which the gods Imuthes (Imhotep), Isis,[22] and Bes play a particular role. Numerous evocations of dreams are also found in the magical texts.[23] In the later period there was an intimate relationship between Greek and Egyptian oneiromancy.[24] Egyptian dream interpretation obviously was held in high esteem, as is illustrated by Claudianus' late mention of "*aegyptia somnia*."[25]

Bergman

2. *Mesopotamia, Hittites, Mari.* In Sumerian, "dream" is *ma-mú* or *ù*, in Akkadian, *šuttu* (from the same root as *šittu*, "sleep" [→ ישן *yšn*]), as well as *munattu*, *ḫiltu*, and *tabrīt mūši*, "nocturnal revelation," from *barû*, "see." In Hittite texts we find both Sum. *ù* and Hitt. *tešḫaš*. The verb *tešḫanna*, "appear in a dream," is used of gods revealing themselves.

Dreams are discussed in royal inscriptions (Gudea, Ashurbanipal, Nabonidus, autobiography of Hattusilis), letters, and epics (the dreams of Dumuzi, Gilgamesh).

In Akkadian, a dream is normally "seen" (verbs: *amāru*, *naṭālu*, also *naplusu* and *šubrû*, "cause to see," with a deity as subject). The dream narratives almost always follow a fixed schema: the dream itself is set in a framework that records the identity of the dreamer, the time (usually *ina šāt mūši*, "in that night"), the place, and the circumstances. The narrative concludes with the sudden awakening of the dreamer, and often with his reaction.

The dreamer is passive. The deity may appear to him in various ways: entering and

---

[18] Volten, 5f.
[19] Pp. 66–73.
[20] Bonnet, 837f.; Sauneron, 40–47.
[21] Sauneron, 48ff.
[22] Diodorus Siculus i.25.
[23] Bonnet, 838.
[24] Volten, 69.
[25] *In Eutropium* i.312.

leaving (*erēbu-aṣû*), standing at his head, placing its hand on his. Conversation with the dreamer is rare. Occasionally demons also appear, wishing to harm the dreamer. There is also a "god of dreams" (^{d}*Ma-mú*, ^{d}*Zaqīqu*).

Dreams can be classified according to their content. Frequently (and perhaps originally) the dream comes during incubation, i.e., a visit to a temple to receive a dream oracle. Only rarely is the healing of a disease involved, but a Hittite text tells of a man who was healed of impotence.[26] When incubation is involved, the dreamers are usually kings or priests. The dream is preceded by sacrifice and prayer. An example is the second dream of Gudea,[27] in which he receives an interpretation of his first dream about building a temple.[28] In difficult situations, kings resort to incubation in order to seek counsel, for instance, in the Hittite version of the legend of Naram-Sin,[29] Ashurbanipal during the attack of the Elamites,[30] and Nabonidus after Nebuchadnezzar has appeared to him and interpreted another dream.[31] It is reasonable to conjecture that the *bārû* priests and *šāʾilu* priests received oracles through dreams.[32] The dreams that come during incubation are not symbolic; the message from the deity is transmitted in clear wording and does not need special interpretation.

Certain dreams require the performance of some action: the placing of a statue in the temple (Ammiditana),[33] the offering of votive sacrifice (Nabonidus). A dream can furnish the inspiration for a work of art (e.g., in the epilogue to the Akkadian epic of Erra). Something analogous may lie behind 1 Ch. 28:11-19; Ex. 25:9; Nu. 8:4.

The message of a dream can appear as a miracle. During the civil war between Ashurbanipal and his brother, a youth saw in a dream an inscription predicting the fall of Babylon on the pedestal of a statue of Sin[34] (cf. Dnl. 5).

Certain dreams were considered to derive not from divine revelation but from the psychological state of the dreamer. These could be either pleasant (*šunāte damqāte*, "good dreams") or unpleasant (*limnu*, "evil," *pardu*, "confusing," *aḫû*, "remarkable," *eklu*, "black," *lā ṭābu*, "not good"). If someone has had bad dreams, he prays for good dreams.[35]

Dreams announcing the death of the dreamer create consternation. In Sumerian literature, we read that Dumuzi had such a dream; he seeks to remove its effect and escape his fate, but is unable to.[36] Enkidu's dream of death on tablet VII of Gilgamesh is, psychologically speaking, an anxiety dream; it depicts a descent into the nether

---

[26] Oppenheim, 194.
[27] *SAHG*, 141f.
[28] Oppenheim, 212.
[29] H. G. Güterbock, "Die historische Tradition und ihre literarische Gestaltung bei Babyloniern und Hethitern bis 1200," *ZA*, N.S. 8 (1934), 86-91.
[30] Oppenheim, 201f.
[31] *Ibid.*, 204ff.; *ANET*, 308ff.
[32] Oppenheim, 199, 221f., 224; *ANET*, 394-96.
[33] Oppenheim, 192.
[34] *Ibid.*, 201f.
[35] *Ibid.*, 230.
[36] *Ibid.*, 236.

world. A similar theme is treated in the so-called vision of the Underworld by an Assyrian crown prince.[37]

Symbolic dreams are obscure in content and need interpretation, which constitutes part of the dream account. In the first dream of Gudea, the building of the temple is represented by symbols: a plan of the building, a basket, and a brick mold.[38] In Dumuzi's death dream there appear symbols such as stalks of grass and reeds that attack each other, and a falling tree.[39]

The significance of a dream can be underlined by repetition. Gilgamesh receives news of Enkidu's coming in a sequence of two parallel dreams.[40] A series of three dreams also appears in Gilgamesh[41] and *Ludlul bel nēmeqi*.[42] There are analogous accounts of two or more people having the same dream simultaneously, so-called double dreams,[43] for example, Ashurbanipal and Nabonidus.[44]

A symbolic dream demands interpretation. The verbs used are Sum. *bur,* Akk. *pašāru*. But these terms can also have a different meaning: "undo" a dream, i.e., negate its evil effects.[45] A dream can be interpreted in three different ways: (a) intuitively through the agency of a qualified individual; (b) through the use of collections of dream omina; (c) through appeal to a deity. A *šā'ilu* or *bārû* priest can function as an interpreter of dreams; women having this function also appear.

Dream omina are attested from the Old Akkadian period on. During the seventh century B.C., Assyrian scholars produced a dream book.[46] It is couched in the usual omen form, with a protasis containing the dream and an apodosis providing the prediction. An appendix contains a collection of rituals for "undoing" bad dreams.[47] But the omina obtained by extispicy were much more important. There were no dream interpreters attached to the court, as in Egypt. It is recorded that Egyptian dream interpreters (*ḫardibi,* i.e., *ḥry-tp* [→ חרטם *charṭōm*]) were summoned to the Assyrian court.[48]

Ottosson

At Mari, a dream (*šuttum*) is a frequent means of revelation to both cultic officials and laymen. While there is no distinguishable difference between dreams and visions (*pānū*), a distinction seems necessary in the case of incubation dreams[49] with their

[37]W. von Soden, "Die Unterweltsvision eines assyrischen Kronprinzen," *ZA,* N.S. 9 (1936), 1-31; Oppenheim, 213f.

[38]*SAHG,* 142.

[39]Oppenheim, 212f., 246.

[40]Gilg. I, 5, 25ff.; 6, 24ff.

[41]Oppenheim, 215f.

[42]*Ibid.,* 217, 250.

[43]Wikenhauser.

[44]Oppenheim, 209.

[45]*Ibid.,* 302f.

[46]*Ibid.,* 256ff.

[47]*Ibid.,* 295ff.

[48]*Ibid.,* 238; *ANET,* 293.

[49]*ARM,* X, 100.

desire for information, abstinence rituals, and sleep in the temple. The revelation received in a *šuttum* comes through vision;[50] hearing can also be involved[51] or even replace vision.[52] The nature of the message (success, disaster, information) is not determined by the nature of the *šuttum,* nor can it be specified with certainty that the temple was the site of the dream. The content of what is revealed in the *šuttum* is, as a rule, not meant for the dreamer himself, but must be transmitted to the king.[53]

Botterweck

3. *West Semites.* In the Ugaritic texts, we find two detailed accounts of dreams. The epic of Keret[54] tells how Keret weeps and sighs in his chamber (*ḥdr*) and then lies down. El appears to him in his sleep: "In his dream (*ḥlm*) El came down, in his vision (*d̲hrt*) the father of mankind approached."[55] El asks him why he weeps; Keret replies, and El instructs him in what he must do to receive a son.[56] Then Keret awakens: "Keret saw and it was a dream, the servant of El and it was a *ḥdrt*"[57] (theophany? [→ הדר *hādhār*]). The literary form of the account exhibits the usual framework. Whether incubation is involved is not clear, since *ḥdr*[58] probably does not refer to a room in the temple.

The other text, however,[59] does appear to describe an incubation, although the word *ḥlm* does not appear in the extant text. Dan'el eats, drinks the *ʒzr* of the gods (food-offerings?), and lies down to sleep. On the seventh day, Baal appears and promises him a son. Later El appears also to have revealed himself and announced that Dan'el's wife was pregnant.

In addition, the word *ḥlm* occurs in the myth of Baal,[60] where we read that after the revival of Baal it is seen in a dream and a vision (*d̲rt*) how the heavens rain oil and the ravines flow with honey.

In the Sefire treaty, if the text is correct, the word *ḥlm* appears once in a simile:

---

[50] *Ibid.,* 10.

[51] *Ibid.,* 50f.

[52] *ARM,* XIII, 112.

[53] Cf. F. Ellermeier, *Prophetie in Mari und Israel* (1968), 85-92, 178f.; F. Nötscher, "Prophetie im Umkreis des alten Israel," *BZ,* N.S. 10 (1966), 161-197, esp. 178-189; C. Westermann, "Die Mari-Briefe und die Prophetie in Israel," in his *Forschung am AT,* I. *ThB,* 24 (1964), 171-188, esp. 177ff.; A. Malamat, "Prophetic Revelation in New Documents from Mari and the Bible," *Volume de Congrès, Genève, 1965. SVT,* 15 (1966), 207-227, esp. 221f. = his *Mari and the Bible* (Jerusalem, 1973), 62-82; J. F. Craghan, "Mari and its Prophets," *BTB,* 5 (1975), 32-55.

[54] *CTA,* 14 [I K], I, 26ff.

[55] *Ibid.,* 35-37.

[56] *Ibid.,* II, 9ff.

[57] *Ibid.,* III, 50f.

[58] *Ibid.,* I, 26.

[59] *CTA,* 17 [II D], I, 1ff.

[60] *CTA,* 6 [I AB], III, 4, 10.

"Then shall the kingdom become like a sand kingdom, like a dream kingdom ruled by Assyria."[61] Possibly we have a dittography: *kmlkt ḥl mlkt ḥlm.*

An ostracon from Elephantine (3rd century B.C.) speaks of a "first dream that I saw" (*ḥlm ḥzyt*).[62]

II. 1. *Etymology.* The etymology of *ḥlm* has not been completely explained. A verb *ḥlm* with the meaning "dream" is found in Ugaritic,[63] Aramaic (Jewish, Christian-Palmyrene, Samaritan, Mandaic), Arabic, and Ethiopic. There is also a *ḥlm* with the meaning "be strong": Syr. *ḥᵉlîm,* "powerful," Arab. *ḥalama* and Tigré,[64] "come of age." *GesB* and *BDB* suggest two different roots. KBL^2 and KBL^3 see a semantic development from "come of age" through "have sexual dreams" to "dream" in general. This development seems a bit forced; there is much to support the hypothesis of two roots.

2. *Occurrences.* The verb *chālam* is attested 24 times in the qal and twice in the hiphil (Isa. 38:16; Jer. 29:8). The noun *chᵃlôm,* "dream," occurs 60 times, 20 of which are as cognate object with the verb. Dream narratives appear primarily in Genesis and Daniel; elsewhere dreams are mentioned only sporadically. In many cases it is hard to distinguish dreams from dreamlike states, since Hebrew can use other more or less synonymous expressions: *chᵃzôn/chezyôn lailāh,* "night vision" (Isa. 29:7; Joel 3:1 [Eng. 2:28]; Job 4:13; 7:14; 20:8; 33:15; Dnl. 1:17; 7:1); *mar'āh,* "vision" (Gen. 46:2; Nu. 12:6; 1 S. 3:15); *dābhār,* "word" (Jgs. 7:9; 1 S. 3:10; 15:10ff.; 2 S. 7:4; Dnl. 10:11). The auditory element appears frequently, in both dreams and visions.

3. *Form of Dream Narratives.* Dreams normally take place at night: *chᵃlôm h/ballailāh* (Gen. 20:3; 31:24; 40:5; 41:11; 1 K. 3:5).[65] The description involves stereotyped phrases:[66] "he fell asleep" (Gen. 41:5), "he lay down" (Gen. 28:11; cf. Job 7:13; Dnl. 7:1), "he awoke, and behold, it was a dream" (Gen. 41:7; 1 K. 3:15), "he awoke" (Gen. 28:16; Ps. 73:20). The dream itself is usually introduced with *vᵉhinnēh* (Gen. 28:13, etc.). The dreamer is usually passive: he sees (Gen. 31:10; 41:22) and hears. God, however, is active: he "came" in a dream (Gen. 20:3; 31:24), "he appeared" (1 K. 3:5; 2 Ch. 1:7), "he made himself known" (*hithvaddaʿ,* Nu. 12:6), or "spoke" to the dreamer (Gen. 20:3; 31:11), he "stood beside" him (Gen. 28:13; 1 S. 3:10). Incubations can also involve conversations.

III. Significance of Dreams in the OT.

1. *Incubation.* In an incubation, a king or popular leader visits a sanctuary in order

[61] *KAI,* 222 A.25.
[62] *KAI,* 270 A.
[63] See I.3 above.
[64] *TigrWb,* 53b.
[65] Cf. J. T. Willis, "On the Text of Micah 2:1aα–β," *Bibl,* 48 (1967), 537f.
[66] See Richter for an analysis of the form.

to obtain an oracle. There is only one complete account of an incubation extant: 1 K. 3:5-15 par. 2 Ch. 1:6-12. Here is recorded how Solomon betakes himself to Gibeon in order to seek a dream oracle. He offers sacrifice and lies down to sleep. Yahweh appears (*nir'āh*) to him in a dream, and Solomon engages in conversation with God. Afterwards he offers sacrifice again (in Jerusalem). The Chronicler does not use the word *chᵃlôm,* undoubtedly because of a negative estimation of dreams as vehicles of revelation.

Gen. 46:1-5 could be an incubation: Jacob comes to the cultic site at Beer-sheba, offers sacrifice, and converses with God in visions of the night (*bᵉmar'ôth hallailāh*). He is assured of God's protection and a multitude of descendants. Gen. 28:10-22 likewise contains elements of an incubation. Jacob lies down to sleep at a sacred site; God appears to him and promises him the land, descendants, and protection. Jacob offers a libation and promises to build a house of God and offer a tithe. According to Ehrlich,[67] this is not a true incubation, since Jacob does not realize at the outset that the place is sacred. Oppenheim calls the episode an "unintentional incubation."[68]

Certain features of an incubation are also present in Gen. 15.[69] Abraham is probably at Hebron, where he has built an altar. The word of Yahweh comes to him in a vision (*bammachᵃzeh*), undoubtedly at night (v. 5); a conversation ensues, and Abraham receives the promise of descendants and the land. In what follows, however, Abraham is awake and offers sacrifice. In v. 12, sleep falls upon him once more and Yahweh speaks to him. The covenant, however, is not concluded in a dream.[70]

The texts just mentioned are all local traditions associated with cultic sites. They are essentially identical in literary structure. In the Genesis traditions, the theme of the land and descendants stands out (as in Keret).

The dream in which Samuel receives his call (1 S. 3) is sometimes also termed an incubation, but the mere fact that the dream is experienced in the temple is an insufficient criterion. The word *chᵃlôm* is not used, but rather *dābhār, chāzôn* (v. 1), and *mar'āh* (v. 15); the context shows, however, that a dream experience is involved.[71] The auditory element predominates. Yahweh awakens Samuel three times to prepare him for the revelation;[72] then he "stands beside him" (v. 10; cf. *Ludlul bēl nēmeqi* and Nabonidus). Yahweh's message points to Samuel's prophetic role (v. 20), which leads to further visions (v. 21). There is a parallel in the dream of the priest of Ishtar.[73]

It is commonly assumed that there are allusions to incubation in Ps. 3:6(5); 4:9(8); 63:3(2), but the expressions are too vague to permit a definite conclusion.[74] There is a possible allusion in Hezekiah's hymn of thanksgiving (Isa. 38:15f.), if the hiphil of *ḥlm* is translated "cause to dream" rather than "make strong, healthy": "I groan

---

[67] *BZAW,* 73 (1953), 27ff.

[68] P. 187.

[69] Ehrlich, *BZAW,* 73 (1953), 35ff.

[70] *Ibid.*, 39; on the lack of unity in this chapter, see G. von Rad, *Genesis. OTL* (trans. ²1973), 182f.

[71] Contra H. J. Stoebe, *KAT,* VIII/1 (1973), 124f.

[72] "*Wecktraum*"; Oppenheim, 249.

[73] *Ibid.*, 249.

[74] Ehrlich, *BZAW,* 73 (1953), 51.

through the hours of my sleep, in the bitterness of my soul. . . . Revive my spirit of life, let me dream and make me live.'' V. 17 then introduces the turn for the better with *hinnēh*.

2. *Valuation of Dreams*. Dreams are considered a vehicle of divine revelation, even if incubation is not involved. In dreams God ''opens the ears of men'' and gives them his warnings, says Elihu (Job 33:16; cf. Akk. *uznā puttû*). This view is made especially clear in Nu. 12:6-8, where the office of Moses is compared with that of the prophets. With Moses, Yahweh speaks mouth to mouth and visibly, and Moses sees his form; to the prophet, Yahweh makes himself known (*hithvadda*ʿ; → ידע *yādha*ʿ) in visions (*bammarʾōth*); he speaks to them in dreams.[75] The auditory element is also underlined in 1 S. 28:6: Yahweh does not answer (*ʿānāh*) in dreams, or by Urim, or by prophets. Since the prophets are singled out, we can assume that Saul himself tried to obtain a dream oracle.[76]

Nu. 12:6 associated revelations through dreams with the prophets. Joel 3:1(2:28) holds out a similar prospect for the eschaton: ''Your old men shall dream dreams, and your young men shall see visions.'' Dt. 13:1-6(12:32-13:5), on the contrary, warns about dreamers and prophets who will mislead the people into serving other gods. Even if their dreams turn out to be true, they are not to be followed. Jeremiah, too, draws a sharp line between the *dābhār* of the true prophets and the *chᵃlôm* of the false (Jer. 23:25-32). Dreams deceive, but the word of Yahweh is ''like fire and like a hammer which breaks the rock.'' Jer. 27:9f. and 29:8 speak of dreams together with false prophets and all kinds of soothsayers. The same negative estimate of dreams is expressed in Zec. 10:2.

In Eccl. 5:2,6(3,7), we find, not unexpectedly, a very negative evaluation of dreams:[77] Their revelatory nature is denied, and they are associated with nothingness (→ הבל *hebhel*).[78] Later, Sir. 31:1-8 reject dreams in similar fashion as the concern of fools; bad dreams, on the other hand, can disquiet everyone (40:5ff.).

3. *Nonsymbolic Dreams*. In nonsymbolic dreams, the dreamer receives instructions that are immediately comprehensible. God ''comes at night in a dream'' (Gen. 20:3; 31:24) and speaks to the dreamer, who replies (Gen. 20:3; 31:11; 1 S. 3:10; 1 K. 3). Laban receives only the command not to interfere with Jacob (Gen. 31:24). Gen. 20 (E) is the only version of the ''peril of the ancestress'' that contains a dream account (cf. the variant in 1QGenAp 19:14ff.). In Gen. 31:10-13, Jacob receives the command to return to his homeland. In his dream, however, he also sees an image drawn from the ordinary life of herdsmen, promising him in semisymbolic form his future inheritance from Laban. V. 10 contains the word *vᵉhinnēh,* which is typical of symbolic dreams,

---

[75] *Ibid.*, 138f.; Oppenheim, 209f.

[76] Cf. Ehrlich, *BZAW*, 73 (1953), 139f., and the Hittite parallels in the Mursilis text, *ANET*³, 396; cf. also Ehrlich, 57.

[77] Cf. H. J. Schoeps, ''Träume als Ausdruck der Sünde,'' in his ''Symmachusstudien III,'' *Bibl*, 29 (1948), 41f.

[78] For a similar use in an Akkadian wisdom text, see Oppenheim, 227.

but the introductory phrase "I lifted up my eyes and saw" is drawn from visionary style (Zec. 2:1[1:18], etc.; Dnl. 8:3; 10:5). V. 13 recalls Jacob's first dream at Bethel (Gen. 28).

Without the use of the word "dream," similarly structured divine commands appear in Gen. 21:17ff.; 22:1-3; 26:24; Josh. 5:13ff.

4. *Symbolic Dreams*. The most detailed narratives are of the symbolic dreams, which demand interpretation. As in the Akkadian parallels, the interpretation is an integral part of the narrative. "A dream without interpretation is like an unopened letter."[79] Most of the symbolic dreams are found in Genesis and Daniel. A symbolic dream also appears in Jgs. 7:13f.: a Midianite soldier sees a cake of barley bread that tumbles into the camp and overturns the staff tent. A companion interprets the cake as the sword of Gideon and the collapse of the tent as the defeat of the Midianites. For Gideon, who overhears their conversation, this means a convincing divine assurance of victory.

The dreams needing interpretation are almost always experienced by non-Israelites, although the dream is sent by the God of Israel. Upon awakening, the dreamer is troubled (Gen. 40:5; 41:8; Dnl. 2:3) because no one can interpret his dream. The dreams of the butler and baker in Gen. 40 are similar in structure: three vines corresponding to three cake baskets. Joseph interprets the number three as referring to a period of three days within which the Pharaoh will elevate his butler and decapitate his baker. Gen. 41 recounts the dreams of Pharaoh: twice seven cows and twice seven ears of grain, with the number seven symbolizing the number of the good years and the number of the lean years.

The symbolic dreams in Daniel bear the stamp of apocalyptic. The symbols in the dreams of Nebuchadnezzar are fantastic, and derive at least in part from mythological conceptions. In Dnl. 2, the king sees a great image or statue (*tsalmā'*), the various parts of which symbolize four kingdoms. A stone not thrown by human hand breaks down the statue and grows into a mountain that fills the earth. In his second dream (3:31-4:34[4:1-37]), Nebuchadnezzar sees a mighty tree that reaches to heaven; then "a watcher, a holy one" comes down from heaven and proclaims that the tree is to be hewn down. This time the tree symbolizes the king himself. Cf. Pharaoh Merneptah's dream of the great statue of Ptah[80] and the great tree in the death dream of Dumuzi.[81]

The symbolic dreams experienced by Israelites are always self-explanatory, i.e., their meaning is immediately clear. In Joseph's dreams (Gen. 37:5ff.), the symbolism immediately suggests his future exaltation: the sheaves of his brothers bow before Joseph's sheaf; the sun, the moon, and eleven stars bow before him. Daniel's vision of the four beasts and the son of man is characterized as a dream in the introduction (Dnl. 7:1f.). The new element is his writing down what he sees. The vision expands into an apocalyptic panorama, which Daniel at first passively observes. Then, troubled by the incomprehensibility of the dream, he finally has to ask for the "interpretation of the

---

[79] *Ber*. 53a.
[80] Oppenheim, 251.
[81] *Ibid*., 246.

things'' (*p^eshar millaiyā*', 7:16). Although chap. 8 reverts to Hebrew and the word ''dream'' is not used, but rather *chāzôn,* it constitutes to some extent a parallel to the earlier dream (cf. v. 1: *'ach^are hannir'āh 'ēlai batt^echillāh*, and the expression ''I raised my eyes,'' which introduces a dream in Gen. 31:10). Auditory elements appear in both 7:16 and 8:13ff. Although Daniel's ability to interpret dreams is emphasized elsewhere (cf. Symmachus, who calls Daniel *chōlēm,* ''interpreter of dreams,'' in Zec. 6:14[82]), here he does not understand what he sees. Strangely enough, the interpretation is provided in the same vision. It is worth noting that in Daniel's dream he is transported to the fortress of Susa and the river Ulai (cf. Ezk. 11:1, etc.).

Symbolic dreams are often underlined by repetition; the same content appears with variations in a second dream. Examples are Gen. 37:1ff. (sheaves and stars bowing), Gen. 41 (seven cows and seven ears), Dnl. 2–3 (a statue and a tree), Dnl. 7–8 (see above); cf. also 1 K. 9:2: ''Yahweh appeared to Solomon a second time, as he had appeared to him at Gibeon.'' Gen. 41:32 explains the repetition of the dream as a sign that God's decree is fixed.

5. *Interpretation of Dreams.* The interpretation of symbolic dreams constitutes a part of the dream account. It is God who sends dreams (Job 7:14). The dreamer is troubled and frightened (Job 4:13ff.; 7:14), since he does not know what God intends. Only God knows the correct interpretation. Pharaoh and Nebuchadnezzar summon their professional dream interpreters (→ חרטם *charṭōm*) and astrologers (Gen. 41:8, 24; Dnl. 1:20; 2:2), but they cannot interpret the dreams, since they do not know the God who sends the dream. In Ex. 7:11 and elsewhere the *charṭummîm* are represented as professional magicians; in Jer. 27:9, the dreaming prophets are lumped together with all kinds of magicians and sorcerers. As dream interpreters, Joseph and Daniel appear as Yahweh's instruments, demonstrating his superiority over foreign magic. Only in a single instance (Jgs. 7:15) is a non-Israelite capable of interpreting a dream. Here the word *shebher* is used as a term for interpretation; it may mean the ''undoing'' of the dream.

When the butler and baker have had their dreams, they are troubled because there is no *pōthēr* (Gen. 40:8). Pharaoh and Nebuchadnezzar react similarly before they hear the *pittārôn* (or *pishrā*') (Gen. 41:11; Dnl. 2:3; 4:2[5]). The root *ptr/pšr* is cognate with Akk. *pašāru* and is generally translated as ''interpret, explain.'' Since a symbolic dream gives expression to a future reality, *pittārôn* conveys the double meaning of ''both presage of reality and realized presage''[83] (cf. Gen. 41:13; Dnl. 4:25[28]).

In the OT view, human fate was determined by God. Through dreams, Yahweh gave a hint of events to come. If the dream was negative, it could not be undone through magical means. Its interpretation belonged to Yahweh (Gen. 40:8; 41:16, 39; Dnl. 1:17; 2:28; 4:15[18]), and the dreamer must submit (Dnl. 2:46; 4:31ff.[34ff.]). Daniel hesitates because he is afraid the interpretation will be negative (Dnl. 4:16[19]). Joseph, on the contrary, assures Pharaoh of a favorable interpretation (*shālôm,* Gen.

---

[82]Cf. Schoeps, *Bibl,* 29 (1948), 40f.

[83]Rabinowitz, 222.

41:16). Joseph and Daniel play similar roles as dream interpreters; among other things, Daniel is called *m^e phashshar chelmîm* (Dnl. 5:12).

All dream interpretation presupposes that the content of the dreams comes from the realm of the divine and announces the future. Interpretation of symbolic dreams therefore requires divine inspiration. In Mesopotamia, the gods could warn men of their fate so that they could protect themselves by means of apotropaic rites. As a rule, the OT rejects dreams as a means of divination. None of the prophets appeals to a dream oracle. Deuteronomy and Jeremiah in particular have a negative evaluation of dreams.

6. *Dreams in Similes.* Occasionally dreams are used in similes to express unreality and worthlessness. "He [the sinner] will fly away like a dream, and not be found; he will be chased away like a vision of the night," we read in Job 20:8. Ps. 73:20 says much the same of the godless: "They are like a dream when one awakes, on awaking you despise their phantoms." In Isa. 29:7, "the multitude of all the nations that fight against Ariel" are likened to "a dream, a vision of the night"—so fruitless will be their attack. According to v. 8, it will be as though the attackers themselves had merely satisfied their hunger and thirst in a dream: when they awake, they are thirsty and faint.

Only in Ps. 126:1 is "dream" used in a positive simile: "When Yahweh restored the fortunes of Zion, we were like those who dream," so enormous and unreal did the event appear to the devout.[84]

Ottosson

[84]On this passage, cf. esp. S. Speier, "Sieben Stellen des Psalmentargums in Handschriften und Druckausgaben," *Bibl,* 48 (1967), 507f.

חָלַף *chālaph;* חֲלִיפָה *ch^a lîphāh;* חֵלֶף *chēleph;* מַחֲלָפוֹת *machl^e phôth*

Contents: I. Basic Meaning, Occurrences. II. Meaning in OT Hebrew. III. Theological Usage.

I. Basic Meaning, Occurrences. The root *ḥlp* appears to be common to all the Semitic languages with the basic meaning "follow in sequence," "exchange," "replace." It is attested in Akk. *ḫalpu,* "substitute,"[1] Phoenician, Moabite ("succeed," Mesha Inscription[2]), and Arab. *ḫalafa,* "succeed, replace," then "be different, di-

chālaph. N. J. Tromp, "De radice חלף in lingua hebraica," *VD,* 41 (1963), 299-304.

[1]*AHw,* I, 313.
[2]*KAI,* 181, 6.

verge," "transgress (a commandment)." Occurrences in Aramaic appear to be especially frequent, both in Old Aramaic and in the later dialects. In Biblical Aramaic, the peal imperfect *yachl^ephûn* appears in the expression "let seven times pass over," repeated four times (Dnl. 4:13,20,22,29 [Eng. vv. 16,23,25,32]). The word *chēleph*, "in return for," in Nu. 18:21,31 is considered an aramaism (cf. Aram. *ch^alāph*).[3]

In Biblical Hebrew, the root *ḥlp* occurs most often in Job (9 out of 40 occurrences). It appears in early poetry (the Song of Deborah) and early narrative (the Jacob and Joseph traditions; the narratives of Samson, and Elisha and Naaman). It occurs 7 times in Isaiah and 5 in the Psalms. The other scattered occurrences are few in number.

Attempts have been made to distinguish this root (*ḥlp* I) from a root *ḥlp* II, "be sharp." Some evidence for the latter can be cited in other Semitic languages, including postbiblical Hebrew. The word *mach^alāphîm* in Ezr. 9:1 is often derived from this root, with the meaning "sacrificial knives" (RSV "censers"), but the meaning is obscure. Tromp finds *ḥlp* II also in Isa. 2:18 (the idols will be "cut down") and Job 14:7 (if the tree is "cut down"). Driver translates Isa. 9:9(10): "we will 'dress' (carve, trim) cedars.'"[4] In all these cases, however, it is more natural to assume *ḥlp* I; the same applies to Jgs. 5:26 and Job 20:24 (usually rendered "pierce").[5] Only a single root *ḥlp* need therefore be assumed in Biblical Hebrew.

II. Meaning in OT Hebrew. The basic meaning of the root is best illustrated by several verb forms in the hiphil and piel with the concrete meaning "change." In Gen. 31:7,41, Jacob accuses Laban of having "changed" his wages ten times; according to Lev. 27:10, it is forbidden to "exchange" one sacrificial animal for (*b^e-*) another (synonym *yāmîr*); in Isa. 9:9(10), sycamore wood is replaced by cedar (*va'^arāzîm nach^alîph*). In several passages the verb has "clothing" as an accusative object. Changing clothes is mentioned particularly as a way of preparing for religious acts, often accompanied by ablutions: in Gen. 35:2 before Jacob and his family set out for Bethel; in Gen. 41:14 before Joseph's audience with Pharaoh; in 2 S. 12:20 before David enters the temple. Ps. 102:27(26) states figuratively that Yahweh changes the heavens like raiment (*kall^ebhûsh tach^alîphēm*), and they pass away. It has been suggested that this verse is based on the mythological notion of the heavens as the raiment of the deity.[6]

This concrete meaning is incorporated by the verbal noun *ch^alîphāh* (originally expressing an activity; almost exclusively in the plural), which appears most frequently in the expressions *ch^alîphôth ś^emālôth* (Gen. 45:22 [twice]), *ch^alîphôth b^eghādhîm* (Jgs. 14:12f.,19; 2 K. 5:5,22f.): a "change" of clothes, and thus concretely clothes to be changed, festal garments. The expression *ch^alîphôth v^etsābhā'* in Job 10:17 can be taken as hendiadys: "relief armies";[7] the textual emendation proposed by

---

[3]M. Wagner, *Die lexikalischen und grammatikalischen Aramaismen im alttestamentlichen Hebräisch. BZAW*, 96 (1966), 56.

[4]G. R. Driver, "Studies in the Vocabulary of the OT, VI," *JTS*, 34 (1933), 381f.

[5]See below.

[6]R. Eisler, *Weltenmantel und Himmelszelt* (1910), I, 51ff.

[7]Dhorme.

KBL[3] on the basis of the LXX is hardly necessary. Job paints a concrete picture of God's enmity: he sees himself surrounded by hostile troops, constantly relieving each other. He uses the same image of relief in a military context to express an illusory hope that his destiny will be changed for the better: he will persevere in battle until he is relieved (*ʿadh-bôʾ chᵃlîphāthî,* the only occurrence of the singular). The word is used adverbially in 1 K. 5:28(14): Solomon sends laborers to Lebanon in monthly relays (*chᵃlîphôth chōdhesh*). A difficulty is raised by Ps. 55:20(19), which says of the psalmist's enemies: *ʾên chᵃlîphôth lāmô. KBL*[3] here suggests a specialized meaning "agreement," as a synonym to *bᵉrîth* in the next verse. More in agreement with the usual meaning of the verb is the translation "no change is theirs," i.e., they never cease doing evil.

The idea of change is also present in another word with concrete meaning, *machlᵉphôth,* "braided hair" (Jgs. 16:13,19).

The verb also appears in the qal. In these cases it is usually used intransitively in the sense "move from one place to another." Here we often find *ʿābhar* used as a synonym. The movement can involve approach; then it means "come upon" or "come over" someone, and is used of violent natural phenomena and catastrophes, and especially of attacking enemies. In Isa. 8:8, the Assyrians are likened to the Euphrates, sweeping on into Judah and overflowing (*vᵉchālaph bîhûdhāh shāṭaph vᵉʿābhar*); in Isa. 21:1, the armies of the Medes and Elamites are likened to storms that sweep through the desert in the Negeb (*kᵉshûphôth banneghebh lachᵃlōph*); Hab. 1:11 describes the Chaldeans as a wind (*rûach*) that sweeps past and goes on (*chālaph, ʿābhar*). The noun *rûach* also appears in Job 4:15; here we are dealing with a phenomenon accompanying a revelation of the divine word, which causes terror. Perhaps we may translate: "a puff of wind blew over my face." In two passages (Job 9:11; 11:10) God is the subject, and the verb seems to refer to the afflictions God visits upon Job. In the first passage Job compares God to a beast of prey or a robber who falls upon his victim before the victim can see and defend himself (*vᵉyachᵃlōph vᵉlōʾ—ʾābhîn lô;* synonymously *yaʿᵃbhōr ʿālai*). The second passage draws on 9:11f. and appears to have the same meaning.

The verb can also signify movement away from the speaker: "go on" (1 S. 10:3, of Saul), "go past" (Cant. 2:11, of rain). Job 9:26 depicts reed skiffs "going by." Thus we have the specialized meaning "vanish." In Isa. 2:18, the idols "pass away" (reading the plural with 1QIs[a]); in Ps. 102:27(26), the heavens "perish" (punning on the other meaning of the hiphil); in Ps. 90:5f., men "perish" like the grass (text uncertain; v. 6a may be dittography of 5b; on the other hand, a contrasting parallel to 6b is expected).

From the verb "pass away," the verbal noun *chᵃlîphôth* takes on the meaning "past" (Sir. 42:19, contrasting with *nihyôth*).

Used intransitively, the hiphil means "be renewed": Job 14:7, "if a tree is cut down, it can sprout again"; Job 29:20, "my bow is renewed [or: 'drawn again'] in my hand" (*KBL*[3] here translates "sprouts," alluding to Aaron's rod in Nu. 17:23, which appears forced); Isa. 40:31, "they who wait for Yahweh shall renew their strength" (Isa. 41:1 may be dittography of 40:31).

The meaning of some texts is uncertain. In Isa. 24:5, the verb occurs transitively in the qal (*chālᵉphû chōq*). Some scholars read the piel here ("they have changed the statutes"), but the qal provides better parallelism with the preceding *ʿābhᵉrû thôrōth;* elsewhere, too, *ʿābhar* and *chālaph* appear in parallel. The translation could be: "They have turned aside from the statutes." Two other transitive qal forms (Jgs. 5:26 and Job 20:24) are usually derived from *ḥlp* II and translated "pierce, cut through." The actual translation is not really convincing, and it is therefore preferable to assume *ḥlp* I here as well. The context shows that in both cases a movement is signified, involving approach: Jael "struck" Sisera's temple with the hammer (Jgs. 5:26); the bronze arrow will "hit" Job even if he flees (Job 20:24). Totally obscure, finally, is Prov. 31:8, *bᵉnê chᵃlôph* ("departed," "weak," "orphaned"?).

Tengström

*Sometimes *chālaph* appears in legal texts, since (esp. in the hiphil) it can refer to substitution (e.g., in the matter of sacrificial offerings [Lev. 27:19]).

The juridical sense of the term appears more clearly in postbiblical texts, where it can appear in the restitution clause "upon demand I will *replace* the document."[8]

(Fabry)

III. Theological Usage. Theologically significant are the passages that speak of God's active intervention, not only the two cases where God is himself the subject of the verb, but also the other texts where *ḥlp* means "come upon" or "fall upon." In the last analysis, it is Yahweh who causes the enemy to fall upon Israel. Thus *ḥlp* includes a nuance of inescapable violence that characterizes Yahweh's intervention. In the prophetic literature this violence is represented as a just punishment. The book of Job, however, relates the problem of theodicy to the individual; God's actions now appear incomprehensible and seemingly arbitrary.

More important, perhaps, are the meanings "pass away," "vanish." The prophets often speak of idols passing away (cf. Isa. 2:18). Yahweh, contrariwise, is the only true God, represented as the renewer (Isa. 40:31). In Wisdom Literature, the transitoriness of man and the world is an important theme, while God appears as the unchanging one. He is the author of creation and all its transformations (Ps. 102:26f.[25f.]); he himself is exalted above all change (vv. 28f.[27f.]).

Tengström

---

[8]Cf. E. Koffmahn, "Die 'Restitutionsklausel' in den aramäischen Vertragsurkunden von Murabbaʿât," *RevQ*, 14 (1963/64), 421-27.

חָלַץ *chālats*

Contents: I. 1. Root; 2. Etymology. II. 1. *chālats,* "Deliver," in the OT; 2. Verbal Forms; 3. Synonyms; 4. Context; 5. LXX and Vulgate. III. 1. Yahweh as Deliverer; 2. Psalms; 3. Wisdom Literature; 4. Theological and Secular Usage.

I. 1. *Root.* While *KBL*[2,3], *WTM,* and other lexicons[1] cite only a single root *ḥlṣ* with a wide variety of meanings, according to *GesB* we are dealing with three independent homonymous roots. This problem must remain unresolved for now. We shall, however, attempt to distinguish the substantially independent meanings of the root and trace their semantic development.

a. The meaning "take off, lay bare"[2] is attested in Hebrew (Dt. 25:9f. [ritual of shoe removal]; Isa. 20:2; Lam. 4:3), Jewish Aramaic, and Middle Hebrew. It developed in various directions. On the one hand, we find Hebrew piel "take out (stones)" (Lev. 14:40, 43; Gunkel[3] finds a similar usage in Ps. 17:14, emending *ḥlqm* to *ḥlṣm*), Aram. "pull out (fish)."[4] On the other, we find Syriac pael "shear," Ethiop. *laḥaṣa,* "peel," Middle Hebrew niphal "be removed, become detached," hiphil "detach." Yet again, we find Hebrew piel "plunder" (Ps. 7:5 [Eng. v. 4]; cf. *chᵃlîtsāh,* "spoil," Jgs. 14:19 and 2 S. 2:21; in 2 Ch. 28:21, *ḥlṣ* should perhaps be read for *ḥlq*[5]), Christian Palmyrene and Syriac pael "plunder," all probably associated with Arab. *ḫalasa,* "steal."

b. From the meaning "escape, withdraw" attested in Hebrew (Hos. 5:6), Jewish Aramaic, and Arabic,[6] there probably developed the resultative usage of *ḥlṣ* for "deliver, save" ("cause to escape"). For Hebrew, cf. the biblical occurrences[7] and the personal name *chelets.*[8] Cf. also Pun. *pdyḥlṣ ʾš ḥlṣ* (not satisfactorily explained)[9] as

chālats. C. Barth, *Die Errettung vom Tode in den individuellen Klage- und Dankliedern des AT* (Zollikon, 1947), 126-146, esp. 129; E. Jenni, *Das hebräische Piʿel* (Zurich, 1968), 138, 190, 240; J. L. Palache, *Semantic Notes on the Hebrew Lexicon* (Leiden, 1959), 29f.; W. J. Roslon, *Salus hominis in VT* (Warsaw, 1970); W. Rudolph, "Eigentümlichkeiten der Sprache Hoseas," *Studia Biblica et Semitica. Festschrift Th. C. Vriezen* (1966), 313-17; J. Sawyer, "What Was a Mošiaʿ?" *VT,* 15 (1965), 475-486, esp. 479; *idem, Semantics in Biblical Research. SBT,* N.S. 24 (1972).

1 Cf. also Jenni, 138.
2 *GesB ḥlṣ* I.
3 H. Gunkel, *GHK,* II/2 (1926; ⁵1968).
4 *KAI,* 274, 4; 275, 3.
5 *KBL*³.
6 *GesB ḥlṣ* II.
7 See II.1.
8 Cf. *IPN,* 180.
9 *KAI,* 73, 4-5.

well as the personal name *ḥlṣbʿl*[10] and *ʾšmnḥl*[*ṣ*];[14] Old Aramaic pael *ʾḥlṣk;*[12] Middle Hebrew hiphil "deliver"; also Arab. *ḫalaṣa* II and V, with its derivative *muḫalliṣ,* deliverer." Palache considers *ḫlṣ,* "deliver," to be an independent root.

c. The totally independent semantic group "gird," "strengthen,"[13] attested in Hebrew and Middle Hebrew, appears to be connected with the noun → **חלצים** *chᵃlātsayim,* "loins," "hips": cf. the Hebrew passive participle qal *chālûts,* "girded (for battle)," niphal "arm oneself," hiphil "make strong"; Syr. and Mand. *ḥlîṣaʾ,* "ready for battle"; Middle Hebrew hiphil "arm," "strengthen." Akk. *ḫalṣu,* "fortress," "redoubt," probably belongs here as well. Kutscher[14] considers *ḥlṣ,* "be strong," an independent root.[15]

d. None of the meanings listed accounts for the use of the root in the sense "be pure," "be white," found only in Arabic and Akkadian. Cf. Akk. *ḫalaṣu,* "press out," "comb out," *ḫalṣu,* "purified,"[16] as well as OSA and Arab. *ḫalaṣa,* "be pure," "be white," II "make pure," *ḫāliṣ,* "purified," and other derivatives.[17]

2. *Etymology.* Neither "gird," "arm"[18] nor "be pure"[19] suggests any conceivable semantic development that could have led to the meaning "deliver"; Delitzsch's suggestion[20] that Arab. *ḫalaṣa* means "be pure," i.e., "free," is pure conjecture. In the case of "take off," "lay bare,"[21] there are two ways such a development could be plausible. On the one hand, with reference to the meaning "take out" attested in Hebrew and Old Aramaic, there is the possibility of a development from the concrete and specific to the figurative ("pull out"). Following this lead, even Delitzsch almost invariably translated *ḥlṣ,* "deliver," as "*herausreissen,*" "pull out."[22] On the other hand, the meaning "remove," "detach," attested primarily in Middle Hebrew, could be cited, here again with a development from concrete to figurative usage ("remove" > "set free, deliver"). It is this etymology, apparently, that led Buber and Rosenzweig to translate *ḥlṣ,* "deliver," as "*losschnüren,*" "*losmachen*" ("undo"), etc. Unfortunately both etymologies rest on very narrow evidence. The better deriva-

---

[10]*KAI,* 68, 4; 69, 1-2, 19.

[11]*KAI,* 72A, 3; 75, 7.

[12]*KAI,* 202A, 14; possibly *lhṣlty,* 266, 7; *DISO,* 95.

[13]*GesB ḥlṣ* III.

[14]E. Y. Kutscher, "The Language of the 'Genesis Apocryphon': A preliminary study," in *Aspects of the Dead Sea Scrolls. ScrHier,* 4 (²1965), 29.

[15]See *KBL*³.

[16]*CAD,* VI, 50; *AHw,* I, 311 associates "press out" with "pull out."

[17]Cf. H. Ringgren, "The Pure Religion," *Oriens,* 15 (1962), 93-96.

[18]See I.1.c.

[19]See I.1.d.

[20]F. J. Delitzsch, *Biblischer Kommentar über die Psalmen* (⁵1894), on Ps. 6:5(4).

[21]See I.1.a.

[22]*Psalmen.*

tion is probably one that starts from the meaning "withdraw, escape";[23] in this case the road to transitive usage in the sense "deliver" is substantially shorter. The fact that the intransitive qal is found only in Hos. 5:6 could be explained on the basis of regional linguistic features.[24] Whether etymological considerations played any role in the use of *ḥlṣ* in the sense of "deliver" can no longer be determined.

II. 1. *chālats, "Deliver," in the OT*. The verb *chālats* appears 15 times with the meaning "deliver." Twelve of these occurrences are in the Psalms or in psalmlike passages; the other 3 are in wisdom texts (Prov. 11:8f.; Job 36:15). The active piel is used 11 times (2 S. 22:20; Ps. 6:5[4]; 18:20[19]; 34:8[7]; 50:15; 81:8[7]; 91:15; 116:8; 119:153; 140:2[1]; Job 36:15), the passive niphal only 4 times (Ps. 60:7[5]; 108:7[6]; Prov. 11:8f.). An additional instance of the piel in the sense of "deliver" is 1QS 11:13.

2. *Verbal Forms*. Especially informative is a survey of the various inflectional forms and suffixes in the 15 or 16 passages cited. Only twice is an act of deliverance in the past mentioned (*vā'achallᵉtsekhā*, Ps. 81:8[7]; *chillatstā naphshî*, Ps. 116:8). Much more common (9 instances) are statements involving the durative present (*yᵉchallᵉtsēnî*, 2 S. 22:20 par. Ps. 18:20[19]; *vaichallᵉtsēm*, Ps. 34:8[7]; *yᵉchallēts*, Job 36:15; *nechᵉlāts*, Prov. 11:8; *yēchālētsû*, Prov. 11:9) or the future (*'achalletskhā*, Ps. 50:15; *'achallᵉtsēhû*, Ps. 91:15; cf. *yᵉchallēts naphshî*, 1QS 11:13). Imperative forms occur 3 times: *challᵉtsāh*, Ps. 6:5(4); *challᵉtsēnî*, Ps. 140:2(1); *vᵉchallᵉtsēnî*, Ps. 119:153; the form *yēchālᵉtsûn* in Ps. 60:7(5) (par. 108:7[6]) is also in an imperative context.

Of the pronominal suffixes, the 1st person singular is most frequent (6 occurrences, including 2 of *naphshî*), followed by the 2nd singular (2) and the 3rd singular and 3rd plural (once each).

3. *Synonyms*. In the immediate or more extended context we usually find synonymous verbs meaning "save." The verb → נצל *nṣl* hiphil, "save," literally "pull out," appears especially close to *ḥlṣ*, "save" (cf. 2 S. 22:20 par. Ps. 18:20[19] with v. 18[17]; Ps. 34:8[7] with vv. 5, 18, 20[4, 17, 19]; 91:15 with v. 3; Prov. 11:8f. with vv. 4, 6; and the variant of Ps. 116:8a in Ps. 56:14aα[3aα]). The hiphil of → ישע *yšʿ*, "save," literally perhaps "make room for someone,"[25] is also frequently used in parallel (cf. Ps. 6:5a[4a] with b; 34:8[7] with 7[6]; 116:8 with 6; 60:7a[5a] par. 108:7a[6a] with b). Other parallel terms include → משה *māshāh*, "draw out" (Ps. 18:20[19] with 17[16]); → לקח *lāqach*, "take, remove" (Ps. 18:20[19] with 17[16]); → פלט *pālaṭ* and → מלט *mlṭ* piel, "rescue" (Ps. 91:15 with 14; 116:8 with 4); → גאל *gā'al*, "redeem" (Ps. 119:153 with 154); as well as the verbs somewhat further removed conceptually → חיה *chāyāh* piel, "heal, give life" (Ps. 6:5[4] with 3[2]; 119:153 with 154); → נצר *nātsar*, "guard"; → שמר *shāmar*, "watch" (Ps. 140:2[1] with 5[4]); and → סגב *sāghabh*, "protect" (Ps. 91:15 with 14).

---

[23]See I.1.b.

[24]Rudolph.

[25]See Sawyer, *Semantics*, 9.

4. *Context.* The contexts in which *ḥlṣ,* "save," is used contain information about the particular situation to which the act of deliverance refers. Only in a few passages are these statements connected directly with the verb (*min* plus a noun naming the enemy or affliction): *mitstsārāh,* Prov. 11:8; *mē'ādhām rā',* Ps. 140:2(1); *mimmāveth,* Ps. 116:8; *mishshachath,* 1QS 11:13. In other cases *ḥlṣ* appears to be used absolutely, but the reference can be derived from parallel verbs (Ps. 18:20[19] from vv. 18[17] and 49[48]: *mē'ōyᵉbhî;* Ps. 34:8[7] from vv. 5[4], 7[6]: *mikkol-mᵉghûrôthāi/tsārôthāv*) or other information in the context (Ps. 50:15[13]; 81:8[7]; 91:15; Job 36:15; in Ps. 6:5[4], cf. vv. 9–11[8–10]; in 119:153, cf. vv. 154, 157). In Ps. 60:7(5), too, the deliverance refers to the affliction described in vv. 3–6(1–4). Only with reservations, therefore, can we speak of an "absolute" use of *ḥlṣ,* "deliver," like that attested for the hiphil of *yṣ'*.

5. *LXX and Vulg.* Among the ancient versions, the LXX usually translates *ḥlṣ* with *exaireín* (6 times) or *rhýesthai* (6 times); there is nothing to suggest why one or the other was chosen. Since the piel forms in Lev. 14:40,43 are also translated with *exaireín,* the use of this verb in the sense of "deliver" may have been motivated by an etymology of "taking out";[26] but cf. below.

The Vulgate translates *ḥlṣ,* "deliver," with *eripere* (6 times) or *liberare* (4 times), once with *eruere* (Ps. 50:15; also Lev. 14) and *salvum facere* (Ps. 18:20[19]). Jerome, by contrast, prefers *eruere* (7 times) or *liberare* (4 times), but never uses *eripere.* The figurative use of *eruere* in the sense of "deliver" does not appear to be found in classical Latin.

Comparison with the translation of other verbs of deliverance in the LXX and Vulg. shows that no fundamental semantic difference was felt between *ḥlṣ* piel, *yš'* hiphil, *plṭ/mlṭ* piel, *pṣh,* and *g'l.* In this case, therefore, it is not desirable to attach much importance to the ancient versions in trying to determine a "fundamental meaning."

III. 1. *Yahweh as Deliverer.* The theological relevance of *ḥlṣ,* "deliver," resides not so much in the word itself as in the way it is used. In all the passages, the subject who performs the act of deliverance is Yahweh. An apparent exception is Ps. 34:8(7), which says that the *mal'ākh yhvh* surrounds the devout like an encampment in order to deliver them. The passive forms in Ps. 60:7(5); 108:7(6); Prov. 11:8f. do not mention any subject explicitly, but the context admits no doubt: it is Yahweh alone who sees that men "are delivered."

That there is no deliverer but Yahweh is the central confession of Israel; to formulate it, *ḥlṣ* and many other verbs are available.[27] In the region of West Semitic, there are instances of an analogous use of *ḥlṣ,* "deliver" (cf. Old Aram. *w'nh 'ḥṣlk,* "and I will deliver you,"[28] and the Punic personal name dating from *ca.* 250 B.C.),[29] which

[26]See I.1.a.
[27]See II.3.
[28]Zakhir Stela, *ca.* 800 B.C., *KAI,* No. 202A, 14.
[29]See I.1.b.

make confession of the deliverance accomplished by Baal and Eshmun. Even the reference to divine deliverance in situations of affliction (e.g., at the hands of enemies)[30] is precisely analogous to the context of the occurrence in the Zakhir Inscription. Israel must have been familiar with such instances. The only difference to be seen is in the demonstration of Yahweh's uniqueness.

2. *Psalms*. The earliest form in which *ḥlṣ*, "deliver," was used theologically is probably the salvation oracle. The Zakhir Stela makes it certain that this form is preexilic. Its primacy is suggested by the fact that the bulk of OT use occurs in psalmody,[31] and even more clearly by our survey of the verbal forms,[32] among which, besides prayer and confession, divine assurance occupies a considerable space. Two typical examples of such oracles occur in Ps. 50, a "judgment liturgy," and Ps. 91, a didactic and parenetic poem. Common to both is the statement that Yahweh hears the call (*qārā'*) of someone in trouble (*beṯsārāh*) and assures him of deliverance (*'achalletskhā,* 50:15; *'achalletsēhû,* 91:15). In 34:8(7), too, the act of deliverance follows the cry of the afflicted (vv. 4[3] and 7[6]). A further example is contained in Ps. 81, a "judgment liturgy" similar to Ps. 50; here, however, the traditional sequence of a cry of distress followed by an assurance of deliverance has been transformed into a reminiscence of the exodus story (*batstsārāh qārā'thā vā'achalletsekhā*).

The use of *ḥlṣ,* "deliver," in laments and thanksgivings of the individual (Ps. 6:5[4]; 140:2[1] for the former, Ps. 18:20[19] par. 2 S. 22:20; Ps. 116:8 for the latter), as well as in communal laments (Ps. 60:7[5]; 108:7[6]—under the influence of the section of Ps. 57 that precedes it, the verse in Ps. 108 appears in individualized form), would be explained easily on the basis of its traditional use in oracles of salvation. The fact that in Ps. 18 (par. 2 S. 22) we are dealing with a thanksgiving of the king (cf. the Zakhir Stela!) might be significant for the history of the word.

3. *Wisdom Literature*. In the use of *ḥlṣ,* "deliver," in Israelite Wisdom Literature (Prov. 11:8f.; Job 36:15; in part also Ps. 34:8[7]; 91:15) the influence of the language of the Psalms is unmistakable. On the basis of personal experience, the assembled community was already addressed and even instructed in individual thanksgivings; now the deliverance of the faithful in general comes to the fore as the subject of monitory instruction. Job 36:15 gives voice to a new idea to the extent that here God (cf. v. 5!) no longer delivers the sufferer "from" his affliction, as was formerly said (e.g., Prov. 11:8: *mitstsārāh*), but rather "by" his affliction (*yechallēts ʿānî bheʿonyô*), i.e., guiding him to insight and salvation.

4. *Theological and Secular Usage*. In retrospect it must be emphasized once more that *ḥlṣ,* "deliver," is far from being exclusively a theological term. It is true that in all 15 occurrences[33] we are dealing with theological usage; nontheological usage of

[30]See II.4.
[31]See II.1.
[32]See II.2.
[33]See II.1.

this *ḥlṣ* therefore cannot be illustrated from the OT. This circumstance, however, is explained satisfactorily by the observation that the piel of *ḥlṣ* had other meanings as well, and that there were enough other words available for "deliver" in its everyday sense. The crucial point is that this everyday sense of "deliver" was expressed by *ḥlṣ* even in Old Aramaic,[34] as well as in Middle Hebrew and Arabic.

Barth

[34] *KAI*, No. 266, 7; but *KAI*, II, 314 prefers a derivation from *nṣl*.

חֲלָצַיִם *chªlātsayim;* מָתְנַיִם *mothnayim;* יָרֵךְ *yārēkh;* כֶּסֶל *kesel*

Contents: I. Occurrences and Meaning. II. Girding One's Loins. III. Metaphorical Use. IV. Loins as Locus of Strength. V. Coming Forth from the Loins. VI. *kesel*. VII. Conclusions.

I. Occurrences and Meaning. The noun *chªlātsayim* occurs only 11 times in the OT. The Aramaic equivalent is *chartsā'* (Dnl. 5:6; Targumim), Syr. *ḥaṣṣā*, Arab. *ḥaṣr*. In Akkadian synonym lists we find *ḫanṣātu* and *ilṣu*.[1] The Hebrew dual means "the (two) loins," i.e., "the body between the ribs and the hip bones."[2] Since the terms for parts of the body are for the most part very ancient—although occurrences do not go back before Isaiah—the verb *ḥlṣ* is probably denominative, exhibiting the following semantic development: place about the hips > gird > strengthen, → חלץ *chālats;* cf. Isa. 58:11: *yachªlîts*, "he will make strong."[3]

Much more frequently attested (46 times) is the ancient term *mothnayim* (likewise found only in the dual), Ugar. *mtnm*, Akk. *matnu*, "the (external) region of the loins, including the hips and the small of the back."[4] A clear terminological distinction cannot be made between loins and hips. More precise terminology appears only in Dnl. 5:6, where *qiṭrê chartsēh* means "his hip joints," something like Gen. 32:26,33 (Eng. vv. 25,32) (J), *kaph-yārēkh;* Ex. 28:42 (P), where the linen breeches of the priests are to reach from the loins/hips (*mtnym*) to the thighs (*yrkym*); and Sir. 30:12, where a

[1] *AHw*, I, 321, 373; *KBL*³, 309.

[2] *KBL*³.

[3] But *KBL*³ reads *yachªlîph* (p. 308); cf. E. Y. Kutscher, "The Language of the 'Genesis Apocryphon': A preliminary study," in *Aspects of the Dead Sea Scrolls. ScrHier*, 4 (1958), 29: 1QGenAp 2:8: *bḥlṣ*, "in strength," Syr. *ḥelîṣûṭā'*, "strength."

[4] *KBL*³, 619.

boy is to be struck on the *mtnym*. For both words the LXX prefers *osphýs,* the Vulg. *lumbus.*[5]

II. Girding One's Loins. "Girding one's loins" is a widespread practice and literary formula (for adornment: Dnl. 10:5). At home and at rest, the belt around the long outer garment was taken off; putting it on and tucking up the garment made its wearer ready for activity, and was done before setting out on a journey or going to work.[6] In particular, warriors tucked up their skirts before battle and girded their weapons, especially their swords, about their hips (*mothnayim,* 2 S. 20:8; 1 K. 2:5; Ezk. 23:15; Neh. 4:12[18]; *yārēkh,* Ex. 32:27; Jgs. 3:16,21; Ps. 45:4[3]; Cant. 3:8). Thus the girding of loins became a symbolic expression for strength and vigorous intervention. Literal girding of the loins is still meant in connection with the eating of the Passover lamb (Ex. 12:11) and in preparation for running (1 K. 18:46; 2 K. 4:29; 9:1). Figurative language is used in Jer. 1:17, "Gird up your loins (*mothneykā*)"; Job 38:3 and 40:7, "Gird up your loins (*ch*ᵃ*lāts*) like a man." The connection between girding and strength is illustrated particularly by the use of the verb → חזק *chāzaq:* Nah. 2:2(1): "gird (*ḥazzēk*) your loins (*mothnayim*)"; similarly Isa. 22:21: "I will gird him (*'ᵃchazzᵉqennû*) with your sash."[7] Obversely, loosing the belt about the hips is a sign of weakness: Job 12:21; with *ch*ᵃ*lātsayim,* Isa. 5:27; with *mothnayim,* Isa. 45:1.

Totally different is the practice of girding one's loins with sackcloth (*śaq*); it is an expression of humiliation. The phrase appears in conjunction with *mothnayim* in Gen. 37:34 (J); 1 K. 20:31f.; Isa. 20:2; Jer. 48:37; Am. 8:10 (Jth. 8:5; 2 Macc. 10:25). The context suggests that Isa. 32:11 should be translated: "Gird sackcloth [the LXX correctly adds *sáddous*] upon your loins (*ch*ᵃ*lātsayim*)." Job 12:18 is also meant pejoratively: God binds a waistcloth on the loins (*mothnayim*) of kings—here equivalent to stripping.

III. Metaphorical Use. We are dealing with purely metaphorical use when it is an abstraction that is "girded" about one's loins. Here the image suggests moral proximity, the state of being closely encompassed by some attribute (Jer. 13:11). The good wife girds her loins (*mothnayim*) with strength (Prov. 31:17). When the messianic king comes, righteousness will be the girdle of his *mothnayim* and faithfulness the girdle of his *ch*ᵃ*lātsayim* (Isa. 11:5, borrowed in part and applied to the faithful in Eph. 6:14). The nouns *mothnayim* and *ch*ᵃ*lātsayim* are completely parallel; the LXX translates the former by *osphýn,* the latter by *pleurás* ("side, flank, rib"). In 1 K. 8:19, too, *ch*ᵃ*lātsayim* is rendered as *pleurṓn;* the equivalent passage 2 Ch. 6:9 uses *osphýos.* In Sir. 30:12, *pleurás* stands for *mothnayim.*

The same image is suggested even when the loins are not mentioned explicitly: "Thou has girded me with gladness" (Ps. 30:12[11]); "the hills gird themselves with joy" (65:13[12]); the curse surrounds the wicked man like a belt (109:19); "the feeble

---

[5]Cf. H. Seesemann, "ὀσφύς," *TDNT,* V, 496f.

[6]Dalman, *AuS,* V (1937), 232-240.

[7]Cf. J. L. Palache, *Semantic Notes on the Hebrew Lexicon* (Leiden, 1959), 29f.; *KBL*³, 291.

gird on strength'' (1 S. 2:4); ''God has girded me with strength'' (2 S. 22:33,40 = Ps. 18:33,40[32,39]); God has girded himself with might (Ps. 65:7[6]; 93:1).

IV. Loins as Locus of Strength. The concrete and symbolic use of ''girding'' was so common that in a later stage of linguistic development the actual verb of ''girding'' did not have to be expressed. Then the girding is no longer symbolic of strength; the loins themselves are viewed as the locus of physical strength, as we read of the hippopotamus: *kōchô bhᵉmothnāv* (Job 40:16). ''My little finger is thicker [stronger] than my father's loins (*mothnayim*)'' (1 K. 12:10 = 2 Ch. 10:10). The negative metaphorical sense of the loins as the center of strength could also be expressed: the loins (*mothnayim*) are in anguish (Isa. 21:3; Nah. 2:11[10]), they ''tremble'' (Ps. 69:24[23]; Ezk. 29:7); probably also Isa. 15:4: ''the loins (*chᵃlātsayim*) of Moab tremble'';[8] Dt. 33:11: ''crush the loins (*mothnayim*)''; similarly Ezk. 21:11(6) and Sir. 35:22. To be taken more literally is the Aramaic passage Dnl. 5:6 mentioned above (see I): ''the joints of his hips grew loose.'' According to Jer. 30:6, every man places his hands on his loins (*chᵃlātsayim*)—indicating pain—like a woman in labor. ''Smiting one's thigh'' (here *ʿal-yārēkh*) is likewise an expression of inward pain (Jer. 31:19; Ezk. 21:17[12]).

V. Coming Forth from the Loins. Another formula is used for physical procreation: ''come forth (*yātsāʾ*) from the loins.'' It does not appear in conjunction with *mothnayim*, which may indicate that *mothnayim* refers more to the hard external portions of the hip and pelvic bones. The phrase is used in conjunction with *chᵃlātsayim* in Gen. 35:11 (P); 1 K. 8:19 = 2 Ch. 6:9, and with *yārēkh* in Gen. 46:26 (probably P); Ex. 1:5 (P); Jgs. 8:30.[9] It is an ancient custom for someone taking an oath to place his hand ''under the thigh'' (*tachath yārēkh*) of the other party (Gen. 24:2, 9; 47:29 [probably J]). The thighs of a woman struck by the curse fall away (Nu. 5:21f., 27).[10]

VI. kesel. The word *kesel* with the meaning ''loins,'' ''fat or muscle of the loins,'' occurs 9 times in the OT. For the etymology, cf. Akk. *ka/islū*, ''loins (muscle),''[11] and Ugar. *ksl*, ''loins,'' ''back.''[12] In the OT, *kesel* refers primarily to the ''fat of the loins'' (Lev. 3:4), the ''loins muscle'' that begins at the kidneys (cf. Job 15:27, ''fat upon his loins'').[13] Ps. 38:8(7) reads: ''My loins (*kᵉsālai*) are filled with burning'' (cf. the similar expression with *mothnai* in Isa. 21:3); cf. also Lev. 3:10,15; 4:9; 7:4. Prov. 3:26 is frequently interpreted as ''Yahweh will be your confidence (*bᵉkhis-*

---

[8]Cf. P. Wernberg-Møller, ''Studies in the Defective Spelling in the Isaiah-Scroll of St Mark's Monastery,'' *JSS*, 3 (1958), 246.

[9]On the ancient word *yārēkh*, see above and *KBL*³, 419.

[10]Cf. É. Dhorme, *L'emploi métaphorique des noms de parties du corps en hébreu et en akkadien* (Paris, 1923, repr. 1963), 98f., 132.

[11]*AHw*, I, 486f.

[12]*WUS*, No. 1357; cf. *KBL*³, 466, and M. Saebø, ''כְּסִיל *kᵉsīl* Tor,'' *THAT*, I, 836.

[13]Cf. also M. Dahood, review of J. Lévêque, *Job et son Dieu* (Paris, 1970), in *Bibl*, 52 (1971), 437.

lekhā).[14] But the addition of the prefix b^e- suggests rather the meaning "by your side."[15] The word is also attested with the meaning "sexual organs" in Sir. 47:19: "You [Solomon] gave your *kslym* to the women" (cf. Prov. 31:3: conj. *yrkyk*).

VII. Conclusions. From the perspective of idiom and anatomy, several nouns were available to designate the place of girding, the locus of strength, and the site where procreation begins. It is theologically noteworthy that God can readily be the subject of the action of girding or ungirding (2 S. 22:33,40; Isa. 22:21; 45:1,5; Am. 8:10; Ps. 30:12[11]; Job 12:18,21; Sir. 35:22). This follows from his omnipotence and omnipresent activity, which occasion all human acts, both outward and inward. It is also probably not by chance that, despite the literary predilection for anthropomorphisms, God is never described as having "loins" or "thighs." They were probably too closely associated with purely physical functions. Nothing more is said than that he "girds" himself with might or strength, and this only in Ps. 65:7(6) and 93:1.

Hamp

[14]Cf. M. Held, "Studies in Comparative Semitic Lexicography," in *Studies in Honor of B. Landsberger* (1965), 401-406: *ksl,* "sinew, tendon, [inner] strength, confidence."

[15]Cf. M. Dahood, "Hebrew-Ugaritic Lexicography III," *Bibl,* 46 (1965), 330; a different interpretation is given by F. Vattioni, "Proverbi 3_{26}," *Aug,* 6 (1966), 324f.: "foot."

חָלַק *chālaq* I; חָלָק *chālāq;* חֵלֶק *chēleq;* חַלּוּק *challuq;* חֶלְקָה *chelqāh;* חֲלַקְלַקּוֹת *chᵃlaqlaqqôth;* מַחְלְקוֹת *machlᵉqôth*

Contents: I. 1. Etymology, Occurrences; 2. Meaning. II. Secular Usage: 1. General; 2. Toponymic. III. Religious and Cultic Use: 1. Prophets; 2. Psalms.

I. 1. *Etymology, Occurrences.* The root *ḥlq* appears in the OT with two basic meanings: "be smooth," and "divide." Whether further basic meanings can be distinguished, as suggested by Kamhi, is not clear. In the sense "be smooth," *ḥlq* has analogous Semitic parallels in Arab. *ḫalaqa, ḫaluqa,* and *ḥalaqa.* The word is also attested with this meaning in Middle Hebrew. In addition to its use as a verb (in the qal and hiphil), the root finds use in several derivative nouns and adjectives.

2. *Meaning.* With the basic meaning "be smooth," "smoothness" as the starting-point (Ps. 55:22 [Eng. v. 21]; Prov. 5:3; Gen. 27:11), this group of words developed in

chālaq. D. J. Kamhi, "The Root *ḤLQ* in the Bible," *VT,* 23 (1973), 235-39; J. L. Palache,

one direction the meaning "be slippery," "slipperiness" (Jer. 23:12; Ps. 35:6; 73:18). At the same time, there developed in another direction three metaphorical meanings, constituting the bulk of the occurrences: (1) "flatter," "flattery" (Prov. 6:24; 29:5; Isa. 30:10); (2) "be hypocritical or deceptive," "hypocrisy," "deceit" (Ps. 5:10[9]; Ezk. 12:24; Prov. 26:28; Dnl. 11:21); (3) "be bare," "bareness" (2 Ch. 28:21; Josh. 11:17; 1 S. 23:28).

II. Secular Usage.

1. *General.* Independently of differences in meaning, all 36 occurrences of the word group in the OT illustrate secular usage. Solely the relationship of the context to secular or religious and cultic actions or states enables us to make a distinction.

a. Basic to the use of the group in its fundamental meaning "be smooth" is its association with objects that are "smooth" by nature. For example, in Ps. 55:22(21) and Prov. 5:3 "butter" and "oil" respectively are used in similes. The group is applied by analogy to parts of the human body characterized by "smoothness," for instance, the neck (Gen. 27:16) and the tongue (cf. Prov. 6:24 and section c. below). Above all, it is frequently applied to objects that become "smooth" through working, use, or wear. In Isa. 41:7, for example, the hiphil of the verb is used with the meaning "make smooth" in connection with the working of metal, while in 1 S. 17:40 the adjective form *challuqê*[1] or *challᵉqê* (conj.)[2] with the two following nouns describes stones that have been worn smooth by the water in a stream. In similar fashion on the basis of this passage the *challᵉqê-nachal* of Isa. 57:6—though without the attribute *ʾᵃbhānîm*—can be interpreted as smooth stones lying in a stream bed.[3] Weise and Fohrer[4] think here instead of rock walls that have been gradually worn smooth or stripped of vegetation by rainstorms.[5]

b. The meaning "slippery" probably developed in close association with the fundamental meaning of the root. As soon as the attribute of "smoothness" was applied to the image of a path or the ground, the notion of "slipperiness" was the necessary result. This is shown by Jer. 23:12 and Ps. 35:6, where the noun *chᵃlaqlaqqôth* is combined with *derekh,* as well as by Ps. 73:18, where the noun *chālāq* occurs alone. Although these three passages all speak of the wicked or those who forsake Yahweh, they are using a secular image, which, however, is to be understood in a figurative sense.[6]

Semantic Notes on the Hebrew Lexicon (Leiden, 1959); A. Schwarzenbach, *Die geographische Terminologie im Hebräischen des ATs* (Leiden, 1954); M. Weise, "Jesaja 57 [5]f.," *ZAW,* 72 (1960), 25-32.

[1]Cf. *BLe,* § 61sγ.

[2]*BLe,* § 20k.

[3]Following *KBL*[3], 310, and C. Westermann, *Isaiah 40-66. OTL* (trans. 1969), 322.

[4]G. Fohrer, *Das Buch Jesaja III* (Zurich, 1964), 194-98.

[5]For the cultic interpretation of this passage, cf. III.1 below.

[6]Cf. III.2 below.

c. The metaphorical meaning "flatter" appears in the hiphil of the verb as well as in the nouns *chālāq, chēleq,* and *chelqāh;* most of the occurrences are in Proverbs. On the basis of the smooth nature of the tongue,[7] the group of words is often used in connection with the noun *āshôn* (Prov. 6:24; 28:23; Jer. 23:31 conj.): to make smooth the already smooth tongue—understood by the OT as the organ of speech (cf. Isa. 28:11)—meant to speak extremely smoothly, i.e., to flatter. The association of the verb with *'ᵃmārîm* (Prov. 2:16; 7:5) confirms this analysis totally. Flattering speech is attributed more specifically to the so-called false prophets (Isa. 30:10; Jer. 23:31 conj.) and the wicked (Ps. 36:3[2]), as well as adulterous and foreign women (Prov. 7:21; 2:16; 6:24; 7:5). The flatterer is always judged negatively.

d. Contrary to *KBL*³, a distinction is made between the meaning "be hypocritical or deceitful," which is likewise metaphorical, and "flatter," on the grounds that the former expresses a new element of "falseness" or "deception" that is even more negative. This is clear above all where the root and its derivatives stand in parallel to → שׁוא *shāv'*, → שׁקר *sheqer,* or → רע *raʿ* (Ezk. 12:24; Ps. 12:3[2]; Prov. 26:23 conj.; 26:28). This meaning appears in the qal and hiphil of the verb, as well as in *chālāq* and *chᵃlaqlaqqôth*; it is often associated with *lēbh* (Hos. 10:2), *lāshôn* (Ps. 5:10[9]), *peh* (Prov. 26:28), and *śāphāh* (Ps. 12:3f.[2f.]; Prov. 26:23 conj.). All the occurrences refer to human conduct, which is always judged negatively. Those who engage in such deception include Israel (Hos. 10:2), false prophets (Ezk. 12:24), the wicked of Israel (Ps. 5:10[9]; 12:3f.[2f.]), and foreign kings (Dnl. 11:21,32 conj.).

e. The metaphorical sense "be bare" is suggested by Kamhi on the basis of 2 Ch. 28:21, where the verb is used with the meaning "plunder."

2. *Toponymic.* The use of the root in toponyms is related to the meaning mentioned in e. above. The phrase *hāhār hechālāq* (Josh. 11:17; 12:7), "Bare Mountain,"[8] refers to an elevation in Edom; *chelqath hatstsiddîm* (2 S. 2:16 conj.; cf. LXX), "Field of Sides," is a region in Benjamin, and *chelqath . . . 'āshēr* (Josh. 19:24f.; 21:30f.; 1 Ch. 6:59f.[74f.] conj.), "the bare (scil. city)," is a town in Asher. Probably *selaʿ hammachlᵉqôth* (1 S. 23:28), located in Judah, also belongs in this context and should be translated "Bare Rock" rather than "Rock of Escape."[9]

III. Religious and Cultic Use.

1. *Prophets.* The strongest evidence linking this group of words with religious or cultic activity is found in Isa. 57:6. Apart from the question of whether we are dealing here with stones in a wadi or with its rock walls,[10] the context links the *challᵉqê-nachal*

---

[7]Cf. II.1.a above.

[8]Schwarzenbach.

[9]On the topography, see F.-M. Abel, *Géographie de la Palestine,* I (Paris, 1938), 453; J. J. Simons, *The Geographical and Topographical Texts of the OT. StFS,* 2 (Leiden, 1959), §§ 506f.

[10]Cf. II.1.

with an illegitimate sacrificial cult against whose practitioners the prophet proclaims judgment. (Palache, Volz, and Duhm argue for a cultic interpretation of the *chᵃlāqîm* themselves.) Similarly, Hosea says that Israel's heart is "false" when the people set up a wealth of altars and pillars (Hos. 10:2), "for they do not seek the will of Yahweh but rather their own opportunities for religious mastery of their own fate . . . [and] the pleasure of cultic celebration."[11] Like the people, the priests and prophets, too, are threatened with judgment when they depart from Yahweh's instruction (Jer. 23:12) and speak flattery or falsehood (Isa. 30:10; Jer. 23:31 conj.; Ezk. 12:24).

2. *Psalms.* In the Psalms, too, this group of words refers exclusively to situations that are negative theologically. The way of those who persecute the devout is to be "slippery" (Ps. 35:6; 73:18); the godless man "flatters" himself (Ps. 36:3[2]), and the enemies of the man who fears God speak "deceitfully" (Ps. 5:10[9]; 12:3[2]), so that Yahweh is asked to cut off all "false" lips (Ps. 12:4[3]).

Schunck

[11]H. W. Wolff, *Hosea* (trans. 1974), 174.

חָלַק *chālaq* II; חֵלֶק *chēleq;* חֶלְקָה *chelqāh;* חֲלֻקָּה *chᵃluqqāh;* מַחֲלֹקֶת *machᵃlōqeth*

Contents: I. Etymology. II. Meaning: 1. OT; 2. Sirach.

I. Etymology. The root *ḥlq,* "divide," "apportion," is attested in Hebrew (Biblical and Middle Hebrew) and Aramaic (all the ancient and middle dialects for which the amount of source material allows us to judge). Whether it is represented in Arabic and Ethiopic by *ḫlq,* "measure off," "be/make equal"; "count up," is dubious (but cf. Dt. 18:8 for the meaning "be/make equal"; the Arabic word is discussed further at the end of this article). It would be represented in Akkadian by *eqlu,* "field," if the same could be said for Aram. *ḥᵃqal,* as well as Arab. *ḥaql,* OSA *ḥql,* and Ethiop. *ḥaql,* likewise meaning "field."[1] This hypothesis must be rejected, however, since it demands a series of most improbable assumptions. The metathesis of the root, limited to this single word(!), would have had to take place independently at two different times and in two different places; for Akk. *eqlu* with its initial vowel cannot have been

chālaq. W. Foerster, "κλῆρος," *TDNT,* III, 758-764; H. H. Schmid, "חלק *ḥlq* teilen," *THAT,* I, 576-79.

[1]*GesB,* 237f.

the predecessor of Aram. *h^a^qal* with its initial consonant. Neither can the Akkadian word derive from the Aramaic, since it is attested as early as the Sargonic period (*ca.* 2334-2193, using intermediate chronology), and Aramaic influence on Akkadian is not attested until a much later period. And to avoid having to assume that the same word for "field" underwent repeated spontaneous metatheses, we would have to turn Aram. *ḥ^a^qal* into a "wanderer" that made its way as far as Southern Arabia and Abyssinia. It is quite possible, however, that Aram. *ḥ^a^qal,* "field," influenced Heb. *chelqāh* and possibly *chēleq,* of similar meaning: the frequent combination *chelqath haśśādheh* (never **chēleq haśśādheh*) looks like an attempt to clarify the meaning of the Aramaic loanword, whose phoneme sequence had already been accommodated to that of an indigenous word, by means of a common synonym.

II. Meaning.

1. *OT.* In Hebrew, the root has primarily the socially defined meaning "(give or receive) the portion coming to one by law and custom." From this meaning develops the meaning "the portion in life determined by God," "destiny." The high frequency of the meanings with social and religious overtones may be due in part to the social and theological concerns of the Bible. It is nevertheless striking how rare in the OT are specific expressions for neutral division, words expressing nothing more than the subdivision of a whole without regard for the interest and profit that someone may have in the resulting portions.

First we must mention the verb *chātsāh,* which means "divide," usually into two parts, sometimes into three (Jgs. 7:16; 9:43) or four (Dnl. 11:4). It can mean "apportion," but has no social component. From the rare root *plg* we have the niphal, "be divided" (Gen. 10:25, an etiology of the name "Peleg"), and the nouns *p^e^laggāh* (Jgs. 5:15f.), *p^e^luggāh* (2 Ch. 35:5), and *miphlaggāh* (2 Ch. 35:12), all meaning "section" and all in the plural.

In the piel, the verb *chālaq* can have the neutral meaning "divide," "separate into portions" (Ezk. 5:1), "distribute" (1 K. 18:6), and "divide and scatter" (Gen. 49:7; possibly also Lam. 4:16). The niphal furnishes the reflexive: "divide up" (troops, etc.: Gen. 14:15; 1 K. 16:21; light: Job 38:24). The qal (1 Ch. 24:4f.; 2 Ch. 23:18) and two forms with uncertain pointing (1 Ch. 23:6; 24:3), "organize by divisions," probably belong here as well. The corresponding substantive is *mach^a^lōqeth.*[2] Substantives in which the notion of a "portion" plays no role include *chēleq,* "military division" (1 S. 30:24); *ch^a^luqqāh* (2 Ch. 35:5); and *machl^e^qôth* (Neh. 11:36, and frequent in Chronicles, e.g., 1 Ch. 23:6), both meaning "division," "small group."

In its primary meaning, *ḥlq* has social overtones. Its concrete referent, the "portion," is something in which giver and receiver, the individual or small group and the community, have an equal interest. The portion (defined in economic or other terms) maintains the individual or small group, and society is based on the totality of all portions. When the community is reorganized, Nehemiah explicates the meaning of

---

[2]See below.

chēleq, "portion," in Jerusalem by the addition of *ts^edhāqāh,* "right," and *zikkārôn,* "memorial [i.e., future?]" (Neh. 2:20).

The structure and development (not to be understood in a chronological sense) of the primary meaning can be illustrated by the extant material. On very rare occasions, the piel of *ḥlq* can mean the "distribution" of gifts (2 S. 6:19) or land (the Seleucids for a price, Dnl. 11:39), as well as the "division" of stolen property (qal: Prov. 29:24; piel: Ps. 22:19 [Eng. v. 18]). In Job 27:17, where there is no mention of a number of people doing the dividing or receiving, and both context and style demand a singular, the qal of *ḥlq* has lost all precision: it means "receive," and not just a portion, but everything. In this respect it is precisely analogous to Akk. *zittu,* "part" and "whole" (of an inheritance).[3]

The frequent use of *ḥlq* to refer to the "division" of spoil (qal: Josh. 22:8; piel: Ex. 15:9, etc.; pual: Zec. 14:1; *chēleq*), where equal participation in the battle means equal participation in the spoil (→ שׁלל *shālal*), leads to the specialized meaning of *ḥlq*. This appears clearly in the "portion" in the royal house, i.e., the regime in power; the "portion" indicates that a group shares in the common life of the community (2 S. 20:1; 1 K. 12:16).

But when land is divided or apportioned by the community, we see *ḥlq* in its most specialized meaning. In this case, "division" refers both to the allotted fields and the apportioned inheritance; the concept is rooted in an agricultural society organized by clans as nowhere else. Thus on the one hand *chēleq* refers to the "arable land" in the plain surrounding a settlement, in contrast to *mighrāsh,* which is common pasture (see, e.g., Josh. 14:4).[4] It is not *mighrāsh* land but *chēleq* land that the Levites are forbidden to own. Unlike *chēleq, mighrāsh* does not count as a fundamental necessity of life or as a sign of belonging to the clan or people. On the other hand, therefore, *chēleq* is frequently associated with → נחלה *nach^alāh,* usually in an hendiadys, sometimes in parallelism extending over a distich or in a looser relationship. But since Yahweh is the original owner (and testator) of Palestine (e.g., Dt. 12:10), whoever receives a portion of the land (niphal: Nu. 26:53; piel: Josh. 19:51; hithpael: Josh. 18:5 [with the recipient always expressed by the dative]; *chēleq*) has a portion in Yahweh's own property (inheritance), and whoever renounces his portion of the land has no portion in Yahweh (Josh. 22:25, 27).[5] A similar idea, stated in terms of *nach^alāh,* appears in 1 S. 26:19.

The qal of *ḥlq* is used generally for inheritance within a family (Prov. 17:2; Neh. 13:13; not far removed is 2 S. 19:30[29]). The word *chelqāh,* the feminine equivalent to *chēleq,* always means "field, meadow." This semantic restriction may be due to Aramaic influence.[6] In Jer. 12:10, the meaning is applied by poetic metaphor to Palestine. In Ezk. 48:29, *machl^eqôth* means "portion," as it probably does in

---

[3] *CAD,* XXI, 146f. (No. 4) and 148.

[4] For a discussion of the whole subject, see F. Horst, "Zwei Begriffe für Eigentum (Besitz): *naḥ^alāh* und *'^aḥuzzāh,*" *Verbannung und Heimkehr. Festschrift W. Rudolph* (1961), 145.

[5] See G. von Rad, "The Promised Land and Yahweh's Land in the Hexateuch," *ZDPV,* 66 (1943), 191f. = *The Problem of the Hexateuch and Other Essays* (trans. 1966), 87f.

[6] See I above.

Josh. 11:23; 12:7; 18:10. In the case of the hiphil (qal?) in Jer. 37:12, we are not dealing with a division of land among the people, but with an attempt on Jeremiah's part to mix with the people and thus "escape" (*ḥlq* III).[7]

The Levites have no *chēleq,* "portion," in Palestine, i.e., they are not entitled to own land (Nu. 18:20; Dt. 10:9; 12:12; 14:27,29; 18:1; Josh. 14:4; 18:7); God is their portion (Nu. 18:20: *chelqᵉkhā vᵉnachᵃlathᵉkhā,* said to Aaron; elsewhere only *nachᵃlāh,* e.g., Ezk. 44:28). The immediate concrete consequence is that the priests have a right to certain "portions" of the sacrifices (Lev. 6:10[17]; cf. Dt. 18:8). This principle is based, however, on the ideal notion that God is the "portion" of the devout, i.e., that he is their personal possession, as is expressed in the name *chilqîyāh(û),* "Yahweh is my portion." This name is first attested as the name of a man who cannot have been born later than the middle of the eighth century (2 K. 18:18; Isa. 22:20); then it appears as the name of Jeremiah's father, some eighty years later (Jer. 1:1); it is also the name of a man who can hardly have been born after 640 (Jer. 29:3). Nothing suggests that the first and third of these had any clerical rank, and the silence of the texts with reference to such status and descent makes such an assumption quite unlikely.

In this connection a small number of Neo-Babylonian and Late Babylonian personal names are of interest: they are analogous in meaning,[8] as can be seen from the names Ea-zittišu,[9] "Ea is his portion," and Mannu-lū-zitti, "Who indeed will be my portion."[10] Since the statement made by the name *chilqîyāhû* is extremely concise, it is impossible to say with any confidence whether and in what way certain Psalm passages (16:5; 73:26; 119:57; 142:6[5]; also Lam. 3:24) go beyond what the name says. It may be noted that at least the authors of Pss. 73 and 142 say more to God than "Thou art my possession"; they say: "Thou art my only possession." The conclusion of Ps. 73 is probably the most impressive expression of the idea "God is my portion" in the entire OT.

It is certainly wrong to call these psalms "levitical hymns,"[11] even in a partial or derivative sense; if nothing else, the nonlevitical "portion" names from Israel and Babylonia rule out this suggestion.

The very ancient personal(?) name *chēleq* (Nu. 26:30; Josh. 17:2) defies interpretation and even assignment to a specific root (*ḥlq* I, II, or III). The name *chelqai* (Neh. 12:15) is likewise unexplained.

Only seemingly related to the idea that Yahweh is the "portion" of an individual or group are two passages from Deuteronomy according to which he "apportioned" (qal, Dt. 4:19; 29:25[26]) the other gods to other nations. Here we have in the background the totally different idea of a primordial division and ordering of the world; the complex variety of bonds between nations and religions observed in the present was the intentional consequence of this division. Analogous to this notion is the complemen-

---

[7]The interpretation of Redaq; Gesenius; and J. Sperber, "Zu Jer. 37, 12," *OLZ,* 19 (1916), 131f.; cf. Akk. *ḫalāqu,* "run away."

[8]Contra *AN,* 371.

[9]*IPN,* 163 and *CAD,* XXI, 141b: *ᵈé-a*-ḪA.LA-*š*[*u*]; *BE,* IX (1898), No. 86a (Plate 71), upper edge.

[10]For additional *zittu* "portion" names, see *IPN,* 163, and *CAD,* XXI, 141.

[11]Contra H.-J. Kraus, *BK,* XV (⁴1972), 123 (570, 821, 933).

tary idea that Yahweh (then) retained Israel as his own *chēleq,* while conferring the other nations upon the other gods (Dt. 32:8f., Qumran, LXX; closely related is Ex. 19:5, → סגלה *s^eghullāh*).

Related to these two last passages is the use of *ḥlq* in the broader sense of a primordial apportionment of things, attributes, and destinies, with more or less emphasis on the notion of creation. Instances include "food" (*chēleq,* Hab. 1:16), "wisdom" (qal: Job 39:17), the portion or "lot" of individuals and nations (Job 20:29; Isa. 17:14; Jer. 10:16), often a lot that is brought to pass by their own conduct (→ גורל *gôrāl,* → נחלה *nach^alāh*).

Peculiar to Ecclesiastes is *chēleq* in the sense of "the space allotted to human life" (2:10; 3:22; 5:17f.[18f.]; 9:6,9).[12] As has just been suggested, this meaning stands in contrast to the view of passages that are much more characteristic of the OT, namely, that man not only receives his "portion" passively, but can take possession of it by his own initiative (Ps. 50:18; Isa. 57:6; cf. Job 27:13; 31:2).

2. *Sirach.* In Sirach, finally, the meaning "creation" appears fully developed. In at least three passages, *ḥlq* (qal?, niphal) means "create" (34:13[31:13]: the [evil] eye; 34:27[31:27]: wine; 38:1: the physician).[13] This is not only the (correct) translation of the LXX (*ktízō*) and Peshitta (*br'*), but also the interpretation exhibited by the manuscript variants *br'* (34:13[31:13]) and *nwṣr* (34:27[31:27]). In other passages (e.g., 39:25; 40:10), it is hard to decide between "create" and "apportion." In a third group, including, for example, 7:15 and 15:9, "apportion" is the only appropriate meaning. These variations of meaning condemn in advance all attempts to explain creation as meaning "division" or "distribution," after the example of Marduk, who splits the body of Tiamat and makes heaven and earth from the parts.[14] Creation is rather "apportionment." The author's interest focuses on how the existing world is used or its role in life; the question of existence itself and how the world came to exist retreats into the background. This is a semantic development of *ḥlq* that is already suggested in OT Hebrew. Middle Hebrew continues the development; *chēleq* comes to mean "character," "disposition."[15] The meanings found in the Apocrypha and in Middle Hebrew also appear in Arabic: *ḫlq,* "create" (I), *ḫalq,* "creation," and *ḫulq,* "character," "disposition." Here we may be dealing with the influence of Middle Hebrew.

Tsevat

חֶמְאָה *chem'āh* → חָלָב *chālābh*

---

[12]K. Galling, *HAT,* 18 ([2]1969), 89.

[13]R. Smend, *Die Weisheit des Jesus Sirach* (1906), 277, suggests a somewhat different interpretation.

[14]EnEl, IV, 136-38; V, 65, 119ff.

[15]Jer. *Ber.* iv.2 (=7d); Jer. *Sanh.* i.4 (=19c), both prayers. This observation was already made by Ben Yehuda, *Wörterbuch,* 1596, upper right. In N. Peters, *Der jüngst wiederaufgefundene hebräische Text des Buches Ecclesiasticus* (1902), 168 top, the whole discussion is wrong.

חָמַד chāmadh; חֶמֶד chemedh; חֶמְדָּה chemdāh; חֲמֻדוֹת chamudhôth; חֶמְדָּן chemdān; מַחְמָד machmādh; מַחְמֹד machmōdh

Contents: I. 1. Etymology; 2. Distribution; 3. Related Concepts; 4. Meaning (LXX). II. General Usage: 1. Negative; 2. Neutral; 3. Positive. III. 1. Usage in Theological Ethics; 2. The Ninth (Tenth) Commandment; 3. The "Evil Eye." IV. Responsibility for Desire in Early Jewish Literature.

I. 1. *Etymology*. The root *ḥmd* has not been the subject of etymological study. Possibly, if the middle radical is ignored as a liquid (*l, m, n, r*), it is connected with an originally biliteral root *ḥd,* a rare root[1] from which Biblical Hebrew derives the verb *ḥdh* I, "rejoice (qal)," "make happy (piel),"[2] and the noun *chedhvāh,* "joy."[3] The relationship between *ḥdh* II, "see," "look at something," and *ḥmd* must remain an open question.[4]

The following are examples of such an elimination of a liquid middle radical from a verb: *gālam,* "wrap together," *gam,* "also," Arab. *ǧamma,* "assemble," X "concentrate," "rest"; *pālach,* "cleave," *pach* II, "thin plate"; *pls,* "make level," *pas,* "flat"; *šmd,* "destroy," *šōdh,* "violence," "devastation," *shādhadh,* "devastate"; *'bb,* "be fruitful," *'ēbh,* "bud," Akk. *inbu,* Jewish Aram. *'inbā',* "fruit"; *'nḥ,* "groan," "sigh," *'āch,* "alas"; *'ānaph,* "be angry," *'aph* II, "nose," "anger,"

---

chāmadh. → אָוָה *'āvāh;* → הַוָּה *havvāh;* → חָשַׁב *chāshabh;* A. Alt, "Das Vergot des Diebstahls in Dekalog," *KlSchr,* I (1953), 333-340; F. Büchsel, "ἐπιθυμία, ἐπιθυμέω," *TDNT,* III, 168-172; T. Canaan, *Aberglaube und Volksmedizin im Lande der Bibel* (1914), 28-32; J. R. Coates, "'Thou Shalt not Covet,'" *ZAW,* 52 (1934), 238f.; H. G. Enelow, *The Mishnah of Rabbi Eliezer* (1933); E. Gerstenberger, "חמד *ḥmd* begehren," *THAT,* I, 579-581; C. H. Gordon, "A Note on the Tenth Commandment," *JBR,* 31 (1963), 208f.; J. Herrmann, "Das zehnte Gebot," *Festschrift E. Sellin* (1927), 69-82; B. S. Jackson, "Liability for Mere Intention in Early Jewish Law," *HUCA,* 42 (1971), 197-225; B. Jacob, "The Decalogue," *JQR,* N.S. 14 (1923/24), 141-187; A. Jepsen, "Beiträge zur Auslegung und Geschichte des Dekalogs," *ZAW,* 79 (1967), 275-304; W. Keszler, "Die literarische, historische und theologische Problematik des Dekalogs," *VT,* 7 (1957), 1-16; L. Köhler, "Der Dekalog," *ThR,* N.S. 1 (1929), 161-184; R. Kriss and H. Kriss-Heinrich, *Amulette, Zauberformeln und Beschwörungen. Volksglaube im Bereich des Islam,* II (1962); J. Lewis, *The Ten Commandments* (1946), 577-581; E. Nielsen, *The Ten Commandments in New Perspective. SBT,* N.S. 7 (trans. 1968); H. van Oyen, *Ethik des ATs. Geschichte der Ethik,* 2 (1967); A. Phillips, *Ancient Israel's Criminal Law* (1970); H. H. Rowley, "Moses and the Decalogue," *BJRL,* 34 (1951/52), 81-118 = his *Men of God* (London, 1963), 1-36; J. J. Stamm with M. E. Andrew, *The Ten Commandments in Recent Research. SBT,* N.S. 2 (trans. [2]1967); M. Wagner, *Die lexikalischen und grammatikalischen Aramaismen im alttestamentlichen Hebräisch. BZAW,* 96 (1966); P. Wechter, *Ibn Barūn's Arabic Works on Hebrew Grammar and Lexicography* (1964).

[1]Wagner, 51, Nos. 83-87.

[2]*KBL*[3], 280.

[3]*Ibid.*

[4]Cf. *ibid.*

Arab. *'anf;*[5] *kānas,* "assemble," *kîs*(?), "bag"; *pāraś,* "spread out," *pāśāh,* "spread."

2. *Distribution.* The root *ḥmd* appears in Biblical Hebrew in the qal (16 times), the niphal participle (4 times), and the piel and hiphil (once each). It is also attested generally in the other West Semitic dialects: Egyptian Aramaic, Jewish Aramaic, Samaritan, Old South Arabic,[6] Mandean,[7] Ugaritic,[8] Phoenician,[9] and the Amarna letters.[10] This root does not appear in East Semitic, which makes use instead of other roots with various nuances: *erēšu,* "wish"; *ḫašāšu,* "need," "yearn for";[11] *manû,* "count on," *manû arda,* "desire a woman";[12] *ṣamāru,* "have in mind," "wish" (*ṣimertu libbi,* "secret wish"). Egyptian uses the roots *ḥḥy* (Old Egyptian), "seek someone or something," *mry* (Old Egyptian), "love (someone)," "want (something)," or *wḫ3* (Middle Kingdom and afterward), "seek," "summon."

3. *Related Concepts.* As we shall see, all these roots coincide only partially with the semantic content of Heb. *ḥmd.* In contrast to simple "rejoicing" (*chādhāh*), *ḥmd* expresses the notion of "finding something desirable or precious on account of its form or splendor." It is thus closely related to → אוה *'āvah,* which means "wish for, desire," and often stands in parallel with *ḥmd* (Gen. 3:6; Prov. 6:25; Ps. 68:17 [Eng. v. 16])[13] or even alternates with it (Ex. 20:17 = Dt. 5:21). In a sense, → הוה *havvāh* is similar in meaning to *ḥmd,* but it always refers to evil desire that is contrary to God's will. There is no semantic connection with → אבה *'ābhāh,* "be willing," but there is with → בחר *bāchar,* "choose for one's own needs from (various) possibilities, objects, persons, nations, or even idols." In fact, both *chāmadh* and *bāchar* are associated with *lāqach,* "take to oneself something desirable or chosen."[14] There is also a connection with → חשׁב *chāshabh,* referring not to emotional but to rational appreciation, to planning that leads up to deliberate action, thus touching on the conceptual domain of *ḥmd.*

The range of use of *ḥmd* and its derivatives is great. They are found in the various types of literature: narrative, didactic, poetic, prophetic, even apocalyptic. In the last (Daniel), in fact, they even find special favor. Outside of Biblical Hebrew, they appear in the book of Sirach as well as in the Dead Sea Scrolls.[15]

---

[5] *Ibid.,* 74a.

[6] Cf. *ibid.,* 312.

[7] *MdD,* 149.

[8] *WUS,* No. 936.

[9] *DISO,* 90.

[10] EA, 138, 126, glossing *iapu* = *yph.*

[11] *AHw,* I, 322f.; *CAD,* VI, 134ff.

[12] *AHw,* I, 604f.

[13] See G. Mayer, "אָוָה *'āvāh,*" *TDOT,* I, 135.

[14] Cf. H. Seebass, "בָּחַר *bāchat,*" *TDOT,* II, 74.

[15] 4Q158 7f.; 163 3:32 (*DJD,* V, 3, 26); 1QH fragment 11:6, where the small amount of text involved makes it difficult to determine the precise nuance intended.

4. *Meaning (LXX).* The word *chāmadh* refers not to the "desire" that is inherently human (concupiscence), but to the specific act of desire that is generated by emotion. This act begins with the visual impression made by the desired object or person: "the eye desires grace and beauty" (Sir. 40:22). This is also the sense of the expression *machmadh ʿēnayim* or *machᵃmaddê-ʿayin* (1 K. 20:6; Ezk. 24:16,21,25; Lam. 2:4). Ugliness, contrariwise, awakens not desire but loathing, making someone totally unwelcome (2 Ch. 21:20).

Consequently the qal passive participle of *chāmadh* is applied to things that seem especially valuable, i.e., desirable (Isa. 44:9; Ps. 39:12[11]; Job 20:20). The niphal participle likewise means "desirable by virtue of appearance or nature": fruit (Gen. 2:9; 3:6 [LXX *hōraíos,* "ripe"]), provisions (Prov. 21:20), the works of God (Sir. 42:22), all striking the eye. In similar fashion, all the derivatives of *ḥmd* refer to outward appearance, the beautiful exterior that suggests high value: *chemedh:* pleasant fields (Isa. 32:12), pleasant vineyards (Am. 5:11), attractive young men (Ezk. 23:6, 12,23); *chemdāh:* a pleasant land (because it is Yahweh's; Jer. 3:19; Zec. 7:14; Ps. 106:24), Yahweh's pleasant portion (Jer. 12:10), pleasant houses (Ezk. 26:12), beautiful ships (Isa. 2:16), precious objects (Hos. 13:15; Jer. 25:34; Nah. 2:10[9]; 2 Ch. 32:27; 36:10; Dnl. 11:8), all that is desirable in Israel (1 S. 9:20) or in the gentile world (Hag. 2:7), magnificent treasures (Sir. 41:12); *chᵃmudhôth:* an attractive garment (Gen. 27:15), delicious food (Dnl. 10:3), precious vessels (Ezr. 8:27), objects made of precious metal (Dnl. 11:38,43; 2 Ch. 20:25), a beloved person (Dnl. 9:23; 10:11,19); *machmādh:* describing the sanctuary (Ezk. 24:21) or its cultic furnishings (Isa. 64:10[11]; Lam. 1:10; 2 Ch. 36:19), considered as Yahweh's treasures, then applied to human property (Hos. 9:6; Lam. 1:7,11: *machmōdh*) and finally to the high value and beauty of human life (Hos. 9:16,25; Cant. 5:16). The same meaning, finally, attaches to the personal name *chemdān,* attested in various Semitic dialects (Gen. 36:26; cf. 1 Ch. 1:41; also "Muhammed").[16]

The semasiological range of *ḥmd* covers the entire human sequence from viewing through perception of pleasure or even delight and inward longing to the desire to possess and the act of possession. Achan confesses: "I *saw* among the spoil a beautiful mantle from Shinar, and two hundred shekels of silver, and a bar of gold weighing fifty shekels, then I *coveted* them, and *took* them" (Josh. 7:21a). It is disputed whether in every case the actual taking possession is implicitly included. But the desire for an object or a person expressed by *ḥmd* has such possession as its goal. Sometimes this is the express meaning: "Neither shall any man desire your land, when you go up to appear before Yahweh your God three times in the year" (Ex. 34:24b). This is also the sense in which the root *ḥmd* is used in the Phoenician Karatepe inscription: "But if a king among kings or a dignitary among dignitaries, if someone who is respected . . ., if he so much as desires this city or tears down this gate, . . ., whether he destroys it out of covetousness (*ḥmdt*) or destroys it out of hatred or malice, . . ."[17]

---

[16]For bibliography, see *KBL*³, 313.

[17]*KAI,* 26 III.12–IV.1.

In Hebrew, the process involved in coveting can be expressed without the actual use of *ḥmd.* Sarai was beautiful to behold (*'ishshāh y^ephath-mar'eh,* Gen. 12:11,14). Thus the officials of Pharaoh praised her attractiveness and she was taken (*vattuqqach,* v. 15) into Pharaoh's palace. It was this very desire that Abram feared and made him take precautions.

Our survey has shown that *chāmadh* and its derivatives refer primarily to persons or things visible to the eye. It is only rarely or late that they are applied to abstractions, such as the ordinances of Yahweh (Ps. 19:11[10]). Especially clear in this regard is the distinction between *ḥmd* and *'wh,* stated thus by Jacob: "The difference is this that the occasion for חמד is inspection, for אוה imagination. . . ."[18] The subject of the piel of *'wh* is invariably *nephesh,*[19] ". . . therefore both חמד, the covetous observation and התאוה, the imaginary desire, apply to all the objects, and it becomes evident that this is not merely a commentary but also a further development of the idea."[20] Not until Sirach is the root commonly applied to abstraction, such as evil desire (*ra'*) per se (Sir. 5:12; 14:14) or grace and beauty (40:22, the only occurrence of the hiphil). The meaning of *ḥmd* can thus approximately be represented by the English expression "have one's eye on something."

In translating *ḥmd,* the LXX placed most emphasis on the effect the attraction has on the beholder, who sets his *thymós,* "heart," on something or covets it (*epithyméō, epithymía*). Only rarely are other terms used, such as *eklektós,* "choice," *hōraíos,* "ripe" (of fruit), or *eudokētós,* "pleasing." On the other hand, the LXX also uses *epithyméō* for such other Hebrew roots as → אָבָה *'ābhāh,* → חָפֵץ *chāphēts,* and → רָצָה *rātsāh.*

II. General Usage. In Biblical Hebrew it is difficult to distinguish purely secular usage of *ḥmd* from theological and ethical usage, since it always describes vision followed by desire that has a specific act as its goal, which ultimately involves responsibility (cf. Achan's theft). The fact that desire is predicated of Yahweh himself (Ps. 68:17[16]) does not in itself imply theological content.

1. *Negative.* On the one hand, the general usage of *ḥmd* can have a negative component.

a. Various opprobrious persons are named as the subject: the wicked (*rāshā',* Prov. 12:12), the scoffer (*lēts,* Prov. 1:22), the godless (*chānēph,* Job 20:5,20), those who devise wickedness and work evil (*chōsh^ebhê 'āven, pō'^alê rā',* Mic. 2:1f.).

b. A negative sense can also be suggested by viewing the desire in conjunction with an opprobrious act (Josh. 7:21a; Mic. 2:2: *gāzal, 'āshaq*) or by describing it as base and impetuous per se (Sir. 5:2; 14:12).

---

18 P. 170.

19 Cf. Mayer, *TDOT,* I, 135.

20 Jacob, 172.

c. The object of desire itself may indicate negative evaluation, as in the case of idols and lovers (Isa. 1:29; 44:9; Ezk. 23:6,12,23).

d. Finally, condemnation of the desire can be expressed by its being incorporated into a prohibition or vetitive (Ex. 20:17 = Dt. 5:21; Prov. 6:25).

2. *Neutral.* On the other hand, desire can be considered ethically neutral when it refers quite generally to certain goods the possession of which is pleasant: lovely garments (Gen. 27:15), delicious food (Dnl. 10:3), glittering treasures (Ps. 39:12[11]; Dnl. 11:38, 43; cf. Ezr. 8:27; Ezk. 26:12; 2 Ch. 20:25; 32:27; etc.). Ugaritic speaks of "desirable" cedars.[21] When the term is applied to persons it is no longer neutral, especially when the person is beloved of God (Dnl. 9:23; 10:11,19).

But such desirable treasures are reduced in value by virtue of the fact that in times of peril, especially when the judgment of God's wrath is threatened, they guarantee no protection or security, but are as cheap as the life of those who rely on them (1 K. 20:6; Isa. 2:16; 32:12; 64:10[11]; Jer. 12:10; 25:34; Ezk. 24:16,21,25; 26:12; Hos. 13:15; Joel 4:5[3:5]; Zec. 7:14; Ps. 39:12[11]; Job 20:20; Lam. 1:7,10; 2:4; Hos. 9:6, 16; 2 Ch. 36:10,19). Thus the predominant use of the term appears to have disparaging or at least devaluing overtones, not in the sense of documenting a fundamental element of sinfulness but rather underscoring the conditional nature of all values.

3. *Positive.* Thus the number of positive occurrences turns out to be surprisingly small. These appear wherever the object of desire is something worthwhile in itself: the ordinances of Yahweh (Ps. 19:11[10]), sufficient provisions (Prov. 21:10), the shadow of one's beloved (Cant. 2:3, the only instance of the piel). Indeed, Yahweh himself can be the subject of the verb when he desires the mountain of his sanctuary (Ps. 68:17[16]).

III. 1. *Usage in Theological Ethics.* Desire becomes a problem of theological ethics when it offends not only against human behavioral norms but also against God's own decrees. This is the case in the story of the "Fall." In the garden of God, Yahweh causes trees to grow that not only are lovely to look at (*nechmādh l^emar'eh*) but also have the virtue of providing with their fruit sufficient food for man (*ṭôbh l^ema'^{a}khāl*). Yahweh nevertheless forbids eating from the tree in the midst of the garden (Gen. 2:9). Only after the tempting question of the serpent does there awaken within Adam's wife a sense of how desirable this tree is. Not only does it provide good food and delight (*ta'^{a}vāh*) for the eyes, it is extremely desirable because it promises insight (*nechmādh l^ehaśkîl*). "She took (*vattiqqach*) of its fruit and ate, and she also gave some to her husband, and he ate" (Gen. 3:6). Because of the words of the serpent, the pure sight of the fruit of the tree was no longer simple observation, but was burdened by knowledge of the ability to distinguish good from evil, withheld by Yahweh. Thus the simple act of seeing (*rā'āh*) became covetous observation (*chāmadh*), leading, in full knowledge

[21] *CTA*, 4 [II AB], VI, 19, 21.

of Yahweh's instruction not to eat of this fruit (Gen. 3:2), to disobedience toward the divine commandment. Only at this point does the statement acquire theological relevance. The verb *chāmadh* reflects the suggestive power of observation, which takes possession of someone and incorporates the deed within itself, despite the best will and intentions. It is undoubtedly in this sense that the word *t^eshûqāh* (4:7) should be understood.

The Apocalypse of Moses (19:3) adds to the Genesis account the statement that the serpent in Paradise made Eve give her oath that she would also give Adam the fruit of the tree of knowledge. Then the serpent sprinkled the fruit with the poison of guilt, namely, desire (*epithymía*), the root and beginning of all sin. This addition of course dissolves the fateful nexus of desire. The combination of seeing, desiring, and taking expressed by *chāmadh* was clearly unknown to the later writer.

2. *The Ninth (Tenth) Commandment.* The word *chāmadh* takes on particular theological relevance in the last commandment of the Decalog, which prohibits the coveting of a neighbor's wife, as well as his manservants, maidservants, cattle, and possessions (Ex. 20:17; cf. 4Q158 7–8:2). Dt. 5:21, however, uses the root *ḥmd* only for coveting the wife; the desire for the neighbor's house, field, manservant, maidservant, ox, ass, or other property is expressed by means of *'wh*. It is not immediately clear why Dt. 5:21 replaced *ḥmd,* which is probably primary, with *'wh* in this passage. The purpose is certainly not to limit the term *ḥmd* to sexual desire for a married woman; such a restriction would contradict OT usage in general and Deuteronomic usage in particular—as in Dt. 7:25, which speaks of coveting silver and gold, so that the term cannot refer exclusively to sexual desire. Neither can sexual lust as such be meant by the Deuteronomic formulation of the tenth commandment, for adultery (→ נאף *nā'aph*), sexual relationships between a man and the wife or the betrothed of someone else, has already been prohibited in Ex. 20:14 = Dt. 5:18. Neither, however, can the tenth commandment mean desire for the wife or property of one's neighbor with the intention of stealing them, since theft has been dealt with in Ex. 20:15 = Dt. 5:19. Whether or not Alt is right that the prohibition refers exclusively to the theft of persons, it is probably impossible to interpret "desire" in the tenth commandment as meaning the wish to steal. The only remaining possibility, then, is to interpret *chāmadh* within the framework of an ethics of pure intention. This is how Jesus interprets the commandment in Matt. 5:28. Characteristically, he, too, interprets desire as beginning with vision (*ho blépōn gynaíka prós tó epithymēsai*). But this cannot have been the original or only meaning in the tenth commandment, since *chāmadh* is applied in the same context (at least in Ex. 20:17) to objects as well as to the neighbor's wife, menservants, and maidservants.

This raises the problem of whether *ḥmd* in Ex. 20:17 = Dt. 5:21 is to be interpreted as defining an ethics of intention, as is often assumed. If so, desire is sinful in itself. But as we have seen above,[22] Herrmann has pointed out that there is a connection between *chāmadh* and *lāqach;* he refers to the passages Dt. 7:25; Josh. 7:21; and Prov.

[22] See I.3.

6:25, which we have already discussed. Similar in content are Ex. 34:24 and Ps. 68:17 (16), while in Mic. 2:2 *gāzal, nāśā'*, and *'āshaq* are used instead of *lāqach*. More recently, the Karatepe inscription has confirmed this interpretation.[23] Jepsen, Keszler, Köhler, Nielsen, Noth,[24] van Oyen,[25] and Stamm all follow Herrmann in interpreting the tenth commandment thus. What is forbidden is the desire that marks the beginning of an attempt, insidious or open, to gain possession of something that belongs to another. Cassuto[26] does not follow this interpretation. Coates has also rejected it on the grounds that it is at odds with the meaning of Arab. *ḥamida,* which means "praise." Wechter,[27] however, says that *ḥmd* in Ps. 68:17(16) "is similar to *ḥamida* and *aḥmada* 'to find a thing praiseworthy', of the same meaning is *ḥimmaḏtî* (Ct. 2, 3). The meaning of *b^eṣillô ḥimmaḏtî w^ejāšaḇtî* (ib.) would then be: 'I considered this praiseworthy and therefore I stayed in it'; of the same meaning is *ḥmd* (Ez. 23,6) and all of its derivatives."

3. *The "Evil Eye."* Other considerations also contradict the view of Coates. As Gen. 2:9; 3:6; and Josh. 7:21 show,[28] *chāmadh* is associated with desire inspired by vision. At this point we are close to the Islamic popular belief in the "evil eye." Now we can ask whether this notion can be used to illuminate the use of *chāmadh* in the tenth commandment. Kriss and Kriss-Heinrich state: "Envy and the evil eye belong together and are inseparably linked. The evil effect of the eye is especially dangerous when the envious person dissembles and cloaks his jealousy in friendly or familiar expressions of admiration."[29] If Heb. *chāmadh* is connected with eye magic, so, too, is Arab. *ḥamida,* "praise," connected with the closely related "speak too soon of," which likewise has a negative effect on the admired object.[30] This parallel from the Islamic world is impressive, because the idea of the "evil eye" is not alien to the OT, as Dt. 15:9; 28:54, 56; Prov. 28:22 (cf. Sir. 14:8) show, where jealousy is revealed by the look in the eye.[31]

Without following Lewis in claiming a magical effect for *chāmadh,* the transpersonal effect of desiring or "speaking too soon" remains an element of the word. The greed and possessiveness that necessarily lead to action can here be seen as the background of the meaning of *chāmadh,* directed toward the property of others. Thus Luther is right in his explanation in the first part of his Small Catechism when he interprets the ninth / tenth commandment as follows: "We should fear and love God, that we may not estrange, force, or entice away from our neighbor his wife, servants, or cattle. We should fear and love God, that we may not desire by craftiness to gain possession of our neighbor's inheritance or home, or to obtain it under pretext of a legal right."

---

[23] *Ibid.*
[24] M. Noth, *Exodus. OTL* (trans. 1962, ²1977), 264.
[25] Pp. 126f.
[26] U. Cassuto, *A Commentary on the Book of Exodus* (Jerusalem, trans. 1967), *in loc.*
[27] P. 68.
[28] See I.3.
[29] P. 17.
[30] S. Seligmann, *Der boese Blick und Verwandtes* (1910), 21–24; cf. also Canaan, 28–32, esp. 29.
[31] G. Fohrer, "Blick, böser," *BHHW,* I, 257.

The tenth commandment of the Hebrew Decalog, by the very multiplicity of the possessions mentioned (expanded by Dt. 5:21), thinks concretely of the prosperity and happiness of the person envied, which appear desirable and arouse jealousy. This jealousy leads to plots that do injury to one's neighbor and detract from his happiness. The conditions for theft are not fulfilled, because the tenth commandment does not necessarily think in terms of thievery as legally defined. "Coveting" can employ a position of power (Gen. 12:10-15), legal means, or unfair competition to acquire the desired property. According to 2 S. 15, Absalom lays the groundwork for his revolt against his father David by turning from his father the hearts of the Israelites who come seeking justice. Theft in the formal legal sense can hardly be involved here. This is also the sense in which the saying of the worshipper in the Egyptian Book of the Dead is to be taken: "O Nosey, who comes forth from Hermopolis, I have not been covetous [*ʿwn ỉb,* "deceit of heart," "be greedy," "be envious"]."[32] This statement comes between "I have not stolen"[33] and "I have not robbed";[34] it has something in common with these two circumstances, but is obviously not identical with either. It likewise seems appropriate to interpret thus the Babylonian hymn to the sun,[35] which praises the all-embracing power of Shamash, which brings justice: "Spread out thy wide net [to catch the man] who has lifted up [his eyes] to the wife of his comrade (*ša ana alti tappišu iššu*)."

It is undoubtedly true that in Egypt, Sumeria, Babylonia, and throughout the ancient Near East desire for the wife or other property of another man was considered contrary to the norms of religious ethics. If Ebeling is correct in reconstructing "his eyes,"[36] the connection between vision and desire was apparent to the Babylonian sense of language as well. Of course this in itself implies nothing about "taking."

IV. Responsibility for Desire in Early Jewish Literature. While recognizing the conclusion that desire and its consequent conduct form a semantic unity, Jackson[37] nevertheless maintains that in the tenth commandment, the only passage in the OT where *chāmadh* occurs in the context of a divine command, the very act of desire involves liability before God for the mere intention. But the Rabbinic literature he cites in support of his position is not favorable to his hypothesis.

The Mekilta on Ex. 20:17, referring to Dt. 7:25, states: "Just as there the conversion of someone's desire into an act is forbidden, so here, too, the conversion of desire into act is forbidden."[38] It is not the desire itself that is forbidden, but its execution. The *Fragmententhargum*[39] speaks of a sin of desire (*ḥwby ḥmdy*ʾ), obviously also meaning the act as carried out. Enelow[40] interprets the Mishnah of Rabbi Eliezer in the same

[32]Chap. 125, B3; J. A. Wilson in *ANET,* 35a.
[33]Chap. 125, B2.
[34]*Ibid.*, B4.
[35]*AOT,* 245; *ANET,* 388b.
[36]*AOT,* 245.
[37]Jackson, 207.
[38]*Ibid.*, 209.
[39]M. Ginsburger, ed., *Das Fragmententhargum* (1899; Jerusalem, ^{2}1968/69), 42.
[40]P. 163.

sense. Here, too, the plan (*mach^{a}shābhāh*) is firmly linked with the criminal act, even if the latter is not fully executed. Jackson describes the debate between the schools of Shammai and Hillel.[41] While the former, for example, condemns the very intention (*chôshēbh*) to misappropriate property that has been entrusted to one, the latter prefers to consider criminal only the actual act. A kind of compromise is represented by the statement of the Palestinian Talmud cited by Strack-Billerbeck in commenting on Mt. 5:28,[42] to the effect that God does not take evil intentions (*mach^{a}shābhāh rāʿāh*) into account, but does take good intentions (*mach^{a}shābhāh ʾtôbhāh*) into account. Thus the execution of an intention plays an important part in how the intention is evaluated.

The views expressed by Hellenistic authors tend in the same direction. Philo, for example, discussed this problem at length in his tractate on the Decalog.[43] Here he terms *epithymía* the worst of all the passions (*páthēma*). He is following the Stoic tradition of treating desire as a disquiet of the soul (*psychḗ*): (a) the soul suffers in the form of anxiety when desire is unfulfilled; and (b) desire for unattained or perhaps unattainable happiness wears down both individuals and entire nations, which ravage each other in a passionate struggle for wealth and power. In this sense Philo considers *epithymía* harmful and thus irrational, though without excluding the connection between desire and act: "The tragic battles of the Hellenes and the barbarians, which they fought among themselves and against each other, all flowed from the same source, the desire (*epithymía*) for treasure or fame or pleasure (*hēdonḗ*), for toward these things the concern of the human race is directed."[44] Thus the desire for wealth and power is the root of the devastating military actions that are for the most part mutually incited. Thus Philo's discussion of the tenth commandment likewise is seen to contradict an interpretation in the form of an ethics of intention.

Philo's tractate *De confusione linguarum* points in the same direction; we read: "Thus when someone attempts (*epicheiréō*) to kill someone from ambush but was unable to cause his death, he is none the less liable for the punishment of manslaughter (*bouleúsai tón phónon*), as the relevant law states."[45] In *De specialibus legibus* he states: "If someone raises his sword (*epanateínō*) with the intention to kill, even if he has not carried out the murder he is culpable, for his purpose (*proaíresis*) makes him a murderer."[46] Each case speaks of intent to kill; but in each case the intention issues in an attempt to carry out the action. This attempt, although unsuccessful, is termed culpable. These citations, too, are insufficient to establish an ethics of intention. It is not by accident that Philo here avoids the use of *epithyméō* and instead uses *epicheiréō*, which is more accurately translated "set one's hand on something," or uses other terms entirely to describe the attempted act.

Neither do the quotations from Josephus point in the direction of an ethics of intention. *Contra Apion.* deals with lewd conduct, adultery, violation of young girls,

---

[41] P. 217: *B. Metzia* iii.12.
[42] St.-B., I, 298-301, citing Jer. *Pes.* i.16b, 5.
[43] *De decalogo* xxviii.142-153.
[44] *Ibid.*, 153, following Cohn.
[45] *De confusione* 160.
[46] *De spec. leg.* iii.86.

and the active or passive attempt (*tolmáō peíran*) to engage in male homosexual conduct. All these actions are designated as capital offenses by the legislator. In ii.217 we read: "In cases of abuses of parents or of blasphemy against God, someone is executed at once if he is even on the point (*kán mellḗsē*) of committing such an act." Josephus' position is expressed even more clearly in *Ant.* xii.358, according to which the historian Polybius records that Antiochus died when he attempted (*boulēthénta*) to plunder the temple of Artemis in Persia. Polybius then goes on to say, however, that a person is not culpable if he has not carried out what he intended (*mēkéti poiḗsai tó érgon bouleusámenon*); punishment is thus incurred only for an act that is performed, not for one that is merely intended or planned.

Not all these quotations can be associated with the Hebrew root *ḥmd,* but they do follow the same path in treating intention. They show unmistakably that an action is culpable even if it is only attempted unsuccessfully. With respect to the interpretation of the tenth commandment, the point is this: it is not the desire for another's wife or property and envy of his happiness and prosperity that are castigated as such, but rather the secret or open attempt to impugn the other's property, to "steal the hearts" of his wife and servants (2 S. 15:6), selfishly to acquire the other's property by ignoble means, possibly not themselves demonstrably illegal.

Thus the term *ḥmd* attains its fullest force and breadth in the last commandment of the Decalog. Sight of a neighbor's prosperity, his happiness over his wife and possessions, issues in envy of his social position within the community. Then the disquieting power of jealousy leads to the development and finally the realization of dark plots and intrigues. But this is at odds with the understanding of property and of personal inviolability found in the Decalog and in the OT as a whole, which strives to guarantee for every individual, both God and man, inviolability of being and possessions. Under no circumstances must the expansion of one's own wealth, of one's own way of life, be bought at the price of another's detriment—neither through adultery, nor through theft, nor through envious greed, all of which ignore the well-being of others.

In 4 Macc. 2:2-4, Joseph is presented as a model in overcoming the desires of the flesh. Although young in years, the wise Joseph overcomes (*perikratéō*) sensual pleasure through understanding (*diánoia*). For understanding (reason: *logismós*) appears not only to overcome incitement to lust, but to conquer every desire (*pásē epithymía*). Here responsibility toward God has been replaced by reason, which interrupts the path from vision through desire to act by overpowering desire itself. The OT's sense of human susceptibility to the allures of sight and experience, which urge to action, has been replaced by a search for human autocracy achieved through insight.

Wallis

חֵמָה chēmāh

Contents: I. 1. Etymology; Ancient Near East; 2. Meaning. II. Human Wrath: 1. Origin; 2. Expression; 3. Evaluation. III. Divine Wrath: 1. Occasion; 2. Expression; 3. Valuation.

I. 1. *Etymology; Ancient Near East.* The noun *chēmah* probably derives from the root *yḥm,* "be hot," "be ardent," which in turn is probably associated with the root → חמם *ḥmm,* "be warm," from which derives the substantive *chammāh,* "glow," "sun." Behind *chēmāh* may stand the form **chimat,*[1] attested with minor variations in almost all the Semitic languages.[2] Thus we find Akk. *imtu;* Ugar. *ḥmt;* Aram. *ḥēmtā',* *ḥm';*[3] Biblical Aram. *ch^amā'* (Dnl. 3:13,19); Syr. *ḥēmtā';* Mand. *hymt';* Arab. *ḥumat, ḥummayyā, ḥamiyyat;*[4] Ethiop. *ḥamōt, ḥamt.* In Hebrew, under the influence of Aramaic, the spelling *chēmā'* was used alongside *chēmāh* (Dnl. 11:44).

2. *Meaning.* The Akkadian parallel has the meaning "poison, venom." For the analogous words in Ugaritic, Aramaic, Syriac, and Arabic, the meaning "poison" is attested, while Ethiop. *ḥamōt* means "gall." In Aramaic, Syriac, and Arabic, we find the additional meaning "excitement," "anger," which developed further into the sense of "pride" in Ethiopic.[5] Arab. *ḥumayyā* also attests to the meaning "wine."[6]

Correspondingly, we find in the OT three meanings: (a) the ancient Semitic meaning "poison" (Dt. 32:24,33; Ps. 58:5 [Eng. v. 4]; 140:4[3]; Job 6:4); (b) the meaning "heat (of wine)," "fiery wine" (Isa. 27:4; Hos. 7:5; Hab. 2:15; Job 36:18); and (c) the meaning "excitement," "anger," "wrath" (Isa. 34:2; Jer. 6:11; Prov. 15:18; etc.). While the first meaning is attested only 6 times and the second 4 times in the OT, *chēmāh* occurs 110 times with the third meaning. The notion of "being hot" (through the action of poison, wine, or excitement) probably furnishes the point of departure for all three meanings.

---

chēmāh. H. A. Brongers, "Der Zornesbecher," *OTS,* 15 (1967), 177-192; G. R. Driver, "On *ḥēmāh* 'hot anger, fury' and also 'fiery wine,'" *ThZ,* 14 (1958), 133-35; W. Eichrodt, *Theol. OTL.* I (trans. 1961), 258-269; J. Fichtner and O. Grether, "ὀργή," *TDNT,* V, 392-412; J. Gray, "The Wrath of God in Canaanite and Hebrew Literature," *Journal of the Manchester University Egyptian and Oriental Society,* 25 (1947/53), 9-19; H. M. Haney, *The Wrath of God in the Former Prophets* (1960); H. Ringgren, "Vredens kalk," *SEÅ,* 17 (1952), 19-30; *idem,* "Einige Schilderungen des göttlichen Zorns," *Tradition und Situation. Festschrift A. Weiser* (1963), 107-113; G. Sauer, "חֵמָה *ḥēmā* Erregung," *THAT,* I, 581-83; R. V. G. Tasker, *The Biblical Doctrine of the Wrath of God* (London, 1951); P. Volz, *Das Dämonische in Jahve. SgV,* 110 (1924).

[1] *BLe,* § 61j.

[2] P. Fronzaroli, "Studi sul lessico commune semitico," *AANLR,* 19 (1964), 250, 264, 276.

[3] Hadad inscription, *KAI,* 214, 33.

[4] P. Wernberg-Møller, review of P. Wechter, *Ibn Barun's Arabic Works on Hebrew Grammar and Lexicography* (1964), *JSS,* 11 (1966), 125.

[5] *TigrWb,* 62b.

[6] Wehr, 208.

This basic meaning probably accounts for the specific focus and usage of the word *chēmāh* alongside other terms in the semantic field of "anger" in the OT: originally, *chēmāh* probably lent expression to the hot inward excitement accompanying anger. This also explains the notion that *chēmāh* "is kindled" (2 K. 22:13,17), "burns" (Jer. 7:20), or blazes like a fire (Jer. 4:4; 21:12; Nah. 1:6; Ps. 89:47[46]).

II. Human Wrath. In the OT, *chēmāh* is used 25 times[7] to designate human excitement or anger; it is especially common in Proverbs (9 occurrences) and Esther (6 occurrences), and in exilic and postexilic texts in general. It is also noteworthy that *chēmāh* frequently occurs in combination with the parallel word → אף *'aph* (7 occurrences).

1. *Origin.* Human *chēmāh* is predicated of both individuals (Gen. 27:44; Ps. 37:8; Prov. 6:34; Est. 3:5) and groups or nations (Isa. 51:13); it is always directed against other individuals (Gen. 27:44; 2 K. 5:12; Est. 5:9) or another group (Isa. 51:13; Dnl. 8:6; 11:44). Accordingly, the reason for human *chēmāh* is found in someone's feeling that he has been offended, insulted, or deceived by someone else (Gen. 27:44; 2 K. 5:12; Est. 1:12; 2:1; 3:5; 5:9; 7:7; etc.), his jealousy toward someone else (Prov. 6:34), or his realization that someone's conduct has been wrong (2 S. 11:20; Job 13:13 conj.).

2. *Expression.* Closely associated with the particular occasion for human *chēmāh* stands the form in which it finds expression. Thus *chēmāh* arises in someone (2 S. 11:20) or burns within him (Est. 1:12), it fills him (Est. 3:5; 5:9) or goes with him (Ezk. 3:14). Analogously, *chēmāh* can turn away (Gen. 27:44; Est. 2:1; 7:10) or be turned away (Prov. 15:1; 21:14), one can refrain from it (Ps. 37:8) or give it up (Job 13:13 conj.). By nature wrath is cruel and merciless (Prov. 27:4); someone in its grip is an *'îsh (baʿal) chēmāh (chēmôth)* (Prov. 15:18; 22:24; 29:22). It is noteworthy that *chēmāh* is never predicated of a woman or described as being directed against a woman.

3. *Evaluation.* To the extent that a judgment is expressed, human *chēmāh* is always evaluated negatively. This is especially clear in proverbial literature. The negative evaluation is implicit in the description of wrath as cruel and unbending (Prov. 27:4) and in its association with jealousy (6:34). Prov. 15:18; 29:22 state that a wrathful man stirs up strife and transgression, and Prov. 19:19 declares that a man of great wrath (who acts accordingly) will pay the penalty. Prov. 22:24 warns similarly against having anything to do with a wrathful man, while Ps. 37:8 warns in general to refrain from anger, because it tends only to evil. This uniformly negative evaluation of *chēmāh* is confirmed by the opposite observation, that it is good to turn aside anger,

---

[7]Including Job 13:13, where *chēmāh* is to be read on the basis of the LXX (*KBL*[3], 313), and omitting Ps. 76:11a(10a), where *chᵃmath* is to be read (O. Eissfeldt, "Psalm 76," *ThLZ,* 82 [1957], 806f. = *KlSchr,* III [1966], 453-56).

whether by means of a soft answer (Prov. 15:1) or a gift in secret (21:14), and by the contrast between the wrathful man and the positive figure of the wise man (16:14).

The only exception to this negative evaluation is Ezk. 3:14, which treats human *chēmāh* as something positive. Here, however, we are dealing with the disturbed state of a prophet, which is to be understood as a consequence of being seized by the spirit of Yahweh.

III. Divine Wrath. The primary use of *chēmāh* in the OT is as a term for divine wrath; the word occurs 85 times with this meaning (omitting Isa. 42:25; 63:5; Job 19:29, where emendation to another word is required). It is especially common in Ezekiel (31 times), Jeremiah (17 times), and Psalms (9 times).

1. *Occasion.* To the extent that a reason is given, the occasion of Yahweh's *chēmāh* is always seen to lie in human conduct. In the preexilic period, his wrath seems primarily to be aroused by the misconduct of his own people, against whom it is therefore directed (2 K. 22:13; Ps. 89:47[46]; Jer. 4:4). In the exilic and postexilic period, the primary provokers and objects of divine wrath are the foreign nations (Ezk. 25:14,17; 30:15; Isa. 34:2; 63:3,6; Mic. 5:14[15]; Ps. 79:6), but also individual sinners among his own people (Ps. 6:2[1]; 38:2[1]; 88:8[7]; 90:7; Job 21:20). The reason for the expression of wrath varies from case to case. The most important reasons are the breaking of the covenant between Yahweh and his people, and the failure to fulfil the obligations arising out of this covenant (Dt. 29:27[28]; 2 K. 22:13; 2 Ch. 34:21; Ezk. 20:13,21). Other causes include sinful conduct of the people in general (Lev. 26:28; Jer. 4:4; 32:31; 33:5), as well as specific transgressions such as turning aside to foreign gods (Nu. 25:11; Dt. 9:19; 29:27[28]; 2 K. 22:17; 2 Ch. 34:25; Jer. 7:20; 44:6; Ezk. 20:8; 36:18) or false prophecy. Similarly the overt hostility of another nation toward Yahweh's people and land can provoke his *chēmāh* (Ezk. 36:6).

2. *Expression.* Divine wrath, too, is expressed primarily in terms of burning or flaring up (2 K. 22:13,17; Jer. 4:4; 7:20; 44:6; Ps. 89:47[46]; Lam. 2:4). We also find the image of wrath being poured out like water (Jer. 6:11; 42:18; 44:6; Ezk. 7:8; 14:19; 20:8; Ps. 79:6; 2 Ch. 12:7; 34:21,25), which underwent a specialized development in the image of the cup of wrath (Isa. 51:17,22; Jer. 25:15) held out like a cup of wine by Yahweh (cf. Hab. 2:15f.). Both groups of images are supplemented by statements about the effects of divine *chēmāh:* since Yahweh's wrath means his turning away from men (Ps. 89:47[46]), and since wrath and punishment are closely related (Ps. 6:2[1]; 38:2[1]), the wrath of Yahweh leads to afflictions for the land (Dt. 29:22[21]), to being scattered abroad (Jer. 32:37), and ultimately to destruction (Dt. 9:19; Ezk. 13:13; Ps. 59:14[13]). This destruction can be carried out by Yahweh himself (Ezk. 13:13; Lam. 2:4), or by an instrument of his wrath (Ezk. 25:14; 2 Ch. 12:7; 28:9).

3. *Valuation.* Unlike human wrath, the wrath of Yahweh is mostly viewed positively. The primary reason is that this wrath is a reaction to human misconduct contrary to Yahweh's will, and is a corollary to his sovereignty and power. It is natural therefore that Yahweh's *chēmāh* should strike the wicked (Jer. 23:19; 30:23) or the nation (2 K.

22:13; Jer. 4:4; 36:7). But it is felt to be no less justifiable that Yahweh's wrath should also be directed against his adversaries (Nah. 1:2) and the enemies of his people (Ps. 79:6; Ezk. 25:14,17; Isa. 34:2). Indeed, the psalmist prays explicitly for Yahweh to show forth his wrath (Ps. 59:14[13]; 79:6), because it destroys the enemy and thus leads to deliverance (Isa. 34:2).

The fundamental affirmation of Yahweh's *chēmāh* does not, however, stand in the way of an equally positive estimation when Yahweh restrains his anger against his own people (Ps. 78:38) or turns it away once more (2 Ch. 12:7). Yahweh may turn away his anger through the intervention of human agents (Nu. 25:11; Ps. 106:23), but it is ultimately an act of Yahweh's compassion (Ps. 78:38; Dnl. 9:16).

A critical estimate of divine *chēmāh* is found only in a few passages; in Lam. 2:4, for example, the wrath of Yahweh leads to the excessively cruel persecution and destruction of his people, or Ps. 88:8(7); 89:47(46), where the psalmist does not understand Yahweh's wrath and asks, "How long. . .?"

Schunck

חֲמוֹר *chᵃmôr*

Contents: I. Lexicography. II. 1. Meaning and Occurrences in the OT; 2. Secular Usage; 3. Sacral and Legal Usage. III. Metaphorical Usage.

I. Lexicography. The word *ḥmr* with the meaning "ass" is relatively common in the Semitic languages. It appears in Akk. *imēru,*[1] where the logogram *ANŠE,* like

chᵃmôr. W. Bauer, "The 'Colt' of Palm Sunday (Der Palmesel)," *JBL,* 72 (1953), 220-29; E. Bickermann, "Ritualmord und Eselskult," *MGWJ,* 71 (1927), 225-264; J. Boessneck, *Die Haustiere in Altägypten. Veröffentlichungen der Zoologischen Staatssammlung München,* 3 (1953); B. Brentjes, "Onager und Esel im Alten Orient," *Beiträge zu Geschichte, Kultur und Religion des Alten Orients. Festschrift E. Unger* (1971), 131-145; G. Dalman, *AuS,* II (1932), 112-165; A. Deimel, *Sumerische Tempelwirtschaft zur Zeit Urukaginas und seiner Vorgänger. AnOr,* 2 (1931), 93f.; *idem,* "Die Viehzucht der Šumerer zur Zeit Urukaginas," *Or,* 20 (1926), 16f.; J. Döller, *Die Reinheits- und Speisegesetze des ATs in religionsgeschichtlicher Beleuchtung. ATA,* 7/2-3 (1917); G. Dossin, "Les archives épistolaires du palais de Mari," *Syria,* 19 (1938), 108f.; W. H. Gispen, "The Distinction between Clean and Unclean," *OTS,* 5 (1948), 190-96; H. Grapow, *Vergleiche und andere bildliche Ausdrücke im Ägyptischen. AO,* 21/1-2 (1920); P. Haupt, "Die 'Eselstadt' Damaskus," *ZDMG,* 69 (1915), 168-172; G. Heinz-Mohr, *Gott liebt die Esel* (1972) [popular]; A. Jeremias, *The OT in the Light of the Ancient East* (trans. 1911), see index under "ass"; K. Kerényi, *Die griechisch-orientalische Romanliteratur in religionsgeschichtlicher Beleuchtung* (1927, repr. 1962), 151-205; H.-W.

continued on p. 466

[1]*AHw,* I, 375f.; *CAD,* VII, 110-15.

Heb. *chamôr,* as a rule refers to the male animal. Occasionally *ANŠE* can be used as a unit of measure or weight (roughly 100 liters; cf. Lat. *onus,* "weight"). As a personal name it appears in Old Akk. (Ur III) *I-ma-ru-um* or *E-ma-ru-um,* like *ḥmwr* in Gen. 34; for Gk. *ónagros* as a personal name, cf. *CIG,* III, 5875[e]. In Imperial Aramaic, *ḥmr'* is attested; it appears at Elephantine, as well as in Syr. *ḥmr'/ḥemārā'* and Palm. *ḥmr.*[2] Egypt. *ỉmr* is a West Semitic loanword.[3] In Arabic, too, besides *ʿair* and *'atān, ḥimār* means "ass."

In Phoenicia and Syria, it is unlikely that the ass was considered sacred;[4] there is no evidence for its use as a sacrificial animal. It nevertheless appears at Ugarit as the mount of the goddess Aṯrt,[5] and at Mari it was used to draw the processional chariots during the *akītu* festival.[6] In the cult of Dionysus it was considered the mount of the god.[7] In Egypt the ass[8] was considered proverbially stupid and stubborn. Someone who cannot write is "like an ass"; a disobedient child is "like a deaf ass."[9] Sacred to the desert- and storm-god Seth-Typhon, who was hated by men as the enemy of Isis and the murderer of Osiris, the ass was considered unclean in Egypt, as Seth's mount.[10]

An etymological connection has been suggested with the common Semitic root *ḥmr* II, "red, reddish, clay-colored,"[11] so that *ḥmwr* would be a nominal derivative[12] meaning "the reddish one," like Akk. *imēru.* By analogy to the connection of *pr',* "wild ass," with the root *pr',* "agile," there could also be a connection between *ḥmwr* and → חמר *ḥmr* I (qal), "be frenzied," so that the word *ḥmwr* would suggest the refractory nature of the ass and its unwillingness to work. Something

---

Kuhn, "Das Reittier Jesu in der Einzugsgeschichte des Markusevangeliums," *ZNW,* 50 (1959), 82-91; M. Landmann, *Das Tier in der jüdischen Weisung* (1959); B. Landsberger, *Die Fauna des alten Mesopotamien nach der 14. Tafel der Serie Ḫar-ra = ḫubullu. ASAW,* 42/6 (1934); R. Largement, "Les oracles de Bile'am et la mantique suméro-akkadienne," *Travaux de l'Institut Catholique,* 10 (1964), 37-50; J. Leibovitch, "The Cult of the Ass in Antiquity," *BIES,* 18 (1954), 129-134; E. Nielsen, "Ass and Ox in the OT," *Studia Orientalia. Festschrift J. Pedersen* (Copenhagen, 1953), 263-274; M. Noth, "Das alttestamentliche Bundschliessen im Lichte eines Mari-Textes," *Mélanges Isidore Lévy. Annuaire de l'Institut de Philologie et d'Histoire Orientales et Slaves,* 13 (Brussels, 1953 [1955]), 433-444 = *GSAT,* I. *ThB,* 6 ([3]1966), 142-154; F. Olck, "Esel," *PW,* VI (1907), 626-676; I. Oppelt, "Esel," *RAC,* VI (1966) 564-595; J. Pedersen, *ILC,* III-IV, 317f.; A. Salonen, *Hippologica accadica, AnAcScFen,* B, 100 (1955), 44ff.; A. Schott, *Die Vergleiche in den akkadischen Königsinschriften. MVÄG,* 30 (1926); E. Schürer, *A History of the Jewish People* (Edinburgh, trans. 1891, [2]1973), II/2, 294, II/3, 266; J. Supervieille, *The Ox and the Ass at the Manger* (London, trans. 1945); J. Ziegler, "Ochs und Ezel an der Krippe," *MThZ,* 3 (1952), 385-402.

[2] *DISO,* 91; *LidzNE,* 277.

[3] Cf. W. A. Ward, "Notes on Some Semitic Loan-Words and Personal Names in Late Egyptian," *Or,* 32 (1963), 417.

[4] Cf. for Ugar. *ḥmr WUS,* No. 942; *UT,* No. 879; *CTA,* 14 [I K], 121, 225.

[5] *CTA,* 4 [II AB], IV-V, 3-15.

[6] *ARM,* I, No. 50, 11-20, naming *damdammu,* mule, and horse.

[7] W. F. Otto, *Dionysus: Myth and Cult* (trans. 1965), 170.

[8] *ʿ3, WbÄS,* I, 165, or *šw, WbÄS,* IV, 433.

[9] Grapow, 19.

[10] Cf. E. Brunner-Traut, "Esel," *LexÄg,* II/1 (1975), 27-30.

[11] *GesB,* 240; *KBL*[3], 314; *LexLingAeth,* 75f.

[12] J. Barth, *Die Nominalbildung in den semitischen Sprachen* ([2]1894), §128c.

similar—albeit with positive overtones—is found in Greek with the association between *ónos,* "ass," and the verb *onásthai,* "be useful." The word *chamôr* clearly refers primarily to the domesticated wild ass of western Asia (*Equus onager*), while in Egypt it was the ass of the Nubian steppes (*Equus taeniopus*) that was domesticated, primarily as a beast of burden.[13] In Akkadian similes only wild asses appear; the horse is rare as an image in similes.[14]

II. 1. *Meaning and Occurrences in the OT.* Besides *chamôr* (*ónos*), which everywhere in the OT except 2 S. 19:27 refers to the male animal, Hebrew has the terms *'āthôn,* "she-ass" (Nu. 22:23; 1 S. 9:20; Job 1:3; 42:12; cf. LXX *ónos thḗleia*); *b^e^khōrāh,* "young she-ass" (Akk. *bakru,* "foal [of an ass]");[15] *ʿayir,* "jackass" (Isa. 30:24; Zec. 9:9; cf. LXX *pṓlos,* Akk. [Mari] *ḫayarum,* Ugar. *ʿr*);[16] and *peredh,* "mule" (1 K. 1:33,38; 2 K. 5:17; etc.). The word for "wild ass," *pereʾ,* from *prʾ,* "wild," "agile(?)," probably suggests the rage for freedom that is characteristic of this species, which inhabits the steppe and salt desert (cf. Job 39:5; Gen. 16:12; Hos. 8:9). All in all, the wealth of terms for "ass" found in Hebrew from the very earliest strata of the OT clearly shows how widespread and valued this animal was in Palestine, where ass nomadism was indigenous (cf. the use of *yādhaʿ* in Isa. 1:3, indicating the good relationship between the ass and its owner).

Together with the swine (*chazîr*), the ass is among the earliest domesticated animals of the ancient Near East. It is the traditional caravan animal of the seminomadic Semites during the prehistoric period and the Bronze Age; as such, it is well attested in the OT—in contrast to the camel Bedouins—for the patriarchs (Gen. 12:16 [J]; 22:3,5 [E?]).

The singular *chamôr* occurs 62 times in the OT, the plural *chamōrîm* 35 times; the distribution of the 97 occurrences does not exhibit any peculiarities.

2. *Secular Usage.* The *chamôr* serves the Israelite as a beast of burden (Gen. 42:26; 44:13; 45:23; 1 S. 16:20; 2 S. 16:1; 1 Ch. 12:41 [Eng. v. 40]; Neh. 13:15), for plowing (Dt. 22:10; Isa. 32:20) and threshing,[17] but also for turning a mill.[18] Together with the ox (*shôr*) the ass stands paradigmatically for all domestic animals,[19] and as the object of jealousy (Ex. 20:17; Dt. 5:21; Job 24:3). The fixed combination of ox and ass appears above all in the Covenant Code and Deuteronomy (Dt. 22:4,10); the triad "wife, ox, and ass" is already attested in the Nuzi texts. Along with the sheep (*śeh*) the ass is considered the domestic animal par excellence by the Israelite (1 S. 9:3; 1 Ch. 27:30; Neh. 7:68; in CH § 8, movable property in general is designated by the words "ox or sheep, ass or swine, or a ship").

As a means of personal transport the ass was saddled (Gen. 22:3; Jgs. 19:10; 2 S.

[13]Boessneck, 19f.
[14]Schott, 121; *AHw,* II, 1052a; for Egypt, see Grapow, 59.
[15]Cf. M. Tsevat, "בְּכוֹר *b^e^khôr,*" *TDOT,* II, 121f.
[16]*KBL*³, 56.
[17]Josephus *Contra Apion.* ii.7 (87).
[18]St.-B., I, 775; *AuS,* III (1933), 233-35; cf. Mt. 18:6: *mýlos onikós,* "ass-mill."
[19]As early as EA 280, 28.

16:1); occasionally the team was accompanied by a driver (Nu. 22:22; 2 K. 4:24; cf. Ex. 4:20).[20] Prominent people valued white she-asses as mounts (Jgs. 5:10), for the breeding of which Damascus and Bagdad were especially famous. Both cities are also key junctions in the transportation system, which relied in large measure on asses. The *'ᵃthōnôth tsᵉchōrôth* praised in the Song of Deborah (Jgs. 5:10), usually translated "tawny" or "white" (she-)asses, may refer to ordinary asses decorated with white ribbons.[21] In war, asses carried supplies and equipment in the baggage train (2 K. 7:7) and also served as mounts for soldiers (Isa. 21:7).

3. *Sacral and Legal Usage*. According to Ex. 13:13; 34:20; and Dt. 22:10, the ass was considered unclean in ancient Israel, and its tasty flesh could not be used for either food or sacrifice.[22] This helps explain (cf. Lev. 11:1ff.; Dt. 14:4ff.) why Ex. 13:13 provides a substitute for the first-born of an ass: "Every firstling of an ass you shall redeem with a lamb, or if you will not redeem it you shall break its neck. Every first-born of man among your sons you shall redeem." Concerning this juxtaposition of the firstling of an ass with a first-born human child, Nielsen states correctly that this may "most safely be regarded as a compromise between the general Semitic attitude toward the ass (unclean animal), and the fact that the ass as domestic animal was quite indispensable for the Israelites."[23] Pedersen observes similarly: "Thus Israel combines the requirements of the time with an impregnable tradition."[24]

Now 2 K. 6:25 admittedly shows that in times of need the flesh of asses was eaten despite all prohibitions, and that an ass's head could command the princely sum of 80 shekels of silver, whereas in peaceful times the price of a whole ass was between 10 and 60 shekels.

In the Mari texts we find reference to the practice of slaughtering an ass at the making of a covenant. In one passage[25] we find the striking phrase *ḫayarum mār atānim* applied to this animal, which has an OT equivalent in the *ʿayir ben-'ᵃthōnôth* of Zec. 9:9. As Noth suggests,[26] probably correctly, this may mean a pure-bred ass in contrast to a bastard brought forth by a female horse. Since the Mari passages speak only of "slaughtering" (*qatālum*), not "sacrificing," it can be stated that in Mesopotamia, too, the ass did not play any significant role as a sacrificial animal; more likely, as in Egypt, Israel, and Canaan, it was considered unclean.[27]

III. Metaphorical Usage. The she-ass in the story of Balaam, Nu. 22–24, plays a special role. The motif of the speaking ass, which belongs to the realm of fairy tales

[20] On the *asinarri*, cf. E. Ziebarth, "'Ονηλάτης," *PW*, XVIII (1939), 459.
[21] F. Vigouroux in *DB*, I (1895), 567.
[22] Döller, 194f.; Noth, 144; Gispen, 190–96.
[23] P. 274.
[24] P. 318.
[25] *ARM*, II, 37, 11.
[26] P. 146.
[27] Cf. R. E. Clements, "Baal-Berith of Shechem," *JSS*, 13 (1968), 21–32.

and gives the impression of being very ancient, has distant extrabiblical parallels.[28] The episode has certain similarities with the ride of the man of God in 1 K. 13:11-29. In both stories, permeated with death, the mount is never in danger.

A harsh image occurs in Jer. 22:19, where the Davidic king Jehoiakim is promised "the burial of an ass" (*qᵉbhûrath chᵃmôr*): "With the burial of an ass he shall be buried, dragged and cast forth beyond the gates of Jerusalem." From this description of an ass's burial, the culmination of the threat uttered against a potentate indulging in luxury, we may conclude that it was generally not customary to bury asses (unclean animals), but rather to leave their bodies lying in the open fields as carrion.[29]

In Gen. 49:14f., Issachar is called a "bony ass" (*chᵃmōr gārem*):[30] "Issachar is a bony ass, crouching between the sheepfolds; he saw that a resting place was good, and that the land was pleasant; so he bowed his shoulder to bear, and became a slave at forced labor." We obviously have here an image for the forced labor of the tribe of Issachar (mockery of a tribal symbol showing an ass?[31]), which demeaned itself to the status of an ass (bearing tribute). Tyrtaeus similarly compares the Messinians oppressed by the Spartans to asses.[32] By contrast, in Akkadian the ass is proverbially considered as nimble as the ibex.[33]

In the episode recounted in Jgs. 15:14f., in which Samson is said to have slain a thousand Philistines with the fresh jawbone of an ass, it appears that we are ultimately dealing with a local etiology, so that the phrase *vaiyimtsāʾ lᵉchî chᵃmôr,* "and he found an ass's jawbone. . . ," suggests a play on Lehi (*lᵉchî*), the name of the site where the event took place.

In contrast to the horse, which was used primarily for military purposes (2 S. 8:4), the ass was considered a symbol of peace. On the basis of this usage it found a place among the requisites of the Messiah. As early as the history of the Solomonic succession (1 K. 1:33,38), the propagandistically exploited choice of a mule (*peredh*) in preference to a horse is striking. The formula *vayyaʿaś* (PN) *lô merkābhāh vᵉsusîm vachᵃmishshîm ʾîsh rātsîm lᵉphānāv* (2 S. 15:1; 1 K. 1:5) associates the latter closely with the reprehensible conduct of a pretender to the throne. Above all, the messianic prince of peace rides upon a *chᵃmôr* (Zec. 9:9; cf. Gen. 49:10f.), while Nehemiah in his apologia avoids any concrete reference to his mount and bars any messianic association by calling his mount a *bᵉhēmāh* (Neh. 2:12,14). Similarly, it is probably possible to interpret the asses that Saul is bring back in 1 S. 9:3ff. as an allusion to his being chosen king.[34]

28H. Gressmann, *Mose und seine Zeit. FRLANT,* N.S. 1 (1913), 327; H. Ewald, *The History of Israel* (London, trans. 1869), II, 215, n. 1; Largement.

29Cf. Jerome on Isaiah, iv.22, 19 in *MPL,* XXIV (Paris, 1845), 815d.

30For a different view, see S. I. Feigin, "Ḥamôr gārîm, 'Castrated Ass,'" *JNES,* 5 (1946), 230-33.

31L. Ginzberg, *The Legends of the Jews* (trans. 1909-1938), VI, 83.

32In Pausanias iv.14.3.

33Schott, 102.

34M. Bič, "Saul sucht die Eselinnen [1 Sam ix]," *VT,* 7 (1957), 92-97; but cf. the justified criticism by H. W. Hertzberg, *I & II Samuel. OTL* (trans. 1964), 80f.

During the intertestamental period, the Jews were falsely accused of worshipping an ass's head.[35] In fact the reference is probably to a rare form of Seth worship. The same accusation was directed against the early Christians, probably through motif transference.[36]

In the NT, *ónos* appears only 6 times, primarily as a messianic proof based on Zec. 9:9.[37] The image of the ox and ass at the manger probably derives from Isa. 1:3.[38]

In der Smitten

[35]Josephus *Contra Apion.* ii.7; ii.80; Plutarch *Symposiaca* iv.5; Tacitus *Hist.* v.3-4.
[36]Citations in Oppelt, *RAC,* VI, 592-94; cf. also the fanciful interpretation in N. Walker, "The Riddle of the Ass's Head, and the Question of a Trigram," *ZAW,* 75 (1963), 225-27.
[37]Cf. St.-B., I, 842; O. Michel, "ὄνος," *TDNT,* V, 283-87.
[38]Heinz-Mohr, 78-95.

חָמַל *chāmal;* חֶמְלָה *chemlāh*

Contents: I. Etymology and Occurrences. II. Meaning.

I. Etymology and Occurrences. The root *ḥml* is not definitely attested outside of Biblical Hebrew. Arab., OSA, and Syr. *ḥml,* "carry," have been considered related,[1] but there is no semantic shift from "carry" to "have compassion on, spare" before medieval Hebrew, and there is no reliable evidence for such a shift in the other Semitic languages (Arab. *ḥml* VIII, "tolerate, endure," *ḥamūl,* "forbearing," and the phoneme sequence *ḥml* in Tigré, appearing in various words with the meaning "smooth, gentle, kind," deserve consideration). Somewhat more likely is the earlier view that associates the root with Arab. *ḥlm,* a fairly well represented phoneme group that appears as noun, adjective, and verb in several stems with the meaning "gentle, compliant."[2] A similarly uncertain claim could be made on behalf of the common Middle Hebrew *mḥl,* "forgive," "forgo."

If the second or third of these etymologies is correct, the word *machmāl* (Ezk. 24:21) is not related to the group of words under discussion; if the first is correct, it is related only indirectly. In any case this word is directly associated with Arab., OSA, and Syr. *ḥml,* "carry," as is shown by the almost literal repetition of the text in v. 25, where we find *maśśā'* instead of *machmāl.*[3]

[1]E.g., *GesB,* 240.
[2]*KBL*[3], 315.
[3]See L. Kopf, "Arabische Etymologien und Parallelen zum Bibelwörterbuch," *VT,* 8 (1958), 172.

The origin and fundamental meaning of *mḥl* are disputed.[4]

In post-Biblical Hebrew, this group of words occurs 4 times in Sirach (13:4, 12; 16:8f.); to the extent shown by the available concordances, it does not occur at all in regular Middle Hebrew. Sir. 13:4,12 are so difficult that the text may well be corrupt. In Tosefta *Ber.* 3:7, *ḥml* found a place in the slightly archaizing language of a prayer; Talmud *Men.* 53b uses it in a play on words involving *hamullāh* (Jer. 11:16). The reading [*wlḥ*]*mwl* in 1QH 15:15 suggested by Habermann[5] is highly questionable.

In the OT, *ḥml* is attested 41 times as a verb (42 times if we count the simplifying 1QIs[a] text of Isa. 9:16 instead of the *yiśmach* of the Masoretic text), to which may be added the 2 occurrences of the noun *chemlāh*. The root appears in the biblical personal name *chāmūl* and 2 names found in inscriptions: *yḥmlyhw* (Palestine, between the 8th and 6th centuries B.C.)[6] and *yḥmwl* (Egypt, late 5th century B.C.).[7]

II. Meaning. The verb *ḥml* means "have compassion on, be sorry for," comprising both emotional reaction and active conduct. The noun should probably be translated as "pity." The simple meaning of the verb, i.e., a meaning not influenced by a specific situation or idea, is found, for example, in Nathan's parable of the rich man who "was sorry" (*vaiyachmōl*) to have to give up his own property and instead took the property of the poor man (2 S. 12:4). Or there is the story of Pharaoh's daughter, who "took pity" on the child exposed on the river (*vattachmōl,* Ex. 2:6). If these verses may be cited as instances of the meaning "be sorry (for)," others belong to the semantic field of "spare." Of the animals taken from the Amalekites, the people "spared" (*chāmal*) the best for sacrifice (1 S. 15:15), subjecting the rest to the ban. On account of the oaths of fidelity and friendship between David and Jonathan, David "spared" (*vaiyachmōl*) Jonathan's son (2 S. 21:7). For the most part, however, the verb is used in a negative sense (30 times—including the rhetorical question of Jer. 15:5—out of 41). In addition, a survey of occurrences shows that in the majority of the passages God is the subject of the verb. But too much theological significance should not be attached to these facts.

In the first place, negative *ḥml* clauses often serve to characterize someone as pitiless or even merciless, as in Hab. 1:17: "Is he [the enemy] then to keep on . . . mercilessly (*lō' yachmôl*) slaying nations?" In particular, since the prophets depict a terrible and inescapable destiny for the future or the present, and since it is God who brings this destiny to pass, the combination of the two phenomena, i.e., negative *ḥml* clauses with God as subject, appears with some frequency in the prophetic writings. For example: "I will no longer have pity on (*lō' 'echmôl*) the inhabitants of this land" (Zec. 11:6).

---

[4]See E. Y. Kutscher, *Archive of the New Dictionary of Rabbinical Literature,* I (Tel Aviv, 1972), 66, n. 154 (in Hebrew).

[5]A. M. Habermann, *Megilot Midbar Yehudah* (Tel Aviv, 1959), 131.

[6]Reproduced, e.g., in *AOB,* No. 589; for bibliography, see D. Diringer, *Le iscrizioni antico-ebraïci Palestinesi* (Florence, 1934), 208; F. Vattioni, "I sigilli ebraici," *Bibl,* 50 (1969), 366 (the personal name *yḥmlyh*[!] mentioned in this article is hardly legible).

[7]Cowley, *AP,* 22, 89(?), 97.

Within the prophetic literature, the book of Ezekiel stands out with 8 occurrences of *ḥml,* 7 of which have in common a negative formulation and a reinforcement by means of the synonym *chûs,* "pity," so that they announce a "pitiless and merciless" event. In 6 of these, God is the subject (including Ezk. 9:5, where heavenly agents act on his behalf). It appears, however, that several of these passages are based on later additions, so that in this case statistics and comparisons might give a distorted picture. With all caution in the use and interpretation of numbers and proportions, it is still appropriate to note that Lamentations uses *ḥml* 4 times in the manner of Ezekiel (albeit without *chûs*), but the book where one would most expect to find the word group, the book of Psalms, does not use it at all. Neither does it occur in any other biblical prayers, with the exception of the occurrences in Lamentations. Perhaps this is because *ḥml* is not a native Semitic word and has no place—as far as we know—in the literature of the Northwest Semites.[8]

The few occurrences of *ḥml* used positively with God as subject and man as object are quickly listed. The verb appears in Joel 2:18; Mal. 3:17; 2 Ch. 36:15; the noun appears in Gen. 19:16 and Isa. 63:9—almost all late passages. The word makes a final appearance in the Tosefta, as mentioned above (verb and noun; in Tannaitic prayers, the resort to biblical expressions—of whatever origin—is always archaizing). Also in line with this picture is the very infrequent use of the root in personal names, with God always named or intended.

In summary, we may state that the religious significance of *ḥml* is slight. It is rarely used in a positive sense, and the passages where it is used positively are comparatively insignificant religiously. In a negative sense it exhibits a uniformity of usage that can be explained in part on the basis of textual history (Ezekiel) and in part on the basis of stylistic considerations, where a negated *ḥml* does not itself constitute the central statement but serves primarily to intensify another statement ("mercilessly").

Tsevat

---

[8]For a general discussion of this question, see M. Tsevat, *A Study of the Language of the Biblical Psalms. JBL Monograph Series,* 9 (1955).

חמם *ḥmm*; חֹם *chōm*; חָם *chām*; חוּם *chûm*; חַמָּה *chammāh*; חַמָּן *chammān*

Contents: I. Distribution and Meaning. II. 1. The Verb *ḥmm*; 2. The Noun *chōm*; 3. The Adjectives *chām* and *chûm*; 4. The Noun *chammāh*. III. The Meaning of *chammān*. IV. Toponyms and Personal Names Derived from *ḥmm*.

I. Distribution and Meaning. The root *ḥmm* and the nouns and adjectives derived from it are widespread in the Semitic languages.[1] The OT, however, exhibits a multiplicity of different types of use that is unparalleled in the other languages. The basic meaning is "be or become hot or warm," which hardly admits a specifically theological usage.[2] The term *chammān,* however, has religio-historical significance.[3] The vocabulary of Ugaritic includes the noun *ḥm* with the meaning "heat" in the meteorological sense,[4] as well as the verb in the form *ḥmḥm,* which has a specifically psychological nuance, namely, as an expression of sexual experience in the sense "grow hot," i.e., "glow with love."[5] This form does not occur at all in the OT, nor does the derived noun *ḥmḥmt,* "heat of passion."[6] The occurrence in Aramaic (Elephantine) also uses this verb in a psychological sense to describe the uneasiness occasioned by a dream.[7] In post-biblical Hebrew and Aramaic likewise there is no trace of the use of *ḥmm* for the heat of the sun,[8] so common in Biblical Hebrew.

ḥmm. A. Alt, "Eine galiläische Ortsliste in Jos 19," *ZAW,* 45 (1927), 59-81; W. Baudissin, "Sonne," *RE*³, XVIII (1906), 489-521, esp. III.2.d, "Baal Chamman und Chammanim"; F. Cumont, "Hammo," *PW,* VII/2 (1912), 2310f.; K. Elliger, "Chammanim = Masseben?" *ZAW,* 57 (1939), 256-265; *idem,* "Der Sinn des Wortes *chammān*," *ZDPV,* 66 (1943), 129-139; K. Galling, "Altar," *BRL,* I/1, 13-22; R. Gradwohl, *Die Farben im AT: Eine Terminologische Studie. BZAW,* 83 (1963); H. Ingholt, "Le sens du mot Ḥammān," *Mélanges Syriens offerts à Monsieur René Dussaud* (Paris, 1939), II, 795-802, Fig. 1; L. Köhler, "*Ḥūm heiss, läufig,*" *ThZ,* 5 (1949), 314f.; J. Lewy, "The Old West Semitic Sun-God Ḥammu," *HUCA,* 18 (1943/44), 429-488; J. Lindblom, *Die Jesaja-Apokalypse, Jes. 24-27. LUÅ,* N.S., avd. 1, 34/3 (1938), 91-100: "6. Die Chammanim"; E. Littmann, *Nabataean Inscriptions from the Southern Ḥaurân. Publications of the Princeton University Archaeological Expeditions to Syria in 1904-1905 and 1909,* IV/A (Leiden, 1914); E. Meyer, "Untersuchungen zur phönikischen Religion," *ZAW,* 49 (1931), 1-15, esp. 8-11; M. Noth, "Studien zu den historisch-geographischen Dokumenten des Josuabuches," *ZDPV,* 58 (1935, repr. 1972), 185-255 = his *Aufsätze zur biblischen Landes- und Altertumskunde* (1971), I, 229-280; J. Simons, *The Geographical and Topographical Texts of the OT. StFS,* 2 (Leiden, 1959); → חמה *chēmāh.*

[1] See the citations in *KBL*³; *WUS,* No. 935; *DISO,* 90.
[2] See II.4 below.
[3] See III below.
[4] *CTA,* 19 [I D], I, 40; see II.2 below: Gen. 8:22; Jer. 17:8; Job 24:19.
[5] *CTA,* 17 [II D], I, 41.
[6] *CTA,* 23 [SS] 51, 56.
[7] *CIS,* II, 1, No. 137A, line 4; *ḥmm* par. *šg'*.
[8] See II.1.a below.

II. 1. *The Verb ḥmm.*

a. The verb *ḥmm* serves in the first instance to describe the period of the day that is warm or hot by virtue of astronomical and physical conditions, i.e., the heat of midday (Gen. 18:1; Ex. 16:21; 1 S. 11:9,11; 2 S. 4:5; Isa. 18:4; Job 6:17; Neh. 7:3).

b. The following passages use the verb *ḥmm* for the warming of the body through external influence: We read in 1 K. 1:1f. how the aged king David was covered with clothes *v^e^lō' yēcham lô,* so that the young Shunammite Abishag was placed beside him *v^e^cham la'dhōnî hammelekh.* This procedure is confirmed by the piece of practical wisdom recorded in Eccl. 4:11: *'im-yishk^e^bhû sh^e^nayim v^e^cham lāhem ûl^e^'echādh 'êkh yēchām.* The revival of the son of the Shunammite woman through the intervention of Elisha is signaled by the fact that "the flesh of the child became warm" (2 K. 4:34). The distress in the period of the prophet Haggai is described in terms of general poverty and the fruitlessness of all efforts; *lābhôsh v^e^'ên-l^e^chōm lô* (Hag. 1:6). In his mockery of idolatry, Deutero-Isaiah describes how men use the same wood from which they have made the idols they worship to make a fire to warm themselves (Isa. 44:15f.). During the feast of sheepshearing, any poor man who sought help in Job's house was able to warm himself by the fire (Job 31:20). The sentence of destruction upon Jerusalem is depicted by the prophet Ezekiel in terms of a pot that is set on the fire emptied of its contents, to be cleansed by becoming hot and having its impurities consumed (Ezk. 24:11). Here, too, belongs the description of the behavior of the ostrich, which buries its eggs in the earth to warm and be hatched (Job 39:14).

c. This expression for the physical state of warmth can also be used to describe an inward sense of warmth. Just as wrath is kindled (→ חרה *chārāh*), so the avenger of blood feels his heart become hot with anger when he pursues someone who has unintentionally slain one of his household (Dt. 19:6). In Hos. 7:7, the prophet describes the revolutionary activity of certain circles in Samaria; a variety of images states that their hearts are hot as an oven. The same meaning is probably intended in Jer. 51:39, where *ḥmm* describes the high spirits of Babylon even as destruction approaches. We are brought to the religious realm by Isa. 57:5, which states that those who turn their backs on Yahweh burn with lust to pursue their fertility rites (*hannēchāmîm bā'ēlîm tachath kol-'ēts ra'^a^nān*). All of these emotions described by *ḥmm* are ethically or morally negative. In Ps. 39:4 (Eng. v. 3), on the other hand, it is inward distress that makes the heart grow hot, like the inward uneasiness occasioned by the dream vision described in *CIS,* II, 1, No. 137A.[9]

2. *The Noun chōm.* The noun *chōm* refers to heat as a meteorological phenomenon, and can therefore be used in parallel with various synonyms: *chōm,* "heat" par. *sh^e^nath batstsōreth,* "year of drought" (Jer. 17:8); *tsîyāh,* "drought" par. *chōm,* "heat" (Job 24:19), or in contrast *qōr vāchōm,* "cold and heat" (Gen. 8:22). As

[9]See I above.

a physical description we find *chōm* in combination with *lechem* (cf. Josh. 9:12[10]): "bread of heat," i.e., fresh bread, is offered constantly as a sacrifice to Yahweh in the sanctuary at Nob (1 S. 21:7[6]).

3. *The Adjectives chām and chûm*. The adjective *chām* describes the state of objects that have been heated through external influence. Thus the Gibeonites who bring dry and moldy bread to Joshua insist that it was still warm (*chām*) from the oven when they set out (Josh. 9:12), and Job's friend Elihu seeks to portray Job's impotence and dependence on Yahweh in vivid terms by reminding him that his clothing becomes hot when the sun blazes upon the earth at midday, and he can do nothing about it (Job 37:17).

In the context of the story of Jacob and Laban as herdsmen (Gen. 30:32f.,35,40), the adjective *chûm* must refer to a specific color. It probably means "brownish," "blackish," "blackish brown," and can easily be derived from *ḥmm*, because "what is heated, especially anything heated by fire, is darkened in color."[11] In modern Hebrew, *chûm* is the word for brown. The rendering "hot," "excited," "in heat," "ready for mating"[12] has been dropped again in *KBL*³.

4. *The Noun chammāh*. The noun *chammāh*, "incandesence," "sun," derives from *ḥmm*. Ps. 19 describes the glory of Yahweh, which is reflected in the natural phenomena of the heavens, especially the course of the sun: "there is nothing hid from its heat" (Ps. 19:7[6]). The designation of the sun as "the hot one" (→ אור *'ôr* II.1.a) is a poetic expression comparable to the use of the word *lᵉbhānāh*, "the white one," for the moon. Cant. 6:10 uses both expressions together as a simile to describe the woman. Poetic usage also appears in the symbolic use of light and dark. Thus Job laments (Job 30:28): "In mourning I go where there is no sun" (*bᵉlō' chammāh;* Fohrer[13] reads instead *bᵉlō' nechāmāh*, "where there is no comfort"), describing his unfortunate and agonizing situation.

But it is not so much this metaphorical usage that is of theological relevance as the purely astronomical, because it merges into cosmological eschatology. Here we find two contrasting statements. In the Apocalypse of Isaiah (Isa. 24:23), sun and moon pale into insignificance when Yahweh manifests his glory as king upon Mt. Zion (cf. Isa. 60:19f.; Rev. 22:5). On the other hand, Isa. 30:26 depicts the eschaton in such terms that sun and moon are multiplied in intensity, and thus symbolize the sovereignty of Yahweh: *vᵉhāyāh 'ôr-hallᵉbhānāh kᵉ'ôr hachammāh vᵉ'ôr hachammāh yihyeh shibhᶜāthayim*.

III. The Meaning of chammān. The noun *chammān* occurs 8 times in the OT (Lev. 26:30; Isa. 17:8; 27:9; Ezk. 6:4,6; 2 Ch. 14:4[5]; 34:3,7). It designates a "cult

---

[10]See II.3 below.

[11]Gradwohl, 50.

[12]Köhler, 315; cf. G. Lisowski, *Konkordanz zum hebraïschen AT* (²1966), 468.

[13]G. Fohrer, *KAT*, XVI (1963), 412.

object''[14] belonging to the negatively judged high places (→ במה *bāmāh*), and is translated either ''sun stela'' (following Rashi) or ''incense altar'' (following Hugo Grotius). The *chammānîm* are frequently mentioned in combination with asherahs (→ אשרה *ʾashērāh*, Isa. 17:8; 27:9; 2 Ch. 14:2–4[3–5]; 34:4,7), and the manner of their destruction is indicated by means of the same verb (*gādhaʿ;* cf. 2 Ch. 34:4,7 with Dt. 7:5; 2 Ch. 14:2[3]; 31:1). It follows that the *chammānîm* are associated with an idolatrous alien cult, and probably exhibit a form similar or identical to the stelae of the asherahs. The translation of *chammān* in the versions (LXX, Vulg., Targumim, Peshitta) varies considerably, which shows that the actual meaning of the word was unknown to the translators. In this connection, attention should be called to Levy's rendering of *chammān* in post-biblical Hebrew and Aramaic as a ''statue set up in honor of the sun-god Baʿal.''[15]

Neither archeology nor epigraphy provides a final answer to the question of what *chammān* means. The word appears in Nabatean[16] and Palmyrene[17] inscriptions, but they do not provide a clear indication of what the word refers to. Probably what is involved is a stelalike cult object serving as an incense altar, to be thought of as resting on the ground,[18] possibly upon an altar.[19]

Since the inscriptions that speak of stelalike cult objects also use the terms *nᵉtsîbh* or *matstsābh/matstsēbhāh,* it is possible that the *chammānîm* served a particular cult. But the question of what deity was worshipped by means of the *chammānîm* has not been answered satisfactorily. Since in one case[20] the cult object interpreted as a *chammān*—although not so designated—is dedicated to the Phoenician Baal Hammon, a close relationship between the *chammān* and Baal Hammon has been suggested.[21] Either the deity takes his name from the *chammān,* in which he is conceived as dwelling,[22] or the object called a *chammān* serves as a symbol of the god Baal Hammon.[23] The other *chammānîm* attested in inscriptions make no reference to any deity or else refer only to an entity other than Baal Hammon. The inscription *CIS,* II,3 No. 3978, from Palmyra, deserves special attention. According to it, the *chammān* that is spoken of (and probably also depicted) is dedicated to the sun-god *šmš,* who was highly honored among the Arameans and especially in Palmyra. A connection between the *chammānîm* and the sun cult is also suggested by other observations: the phonetic similarity of *chammān* to *chammāh,* ''sun,''[24] and—to the extent that there actually is a connection between *chammān* and Baal Hammon—the association or even identifica-

---

[14] *GesB,* 241.

[15] *WTM, s.v.* חמן.

[16] *RES,* No. 2053, 2115.

[17] *CIS,* II,3, No. 3917, 3978; J. Starcky, ''Autour d'une dédicace palmyrénienne à Šadrafa et à Duʿanat,'' *Syr,* 26 (1949), 45; citations from *DISO,* 90.

[18] Ingholt, 798f., Fig. 1.

[19] Cf. *CIS,* I, No. 138, Plate XXIX.

[21] Elliger, *ZAW,* 57 (1939), 264, notwithstanding.

[22] Meyer, 9.

[23] Ingholt, 800.

[24] See II.4 below.

tion of Baal Hammon with the sun-god.[25] The OT, too, mentions an alien cult of the sun (2 K. 21:3), to which Josiah put a temporary end with his reforms (2 K. 23:11), although it continued to exist later (Ezk. 8:16); it can be traced to either the Assyro-Babylonian or the Aramean sphere. The sun cult could also have made use of the *chammānîm,* which are therefore expressly mentioned alongside the altars and images dedicated to other deities and also the asherahs. The scanty OT and epigraphic information thus definitely admits the possibility that in the *chammānîm* we have cultic objects in the form of stelae, used as incense altars and used in the cult of a solar deity. If so, the two current translations "sun stela" and "incense altar" would both be correct, in that the former would speak of the form of the object and deity associated with it, whereas the latter would merely describe its function.

IV. Toponyms and Personal Names Derived from ḥmm. The root *ḥmm* is also clearly present in two toponyms in the tribal territories of Naphtali and Asher. The site in Naphtali has various names: *chammāth* (Josh. 19:35), *chammôth dôr* (Josh. 21:32), and *chammôn* (1 Ch. 6:61[76]); it is certain, however, that the same place is involved in each case.[26] The name derives from the fact that warm springs are found in the area.[27] According to Simons, however, the identification is not absolutely certain: "the place does not seem to be of sufficient antiquity."[28] The *chammôn* in the territory of Asher is identified with *ḫirbet umm-el-ʿawāmīd* on the basis of a stela discovered there dedicated to Baal Hammon,[29] or else with *wādi ḥāmūl,*[30] likewise located north of *rās-en-nāḥūra.* In any case, it is necessary to consider the possibility of deriving the toponym from Baal Hammon or the sun-god Ḥammu,[31] who likewise appears to be associated with the root *ḥmm.*[32] The same may be true of the biblical personal name *chammûʾēl* (1 Ch. 4:26), which, according to Lewy,[33] is to be rendered "The Sun is El."[34]

Beyse

---

25 Baudissin, 496; Lindblom, 98.
26 W. Rudolph, *HAT,* 21 (1955), 62.
27 See Josephus *Ant.* xviii.2.3.
28 Simons, § 335, 3.
29 Contra Simons, § 332B.
30 Alt, *ZAW,* 45 (1927), 71, 1.
31 Lewy, *HUCA,* 18 (1943/44), 455, 142.
32 See III above.
33 P. 434.
34 Contra *IPN,* 243: "The first element is inexplicable." Cf. also 79.

חָמָס chāmās

Contents: I. Occurrences: 1. Ancient Near East; 2. OT. II. Meaning: 1. Verb; 2. Noun: a. Parallel Terms; b. LXX; c. Usage; d. Range of Meanings. III. Context: 1. Society; 2. Law; 3. Killing; 4. Human Sin; 5. Glosses. IV. Theology: 1. Against Yahweh; 2. Yahweh's Intervention; 3. Yahweh's Deliverance. V. Qumran.

I. Occurrences.

1. *Ancient Near East*. The root *ḥms* is scarcely attested outside Israel. The Zenjirli inscription[1] contains an instance of *ḥms* in the singular absolute; the inscription, which dates from the mid-eighth century B.C., is fragmentary, and *KAI* supplies the missing context: "[Whoever] lays hand to sword and [commits] violence." It is certain that *ḥms* is here associated with murder. According to Friedrich and Röllig,[2] the language of the inscription is Ya'udic.

There is also an occurrence in Imperial Aramaic in the phrase *šhd ḥms,*[3] which probably corresponds to Heb. *ʿēdh chāmās,*[4] thus meaning "accuser of violence," i.e., an accuser who intends injury.[5] For Ugaritic, *yḫms* from *ḫms,* "do wrong," may be cited.[6]

2. *OT*. The verb *ḥms* occurs 8 times in the OT: 7 times in the qal (Job 15:33; 21:27; Prov. 8:36; Jer. 22:3; Lam. 2:6; Ezk. 22:6; Zeph. 3:4), once in the niphal (Jer. 13:22). In Job 21:27, emendation to *hms* or the assumption of a root *ḥms* is not necessary.[7]

The noun *chāmās* occurs 60 times; Mandelkern cites 61 occurrences in his concordance, since he prefers the reading *vattimmālēʾ hāʾārets chāmās* to *vattimmālēʾ hāʾārets dāmîm* in Ezk. 9:9, although *dāmîm* is probably the original reading.[8] Of the 60 passages, 14 are found in the Psalms, 7 in Proverbs, 6 each in Ezekiel and Habak-

---

chāmās. H. J. Boecker, *Redeformen des Rechtslebens im AT*. *WMANT*, 14 (1964, ²1970); R. Knierim, *Studien zur israelitischen Rechts- und Kultusgeschichte* (diss., Heidelberg, 1957), 125–146; *idem, Die Hauptbegriffe für Sünde im AT* (²1967); I. L. Seeligmann, "Zur Terminologie für das Gerichtsverfahren im Wortschatz des biblischen Hebräisch," in *Hebräische Wortforschung. Festschrift W. Baumgartner*. *SVT*, 16 (1967), 251–278, esp. 257–59, 263; H. J. Stoebe, "Das achte Gebot (Exod 20, Vers 16)," *WuD*, N.S. 3 (1952), 108–126; *idem*, "חָמָס *ḥāmās* Gewalttat," *THAT*, I, 583–87; L. van den Wijngaert, "Die Sünde in der priesterschriftlichen Urgeschichte," *ThPh*, 43 (1968), 35–50.

[1] *KAI*, 214.26.

[2] J. Friedrich and W. Röllig, *Phönizisch-punische Grammatik*. *AnOr*, 46 (1970), 1, n. 1.

[3] Ahikar, 140.

[4] See III.2 below.

[5] Cf. also *DISO*, 90: "un témoin malveillant."

[6] RS 20.401 Ab 2 (*KTU* 6.48, 2); M. Dietrich and O. Loretz, *Die Elfenbeininschriften und S-Texte aus Ugarit*. *AOAT*, 13 (1976), 7; cf. *KTU*, I, 142.

[7] See II.2 below.

[8] See C. H. Cornill, *Das Buch des Propheten Ezechiel* (1886), 228f.; W. Zimmerli, *Ezekiel* (trans. 1979), 225; Seeligmann, 258.

kuk, 4 each in Genesis and Jeremiah, and 3 in Isaiah; the rest are scattered elsewhere. Hab. 2:8 is a doublet of 2:17 (primary), Prov. 10:6 a doublet of 10:11 (primary), and 2 S. 22:49 a doublet of Ps. 18:49 (Eng. v. 48), although 2 Samuel uses the plural. The occurrence of *chāmās* is disputed in the obscure verse Ezk. 7:11, where *hechāmās qām* is a "later addition."[9] Aalders[10] maintains that the verse is original and comprehensible. In Ezk. 8:17, too, the charge "they have filled the land with *chāmās*" in a list of cultic transgressions is probably a later addition.

The noun occurs 21 times as an accusative object (7 times as the object of *mālē'*, 3 times as the object of *kāsāh*), 16 times as an attributive genitive. Only in this genitive combination do we find the plural of *chāmās:* 3 times in the phrase *'îsh chamāsîm* (2 S. 22:49; Ps. 140:2,5[1,4]), once in *yên chamāsîm* (Prov. 4:17). The plural occurs only in poetic texts. There is no discernible difference in meaning between the singular and the plural; the plurals might be called plurals of quality or amplification.[11] The phrase *'îsh chāmās* occurs 4 times (Ps. 18:49[48]; 140:12[11]; Prov. 3:31; 16:29); *'ēdh chāmās* occurs 3 times (Ex. 23:1; Dt. 19:16; Ps. 35:11). Noteworthy is the expression "With what *chāmās*-hatred they hate me" (Ps. 25:19). The noun appears as subject 11 times; as subjects we also find the suffixed formed *chamāsî* (twice, with the suffix as object) and *chamāsô* (once, with the suffix as agent). The preposition *min* introduces *chāmās* 8 times, 5 times with the meaning "on account of," 3 times with the meaning "from." Only in the difficult passage Ezk. 7:11 and in Jonah 3:8 do we find *chāmās* with the article. There is one occurrence of the compound *lechāmās,* introduced by *bô'*. When a genitive follows *chāmās,* it designates the object on which *chāmās* is inflicted: human beings (Jgs. 9:24; Joel 4:19[3:19]; Ob. 10) or nature (Hab. 2:8,17).

II. Meaning.

1. *Verb.* For the verb, we may take as our starting-point Zeph. 3:4, a sermon detailing the offenses of various classes, in which the priests do *ḥms* to the law. The context as a whole points to wronging of the powerless, to whose disadvantage the religious law is bent. The socio-ethical aspect of *ḥms* stands in the foreground from the very outset. The same is true of the incorporation of Zeph. 3:4 in Ezk. 22:26, which has the effect of an expanded quotation. Here *ḥms* refers to the arbitrary and autocratic appropriation of what belongs to God or one's neighbor. They use "the divine instruction . . . arbitrarily for their own benefit."[12] The same socio-ethical wrongs are implied by *ḥms* in Jer. 22:3 (par. *ynh*), where the subject matter is brutal exploitation of helpless aliens, orphans, and widows; here, however, the continuation "nor shed innocent blood in this place" introduces the notion of assault on the life of one's neighbor, which is often designated by *chāmās*. Jer. 13:22 (niphal), by contrast, speaks of physical assault on a woman ("skirts" standing euphemistically for pudenda). But there is no reason to derive the meaning "lay bare" for *ḥms* on the basis

[9] Zimmerli, *Ezekiel,* 197.
[10] G. C. Aalders, *Ezechiël. COT* (Kampen, 1955), I, 139.
[11] *GK*[28], §§ 124d, e.
[12] Zimmerli, *Ezekiel,* 468.

of this verse and emend *chāmās shōtheh* in Prov. 26:6 to *chōmēs shēthô,* "he uncovers his buttocks."[13] In Prov. 8:36, *ḥms* has the neutral sense "injure," while in Job 15:33, the vine "does violence to" its grapes by casting them off unripe.

Textual problems are raised by Lam. 2:6 and Job 21:27. Despite uncertainty in detail, however, the meaning of Lam. 2:6 is clear, and the verb *ḥms* should not be emended. In parallelism with *šḥt* (piel), *ḥms* means "do (physical) violence to," "destroy by force." In Job 21:27, the majority of commentators emend *ḥms* to *hms*[14] or postulate a root *ḥms* II.[15] But quite apart from the fact that *hms* would be a hapax legomenon in the OT, the Masoretic text yields perfectly good sense: "I know your thoughts and your (wicked) schemes with which you do violence against me," i.e., "wrong me," "resist me" (cf. RSV). It is already apparent here that all *chāmās* is ultimately directed against Yahweh.

2. *Noun.*

a. *Parallel terms.* The wide range of meanings of the noun *chāmās* can be seen from the variety of its synonyms. It occurs in parallelism with → און *'āven,* "iniquity" (Ps. 55:11[10]; Isa. 59:6f.; Hab. 1:3); *ga'ᵃvāh* (→ גאה *gā'āh*), "pride" (Ps. 73:6); → דם *dām,* "blood" (Jgs. 9:24; Ps. 72:14; Jer. 51:35; Ezk. 7:23; Hab. 2:8,17; cf. Isa. 59:3, 6f.; Joel 4:19[3:19]); *derekh rā'āh,* "evil way" (Jonah 3:8); → הוה *havvāh,* "ruin" (Ps. 55:12[11]); *chēlebh,* "fatness," "insensitivity" (Ps. 73:7); *chᵒlî,* "sickness" (Jer. 6:7); *mādhôn,* "contention" (Hab. 1:3); *mᵉhûmāh,* "panic" (Am. 3:9f.); *makkāh,* "wounds" (Jer. 6:7); *maśkîyôth lēbhābh,* "(wicked) plans of the heart" (Ps. 73:7); *mirmāh,* "fraud" (Ps. 55:12[11]; Isa. 53:9; Zeph. 1:9); *'āmāl,* "mischief" (Ps. 7:17[16]; 55:11[10]; Hab. 1:3); *'āvel,* "dishonesty" (Ps. 58:3[2], emended); *'avlāh,* "wickedness" (Isa. 59:3); *'āvōn,* "iniquity" (Isa. 59:3); *'ōsheq,* "oppression (of the poor)" (Ps. 73:8; Jer. 6:6f.); *'ᵃshûqîm,* "oppressions" (Am. 3:9f.); *rā',* "malice" (Ps. 73:8); *rā'āh,* "wickedness" (Jer. 6:7); *rîbh,* "strife" (Ps. 55:10[9]; Isa. 59:6; Hab. 1:3); *rᵉmîyāh,* "lies" (Mic. 6:12); *resha',* "wickedness" (Prov. 4:17); *shebher,* "destruction" (Isa. 59:6f.; 60:18; Jer. 51:35[?]); *sheqer,* "lies" (Isa. 59:3; Mic. 6:12); *tōkh,* "oppression" (Ps. 55:12[11]). In Ezk. 28:16, "be filled with *chāmās*" is synonymous with "sin" (*ḥṭ'*).

The most common synonym of *chāmās,* however, is *shōdh* (→ שדד *shādhadh*) (Isa. 59:6f.; 60:18; Hab. 2:17 [twice]), which means primarily oppression of the *'ᵃnîyîm* and *'ebyônîm* (Ps. 12:6[5]) and even suggests that this is the basic meaning of *chāmās.* The pair *chāmās* and *shōdh* seems almost to have been felt to constitute a single concept. We find *chāmās vāshōdh* in Jer. 6:7; 20:8; Ezk. 45:9; Am. 3:10, *shōdh vᵉchāmās* in Hab. 1:3. It would be difficult to maintain the distinction between *shōdh,* which means violence against property and possession, and *chāmās,* which signifies an

---

[13]N. H. Tur-Sinai, *The Book of Job* (Jerusalem, ²1967), 260, citing his "Nachträge und Berichtigungen zu meinen Proverbiastudien ZDMG, 71, 99–118," *ZDMG,* 72 (1918), 156; B. Gemser, *HAT,* 16 (²1963), 113; *KBL*³.

[14]*BHK, BHS,* Fohrer, Hölscher, Tur-Sinai, Weiser.

[15]Dhorme, *KBL*³.

attack on human life.[16] Stoebe[17] sees the difference in the fact "that the emphasis in the case of *shōdh* is on the act itself, whereas in the case of *chāmās* it is on the nature and consequences of the act."

Although *chāmās* can be done by a woman (Gen. 16:5), it is usually done by a man. Ancient Israel uses the term *'ēsheth chayil* (Prov. 31:10), but not *'ēsheth chāmās;* we find only *'îsh chāmās* (Ps. 18:49[48]; 140:12[11]; Prov. 3:31; 16:29) or *'îsh ch^{a}māsîm* (2 S. 22:49; Ps. 140:2, 5[1, 4]). The phrase *'îsh chāmās* is synonymous with *'ādhām ra'*, "evil man" (Ps. 140:2[1]; cf. Prov. 4:14); *'ôyēbh*, "enemy" (Ps. 18:49[48] par.); *'îsh b^{e}lîya'al,* "worthless man" (Prov. 16:27); *'îsh lāshôn,* "slanderer" (Ps. 140:12[11]); *'îsh tahpukhôth,* "perverse man" (Prov. 16:28); *k^{e}sîl,* "fool" (Prov. 3:35); *lēts,* "scorner" (3:34); *nālôz,* "perverse man" (3:32); *nirgān,* "whisperer" (16:28); *qām,* "adversary" (Ps. 18:49[48] par.); *rāshā'*, "wicked man" (Ps. 140:5[4]; Prov. 3:33; cf. Prov. 4:14,19). Besides the *'îsh chāmās* there is also the *'ōhēbh chāmās* (Ps. 11:5), who corresponds to the *rāshā'* and is the opposite of the *tsaddîq*.

Set in contrast to *chāmās* we find *b^{e}rākhôth,* "blessings" (Prov. 10:6); *ṭôbh,* "good" (Prov. 13:2); *y^{e}shû'āh,* "salvation" (Isa. 60:18); *mishpāṭ,* "justice" (Isa. 59:6,8); *n^{e}khōchāh,* "right" (Am. 3:10); *shālôm,* "peace" (Isa. 59:6,8); *t^{e}hillāh,* "praise" (Isa. 60:18). In contrast with *chāmās vāshōdh* we find *mishpāṭ ûts^{e}dhāqāh* (Ezk. 45:9).

b. *LXX*. Hardly less varied is the vocabulary of the LXX (to the extent it follows the Masoretic text). For the noun *chāmās,* the most common though more remote rendering involves the group *adikía* (17 times), *tó ádikon* (4 times), and *adikéomai* (Gen. 16:5; Hab. 1:2).[18] But *asébeia* is used 7 times (as well as the double expression *sphagḗ kaí asébeia* in Ob. 10 and the personification *asebeís* in Hab. 1:9), and *anomía* 4 times. Once each we find *athesía* (Jer. 20:8), *apṓleia* (Prov. 10:1); *hoi móchthoi* (Jer. 51[28]:35), *óneidos* (Prov. 26:6), and *pénthos* (Prov. 10:6). The *'îsh chāmās/ch^{a}māsîm* is *anḗr ádikos* (4 times) or *adikēmátōn* (2 S. 22:49), *anḗr kakós* (Prov. 3:31), or *anḗr paránomos* (Prov. 16:29). For *yên ch^{a}māsîm* we find *oínos paránomos,* for *'ēdh chāmās* always *mártys ádikos*. For the verb *ḥms, asebéō* prevails (Prov. 8:36; Jer. 22:3; Zeph. 3:4); Lam. 2:6 uses *diapetánnymi,* and Ezk. 22:26 uses *athetéō*. From these data, we can conclude that Hellenistic Jews heard less of brutality and killing in *ḥms* than of injustice and disobedience to the law.

c. *Usage*. In one single instance (Job 19:7) the subject of *chāmās* is God; elsewhere it is always man: Israelites as well as aliens, indeed mankind from the beginning (Gen. 6:11,13) to the eschaton (Jer. 51:46). Within Israel there are singled out Simeon and Levi (Gen. 49:5), Abimelech (Jgs. 9:24), the princes of Israel (Ezk. 45:9), and the rich (Mic. 6:12; Isa. 53:9).[19] Foreigners who do *chāmās* include the Egyptian Hagar (Gen. 16:5), Tyre (Ezk. 28:16), Edom (Joel 4:19[3:19]; Ob. 10), Egypt (Joel 4:19[3:19]), the people of Nineveh (Jonah 3:8), the Chaldeans (Hab. 1:3,9, although

[16] Seeligmann, 257; similarly H. W. Wolff, *Joel and Amos* (trans. 1977), 193f.
[17] *THAT*, I, 584.
[18] G. Schrenk, "ἄδικος," *TDNT,* I, 149-163.
[19] See III.1 below.

the subject cannot be identified with certainty; see the commentaries), Babylon (Jer. 51:35; probably also Ps. 74:20). But Job, also a foreigner, who himself suffers *chāmās* at Yahweh's hands (Job 19:7), can swear that he has never done *chāmās* (Job 16:17).

Exceptionally, the object of *chāmās* can be Yahweh (Job 21:27)[20] and his *tôrāh* (Ezk. 22:26; Zeph. 3:4)[21]; as a rule, however, it is a human being. On rare occasions it is nature: the brutal deforestation of Lebanon is called *ch^{a}mas l^{e}bhānôn* in Hab. 2:17a; and Hab. 2:8 (gloss) and 2:17b speak of *chāmās* to the earth, the city, and its inhabitants with reference to Nebuchadnezzar's devastation of Judah and destruction of Jerusalem.

d. *Range of Meanings*. The source of *chāmās* is either greedy desire (*havvāh,* Prov. 10:3; *nephesh,* Prov. 13:2), when exploitation of the socially helpless is involved,[22] or hate, especially in the case of false accusation.[23] Therefore a man who is filled with hate is said to "breathe out" *chāmās* (Ps. 27:12, emended); indeed, the ultimate hatred, exploding in *chāmās,* is called *chāmās* hatred (Ps. 25:19).

The noun *chāmās* designates an action (*pōʿal,* Isa. 59:6) that is done (*ʿāśāh,* Isa. 53:9; cf. Ezk. 45:9: instead of *chāmās,* the princes are to execute [*ʿāśah*] *mishpāṭ* and *ts^{e}dhāqāh*). The use of physical violence is not necessarily, or at least not directly involved. The mouth can also do *chāmās* (Prov. 10:6; leading astray into evil conduct: Prov. 16:29; humiliation through impudent self-aggrandizement: Gen. 16:5; unjust judgment: 2 S. 22:3). In Prov. 26:6, *chāmās* has the general sense of trouble or injury. Often, however, the hand is the agent of *chāmās;* it is "in the hands" (1 Ch. 12:18[17]; Job 16:17; Isa. 59:6; Jonah 3:8 [*kaph*]), hands deal out *chāmās* (Ps. 58:3[2] [*yādh*]). This physical violence can go so far as the physical destruction of the enemy, so that *chāmās* can take on the meaning "bloodshed." Thus the slaughter of the Shechemites by Simeon and Levi is called *chāmās* (Gen. 49:5), as is Abimelech's slaying of his seventy brothers (Jgs. 9:24). See also the passages where *chāmās* stands in parallelism with *dām*.[24] A city or country can be "filled" with *chāmās* (Gen. 6:11,13; Ezk. 7:23; 8:17; 28:16), as can a house (Zeph. 1:9) or even the man who does *chāmās* (Mic. 6:12). It can be "heard" (Jer 6:7 and the allusion in Isa. 60:18). The doing of *chāmās* can become second nature, so that it can cover a man like a garment (Ps. 73:6). One can speak of the "habitations" (*n^{e}ʾôth*) of personified *chāmās* (Ps. 74:20; cf. *n^{e}vēh tsedheq,* Jer. 31:23; 50:7). Thus *chāmās* is cold-blooded and unscrupulous infringement of the personal rights of others, motivated by greed and hate and often making use of physical violence and brutality.[25]

---

[20]See II.1 above.
[21]See II.1 above.
[22]See III.1 below.
[23]See III.2 below.
[24]See II.2.a above.
[25]G. von Rad, *OT Theol,* I (trans. 1962), 157, n. 34: violent breach of a just order.

III. Context.

1. *Society.* The primary context of *chāmās* is society.[26] Amos (3:10) accuses the prosperous society in Samaria of storing up *chāmās vāshōdh* in their magnificent houses, i.e., treasure and provisions acquired through illegal "oppression and exploitation" of the poor.[27] In 6:1-3, he charges the notable men who are at ease in their fortress—i.e., the military elite and members of land-owning families[28]—with *chāmās*. Mic. 6:12 and Isa. 53:9 likewise indicate that *chāmās* involves primarily the rich and powerful (*ʿāshîr;* Eccl. 10:20 uses this term in parallelism with *melekh*): they are full of *chāmās*. In Zeph. 1:9, *chāmās* infects the officials, princes, and chamberlains of the royal court, i.e., the peak of the social hierarchy; once again, the reference is to wealth acquired unjustly. In Ps. 73:6, too, the image of garment and necklace shows that we are dealing with rich men who oppress the "lowly"; and in Ps. 72 the victims of *chāmās* (v. 14) are the poor (*ʿānî,* vv. 2, 4), the needy (*ʾebhyôn,* vv. 4, 12f.), the weak (*dal,* v. 13), and he who has no helper (*ʾên ʿōzēr lô,* v. 12). In Ps. 140, likewise, the one who is oppressed by the *ʾîsh chāmās* is identical with the *ʿānî* and the *ʾebhyôn,* while in Ps. 74:19-21 the two terms are extended to the entire nation as the victims of *chāmās*. Envy of the *ʾîsh chāmās,* against which Prov. 3:31 warns, can only be concerned with his wealth that is wrung from others; therefore he eats the "bread of wickedness" and drinks the "wine of *chᵃmāsîm*" (Prov. 4:17). In Prov. 10:6, the *chāmās* of the *rᵉshāʿîm* is defined as greed (*havvāh,* v. 3; cf. 13:2: *nephesh*)[29] and treasures gained by wickedness (*ʾôtsᵉrôth reshaʿ,* v. 2), and contrasted with the wealth of the righteous, which is gained through diligence (vv. 3f.). In Prov. 16:29, the *ʾîsh chāmās* is described in general terms as one who leads others astray (*pth* piel); but 1:10ff. show that this refers primarily to unjust enrichment. To drink *chāmās* is tantamount to cutting off one's own feet (Prov. 26:6), to losing out, to falling on evil days. Even in Ezekiel and his redactors the social component of *chāmās* cannot be missed (esp. 12:19; 45:9).

2. *Law.* A favorite instrument of *chāmās* is false accusation and unjust judgment. Especially in the Psalms, *chāmās* appears in the context of the manifold afflictions of the unjustly persecuted psalmist who cries out to Yahweh and demands justice from him. The threat of *chāmās* on the part of his enemies drives the petitioner of Ps. 11 into the temple, where he can commit his cause to Yahweh (v. 5). In Ps. 7:17(16), *chāmās* is the false accusation that demands the life of the innocent. In Ps. 25:19,[30] too, the speaker, who is persecuted with *chāmās* hatred, appears to be unjustly accused. The Levite—for such we may consider him—who laments in Ps. 55 that there is *chāmās* and *rîbh* in the city (v. 10[9]), *tōkh* and *mirmāh* in the marketplace (v. 12[11]), i.e., where court is held, is the victim of calumny and false accusation (vv. 4,10a[3,9a]);

---

[26]Contra Knierim and Stoebe.
[27]W. Rudolph, *KAT,* XIII/2 (1971), 164.
[28]A. Weiser, *ATD,* XXIV ([5]1967), *in loc.;* cf. Wolff, *Joel and Amos,* 274f.
[29]See II.2.d above.
[30]See II.2.d above.

and "Ps. 140 is the song of an *ʿānî* who does not receive justice from others."[31] In Ps. 58:3(2), *chāmās* refers explicitly to unjust judges (v. 2[1]), while the king of the age of salvation will deliver the poor and helpless[32] from *chāmās* through his righteous judgment (Ps. 72:14; cf. vv. 1f.). When Isa. 59:6 charges a powerful group in Jerusalem with *pōʿal chāmās,* he is again thinking primarily of abuse of the judicial process (see esp. v. 4). The textually dubious passage Ezk. 7:11a probably also belongs here.[33] In Ps. 18 = 2 S. 22, the thanksgiving of a king after victory, v. 49c(48c), "thou didst deliver me from men of *chāmās*," destroys the continuity.

That the accused should experience *chāmās* in court is all the more perverse, because it is in court that he should find protection from *chāmās*. He appeals to the court just because he feels threatened by *chāmās*. This accounts for the use of "*chāmās*" as a cry of distress, rather like English "Help!" In this sense *chāmās* is associated with → זעק *zāʿaq* (Jer. 20:8; Hab. 1:2) or *tsāʿaq* (Job 19:7). It is the cry of the victim of an attack (cf. Dt. 22:24, where the betrothed virgin attacked in the city is accused *ʾasher lōʾ tsāʿaqāh bhāʿîr*) who can see no escape and cries "*chāmās*" for help. Thus this cry is closely associated with legal language.[34]

Job cries "*chāmās*" because he seeks justice; he appeals to God as the "defender of justice" (Job 19:7).[35] But he does not receive the justice he deserves (*veʾên mishpaṭ*). Here we find *chāmās* as the cry of one who seeks help, who knows he is in the right and thus cries out for righteous judgment. Thus "*chāmās*" becomes the cry that begins an indictment. This usage explains the idiom "hear (*shāmaʿ*) *chāmās.*" When *chāmās* is heard, oppression reigns (Jer. 6:7), justice and law languish (Hab. 1:2f.). When *chāmās* is no longer heard, the time of peace and righteousness has come (Isa. 60:18).

The phrase *ʿēdh-chāmās* (Ex. 23:1; Dt. 19:16; Ps. 35:11) also points clearly to the sphere of law and justice. The person called *ʿēdh-chāmās* is one who plans or commits *chāmās* through his appearance as *ʿēdh*. It must be remembered, however, that *ʿēdh* often does not have the technical sense of "witness" in our legal vocabulary. This meaning may be present in Ps. 35:11; it is certainly intended in the Decalog (Ex. 20:16 par.). Often, however, the *ʿēdh* is "more plaintiff than witness."[36] In Dt. 19:16, for instance, the *ʿēdh-chāmās* is the plaintiff, who with his false accusation "is making an attempt on the defendant's life."[37] That lying is involved in the case of an *ʿēdh-chāmās* is shown by Ps. 27:12, where *ʿēdhê-sheqer* breathe out *chāmās* against the petitioner. If it can be proved that such a plaintiff is lying (*ʿēdh-sheqer hāʿēdh*), he is to be put to death, as the formula in Dt. 19:18f. shows (*ûbhiʿartā hārāʿ miqqirbekhā*). The *ʿēdh-chāmās* in Ex. 23:1 should probably also be taken in this sense. Here, too, we are dealing not so much with false witness as unjust accusation that intends the destruction of the defendant.

---

[31]H.-J. Kraus, *BK*, XV/2 (⁵1978), *in loc.*
[32]See III.1 above.
[33]See I.2 above.
[34]See Boecker, esp. 57-66.
[35]G. Fohrer, *KAT*, XVI (1963), 313.
[36]Stoebe, "Gebot," 119.
[37]Seeligmann, 263, citing 1 K. 21:10ff. as an example.

3. *Killing.* In both the social and the legal context, brutality can reach the point of physical destruction of one's enemy. This meaning is particularly suggested in passages where *chāmās* is used in combination with *dām* or *dāmîm* (Ezk. 7:23, etc.).[38] Then *chāmās* takes on the meaning "slaying" or "bloodshed." Something similar is intended by *ʿēdh-chāmās* in Dt. 19:16-19.[39]

4. *Human Sin.* We find *chāmās* used in a strictly theological sense in the introduction to the Priestly account of the Deluge (Gen. 6:11, 13), although the original sense is preserved of "an act of violence or crime involving the shedding of blood, criminal assault, oppression, or the like."[40] This "violent highhandedness"[41] is the means whereby man as the image of God does as he pleases within the creation entrusted to him (Gen. 1:26-28), corrupting, as is underlined with threefold repetition, the good creation of God (6:11f., niphal and hiphil of *šḥt*) and thus laying it open to destruction (v. 13, hiphil of *šḥt*). Man cannot exonerate himself; neither—as in the Yahwist (Gen. 8:21)—is he exonerated by Yahweh. He must accept full responsibility (*mippᵉnêhem,* v. 13). Once man has fallen into *chāmās,* only two ways lie open to salvation: God may endure the earth, full of *chāmās* as it is, with merciful patience for the sake of his *bᵉrîth* (Gen. 9:8-17), or he may deliver it from *chāmās* through his epiphany (Isa. 60:18).

5. *Glosses.* In Ezk. 7:11 and 8:17, we obviously are dealing with glosses that are no longer intelligible.[42] For a discussion of Ps. 18:49c(48c) par., see III.2 below.

IV. Theology.

1. *Against Yahweh.* According to the secular tradition of Israel (see Gen. 4:9-12 and Ex. 22:26), *chāmās* as social crime, unjust judgment, and above all bloodguilt is directed ultimately against Yahweh and provokes his judgment, which comes to pass without human intervention on the basis of Yahweh's holiness and righteousness. Yahweh hides his face (Isa. 59:2), turns his face (Ezk. 7:22), scatters sinners (Gen. 49:7), sends them into exile (Am. 6:7), destroys them (Gen. 6:13; Ob. 10), and gives their land to a curse (Mic. 6:13-15), plunder (Jer. 6:1-8; Am. 3:11f.; Zeph. 1:12), and desolation (Ezk. 12:19; Joel 4:19[3:19]). The *chāmās* to which mankind pledged its soul in its youth even abrogates God's affirmation of his whole creation (Gen. 6:11-13).

2. *Yahweh's Intervention.* It is in this light that we must understand the passages that speaks of *chāmās* "coming" (→ בוא *bô'* III) upon (*ʿal*) the doer, returning to punish him (Gen. 16:5; Jgs. 9:24; Ps. 7:17; Jer. 51:35). As Jer. 51:35 shows, we are

---

38 See II.2.a, d above.
39 See III.2 above.
40 C. Westermann, *BK,* I/1 (1974), 559.
41 G. von Rad, *Genesis. OTL* (trans. ²1973), 127.
42 See I.2 above.

dealing with the same theologoumenon as that which speaks of blood being on the head of the offender (→ דם dām). Even if it is true that "Israel saw no conflict between the concept of deed and consequence and belief in a providential guidance of Yahweh,"[43] the emphasis is clearly still on Yahweh's intervention through the latter. That Yahweh binds the human conscience to his will and responds to obedience or disobedience in sovereign freedom with life or death, blessing or curse, is a fundamental pillar of Yahwistic theology.

In Gen. 16:5, Sarai appeals first to Abram, who is responsible for seeing that justice is done, for eradicating the injustice that has been done her by her maid Hagar, and for seeing to it that the rights and position that are justly hers are restored[44] (cf. also CH §195, which stipulates that in such a case the maid is to be degraded once more to the status of a slave). But Sarai goes further and "imposes the burden of the injustice done her as guilt upon Abram."[45] Sarai's concluding statement, "May Yahweh judge between you and me," shows clearly that the *chāmās* of Hagar, which Abram tolerated and for which he is therefore responsible, will come upon him not automatically of its own accord but through the intervention of Yahweh acting as judge.

The deuteronomistic redactor of Jgs. 9:24 likewise ascribes the coming of *chāmās* to the sons of Jerubbaal and the laying of their *dām* upon Abimelech to the evil spirit sent by Yahweh. Above all, the petitioner in Ps. 7, through his repeated protestations, leaves no doubt that it depends solely on Yahweh's judicial intervention whether *chāmās* descends (*yāradh*) on the pate of the enemy who is persecuting him: "Awake, arise, appoint a judgment" (v. 7[6]), "Judge me" (v. 9[8]), "God is a righteous judge" (v. 12[11]), "I will give to Yahweh the thanks due to his righteousness" (v. 18[17]). Because Yahweh hates the *'ōhēbh chāmās,* he rains fire and brimstone on him (Ps. 11:5f.). In Hab. 2:15-17, a political opponent must drink the cup of judgment from Yahweh's hand on account of the *chāmās* he has done.

3. *Yahweh's Deliverance.* Because Yahweh's sovereignty alone can triumph over human *chāmās,* we find in the Psalms those passionate appeals in which Yahweh is adjured by the victim of *chāmās* to judge (*shāphaṭ,* Ps. 7:9[8]; 58:12[11]), to save (*yš'* hiphil, 2 S. 22:3; Ps. 7:11[10]; 55:17[16]; Mal. 1:2; *plṭ* piel, Ps. 18:49[48] par.; *ḥlṣ* piel, Ps. 140:2[1]), to deliver (*nṣl* hiphil, Ps. 18:49[48] par.; 25:20), to preserve (*nātsar,* Ps. 140:2[1]; *shāmar,* Ps. 140:5[4]), to redeem (*pādhāh,* Ps. 55:19[18]; *gā'al,* Ps. 72:14). See also Hab. 1:2, where the cry of "*chāmās*" is addressed not to a human court, but to Yahweh: "I cry '*chāmās,*' and thou dost not save (*yš'* hiphil)."

V. Qumran. At Qumran, too, *chāmās* is in the first instance an expression meaning violent oppression. Thus 1QpHab 8:11 speaks of the Wicked Priest: *wyqbwṣ hwn*

---

[43] H. D. Preuss, "בּוֹא *bô'*," *TDOT,* II, 26. See the controversy between H. Graf Reventlow, "'Sein Blut komme über sein Haupt,'" *VT,* 10 (1960), 311-327, and K. Koch, "Der Spruch 'Sein Blut bleibe auf seinem Haupt' und die israelitische Auffassung vom vergossenen Blut," *VT,* 12 (1962), 396-416.

[44] Von Rad, *Genesis,* 191f.

[45] Knierim, *Studien,* 136.

'nšy ḥms, "he collected the wealth of the men of violence." The plundering of the cities of Judah is also called *chāmās* in 1QpHab 12:9. In 4QTest 25, we read (probably with reference to Simeon and Levi) "that they will both become instruments of violence" (*kly ḥms,* cf. Gen. 49:5). By contrast, the devout man promises the community that he will not strive after wickedness or possessions gained through violence (*rš'h wlhwn ḥms lw' t'wh npšy;* 1QS 10:19); and 4Q158, 1-2, 8 (a paraphrase of Gen. 32:20) express the wish: "May Yahweh . . . save you from all *ḥms.*" In 1QH 6:5, the righteous man thanks God for having preserved him from the company of the violent (*mswd ḥms*). Here (as in 11QPs[a]*Zion* 22:6: *ṭhr ḥms mgwk*) we may have a warning against doing violence to pure doctrine.[46]

H. Haag

[46]See J. D. Amoussine, "Observatiunculae Qumraneae," *RevQ,* 7 (1969/71), 533-552, esp. 542-45; see II.2.c. above.

חמץ *ḥmṣ;* חָמֵץ *chāmēts;* חֹמֶץ *chōmets;* חָמוּץ *chāmûts;* חָמִיץ *chāmîts*

Contents: I. 1. Etymology; 2. Occurrences. II. Usage in the OT: 1. Leaven; 2. Vinegar; 3. *chāmûts*; 4. *chāmîts*.

I. 1. *Etymology.* The root *ḥmṣ* is attested in Akkadian as *ēmēṣu,*[1] "be sour," adj. *emṣu,*[2] "sour" (wine, vinegar, beer, fruit) or leavened bread, and *umṣatu,* "sorrel."[3]

In Ugaritic, the root appears only in a single text, a ration list,[4] where *ḥmṣ* stands in parallel with wine as a beverage, though probably like Heb. *chōmets,* "vinegar."[5] For Phoenician and Punic, *amoutim* is attested[6] as a term for sorrel.[7] In later Aramaic,

ḥmṣ. J. Colin, "Essig," *RAC* (1966), VI, 635-646; H. W. Heidland, "ὄξος," *TDNT,* V, 288f.; L. Köhler, "Archäologisches. Nr. 16. בליל חמיץ Jes 30[24]," *ZAW,* 40 (1922), 15-17; G. Schrot, "Essig," *KlPauly,* II (1967), 378f.; N. Snaith, "Exodus 23:18 and 34:25," *JTS,* N.S. 20 (1969), 533f.; H. Windisch, "ζύμη," *TDNT,* II, 902-906.

[1]*AHw,* I, 214.

[2]*Ibid.,* 215; *CAD,* IV, 152f.

[3]H. Holma, *Kleine Beiträge zum Assyrischen Lexikon. AnAcScFen,* B, 7/2 (1913), 61f.; cf. also B. Landsberger, "Keilschrifttexte nach Kopien von T. G. Pinches: Texte zur Serie ḪAR.ra=ḫubullu," *AfO,* 12 (1937/39), 139, n. 26.

[4]*PRU,* II, 99, lines 27, 28, 35.

[5]*CTA,* 19 [I D], I, 17 does not contain the root *ḥmṣ*.

[6]Dioscorides Pedanius *De materia medica* ii.114.

[7]See the discussion of *chāmîts* below.

phonetic laws would lead us to expect a root *ḥmʿ*, which is in fact well attested in Jewish, Samaritan, and Christian Palestinian Aramaic, as well as Syriac. The meanings can be derived from "be fermented." But there is also a root *ḥmṣ* attested in Syriac with the meaning "be of sour taste." According to Brockelmann,[8] the *ṣ* is the result of dissimilation caused by the preceding *ḥ*. Similar irregularities in phonetic laws in Aramaic are commonly explained as Canaanisms.[9] Since, however, the sequence of *ḥ* as the first radical and *ʿ* as the third radical cannot appear in a Semitic verbal root,[10] there was probably a tendency to avoid a verb *ḥmʿ* as a secondary development, or to replace it with *ḥmṣ*. There is therefore no justification for following *KBL*[3] in assigning Syr. *hmʿ* and *ḥmṣ* to Heb. *ḥmṣ* I and II.

South Semitic is represented primarily by Arab. *ḥamu/aḍa* in the sense of "sour, sharp, acid" in taste, like vinegar or sour milk.[11] In Amharic we find *homäṭṭäṭä*, "be sour."[12] Finally, Late Egyp. *ḥmḏ*, "vinegar,"[13] and its Coptic equivalent *hmoč*, "vinegar,"[14] should probably also be assigned to the Semitic root *ḥmḍ;* a Semitic borrowing may be involved. It is unlikely that Egyp. *ḥm3.t* and Coptic *hmū*, "salt," belong here;[15] they are more likely associated with the root *ḥmr*.

For Hebrew, a root *ḥmṣ* II must also be postulated, as etymological parallels show: primarily Akk. *ḫamāṣu*, "strip, rob,"[16] and Imperial Aram. *ḥmṣ*[17] in the sense "take something from someone unjustly," but also Mand. *hmṣ*, "oppress, subject,"[18] and OSA *ḫmṣ*, "deface, obliterate (an inscription)."[19] Ethiop. *ʿamaḍa*, "treat unjustly,"[20] may also be cited. This root *ḥmṣ* II is attested in Hebrew in Isa. 1:17 in the agent noun *chāmôts*, "violent," or better the passive *chāmûts*, with the versions; in Ps. 71:4 as the participle *chômēts*, "wicked man, oppressor" (par. *m*[eʿ]*avvēl*); and in Isa. 16:4 instead of *hmṣ* (cf. 1QIs[a]).[21] A connection with the root → חמס *chāmās* was already proposed by Gesenius.[22] Fraenkel,[23] on the other hand, suggests that "the meaning of the word 'sharp,' . . . influenced by the phoneticly similar *ḥms*, became differentiated

---

[8] *VG*, I, 135.

[9] E.g., by C. Brockelmann, *LexSyr*, 240b, and P. Jensen, *KB*, VI/2, 4*.

[10] See J. Kuryłowicz, *Studies in Semitic Grammar and Metrics* (Krakow, trans. 1972), 21.

[11] See Lane, I/2, 644f.

[12] See W. Leslau, *Contributions*, 21; *idem*, *Hebrew Cognates in Amharic* (1969), 45.

[13] *WbÄS*, III, 99.

[14] W. E. Crum, *A Coptic Dictionary* (Oxford, 1939), 682f.

[15] Contra *WbÄS*, III, 93f.

[16] *AHw*, I, 315b.

[17] *AP*, 45, 3.

[18] *MdD*, 150a.

[19] Ja 1028, 12.

[20] *LexLingAeth*, 958.

[21] But see L. Delekat, *Asylie und Schutzorakel am Zionheiligtum* (Leiden, 1967), 93, n. 4; Delekat rejects a root *ḥmṣ* II and starts with the meaning "sour" even in Isa. 1:17 and Ps. 71:4.

[22] F. Gesenius, *Thesaurus philologicus criticus linguae hebraeae et chaldaeae Veteris Testamenti* (1829), 492.

[23] S. Fraenkel, "Zum sporadischen Lautwandel in den semitischen Sprachen," *BAss*, 3 (1898), 62.

in the direction of the latter's specialized meaning." This theory is opposed by Barth, however, on the basis of Ethiopic.[24]

It is also uncertain whether there is any connection between *ḥmṣ* I or II and the Hebrew root → אמץ *'āmats,* "be strong,"[25] not otherwise attested except for Ugaritic.

The hypothesis of an independent root *ḥmṣ* III, as proposed by *BDB,* with the meaning "be red," for Isa. 63:1 and Ps. 68:24 (Eng. v. 23) conj. (in place of *tmḥṣ*), on the basis of Syr. *ḥmṣ* ethpael, "grow red," "be overcome with shame," is impossible because the meanings "sour, sharp, painfully hot, fiery red" belong to a single semantic sphere; cf. Lat. *acer*. Even if the litmus effect was unknown in antiquity, the path from "sour" to "red" is not insuperable.

2. *Occurrences.* If on the basis of the etymological parallels cited above we eliminate the rare occurrences of *ḥmṣ* II in Ps. 71:4; Isa. 16:4 (conj.); and Isa. 1:17, we are left with 25 occurrences of *ḥmṣ* I. The verb appears 6 times: the qal, "be leavened," in Ex. 12:34,39 and the infinitive with suffix in Hos. 7:4; the hiphil only participially (*machmetseth,* "leavened, sour") in Ex. 12:19f.; and the hithpael, "be embittered," in Ps. 73:21.

The noun *chāmēts,* "leavened bread, leaven," appears 11 times: Ex. 12:15; 13:3,7; 23:18; 34:25; Lev. 2:11; 6:10; 7:13; 23:17; Dt. 16:3; Am. 4:5. Another noun *chōmets* with the meaning "vinegar" appears 5 (or 6) times: Nu. 6:3 (twice); Ps. 69:22(21); Ruth 2:14 (see below); Prov. 10:26; 25:20. There is also a *qāṭûl* form in Isa. 63:1 and a *qāṭîl* in Isa. 30:24. It is not easy to decide whether the verb or a nominal form stands at the beginning of the root's development. Possibly the *qaṭil* form *chāmēts* with the meaning "sour (to the taste)" can be labeled the starting-point. All the more specialized meanings in Hebrew can be derived from the basic meaning "sour."

II. Usage in the OT.

1. *Leaven.* In the OT, the word *chāmēts,* "that which has been leavened," is not a parallel to *śᵉ'ōr,* "leaven" (Ex. 12:15,19; 13:7; Lev. 2:11; Dt. 16:4), although the LXX suggests such an identification by its rendering *zýmē*. Instead, as the phrase *lechem chāmēts* (Lev. 7:13) shows, it is an elliptical term for bread that has been baked with sourdough, a leaven consisting of yeast and lactic acid. The sourdough itself (*śᵉ'ōr*) is not eaten. According to Hos. 7:4, the baker stops stirring the *tannûr* from the kneading of the dough until it is thoroughly leavened (*ʿadh-chumtsāthô*) so that no valuable fuel will be wasted unnecessarily. We may conclude that the dough took long enough to rise that it paid to let the fire in the oven go out.

The earliest occurrences of *chāmēts* are Ex. 34:25 and 23:18. If in 34:25a and 23:18a[26] we have what was originally an independent sentence (without the interpretive

---

[24] J. Barth, *Wurzeluntersuchungen zum hebräischen und aramäischen Lexicon* (1902), 57.

[25] See, e.g., A. Neher, *Amos: Contribution à l'étude du prophétisme* (Paris, 1950), 95.

[26] On the minor differences between the two formulations, see Snaith, *JTS,* N.S. 20 (1969), 533f.; H. Horn, "Traditionsschichten in Ex 23, 10-13 und Ex 34, 10-26," *BZ,* N.S. 15 (1971), 212.

second half of the verse) incorporated into a Decalog, then the prohibition against offering bloody sacrifice on leavened bread probably derives from nomadic traditions,[27] since unleavened cakes are the nomadic form of bread. The present combination of 34:25a and 23:18a with the second half of the verse suggests that both prohibitions were related to the Passover Festival.[28] Since unleavened bread (*matstsôth*) probably always played a role in the ritual of Passover, it was easy for Passover and the Festival of Unleavened Bread to coalesce into a single festival, since the eating of unleavened bread for seven days was a constitutive element of the Festival of Unleavened Bread. It should be noted that only the eating of *chāmēts* is prohibited (cf. Ex. 12:34, 39 [verbal forms of *ḥmṣ*], early source; Ex. 13:3,7; Dt. 16:3; and for P Ex. 12:15,19,20 [the last two with the hiphil participle]); nothing is said about the possible offering of *chāmēts* or *matstsôth*.

Now it is clear from Am. 4:5 that in the thank-offering (*tôdhāh*) leavened *chāmēts* was offered to Yahweh; the attempts to interpret the text otherwise are not convincing.[29] In the legislation of P, however, the use of leavened bread for sacrifice is explicitly forbidden (see Lev. 2:11 and 6:10[17]). The prohibition of *chāmēts* in combination with honey as a cereal-offering in Lev. 2:11 is usually explained by reference to the decomposition (and therefore corruption) brought about by fermentation.[30] But Schlatter[31] already pointed out that this explanation can hardly be correct, since no one had ever considered leavened bread to be spoiled. A more likely explanation for the prohibition of leavened bread and honey in the cult of Yahweh is that both were popular as sacrifices to Canaanite deities and were therefore explicitly forbidden to be used as burnt sacrifice to Yahweh. In the Greek and Roman cult, too, normal leavened bread and honey play an important sacrificial role, especially for chthonic deities.

Even in P, however, when a *tôdhāh* is involved in a sacrificial meal (*zbḥ twdt šlmyw;* cf. Am. 4:5), rounds of leavened bread can be offered. Presumably this practice, as well as the ordinance in Lev. 23:17 that requires the offering on the Feast of Weeks of two rounds of bread baked with leaven as firstfruits, is intended to allow the clergy to receive leavened bread in addition to unleavened as part of their priestly perquisites.

2. *Vinegar.* Vinegar (*chōmets*) is produced by the fermentation of alcoholic liquids, in the OT period, like today, primarily wine. Beer (*shēkhār*) was also used (*chōmets shēkhār,* Nu. 6:3, corresponds precisely to *šikaru emṣu,* sour beer[32]). In Nu. 6:3, which prohibits the use of alcohol by the Nazirites, the pure beverages *yayin* and *shēkhār* are listed together with their soured forms *chōmets yayin vᵉchōmets shēkhār;*

[27] See Horn, "Traditionsschichten," 212, 221.

[28] See F.-E. Wilms, *Das jahwistische Bundesbuch in Ex 34. StANT,* 32 (1973), 172.

[29] See T. H. Robinson, *HAT,* 14 (^{3}1964), 86, and even earlier N. H. Snaith, *The Book of Amos* (London, 1946), 71-73.

[30] See, e.g., L. R. Stachowiak, "Sauerteig," *BL*^{2}, 1528.

[31] *Calwer Bibellexikon* (^{3}1912), 645.

[32] See W. Röllig, *Das Bier im alten Mesopotamien* (1970), 37.

the latter can hardly be mentioned on account of their intoxicating effect, but rather in an effort to formulate the prohibition as inclusively as possible.

According to Prov. 25:20, a song has the same effect on a heavy heart that vinegar has on soda. It is suggested that the point is to characterize song as being inappropriate to cure melancholy;[33] this interpretation is not uninfluenced by the LXX. If we begin, however, with the observation that vinegar as an acid neutralizes soda as an alkali, then Prov. 25:20 should rather be interpreted in the sense of 1 S. 16:17-23, where David's playing succeeded in dispelling the *rûach hārāʿāh* that had come upon Saul.

Vinegar is thought of as something unpleasant in Prov. 10:26, which states that the sluggard is to the one who sends him like vinegar to the teeth and smoke to the eyes. The explanation of this passage in Talmud *Shab.* 111a states on the one hand that vinegar made from (unripe) fruit is so sour that it is unpleasant to drink, and on the other that the passage has in mind a sore (in the mouth) that makes the drinking of vinegar unpleasant.

In Ps. 69:22(21), the sufferer laments that his enemies have poisoned his food and given him vinegar for his thirst. The parallelism shows that vinegar is considered as unpalatable as poison.[34] The passage became part of the passion narrative in the NT (Mt. 27:34 conj., 48; Mk. 15:36; Lk. 23:36; Jn. 19:29f.), but there is no exegetical consensus whether the Gospels use *óxos* to mean the *posca* of the Roman soldiers, which would indicate an act of kindness toward Jesus, or whether vinegar in the sense of Ps. 69:22(21) represents an additional insult and torment.

We do not find *chōmets* in such texts as the Samaria ostraca. This is understandable, because, probably more often than the recipients would have liked, the wine would turn during or after shipment, so that it could only be used for vinegar or in a *posca*.

At Arad, nevertheless, *ḥmṣ* is among the supplies apportioned to the *kittiyîm,* as we learn from an unpublished ostracon in the Israel Museum, Jerusalem,[35] addressed to Elyashib. There we read, after the allotment of bread and wine: *w'm ʿwd ḥmṣ wntt lhm,* "and if there is any *ḥmṣ* remaining, give it to them."[36]

In Talmud *B. Metzia* 83b, *ḥwmṣ bn yyn* can be used as a term of abuse.

Ruth 2:14 tells how Boaz calls Ruth to join in the meal of the harvest laborers, which includes dipping her morsel in *chōmets*. We may assume that this was the usual practice of the laborers when eating. Although the text does not say so explicitly, it is reasonable to suppose that the morsels to be dipped were bread. Morsels dipped in pure vinegar or vinegar diluted with water should be understood as a thirst-quenching form of refreshment, as suggested by Rudolph,[37] who refers to the *posca,* a vinegar-based beverage of the Roman soldiers, although Dalman[38] points out that there is no

---

[33] B. Gemser, *HAT,* 16 (1937), 92.

[34] See L. Delekat, *Asylie,* 136, 139.

[35] Nos. 67-625.

[36] See R. Hestrin, Y. Israeli and Y. Meshorer, eds., כתובות מספרות (*Inscriptions Reveal: Documents from the Time of the Bible, the Mishnah, and the Talmud*) (Jerusalem, 1973), No. 50.

[37] W. Rudolph, *KAT,* XVII/1 (1962), 49.

[38] *AuS,* IV (1935), 388.

vinegar-based beverage in modern Palestine. Reed[39] therefore made the illuminating suggestion of seeing in the *chōmets* of Ruth 2:14 the popular chick-pea paste of Palestine *chummuts,* into which bread is dipped. Since Arab. *ḥummuṣ* (Classical Arab. *ḥimmaṣ*) is an Aramaic loanword and Syr. *ḥemṣē'* would appear in Hebrew as *ḥmṣ,* there are no linguistic objections, and no knowledgeable person would hesitate if given the choice of dipping his bread in vinegar or in *chummuts.*

The word appears only once at Qumran: in 1QH 4:11, alluding to Ps. 69:22b(21b), it is said that the enemies of the community withhold the draught of knowledge from the thirsty and give him instead *chōmets,* "vinegar."

Except in Prov. 10:26 (where we find *ómphax,* "sour grapes"), the LXX always renders *chōmets* as *óxos;* it should be remembered that for Greek authors *óxos* can include *oxýkrama, posca.*

3. *chāmûts.* In Isa. 63:1-6, the vision of the advancing wine-press treader, there appears in line 1 the phrase *ch^{a}mûts b^{e}ghādhîm* describing his clothes. The word *ch^{a}mûts* is the passive qal participle of *ḥmṣ* in the construct.[40] The interpretation of the phrase is disputed.

a. Starting from the observation that "sour" can pass into "sharp" (cf. Lat. *acerbus* and Ps. 73:21, *ḥmṣ* hithpael, "show oneself sour, sharp = embittered"), Dalman[41] has suggested for *chāmûts* the meaning "sharply = brilliantly colored"; Gradwohl[42] has similarly suggested "garishly (clothed)."

b. The LXX and Syriac find in *chāmûts* the color red, as do *BDB* and Zorell, citing the ethpael of Syr. *ḥmṣ*. The question in v. 2 does not of itself allow the conclusion that *chāmûts* in v. 1 means "red."[43] It is more appropriate to interpret *chāmûts* on the basis of the parallel *chādhûr.*

c. The two interpretations can be combined to yield the meaning "bright red"[44] or "crimsoned."[45]

d. Guillaume's citation of Arab. *ṣuḥmat,* "varicolored,"[46] does not hold water. Even if the transposition of the last two radicals could be explained, Fischer's state-

---

[39]W. L. Reed, "Translation Problems in the Book of Ruth," *College of the Bible Quarterly,* 41/2 (1964), 8-10.

[40]See C. Brockelmann, *Synt.,* §§ 77f.

[41]*AuS,* IV, 369.

[42]R. Gradwohl, *Die Farben im AT: Eine terminologische Studie. BZAW,* 83 (1963), 22f.

[43]*KBL*[3]; J. Morgenstern, "Further Light from the Book of Isaiah upon the Catastrophe of 585 B.C.," *HUCA,* 37 (1966), 1-28.

[44]K. Budde in E. Kautzsch and A. Bertholet, *HSAT* ([4]1922/23), *in loc.*

[45]E.g., C. Westermann, *Isaiah 40-66. OTL* (trans. 1969), 380.

[46]A. Guillaume, "Hebrew and Arabic Lexicography: A Comparative Study," *Abr-Nahrain,* 1 (1959/60 [1961]), 24.

ment[47] that *ṣḥm* is a dialectic variant of *sḥm* is proof enough that Arab. *ṣuḥmat* has nothing to do with Heb. *chāmûts*.

e. Jerome's interpretation in the Vulgate (like the Arabic translation in the Polyglot), *tinctis vestibus,* "with dyed garments," can be connected with *ḥmṣ,* "sour"; for even today wool dyes are acid.

f. The Targum's rendering, *prʿnʾ tqypʾ,* "mighty vengeance," may be thinking of *ḥmṣ* II.

If we attempt to determine the meaning of *chāmûts* from the context, the battle dress of a warrior seems to be intended, which was red in the case of the Greeks and Romans.[48]

4. *chāmîts*. In Isa. 30:18-26, a promise concerning the coming age of salvation, the *chāmîts* spoken of in v. 24 as a special delicacy for oxen and asses is likewise connected with the root *ḥmṣ,* "sour." Köhler,[49] citing primarily the Punic gloss *amoutim* in Dioscorides, was able to show that *b^elîl chāmîts* refers to mixed fodden containing sorrel. The Syriac, Arabic, and Akkadian words for sorrel (=*Rumex*), which come from the same root, demonstrate the correctness of this interpretation.

D. Kellermann

---

[47] W. Fischer, *Farb- und Formbezeichnungen in der Sprache der altarabischen Dichtung* (1965), 378f.

[48] See E. Wunderlich, *Die Bedeutung der roten Farbe im Kultus der Griechen und Römer. RVV,* 20/1 (1925), 73ff.

[49] Köhler, *ZAW,* 40 (1922), 15-17.